Encyclopedia of

# GARDENS

History and Design

CHICAGO BOTANIC GARDEN

*Encyclopedia of*

# GARDENS

History and Design

Volume 1

A–F

*EDITOR*

CANDICE A. SHOEMAKER

FITZROY DEARBORN PUBLISHERS

CHICAGO   LONDON

Copyright © 2001 by
FITZROY DEARBORN PUBLISHERS

All rights reserved including the right of reproduction in whole or in part in any form.
For information write to:

FITZROY DEARBORN PUBLISHERS
919 N. Michigan Avenue, Suite 760
Chicago, Illinois 60611
USA

or

FITZROY DEARBORN PUBLISHERS
310 Regent Street
London W1B 3AX
UK

**Library of Congress and British Library Cataloging in Publication Data are available.**

ISBN 1-57958-173-0

First published in the USA and UK 2001

Index prepared by Hughes Analytics, Chicago, Illinois
Typeset by Argosy Publishing, Waltham, Massachusetts
Printed by Edwards Brothers, Ann Arbor, Michigan
Cover design by Chicago Advertising and Design, Chicago, Illinois

Cover illustration: Vaux-le-Vicomte, Seine-et-Marne, France. Copyright Robert M. Craig.

# CONTENTS

# EDITOR'S NOTE

The history of gardens is as old as the history of civilization: the earliest garden found to date, a grove of trees beside the 4th Dynasty pyramid of Seneferu at Dahshur, is from approximately 2613 B.C. As such, garden history is a rich and complex subject touching on the disciplines of architecture, the various fine arts, botany, horticulture, and history. Over time gardens have played a series of differing roles, from a place providing food and medicine to a space demonstrating power and wealth. Equally as important as their function, gardens reflect the cultural and artisitic values of their creators and even the societies in which they were built. Each period in garden history is culturally specific and influenced as much, if not more, by the political, social, economic, and religious ideas and events of its era as by the horticultural or architectural innovations of its time. The study of gardens and garden design is therefore interdisciplinary, exploring the relationships between art and nature as they are expressed in the literary and visual cultures of different periods and societies. The grand formality of Versailles or the intimate arrangement of borders and flowers at Munstead Wood are equally revealing as documents of changing tastes and ideas that reveal how gardens can be interpreted as works of art with complex social, aesthetic, and intellectual meanings.

The overall aim of the *Encyclopedia of Gardens: History and Design* is to provide description and analysis of a range of subjects and individuals related to the history of gardens and garden design. The entries are arranged in alphabetical order and fall into three broad categories: those on individuals (architects, designers, plant collectors, patrons, and writers), those on places (countries, regions of the world, and specific gardens), and those dealing with topics (garden elements, periods, and styles).

The final selection of entries for the *Encyclopedia of Gardens* was the result of a long process of refining an original much longer list of suggestions on the basis of views and ideas put forward by the project's advisers, the contributing authors, and other scholars. The principal criterion employed in the selection of articles on individuals and gardens was that they had an especially strong or lasting impact on the history of gardens or garden design. In an attempt to represent a full range of styles and types of gardens, public and private gardens as well as gardens that no longer exist have been included. Both small gardens of less than a hectare in size and large gardens such as Versailles have been included because both have contributed to the development of garden design. It has not, however, been possible to include every architect, designer, or garden of note, and the *Encyclopedia* does not claim to do so.

Every effort has been made to create a work that is international in scope; in spite of this, the *Encyclopedia of Gardens* is undeniably Eurocentric. This is due primarily to the fact that there is comparatively less research into the history of gardens and gardening traditions outside Europe. It is hoped, however, that the country and regional survey articles as well as the individual garden entries from virtually every major gardening tradition will provide a starting point for further study.

Each entry consists of a critical essay, a summary biography and list of principal works (entries on individuals), a chronological synopsis of major developments in a site's history (entries on specific gardens), and a list of further reading. The essays on individuals focus on that person's contribution to gardens and garden design. Essays on individual gardens—both public and private—focus on the gardens' significance to the history of gardens as well as on descriptions of the important features of the sites. Essays on countries and regions focus on the history and development of gardens, designs, and methods within these specific geographic and cultural areas. Finally, essays on topics focus on a wide range of subjects including types and styles of gardens, tools and techniques, and surveys of the traditions of specific eras, cultures, and schools of thought.

This project has been completed over a three-year period, which for a work of this scope is an astoundingly short period of time. Certainly there is still much more that could and should be written on gardens and garden design, and it is hoped that this *Encyclopedia of Gardens* will be a useful resource for future work.

## Acknowledgments

A work of this size is not possible without the help, advice, and support of many people. First of all I would like to thank my staff and colleagues at the Chicago Botanic Garden, who with patience, understanding and support, accepted my frequent absences from the garden so that I could work on the encyclopedia. I am also deeply grateful to the Editorial Advisory Committee—Erik de Jong, Géza Hajós, Linda Cabe Halpern, Martin Hoyles, Wilhelmina F. Jashemski, Mark Laird, Cecilia Mejia, E. Charles Nelson, D. Fairchild Ruggles, Dmitry Shvidkovsky, Paul D. Spreiregen, Marc Treib, Gabrielle Van Zuylen, Joseph C. Wang, and Joachim Wolschke-Bulmahn—who tackled the daunting task of helping to shape the final list of entries, recommended many of the contributors, and prepared entries. No less deserving are the hundreds of scholars and specialists who have written for the book and generously shared their expertise. It was a great pleasure to work with Julie Laffin who served as photo researcher and her assistants Karen Hanmer and Cathy Melloan, all who were very creative in finding the wonderful illustrations for the book. Last but not least is gratitude to and acknowledgment of the staff at Fitzroy Dearborn.

CANDICE A. SHOEMAKER

# ADVISERS

Erik de Jong
*Vrije Universiteit*

Géza Hajós
*Monument Office of Austria*

Linda Cabe Halpern
*James Madison University*

Martin Hoyles
*London*

Wilhelmina F. Jashemski
*Silver Spring, Maryland*

Mark Laird
*Toronto, Ontario*

Cecilia Mejia
*Bogotá*

E. Charles Nelson
*Outwell, Wisbech*

D. Fairchild Ruggles
*Cornell University*

Dmitry Shvidkovsky
*Moscow Institute for Architecture*

Paul D. Spreiregen
*Washington, D.C.*

Marc Treib
*University of California, Berkeley*

Gabrielle Van Zuylen
*Paris*

Joseph C. Wang
*Virginia Polytechnic Institute*

Joachim Wolschke-Bulmahn
*Universität Hannover*

# CONTRIBUTORS

Barbara Abbs
Arnold R. Alanen
Paul Armstrong
Diana Baskervyle-Glegg
Robert A. Benson
Michael J. Bevington
Lynn Bjorkman
Brian Black

Joseph C. Blalock, Jr.
Charles Boewe
Patrick Bowe
Georgene A. Bramlage
C. Stephen Briggs
John Trevor Brighton
Juan Antonio Bueno
Jon Bryan Burley

Peter Butler
Susan Campbell
David Cast
Cheng Liyao
Elizabeth Cernota Clark
Terry L. Clements
David Coffin
Jill Collett
Caroline Constant
Allan Correy
Sarah Couch
Fiona Cowell
Robert M. Craig
Howard Crane
Victor Crittenden
Gillian Cull
Stephen Daniels
Stevie O. Daniels
Jana Das
Nirmal Dass
Stéphanie de Courtois
Erik A. de Jong
Peter Del Tredici
David Dernie
Steven Desmond
M.F. Downing
Nigel Dunnett
John Edmondson
Marek Ehrlich
Susan Toby Evans
Valery Ezhov
Linda Farrar
Kristóf Fatsar
Gennady A. Firsov
Margrethe Floryan
Eijiro Fujii
Isobel Gabites
David Allan Galbraith
Kartik Ram Ganapathy
Nikolay B. Gaponenko
Anne Garland
Judith Gerber
Ute-Harriet Gladigau
Kathryn L. Gleason
John Glenn
Emily N. Goodman
Tilman Gottesleben
Katja Grillner
Gert Gröning
Carol Grove
Hazel Hahn
Beatrix Hajós
Géza Hajós
Linda Cabe Halpern
Dianne Harris

Vroni Heinrich
Kenneth Helphand
Paula Henderson
Susan Herrington
Sherman J. Hollar
Martin Hoyles
Vena Hrdličkova
Martha A. Hunt
Jane Hutcheon
Marie Iannotti
Richard R. Iversen
Wilhelmina F. Jashemski
Charlotte Johnson
Lauri MacMillan Johnson
David Jones
Tresa Jones
Karsten Jorgensen
Evie T. Joselow
Brian Katen
Marc Peter Keane
Richard Kenworthy
Julia King
Ludmila Kiriushina
Vernon N. Jr. Kisling
Ebba Koch
Marcus Köhler
Alenka Kolšek
Ann E. Komara
Rebecca Krinke
Alon Kvashny
H. Walter Lack
Mark Laird
Sylvia Landsberg
Michael Laurie
Iris Lauterbach
André Lawalree
Helen Leach
Prudence Leith-Ross
Anthony H. T. Levi
Valencia Libby
A. R. Littlewood
Margaret Livingston
Alexander Luferov
Kjell Lundquist
Loubov I. Lyashenko
Fernando Magallanes
Marilyn Magnuson
Judith K. Major
William A. Mann
Martin J. Manning
John Martin
Susan Garrett Mason
David Mawson
Henrietta McBurney
David McClintock

Donal P. McCracken
Lorna Anne McNeur
Eleanor M. McPeck
Elizabeth R. Messer Diehl
Karen Meyers
Paul Meyers
William C. Miller
Frank Mills
Sandra Morris
Ulrich Müller
Kenneth Hall Murta
Mary E. Myers
Daniel Joseph Nadenicek
Lance M. Neckar
E. Charles Nelson
Sandra Nicholson
Fran Nolan
Zdenek Novák
Lisa Nunamaker Orgler
Božena Pacáková-Hošt'álková
Danilo Palazzo
Artyom Parshin
Allen Paterson
Marie Pavlátová
Marc Perrotta
Douglas Ellory Pett
Dan Philippon
Wendy Pullan
Anne Purchas
Richard Quaintance
Beate Räckers
Paul Rich
Christopher Ridgway
Edward A. Riedinger
Dušan Riedl
Juan Luis de las Rivas Sanz
Michael Rohde
D. Fairchild Ruggles
Eeva Ruoff
Cecilia Rusnak
Keli Rylance
John Sales
Walter Salmen
Eugenia Salza Prina Ricotti
Thomas Scheliga
Angela Schwarz
Mladen Obad Scitaroci
Galina Semenova
Zheng Shiling
Candice A. Shoemaker

Ekaterina Shorban
Dmitry Shvidkovsky
Paul C. Siciliano, Jr.
Marek Siewniak
Jeannie Sim
Barbara Simms
Iona Sinclair
Manu Sobti
David Solman
Frederick Steiner
David C. Streatfield
Jack Sullivan
Antonín Marián Svoboda
Simon Swaffield
Malgorzata Szafrańska
Judith B. Tankard
Hilary A. Taylor
Catharine Ward Thompson
Mine F. Thompson
William H. Tishler
Ludwig Trauzettel
Vesselina Troeva
David Underwood
Isabelle van Groeningen
Anne Marie Van Nest
Gabrielle van Zuylen
Věra Vávrová
Nancy Volkman
Ulrich von Rath
Joseph C. Wang
Pamela J. Warner
Teresa S. Watts
Karol K. Weaver
Constance A. Webster
Udo Weilacher
Gunnar Weimarck
Richard Westmacott
Robin Whalley
Agnieszka Whelan
David Whitehead
Elisabeth Whittle
Alix Wilkinson
Clemens Alexander Wimmer
John Winter
Joachim Wolschke-Bulmahn
May Woods
Jan Woudstra
Kristin Wye-Rodney
Xu Dejia

# LIST OF ENTRIES

# GENERAL BIBLIOGRAPHY

## Dictionaries, Encyclopedias, and Reference Guides

Brickell, Christopher, editor, *The American Horticultural Society Encyclopedia of Garden Plants,* London: Dorling Kindersley, and New York: Macmillan, 1989; revised edition, as *The American Horticultural Society A–Z Encyclopedia of Garden Plants,* edited by Brickell and Judith D. Zuk, New York: DK, 1997

Conan, Michel, *Dictionnaire historique de l'art des jardins,* Paris: Hazan, 1997

Desmond, Ray, *Dictionary of British and Irish Botanists and Horticulturists: Including Plant Collectors and Botanical Artists,* London: Taylor and Francis, 1977; revised and updated edition, by Desmond and Christine Ellsworth, London and Briston, Pennsylvania: Taylor and Francis, 1994

Everett, Thomas H., *The New York Botanical Garden Illustrated Encyclopedia of Horticulture,* 10 vols., New York: Garland, 1980–82

*Garden Literature: An Index to Periodical Articles and Book Reviews* (1992– )

Goode, Patrick, and Michael Lancaster, editors, *The Oxford Companion to Gardens,* Oxford and New York: Oxford University Press, 1986

Hadfield, Miles, Robert Harling, and Leonie Highton, *British Gardeners: A Biographical Dictionary,* London: Zwemmer, 1980

Huxley, Anthony Julian, *An Illustrated History of Gardening,* New York: Paddington Press, 1978

Huxley, Anthony Julian, editor, *The New Royal Horticultural Society Dictionary of Gardening,* 4 vols., London: Macmillan, and New York: Stockton Press, 1992

Morrow, Baker H., *A Dictionary of Landscape Architecture,* Albuquerque: University of New Mexico Press, 1987

Symes, Michael, *Glossary of Garden History,* Princes Risborough, Buckinghamshire: Shire, 1993

Wilkinson, Elizabeth, and Marjorie Henderson, editors, *The House of Boughs: A Sourcebook of Garden Designs, Structures, and Suppliers,* New York: Viking, 1985; revised edition, as *Decorating Eden: A Comprehensive Sourcebook of Classic Garden Details,* San Francisco: Chronicle Books, 1992

## Monographs

Adams, William Howard, *Nature Perfected: Gardens through History,* New York: Abbeville Press, 1991

Adams, William Howard, *Grounds for Change: Major Gardens of the Twentieth Century,* Boston: Little Brown, 1993

Alaimo, Marilyn K., and Priscilla P. deVeer, editors, *Stewards of the Land: A Survey of Landscape Architecture and Design in America,* St. Louis, Missouri: National Council of State Garden Clubs, 1999

Berrall, Julia S., *The Garden: An Illustrated History,* New York: Viking Press, 1966; as *The Garden: An Illustrated History from Ancient Egypt to the Present Day,* London: Thames and Hudson, 1966

Birnbaum, Charles A., and Robin Karson, editors, *Pioneers of American Landscape Design,* New York: McGraw-Hill, 2000

Clifford, Derek Plint, *A History of Garden Design,* London: Faber and Faber, and New York: Praeger, 1962

Conan, Michael, editor, *Perspectives on Garden Histories,* Washington, D.C.: Dumbarton Oaks Research Library and Collection, 1999

Crandell, Gina, *Nature Pictorialized: "The View" in Landscape History,* Baltimore, Maryland: Johns Hopkins University Press, 1993

Crowe, Sylvia, *Garden Design,* London: Country Life, 1958; New York: Hearthside Press, 1959

Desmond, Ray, *Bibliography of British Gardens,* Winchester, Hampshire: St. Paul's Bibliographies, 1984

*The Garden Book,* London: Phaidon, 2000

Gothein, Marie Luise Schroeter, *Geschichte der Gartenkunst,* Jena, Germany: Diederichs, 1914; 2nd edition, 1926; as *A History of Garden Art,* 2 vols., edited by Walter P. Wright, translated by Mrs. Archer-Hind, London: Dent, and New York: Dutton, 1928; reprint, New York: Hacker Art Books, 1979

Hadfield, Miles, *Gardening in Britain,* London: Hutchinson, 1960; as *A History of British Gardening,* London: Penguin, and Newton, Massachusetts: Branford, 1985

Harvey, John Hooper, *Mediaeval Gardens,* London: Batsford, and Beaverton, Oregon: Timber Press, 1981

Henrey, Blanche, *British Botanical and Horticultural Literature before 1800: Comprising a History and Bibliography of Botanical and Horticultural Books Printed in England, Scotland, and Ireland from the Earliest Times until 1800,* 3 vols., London and New York: Oxford University Press, 1975

Hobhouse, Penelope, *Plants in Garden History,* London: Pavilion Books, 1992; as *Penelope Hobhouse's Gardening through the Ages,* New York: Simon and Schuster, 1992

Hunt, John Dixon, *Gardens and the Picturesque: Studies in the History of Landscape Architecture,* Cambridge, Massachusetts: MIT Press, 1992

Hunt, John Dixon, editor, *Garden History: Issues, Approaches, Methods,* Washington, D.C.: Dumbarton Oaks Research Library and Collection, 1992

Hyams, Edward S., *A History of Gardens and Gardening,* New York: Praeger, and London: Dent, 1971

Jellicoe, Geoffrey, and Susan Jellicoe, *The Landscape of Man: Shaping the Environment from Prehistory to the Present Day,* London: Thames and Hudson, and New York: Viking Press, 1975; 3rd edition, expanded and updated, New York: Thames and Hudson, 1995

King, Ronald, *The Quest for Paradise: A History of the World's Gardens,* Weybridge, Surrey: Whittet/Windward, and New York: Mayflower Books, 1979

Le Dantec, Denise, and Jean-Pierre Le Dantec, *Le roman des jardins de France: Leur histoire,* Paris: Plon, 1987; as *Reading the French Garden: Story and History,* translated by Jessica Levine, Cambridge, Massachusetts: MIT Press, 1990

Mann, William A., *Space and Time in Landscape Architectural History,* Washington, D.C.: Landscape Architecture Foundation, 1981; revised edition, as *Landscape Architecture: An Illustrated History in Timelines, Site Plans, and Biography,* New York and Chichester, West Sussex: Wiley, 1993

Millichap, Gordon T., and J. Gordon Millichap, *The School in a Garden: Foundations and Founders of Landscape Architecture,* Chicago: PNB, 2000

Mosser, Monique, and Georges Teyssot, editors, *L'architettura dei giardini d'Occidente,* Milan: Electa, 1990; as *The Architecture of Western Gardens,* Cambridge, Massachusetts: MIT Press, 1991; as *The History of Garden Design,* London: Thames and Hudson, 1991

Newton, Norman T., *Design on the Land: The Development of Landscape Architecture,* Cambridge, Massachusetts: Harvard University Press, 1971

Nichols, Frederick Doveton, and Ralph E. Griswold, *Thomas Jefferson: Landscape Architect,* Charlottesville: University Press of Virginia, 1978

Ogrin, Dušan, *The World Heritage of Gardens,* London: Thames and Hudson, 1993

Oldham, John, and Ray Oldham, *Gardens in Time,* New York and Sydney: Lansdowne Press, 1980

Ottewill, David, *The Edwardian Garden,* New Haven, Connecticut: Yale University Press, 1989

Pizzoni, Filippo, *Il giardino, arte e storia: Dal Medioevo al Novecento,* Milan: Leonardo Arte, 1997; as *The Garden: A History in Landscape and Art,* translated by Judith Landry, New York: Rizzoli, and London: Aurum Press, 1999

Pregill, Philip, and Nancy Volkman, *Landscapes in History: Design and Planning in the Western Tradition,* New York: Van Nostrand Reinhold, 1993

Punch, Walter T., editor, *Keeping Eden: A History of Gardening in America,* Boston and London: Little Brown, 1992

Thacker, Christopher, *The History of Gardens,* London: Croom Helm, and Berkeley: University of California Press, 1979

Thomas, Graham Stuart, editor, *Recreating the Period Garden,* London: Collins, 1984; Boston: Godine, 1985

Tishler, William H., editor, *American Landscape Architecture: Designers and Places,* Washington, D.C.: Preservation Press, 1989

Tobey, George B., *A History of Landscape Architecture: The Relationship of People to Environment,* New York: American Elsevier, 1973

Vercelloni, Virgilio, *Atlante storico dell'idea del giardino europeo,* Milan: Jaca, 1990; as *European Gardens: An Historical Atlas,* New York: Rizzoli, 1990

Wengel, Tassilo, *Gartenkunst im Spiegel der Zeit,* Leipzig: Edition Leipzig, 1985; as *The Art of Gardening through the Ages,* translated by Leonard Goldman, Leipzig: Edition Leipzig, 1987

**Journals**

*A Bulletin of American Garden History* (1985– )
*Garden History* (1972– )
*The Historical Gardener* (1992–95)
*Journal of Garden History* (1981–97); as *Studies in the History of Gardens and Designed Landscapes* (1998– )

*Journal of the Australian Garden History Society* (1980– )
*Journal of the New England Garden History Society* (1991– )
*Magnolia: Bulletin of the Southern Garden History Society* (1984– )

# A

## Aalto, Alvar 1898–1976

## Finnish Architect and Designer

During Alvar Aalto's 50-year career, his architecture embraced Finnish national romanticism, Nordic classicism, and European modernism before evolving into what is recognized as his uniquely personal mode of expression. Within this evolution his work always exhibited clear organizational strategies, yet revealed a certain roughness, irregularity, and variation in realization. While following a similar organizational pattern in his buildings, he nonetheless managed to create a rich and varied set of spaces and forms.

Unlike his European contemporaries—Le Corbusier, Mies van der Rohe, and Walter Gropius—Aalto tired quickly of modernism's reliance upon industrial processes as the primary source of architectural expression and order. Upon visiting Italy early in his career, he began developing a sensibility to the landscape and the way in which architecture could interact with it. This sensibility influenced his entire corpus of work. The creation of architecture was, in part, for Aalto a dialogue between nature and building that created an interactive, reciprocal response. But unlike his American counterpart Frank Lloyd Wright, he was not seeking to create an architectural metaphor of organic unity with nature. Aalto's interest in nature and the expressive variety inherent in the natural order was intended to result in an architecture embracing a range of spatial and formal variation similar to that found in nature.

For Aalto natural organic life understood through biological processes became a metaphor for his architectural production. This is seen in his writings and witnessed in his work: "Architecture's inner nature is a fluctuation and a development suggestive of natural organic life," Aalto wrote in 1938. Nature was biology for Aalto, and the basic element in creation was the biological cell: the infinite variety of forms and types characterizing nature's diversity evolved from the cell. For Aalto, the cell was a generic module, a small building unit or element, with unlimited capacity for variation and richness in its type, shape, and configuration. Aalto desired to create an architecture that displayed the same infinite variation—that is, to compose an architecture yielding unlimited opportunities for variety in organization, arrangement, and expression.

Aalto achieved this goal at two levels in his work. The first is evident in his design sketches, which capture the essence of Aalto's architectural production at all levels. Aalto's furnishings, paintings, and applied designs exhibit an uncanny resemblance to the formal and spatial configurations found in his buildings. They appear to be small "cells" awaiting full realization in the larger organic whole of a building. The second is found in the design strategy he used in developing his buildings and complexes. This was a simple tactic that over the course of his career yielded, in a manner akin to nature's building up of intricate multi-cellular structures, a rich and varied series of architectural realizations.

In designing a building complex, Aalto often first sought to create a space within nature that would be qualitatively different from the surrounding landscape. This space was often a courtyard or piazza that defined a realm for human action. He would then differentiate the "honorific" activities of the architectural program from the utilitarian ones. Honorific activies are those spaces of particular importance—concert and lecture halls, council chambers, reading rooms, church sanctuaries, and the like—which are articulated using sinuous or curved shapes and positioned as strong architectural forms within the landscape as well as the complex. This strategy, simple though it was, yielded a rich range of architectural results. From Aalto's earliest works—the Seinäjoki Defense Corps Complex (1924) and church competitions from the 1920s—to his later ones—the Säynätsalo Town Hall (1949) (see Plate 1), the National Pensions Institute (1952), and Rovaniemi City Center

1

Complex (1961–85)—this was an ordering sensibility that informed much of his architectural design, irrespective of program or size.

The courtyards or piazzas that Aalto used to order works from dwellings to civic centers not only established place in the Finnish forest but provided a setting for communal activity, whether familial or public. Moreover, it is akin to a mnemonic device, recalling the exterior courtyards around which Finnish farm complexes and city houses were traditionally organized. Rooting his buildings to their sites as well as to cultural traditions, Aalto's domestic and civic courtyards are grass surfaced, continuing the evocation of the grass courts in traditional Finnish dwellings. The organization of Aalto's house, the Villa Mairea, and his office and studio, as well as that of the Säynätsalo Town Hall, the Seinäjoki Civic Center, and the Rovaniemi City Center bear witness to the diverse realizations this strategy embraced.

The jutting and ragged profiles produced by the volumetric massing of Aalto's buildings achieves a picturesque composition that is both irregular and asymmetrical. Important rooms are articulated through unique shaping in plan, section, and volume, and they stand unsuppressed within the common, ordinary order accorded the remaining spaces. That Aalto uses figural or undulating forms and shapes to signify these important rooms reinforces their prominence and position in his compositions. Again, the Säynätsalo Town Hall, the Seinäjoki Civic Center, the Main Building at the Technical University, and Finlandia Hall of 1967–71, as well as his residential work demonstrate this quality.

In contrast to the conventional wisdom of modernist architectural thought, Aalto used a substantial and varied number of materials and textures in his buildings. Through this range of materials he made use of both a material's associative value and its corporeal nature (a material has specific properties that can be treated or displayed in certain ways). For Aalto, the selection of building materials was as much for propriety (that is, to convey essential knowledge about the structure's task and purpose) as it is for sensory, experiential qualities. Coupled with this characteristic use of materials is the presence of planting on the surfaces and within the structure of his buildings. It appears as if Aalto was considering the impact of aging and time upon his works. Nature is allowed to engage the built form, a reminder that is always present to reclaim our works if we are careless in our stewardship of the environment.

The courtyard, the differentiation of honorific from utilitarian spaces, the use of multiple textures and materials, the introduction of planting into the architectural scheme, and the creation of undulating surfaces and forms are all hallmarks of Aalto's mature style. These are often made manifest in his lyrical, sensuous design drawings. The painterly lines of these drawings, which poignantly record his process of generating space and form, expressively describe the emergent, sinuously shaped spaces and forms of his buildings, their courtyards and interior spaces. His sketches further incorporate images of landscape and planting, showing building and nature interacting at the inception of the design. Marked by a rich and complex architectural language that explored the full range of expressive means available to the architect, Aalto's was an architecture that was extremely humane yet profoundly tangible.

## Biography
Born in Kourtane, near Jyväskylä, Finland, 3 February 1898. Studied architecture at Helsinki Polytechnic, 1916–21; worked in Göteborg, Sweden, and in Tampere and Turku, Finland, before starting his own architectural practice in Jyväskylä, 1923–27; Turku, 1927–33, and Helsinki, 1933–76; worked in partnership with wife (m. 1924; d. 1949), architect and designer Aino (Marsio) Aalto, 1924–49; in partnership with wife (m. 1952; d. 1994), architect and designer Elissa (Mäkiniemi) Aalto, 1952–76; designed furniture and applied designs from ca. 1920; founded ARTEK to mass produce furniture and textile designs, 1935; professor, Department of Architecture, Massachusetts Institute of Technology, Cambridge, 1940 and 1946–47; member, Academy of Finland, 1955; honorary member, Akademie der Künste, Berlin; honorary fellow, 1958, and Gold Medal, 1963, American Institute of Architects; Gold Medal, Royal Institute of British Architects, 1957. Died in Helsinki, 11 May 1976.

## Selected Designs
A vast collection of original drawings, designs, correspondence, cuttings, and models is contained in the Alvar Aalto Archive, Alvar Aalto Foundation, Munkkiniemi. Additional materials are in the Alvar Aalto Museum, Jyväskylä, the Finnish Museum of Architecture, and the Finnish Museum of Applied Arts, Helsinki. For a guide to other collections, see Weston. A complete catalog of Aalto's architectural and design work appears in Schildt (1994).

| | |
|---|---|
| 1924–29 | Defense Corps Building, Seinäjoki, Finland |
| 1926–28 | South-Western Agricultural Co-operative Building and Theater, Turku, Finland |
| 1929 | 700th Anniversary Exhibition (with Erik Bryggman), Turku |
| 1929–33 | Tuberculosis Sanatorium, Paimio, Finland |
| 1933–35 | Library, Viipuri, Finland |
| 1934–35 | Aalto house and studio, Munkkiniemi, Finland |
| 1936–37 | Pulp Mill, Sunila, Finland |
| 1937 | Finnish Pavilion, World's Fair, Paris, France |

| | |
|---|---|
| 1938–39 | Finnish Pavilion, World's Fair, New York, United States |
| 1938–41 | Villa Mairea, Noormarkku, Finland |
| 1947–48 | Baker House Dormitory, Massachusetts Institute of Technology, Cambridge, Massachusetts, United States |
| 1949–52 | Town Hall, Säynätsalo, Finland |
| 1952–55 | Rautatalo office building, Helsinki, Finland |
| 1952–56 | National Pensions Institute, Helsinki, Finland |
| 1952–57 | Pedagogical University (now Jyväskylä University), Jyväskylä, Finland |
| 1953 | Aalto summer house, Muuratsalo, Finland |
| 1955–56 | Aalto office and studio, Munkkiniemi, Finland |
| 1955–66 | Main building, Technical Institute, Otaniemi, Finland |
| 1957–59 | Vuoksenniska Church, Imatra, Finland |
| 1958 | House of Culture, Helsinki, Finland |
| 1958–66 | Cross of the Plains Church and parish center, Seinäjoki, Finland |
| 1959–62 | Enso-Gutzeit Headquarters, Helsinki, Finland |
| 1960–63 | Cultural Center, Wolfsburg, Germany |
| 1961–65 | Town Hall and Library, Seinäjoki, Finland |
| 1961–85 | Rovaniemi City Center Complex, Rovaniemi, Finland |
| 1964–69 | Library, Technical Institute, Otaniemi, Finland |
| 1965–70 | Library, Mount Angel Benedictine College, Mount Angel, Oregon, United States |
| 1966–69 | Academic Bookstore, Helsinki, Finland |
| 1966–76 | Parish Church, Riola, Italy |
| 1967–71 | Finlandia Hall, Helsinki, Finland |
| 1971 | Alvar Aalto Museum, Jyväskylä, Finland |

**Selected Publications**

*Post-War Reconstruction: Rehousing Research in Finland,* 1940

"The Humanizing of Architecture," *Technology Review* (November 1940)

"The Trout and the Mountain Stream," *Arkkitehti* no. 1–2(1948)

*Alvar Aalto in His Own Words,* edited and annotated by Göran Schildt, 1997

**Further Reading**

Aalto, Alvar, *Viiva: Originaalpiirustuksia Alvar Aatto arkistosta; Linjen: Originalritningar ur Alvar Aalto arkiv; The Line: Original Drawings from the Alvar Aalto Archive* (bilingual Finnish-Swedish-English edition), Helsinki: Suomen Rakennustaiteen Museo, 1993

Aalto, Alvar, *The Architectural Drawings of Alvar Aalto, 1917–1939,* 11 vols., New York and London: Garland, 1994

*Alvar Aalto,* London: Academy Editions, 1978; New York: Rizzoli, 1979

*Alvar Aalto Houses: Timeless Expressions,* Tokyo: A + U, 1998

*Alvar Aalto in Seven Buildings: Interpretations of an Architect's Work,* Helsinki: Museum of Finnish Architecture, 1998

Fleig, Karl, editor, *Alvar Aalto: The Complete Works,* 3 vols., Zurich: Artemis, 1990

Futagawa, Yukio, editor, *Villa Mairea, Noormarkku, Finland 1937–1939,* Tokyo: A.D.A. Edita, 1985

Mendini, Alessandro, "L'opera di Alvar Aalto," *Casabella* 299 (November 1965)

Miller, William C., *Alvar Aalto: An Annotated Bibliography,* New York: Garland, 1984

Pallasmaa, Juhani, editor, *Alvar Aalto: Villa Mairea,* Helsinki: Alvar Aalto Foundation and Mairea Foundation, 1998

Pearson, Paul David, *Alvar Aalto and the International Style,* New York: Whitney Library of Design, 1978

Quantrill, Malcolm, *Alvar Aalto: A Critical Study,* London: Secker and Warburg, 1983

Reed, Peter, editor, *Alvar Aalto: Between Humanism and Materialism,* New York: Museum of Modern Art, 1998

Ruusuvuori, Aarno, editor, *Alvar Aalto, 1898–1976,* Helsinki: Museum of Finnish Architecture, 1978

Schildt, Göran, *Alvar Aalto: The Early Years,* New York: Rizzoli, 1984

Schildt, Göran, *Alvar Aalto: The Decisive Years,* New York: Rizzoli, 1986

Schildt, Göran, *Alvar Aalto: The Mature Years,* New York: Rizzoli, 1991

Schildt, Göran, *Alvar Aalto: The Complete Catalogue of Architecture, Design, and Art,* New York: Rizzoli, 1994

Schildt, Göran, *Alvar Aalto: Masterworks,* New York: Universe, and London: Thames and Hudson, 1998

Trencher, Michael, *The Alvar Aalto Guide,* New York: Princeton Architectural Press, 1996

Weston, Richard, *Alvar Aalto,* London: Phaidon, 1995

WILLIAM C. MILLER

# Abelin, Carl Rudolf Zacharias 1864–1961

## Swedish Gardener, Garden Designer, and Pomologist

Rudolf Abelin's achievement in Swedish parks and gardens for half a century, from the 1890s to 1941, rested on the maxim he learned from Erik Schwartz, the squire of Stenkullen: "Nature is the Mother of Art." Abelin wrote in 1921, "However chiseled and artistic landscape gardening is, to me it is a completely dead entity unless the sound elements of nature itself is woven into it."

Abelin became one of Sweden's most prominent ambassadors for the classic values and expressions of gardens, while at the same time he was modern and progressive. His ambitions were high: to educate, to elevate, to reform, and by those means, to create comfort and well-being. He committed himself to the benefits and the economically profitable production of gardens—horticulture—as well as to their aesthetic organization and arrangements through landscape gardening. He pursued his mission with great zeal by writing books, giving lectures, teaching at schools of horticulture and gardening, and giving advice on gardening, as well as through his own garden design. His resourceful interpretative and consultative work can be found in some 35 grounds in Sweden, mostly country estates and large private houses. The real number, however, is probably considerably higher.

Abelin's importance in the history of gardening in Sweden is manifold. He modernized Swedish fruit and nut growing in terms of variety as well as cultivation and economy. He won numerous prizes (including the gold medal at the World Exhibition in Paris and major distinctions at the Scandinavian Exhibition in Copenhagen). He cultivated more than 5,000 fruit trees of several hundred different varieties and even more large hazelnut bushes at his estate, Norrviken. He reformed horticultural instruction, started a horticultural school for female students at Björnviken, developed the horticultural school at Adelsnäs (Östergötland), and founded a new horticultural school at Norrviken. In his writings he argued for the importance of the kitchen garden in the national economy and for "the rebirth and rational maintenance of the country estate." Together with Anna Lindhagen, Abelin was one of the leading advocates of allotment gardens in Sweden.

The name of Rudolf Abelin is inseparably associated with Norrviken, the estate he acquired in 1906 in the northwestern part of the province of Skåne near Båstad, by the sea, to which he devoted all his time until it was sold in 1941. Norrviken became Abelin's primary mission in life, and these grounds illustrate Abelin's entire horticultural achievement. Here, he emphasized the importance of fruit and nut growing from an economic point of view and also carried out experiments on the control of fungus diseases and insects, as well as experiments with pruning and hardiness.

At Norrviken Abelin aimed aesthetically to create a field for object lessons, "where the visitor could get the most widely differing ideas and see the effects of them in the field." Abelin hoped that Norrviken would bring back the larger perspectives, the volume of leaves, and the outlines of the ground in landscaping that had been ignored in favor of what he saw as an overemphasis on details, especially flowers and flower beds. Terraces and parterres took precedence, but Abelin created them to be more open and to have an obvious and well-arranged outline. Everything would merge in the crucible of the new Norrviken.

The front garden of Norrviken became a French palace garden with a large pool and a mile-long (1.6-km) perspective. The opposite side of the manor, which was surrounded by medieval-style buildings on three sides, was continued by a Renaissance garden with box hedges more than a mile-and-a-half (2.4 km) long. The perspective continued infinitely across the Kattegat shoreline, fading into blue. Abelin laid out a free natural garden at right angles to the north, in a Japanese style; in the opposite facade was a half-English, half-Italian rose and rhododendron parterre with avenues of yew trees arranged in columns and a perspective toward the ridge in the south. This part, with its niched wall, water cascades, and gates, constituted the entrance to the large natural park, which demonstrated new possibilities in dimensions, terrain, and vistas. At the entrance, in "The Valley of Death," was the cemetery, which was meant to give peace and confidence, accompanied by the murmur of the brook and bird song and away from artificiality and banalities. A smaller swamp and rock garden were also laid out, as well as a small oriental garden. Pedagogically, Abelin aimed to make Norrviken useful in the area of education and in the training of country estate gardeners.

Abelin dedicated his life's work to landscape gardening at a time when the older traditions in Sweden, primarily from country estate gardens, had not been maintained and when there was a decided lack of skilled professional gardeners. As such, he became pioneer and innovator, greatly influencing Swedish garden culture during his lifetime. At the time of his death, at the age of 97, most people had forgotten Abelin, but he was appreciated and devotedly beloved by a small circle of friends.

Pool at Norrviken, Skåne, Sweden
Courtesy of Byggförlaget

## Biography

Born in Malmö, Sweden, 30 May 1864, only son of
Gustaf Rudolf Abelin, general, minister of war, and
commander in chief. Spent childhood in Stockholm;
moved to Bjärka-Säby manor (Östergötland), 1872;
moved to Norsholm and Björnsnäs, 1878, by Bråviken
Bay in the Baltic; seriously interested in gardening from
youth; studied law at Uppsala University; contracted
incurable eye disease and went to clinic in Copenhagen;
several trips to Europe (Italy); graduated as gardener
from Rosenborg Have, Copenhagen, 1888; moved back
to Björnsnäs and took over father's tenancy, including
all kinds of practical garden work; came to Adelsnäs
School of Gardening, 1901 (Östergötland), as
superintendent, by invitation of Baron Theodor
Adelswärd; published approximately ten books on
gardening, 1900–1915, several published in later
revised editions; bought Norrviken, Båstad, 1906, along

the Kattegat shoreline, Norrviken opened to public,
1920, and sold, 1941; started gardening school. Died at
Norrviken, 2 January 1961.

## Selected Designs

| | |
|---|---|
| 1890s | Björnsnäs, Östergötland, Sweden |
| 1903 | Löfstad, Östergötland, Sweden |
| 1904–5 | Rockelstad, Sörmland, Sweden |
| 1906–41 | Norrvikens trädgårdar, Skåne, Sweden |
| 1920s | Adelsnäs, Östergötland, Sweden; Bjärka-Säby, Östergötland, Sweden |

## Selected Publications

editor, *Trädgårdsskötseln: Tidskrift för trädgårdsodling
och dess bigrenar*, 1895–96
*Fruktodlingsfrågan 1899: Återblick, önskemål*, 1900
*Om frukt och fruktträdsodling: En handbok för
Sveriges fruktodlare*, 1901; 2nd edition, 1906

NORRVIKEN.

Plan of Norrviken, 1920–30, Skåne, Sweden
Courtesy of Byggförlaget

*Den mindre trädgården: En bok för täppan och torpet*,
  1902; 8th edition, 1932
*Villaträdgården: En bok för sommarställen och
  stadsgårdar*, 1903; 2nd edition, 1915
*Trädgården inomhus, i krukor och jord, i glas och
  vatten: En bok för kvinnan och hemmet*, 1904; 4th
  edition, 1933
*Lekstugans trädgård: En sommarbok för ungdom och
  smått folk*, 1906
*Koloniträdgården: En bok för stadsbor och
  industrisamhällen*, 1907
*Herrgårdsträdgården: En principbok om och för de
  större trädgårdarne på landet*, 1915

"Norrviken," *Lustgården* (1922)
editor, *Föreningen Norrvikens trädgårdar*,
  1924

**Further Reading**

Waern, Kolbjörn, "Rudolf Abelin (1864–1961),"
  in *Svensk trädgårdskonst under fyrahundra år*,
  edited by Thorbjörn Andersson, Tove Jonstoij,
  and Kjell Lundquist, Stockholm: Byggförlaget,
  2000

KJELL LUNDQUIST

# Adam, William 1689–1748

## Scottish Architect and Landscape Designer

William Adam was descended on his father's side
from a line of minor Scottish aristocrats, or lairds, holding estates near Forfar, in Angus. His wife's father, Lord
Cranstoun, had been a judge. William's own father, the
second son in the family, had taken up the business of a
mason. He settled at Linktown of Abbotshall beside
Kirkcaldy, Fifeshire. Here he seems to have continued

trade involving building work and acting as a local
builder-architect on a small scale.

Adam himself is thought to have attended the Kirkcaldy Grammar School, which, contemporary records
suggest, maintained high academic standards. He
apparently left there in 1704 at the age of 15 and completed his indentures in the masonry trade. He then

undertook a tour of the Low Countries, during which he showed great interest in construction and engineering. He returned to Scotland with ideas for setting up a tile works to manufacture pantiles. He had also investigated the locks on the Ostend-Bruges Canal with a view to copying them in Scotland and brought home, among other things, a model of a barley mill. Although he is primarily known as an architect, his interest in these other areas marks him as one who would become a significant entrepreneur in addition to his other activities.

In 1714 he went into partnership with William Robertson, whose daughter Mary he was to marry two years later. The partnership continued until 1728, when his father-in-law died, and the Adams moved to Edinburgh. By this time Adam's own architectural expertise had become well recognized throughout the country among the aristocracy and gentry. In the majority of cases his landscape work followed his commissions for buildings, and it is the latter that survive in any recognizable form and for which he is most generally known. His *Vitruvius Scoticus*, a collection of architectural drawings, features his own work prominently. The idea for the book came to Adam in 1726, and by 1727 subscriptions were being sought. Although the single sheets of drawings that were to make up the book were being drawn and engraved in the 1730s, and many of the individual sheets were printed in the 1740s, the volume was not published until 1812.

Adam's first major architectural commission was in 1721 at Floors Castle for the Duke of Roxburghe. This great house, the basic structure of which exists to this day, though castellations were added to the elevation in the late 19th century, was intended to be the centerpiece of a new landscape park. There is, however, no evidence of Adam's involvement in designing the latter. In the same year, he was called to Hopetoun House, where he carried out additions to and remodelling of the building and continued by producing plans for the gardens and park. These were in the formal style and included, for example, an extensive and elaborate parterre in front of the house. Although almost all of his work continued predominantly in the formal style, he is credited with introducing elements of the informal—perhaps where his clients were amenable—and certainly with advocating the adoption of a style that by the time of his death was establishing a firm hold further south in England. As early as 1720 he sketched out a serpentine riverside walk. This was in his plans for Taymouth Castle, at the eastern end of Loch Tay in Perthshire, where he had been commissioned by Lord Breadalbane to design and build some pavilions (dismantled in the same century). His landscape work, though considered rather heavy handed, was more lasting, consisting of, in addition to a parterre garden, extensive avenues north and south and rides at 45 degrees marked out by a series of woodland blocks. The castle itself was sited in a bow of the river,

and it was along its meandering bank that a serpentine walk was incorporated into the design. The plan, attributed to Adam and dated to approximately 1720, also shows irregular blocks of woodland laid out between the avenues and rides. This plan is evidence that where his client's taste would accept it, he would introduce a softening of the formal baroque style in which he had been brought up. Another much later illustration of his leaning toward the more informal landscape style is found in the work he undertook for the duke of Hamilton at Hamilton Palace in Lanarkshire, Scotland. The estate had been laid out at the beginning of the century, and Adam was employed to design grand staterooms for the palace. At the same time he undertook the design of a great parterre. In the context of the overall geometry of the estate layout, he placed the dog kennels—a flamboyant range of buildings given the grand name of Chatelherault and including such features as a dining room for the duke—on the rim of a precipice, affording a view that was a dramatic departure from the ordered landscape of the park. This innovation seems to have met with the full approval of his client.

A great deal of the difficulty of assessing Adam's contribution to landscape design results from the lack of remaining evidence of his landscape work, particularly on the ground. His status as an architect has long been debated, and until fairly recently he was dismissed as merely the father of his three well-known architect sons, especially the brilliant Robert. In the last 20 or so years, however, his work has been reassessed as a result of the reprinting of *Vitruvius Scoticus* and in the light of the many buildings he completed that are still standing, though in some cases—Floors Castle, for example—altered and enhanced. Appreciation of his landscape work must depend on a few plans, some notes, and in some instances the outline of former designs revealed through aerial photography. At Newliston (1725), where no house existed before that built by Robert Adam in 1792, and Castle Kennedy, where the garden was laid out around the ruins of the castle, formal gardens were created for the earl of Stair for their own value. At Buchanan (ca. 1725) in Stirlingshire, for the duke of Montrose, he produced a plan that is rigidly geometrical but bounded on the west by a meandering river and featuring serpentine woodland walks, a plan whose form seems, despite its formality, to respond to the landscape in which it was set.

## Biography

Born and baptised in Abbotshall, near Kirkcaldy, 24 October 1689. Father John a stone mason builder, mother daughter of Session Court judge; brought up to follow father in business and did so after travels in Holland; on death of father, set up partnership with William Robertson, adding manufacture of bricks and tiles to masonry work; responsible for introducing manufacture of Dutch pantiles to Scotland, one of several continental processes and ideas he is credited with importing; began designing buildings approximately 1720; designs for Floors Castle, 1721; principally remembered as architect, also entrepreneur and landscape gardener; sons John, Robert, and James all highly distinguished architects. Died in Edinburgh, Scotland, 1748.

### Selected Designs

| | |
|---|---|
| 1720 | Taymouth, Perthshire, Scotland |
| ca. 1726 | Arniston House, Midlothian, Scotland |
| ca. 1730 | Castle Kennedy, Wigtownshire, Scotland; Culhorn, Wigtownshire, Scotland |
| ca. 1731 | Newliston, West Lothian, Scotland |
| 1735 | Hamilton House, Hamilton, Lanarkshire, Scotland; Chatelherault, Lanarkshire, Scotland |
| 1742 | Cally, Kirkcudbrightshire, Scotland |
| 1745 | Buchannan House, Stirlingshire, Scotland |

### Selected Publications
*Vitruvius Scoticus,* 1812

### Further Reading

Gifford, John, *William Adam, 1689–1748: A Life and Times of Scotland's Universal Architecht*, Edinburgh: Mainstream, 1989

Howard, Deborah, editor, *William Adam*, Scotland: Edinburgh University Press, 1990

Tait, A.A., *The Landscape Garden in Scotland, 1735–1835*, Edinburgh: Edinburgh University Press, 1980

M.F. DOWNING

# Addison, Joseph 1672–1719

## English Writer and Statesman

Joseph Addison is probably best known as a writer and statesman. He held such positions as secretary to the lord lieutenant of Ireland and was elected a member of Parliament. In addition, however, he exerted great influence on British gardeners through his essays on landscape gardening published in the *Spectator*, although he does not appear to have had much practical interest in horticulture. In 1712 he bought Bilton Hall near Rugby with its 1,000-acre (405-ha) estate more as an attestation of his status as a writer (he was cofounder of the *Spectator*) and a statesman than through any great love of gardening. Buying a country estate to escape politics and London during the summer, as well as to prepare for retirement, was the accepted thing to do in his circle.

Addison also had a general love of nature despite being extremely derisive of those people who got too involved in the minutiae of, for example, butterfly collecting. Although few books about natural history were available at the time, he read as extensively as he could and attempted to place humankind within the idea of the natural system. He placed the study of nature above that of metaphysics and speculated on the relationship between nature and religion.

The eldest son of a country parson, Addison excelled at school and went to Queen's College, Oxford, at age 15. His classical scholarship, especially his knowledge of Latin poetry, attracted notice, and he became a fellow in 1698. He was highly thought of by his contemporaries, including Jonathon Swift. He acquired a pension of 300£ per year in 1698, which allowed him to travel throughout Europe. After more than a year in France, spent perfecting the language, he traveled to Italy and then to Switzerland, Austria, Germany, and Holland before returning to England after hearing of his father's death.

After Addison had begun planting and laying out his garden on his estate at Bilton Hall for the first time in 1712, he wrote as the "Humorist in Gardening" in the *Spectator*. Gardeners at this time followed the practices of the French landscape gardener André Le Nôtre. Addison, however, preferred the "carefully studied negligence of Fontainebleau to the formalism of Versailles." He was the first English writer to publicly disapprove of Le Nôtre's formal style when he condemned the prevailing horticultural fads in the *Spectator*. He was also unimpressed by Italian gardens. In particular he was scathing of the excesses of topiary: "Our British Gardeners . . . Instead of humouring Nature, love to deviate from it as much as possible. Our trees rise in Cones, Globes and Pyramids. We see the Marks of the Scissors upon every Plant and Bush" (*Spectator*, 1712).

Addison knew that he was at odds with prevailing fashions and opined that there were as "many kinds of Gardening as of Poetry." He was also one of the first, albeit minor, exponents of the school of gardening that produced the grotto, the wild garden, the water garden, and the rockery: "I have several Acres about my House, which I call my Garden, and which a Skillful Gardener would not know what to call. It is a Confusion of Kitchen and Parterre, Orchard and Flower Garden, . . . a natural Wilderness, and one of the uncultivated Parts of our Country"(*Spectator,* 1712). Addison's garden was also bird friendly. He had a lifelong affection for birds and valued his garden more for being full of blackbirds than of cherries; one part of his garden contained a wooden summerhouse so that he could sit and enjoy the bird songs. Not everyone heeded Addison's condemnation of formal gardens, as Canons, in Middlesex, probably the most ornamented of all English formal gardens, was not started until 1713.

Addison planted *Taxus* in his garden in what became known as the Bilton Taxodium. An exceedingly rare tree in England at the time, its seeds were probably sent by a friend in America. He also planted *Taxus* hedges. In addition, he grew a number of *Ilex,* from seeds brought back by a friend from Spain, which were among the first to be established in England.

Addison's writings marked the start of an English informal landscape style that within the next half century had crossed to mainland Europe as the popular *jardin anglais.*

## Biography

Born in Milston, Wiltshire, England, 1672. Studied at Oxford University, 1687; gained reputation as classicist and poet; fellow of Oxford, 1698; embarked on grand tour, 1699; returned to England, 1703, on death of father; continued as writer and poet while embarking on career in politics; bought estate of Bilton Hall, Warwickshire, England, 1712; among first to plant *Taxus* and *Ilex* in England, seeds of which he was sent by friends. Died in London, 1719.

## Selected Designs

1712    Garden, Bilton Hall, Bilton, Warwickshire, England

## Selected Publications

*Remarks on Several Parts of Italy in the Years 1701, 1702, 1703, 1705;* 2nd edition, 1718

[essays], *Spectator* (1711–12) (as the "Humorist in Gardening")

"On the Pleasures of the Imagination," *Spectator* no. 414 (1712)

## Further Reading

"Addison, Joseph," in *Dictionary of National Biography,* edited by Leslie Stephen and Sidney Lee, vol. 1, London, 1885; reprint, Oxford: Oxford University Press, 1973

Batey, Mavis, "The Magdalen Meadows and the Pleasures of Imagination," *Garden History* 9, no. 2 (1981)

Hadfield, Miles, Robert Harling, and Leonie Highton, *British Gardeners: A Biographical Dictionary,* London: Zwemmer, 1980

Leatherbarrow, David, "Character, Geometry, and Perspective: The Third Earl of Shaftesbury's Principles of Garden Design," *Journal of Garden History* 4, no. 4 (1984)

Nelson, E. Charles, and Eileen M. McCracken, *The Brightest Jewel: A History of the National Botanic Gardens, Glasnevin, Dublin,* Kilkenny, Ireland: Boethius Press, 1987

Smithers, Peter, *The Life of Joseph Addison,* Oxford: Clarendon Press, 1954; 2nd edition, 1968

JANE HUTCHEON

---

# Adriana, Villa

## Tivoli, Lazio, Italy

**Location:**   approximately 15 miles (24 km) east-northeast of Rome, and 1 mile (1.6 km) southwest of Tivoli

When, in the middle of the 16th century, Pirro Ligorio, Ippolito d'Este's architect, was sent to survey and excavate Villa Adriana, an imperial residence that occupied 500 acres (202 ha) of a hilly countryside, the majesty and the beauty of the ruins duly impressed him. He described them in a manuscript titled *Descrittione della superba et magnificentissima Villa Hadriana* (Description of the Superb and Very Magnificent Villa of Hadrian), in which he wrote that in its borders were 90 "Piazzas." This may have been an overstatement as recent research has found 45, and almost all were gardens. Villa Adriana, or Hadrian's Villa, the largest and most elaborate architecture that spotted the Roman countryside from the late Republic to late antiquity, represents Roman architecture at its creative best.

The Emperor Hadrian erected an ensemble of monuments between A.D. 118 and 138 on land lying between two valleys, and facing south and west. In size and splendor his villa resembled a small town rather than a palace. Unfortunately, robbery and misuse of the villa's ornaments and statuary likely began not long after Hadrian's death in 138 A.D. During the Middle Ages, the complex suffered more neglect and abuse, its building materials and marbles carted off to nearby sites for reuse or burnt for lime. Between its "rediscovery" in 1461 by Pope Pius II and the humanist Flavio Biondo and the first scientific, comprehensive plan drawn up almost two hundred years later in 1668 by Francesco Contini, the villa served along with other Roman antiquities as a source of inspiration for a multitude of Renaissance artists and architects, including Francesco di Giorgio, Donato Bramante, Andrea Palladio, Philibert Delorme, and Pirro Ligorio. Descriptions and comprehensive site plans of the villa in print, however, did not appear until the mid-17th century. The villa was a curiosity and not a reliable model of antiquity. Architects of the 17th century, who must have found much that was exciting in the villa's novel forms, used the plans as inspiration and a sort of artistic justification for their own highly creative work. After the unification of Italy in 1870, the Italian government purchased the villa, and the destruction of the villa was arrested.

Gardening in Hadrian's Villa was not an easy task. The villa was built on a tufa platform, and large holes and trenches had to be cut in the rock to plant trees and shrubs. It included peristyle gardens, terraced gardens, and even a garden shaped like a stadium, the last craze of the time. They were mostly green gardens surrounded by flower beds bordered by long rows of box hedges or framed by lines of low, well-groomed trees, pruned in the shapes of the most fashionable topiary. Water made the gardens special: lying in basins, moving slowly in canals, sliding as a mobile silvery veil on the marble steps of the typical Roman waterfalls, or sprinkling from small fountains to refresh the air. The amount of water throughout the gardens and the spectacular ways it was used were unique for the times.

The Pecile, measuring 233 meters by 133 meters (255 yd. by 146 yd.), is one of the largest gardens in the villa. A long wall, around which once ran the double portico used by the emperor for his daily exercise, limits its north side. On the south and west sides, a high terrace dominates the plain below, with Rome seen in the distance. The most striking feature of the Pecile is the large pond that occupies its center, a deep basin 117 meters (128 yd.) long and 33 meters (36 yd.) wide.

The Canopus is considered the most impressive of Hadrian's gardens. In ancient time the Canopus was the first glimpse important visitors and guests coming from Rome saw of Hadrian's Villa. It occupied the whole area of a narrow valley set at the south side of the villa's principal entry. A huge canal ran along all the length of the dell. Columns and white marble statues reflected in its blue water, and two statuary groups, both representing Scylla in the act of killing Ulysses's mates, emerged from the canal. A portico ran along one of its banks, and the garden framed the canal with its well-cut hedges of box tree, while high terraces rose at its two sides scaling the surrounding hills. Completing the landscape was a monumental exedra, set at the end of the valley, with numerous marble and colorful mosaics. Its niches contained imposing statues and large waterfalls; at the end of a central deep gallery, a powerful cascade fed the outlying waterway.

Nearby, in a small peristyle garden, a path with a ring-shaped space in the middle—probably to display a marble sculpture—divided two flower beds cut in the tufa. In this villa tests on ancient pollens did not produce results to clearly identify the plant materials; however, studies at Pompeii and the writings of Pliny the Elder suggest possible plantings. The Roman garden was essentially a green garden. Few flowers were used (primarily roses and violets). It was not at all unusual in antiquity to give the same name to entirely different plants. Pliny mentions many kinds of violets, including "the purple, white and yellow."

Not far from the small peristyle garden was a garden shaped like a stadium. On one end was the hemicycle, usually occupied by the public, represented here by a splendid *nymphaeum,* eight small waterfalls flowed over white marble steps; hedges of box trees, neatly cut and set in big mortar containers, took the place of the spectators' seats. At the bottom, in a small grotto, a fountain collected the falling water, which emptied into a semicircular basin. Two tricliniar pavilions set on both sides of a square "piazza" occupied the central part of the garden, while at the other end a small canal flanked by two flower beds reflected the encircling architecture.

The Palace Nymphaeum was a garden shaped like an auditorium. A monumental apsidal entry hall led the way to a large paved area. A hemicycle concluded the arrangement and rose to meet the higher grounds at its back. The decoration was the same as the Stadium Garden: waterfalls on white marble steps and hedges of box trees set in big mortar containers. Water flowed down from a cistern set on the roof of an adjoining building and was collected in a large basin. Two oval flower beds—or basins—in the middle of the paved courtyard gave a touch of color to this open space.

Set on the usual platform of tufa, the Piazza d'Oro Garden was bordered by a double line of deep holes in which trees were planted. Romans used cypresses, plane trees, pine trees, pomegranates, oleanders, laurels, and at the end of the Republic, even lemon trees in their gardens. Laurels, which grow well in the area, were likely used here. Flowering shrubs and perhaps Pliny's violets set in decorative designs were grown in the central part of the garden. In the middle of the area, a beautiful white marble canal was set between the entrance hall on one side and the tricliniar pavilion with all its fountains on the other. In ancient times the reflection of the encircling buildings with their gleaming walls in its water must have been similar to the celebrated view of the Taj Mahal gardens at Agra.

A particularly distinctive canal crossed the Libraries' Garden, on a large terrace: a low strip of water that at its two ends was concluded by two large octagons, in the centers of which two flower beds emerged from the water, producing a pleasant and original effect. The platform stood on a sustaining wall, two meters high and more than one hundred meters long (109 yd.), decorated with 25 niches that in ancient times likely held as many statues. The Libraries' Garden overlooked an ample stretch of land that was probably kept as a park. On the opposite side two paths bordering an ancient nympheum connected the Libraries' Garden with the Libraries' Courtyard, a large and traditional peristyle garden dating back to the Republican period. The buildings of the libraries were thus immersed in lush vegetation and open-air arrangements.

The so-called Throne Hall Garden was not a throne hall at all. Current excavation has revealed that it contained two flower beds, divided by a central alley, a large path leading to a podium set in an ample apse. A series of niches lined by chunks of pumice, tinged with green and bluish hues to imitate the grottoes' rocky walls, decorated this hemicycle. The arrangement was evidently created to expose some particularly beautiful piece of sculpture in a garden setting. The flower beds, excavated in the tufa platform, had a simple square shape, but a curved edge may have accompanied the contour of the apse. During recent excavation a small flowerpot was found in the northern flower bed; its size and shape reveal it to have contained some plant of the kind called a viola by Pliny. Thus the flower beds must have been colorful and cheerful.

The Inferi Garden, on the other hand, could never have been described as cheerful. Hadrian probably created it as a memento of the Eleusinian mysteries, a religion connected with death and resurrection to which he had been initiated. One of the important landmarks of this cult was the so-called Plutonium Grotto, a cavity representing the chasm leading to the dark recesses of Pluto's kingdom. The garden consisted of a narrow vale going deep into the ground, leading the way to a small, dark, and ominous cave that had the same dimension as the one at Eleusis. Referring to this garden when listing all the marvels of Hadrian's residence, the historian Spartianus wrote, "and in order not to omit anything, he even made a Hades."

Hadrian's Villa also included elegant pavilions and exedras where one could pause and take a rest, read, or converse. These types of structures, as important for vast imperial gardens as flowering shrubs and flower beds were for smaller ones, are found in all the lavish residences of ancient Rome. The Belvedere of the Venus of Cnidus at Hadrian's Villa is one of the most charming. It was located on a hillock overlooking the so-called Valley of Tempe. Two large exedras were placed on one of its sides. A round temple sheltering a copy of the *Venus of Cnidus* by Praxiteles stood in its center, and from it, the view ranged over Tivoli and the Apennines in the background.

Hadrian's Villa contained numerous gardens, of which many remain to be studied. The few that have been examined provide an idea of the magnificence of the place and unveil the enormous influence that Hadrian's Villa had on Renaissance gardens. By the end of the 16th century, many gardens were planned by architects impressed by the majestic green gardens and unforgettable water display of the Villa d'Este, which Ligorio created after his survey of Hadrian's Tivoli residence and its waterworks. As a result all the princely residences of the end of the Renaissance and of the baroque period were surrounded by parks with thickets of high trees, box hedges, and above all, as in Tivoli, on a multitude of basins, canals, fountains, and roaring waterfalls.

## Synopsis

A.D. 118–38    Gardens created by Roman emperor Hadrian

mid-16th C.    Site surveyed by Pirro Ligorio, garden designer and architect to Ippolito II, Cardinal d'Este

## Further Reading

Jashemski, Wilhelmina F., and Eugenia Salza Prina Ricotti, "Preliminary Excavations in the Gardens of Hadrian's Villa: The Canopus Area and the Piazza d'Oro," *American Journal of Archaeology* 96, no. 4 (1992)

MacDonald, William Lloyd, and John A. Pinto, *Hadrian's Villa and Its Legacy*, New Haven, Connecticut: Yale University Press, 1995

Pinto, J., "Patoral Landscape and Antiquity: Hadrian's Villa," *Studies in the History of Art*, 36 (1992)

Salza Prina Ricotti, Eugenia, *Villa Adriana, il sogno di un imperatore*, Rome: Bretschneiders, 2001

EUGENIA SALZA PRINA RICOTTI

# Africa

Africa is the second-largest continent, embracing one-fifth of Earth's land area, and in general is still a developing continent. The only exceptions are South Africa and the northern countries along the Mediterranean. The sub-Saharan region lies between the Sahara Desert in the north and the group of five countries at the southern tip of the continent and is almost equally divided by the equator. The major countries in sub-Saharan Africa include Ghana, Nigeria, Burkina Faso, Ethiopia, Kenya, Somalia, Sudan, Cameroon, Gabon, Democratic Republic of the Congo, Central African Republic, Uganda, and Tanzania. Although it is the least urbanized area in the world, during recent decades this region has known the most rapid growth of people moving into urban areas, where approximately 40 percent of the population now resides.

In the tropical climate of sub-Saharan Africa, temperatures are high most of the year and rainfall is the crucial factor for agricultural activity. Closest to the equator is the wet tropics, which has no dry season; the area just beyond is the wet/dry tropics (monsoon rainforest), which has the most rainfall in the summer and a dry season in the cooler months; the next section is the dry tropics (tropical savanna), with hot, dry desert conditions where crops cannot be grown without irrigation.

In the wet tropics vegetation is lush and grows on weathered soils. If soil is left undisturbed, it supports the natural vegetation, but when cultivated, the soil loses organic matter very quickly. In these humid tropical forests the main agricultural crops are rubber, coconuts, coffee, cocoa, and rice. In the wet/dry tropics, or humid savanna areas, the main agricultural crops are cotton, groundnuts (peanuts), maize (corn), and coffee.

Only about 6 percent of the continent is arable, while 25 percent is forested. Although agriculture is the most important sector of the economy in most countries, many still do not produce sufficient crops to meet the needs of the people. Gardening as an aesthetic arrangement of plants done mostly as a leisure activity is rarely found. For the most part plots of arable ground are used for growing food and other useful crops. Traditional farming, done on small plots (from one-tenth to one-half hectare [0.2 to 1.2 acres]), predominates. Many of the small farmers are women. Because of the small scale and the techniques used, the practice is closer to gardening than agriculture.

In the sparse documentation that exists about gardening in sub-Saharan Africa, a particular style emerges that is common across the region—intercropping, a multistoried, layered method of combining crops. Intercropping diversifies production on a small plot, uses ground area most efficiently, shades crops to conserve water, and reduces labor. Vegetables, herbs, and fruit trees are grown together in such a way that they do not compete for nutrients or space. For example, sweet potato, cocoyam, pineapple, millet, sorrel, pigeon pea, and bush greens may be grown beneath papaya, pear, and baobab trees. The appearance may seem random, but plants are carefully located based on light and water requirements. Combining annual, perennial, and semiperennial plants means that they take up different nutrients at different times and from different soil layers.

In the late 19th and early 20th centuries, having carved Africa into colonies, Europeans attempted to force the native peoples to grow cotton in plantation-type regimes. For Africans, who were accustomed to obtaining food from managing wild stands of certain plants or by cultivating plants around their homes, planting one crop by itself in long rows made no sense. The labor that it required interfered with the work of their daily lives—fishing, foraging for food, and managing their home grounds. The Germans went so far as to outlaw the traditional methods and dictate when cotton could be planted and when it had to be uprooted, even making it illegal to intercrop cotton with food crops. This tactic led to poverty and hunger among the Africans by disrupting a centuries-old method of producing sufficient food.

Although the traditional methods survived and persisted after the colonial period (ending in the 1950s), even today many of the developing countries do not produce enough food for their populations. Successive governments before and since independence have stressed the need to increase domestic food production.

Until the 1990s, when commercial farming was introduced in West Africa, the main sources of food were peasant farms and home gardens.

African farming systems are ecologically well adapted to the harsh conditions that pervade the continent. Fortunately, Western development specialists who have tried to help as agricultural advisers are working now to improve rather than replace traditional practices. The focus of these improvements has been irrigation, quality hand tools and small-scale machinery, and improved seed quality.

The development of home gardening in Ghana can be traced from the early 19th century when British administrators, European traders, and missionaries planted well laid out gardens around their homes, particularly in such towns as Arburi, Mampong, and Akropong. In 1890 the Aburi Botanical Garden opened. Although the grounds cover 160 acres (64 ha), only 12 acres (4.9 ha) are cultivated. In 1939, when a major earthquake left many homeless, the government built estate houses with individual compounds. With room to garden, people planted hedges, herbaceous borders, and shade and fruit trees. Commercial nurseries also developed in urban areas at this time. Approximately 2,500 indigenous plants are regularly eaten—whether gathered from the wild or cultivated on home grounds. The main food crops are millet, sorghum, maize, beans, mango, taro, cocoyam, plantain, cowpeas, casava, bananas, dates, oranges, pineapples, okra, watermelon, and a variety of greens.

Gardens around a home include plants for various purposes—fruits; vegetables; herbs for seasoning, medicines, and dyes; wood for fuel and building; fiber plants; flowers; gourds for containers; and loofahs. Trees are planted to help modify the climate; they provide shade during the dry season and cool the cultivated garden soil. They also provide many products. For example, the African elemi (*Canarium schweinfurthii*) provides fruit, its stones (pits) are used for handcrafts or flooring, its fragrant resin is used as incense or to light fires, caterpillars that live on the leaves can be cooked and eaten, and the hardwood is used for fuel when the tree is cut down.

Another special technique reported by Hughes Dupriez and Philippe de Leener is the mixing of different varieties of seeds for a planting of one crop. At a site in Rwanda they observed a farmer making mixtures of a selection of 18 varieties of beans to be planted in three plots. One mixture was to be planted beneath bananas and another in a plot that was known to be less productive. The different varieties exhibited a range of characteristics such as early and late maturing, staggered harvest, creeping habit, resistance to drought, and resistance to a certain pest. Sowing such a mixture ensures that the entire crop won't be lost because of weather conditions or a pest attack.

In the large cities of sub-Saharan Africa, urban agriculture has become widespread. Urban agriculture is the practice of growing food crops and raising animals on small plots of land next to the home or on public land along railways and roads, under power lines, and in school yards. Studies show that although this practice has increased as a result of the influx of migrants from rural areas, not just the urban poor grow their own food. The declining economic situation has impacted people at all income levels. In Nairobi, Kenya, estimates show that about 55 percent of the 1.5 million residents in 1993 lived in the slums or shantytowns of the urban poor.

Urban agriculture has become a primary aspect of the informal economy and a practice that is essential to survival in the city. In the early years municipal governments tried to forbid farming in city boundaries, but enforcement was not realistic. The present goal is to find ways to integrate urban farming into long-term planning. Nakura, Kenya, is one of three towns in the world where a plan, Localising Agenda 21: Action Planning for Sustainable Urban Development, is currently being implemented. A study for this project (Dick Foeken and Samuel Owuor) found that one-fourth of the population in Nakura is cultivating crops in town, and many people are raising one or more animals for food. Plot size ranges from two to three square meters to 1.6 hectares (2.4–3.6 sq. yd. to 4 acres). The most common crops are maize, kale, beans, onions, spinach, tomatoes, Irish potatoes, cowpeas, and bananas. The family consumes most of what is produced; very little is sold. Some urban dwellers also grow crops in rural areas where they came from and still have access to land.

In Ibadan, Nigeria, the National Horticultural Research Institute has sponsored several conferences to discuss the production of fruits and vegetables and what can be done to help small farmers improve their seed stock and handle pest and disease problems.

Although the majority of gardening in sub-Saharan Africa is done to produce food and other useful crops, the native landscape is filled with thousands of ornamental herbaceous perennials, shrubs, and trees. In fact, botanists have pointed out that Africa has more than 30,000 species compared with 11,000 in Europe, although it has only 40 botanical gardens for conservation and research compared with more than 450 in Europe. Some favorite ornamentals are planted around homes and in major cities, parks, and botanical gardens.

Noted garden designer Ato Sebhatu Gebre Yesus of Addis Ababa, Ethiopia, president of the Horticultural Society of Ethiopia, landscaped the gardens of Africa Hall in Addis Ababa, designed by the Italian architect Mezzedimi. Sebhatu also planned and designed landscapes for many of the capital's institutions, including the Commercial Bank of Ethiopia, Ethiopia Hotel, the

Addis Ababa Hilton, and Wabe Shebelle Hotel. He also established the country's first botanical park, Behere Tsige (country of flowers), in 1967. He was responsible for advising the use of *serdo* for lawns, a local grass that provides better cover than imported grass. Sebhatu campaigns for the importance of protecting natural areas, putting emphasis on conservation rather than reforestation.

In Ethiopia botanists and foresters have been working to document the more than 1,000 native trees and shrubs, many of which offer food and medicines and perhaps have other uses not yet discovered. Deforestation, livestock grazing, and invasion of exotic species threaten the survival of native plants. Part of the difficulty in this work is that no one language is common to all of the people of Ethiopia, although Amharic is widely understood. More than 17 languages are used for vernacular names of the same species.

In Ghana the Department of Parks and Gardens is responsible for planting decorative gardens in all of the regional capitals and major towns. In addition to Aburi Botanical Gardens, others have been created at the University of Ghana, Legon; the University of Science and Technology, Kumasi; and the University of Cape Coast. Approximately 13 other botanical gardens currently exist in sub-Saharan Africa, some of which are in decline or have closed due to economic difficulties.

In the tropics especially, trees are important for the shade they provide from the scorching sun and are planted in recreational areas, markets, and school yards. Some examples include red sandalwood (*Adenanthera pavonina*), Persian lilac (*Melia azedarach*), and *Berlinia grandiflora*. Plants used for hedges include anatto (*Bixa orellana*), Alexandra laurel (*Calophyllus inophyllum*), and golden dewdrop (*Duranta repens*).

Examples of ornamental trees planted along avenues throughout sub-Saharan Africa include the deciduous African tulip tree (*Spathodea campanulata*), with fiery orange red clusters followed by woody capsules; *Acacia albida*, a deep-rooted tree that fixes nitrogen and is often intercropped with sorghum and millet and which has large compound leaves and fragrant creamy spikes

in bloom followed by thick, hard shiny pods (containing seeds used for flavoring) that ripen by the end of the dry season; and *Millettia thonningii,* which has purple flowers at the beginning of the first rains.

*See also* African-American Gardening; Egypt; Islamic Gardens; Kirstenbosch National Botanical Garden; South Africa

**Further Reading**

Abbiw, Daniel K., *Useful Plants of Ghana: West African Uses of Wild and Cultivated Plants,* London: Intermediate Technology, and Royal Botanic Gardens, Kew, 1990

Bekele-Tesemma, Azene, Ann Birnie, and Bo Tengnäs, *Useful Trees and Shrubs for Ethiopia: Identification, Propagation, and Management for Agricultural and Pastoral Communities,* Nairobi, Kenya: Regional Soil Conservation Unit, Swedish International Development Authority, 1993

Dupriez, Hughes, and Philippe de Leener, *Jardins et vergers d'Afrique,* Nivelles, Belgium: Terres et Vie, 1987; as *African Gardens and Orchards: Growing Vegetables and Fruits,* translated by Bridaine O'Meara, London: Macmillan, 1989

Epenhuijsen, C.W. van, *Growing Native Vegetables in Nigeria,* Rome: Food and Agriculture Organization of the United Nations, 1974

Isaacman, Allen F., and Richard L. Roberts, editors, *Cotton, Colonialism, and Social History in Sub-Saharan Africa,* Portsmouth, New Hampshire: Heinemann, 1995

Ojehomon, O. Ojeaga, P.A. Town, and K. McLean, editors, *Proceedings, Recommendations, and Papers: First National Seminar on Fruits and Vegetables, Ibadan, 13–17 October, 1975,* Ibadan, Nigeria: National Horticultural Research Institute, 1976

Sekyi, P.E., "The Development of Individual Home Gardens in Ghana," *Acta Horticulture* 53 (April 1977)

STEVIE O. DANIELS

# African-American Gardening

African-American traditions of gardening developed in rural areas of the South first in slavery, then in oppression. In less than 50 years, African-American society in the United States has changed from being predominately rural to mainly urban. A few of the rural traditions can be found in the city, mostly in community gardens. But a distinctive African-American tradition of urban or suburban garden art has not yet emerged as a recognizable form, as say, the blues have developed from their rural origins into a thoroughly urban expression.

There is very little documentation of slave gardens, although a few visitors to the South recorded their observations. One was Frederick Law Olmsted in the *Cotton Kingdom* (1861). Probably most slaves were allowed to have gardens, and some even kept a few chickens and pigs. The garden supplemented the slaves' diets and gave them an opportunity to assert some measure of independence.

After slavery the garden became critical for subsistence and survival. Many African-Americans stayed on the land as sharecroppers, but as such they had no security of tenure. Raper found in 1936 that in one Georgia county more than 33 percent of the black population had lived in the same house for less than one year, a condition of transience hardly conducive to gardening. However, a combination of factors, especially the mechanization of agriculture and World War II, resulted in a huge number of landless African-Americans leaving the countryside. Most had little reason to espouse agrarian values. Many of those who remained had acquired some land, which gave them the basis for self-sufficiency and financial independence. That was the situation of most of the rural subjects in Westmacott's *African American Gardens and Yards in the Rural South* (1992), and they voiced agrarian values probably not representative of African-American society as a whole.

Even in the days of sharecropping, many rural African-American families apparently found time to have flower gardens, gestures of defiant graciousness, despite the conditions of extreme hardship. African-Americans in the South refer only to the vegetable garden as their "garden." Flowers are grown in the yard, which in rural homesteads is always in front of the house. Privacy is not a criterion in either its location or design. It is rather the opposite, as the flower yard usually contains a shaded sitting area from which passing cars can be hailed. The yard is a display, an invitation to stop and visit. The display is principally of flowers arranged and rearranged; hence, plants are often in containers, but the display includes other decorative objects and assemblages. Yards may appear at first sight to be symmetrical, but then there is something quite unexpected. In this respect garden art has much in common with African-American quilting, a craft associated with a discipline but one that is not applied too strictly, resulting in designs that have rhythmic qualities but are full of surprises.

West African cultures in precolonial times did not use flowers for decorative purposes. There were no flowers for ornament around dwellings, for ceremonial purposes, for decorating the body, or as motifs in textiles or painting. The practice appears to have been adopted and developed in the Americas, but the arrangement of decorative plants by African-Americans is distinctly different from arrangements derived from European traditions. Plants are not massed for "structural" purposes.

Clara Edwards using a dogwood brush broom to sweep her daughter's yard in Hale County, Alabama
Photo by Richard Westmacott

They are rarely used as ground cover, for edging, for foundation planting, or massed to create a background. Plants are appreciated and displayed as individuals and are often grown in containers, allowing displays to be changed to suit the occasion.

In rural gardens in the United States, African-Americans show a strong preference for colorful flowers. But no recurring pattern in the arrangement of color has been observed as, for instance, in textile design, where colors are often deliberately clashed. In temperate regions foliage plants are rarely grown, but in the tropics there are many colorful foliage plants that are widely used with favorite flowers such as oleander (*Nerium oleander*), hibiscus (*Hibiscus rosa-sinensis*), and bougainvillea.

A feature of gardens and yards throughout the South and the Caribbean was that they were swept. This was true for both white and black families at all levels of society. But the practice has persisted for longer in African-American rural society. Sweeping the spaces around dwellings was practiced throughout Africa, and it was eminently practical for the kitchen yard that until quite

Farm Security Administration photograph of the yard of an African-American family in North Carolina, ca. 1939
Photo by Dorothea Lange, courtesy of Library of Congress

recently was found behind the houses of poorer families throughout the South. The yard usually contained the wellhead, an open fire, and shady places where the family carried out washing and various chores. It was safe and neat to sweep the "hearth" into the fire after each meal. The practice was also used in other areas around the house that were in constant use and became an accepted tradition that was only abandoned when power mowers made grass a feasible alternative. In the Cayman Islands, as in much of the Caribbean, the swept yard is traditional, but the spreading of clean white sand has become a yearly ritual.

Writing in 1941, Herskovitz criticized scholars in the United States for denying rather than investigating the survival of Africanisms. The extent to which gardening practices are African survivals or are the result of assimilation of cultural and environmental influences in new surroundings has not been fully explored by a scholar with a broad knowledge of West African cultures. The lack of documented evidence of the lives of African-Americans also makes tracing survivals from Africa difficult. It is indicative of how little was recorded about how African-Americans used the spaces around their dwellings that much of what we know today comes from historical archaeologists.

Gardeners anticipate change with pleasure. They enjoy the garden by walking around it to see what changes have occurred. Constant change is characteristic of vernacular gardens, and African-American gardens are no exception. Scholars in several branches of the arts have pointed out the extraordinary adaptability to change and innovation shown by African-Americans, frequently using creative improvisation as an example of such adaptability. However, the persistence of poverty among African-Americans, particularly in the rural South, makes it questionable to ascribe creative improvisation to ethnicity rather than to socioeconomic circumstance, and this caveat must apply to some characteristics of African-American gardens as well.

**Further Reading**

Blassingame, John W., *The Slave Community: Plantation Life in the Antebellum South,* New York: Oxford University Press, 1972; revised and enlarged edition, 1979

Genovese, Eugene D., *Roll, Jordan, Roll: The World the Slaves Made,* New York: Pantheon Books, 1974
Goody, Jack, *The Culture of Flowers,* Cambridge and New York: Cambridge University Press, 1993
McDaniel, George W., *Hearth and Home: Preserving a People's Culture,* Philadelphia, Pennsylvania: Temple University Press, 1982
Olmsted, Frederick Law, *The Cotton Kingdom* (1861): *A Selection,* Indianapolis, Indiana: Bobbs-Merrill, 1971
Pulsipher, Lydia M., "The Landscapes and the Ideational Roles of Caribbean Slave Gardens," in *The Archaeology of Garden and Field,* edited by Naomi F. Miller and Kathryn L. Gleason, Philadelphia: University of Pennsylvania Press, 1994
Raper, Arthur Franklin, *Preface to Peasantry: A Tale of Two Black Belt Counties,* Chapel Hill: University of North Carolina Press, 1936
Thompson, Robert Farris, *Flash of the Spirit: African and Afro-American Art and Philosophy,* New York: Random House, 1983
Vlach, John Michael, *The Afro-American Tradition in Decorative Arts,* Cleveland, Ohio: Cleveland Museum of Art, 1978
Vlach, John Michael, *Back of the Big House: The Architecture of Plantation Slavery,* Chapel Hill: University of North Carolina Press, 1993
Walker, Alice, *In Search of Our Mothers' Gardens: Womanist Prose,* San Diego, California: Harcourt Brace Jovanovich, 1983
Westmacott, Richard Noble, *African-American Gardens and Yards in the Rural South,* Knoxville: University of Tennessee Press, 1992

RICHARD WESTMACOTT

---

# Agra Fort

## Agra, Uttar Pradesh, India

**Location:**  approximately 100 miles (161 km) south-southeast of Delhi

A pristine example of multilevel architecture interspersed with landscaped gardens, bodies of water, and built palaces, the Agra Fort was constructed in the second half of the 16th century by the Mogul emperor Akbar (r. 1556–1605) in several phases of construction spanning over nine years. Of Akbar's original endeavor,

its crenellated red sandstone walls and two impressive gateways—the Dilli Darwazah and the Akbar Darwazah—remain. Emperor Shah Jahan (r. 1628–58) substituted most of its early sandstone buildings with marble palaces.

As a fortified camp palace, the Agra Fort is an example of a palace garden. It was not meant to be a principal garden site for entertainment or public gathering but rather an offshoot of the residential lawn; the gardens served as evening retreats or relaxation spots for the emperor or his harem, situated alongside the respective living quarters. The fort's two main garden sites were the Anguri Bagh (Grape Garden) and the Machchi Bhawan (Fish Square). The other landscaped areas defined entry, transition, or public areas.

Often reminiscent as the grieving dais during Shah Jahan's imprisonment by his son Aurangzeb, the gardens of the fort provide one of the finest views of one of the greatest architectural marvels—the Taj Mahal—across the vast expanse of the almost-dry Jumna River. The fort consists of five distinct areas: the Diwan-i-Am (public court), the Machchi Bhawan, the Anguri Bagh, Diwan-i-Khas (private ministers' court), and the Moti Masjid (pearl mosque). Other structures include the Jehangir and the Akbar Mahal, residential palaces toward the south, facing the river. The fort is equivalent to a miniature township, with courtyards, mosques, palaces, and gardens.

The traditional layout of Islamic gardens is based on order, geometry, and symmetry, comprising basically linear paths with adjoining square gardens and rectilinear bodies of water. The simplest prototype consists of deliberate divisions and subdivisions of the common square grid. Differing in scale and shape, they entice the visitor through linear paths to elements of surprise, such as monuments or terraced gardens. The resulting four square blocks with two linear paths from one end to the other, usually following the cardinal axes, define the typical chahar-bagh (four gardens) pattern.

All the palaces contained gardens with running water, which flowed in channels into reservoirs of stone, jasper, and marble. The rooms and halls of the palaces ordinarily contained fountains or reservoirs of the same stone and of proportionate size. The gardens always contained flowers planted according to the season. The gardens had no large fruit trees of any sort, so as not to hinder the open view. The palaces also contained seats and private rooms, some in the midst of running water stocked with fish.

Although the prototype plan was almost flat and two-dimensional, the terraced levels of the fort added a third dimension to the viewpoints to and from the Anguri Bagh and the Machchi Bhawan. Mogul gardens did not consist solely of vegetation; the surrounding structures also were part of the landscape. Motifs, carvings, and inlay work blanketed the adjoining structures and garden furniture in the form of trees, flowers, and creepers. Water chutes, cascades, and fountains helped transform the dry desert climate into an oasis environs.

The Anguri Bagh consisted of a square pool connecting the Khass Mahal with the garden. Laid out in geometrical stone-edged parterres, it contained four terraced walks radiating from a central pavilion, with a raised tank. Surrounded by the four compartments of the chahar-bagh, the tank has a cusped and foiled border with steps leading to it on the east and west sides. Originally, a stone trellis enclosed the flower beds, presumably supporting vines, but the name Anguri Bagh derived from the precious vine-pattern decoration constructed by Shah Jahan near the Jasmine Tower. Toward the river is situated the Khass Mahal, which consists of Shah Jahan's sleeping pavilion (Khwabgah), flanked on both sides with pavilions with curved-up roofs. Toward the north of the Khwabgah is the Bangla-i-Darshan, and toward the south is the Bangla-i-Jahanara, both of which were completed in 1637. In front of the Khass Mahal a shallow channel of water cascaded over carved niches into a small pool.

The garden, intimate in scale, is divided into four parts. Elaborate carvings are made from marble, while the flower beds are intricately outlined in sandstone. A rich variety of flowers and low shrubs grew in the chahar-bagh.

The Institutes of Akbar (Ain-i-Akbari), a 16th-century document, lists the customs and regulations of the Mogul Empire, including the names of garden plants, such as roses, violets, sunflower, and jasmine. Mogul illustrations of this period also define the type of plantation. The Anguri Bagh included four dark cypress spires planted at angles of the paths around the small central pavilion, repeating the lines of the corner slender pillars. The feathery heads of palms towered high above the outer walls, the walks were bordered by sweet scented tuberoses and hollyhocks planted alternately, and close to the fountain, a bed of poppies made a solid mass of color, softening the harsh edge of the white marble platform with their frail transparent flowers. In the larger gardens at the approach to the Diwan-i-Am, cypress trees alternated with the rosy almond tree or the silvery plum.

Akbar constructed the apartments on three sides of the Anguri Bagh essentially for the woman attendants of the household. Diverse areas within the fort included the adjacent Machchi Bhawan, which contained fish tanks surrounded by flower beds, fountains, and channels. Having been ransacked by the Jats in the 18th century, its two-story arcade today merely encloses a grassed space, apart from the open terrace overlooking the Jumna River.

Large grass lawns with bordering trees appear to the foreground of the Diwan-i-Am and the entrance to the Akbar and Jehangir Mahal. Another garden patch exists at the entrance to the Moti Masjid, constructed by Shah Jahan and the finest marble structure at the fort. Its massive columns of hewn marble and three well-proportioned domes face a simple courtyard and an ablution tank. Built on the highest ground, the Moti Masjid reigns supreme as a place of worship.

Unfortunately, the gardens have not been maintained in their original pristine form. Visitors to the site gain lit-

Agra Fort, Agra, Uttar Pradesh, India
Copyright Ken Gibson/Garden Matters

tle insight into the living environs during the reign of the Mogul emperors. Except for grassy lawns and peripheral trees of cypress, mango, and neem, little effort has been made to replant similar vegetation. Nonetheless, notwithstanding the dry water channels and fountains, this site holds ample hope for proper conservation.

**Synopsis**

| | |
|---|---|
| 1565 | Mogul Emperor Akbar destroys the old fort of Sikander Lodi |
| 1565–74 | Akbar constructs Agra Fort |
| 1566–67 | Akbar Darwazah completed (today called Amar Singh Gate) |
| 1568–69 | Principal gateway to fort, Dilli Darwazah, constructed |
| 1569 | Newly constructed Bengali Mahal inaugurated |
| 1574 | Red sandstone Agra Fort completed with palaces and gardens |
| 1619 | Mogul Emperor Jehangir constructs Jehangir Mahal, the palace between Machchi Bhawan (Fish Square) and Mussaman Burj; Bangla-i-Darshan (Hall of Consultations) and Bangla-i-Jahanara (Queen's Palace) completed |
| 1627–55 | Mogul Emperor Shah Jahan converts red sandstone structures into marble palaces |
| 1627 | Shah Jahan demolishes some buildings and replaces them with Diwan-i-Am (Hall of Public Audience) |
| 1637 | Shah Jahan builds Diwan-i-Khas (Hall of Private Audience), with double row of columns |

| 1637 | Bangla-i-Darshan and Bangla-i-Jahanara completed |
| 1648–55 | Moti Masjid (Pearl Mosque) completed |
| 1700s | Jats of Bharatpur ransack fort causing substantial damage to gardens |
| ca. 1900 | Lord Curzon orders reconstruction of Agra Fort and gardens |

**Further Reading**

Brown, Percy, *Indian Architecture,* vol. 1, *The Islamic Period,* Bombay: Taraporevala, 1942

Hambly, Gavin, *Cities of Mughul India: Delhi, Agra, and Fatehpur Sikri,* London: Elek, and New York: Putnam, 1968

Koch, Ebba, "The Lost Colonnade of Shah Jahan's Bath in the Red Fort at Agra," *The Burlington Magazine* 124 (1982)

Lehrman, Jonas Benzion, *Earthly Paradise: Garden and Courtyard in Islam,* London: Thames and Hudson, and Berkeley: University of California Press, 1980

Mehta, Rustam Jehangir, *Masterpieces of Indo-Islamic Architecture,* Bombay: Taraporevala, 1976

Michell, George, and Philip H. Davies, *The Penguin Guide to the Monuments of India,* 2 vols., London: Penguin, and New York: Viking, 1989; see especially vol. 2, *Islamic, Rajput, and European,* by Davies

Moore, Charles Willard, William John Mitchell, and William Turnbull, Jr., *The Poetics of Gardens,* Cambridge, Massachusetts: MIT Press, 1988

Nath, R., *History of Mughal Architecture,* 3 vols., New Delhi: Abhinav, 1982; see especially vol. 2, *Akbar*

Petersen, Andrew, *Dictionary of Islamic Architecture,* London and New York: Routledge, 1996

Petruccioli, Attilio, editor, *Gardens in the Time of the Great Muslim Empires: Theory and Design,* Leiden, The Netherlands, and New York: Brill, 1997

Smith, Edmund W., *The Moghul Architecture of Fathpur-Sikri,* Delhi: Caxton, 1985

Smith, Vincent Arthur, *Akbar, the Great Mogul, 1542–1605,* Oxford: Clarendon Press, 1917; 2nd edition, revised, 1919

Toy, Sidney, *The Fortified Cities of India,* London: Heinemann, 1965

Villiers-Stuart, Constance Mary, *Gardens of the Great Mughals,* London: Black, 1913; reprint, New Delhi: Cosmo, 1983

KARTIK RAM GANAPATHY

---

# Aiton, William 1731–1793

## Scottish Gardener

William Aiton described himself as "gardener to His Majesty," but he was much more than this; in fact he may be said to have founded the reputation that the Royal Botanic Gardens, Kew, has enjoyed ever since. Unfortunately, the Aiton family papers and gardening correspondence were burned when Aiton's younger son, John, inherited them on the death of the elder son, William Townsend Aiton. Therefore, much of the information about William Aiton can only be ascertained through the letters of others.

Like many other Scottish gardeners of his time, Aiton moved south as a young man to find employment in England. Scottish gardeners were in demand as they were educated and highly skilled. Aiton seems to have had very little money and may have walked to London from Lanarkshire with a friend. Aiton appears to have had a letter of introduction to Philip Miller of the Chelsea Physic Garden. Miller, who was from a Scottish family, had the reputation of being a likely employer of Scottish gardeners. Chelsea Physic Garden was England's main center for receiving and sending to other gardens exotic plants that came from abroad, making it an outstanding learning place for a young gardener. In fact, Chelsea Physic Garden during Miller's time as head gardener came to rival the gardens at Leiden and Paris. Aiton worked at Chelsea from 1754 to 1759.

Armed with a letter of recommendation from Miller, Aiton arrived at Kew in 1759. The Royal Botanic Gardens now consisted of two estates that once belonged to the royal family. Augusta, dowager Princess of Wales, started a garden of about nine acres in 1751, with the help of Lord Bute, her botanical adviser. Aiton had by this time great experience cultivating a wide range of plants, and under the direction of Bute he soon raised the profile of the garden. To begin, Aiton was only responsible for the botanic, or "physic," garden section of the Kew House (or White House) estate. It was called the botanic or physic garden because it contained herbaceous plants including those thought to have medicinal uses. The "pleasure ground" area, along with the Richmond Lodge gardens, was under the curatorship of John Haverfield. That Aiton was clearly junior in status to Haverfield is shown by the household accounts, which state that Haverfield earned £700 per annum and Aiton only £120.

On the death of his mother, Princess Augusta, in 1772, George III amalgamated the two gardens. However, it was not until the death of Haverfield in 1784 that Aiton became head gardener. Sir Joseph Banks became the unofficial director, and he and Aiton worked well together to make the garden famous; Banks frequently left on voyages of discovery while Aiton controlled the garden's operations.

Together with Banks, Aiton was responsible for establishing the tradition at Kew of sending members of staff on plant-hunting expeditions. In 1772 a young Scottish gardener, Francis Masson, who was selected on the basis of his health and fitness, was sent out to the Cape, South Africa, for the purpose of collecting plants and bulbs. Masson collected a specimen of *Encephalartos altensteinii* that is still grown at Kew. Aiton described several new species from the material sent to him, including two species of the succulent *Stapelia*. Proteas, crassulas, mesembryanthemums, ericas, pelargoniums, ixias, and gladioli all arrived for Aiton at Kew courtesy of Masson's expeditions. Aiton adeptly organized the exchange of seeds and plants from these expeditions. Carl Linnaeus named the genus *Aitonia*, discovered by the Swedish botanist Carl Thunberg, after Aiton. *Aitonia*, now called *Nymania*, is a genus of one species of evergreen shrub from the hot dry areas of South Africa's eastern Cape.

Aiton's only publication, *Hortus Kewensis* (A Catalog of Plants Cultivated in the Royal Botanic Garden at Kew [not to be confused with Sir John Hill's one-volume *Hortus Kewensis*]), was published in three volumes in 1789 and sold out within two years. Aiton dedicated the volumes to George III. The title page states that "small as the book appears the composition of it has cost [Aiton] a large portion of the leisure allowed by the daily duties of his station, during more than sixteen years." There is some debate as to how much of these volumes was the work of Aiton himself. It seems likely that Jonas Dryander, Daniel Solander, and Robert Brown (all eminent scientists), whose names do not appear on the title page, had far greater input than Aiton. Aiton did, however, acknowledge that the work would not have been possible without "the assistance of men more learned than himself." Ker Gawler in the *Botanical Register* of 1823 describes *Hortus Kewensis* as a "monument to the taste and criticism of Solander and Dryander, the worthy disciples of Linnaeus."

Aiton's book is much more than merely a list of the plants then cultivated at Kew. It gives diagnoses in Latin—following Linnaeus's binomial method of description—for over 5,500 plants, almost all the species cultivated in England at that time. The work is a combination of practical and scientific information. Besides giving a means of recognizing the plants, it also established as accurately as possible the dates and who had introduced them to English gardens. It describes for the first time many new species, including over 500 species brought back by Masson.

The specimens from Kew that were the basis for *Hortus Kewensis* were dried and added to Banks's herbarium. They are now in the Natural History Museum, in London. When Aiton died in 1793, he was buried in Kew Churchyard, and his pall was supported by Banks and Dryander, among others. Aiton House, named in honor of William Aiton, opened at Kew in June 1977. The building houses office accommodation for the curator and his deputy, the technical propagation unit, plant records, and the planning and information unit. It is appropriate that the building should be named after the first head gardener of the Royal Botanic Gardens, Kew.

*See also* Kew, Royal Botanic Gardens

**Biography**
Born in Boghall, Carnwarth, Lanarkshire, Scotland, 1731. Son of a farmer, he moved with his family to Shawfield estate near Airdrie, where he and two brothers trained as gardeners; moved south to London and took up employment at Chelsea Physic Garden with Philip Miller, 1754; commenced work at Kew, 1759, becoming Superintendent of Kew, 1784; published his three-volume catalog of Kew, *Hortus Kewensis*, 1789. Died in Kew, Surrey, February 1793 and was buried in Kew churchyard. Succeeded at Kew by his son William Townsend Aiton.

**Selected Publications**
*Hortus Kewensis*, 3 vols., 1789

**Further Reading**
Desmond, Ray, *Kew: The History of the Royal Botanic Gardens*, London: Harvill Press, 1995
"The Elder Aiton," *Kew Bulletin* (1891)
King, Ronald, *Royal Kew*, London: Constable, 1985
Pagnamenta, Frank, *The Aitons: Gardeners to Their Majesties, and Others*, London: Richmond Local History Society, 1999
"The Tomb of William Aiton," *Kew Bulletin* (1910)
Turrill, William Bertram, *Royal Botanic Gardens, Kew: Past and Present*, London: Hubert Jenkins, 1959

JANE HUTCHEON

# Alberti, Leon Battista 1404–1472

## Italian Architect and Scholar

Leon Battista Alberti, a member of an old, distinguished Florentine Family, was the only 15th-century Italian artist to have attended a university and to have received an advanced degree in law. Beginning early in his career, he wrote numerous treatises on a variety of subjects, including each of the three major arts, architecture, painting, and sculpture. Later in life he became a famous architectural designer while serving as secretary in the papal court at Rome. In all of his writings and his architectural designs, he took ancient Roman culture as a model.

Alberti's most famous and influential writing was his architectural treatise *De re aedificatoria* (On Building), completed in the mid-15th century but first printed in 1485. Throughout his book Alberti considers gardens as particularly important to create a pleasurable ambience for human living. As a consequence, there are frequent references to the desirability of gardens or small green areas (*hortuli*) in association with recreational areas such as racecourses and swimming pools or with other centers of human activity, such as a "palestra for philosophical disputations." Even city residences should "feature delightful gardens," and "green gardens" are a requirement for all summer dining rooms. None of the references to gardens, however, convey any idea of their form or planting. Only in Alberti's discussion of the "suburban *hortus*," or suburban villa, in book 9 does he consider the nature of a garden: he states that it should have rare and exotic plants such as Lorenzo de' Medici had later at his villa at Careggi.

Alberti offers some slight advice on the care of some plants, quoting the ancient Greek writer Theophrastus: box hedges must be sheltered and not exposed to the wind or sea spray, and myrtle, laurel, and ivy prefer shade; laurel, citrus, and juniper may have their branches pleached; rows of trees must be planted in the ancient form of the quincunx, using a module of five trees so that there are straight rows of trees not only at right angles but also on the diagonal. Without citing Pliny the Younger, Alberti notes that ancient Romans traced the names of the masters of the house in boxwood or herbs similar to what the Medici did in 1459, when their gardener planted the rear garden of their palace at Florence with the Medici insignia and that of a visiting Sforza prince.

Alberti is apparently ambivalent regarding statues in gardens. Early in the treatise he derides the "absurd garden statues of scarecrow gods," but later he approves of "comic statues in the garden . . . provided they are not obscene."

Alberti's most important contribution to Renaissance gardening was to revive the idea of a grotto as a garden feature. He describes how the ancients revetted their grottoes with "pumice chips, or travertine foam" that was daubed with green ochre in order to imitate "bearded moss." In one ancient grotto the interior surface was covered with a pattern of seashells.

There is no record of Alberti ever designing any specific garden. Occasionally the garden of the villa at Quaracchi near Florence of Giovanni Rucellai, Alberti's principal architectural patron in Florence, has been associated with Alberti without any evidence or probability.

Alberti's ideas have had a long and positive influence. At the end of the 16th century, the Florentine horticultural writer Giovanvittorio Soderini repeated most of Alberti's few comments on the garden, and Jacques Boyceau, the first French writer on the theory and design of ornamental gardening, wrote in 1638 that a garden must be considered as a complete unity, with all of its parts contributing to the harmony of the whole, a statement that echoes the main thesis of Alberti's treatise.

## Biography

Born in Genoa, Italy, 1404. Attended University of Bologna; wrote treatises on many subjects; wrote *De re aedificatoria*, 1485, outlining his views on gardens and sketches basic principles of Renaissance garden. Died in Rome, 1472.

## Selected Publications

*De re aedificatoria,* 1485; as *Ten Books on Architecture,* translated by James Leoni, 1755

## Further Reading

Alberti, Leon Battista, "Villa," in *Opere volgari*, edited by Cecil Grayson, Bari, Italy: Laterza, 1960

Alberti, Leon Battista, *De re aedificatoria,* Florence, 1485; as *The Architecture of Leon Battista Alberti in Ten Books,* translated by James Leoni, London: 1755; reprint, as *The Ten Books of Architecture: The 1755 Leoni Edition,* New York: Dover, 1986; also translated as *On the Art of Building in Ten Books,* translated by Joseph Rykwert, Neil Leach, and Robert Tavernor, Cambridge, Massachusetts: MIT Press, 1988

Lücke, Hans-Karl, *Alberti Index: Leon Battista Alberti, De Re Aedificatoria, Florenz, 1485: Index Verborum,*

2 vols., Munich: Prestel, 1975; see especially vol. 2

Perosa, Alessandro, editor, *Giovanni Rucellai ed il suo zibaldone,* London: Warburg Institute, 1960

Tavernor, Robert, *On Alberti and the Art of Building,* New Haven, Connecticut: Yale University Press, 1998

DAVID COFFIN

# Aldobrandini, Villa

## Frascati, Lazio, Italy

**Location:**  in the Alban Hills, approximately 10 miles (16 km) southeast of Rome

Since ancient times Frascati has been famous for good air and beautiful views, and it was a popular place for the Roman *villeggiatura* (country retreat) since the 16th century. The Villa Aldobrandini, realized in a short period of time in the early 17th century, marks an important point in the development of baroque garden architecture and waterworks. It was dramatically remodeled under the ownership of Cardinal Pietro Aldobrandini. The villa, also called Villa del Belvedere, is situated on a steep hillside offering a remarkable view over the *campagna* (open countryside) towards Rome and the Mediterranean in the distance. For the visitor approaching from the village, the *casino* (ornamented building) appears elevated above terraces and substructures. The lower garden is organized by three axes radiating from a single point; this *patte d'oie* recalls the earlier Villa Montalto in Rome. A large hippodrome-like area just below the building could have been used for open-air plays and tourneys. A *giardino segreto* (secret garden) with parterres was south of the building on the same level because of the lack of space.

The main attraction of the villa is the famous waterworks disposed along the main axis of the upper part of the garden. Construction began in 1601 using plans by Giacomo Della Porta, but the project was enlarged and realized by Carlo Maderno and Giovanni Fontana. The full supply of water was not secured until the beginning of 1604. Fountains in the lower garden include *nicchione* (niche) fountains (fountains in the form of a ship), *scherzi d'acqua* (surprise water jets), *fontane rustiche* (rustic fountains), and a cascade along the main axis; combined, they display a great variety of artificial water effects. Loggias on each level of the building give the opportunity to enjoy a panoramic view as well as the optical and acoustic effects of the waterworks on the hillside. "Canalized" by high hedges, the water from the *Monte Algido* (also known as the *Acqua Algida*) falls down the hillside in several steps and cascades before it comes out in the exedra (semicircular backdrop) of the *teatro delle acque* (water theater), close to the facade of the pavillion. The Aldobrandini star that sprays water over the central niche has a heraldic meaning, while the sculptural decoration (not completely conserved), including statues of Atlas and Hercules in the central niche of the *teatro delle acque* as well as two monumental columns on top of the cascade, is based on the myth of Hercules. Rooms in the lateral wings of the *teatro* contained a chapel, and in the *stanza de' venti* (room of winds), decorated by Domenichino's frescoes (now in the National Gallery, London), was a sculptural group representing Apollo and the Muses on Mount Parnassus. The water effects, including water music and other acoustic phenomena, are as elaborate as those in the mannerist garden of the Villa d'Este in Tivoli. Their dramatic concentration on the main axis and the spectacular bursting forth in the *teatro delle acque* further the perspective organization of the garden space and the garden's orientation toward the building, both of which are baroque features that influenced the further development of garden art.

The villa and its waterworks were described by many visitors to the region and later illustrated by Dominique Barrière's (1647) and Giovanni Battista Falda's (ca. 1670) plates. The Villa Aldobrandini inspired not only other villas in Frascati, such as the Villa Ludovisi and Villa Borghese di Mondragone, where similar fountains were added, but also gardens of Italophile patrons and artists north of the Alps and theater decoration.

**Synopsis**

| | |
|---|---|
| ca. 1574 | Small casino built on site for Antonio Contugio or ca. 1588 for Domenico Paolo Capranica |
| 1598 | Villa given to Cardinal Pietro Aldobrandini by his uncle Pope Clement VIII |

Upper cascade, Villa Aldobrandini, Frascati, Lazio, Italy
Copyright Alinari/Art Resource, New York

| | | |
|---|---|---|
| 1599–1600 | Aldobrandini makes efforts supply enough water for site | |
| 1601 | New casino built, designed by Giacomo della Porta (includes older building) | |
| 1602 | *Palazzo et fontana* begun; della Porta dies soon afterward | |
| 1603 | Payments to architect Carlo Maderno and to specialist for water works, Giovanni Fontana | |
| 1603 | Casino and lower garden structure completed | |
| 1604 | Water supply ensured | |
| 1603–4 | Upper garden buildings (water theater and adjoining wings) and fountains realized, | |

designed by Maderno and Giovanni Fontana

ca. 1610–ca. 1620   *Teatro* and fountains finished, designed by Maderno, with collaboration of specialist for water works, Horatio Olivieri; frescoes by Domenichino for *stanza de' venti*; construction of upper, third belvedere loggia

after 1620   Construction of building north of casino for conservation of delicate plants in winter

1621   Pietro Aldobrandini dies

**Further Reading**

Barrière, Dominicus, *Villa Aldobrandina Tusculana sive Varij Illius Hortorum et Fontium Prospectus*, Rome, 1647

Berger, Robert W., "Garden Cascades in Italy and France, 1565–1665," *Journal of the Society of Architectural Historians* 33 (1974)

Coffin, David R., *Gardens and Gardening in Papal Rome,* Princeton, New Jersey: Princeton University Press, 1991

D'Onofrio, Cesare, *La Villa Aldobrandini di Frascati,* Rome: Staderini, 1963

Falda, Giovanni Battista, *Le fontane delle ville di Frascati nel Tusculano,* Rome, s.d.

Franck, Carl L., *Die Barockvillen in Frascati,* Munich: Deutscher Kunstverlag, 1956; as *The Villas of Frascati, 1550–1750,* London: Tiranti, and New York: TransAtlantic Arts 1966

Frezzotti, Stefania, "I teatri delle acque nelle ville di Frascati," *Studi romani* 30 (1982)

Lauterbach, Iris, "Die Brunnenserie von Giovanni Battista Falda und Giovanni Francesco Venturini," in *Le fontane di Roma,* by Giovanni Battista Falda and Giovanni Francesco Venturini, Nördlingen, Germany: Uhl, 1996

Percier, Charles, and Pierre François Léonard Fontaine, *Choix des plus célèbres maisons de plaisance de Rome et de ses environs,* Paris, 1809

Schwager, Klaus, "Kardinal Pietro Aldobrandinis Villa di Belvedere in Frascati," *Römisches Jahrbuch für Kunstgeschichte* 9/10 (1961/62)

Steinberg, Robert Martin, "The Iconography of the Teatro dell'Acqua at the Villa Aldobrandini," *Art Bulletin* 47 (1965)

IRIS LAUTERBACH

# Alexandria, Gardens of Ancient

Alexandria, Egypt, is the only existing city in the world that can still claim to have been founded by Alexander the Great. Long before Alexander set foot in Egypt, however, the Greek poet Homer mentioned the island of Pharos in the *Odyssey.* Substantiating the antiquity of this area, the remains of a prehistoric harbor have been found near the peninsula of Ras-el-Tin.

On the Egyptian mainland, opposite the island of Pharos, was a small fishing village, probably located around the area where Pompey's Pillar now stands. This village was called Rhakotis, where remnants of settlement have been found dating back to the 13th century B.C. Little is known about Pharos and Rhakotis from the time of the pharaohs, since Egyptian civilization was thoroughly centered around the Nile River. Rhakotis was likely little more than a remote fishing village for most of its existence. But its standing changed with the coming of Alexander the Great in the fourth century B.C. He was gladly received by the Egyptians, who saw him as a liberator from the rule of the Persians. Having swept through Greece, Asia Minor, and Syria, he had plans to march eastward to India. He first rested in Egypt and sought to consult the famous oracle of Ammon in the Oasis of Siwa.

On his way to Siwa, Alexander stopped at a stretch of land between the Mediterranean Sea and Lake Mareotis, with the nearby island of Pharos. Alexander admired the area and ordered a city to be founded there to serve as the regional capital and as the meeting point of Greece across the Mediterranean and all of Egypt. The Greek architect Dinocrates drew up plans, and leg-

end has it that Alexander himself marked out where the outer walls of the city were to stand. In April 331 B.C. the new capital of Egypt, Alexandria, named after the ruler, was founded. He went on to found other Alexandrias (17 in all), none of which now survive. Although Alexander never saw one building of the city that eventually arose, he would be buried there.

Alexandria reached its zenith during the Ptolemaic period (330–23 B.C.), by which time it had become an important cultural, intellectual, economic, and political city, where were built the Lighthouse (one of the Seven Wonders of the Ancient World), the Great Library, and the Serapeum (where the sacred bulls of Apis were buried). Many gardens also flourished in Alexandria, for ancient Egypt was known for its elaborate gardens. Indeed, the city saw a synthesis of styles—the Greek merging with the Egyptian, with a strong admixture in later times with the more elaborate Roman garden styles. Gardens could be found around the temple and palace complexes, including the Temple of Poseidon, the Temple of Isis on Pharos, the Temple of Isis on the mainland, the Serapeum, the Caesarium, and the Island Palace.

The Egyptians were the first to design and cultivate formal and domestic ornamental gardens, perhaps as early as 2800 B.C. The oldest surviving garden plan dates to 1400 B.C. Egyptian tomb paintings show gardens within walled enclosures, where fig and date trees flourished and where trellises supported grapevines and roses. Often the well-arranged garden plots surrounded a rectangular fishpond. Greek gardens, on the other hand, were simple in design and practical in purpose. They were also cultivated within enclosing walls and colonnaded central courtyards of homes. Most plants were grown in pots, since the main emphasis was on propagating vineyards, olive groves, and fruit trees.

The Romans, however, developed agriculture to a high degree and made gardening into a unique science, namely, horticulture (the word derives from Latin and means "garden cultivation"). The Romans based their peristyle gardens on the Greek model but made them far more sensual and elaborate. They incorporated pools, fountains, running water, waterfalls, walkways among the plants, and ornate trellises with exotic vines, creepers, and climbers. In short, the Romans invented the science of landscaping, where gardens were no longer practical places to grow food (as with the Greeks), or quiet spots where one could rest (as in Egyptian gardens) but rather an extension of living space—a place where civilized people could enjoy the gracious harmony of structured nature.

All these major influences could be found in the gardens contained in the palaces and temples of Alexandria. It is now difficult to gain a clear picture of the extent of the gardens found in the city because most of the city now lies under the Mediterranean.

Approaching from the Mediterranean Sea, at the western point of Pharos Island, stood the Temple of Poseidon. The area at the present time includes the modern lighthouse, a hospital, and the Palace of Ras-El-Tin. On the eastern edge of Pharos stood the famed Lighthouse. Not far from the Lighthouse, on shore, was the site of the Temple of Isis, possibly opposite the Abul-Abbas Mosque or near the Marine Scouts Club. Another Temple of Isis stood on the mainland, located near the tip of the promontory of Silsila. The center of the city was further inland, where could be found the Ptolemaic Palace, probably stretching from Silsila to Raml Train Station. Connected to the palace was the famous Library or the Mouseion, which included many schools, laboratories, gardens, and a zoo. Nearby stood the Shrine of Pompey, Cleopatra's Needles, and the Caesarium, and further to the south was the famous Serapeum and Pompey's Pillar (which actually commemorates the Emperor Diocletian).

The Tomb of Alexander the Great (known as the "Soma") was located in the city, but its whereabouts are impossible to know. Some scholars believe it lies near the intersection of Horreya (Fouad) Street and Nebi Daniel Street. Others believe that the Soma lies underneath the mosque of Nebi Daniel.

Gardens played an important civic and religious role in Alexandria. All the temples and official buildings contained gardens; plants were not only ornamental but also imbued with mystical efficacy and mythical meaning. For example, Egyptians regarded the sycamore as a manifestation of the goddesses Nut, Isis, and Hathor and as such planted them near tombs and mausoleums. The persea (a deciduous tree) was sacred to the sun and was said to tolerate no water but that of the Nile. The willow was sacred to Osiris, and therefore most temples contained sacred willow groves. In Egyptian temples terraced gardens were planted in imitation of the paradise of Ammon; myrrh trees intermingled with date palms (trees that symbolized fecundity and victory) surrounded these terraces. This tradition survives still in Christianity, where Christ's victory over death is signified by the palm branch.

Sacred trees were a feature common to Greek temples as well, where plane and ash trees were abundantly grown. In addition, the oak, olive, and myrtle were cultivated. The oak was sacred to Zeus and to the god Pan, the olive represented the goddess Athena, and the myrtle was consecrated to Aphrodite.

Another feature common to both Greek and Egyptian temples was the reproduction in stone of an idealized, sacred landscape. Thus columns were representations of sacred trees, where the drama of creation, death, and rebirth was perpetually played out. The Romans freely adapted the ideas of the Greeks and Egyptians and put their own mark on their garden landscapes.

In order to support their sacred and civic gardens, the Egyptians, Greeks, and Romans developed various technologies. The Egyptians conceived the concepts of drainage and irrigation, land preparation, and the planned garden. The Greeks added to these ideas by creating the science of studying plants, their function, description, cultivation, and sexual reproduction, exemplified by the work of Theophrastus. Indeed, Alexander consistently sent back to Athens new plants that he encountered in his conquests.

The Romans borrowed whatever they found useful in terms of garden craft, while creating the science of landscaping. They developed sophisticated ornamental gardens (the peristyle), as well as the craft of grafting and budding, the use of cultivars, legume rotation, and even the greenhouse. All of these features were prominent in Alexandria. The temples of Isis, Poseidon, and the Serapeum were filled with terraces, sacred groves, and holy pools, while the palaces afforded artificial oases where one could enjoy privacy and intimacy in a cool, leafy and shady setting. The cultivated places in Alexandria, its temple and palace gardens, were places to refresh oneself spiritually and physically.

Unfortunately none of these gardens survive today. But one can still well imagine the splendorous verdure of Alexandria, which ranked it as the center of the Greco-Roman world.

## Synopsis

| | |
|---|---|
| 332 B.C. | Founded by Alexander the Great |

331 B.C.         Construction of city proper,
                   planned by architect Dinocrates
323–30 B.C.      Ptolemaic period
30 B.C.–A.D. 641  Roman period
A.D. 642–1798    Arab period
1798–present     Modern period

**Further Reading**

Brosse, Jacques, *Mythologie des arbres,* Paris: Plon,
  1989
Fraser, Peter Marshall, *Ptolemaic Alexanderia,* 3 vols.,
  Oxford: Clarendon Press, 1972
Lethaby, William Richard, *Architecture, Mysticism, and
  Myth,* London, 1891; reprint, New York: Braziller,
  1975
Parke, Herbert William, *The Oracles of Zeus: Dodona,
  Olympia, Ammon,* Cambridge, Massachusetts:
Harvard University Press, and Oxford: Blackwell,
  1967
Schama, Simon, *Landscape and Memory,* New York:
  Knopf, 1995
Smith, Earl Baldwin, *Egyptian Architecture as Cultural
  Expression,* New York and London: Appleton
  Century, 1938
Vannucci, M., "Sacred Groves or Holy Forests," in
  *Concepts of Space Ancient and Modern,* edited by
  Kapila Vatsyayan, New Delhi: Abhinav, 1991
Yehya, Lutfi A.W., "Alexandria and Rome in Classical
  Antiquity. A Cultural Approach," in *Roma e l'Egitto
  nell'antichità classica,* edited by Giovanni Pugliese
  Carratelli, Rome: Istituto Poligrafico e Zecca dello
  Stato, 1992

NIRMAL DASS

---

# Alhambra

## Granada, Spain

**Location:** on a hill immediately east of the city of
            Granada

The *Calat* Alhambra, or red castle, is a pink-gold palace
built on a hilly terrace immediately east of Granada.
There are three different groups of buildings on the hill:
the 11th-century Alcazaba fortress to the west, the Generalife gardens to the east, and in the center the complex
of buildings constituted essentially by the amalgamation
of the Moorish palace of the Nasrid dynasty, with its decoration of marvelously delicate but complex tracery, and
the unfinished square 16th-century palace of Charles V.

The walled enclave Alcazaba covers about 14 hectares
(34.5 acres) and overlooks the Darro River to the west.
Neglected, vandalized, and ruinously restored since the
13th century, the Alhambra still contains Europe's most
perfect example of Moorish art at the peak of its development, liberated from the Byzantine influences still
observable in Córdoba, and more elaborate than the
Giralda at Seville.

The entry from the town is through the massive 16th-
century triumphal gateway, the Puerta de las Granadas,
from which two paths to the right lead to the Alhambra
Park, lying to the south of the walled enclave and
planted by the Moors with roses, oranges, and myrtles
and superseded in 1812 by a dense wood of English
elms brought over by the duke of Wellington. Its fountains and cascades, fed from a five-mile (8 km) conduit
from the Dorro above Granada, reinforce the feeling of
coolness, and the park is still famous for its nightingales.
The paved left-hand footpath from the gate ascends
steeply up the wooded slope through the shrubbery past
an enormous fountain of 1554 to the magnificent Moorish horseshoe-shaped Puerta de la Justicia, whose square
tower forms part of the ramparts. The gateway, erected
in 1340, is decorated with Muslim symbols. From the
fountain, a right-hand path climbs to the perimeter towers of the southwest-facing wall, some of which may
date back to the eighth century, while a left-hand path
leads past the 1345 Wine Tower (Torre del Vino), used
in the 16th century as a cellar, to the Plaza de los Aljibes,
the central "Cistern Court" between the ruins of the
Alcazaba to the west and the gully west of the royal palaces of the Nasrids and of Charles V to its east.

The Alcazaba is dominated by its 26-meter (28.5-yd.)
watchtower, the Torre de la Vela, whose turret and bell
were added in the 18th century. Charles V nearly made
Granada his capital and undertook much construction
work within the enclave, including the palace, whose
construction was begun in 1526 and abandoned in 1650.

The decorative skill and architectural ingenuity of the
Nasrid complex is chiefly to be seen in the 14th-century
interiors, covered in filigree stucco, tiling, and marque-
try and supported by exquisitely carved marble pillars.

Courtyard with reflecting pool, Alhambra, Granada, Spain
Copyright Paul Miles Picture Collection

In the center of the Nasrid complex is the Patio de los Arrayanes (Court of the Myrtles). It has an oblong central pool sunk in marble, lined with myrtles, and enclosed by multistoried buildings, reflecting the imposing Comares Tower to its north. On its north and south sides are galleries over slender-pillared colonnades open to the sun and air and with a series of arches echoing one another's shapes. Most of the color has faded, but the decorative elements of the intricately woven arabesques include much foliage, Arabic inscriptions, and geometric patterns, the walls faced by painted tiles.

The Patio de los Leones (Court of Lions) at the center of another part of the complex is, at 35 by 20 meters (38.3 by 22 yd.), a little smaller than the Court of the Myrtles (42 by 22 meters [46 by 24 yd.]). It also derives from the 14th century and is surrounded by a gallery supported by 124 irregularly placed marble columns. It has at its center the famous lion fountain, made of a large low-slung alabaster basin supported by 12 roughly carved white marble lions symbolizing strength and stability. Four streams flow from the fountain to the center of each side of the court, which was designed as an interior garden and deliberately filled with aromatic herbs

between the shrubs. Pavilions project into each end of the court, emphasizing by their filigree wall decoration and elaborately ornamented roofs the gracefulness of the whole ensemble, once the residence of the Nasrid royal family.

East of the Nasrid palace complex are the terraces of the Partal gardens, which descend to the porticoes of the Torre de las Damas (Ladies' Tower) on the north perimeter. They are marked by the same absence of curves as characterizes the architectural ground plan of the whole Nasrid complex. Everywhere among the Moorish buildings are graceful fountains, pools, offices, and apartments, with trees, shrubs, and bushes among the patios, pools, fountains, arches, and cupolas, mingling decorative planting with impermanent stucco stalactites that each generation was expected to replace, with sometimes enameled banding and more permanent stucco filigree and arabesques based on foliage, geometric patterns, Arabic inscriptions, and illegible patterns taken from verses from the Koran. The designs are intended to encourage the mind to empty itself of its logically organized focuses and to allow it to return, like the gardens, to a cultivated state of natural rhythm and harmony.

The 16th-century palace of Charles V, for which he tore down a whole wing of the Nasrid building, contains the only round courtyard of the complex. Fernando and Isabella lived for a while in the Alhambra, converting the mosque but leaving the structure unaltered. Reached by a wisteria-covered path, the neoclassical building of Charles V was in that setting insensitive. By the 18th century, the royal palace was being used as a prison, and the whole complex was occupied and looted by Napoléon's forces, who attempted to blow it up when forced to retreat. It was saved by a crippled soldier who removed the fuses, and it is now a national monument with a plan in place to restore the Moorish elements in the enclave.

**Synopsis**

| | |
|---|---|
| 1238 | Ibn el-Ahmar establishes independent Moorish kingdom in Granada |
| 1248 | Construction of Alhambra palace begun; Alcazaba rebuilt, walls erected |
| 1275 | Death of Ibn el-Ahmar |
| 1334–54 | Reign of Yusef I; royal palace built |
| 1345 | Torre del Vino |
| 1354–91 | Reign of Mohammed V, son of Yusef I |
| 1365 | Council chamber completed |
| 1492 | Boabdil, last Muslim prince, surrenders Alhambra to Ferdinand and Isabella |
| 15th C. | Building of Puerta de las Granadas triumphal arch |
| 1526 | Construction of new palace begins |
| 1554 | Building of Pillar of Charles V |
| 1700–1746 | Further destructive adaptations by Philip V |
| 1812 | Occupation by Napoléon's army |
| 1881 | Addition of turret and bell to Torre de la Vela |

**Further Reading**

Burckhardt, Titus, *Die maurische Kultur in Spanien,* Munich: Callwey, 1970; as *Moorish Culture in Spain,* translated by Alisa Jaffa, London: Allen and Unwin, and New York: McGraw Hill, 1972

Fletcher, Richard A., *Moorish Spain,* London: Weidenfeld and Nicolson, and New York: Holt, 1992

Goury, Jules, Owen Jones, and Pasqual de Gayangos, *Plans, Elevations and Details of the Alhambra,* 2 vols., London, 1842–45

Harvey, Leonard Patrick, *Islamic Spain, 1250 to 1500,* Chicago: University of Chicago Press, 1990

Irving, Washington, *The Alhambra: A Series of Tales and Sketches of the Moors and Spaniards,* Philadelphia, 1832; reprint, New York: Avon, 1965

ANTHONY H.T. LEVI

---

# Allé. *See* Avenue and Allé

---

# Allinger, Gustav 1891–1974

## German Landscape Architect

Gustav Allinger was an important landscape architect in 20th-century Germany. Numerous gardens, parks, cemeteries, school and sports grounds, and garden exhibitions are evidence of his outstanding qualities as a garden designer. His impact on German landscape architecture was equivocal. Driven by his enormous ambition, Allinger played a dubious role in the development of the profession, particularly during the time of National Socialism.

Allinger's professional career began at the end of the imperial *Reich* and covered the periods of the Weimar Republic (1918–33), National Socialism (1933–45), and the Federal Republic of Germany (after 1945). He started in 1907 as an apprentice in the architectural firm of J. Saame in Heilbronn and worked from 1909 to 1911 in architectural firms in Heilbronn and Heidelberg. From 1911 to 1913 he apprenticed in the parks department of Cologne under Fritz Encke, one of the most important landscape architects and park directors of the late 19th and early 20th centuries. Allinger's career, interrupted by four years of service during World War I, continued with his appointment as *Gartentechniker* (garden technician) under Encke in Cologne until 1920. From 1920 to 1921 he worked for the parks and cemetery department in Dortmund. He ended this phase of his career as assistant head of the garden design office of the Späth Nursery in Berlin, where he worked from 1921 to 1925. The nursery of Ludwig Späth was one of the most important nurseries in Europe and had a large garden design office with commissions all over Europe. Numerous German landscape architects started their careers in the Späth office.

The second phase of Allinger's career began in 1926, when he won the competition for the Jubiläums-Gartenbau-Ausstellung Dresden 1926 (Jubilee Horticulture Exposition) (see Plate 2) and became artistic director for the exposition. In 1927 he was appointed artistic director for the Deutsche Gartenbau- und Schlesische Gewerbe-Ausstellung Liegnitz (German Horticulture and Silesian Trade Exhibition). His contributions to garden expositions are perhaps the most remarkable facet of his life's work. The 1926 exposition in Dresden was a milestone in the evolution of garden expositions in Germany and reflects Allinger's design and organizational talents. His *Kommender Garten* (garden of the future) was one of the most commented on gardens of its period. On the one hand, it was a masterpiece of garden design; on the other hand, it clearly represented Allinger's willingness to adjust his ideas to suit the trends of the time. So ambiguous was the overall effect of Allinger's garden that it might be viewed as an attempt to avoid any clear statement about design. Allinger left open the possibility for various interpretations, claiming that this garden was designed

> for a creative person, who has in himself a great respect for the beauty of plants and a strong feeling of nature. For men who love the German home, but do not want to miss its completion by exotic plants, who have travelled widely, who have seen a lot, whose thoughts and emotional remembrances become newly enlivened by the contents of this garden.

Allinger integrated on a very small scale formal and informal elements in garden design. The 1920s were marked by a highly emotional and ideological debate about the future of garden design in Germany. One of the most hotly contested issues was the struggle between formal and informal styles. Allinger's *Kommender Garten* focused attention on the debate over the future of garden design in Germany. In the following years several articles appeared under the title *Kommender Garten*, among them articles by landscape architect Leberecht Migge and Gunnar Nyle Brands, both in 1927.

In his attempt to be in vogue, Allinger also incorporated other trends from the arts. For example, he tried to introduce expressionist art forms into garden design. His sketches "Auf dem Kristallberg" (Atop the Crystal Mountain) for a 1924 exposition of the Verband Deutscher Gartenarchitekten (Association of German Garden Architects) closely resemble earlier designs of the German architect Bruno Taut's so-called Alpine architecture.

Allinger was garden director of the new town of Hindenburg in Upper Silesia from 1928 to 1931, and he created comprehensive plans for its parks, gardens, and other urban open spaces. In 1932, together with Hermann Rothe, he founded the firm Deutsche Park- und Gartengestaltung (German Park and Garden Design) Allinger und Rothe and worked as a freelance landscape architect. In 1933 he headed the Deutsche Gartenbau-Ausstellung (German Horticulture Exposition) in Berlin and in 1934 the exposition Sommerblumen am Funkturm (Summer Flowers at the Radio Tower) in Berlin.

Allinger tried to use the ascendancy of National Socialism in 1933 to become the dominant garden designer in Germany. He closely collaborated with Nazi agencies and took a leading role in bringing the professional landscape architecture organizations into line. He became a member of the Nationalsozialistische Deutsche Arbeiterpartei (NSDAP; National Socialist German Workers Party) and from 1933 to 1934 was president of the then leading garden association, the Deutsche Gesellschaft für Gartenkunst (DGfG; German Society for Garden Art). From 1934 to 1935 he was vice president of the Deutsche Gesellschaft für Gartenkultur (German Society for Garden Culture). His unscrupulousness was seen in a court-of-honor case at the Nazi Reich Chamber of Fine Arts, when he reproached a colleague for displaying a garden designed for a Jewish client at a March 1935 exposition.

Besides his work as a landscape architect, Allinger became a "landscape attorney" in 1934 and acted as a consultant for the construction of the *Reich*'s highways. He worked under the supervision of Alwin Seifert, one of his rivals for the leadership of landscape architecture in Nazi Germany. This collaboration ended in 1938. One reason was that Seifert had criticized Allinger's plant selection for the highway between Berlin and Stettin. Seifert, a fanatic anti-Semite and ardent follower of the Nazi blood-and-soil ideology, argued that only plants considered native to the various landscapes in Germany would be appropriate for the German "race" and could be used in German landscapes. Allinger, less ideological and much more pragmatic, also used nonindigenous species.

During World War II Allinger was entrusted with such special tasks as designing camouflage for the army, the armament industry, and the administrative office (Verwaltungsamt) of the Weapon-SS.

After World War II Allinger continued his career as a landscape architect. He worked for garden expositions in Erfurt, East Germany, in 1945 and 1946 and as consultant for state and communal agencies and for industrial firms in North Rhine Westphalia. From 1948 to 1954 he was vice president of the Bund Deutscher Gartenarchitekten (BDGA; Association of German Garden Architects) and became an honorary member in 1954. Despite his National Socialist background and lack of special academic qualifications, in 1952 he was offered the position of professor and director of the Institute for Garden Art and Landscape Design at the Technical University in Berlin. He headed the institute until 1959. In 1965 he became a guest professor at the Aegian University in Izmir, Turkey. During his professional career Allinger was active as the author of garden books and numerous articles on landscape architecture and garden design. He died in 1974 in Bonn.

## Biography

Born in Lauffen, Germany, 1891. Apprenticed to architectural firm in Heilbronn, Germany, and parks department of Cologne, 1911–13; worked for parks department of Cologne, then Dortmund, Germany, 1920-21; held leading position in Department of Garden Art, Späth Nursery, Berlin, 1921–25; won many prizes in garden design competitions; head of parks department of city of Hindenburg, 1928–31; founded a design firm with Hermann Rothe, 1932; collaborated closely with Nazi agencies and took leading role in bringing professional organizations in field of landscape architecture into line with Nazi ideals; worked during Nazi regime as "landscape attorney," as consultant for construction of Reich motor highways; undertook special assignments for National Socialist Wehrmacht and other Nazi agencies; worked as landscape architect for garden exhibitions in Erfurt, Germany, 1945 and 1946; consultant for various state and communal agencies and for industrial firms in North Rhine-Westphalia, 1950–51; professor and director of Institute for Garden Art and Landscape Design at Technical University, Berlin, 1952–59. Died in Bonn, 1974.

## Selected Designs

| | |
|---|---|
| 1920 | Hauptfriedhof Dortmund (Central Cemetery Dortmund), Dortmund, Germany |
| 1926 | "Coming garden," Jubilee Horticulture Exposition, Dresden, Germany |
| 1928 | Parks and Sachsenring stadium of spa, Elster, Germany; gardens of Höhere Staatslehranstalt für Gartenbau (Horticultural College), Pillnitz, Germany |
| 1928–31 | Green-space plan (Grünflächenplan), Hindenburg, Germany |
| 1932 | Parks, Richard Wagner Concert Hall (Festspielhaus), Bayreuth, Bavaria, Germany; gardens, state hospital, Zwickau, Saxony, Germany |
| 1932–34 | Gardens, Forschungssiedlung (research settlement) Haselhorst, Berlin, Germany |
| 1932–36 | Richard Wagner grove, Palmengarten (Palm Garden), and promenades (with Ulrich Wolf), Leipzig, Saxony, Germany |
| 1933 | Deutsche Gartenbau-Ausstellung, Berlin, Germany |
| 1934 | Garden show "Sommerblumen am Funkturm," Berlin, Germany |
| 1938–41 | Sports park and woods, Junkers airplane and motor factory, Dessau, Germany |
| 1955–60 | Clinic, University of Cologne, Cologne, Germany |
| 1960–66 | Landscape, Bigge barrage, North Rhine-Westphalia, Germany |

## Selected Publications

"Vom Planen und Bauen neuer Friedhöfe," *Die Gartenwelt* 26 (1922)

"Auf dem Kristallberge," *Die Gartenkunst* 37 (1924)

*Die Jubiläums-Gartenbau-Ausstellung Dresden 1926,* 1926

"Deutsche Gartenbau- und Schlesische Gewerbe-Ausstellung Liegnitz 1927," *Behörden-Gartenbau* 4, no. 1 (1927)

"Die neuen Frei- und Grünflächen der Stadt Hindenburg O.S.," *Die Gartenkunst* 41, no. 9 (1928)

"Neuordnung des Gartenbauwesens," *Die Gartenkunst* 46, no. 9 (1933)

"'Die Deutsche Gartenbauausstellung, Berlin 1933' als künstlerische Einheit," *Die Gartenkunst* 46, no. 9 (1933)

"Die zukünftigen Aufgaben der Berliner Stadtgartenverwaltung," *Die Gartenkunst* 47 (1934)

"Sport- und Waldpark eines Werkes in Dessau," *Die Gartenkunst* 54 (1941)

*Das lebendige Grün in Bauentwürfen, Bäume und Bauten,* 1946

*Der deutsche Garten, sein Wesen und seine Schönheit in alter und neuer Zeit,* 1950

*Das Gartenheim,* 1953

*Schöne Wohngärten in Stadt und Land,* 1955

*Das Hohelied von Gartenkunst und Gartenbau; 150 Jahre Gartenbau-Ausstellungen in Deutschland,* 1963

## Further Reading

Architekten- und Ingenieur-Verein zu Berlin, editor, *Berlin und seine Bauten,* vol. 4, part C, *Wohnungsbau,* Berlin: Ernst, 1975

Gröning, Gert, and Joachim Wolschke-Bulmahn, *Grüne Biographien: Biographisches Handbuch zur*

*Landschaftsarchitektur des 20. Jahrhunderts in Deutschland*, Berlin: Patzer-Verlag, 1997

Gröning, Gert, and Uwe Schneider, "Nachlässe von Gartenarchitekten des 19. und 20. Jahrhunderts als Grundlage freiraumplanerischer Forschung," *Die Gartenkunst* 8, no. 1 (1996)

Werner, F.W., "Prof. Gustav Allinger 75 Jahre," *Der Gartenbauingenieur* 12, no. 1 (1967)

Wolschke-Bulmahn, Joachim, "The Peculiar Garden: The Advent and the Destruction of Modernism in German Garden Design," in *The Modern Garden in Europe and the United States*, edited by Robin S. Karson, Cold Spring, New York: Garden Conservance, 1994

JOACHIM WOLSCHKE-BULMAHN

# Allotment

An allotment is a small portion of land rented by an individual for the purpose of cultivation. The practice of tenant farming dates back to medieval times. In Britain provision of land for allotments came about at the time of the Enclosures Acts in the 18th and 19th centuries. Enclosure of more than 3 million acres of land, including common land (community land on which some livestock grazing was allowed), deprived people of land on which to live, grow food, and graze livestock. Concern for poor people in rural areas led to land for allotment use being provided by parish councils, private landowners, and charities. Private institutions such as the railway companies and water boards were also to provide land. The 1845 Enclosure Act made it mandatory for land to be set aside for "allotments for the labouring poor," which were administered by the enclosure officers.

Toward the end of the 19th century the first allotment legislation was introduced in England empowering local authorities to acquire land, by compulsory purchase if necessary, for the provision of allotments. Legislation also required local authorities to provide allotments if there was a proven demand and if such lands were not available privately. Thus, local authorities became the main providers of allotments.

In the beginning of the 20th century, no distinction was made between allotments and smallholdings, or in other words, land cultivated for food for domestic use and land on which crops were raised for commercial sale. The newly formed Agricultural Organizations Society was made up of allotment holders, smallholders, and farmers. The 1908 Smallholdings and Allotments Act consolidated all previous legislation and remains the basic legislation for allotments (along with the 1922 and 1925 Allotment Acts). It still requires local authorities to provide allotments where demand is proven, such demand being defined as representation from six or more resident registered electors.

Although many allotments were in rural areas, the early 20th century saw a demand for allotments in urban areas. This demand increased during World War I, when many people were introduced to allotment gardening for the first time. In order to meet the need, land had to be requisitioned and then, after the war, returned to the original owners. This practice led to legislation to give allotment holders some measure of security against "arbitrary ejection" and compensation for disturbance.

Interest in allotment gardening remained high after the war. No longer were plots provided solely for the laboring poor, and the recreational aspects of allotment gardening began to be recognized. At a time of high unemployment and increasing vegetable prices, allotment gardening became an essential feature of many households and a part of working-class tradition.

In the 1920s and 1930s, with the passage of further legislation and the formation of the National Allotment Society, allotment provision and management became better organized. Three types of allotment sites existed: statutory sites, where land was acquired specifically for allotments; temporary sites, where land was leased or bought for another purpose but used for allotments in the interim; and private sites, which were not provided by the local authority. Local authorities could not dispose of statutory sites without the prior permission of the secretary of state for the environment.

With the outbreak of World War II demand for allotments increased once again. "Dig For Victory" campaigns began, and local authorities were empowered to use vacant land under the Cultivation of Lands (Allotments) Order of 1939. Literature appeared to help educate novice gardeners on the cultivation of crops. By the end of the war there were an estimated 1.5 million allotments. This number soon declined, however, as requisitioned sites were returned to their owners, new houses were built with their own gardens, and general postwar development made land less available.

In 1947 the National Allotment Society, which had been very active during the war, changed its name to National Allotment and Gardens Society. The following

Example of allotments ca. 1967 in Cowley, Oxford, England
Courtesy of Mary Evans Picture Library

year the Society submitted evidence to the government's Allotment Advisory Committee urging that four acres (1.6 ha) of allotment land should be provided for every 1,000 people. This recommendation was incorporated into legislation that also stated the need for local authorities to make such a provision.

In the 1960s the Labour government established a committee to examine allotment policy and suggest any necessary changes. The Thorpe Report was published in 1968 with several recommendations. Allotment legislation was to be updated and consolidated into a single Act. The term *allotment* would be replaced with *leisure garden* to convey a more suitable image. The distinction between statutory and nonstatutory sites should be abolished and replaced with established (life expectancy

of 21 years) and nonestablished sites. Local authorities would agree to a minimum standard of provision and would be able to borrow money for provision of allotments. Rents would be "fair" and based on the administrative and maintenance costs. A development program would be drawn up. And unless they had the approval of the secretary of state to do otherwise, authorities would be obliged to use receipts from the sale of leisure garden land for allotment purposes. However, these recommendations were not implemented.

In the 1970s new legislation allowed local authorities to dispose of allotment land with permission from the Secretary of State for the Environment, providing that alternative land was provided for dispossessed tenants and some of the sale proceeds were used to improve existing sites. The National Allotment and Garden Society changed its name to become the National Society of Allotment and Leisure Gardens, which reflected the change in allotment use at this time. Demand for plots increased in the short term as a result of growing ecological awareness, the oil crisis, and an increase in the price of potatoes, but this demand declined in the 1980s. However, sites with good facilities were—and still are—sought after. In the early 1980s legislation was passed allowing local authorities to decide for themselves, without seeking permission of the secretary of state, whether money from the sale of allotment land is surplus to requirements and may thus be spent for non-allotment purposes.

Allotment gardening today is very different from the days when allotments were used to provide food for the family. With fresh fruits and vegetables readily available from supermarkets, the reasons for having an allotment have changed. Allotment gardening is regarded as a leisure pursuit, an opportunity for fresh air, relaxation, exercise, and socializing. The range of crops grown on the plots has been extended from traditional crops to include flowers, soft fruits, and "exotic" vegetables. The traditional image of the allotment gardener as a retired working-class male is also changing as a more diverse range of people take on plots. Younger and more middle-class people are becoming allotment gardeners, and inner-city sites are multicultural. Although allotment gardening is still male dominated, more women are participating today, and some sites are family oriented.

Allotment sites are mainly provided and managed by local authorities, although a few private sites still exist. In many cases day-to-day management responsibilities have been delegated to an allotment association based on site. Allotment holders now expect a greater level of provision—for example, security features, parking spaces, plots with sheds, access to running water and toilets—although levels of investment by local authorities do not always match expectations. Receipts from sale of extra sites can be used to improve remaining sites, providing roadways, water, and sheds. For purposes of uniformity many local authorities prefer to offer allotments with a standard shed, although structures built by allotment-holders often have a certain idiosyncrasy and are good examples of recycling. Literature is often provided that gives new plot-holders help with planning their crops and other useful advice. Allotment associations, in conjunction with the local authority, often run winter activity programs providing an opportunity to socialize and learn.

Distribution of allotment sites within the local authority's jurisdiction does not always match demand; thus, there may be vacant plots on some sites and waiting lists for others. Vacant plots cause problems such as weeds seeding to adjacent plots, and potential tenants are reluctant to take on neglected plots. The result can be a poor image that only exacerbates the problem. Some solutions include grouping of vacant plots together to make a landscaped parking lot or an area for toilets or playgrounds; another alternative is to create communal gardens. Vacant plots are less likely to occur on well-managed sites. Vandalism also discourages people from taking on allotments; secure sites with good facilities are far more attractive to potential plot-holders. Theft from allotments has become an increasing problem.

Current legislation in Britain supports only the traditional allotment rather than the continental style of leisure garden. Rental agreements specify the types of crops that may or may not be grown. Restrictions often apply to permanent crops such as fruit trees or practices such as the growing of flowers or single crops for commercial sale. However, there may be some latitude if the relaxation of rules results in well-tended plots. Flower growing and soft fruit cultivation are often permitted, and some authorities actively encourage landscaping around sheds.

Allotments still have statutory protection but are under constant threat of development, despite being recognized as an important form of public open space and mentioned in British government policy initiatives such as *Greening the City* (1996). Allotment holders can be moved from a statutory site provided they are offered an alternative site. They may find, however, that the alternative site does not have the same statutory protection and is offered only on a short-term lease. The average rate of loss in the 1990s was said to be in the region of 50 sites per year. Yet allotments are an important part of sustainability, and the British government has stated that it recognizes that allotments can form part of sustainable regeneration of towns and cities. At the end of the 20th century the future of allotments in England was under active discussion. A House of Commons select committee began an inquiry in 1998. Allotment associations were fighting to protect their sites from development and presented evidence at the inquiry, as did the National Society of Allotment and Leisure Gardeners.

In the United States the community garden is the equivalent to the British allotment site although very different in style. Community gardens began to develop during World War II. There are similarities in that the gardens may be established on permanent sites or on sites with varying length of lease or sometimes no lease at all. City councils, institutions, or private owners may own the land, with the gardens being managed by community groups. Many sites are often under threat of development. There is greater emphasis on ornamentation than on a British allotment site, with permanent planting of trees, shrubs, and perennials, but the garden plots are also highly productive. Communal areas are important features. Organizations exist to help groups establish and manage community gardens.

Leisure gardens rather than allotments are to be found on the Continent. They are regarded much more as a form of recreation than in Britain, although their original purpose was not dissimilar. In Germany the *Kleingärten* is the family garden for those people who live in apartments. Fruit and vegetables are grown, but part of the plot is planted with ornamental plants. The plot also has a chalet for the storage of tools and materials (chalets may also be used for the occasional overnight stay). Permanent residence in chalets is not permitted, and the authorities have much say in the appearance and design of the chalet. There are parallels to the situation in Britain in that demand for allotments fell in the 1970s, and allotment holders tended to be older people. Today, likewise, demand has increased and families are involved, encouraged by facilities such as clubs, play areas, and organized activities.

## Further Reading

Ahrens, Caroline, and Brita von Schoenaich, "Community Spirit," *The Garden* 119, no. 8 (1994)

Crouch, David, *English Allotments Survey: Report of the Joint Survey of Allotments in England,* Corcky, Northamptonshire: National Society of Allotment and Leisure Gardeners Limited and Anglia Polytechnic University, 1997

Crouch, David, and Colin Ward, *The Allotment: Its Landscape and Culture,* London: Faber, 1988

Garnett, Tara, *Growing Food in the Cities: A Report to Highlight and Promote the Benefits of Urban Agriculture in the United Kingdom,* London: National Food Alliance, 1996

*The Government's Response to the Environment, Transport, and Regional Affairs Committee's Report: The Future for Allotments,* London: HMSO, 1998

Hyde, Michael, *City Fields, Country Gardens*, edited by David Crouch and Martin Stott, Nottingham: Five Leaves Publications, 1998

Hynes, H. Patricia, *A Patch of Eden: America's Inner City Gardeners,* White River Junction, Vermont: Chelsea Green, 1996

Larkcom, Joy, "Community Service," *The Garden* 121, no. 3, (1996)

Parliament, House of Commons Environment, Transport, and Regional Affairs Committee, *The Future for Allotments,* 2 vols., London: HMSO, 1998

Stokes, Geoff, "Plotting for the Future," *The Garden* 122, no. 3, (1997)

Stott, Martin, "Don't Lose the Plot," *Town and Country Planning* 167, no. 2 (1998)

SANDRA NICHOLSON

# Alphand, Jean-Charles Adolphe 1817–1891

## French Engineer and Landscape Designer

Between 1854 and 1870 J.C.A. Alphand's hand touched every quarter of Paris; the parks, gardens, squares, and boulevards on which he worked are the tangible evidence of Napoléon III's transformation of Paris from a teeming, dense medieval city into a preeminent European capital filled with "light and air" and acknowledged as a model of urban design. Alphand's numerous works reflect not only his technical training as an engineer and his understanding of landscape traditions but also the skills of his associates within Paris's Department of Parks. The boulevards and squares display sophisticated design strategies for defining urban spaces. In contrast to these highly ordered geometric lines and moments interwoven into the urban fabric, Alphand's work on five major parks embraced concepts rooted in popular picturesque imagery. Massings of plants arranged on circuit drives and promenades contribute to the visual experience of these parks, yet much of their scenic quality must be attributed to Alphand's remarkable technological innovations, particularly at the Parc des Buttes-Chaumont, one of the crowning design achievements of his tenure. Like the work of his American counterpart, Frederick Law Olmsted, Sr., Alphand's major urban parks can be appreciated as examples of highly engineered "natural" landscapes that engage the full range of 19th-century construction techniques and materials to achieve their image.

Alphand was born in Grenoble, Switzerland, where his father was a colonel in the French artillery force. Alphand ventured to Paris in 1834 to complete his advanced studies at the Lycée Charlemagne. In the following year he entered the École Polytechnique. Upon matriculating in 1838 he entered into his specialized training for civil and structural engineering at the École des Ponts et Chaussées, a school established in 1744. The influential head of the school during Alphand's time was Gaspard François Prony, who formerly associated closely with the engineer Jean Rodolphe Peronnet in the design and construction of some of the latter's finer bridges. As a result Alphand's training engaged the most up to date technology and design theory for bridges. Another influential faculty member was C.L.M. Navier, whose textbook *Leçons sur l'application de la mechanique* (1826; Lessons in Applied Mechanics) provided Alphand with a solid foundation in mechanics and hydraulics—skills he employed throughout his career.

Some time shortly after his graduation in 1843, Alphand took a position as an engineer of roads and bridges at Bordeaux. For the next ten years he worked through a period of apprenticeship and developed his technical skills working on several projects, most notably the design and construction supervision for the harbor basin and quays. The coup of 1851 turned political tides, and Emperor Napoléon appointed Baron Georges-Eugene Haussmann as prefect of the Seine. Under Haussmann's orchestration Alphand designed a grand triumphal setting for a reception honoring Napoléon III held in October 1852. The event proved seminal for Alphand's political future; he gained not only his superior's approval but also the notice of the future emperor. In November 1854 Alphand arrived in Paris as Haussmann's protégé. His quick rise through the ranks of the prestigious civil service began on 5 December 1854, when he replaced the horticulturist Louis-Sulpice Varé to become the engineer in charge of the Bois de Boulogne project.

The transformation of the Bois de Boulogne's 2,000 acres (809 ha) from hunting park to civic grounds initiated Napoléon III's urban campaign. Following the emperor's wishes, the intentions for the redesign of the park embraced the picturesque image of the garden parks found in England beginning in the 18th century. In addition, the park was to be a place where the citizens of Paris could benefit from the fresh air and enjoy the civic interaction afforded during the promenade. The work on the park fit into the larger urban design goals laid out by the emperor, which included improving the health of the citizens and visitors, improved internal movement systems within the city, and the enhancement and addition of green spaces.

In all of these endeavors Alphand plays a significant role, but isolating his part in the overall design ideas and concepts from Haussmann's within this urban milieu is problematic. The process of clarifying their roles as set forth in Haussmann's memoirs and Alphand's book *Les promenades de Paris* (1867–73; The Promenades of Paris) is complicated because the vast majority of civic-planning and financial records from this era were burned or destroyed during the overthrow of the Communards in the early 1870s. Nonetheless, one can discern Alphand's hand within the individual projects. At the Bois de Boulogne his engineering skills are revealed in the construction of the water features. In striving to accede with the emperor's wishes for a body of water, the original engineer had designed a large lake that immediately drained because of porous soils and improper elevations. Alphand's ingenious solution called for an elaborate pump system to bring water to the Lac Supérieur (upper lake) and the Lac Inférieur (lower lake), which were fully excavated and the beds prepared with a newly tested cementitious concrete lining. Other features and elements at the Bois de Boulogne that became Alphand signatures throughout his ensuing works include a grotto, running rivulets and rills of water, an irrigation watering system, rock work called *rocaille,* and the collection of details and structures such as railings, benches, bridges, kiosks, iron grates, and lights.

Alphand was particularly skillful at marrying his engineering skills with an aesthetic in the parks. As at the Bois de Boulogne, the results at the Bois des Vincennes, the Parc Monceau, Parc du Trocadéro, Parc des Buttes-Chaumont, and Parc Montsouris are picturesque parks fully constructed to exploit—and even show off—the designer's technological skill and use of innovative materials. At Buttes-Chaumont and Montsouris, two new parks created in what were then outlying arrondissements, Alphand created landscapes featuring promenades and paths that follow the curves and forms of the ground to provide a series of shifting visual scenes and experiences. At Buttes Chaumont the strongly contoured shape arose from the vestiges of an old gypsum quarry that Alphand accentuated and reiterated as a series of high points within the park. The cascading water features, rock work, and bridges at both parks reveal the latest technology in hydraulic pumps, reinforced concrete, and cast-iron detailing. In this respect Alphand's landscape designs merge his training with the picturesque images.

In planting the parks and boulevards, Alphand worked closely with a team of experts, most notably Jean-Pierre Barillet-Deschamps, a horticulturist trained at the Jardins des Plantes whom Alphand brought back to Paris around 1860. They used both local and exotic plant materials arranged to highlight the spaces and scenes initiated through the contouring of the ground. At the Parc Monceau this collaboration successfully emerges as a garden with a rich palette. Massed shrub beds form the spaces, highlighted by floral displays and sculptural elements. Specimen trees such as a copper beech and weeping willow accentuate the long vistas that flow the length of the park.

Tree planting on the boulevards and in the formal squares takes on a different character with a plant list focused on street trees such as horse chestnut, sycamore, and linden. The precise geometric layout contributes greatly to the feeling of order and space within the new urban street system. In particular, the street-tree planting program must be recognized for the qualities it offers in the sectional design of broad sidewalks and tree borders flanking the road and the added layer of trees reinforcing the regularity of the Haussmannian architecture. The result is the effect of long perspective vistas linking the key moments within the urban fabric, a signature of the French urban design tradition within which Alphand falls.

Alphand documented his contributions to the redesign and creation of "modern" Paris in his book *Les promenades de Paris,* which carefully catalogs the tools, techniques, materials, methods, and history of garden design, showing everything from details of artesian wells and sewer sections to planting bed and street-tree layouts, building elevations, and park furnishings. The book extensively supports the explanations of his projects with data on costs and construction issues, as well with many plans, perspectives, and details. *Les promenades de Paris* proved extremely influential; it was distributed as a gift to the heads of state and significant leaders in capitals throughout Europe and the United States. Indeed, the design of such cities as Berlin, Barcelona, Vienna, and Washington, D.C., all show some influences garnered from Alphand's Paris. Today, both the city and the book stand as testimony to the efforts and vision of Emperor Napoléon, Baron Haussmann, and their chief designer, J.C.A. Alphand.

*See also* Bois de Boulogne; Buttes Chaumont; Parc Monceau

## Biography

Born 26 October 1817 in Grenoble, Switzerland. Trained at École Polytechnique, Paris, beginning 1835; began working as government engineer of roads and bridges, Bordeaux, where he constructed harbor basin and orchestrated grand setting for reception honoring Louis-Napoléon Bonaparte, 1854; called to Paris as the protegée of Baron Georges-Eugene Haussmann and appointed to Corps des Ponts et Chaussées, late 1854; as Haussmann's assistant, chiefly responsible for parks and landscaping; responsibility for creating city's greenhouses and nurseries, 1855–59; chief engineer of parks, 1867; director of streets and parks, 1869; director of works for City of Paris, 1878–91. Died in Paris, France, 6 December 1891.

## Selected Designs

| | |
|---|---|
| 1843–53 | Harbor basin and quays, Bordeaux, France |
| 1854–58 | Redesign of Bois de Boulogne, Paris, France |
| 1855 | Champs-Élysées, Paris, France |
| 1856 | Square de la Tour Saint-Jacques, Paris, France |
| 1860–65 | Redesign of Bois des Vincennes, Paris, France |
| 1860–61 | Redesign of Parc Monceau, Paris, France |
| 1862 | Square des Innocents, Paris, France |
| 1862–70 | Boulevards, including Saint-Germaine, Saint-Michel, Arago, and Richard-Lenoir, as well as L'Avenue de l'Impératrice and L'Avenue de L'Observatoire, Paris, France |
| 1864–67 | Parc des Buttes-Chaumont, Paris, France |
| 1866–67 | Place du Roi-de-Rome, International Exposition grounds, and Parc du Trocadéro, Paris, France |
| 1867–78 | Parc Montsouris, Paris, France |

## Selected Publications

*Les promenades de Paris,* 1867–73
*L'art des jardins, parcs, promenades* (with Baron Alfred Auguste Ernouf), 1889

## Further Reading

Choay, Francoise, "Haussmann et le systeme des espaces verts parisien," *Revue de l'art* 29 (1975)

Conan, Michel, and Isabelle Marghieri, "Figures on the Grass: The Public Gardens of Paris," *Landscape* 31, no. 1 (1991)

Grumbach, Antoine, "The Promenades of Paris," *Oppositions* 8 (Spring 1977)

Lafenestre, Georges, "La vie et les oeuvres de M. Alphand," *L'ami des monuments et des arts parisiens et français* 14, no. 77 (May 1900)

Marceca, Maria Luisa, "Reservoir, Circulation, Residue: J.C.A. Alphand, Technological Beauty, and the Green City," *Lotus International* 30 (1981)

Merivale, John, "Charles-Adolphe Alphand and the Parks of Paris," *Landscape Design* 123 (August 1978)

Meyer, Elizabeth K., "The Public Park as Avante-Garde (Landscape) Architecture: A Comparative Interpretation of Two Parisian Parks, Parc de la Villette (1983–1990) and Parc des Buttes Chaumont (1864–1867)," *Landscape Journal* 10, no. 1 (Spring 1991)

Pinkney, David H., *Napoleon III and the Rebuilding of Paris,* Princeton, New Jersey: Princeton University Press, 1958

Robinson, William, *The Parks, Promenades, and Gardens of Paris, Described and Considered in*

*Relation to the Wants of Our Own Cities and the Public and Private Gardens*, London, 1869; 3rd edition, as *The Parks and Gardens of Paris*, 1883

Strauss, M. Paul, "M. Alphand et les travaux de Paris," *Revue politique et litteraire: Revue bleue* 48 (1891)

ANN E. KOMARA

# Alpine Garden

Ancient rock gardens, carefully arranged with blocks of stone forming natural towers and sparsely planted, still exist in China. In Japanese gardens, stones have been used as garden features for at least the last 1,500 years. However, the first rock gardens, as we know them today, are considered to have been developed in the 18th century.

The rockery created in a greenhouse at Chelsea Physic Garden, built in 1772, is probably the first rock garden. It was constructed of 40 tons of old Portland stone from the Tower of London to which flints, pieces of chalk, and volcanic lava brought from Iceland were added. Some of it still exists in modified form, although much of the Portland stone has been removed, and the original rocks now form a rock garden around a bust of Sir Hans Sloane, who leased the garden in 1772 from the Worshipful Company of Apothecaries, which had laid it out in 1673.

The exploration of the world's mountainous areas beginning in the late 18th century led to the discovery of novel flora, often with flowers of jewel-like intensity, that influenced the initial interest in rock gardens. Drs. John Fothergill and William Pitcairn, English physicians and botanists, sponsored the first known expedition to collect alpine plants with a view to cultivating them. In 1775, Fothergill and Pitcairn jointly commissioned Thomas Blaikie for a plant-collecting expedition to the Alps and Switzerland. Blaikie collected 447 different species from the Alps and the Jura on this trip that were planted in Fothergill's botanical garden at Upton House, West Hamm. Many of the plants he brought back began to appear at flower shows and in alpine houses, and as a result, a fashion for growing these plants began to develop, resulting in the construction of gardens for their care and display.

By the 1830s, the growing of alpines in pots was sufficiently common for Joseph Paxton's *Magazine of Botany* to recommend, under the heading "Operations for October," that "the various kinds of alpine plants should be removed to their winter quarters and introduced into the cold frame or pit, where a dry floor has previously been made with coal ashes." More ambitious attempts were the imitations of mountain scenery, first evidenced at Hoole House, Cheshire, in the 1830s, where Lady Broughton's rockery re-created the mountains of Chamonix with the snow-covered summits and glaciers being represented in white spar. American landscape gardener Andrew Jackson Downing wrote about rockeries in his 1841 *A Treatise on the Theory and Practice of Landscape Gardening*, which suggests that rockeries were also being developed in the United States at this time.

The success of cultivating the alpine plants in these rock gardens was a challenge. Some botanic gardens were developing alpinums to study, cultivate, and display alpine plants. Study of these alpine plants indicated that many required specific environmental conditions to thrive. Many alpine plants thrive under an unvarying annual cycle of up to six months' snow cover, while lowlands, where the rock gardens were being established, typically have a fluctuating winter climate. Some alpine plants thrive in the rock debris continually flaking off by the action of the frost that is found on the sides of mountains—the unstable "scree." Scree beds are now a feature of many rock gardens. Austrian botanist Anton Kerner von Marilaun successfully established an alpinum at the Botanic Garden in Innsbruck with the plantings in scree conditions segregated according to the valleys of the Tyrol. He also established alpine research gardens at elevations ranging from 1,524 to 2,133 meters (1,666 to 2,332 yd.). His book *The Cultivation of Alpine Plants,* published in 1864, stimulated the interest of private gardeners and botanic gardens to establish alpinums. Irish gardener William Robinson's book *Alpine Flowers for English Gardens,* published in 1870, was also influential. By the end of the 19th century, significant rock gardens could be found at the Royal Botanic Gardens at Kew and Edinburgh and at Backhouse Nurseries, York.

English plant collector Reginald Farrer was the leading figure in the development of rock gardens in the early 1900s. His book *The English Rock Garden* (two volumes, 1919) is still considered a classic book on the subject. Farrer promoted the use of imitation moraines as the growing medium for alpine plants. The rockery of the 1920s and 1930s was characterized by the use of moraines and scree beds, so interest switched more to the plants and away from the rock structures.

Today, as urban areas continue to expand, usually with smaller garden spaces than in the past, the demand for alpine and rock-growing plants, most of which are dwarf, has grown considerably. A review of current popular garden books provides further evidence of the continued popularity of rock gardens.

**Further Reading**

Cabot, Francis H., "As It Was in the Beginning," *Bulletin of the American Rock Garden Society* 42, no. 5 (1984)

Farrer, Reginald, *The English Rock Garden,* London: Jack, 1919; reprint, Sakonnet, Rhode Island: Theophrastus, 1975
Robinson, William, *Alpine Flowers for English Gardens,* London, 1870
Thomas, Graham Stuart, *The Rock Garden and Its Plants: From Grotto to Alpine House,* Portland, Oregon: Sagapress/Timber Press, 1989

CANDICE A. SHOEMAKER AND PAUL MILES

# American Garden

During the 18th century, the importation into Britain of plants from eastern North America gave rise to two types of planting within the English landscape garden: the "shrubbery" and the "American garden." Beginning in 1735, a London merchant, Peter Collinson, made an agreement with John Bartram of Philadelphia to collect and send seeds of American plants to his subscribers in England. This influx coincided with moves to informalize garden design; the clipped hedges of the geometric "wilderness" were replaced by tiered arrangements of flowering shrubs that included American exotics. In the 1750s these graduated Picturesque plantations acquired the name *shrubbery.* Some American plants, however, were better suited to shady woodlands where leaf mold was abundant. Thus in the mid-18th century, Lord Botetourt and Dr. John Fothergill experimented with planting magnolias, kalmias, and rhododendrons beneath existing oaks and yews. Only around 1800, however, were such specialized woodland gardens called "American gardens."

One of the most famous American gardens was that at Fonthill, created from the 1780s by William Beckford. It was described by John Rutter in 1823. Among the "groves of the loftiest rhododendrons" were winding paths lined with Carolina rose (*Rosa carolina*), allspice (*Calycanthus floridus*), strawberry tree (*Arbutus unedo*), and Portugal laurel (*Prunus lusitanica*). The presence of European species indicates how an "American garden" could contain plants from areas other than America. Thus in John Claudius Loudon's *Encyclopaedia* of 1822, the entry "Select American and other Peat-Earth Shrubs" listed "Cistus, Arbutus, Vaccinium, Andromeda, Erica, Daphne" along with "Magnolia . . . Rhododendron, Azalia, Kalmia" from America.

Loudon described different ways of using these plants: hardy rhododendrons placed on the margins of woodland in pits of peat and leaf mold; herbaceous plants used at the front of a "sloping phalanx of American trees"; or "low species of heaths and other bog undershrubs" substituted for flowers in an "American shrubbery." In this sense, many woodland American gardens were hybrids, evolving out of the graduated shrubberies of the mid-18th century. Where a canopy had formed after 50 years' growth, a new American understory could be added. One such example was Lancelot "Capability" Brown's wilderness of the 1750s at Petworth, replanted in the late 18th century. By 1810 one visitor, Louis Simond, having spent several years in America, could describe this pleasure ground as "planted with the largest trees, close together, something like a heavy-timbered American forest." In such woodland gardens some American plants became naturalized; Loudon referred to the "extensive woods of Fonthill, where, as also at King's Weston near Bristol, Kenwood at Hampstead, etc., many of the plants shed their seeds, and young rhododendrons and azalias spring up in abundance."

The provision of shade or partial shade, a peaty, humus-rich soil, and constant watering simulated conditions found in America. In James Mean's revised edition of Abercrombie's *Practical Gardener* of 1817, an account links cultivation to habitat:

> Most of the exotic shrubs brought from America, were originally found growing on tracts of ground resembling our beds of peat, except that the alluvial soil there extends along a greater surface, and the body of vegetable mould embedded in the swamp is richer and deeper. . . . The luxuriance of the vegetables may . . . partly be ascribed to the excessive moisture which is peculiar to the climate of America.

One way to reduce the risk of drought was to give the American shrubs a northern or eastern exposure.

W. Hughes, "A View of the Scenery of the American Plantations," from J. Rutter, *Delineations of Fonthill*, 1823
Courtesy of Dumbarton Oaks, Studies in Landscape Architecture, Photo Archive

Fothergill placed his collection of small American shrubs and herbaceous plants beneath a north wall in rich black soil mixed with sand. Plentiful watering in summer and a warm covering of ferns in winter ensured a good survival rate.

Fothergill's two types of American garden—the woodland garden and the north border—reflect divergent possibilities in organizing a collection of American plants: on the one hand, the attempt to make a "wild garden," simulating conditions found in North American forests, and on the other, a concern for organizing a group of plants of distinct geographical origin into an artificial setting that suited their cultural needs. In some sites, American gardens were little more than a botanical display of American and ericaceous plants. When, for example, the Rev. Arthur Young visited Lord Coventry's Croome Court in 1801, he found

> a part of the flower garden . . . dedicated to the growth of American shrubs and plants, hence called the American Border: it contains every variety of the azalea, Kalmia, and rhododendron, ledum and vaccinium genus; 15 varieties of Andromeda, and all the hardier heaths. The soil

for this border (a black sand) was brought, at a considerable expence, by the Severn, from Bewdley Forest.

Young emphasized that the border was not exclusively for American plants. The hardy heathers represented the European ericaceous plants. The "American Border" at Croome formed part of an extensive pleasure ground in which other exotics, tender and hardy, were displayed. Thus, in William Dean's description of the Croome flower garden in 1824, plants from the Indies, the Cape of Good Hope, China, and the South Seas were kept in hothouses alongside "two borders of American plants."

There was an American garden on the Liston estate, Millburn Tower, in Scotland. In 1805 Lady Liston wrote that her "American Garden has received a great accession of Plants, some for *love,* some for *money.*" Plants were exchanged with Thomas Johnes at Hafod in Wales, where an American garden was in the making after 1799. But Lady Liston was also in touch with the large Lee and Kennedy nursery in London. In 1810 she was sent plants by her neighbor, Lord Torphichen of Calder House: "Sumachs, Viburnum, Cheliones, Jessamaines, Broad-leafed Spirea, Nappea, Rudbeckia

Nitida, Diervilla, Bladder Nut, dwarf horsechestnut, tall Phlox, Persimon, Fringe tree, Caster oil nut." Even hardy Australian plants made it into these two "American" gardens.

In the 1790s, when the English landscape designer Humphry Repton converted the wilderness at Bulstrode into an American garden, he followed the woodland style. Yet his American garden at Ashridge (1813) took the form of a hemisphere with radial beds. This duality of styles reflects the dichotomy of the American garden: from naturalness to artificiality. Planting methods were similarly divided into two schools. According to Loudon, American gardens might be "arranged in the mingled manner, or grouped or classed according to some system." In this sense, it shared common ground with the shrubbery and flower border, which were likewise disposed in either a "mingled" or a "grouped" system. By 1843 Loudon's American garden at Coleshill reflected a style loosely associated with the term *gardenesque*. Thus, just as the epithet "American" was fluid enough to include non-American plants, so the appellation "American garden" was vague enough to allow modifications in taste and purpose. By the early 20th century, this distinctive yet diverse type of gardening would die out, as the hardy plants of Asia Minor and Asia gained supremacy over American specimens in English woodland gardens.

**Further Reading**

Dean, William, *An Historical and Descriptive Account of Croome d'Abitot, the Seat of the Right Hon. the Earl of Coventry,* Worcester, 1824

Laird, Mark, "Approaches to Planting in the Late Eighteenth Century: Some Imperfect Ideas on the Origins of the American Garden," *Journal of Garden History* 11, no. 3 (1991)

Laird, Mark, *The Flowering of the Landscape Garden: English Pleasure Grounds, 1720–1800,* Philadelphia: University of Pennsylvania Press, 1999

Loudon, John Claudius, *An Encylopaedia of Gardening,* 2 vols., London, 1822; reprint, New York: Garland, 1982

Rutter, John, *Delineations of Fonthill and Its Abbey,* Shaftsbury, Dorset, and London, 1823

Tait, A.A., "The American Garden at Millburn Tower," in *British and American Gardens in the Eighteenth Century,* edited by Robert P. Maccubbin and Peter Martin, Williamsburg, Virginia: Colonial Williamsburg Foundation, 1984

MARK LAIRD

# Ammann, Gustav 1885–1955

## Swiss Garden Architect

Gustav Ammann, one of the most renowned Swiss garden architects of the first half of the 20th century, had a strong influence on postwar Swiss landscape architecture. After high school Ammann learned the gardening profession at the renowned firm Froebels Erben in Zürich between 1901 and 1903. In the following two years he continued his professional education working at the Zürich Botanical Gardens and attending lectures at University of Zürich. Between 1905 and 1911 he attended the College of Arts and Crafts in Magdeburg, Germany, and worked with renowned German garden architects. Study trips led him to London, Paris, and Florence. Working with the famous German garden architect Leberecht Migge in Hamburg was especially important for the young Swiss garden architect. From Migge he learned about the new functionalistic architectonic garden style and about the connection between modern, public-spirited urban planning and garden architecture.

In 1911 Ammann became the executive garden designer for Froebels Erben. For more than 20 years, until the company closed in 1933, he was responsible for the design of many of Froebels Erben's most popular gardens. During this time he also taught young Swiss garden architects such as Ernst Cramer. He even strongly influenced the internationally renowned architect Richard Neutra, who began working with the garden architecture firm as a young apprentice in 1918 and helped to deepen Neutra's understanding of the relationship between architecture and the landscape. The two became close friends.

In 1934 Ammann created his own garden architecture office in Zürich, one that for the first time was not associated with particular nursery or gardening firm. During these years he worked with many prominent modern Swiss architects of the time, including Max Ernst Haefeli, Werner M. Moser, Rudolf Steiger, Max Frisch, and Albert H. Steiner. Besides numerous private garden projects Ammann also designed public swimming pools, schools, and cemeteries. Among his most famous projects in Zürich are the garden design for the first Swiss Werkbund housing project, Neubühl (1929–30), and the public swimming pools Allenmoos (1939) and Letzigraben (1949). Ammann was also the leading garden architect for the Zürich garden exhibition (ZÜGA) in 1933 and the Swiss national exhibition (Landi) in 1939, also in Zürich. On both occasions he stressed that garden architecture in Switzerland should not get mired in an overly traditional style. Instead of developing a modern garden style, the so-called *Heimatstil* (traditional rustic garden style) became increasingly more important in Switzerland especially during and shortly after World War II.

In addition to his practical work, Ammann wrote a large number of scientific articles in professional magazines and was active in professional associations and commissions. He was one of the founding members and later president of the Swiss Federation of Landscape Architects (BSG/BSLA) and was also a member of the Swiss Werkbund and secretary general of the International Federation of Landscape Architects (IFLA). As a teacher he was active at the Arts and Crafts School in Zürich and at the School of Horticulture in Niederlenz. Although Ammann consistently emphasized the need for a contemporary, simple garden architecture, his garden designs were rather moderately traditional, especially compared with the work of his former apprentice Ernst Cramer.

## Biography

Born in Zürich, Switzerland, 1885. Apprenticeship as gardener at Froebels Erben, Zürich, 1901–3; education at botanical garden, Zürich, and attendance at lectures at University of Zürich; worked in Germany with garden architect R. Hoemann in Düsseldorf and attended arts and crafts school, Magdeburg, 1905–11; years of travel in England (London), France (Paris), and Italy (Florence); executive garden designer for Froebels Erben, Zürich, 1911–33; own office for garden architecture, 1933–55; taught at arts and crafts school, Zürich, and at school of horticulture, Niederlenz; cofounder and later president of Swiss Federation of Landscape Architects; cofounder and member of the Swiss Werkbund, 1917–55; secretary general of the International Federation of Landscape Architects. Died 1955.

## Selected Designs

| 1913 | Zürich, park of villa Zum Fels, Zürich, Switzerland |
| --- | --- |
| 1930–32 | Private gardens for first Swiss Werkbund housing project "Neubühl," Zürich, Switzerland |
| 1932 | Garden design for college of arts and crafts, Zürich, Switzerland |
| 1939 | Open-air swimming pool Allenmoos, Zürich, Switzerland |
| 1948 | Cemetery Hoenggerherg, Zürich, Switzerland |
| 1948 | School in Adliswil, Switzerland |
| 1949 | Open-air swimming pool, Letzigraben, Switzerland |
| 1953 | Garden design for hospital "Waidspital," Zürich, Switzerland |

## Selected Publications

"Begleitworte zu den Arbeiten von Otto Froebels Erben, Zürich," *Das Werk* 4 (1919)

"Der Garten—Ein Rückblick und Ausblick," *Das Werk* 4 (1919)

"Mensch, Bauwerk und Pflanze im Garten," *Das Werk* 6 (1926)

"Sollen wir die Form ganz zertrümmern?" *Die Gartenkunst* 39 (1926)

"Das Raumgesicht," *Die Gartenkunst* 6 (1929)

"'ZÜGA': Die Zürcher Gartenbau-Austellung 1933: Die Gartenanlagen," *Schweizerische Bauzeitung* 10 (1933)

"Die Gärten der Schweizerischen Landesausstellung 1939," *Schweizerische Bauzeitung* 18 (1939)

"Das Landschaftsbild und die Dringlichkeit seiner Pflege und Gestaltung," *Schweizerische Bauzeitung – Sonderheft über Landschaftsgestaltung* 15 (1941)

"Ist das 'Natürliche' ein Form-Ersatz?" *Schweizer Garten* 2 (1945)

"Die Entwicklung der Gartengestaltung," *Garten und Landschaft* 4 (1952)

"Alles fliesst (Heraklit)," *Garten und Landschaft* 1 (1953)

*Blühende Gärten; Landscape Gardens; Jardins en fleurs,* 1955

## Further Reading

Bucher, Annemarie, *Vom Landschaftsgarten zur Gartenlandschaft: Gartenkunst zwischen 1880 und 1980 im Archiv für Schweizer Gartenarchitektur und Landschaftsplanung,* Zurich: Hochschulverlag AG an der ETH, 1996

UDO WEILACHER

# Amphitheater/Theater

An amphitheater is an outdoor theater that typically has an inclined, semicircular curved group of seats facing a level performance space. Designed to take advantage of natural inclines, amphitheaters developed in ancient Greece and became common features of both Greek and Roman imperial cities. Abandoned until the Renaissance, amphitheaters then became common features in formal private gardens, university campuses, and public gardens. In addition to their simple and functional design, amphitheaters possess an inherent relationship with nature and a sculptural quality that makes them a popular feature in many historic and contemporary gardens.

The relationship between amphitheaters and the landscape has existed since their initial development in ancient Greece. Their architectural form developed out of naturally formed hollows and bowl-like hillsides that overlooked a level area containing space to dance, sing, and erect an altar for the cult of Dionysus. As the popularity of these ritual performances grew, the Greeks soon developed a permanent architectural model that employed stone seats on an artificially banked hillside, the circular performance space, called the orchestra, and a semipermanent backdrop. In addition to the rites of Dionysus, amphitheaters were also used for public meetings and musical, literary, and dramatic performances.

The Greek amphitheater remained largely unchanged until the appearance of the Romans, who soon altered the Greek amphitheaters to host the outlandish and violent spectacles that they craved. With the dissolution of the Roman Empire, the construction of amphitheaters fell victim to the Christian distaste for pagan Roman culture.

During the European Renaissance amphitheaters returned to the landscape as an attribute of garden design. Not only did this period introduce a new fascination with gardening, but designers used principles of classical art, architecture, and mythology in the hopes of regaining a classical mysticism and philosophy of nature. As a result, amphitheaters were used as a classical embellishment and as a place for outdoor gatherings and entertainment. One of the most famous amphitheaters built during the Renaissance is found in the Boboli Garden in Florence. Situated behind the Pitti Palace, this large amphitheater is ornamented with several niches filled with neoclassical statuary and a centrally located obelisk. Built by one of Florence's most influential families, the Medici, the Boboli Garden amphitheater also hosted private spectacles, such as a naval battle in 1589, and public events that attracted most of Florence.

Baroque garden designers continued to favor classical motifs. In Italy amphitheaters were popular features in many elaborate gardens, such as that found on the Isola Bella (1671), on Lake Maggiore. Similar to the Boboli Garden amphitheaters, niches filled with neoclassical figures and a central statue of Hercules dominate the amphitheater's backdrop.

The baroque period also introduced amphitheaters that are indebted more to innovative garden design than to historic precedents. For example, the *theatre de verdure,* or green theater, is a garden theater that employs stages and backdrops formed of vegetation. Baroque designers also incorporated elaborate water treatments in garden theaters, a notable example of which exists among the canals and alleys at the garden of Versailles. Here, André Le Nôtre hid a water theater, Le Salle de Bal (1683), within a bosquet, an outdoor space enclosed with hedges and trees. This intimate and decorative amphitheater includes several fountains and water that cascades down its semicircular seating area. Nonetheless, Le Salle de Bal also maintains its attachment to classical antiquity with several neoclassical urns and statuary.

During the early 18th century classical architectural features remained common contrivances for English garden designers. The extensive, pastoral grounds of large country houses during this period provided an opportunity to re-create the noble tranquillity of the antique landscape, such as the Greco-Roman amphitheater built at Claremont in Surrey. Here, the design reduces the theater form to natural, almost abstract elements: grass replaces the stone architecture, and a circular pond replaces the orchestra.

Amphitheaters were found in elaborate, private gardens until the early 20th century. Amphitheaters, which now relied on the classicism of the Renaissance and baroque eras, were also popular in the gardens that surrounded the private houses of wealthy American industrialists, such as Villa Vizcaya (1912) and the James Deering estate in Miami, Florida. In the United States public or nonprofit organizations, such as Red Rocks Amphitheater, a municipally owned theater built outside of Denver, Colorado, in the early 1940s, created and operated most amphitheaters. In addition, several amphitheaters began to appear on college and university campuses, such as the Browning Amphitheater at Ohio State University (1925) and the Scott Outdoor Amphitheater at Swarthmore College (1942).

After the 1980s amphitheaters became common projects for large U.S. cities seeking cultural revitalization and revenue. The one in the North Carolina Museum of Art exemplifies the amphitheater's cultural and educational role. Completed in 1998, the 600-seat amphitheater, which can present both videotaped and live performances, incorporates a large earth sculpture by artist Barbara Kruger. Amphitheaters can also enhance the viewer's understanding about the landscape itself. A few contemporary public gardens, such as the 100-seat amphitheater in the Chihuahuan Desert

Garden in northern Mexico, use amphitheaters to educate visitors about horticulture and the environment.

In addition to their educational use, amphitheaters continue to be a highlight of public gardens. A contemporary example is found in a garden completed in 1998 in Terrasson-La-Villedieu, France. Here, an amphitheater is a place of rest and impromptu performance. Using no defining edges or architectural components, the amphitheater comprises a stepped, grassy hillside with simple curved benches of silver metal. Several trees, left to grow in between the benches, enhance the amphitheater's dialogue with nature. This relationship also illustrates how little the ancient architectural form has changed. Despite different uses and settings, the amphitheater remains a place of gathering and performance, as well as an ideal location to enjoy the splendors of a well-planned garden.

## Further Reading

Gebhard, Elizabeth R., *The Theater at Isthmia,* Chicago: University of Chicago Press, 1973

Hobhouse, Penelope, and Patrick Taylor, editors, *The Gardens of Europe,* New York: Random House, and London: Philip, 1990

Hucliez, Marielle, *Jardins et parcs contemporains: France,* Paris: Telleri, 1998; as *Contemporary Parks and Gardens in France,* translated by Rubye Monet, Paris: VILO, 2000

Lawrence, Arnold Walter, *Greek Architecture,* London and Baltimore, Maryland: Penguin, 1957

Quinn, Lawrence, "Encore for Amphitheaters," *Planning* 454 (1988)

Rainero, Enrico, *Giardini, labirinti, paradisi,* Florence: Studio E. Rainero, 1985; as *Gardens, Labyrinths, Paradise,* translated by Patricia Schultz, Florence: Studio E. Rainero, 1985

Reboli, Michele, "A Park for the New World," *Casabella* 62, no. 654 (1998)

Taylor, William, *Greek Architecture,* New York: Day, and London: Barker, 1971

Triggs, Harry Inigo, *The Art of Garden Design in Italy,* London and New York: Longmans Green, 1906

Turner, Tom, *English Garden Design: History and Styles since 1650,* Woodbridge, Suffolk: Antique Collectors Club, 1986

Walton, Guy, *Louis XIV's Versailles,* Chicago: University of Chicago Press, and London: Viking, 1986

Ward-Perkins, Bryan, *From Classical Antiquity to the Middle Ages: Urban Public Building in Northern and Central Italy, AD 300–850,* Oxford and New York: Oxford University Press, 1984

MARC PERROTTA

# Amsterdamse Bos

## Amsterdam, Netherlands

**Location:** in southern suburb of Amstelveen, near Schiphol International Airport

Het Amsterdamse Bos, literally the Amsterdam Forest, was conceived in the early years of the 20th century, the idea appearing first in the south extension plan for the city of Amsterdam prepared in 1917 by the architect Hendrik Petrus Berlage, who had also produced a plan for the South Park in The Hague, the Dutch capital, nine years earlier. Amsterdam was rapidly expanding as a city and had very limited open space for the recreation and enjoyment of its inhabitants. Between 1870 and 1938 its population tripled, and city authorities from quite early in the century decided that, in view of the actual and anticipated continuing expansion, some provision for such open spaces should be made. By 1938 the city's population had reached 800,000, while the available area of parks and so on was only about 400 acres (162 ha)—half an acre per thousand people. The Bos Park is on the south side of the city within three-and-a-half miles (5.6 km) of the center; it extends over 2,250 acres (936 ha). The estimated average annual level of visitors in the 1990s was 4.5 million; approximately 95 percent of these come from Amsterdam and its immediate suburbs, and almost all from within a six-mile (9.7 km) radius. Such a large number of visitors calls for a robust park that will develop and regenerate easily and quickly. The park is bordered on the east by housing, part of the city's southern expansion area; to the west is Schiphol Airport. The northern boundary is formed by the Nieuw Meer, a favorite area for small-boat sailing, to the east of which is the 40,000-capacity sports stadium and other athletic facilities created for the 1928 Olympics.

The plan for the Bos Park can reasonably be described as pragmatic. The creation of a park on this scale for public recreation and the enjoyment of nature necessitated the optimization of the site's conditions, the use of ecological principles in planting, and the development of a natural self-sustaining balance in order to minimize the complexities of management. The site was on clay, although extensively overlain with peat, and the water table was very high, an impediment to tree growth. The first step was to reduce the level of the water table by developing an underdrainage system that discharged into pools connected by waterways through the site and beyond. An ecological study was undertaken to establish which species would best grow in the conditions being created; this was based on the natural vegetation of the polder regions. Various mixes were planted in different areas depending on the conditions; these were intended to achieve over time the same mixture of vegetation as would develop under natural conditions. Oak (35 percent), beech (20 percent), ash (15 percent), maple (10 percent), lime, hornbeam, birch, willow, poplar, and alder have formed the top story in different parts, with cornus, elder, hazel, holly, and yew forming a lower layer. Elm, as expected in an ash-elm forest, has not been planted except in small numbers because of the dangers of Dutch elm disease. Regeneration in the main comprises ash and maple. Of the 936 hectares of the park, 420 are forest, 215 meadows, 135 water, 70 described as wet hayland, and 65 are roads and paths.

The principal function of the park is recreation primarily related to the enjoyment of nature; thus, nature conservation is an important objective. In terms of habitat the park is particularly noted for the large population of birds of prey, which in turn indicates the presence of the small mammals on which these birds depend. Access for cars is carefully limited, and circulation is mainly on foot and, predictably in Holland, by bicycle.

Walking and cycling are, in fact, the main recreational activities of the park, with associated picnicking and sunbathing. There are also swimming facilities, a goat farm, and a restaurant. The Olympic-standard rowing lake at the northern end provides a center for water sports—it is 2,428 yards (2,220 meters) long and 71 yards (65 meters) wide. It was opened in 1937, at the time and for a number of years the largest such course created.

The capacity of the park was one of the issues that predominated from the earliest years of its planning, and early reports included estimates of the numbers that could be accommodated in different areas and at different facilities, although the promotion of the appreciation and enjoyment of nature required that this be balanced with care for conservation.

In recent years the policy of management at the Bos Park has evolved in two ways. First, the view has developed that traditional management resulted in a too well kept look, and proposals are in hand to create a more wild and natural appearance. To that end, about 247 acres (100 ha) of the meadows will be grazed by high-

land cattle rather than mown by machine. The banks of the canals are now thought to be too heavily planted with hardwoods, which will be thinned to create a more natural transition between land and water. A third element of this planned change relates to the management of the woods, where traditional thinning methods resulted in a uniform managed appearance. A method described as transformation management has been adopted, where, instead of suppressing the competitors of the intended final crop throughout, competitors are allowed to grow in some areas, some glades are created, and a much more varied and random age structure is achieved, resulting in a more natural appearance. This transformation management program is scheduled to be completed by 2005 and will be succeeded in some areas by what is described as "do-nothing management."

Coupled with these changes in the treatment of specific areas is a new zoning of different areas of the park into four zones as follows: the *park forest* zone, favoring general casual recreation; the *nature forest* zone, with an emphasis on nature-related leisure; the *nature* zone, in which nature is supreme; and the *urban fringe* zone, important for human use and managed in the same way as the park forest zone.

This remarkable and unique park, which has served the population of Amsterdam and its suburbs so well for over half a century, is a testament to the foresight and wisdom of the city authorities and the landscape designers involved in its creation.

## Synopsis

1917    Berlages plan for the extension of Amsterdam South

1928    City Council confirms intention to develop the park

1929    Setting up of Committee for the Boschplan

1937    Van Eesteren, J.H. Mulder et al. produce Bos plan; planting begins

## Further Reading

Boer W.C.J., "Changing Ideas in Urban Landscape Architecture in the Netherlands," in *Learning from Rotterdam: Investigating the Process of Urban Park Design,* by M.J. Vroom and J.H.A. Meeus, London: Mansell, and New York: Nichols, 1990

Chadwick, George, *The Park and the Town: Public Landscape in the 19th and 20th Centuries,* London: The Architectural Press, 1966

Royal Institute of British Architects, "The Amsterdam Boschplan," *Journal of the Royal Institute of British Architects* 45, no. 14 (23 May 1938)

M.F. DOWNING

# Amusement Park

The amusement park industry began with the pleasure gardens of medieval Europe. Located on the outskirts of major European cities, pleasure gardens featured live entertainment, fireworks, dancing, games, and early amusement rides. Although they were enormously popular, political unrest led to the closure of most of these parks after 1700, although one, Bakken (north of Copenhagen), opened in 1583 and remains the world's oldest operating amusement park.

The era of prosperity in the post-World War II United States expanded the scale and scope of many leisure activities. Consumers after 1950 became increasingly willing to spend considerable sums of money on activities that provided amusement and diversion. This trend culminated in a form created when amusement mixed with destination tourism. The amusement park, which began in the 20th century as a privately owned, small-scale enterprise, has become a multibillion dollar corporate endeavor. The organizing device of each landscape form for the amusement park is escapism.

Such landscapes of imagination fused two 19th-century developments into one. The pleasure garden had been popularized in the form of rural cemeteries, city parks, and rooftop gardens and offered one of the first landscape forms organized permanently around leisure recreation, usually strolling or walking. As the desire for such sites extended from the more elite classes to include the working class, entrepreneurs began integrating devices of new technology intended to thrill the audience, such as the carousel, roller coaster, and Ferris wheel. These two forms converged at the end of the 19th century in one of the most famous landscapes in the United States, the 1893 Columbian Exposition.

The Columbian Exposition of 1893, held in Chicago, Illinois, was one of the most important events in U.S. cultural history; most significant among its contributions was the White City, the landscape created to house the world exposition. Ironically, the White City—completed with grounds designed by Frederick Law Olmsted and buildings by Louis Sullivan, Frank Lloyd Wright, and others—was designed to be a temporary landscape. In its sprawling cacophony of amusements and aesthetic beauty, however, the form of the White City, derived from the ancient arcade, began the development of the American amusement park. The center of the design was the Court of Honor, a dazzlingly white area circling an approximately 833-yard (762-m)-long reflecting pool. At one end lay the Peristyle, 48 Corinthian columns with 85 allegorical figures; toward the other was the 33-yard (30-m)-tall Republic statue (roughly as tall as the Statue of Liberty), which rose out of the water and faced west. Most important, the White City offered an example of the American ability to plan and design an integrated landscape that operated as an oasis from its surroundings. It suggested that technology joined with art and a progressive spirit could create a garden city out of the wilderness.

During an era of rapid technological development, ensuing landscapes veered drastically toward amusement and away from aesthetic beauty. The most popular attraction of the early 20th-century United States, Coney Island, brought the Ferris wheel from the Columbian Exposition to a permanent home outside of New York City. In an effort to attract working-class patrons of many nationalities, the developer, George Tillyou, emphasized thrills with rides such as the Steeple Chase. From the hot dog to the demeaned midget, nearly every detail of the amusement park sought to break down social barriers. Sudden disorientation, loss of balance, exposure of flesh, unaccustomed and rather intimate contact with strangers, public shame, and strenuous physical activity resulted in a tremendous sense of release. Coney Island re-created the escape and release of the traveling circus or the World's Fair and gave it a permanent home.

In 1956 Walt Disney raised amusement parks to a new level with Disneyland in California. A permanent theme park based more on escapism than thrill, Disneyland, and later Disney World in Florida (1965), sought to create a world apart for visitors. An air of fantasy defined the visitor's experience, and each component of the park was crucial. The landscape quickly became an important tool for Disney's designers. Disney World re-creates the tensions and oppositions that organized earlier fairs to anticipate advertising and design strategies at work throughout the North American landscape. Whether visualizing the city, the country, the public, the private, or the natural, Disney sought a world that would present ideal visions for future development. Most important, the more traditional park of Disney World bred EPCOT (Experimental Prototype Community of Tomorrow) in 1982.

Unlike any theme park before it, EPCOT includes housing developments, water parks, a monorail system, a conservation area, artificial lakes and streams, hotels, resorts, freeways, parking lots, a wilderness area, ancient cities, and modern shopping areas. The goal was to re-create the American community. While structurally it contains many referents to Le Corbusier, whose designs would define modern architecture as an urban enterprise, the dominant form is not the city but the amorphous continuum of the exurb. Monorail and freeway link the various areas of the park, as though demarcated as city, suburb, country, and wilderness. Yet each of the spaces is structurally identical to the others. Emptied of their historical function, they can only be distinguished by the themes assigned to them. The swamp of this region was massively developed and then "renaturalized" to appear aesthetically attractive. "Whimsification," as Disney designers refer to it, includes canals that cross over a road on a bridge and endless hedges clipped into topiary of Disney cartoon characters. The latter may, in the end, be the most effective summary of the Disney landscape.

As the status of the United States in world affairs has grown since 1970, so has its dominance over the emerging global mass culture. The amusement park has become a mainstay of this influence, with Euro Disney in France and Disney World in Japan the primary examples. Each park has weathered initial local reluctance to become attractions similar to Disney's parks in the United States. The utopian, escapist mission of such theme parks has proven to have transcultural success. Coney Island demonstrated that thrill rides appeal to any ethnic group; Disney has shown that the release of escaping to a world of magic and fairy tales appeals as well. It has also shown that Disney's characters, films, and marketing have a worldwide audience.

The universal allure of such contemporary theme parks, however, goes beyond attraction to cartoon characters. Disney planners and designers have also mastered the form of a landscape of leisure amusement. Sprawling sites that lead visitors through lands of magic and cartoon characters also maintain a pleasant aesthetic. Most visitors first notice the parks' cleanliness. Additionally, Disney mixes the natural elements of an outdoor park, including lakes, ponds, and water fowl, with the meandering walkways necessary for travel. Designers have used natural elements of every sort to mimic the appearance of specific foreign nations in parks such as EPCOT. Walkways are also planted with carefully manicured shrubs and trees to create an ambience reminiscent of the European pleasure gardens. In this instance, however, such pleasure provides respite from each barrage of roller-coaster-like thrills.

While it has a core of utopian planning, Disney World remains an amusement park designed to thrill and intrigue the educated visitor, who is always viewed as a consumer. Although the totality of the experience proves a distant connection to the Columbian Exposition of 1893, the landscape's intention remains the creation of a world apart.

**Further Reading**

Adams, Judith A., *The American Amusement Park Industry: A History of Technology and Thrills,* Boston: Twayne, 1991

Dunlop, Beth, *Building a Dream: The Art of Disney Architecture,* New York: Abrams, 1996

Kasson, John, *Amusing the Million: Coney Island at the Turn of the Century,* New York: Hill and Wang, 1978

Wilson, Alexander, *The Culture of Nature: North American Landscape from Disney to the Exxon Valdez,* Toronto: Between the Lines, 1991; Cambridge, Massachusetts: Blackwell, 1992

BRIAN BLACK

# Andersson, Sven-Ingvar 1927–

## Swedish Landscape Architect

Swedish landscape architect Sven-Ingvar Andersson is well known for a number of successful designs and awards. He became professor of landscape architecture at the Royal Academy of Fine Arts in Copenhagen in 1963, after Professor C.Th. Sørensen's retirement. Andersson has, through honorary positions, articles, books, lectures, and projects, been a leading figure in Scandinavian and European landscape architecture for more than 30 years. His own topiary garden in Södra Sandby, Sweden, with its "Hen Garden," expresses his playful approach to the profession. At the same time he always emphasizes the ecological and social dimensions of landscape architecture.

Andersson was born in Södra Sandby, Sweden, in 1927. His parents were farmers, but Andersson left farming to study at Lund University and the Agricultural University in Alnarp. He graduated in 1954 with a degree in horticulture from the Swedish Agricultural University and a degree in art history from Lund University. It was a good combination for a landscape architect, and necessary, because a separate study program in landscape architecture was not yet established in Sweden. He started working at the office of Sven A. Hermenlin and Inger Wedborn in Stockholm in 1954 and stayed there until he was offered a position at the parks department in Helsingborg in 1957. From 1959 he worked as a lecturer at the Royal Academy of Fine Arts in Copenhagen. He also established his own practice in 1959, first in Helsingborg, and later in Copenhagen. In 1963 he was appointed professor of landscape architecture at the Royal Academy, a position he held until his retirement in 1994. He has published four books and numerous essays and articles in books and magazines. His articles discussing the principles of restoring garden art are well known and have been used by many garden historians. In one such article he underlines the importance of understanding the creation of gardens in order to "re-create" them. He introduces three notions for the creation of garden art: *locus amoenus*, the garden as the place for sensual pleasure; *genius loci*, the garden as the realization of the potential of the place; and *teatrum orbi*, the garden as a stage for life. Similarly, he introduces three approaches to garden restoration: reconstruction, renovation, and free renewal (*Landskab*, 1993).

In some of Andersson's restoration projects, one can see his principles for garden restoration realized. At Sophienholm near Copenhagen (ca. 1967), all three approaches can be traced. The place is a landscape park dating from the 19th century, and today it is used by the municipality for exhibitions and concerts. At Ronneby in Sweden, Andersson restored a landscape garden from the late 19th century; his additions included a scent garden and a Japanese garden. In Damsgaards Have (ca. 1983), a small rococo palace in Bergen, his approach was to reconstruct the Renaissance-style garden that most likely surrounded the house in 1783. When Andersson presented the plan in Oslo 1994, he emphasized the *locus amoenus* motive: "garden art is the most sensual of all the arts," he claimed. The garden speaks directly to the senses: the flowers please the eyes and the sparkling water delights the ears. Both the olfactory and taste senses are gratified by the edible products from the garden, and the tactile and kinesthetic senses are stimulated by the changing texture and terrain of the garden. At Uranienborg on the island of Hven (ca. 1992), Andersson used the free-renewal approach, based on both archaeological findings and his own artistic skill, to create the illusion of the 16th-century observatory founded by the Danish astronomer Tycho Brahe.

Andersson has designed several public spaces and plazas. At Stadshuset, Town Hall Plaza in Höganäs (ca. 1958), he designed a large pool covering most of the plaza, surrounded by a loggia connecting the buildings. In the shallow rectangular pool is a fountain with water and light; it is paved with the same cobblestones that are used in the surrounding area. This links the pool with the space beyond and makes it accessible during the winter when the pool is empty. At Havnetorget (Harbor Plaza) in Helsingborg (ca. 1993), the harbor itself is the central pool, and the fountain is like an earring at the quay with a spray into the sea. At Karlsplatz in Vienna (ca. 1971), the design is built up by a number of large ellipses containing greenery or water. The design for Rådhuspladsen (City Hall Plaza) in Copenhagen (ca. 1979) treats the whole plaza as one continuous carpet, with a few elements such as trees and sculptures to accompany the main focus of the plaza: the people passing or stopping to look or talk. At Tête Défense in Paris (ca. 1984–86), Andersson designed the surroundings of *The Cube,* designed by architect Johan Otto von Spreckelsen. The main elements were to be a long marble walkway, a canal with water and vegetation, and light constructions with pergolas and roofs of different shapes. The project was not realized as designed.

## Biography

Born in Södra Sandby, Sweden, 1927. Graduated as landscape architect, Agricultural University of Sweden, 1954; degree in history of art, University of Lund, 1954; worked with landscape architect Sven Hermelin, 1955–56, and in municipality of Helsingborg, Sweden, 1957–59; established own practice in Helsingborg, 1959, and from 1963 in Copenhagen, Denmark; appointed lecturer, Royal Academy of Fine Arts, Copenhagen, 1959, and from 1963, professor of landscape architecture; won first prize in competition for Karlsplatz, Vienna, 1972 (with Odd Brochmann), and one of nine first prizes in competition for Parc de la Villette, Paris, 1982 (with Steen Høyer, Vibeke Dalgas, and Johan Otto von Spreckelsen); retired from professorship, 1994, but still active as designer, writer, and lecturer.

## Selected Designs

| | |
|---|---|
| 1961 | Höganäs Town Hall, Höganäs, Sweden |
| 1963 | Villanden, residential area, Landskrona, Sweden |
| 1969 | Sophienholm, restoration plan for historical garden, Lyngby, Denmark |
| 1970 | Ådalsparken, residential area and park, Ådal, Denmark |
| 1970 | Eremitageparken, residential area, Lyngby, Denmark |
| 1971–78 | Karlsplatz-Resselpark, city plaza and park, Vienna, Austria |
| 1980 | Rådhuspladsen, city hall plaza, Copenhagen, Denmark |
| 1983 | Damsgaard Hage, restoration of historical garden, Bergen, Norway |
| 1993 | Museumsplein, urban park, Amsterdam, Netherlands |
| 1993 | Havnetorget, harbor plaza, Helsingborg, Sweden |

## Selected Publications

"En udstilling om haver og havekunst," in *Havekunst Sophienholm,* 1977

*Parker og haver i København og omegn* (with Hjørdis
  Hass Christiansen and Bente Hammer), 1979
*Parkpolitik: boligområderne, byerne og det åbne land*
  (with Annelise Bramsnæs and Ib Asger Olsen), 1984
"Garden of Sven-Ingvar Andersson near Lund," *Anthos*
  27, no.1 (1988)
"Havekunsten i Danmark," *Arkitektur* 4 (1990)
*Havekunst i Danmark; Landscape Art in Denmark*
  (with Annemarie Lund; bilingual Danish-English
  edition), 1990
*C.Th. Sørensen: En Havekunstner* (with Steen Høyer),
  1993

"Prinsipper for bevaring," *Landskab* 74, no. 6/7
  (1993)

**Further Reading**
Høyer, Steen, Annemarie Lund, and Susanne Møldrup,
  editors, *Festskrift Tilegnet Sven Ingvar Andersson,*
  *September 1994,* Copenhagen, Denmark: Arkitektens
  Forlag, 1994
Olsen, Ib Asger, "Sven-Ingvar Andersson: 60 år,"
  *Landskab* 68, no. 8 (1987)

KARSTEN JØRGENSEN

---

# André, Edouard François 1840–1911

## French Landscape Gardener

Art historians and practitioners have recently rediscovered Edouard André and his extensive body of work. While research is still a long way from recovering all the details of his career, it has already revealed the great richness and creativity of André's work.

In France the second half of the 19th century saw a developing interest in the plant kingdom on the part of large sections of the population, and with it the creation of public and private gardens. The Parisian experiment carried out by the group established by Baron Haussmann around Adolphe Alphand and Jean-Pierre Barillet-Deschamps, in which André participated at the beginning of his career, led to numerous orders for parks in large and small provincial towns and in foreign capitals. Political stability and growing wealth were also transforming French society, and many people aspired to a bourgeois lifestyle. Whether in town or country, the garden was an essential element of this lifestyle, and demand grew steadily, as people commissioned designers to create schemes in the English, or landscape, style that reflected new ideas of society and art. People turned to established designers or learned about innovations in taste, techniques, and available plants from the specialist press, which enjoyed an astonishing growth beginning in 1860.

André played an essential part in the landscape movement, which he supported just as much as he gave rise to it. A horticulturist by training, a botanist thanks to his voyages of exploration to South America, with a love for the plant world, which he studied all his life at his properties in Touraine and on the Côte d'Azur, he engaged in intense creative activity, planning over 200 parks in France and abroad.

As a number of André's landscape schemes have been reaching maturity, their restoration and maintenance have drawn attention to his compositional principles, choice of plants, and the people who commissioned parks from him. An international conference arranged in 1998 enabled various specialists to pool their knowledge concerning the great diversity—geographical as much as thematic—of André's work. This review and various studies have restored André to the key position that he occupied in the field of landscape gardening between 1860 and 1906, when he was forced to cease his activities, and have made clear his extraordinary influence on the development of horticulture and landscape art in France and abroad.

As the designer of so many parks, André was able to experiment with gardens in numerous styles, including small gardens in towns, by the sea, or in a Mediterranean climate, as well as parks in spa towns, rose gardens, country parks, botanical gardens, and so on. Especially important were commissions for public parks. His scheme for Sefton Park in Liverpool, for example, which won a competition in 1867 and launched his career as a practitioner in his own right, incorporated a variety of activities into the park, as well as a scheme of development land linked to the surrounding city. He also received the commission to transform the former bastions of Luxembourg into a large urban park and provided in his "Couronne verte" a variety of intimate spaces, vistas out toward the countryside, interesting connections with the city, and several special areas such as a rose garden and a bandstand. His collaboration with his son René-Edouard André, who had trained as an engineer, led him to work with urban development plans, in particular that for Montevideo in Uruguay, where he planned a system of public squares and gardens that would allow for the future development of the city.

In all his projects André gave plants a key role. Made famous by the introduction into Europe of *Anthurium andraeanum,* he was always interested in newly discovered plants and hybrids, although in his designs he also used native species. At Luxembourg he went so far as to create a botanical garden of native species—the antithesis of the practice of his contemporaries, whose misuse of exotic plants he deplored. He employed an extremely wide palette of plants, including alpine plants, aquatic plants, and broad-leaved and coniferous trees, which can easily be recognized in his parks today.

André produced a text that remains a key work for today's practitioners, the *Traité général de la composition des parcs et jardins* (1879; General Textbook of Park and Garden Design). Drawing on 20 years' experience, it attests to the range of André's knowledge, to the deep historical sense that was fundamental to his art, to his interest in practical techniques, and to his desire to control every aspect of a park, from the choice of plants to the design of the buildings and ornaments.

This highly successful work contributed greatly to André's fame and to the dissemination of the landscape style. However, it represents no more than a stage in André's career; he continued to develop throughout the following 20 years. In fact, he sketched out in the *Traité général* a new form of design—the composite or mixed style—of which he is considered to be the first proponent. He defines it thus:

> It is from the intimate union of Art and nature, of Architecture and landscape, that the best garden designs will arise in the course of time, as the public's taste becomes more refined. The surroundings of palaces, castles, and monuments situated in huge parks, handled according to the laws of architecture and geometry, and shading gradually into the distant parts where wild nature regains its dominance—this is what may inspire the exertions of the landscape designers of the future.

Among the first parks in this mixed style was that at Weldam in the Netherlands. This park, still beautifully maintained, combines box-edged parterres inspired by 17th-century Dutch gardens around the castle with a park in a style that becomes progressively freer the farther one moves from the building. Thereafter, the mixed style enjoyed a rapid development, becoming particularly popular with private landowners anxious to avoid the monotony of the landscape style, which had grown hackneyed as a result of being imitated, simplified, and distorted.

André also played an important part in establishing a proper professional milieu for horticulturists and landscape designers. Beginning in 1860 he wrote numerous articles and later became editor-in-chief of the highly respected *Revue horticole,* a position he held between 1882 and 1906. As editor-in-chief he exerted considerable influence on both amateurs and professionals, as well as political circles: although a horticultural journal, the *Revue horticole* also addressed landscape design and botany, encouraged the creation and dissemination of new vegetables, and supported calls for more favorable legislation. As a jury member of numerous international exhibitions, and as an associate of several foreign professionals whose articles he arranged to be translated, André also contributed to the spread of French horticultural art. He established numerous contacts in the United States, in particular with Charles Sprague Sargent and Frederick Law Olmsted, and on several occasions welcomed American landscape gardeners to France to complete their training.

The heir of Alphand and Barillet-Deschamps, with whom he had trained in Paris, André was a contemporary of the brothers Bühler and the Duchênes. He himself trained a whole generation of architects and landscape gardeners—who frequently went abroad to disseminate the French style—both through his publications and as a teacher of garden and glasshouse architecture at the National Horticultural School at Versailles between 1892 and 1906. Supported and then relieved in his activities by his son, he thus left a lasting mark on the designs of the early 20th century.

## Biography

Born at Bourges, Cher, France, 1840. Trained with nurseryman Leroy at Angers, Maine, France, then at Museum of Natural History, Paris, 1858–60; chief gardener of City of Paris, where he worked in particular at Buttes-Chaumont, 1860–68; built up very significant private and public clientele, both in France and abroad, after 1868; extended activities further when he was joined by his son, 1892, enabling him to devote himself to various roles as publicist, botanist, and teacher; ceased working, 1906; his son carried on activities of business until 1942. Died in 1911.

## Selected Designs

| | |
|---|---|
| 1867–72 | Sefton Park, Liverpool, England |
| 1872–1906 | Luxembourg city public park, Luxembourg |
| 1874 | Ebenrain, Switzerland |
| 1880 | Public gardens of Casino, Monte-Carlo, Monaco |
| 1880–1903 | Le Lude, Sarthe, France |
| 1886 | Weldam, Hengelo, Overijssel, Netherlands |
| 1888–1912 | Royal park of Euxinograd, Varna, Bulgaria |

| 1890 | City plan of Montevideo, Uruguay |
| 1895–1900 | Parks of Waka, Trakaï, Palanga, Lentvaris, Lithuania |
| 1895–1902 | Parc de Baudry, Indre-et-Loire, France |
| 1896–1900 | Parc du Champ de Mars, Montpellier, Hérault, France |
| 1899 | Rose garden, L'Haÿ-les-Roses, Seine-et-Marne, France |

## Selected Publications

*Traité des plantes ornementales,* 1866

*Les Fougères* (with Vilmorin-Andrieux), 1867

*Notes de voyage: Un mois en Russie,* 1870

*Traité général de la composition des parcs et jardins,* 1879

*Bromeliaceae Andreanae,* 1899

## Further Reading

André-Kaeppelin, Florence, "Le parc de La Croix, un jardin autobiographique," diss., École d'Architecture de Versailles, 1999

André, Florence, and Stéphanie de Courtois, *Edouard André, un paysagiste-botaniste sur les chemins du monde,* Besançon, France: Éditions de l'Imprimeur, 2001

Berjman, Sonia, *Plazas y parques de Buenos Aires: La obra de los paisajistas franceses, Andre, Courtois, Thays, Bouvard, Forestier, 1860–1930,* Buenos Aires: Fondo de Cultura Economica de Argentina, 1998

Courtois, Stéphanie de, *Edouard André et la société de son temps,* diss., Panthéon Sorbonne, 1996

STÉPHANIE DE COURTOIS

# Andromeda Gardens

## Barbados

**Location:** northeast coast of the island, above Trents Bay, approximately 10 miles (16.1 km) north of the airport

The Andromeda Gardens are well known among horticulturists worldwide not only for their beauty but also because of their tremendous collection of unusual plants, collected from around the world by Iris Bannochie. The site of the garden is striking—high above the sea and rocks of the east shore of Barbados, which receives the prevailing wind. The site and the plants, rather than a real plan or design, guided the development of the gardens. The site is also an old one horticulturally; excavations have turned up Arawak Indian tools and other traces of previous cultivation. Like other gardens in Barbados, the Andromeda Gardens are on a steep hillside. A stream running through it has been most imaginatively harnessed for use in the gardens. The soil is a rich clay that in places is over 90 meters (98.5 yd.) deep. The land has belonged to the McConney family since about 1740, and Bannochie inherited her share in 1953. The house was built soon after, and the garden started at the same time.

Signs on the land point to its previous use: trees of breadfruit (*Artocarpus incisus*) and coconut (*Cocos nucifera*), a large bearded fig or banyan (*Ficus citrifolia*), and fustic trees (*Chlorophora tinctoria*). There were also whitewood trees (*Tabebiua pallida*) used for boat building, pop a gun trees (*Cecropia peltata*) for medicinal use, and small fruit trees such as guava (*Psidium guajava*), soursop (*Annona muricata*), custard apple (*Annona reticulata*), avocado (*Persea americana*), and Barbados cherry (*Malphigia glabra*).

The layout of the garden consists of small winding paths joining open areas of lawn or rooms, each one surrounded by collections of plants. The numerous boulders and rocks to a certain extent dictated the plantings. Bannochie replaced weeds in the crevices with desired plants instead. The needs of the plants were paramount in the planning of the garden. She established a level area near the house to set it off; the resulting hole was turned into a lily pond divided by a bridge. It contains several types of lily, including the Amazon lily (*Victoria amazonica*), and a *Lotus*. Several bridges cross the stream, and many paths zigzag across the hillside.

The many microclimates and varying soil conditions in the garden meant that plants needing similar cultural conditions needed to be grouped together. The result is a series of gardens, such as a heliconia garden, hibiscus garden, orchid garden, and palm garden. At the main entrance to the gardens is a shade house full of orchids, some hanging on the outside of the house. In fact, orchids grow on trees throughout the garden, including some down in the more humid valley. From the orchid house the walk leads up the hill through a shaded area, with heliconias and torch lilies on either side. The larger trees provide the shade that these plants need. At the top of the path is a huge old ficus (*F. citrifolia*) surrounded with rocks, all with their complement of plants in the crevices. Below it is another small lily pool with water lilies (*Nymphaea*) and wandering Jews (*Tradescantia fluminensis*) on the edging rocks. Down the hill one reaches one of the hibiscus gardens and below that, more orchids and the palm garden. Here is the large talipot palm, which grows to a great height over about 60 years, puts out a giant inflorescence, and then dies. The garden contains some young ones as well. The palm garden also includes *Licuala grandis* with its large leaves, the sealing wax palm (*Cyrtostachys renda*) from Malaysia, so named because of its bright red leaf bases and petioles. There is also a palm that almost looks like an animal with its hairy prickly trunk, the macaw palm (*Aiphenes*). The garden also contains a fishtail palm (*Caryota mitis*) and some of the more common palms such as the Fiji fan palm (*Pritchardia pacifica*) and the date palm (*Phoenix*).

Beyond the palm garden is a buttercup tree (*Cochlospermum vitifolium*), which flowers in the spring before any leaves appear. The blossoms are indeed like giant buttercups. Through a shady area one arrives at the lily pool. It is almost impossible to describe all the plants that crowd the gardens.

Bannochie was a well-known collector and traveled widely to find new treasures for the gardens. She won many awards for her displays at the Chelsea Flower Show as well as some of the most prestigious medals and awards by the Royal Horticultural Society of England. She died in 1988, and her husband John died a few years later. She left the garden to the Barbados National Trust.

## Synopsis
1954  Iris Bannochie begins designing and
      constructing gardens
1988  Death of Iris Bannochie; Barbados National
      Trust assumes responsibility for care of
      gardens

## Further Reading
*Barbados*, Bridgetown, Barbados: Barbados Board of Tourism, 1991

Hobhouse, Penelope, and Elvin McDonald, editors, *Gardens of the World: The Art and Practice of Gardening*, New York: Macmillan, and Toronto: Collier Macmillan Canada, 1991

Smiley, Nixon, *Tropical Planting and Gardening for South Florida and the West Indies*, Coral Gables, Florida: University of Miami Press, 1960

JILL COLLETT

# Anet

## Eure-et-Loir, France

**Location:** approximately 47 miles (75.6 km) west of Paris

Created during the Renaissance in France, the Château d'Anet is a superb example of the house and garden unified on a central axis. It was built for Diane de Poitiers (1499–1566), widow of Louis de Brézé and lady-in-waiting to Claude, wife of François I. Diane was a patron of the arts and an excellent hunter. Soon after her arrival at court, she became attached to François's second son, Henri, who was 20 years her junior. When Henri became king, she became his mistress. Diane used her position as courtesan to build gardens at Chenonceau and Anet. Although not the designer, she served as patron and inspiration for the designs and had the king's architect, Philibert de l'Orme, at her disposal. She engaged de l'Orme to build a new château and garden

at Anet, a property she had inherited from her husband. Two châteaus had previously stood on the site.

Conceived as a royal hunting lodge for herself and the king, Anet became Diane de Poitiers's main residence for the rest of her life. The project began in 1546, one year before Henri became king. De l'Orme was a respected architectural theoretician and had traveled to Rome to study Italian Renaissance architecture. His thorough knowledge of construction and classicism was brought to fruition at Anet. The building, constructed of brick and stone, featured the correct use of classical elements such as pilasters and columns, previously misunderstood by French architects. De l'Orme's deep understanding of classicism helped to guide the organization of the entire site. The unification of the house and garden at Anet would become characteristic of the French formal garden for the next 200 years.

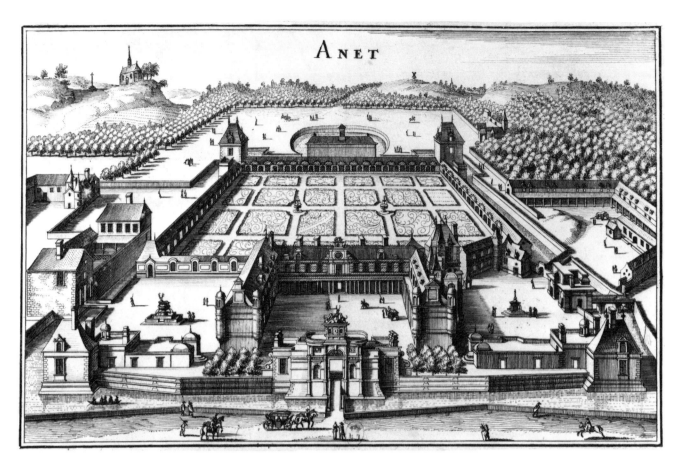

Château at Anet, Eure-et-Loir, France
Courtesy of Bibliothèque Nationale de France

The walled complex was surrounded by a moat, fed by the river Eure. The original site was marshland, making it necessary to drain the water and contain it in moats, fountains, and basins in the formal gardens and canals in the park beyond. The entry portal, completed in 1552, was constructed in the form of a triumphal arch with black-and-white marble detailing to match the colors of Diane's clothing. Over the entrance portal was a bronze sculpture of the goddess *Diana* by Benvenuto Cellini, topped with another symbol of the hunt, a deer surrounded by four hounds. Originally the deer counted out the hour with its hoof, while the dogs barked. To complete the iconographic imagery of Diane as goddess, groves of trees on elevated terraces, representing Ovid's mythical account of Diana bathing in a grove, flanked the entry.

The original plan contained three courtyards within the building complex, the formal garden beyond the Corps de Logis surrounded by galleries, and the park. The outer courtyards had fountains in the center, the most famous of which was of the goddess Diana and her stag surmounted on a sarcophagus. The formal garden featured two fountains and was divided into 24 squares,

each with a different decoration, with arabesques formed by boxwood, grass, aromatic herbs, and flowers such as jasmine, violets, jonquils, lilies of the valley, stock, and violets. Of the gardens at Anet, the 16th-century poet Olivier de Magny wrote, "Monograms and mottoes the whole in plants so well feigned one would almost say it was painted" (Woodbridge). The garden terminated with a circular canal that was used as a bathing pool (Diane was well known for taking cold baths nightly to preserve her beauty), and at each end of the garden wall were two small pavilions where trumpeters and horn players could entertain revelers in the park. Other amenities in the park included an orangery, an aviary, fishponds, small canals, and paths connecting each space.

Through the centuries revisions to the gardens at Anet have obscured the original design. André Le Nôtre, or possibly his nephew Claude Desgots, removed much of the garden in 1685 in an attempt to "rejuvenate" the property. The formal gardens were transformed into grand parterres and a long vista, characteristic of the 17th-century garden. After the Revolution the garden was neglected for 50 years. In 1850 the landscape architect Bülher redesigned the park in the Picturesque style. The entry portal with adjoining walls and structures, the left wing of the château, and the chapel are the only original structures on the property. The Diana fountain and the original Cellini bronze are in the Louvre, and the facade of the Corps de Logis is in the courtyard of the École des Beaux-Arts in Paris. The restoration effort at Anet continues.

## Synopsis

| | |
|---|---|
| 1546 | Construction of new château and garden by Philibert de l'Orme begins |
| 1685 | André Le Nôtre redesigns garden in classical style |
| 1790s | Château taken over during French Revolution and its contents removed |
| 1804 | Demonti *fils* demolishes most buildings and destroys park |
| 1840 | Count Adolphe de Caraman begins restoration |
| 1850 | Landscape architect Bühler redesigns park |

## Further Reading

Adams, William Howard, *The French Garden, 1500–1800*, New York: Braziller, 1979

Blunt, Anthony, *Art and Architecture in France, 1500–1700*, Baltimore, Maryland: Penguin, 1954

Blunt, Anthony, *Philibert de l'Orme*, London: Zwemmer, 1958

Hautecoeur, Louis, *Histoire de l'architecture classique en France*, Paris: Picard, 1943

Roussel, Pierre Désiré, *Histoire et déscription du Château d'Anet*, Paris, 1875

Ward, William Henry, *The Architecture of the Renaissance in France: A History of the Evolution of the Arts of Building, Decoration, and Garden Design under Classical Influence from 1495–1830*, 2 vols., London: Batsford, 1911; 2nd edition revised, 1926; reprint, New York: Hacker Art Books, 1976; see especially vol. 1

Woodbridge, Kenneth, *Princely Gardens: The Origins and Development of the French Formal Style*, London: Thames and Hudson, and New York: Rizzoli, 1986

Yturbe, Charles de, *Le Château d'Anet*, Paris: Nouvelles Editions Latines, 1980

CONSTANCE A. WEBSTER

---

# Anhalt-Dessau, Franz von 1740–1817

## German Prince, Patron of the Arts, and Garden Designer

Leopold III Friedrich Franz of Anhalt-Dessau played an especially significant role not only in the development of a new artistic taste in architecture and landscape design in Germany but also in the introduction of the landscape garden to central Europe. As a head of state with enlightened views, he brought about changes in living conditions throughout his entire principality of Anhalt-Dessau, one of around 300 such small states in 18th-century Germany. In addition to initiating numerous improvements in lifestyle, trade, agriculture, education, and social conditions, he led a drive for the aesthetic improvement of his state, resulting in new forms of architecture and garden design based predominantly on English and Italian precepts.

During his reign (1758–1817) the prince laid out perhaps the earliest large-scale ornamental landscape program in Central Europe, transforming his principality on the banks of the Elbe into a "garden kingdom." He was assisted in this endeavor by his friend, adviser, and architect Friedrich Wilhelm von Erdmannsdorff, along with various gardeners and other assistants. Influenced primarily by the gardens and country houses of England but also by the philosophy of Jean-Jacques Rousseau and his mentor Johann Joachim Winckelmann, Prince Franz created a synthesis of wide-ranging English developments drawn from the work of the landscape designers Henry Hoare, Lancelot "Capability" Brown, William Kent, and Sir William Chambers. The resulting landscape is largely extant today and has undergone extensive restoration since 1982, so that it can once more be experienced in its intended form. Thus, classical, Gothic, chinoiserie, and other stylistic characteristics of the 18th century English landscape garden found a new home in Germany two generations before the advent of the German landscape designer Karl Friedrich Schinkel and established a pattern for the further development of this art form in central Europe.

Succeeding to power in his little state at the age of 18, the anglophile Franz had initially intended to marry his childhood sweetheart and spend his life as a country gentleman in England, handing the reins of power to his younger brother Johann Georg. This plan had to be abandoned owing to political pressure from Frederick the Great of Prussia (1712–86), on whom Anhalt-Dessau was politically dependent. In 1767 therefore Franz instead married his cousin Henriette Wilhelmine Luise of Brandenburg-Schwedt according to Frederick's requirements. Franz's politics, however, took an independent route, rejecting the family tradition of Prussian military service and pursuing instead the aims of an enlightened humanist.

Franz was the hereditary landowner of his principality, which at the time of his improvements encompassed a land area of around 700 square kilometers (270 sq. mi.) The present area of the "garden kingdom" under conservation protection covers some 145 square kilometers (60 sq. mi.). Through his approach of enlightened humanism he acquired the nickname "Father Franz" and, as described by Goethe, "led by shining example, and promised his servants and subjects a golden age." As part of his efforts to develop the cultural life of his state he was an active garden artist and landscape designer, but he was also active as an improver of flood-protection dikes, watercourses, and roads; a promoter of new agricultural methods; and an arboriculturist and pomologist (grower of fruit trees). He introduced new economic crops, timber trees, and fruit cultivars into Germany and applied himself to any new venture he felt might benefit his state's economy, such as silk culture and the cultivation of clover and madder.

The garden buildings of Wörlitz were intended from the outset to usher in a revolution in central European garden taste, a change of direction in favor of the landscape garden. The ornamental garden features, set in the context of a feeling for nature, are no mere whimsical objects: the grounds and buildings, open to the public from the outset, were laid out according to a definite program and combine functional, educational, and recreational objectives alongside their decorative role. They were intended to inform the local population as well as interested guests, who, according to the earliest records, were numerous. The program of the gardens, as well as their spatial composition, was chiefly the work of the gardeners Johann Leopold Ludwig Schoch the Elder, Johann Georg Schoch the Younger, and Johann Friedrich Eyserbeck, who transferred the designs onto the existing meadow landscape, each with his own defined role. Other gardeners, foresters, and farmers contributed to the formation of the wider garden kingdom. At that time the gardeners still worked as planters in the manner of their contemporaries in baroque gardens elsewhere in Germany: landowners and architects would determine the ideas and layouts,

and the gardeners would implement them. Avenues, green walls, and viewpoints, garden enclosures and sight lines were all constructed with the building blocks of vegetation, just as stonemasons or carpenters used tiles, stone, boards, and beams in their work.

The prince began to implement his landscape improvement measures soon after his accession to power in 1758, which continued until his death in 1817. The meadow landscape along the Elbe reminded the prince of the richly gardened scenes along the Thames near London, and he gradually developed a series of six landscape gardens and numerous buildings in the new taste of the time. The existing baroque layouts were altered in accordance with the prince's ideas and seamlessly merged into the extensive designed landscape. After the completion of the works in the early 19th century, the 700-square-kilometer (270 sq. mi.) garden kingdom consisted of the gardens at Kühnau, Mosigkau, and the Georgium to the west of the residence city of Dessau, with the eastern "park" taking in the grounds at the Luisium, the Sieglitzer Berg, Wörlitz, the Krägen, Oranienbaum, and the Tiergarten. Further designed features, such as bridges, seats, monuments, and individual buildings, served to decorate the wider landscape. New roads and stretches of flood dike with decorative plantings, avenues, and orchards connected the ornamental estates with one another. Avenues of decorative and fruit trees were planted along the newly built "English country roads" in addition to the land in front of the dikes, and the fields and woodland margins were adorned with ornamental viewpoints.

Franz had a complete understanding of the implications of the genius loci, or pervading spirit of the place, and of the (English) principles underpinning the improvement of the existing meadow landscape. According to these tenets, none of the designs were to strike the visitor as artificial: everything was to appear as the work of nature. All designs were to adhere to the Roman poet Horace's principle of combining the useful with the beautiful, a motto well understood in England. Nothing was to be laid out without a practical function, and the entire garden kingdom was to be understood as an educational program reflecting the intentions of its creator. Pastureland and arable fields were incorporated into the gardens themselves; orchards and herds of livestock contributed, along with the routine work of the countryside, to the decorative picture. The visitor was led through the countryside and the gardens along a network of paths and drawn into the design program by observing features such as buildings, garden scenes, and so forth, whose thought-provoking significance was intended to educate and develop the tastes of the enlightened contemporary visitor. Thus the 51 different bridges of the garden kingdom were to demonstrate to the visitor the historical development of bridge building and to illustrate different construction techniques and variations. The latest technology, represented by Wilkinson's Iron Bridge (in Shropshire, England) was reconstructed in a scaled-down copy to cross a stream next to a ford, the most primitive form of river crossing. Mythological references, allegories, vignettes of garden scenery, and inscriptions combined to clarify the set of ideas incorporated into the layout and served to imbue the visitor with the spirit of enlightenment and humanism espoused by Prince Franz and his collaborators.

### Biography
Born in Dessau, Germany, 10 August 1740. Eleven when both parents died, he was brought up by his uncle and guardian Dietric of Anhalt-Dessau (1702–1769), who acted as regent until, declared of age by the emperor, Franz assumed power, 1758; following extensive tours of Europe and England, 1763–4, 1765–67, 1775, and 1785; implemented a comprehensive policy of social reform throughout the state based on principles of the Enlightenment; within this framework a progressive program of landscape improvement developed, 1764–1800. Died in Dessau, 9 August 1817.

### Selected Designs

| | |
|---|---|
| ca. 1760– | Transformation of state of Anhalt-Dessau into a garden kingdom |
| 1765–1817 | Worlitz Park, Halle, Germany |
| 1774–97 | Luisium, Halle, Germany |
| 1777–93 | Sieglitzerberg, Germany |
| 1793–97 | Anglo-Chinese garden at Oranienbaum, Halle, Germany |
| after 1780 | Assisted brother Johann Georg at the park of the Georgium |

### Further Reading
Bode, Ursula, Michael Stürmer, and Thomas Weiss, *For the Friends of Nature and Art: The Garden Kingdom of Prince Franz of Anhalt-Dessau,* Ostfildern-Ruit, Germany: Hatje, 1997

Günther, Harri, editor, *Gärten der Goethezeit,* Leipzig: Edition Leipzig, 1993

Hirsch, Erhard, *Dessau-Wörlitz,* Munich: Beck, 1985; 2nd edition, Leipzig: Koehler and Amelang, 1987

Rode, August, Hartmut Ross, and Ludwig Trauzettel, *Der Englische garten zu Wörlitz,* Berlin: Verlag für Bauwesen, 1987; 2nd expanded edition, 1994

Trauzettel, Ludwig, "Wanderer, achte Natur und schone ihrer Werke: Ideengehalt und Wiederherstellung der Wörlitzer Anlagen," in *Garten, Kunst, Geschichte: Festschrift für Dieter Hennebo zum 70. Geburtstag,* edited by Erika Schmidt, Wilfried Hansmann, and Jörg Gamer, Worms, Germany: Werner, 1994

Trauzettel, Ludwig, "Die Wörlitzer Anlagen," in *Das Gartenreich Dessau-Wörlitz: Ein Reiseführer,* Hamburg, Germany: L und H Verlag, 1996

Trauzettel, Ludwig, "Wörlitz: England in Germany," *Garden History* 24 no. 2 (1996)

Trauzettel, Ludwig, "Fürst Leopold III. Friedrich Franz von Anhalt-Dessau: Initiator neuer Gartenkunst in Mitteleuropa," *Stadt und Grün* 12 (1998)

Weiss, Thomas, and Frank-Andreas Bechtoldt, editors, *Weltbild Wörlitz: Entwurf einer Kulturlandschaft,* Stuttgart, Germany: Hatje, 1996

Weiss, Thomas, *Sir William Chambers und der englisch-chinesische Garten in Europa,* Stuttgart, Germany: Hatje, 1996

LUDWIG TRAUZETTEL
*TRANSLATED BY STEVEN DESMOND*

# Animals in Gardens

Throughout most of history live animals have been an integral part of gardens. Whether considered as beautiful, curious, natural looking, or a source of food, animals belong to the idea of the garden as a managed landscape that provides all the blessings of nature in a controlled environment.

Among the first gardens anywhere were the wild game parks belonging to princes and wealthy families of many ancient cultures, including China and Mesoamerica. Such parks were first described to the West by the Greek general Xenophon, who discovered them in Persia. These vast walled enclosures, called *pairidaezas,* were stocked with fruit and ornamental trees, flowers, birds, fish, and mammals and were used chiefly as hunting grounds for the education of young princes. The young Cyrus the Great, for example, hunted bears, boars, lions, leopards, deer, gazelles, wild sheep, and wild asses in his *pairidaeza.*

The fashion caught on in ancient Rome, where the great estates of the wealthy often included large hunting preserves. In some cases the animals were clearly considered ornamental rather than a source of sport. Cicero's contemporary, the orator Hortensius, had at his villa a vast park stocked with many kinds of tamed

ON THE TERRACE—THE LATE EARL'S FAVOURITE WALK

Peacocks as garden ornaments in an engraving of Benjamin Disraeli in his garden at Hughenden, Buckinghamshire
Courtesy of Mary Evans Picture Library

animals. During dinner parties, for the amusement of the guests, a slave dressed as Orpheus played a lute, and the animals would cluster around him.

Wall paintings at Pompeii suggest that Romans of more modest means also associated gardens with birds and animals. Many paintings depict fountains, trees, flowers, and birds; others show mountainous landscapes with lakes and streams through which wild animals are roaming. There even survive some paintings of near-life-size animals. Apparently city dwellers were eager to create the illusion of having their own *pairidaeza*.

In medieval Europe gardens served both decorative and practical purposes: they provided fruits, vegetables and herbs, fish from the pond, birds from the aviary, and game and timber from the hunting park. Usually, one or more small gardens resided within the castle walls and numerous larger gardens and parks nearby. A 14th-century Welsh poem describes a manor with an orchard, vineyard, rabbit park, deer pasture, stone dovecote, fishpond, and a lawn for food birds, including peacocks and heron.

The "small park" or pleasure park was one of three standard types of pleasure garden, according to Piero de' Crescenzi of Bologna in his *Ruralium commodorum liber* (1305; Book of Rural Interests). In contrast to the "great park," which was used for hunting and available only to the wealthiest kings and nobles, the small park was a kind of open menagerie populated with harmless animals to look at for pleasure (such as stags, roebucks, wild goats, and rabbits) and was within the means of both upper and middle classes. The park included rivers and pools for fish and waterfowl, as well as trees and shrubberies for pheasants, partridges, and songbirds. Crescenzi directs that plantings of trees and shrubs, in which the wild creatures might nest and hide, should be interspersed with open grassy areas to permit them to be seen. The pleasure park was also to include a timber-framed summer pavilion for comfortable viewing. Many royal sites apparently included both great and small (or hunting and pleasure) parks.

Dovecotes have been common garden features in every age. The doves themselves were often raised to be eaten, and their droppings could be used as garden manure. The birds were also appreciated for their aesthetic appeal, as is proven by the beauty and detail of the structures housing them. Some dovecotes are of fantastic size, housing thousands of nesting pairs of birds.

By the beginning of the 16th century, a *volary* had become a common garden feature; it was an elegant structure of copper wire built around trees and serving as an aviary for rare or decorative birds. (Falcons and other hunting birds were usually kept in quarters quite separate from the garden.) Princely houses were also eager to collect rare animals for menageries; Renaissance and 17th-century records mention giraffes, zebras, camels, rhinoceroses, and elephants.

In China and Japan gardens were often the abodes of birds, fish, and turtles, but in general the interest in animals seems to have been expressed more by shaped rocks than by the actual cultivation of live animals in the garden. A description of the 11th-century garden of the Chinese statesman Hsi-Ma-Kuang mentions islands in his lake on which special houses were built to accommodate birds. The koi (goldfish) that are such a typical feature in Japanese gardens are often said to take the place of flowers.

In 18th-century Europe the revolution in garden taste married gardens to hunting parks for the first time and attempted to make the unified whole as much like "nature," that is, the surrounding countryside, as possible. The presence of livestock, birds, and even squirrels was considered to grace a scene with movement and naturalness, although often the effect was carefully constructed. Horace Walpole kept at his home "some Turkish sheep and two cows, all studied in their colours for becoming the view," and the famous designer Humphry Repton suggested that one should have three cows rather than two because "two can never compose."

Victorian gardens borrowed influences and ideas from many times and lands, and animal features became increasingly popular with the development of public zoos and menageries starting in the early 19th century. Elaborate aviaries and fishing pavilions were constructed in "Chinese" and other architectural styles. However, the trend was toward smaller gardens as populations expanded and more people lived in cities or suburbs. By the late 19th and early 20th centuries, therefore, the use of living animals as garden features had diminished.

With increasing concern about the disappearance of wildlife habitats, the later 20th century saw an upsurge of interest in designing "natural" gardens using native plant species, some of them created principally to attract birds, butterflies, and other wildlife. Indeed, bird gardens and butterfly gardens have become recognized types. Although they began as controlled natural sites that contained animals for food or pleasure, many gardens are now deliberately designed to mirror the natural surroundings in order to preserve animals and their now endangered homes.

**Further Reading**

Clifford, Derek Plint, *A History of Garden Design,* London: Faber and Faber, 1962; New York: Praeger: 1963; revised edition, 1966

Cowell, Frank Richard, *The Garden As a Fine Art, from Antiquity to Modern Times,* Boston: Houghton Mifflin, and London: Weidenfeld and Nicolson, 1978

Landsberg, Sylvia, *The Medieval Garden,* New York: Thames and Hudson, and London: British Museum, 1996

Moynihan, Elizabeth B., *Paradise As a Garden in Persia and Mughal India,* New York: Braziller, and London: Scolar Press, 1979

EMILY N. GOODMAN

# Annevoie, Jardins d'

## Belgium

**Location:** approximately 40 miles (64.3 km) southeast of Brussels, 10 miles (16 km) south of the city of Namur

The gardens of Annevoie are sited in the remote wooded valley of the Rouillon stream, high above the steep valley of the River Meuse in Belgium. It is a wooded landscape of mists and water, which the 11-hectare (27-acre) park has appropriated in its design. For almost 250 years, the gardens have been built and maintained by one family. Ten generations of de Montpelliers have lived at Annevoie since they inherited the property in 1696. Parts of the garden are now protected as a recognized national site, while others continue to be developed by the park's owners.

It was Charles-Alexis de Montpellier, an iron master and elder of the Court of Iron Merchants, who between 1758 and 1776 used his fortune to develop and enlarge the château and to lay out the original gardens. After his death, the garden was extended by his son Nicolas-Charles. Charles-Alexis de Montpellier was an 18th-century man of taste and culture who traveled widely and would have been familiar not only with the fashionable gardens of France, Italy, and England, but also with current thinking on landscapes as published in the writing of Dézallier d'Argenville (1680–1765) in France and Alexander Pope (1688–1744) and William Shenstone (1714–63) in England.

At Annevoie Charles-Alexis introduced a range of garden features borrowed from fashionable European gardens, but his overriding inspiration was undoubtedly the site itself. In its shaded valley, the theme of the garden is water, and what is most remarkable is the fact that the fountains and cascades have continued to run without the help of pumps or machinery since the day they were installed. The water gardens are fed by four springs, and the little stream the Rouillon. The water, flowing partly underground, maintains a constant temperature of 10 to 14 degrees Celsius (50 to 57 degrees Fahrenheit), even when the River Meuse is frozen.

The regular flow of the fountains depends entirely on a careful manipulation of changing water levels. The Grand Canal, cut into the hillside to the south (365 meters long and 7 meters wide (400 by 8 yards), acts as the principal reservoir. Its water is brought from the opposite slope in 1.6-meter-diameter (5-ft.) pipes, sometimes laid on 10-meter-high (33-ft.) dikes to compensate for differences in level. The steeply sloping site and use of fountains recalls the water displays of the Villa d'Este at Tivoli (1565). But these depended on an aqueduct and a conduit to divert water from the River Aniene. The important waterworks at Versailles completed by Le Nôtre in 1685 would have been another familiar reference; but there again, they required the construction of a massive watermill at Marly, which lifted the water from the Seine and transported it several miles by means of a viaduct, to ensure their operation. Today, the fountains at Versailles play very rarely. But at Annevoie, as a result of the constant maintenance of the conduits and lead fittings, the water garden is the only one in Belgium to have remained in perfect order.

The garden is laid out on three different axes, of which the first, built by Charles-Alexis, lies to the southeast of the château. Its symmetry is borrowed from the French classical style of Le Nôtre, and the first feature is known as the French Waterfall. It falls into an octagonal pond, in the middle of which is the Great Geyser, a jet of water over 7 meters (23 ft.) high. Alongside this formal feature, and in marked contrast, is the so-called English Waterfall, introduced by Nicolas-Charles toward the end of the 18th century, together with Neptune's Grotto to the west and a hermitage to the east (which is not open to the public). All these features reflect a change in fashion in favor of the Picturesque style expressed in the work of Jean-Jacques Rousseau and the English Romantics. Both of these waterfalls are fed by the same reservoir: the lake in front of the château. This "mirror" of water, another feature borrowed from the French classical garden, has been carefully calculated so that the slightly curved facade of the building is reflected in its entirety, together with a small sliver of sky.

Perhaps the most pleasing feature of the garden is the *Buffet d'eau,* which lies on the northwest-to-southeast axis that cuts through the château and its courtyard, providing a view from the house to the top of the slope, where a statue of Minerva stands at the end of an avenue of limes, on the far side of the Great Canal. Plumes of water, five to the left and five to the right, climb the slope, rising as if by magic directly out of the ground. A line of six jets at the front are placed closer together and provide a gap in the middle through which to view the statue of Neptune and Amphitryon above. The alignment of the jets and positioning of the lime trees are adjusted as the slope rises, in order to provide a "false" perspective.

The original cast-iron statues, now replaced by copies, were made in local foundries. One of the most delightful is the Wild Boar, a copy of the *porcellino* designed by Pietro Tacca for the piazza outside the Uffizi Palace in Florence. Placed on a mound within a pool and surrounded by a covered gallery of hornbeam, this green room or bosquet is one of many in the garden that provide the shady intimate spaces that contrast with the brighter sunlit spaces of the canals. One such "room," a grotto-like space cut out of the rock in the English Picturesque style, contains a statue of Minerva by the Liège sculptor De Tombay. Typical of this particular region are the two-dimensional trompe l'oeil heads of Roman emperors and vases in cast iron.

The visitor is invited to follow a prescribed route through the gardens, similar to that proposed at Leasowes, the home of the poet William Shenstone. It offers a series of contrasting scenes, alternating light and shadow, intimacy and grandeur, and provoking those feelings of pleasure and fear, awe and even terror, that are essential elements of the Picturesque. The journey by traditional boat that carries the visitor along the straight stretch of the Great Canal no longer leads him to the Woods of the Hermitage, where the buildings survive, although in a ruinous state. It does however offer a spectacular view over the valley of the Meuse, giving the feeling of boating on a mountaintop. Next the canal changes abruptly into a sinuous passage that ends in a circular pool. Continuing on foot into the dense shade of the wood, the visitor is forced to pass through two gloomy tunnels, one a vaulted cave built as a semi-ruin that leads to an "abyss" crossed by a narrow arched bridge. The hermitage chapel is discovered in a clearing, built in artificial stucco to look like rough-hewn stone, with a thatched roof and a small belfrey; the whole ensemble is reminiscent of the paintings of Salvator Rosa. Inside is a dark room like a rustic cave, and in the room opposite what appeared to be the silhouette of a hermit—in fact, a puppet to be manipulated by the unseen hand of the gardener. Beyond, the chapel opens onto an elegant room with three windows, offering another splendid view over the Meuse Valley. It is this contrast between the natural and the artificial, the symbolic play of light and shade, that constitutes the inner landscape of Annevoie.

Huge copper beeches bordering the gardens are over 200 years old and are grafted onto the stock of the common beech. In the last 50 years a flower garden, planted with roses in the English style, has been introduced at the northeast end of the garden near the present visitor entrance and garden center. The original gardens, which begin at the Octagon Pool, are classified and protected by the Belgian Commission Royale des Monuments et des Sites.

## Synopsis

| | |
|---|---|
| 1696 | Jean de Montpellier inherits property at Annevoie, and enlarges existing 15th-century building |
| 1750 | Charles-Alexis de Montpellier inherits property from father |
| 1758–76 | Present house built in local stone, and gardens laid out in style of Louis XIV |
| | by Charles-Alexis, using fortune made from his local foundries |
| 1776 | Charles-Alexis's son, Nicolas-Charles de Montpellier, carries on work in gardens, in Picturesque style, adding hermitage with hermit (long since disappeared) |
| 1815–75 | Frédéric de Montpellier attempts to anglicize gardens in contemporary style |
| 1928 | Pierre de Montpellier restores avenues to original form, adding large number of statues |
| 1950s | Kathleen de Montpellier designs floral wall alongside small canal in upper gardens |
| 1952 | Pierre de Montpellier lays out new flower gardens to the northeast |
| 1985 | On death of father, Pierre, estate taken over by his son Jean |
| present day | Gardens and house continue to be maintained by Nicolas de Montpellier and his wife, Véronique |

## Further Reading

Dézallier D'Argenville, Antoine-Joseph, *La théorie et la pratique du jardinage*, Paris, 1709

Pechère, René, *Parcs et jardins de Belgique*, Brussells: Rossel, 1976

Shenstone, William, "Unconnected Thoughts on Gardening," in *The Works in Verse and Prose*, by Shenstone, vol. 2, edited by Robert Dodsley, London, 1764; 2nd edition, London, 1765; reprint, London: Hughs, 1968

SANDRA MORRIS

# Anuradhapura Gardens

## Anuradhapura, Sri Lanka

**Location:** 90 miles (145 km) north of Kandy

Anuradhapura is an ancient city—renowned for its past as a Buddhist epicenter and today a heavily trafficked pilgrimage and tourism site. Some historians and archaeologists attest that its importance rivaled that of Niniveh and Babylon centuries ago, but it is most popularly recalled as the first capital of Sri Lanka and the base from which the Sinhalese kings ruled the island for over 1,000 years. Today the excavated old city contains the remnants of a sprawling monastic complex replete with ghostly court gardens, bell-like stupas (Buddhist commemorative shrines, also called dagobas), ancient reservoirs, and the still majestic Brazen Palace. Larger and more organized botanical collections certainly exist in the northern region of the island, particularly at

Peradeniya (established in 1821) and Hakgala, but Anuradhapura, abandoned for centuries after its tenth-century invasion, has the lure of an evocative and recovered history.

First settled around 500 B.C., the city was established as the capital of the new Sinhalese kingdom by King Pandukabaya (437–367 B.C.), a prodigious civic planner who quickly transformed the hamlet into a small metropolis that would eventually emerge as one of the largest regional centers of Buddhism. Both King Pandukabaya and his successor, Muta Siva, not only established parks and pleasure gardens but also sponsored extensive landscape development programs. Maha Megha, a royal pleasure garden with fruit and flowering plants, was one of these efforts wherein lay perhaps the most famous resident of Anuradhapura—the Sacred Bo-Tree (*Ficus religiosa*).

Purportedly grown from a limb of the pipal tree under which the Buddha achieved enlightenment, the Bo-Tree is undeniably the city's holiest artifact. According to legend, the branch was delivered to Sri Lanka from India in the third century B.C. (the approximate time period that marks the arrival of Buddhism to the island). The tree remains today as an important and cherished shrine, and precautions have been exercised throughout the centuries to protect the tree from both human and animal contact (it is currently girded by an iron fence). Some claim that it is the oldest documented tree in the world with a historical record dating back to its planting in 245 B.C. Certainly the Bo-Tree inspires the annual pilgrimages and festivals that draw thousands of outsiders to Anuradhapura.

Significantly, the city's gardens benefit from a northern climate that is consistently hot and dry. Although this allows for the cultivation of plants that are intolerant of excessive humidity, a need for an extensive irrigation system was realized early on, and King Pandukabaya quickly mandated two main water reservoirs during his reign: Abaya Wewa and Jaya Wewa. These tanks were supplied with water through a channel system that collected the periodic and short-lived monsoon rains and disbursed them through an irrigation network to service the whole city. This arrangement benefited the municipal gardens as well and provided much-needed water for rice cultivation. Later, huge man-made cisterns—such as the Nuwarawewa, Tissawewa, and Basawakkulame—were also constructed.

With these introduced water reserves and the city's predictable climate, fruit orchards and groves of mango, jambu, and frangipani thrived. Cultivated flower gardens flourished along the Kadamba River and may have included endemic varieties of flowering orchids. Several types of bamboo, palm, eucalyptus, silk oak (*Grevillea robusta*), and dadop are all natural inhabitants of the upland area, and rich rhododendron forests blanket much of the region. In later years under the ruler Bhatika Abaya, jasmine creepers were planted along the main arteries of the city for ornamental decoration while serving the auxiliary purpose of supplying ceremonial flowers for monks at the *viharas* (monasteries).

The garden complex, gradually being enhanced to reflect the splendor of its prime, presently covers about 40 acres (16.2 ha) that for the most part are considered an adjunct to the Peradeniya Botanical Gardens farther to the south. Even so, many classical garden features, such as moonstones, elephant friezes, and bathing pools (in particular the twin bathing ponds for monks known as the Kuttam Pokuna), evoke the strong Buddhist flavor of the old city and its ever present emphasis on water.

Throughout the old city lie the stupas, which are more rustic than their lavish counterparts in neighboring India and survive today as mounds of masonry complementing the natural beauty of the outlying gardens. Constructed of sun-dried bricks and usually more than 33.3 yards (30.5 m) in height, these ancient monasteries include the Brazen Palace, which was originally covered with a roof of plated copper; the Thuparamaya Dagoba, one of the oldest temples and rumored repository for the right collarbone of the Gautama Buddha; the Jetavanarama Dagoba, the largest remaining structure that is believed to have once housed several thousand resident monks; and the plastered Ruwaneli Dagoba, a temple that suffered much abuse over 1,000 years ago by the marauding Cholas (a tribe intolerant of Buddhism).

Indeed, it is almost certain that the beginning of Anuradhapura's decline is coincident with this invasion by the Cholas in A.D. 933, when the Hindu clan from neighboring India sacked and burned the city. Over the next century, the monks were eventually displaced, and Anuradhapura was abandoned to the encroaching jungle. The buried complex and others like it lay ignored by the Portuguese and Dutch trade missions in their singular pursuit of spices, but British archaeologists began to penetrate the site in 1823. Astonishingly, a resident Buddhist priest had already dedicated himself to exhuming and restoring the Ruwaneli stupa, and later he worked in collaboration with the British to excavate Anuradhapura's civic center.

Today the old city is a popular destination for both its ruins and its resurrected gardens. Curiously, both the British occupation of the early 20th century, with its attendant respect for preservation, and the recent tourism surge have had the effect of buffering Anuradhapura from exploitation as conservation needs have been increasingly recognized.

## Synopsis

543 B.C.    City named after Anuradha, minister and founder of Sinhalese race

| | |
|---|---|
| 437 B.C. | King Pandukabaya establishes Anuradhapura as Sinhalese capital |
| 245 B.C. | Sacred Bo-Tree planted |
| A.D. 933 | Anuradhapura destroyed by Hindu Chola empire |
| 1823 | British archaeologists begin to excavate old city |
| 1948 | Sri Lanka (formerly Ceylon) gains independence; "New Anuradhapura" dedicated |

**Further Reading**

Brookes, John, *Gardens of Paradise: The History and Design of the Great Islamic Gardens,* New York: New Amsterdam, and London: Weidenfeld and Nicolson, 1987

MacMillan, Hugh Fraser, *A Handbook of Tropical Planting and Gardening, with Special Reference to Ceylon,* Colombo, Ceylon: Cave, 1910; 5th edition, as *Tropical Planting and Gardening, with Special Reference to Ceylon,* London: Macmillan, 1943; New York: St. Martin, 1956

McConnell, Douglas John, *The Forest-Garden Farms of Kandy, Sri Lanka,* Rome: Food and Agriculture Organization of the United Nations, 1992

Perera, H.R., *Buddhism in Ceylon: Its Past and Present,* Kandy, Ceylon: Buddhist Publication Society, 1966; as *Buddhism in Sri Lanka: A Short History,* Kandy, Sri Lanka: Buddhist Publication Society, 1988

Witane, Godwin, "Anuradhapura: Its Origin, Fall, and Revival," *Sri Lankan Sunday Observer* (9 April 2000)

KRISTIN WYE RODNEY

# Aranjuez

## Aranjuez, Madrid Province, Spain

**Location:** approximately 25 miles (40.2 km) southeast of Madrid

Aranjuez consists of a royal town, palace, and gardens and occupies an extensive vale at the confluence of the rivers Jarama and Tagus, almost due south of Madrid. Although a fragment of the present garden is datable to the 15th century, the surviving layouts around the royal palace are of two main traditions: baroque and 18th-century informal. Aranjuez shared some 16th-century architects in common with the Escorial, whose more robust formal architecture contrasts with the other's modest scale.

The origins of Aranjuez go back 800 years. Following his conquest of the Toledo kingdom, the Castilian Christian king Alfonso VI gifted this area to the Grand Masters of the Military Order of Santiago at the end of the 11th century. There they established a pleasure palace. When, at the end of the 15th century, the Crown absorbed this military order, their Aranjuez site became one of several royal palaces belonging to Queen Isabella.

The area was firmly established as a rural residence for the king's recreation under royal warrant in Carlos V's time (1544). Because a particularly benign microclimate fitted the place to spring and autumn residence, it developed as a seasonal royal home, a role it was to play from Felipe II's day (r. 1556–98) until the late 19th century. At Aranjuez imaginative manmade features were designed for a floodplain and its river. As the landscape design matured over time, it became celebrated as a fine example of natural beauty reserved as a paradise for the King of Spain. It was painted by Spain's leading artists (Velázquez, Goya, and Maella) and celebrated by its poets. Alluded to most favorably by Schiller in his *Don Carlos,* its genius loci is known to a musical public from the eponymous popular guitar concerto of Rodriguez.

Whereas the park's evolution and overall form were molded by riverine topography, the location and architecture of the palace have strongly influenced the design of its formal garden nucleus. From the very beginning running water was harnessed ingeniously. Dams and drainage features were contrived functionally for irrigation and decoratively for display. Consequently, there is an outstanding wealth of fountains, some sites surviving from the 16th century, although most are of a later date.

Under Carlos V (r. 1519–56) Flemish gardens were introduced onto the river island adjacent to the palace. The first botanic garden in Spain was planted with medicinal herbs here in 1555, following Dr. Laguna's dedication of his translation of Dioscorides's *De materia medica* to Felipe II. This demonstrated Laguna's concern for maintaining the king's health as well as for

Aranjuez Island Garden, Madrid, Spain
Copyright Paul Miles Picture Collection

educating the public. Felipe II planted English elms (*Ulmus procera*) in the later 1550s and introduced new Renaissance designs to the Island Garden in 1562, bringing in fountains, tree-lined avenues (*calles*), and fruit trees. These formed part of a wider plan that involved developing the palace to designs by Juan Bautista de Toledo and Juan de Herrera.

Felipe IV (r. 1631–65) brought Cosimo Lotti from Florence, with two gardeners from the Boboli gardens, to continue developing high Renaissance horticultural tradition on the site. He introduced a further wealth of fountains and ornaments with fashionable water tricks to the island, which was by then well endowed with groves of trees.

By the later 17th century the palace environs consisted of a geometrically planned landscape with radiating vistas. The palace and formal gardens lay mainly within and were suspended by smaller garden designs from two river meander cores toward the west. Further improvements and enlargements followed under Felipe V (r. 1700–24). Today the general southern aspect of this earlier plan is subsumed by the town, which became integral to the overall design concept later in the 18th century under Fernando VI (r. 1724–59) and Carlos III (r. 1759–88). Royal management of the estate continued effectively until the mid-19th century, after which dramatic political and economic changes conspired to arrest its growth, leaving only the major essentials of its garden nucleus to be managed by the Patrimonio Nacional since the early 1980s.

Aside from the town, the palace setting still retains three main recognizable components significant to European garden history. The first is the Parterre and King's Garden. These form an impressive axial approach to the palace's south facade. The second is an extensive regular grid infill in the more westerly river meander core. Detached by a canal, it is known as the Island Garden (El jardin de las Isla). The third and largest surviving component is the Prince's Garden (El jardin del Principe), an extensive parkland, punctuated by buildings and follies, still recognizable as an important 18th-century landscape garden.

Although generally speaking time has been kind to the appearance and condition of both the palace and grounds, a train station was placed adjacent and to the west of the site in 1851. Subsequently, in the 1990s a roadway and new bridge were carved out close to the Parterre frontage. These developments may distract visitors' first impressions of the place.

The Parterre was ordered by Felipe V in 1727 to a typically French design by the engineer Etienne Marchand. Sancho (1996) perceives it to be a compromise between the French parterre and the many pre-existing and natural conditions of the site: "[The] restrained river was used here in a picturesque manner as a transition and frontier between wild nature and the area submitted to etiquette." Its boxwood hedges and flowers were removed about 1850, and the garden later modernized.

The main palace approach is along the main axis of rose beds laid out to the simplest baroque design. Its principal elements include two fountains, which replaced generations of earlier water features. Statues of Hercules and Antaeus now occupy the first fountain in a round pond near the entrance. They are followed by a group of Ceres placed centrally in an oval pond midway toward the palace. In both cases their sculptural composition results from changes made within the last two centuries.

Overlooked by the royal apartments, the King's Garden, the oldest surviving formal garden at Aranjuez, made up of eight square beds, lies on the south side of the palace. Conceived by Juan Bautista de Toledo for Philip II and built by Juan de Herrera around 1577, it was finished with the installation of a green jasper fountain carved by Roque Solario in 1582. Both garden and fountain were entirely restored in 1986.

Marble gateways and irrigation canals were established on the island by Gaspar de Vega and Alonso de Covarrubias in 1550, during Carlos V's reign. Although Carlos V introduced changes during his regency, it was after Felipe II's ascension that Juan Bautista de Toledo was engaged to draw up a plan for the Island Garden. Numerous foreign gardeners became involved, including the Fleming Juan Holvecq and the Italian Jeronimo de Algora. Designed to enhance an appreciation of contemporary landscape perspective, the resulting initiative saw the site laid out in a grid pattern of larger rectangles accommodating smaller squares, divided by "streets" interspersed with fountains (after 1582) and piazzas. Ingenious plant-covered trelliswork helped integrate the piazzas, highlighting their classical sculptures, with shady, greener places and plantings. Also included were features where unsuspecting visitors could be trapped and soaked by water games. Plants were imported from Flanders and France; fruit trees from Andalusia and Valencia.

Ascribing a particular style to this early phase is difficult. It owed something to the Islamic garden (the low fountains and geometric form), to the Italian mannerist garden (its mythological allusion), and to the Flemish garden (the low parterres, especially of roses).

The Island Garden evolved, and in 1660 Sebastian de Herrera Barnuevo, Master of the Royal Works, began installing new fountains. New piazzas, benches, and columns of Colmenar stone designed by Sabatini in 1782 became focal to the later 18th-century landscape. Curiously, by that time neglect had become crucial to the aesthetic sensibility of the place, its mature 16th- and 17th-century trees conveying the idea of a fashionable "natural garden." The current intention is to restore this garden to its earlier Renaissance splendor.

The Prince's Garden is located between the river Tagus on the north and a tree-lined east-running avenue on its south, the Calle de la Reina (Queen's Avenue), which dates from Felipe II's day. Juan Bautista de Toledo intended it to enclose orchards, gardens, and a grove of trees. These survived into the 18th century.

Although having earlier origins, the surviving Prince's Garden dates mainly from the mid- to late- 18th century. It was conceived by Carlos IV before he ascended the throne (hence its name). During the 18th century the site grew to encompass an enormous and unusual combination of landscape garden and parkland. At present it incorporates both garden and arboretum and includes many elements reworked over the past two centuries.

On the whole it reflects well Carlos's vision for a landscape of English and French influences. It still includes over a dozen recognizable gardens, or complexes of garden or royal estate features, and incorporates several magnificent gateways, fountains, and pavilions, set within a park running roughly west to east.

Entered through its quadricolumnar gateway (Puerta del Embarcadero), the Calle del Embarcadero runs north, passing Felipe II's orchard site to the right, before passing the First, or Spanish, Garden, beside the Tagus on the left, and the Second Garden on the right. Farther on, still on the left, is the Landing Stage of Ferdinand VI, with its grouping of five pavilions (created for Ferdinand VI and Charles III) and an adjacent Picturesque fort complete with cannons. Beyond that stands an incomplete Picturesque ruined castle, built as a mirador, or viewing point. Adjacent is the Royal Barge Museum built in 1963 to a design of Ramon Andrada, facing the grove of the Casa de Marinos on the opposite bank.

Turning eastward, the Narcissus Fountain is central to the Third Garden, while the Fourth Garden houses the Ceres Fountain and faces across an avenue the Fifth Garden. Riverward, to the north, stands the Apollo Fountain alongside the east-west Calle de Apolo. Between these three features and the Real Casa del Labrador (King's Lodge) are three more gardens, beginning with a pond and features originally in the Chinese style (the Sixth Garden). The Seventh and Eighth Gardens lie between this and the Royal Lodge, which at one time was isolated from the park by a meander in the Tagus. Beyond the lodge is the now inaccessible and overgrown Miraflores Park designed in the English style for Isabel II's palace governor, the Marques de Miraflores in 1848, by J. Whitby.

The progenitor of this 18th-century work was Pablo Boutelou, who designed the first five gardens between 1775 and 1784. Of a minor gardening dynasty, his grandfather Esteban I had worked at Aranjuez from around 1716, and the gardens owe much of their present splendor to his father, Esteban II, head gardener under Fernando VI and Carlos III. Pablo built on his family's experience by traveling abroad. The Boutelous were to continue the family tradition at Aranjuez well into the 19th century. These first gardens were separated from the parkland by a ha-ha.

In 1785 work started on the Sixth, or Anglo-Chinese, Garden, at which point the architect Juan de Villanueva became involved. The combined talents of Villanueva and Boutelou on this project produced one of the most exciting contrasts of garden sculpture of its day. It included a Chinese gazebo, a rotund pillared temple, fountains, statues, and ornamental rock formations to achieve novel effects with moving water.

Also reflecting contemporary mode, the Seventh Garden—Islas Americanas and Asiaticas—was landscaped in an informal style in 1793. Its 19th-century title reflects the considerable renown achieved by Carlos IV's overseas botanical collecting.

Construction began on the Royal Lodge in 1791, originally to designs by Villanueva. It was completed in 1803, probably under his successor, Isidro Gonzales Velázquez. The interior is decorated in the most sumptuous manner imaginable, reflecting how its several designers combined the techniques of inlaying numerous colored marbles and ornamental stone with the skills of plastering and painting in one of the most interesting interiors of its time.

## Synopsis

| | |
|---|---|
| pre-1200 | Alfonso VI of Castile donates Aranjuez to Holy Military Order of Santiago |
| 1469–92 | Palace adopted as residence by Ferdinand and Isabella |
| 1544 | Warrant establishing Aranjuez as rural residence for King Charles V's recreation |
| 1550 | Marble gateways and irrigation canals established on Island Garden (El jardin de las Isla) by Gaspar de Vega and Alonso de Covarrubias |
| 1555 | Spain's first botanic garden established at Aranjuez |
| 1562 | Elms and fountains established on Island Garden, allées and fruit trees planted under direction of Philip II |
| ca. 1577 | Juan Bautista de Toledo and Juan de Herrera create King's Garden |
| late-16th century | Involvement of gardeners Juan Holvecq and Jeronimo de Algora |
| 1582 | Roque Solario installs green jasper fountain in the King's Garden |
| ca. 1650–60 | Cosimo Lotti comes from Florence with two gardeners from Boboli gardens |
| 1660 | Sebastian de Herrera Barnuevo installs new fountains in Island Garden |
| 1716 | Esteban Boutelou I works in garden |
| 1727 | Etienne Marchand designs parterre for Philip V |
| 1754 | Bonavia builds Royal Pavilion in Pavilion Garden |
| 1775–84 | Pablo Boutelou designs five gardens for Prince's Garden |
| 1782 | Sabatini designs new piazzas, benches, and columns for Island Garden |
| 1785 | Pablo Boutelou starts work on Anglo-Chinese Garden with Juan de Villanueva (1739–1811) |
| 1791 | Work begins on Casa Real de Labrador |
| 1793 | Charles IV commissions Islas Americanas and Asiaticas exotic botanic landscape |
| 1827–28 | Joachim Dumondre rebuilds Narcissus Fountain and Ceres Fountain in Prince's Garden |
| 1848 | Mirafiores Park designed by J. Whitby |
| 1963 | Royal Barge Museum built to design of Ramon Andrada |
| 1982 | Ongoing restorations |
| 1986 | Restoration of King's Garden and green jasper fountain |

## Further Reading

Anon (Feliu), Carmen, "Nature and the Idea of Gardening in Eighteenth Century Spain," in *The History of Garden Design: The Western Tradition from the Renaissance to the Present Day*, edited by Monique Mosser and Georges Teyssot, London: Thames and Hudson, 1991

Casa Valdes, María Teresa, *Jardines de Espana*, Madrid: Aguilar, 1973

Gromort, Georges, *Jardins d'Espagne*, 2 vols., Paris: Vincent, 1926

Sancho, Jose Luis, "El Palacio Real de Aranjuez," in *Palacios Reales en Espana: Historia y arquitectura de la magnificencia*, Madrid: Fundación Argentaria, 1996

*Visitor's Guide to Aranjuez: The Royal Seat of Aranjuez*, Madrid: Editorial Patrimonio Nacional (1998)

C. STEPHEN BRIGGS

# Arbor

The word *arbor* has had several meanings in connection with gardens. Derived from the word *herber*, an arbor once referred to any place covered with grass or to an orchard or herb garden. Today, however, the word is most commonly applied to certain garden structures or retreats formed entirely of living plants or of plants trained to climb a framework of stone, metal, wood, or living materials. Arbors can be built in a variety of shapes: a single arched arbor, a long tunnel-arbor (the Italian pergola or the French *berceau*), or an enclosed chamber or bower. Arguably the oldest form of garden architecture, the arbor is the simplest type of garden building to construct but the most difficult to maintain. As a result, few historic arbors survive.

Arbors were found in the very earliest gardens: they are depicted in Egyptian tomb paintings (Tomb of Neb-Amun, Thebes) and in Assyrian reliefs (King Ashurbanipal feasting in a grape arbor, 660 B.C., British Museum). Pliny mentions them in his accounts of Roman gardens. Illuminated manuscripts (such as the Limbourg brothers' *Trés Riches Heures de Duc de Berry,* ca. 1416; The Book of Hours of Jean, Duc de Berry) demonstrate that both bowers and tunnel-arbors were common in the medieval pleasure garden.

The earliest printed garden books make it clear that the building of arbors was considered a basic skill of a good gardener. Thomas Hill, who published books on gardening from 1563, included lengthy discourses on arbors. Arbors constructed of juniper, he wrote, would last ten years, while those built of willow would have to be repaired after only three years. The arbor could be built in "a square forme, or in arches manner winded, that the braunches of the Vine, Melone, or Cucumbre, running and spreading all over, might so shadowe and keepe both the heate and Sunne." The structural material was "carpenter's work"; later it would be called a lattice or trellis, and if quite grand, as it often was in France, it was referred to as treillage.

As suggested by Hill, the plants used to cover arbors were most often the grapevine or fast-growing fruits and vegetables. In the most delightful pleasure gardens, however, roses, honeysuckle, jasmine, and other fragrant plants were chosen. Boccaccio, in the *Decameron,* describes spacious alleys and bowers built with a trellis of vines, covered with red and white roses and with jasmine, providing both shade and delicious scent.

It was during the Renaissance that arbors had their greatest impact on garden design. Long tunnel-arbors running through or on the sides of garden compartments emphasized axial divisions of the garden and sometimes provided an evergreen geometric framework. At the Villa d'Este, Tivoli, the lowest garden compartment was divided into quadrants by long tunnel-arbors. A tall two-story octagonal bower stood at the intersection of the pergolas; smaller bowers were placed at the center of each walk. This great emphasis on the various arbor forms was found in other Italian gardens and became fashionable in northern Europe. Gardens shown in the publications of Crispjin Van de Passe and others are frequently dominated by long arbors running around and through the gardens. In keeping with the mannerist architecture of the period, arbors were often supported on grotesque terms and caryatids. Similarly, the influential gardens at Wilton House in England, designed by Isaac de Caus in the 1630s, had tunnel-arbors approximately 90 meters (98.4 yd.) long, as well as quadrangular bowers.

It was also during the Renaissance that the most dramatic variation of the arbor—the tree house—reached its peak. Known from antiquity (Pliny the Elder wrote of a tree house built by Emperor Caligula, with a dining room large enough for 15 guests and servants), tree houses were built on an even more elaborate scale in the 16th and early 17th centuries. At the Medici villa at Pratolino, two great ramps wound around a giant oak tree (known as *La fontana della Rovere*) up to an immense platform, visible in illustrations of the garden by Utens, Stefano della Bella, and others. At Castello, the tree house (described by Vasari in his account of the life of the sculptor Niccolo, il Tribolo, designer of the garden) had a table on which stood a marble vase with hidden spouts of water that sprinkled unwary visitors. The tree houses at Castello and Pratolino no longer exist, but there are remains of a stairway encircling an oak at Villa Petraia, near Florence, Italy.

Typically, the practice spread north. By 1629 John Parkinson (in *Paradisi in Sole, Paradisus Terrestris*) was describing a three-story tree house at Cobham Hall in Kent that could hold "halfe an hundred men at the least." Pieter Brueghel's engraving of *Spring,* first published in 1570, shows gardeners toiling in a garden and weaving vines onto an elaborate tunnel-arbor. In the background aristocratic couples dance and feast in a multistory arbor built around a spindly tree.

The great popularity of the arbor in the Renaissance might be explained by its ancient pedigree, but it was also the perfect collaboration between art and nature, which was so admired in the intellectualized gardens of the period. Trompe l'oeil arbors even crept into interior design, with rooms in great houses painted in imitation of the woven branches of arbors, complete with fruit, flowers, and birds.

By the latter part of the 17th century, however, the arbor began to play a less dominant role in garden design, and some writers (John Worlidge, for example) complained that arbors were damp and difficult to maintain.

Dome of St. Peter's Arbor Garden, Vatican City
Copyright John Bethell/Garden Picture Library

While there was no structural role for the arbor in the English landscape garden, its evocative qualities were recognized. In 1755 Thomas Wright of Durham published *Universal Architecture, Book I: Six Original Designs of Arbors,* in which he constructs highly imaginative arbors for druids and hermits supposedly dwelling in the garden. The Victorians picked up on this romantic interpretation of the arbor, building suitably gloomy rustic retreats of living materials (arbors shrouded with greenery were particularly apposite to a society that dwelled on death). Today it is possible to purchase ready-made frames of wood or metal from many modern garden suppliers. It is testimony to the enduring love of the arbor (and to its great resurgence in the 20th century) that among the most photographed garden features in modern Britain is Rosemary Verey's laburnum walk at Barnsley House in Gloucestershire.

**Further Reading**

Henderson, Paula, "Tree-Top Conceits," *Country Life* (25 December 1986)

Hill, Thomas, *The Proffitable Arte of Gardening,* London, 1568; reprint, London: Marsh, 1983

Jekyll, Gertrude, *Garden Ornament,* London: Country Life, and New York: Scribner, 1918; reprint, Woodbridge, Suffolk: Antique Collectors' Club, 1994

Van de Passe, Crispjin, *Hortus Floridus,* Utrecht, The Netherlands, 1614; as *Hortus Floridus: The Four Books of Spring, Summer, Autumn, and Winter Flowers,* translated by Spencer Savage, London: Minerva, 1974

Wilkinson, Elizabeth, and Marjorie Henderson, *The House of Boughs: A Sourcebook of Garden Designs, Structures, and Suppliers,* New York: Viking, 1985

Worlidge, John, *Systema Agriculturae: The Mystery of Husbandry Discovered,* London, 1669

Wright, Thomas, *Universal Architecture: Arbours and Grottoes,* London, 1755

PAULA HENDERSON

# Arboretum

An arboretum is a garden or part of a garden containing a collection of trees and shrubs. The Latin term *arboretum* has been known since the Renaissance but was used in those times only metaphorically—for example, *Arboretum sacrum* referred to the trees in the bible—or poetically (*arborets* in Milton refer to groves). There is no evidence that the term *arboretum* was used for a garden before the 18th century. It also seems that the earliest dendrological collections in England (Fulham, Chelsea, Kew, etc.) and Germany (Schwöbber near Hameln, Harbke near Brunswick, Kassel, Mannheim, Hohenheim near Stuttgart) were not termed *arboretums*. The first recorded example for a tree collection called an arboretum is a part of a garden at Schönbrunn, Vienna, about 1753. Johann Georg Krünitz used the term in 1774 as an equivalent to *Baum-Schule* (nursery). F.L. Sckell created in 1776 for the Palatine elector at Schwetzingen an Arborium Thedoricum, also called Arboretum.

The term became more wide spread in the 19th century. John Claudius Loudon discussed arboretums in his *Treatise on Country Residences* (1806), in his *Encyclopaedia on Gardening* (1822), in *The Gardener's Magazine* (1826; Loddiges's Arboretum, Hackney), and in his *Arboretum Britannicum* (1838). In the latter work he declared, "We trust that the time will soon come when there will be no gentleman's seat of any extent without one [arboretum]." Charles M'Intosh complained in his *Practical Gardener* (1828) that there were still too few arboretums. Loudon was the greatest promoter of the arboretum idea in Britain. German encyclopedias did not record the term before 1842 (*Meyer's Conversations-Lexicon*).

Arboretums may be designed in several manners. There were strictly systematic collections with trees planted in straight rows as found at Harbke, Hohenheim (1772), Kleve (1782), Schönbrunn (1788), and Potsdam (1790). Conrad Loddiges at Hackney (1816) arranged his specimens in a snail-like curved line. A similar pattern is described in Gottlieb Becker's *Taschenbuch für Gartenfreunde* (1798; Garden Friend's Pocketbook). The collections at Hackney and Potsdam were alphabetically arranged. Other collections were designed according to the landscape style (Painshill, Woburn Farm, Kew, Schwetzingen, Machern near Leipzig, Derby Arboretum).

The plantings for most 19th-century arboretums followed Bernard and Adrien de Jussieu's, Alphonse de Candolle's, or John Lindley's botanical system. This so-called natural system was regarded as a way to combine science and design (e.g., by Loudon, Joseph Paxton, Charles H. Smith, M'Intosh, Gustav Meyer, and Eduard Petzold). After Charles H. Smith, the first systematically planted arboretum was at Turnham Green near London (1823).

Although Loudon warned not to mix exotic species indiscriminately, he could not stop the exuberant collecting of exotics that took place without taking into consideration the harmony of specimen forms. Julius Bosse of Oldenburg recognized in 1840 aesthetic planting and botanical collecting to be incompatible and destructive to aesthetics. M'Intosh felt the same and recommended in 1836 planting species of only one order together. Sufficient space is needed to plant species of the same family together in large numbers. If space or money were restricted, he advised to take only conifers, *Corylaceae* (oaks, beaches, chestnuts, hazels), or *Salicaceae* (willows and poplars).

M'Intosh also referred in 1853 to a new manner of arboretum arranging. Messrs. van Mallen in Brussels had arranged their extended collection of conifers according to their geographical distribution, and John Spencer designed a geographically arranged pinetum for the marquis of Landsdowne at Bowood in 1850. As Spencer noted, this arrangement exclusively permits one to display the general character of a species, its size, and habit.

As far as is known, planting according to geographic patterns was first mentioned by Carl Gottlob Rössig in 1800, as a garden vision. Humphry Repton proposed in 1802 planting a garden with Chinese plants around a Chinese pavilion at Woburn Abbey, as well as a garden with American plants. (An "American garden" was generally considered only as a garden with bog-loving plants.) The most important promoter of plant geography was Alexander von Humboldt, who established this science in 1805. In a later work (*Kosmos* [1845]) he related to gardening as a matter of understanding the biologic unity in diversity and recommended that the landscape designer regard realistic plant physiognomy and contrast, maintaining that the physiognomic beauty of plants is important in landscape gardening. Humboldt's writings received worldwide acknowledgment, even by landscape gardeners.

In 1841–48 George Fleming planted geographical groups (called Mexico, America, Italy, and Ireland) at Trentham Arboretum in England. Thereafter James Bateman created his famous "China" at Biddulph Grange, which contained both Chinese buildings and Chinese plants. Eduard Petzold planted geographic areas in the Muskau Arboretum, Saxony, Germany (1859). After the Royal Botanic Gardens, Kew, he regarded this arboretum as the most complete one concerning species; with regard to landscaping, however, he emphasized better design. Gustav Meyer from Berlin published his layout for a dendropomological garden in the *Gardener's Chronicle* (1871). Charles Sprague Sargent's Arnold Arboretum in Boston (1883) followed some of William

Robinson's ideas pertaining to Impressionistic design. The genera were planted according to Bentham and Hooker's *Genera Plantarum* (1862–83) and the species were geographically planted. In the Berlin Botanical Garden (1895), which was designed in the landscape style, vast geographical divisions were laid out along with the systematically arranged arboretum. This was the first great public arboretum in Germany. Other efforts at national arboretums in Germany, Austria, and Czechoslovakia were not successful. Other famous private arboretums were laid out at Les Barres (1821) and Segrez (1857) in France, at Trompenburg, in Netherlands (1859), at Sychrov (1820) and Pruhonice (1885) in Bohemia, and in Chicago (Morton Arboretum, 1922) in the United States. The arboretum of the Berlin Botanical Garden (1906) functioned as a national collection.

In Europe most private arboretums ceased in the early 20th century, due to the restrictions of wealth after World War I. The newly created national arboretums after 1945 emphasized practical dendrology and forestry and primarily used a landscaped layout. Woodland arboretums were planned in England, Scotland, and Wales. A German forestial-botanic garden was created near Cologne in 1963. Outside its landscaped area with single specimens are experimental forest plantations, for example, from *Sequioadendrons* and *Prerocaryas*. The Thimm nursery arboretum at Thiensen (near Hamburg, Germany, 1956) was given to the district government in 1983. A national dendrological garden was founded in 1972 near the old private park at Průhonice, Czechoslovakia. Vast divisions for creepers, hedge plants, and ground covers can be seen. In France the arboretum of Chevreloup near Versailles was founded in 1960 as a division of the Natural History Museum in Paris. Tropmenburg Park near Rotterdam, the Netherlands, was converted into an arboretum beginning in 1920. The 300-hectare (741 acre) Morton Arboretum in Chicago (1922), belonging to a private foundation, may be considered as an outstanding U.S. example, covering multiple aspects of dendrology, ecology, and landscape planning.

Specialized arboretums include the pinetum, *salicetum, quercetum,* and *rosarium,* which are each dedicated to one genus. A pinetum is usually considered to be a collection of conifers, including *Ginkgo.* This idea derives from early references by Joseph Addison (1712), who recommended evergreen planting schemes. Richard Bradley, Lord Petre, and Philip Miller made first use of such schemes around 1730. Loudon referred to the duke of Argyll, who had a collection of conifers as early as 1720 to 1730 at Whitton. He also mentioned other early collections at Mill Hill, Sion House, and Kew. In France Duhamel de Monceau (1755) and Jean-Marie Morel (1776) recommended winter bosquets. In Germany Hirschfeld proposed winter gardens, and Count Finckenstein realized an evergreen mountain at Alt-

Madlitz Park, Brandenburg, around 1780. But these so-called winter gardens were integrated parts of a designed entity and aimed more toward aesthetics than to scientific collections, as the evergreen assortments were too restricted before the 19th century. The term *pinetum* was not used during these times.

The earliest peculiar pineta were established at Dropmore, Berkshire, in 1796 (which Loudon called the most important), Glasnevin near Dublin in 1798, Paris in 1800, Dublin in 1808, and in Berlin in 1816. A.B. Lambert and F. Bauer published the influential *A Description of the Genus Pinus* (1803–7). The duke of Bedford founded one of the most famous pineta at Woburn Abbey in 1836. The enthusiasm for pineta reached its peak around 1840 in Britain. Conifers such as *Abies procera, Chamaecyparis lawsoniana, Pseudotsuga, Sequoia,* and *Sequoiadendron,* discovered between 1829 and 1854, gave more impetus for such collections. Conifers were more esteemed than deciduous trees, and Charles H. Smith regarded pineta in 1852 as the most important tree collection type. Loddiges's nursery at Hackney offered the greatest assortment of conifers, followed by Booth's near Hamburg. The pinetum trend spread rapidly to France and Germany. The National Pinetum of Britain at Bedgebury was established in 1924 as an outpost of the Kew National Tree collection.

After 1875 the intrinsic pinetum was replaced by a more diversified evergreen garden type, enriched by new evergreens such *Cotoneaster, Skimmia, Mahonia, Berberis,* and *Viburnum* species, along with *Rhododendron* and *Prunus laurocerasus* cultivars. Beginning in 1892 Baron Ambrózy Migazzi created a park containing more than 6,000 evergreen deciduous trees and shrubs in Mlany, Slovakia.

**Further Reading**

Elliott, Brent, *Victorian Gardens,* London: Batsford, and Portland, Oregon: Timber Press, 1986

Hay, Ida, *Science in the Pleasure Ground: A History of the Arnold Arboretum,* Boston: Northeastern University Press, 1995

Humboldt, Alexander von, *Kosmos: Entwurf einer physischen Weltbeschreibung,* 4 vols., Stuttgart, Germany, 1845–58; reprint, Stuttgart, Germany: Brockhaus, 1978; as *Cosmos: A Sketch of a Physical Description of the Universe,* 5 vols., translated by Elise C. Otté, London, 1848–58; New York, 1850–59; reprint, 2 vols., Baltimore, Maryland, and London: Johns Hopkins University Press, 1997

Loudon, John Claudius, *Observations on the Formation and Management of Useful and Ornamental Plantations,* Edinburgh, 1804

Loudon, John Claudius, *An Encyclopaedia of Gardening,* 2 vols., London, 1822; new edition, 1835; reprint, New York: Garland, 1982

Loudon, John Claudius, "On Mixing Herbaceous Flowering Plants with Trees and Shrubs," *The Gardener's Magazine* 11 (1835)

McIntosh, Charles, *The Practical Gardener, and Modern Horticulturist*, London: Kelly, 1828; new edition, as *The New and Improved Practical Gardener, and Modern Horticulturist*, London: Kelly, 1847

McIntosh, Charles, *The Book of the Garden*, 2 vols., Edinburgh and London, 1853–55

Petzold, Eduard Carl Adolf, and Gerhard Kirchner, *Arboretum Muscaviense*, Gotha, Germany, 1864

Rössig, Carl Gottlob, "Ueber die Anordnung der Holzpflanzen und anderer Gewächse in Lustanlagen nach ihrem Vaterlande," in *Taschenbuch auf das Jahr 1801 für Natur- und Gartenfreunde*, Tübingen, Germany: Gotta, 1800

Sargent, Charles, "The Artistic Aspect of Trees," *Garden and Forest* 1 (1888) and 2 (1889)

Smith, Charles H.J., *Landscape Gardening; or, Parks and Pleasure Grounds*, New York, 1853; reprint, New Haven, Connecticut: Research Publications, 1972

Wimmer, Clemens A., *Bäume und Sträucher in historischen Gärten*, Dresden: Verlag der Kunst, 2001

CLEMENS ALEXANDER WIMMER

# Archaeology

Archaeology is an established tool of historic garden-conservation management and interpretation. It is of particular value for informing restoration and re-creation. Its use to unravel the complex aspects of landscape history is nevertheless a relatively recent development. Beginning in the 20th century, this investigational method has grown slowly from roots in influential projects such as the restoration of Colonial Williamsburg, Virginia, United States and the installation of a Renaissance-style garden at Kirby Hall, Northants, England, during the 1930s. However, in the United States, at least, the integrity of stratigraphic recording in such projects was not fully realized until the late 1950s and 1960s.

Excavating gardens is only one aspect of a broadening investigational discipline that today also includes precise mensuration, remote sensing for landscape reconnaissance, principally by aerial photography but including nondestructive ground penetration, and analytical laboratory techniques. One can use all these techniques to supplement or substitute for deficient or absent written or graphic evidence for garden evolution and function.

Ever since the inception of flight, aerial archaeology has made a deep impact on European archaeology in general. Post–World War II aerial photography programs have produced important visual records of country-house estate gardens throughout the British Isles, demonstrating how generations of lost or buried garden designs can lie buried but recognizable from above, defined by palimpsest crop or parch marks in the soil. Important images of extensive earth works testifying to abandoned medieval and Renaissance settlements, gardens, and landscapes have also been captured from the air in raking light or under powderings of snow. Similarly, images have been made of the more recent utilitarian plots and plant beds that surrounded abandoned cottages or that now define lost farm gardens. Studies of these photographs can sometimes help shed light on early horticultural practice.

Overall, aerial photographic records enable useful documentation of evolving estate and parkland patterns. Along with historic maps and plans, a growing archive of large-scale governmental vertical or purpose-taken oblique images (many derived from defense programs) now offer great potential to realize Geographic Information Systems (GIS) plotting techniques by depicting "layered" period estate plantings and evolving garden-design plans.

Aerial reconnaissance has developed more slowly outside England and Germany, although since glasnost fertile ententes between Eastern and Western scholars have greatly extended both the techniques and their geographical milieus. The knowledge so gained should eventually enable cultural research evaluation of later medieval and Renaissance garden and landscape-design fashions well into the Mediterranean, Polish, and Russian heartlands. In the United States aerial photography has notably provided evidence for the form of lost gardens at Colonial Williamsburg.

The motive to study early earthwork garden sites by field survey arose to some degree from the successes of aerial photographic discovery. Between approximately 1965 and 1995 initiatives by field-workers within the former Royal Commission on Historic Monuments in England (now part of English Heritage) resulted in the production of detailed plans of approximately 100 extensive or partially preserved garden earth works

Excavation of a flower bed in the Canopus Garden, Villa Adriana,
Tivoli, Italy
Copyright Eugenia Salza Prina Ricotti

dating from the later 16th to the 19th and even 20th
centuries. A majority of these sites had originally been
created to adorn high-status houses. The nuclear areas
of discovery have been mainly in the Midlands and eastern England, where agricultural conditions enabled
good preservation. The County Inventories of Ancient
Monuments for Northamptonshire and Cambridgeshire
published many of these sites during the 1970s and
1980s. Archaeologists have now made discoveries and
surveys of similar sites, more modest in numbers,
throughout most settled parts of England and Ireland.

Antiquarian digging in gardens informed a basic
understanding of Roman villas and their environs in
Italy and beyond over several centuries. Such digging
was probably inspired more by architectural and statuary collectors' whims than by any motive to describe
planting patterns or to understand tastes in landscape
style. In 20th-century Europe one of the first applications of more systematic, scientific archaeology in this

regard was on the Roman Palace at Fishbourne,
England, during the 1960s. Here, palynology directly
informed both the plan and flora of its restored garden.
Through parallel developments at Colonial Williamsburg in the United States, garden archaeologists also
used analytical techniques to identify original plantings
for restoration purposes. Since then, researchers have
employed increasingly sophisticated scientific methods
for deciphering gardens of all periods.

During the early 1930s Arthur A. Shurcliff researched
the landscapes and gardens of Colonial Williamsburg as
part of an architecture-led approach to conservation
and restoration. Although exploratory excavations
were undertaken in gardens (including the Governor's
Palace), archaeology played little role in the landscape
reconstruction, and the restorers did not involve professional archaeologists in research. In fact, at first the
restorers recorded and interpreted only buried walls and
the more obvious structures. Apparently, stratigraphies
were not recognized.

The situation at Colonial Williamsburg changed with
the introduction of area excavation by Ivor Noel Hume
during the 1960s. At first this technique was not particularly productive for garden archaeology. However, by
the 1970s waterlogged plant remains carefully recovered from Williamsburg gardens could be used to demonstrate their historic floras. Also about the same time,
William Kelso first dug at Carter's Cove and later at
Monticello, where he painstakingly conducted large-
scale excavations to maximize interpretation of the evidence. Then, during the 1980s Luccketti's work at
Bacon's Castle in Surry County illuminated one of the
most complete Virginian tidewater gardens of the later
17th century.

Since the 1980s Colonial Williamsburg has adopted
the full gamut of garden-archaeology technique. Aerial
photography, close-interval contour mapping, and
searching for relevant "ecofacts" such as seeds, pollen,
and phytoliths found in the layers, features, and fill
deposits related to gardening have all contributed.
Through the use of these techniques, attitudes to the
Williamsburg landscape have changed radically. Fundamentally, the distinction between decorative flower borders and functional vegetable beds has been made
possible, even resulting in such detail as the precise recognition of a bed for *Asparagus officinalis*. Investigation
continues with constant refinement of technique.

The archaeology commissioned to inform the restoration of the Royal Privy Garden at Hampton Court Palace
in England between 1992 and 1995 arguably provides
the story of the most effective excavation on the most
important historic garden so far undertaken. Although
first established as a Privy Garden under Henry VIII, the
parterre underlying the surviving enclosure in 1990 was
almost entirely the creation of William III and dated

from 1701. This rectangular walled enclosure runs north-south from the palace to the Thames. It encloses a long sunken garden terraced down from the palace end and overlooked on either side by raised walkways.

Since Victorian times this garden enclosure had been maintained as a visitor feature, cluttered with numerous overmature trees, and had come to represent a variety of garden styles. The decision to take the garden back to its original planting date of 1701, undertaking restoration as authentically as possible, drove excavation initiatives. Archaeology was only part of a well-orchestrated investigation that included detailed historical research on both the form and planting of the area. Together, these elements provided a quite comprehensive story. On the broader front the restorers intended the excavation to examine the origins and development of the terraces, identify the positions of steps, investigate the relationships of boundary walls, and examine tree-pit positions. More specifically, they wanted to resolve a number of practical problems that arose from the interpretation of historic documents.

Initial trenching began in 1991. On the ground hand digging was combined with machine clearance, all closely supervised. Archaeologists located traces of built features—including two Tudor garden towers—associated with Henry VIII's lost Privy Garden and his long-dismantled Water Gallery, although only a limited amount could be ascertained about the sequence of gardens that occupied the area prior to 1701.

Excavation clearly demonstrated how William III's garden had been extended beyond the bounds of its Tudor predecessor. Restorers were also able to illustrate the form of a long wooden pergola feature that had been known as Queen Mary's Bower. Trenches cut tangentially across the southern terminals of the two north-south terraces demonstrated an absence of any footings for stone steps and thus suggested how, for a limited period after the garden's construction, ascension had been on wooden treads.

Detailed pollen and soil analytical studies helped confirm what was already conjectured from historical sources about the varieties of shrubs used and the ways in which they had been planted. Researchers also found and scrutinized numerous artifacts to gain clearer insights into postmedieval gardening practices on royal sites. The outcome of this collaborative investigation was the complete reinstatement of the site, which was opened to the public by Prince Charles in July 1995. Archaeology provided the main intellectual authority to confidently undertake such a radical restoration.

Geophysical survey and soil resistivity are nondestructive reconnaissance tools now commonly used to map features underlying the present soil surface. Such mapping can be used to provide accurate plans of the formal layouts surrounding the houses of the gentry and

nobility, which were so often lost at the expense of 18th-century (and later) parkland landscaping introduced to intentionally erase the taste for formality.

Scientists have long employed dendrochronology effectively for the accurate dating of medieval and post-medieval buildings in Europe, usually from their structural timbers. At Hampton Court the technique assisted an understanding of yew and holly growth over a 300-year sequence within the Privy Garden. This dating offered no significant surprises to garden historians. More significantly, at Aberglasney, Wales, a sequence of cores taken from the live yews of a garden grove surprisingly demonstrated an age no greater than 250 years, in contrast to claims that had been made for a planting date of approximately 1000 A.D.

The analysis of garden soil to recover pollen and plant macrofossils, particularly seeds and pollen, is now a significant aid to garden history. Unfortunately, continuous waterlogging is important so that soil can be an effective medium of preservation. Damp or dry soils can suffer bacterial or biochemical action that eventually destroys its organic content beyond even microscopic recognition. But size particle analyses, the chemical analysis of soils, and particle analysis of path gravels and tree holes may provide indicative data that can be considered critically alongside structural information about early gardens.

Because thorough investigation can be an expensive exercise, and because archaeological activity may slow down building or restoration developmental work, garden archaeology is not yet universally accepted. Although in Europe the technique is promoted as an important aid to restoration and interpretation, planning laws differ from state to state, and the degree to which monuments are protected is inconsistent. Even in England, where so many innovations have been adopted in garden research, some important gardens still escape thorough archaeological scrutiny.

Tensions may also arise among fellow investigators when historic documents and archaeology are found to be at variance and when the definition of what actually constitutes evidence is effectively questioned. For example, in the absence of historical research, archaeologists working in 1989–92 at Castle Bromwich Hall, near Birmingham, England, suggested an exclusively 19th-century date for its "Holly Walk," a feature that had at one time joined two pavilion-like features across an 18th-century terrace. Although documentation later emerged demonstrating its existence in 1745, the archaeologists have still argued for the later date.

Aberglasney, Wales, offers a more complex case history whereby aesthetic and literary historians have promoted a 16th-century date and Italian inspiration for a supposed garden walkway raised on arches. Historical research, however, favors the theory that it was built atop an 18th-century farm building, while digging archaeology has located no credible evidence for any garden layout or plantings before approximately 1770–1800.

Through improved understanding of the archaeological potential of gardens and through cooperative restoration ventures and collaborative research studies, differences of approach and conflicts about interpretation should ideally resolve into open and constructive debates, which would in turn advantage restoration projects, scholarly research, and educational needs.

## Further Reading

Briggs, C.S., "Aberglasney: The Theory, Archaeology, and History of a Post-Medieval Landscape," *Post-Medieval Archaeology* 33 (1999)

Brown, Anthony Ernest, editor, *Garden Archaeology: Papers Presented to a Conference at Knutson Hall, Norhamptonshire, April 1988,* London: Council for British Archaeology, 1991

Currie, C.K., and M. Locock, "Excavations at Castle Bromwich Hall Gardens, 1989–91," *Post-Medieval Archaeology* 27 (1993)

Dix, Brian, "The Excavation of the Privy Garden," in *The King's Privy Garden at Hampton Court Palace, 1689–1995,* edited by Simon Thurley, London: Apollo Magazine, 1995

Dix, Brian, "Of Cabbages—And Kings: Garden Archaeology in Action," in *Old and New Worlds: Historical/Post-Medieval Archaeology Papers from the Societies' Joint Conferences at Williamsburg and London 1997 to Mark 30 Years of Work and Achievement,* edited by Geoff Egan and Ronald L. Michael, Oxford: Oxbow Books, 1999

Dix, Brian, I. Soden, and T. Hylton, "Kirby Hall and Its Gardens: Excavations in 1987–1994," *Archaeological Journal* 152 (1995)

Hayden, P., "Castle Bromwich Hall Gardens: An Alternative Date," *Post-Medieval Archaeology* 27 (1993)

*Journal of Garden History* 17, no. 1 (1997) (special issue edited by D. Jacques entitled "The Techniques and Uses of Garden Archaeology")

Kelso, William M., *Kingsmill Plantations, 1619–1800: Archaeology of Country Life in Colonial Virginia,* Orlando, Florida: Academic Press, 1984

Kelso, William M., and Rachel Most, editors, *Earth Patterns: Essays in Landscape Archaeology,* Charlottesville: University Press of Virginia, 1990

Landsberg, Sylvia, *The Medieval Garden,* London: British Museum Press, 1995; New York: Thames and Hudson, 1996

Miller, Naomi Frances, and Kathryn L. Gleason, editors, *The Archaeology of Garden and Field,* Philadelphia: University of Pennsylvania Press, 1994

Morgan Evans, David, Peter Salway, and David Thackray, editors, *The Remains of Distant Times: Archaeology and the National Trust,* Woodbridge, Suffolk, and Rochester, New York: Boydell Press, 1996

Noël Hume, Audrey, *Archaeology and the Colonial Gardener,* Williamsburg, Virginia: Colonial Williamsburg Foundation, 1974

Noël Hume, Ivor, *Digging for Carter's Grove,* Williamsburg, Virginia: Colonial Williamsburg Foundation, 1974

Pattison, Paul, editor, *There by Design: Field Archaeology in Parks and Gardens,* Oxford: Archaeopress, 1998

Taylor, Christopher C., *The Archaeology of Gardens,* Aylesbury, Buckinghamshire: Shire, 1983

Thurley, Simon, *The King's Privy Garden at Hampton Court Palace, 1689–1995,* London: Apollo Magazine, 1995

C. STEPHEN BRIGGS

# Archangelskoye

## Krasnogorsk District, Moscow Region, Russia

**Location:** approximately 10 miles (16 km) west of Moscow

Archangelskoye is one of the most remarkable sights in Moscow Region. It is a stately home, approximately 12 miles (19.3 km) from the capital city of Russia, and it represents a wonderful combination of garden and architectural art with fine artwork inside its palace and park. It sits on a high bank of the river Moskva, and its area exceeds 100 hectares (247 acres). Archangelskoye was a residence of Russian aristocracy beginning in the 16th century. Its present appearance was essentially created by its 18th- and 19th-century owners, Princes Golitsin and Yusupov.

In the early 18th century, when Archangelskoye belonged to Peter the Great's adherent, Prince Dimitri Golitsin, a wooden palace was built on the top slope of the river Moskva. The vast area in front of the palace was laid out as a geometric network of straight paths bordered with rows of clipped trees. Contemporary documents mention greenhouses containing exotic plants such as pineapple, orange, laurel, fig, and oleander.

This geometric pattern became the base of the formal garden of Archangelskoye. In the late 18th century the wooden palace was torn down and Prince Dimitri's grandson Nicolay had a new brick palace built almost at the same place. This "Great House," designed by French architect Charles Guern, was larger and had two wings linked with the main palace by colonnades of white stone. The formal garden was widened and improved, and two terraces with a grotto and numerous statues of Greco-Roman gods and heroes were placed in front of the palace, designed by the Italian architect Giacomo Trombaro. Fountains were arranged there as well, the project of Swedish engineer F. Norberg. The name of the garden designer is unknown, but he was certainly an expert and used the natural shape of the river slope quite skillfully. His creation was inspired by the main traits of André Le Nôtre's style. Contemporaries called this country seat of Archangelskoye the "Russian Versailles."

During the same period another, much smaller, palace was built in the west part of the garden. It was called the "Caprice." A tiny garden, corresponding to the palace's size, was created in front of the Caprice. It was fenced and decorated with marble statues and vases. Near it a spacious building for the prince's outstanding library was erected, designed by Giovanni Pettondi.

In 1810 the estate was bought by Prince Nikolay Borisovich Yusupov, a wealthy, well-educated Russian nobleman who was also a famous art collector. The new owner declared that Archangelskoye was not an income village but a place for joy and pleasure. Accordingly, he steadily followed this principle, spending a lot of money to make the palace and park a wonderful place. He bought many rare works of art and instructed his servants to purchase the best things, "better than the ones others had." Prince Yusupov had the park decorated with many sculptures, busts, and vases. Two large terraces in front of the Great House were rebuilt, and the fountain system and greenhouses were improved.

The present appearance of the French formal garden at Archangelskoye was in place by the late 1820s. Its principal axes are the majestic Emperor's Alley that leads to the park through the entrance archway, the main courtyard, and the palace. The garden gradually descends with the principal stairs of both terraces and turns to the huge parterre (270 by 70 m [295 by 76 yd.]). The hedges of trellis-works, pergolas, and clipped lime trees border the sides of the parterre. These lines are mirrored by rows of marble statues, which were created by Italian sculptors in the 18th and early 19th centuries. After the parterre the main axis rises slightly at the terrace between two buildings of former greenhouses on the edge of the river bluff. The magnificent panorama with picturesque sweep of fields, meadowlands, and forests is revealed from here.

The general size of the formal garden is optimum for its embrace of simultaneous views from any vantage point. It is decked by monumental temples and columns, in honor of czars' visits, as well as pavilions, statues, obelisks, and fountains memorializing important events of Prince Yusupov's life. The upper terrace is the best vantage point from which a visitor can cast a glance over the park and appreciate the marvelous effect of the fusion of all these elements with nature.

At the time of Nikolay Yusupov, formal gardens were out of fashion, although this did not discourage the retired prince. Such gardens reminded him of the time of his youth and glory. Nonetheless, he gave the new trends their due as well. The old formal garden was surrounded by a spacious landscape park with its natural views of picturesque scenes: the river, ponds, thick groves, and clearings. Thousands of limes, firs, birches, mountain ashes, larches, and various bushes were planted there. Each grove received its own name (e.g., Apollo, Raspberry, Prussian, Mohammedan, etc.), and there was a kind of zoo with llamas, camels, pelicans, and so on. In the 1810s a wooden theater was built in one of the groves for the production of theatrical scenes by the well-known Pietro Gottardo Gonzaga. It was a modest building with plain walls and small portico, but inside it was very sumptuous.

Archangelskoye stands on the crossroads of two artistic styles. But its two parks don't contradict one another. Arranged at almost the same time, they demonstrate the basic identity of two types of garden culture (formal and landscape), which meet and find harmonious agreement here.

Prince Yusupov's time at Archangelskoye was a time of prosperity for the estate. After his death, his heirs did not add much to Archangelskoye. On the contrary, they took numerous sculptures and paintings to their St. Petersburg palace and sold many exotic plants from the greenhouses. Most of the works of art, however, were returned when the National Museum was set up in Archangelskoye in 1919. Since 1934 the museum has been sharing the territory of the former Archangelskoye estate with a Military Health Center (sanatorium). This organization created some new buildings for its own needs, which has changed the appearance of the park somewhat (e.g., in 1937 two new hotels replaced the greenhouses). Nonetheless, the formal garden has been carefully looked after. It was partly restored in the early 1980s. Restoration of the main palace began in the early 1990s.

## Synopsis

| | |
|---|---|
| early 18th C. | Palace built and gardens laid out for Prince Dmitry Golitsyn |
| late 18th C. | Palace torn down and replaced by "Great House," designed by French architect Charles Guern; formal garden widened and improved; landscape park partly constructed around it (executed after Prince Nicolay Alexeyevich Golitsin's conception) |
| 1810 | Archangelskoye estate bought by Prince Nikolay Borisovich Yusupov; his art collections transported to palace |
| 1813–late 1820s | Palace and gardens restored after war of 1812; many improvements to gardens, landscape park widened; theater built in one of groves |
| 1919 | National museum established at Archangelskoye |
| 1980s | Partial restoration of the formal garden |

## Further Reading

Bezsonov, Sergei Vasil'evich, *Arkhangel'skoe: Podmoskovnaia usad'ba,* Moscow: Izd-vo Vsesoiuznoi Akademii Arkhitektury, 1937

Rapoport, Valerie Leonidovich, *Arkhangelskoye: A Country Estate of the 18th and 19th Century,* Leningrad: Aurora Art, 1984

LUDMILA KIRIUSHINA

# Arkadia

## Łowicz, Skierniewice, Poland

**Location:**  50 miles (80.6 km) west of Warsaw

The landscape park of Arkadia, created by Princess Helena Radziwill between 1778 and her death in 1821, is one of the finest examples of Polish Enlightenment garden design. It lies about 3.7 miles (6 km) from the palace of Nieborów, which was bought by the Radziwills in 1774 as their summer residence. Helena wished to create a private retreat in the English style, separate from the palace but close enough for frequent visits, a garden of sweet melancholy in which to enjoy fashionable sorrow and worship worthy ideas. A suitable piece of land, with the essential element of a river, was found near the village of Łupia.

Helena initially engaged the leading architect and landscape designer of the day, Symon Bogumił Zug, who had been closely connected with the introduction into Poland of the ideas of the English garden. He wrote a section on the progress of landscape gardening in Poland for Christian Hirschfeld's *Théorie de l'art des jardins* (French edition, 1784) and provided illustrations (now lost or dispersed) for August Moszynski's manuscript treatise, which itself was largely based on the French translation of Thomas Whately's *Observations on Modern Gardening.* Zug was therefore well practiced in the version of the English style current in Europe. He designed many gardens in the environs of Warsaw, starting with Solec (ca. 1772) and including Powazki (destroyed in the Prussian siege of 1794) for Helena's friend and rival Izabela Czartoryska. Of all these, Arkadia is the sole survivor. Just as Arkadia embodied the attitude of regret, yearning, and elegiac sorrow, which represented the condition of Poland at the time as well as suiting Helena's personal preferences, so Puławy, developed for Czartoryska by Chrystian Piotr Aigner, came to symbolize the defiant nationalism of a Polish nation that refused to die. Arkadia and Puławy were the two great gardens of Poland that were to be included in Jacques Delille's poem *Les jardins,* but Helena was so late submitting her text that it had to be inserted in the notes of the last edition.

Although Arkadia extended to 74 acres (30 ha), no residence was built in the park, and all the features had to be easily accessible during a visit from Nieborów. Zug concentrated his design in the southeast section, where both the entrance and exit were situated. The layout was made with the intention that the visitor should follow a predetermined route that would give an impression of greater size and variety than actually existed. To ensure that this correct route was followed,

Temple of Diana seen through the Greek Arch at Arkadia, ca. 1789, by Jean-Pierre Norblin
Courtesy of private collection

Helena published in 1800 a *Guide d'Arcadie,* which was also intended to evoke the emotions that visitors should be experiencing as they walked through the groves and buildings. (No original volume of this book has been found; the text is known only from the edited version in *Les jardins* and an obscure translation into archaic Polish, printed in *Album Literackie* in 1848.)

The first major undertaking, started even before the purchase transaction was finalized, was the excavation of the lake, the focal point of the design. The Temple of Diana, the main feature of Arkadia, was one of the earliest structures to be built (1783). Its apparent simplicity belies its sophistication. The interior combines pantheon (where Freemasonic activities were held), sleeping quarters, shrine, and museum, where most of the exhibits were painted on the walls. However, the great skill of the design lies in the fact that three of the four facades, viewed from various points on the circuit, seem to be three different buildings: the east side, seen through the Greek arch, gives the impression of a circular colonnaded temple; the west side, best viewed from the opposite bank of the lake, has an Ionic portico with pediment surmounting the rectangular facade; and the south side is transformed into a shrine by a canted projection with a niche for a statue of Pan. Only the north wall was left blank, heavily screened by trees.

Each of the garden features contributed to the overall program, although the emphasis changed slightly over the course of Helena's lifetime: the Freemasonic overtones persisted, reflecting her affiliation with the Society of Mopses (an Order of Freemasonry that admitted women, founded 1740), but the aspect of garden cemetery, which had originally consisted only of a fashionable "Tomb of Rousseau" on an island of poplars, became more pronounced with her real sorrow over the successive early deaths of three of her daughters. The themes embraced by Arkadia were designed to inspire the visitor with lofty emotions. Generosity and hospitality were expressed by the cottages of Baucis and Philemon at the entrance; offerings of flowers, picked in the cottage gardens, could be laid on altars dedicated to Love, Friendship, Hope, Gratitude, and Remembrance on the Island of Feelings. Further on, the visitor climbed a rocky path in the dark through the Sybil's Grotto (1796) to arrive at the Gothic House (1797), "sanctuary of adversity and melancholy." One then walked through an open gallery to the Greek arch, a massive brick structure of Roman rather than Greek design, which was seen as steadfast "against the ravages of revolution." Attached to a side of the arch was the Margrave's House, which in form could have been an Italian farmhouse from a painting by Claude Lorrain, but in name suggested a nationalistic border defense. The Greek arch provided an artistic frame for the Temple of Diana, a view that was much admired and drawn. After walking through the temple, the visitor came to the aqueduct, an imposing "Roman" feature used by Zug to balance the importance of the Island of Feelings at the other end of the lake. The House of the High Priest held an important place in the emotive program. It was constructed as the elaborate mock ruin of a once-grand building, which had been adapted by the shepherds of Arkadia to serve as sheep pen and shelter.

By the late 1790s Zug's place was taken by Henryk Ittar, whose severe neo-classicism was used for the later buildings in Arkadia: a black marble mortuary chapel, an amphitheater, and a circus. Of these, only Ittar's designs remain and the outline of the circus. Helena was still designing additions to Arkadia at the time of her death, and Czartoryska called it "that beloved place with which she was never satisfied."

Although the greatest emphasis in Arkadia was on its iconography, flowers also played a part, particularly in the orchard by the High Priest's House. The low wall was surmounted with trellis, covered with scented and climbing plants–lilac and double clematis are mentioned. Much of the screening planting included acacias, the fragrance of which contributed to the perfume.

Arkadia was described rapturously by its many visitors, although most of the written comments refer to its beauty and novelty rather than to its high moral tone. With brief periods of use through the 19th century, the garden gradually fell into decay, but was rescued in the 1950s by Gerard Ciołek of the National Museum of Warsaw. After desultory attempts at restoration, a serious program was started in the 1980s and continues as and when funds allow.

## Synopsis

| 1778 | Gardens established by Helena Radziwill at Lowicz |
|---|---|
| 1783–90 | Symon Bogumił Zug designs buildings, including Sanctuary of the High Priest, Temple of Diana, cottages of Baucis and Philemon, aqueduct, Knight's Tent (otherwise known as *Salon de Cristal*), and island of poplars with Tomb of Rousseau (later adapted to be tomb for Helena) |
| 1783 | Temple of Diana built |
| 1796–97 | Sybil's grotto and Gothic house constructed |
| 1797 | Henryk Ittar takes over design of buildings |
| 1821 | Death of Helena Radziwill |
| 1869 | Radziwill family sells Arkadia; Temple of Diana used as Catholic chapel, and Gothic house turned into Orthodox church |
| 1914–18 | German soldiers occupy Arkadia, inflicting damage on all surviving buildings |
| pre-1940 | Further wartime damage |
| 1945 | Arkadia becomes department of National Museum of Warsaw |
| 1950s | Gerard Ciołek begins restoration |
| 1980s | Further efforts at restoration |

## Further Reading

*Arkadia: The Illusion and the Reality: An Eighteenth-Century Polish Garden under Restoration* (exhib. cat.), London: Polish Cultural Institute, 1995

Ciołek, Gerard, *Ogrody Polskie,* Warsaw: Arkady, 1952; 2nd edition, 1978

Curl, James Stevens, "Arkadia, Poland: Garden of Allusions," *Garden History* 23, no. 1 (1995)

Delille, Jacques, *Les jardins,* Paris, 1824

Jablonski, Krzysztof, and Wlodzimierz Piwkowski, *Nieborów, Arkadia,* Warsaw: Wydawn, 1988

Knox, Brian, "The English Garden in Poland," in *The Picturesque Garden outside the British Isles,* edited by Nikolaus Pevsner, Washington, D.C.: Dumbarton Oaks, 1974

Lorentz, Stanislaw, and Andrzej Rottermund, *Neoclassicism in Poland,* Warsaw: Arkady, 1986

Mikocki, Tomasz, editor, *Arcadiana: Arcadia in Poland: An 18th-Century Antique Garden and Its Famous Sculptures,* Warsaw: Institute of Archaeology, Warsaw University, 1998

Zamoyski, Adam, *The Last King of Poland,* London: Jonathan Cape, 1992

FIONA COWELL

# Arnold Arboretum

## Jamaica Plain, Massachusetts, United States

**Location:** 125 Arborway, adjacent to the Forest Hills stop on Boston's Orange Line subway station

The Arnold Arboretum was established in 1872 when the trustees of the will of James Arnold, a wealthy merchant from New Bedford, Massachusetts, transferred a portion of Arnold's residual estate to the president and fellows of Harvard College. The income from this bequest was specified for the establishment, development, and maintenance of an arboretum to be known as the Arnold Arboretum and the appointment of a director who would serve as Arnold Professor of Dendrology at Harvard College. According to the terms of the bequest, the Arnold Arboretum was to contain, "as far as practicable, all the trees [and] shrubs . . . either indigenous or exotic, which can be raised in the open air."

Charles Sprague Sargent was appointed as Arnold Arboretum's first director in 1873 and for 54 years was responsible for shaping and formulating the policies and programs of the arboretum. The development, activities, and achievements of the arboretum since its inception have largely served as the standard by which similar institutions have been modeled and judged, both in North America and elsewhere. The successes of Sargent's administration were based in part on his ability to raise the funds necessary to implement his plans and in part on a creative lease agreement that was forged between the city of Boston and Harvard in 1882. According to the terms of the 1,000-year lease, Harvard-owned land comprising the Arnold Arboretum in the Jamaica Plain section of Boston became part of the city park system, but control of the collections and their development would still reside with the Arboretum staff. The city agreed to maintain the perimeter walls, gates, and roadway system and to provide police surveillance, while the arboretum agreed to keep the grounds open, free of charge, to the general public every day of the year from sunrise to sunset. As a result of this unique arrangement, the arboretum became a part of the famous "Emerald Necklace," the seven-mile (11 km)-long network of parks and open lands that Frederick Law Olmsted laid out for the Boston Park Department between 1878 and 1892.

The design of the arboretum itself was the result of a close collaboration between Sargent and Olmsted, who laid out the path and roadway system and delineated areas within the arboretum for specific groups of plants. Early on Sargent decided to arrange the plant collections by family and genus following the then currently accepted classification system of George Bentham and Joseph Hooker. As Sargent envisioned it,

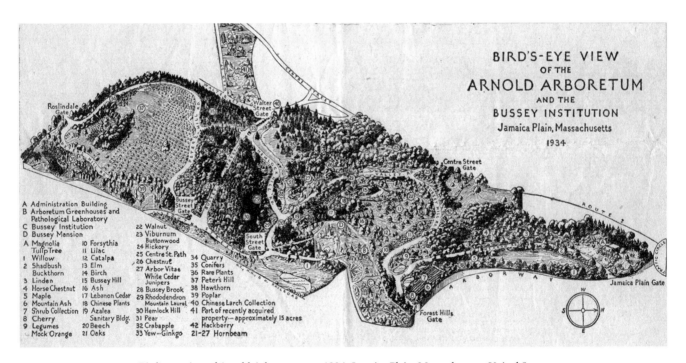

Bird's eye view of Arnold Arboretum, ca. 1934, Jamaica Plain, Massachusetts, United States
Courtesy of Archives of Arnold Arboretum

a visitor driving through the Arboretum will be able to obtain a general idea of the arborescent vegetation of the north temperate zone without even leaving his carriage. It is hoped that such an arrangement, while avoiding the stiff and formal lines of the conventional botanic garden, will facilitate the comprehensive study of the collections, both in their scientific and picturesque aspects.

Another aspect of Sargent's success as an administrator centered on his realization of the research potential of the institution he headed. As the era's most distinguished dendrologist, Sargent authored *The Silva of North America* (14 vols.; 1890–1902) and *Manual of the Trees of North America* (1905; second edition, 1922), both of which remain standard references. By developing a comprehensive library devoted to botany, horticulture, and dendrology, an equally noted herbarium as a repository for specimens representing the woody plants of the world, and a series of scholarly and semipopular publications, Sargent established the Arnold Arboretum as a leading scientific institution. In addition, the arboretum's direct involvement with botanical and horticultural exploration of the floras of the world, with particular emphasis on those of eastern Asia, resulted in the introduction of many new plants into cultivation and an expanded knowledge of their evolution and systematics.

The Arnold Arboretum occupies 265 acres (107 ha) of land in the Jamaica Plain section of Boston and is administered as an Allied Institution within the central administration of Harvard University. As of January 2000, the living collections consist of some 7,082 accessioned plants representing 4,544 botanical and horticultural taxa, with emphasis on the woody species of North America and eastern Asia. Historical collections include the plant introductions from eastern Asia made by Sargent, Ernest "Chinese" Wilson, William Purdom, and Joseph Rock. In addition, the arboretum's herbarium collection contains over 1.5 million specimens, and its library holdings include over 100,000 volumes, some located in Jamaica Plain and some in Cambridge as part of the Harvard University Herbaria. The arboretum also maintains an extensive photographic archive in Jamaica Plain, along with general archival collections relating to its history and the history of botany and horticulture in North America.

The Arnold Arboretum continues to maintain a comprehensive collection of hardy, woody plants in the naturalistic style originally established by Sargent and Olmsted, with particular emphasis on *Acer, Fagus, Lonicera, Magnolia, Malus, Quercus, Rhododendron,* and *Syringa.* For the most part—diseases and insects notwithstanding—the living collections are still planted according to the Bentham and Hooker classification system, and the arboretum continues its tradition of plant

exploration, having sponsored seven major collecting trips to eastern Asia since 1977.

From the time of its founding, the Arboretum has maintained a complete record system that tracks the name and origin of every plant on the grounds and assigns it a standardized accession number. These records are currently maintained on a computerized database linked to a computerized mapping program. This detailed record system facilitates research use of the collections by staff and outside scientists.

Current areas of active research that use the living collections include molecular systematics, plant physiology and morphology, vegetative propagation of woody plants, and evaluation and selection of new cultivars of woody plants with ornamental merit. Research on plant pathology and integrated pest management is ongoing and relates directly to the maintenance of the living collections. Herbarium-based research focuses on the systematics and biodiversity of both temperate and tropical Asian forests, as well as their ecology and sustainable utilization. The arboretum's education programs offer school groups and the general public a wide range of lectures, courses, and walks focusing on the ecology and cultivation of plants, and its quarterly magazine *Arnoldia,* established in 1911, provides in-depth information on horticulture, botany, and garden history.

**Synopsis**
1872   Harvard College accepts James Arnold bequest, executes indenture of Arnold Arboretum, and agrees to locate Arboretum on Bussey estate in West Roxbury
1873   Charles Sprague Sargent appointed director of both Harvard Botanic Garden and Arnold Arboretum
1874   Harvard officially allocates portion of Bussey estate, West Roxbury (137 acres [55.5 ha]), as site for Arnold Arboretum
1875   Sargent commissions Frederick Law Olmsted to produce design for Arnold Arboretum
1879   Sargent resigns as director of Harvard Botanic Garden; Olmsted completes initial design for Arnold Arboretum
1882   Harvard transfers Arboretum land to City of Boston, which leases it back to Harvard for 1,000 years
1885   Permanent tree planting begins with installation of beech, ash, elm, and hickory collections
1888   Sargent launches publication of journal *Garden and Forest*
1892   Sargent collects plants in Japan for Arboretum
1894   Peters Hill tract added to Arboretum under second indenture with City of Boston

1902    Alfred Rehder appointed to staff of Arboretum as taxonomist

1905    Herbarium wing added to administration building; Arboretum dendrologist J.G. Jack collects plants in Japan and Korea

1906    Ernest Henry Wilson hired to collect seeds and herbarium specimens for Arboretum in China

1910    Wilson returns to China on second expedition for Arboretum

1924    Joseph Rock commissioned to collect for Arboretum in China and Tibet

1927    Sargent dies; Oakes Ames appointed director; Wilson appointed Keeper

1929    Elmer D. Merrill appointed director; Donald Wyman appointed Horticulturist

1930    Arboretum receives donation of Larz Anderson bonsai collection

1931    Hurricane of September 21 decimates living collections

1942    Arboretum acquires Case Estates in Weston, Massachusetts

1946    Karl Sax appointed director

1954    Richard A. Howard appointed director; major portions of Arboretum's herbarium and library moved to new Harvard Herbaria building in Cambridge (along with curators)

1963    Charles Stratton Dana greenhouses constructed

1978    Peter S. Ashton appointed director

1980    Arboretum participates in Sino-American Botanical Expedition to China

1985    Bradley Collection of Rosaceous Plants dedicated on site of former shrub and vine collection

1989    Oversight of the Arnold Arboretum within Harvard transferred from Faculty of Arts and Sciences to the Office of the Vice President for Administration; Robert E. Cook appointed director

2001    New Shrub and Vine Garden constructed below the Dana Greenhouses

## Further Reading

Connor, Sheila, *New England Natives*, Cambridge, Massachusetts: Harvard University Press, 1994

Hay, Ida, *Science in the Pleasure Ground: A History of the Arnold Arboretum*, Boston: Northeastern University Press, 1995

Rehder, Alfred, *Manual of Cultivated Trees and Shrubs*, New York: Macmillan, 1927; 2nd edition, 1940

Sargent, Charles S., "The First Fifty Years of the Arnold Arboretum" *Journal of the Arnold Arboretum* 3 (1921)

Spongberg, Stephen A., *A Reunion of Trees: The Discovery of Exotic Plants and Their Introduction into North American and European Landscapes*, Cambridge, Massachusetts: Harvard University Press, 1990

Sutton, Silvia Barry, *Charles Sprague Sargent and the Arnold Arboretum*, Cambridge, Massachusetts: Harvard University Press, 1970

Wilson, Ernest H., *America's Greatest Garden: The Arnold Arboretum*, Boston: Stratford, 1925

Zaitzevsky, Cynthia, *Frederick Law Olmsted and the Boston Park System*, Cambridge, Massachusetts: Belknap Press, 1982

PETER DEL TREDICI AND STEPHEN A. SPONGBERG
Part of this essay originally appeared in "Arboreta" by Stephen A. Spongberg in *Encyclopedia of Environmental Biology*, vol. 1, copyright 1995 by Academic Press; reprinted by permission of the publisher.

# Arts and Crafts Gardening

In the second half of the 19th century, under the leadership of men such as John Ruskin, William Morris, and Philip Webb, there was a reaction to the uniformity of the machine-made goods of the industrial revolution and a movement toward the individual qualities of more traditional crafts products. This became known as the Arts and Crafts movement, a movement devoted to design and construction eclectic in nature but based on the principles of reuniting the arts and restoring the craftsman to his rightful place in the community. In domestic architecture, the emphasis was on functional designs that drew inspiration from historical styles and reflected the traditional vernacular by using locally available building materials. Red House in Kent, designed by Webb in 1859 for William Morris, was the first Arts and Crafts house built according to these principles and was the most influential Arts and Crafts architectural design over the next half century. Other prominent architects, such as W.R. Lethaby, George Devey, Reginald Blomfield, C.F.A. Voysey, Robert Lorrimer, Sir Edwin Lutyens, E.S. Prior, and

H.M. Baillie Scott, interpreted Arts and Crafts principles in a variety of ways to produce houses designed to both meet the needs of family life and sit well in the landscape.

This principle of design unity led many architects to extend their design skills to both the interior of the house and its garden, which was a controversial move, as it often precluded the creative input of local craftsmen. There were those, primarily architects led by Reginald Blomfield and John Sedding, who believed that a house and its garden should be an architectural whole. In his celebrated publication *The Formal Garden in England* (1892), Blomfield states that "The formal treatment of gardens . . . consists in the extension of the principles of design which govern the house to the grounds which surround it." This point of view was in direct opposition to the opinions expressed by horticulturists and horticultural writers such as William Robinson and Gertrude Jekyll, who promoted the concept of the wild, informal garden in harmony with, but not necessarily designed as part of, the house. Their dislike of control and artificiality in the garden environment was, in large part, a reaction against the use of garishly colored, mass-produced bedding plants, which had become popular during the mid-19th century.

Many Arts and Crafts designers who subscribed to the informal garden style considered that the "cottage garden" model embodied the spirit of a vernacular style. William Morris had suggested that a garden should contain flowers "that are free and interesting in their growth, leaving nature to do the desired complexity" (Morris). Both Robinson and Jekyll enjoyed the simplicity and beauty of a traditional cottage garden, which contained a mixture of native flowers, fruits, and vegetables. Jekyll had been a follower of Morris since her early years, as her love of the colors and variety of nature can be found in her paintings, silverwork, embroidery, and gardens. However, Robinson's work with hardy herbaceous plants and wildflowers at the Royal Botanic Gardens, Regent's Park, led him to propose in *The Wild Garden* (1870) "placing plants of other countries, as hardy as our hardiest wild flowers, in places where they flourish without further care or cost." Jekyll agreed, and in her planting plans she created colorful borders using a mixture of old-fashioned plants, improved varieties of herbaceous perennials, and newly introduced hardy plants.

To ensure the conception of the house and garden as an architectural whole, Blomfield and his colleagues were emphatic that the architect rather than the horticulturist should have the main input concerning the layout of a garden. House and garden were to be constructed from the same local building materials, and structural features, such as pergolas, were to extend the house into the garden. The garden was to be laid out with regularity and symmetry, based on a strong axial design. Despite the earlier emphasis on the tripartite

relationship between the house, the garden, and the surrounding landscape, the architectural garden tended to be enclosed, although vistas continued to be used as design features.

The garden was often divided into a number of different compartments incorporating a wide variety of planting styles, a later well-known example being Hidcote Manor Garden in Gloucestershire. The garden at Hidcote was developed in the early 20th century, but unlike many grand gardens, it was designed by an amateur, the owner Lawrence Johnson. The structural framework of the formal part of the garden is provided by clipped yew hedges, alleys of pleached limes, pergolas, and the use of long grassy walks and vistas. By contrast, there are areas with a cottage garden feel, with old-fashioned borders and plants tumbling over walls. Designs along Arts and Crafts principles for smaller gardens, such as the Orchard at Harrow, were available from popular magazines such as *The Studio* or in publications including *The Art and Craft of Garden Making* (Thomas Mawson, 1900) and *Houses and Gardens* (H.M. Baillie Scott, 1906).

By the beginning of the 20th century, the gap began to close between these opposing views on garden design through the partnership of the architect Sir Edwin Lutyens and Gertrude Jekyll. Jekyll and Lutyens first met in 1889, and by 1894 Jekyll had commissioned Lutyens to build a new house in her existing garden at Munstead Wood, Surrey. Both had a deep understanding of traditional craftsmanship and materials, and between them they developed a vernacular house and garden style that, to some extent, united the architectural garden requirements of Blomfield and the planting aspirations of Robinson. At Munstead Wood, Lutyens's imposing architectural framework is clear in the geometrically aligned courtyards, terraces, pergolas, pools, steps, and paths in traditional materials. This hard landscaping was softened by Jekyll's informal and exuberant mixed plantings and her use of continuous color sequences to provide interest throughout the year. These features were integral to what became the celebrated "Surrey Style." Gertrude Jekyll was a prolific writer, and her planting theories and experiments at Munstead Wood are recorded in a number of her books, such as *Wood and Garden* (1899) and *Colour in the Flower Garden* (1908). Jekyll and Lutyens collaborated on approximately 100 gardens between 1897 and 1928; a supreme example of their work being Hestercombe, in Somerset.

The Arts and Crafts movement continued in popularity throughout the early 20th century, and many of the influential gardens of the time were featured in the magazine *Country Life*, which was first published in January 1897. Some notable gardens include Lees Court, Kent; Rodmarton Manor, Gloucestershire; and Coleton Fishacre, Devon. The gardens featured "green architecture," with the emphasis on form: neatly clipped yew hedges and plants trained as standards and topiaries; garlands of wisteria, roses, and laburnum tumbling over walls and pergolas; plants growing through paving and steps; irregular masses of plants and vertical layering in the herbaceous border; and drifts of progressive colors throughout the year, all legacies of Gertrude Jekyll. Such a rich tapestry of planting was the principal characteristic associated with gardens of the Arts and Crafts movement.

*See also* Hidcote Manor Garden; Jekyll, Gertrude; Lutyens, Edwin; Munstead Wood

**Further Reading**

Blomfield, Reginald T., and F. Inigo Thomas, *The Formal Garden in England,* London, 1892

Cumming, Elizabeth, and Wendy Kaplan, *The Arts and Craft Movement,* New York: Thames and Hudson, 1991

Elliott, Brent, *The Country House Garden: From the Archives of Country Life, 1897–1939,* London: Beazley, 1995

Jekyll, Gertrude, *Wood and Garden: Notes and Thoughts, Practical and Critical, of a Working Amateur,* London and New York, 1899

Jekyll, Gertrude, *Colour in the Flower Garden,* London: Country Life, 1908

Mawson, Thomas, *The Art and Craft of Garden Making,* London: Batsford, 1900

Morris, William, *Hopes and Fears for Art,* Boston, 1882

Ottewill, David, *The Edwardian Garden,* New Haven, Connecticut: Yale University Press, 1989

Robinson, William, *The Wild Garden,* London, 1870; 5th edition, 1903

Robinson, William, *The English Flower Garden,* London, 1883; 15th edition, London: Murry, 1933; reprint, Sagaponack, New York: Sagapress, 1995

Scott, Mackay Hugh Baillie, *Houses and Gardens: Arts and Crafts Interiors,* London: Newnes, 1906

Sedding, John, *Garden-Craft Old and New,* London, 1891

BARBARA SIMMS

# Atget, Eugène 1856–1927

## French Photographer

Jean Eugène Auguste Atget was one of the pioneers of documentary photography. He was born in Libourne near Bordeaux in 1856 and died in obscurity in Paris in 1927. In 1897 he abandoned a career in acting and briefly experimented with painting before turning to the emerging art of photography. Over a 30-year period he documented Paris, the older suburbs, and the outlying royal parks of the ancien régime, accumulating an inventory in excess of 20,000 glass negatives.

From 1852 Paris was in the process of a radical reconstruction, inspired by Napoléon III and directed by Baron Haussmann. Its medieval confusion of tortuous streets, unsewered courts, and ramshackle buildings was being transformed into a modern city with broad, straight, tree-lined boulevards lined with uniformly elegant buildings. Many architectural photographers, including Atget's predecessor, Charles Marville, documented the destruction and reconstruction; most are forgotten. Atget, however, has enjoyed a modern revival because his pictures transcend mundane documents, creating a collection of images of the artistic and picturesque in Paris and its environs. He had the rare ability to combine fact and the picturesque often with a sense of melancholy for the changes he felt had destroyed the social and physical fabric of the Paris he loved.

Atget sold prints to the Bibliothèque Nationale, the Caisse Nationale des Monuments Historiques, the Bibliothèque Historique de la Ville de Paris, and the Musée Carnavalet, the latter created especially to preserve fragments of the city's history. Four hundred prints went to the Victoria and Albert Museum in London. He supplemented his income from the sale of these prints by supplying "Documents pour artistes" (Information for Artists), as the sign to his fifth floor Montparnasse garret read. Street scenes, a commissioned series on lowly occupations, and urban and landscape details were all of use to artists needing accurate backgrounds and models from vernacular life for their subject matter, saving them the inconvenience of sketching in the open air.

A conservative, out of sympathy with the city's improvements, Atget preferred to document the transient character of the old, organic, and human-scale city. Disdaining modern photographic techniques and materials, he used a heavy, old-fashioned view camera using 7.1 by

9.4 inch glass plates, the whole steadied on a tripod because of the long time exposures. His living room was his darkroom; he exposed his Aristotype paper prints by natural light on his windowsill, adding a toner of gold chloride. He photographed in the early morning as much for the quality of the light as for the emptiness of the streets and gardens, employing theatrical craft to place himself mentally in an environmental theater. Like Sebastiano Serlio's designs for stage scenery, Atget regarded the dawn streets as empty stages awaiting the tragedy and comedy of each day's life. These surviving urban pockets were theaters of nostalgia, secreted within the armature of the new Paris. Early morning photography had practical advantages as well; his scenes were uncorrupted by the hectic pace of contemporary life, and it was too early for the looming buses and lumbering wagons that would have blocked his views. There were also fewer pedestrians to leave disfiguring blurs across his images. Absent also were the curious who would have deflected concentration from his upside-down images.

Atget is at his most elegiac in his documents of the urban and the grand royal palace parks such as Versailles and the overgrown remnants of André Le Nôtre's Sceaux and Saint-Cloud. It was to these suburban fringes that Atget turned increasingly during and after World War I, weary of being mistaken for a spy and fearful of aerial bombardment. These are his most mature and lyrical images, his response to the melancholy peace of deserted gardens and the abandoned landscapes that were once the envy of the Western world. The allegorical meanings of the surviving sculptures are largely lost, in the absence of a classical education. The lichen-stained Pomonas and Apollos and the empty urns survive as aesthetic accents amid the foliage. The weathered and broken condition of startling presences discovered terminating overgrown allées or presiding over weed-choked pools add character to their vapid overabundance.

The Montparnasse district was Atget's quarter, and the studios he visited energized and informed his artist's eye. He knew the Postimpressionist Maurice Utrillo, whose White period demonstrated the latent poetry in Montmartre's slums. A neighbor was the surrealist painter and photographer Man Ray and his assistant Berenice Abbott, who tried to convince Atget, without success, to use more convenient modern equipment.

Despite Atget's antiquated and cumbersome gear, his sympathetic lens saw character and vitality in working-class occupations. He had a modern eye for the texture of peeling paint, of sinuous wrought iron and gleaming stone-paved streets. His lyric view captured the mirror qualities of water; the gently agitated reflections followed the progress of billowing clouds, often mingling with the soft forms of ancient trees. His sense of composition was exquisite, often rising to a surreal statement about relationships: of human forms and the tracery of winter branches.

**Biography**

Born in Libourne, France, 1856. Abandoned career in acting and took up photography, 1897; over the course of 30 years, documented Paris, its outer suburbs, and outlying royal parks, creating an archive of 20,000 glass negatives. Died in Paris, 1927.

**Further Reading**

Adams, William Howard, *Atget's Gardens: A Selection of Eugène Atget's Garden Photographs*, Garden City, New York: Doubleday, and London: Gordon Fraser, 1979

Atget, Eugène, *Eugène Atget: Paris,* translated by Anne Heritage, New York: Te Neues, 1998

JOHN MARTIN

# Australia

The Aboriginal people of Australia had lived on the continent for thousands of years, but they did not develop gardens in the Western sense. Aboriginal gardening took the form of organizing the growth of some edible plants in particular locations, a task undertaken largely by women, but this practice was not universal.

The first European type of garden was established in 1788 in Sydney on the arrival of the settlers who set up the colony of New South Wales, often referred to as Botany Bay. The ground was hoed, and plants and seeds that were brought from England, Rio di Janeiro, and Cape Town were planted in the dry, sandy soil around Sydney Cove. These gardens consisted of vegetables needed for survival; only a few geraniums were planted as the first exotic flowers. Vegetable and primitive flower plots were eventually established in the gardens in the front of the first constructed huts in Sydney Town. The house built by Governor Phillip, called Government House, was the site of the first garden that led down to the waters of the harbor, while another garden or small farm was established over the hill in what was to become Sydney's Botanic Garden.

Australian native plants were collected by the first settlers and grown in pots to send back to England, and the governor wrote about them to Sir Joseph Banks. A few of the native plants found their way into the local gardens, although none of the native plants were obviously suitable for food except for a type of native spinach.

Fruit trees, especially the orange and stone fruits, such as the peach, took root and flourished in the Sydney climate, while grapes were available within a couple of years in the Government House garden. In Van Diemen's Land (Tasmania), it was the apple and pear trees that dominated the fruit trees of that island colony.

The first signs of change came in 1809 with the arrival of Governor Macquarie. The garden lost its vegetable character and was laid out like a small English park. One noticeable native plant used was the Norfolk island pine tree (*Araucaria heterophylla*), which became popular in Sydney and in Van Diemen's Land. In 1816, Governor Macquarie established the Sydney Botanic Gardens and appointed Charles Fraser to manage it. This became the primary center for the introduction of new plants into the colony.

Throughout the 19th century, the pattern of Australian gardens followed the design concepts of Great Britain. Many of the first gardeners and nurserymen came from Scotland, as did Thomas Shepherd, who arrived in 1826. Shepherd was a follower of the landscape garden ideas of the Englishman Humphry Repton. These garden concepts did not develop a great following because the colony consisted of many small farms instead of the large plantations needed for grand landscape designs to take root. Shepherd wrote the first gardening books concerning the region in *The Horticulture of New South Wales* and *Landscape Gardening in Australia*. Two gardens were of importance in this early period: Alexander McLeary's garden at Elizabeth Bay and the garden of William Macarthur at Camden Park. Both were prominent in the importing of new plants from various parts of the world, and both developed extensive gardens. Another harborside garden in this landscape tradition was Henriette Villa on Point Piper.

In the early colonies most gardens were essentially of the cottage garden type, and this became the general pattern, because every house in the town was of a single story built back from the street, thus creating a "front garden." In Sydney there was often a geranium hedge along the street front, a feature commented upon by many early writers. Gardens for larger houses such as that at Brownlow Hill or Clarens at Potts Point became much more sophisticated and elaborate, with stairs and urns and an occasional statue. The greatest influence on these designs was the English garden writer J.C. Loudon, whose influence was apparent in all the colonies. Toward the end of the 19th century, Melbourne and

Adelaide quickly developed a great gardening tradition that was also dominated by the English garden type.

It was local nurserymen who exercised a strong influence as to the type of garden and the varieties of plants grown. Daniel Bunce, first in Van Diemen's Land and then in Victoria at the Geelong Botanic Gardens, was of importance while the great botanist Ferdinand von Mueller and later William Guilfoyle at the Botanic Gardens in Melbourne played an increasingly important role in planting exotic trees in a natural type of setting. Guilfoyle transplanted many of the large trees established by his predecessor. Native Australian trees, such as wattles cedars (*Acacia*), the bunya-bunya (*Araucaria bidwillii*) and Moreton Bay fig trees were increasingly used during the 19th century, especially in larger gardens in Brisbane and Sydney. The gum trees (eucalyptus) were not used extensively as they tended to destroy the idea of a neat and organized garden so popular in the colonial period. This was the period of brilliantly colored annuals in patterned garden beds. An Australian shadehouse or greenhouse was developed and was called the bush house, and even small suburban gardens often had one built with local bush materials containing some of the native ferns available. Retreats to the mountains in the hot summer months resulted in gardens grown up around the verandaed houses of the Blue Mountains in New South Wales, the Dandenongs and Mount Madecon in Victoria, and the Adelaide Hills.

With the beginning of the 20th century and the federation of the states into the commonwealth of Australia, garden styles gradually changed. The English influence of Gertrude Jekyll and William Robinson was spread by enthusiasts in Australia such as Carl Bogue Luffman and Edna Walling. These English influences were altered somewhat by the different plant materials available and the more temperate climate as well as the gradual increase in the use of native Australian plants. A minor controversy developed between those advocating formal gardens and those who favored gardens of natural design, the latter approach strongly advocated by Luffman. Many fine gardens were developed during this period, such as the garden at Eryldene in Sydney, where Professor E.G. Waterhouse filled his garden with the camellias that had made his name world famous. William Hardy Wilson, the architect of Eryldene, designed the structures in the garden.

By the 1950s, the idea of a garden made up completely of plants native to Australia had begun to emerge, with Edna Walling leading the way. Other landscape designers, such as Paul Sorensen, were increasingly important. Sorensen made greater use of trees and shrubs in a simple grassed landscape, placing the more formal parts of the garden closer to the house (the Everglades in the Blue Mountains is generally regarded as his masterpiece).

There are now many beautiful gardens that have been established in recent times. Edna Walling's gardens are now carefully treasured and preserved, such as Markdale in New South Wales and Dame Elizabeth Murdoch's garden Cruden Farm in Victoria. Others, such as Naroo at Mount Wilson, have achieved the distinction of being reproduced on Australian postage stamps. Tasmania has such historic gardens as Beaufront, Brickenden, and Woolmers, among hundreds of others. In South Australia, gardens such as Beechwood are now owned by the Adelaide Botanic Gardens. The tropical state of Queensland has a wide range of gardens in Brisbane, Toowoomba, and more recently the Gold Coast.

The domestic front garden found in the city continued to change from a cottage garden type to a more formal lawn with paths, rose beds, and beds of annuals. These gardens began to incorporate more natural use of trees and shrubs, eventually developing into front gardens devoted entirely to native plants with no lawn at all. Although these gardens have become quite popular, the early concept of the front garden has not been completely superseded. Most common at present is a mixture of native and exotic species within the same garden.

Gardens in Australia remain European in concept, although the influences of China and Japan are sometimes evident, especially in the use of pebbles and rocks. Worldwide influences are seen in the wide variety and use of plants from different parts of the world. In this respect, Australia is no different from America and Europe, and in recent times, there has been an increase in American influence. This is more apparent in the back gardens that now often contain a swimming pool, paved areas with outdoor furniture, and a barbecue, which has taken over from the messy back yard with its clothes line and vegetable patch.

Some aspects of Australian gardens, although European in appearance, are distinctly native. Unlike American gardens, Australians have a front fence and a solid wood paling back and side fences. There is a front gate and a mail box with a path to the front door. The gate for the car and driveway is usually on one side of the block. Only in Canberra, the capital of Australia, which was designed by the American Walter Burley Griffin, are there no front fences, although there are protests from time to time against this restriction. Burley Griffin made the whole city a garden. The landscape takes in the surrounding hills (which are not to be built on), and the series of lakes and the heavy tree cover makes the city a landscape design with buildings partly hidden among the foliage. Early designers such as Weston, who created the tree cover, and Richard Clough, who carefully landscaped the surrounding parkland of Lake Burley Griffin,

maintained the original designer's feeling for the setting of the city. The Commonwealth Park by the lake, created from plans by Sylvia Crowe, the English landscape designer, and developed by Australian designers, created the ideal setting for Canberra's annual Floriade. The Australian National Botanic Gardens in Canberra differs from the much older and important botanic gardens in each of the states' capitals in that it has only Australian native plants in its garden and natural settings. This is an exciting new development for gardens in Australia and leads the way in displaying how native plants can be used with stunning effect in garden design.

*See also* Forest Lodge; Sydney, Royal Botanic Gardens

**Further Reading**

*An Australian Gardener's Anthology*, Adelaide and New York: Rigby, 1982

Baskin, Judith, and Trisha Dixon, *Australia's Timeless Gardens*, Canberra: National Library of Australia, 1996

Bligh, Beatrice, *Cherish the Earth: The Story of Gardening in Australia*, Sydney: Ure Smith, 1973

Crittenden, Victor, *The Front Garden: The Story of the Cottage Garden in Australia*, Canberra: Mulini Press, 1979

Crittenden, Victor, *A History of Australian Gardening Books and a Bibliography, 1806–1950*, Belconnen, Capital Territory: Canberra College of Advanced Education Library, 1986

Gilbert, Lionel, *The Royal Botanic Gardens, Sydney*, New York: Oxford University Press, 1986

Lothian, Noel, and Ivan Holliday, *Growing Australian Plants*, Adelaide: Rigby, 1964

Luffmann, Carl Bogue, *Principles of Gardening for Australia*, Melbourne: Book Lover's Library, 1903

Pescott, Richard Thomas Martin, *W.R. Guilfoyle, 1840–1912: The Master of Landscaping*, New York: Oxford University Press, 1974

Ratcliffe, Richard, *Australia's Master Gardener: Paul Sorensen and His Gardens*, Kenthurst, New South Wales: Kangaroo Press, 1990

Simons, Phyl Frazer, *Historic Tasmanian Gardens*, Canberra: Mulini Press, 1987

Stones, Ellis, *Australian Garden Design*, South Melbourne: Macmillan, 1971

Watts, Peter, *The Gardens of Edna Walling*, Melbourne: National Trust of Australia Women's Committee, 1981; 2nd revised edition, as *Edna Walling and Her Gardens*, Rozell, New South Wales: Florilegium, 1991

VICTOR CRITTENDEN

# Austria

Austria's earliest gardens of repute originate from the 16th century. Vienna, the imperial residence town, attracted many foreigners. Other important cities include Salzburg (seat of an Archbishop), Graz, and Innsbruck (residences of Habsburg collateral lines), where aristocratic gardens were created from the 16th century to the 18th century. In the 16th and 17th centuries, the influences came mainly from Italy, but the Netherlands was also of great importance from the 16th to the 18th century, especially for planting and botanic concerns. From about 1700 on, several French garden architects worked in Austria (Trehet, Girard, Gervais). In the late 18th century, the Irish general Lacy and the Scottish general Loudon were the first patrons of English gardens. There was also a lively exchange of ideas and garden experts with the German countries in the second half of the 18th century. About 1900 the ideas of the cottage movement impressed the group of Austrian architects around Otto Wagner. From the 18th century until 1918, Viennese garden architecture radiated into the countries of the monarchy in Austria, Czechia, Hungary, and on the Balkan Peninsula.

The first Austrian sovereign with a great passion for gardens was Emperor Maximilian I (r. 1493–1519), who advised that instructions concerning how to maintain his gardens be written down. This important document was published in 1567 in Ambras, with the title *Imperatoris Maximiliani I. opuscula quatour quorum tituli Germanici: Gartnerey, Falknerey, Jagerey, Kellerey.* In his spring residence in Laxenburg, Maximilian laid out a Dutch pleasure garden (the southern Netherlands, now Belgium, was part of the Habsburg Empire from 1477, the year of Maximilian's marriage to Mary of Burgundy, until 1815). Maximilian also furnished the gardens of the Hofburg, his residence in Vienna, with several buildings and sculptures. These gardens were at their most splendid under Ferdinand I (r. 1531–64), but nothing from this time exists any more.

Austria's most eminent gardens of the 16th century were at the palace Neugebäude in Vienna, erected under Maximilian II (r. 1564–76), and in Innsbruck and Ambras, laid out under Maximilian's brother, the Archduke Ferdinand II, governor of Tirol 1564–95.

The garden palace Neugebäude was begun in 1567–68 and was enlarged in several phases until the early death of Maximilian II in 1576. The main building, a 144-meter-long (158 yd.) banqueting hall, which was also meant to contain a collection of antique sculptures, was designed by the architect Jacopo da Strada in Italian Renaissance style but was never finished and exists today in a rather ruined state. This building, extending in an east-west direction, was the center of terraced flower gardens with ornamental beds, game enclosures,

and a hunting park. Two etchings, one from 1649 by Merian and the other ca. 1700 by Fischer von Erlach and Delsenbach, give some information on the grounds. The northern terraced flower garden ended at a rectangular pond; the southern flower garden was surrounded by four pleasure towers connected by elevated walks to give a better view of the elaborate flower beds. In the east of the main building was a menagerie where exotic animals such as monkeys, lions, and an elephant were kept. A great deal of the southern garden is now occupied by a cemetery. From the northern garden the terraces still exist, and there are plans for a reconstruction.

Important garden prefects came from the southern Netherlands, first Augier de Busbecq, who went to Turkey as imperial ambassador 1554–62 and brought back antiquities and new plants (such as the tulip and lilac) to Vienna. Later, the great Flemish botanist Carolus Clusius worked at the Neugebäude gardens, from 1573 to 1576. He also explored the alpine flora of Lower Austria and Styria and the Pannonian flora of Hungary before returning to the Netherlands in the 1590s.

In Tirol the Archduke Ferdinand II erected the Hofgarten (the residential garden) in Innsbruck beginning in 1564. There were different sections with a ballgame house, conservatories, pleasure pavilions, sculptures, a lion's house, a pheasantry, and more. The gardens still exist, but they were reduced and transformed in the 18th and 19th centuries. The gardens of Ambras castle near Innsbruck were laid out between 1566 and 1572. In spite of some transformations in the 19th and 20th centuries, the area in front of the "Spanish banqueting hall" still has the original ground modeling and also a grotto and a tower. A report by Stephan Phigius from 1574 gives an exact description of some machines—for example, a table that turned via a hydraulic mechanism.

The most important garden of the 17th century was the garden-palace Hellbrunn in Salzburg, created between 1612 and 1619 as the first *villa suburbana* north of the Alps by Santino Solari for the Archbishop Markus Sittikus von Hohenems. It included mannerist hydraulic jokes, a baroque water parterre, and the Felsentheater (the first open-air theater north of the Alps).

Of great importance for the development of Austrian garden architecture in the baroque era were the gardens of Prince Eugene of Savoy, created in the first four decades of the 18th century. The prince, commander in the victorious war against Turkey, was rewarded generously by the emperor and was thus able to build several palaces, such as the Belvedere in Vienna, as well as Obersiebenbrunn and Schloßhof in Lower Austria. All three gardens were created by the same team, consisting of the architect Johann L. von Hildebrandt, the garden designer Dominique Girard (a pupil of Le Nôtre), and the gardener Anton Zinner. The Lower Belvedere was completed in 1716, the Upper Belvedere in 1732. The garden's main features are three slightly sloped terraces connected by water cascades. Only parts of the sculptures and the iconographic program are left. The Belvedere was meant to be the home of the glorious warrior Prince Eugene and to celebrate him as equivalent to Hercules and Apollo. The important orangery has been transformed, and the semicircular ground structure of the menagerie can still be seen. The gardens of Schloßhof from about 1725 had seven terraces. About 1760 Bellotto documented them meticulously in three great paintings (in the Kunsthistorisches Museum, Vienna). The structure of the terraces, some stairs, gates, and sculptures still exist. After very successful garden-archaeological research, a step-by-step reconstruction of the planting was begun in 1993.

After the raising of the Turkish siege of Vienna in 1683, a "wrest of gardens" developed outside the fortifications in the suburbs of Vienna. Many aristocratic families created splendid gardens (e.g., Althan, Liechtenstein, Harrach, etc.). The oldest from this period is the imperial *Augarten*, whose clipped alleys still exist. A group of four adjoining gardens along the Rennweg in Vienna's third district still gives an idea of Vienna's suburban "garden wrest." There are, from east to west, the botanical garden (founded in 1754, transformed in the 19th century), the gardens of the Salesian nunnery (transformed and reduced), Prince Eugene's Belvedere, and the Schwarzenberg Gardens (initiated about 1700, probably by Jean Trehet). In the 1730s Salomon Kleiner published a great number of etchings that show many details of these vanished gardens.

Austria's largest garden of the 18th century is the imperial park of Schönbrunn in Vienna. The first garden was laid out by Jean Trehet about 1700. It was extended and modernized ca. 1750–65 in the style of J.F. Blondel by garden designers from Lorraine and gardeners from the Netherlands. In this period the large and still well-preserved rococo bosquet area with the radial system of avenues was laid out, and the menagerie, botanical garden, and orangery were created. In the 1770s the park was decorated with follies and sculptures.

In Salzburg the Mirabell Gardens got a new layout beginning in 1687 by the architect J.B. Fischer von Erlach and the garden engineer Matthias Diesel. The main axis of the large parterre is oriented so that the fortress on the opposite side of the town is its focal point. Several other garden areas still retain the Renaissance character of an ensemble of isolated elements. In 1730 Franz A. Danreiter transformed the garden into rococo style.

A number of other baroque gardens in Austria's different provinces from the 17th and 18th centuries, all more or less well preserved, should be mentioned: Draßburg and Halbthurn (in Burgenland), Annabichl and Zwischenwässern (in Carinthia), Greillenstein, Salaberg near Haag, Schönborn near Göllersdorf and the abbey of Melk (in Lower Austria), the abbey of Kremsmünster (in Upper Austria), the abbeys of Admont and of St. Lambrecht (in Styria), and Mühlau near Innsbruck (in Tirol).

The emperor Joseph II (r. 1765–90) admired the ideas of the Enlightenment and especially of Jean-Jacques Rousseau. In 1777 the emperor visited Rousseau in Ermenonville and saw the Marquis de Girardin's modern natural gardens with sceneries inspired by Rousseau. Already in 1766 Joseph II had opened the hunting park Prater to the public (with an avenue of four kilometers, forest aisles, a pleasure pavilion, and a playground), and in the 1770s he made several baroque imperial gardens (Augarten, Belvedere, Schönbrunn) accessible to all citizens.

The first large English park in Vienna was laid out in 1766 in Neuwaldegg by the field marshal Duke Moritz Lacy, who had been counseled by the English Lords Grenville (Stowe) and Spencer (Blenheim). In Bruck on Leitha an important landscape park still exists, which was executed with very modern planting of various indigenous and foreign trees beginning in 1789 by the gardener Christoph Lübeck from Anhalt for Earl Ernst J.N. Harrach. In Schönau on Triesting the theater director and manufacturer P.F. von Braun owned a very curious garden beginning in 1796, with a grotto mountain containing a "Temple of Night," where the visitors had to absolve a path of examination that recalls Mozart's *Zauberflöte* (*Magic Flute*). The park of Pötzleinsdorf in possession of the bank owner J.H. Geymüller was begun in 1799 by the gardener Konrad Rosenthal and is today one of Vienna's most beautiful English gardens.

Emperor Joseph II had promoted a new love of nature, but he was not the first to initiate a modern English garden. When he modernized the baroque hunting park of his summer residence in Laxenburg (1782–83), the design of his architect Isidore Ganneval (Cannevale) retained many formal features (the same layout was much appreciated by the garden theorist Hirschfeld in 1785).

Under the government of Emperor Franz II (r. 1792–1835), gardening became an important part of cultural life. As each male member of the imperial family had to learn a practical trade as part of his education, Franz II chose to become an apprentice of gardening. During his government a flowery house-garden culture developed in the Austrian provinces. Beginning in the 1790s the emperor and his wife, Marie Therese of Naples, transformed the hunting park of Laxenburg into a Picturesque landscape park with numerous pastoral and neo-Gothic follies. The concept was worked out by the emperor himself and by Michael Riedl, chief surveyor of the buildings and gardens of

Laxenburg from 1798 to 1849. In Eisenstadt (Burgenland) Prince Nikolaus Esterházy's baroque garden was transformed into a landscape park between the late 18th century and ca. 1830 by the architect Charles Moreau. Its most splendid scenery is the pond with a circular temple high up on a rock.

After 1850 the imperial family erected several important landscape gardens with arboretum planting and fashionable carpet beds near the house. These include the park of Artstetten castle (Lower Austria) begun 1861 for Archduke Karl Ludwig; the park of Hernstein (Lower Austria) with a neo-Gothic palace by the architect Theophil Hansen, erected 1856–80 for the Archdukes Rainer and Leopold; the park of the imperial villa in Bad Ischl (Upper Austria), created 1855–60 by the architect Antonio Legrenzi and the gardener Franz Rauch, a present for the young Emperor Franz Joseph I and Elisabeth of Bavaria on the occasion of their engagement; the gardens of Ambras castle in Innsbruck, transformed 1856–62 for Archduke Karl Ludwig; and finally the Burggarten in Vienna, which received a new landscaped layout in two phases about 1847 and 1863 by the gardener Franz Antoine the Younger for Emperor Franz Joseph I. Its famous neoclassical glasshouse, built in 1822 by Ludwig von Remy, was later demolished to make room for the *Jugendstil* palm house by the architect Friedrich Ohman from 1902 (the palm house was restored in 1994–98). A particularly ambitious garden patron was the successor to the throne Archduke Franz Ferdinand, who erected the park of Eckartsau (Lower Austria) in the late 19th century and modernized Artstetten (Lower Austria) about 1900.

Even in the rather conservative Austrian monarchy, the public demanded gardens for its use (the activities of Joseph II in this concern have already been mentioned). In the years of occupation by Napoléon shortly after 1800, the creation of urban parks and promenades in the provinces was mainly organized by civic "societies for the improvement of local amenities." In Vienna it was the emperor Franz II who erected the Volksgarten (people's garden) in 1819–23 at the site of the old fortifications that had been demolished by Napoléon's troops. It was not an English garden but designed in a formal neoclassical style (with the Temple of Theseus by Pietro Nobile in a grove of poplars) because this type of garden seemed more apt for a promenade where people wanted to see and to be seen. From the very beginning, about 1819, the Volksgarten was part of a great concept designed by Ludwig von Remy for the open spaces between the western front of the imperial Hofburg and the fortifications of the town, which was divided in three parts with different functions. The central area, the Äußere Burgplatz (today, Heldenplatz) ending at a town gate, the Äußere Burgtor (finished by Nobile in 1824), was a representative square for public events. On one side it was flanked by the Volksgarten, and on the other side by the Burggarten, at this time the emperor's private garden with fruit trees planted in rows and a large glasshouse by Remy.

Only when Vienna's Ringstraße (a circular boulevard with alleys surrounding the city in place of the old fortifications) had been carried out in the 1850s under the emperor Franz Joseph I was a real municipal park, the Stadtpark, initiated by the civic community (1860–63), designed in landscape style by the painter Joseph Selleny and carried out by the municipal gardener Rudolph Siebeck. In 1863 a special part was dedicated to children. About the same time (1857–84), the gardener Franz Antoine the Younger added a neo-baroque section to the Volksgarten. In 1872–73 the Rathauspark (park of the city hall) was carried out in a picturesque design by Rudolph Siebeck. Thus, the parks along the Ringstraße represent the rivalry between formal and landscaped garden design. The highest degree of formalism can be found in the garden on Maria Theresien-Platz, with its formal ground modeling, globe- and cone-shaped topiaries, the memorial of Empress Maria Theresia by C. Zumbusch, and fountains with very good sculptures. It was designed by the architect C. Hasenauer and carried out with some modifications of the planting by the imperial garden administration in 1884–85. In the hills of western Vienna, the Türkenschanzpark was carried out as the center of a villa colony by the municipal gardener Gustav Sennholz in 1885–88, with a great variety of exotic and indigenous trees. In 1902–9 the park was considerably extended.

Vienna's Stadtpark released a whole wave of municipal parks all over the monarchy, many of them founded on the occasion of the emperor's anniversaries of government and initiated by savings banks and societies for the improvement of local amenities. The most interesting municipal park outside Vienna was carried out in Graz (Styria) in 1878–88. The designer was the gardener Franz Marouschek.

The spa parks also were important for public recreation. In Baden near Vienna such a park was already laid out in the late 18th century. It reached its maximum splendor in the 1820s (when Beethoven and Grillparzer used to stay in Baden) and is still a great attraction for visitors and locals alike. The spa park in Bad Ischl (Upper Austria) was founded in 1838 and extended in 1873–75. Beginning in the middle of the 19th century, Franz Joseph I spent his summers in Bad Ischl every year; many of Vienna's bourgeois followed his example. All these parks were continuously developed and enriched during the second half of the 19th century with spa houses, music pavilions, promenades, and so on.

In the 1890s the architect Otto Wagner and the artist's group of the Wiener Secession began to propagate new ideas for the house garden and public green. Before 1890 the garden architect Lothar Abel had been the only advocate of formal (neo-baroque) gardens, but now functionalist principles caused a decline of the pseudo-landscape design in the second half of the 19th century, especially for smaller gardens. For the generation of the architects Joseph Hoffmann and Adolph Loos, the villa garden was the new issue—they wanted to connect its form and its social function with the house. The baroque style also saw a renaissance in the writings of Franz Lebisch and Joseph A. Lux. The architect Joseph M. Olbrich dealt with "color gardens" (the composition and symbolism of colors), and the architect Friedrich Ohman created the most important gardens of the Jugendstil period, including the section with the Empress Elisabeth monument in the Volksgarten (1898–1907) and the vaultings of the river Wien in Vienna's Stadtpark, done together with Joseph Hackhofer in 1902–7.

The conception of the formal garden continued in the period between the world wars. About 1930 the garden architects Albert Esch and Joseph Wladar designed many villa gardens. Also the large blocks of flats that were built and owned by the municipal community of Vienna received well-designed gardens, but in contrast to those in Germany, they did not very much consider the social functions.

After World War II two great garden expositions gave the occasion to create large green spaces at the outskirts of Vienna, the Donaupark (1964, planned by the municipal garden administration) and the Kurpark Oberlaa (1974, the leading architect was Erich Hanke). At the site of old loam pits and brick kilns, the Wienerberg-Park was planned by Wilfried and Maja Kirchner beginning in 1983 as an ecological recreation area. The largest project was begun in 1972 and finished only in the 1990s. In connection with precautions for flood protection at the Danube, the "Danube-Island" (a dam, about 20 kilometers [12.4 mi] long and 200 meters [218.7 m] wide) was shaped into a new and popular recreation area by the landscape architects Hansjakob, Heiss, and Kirchner.

*See also* Belvedere Palaces; Hellbrunn; Laxenburg; Schönbrunn; Stadtpark, Vienna

## Further Reading

Auböck, Maria, "Zur Gartenarchitektur der Otto Wagner-Schule und ihrer Zeit," *Die Gartenkunst 7,* no. 2 (1995)

Auböck, Maria, and Gisa Ruland, *Grün in Wien,* Vienna: Falter, 1994

Auböck, Maria, Gisa Ruland, and Ingrid Gregor, *Paradiesträume: Parks, Gärten und Landschaften in Wien,* Vienna: Holzhausen, 1998 (with English and Japanese summaries)

Frenzel, Monika, *Gartenkunst in Tirol: Von der Renaissance bis heute,* Innsbruck, Austria: Tyrolia, 1998

Hajós, Géza, *Romantische Gärten der Aufklärung: Englische Landschaftskultur des 18. Jahrhunderts in und um Wien,* Vienna: Böhlau, 1989

Hajós, Géza, "Renaissance Gardens in Austria: Current Research Findings and Perspectives of Conservation," in *The Authentic Garden,* edited by L. Tjon Sie Fat and E. de Jong, Leiden: Clusius Foundation, 1991

Hajós, Géza, editor, *Historische Gärten in Österreich: Vergessene Gesamtkunstwerke,* Vienna: Böhlau, 1993

Lietzmann, Hilda, *Das Neugebäude in Wien: Sultan Süleymans Zelt, Kaiser Maximilians II. Lustschloß: Ein Beitrag zur Kunst- und Kulturgeschichte der zweiten Hälfte des sechzehnten Jahrhunderts,* Munich: Deutscher Kunstverlag, 1987

Loidl-Reisch, Cordula, "Wiener Stadtparks um 1900, am Beispiel von Türkenschanzpark und Elisabeth-Denkmal (Volksgarten)," *Die Gartenkunst 7,* no. 2 (1995)

Mang, Brigitte, "Josef Oskar Wladar, die frühen Arbeiten des österreichischen Gartenarchitekten," *Die Gartenkunst 7,* no. 2 (1995)

Neubauer, Erika, *Wiener Barockgärten,* Dortmund, Germany: Harenberg, 1979

Schmidt, Stefan, "Albert Esch, ein österreichischer Gartenarchitekt der Ersten Republik," *Die Gartenkunst 7,* no. 2 (1995)

GÉZA HAJÓS AND BEATRIX HAJÓS

# Automata

In combination with the science of hydraulics, self-propelled mechanical devices propelled by the movement of water, called *automata,* have played a crucial role in the history of garden design. While hydraulic devices facilitated the transportation of water across large distances and over difficult terrain, automata or automatons primarily served as elements of visual delight within the garden environment. They frequently took diverse forms such as elaborate sprays, fountains, and other ingenious machines incorporating motion, sound, music, or even patterns of light and were made up of a large number of moving parts and interconnected gears.

Interest in automata and their extensive use in the garden environment dates back to ancient times. The first possibility of their use comes from the Hanging Gardens of Babylon, thought to have been completed under Nebuchadnezzar II in the sixth century B.C. Because the entire ensemble was located on hilly terrain, massive machines must have transported water to its highest terraces. Besides facilitating the passage of water, these machines must have to some extent functioned as visual curiosities, groaning and screeching as vast quantities of the precious liquid were moved. In all probability some moving parts were disguised to blend against the backdrop. Similarly, sophisticated automata also facilitated high priests in ancient Egypt to command the rise and ebb of the ceremonial fire through a set of concealed controls, much to the awe and horror of the believers. Automata evidently added to the atmosphere in each case. Hero's experiments with enchanting automata in the gardens at Alexandria in the first century B.C. continued the emphasis on aesthetics and visual delight. His amusing inventions anticipated the steam engine, employing moving water and steam to make artificial animals move and hiss, birds to sing, and leaves to rustle. At Pompeii the Augustan aqueduct fed into dwelling courtyards, and lead pipes caused jets of water to emerge from elaborate fountain statues. This legacy continued unbroken to Byzantium, where the flow of water through metal pipes of varying lengths produced music in an elaborate organ or *al-urgana* at the court of Emperor Basil I in 867 A.D. Legends also spoke of the famous bronze tree with singing birds that formed part of the Byzantine emperor's Throne of Solomon.

Within the Islamic world literary accounts boasted of several mechanized devices (*hiyal*) within the garden environment. These included the legendary jewel-studded tree at the court of the caliph in Baghdad and the Birkat al-Mutawakkil at Hayr al-Wuhush Palace in Samarra, where animal-shaped (zoomorphic) fountains made of precious materials decorated several courtyards. Exotic and visionary automata are also known from the 11th-century treatises of Banu Musa and the 1206 work of Banu al-Jazari. While certainly influenced by the writings of Hellenistic inventors, particularly Philon and Heron, their innovations incorporated substantial improvements. Essentially based on the principles of the *naura* or *noria* (water wheel) and the *saqiya*, a water-elevating machine—standard technologies in Islamic gardens through the Middle Ages—these were advanced versions, concentrating on the visual versus the functional aspects of these devices. In one water-elevating mechanism explained by al-Jazari, water from a nearby lake filled a tank whose bottom contained a

drain that discharged a steady stream of water over a mechanism concealed in a lower basin. This water in turn turned a wheel with scoops, setting it in motion. Through a system of meshed gears, this motion was transferred vertically to a mechanism that dipped into the top tank and in turn carried water to a channel, which emptied into the lake as a cascade. All that the amazed crowds of viewers would see, however, was a *saqiya*, which appeared to be propelled by a model of a wooden cow, since all of the lower mechanism was cleverly hidden from the sight.

The nomadic Mongols were so awed with automata devised in western Europe and the Islamic world that the Muslim kingdoms presented a musical organ to Kublai Khan between 1260 and 1264. Since several of these early organs employed water power as a means of operation, they were necessarily placed within or close to outdoor environments. Foreign envoys visiting the court of Mongke at Karakorum around 1345 remarked on the amazing Fountain Tree in the entrance courtyard to the royal palace. Serpentine conduits wrapped around the tree to produce a choice of four drinks, at the blow of an angel's trumpet, located within the ensemble. Concealed pumps and tubes allowed servants some distance away to refill these drink conduits. Evidence that writings and concepts on automata had in fact survived the hiatus created by the Mongol invasions in the early 13th century comes from Clavijo's descriptions of a golden tree with bejeweled fruit and golden birds on its branches within the trellis tent of Saray Mulk Khanum, Tamerlane's principal wife.

Accounts of developments in the Islamic world, such as the travel sketches of Guillaume Baucher in 1345, later reproduced in the *Voyages faites principalement en Asie dans les XII, XIII, XIV, et XV siecles* (1735), added to western Europe's interest in hydraulics and waterworks. The early water clocks, or *clepsydras*, gave way to Leonardo da Vinci and Machiavelli's fantastic scheme to build a system of canals that would extend the Arno to the sea. Building on Leonardo's work, Ramelli's *Le diverse et artificiose machine* (1588; Diverse and Ingenious Machines) illustrated the rotary pump, mechanical details of windmills, and a cofferdam of interlocking piles. Salomon de Caus's *Les raisons des forces mouvantes avec diverses machines tant utiles que plaisantes* (1615; The Relations of Motive Forces, with Various Machines as Useful as They Are Pleasing) demonstrated schemes for pleasure gardens incorporating elaborate grottoes and fountain equipment, including the mechanism of hydraulic singing birds. Montaigne's account of the best 16th-century examples of ingenious hydraulic and pneumatic devices in Italy included the Villa d'Este at Tivoli and the archducal Villa of Scarperio in Tuscany. At Tivoli, in addition to the fine statuary adorning the villa and gardens, he was impressed by the organs that played music to the accompaniment of the fall of water. His descriptions of Scarperio included mills motivated by waterpower to operate small church clocks, animals, soldiers, and other automata.

## Further Reading

Al-Hassan, Ahmad Yusuf, and Donald Routledge Hill, *Islamic Technology: An Illustrated History,* Cambridge and New York: Cambridge University Press, and Paris: UNESCO, 1986

Bedini, Silvio A., *Patrons, Artisans, and Instruments of Science, 1600–1750,* Aldershot, Hampshire, and Brookfield, Vermont: Ashgate/Variorum, 1999

Clark, William, Jan Golinski, and Simon Schaffer, editors, *The Sciences in Enlightened Europe,* Chicago: University of Chicago Press, 1999

Glick, Thomas F., *Irrigation and Society in Medieval Valencia,* Cambridge, Massachusetts: Harvard University Press, 1970

Goblot, Henri, *Les qanats, une technique d'acquisition de l'eau,* Paris and New York: Mouton, 1979

Hill, Donald Routledge, *Arabic Water-Clocks,* Aleppo, Syria: University of Aleppo, Institute for the History of Arabic Science, 1981

Hill, Donald Routledge, editor and translator, *On the Construction of Water-Clocks,* London: Turner and Devereaux, 1976 (translation of a treatise ascribed to Archimedes)

Masters, Roger D., *Fortune Is a River: Leonardo da Vinci and Niccolò Machiavelli's Magnificent Dream to Change the Course of Florentine History,* New York: Free Press, 1998

Macdougall, Elisabeth B., editor, *Fons Sapientiae: Renaissance Garden Fountains,* Washington, D.C.: Dumbarton Oaks Trustees, 1978

Macdougall, Elisabeth B., and Wilhelmina F. Jashemski, editors, *Ancient Roman Gardens,* Washington, D.C.: Dumbarton Oaks Trustees, 1981

Petruccioli, Attilio, editor, *Gardens in the Time of the Great Muslim Empires,* Leiden, Netherlands, and New York: Brill, 1997

Schiøler, Thorkild, *Roman and Islamic Water-Lifting Wheels,* Odense, Denmark: Odense Universitetsforlag, 1973

Turner, Howard R., *Science in Medieval Islam,* Austin: University of Texas Press, 1995

Vercelloni, Virgilio, *Atlante storico dell'idea del giardino europeo,* Milan: Jaca, 1990; as *European Gardens: An Historical Atlas,* New York: Rizzoli, 1990

MANU P. SOBTI

---

# Avenue and Allée

In many ways the history of avenues and allées reflects the history of garden design itself. Walks and avenues have been known since antiquity in many cultures. In ancient Egypt, Mesopotamia, Greece, and Rome, trees were planted for shade and sometimes for fruit. Illustrations from Thebes dating from as early as 1400 B.C. show rows of trees in a geometric garden. There was also a long tradition of roadside planting in much of Europe, for both timber and shade.

The origins of the great period of geometric landscape design may be traced to the Roman era. The designers of the Italian Renaissance looked back to Roman sources, such as Pliny's descriptions of country villa gardens. Roman imperial town planning may be seen as the forerunner of the geometric style of gardening, of which avenues and walks formed the fundamental structure. The celebrated 16th century Italian architect Andrea Palladio wrote that outside the cities the streets were "adorn'd with trees; which being planted on each side of them, by their verdure enliven our minds, and by their shade afford very great conveniency." In *I quattro libri dell'Architettura* (1570; *The Four Books of Architecture*), Palladio illustrated the Villa Emo near Venice, depicting long avenues of poplars (*Populus*) extending the main axis to the front and rear of the villa, an idea taken up in the 17th century by the French garden designer and writer André Mollet.

Many of the essentials of this movement in gardening were set down in the 17th century, first in Italy, then in France. In 1615 Vincenzo Scamozzi described a double approach avenue terminating in a half moon. Pedestrians could walk along the shaded side, or counter walk, while carriages used the central drive, turning in the large area described by the half moon. This design became one of the key features of the geometric garden layout. An early example at Honselarsdijk in the Netherlands was laid out in 1625. In England this arrangement of an avenue terminating in a half moon was seen at Twickenham Park as early as about 1609–18 and New Hall in Essex in 1623.

In France Jacques Boyceau's *Traité du jardinage* (Treatise on Gerdening) of 1638 was the first book to set out the proper dimensions for tree-lined walks, devoting a whole chapter to allées. However, his ideas of proportion were not popularized, and certainly not in England, until the publication of Mollet's *Le jardin de plaisir* (1651; *The Garden of Pleasure*), which was translated into English in 1670. Mollet, influenced by Scamozzi and his experience at Honselarsdijk, advocated extensive axial avenues and walks laid out in exact proportions. He rated the provision of an avenue leading to the house second in importance only to its situation. He proposed "a great Walk of double or treble rank either of female Elms, or of Lime Trees, which are the two sorts of Trees which we esteem the fittest for this purpose." From the middle of the 17th century these grand approaches became common in France and, after 1660, in England. Mollet's ideas were put into practice at St. James Palace in 1660 and Hampton Court in 1661. At Hampton Court a vast "goose foot" of avenues radiated across the landscape from the half moon, separated from the parterre by canals and screens.

The English country gentleman and diarist John Evelyn is credited with the first use of the word *avenue* to mean a special tree-lined approach walk, as opposed to a simple approach or a tree-lined garden walk. The Oxford English Dictionary dates this usage to an entry in Evelyn's *Diary* from 25 August 1654, and the term was further defined by him in *Sylva* (1664): "Let them read for avenue, the principal walk to the front of the house." From this description avenue is taken to mean a designed drive or walk, with regularly planted trees in straight rows. The definition can also be widened to include drives planted with "platoons," or regular clumps of trees, rides cut through woodland, or the later curving, tree-lined drives.

It was the use of rows of trees, however, that preoccupied the influential garden writers of the day. In England the relatively settled period following the restoration of the monarchy in 1660 saw the start of a series of books promoting the planting of trees and a corresponding increase in the creation of large geometric layouts defined by avenues. The primary design influence came from France, and many English books were a direct translation from the French. Evelyn's *Sylva*, however, was published in many editions from 1664 into the 19th century and was much plagiarized. The book drew on examples of avenues in France, Spain, and the Netherlands, its primary intention being to encourage large-scale tree planting while advocating French-inspired axial designs.

The planting of regular rows of trees across a landscape was a highly visible expression of social and economic power, of man's imposition of order over nature, the landscape, and its inhabitants. The avenues served many functions: providing access for pedestrians, riders, or carriages; framing views of the house from outside; framing views of buildings and monuments seen from the house; linking different areas either physically or visually; affording hunting grounds.

In the literature of garden design, walks or allées were described in the earliest gardens. There was a long-standing tradition of planting walks with trees, and the term *walk* has been defined as an avenue bordered by trees, as portrayed in Edmund Spenser's allegorical poem *The Faerie Queene* (1596), which described even ranks of trees along the walks and alleys and in John Smythson's plan of Wimbledon gardens, dated 1609, which included a walk planted with lime trees "both for shade and sweetness." It is notable that many writers drew no distinction between the terms *walk* and *avenue* at this time.

Recommendations for setting out walks and avenues were given at length; the essential element was the wide axial approach, although topography and preexisting features often precluded the ideal layout. Great attention was given to the correct dimensions and proportions. Mollet and other French writers described the placing of trees using the French dimension the *toise*, or six French feet (6.4 ft. [2 m]), and multiples of three feet were common. English writers used multiples of three feet, five feet, and the rod (a unit of measurement equal to 16.5 ft. [5 m]). The width of an approach avenue was recommended by Evelyn, Moses Cook, and Batty Langley to relate to the length of the approach and to the width of the building to which it led. Counter walks, or side avenues, were generally recommended, their width to be half the width of the main walk; trees were to be planted either on the square or in quincunx (i.e., one at each corner and one in the center, as the five on a die), a staggered layout, giving diagonal views. The trees would be spaced according to the species and the type of walk.

Dézallier d'Argenville's *La théorie et la pratique du jardinage* (The Theory and Practice of Gardening) of 1709 was translated by John James in 1712 and became a major source for the design of walks. D'Argenville differentiated between walks in the various parts of the garden, "the Close and the Open, the Single and the Double." The principal walks were "those that face a Building, Pavilion, Cascade, or the like"; they should be of the open type, wider than other walks to allow a view and preferably with "close" counter walks on either side to provide much sought after shade. "The two middle rows," according to D'Argenville, "should be planted with Trees detached, that is to say not shut up with a Palisade, but free, that you may go round them; and the two other Rows should be filled up and edged with Palisades. As double Walks are the most esteemed, so they are generally made to possess the finest Parts of a Garden." Trees were planted as closely as 12 feet (3.7 m) apart. Walks in the wilderness or grove ranged from ridings cut through woods to palisaded (i.e., hedged) walks through groves. The groves that open into compartments were to have allées planted with lime or horse chestnut set with a low palisade about three feet (1 m) high, allowing a view into the compartments. These walks could be either "open" or "close." An analysis of sites containing trees that are thought to be original reveals that the planters of the period from approximately 1650 to 1750 followed the guidelines on spacing and layout very closely. Unless regularly replanted, as for instance at Versailles, walks within gardens have survived much less well than avenues in the park.

The most highly prized trees for the planting of walks and avenues were the lime, preferably the Dutch lime. Both these trees had the advantage of being easily propagated from suckers, giving trees of identical genetic material and being suitable for pruning into palisades for walks as well as forming an attractively shaped avenue tree. The horse chestnut and plane were popular in France. The use of the plane for avenues has ancient origins: the Romans had imported the plane from Greece, and it was used extensively in Roman gardens, along with umbrella or stone pines and cypress. The beech could be used in a similar way to the elm and lime for walks, palisades, and avenues. A wide range of other trees were recommended and used including oak, walnut, ash, fir, and pine, the more spreading trees being used for larger parkland avenues.

The planting of extensive layouts of walks and avenues required the supply of great numbers of suitably raised trees. The nursery trade grew in response to this fashion, and the Dutch lime was exported in great numbers from the Netherlands in the 17th century. Many large estates would also grow their own trees, and advice was at hand from writers such as Stephen Switzer, who described the method for propagating from layers, using a transplanted stool as a mother plant. Careful nursery training was needed to achieve a correctly shaped tree. In addition to pruning to select a strong leader, it is clear that it was common practice to "head," "top," or cut off the crowns of young trees when they were set out in avenues or walks. There were several reasons for heading: if the tree was transplanted bare-rooted or over about seven feet in height; to encourage branching and crown growth; or to create a standard-height tree when planted. Surviving avenue trees of the period display marks of old pruning, particularly trees on the inside of narrow avenues, which may have been "plashed" (i.e., pleached) at some stage (see Plate 3).

The surface of these walks also required great attention. Again, James set out recommendations for walks, including keeping down weeds by hoeing or even plowing and raking, although he recommended that wide middle walks could be grassed and mown. When laying gravel he recommended beating the rubble base and beating and watering a layer of fine dust before laying and beating the gravel. Most walks in France were sand or gravel.

During the early part of the 18th century, the approach to garden design was changing, and this time the impetus was from England. Switzer was at the forefront in advocating "rural and extensive gardening" in his *Nobleman's Recreation* of 1715. The ostentation of the baroque landscape was giving way to the concept of rural improvement and an idealized vision of natural beauty. Charles Bridgeman is seen as the major exponent of this new style, which embodied irregularity but in which avenues and straight walks still played a major part within and encircling the garden. During the second half of the 18th century, the search for an affordable, universal landscape style led to the rejection of the formal layout. Lancelot "Capability" Brown was the leading exponent of the resulting English landscape style, which was widely imitated. Brown is often seen as the great destroyer of avenues, although he allowed them to remain in major landscapes such as at Blenheim and Stowe. There was an understandable reluctance to remove mature trees: at Langley, the English landscape designer Humphry Repton recommended breaking the line of the avenue rather than removing it completely.

The writers of the later 18th century revealed a lingering affection for the avenue, and by 1800 the subject was again being debated. Uvedale Price, the leading theorist of the Picturesque, extolled the architectural and meditative qualities of the avenue. As many trees were aging, their repair became one of the foremost issues for garden conservation. The tide of taste was turning, and from the 1850s on, not only were avenues being repaired, but new avenues were being planned in an extraordinary range of newly introduced exotics. In the later 20th century the difficult issue of the conservation of avenues again became a subject for debate, since many of the surviving trees from the great age of avenue planting of the late 17th and early 18th centuries were at the end of their life.

## Further Reading

Cook, Moses, *The Manner of Raising, Ordering, and Improving Forrest-Trees,* London, 1676

Dézallier d'Argenville, Antoine-Joseph, *La théorie et pratique du jardinage,* Paris, 1709; as *The Theory and Practice of Gardening,* translated by John James, London, 1712; reprint, Farnborough, Hampshire: Gregg, 1969

Duhamel du Monceau, M., *Des semis et plantations des arbres, et de leur culture,* Paris, 1760

Evelyn, John, *Directions for the Gardiner at Says-Court but Which May Be of Use for Other Gardens,* edited by Geoffrey Keynes, London: Nonesuch Press, 1932

Evelyn, John, *The Diary of John Evelyn,* 6 vols., edited by E.S. de Beer, Oxford: Clarendon Press, 1955

Evelyn, John, *Sylva; or, A Discourse of Forest-Trees,* London, 1664; reprint, Menston: Scolar Press, 1972

Gentil, François, *Le jardinier solitaire,* Paris, 1704; as *The Retir'd Gardener,* translated by George London and Henry Wise, London, 1706; reprint, 2 vols., New York: Garland, 1982

Hadfield, Miles, *A History of British Gardening,* London: Hutchinson, 1960

Harvey, John Hooper, *Early Nurserymen: With Reprints of Documents and Lists,* London: Phillimore, 1974

Hazlehurst, F. Hamilton, *Jacques Boyceau and the French Formal Garden,* Athens: University of Georgia Press, 1966

Jacques, David, and Arend Jan van der Horst, *The Gardens of William and Mary,* London: Helm, 1988

Langley, Batty, *New Principles of Gardening,* London, 1728; reprint, New York: Garland, 1982

Mollet, André, *Le jardin de plaisir,* Stockholm, 1651; reprint, Paris: Éditions du Moniteur, 1982; as *The Garden of Pleasure,* London, 1670

Palladio, Andrea, *I quattro libri dell'architettura,* Venice, 1570; as *The Four Books of Architecture,* London, 1738; reprint, as *The Four Books on Architecture,* translated by Robert Tavernor and Richard Schofield, Cambridge, Massachusetts: MIT Press, 1997

Pigott, C.D., "Estimation of the Age of Lime-Trees (*Tilia* spp.) in Parklands from Stem Diameter and Ring Counts," *Arboricultural Journal* 13 (1989)

Richens, Richard Hook, *Elm,* Cambridge and New York: Cambridge University Press, 1983

Scamozzi, Vicenzo, *Dell'idea della architettura universale,* Venice, 1615

Switzer, Stephen, *The Nobleman, Gentleman, and Gardener's Recreation,* London, 1715; new edition, as *Ichnographia Rustica: The Nobleman, Gentleman, and Gardener's Recreation,* 3 vols., London, 1718; reprint, New York: Garland, 1982

Woodbridge, Kenneth, *Princely Gardens: The Origins and Development of the French Formal Style,* New York: Rizzoli, and London: Thames and Hudson, 1986

SARAH COUCH

# Aviary

An aviary is a fancy garden construction for housing and displaying birds that is usually highly artistic. Aviaries are commonly decorated with sculpture and bas-relief. The birds themselves are decorative, because of their appearance and size, colorful feathers, singing, and distinctive behavior. They easily adapt to cage rearing and are capable of breeding under these conditions. Birds entered the decorative garden repertoire as part of the paradise garden archetype. Some birds were allowed free range (e.g., peacocks, turkeys, and native wild birds), but others required specially adapted environments. In this way, native and exotic birds could be kept separate from birds of prey such as falcons, eagles, hawks, owls, and ravens.

Aviaries, unlike cages, were made large enough to allow flying. To allow a view of the birds inside, the construction was usually transparent: glass, wire mesh, or fish net. In Russia, aviaries were covered with silk. There also were aviaries of interlaced branches and fretwork. In the second half of the 19th century aviaries were made from cast iron. Inside the structures were small compartments, watering troughs, feeding troughs, branches of dried trees, rocks or resting shelves, and other accessories; large aviaries were partly roofed. Birds were viewed from the outside or from special rooms that were an integral part of the aviary.

Aviaries are found during all periods of garden art development. They were a frequent decorative motif in ancient Egyptian gardens and were made for guest entertainment in the villa gardens of imperial Rome. Aviaries could also be found at small villas as little or slightly larger cages, such as those known from Pompeii. In medieval gardens aviaries were always found in association with animal parks, and in Renaissance gardens they acquired a more decorative appearance as pavilions situated near the villa or palace. In the baroque period, aviaries could be found in association with animal parks, menageries, and *entre eventail et etoile* (a fan-shaped menagerie, hunting lodge, and deer park). They also posed as very attractive buildings near palaces. They were gladly introduced into landscape, classical, and especially romantic gardens in the 18th and 19th centuries.

Aviaries became especially popular in many European countries beginning in the 18th century. They took the form of decorative garden pavilions, follies, or bowers, in the classical, Chinese, or rustic style. Those known as an eagle's cage or raven's cage were formed as a big semi-spherical enclosure. A fowler was usually employed to look after the birds in such aviaries. The use of aviaries was wide-ranging; they were attached to noble mansions, large urban winter gardens, and middle-class apartments. They gained new meaning when zoological gardens and menageries started appearing. They were popular in the parks created for culture and recreation during the 19th and 20th centuries, where they provided a chance of viewing birds safely at the closest possible distance.

Special aviaries for rearing various species of birds were found at granges as well as decorative gardens. The pheasantry is a decorative construction in the form of a large wooden or cast iron aviary protected by a net. The decorative exotic species of pheasants were among the fashionable birds kept in such aviaries. Their popularity peaked during the second half of the 18th century and the first half of the 19th century. The pheasantry was used to domesticate *Colchician* pheasants. Similar aviaries were used for rearing partridges, quail, thrushes (robins), and fieldfares. Such aviaries were usually set up near stately hunting lodges. Similarly, peacock houses were built for peacocks.

The columbarium (pigeon house or dovecote) is a decorative garden construction usually placed on a tower made of wood, brick, or stone. It was related to the medieval tradition of pigeon rearing in which squabs were kept for food and their manure was used in vegetable or melon cultivation. The number of nesting holes in a columbarium was usually large, up to 1,000. During the time of landscape parks, they were a popular part of country estates. A classical columbarium designed by S.B. Zug in Mokotów, Warsaw, was connected with a gatehouse and also served as a watchtower.

The poultry-house or fowl-house is a large decorative building meant for poultry including chickens, ducks, geese, turkeys, and peacocks. The fowl-house was both decorative and utilitarian, as a home to exotic, decorative poultry and as a place for meat, egg, and feather production. Columbariums and fowl-houses were common features near mansions.

The ornithon is a special roofed garden building constructed in villa gardens in ancient Rome, which posed as an interesting variation of the aviary. The front part of this construction was decorated with a portico of stone columns interlaced with single trees. The inside contained two fish ponds. A rotunda in the interior was surrounded by a double colonnade with a basin in the middle. A miniature island was placed in the basin with a small column serving as support for a round table top where feed was left for aquatic birds. The rotunda was covered with a semi-spherical dome. A sundial and the wind directions were marked on the outer surface of the dome. Such buildings were usually located in a big park with freely roaming animals.

## Further Reading

Coppa and Avery Consultants, *The Architecture of Zoological Gardens and Aviaries,* Monticello, Illinois: Vance Bibliographies, 1984

Enehjelm, Curt af, *Kafige und Volieren,* Stuttgart, Germany: Franckh, 1969; as *Cages and Aviaries,* translated by U. Erich Friese, Hong Kong: T.F.H., 1981

Pearce, David William, *Aviary Design and Construction,* Poole, Dorset: Blandford Press, 1983

Thacker, Christopher, *The History of Gardens,* Berkeley: University of California Press, and London: Croom Helm, 1979

Vriends, Matthew M., *Aviaries: A Complete Introduction,* Neptune, New Jersey: T.F.H., 1987

MAREK SIEWNIAK

# B

## Baba Wali, Garden of

### Qandahar, Afghanistan

**Location:** approximately 3 miles (6.5 km) west of Qandahar

The Garden of Baba Wali (or Bagh-e-Baba Wali) is one of the earliest examples of a Persian paradise garden (*chahar-bagh*) in Afghanistan. The garden contains the shrine of the Sufi saint Baba Wali (also known as Baba Hasan Abdal Qandahari, a shrine to whom can also be found in Hasan Abdal, Pakistan), who flourished in the early part of the 15th century and is thought to have died around 1480. The present shrine dates from the early 16th century.

The shrine lies enclosed in an old, ruined garden approximately three miles (6.5 km) west of the modern-day city, among the remains of old Qandahar, which was sacked and razed in 1714 by the Iranian conqueror Nadir Shah. The current condition of the garden is extremely dilapidated, being mostly half-buried, and it is difficult to determine the structure and form of the original. Encircled by a rocky ridge, the garden is discerned only by the small citadel of Baba Wali's shrine, which still attracts Muslim, Hindu, and Sikh pilgrims.

Although the shrine to Baba Wali existed during Timurid times (the Timurid dynasty ruled the area now called Afghanistan from the 13th century to the early 16th century), the garden itself was only built after the conquest of Qandahar in 1522 by Babur, the first Mogul ruler of India. His son Mirza Kamran completed the garden around 1531. Local legend has it that it took 70 men nine years to complete the garden.

The design was a classic paradise garden or *chahar-bagh*, with four raised water channels merging into a central pool; these intersecting channels divided the garden into four sectors in which various shrubs and plants were planted, especially jasmine, delphinium, narcissus, saffron, and carnation. On the outer edges of the garden were planted mulberry trees, with grapevines entwining each tree. Water was sourced from the Argandab River, which flows between Qandahar and Khalishak, by way of canals.

The design of the garden is flat, although the natural rise of the land could power two small waterfalls. Evidence also indicates that small gazebos stood at the four corners of the garden, from where the flow of the water could be enjoyed. Behind these gazebos stood fruit trees, especially apricot, apple, peach, and pomegranate. A wall surrounded the entire garden, which kept the dust of the plain at bay, while affording privacy and protection.

The northeast part of the garden includes a series of massive steps (40 in all) made of limestone that lead up to a vaulted chamber cut into the ridge that faces the ruins of old Qandahar. Babur also constructed this chamber after 1522 to commemorate his conquest of northern India. Locally, this chamber is known as *rawaq* (portal or gateway). At the foot of the steps once stood two crouching tigers (metaphoric references to Babur, whose name means "tiger"). The tigers have disappeared, and only the plinths on which they stood are now visible. Inside the dome of the chamber is an inscription in relief stating in verse that Babur took possession of Qandahar on 1 September 1522 and that same year he constructed the garden and chamber. Babur's grandson, Emperor Akbar, added a second, later, inscription (dated 1598).

Although Baba Wali's shrine survived the sack of the old city of Qandahar, the garden itself never recovered from the devastation and remains a ruin to this day.

### Synopsis

| | |
|---|---|
| 15th C. | Baba Wali flourishes |
| 1522 | Babur conquers Qandahar; constructs garden and chamber |
| 1531 | Babur's son completes garden |
| 1714 | Nadir Shah razes the city of Qandahar |

**Further Reading**

Fergusson, James, *History of Indian and Eastern Architecture*, London, 1876; 2nd edition, 2 vols., edited by James Burgess and Richard Phené Spiers, London: John Murray, 1910; reprint, Delhi: Munshiram Manoharlal, 1968

Jairazbhoy, Rafique Ali, "Early Garden-Palaces of the Great Mughals," *Oriental Art* 4 (1958)

Vigne, Godfrey Thomas, *A Personal Narrative of a Visit to Ghuzni, Kabul, and Afghanistan, and of a Residence at the Court of Dost Mohamed: With Notices of Ranjit Singh, Khiva, and the Russian Expedition,* London, 1840; reprint, Delhi: Gian, 1986

NIRMAL DASS

# Babur 1483–1530

## Mogul Ruler and Garden Designer

Soldier of fortune, diarist, poet, horticulturist, garden designer, and founder of the Mogul dynasty (1526–1858) in Central Asia and India, Babur was born on 14 February 1483 in Andijan, Uzbekistan. He was a lineal descendant of Timur (Tamerlane) and of the Mongol conqueror Genghis Khan. Following the death of his father in 1494, Babur was forced to relinquish his patrimony in Fergana and for several years led a free-booting existence with a small band of followers in remote areas of Central Asia. In 1504 he occupied Kabul and asserted control over the surrounding Afghan tribes, and over the next 15 years, between 1507 and 1522, he carried on a series of inconclusive struggles with his neighbors in Central Asia, the Punjab, and eastern Iran. Finally in 1526, taking advantage of rivalries between different branches of the ruling Lodi dynasty in northern India, he attacked Delhi. After defeating Sultan Ibrahim's forces at Panipat in the Punjab (April 1526), he went on to occupy Delhi and Agra before advancing eastward down the Ganges to the frontiers of Bengal. By his death four years later (26 December 1530), he had established himself as ruler of much of northern India and had founded a new ruling house in the subcontinent, the Mogul dynasty, which would survive until the middle of the 19th century. He was first buried in the Aram Bagh (Garden of Rest) in Agra, popularly held to have been on the site of the present-day Ram Bagh, later in the Bagh-i Babur in Kabul, to which his remains were removed sometime between 1530 and 1544.

Given his Timurid heritage, it is hardly surprising that Babur should have given high priority to the construction of gardens. Since none of these remain intact, however, it is impossible to define the relationship between Babur's foundations and their earlier Central Asian and Persian antecedents. Sources for the study of their form and function as well as of Babur's horticultural activities are therefore largely limited to his extraordinary auto-biographical memoirs, the *Babur Name* (Book of Babur) (see Plate 4), and to archaeological surveys that have been conducted on several of his garden sites.

According to Babur's own testimony, his earliest landscape design activities date back to his youth, when, in 1496, he ordered the construction of a summer house (*hujra*) on the slopes overlooking the town of Ush in Fergana. His subsequent garden-building activities were divided between Afghanistan and the Indian subcontinent and included both residental gardens in the suburbs of his capitals and landscape gardens located in scenic spots he encountered in the course of his campaigns and travels.

Babur's earliest effort of this latter sort was the Bagh-i Wafa (Garden of Felicity) opposite Fort Adinapur (Jalalabad) on the road between Kabul and the Khyber Pass, founded in 1508–9. Although traces of the garden could still be identified in the mid-19th century, neither its exact site nor its layout or plantings can today be established. Babur describes it as located on sloping ground with a stream flowing through it to a reservoir. He adds that it was divided into four plots (*chahar-bagh*), although whether this should be taken to mean that it was symmetrically partitioned into quadrants or consisted of four descending terraces is unclear. Plantings included orange trees and pomegranates around the reservoir, plus bananas and sugarcane. A well-known painting of the garden in a dispersed manuscript of the *Babur Name* dating to the end of the 16th century and today in the Victoria and Albert Museum in London depicts the Bagh-i Wafa as a walled rectangle divided into four quarters by axial watercourses in the manner of later Mogul gardens. However, this arrangement finds no basis in Babur's own text and may well be an anachronism.

Other landscape gardens built by Babur in Afghanistan include the Bagh-i Kalan (Great Garden) in Istalif, and north of Kabul, the Nazar-gah (Observation Place, known also as Khawaja Basta) north of Charikar, and an otherwise unidentified garden in Qandahar. While details of the latter are lacking, Babur describes the Istalif garden as located on a hillside overlooking the Kuh-Daman Valley and cut by a tree-lined stream that Babur had caused to be straightened. Architectural features included a cistern and a large circular seat; willows are mentioned as among the plantings. Likewise, the Nazar-gah is described as containing a reservoir with plantings that included trees, lawns and "borders of sweet herbs and flowers of beautiful color and scent."

Babur's initial raids into the Indian plain were followed by construction of landscape gardens in the Punjab and the Delhi-Agra region. In 1519, at the time of his first crossing of the Indus, Babur built the Bagh-i Safa (Garden of Purity), overlooking Lake Kalda-Kahar in the Chakwal district of Pakistan. He describes it as located in a meadow, in fact, on an alluvial fan, sloping down to the lake, with a spring in the heights above. Archaeological surveys reveal no evidence of either a surrounding wall or of a formal, regularized layout.

Other Indian landscape gardens mentioned by Babur in passing include *chahar-bagh* at Chitr (1526), Panipat (1526–29), and Gwaliyar (1528), none of which have been fixed as to location, and the Bagh-i Fath (Garden of Victory) at Fathpur Sikri, built in 1527–28 to commemorate his victory at Khanwa. Although the precise location of the latter is a matter of some controversy, it was probably situated in the southwestern part of the town, near the Ajmeri Gate.

The most fully documented and best preserved of Babur's Indian landscape gardens, however, is the Bagh-i Nilufar (Lotus Garden) in the village of Jhor, about two miles west of Dholpur on the Agra-Gwaliyar road. Babur states that he ordered work on the garden begun in late 1527 by his architect, Ustad Shah Muhammad, and that he subsequently visited it on repeated occasions in order to supervise the work, which was still continuing as late as 1529. Babur's memoirs describe the garden as including a dam (*band*), an octagonal roofed cistern or tank (*hauz*), a pool (*ab-khana*), an audience chamber (*suffa, talar*), a well (*chah*), mosque (*masjid*), and bath house (*hamam*), and a leveled platform cut as a single piece out of a rock with a pool at the center. Several of these structures can still be identified. The garden, which apparently was not walled, is described as thick with trees, mangoes, and *jaman* (*Eugenia jambolana*).

In addition to landscape gardens, Babur also describes residental gardens that he built in the suburbs of Kabul and Agra. At Kabul he mentions building a *chahar-bagh* outside the city walls in 1504–5 and notes that it con-

tained an audience hall (*divankhana*), a picture gallery (*suratkhana*) over the gate, stables, and a place for Babur's tent. It is at Agra, however, that he built his most elaborate residential garden, the Bagh-i Hasht-Bihisht (Garden of the Eight Paradises). A *chahar-bagh* located on the east bank of the Jumna, possibly on the site of the present-day Ram Bagh, it was laid out within a few days of Babur's first entry into the city in 1526 and is described as including a well (*chah*), large tank (*hauz*), bath house (*hamam*), audience chamber (*talar*), private apartments (*khilwat-khana*), and various other buildings. Plantings are described as laid out in orderly and symmetrical borders and parterres and included roses, narcissus, and grapes.

Despite the often imprecise and fragmentary character of much of the available information, it is apparent that Babur took an active part in the designing and laying out of his gardens. Unfortunately, he nowhere gives a systematic account of the principles that guided him in his landscape designs. It is nonetheless clear from his memoirs that he had an abiding interest in plants and landscape and that he deeply admired Timurid-Persian gardens such as those he encountered as a young man in Samarkand and Herat, the old Timurid capitals. In Samarkand, which he occupied in 1497, he praises the gardens of Timur, of Ulugh Beg, and of Sultan Ahmad Mirza—the Bagh-i Dilkusha (Joy-giving Garden), Naqsh-i Jahan (Image of the World), Bagh-i Chanar (Plane-Tree Garden), and others—and describes various of their architectural features and plantings. He admires the *chahar-bagh* of Darwesh-Muhammad Tarkhan, for example, for its location on a sloping site with a fine view, for its symmetrical arrangement in a series of terraces one above the other, and for its plantings, which included elm, cypress, and white poplar. Its one defect, he notes, was its lack of a large stream.

Similarly, Babur's critiques of Indian gardens shed light on his landscape and design aesthetic. These he describes as characterized by irregularity, a lack of symmetry, and an absence of running water but continues that in designing his gardens in Agra, he laid them out "with order and symmetry, with suitable borders and parterres in every corner and in every border rose and narcissus in perfect arrangement . . . [Indeed] the people of Hind . . . had never seen grounds planned out so symmetrically and thus laid out."

Despite the generalities in which Babur describes his garden designs, it is nonetheless possible, when his writings are combined with archaeological evidence, to develop a picture of some of the principles behind Babur's garden designs and, by analogy, of early Mogul gardens in general. First, it seems that gardens were often sited on sloping ground that provided an attractive view of the surrounding landscape (Osh, Istalif, Jalalabad, Kalda Kahar). While later Mogul gardens were generally in the form of walled rectangles, and although walled enclosures are mentioned in Agra and are implied (by reference to a gatehouse) in Kabul, evidence for this sort of arrangement is lacking at many of his landscape gardens, such as those of Jalalabad, Kalda Kahar, and Dholpur.

Babur refers to a number of his gardens as *chahar-bagh*, a term that has come to be associated with square or rectangular sites partitioned into quarters by axial systems of paths, running water, and plantings. Given that several scholars have now shown that the term *chahar-bagh* was sometimes applied to rectilinear terraced layouts, however, and that Babur himself described the *chahar-bagh* of Darwish-Muhammad Tarkhan at Samarkand as "arranged symmetrically, terrace above terrace," it is unclear whether Babur is describing a garden of four terraces or four symmetrical quadrants when he applies the term to one or another of his landscape projects.

Running water was clearly an important feature of Babur's garden designs. Sites were chosen for springs and natural streams, which in some cases (e.g., Istalif) were straightened and lined with stone. Dams and water wheels were constructed to insure a continuous supply of running water and, within gardens, cisterns, tanks, and rock-carved pools were constructed.

Finally, although the original plantings of Babur's gardens are only vaguely described in his memoirs, it is clear that he made little distinction between ornamental and economically important plants. Plantings were arranged symmetrically around and along the borders of watercourses and pools and included such stalwarts of Persian gardens as the cypress, rose, and narcissus, as well as plants and trees of south Asian origin such as bananas, sugarcane, oranges, and mangoes. Thus, Babur's gardens were horticultural environments in the broadest sense, for which sweet herbs and flowers of beautiful scent and color were chosen eclectically from a variety of sources.

As was the case with the Timurids, so too Babur's gardens were associated with the paradisaic imagery long characteristic of the Iranian world and were intended to serve as settings for a variety of activities. Thus, following well-established Timurid practice, Babur used his gardens as royal residences and encampments. It was here that he pitched his tent, held audience, and conducted state affairs. The *Babur Name* makes clear, however, that they were also used for less formal activities—as rest stops during Babur's travels, as places for viewing the landscape, and as settings for drinking parties. Ultimately, however, there is reason to believe that Babur's gardens had another, metaphoric significance, as symbols of imperial conquest, transforming the Indian landscape into one with Timurid and Central Asian associations. Significantly, a number of Babur's gardens were built on the sites of his greatest victories (Panipat, Khanwa, Qandahar) and served in part to commemorate his most important military triumphs and mark his imperial conquests. Certainly, their four-part, ordered arrangement represented a Central Asian and Timurid tradition, even in the eyes of Babur's Indian subjects, as can be surmised from the fact that the quarter in which Babur's Agra garden stood was known to the local inhabitants as Kabul and the area in which his Panipat garden was located is still referred to locally as Kabuli Bagh.

### Biography

Born in Andijan, Uzbekistan, 14 February 1483. Descendant of Timur (Tamerlane) through father Umur Shaykh, prince (*mirza*) of Fergana, and of Chengiz Khan on side of mother, Kutluk Nigar Khanum; succeeded father as ruler of Andijan, 1494, but lost patrimony, 1501; wandered with small band of supporters; occupied Kabul, 1504; after years of raiding in Punjab, occupied Delhi and Agra, 1526; subsequent campaigns enlarged his holdings in Northern India east to Bengal. Died 26 December 1530.

### Selected Designs

| | |
|---|---|
| 1508–9 | Bagh-i Wafa (Garden of Fidelity), Jalalabad, Afghanistan |
| 1519 | Bagh-i Kalan (The Great Garden), Istalif, Afghanistan (perhaps only restoration); Bagh-i Safa (Garden of Purity), Kalda-Kahar Lake, Pakistan (possibly only restoration) |
| 1526 | Bagh-i Hasht-Bihisht (Garden of Eight Paradises) or Bagh-i Gulafshan (Flower-Scattering Garden), Agra, India |
| 1526–29 | *Chahar-bagh*, Panipat, India |
| 1527–28 | Bagh-i Fath (Garden of Victory), Skiri, India |
| 1527–29 | Bagh-i Nilufar (Lotus Garden), Dholpur, India |
| 1528 | *Chahar-bagh*, Gwaliyar, India |
| before 1529 | Bagh-i Khiyaban (Avenue Garden), Kabul, India (perhaps only restoration); Nazar-gah (Observation Place), Charikar, Afghanistan |

### Selected Publications

*Babur Name* (written early 16th C.); as *Baburnama*, translated, edited, and annotated by Wheeler M. Thackston, 1993

### Further Reading

Asher, Catherine, "Babur and the Timurid Char Bagh: Use and Meaning," *Environmental Design* 11 (1991)
Crane, Howard, "The Patronage of Zahir al-Din Baburt and the Origins of Mughal Architecture," *Bulletin of the Asia Institute* 1 (1987)

"Gardens versus Citadels: The Territorial Context of Early Mughal Gardens," in *Garden History: Issues, Approaches, Methods,* edited by John Dixon Hunt, Washington, D.C.: Dumbarton Oaks Research Library and Collection, 1992

"Landscapes of Conquest and Transformation: Lessons from the Earliest Mughal Gardens in India, 1526–30," *Landscape Journal* 10 (1991)

Moynihan, Elizabeth, "The Lotus Garden Palace of Zahir al-Din Muhammad Babur," *Muqarnas* 5 (1988)

Nath, R., "Babur's Jal-Mahal at Fatehpur Sikri," *Studies in Islam* 18, nos. 3–4 (1981)

Wescoat, James L., "Picturing an Early Mughal Garden," *Asian Art* 2 (Fall 1989)

Zayn al-Din Wafa'i Khwafi, *Zain Khan's Tabaqat-i Baburi,* translated by S. Hasan Askari, Delhi: Idarah-i Adabiyat-i Delli, 1982

HOWARD CRANE

# Bacon, Francis 1561–1626

## English Statesman and Philosopher

The opening lines of Sir Francis Bacon's 1625 essay "Of Gardens"—"God Almighty first planted a Garden. And indeed it is the purest of human pleasures. It is the Greatest Refreshment to the Spirits of Man"—have inspired many subsequent garden writers, who have often quoted him. Bacon describes in this essay an ideal garden meant to complement the "princely palace" that he describes in another 1625 essay, "Of Building." A close reading of his essay on gardens suggests that the garden described is not wholly representative of the gardens of the period, nor does it conform to what we now know of Bacon's own gardens. Nonetheless, the essay remains a unique attempt to describe an ideal garden of the early 17th century and provides important information on the types of plants common in early Stuart gardens.

The princely garden, according to Bacon, must be large (approximately 30 acres [12 ha]) with a "Greene" of about 4 acres of "finely shorne" grass with a "fair alley in the midst" closest to the house, a large "Maine Garden" of 12 acres (5 ha), and a "Heath or Desart" (wilderness) of 6 acres (2.5 ha) flanked by two 4-acre (1.6-ha) side grounds, ending in a terrace with mounts at the corners farthest from the house. In size and in its essentially tripartite form, the garden resembles other important contemporary gardens (e.g., the garden of Robert Cecil, first earl of Salisbury, at Hatfield House in Hertfordshire). The use of "alleys" (covered walks either of arched trelliswork or hedges) to provide shade and structure to the individual compartments was also typical.

Slightly old-fashioned elements include a large central mount with a banqueting house (such as the one built by Henry VIII at Hampton Court a century earlier). Bacon also diverged from contemporary fashion when he dismissed knots as mere "Toyes," as well as "Images

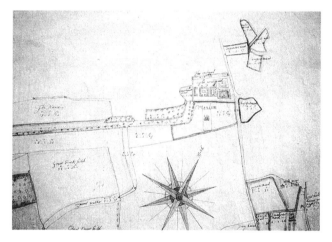

17th-century estate map, showing the water gardens Francis Bacon created for Gorhambury, Hertfordshire, England
Courtesy of Gorhambury Estates

Cut out in Juniper" (topiary), both often considered quintessential elements of early Stuart gardens. He was also critical of sculpture, which he felt added "nothing to the true Pleasure of a Garden," at a time when Charles I and the earl of Arundel were creating their highly praised museum gardens. Bacon's dismissal of ponds because they "make the garden unwholesome, and full of flies and frogs" is surprising in light of his own work at Gorhambury in Hertfordshire.

Among the most imaginative ideas in Bacon's garden essay is the placement of hidden cages for birds (aviaries) in the arches of the hedges. Bacon also suggested putting into the hedges small pieces of colored and gilded glass for "the Sunne to Play upon," a touch that might appear gaudy to the modern observer but that would have been very much in keeping with the Jacobean aesthetic, with its love of pattern and bright colors. The "Heath" or "Naturall wildnesse" at the end of the garden, like the grassy lawn near the house, suggests an interest in nature and natural form within the garden that anticipates aspects of the 18th-century English landscape garden.

Bacon's love of plants is revealed in the extensive list of flowers, herbs, and trees that provide beauty throughout the year. Evergreen plants such as ivy, holly, yew, cypress, lavender, and periwinkle enhance the garden in December and January, followed by crocus, primroses, anemones, and bulbs (e.g., tulips, hyacinths, and fritillaries) for late winter months and early spring. Violets, daffodils, daisies, and flowering fruit trees embellish the spring garden, and pinks, roses, honeysuckles, columbines, and many other blooms fill the summer garden. August and September are graced with fruits and nuts from the garden and orchard. Native plants dominate, but there are also references to more exotic or fragile plants, such as orange and lemon trees, which were clearly meant to be grown in special conditions. Bacon was as fascinated by fragrance as he was by visual beauty and described in loving detail the "Breath of Flowers." He did not, however, attempt to give planting schemes or designs.

As important as Bacon's essay is, his own gardening efforts have only recently been investigated. Bacon occupied a number of houses during his lifetime, including Twickenham House in Middlesex, which he leased in the late 1590s. The elaborate geometric garden with mounts in each corner recorded in a plan by the architect Robert Smythson (ca. 1609; now at the Royal Institute of British Architects, London) may well represent Bacon's work there. While treasurer of Gray's Inn in London (from 1608), Bacon improved the gardens, erecting a high mount with a banqueting house at the center of the garden.

At about the same time, Bacon began to plan alterations to the gardens at Gorhambury, the family seat that he had unexpectedly inherited in 1601. A memo dated 1608 gives details of a "place of pleasure" or water garden to be created about a mile from the house, terraces, a grotto, an arbor of musk roses, a banqueting house, and, surprisingly, statuary. The water gardens he eventually created there some years later are visible in an estate map of 1634 (Hertfordshire Record Office). Set into a rectangular enclosure of approximately 4 acres (1.6 ha), Bacon's water garden was adjacent to medieval fishponds and fed by the river Ver. In the middle was a square pond with an island at the center, which had a "curious banquetting-house of Roman architecture," according to John Aubrey, who visited in 1656. The channels that formed the water gardens were lined with pebbles of different colors, some made into mosaic figures, particularly in the form of fish. Over-looking the pond gardens was Verulam House, an architecturally precocious summerhouse, probably designed by Bacon himself so that he could climb to the roof and enjoy the views down over the ponds. Bacon's water gardens were already in decline when Aubrey visited them. Today all that survives of any of Francis Bacon's gardens are the earthworks of the water gardens at Gorhambury.

## Biography

Born in The Strand, London, 1561. Younger son of Sir Nicholas Bacon (1509–79), Lord Keeper of the Seal; inherited family seat at Gorhambury, Hertfordshire, 1601, where he designed a water garden, from 1608; knighted, 1603; held important positions in the court of James I, including that of attorney general and eventually of lord chancellor, 1618–21; became Viscount St. Albans, 1621; charged with bribery and dismissed from office, 1621. Bacon was a prolific writer of influential and highly original philosophical works and essays. Died in Highgate, London, 1626.

## Selected Designs

late 1590s    Bacon's Twickenham House, Twickenham, Middlesex, England
after 1608    Garden, Gray's Inn, London, England
from 1608    Water garden, Gorhambury, Hertfordshire, England

## Selected Publications

"Of Gardens," in *The Essayes or Counsels, Civill and Morall,* by Francis Bacon, 3rd edition, 1625
*The Works of Francis Bacon,* edited by James Spedding, Robert Leslie Ellis, and Douglas Denon Heath, 14 vols., London, 1858–74; see especially vol. 6

## Further Reading

Henderson, Paula, "Sir Francis Bacon's Water Gardens at Gorhambury," *Garden History* 20, no. 2 (December 1992)
Henderson, Paula, "Secret Houses and Garden Lodges: The Queen's House, Greenwich, in Context," *Apollo* (July 1997)
Jacques, David, "The 'Chief Ornament' of Gray's Inn: The Walks from Bacon to Brown," *Garden History* 17 (1989)
Smith, Hassell, "The Gardens of Sir Nicholas and Sir Francis Bacon: An Enigma Resolved and a Mind Explored," in *Religion, Culture, and Society in Early Modern Britain,* edited by Anthony Fletcher and Peter Roberts, Cambridge and New York: Cambridge University Press, 1994

PAULA HENDERSON

# Bailey, Liberty Hyde 1858–1954

## United States Botanist and Horticulturist

Known as the "father of American horticulture," Liberty Hyde Bailey was a botanist and horticulturist whose achievement in these fields was matched by his success as an educator and administrator, a philosopher and rural sociologist, and a writer and editor. As a scientist he made substantial contributions to taxonomic botany, helping to transform the art of gardening into the science of horticulture; as an educator and administrator he oversaw the development of the New York State College of Agriculture at Cornell University into one of the foremost agricultural colleges in the nation; as a philosopher and rural sociologist he was a vocal advocate for country life and a forward-thinking spokesman for environmental awareness; and as a writer and editor he brought hundreds of books and articles to publication that were read not only by his fellow botanists and professional horticulturists but also by amateur gardeners and the general public. Through his work in each of these realms, Bailey combined his interests in the application of botanical concepts and methods to horticulture with his concern for the social and cultural implications of scientific progress.

Born in South Haven, Michigan, Bailey was the son of Liberty Hyde Bailey, Sr., a farmer and fruit grower, and Sarah Harrison. As a youth he wandered the fields and forests of Michigan, which sparked his interest in agriculture, and he read Charles Darwin's *On the Origin of Species by Natural Selection* (1859) and Asa Gray's *Field, Forest, and Garden Botany* (1868), which directed his attention to evolutionary biology and systematic botany. After attending a one-room schoolhouse in South Haven, Bailey enrolled in the Michigan Agricultural College (now Michigan State University), one of the earliest agricultural colleges in the United States, where he studied with the botanist William J. Beal and published his first articles on plant identification in the *Botanical Gazette.* After graduating in 1882 with a bachelor's degree in botany, Bailey traveled to Massachusetts to Harvard, where he worked for two years as Asa Gray's assistant, sorting and classifying plant specimens received from the Royal Botanic Gardens, Kew.

In 1885, when Bailey accepted an offer to return to the Michigan Agricultural College as professor of horticulture and landscape gardening, John Merle Coulter, a fellow student and later an outstanding botanist at the University of Chicago, reportedly told him, "You will never be heard from again." Coulter's comment and Gray's own disappointment at Bailey's career choice were typical of the dichotomy thought to exist at the time between the science of botany and the practice of horticulture. Botanists concerned themselves mostly with wild plants, and horticulturists focused their efforts on domestic varieties; botanists worked in the laboratory, and horticulturists kept to the garden. Bailey attempted to unite the theory and practice of both disciplines: to bring botanical science more fully into horticulture, and to bring the plants of the garden to the attention of more botanists. In a lecture before the Massachusetts State Board of Agriculture in 1885 entitled "The Garden Fence" (published in 1886), Bailey concluded, "If we need one thing more than another, it is that the botanist shall climb the garden fence and include within the realm of his science all the plants which we till." To that end, in 1903 Bailey cofounded the American Society for Horticultural Science, an organization formed "more fully to establish horticulture on a scientific basis," and served as its first president until 1907.

In 1888, at age 30, Bailey became chair of general and experimental horticulture at Cornell University, the institution at which he would remain for the rest of his life. From 1903 to 1913 he served as Dean of the College of Agriculture, which in 1904 became a separate state-supported college within Cornell. As dean Bailey reorganized and expanded the college, establishing several new departments—including plant breeding, plant pathology, plant physiology, and home economics—and increasing enrollment and faculty size tenfold. Bailey also became a champion of the extension service, which brought the fruits of university research and teaching to farmers around the state through lectures, courses, and public-information bulletins. Bailey wrote many of these bulletins himself, including "Some Preliminary Studies on the Influence of the Electric Arc Lamp upon Greenhouse Plants" (1891), which was selected for inclusion in *Classic Papers in Horticultural Science* (1989).

Bailey's interest in disseminating research through teaching and extension work paralleled his concern for encouraging nature study among young people and improving the conditions of rural life. *The Nature-Study Idea* (1903) discusses the need for an extensive rural nature-study program, which he and several collaborators helped to create by producing nature-study leaflets for thousands of teachers and students in the public schools. Based on Bailey's success in this and other endeavors, in 1908 President Theodore Roosevelt appointed him chairman of the Commission on Country Life, which studied the effects of modern society on rural communities around the nation. In 1911 the commission released its report, written largely by Bailey, and its recommendations resulted in the establishment of the U.S. Parcel Post system, a nationwide agricultural extension service, and federal support for rural electrification programs, among other things. Bailey discussed these issues further in *The Country Life Movement in the United States* (1911).

After his retirement as dean in 1913, Bailey continued to botanize, research, and write for another 36 years. He attempted to articulate his social and moral philosophy in what he called his "Background Books," which include *The Holy Earth* (1915), *Wind and Weather* (1916), *Universal Service* (1918), *What Is Democracy?* (1918), *The Seven Stars* (1923), *The Harvest of the Year to the Tiller of the Soil* (1927), and *The Garden Lover* (1928). The most important of these is *The Holy Earth*, in which Bailey articulated an environmental ethic grounded in both religion and science—an idea far ahead of its time. Evolution, he wrote, has revealed that "the living creation is not exclusively man-centered; it is biocentric." Bailey's ecological thinking is said to have influenced Aldo Leopold's formulation of his "Land Ethic" in *A Sand County Almanac* (1949).

The author of more than 60 books—including textbooks on fruit, vegetable, and flower growing, plant breeding, and nursery work—Bailey also wrote more than 100 scientific papers, in which he made substantial contributions to taxonomic botany. Through these publications he became a recognized authority on *Carex*, New World palms, *Brassica*, *Vitis*, *Rubus*, and *Cucurbita*. His most influential edited volumes include the *Standard Cyclopedia of Horticulture* (1914–17), *Manual of Cultivated Plants* (1924), *Hortus* (1930), and *Hortus Second* (1941). Bailey also served as editor of the popular *American Garden* monthly for nearly two years, beginning in 1890, and was the founding editor of *Country Life in America*, from 1901 to 1903, the most widely read suburban periodical in the nation.

Throughout his life Bailey traveled the world collecting plants, and in 1935 he presented his private herbarium of 125,000 specimens and his library of 2,700 volumes to Cornell as the Bailey Hortorium, a word he coined to describe a place for the botanical study of things of the garden. He continued to botanize until the end of his life, taking at least 68 trips between 1919 and 1951 to China, Mexico, Brazil, the West Indies, and other destinations, logging more than 250,000 miles (400,000 km) and collecting more than 275,000 plants. In his pocket at the time of the injury that ended his travels was a set of one-way tickets to tropical Africa, his next planned destination.

## Biography
Born in South Haven, Michigan, 1858. B.S. in botany, 1882, and M.S., 1886, from Michigan Agricultural College, East Lansing, Michigan (now Michigan State University); worked as assistant to Harvard botanist Asa Gray, 1883–84; professor of horticulture, Michigan Agricultural College, 1884–88; professor of horticulture, Cornell University, Ithaca, New York, 1888–1903; founding editor of *Country Life in America*, 1901–3; dean of the College of Agriculture and director of the Agricultural Experiment Station, Cornell University, 1903–13; appointed chairman of the Commission on Country Life, 1908; founder and director of the Bailey Hortorium, Cornell University, 1935–51. Died in Ithaca, New York, 1954.

## Selected Publications
*The Garden Fence*, 1886
*Cyclopedia of American Horticulture*, 4 vols., 1900–1902; revised edition, as *The Standard Cyclopedia of Horticulture*, 6 vols., 1914–17
*The Nature-Study Idea*, 1903
*Cyclopedia of American Agriculture*, 4 vols., 1907–9 (editor)
*The Country-Life Movement in the United States*, 1911
*The Holy Earth*, 1915
*Manual of Cultivated Plants*, 1924; revised edition, 1949 (editor)
*The Garden Lover*, 1928
*Hortus* (with Ethel Z. Bailey), 1930; revised edition, 1935; new edition, as *Hortus Second*, 1941 (compiler)
"Some Preliminary Studies on the Influence of the Electric Arc Lamp upon Greenhouse Plants," in *Classic Papers in Horticultural Science*, edited by Jules Janick, 1989

## Further Reading
Banks, Harlan P., "Liberty Hyde Bailey: March 15, 1858–December 25, 1954," *Biographical Memoirs* 64 (1994)
Bowers, William L., *The Country Life Movement in America, 1900–1920*, Port Washington, New York: Kennikat Press, 1974
Dorf, Philip, *Liberty Hyde Bailey: An Informal Biography*, Ithaca, New York: Cornell University Press, 1956
Elliott, Charles, "The Pioneer of American Horticulture," *Horticulture* 96, no. 6 (1999)
Fox, Stephen, "Liberty Hyde Bailey: The Earth as Whole, the Earth as Holy," *Orion* 2, no. 4 (Autumn 1983)
Lawrence, George H.M., "Liberty Hyde Bailey, 1858–1954: An Appreciation," *Baileya* 3 (1955)
Rodgers, Andrew Denny, *Liberty Hyde Bailey: A Story of American Plant Sciences*, Princeton, New Jersey: Princeton University Press, 1949
Sarver, Stephanie L., *Uneven Land: Nature and Agriculture in American Writing*, Lincoln: University of Nebraska Press, 1999

Seeley, John G., "Liberty Hyde Bailey: Father of American Horticulture," *HortScience* 25, no. 10 (1990)
Wilcox-Lee, Darlene, "Introduction: L.H. Bailey," in *Classic Papers in Horticultural Science,* edited by Jules Janick, Englewood Cliffs, New Jersey: Prentice Hall, 1989

DANIEL J. PHILIPPON

# Ban Mu Yuan

## Beijing, China

**Location:**  Gongxuan alley in the northeast of Beijing

Ban Mu Yuan, situated in Gongxuan alley at the northeastern corner outside of the Forbidden City, was a private garden noted for its elegant exhibits and complex construction.

Ban Mu Yuan was designed by Li Li-weng in the 17th century to house the owner's (Jia Jiao-hou) rock collection. It was called Ban Mu Yuan (Half-Acre Garden) because of its small scale. Ban Mu Yuan was once designed by well-known rock builders to help their reputation. It was later sold and gradually lost its fame, becoming a storage facility. In 1841 the inspector-general Lin Qing, an admirer of Jia Jiao-Hou's style, restored Ban Mu Yuan. Completed in 1843, it retained its original name. Ban Mu Yuan remained in good condition through the 1960s. It no longer exists, destroyed in 1980 during the Cultural Revolution.

Lying straight north to south, Ban Mu Yuan covered about 0.2 hectares (0.5 acre) and was narrow in shape. The garden was sited to the west of the residential quarter, separated from it by a long and narrow pathway without any door connecting the two. The garden was rich with artificial rock hills and numerous splendid pavilions and halls. The main construction was located at the center of the garden, with the Baishixuan, Puhuage, Jinxienjai, Tuisuting, Shiangquanshi halls and pavilions on both the east and the west sides, connected by roofed walkways. The sophisticated courtyards, rockeries, and halls, all surrounding a central pond, were places of literati entertainment. The garden was famous for its fine workmanship, for its magnificent view of the Forbidden City, and for its elaborate elegance.

Ban Mu Yuan also contained important artworks created by the elite of the society and belonging to the owners of the garden, and these works were displayed systematically. These private art collections, which included valuable antiques, paintings, rare books, and exquisite musical instruments, helped make the garden into a cultural environment.

### Synopsis

| | |
|---|---|
| mid-17th C. | At invitation of Jia Jiao-hou, Qing dynasty vice defense minister, renowned garden designer Li Li-weng designs Ban Mu Yuan |
| 1841 | Lin Qing purchases decayed garden and produces new design for old site |
| 1842 | Garden completed and retained name Ban Mu Yuan |
| 1980 | Garden completely torn down, only residential quarters in east remain intact |

### Further Reading

Chi, Ch'eng, *The Craft of Gardens* (1634), translated by Alison Hardie, New Haven, Connecticut: Yale University Press, 1988
Johnston, R. Stewart, *Scholar Gardens of China: A Study and Analysis of the Spatial Design of the Chinese Private Garden,* Cambridge and New York: Cambridge University Press, 1991
Keswick, Maggie, and Charles Jencks, *The Chinese Garden: History, Art and Architecture,* New York: Rizzoli, and London: Academy Editions, 1978
Liu, Tun-chen, *Su-chou ku tien yüan lin,* Beijing: Chung-kuo chien chu kung yeh ch'u pan she, 1979; as *Chinese Classical Gardens of Suzhou,* translated by Chen Lixian, edited by Joseph C. Wang, New York: McGraw Hill, 1993
Tsu, Frances Ya-Sing, *Landscape Design in Chinese Gardens,* New York: McGraw Hill, 1988
Wang, Joseph Cho, *The Chinese Garden,* Oxford and New York: Oxford University Press, 1998

CHENG LIYAO AND JOSEPH C. WANG
*TRANSLATED BY SYLVIA CHOI*

# Baroque Style

The terms *barocco* (in Portuguese, literally, little stone), *baroque* (French), or *barock* (German) originally meant strange, oblique, or irregularly shaped. In the 16th century, especially, pearls were called baroque if they were irregularly shaped. French classicists termed architecture that was old fashioned and overdone at their time "en style baroque," in a pejorative sense. German art historians established the term as a category of style in the late 19th century. Jakob Burckhardt and Wilhelm Lübke were apparently the first to use the term *der Barock* in this sense in 1855, referring to the often curved, dynamic design of Italian 17th-century architecture, sculpture, and painting. Baroque style was considered to be a style of powerful movement, breaking out from the limits of space. Facades, ceilings, and walls were replaced by curved colonnades, windows, and ornately painted cupolas. In the early 20th century, the term *baroque* was also applied to the music, literature, and garden design of the later 17th and early 18th centuries. Joseph August Lux seems to have been the first to write about the "barocke Gärten" in his booklet *Schöne Gartenkunst* (1907).

Baroque-style gardens developed from Renaissance patterns, in which the outlines of the new style were already appearing. The two final periods of the baroque garden in the first half of 18th century can be termed Regence and rococo. The latter was a transitory style, leading to the landscape garden. The baroque style was replaced in the time of Enlightenment by the period of classicism and sentimental style, or Sturm und Drang (storm and stress), which covers the age of the landscape garden.

Historians outside of Germany hesitated to use the term *baroque* as a style category. Some historians had spoken of a geometric style, but this term covers the preceding Renaissance times as well—axiality and symmetry had already been used in Renaissance gardens. The often-used term *formal gardens* seems less appropriate, because every garden design, even a landscaped one, may be formal.

In France, the term *style Louis XIV* refers to this period. The anglophone world prefers the term *French style*. This term may be well founded because French architecture under the Sun King, Louis XIV, never used undulating lines as did the contemporary Italian school of architects. The French preferred classical, straight, but nevertheless powerful and stretching lines. The French court was regarded as the European center of art development. Therefore *French style* may be a useful term—however, it does not consider the vast Italian and

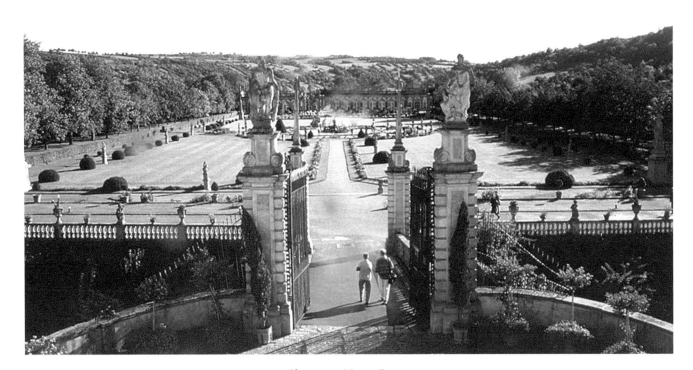

Champs sur Marne, France
Copyright C.A. Wimmer

Dutch influence during the same period. Another term, used mainly in France, the English equivalent of which is *classic style,* is based on some classical sources of this style, but because it can be mistaken for classicism, it should be avoided.

The most famous baroque garden designer was André Le Nôtre, although he had several forerunners, including Claude Mollet and Jacques Boyceau, who developed the style as early as 1600. Le Nôtre also borrowed elements from Italy, such as terraces and the view axes. The Isola Bella in northern Italy, for example, was created in a fully developed baroque style before Le Nôtre's debut as a garden designer. French gardeners and designs were widespread in Europe during the time of Louis XIV, but in some parts of Europe, including southern Germany, Austria, and Bohemia, the Italian influence was immense. This can be seen in the powerfully sculptured stairs and gardens in many northern countries, for example, Gottorf and Großsedlitz in Germany, Belvedere in Vienna, and Powis Castle in Scotland. Unlike their French counterparts, Italian and Dutch garden designers kept characteristic features of the Renaissance garden, such as statues, squares, and enclosures. Therefore, the terms Italian and Dutch gardens were often used as synonyms for the Renaissance garden.

Baroque garden designs are geometric and mostly symmetrical—at least, apparently symmetrical. The *parterre de broderie,* the wide open space, a broad axis into the landscape, and the three-dimensional, symmetrical design of the whole complex, using several levels with highly elaborate optical refinements, can be regarded as essentials of the baroque garden. There were, except in small private gardens, no more restrictions by hedges and walls as in many Renaissance gardens. The formerly used squares were replaced by dynamic oblong forms. Water was used in a more extended way, as in broad channels or tall emerging fountains. The surrounding woodland was connected with the buildings, parterres, and bosquets by using long crossing axes.

The most beloved plants of the baroque garden were limes, elms, hornbeam, horse chestnuts, yew and box for tree architecture, tulips and other bulbs as flowers, and orange trees and other Mediterranean and Cape plants for the greenhouse.

**Further Reading**

Hazlehurst, F. Hamilton, *Jacques Boyceau and the French Formal Garden,* Athens: University of Georgia Press, 1966

Laird, Mark, *The Formal Garden: Traditions of Art and Nature,* New York: Thames and Hudson, 1992

Stammler, Wolfgang, "Barock," in *Reallexikon zur deutschen Kunstgeschichte,* vol. 1, Stuttgart, Germany: Metzler, 1933

Turner, Thomas Leslie, *English Garden Design: History and Styles since 1650,* Woodbridge, Suffolk: Antique Collector's Club, 1986

Wimmer, Clemens Alexander, *Geschichte der Gartentheorie,* Darmstadt, Germany: Wissenschaftliche Buchgesellschaft, 1989

CLEMENS ALEXANDER WIMMER

# Barragán, Luis 1902–1988

## Mexican Architect and Garden Designer

Luis Barragán is best remembered for his contributions to 20th-century Latin-American architecture and landscape architecture. His brilliantly colored walls and poetic spaces are easily recognizable. His landscapes display strong Mediterranean influences incorporated into modern designs. Barragán created walled garden spaces based on Mediterranean ideals as a way to battle the pressures of modern life. People, he thought, were being overwhelmed by the stress that came from fast developing technologies. This provoked a deep concern within him about the well-being of people and the environments they inhabit. Barragán's gardens were sanctu-aries designed to bring the individual's senses back into contact with nature and other humans. His work had a strong, formal presence derived from his personal struggle to blend the variables of poetry, culture, aesthetics, traditions, memory, and materials with an international style as well as with the regional influences of Mexico.

Early in his life, Barragán learned the value of Mexican architectural traditions. Born in Guadalajara, Mexico, he spent most of his childhood on a hacienda developing an appreciation for rural life, popular architecture, horses, ranching, and small towns. Barragán describes his upbringing as a critical stimulant behind his work. It is from these memories of rural landscapes that Barragán derived his understanding of the psychological strengths and possibilities of the garden.

Barragán trained as a civil engineer at the Escuela Libre de Ingenieria de Guadalajara, where he received his degree in 1923. He undertook studies in architecture but failed to complete the exams required to receive his degree. He then decided to travel to Europe. On an initial excursion to Europe in 1924 and during subsequent travel there, Barragán visited Spain, France, Italy, Morocco, and Greece. On his travels he encountered the work of the Modernist French architect Le Corbusier and the French Beaux Arts-trained landscape architect Ferdinand Bac. Le Corbusier and the International Style's modernist theories presented Barragán with a new level of discourse. For example, Barragán would forever debate Le Corbusier's statement that modern architecture was a "machine for living" when working on his own designs. In Bac he found the strong garden design tradition of Mediterraneanism, which Barragán deemed closely akin to his own Hispanic roots. The books *Les Colombières: Ses jardins et ses decors* (1925; The Dove Aviary: Gardens and Descriptions) and *Jardins enchantés: Un romancero* (1925; The Tale of the Enchanted Garden) explain and illustrate Bac's concept of fantasy gardens, rooted in the mythic stories of the Mediterranean. Bac awakened Barragán's passion for gardens and filled him with inspirational thoughts about beauty, magic, and solitude.

The places Barragán visited in Europe would influence him for the rest of his life. Undoubtedly the Mediterranean regions of Europe, and especially Spain's Alhambra and the Generalife, showed Barragán the importance of Islamic garden design. The Alhambra with its compartmentalized garden rooms, bold use of pools and fountains, reddish castle walls, and serene qualities fascinated him. In his 1980 Pritzker Prize speech, he pays tribute to "the esthetic wisdom of the Spanish Moors" for producing what he believed to be the most perfect garden, one that encapsulated "the entire Universe." The Alhambra held within it all the attributes needed in a garden—beauty, serenity, and magic. The Alhambra became the model he aspired to in combating the negative conditions of the early 20th-century architectural environment.

Barragán created his early body of work in Guadalajara, Jalisco. From 1928 to 1935 he began working with elements of Spanish and Islamic design. The 1928 residence of Efrain Gonzalez Luna and the residence of Gustavo R. Cristo are examples of Barragán's exploration into Mediterraneanism. He experimented with arches and columns, textured wall enclosures, the effects of light and shade, the interrelationship of the garden with the architecture, the selection of materials, and the use of water.

In 1935 Barragán moved to Mexico City, where his work matured. He designed residential gardens, the suburban housing developments of Las Arboledas and El Pedregal, the University of Mexico campus grounds, and the Plaza de las Torres Satelite. Through collaborative efforts with other designers such as Andres Casillas and Mathias Goeritz, his designs gained a bold simplicity. He defined volumes of space using walls, color accents, and water that enclosed a person in silence. Through this silence, the spaces stimulated and heightened the senses. Barragán's gardens became places for meditation and living. The individual experienced the elements of sound, light, and air while moving through a series of controlled rooms where Barragán had removed everything that impeded the meditative process. At San Cristobal (the Folke Egerstrom residence), Barragán designed a house, pool, and stable complex held together by a series of walls. The walls vary in size and color to suit separate functions. Barragán's spaces at San Cristobal are animated with the sounds of horses, riders, and water; the visual play of the water; and the changing light and shadows.

At El Pedregal, an existing lava site outside Mexico City, Barragán planned a suburban housing development that exhibited a harmonious contrast between architectural elements and the landscape. He developed this contrast by integrating roads, buildings, fountains, and sculpture into the topography, vegetation, and textures of the rocky volcanic surroundings. He embraced the lava landforms and harmonized his man-made forms around them. Barragán had studied the volcanic landscape and geology by taking long walks with Dr. Atl (Gerardo V. Murillo), a noted Mexican landscape painter, who gave Barragán an awareness of the local soil, colors, history, indigenous trees, and scrub plants.

In 1976 the Museum of Modern Art in New York sponsored an exhibition that catapulted the 74-year-old architect into the international spotlight. The exhibition highlighted most of his architecturally significant works from 1945 to 1968. Photographer Armando Salas Portugal captured the special qualities in Barragán's works in a series of powerful images. The museum also published the book *The Architecture of Louis Barragán*, which combines the photographs with an essay by the architect Emilio Ambasz. The exhibition and book introduced the public to Barragán's boldly colored walled gardens and surrealistic spaces such as had only been imagined in paintings. These works show Barragán's own regional influences, sensitivity to natural context, and poetic design program. They clearly reflect his desire to incorporate historical, cultural, and ideological influences within the landscape garden.

## Biography

Born in Guadalajara, Jalisco, Mexico, 1902. Grew up on hacienda and learned traditional architecture of Mexico; entered Escuela Libre de Ingenieros in

Guadalajara to study engineering, 1919; also enrolled in architecture program but failed to complete final examinations officially recognizing him as an architect; traveled to Europe, 1924–25, then returned to Guadalajara to undertake first commissions and establish himself; moved to Mexico City, 1936; retired from architecture and decided to design gardens, 1940–44; developed Gardens of the Pedregal; designed Arboledas, Plaza de las Torres Satelite, Casa Folke Egerstrom, Casa Francisco Gilardi, 1945–78; exhibition of photographs of his architecture and gardens at Museum of Modern Art, New York City, 1976; received Pritzker Prize, 1980. Died in Mexico City, 1988.

## Selected Designs

| | |
|---|---|
| 1928 | Casa Efrain Gonzalez Luna, Guadalajara, Jalisco, Mexico |
| 1929 | Casa Gustavo R. Cristo, Guadalajara, Jalisco, Mexico |
| 1929 | Casa Ildefonso Franco, Guadalajara, Jalisco, Mexico |
| 1935 | Parque de la Revolucion, Guadalajara, Jalisco, Mexico |
| 1936–40 | Various apartments in Mexico City, Mexico |
| 1940–43 | Ortega House, on Calle Francisco Ramirez, and four private gardens, on Avenida Constituyentes, Mexico City, Mexico |
| 1945–50 | Jardines del Pedregal, San Angel, Mexico City, Mexico |
| 1947 | Luis Barragán residence and studio, Tacubaya, Mexico City, Mexico |
| 1950 | Casa Eduardo Prieto Lopez, Jardins del Pedregal de San Angel, Mexico City, Mexico |
| 1949–54 | Ciudad Universitaria, Mexico City, Mexico |
| 1952–55 | Convento de las Capuchinas, Tlalpan, Mexico City, Mexico |
| 1955 | Casa Antonio Galvez, San Angel, Mexico City, Mexico |
| 1957 | Torres de la Ciudad Satelite (with sculptor Mathias Goeritz), Highway to Queretaro, Mexico City, Mexico |
| 1958–59 | Plaza y Fuente del Bebedero and the Muro Rojo, Las Arboledas, Mexico City, Mexico |
| 1958–61 | Las Arboledas, Mexico City, Mexico |
| 1963–64 | Los Clubes, general planning, Mexico City, Mexico |
| 1964 | Fuente de los Amantes, Los Clubes, Mexico City, Mexico |
| 1967–68 | Cuadra San Cristobal and Casa Folke Egerstrom (collaboration with architect Andrés Casillas), Los Clubes, Mexico City, Mexico |
| 1976 | Casa Francisco Gilardi, Tacubaya, Mexico City, Mexico |
| 1980–82 | Lighthouse of Business, Monterrey, Nuevo Leon, Mexico |

## Selected Publications

*1980 Pritzker Prize Acceptance Speech, June 3, 1980,* S.l.: Hyatt Foundation, 1980

## Further Reading

Ambasz, Emilio, *The Architecture of Luis Barragán,* New York: Museum of Modern Art, 1976

Ambasz, Emilio, and Yukio Futogawa, "Luis Barragán," *GA Global Architecture* 48 (1979)

*Artes de México* 23 (March–April 1994) (special issue entitled "En el Mundo de Luis Barragán")

Buendía, Júlbez, Jose Maria, Juan Palomer, and Guillermo Eguiarte, *The Life and Work of Luis Barragán,* translated by Margaret E. Brooks, New York: Rizzoli, 1997

Kirby, Rosina Greene, *Mexican Landscape Architecture,* Tucson: University of Arizona Press, 1972

*Luis Barragán Morfín, 1902–1988* (exhib. cat.), Sevilla: Conejeria de Obras Publicas y Transportes, 1989

Martínez, Antonio Riggen, *Luis Barragán (1902–1988),* Milan: Electa; as *Luis Barragán: Mexico's Modern Master, 1902–1988,* translated by Christina Bennett, New York: Monacelli Press, 1996

Salas Portugal, Armando, *Barragán: Photographs of the Architecture of Luis Barragán,* New York: Rizzoli, 1992

San Martin, Ignacio, editor, *Luis Barragán: The Phoenix Papers,* Tempe, Arizona: Center for Latin American Studies Press in collaboration with Herberger Center for Design Excellence, Arizona State University, 1997

Smith, Clive Bamford, *Builders in the Sun: Five Mexican Architects,* New York: Architectural Book, 1967

FERNANDO MAGALLANES

# Barth, Erwin 1880–1933

## German Landscape Architect

Erwin Barth was an outstanding personality among the landscape architects of the first third of the 20th century in Germany. He learned gardening in his hometown of Lübeck and worked as a journeyman in one of the large tree nurseries that were being established at the beginning of the 20th century in the city of Elmshorn, some 30 miles (approximately 50 km) north of Hamburg. He graduated from the royal horticultural school for gardening (Königliche Gärtnerlehranstalt) at Wildpark-Potsdam in 1902 and took another exam there as head gardener in 1906. Barth enlarged his professional knowledge in the municipal parks department in Hannover, Lower Saxony, which was headed by the outstanding Julius Trip, who in those days took a very active part in reshaping the Verein deutscher Gartenkünstler (Association of German Garden Artists), the first professional organization of landscape architects in Germany, which had been founded in 1887. Barth also worked with free-lance landscape architects such as Reinhold Hoemann in Düsseldorf and Ernst Finken in Cologne-Rodenkirchen before serving as chief of the municipal parks department in Lübeck, Schleswig-Holstein, from 1908 to 1911. His most famous work from that period was the design for the open space along the Marlistrasse in Lübeck, where he created a number of vantage points from which visitors could enjoy picturesque views of the city. Barth wanted to highlight and frame by means of plants and architecture the best views of Lübeck, as he wrote in the journal *Die Gartenkunst* (*Garden Art*) in 1908.

From 1912 to 1925 Barth was head of the municipal parks department in the city of Charlottenburg, which became incorporated into Berlin in 1920. In this post Barth—who had been awarded a gold medal for his work as garden artist at the jubilee exhibition in Mannheim in 1907 and who had in 1914 received an honorary diploma and a golden medal for his contribution to the horticultural exhibition in Altona near Hamburg—created a series of outstanding public spaces in the densely populated city. These urban spaces, such as Brixplatz, Karolingerplatz, and many others, offer exemplary open-space design solutions that not only feature convincing spatial arrangements but also testify to Barth's interest in serving the social needs of the local residents. On Brixplatz (formerly Sachsenplatz), for example, Barth wanted to show city-dwellers the various kinds of natural plant associations that could be found in the areas around Berlin, such as heath, dune, swamp, and deciduous and conifer forest formation. A plan was developed in 1912, but the former quarry was not turned into Sachsenplatz (later Brixplatz) until after World War I. Although Barth claimed Sachsenplatz to be a people's park, it had none of the many facilities characteristic of such parks and was accessible only via a single circular path that allowed visitors to view the various plant formations. As a result of public pressure in the late 20th century, the maintenance paths had to be opened to visitors, a measure that threatened the survival of some of the park's more sensitive plants.

In 1921 Barth won the competition for the cemetery in the woods in Berlin-Wilmersdorf (Waldfriedhof Wilmersdorf), a further proof of his unique design skills. Whereas the city places are relatively small open spaces primarily serving residents of the surrounding neighborhood, people's parks are large open spaces that attract visitors from an entire region. Barth excelled with his designs for the people's park Jungfernheide (Virgin's Heath) in Charlottenburg, which he started in 1922, and Rehberge (Deer Mountains) in Berlin-Wedding, which was originally designed by Rudolf Germer, the head of the parks department of the borough of Wedding in Berlin in 1922 but seems to have been redesigned by Barth before the plan was finally accepted in 1927. For the Jungfernheide Barth took the people's park in Hamburg as a model. The influence of the designs for Central Park in New York City and Franklin Park in Boston, both by Frederick Law Olmsted, also seems likely. The wading pools (*Planschbecken*) in particular seem to be a feature adapted from American park design. Barth popularized wading pools in Berlin, incorporating them when such city places as Arkonaplatz (1926), Boxhagener Platz (1929), Traveplatz (1929), and others were redesigned. The only one of these pools that can still be seen is in the people's park Jungfernheide.

Barth frequently traveled in the Mediterranean. From 1926 to 1929 he was head of the parks department of Great-Berlin, a new political and administrative unit that had been formed in 1920 and that included a number of communities adjacent to Berlin. Since Barth had thus risen above the borough level, he felt he should review all designs for open spaces in all of Berlin and consequently ran into considerable trouble with the heads of the parks departments of the Berlin boroughs.

The years of the Weimar Republic from 1919 to 1933, when Germany was governed by a democratic constitution for the first time in her history, were essential for the establishment of a university curriculum for landscape architecture. Since 1920 Barth had served as docent and in 1927 had become honorary professor for garden art at the faculty of architecture at the Technical University Charlottenburg in Berlin. After a tough debate in professional circles in the late 1920s over whether landscape architecture should become a university discipline, the first chair for garden art was established at the Agricultural University, Berlin, and given to Barth in September 1929. The first courses actually started in 1930. Barth eagerly grasped this opportunity to teach garden art at the university level. He had a clear perspective on urban if not metropolitan open-space issues. In 1931, well in advance of the creation of pedestrian zones in inner-city commercial and residential areas in the 1970s, Barth developed a scheme for reducing automobile traffic and establishing playgrounds, a wading pool, and lawn areas for streets surrounding a residential block in Berlin-Charlottenburg. Around this time, however, the shadows of National Socialism began to darken Barth's career. National Socialist students disturbed his lectures, and fellow teachers who had joined the movement withdrew their support for him. As if this were not enough, he began to develop vision problems and feared he would lose his sight. These fears ultimately led him to commit suicide in July 1933, only a few months after the National Socialist takeover in January 1933. In 1934 he was succeeded by Heinrich Friedrich Wiepking-Jürgensmann.

## Biography

Born in Lübeck, Germany, 1880. Apprenticeship in gardening enterprise of Philipp Paulig in Lübeck, 1897–99, and tree nursery of J. Timm in Elmshorn, 1899–1900; attended Königliche Gärtnerlehranstalt Wildpark-Potsdam, 1900–1902, and took head gardener exam there, 1906; worked with municipal parks departments in Hannover, 1902, and Bremen, 1902–3, and with private landscape architects Reinhold Hoemann in Düsseldorf, 1904–5, and Ernst Finken in Cologne-Rodenkirchen, 1906–8; head of municipal park administration in Lübeck, 1908–11; awarded gold medal for work as garden artist at jubilee exhibition in Mannheim, 1907, and received honorary diploma and golden medal for contribution to horticultural exhibition in Altona, 1914; head of municipal parks administration in Berlin-Charlottenburg, 1912–25; head of parks department of Great-Berlin, 1926–29; first professor of newly established chair for garden art at Agricultural University Berlin, Germany, 1929–33; member of Verein deutscher Gartenkünstler, Deutsche Gesellschaft für Gartenkunst, Deutsche Dendrologische Gesellschaft, Reichsausschuß für Leibesübungen, and Volksbund Deutsche Kriegsgräberfürsorge. Died in 1933.

## Selected Designs

1908–11  Buniamshof playground, site at Marlistreet, Lübeck, Germany; Hansa place, Lübeck, Germany; urn grove at Vorwerk cemetery Lübeck, Germany; country estate Lindenhof between Warnsdorf near Travemünde and lake Hemmelsdorf, for the German-American Arthur Donner

1912–25  Goslarer Platz, Berlin-Charlottenburg, Germany; Gustav-Adolf-Platz (Mierendorff Platz), Berlin-Charlottenburg, Germany; Karolingerplatz, Berlin-Charlottenburg, Germany; Dernburgplatz, Berlin-Charlottenburg, Germany; Sachsenplatz (Brixplatz), Berlin-Charlottenburg, Germany; Savignyplatz, Berlin-Charlottenburg, Germany; Scholzplatz, Berlin-Charlottenburg, Germany; Teutoburger Platz, Berlin-Charlottenburg, Germany; Schustehruspark, Berlin-Charlottenburg, Germany; Wittenbergplatz, Berlin-Charlottenburg, Germany; site along the western shore of Lietzensee, Berlin-Charlottenburg, Germany; park enlargement at the municipal hospital Westend, Berlin-Charlottenburg, Germany; people's park Jungfernheide, Berlin-Charlottenburg, Germany; allotment garden sites Masurenallee, Berlin-Charlottenburg, Germany

1926–29  People's park Köpenick, Berlin, Germany; Lilienthalpark, Berlin, Germany; people's park Rehberge, Berlin, Germany; people's park Wuhlheide, Berlin, Germany; Luisenstädtischer Kanal, Berlin, Germany; allotment garden site Bleichröder, Berlin, Germany; central cemetery Lichterfelde, Berlin, Germany; Reichskanzlerplatz (Theodor-Heuss-Platz), Berlin, Germany

1929–33  Park around the "Holstentor" (Holsten Gate) in Lübeck, Germany; cemetery and Bismarckplatz and Schraderplatz in Stolp, Pomerania; private parks and gardens in various locations in Germany, including Bergisch-Gladbach, Lübeck, and Berlin

## Selected Publications

"Studie zu einer Villenkolonie," *Gartenkunst* 9 (1907)

"Der Vorwerker Friedhof zu Lübeck," *Gartenkunst* 10 (1908)

"Gartenkünstlerische Gestaltung eines Platzes auf Marly zu Lübeck," *Gartenkunst* 10 (1908)

"Charlottenburger neue Stadtplätze," *Gartenkunst* 15 (1913)
"Der Spielplatz auf Buniamshof in Lübeck," *Gartenkunst* 27 (1914)
"Der Schustehruspark," *Gartenkunst* 32 (1919)
"Ausbildung der Gartenarchitekten an Kunsthochschulen," *Gartenkunst* 33 (1920)
"Der Lietzenseepark in Charlottenburg," *Gartenkunst* 34 (1921)
"Entwurf für einen in Stahnsdorf gelegenen Friedhof der Gemeinde Berlin-Wilmersdorf," *Gartenwelt* 25 (1921)
"Volksparke, Spiel- und Sportplätze," *Gartenwelt* 27 (1923)
"Zwei Platzgestaltungen in Charlottenburg," *Gartenkunst* 37 (1924)
"Gartentheater nach griechischer Art," *Gartenwelt* 29 (1925)
"Berlins Park- und Gartenanlagen," in *Das neue Berlin,* 1929
"Die hochschulmäßige Ausbildung des Gartenarchitekten," *Der deutsche Gartenarchitekt* 7 (1930)
"Eine Gestaltungsmöglichkeit des Reichskanzlerplatzes zu Charlottenburg, Gartenterrassen auf unterirdischen Hallen," *Die Form* (1931)
"Die Entwicklung der Gartenkunst aus der Landwirtschaft," in *Wissenschaft und Landwirtschaft,* 1931
"Die brandenburgische Heimat im Volkspark," *Velhagen und Klasings Monatshefte* 45 (1931)

**Further Reading**

Gröning, Gert, and Joachim Wolschke-Bulmahn, *DGGL, Deutsche Gesellschaft für Gartenkunst und Landschaftspflege e.V.: 1887–1987, ein Rückblick auf 100 Jahre DGGL,* Berlin: Boskett, 1987
Gröning, Gert, and Joachim Wolschke-Bulmahn, *Grüne Biographien: Biographisches Handbuch zur Landschaftsarchitektur des 20. Jahrhunderts in Deutschland,* Berlin: Patzer, 1997
Heicke, Carl, "Urnenhaine," *Gartenkunst* 12 (1910)
Radicke, Dieter, editor, *Erwin Barth, Gärten, Parks, Friedhöfe* (exhib. cat.), Berlin: Universitätsbibliothek, Technische Universität Berlin, 1980
Stürmer, Rainer, "Erwin Barth (1880–1933): Sein Wirken für Berlins Grünanlagen," *Jahrbuch für brandenburgische Geschichte* 34 (1983)
Weber, Klaus Konrad, editor, *Berlin und seine Bauten,* Berlin: Ernst, 1964– ; see especially vol. 11, *Gartenwesen,* 1972

GERT GRÖNING

# Bartram Family

## United States Botanists

John Bartram was the world's greatest "natural botanist" according to Linnaeus, his contemporary. Bartram began planting his eight-acre (3.2 ha) plot in about 1730; located on the west bank of the Schuylkill River at Kingsessing (now a part of Philadelphia), it was not the first botanical garden in the American colonies, but it was the most important one. For more than a century, through his efforts and those of his heirs and successors, it served as the central depot for the exchange of plants between the new world and the old.

There is some disparity in stories about the origin of John Bartram's fascination with plants. The best-known account comes from Crèvecoeur's "Letter XI" in *Letters from an American Farmer,* in which Bartram tells of having laid aside his plow to rest in the shade, where he idly picked a daisy. Looking at its intricate form, he realized that he had been "employed so many years in tilling the earth and destroying so many flowers and plants, without being acquainted with their structures and their uses" and therefore resolved to teach himself botany. Tutored by a local schoolmaster, he learned enough Latin to be able to read Linnaeus. A less homiletic account is that by Bartram's son William, who reported that his father had been interested in plants from about age ten and was encouraged to take up the study of botany by John Parkinson's *Herbal* (1640), a book he received as a gift. In any event, John Bartram was self-trained.

On 102 acres (41.3 ha) bought at a 1728 sheriff's sale, Bartram constructed a dwelling by expanding and modifying a small cottage on the property. This house, placed on the National Register of Historic Places in 1966, served as home for the Bartrams as long as the family controlled the garden. Both Benjamin Franklin and George Washington were visitors there during John Bartram's lifetime, and in 1787 the entire Constitutional

Convention convened at the garden to see the plant treasures the Bartrams had collected. By that time the garden struck Washington as not having been "laid out with much taste," for neither John Bartram nor his son William had any interest in the design elements associated with horticultural art. As systematic botanists and successful seedsmen, their interests were pragmatic; they planted their specimens in straight rows, taking advantage of the various soils afforded by the sloping plot.

Through correspondence John Bartram became acquainted with a fellow Quaker in England, Peter Collinson, and though the two never met in person, this relationship became the nexus for a remarkable exchange. Through their extant letters we know that trees such as the sugar maple and shrubs such as the witch hazel were introduced in England by Collinson from seeds sent to him by Bartram. Bartram also sent novelties such as the skunk cabbage and the Venus flytrap. Moreover, since Collinson shared his American exotics with others, it has been estimated that during the period he and Bartram were collaborating, Bartram probably was responsible for providing as many as 200 new plants in English gardens. Plant materials also traveled in the other direction. In addition to fruit trees, Collinson sent Bartram many ornamentals, including lilies, tulips, roses, and 20 varieties of crocus. Collinson, with other wealthy friends, also subscribed funds to finance Bartram's collecting trips and, in 1765, he secured Bartram's appointment as Royal Botanist to King George III.

Bartram began his plant-hunting travels by exploring the sources of the Schuylkill River in 1736. During the next year he traveled in Delaware; in 1738 he went to Virginia; and yet another trip took him through New Jersey, probably in 1740. He visited the Catskills in 1742, then returned again to New York State and Pennsylvania in 1743–44, the expedition that resulted in his first notable publication, *Observations on the Inhabitants, Climate, Soil... Made by Mr. John Bartram, in His Travels from Pensilvania [sic] . . . to Lake Ontario.* On these journeys Bartram also collected faunal and mineral specimens of interest to his European sponsors. It was possible for him to be away so often because his farm was ably managed by loyal black workmen whom he had freed, paid a decent wage, and who ate at the same table with him and his family.

Meanwhile, his son William had developed a talent for drawing natural objects. The fifth of the nine children born to John and his second wife Ann, William began to travel with his father at age 14. His first trip was to the Catskills in 1753, followed by Connecticut in 1755, and then a longer trip to South Carolina, Georgia, and Florida in 1765–66. William also became the beneficiary of English patronage. Some of his drawings sent by his father to Collinson were passed on to another Quaker botanist, Dr. John Fothergill. It was Fothergill's money that financed William Bartram's major expedition, his lengthy 1773–77 exploration of the southeastern United States that resulted in his remarkable *Travels* (1791), a book that stimulated the imagination of a generation of English romantic poets.

Never successful in his business ventures and unmarried, William stayed on in the Bartram garden after its management passed to his brother John, Jr., who lived only until 1812. Thereafter management passed to William's niece Ann Carr (1779–1858) and her husband Robert Carr. With William's continued help, the garden became a thriving commercial nursery. Its *Catalogue of American Trees, Shrubs and Herbacious Plants*, a broadside issued in 1783, is the earliest American seed list.

John Bartram Carr (1805–39), Ann's stepson and a capable botanist, was the last of the family involved with the garden. In 1850 its ownership passed to a rich industrialist, Andrew M. Eastwick, who so revered the Bartram tradition that he decreed not "a solitary branch" should be cut in the garden. Finally in 1891, through the efforts of Thomas Meehan, who had been Eastwick's gardener, the property was acquired by Philadelphia's park system.

At the peak of their success, the Bartrams were propagating more than 4,000 species. The southern expeditions of both John and William Bartram resulted in rich hauls of plants hitherto unknown in Philadelphia. Situated where hardiness zones 6 and 7 meet, this location proved to be an excellent place to naturalize them. The most famous of these plant discoveries was undoubtedly the Franklin tree (*Franklinia alatamaha*), found in Georgia in 1765 and last seen wild in 1803; all living specimens of this ornamental shrub have descended from those propagated at Bartram's garden.

Today the garden still contains a few plants known to date back to John Bartram's time. Though not introduced by him, one is a male *Ginkgo biloba*. One of the oldest is a yellowwood (*Cladrastis kentuckea*) believed to be the gift of André Michaux in the 1790s, well before it was named by Rafinesque in 1822. The once famous bald cypress (*Taxodium distichum*) no longer survives, but the Bartram oak (*Quercus heterophylla*), a naturally occurring hybrid discovered on the farm itself, does remain. It is an appropriate reminder of the garden's creator, since John Bartram was among the earliest Americans to study hybridity.

## Bartram, John 1699–1777

### Biography

Born near Darby, Pennsylvania, 1699. Began farming land inherited from his uncle, but in 1728 purchased a plot at Kingsessing, on the Schuylkill River, where he laid out a botanical garden; began plant exchange with the Englishman Peter Collinson, ca. 1733; traveled in Virginia, 1738; to the Catskills with son William, 1753; visited the Carolinas, 1760, the Ohio River and western Virginia, 1761, and South Carolina, Georgia, and Florida with William, 1765, the year he was appointed Botanist to King George III. Died in Kingsessing (now Philadelphia), Pennsylvania, 1777.

## Selected Publications

*Observations on the Inhabitants, Climate, Soil . . . Made by Mr. John Bartram, in His Travels from Pensilvania [sic] . . . to Lake Ontario*, 1751
*Description of East Florida, with a Journal by John Bartram*, 1769
*Diary of a Journey through the Carolinas, Georgia, and Florida . . .* , 1942

# Bartram, William 1739–1823

## Biography

Born at Kingsessing (now part of Philadelphia), 1739. Unsuccessful as a merchant in North Carolina; accompanied his father to Florida, 1765, and tried farming there, at which he was also unsuccessful; with funds supplied by John Fothergill in England, explored the southeastern United States, 1773–78, resulting in his one famous book, *Travels*, 1791; until his death, lived at the botanical garden established by his father. Died Kingsessing (now Philadelphia), 1823.

## Selected Publications

*Travels through North and South Carolina, Georgia, East and West Florida . . . together with Observations on the Manners of the Indians*, 1791

## Further Reading

Barnhart, John Hendley, "Significance of John Bartram's Work to Botanical and Horticultural Knowledge," *Bartonia* (1931)
Bartram, John, *Diary of a Journey through the Carolinas, Georgia and Florida: From July 1, 1765 to April 10, 1766*, annotated by Francis Harper, Philadelphia: American Philosophical Society, 1942
Bartram, John, *John and William Bartram's America*, edited by Helen Gere Cruickshank, New York: Devin-Adair, 1957
Bartram, John, *The Correspondence of John Bartram*, edited by Edmund Berkeley and Dorothy Smith Berkeley, Gainesville: University Press of Florida, 1992
Bartram, William, *Travels through North and South Carolina, Georgia, East and West Florida, the Cherokee Country, the Extensive Territories of the Muscogulges, or Creek Confederacy, and the Country of the Chactaws*, Philadelphia, Pennsylvania, 1791; London, 1792; reprint, New York: Library of America, 1996
Bartram, William, *Botanical and Zoological Drawings, 1756–1788*, edited by Joseph Ewan, Philadelphia, Pennsylvania: American Philosophical Society, 1968
Berkeley, Edmund, and Dorothy Smith Berkeley, *The Life and Travels of John Bartram*, Tallahassee: University Presses of Florida, 1982
Brett-James, Norman George, *The Life of Peter Collinson*, London: Dunstan, 1926
Cappon, Lester J., "Retracing and Mapping the Bartrams' Southern Travels," *Proceedings of the American Philosophical Society* 118, no. 6 (1974)
Clarke, Larry R., "The Quaker Background of William Bartram's View of Nature," *Journal of the History of Ideas* 46 (1985)
Coleridge, Ernest Hartley, "Coleridge, Wordsworth, and the American Botanist William Bartram," *Transactions of the Royal Society of Literature* 2nd ser. 27, no. 5 (1907)
Darlingon, William, *Memorials of John Bartram and Humphry Marshall*, Philadelphia, Pennsylvania: Lindsay and Blakiston, 1849; reprint, with a new introduction by Joseph Ewan, New York: Hafner, 1967
Earnest, Ernest Penney, *John and William Bartram, Botanists and Explorers, 1699–1777, 1739–1823*, Philadelphia: University of Pennsylvania Press, 1940
Fagin, Nathan Bryllion, *William Bartram, Interpreter of the American Landscape*, Baltimore, Maryland: Johns Hopkins Press, 1933
Fox, R. Hingston, *Dr. John Fothergill and His Friends; Chapters in Eighteenth Century Life*, London: Macmillan, 1919
Fry, Joel T., "John Bartram Carr, the Unknown Bartram," *Bartram Broadside* (1994)
Harshberger, John William, *The Botanists of Philadelphia and Their Work*, Philadelphia, Pennsylvania: Davis, 1899
Herbst, Josephine, *New Green World*, New York: Hastings House, and London: Weidenfeld and Nicolson, 1954
Klein, William M., Jr., *Gardens of Philadelphia and the Delaware Valley*, Philadelphia, Pennsylvania: Temple University Press, 1995
St. John de Crèvecoeur, J. Hector, *Letters from an American Farmer*, London: Thomas Davies and Lockyer Davis, 1782; reprint, Oxford and New York: Oxford University Press, 1997

Slaughter, Thomas P., *The Natures of John and William Bartram*, New York: Knopf, 1996
Walters, Kerry S., "The Creator's Boundless Palace: William Bartram's Philosophy of Nature,"

*Transactions of the Charles S. Peirce Society* 25, no. 3 (1989)

CHARLES BOEWE

# Beaton, Donald 1802–1863

## Scottish Gardener and Horticultural Writer

Donald Beaton developed his early botanical interests into a career as a gardener after it became clear that, because of both financial and academic limitations (he had difficulty learning English after a Gaelic upbringing), he was not to attend university. In his own words, "[while] I expected everyday to be made a gentleman . . . I began to think seriously of being a gardener instead." Following early employment and training in Scotland, Beaton moved south to England and worked in several established gardens and nurseries during the 1830s, a period of great horticultural discovery and scientific invention.

During the 1840s Beaton was head gardener at Shrubland Park, Suffolk, where he became known for his flower gardening. He had an important influence on the establishment of the bedding system, in particular the practice of "bedding out" tender plants during the warmer months. At this time the debate in the art world over the proper use of color was extending into the world of the flower garden. Beaton advocated the use of a restricted range of highly colored hybridized plants, primarily *Pelargonium, Petunia, Salvia, Calceolaria, Verbena,* and *Lobelia*. These were to be arranged according to a color scheme that took into account the perceived colors of the plants at different times of the day and in varying weather conditions. Beaton also argued for "central neutrality," an arrangement whereby the central parts of a display were subdued colors and bright colors remained on the periphery. This scheme was intended to increase the apparent size of a display by drawing the eye outward from the center.

During the 1850s Beaton was involved in a controversy with John Lindley, assistant secretary of the Horticultural Society of London (later the Royal Horticultural Society). Lindley proposed that plants should be grouped according to the notion of complementary, harmonious colors, a scheme based on the principles of the French research chemist Michel-Eugène Chevreul. This proposal was strongly opposed by Beaton, who believed that the "ground" color provided by the green leaves of a bedding display canceled the effect of complementary colors. Trials using graded sequences of "warm" and "cold" colors in flower beds at Hampton Court and the Horticultural Society's garden at Chiswick supported Beaton's views, and Lindley eventually abandoned the theory of complementary colors.

Throughout most of his professional life Beaton was an entertaining and prolific writer, contributing to gardening journals such as *The Gardener's Magazine, The Gardeners' Chronicle,* and *The Cottage Gardener and Country Gentleman's Companion*. His writings were primarily concerned with the flower garden, but he also wrote controversial articles on gardens and nurseries he had visited and on the exhibitions and policies of the Horticultural Society. Beaton left Shrubland Park when Sir Charles Barry was redesigning its gardens along Italianate lines, obliterating all of Beaton's work except a maze, which still exists. Beaton retired to Surbiton, Surrey, at the age of 50, where he continued to write journal articles and undertake horticultural experiments, producing many new pelargonium hybrids. He was offered the use of the grounds of Grove House, Surbiton, for his experimental garden and published his findings in *The Cottage Gardener* until 1862, when he suffered his first stroke. He died after a second stroke in 1863. His last article, published posthumously, was a continuation of a plant breeding debate with Charles Darwin, who referred to Beaton as "a clever but damned cocksure man" (Darwin).

*See also* Bed and Bedding System; Color

**Biography**

Born in Urray, Ross-shire, Scotland, 8 March 1802. Early work as gardener at Beaufort Castle, Altyre (near Forres), nursery of Messrs. Dickson and Turnbull in Perth, and Caledonian Horticultural Society, Edinburgh, early 1820s; moved to London to work at Clapton Nursery, late 1820s; worked at Haffield House, began plant breeding and writing for horticultural journals, became head gardener at Shrubland Park, Ipswich, Suffolk, early 1830s; retired to Surbiton, Surrey, 1852. A regular contributor to *The Cottage Gardener*, 1848–62. Died at Surbiton, October 1863.

## Selected Publication

"My Autobiography," *Cottage Gardener* 8, no. 322 (1854)

Numerous articles for the journals *Gardiner's Magazine, Gardeners' Chronicle, Cottage Gardener,* and *Country Gentleman's Companion*

## Further Reading

Beaton, Donald, "My Autobiography," *The Cottage Gardener* 8, no. 322 (1855)

Darwin, Charles, *More Letters of Charles Darwin*, 2 vols., edited by Francis Darwin and A.C. Seward, London: John Murray, and New York: Appleton, 1903; see especially vol. 2

Elliott, Brent, *Victorian Gardens*, London: Batsford, 1986

Elliott, Brent, "Donald Beaton: The Greatest Gardening Journalist of the Early 19th Century?" *The Garden* 116 (1991)

BARBARA SIMMS

# Bed and Bedding System

The classical plant bed is an elevated piece of earth between wooden edges or lower plant rows. Authors from antiquity describe the manners of edgings and the width of beds and paths for best weeding. Few alterations to the classical bed type seem to have been made in the Middle Ages.

In the Renaissance the contours of the beds became more sophisticated to construct geometric parterre patterns (see, for example, the books by Francesco Colonna [1499], Charles Estienne [1564], Johann Peschel [1597], William Lawson [1618], Daniel Loris [1629]). Olivier de Serres (1600) recommends putting colored gravel on the surface to enhance the ornamental shapes.

After Jacques Boyceau (1638) the beds became mere ornaments, filled with gravel instead of flowers. This form of bed was later called *broderie* (embroidery, *Laubwerk*) and was generally bordered by dwarf box. Each element of *broderie* had its own French term: The connecting parts formed *quarreaux* or *tableaux* and were bordered with *bordures* (hedges) of one taller plant species (during the Renaissance), dwarf box (after ca. 1590), and finally with *plates-bandes* (borders). By this time flowers were now planted in *plates-bandes*. Bulbs and perennials were arranged in a grid manner, each plant neighbored by another species and another color, the tallest in the middle and the lower ones on the side rows. Topiaries, flowering shrubs, or plants in tubs or vases might be included in the middle. The general planting system of the baroque period was a regular mixture (*heureux mélange*). Flower beds during this period survived in the secret garden hidden by walls. So-called *pièces coupées* contained flowers between box *bordures* as formerly in the Renaissance parterre.

The rococo period had a special love for such flower beds and replaced them in the main parterre. Flower enthusiasts such as John Spencer and William Gilpin created new flower gardens in mid-18th-century England. As was usual in the baroque border, the flowers were mixed together, planted in grids, and arranged by height and color, but elevated shrubs were excluded. Some flower beds during this time found their way from the flower garden to the landscape garden, sparingly scattered around the house near the paths (e.g., the gardens of Humphry Repton). This well-known bed type laying in the turf did not arise before 1760. Round beds were planted in concentric circles or snake lines. Depending on the growth habit of the species, the beds were planted with up to ten specimens. Repetition of species was permitted only on the margin. The aim of such a bed was to display different aspects of flowering and color during the four seasons. As N. Swinden noted in 1778, the more diversified the colors, the more agreeable and pleasant the appearance.

The *mixed* or *mingled manner* goes back to the early 19th century. Beginning in 1804 the young John Claudius Loudon fought for a so-called *select* or *grouped manner*, consisting of the display of one genus, species, or variety in each bed in order to produce a powerful effect. The aim was to highlight one single florist's flower (e.g., hyacinth, tulip, carnation, auricula, dahlia, peony, chrysanthemum, bog-earth plants, etc.) and its form and character. Loudon described this manner in 1822, as it was then established along with the mingled manner. Each flower bed was singularly laid out on the lawn and filled with one species, sometimes with one or two circle borders of a contrasting species. The outline was round or elliptic.

From this point two developments arose. One variation consisted of several beds coming together to form ornaments interspaced with lawn (Loudon). The other variation was to divide one bed into several color segments.

The phenomenon of combining several beds, each of one color, first took place around 1820. The outline of the single bed became more ornamental, producing figures such as a rosette, palmette, trefoil, star, or heraldic flower. Repton's design for Ashridge (1813) is a forerunner of this bed type. Peter Lenné, after a visit to Eaton Hall in England, used these forms at the New Palace Parterre at Potsdam in 1822. Loudon published many such bed patterns beginning in 1830. His followers practiced them up to Victorian times, as Lenné's followers did in Germany up to about 1900. The bed itself could be bordered by willow slips, terracotta tiles, concrete, or cast-iron forms, rising three to four inches above the lawn. Sometimes box was still used. Both concentric and nonconcentric patterns were used. In 1839 Wilhelm Legeler, a pupil of Lenné, published some concentric bed patterns (see Plate 5), which Charles M'Intosh copied in 1853. Characteristic for this type were small lines of lawn between the bed segments. Although a general accepted term for this bed type is lacking, it has been called a *figure bed* (Ernst Levy [1892]) or *pattern bed* (George Eyles [1877]).

In these beds the colors were usually combined according to the color theories of Goethe (1810) and of Michel-Eugène Chevreul (1839): contrasting complementary colors were seen as harmonious, similar ones as disharmonious (e.g., blue plants were contrasted with orange ones, yellow plants with purple ones, etc.).

A new type of bed was created when small ornamental gravel paths were laid around and in between box-edged beds. Repton's *rosary* at Ashridge (1813) can be considered to be a forerunner of this type. Gravel borders became more favored after 1850. "Small beds, bordered with Box and gravel, the whole being on grass" are recorded in the Royal Horticultural Society's garden in 1854. In Germany such beds occurred after 1854. Rudolf Wörmann published the first German bed-pattern book in 1864 in Berlin. He called this bed type *Teppichgärten* (carpet gardens); this is the first record of the term *carpet* being used to relate to flower beds. Some of these new beds were in antique, Gothic, baroque, or rococo styles and sometimes reflected *broderie* patterns; however, they were filled with flowers instead of gravel (M'Intosh [1853]). In 1871 Shirley Hibberd proposed four displays throughout the year, with the *plunging system*, which means continually changing plants in pots, when and where required. Each area was planted with one species only.

The *carpet bed* originated by varying the edging circle borders into ornamental and crossing lines. The carpet bed is a compact entity without grass or gravel inter-spaces. Carpet plants mainly served to constitute the pattern, the individual plant itself being without value. The edges consisted of carpet plants similar to the fillings, rather than of box or dead materials (e.g., tiles). The surface mostly rose from the edge to the middle (height to diameter in a ratio of one to five). It is not clear from which country the carpet bed arose. One of the first examples was seen at Linton Park, Kent, in 1861 and published in *La Belgique Horticole* in 1865. The same volume displays carpet beds from Cologne. The term *Teppichbeet* (carpet bed) first occurred in *Deutsche Gartenzeitung* in 1867. Carpet-bed competitions were organized at Namur and Hamburg in 1869. Fully developed carpet beds were at Kew Gardens and Battersea Park in 1870, Victoria Park, Hyde Park, and Kensington Gardens in 1873, and at Crystal Palace in 1875. Eyles (1877) provides this definition: "Carpet bedding differs chiefly from the pattern-bedding style in the plants being as nearly as may be of one height, so as to represent a textile or woven fabric of uniform texture, or slightly varying in thickness." The French term *mosaïculture* is said to be invented by Jules Chrétien from Lyon. Edouard André and S.J. Mottet published *mosaïculture* designs in France.

Refined carpet beds became more three-dimensional, as in the highly complicated designs of Wilhelm Hampel from Silesia. The outline is mostly rounded, sometimes elliptical, seldom figurelike (e.g., shaped in butterflies, coats-of-arms, texts, or dials). The design could be rendered in any style such as antique, Gothic, Renaissance, or Moorish. Essential elements were the carpet plants themselves. These included some new introductions from South America: *Alternantheras* (introduced 1862) and *Iresines* (1870), *Cuphea ignea* (1845), *Echeveria* (1833), *Begonia,* and *Petunia* (1823), along with older species such as *Chrysanthemum parthenium* var. *aureum, Helichrysum petiolare, Lobelia erinus, Lobularia maritima, Perilla, Coleus, Verbena, Ageratum, Cerastium, Senecio bicolor, Antennaria dioica,* and *Pelargonium,* which were all cultivated under glass. Each segment was densely planted with one species only, with up to 15 species per bed. The center was often accentuated by foliage plants such as *Canna, Colocasia, Fatsia, Yucca, Dracaena, Wigandia, Solanum robustum, Tetrapanax, Ricinus,* or *Chamaerops.*

Shirley Hibberd, William Robinson (1878), and others reacted against the extensive bedding system. According to Robinson, "The beautiful forms of flowers are degraded to the level of crude colour to make a design, and without reference to the natural form or beauty of the plant. . . . The contents, and not the outlines of the beds, are what we should see." In response, modern beds contained more picturesque groups of taller flowers, with carpet plants as borders only, or one-color beds shaped in art nouveau style or expressionistic patterns. After World War I carpet beds disappeared in England and Germany, surviving partly in France and Eastern Europe.

A bed consisting mainly of trees and shrubs is termed a *clump* or *shrubbery*. In early landscape gardens (e.g., Switzer, Kent, Brown) a *clump* contained many tall trees of one species, mostly circularly grouped (or in a square, as in Blenheim Park), nearly equal in its dimensions. The advocates of the picturesque, including Uvedale Price and R. Payne Knight, refused such forms ("this formal lump/Which the improver plants, and calls a clump!"). The clump was bettered as a group of two or more trees, irregularly grouped, and eventually of different species (e.g., Whately, Gilpin). Whately primarily recommended similar but not equal plant forms and structures as neighbors. Deciduous trees and conifers, therefore, did not harmonize. Another improved type of clump containing shrubs as well as perennials was sometimes termed *shrubbery* (W. Mason, Hirschfeld, Repton). As a forerunner of this type, Lord Petre planted diversified clumps in Worksop in 1738. At Monticello Thomas Jefferson used the terms *clump* and *bed* as synonyms. These clumps must have been often clipped and modified.

The term *shrubbery* was first used by William Shenstone at The Leasowes in 1748. The shrubbery developed through transforming mixed planting rows of a rococo garden into round or curved outlines on the lawn. The result was a regular mixed planting, although more irregularly formed, with flowering shrubs, destined less for the park than for the garden. The heights gradually diminished from the middle to the edges. The edges could be planted with perennials or bulbs. There is no sharp margin between the terms *flower garden, shrubbery,* and *pleasure ground*. According to Loudon (1822) the shrubbery is a curved border of perennials, shrubs, and trees. The German equivalent to *shrubbery* is *Lustgebüsch,* the French equivalent *massif*.

The grouping of shrubs of one species or more than one, but related, species in the grouped manner described previously was propagated by Loudon, Nash, Pückler, and Paxton. This praxis made it possible to contrast groups of different colors.

Beds of one species and color persisted during the greater part of the 20th century. Some designers used them to construct abstract patters (Paul Véra, Gabriel Guévrékian, Roberto Burle Marx). During the last decade of the century, however, tastefully mixed beds saw a revival.

*See also* Color

**Further Reading**

Elliot, Brent, *Victorian Gardens,* London: Batsford, and Portland Oregon: Timber Press, 1986

Eyles, George, "Carpet Bedding," *The Gardener's Chronicle* 7 (1877)

Götze, Karl, *Album für Teppichgärtnerei und Gruppenbepflanzung,* Erfurt, Germany, 1892; 4th edition, Erfurt, Germany: Möller, 1902

Hampel, Carl, *Gartenbeete und Gruppen,* Berlin, 1893; 2nd edition, Berlin: Parey, 1901

Hampel, Wilhelm, *Die moderne Teppichgärtnerei,* Berlin, 1880; 7th edition, Berlin: Parey, 1907

Harris, John, "The Flower Garden, 1730 to 1830," in *The Garden: A Celebration of One Thousand Years of British Gardening,* edited by Harris, London: Mitchell Beasley, 1979

Hayward, Charles F., *Geometrical Flower Beds,* London, 1853

Hibberd, Shirley, *The Amateur's Flower Garden,* London, 1871; reprint, London: Croom Helm, 1986

Laird, Mark, *The Flowering of the Landscape Garden: English Pleasure Grounds 1720–1800,* Philadelphia: University of Pennsylvania Press, 1999

Legeler, Wilhelm, *Mathematik, Zeichnenkunst, Physik und Chemie,* Berlin, 1839

Levy, Ernst, *Neue Entwürfe zu Teppich-Gärten,* Berlin, 1875; 2nd edition, 1879

Mottet, Séraphin Joseph, *La mosaïculture,* Paris, 1891; 2nd edition, 1894

Niemann, W.A.C., *Der Teppichgärtner,* Hamburg, 1870; reprint, in *Gartenkunst* 3 (1991)

Paxton, Joseph, "On Planting Showy Shrubs in Masses," *Paxton's Magazine of Botany* 11 (1846)

Phillips, Henry, *Sylva Florifera: The Shrubbery Historically and Botanically Treated,* London, 1823

Puppe, Roland, "Das Teppichbeet," in *Blumenverwendung in historischen Gärten,* Berlin: Kulturbund, 1990

Thompson, Robert, *The Gardener's Assistant: Practical and Scientific,* London and Glasgow, 1878

Wimmer, Clemens A., "Die Kunst der Teppichgärtnerei," *Gartenkunst* 3 (1991)

Wörmann, Rudolf W.A., *Die Teppichgärten,* Berlin, 1864

CLEMENS ALEXANDER WIMMER

# Bei Hai Park

## Beijing, China

**Location:** northeast of the Forbidden City in Beijing

Bei Hai, a large area of parkland formerly called Haiziyuan, was first recorded during the Tang dynasty (618–907) and included the northeast side of Youzhou. Youzhou's name changed to Nanjing during the Liao dynasty (947–1125), and Haiziyuan was reconstructed into the site of an imperial lodge named Yaoyu. During the Jin dynasty (1115–1234) Nanjing was renamed Yenjing and became the dynasty's capital city, called Zhongdu. During this dynasty many artificial island hills, lakes, and a luxurious palace named Dalinggong were built around Yaoyu. The rockery islands were built with Taihu rocks, brought from the Genyu Garden in the Song dynasty capital of Bianliang. It was called Qionghua Island, an imitation of Genyue Garden. Qionghua Island was enlarged during the Yuan dynasty (1271–1368) into a formal imperial garden. The Yuan dynasty renamed Qionghua Island Wansuishan and named the lake Tai Ye Chi. During the Ming dynasty (1368–1644), the capital city moved from Nanjing to Beijing, and a new city was built on the Yuan capital Da Du in 1420. Combining Tai Ye Chi and Wansuishan, the Ming rulers called it Xi Yuan, which became the largest imperial park in Beijing.

The Ming dynasty extended Tai Ye Chi into a long and narrow lake, separated by Qionghua Island, and divided the area into three sections: Bei Hai (North Sea), Zhonghai (Middle Sea), and Nanhai (South Sea). More pavilions and halls were added at that time. The first emperor of the Qing dynasty (1636–1911), Emperor Shunzhi (1651), built a white lama temple at the original site of the Moon Hall located on the top of Qionghua Island. This became the White Dagoba. Qionghua Island was thus also referred to as White Dagoba Hill. At the same time many halls south of the Qionghua Island were demolished, and in their place was erected the temple called Yong An Temple. During the time of Emperor Qianlong, a number of terraces and pavilions were built in the surrounding area of the White Dagoba Hill. Corridors connected this series of buildings facing Tai Ye Chi. The east side of Bei Hai contained some small gardens, such as Huafangzhai Studio, Haopujian Garden, and Guketing. On the north shore of Tai Ye Chi were the Jingqingzhai Garden, Chengguantang Hall, and some Buddhist temples and buildings, such as the Chanfu Temple and Wanfoqiao Bridge.

The legend of Qionghua Island can be traced to the Jin dynasty. Emperors believed the island was inhabited by immortals. Later emperors started construction surrounding the White Dagoba, sited at the center of Qionghua Island. The northern slope of the island hill includes two artificial caves, one of which extends for 50 meters (54.7 yd.). The caves were made out of Taihu rocks, coming mainly from the Genyue Garden in the Song dynasty capital Bianliang. The great beauty of Bei Hai makes it a unique and magnificent landmark among royal gardens in China.

One of the features in Bei Hai is the Jingqingzhai Garden, a garden within a garden, first built in 1758 as an area of study for princes. During the time of Emperor Guangxu (1875–1908), its name changed to Jingxinzhai. The garden is approximately 0.8 hectares (2 acres), with pavilions and halls on the north side and water areas and rock hills on the south. An artificial rockery, lying east to west, is located at the north end of the garden. Standing on the terrace in front of the pavilion on the mountain, one has a panoramic view of the whole garden. The architecture design made the rockery a masterpiece in style and technique.

**Synopsis**

| | |
|---|---|
| 1179 | Emperor of Jin dynasty builds royal resort Daning Gong, excavates man-made lake, constructs Qionghua Island at center of lake, and builds Guangsai Dian Hall on island, patterned after Genyu Garden of Song capital Bianliang |
| 1267 | Yuan emperors build Da Du as capital, encompassing Daning Gong, and expand Qionghua island and surrounding waters; much enlarged lake Tai Ye Chi, along with other scenic elements, formally become constituent part of royal garden |
| 1368 | Name Tai Ye Chi changed to Xi Yuan during early Ming dynasty |
| 1457–64 | Ming ruler expands Xi Yuan by extending man-made lake toward south; distinctive areas of Bei Hai, Zhonghai, and Nanhai created where Qionghua island became center of lakes |
| 1522–1620 | New constructions at Zhonghai and Nanhai |
| 1651 | Emperor Shunzhi builds lama temple pagoda (named Baita Shan) at original site of Guangsai Dian Hall on Qionghua Island and demolishes |

Everlasting Peace Bridge, Bei Hai Park, Beijing, China
Copyright Robert M. Craig

buildings on southern slope of Qionghua Island and replaces them with Yongan Si temple

1736–95　Emperor Qianlong builds series of buildings on Bei Hai designed in imitation of famous Zhenjiang (Jiangsu Province) Jiang Tian Yi Lan scenes

**Further Reading**

Chi, Ch'eng, *The Craft of Gardens* (1634), translated by Alison Hardie, New Haven, Connecticut: Yale University Press, 1988

Johnston, R. Stewart, *Scholar Gardens of China: A Study and Analysis of the Spatial Design of the Chinese Private Garden*, Cambridge and New York: Cambridge University Press, 1991

Keswick, Maggie, and Charles Jencks, *The Chinese Garden: History, Art and Architecture*, New York: Rizzoli, and London: Academy Editions, 1978

Liu, Tun-chen, *Su-chou ku tien yüan lin*, Beijing: Chung-kuo chien chu kung yeh ch'u pan she, 1979; as *Chinese Classical Gardens of Suzhou*, translated by Chen Lixian, edited by Joseph C. Wang, New York: McGraw Hill, 1993

Tsu, Frances Ya-Sing, *Landscape Design in Chinese Gardens*, New York: McGraw Hill, 1988

Wang, Joseph Cho, *The Chinese Garden*, Oxford and New York: Oxford University Press, 1998

CHENG LIYAO AND JOSEPH C. WANG
*TRANSLATED BY SYLVIA CHOI*

# Belgique, Jardin Botanique National de

## Meise, Belgium

**Location:**  approximately 7.5 miles (12 km) from center of Brussels

As a state scientific institution, the Jardin Botanique National de Belgique dates to 1870. It is the successor to the private botanical garden set up by the Société Royal d'Horticulture des Pays-Bas in Brussels at the Porte de Schaerbeek, which opened in 1829. In 1939 it was transferred to the Domaine de Bouchout in the commune of Meise, about 7.5 miles (12 km) from the center of Brussels on the Brussels-Antwerp autoroute.

Botanical gardens existed in Brussels in the 17th and 18th centuries, but they were small private establishments. In 1796 the French regime established the École centrale du Département de la Dyle in the palace of Prince Charles Alexandre of Lorraine (the Ancienne Cour/Hôtel de Nassau, a block bounded by the Montagne de la Cour, the Place du Musée, the rue de Ruysbroeck, and the rue de l'Empereur). The decree of the Département de la Dyle of the 26 Fructidor of Year IV (12 September 1796) stipulated that the stables and riding school of the Ancienne Cour were to be used to accommodate the plants that were to be "taken immediately from the houses of those who have emigrated." Joseph F.P. Van der Stegen de Putte was the Central School's first professor of natural history. He had the garden of the Ancienne Cour transformed into Brussels's first public botanical garden, of which he became the first director. By 1809 this garden contained approximately 1,400 different species and varieties.

In 1826 Guillaume I, king of the Netherlands, ordered developments in this district, which led to the disappearance of Brussels's first botanical garden. On 28 March 1826 plant enthusiasts founded the Société Royal d'Horticulture des Pays-Bas, one of whose objectives was to establish a new garden in Brussels and to move the first botanical garden's collections to it. The new garden was laid out on a piece of land stretching from the present-day Place Rogier to the Porte de Schaerbeek (rue Royale). A competition was announced for the buildings: the neoclassical scheme chosen was the work of the Frenchman P.F. Gineste, the painter of decorative schemes at the Théâtre de la Monnaie, among other places. Meeus-Wouters was responsible for the detailed plans and the choice of materials. Work began in November 1826 with the laying of the foundations of one of the orangeries. On 10 September 1827 the plants were transferred from the Ancienne Cour garden into the newly constructed glasshouses. To mark the inauguration of the new garden, the Société Royal d'Horticulture organized its first exhibition of horticultural products, held from 1 to 3 September 1829. On 3 September there was a banquet, followed by a *fête champêtre* and fireworks. Further construction took place in 1843–44, 1847, and 1852–54, to plans by the architect Tilman François Suys.

About 1830 a portion of the cellars was used to grow mushrooms. The head gardener, Bresiers, used the same cellars to blanch vegetables, including the winter salad *Cichorium intybus* subsp. *sativum.* Some of the plants, on which moist earth had been heaped, formed "hearts"—and so "witloof" (chicory) was born. For a long time its method of production remained a secret known only to a few of the botanical garden's gardeners. After Bresiers's death the art of growing it gradually became public knowledge.

The Société Royal d'Horticulture ("de Belgique" since 1837) continued to own the Brussels Botanical Garden until 1870. It supported itself mainly by selling plants and by hiring out rooms for functions. It experienced periods of both prosperity and decline. In 1841 it sold part of its land, on which the Gare du Nord (among other things) was then built. From an early date it began to build up a botanical and horticultural library, as well as herbaria, such as the one that Henri-Guillaume Galeotti collected in Mexico between 1835 and 1840, before himself being appointed head of the Brussels Botanical Garden.

In 1867 the Société Royal d'Horticulture fell into serious financial difficulties. The amateur botanist Barthélemy Dumortier, an influential politician and the government commissioner to the society since 1837, persuaded the state to buy out the society and turn its garden into a center of botanical research: the sale was confirmed on 28 June 1870.

For 170 years the Brussels Botanical Garden, in addition to its scientific research, fulfilled an important cultural role, looking after the planting of its park (in which Charles Bommer planted many rare trees) and organizing exhibitions both permanent (e.g., the glasshouses and the museum of forestry conceived by Bommer and opened in 1902) and temporary (e.g., seasonal flowers, works by the garden's illustrators, etc.). A well-stocked specialist library was open to the public. Learned societies had their offices there, among them the Société royale de Botanique de Belgique and the Société Royale Linnéenne et de Flore. Public gardening classes were also held there.

From 1894 to 1898 the government, in order to encourage the country's artists, commissioned and had erected in the garden, under the direction of Constantin Meunier and Charles Van der Stappen, 43 statues, which became the pride of the people of Brussels.

In May 1910 the 3rd International Botanical Congress was held in Brussels, partly in the Brussels

Botanical Garden, whose scientific staff played a large part in the congress. The staff at that time included a director, two conservators, a head of cultivation, and an assistant naturalist.

The Domaine de Bouchout, which is part of the commune of Meise, dates to the 12th century. In 1130 Godefroid the Bearded, duke of Brabant and Lower Lotharingia and lord of the manor of Bouchout, built the square tower of the Château de Bouchout, which at this period was surrounded by a moat with five sides.

Subsequently, the Domaine belonged successively to several illustrious families. At the beginning of the 19th century, when it was much more extensive than today, it was inherited by Countess Marie Elisabeth Roose de Baisy, Baroness of Bouchout, who in 1830 married Count Amédée de Beaufort. A highly cultured aesthete, the first director of the Musées Nationaux d'Art et d'Histoire de Belgique and the first president of the Commission Royale des Monuments, Amédée commissioned Tilman François Suys to turn the Château de Bouchout into a manor house in the "English" style, with crenellated towers. Only Godefroid the Bearded's square keep retains its original appearance.

In 1879 King Leopold II bought the Domaine de Bouchout as a home for his sister, Empress Charlotte, widow of Emperor Maximilian of Mexico; she lived in the Château de Bouchout until her death. In 1882 Leopold bought the estate and château of Meise, adjoining the Domaine de Bouchout to the north, from Baron E. Van der Linden d'Hoogvorst and amalgamated the two properties. On 23 December 1938 the Belgian state bought the Domaine, including the château and estate of Meise, from the royal family, along with an adjoining plot of meadow—230 acres (93 ha) in all—in order to preserve this remarkable historic property and create in it a new botanical garden. Work began on 2 January 1939. That year 12 glasshouses were built, and in April the first living plants, those of the open-air ecological collection, were transferred from Brussels to Meise. In March 1940 began the transplantation of interesting trees and shrubs located on the route of the tunnel for the planned Gare du Midi/Gare du Nord railway junction. World War II held up work on the junction considerably: it began on 27 January 1941, cutting the Brussels Garden in two and obliterating a number of interesting plants and several glasshouses. In April 1941 a superb specimen of *Quercus bicolor* (swamp white oak), probably planted at Brussels between 1826 and 1827, was moved along with its ball of earth; despite the care lavished on it, the tree died. The attractive "crowned glasshouse," first erected in the Parc Leopold by the architect Alphonse Balat, then moved to the Brussels Botanical Garden, where it served as the "Victoria Glasshouse," was moved once again and rebuilt at the Domaine de Bouchout.

On 2 December 1944 a fire destroyed the Château de Meise. The Palais des Plantes was completed in 1959. During the 1960s the herbarium and library building was constructed; the growth of the collections and research programs necessitated the addition of a new wing in 1986–87. On 9 August 1967 a royal decree granted the Domaine de Bouchout protected-landscape status, making it safe from property developers. In 1988 the full restoration of the Château de Bouchout was completed, including the fitting out of huge conference and exhibition rooms.

Since 1982 the staff of the National Botanical Garden of Belgium has included 19 scientific members. The garden also benefits from the help of amateurs and botanists from other institutions and collaborates with other botanical gardens in Belgium and abroad. So, for example, the 16th Congress of the Association for the Taxonomic Study of the Flora of Tropical Africa was held at Meise in 2000. For almost a century, moreover, the garden has fought for the protection of the flora and of nature in general.

The garden manages some important scientific collections. The living plant collections include the Herbetum, which contains approximately 1,200 species of herbaceous plants arranged in systematic order around the Balat glasshouse; the Fruticetum, which contains some 2,000 species of shrubs; and the Coniferetum. There are also the collections of rhododendrons, hydrangeas, oaks and maples, the North American forest, and the medicinal plant garden, containing some 350 species.

The Palais des Plantes forms a rectangle 154 meters long by 73 meters wide, covering 11,087 square meters (13,260 sq. yd.), of which 9,776 square meters (11,690 sq. yd.) is usable space. It comprises 13 large glasshouses between 8 meters (8.75 yd.) and 16 meters (17.5 yd.) in height: 12 form the perimeter of the palace, while the 13th is in the middle. These large glasshouses surround two groups of ten small glasshouses each and two small "special" glasshouses (one for bryophytes, the other for insectivorous spermatophytes).

Most of the large glasshouses contain plants grouped by geographical area and laid out in landscape style. The visitor is presented with the flora and vegetation of equatorial, subtropical, and tropical Africa, equatorial America, subtropical North and South America, subtropical Asia, Australia, the Canary Islands, and the Mediterranean basin.

The Victoria Glasshouse, of particular interest to gardeners, contains a central pond of 228.5 square meters (273.3 sq. yd.) of usable surface area whose water, kept at an average temperature of 30 degrees Celsius (86 degrees F.) contains a collection of Nymphaeaceae (including *Euryale ferox* and cultivars of *Nymphaea*, *Victoria amazonica*, and *V. cruciana*), as well as *Eichhornia crassipes* (water hyacinth), *Cyperus papyrus* (papyrus), *Mimosa pudica* (sensitive plant), *Pistia stra-*

tiotes (water lettuce), and *Saccharum officinarum* (sugar cane). Around the edge of the glasshouse is a mixed border of notable plants from hot countries, along with cultivars of *Caladium*. Hanging baskets contain *Nepenthes* and *Orchidaceae* (including *Phalaenopsis amabilis*).

One of the large glasshouses presents useful plants from the tropics arranged according to their properties or products.

The small glasshouses of the Palais des Plantes are essentially devoted to tropical and subtropical species of various families and genera: Araceae (350 species), *Begonia* (including numerous horticultural hybrids), Bromeliaceae (350 species), Cactaceae (600 species) and other succulent plants (800 species), Cycadaceae, ferns (225 species), Marantaceae and Orchidaceae (1,200 species, plus cultivars and hybrids). The number of species and infraspecific taxa represented in the Palais des Plantes by living specimens is estimated at 10,000.

The garden is involved in an international research program on the Phaseolinae, which contains the "haricot bean," with the aim of developing a protein-rich food source for Third World countries. The garden is responsible for conserving the various taxa and making their seeds available to researchers.

The National Botanical Garden's herbarium is one of the 25 largest in the world, with over 2.5 million specimens. It holds among others the personal herbarium of the 19th-century Munich botanist Karl Friedrich Philipp von Martius, containing 60,000 specimens, 20,000 of them from Brazil. It also contains the personal herbarium of roses collected by François Crépin, containing approximately 43,000 specimens.

The garden's library, one of the richest in the fields of botany and horticulture, includes 63,000 books and over 3,300 periodicals, of which 1,300 are still being published. For two days a week the library is open to the public, which has at its disposal a vast reading room and about 3.5 million index cards. Readers may borrow books on certain conditions. The garden also publishes a number of works, some of them purely scientific and others more popular, as well as some intended for children and schools. Many exist in both French and Dutch versions.

## Synopsis

| | |
|---|---|
| 1829 | Netherlands Royal Horticultural Society botanical garden opens |
| 1870 | State buys botanical garden and renames it Jardin Botanique National de Belgique |
| 1894–98 | Constantin Meunier and Charles Van der Stappen oversee creation of 43 statues in garden |
| 1939 | Transfer of garden to Meise begins |
| 1944 | Château de Meise destroyed |
| 1959 | Palais des Plantes completed |
| 1960s | Herbarium and library built |
| 1986–87 | New wing added to herbarium/library building |
| 2001 | Inauguration of the Desert Greenhouse |

## Further Reading

Balis, Jan, Els Witte, and Roland Tournay, *Histoire des jardins botaniques de Bruxelles, 1870–1970*, Brussels: Crédit Communal de Belgique, 1970

Borremans, Paul, Danny Swaerts, and F. Billiet, *Le domaine de Bouchout, du parc seigneurial au Jardin Botanique: 1939–1989*, Meise, Belgium: Ministère de l'Agriculture, 1989

Demaret, Fernand, "La structure et le rôle du Jardin botanique national de Belgique," *Boissiera* 14 (1969)

Ganz, Edwin, *Le domaine royal de Bouchout et ses châteaux*, Meise, Belgium: Van Gijseghem, 1940

Horta, Victor, "Étude objective des auteurs des Serres du Jardin botanique de Bruxelles," *Bulletins de l'Académie royale des sciences, des lettres et des Beaux-Arts de Belgique* 27 (1935)

Jardin Botanique National de Belgique, *Le jardin botanique national de Belgique*, Brussels: Jardin Botanique National de Belgique, 1970

Lettens, Hugo, "De sculpturale versiering van de Kruidtuin te Brussel onder leiding van Constantin Meunier en Charles Van der Stappen: Sculptuur onder toezicht," *De brabantse folklore en geschiedenis* 271 (1991)

Robyns, Walter, "Le Palais des plantes au Jardin botanique national de Belgique," *Bulletin des seances* 4 (1967)

ANDRÉ LAWALREE

# Belgium

Belgium is located at almost the exact center of Europe. Bounded on the north by the Netherlands and the North Sea, on the east by Germany, and on the south and west by France, the land can be divided into three distinct regions: a coastal plain, a central plateau, and the Ardennes highlands. Since the 15th century the land on the coastal plain has been reclaimed for various uses by a series of dykes that prevent continual flooding by the sea. This flat and fertile land is called the *polders*. The central plateau is comprised of rolling hills and is crisscrossed by many waterways. The fertile valleys in this region contain rich alluvial soil. The highlands are heavily wooded; the highest peak in Belgium is located in this area—Mount Botrange, with an elevation of 679 meters (2,228 ft.). The climate throughout Belgium is temperate. The mean annual temperature in Brussels is 50 degrees Fahrenheit (10 degrees C.), and the average annual rainfall is 70 centimeters (27.5 in.).

Belgium did not exist as an independent nation until 1830. Before the uprising that ended with Belgian independence, the country was held at various times by the Spanish, the French, the Austrians, and the Dutch. Because of a shared language and geographical proximity, France has exerted a powerful influence on Belgium, one that can be seen clearly in the development of garden styles. Because of its central location in Europe, Belgium has also been the site of many battles, including the defeat of Napoléon at Waterloo, and its cities and castles have thus been subjected to much destruction over the centuries.

Little is known about Belgian parks and gardens in the Middle Ages. The few available sources suggest that gardens were enclosed, rather small, and quite symmetrical. A fountain or sculptural work sometimes provided a focal point. Plants were grown for food as well as for ornamental value. In the 15th century gardens increased in size, although they still tended to be arranged in straight lines and rectangles. The grounds of the Brussels Court provide a good example of the late medieval garden. Most of the land was left in its natural state, consisting mainly of woodlands. Behind the house were an enclosed private garden, flower garden, fishpond, palm-court, tournament field, and vineyard.

In the 16th century gardens were larger but still tended to be enclosed. Layouts were still symmetrical, but the design became much more complicated, and arbors and *cabinets de verdure* (small garden enclosures, often surrounded by clipped hedges) were added. Often the design had the feel of a labyrinth. For example, about 1520 Emperor Charles V transformed the gardens at the Brussels Court into a labyrinth, with trees of the same type planted and pruned to form allées, or long walks bordered by trees, porticoes, and bowers. Fountains were added to the garden, and a bathing pool was built, in the middle of which stood a summerhouse.

During this period round or polygonal bowers began to appear, in which trees were pruned in layers and supported by small columns. A bower of this sort can still be seen at Macon-Momignies. Also in this period a collection of garden plans published by Jan Vredeman de Vries, *Hortorum virdariorimque formae* (1583), influenced gardens in the northern Flemish provinces. Gardens were still enclosed by hedges or low walls and crossed by parterres, still in geometrical patterns. Foun-

tains, statues, and sculptures were incorporated in arbors and bowers, and an effort was made to integrate the garden with the buildings. Although Italian influences can be detected in gardens of the late 16th century, the flatness of the land in Belgium prevented the incorporation of terraces. Gardens also still remained relatively small.

The rise of Renaissance humanism led to an increased interest in the sciences in general and in botany in particular. Many new species of plants, including the tulip and the lilac, were introduced during this period. In the gardens at Borgerhout, near Antwerp, more than 600 foreign plants could be found. Unfortunately, rebellions in the Netherlands and the Thirty Years' War disrupted life in the region for many years. Many gardens were destroyed, and many garden designers emigrated.

Two new trends emerged in the 17th century. The first was the incorporation of the French *parterres de broderie* (embroidered parterre), complex sweeping patterns of flowers and shrubs. Enclosures, bowers, and arbors began to fall out of fashion, and gardens began to be more open. The goal was to be able to see the entire garden from the house. Unlike the French gardens of the period, however, Belgian gardens still had not entirely integrated the house with the grounds or the outlying grounds with the gardens.

The second new trend was the introduction of rockeries and ornamental waterworks in imitation of Italian gardens. A significant achievement of the century was the Belevedere Garden near Ghent. Although massive and comprised of 20 rectangles separated by straight allées, the garden could be seen in its entirety from the house because of the absence of enclosures. The garden housed a number of sculptures and *fabriques,* or ornamental garden structures, set at the ends of the allées. The crowning achievement of the period, however, was the garden at Enghein. This estate was purchased in 1606 by Prince Charles d'Arenberg, and the gardens were designed by his brother Charles, a Capuchin monk. A member of Louis XIV's court who visited the garden wrote that it was "the most beautiful and extraordinary thing in the world." The garden was extremely large, divided into three spectacular sections, replete with fountains, statues, grottoes, and pavilions. The entrance to Enghein was particularly impressive. One entered the garden through a huge stone arch, beyond which was an allée that led to the central circular garden, at the center of which was a Temple of Hercules, a seven-sided belvedere of stone and marble. Hidden jets of water sprayed guests as they approached the arch.

The 18th century saw many new gardens built in urban areas, particularly in Brussels, Antwerp, and Ghent. Although the French classical style of gardening continued to dominate Belgian gardens, the informal

English garden began to have an influence late in the century. Beloeil is perhaps the best example in this period of the French classical garden, designed by Prince Claude-Lamoral de Ligne and French architect Jean-Baptiste Bergé. De Ligne, whose brief autobiography, *Coup d'oeil sur Beloeil et sur une grande partie des jardins de l'Europe* (1781), sets forth his ideas on gardens and many other subjects, turned his estate into a vast allegory, replete with fountains, *fabriques,* and walks named "the cradle of my childhood" and the "chamber of death." The château faces a large pool with a monumental fountain at the far end. On either side of the pool are gardens laid out in magnificent *parterres de broderie.* De Ligne valued originality in garden construction, writing that "Peruvian huts, Laplanders' shelters, little palaces from the Caucaasus are more striking than eternal parodies of the gods of the Sun, War, and Wine."

Annevoie, which dates from the same period, is much less formal in design and makes spectacular use of water. Charles-Alexis de Montpellier was responsible for much of the original design, creating in essence an aquatic landscape with fountains and cascades. He set up artificial reservoirs to contain water collected from four natural sources in the forest; due to the lie of the land and the resulting water pressure, he needed no pumps to create the spectacular water effects.

During the last quarter of the 18th century, a gardening revolution took place as the informal English garden began to supplant the French formal style. Gardens began to adapt to the natural contours of the land and tended to take in the entire landscape surrounding the estate, not just the lands immediately adjacent. Irregularity replaced symmetry, and the taste of the times turned to picturesque views and vistas. *Fabriques* became ever more fanciful, including Gothic ruins and Chinese pagodas. There was also an increased use of foreign plants; the Lombardy poplar and the rhododendron in particular became quite popular. Many older estates, such as Beloeil, modified some garden areas to adapt to the English style. Moreover, new gardens were designed entirely in the English style. A remarkable example is Laeken, which was begun by the Austrian governors-general in 1781. Considered to be the first Belgian garden done completely in the English style, the garden makes use of meadowland, a meandering stream, and a rolling landscape. It includes pavilions, a hermitage, an artificial grotto, an orangery, a Chinese tower, rare plants, and even an artificial waterfall. The curving lines and complete asymmetry of the design appears extraordinarily casual when compared to the straight lines and balanced layout of the formal French style.

The 19th century saw a vastly increased interest in horticulture in Belgium. Ghent became a center for the cultivation of camellias and azaleas, and Jean Linden, the "father of the orchid," imported orchids from North America and grew many species in Brussels. A new kind of parterre, the *corbeille,* or basket, consisted of large, round, raised flower beds filled with unusual flowers and greenery. Winter gardens, built of metal and attached to the house, became increasingly popular, in part to house such exotic species as palm trees. New tree varieties were introduced, including weeping willow, Lebanon cedar, sequoia, monkey puzzle, and *Ginko biloba,* or maidenhair tree. In the first half of the century, gardens were still created predominantly in the irregular English style, while houses, in contrast, had become increasingly simple and regular in design. As urban populations grew, more municipal parks were built. These new gardens featured oval paths suitable for vehicles, as well as chalets, metal greenhouses, and large ornamental rocks. One of the most important garden designers of the time was Edouard Keilig, who laid out the municipal parks at Brussels, Antwerp, and Ostend.

Some formal classical gardens were also built in the second half of the 19th century, including the Brussels Botanical Gardens, the Kalmthout nurseries, and the square of the Petit Sablon in Brussels. The 1897 international exhibition featured formal gardens at Tervurne. As the century waned, a combination of formal and informal styles predominated. Alpine and Japanese gardens were also popular. More and more frequently, gardens became an integral part of urban planning, with space set aside for green areas within cities.

The 20th century saw a tendency toward eclecticism. Jules Buyssens designed a number of gardens in Belgium; he integrated the house with the garden and built terraces from stone found at the building site in order to establish a strong tie between the site and the design. Buyssens designed the Astridpark in Brussels and the gardens of the Abbaye de la Cambre. Other noted Belgian garden designers of the 20th century include René Pechère and René Latinne. Latinne focuses on ease of maintenance and often uses perennials in combination with water.

*See also* Annevoie, Jardins d'; Belgique, Jardin Botanique National de; Beloeil; Enghien

**Further Reading**

Balis, J., *Hortus Belgicus* (exhib. cat.), Brussels: Albert Ier Bibliotheek, 1962

Bridgeman, Harriet, and Elizabeth Drury, *Visiting the Gardens of Europe,* New York: Dutton, 1979

Coats, Peter, *The House and Garden Book of Beautiful Gardens round the World,* Boston: Little Brown, and London: Weidenfeld and Nicolson, 1985

Ligne, Charles-Joseph, Prince de, *Coup d'oil sur Beloeil et sur une grande partie des jardins de l'Europe,* Beloeil, 1781; 3rd edition, Vienna, 1795; reprint, Paris: Édition de Paris, 1997; as *Coup d'oeil at Beloeil*

*and a Great Number of European Gardens,*
translated and edited by Basil Guy, Berkeley:
University of California Press, 1991

Mosser, Monique, and Georges Teyssot, editors,
*L'architettura dei giardini d'Occidente,* Milan: Electa,
1990; as *The Architecture of Western Gardens,*
Cambridge, Massachusetts: MIT Press, 1991; as *The
History of Garden Design,* London: Thames and
Hudson, 1991

Pechère, René, *Parcs et jardins de Belgique,* Brussels:
Rossel, 1976; 2nd edition, Hainaut, Belgium:
Fédération du Tourisme de la Province de Hainaut,
1987

Thacker, Christopher, *The History of Gardens,*
Berkeley: University of California Press, and London:
Croom Helm, 1979

KAREN MEYERS

# Beloeil

## Hainaut, Belgium

**Location:**  approximately 43.5 miles (70 km) southwest
of Brussels and 11.2 miles (18 km)
northwest of Mons

The estate of Beloeil has been the residence of the
Ligne family since the 14th century. The present château
is a copy of that originally constructed in 1538 (and
embellished in the Renaissance style in the 17th century),
which was destroyed by fire in 1900.

In 1642 Claire-Marie de Nassau Siegen, the widow of
Albert-Henri, the second prince de Ligne, married his
brother Claude-Lamoral I, the third prince. She was the
first key figure in the development of the gardens of
Beloeil. Not only did she create the plan for a part of the
park and oversee the re-laying out of a labyrinth, but
she also introduced into the region copper beeches from
the Black Forest. It was at this time also that the great
lake was first enlarged. It was at the beginning of the
18th century, however, that the grandson of Claude-
Lamoral I, Claude-Lamoral II, laid out the gardens in
the French formal style, giving them the appearance
they have today.

Two French architects, Jean-Baptiste Bergé and Jean
Michel Chevotet, have been mentioned as being
involved in the creation of this *jardin à la française.*
Chevotet, who designed the Hanover Pavilion at
Sceaux, was in service with the seigneur of Beloeil
between 1754 and 1760. He drew plans of the orangery,
the lake, or *Grand Etang,* a cascade, forest paths,
bosquets, and little buildings that punctuate the perspective. He also planned ornamental pools like those at
Versailles. Basil Guy, in his edition of *Coup d'Oeil sur
Beloeil,* comments in a footnote that the famous Belgian
landscape architect, René Pechère, has suggested that
Bergé was responsible for the gardens. Certainly Bergé

is cited by Xavier Duquenne in *The Oxford Companion
to Gardens.* Engravings by La Marcade dating from the
18th century and, later, the drawings and paintings of
Van Wel show the layout of the garden at that time.

All parts of the 18th century design are on a monumental scale: the lake, or *Grand Etang,* measures 453
by 130 meters, or nearly 6 hectares (14.8 acres) in area,
and is divided from the moated château by a grass-
bordered walk. The lake forms the first part of the great
vista from the château, which extended for five kilometers (3.1 mi.) beyond the gardens. The curved end of the
lake is decorated with urns on pedestals and a fine
statue of Neptune flanked by reclining figures and lively
horses by Adrien Henrion. Beyond this, a boundary
canal acts as a ha-ha between the garden and a road,
preventing access but allowing the eye to travel to the
end of the vista.

On either side of the lake are a series of small enclosed
gardens, or bosquets, along parallel axes. Bordering the
enclosures on the east side is the long path known as the
Dean's Lane, or *L'Allée du Doyen,* with hedges six
meters (6.5 yd.) high. The first enclosure, known as *Le
Bassin Vert* or the *Boulingrin,* once included a pool but
is now simply a low mound of grass with gravel. To the
east of this enclosure is the rose garden, which used to
be filled with Bengal roses. Continuing eastward, the
next enclosure is a small children's playground and a
goldfish pond in the center of a newly planted *berceau.*
Next is the oval pool, which is surrounded by hornbeams. The final section to the east of the lake is *Les
Miroirs,* four rectangular pools that reflect the sky and
surrounding trees.

On the west side of the *Grand Etang* a similar series
of bosquets begins with *Le Bassin au Glacé,* or the Ice
Pool, a reflecting pool surrounded by an arbor. The

Statue of Neptune in the gardens of Beloeil, Brussels, Belgium
Copyright Miranda Abbs

Ladies' Pool, or *Bassin des Dames,* is surrounded by hornbeam tunnels recently replanted. There is a cross axis through the Ladies' Pool from the bosquets on the far side of the lake and through to the domed slate-roofed temple of Pomona in the *potagerie,* visible through the oak avenue, *L'Allée du Mail.* In *La Cloître* double hedges of hornbeam enclose a rectangular pool. The final section, at the end of the *Grand Etang* and facing *Les Miroirs,* is the quincunx of copper beeches from which the 19th-century orangery can be seen.

When Charles-Joseph, seventh prince of Ligne, succeeded to the title and the estate in 1766, he made small but significant changes to the gardens. He was the author of *Coup d'oeil sur Beloeil* and one of the most cultivated men of his day, much traveled, well read, and influenced by the new sensibility to nature. He appreciated the French style and comments "the glory of Beloeil is due to my father. . . . Satisfied with the harmony of the majestic proportions that I found in my garden, I have been careful to maintain them, and I have sought to be creative in a different way."

Influenced by the current taste for English or *anglochinois* gardens, where nature was allowed more scope, the prince created a narrow winding stream, Love's Rill (*Le Rieu d'Amour*) near the Dean's Lane on the east

side of the *Grand Etang* in 1770. The stream rises from three springs; a narrow path running along side it emphasizes its sinuous course. In 1775, with the help of François-Joseph Bélanger, a proponent of the *jardin irrégulier* and creator of the landscapes at Folie Saint-James and Méréville and the pavillion and garden at Bagatelle, Charles-Joseph added an English garden to the west of the castle. A brook winds amongst tall trees, and at one end a temple of Morpheus is set as a resting place for visitors to the garden. A folly, a copy of the ruined Temple of the Sibyl at Tivoli, is sited near a cascade. gardens at Bagatelle in Paris. The English Garden is now known as the deer park, *Le Parc au Daims,* and is not open to the public.

In 1787 Charles-Joseph created, with clay and twigs, an exact replica of his estate together with the improvements he wished to make. The layout and improvements depicted in miniature have hardly changed on the ground to this day. As a result of his work at Beloeil the prince became known as a designer and was asked for his advice about other gardens. He is believed to have suggested the idea of the Temple of Love in Marie-Antoinette's garden at Petit Trianon. In 1794, however, all idea of further work at Beloeil ended. The victory of the French revolutionary army at Fleurus forced the prince into exile. He went to Vienna but lived there in relative poverty as his estates, including Beloeil, were confiscated.

In 1804 Napoleon restored the estate to Ligne's second son (his first, Charles, had been killed while fighting the revolutionaries in France; a memorial to him, an obelisk, still stands in the private garden at Beloeil). Charles-Joseph was never to return to Beloeil.

## Synopsis

| | |
|---|---|
| 1538 | Original château constructed at Beloeil |
| 1637 | Land acquired with view to expansion of garden |
| 1721 | Potager laid out on site of Le Mail |
| 1734 | Commencement of water works |
| 1738 | Construction of temple of Pomona |
| ca. 1750 | Grand Etang enlarged to current dimensions |
| 1766 | Adrien Henrion commissioned to sculpt statue of Neptune to stand at head of Grand Etang |
| 1770 | Love's Rill created |
| 1775 | Creation of English garden with assistance of François Joseph Belanger |
| 1830 | Orangery transformed and reconstructed |
| 1900 | Fire destroys Château |
| 1906 | Château rebuilt and furnished with objects saved from fire |

## Further Reading

Ligne, Charles-Joseph, Prince de, *Coup d'Oeil sur Beloeil et sur une grande partie des jardins de l'Europe,* Beloeil, 1781; 3rd edition, Vienna, 1795; reprint, Paris: Édition de Paris, 1997; as *Coup d'Oeil at Beloeil and a Great Number of European Gardens,* translated and edited by Basil Guy, Berkeley: University of California Press, 1991

Scufflaire, Andree, et al., *Le château de Beloeil,* Gand, Belgium: Ludion, and Brussels: Crédit Communal, 1994

BARBARA ABBS

---

# Belvedere Palaces

## Vienna, Austria

**Location:**  Prinz Eugen-Straße 27

A summer residence built during 1713–23 for Prince Eugène of Savoy, the Belvedere palaces were initially situated just outside the city walls of Vienna. The two palaces—the Untere (Lower) and the Obere (Upper) Belvedere—and the garden that connects them have been carefully restored and maintained after suffering great damage during World War II. The garden is considered a major work of the baroque period in Vienna and one of the finest amalgams of Italian and French garden art. Some changes to the lavish design have been made: the orangery has been completely modified, and the menagerie and botanical garden no longer exist.

Prince Eugène (1663–1736) was an influential statesman, personal advisor to three emperors (Leopold I, Joseph I, and Karl VI), and supreme commander of the imperial forces, including during the wars against the Ottoman Empire. Beginning in 1679 the prince bought land on the gently descending grounds just outside the city walls of Vienna. He had the area terraced, effecting a *demi côte* that made waterworks and cascades possible. The beautiful view (hence the name Belvedere) over the spires and roofs of the imperial city added a special flavor to the place (see Plate 6). Starting in 1713 two spectacular summer palaces were constructed; the Untere Belvedere, completed in 1717, and the Obere Belvedere, finished in 1723. The rectangular garden that ingeniously joined the two palaces included parterres, an orangery, a menagerie, stables, as well as a large artificial pond, waterworks, stairways, and sculptures. Together they form a *Gesamtkunstwerk* regarded by many as the quintessence of a baroque summer residence, subtly blending elements from Italian and French garden art.

This elegant creation sprang from the prince's enormous wealth and the collaboration of three remarkable men: architect Johann Lukas von Hildebrandt, garden designer Dominique Girard, and gardener Anton Zinner. Their work is fully documented in J.B. Küchelbecker's *Allerneueste Nachricht vom Römisch-Kayerl. Hofe* (1720; Most Recent Report from the Roman Imperial Court) and two works by S. Kleiner, *Wunder würdiges Kriegs- und Siegs-Lager* (1731–40; Miraculous War and Victory Camp) and *Vorbildung Aller Ausländischen Thiere* (1734; Presentation of All Foreign Animals). Unanimously praised by the prince's contemporaries, the

Belvedere complex was used for political events and evening receptions during which the palaces and gardens were fully illuminated. The prince is said to have had a very personal relationship with his creation, where he fed his favorite animals, cleaned hedges, and took daily walks in the garden. Both the menagerie and botanical garden are reported to have been second only to those at Versailles. The botanical garden contained many rarities, such as pineapples, dragon trees (*Dracaena draco*), and three different palm species (a record at that time). The orangery, with its movable roof, was also famous.

After the death of Prince Eugène, the perhaps inevitable decline of the complex began. His heir, Victoria, later Princess of Sachsen-Hildburghausen, started to dissolve the menagerie, gave away botanical specimens, sold the vast art collection, and finally, in 1752 sold the Belvedere complex itself. The new owner was Maria Theresia, Queen of Hungary and Bohemia, who surprisingly never lived in her acquisition because she preferred the Schönbrunn palace. She opened the gardens to the public, however, and in 1770 invited more than 6,000 guests there to celebrate the marriage of her daughter Marie Antoinette and the dauphin (later King Louis XVI of France). In 1776 the imperial gallery was transferred to the Belvedere palaces and also opened to the public. However, the decline of the garden continued, with the waterworks in ruins and many ornaments demolished. About a century later, in 1888, the imperial gallery was moved out again, and the Belvedere palaces became the Vienna residence of Archduke Franz Ferdinand, who closed parts of the garden to the public and had them altered. After his assassination in Sarajevo, which led directly to World War I, the Belvedere was used by Archduke Maximilian (a brother of Karl I, the last emperor of Austria). Pigs, chickens, and bees were kept in the garden during the famine in Vienna.

With the fall of the Habsburg Empire, the Belvedere complex became property of the Republic of Austria and was again fully opened to the public. Starting in 1923–24 the Untere Belvedere became the home of the Austrian Museum of Baroque Art and the Obere Belvedere that of the Austrian Gallery of 19th- and 20th-century art. The garden now reached its lowest ebb; the water basins went dry and hay was grown on the former parterres. During World War II, the Belvedere complex was abused by Adolf Hitler and Hermann Göring during demonstrations of their power. Later a bunker was built under the artificial lake in front of the Obere Belvedere, and during 1944–45 both palaces were severely damaged by bombs.

Prompt restoration work soon allowed the museums to reopen. In 1955 the Österreichischer Staatsvertrag, an agreement between the Allies and Austria returning the nation's sovereignty, was signed in the Obere Belvedere

while crowds of Viennese celebrated in the garden. The Strategic Arms Limitation Treaty (SALT) talks between the United States and the Soviet Union were formally opened in the palace. On the basis of Kleiner's 18th-century documents a more careful restoration of the garden was undertaken in the 1990s. The resulting recreation of the entire complex as it was planned by Prince Eugène makes the Belvedere palaces a must-see for every visitor to Vienna.

**Synopsis**

| | |
|---|---|
| 1697 | Prince Eugène of Savoy starts buying land for summer residence; Johann Lukas von Hildebrandt commissioned as architect |
| 1717 | Dominique Girard, designer of Belvedere garden, in Vienna for first time; completion of Untere Belvedere |
| 1723 | Completion of entire project |
| 1752 | Maria Theresia, Queen of Hungary and Bohemia, buys complex; first mention of name Belvedere |
| 1760 | Bernardo Bellotto paints view from Obere Belvedere; gradual decline of garden begins |
| 1781–1888 | Both palaces used to house imperial art collections |
| 1899–1974 | Both palaces used as Vienna residence for Archduke Franz Ferdinand |
| 1923–24 | Both palaces again used to house art collections; garden at its lowest ebb |
| 1944–45 | Heavy damage due to bombing; cows and horses grazing on former parterres; early restoration |
| 1955 | Austrian State Treaty signed in Obere Belvedere |
| 1994– | Meticulous reconstruction of Belvedere complex |

**Further Reading**

Aurenhammer, Hans, "Der Garten des Prinzen Eugen: Zu seiner Theorie und Erscheinung," in *Prinz Eugen und sein Belvedere,* Vienna: Österreichische Galerie, 1963

Aurenhammer, Hans, et al., *Das Belvedere in Wien,* Vienna: Schroll, 1971

Fiedler, W., and U. Giese, "Die Menagerie und der Botanische Garten des Prinzen Eugen im Belvedere," in *Prinz Eugen und sein Belvedere,* Vienna: Österreichische Galerie, 1963

Schmidt, S., "Parkpflegewerk Belvedere-Garten in Wien," *Gartenkunst* 4 (1992)

H. WALTER LACK

# Berlin, Tiergarten

## Berlin, Germany

**Location:**   Berlin city center, adjacent to the
Brandenburg Gate

The German term *Tiergarten* (literally translated as "animal garden" or in French, "parc") refers to an aristocratic hunting preserve bordering the city limits. The first written evidence documenting the Berlin Electoral Tiergarten dates back to the first half of the 16th century. In 1697–98 Elector Friedrich III intersected the area with several straight avenues. The main avenue ran from the Berlin City Palace westward toward the newly built summer residence, Charlottenburg. In the center he created a star formed by eight avenues and named the Great Star. On the banks of the Spree River he created two semicircular salons with tree-lined walks radiating out from their center. Today this system of avenues is preserved almost in its original form.

In 1742 Friedrich II's director of palaces and gardens, Georg Wenzeslaus von Knobelsdorff, transformed part of the woodland into a French rococo-style bosquet. He created a labyrinth, an oblong basin dominated by a Venus sculpture, and numerous pathways and rondels, mostly ornamented with sculptures. Each boulevard was bordered by a different species of tree, such as pines, sycamores, acacias, and birch. Since this time the park has been opened to the general public.

Following the influence of the new landscape style, the royal court planter Justus Ehrenreich Sello introduced two small island areas: Rousseau Island in 1792 and Louise's Island in 1809, commemorating, respectively, the French philosopher with an urn and the beloved Prussian queen with a memorial vase. Both monuments have been replaced, the vase by a monumental sculpture of the queen (1877–80), and the Rousseau urn by a Rousseau stela (1987).

Near the Great Star lies the well-kept Bellevue park. Its palace currently serves as the residence for the president of Germany. The park was originally designed in 1784–92 as one of the first gardens in the *anglo-chinois* style in Prussia by the gardener Weil for Prince Ferdinand, the youngest brother of Frederick the Great. The palace is a focal point of one of the older Tiergarten boulevards. On the garden side it had four fan-shaped view axes stretching into the adjacent landscape on the banks of the Spree River. These charming views were the rationale behind the place's name, "Bellevue." Unfortunately, these views are now all obstructed, and a wall between the river and the park has been built under the auspices of President Herzog. Little remains of the original park; it was most recently redesigned in 1958–59 by Reinhard Besserer.

Peter Joseph Lenné transformed the remaining woodland areas of the Tiergarten into the existing great public landscaped park in 1833–40. He extended the rivulets in a picturesque manner and created open meadows within the forest and an inviting undulating network of paths. Crown Prince Friedrich Wilhelm laid out a symmetrical area near the Brandenburg Gate in 1839, containing a salon with a tree for each day in the year. It was redesigned in 1909 into a rose garden. Finally in 1846–47 Lenné designed the irregular-shaped New Lake in the southern part of the park. The first public zoological garden in Germany lies adjacent to the southern border of the Tiergarten and was designed by Lenné in 1844.

During the reign of the German kaisers (1871–1918), many representative and patriotic monuments were erected in the park commemorating famous Prussian kings, German authors, and composers, among others.

Albert Speer, Hitler's main architect, enlarged the east-west axis as one of his monumental axes in 1938–39 and bordered it with neoclassical iron candelabras. He moved the Victory Column, erected originally in 1873 in front of the Reichstag building, into the center of the Great Star. The Victory Column was surrounded with monuments of Bismarck, Moltke, and Roon, which were also moved from their original position near the Reichstag. Speer complemented the ensemble with neoclassical porticos and railings.

During and after World War II, the park's trees and plants were almost totally destroyed. The Soviets erected a victory monument near the Brandenburg Gate with the marble stones remaining from Hitler's Neue Reichskanzlei. The new government in West Berlin planted vast new populations of trees and plants in 1949–50. Fritz Witte and Willy Alverdes elaborated the layouts. Donations for this endeavor were received from throughout West Germany. At this time many rhododendrons were introduced along the waterways and now have reached enormous proportions.

As a special present from the British government to the Berlin people, the so-called English Garden was established near Bellevue in 1951–52. It is accentuated by a formal flower parterre and a reed-covered teahouse.

Since 1987 several parts of the park have been returned to their earlier contours; for example, Louise's Island is now restored to the state it was in in 1880, as are the two semicircular areas with focusing avenues on the banks of the Spree. The Berlin Garden Conservation Department, founded in 1978, supervised the restorations.

In addition, unsuccessful attempts to modify Albert Speer's monumental design have been carried out. The

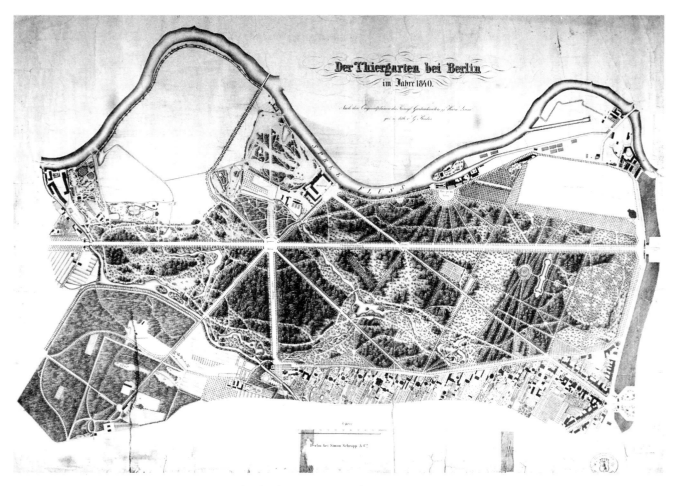

Site plan for the Tiergarten, Berlin, Germany, ca. 1840
Courtesy of Landesarchiv Berlin

width of the east-west axis was narrowed by means of rows of trees, and modern lampposts were erected. The Great Star was decorated with old-fashioned candelabra-style lampposts and street signs to replace the street lighting designed by Speer. The ensuing contradictions hardly can be explained.

## Synopsis

| | |
|---|---|
| early 16th century | First written record of Berlin Electoral Tiergarten (hunting preserve) |
| 1697–98 | First avenues, including the Great Star, cut into the hunting area, by Elector Friedrich III |
| 1742 | Partly transformed according to rococo style by Georg Wenzeslaus von Knobelsdorff |
| 1784–92 | Construction of Bellevue park on the margin, by the gardener Weil |
| 1792 | Rousseau Island introduced |
| 1809 | Louise's Island introduced (memorial to the Prussian queen) |
| 1833–40 | Peter Josef Lenné transforms rest of woodland into public landscape park |
| 1839 | Crown Prince Friedrich Wilhelm lays out area near Brandenburg Gate |
| 1844 | Germany's first zoological park established, designed by Lenné |
| 1846–47 | Lenné designs irregular-shaped New Lake |
| 1938–40 | Main axis enlarged; Victory column erected on the Great Star |
| 1949 | Replanting according to modern designs begun |
| 1958–59 | Bellevue park redesigned by Reinhard Besserer |

| 1987 | Reconstruction into earlier contours begun |
|---|---|

**Further Reading**

*Gartenkunst Berlin: 20 Jahre Gartendenkmalpflege in der Metropole; Garden Art of Berlin: 20 Years of*

*Conservation of Historic Gardens and Park in the Capital,* Berlin: Schelzky and Jeep, 1999

Wendland, Folkwin, *Der große Tiergarten in Berlin: seine Geschichte und Entwicklung in fünf Jahrhunderten,* Berlin: Mann, 1993

CLEMENS ALEXANDER WIMMER

---

# Berlin-Dahlem, Botanischer Garten

## Dahlem, Berlin, Germany

**Location:**  approximately 5 miles (8.3 km) southwest of Berlin city center

The Berlin-Dahlem Botanic Garden is Germany's largest botanical garden and one of the richest in species in the world. Part of a university institution that also comprises a rich herbarium, magnificent library, and Germany's main botanical museum, it is regarded as one of the leading institutions of its kind.

In 1897, limited space and the effects of a growing metropolis led to the decision to transfer the Royal Botanic Garden from Schöneberg, a suburb of Berlin, to a new and much larger site in Dahlem, later to become Berlin-Dahlem. Although this action is usually credited to Adolf Engler, then director of the Royal Botanic Garden and Museum, the driving force behind the move was actually his deputy, Ignatz Urban; the layout was basically the work of Wilhelm Perring and Franz Ledien, the *Garteninspektoren* (technical garden directors) at the time. However, the emphasis on plant geography in the arrangement of large parts of the new garden is clearly due to Engler, who had earlier restructured, according to this scheme, major parts of the Royal Botanic Garden in Breslau (Wrocław) and the Royal Botanic Garden in Schöneberg.

Since its beginning the Berlin-Dahlem Botanic Garden has consisted of several distinct gardens: a large arboretum, a systematic section, an extensive plant-geography section, a section for cultivated plants, a garden for aquatic plants, a medicinal garden, an "Italian garden," and the conservatories. Of these the arboretum, plant-geography section, Italian garden, and the conservatories still remain basically unchanged, making the garden an important garden monument. The large tropical conservatory is also a famous example of early 20th-century steel-and-glass construction. The systematic section, the section for aquatic plants, and the medicinal garden have been remodeled, and the section of cultivated plants has been discontinued. The medicinal garden also changed position within the garden.

The arrangements of plants in the arboretum and systematic section follow taxonomic concepts, in the medicinal garden the plants' uses, and in the aquatic garden ecological considerations. The Italian garden is an attempt to imitate a type of garden found frequently on the lakes south of the Alps—but here the conservatories dominate the garden and not the owner's palazzo. In contrast, the plant-geography section tries to imitate native vegetation: on no less than 23 hectares (57 acres) the visitor can admire the various types of vegetation found in temperate climates and wander through, for example, the Pyrenees, the Alps, mountains of the Apennine and Balkan Peninsulas, the Caucasus, the Himalaya, and the Appalachians. The plant-geography section is regarded as the apotheosis of a garden laid out according to these principles; nowhere else in the world was such a large area planted according to this rigid and scientifically accurate scheme. The plants cultivated in the large tropical greenhouse and several other conservatories are also arranged according to the principles of plant geography and offer impressions of the native vegetation, for example, of the Cap region, of Australia, and of the Mediterranean. In short, a tour through the world's vegetation zones is possible in the Berlin-Dahlem Botanic Garden.

Since Engler's days a considerable proportion of the plants grown were collected on expeditions and are at least partly documented, with a vast number of specimens fully labeled, both in the open and in the conservatories. The Italian garden, the imitation of a Japanese temple, and a long row of lilacs (*Syringa vulgaris*) are among the few concessions to the less botanically minded public.

Although visitors were permitted in the garden as early as 1903, the official inauguration took place in

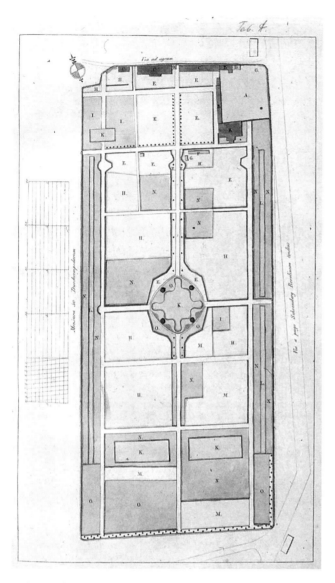

Early site plan of the Berlin-Dahlem Botanic Garden, 1801
Courtesy of Botanischer Garten und Botanisches Museum Berlin-Dahlem

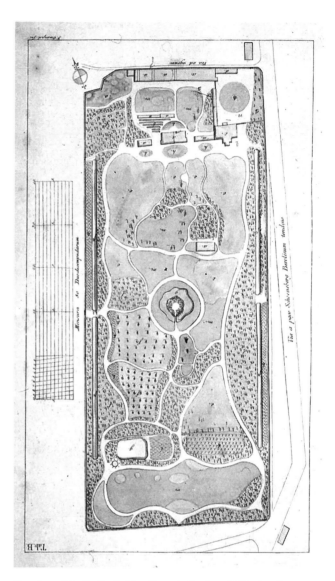

Site plan of the Berlin-Dahlem Botanic Garden, 1812, showing changes to the garden since 1801
Courtesy of Botanischer Garten und Botanisches Museum Berlin-Dahlem

1910. Right from the beginning the layout was universally praised, and the collections of living plants, in particular those grown in the vast conservatories, attracted the masses to Dahlem. In addition to its role in academic teaching, the Royal Botanic Garden in Dahlem acted during the first decade of its existence as a clearinghouse for economic plants from the German *Schutzgebiete* (colonies), much in the same way the Royal Botanic Gardens at Kew fulfilled this function for the British Empire. This came to an end in 1919, when the German Reich lost all its overseas territories.

No major change took place at the botanic garden until the end of World War II. During the last days of the war, heavy fighting on garden grounds, the destruction of the conservatories' glass cover, and the building of trenches caused substantial losses.

Soviet military personnel protected the garden after the armistice. For a starving population cabbage and potatoes were grown during the first summer, but the garden was soon restored and reopened to the public. The reconstruction of the conservatories was finally completed in 1968 with the inauguration of the large tropical conservatory. Subsequently, emphasis was placed on the acquisition of documented plant material collected in the wild, the seed of which is regularly offered in the garden's *Index Seminum*. Conservatories for mosses and *Welwitschia mirabilis* are special new attractions. There is also a small cemetery in the garden, in which some of the most famous German botanists are buried, among them Georg Schweinfurth, Adolf Engler, and his successor, Ludwig Diels.

For obvious reasons there are no monumental trees in the Berlin-Dahlem Botanic Gardens, the oldest specimens being of *Encephalartos altensteinii* from South Africa and *Dioon spinulosum* from Mexico, both cultivated in the large tropical greenhouse and, according to oral tradition, transplanted from the garden's former site. A few popular garden plants have been first introduced into cultivation by the Berlin-Dahlem Botanic Garden, among them *Sedum adolphii* Hamet, also from Mexico.

Due to its size and the richness of its living collections from all parts of the world, this garden is generally regarded as Germany's brightest botanical jewel and merits a visit at all times of the year.

## Synopsis

| | |
|---|---|
| 1897 | Decision by Parliament to transfer Royal Botanic Garden from Potsdamer Strasse to new site in Dahlem |
| 1897–1903 | Layout by Wilhelm Perring and Franz Ledien according to master plan by Adolf Engler |
| 1903 | First visitors admitted to garden |
| 1909 | Construction of conservatories completed |
| 1910 | Official inauguration |
| 1944–45 | Destruction of conservatories and garden grounds by war action |
| 1948 | Reopening of first conservatory |
| 1950 | Reconstruction of garden completed, excluding conservatories |
| 1968 | Reopening of large tropical conservatory |

## Further Reading

Hagemann, Isolde, and Bernhard Zepernick, *Der Botanische Garten Berlin-Dahlem: Führer durch das Freiland und die Gewächshäuser,* Berlin: Fördererkreis der Naturwissenschaftlichen Museen Berlins, 1992; as *The Berlin-Dahlem Botanic Garden: Guide to the Grounds and Greenhouses,* translated by Lowell Smith, 1993

Lack, H. Walter, "Berlin and the World of Botany," in *Proceedings of the XIV International Botanical Congress,* edited by Werner Greuter and Brigitte Zimmer, Königstein, Germany: Koeltz Scientific Books, 1988

Lack, H. Walter, "Berlins grüne Schatzkammer: Botanischer Garten und Botanisches Museum Berlin-Dahlem," in *Theater der Natur und Kunst; Theatrum Naturae et Artis: Wunderkammern des Wissens,* edited by Horst Bredekamp et al., Berlin: Henschel, 2000

Lack, H. Walter, *Botanisches Museum Berlin: Adolf Engler: Die Welt in einem Garten,* Munich and New York: Prestel, 2000

Urban, Ignatz, "Geschichte des Königlichen Botanischen Museums zu Berlin-Dahlem (1815–1913) nebst Aufzählung seiner Sammlungen," *Beihefte zum Botanischen Centralblatt* Abt. 1, 34 (1917)

Zepernick, Bernhard, and Friedrich Karl Timler, *Grundlagen zur 300 Jährigen Geschichte des Berliner Botanischen Gartens,* Berlin: Botanischer Garten und Botanisches Museum Berlin-Dahlem, 1979

H. WALTER LACK

# Bermuda

Bermuda lies 600 miles (968 km) off the coast of North Carolina in the Atlantic Ocean. It is, in fact, a collection of coral islands perched atop an extinct volcano. The archipelago is about 21 miles (34 km), lying northeast to southwest; the biggest islands are at most two and a half miles (4 km) across and are joined by bridges. From a gardener's point of view, Bermuda benefits from a semitropical climate but also has high winds, even hurricanes on occasion, and there are no rivers or streams. There is ample rainfall, but all water must be caught and stored in tanks or the underrock natural water lens, or aquifers, used. The soil comes in pockets of variable depths, some as deep as six feet, others mere inches; but with good cultivation even the shallow soil is productive.

Bermuda was first colonized in a dramatic way. Portuguese and Spanish ships had visited it and left behind pigs and some plants for future shipwrecked travelers. An expedition scattered by a hurricane on its way to Virginia in 1609 managed to land its last ship on the rocks and get all passengers plus their stores and seeds ashore. They spent a year there before setting off in ships they built from cedar trees then covering the island. During that year they planted the seeds they brought with them. Sir George Somers, leader of the expedition, planted "kitchen herbs," lettuces, radishes,

Waterways, Somerset Bridge, Bermuda
Copyright Jill Collett

peas, onions, and muskmelons. Proper colonization followed in 1612 with ships from England, and by 1617 a correspondence had been established between the Rich brothers—Richard in Bermuda and Nathaniel in England—about the gardens in Bermuda. As early as those years, the essential and characteristic walls and palings appeared. It was necessary to enclose gardens against wandering pigs and livestock, as well as to demark ownership. Richard Rich writes:

> Your garden that is payled in is fifty pole square [two hundred seventy five yards square] and a well in the midst of it. Figg trees planted round about the well and vines and one [of] the post dyells [a sundial?] that I brought over with mee sett upp nere unto the well.

He later refers to the bees he has installed in another garden for their honey. These early gardens were what would today be called vegetable gardens, although most plants had medicinal and alternative uses as well. There is adequate evidence that roses grew at the time, and every part of the rose was used medicinally. The 17th century was a busy farming time, and inventories show that most houses had gardens. However, through lack of good husbandry, the land was soon worked out, and the cutting of cedar trees for shipbuilding opened up the islands to the wind and to plant diseases. By the 18th century, in spite of exhortations from England and their own governors, the people of Bermuda concentrated on shipbuilding, trading, and fishing.

At the same time, some handsome houses were built in the 18th century, many of which still stand. Each usually had a walled garden very near the house and some had another garden a short distance away. There were a few big enclosures similar to those in England. Some terracing was done, and so steps are another common garden feature. Also during this century purely decorative plants started to be brought back from the travels of wandering sailors. Trees, too, were imported, and it may have been hoped that some of these would eventually be harvested for lumber. Tamarind arrived from the West Indies and mahogany from British Honduras. The locust tree (*Hymenea courbaril*) formed a magnificent avenue by the early 19th century, according to one writer, and the tree planted along streets in America, *Melia azerdarach*, arrived in 1780, very soon after its arrival in America (it had been brought from Persia by André Michaux). Oleander, now widely used as hedging, arrived about the same time. The Tucker brothers, Henry in Bermuda and St. George in Williamsburg, Virginia, wrote to each other, exchanging and discussing plants, among them *Poinciana pulcherrima*, used in Barbados as fencing. Both *Hibiscus tiliaceus*, good for seaside planting, and *Erythrina coralladendron*, both from the Southern Islands, arrived a few years later. And although the general populace, lacking food, relied heavily on imports, some people continued to grow fruits and vegetables. The island gradually began to accommodate a great variety of trees, shrubs, flowers, and vegetables.

When Governor William Reid arrived in 1839, he was concerned with encouraging agriculture to make the island self-sufficient from a military point of view and reduce its vulnerability to blockades. He sent for plows and Scotsmen to demonstrate their use, imported many vegetables and flowers for the first time, inaugurated agricultural shows, and established the basis for modern agriculture. This period also coincided with the movement of people around the world for many different reasons, mostly economic—the Irish to America, the Indians to Trinidad, and the Portuguese from the Azores to Bermuda. The Azorean Portuguese have formed the hard-working farmer class of Bermuda since then. They still form the largest class of farmers, although a few young Bermudans have turned back to farming. Later in the century Bermuda onions and Easter lilies became popular, and both were exported in large quantities to America and Europe.

The modern garden in Bermuda has a wide variety of plants, including crotons and hibiscus in many colors, plumbago, bougainvillea, gardenias, and frangipani; many gardens have mixed citrus orchards, and some have a small vegetable bed. The British landscape movement never really touched Bermuda—there was not enough space. If there is a derivative style at all, it is Victorian, partly because of the encouragement of the Portuguese gardeners and partly because the neatness appealed to people's sense of order. The early walls and steps remain, and the islands convey the sense of being one big garden.

**Further Reading**

Leighton, Ann, *Early American Gardens*, Boston: Houghton Mifflin, and London: Cassell, 1970

Zuill, William, *Bermuda Sampler*, Hamilton: The Bermuda Book Stores, 1937

Zuill, William E.S., *The Story of Bermuda and Her People*, London: Macmillan, 1973; 2nd edition, London: Macmillan Education, 1983

JILL COLLETT

# Biddulph Grange

## Biddulph, Staffordshire, England

**Location:**  approximately 10 miles (1.6 km) north of Stoke-on-Trent, or 35 miles (56.3 km) south of Manchester

"Not a typical Victorian garden yet very much a garden of its time" is how Peter Hayden describes Biddulph. It was certainly novel, even revolutionary in its design and planting, reflecting the eclecticism of the time and the developing passion for growing exotic plants.

Already an accomplished horticulturist and specialist in orchids, James Bateman moved to Biddulph in 1841 and began simultaneously laying out the garden and redesigning and extending the house. He soon called on Edward Cooke, marine painter and aspiring garden designer, to help him realize his ideas for the house and provide inspiration for the garden. This classic collaboration of a wealthy and imaginative plantsman and a visionary designer resulted in a garden of richness and individuality.

Although Biddulph was entirely original in its purpose and arrangement, ideas were, as always, drawn from nearby gardens of the time, notably Alton Towers, Chatsworth, Derby Arboretum, and Elvaston Castle.

Architectural structure and water, Biddulph Grange, Staffordshire, England
Copyright Paul Miles Picture Collection

Multitiered avenues, rock work and extensive land modeling, eclectic styling, and the liberal use of evergreens were all elements of Bateman's garden. Significantly, the creation of Biddulph coincided with the establishment of the Royal Botanic Gardens, Kew, and Bateman fostered close links with it through its first director, Sir William Hooker, and his son Joseph. Innovation was the order of the day whether it was William Barron moving mature trees or Joseph Paxton designing great greenhouses and ultimately the Crystal Palace.

It was also an exciting time for plant collecting, with new sources such as China and Japan being opened up and the invention of means for importing young plants. Nathaniel Ward's glazed packing case, or Wardian case, which effectively protected plants for many weeks onboard ship, revolutionized plant introduction especially from the Far East. The golden larch (*Pseudolarix amabilis*) growing in the section referred to as China is the sole survivor of the first small batch of seedlings of this species ever grown outside the country China, one of the many plants collected by Robert Fortune and introduced by Loddiges's Nursery of Hackney.

Bateman and Cooke broke new ground in their ambition to grow every possible plant from all over the world, each in an appropriate setting, both culturally and stylistically: hence their eclectic arrangement of contrasting features—China, Egypt, the Rocky Glen, the terraces, etc.—wittily juxtaposed and cleverly separated. They employed a whole range of devices to divide and articulate their asymmetric arrangement while fitting in a maximum of interest and variety.

Edward Kemp, who recorded the garden precisely in a series of articles in *The Gardeners' Chronicle* in 1856 and 1862, reflected intense contemporary interest in the garden, stressing both that it was "a very high achievement of art" and that its "great true secret" lay in "the preparation of a suitable home" for Bateman's growing plant collection.

**Synopsis**

| | |
|---|---|
| 1841 | James Bateman moves to Biddulph Grange and begins work, some initial planting started |
| 1849 | Edward Cooke's first visit to Biddulph Grange |
| 1850–67 | Garden features designed and developed by Cooke in collaboration with Bateman, while Bateman designs and rebuilds house |
| 1856–67 | Terraces, parterres, dahlia walk, cherry orchard, Egyptian court, Cheshire cottage, arboretum, pinetum, "China" (a Chinese garden), "stumpery" (oak stumps and woodland plants), glen, and rhododendron ground completed |
| 1871 | Sale of Biddulph Grange to Robert Heath |
| 1896 | Fire destroys main part of house; rebuilding |
| 1921 | Conversion of house into orthopedic hospital |
| 1939–88 | Accelerating decline and vandalism |
| 1988 | Acquisition by National Trust and start of restoration |

**Further Reading**

Bateman, James, *The Orchidaceae of Mexico and Guatemala*, London, 1837–43; reprint, Richmond, British Columbia: Hamilton, 1994

Coats, Alice M., *The Quest for Plants: A History of the Horticultural Explorers*, London: Studio Vista, 1969; as *The Plant Hunters: Being a History of the Horticultural Pioneers, Their Quests, and Their Discoveries from the Renaissance to the Twentieth Century*, New York: McGraw-Hill, 1969

Conner, Patrick, *Oriental Architecture in the West*, London: Thames and Hudson, 1979

Elliott, Brent, *Victorian Gardens*, London: Batsford, and Portland, Oregon: Timber Press, 1986

Fletcher, Harold Roy, *The Story of the Royal Horticultural Society, 1804–1968*, London: Oxford University Press, 1969

Fortune, Robert, *Three Years' Wanderings in the Northern Provinces of China*, London, 1847; reprint, London: Mildmay, 1987

Fortune, Robert, *A Journey to the Tea Countries of China*, London, 1852; reprint, London: Mildmay, 1987

Hayden, Peter, *Biddulph Grange, Staffordshire: A Victorian Garden Rediscovered*, London: Philip, 1989

Kemp, Edward, *How to Lay Out a Garden*, London 1850; 8th edition, New York: Wiley, 1894

Kemp, Edward, "Biddulph Grange" (two series of articles), *The Gardeners' Chronicle* (1856 and 1862)

Loudon, John Claudius, *The Suburban Gardener and Villa Companion*, London, 1838; 2nd edition, as *The Villa Gardener*, London, 1850; reprint of 1st edition, New York: Garland, 1982

Munday, John, *E.W. Cooke, Marine Painter*, London: Society for Nautical Research, 1967

Murray, Andrew, *The Book of the Royal Horticultural Society: 1862–1863*, London, 1863

JOHN SALES

---

# Bijhouwer, Jan Thijs Pieter 1898–1974

## Dutch Landscape Architect

Jan Bijhouwer was the grandson of a flower grower and the son of a horticulture teacher. This background of both horticulture and teaching seems to have been instrumental in shaping Bijhouwer's career as a landscape architect. Following secondary school he spent part of a year working for the Kriest plant nursery in Amsterdam. He then went to the Agricultural University in Wageningen where he studied horticulture and garden architecture under H.F. Hartogh Heys van Zouteveen (1870–1943), a cultural philosopher by training. Van Zouteveen was the first to use a scientific rather than an artistic base for landscape design, by applying principles of plant geography. This influence encouraged Bijhouwer to work as a research assistant in the Department of Plant Taxonomy and Geography, where he earned his Ph.D. by completing a geobotanic study of the dunes near Bergen that provided evidence of a connection between vegetation and soil conditions. Following a year at the Arnold Arboretum in Massachusetts, he worked as a landscape architect for Better Homes for America.

Returning to the Netherlands in 1930, Bijhouwer temporarily served as editor of the popular home and garden magazine *Onze Tuinen met Huis en Hof* until he

Model of the sculpture garden of the Museum Kröller-Müller, Otterlo, Netherlands
Courtesy of Wageningen UR Library

was offered a position in the Department of City Development in Rotterdam. There he worked on the Kralinger Hout, a large urban woodland project at the edge of the city. In Rotterdam he met various members of Opbouw, the Rotterdam branch of the International Congress of Modern Architecture (CIAM). He joined the group and cooperated on its recreational study of Rotterdam. While working with these progressive functionalist architects, Bijhouwer continued to develop his ideas on landscape design. His motto became: "Back to nature and native art!" With this approach Bijhouwer showed an affinity for more traditional architects such as Professor L.M.J. Granpré Molière of the Technical University of Delft, whose work on the garden village Vreewijk at the edge of Rotterdam Bijhouwer praised repeatedly. As a result, Bijhouwer was asked to organize a lecture course on Dutch landscapes in Delft in 1932 and was appointed landscape architect for the Wiering-

ermeer, the first of the new IJsselmeer polders, where Granpré Molière was the main consultant on aesthetics. This appointment enabled Bijhouwer to embark on a career as a freelance consultant.

Bijhouwer's main works consisted of private gardens for houses designed by various architects. Thus he was able to theorize about the relationship between building and garden, resulting in his seminal essay in *De 8 en Opbouw* in 1938. In 1936 Bijhouwer accepted a lecturing position at the Agricultural University in Wageningen, where he became a reader in 1939. His inaugural lecture concentrated on the issue of contemporary planting design. It clearly indicated his special interest in planting design based on phytogeographical principles, which remained a recurrent issue after the war. The commencement of his academic career meant that there was less time for private practice, and Bijhouwer tended to spend more time theorizing and publishing. He was, however, still to get some of his largest commissions, including the landscape plan for the Noordoostpolder in 1942, followed by further commissions.

In 1946 Bijhouwer was appointed the first professor of garden and landscape architecture in the Netherlands. His inaugural lecture showed a greater commitment to social issues through the topic of neighborhood planning. He identified the role of landscape architects in this work, noting the extent and limitations of their involvement and the need for cooperation between various professions. Some of his most important postwar commissions were his appointment as adviser for the national park Hoge Veluwe, where he designed the Kröller-Müller sculpture garden; other important commissions include the Erebegraafplaats, Overveen, for wartime resistance fighters, and the Memorial Garden in Putten. While the majority of his projects after the war were private gardens, his greatest achievements were in large-scale planning and policy. In the immediate postwar era his name became associated with the functionalistic approach to landscape design, which was known as the School of Bijhouwer. His association with modernism was perhaps strengthened by his second marriage (in 1947) to a former Bauhaus student.

Before the war Bijhouwer had been a valued member of a roadside planting committee (1937–39), which allowed him to explore his interest in planting design. His postwar projects were dominated by planting strategies for various councils. His other commitments show that he enjoyed working with others on large and complicated projects. His lifelong associations with architects and former students provided him with continuing stimulus and work. However, it was as a landscape theorist and critic that he became best known. His prolific output of well over 250 publications in both the popular and professional press showed him to be a sharp observer with a methodological mind. His critical essays were frequently about environmental or social issues, and his books were written primarily for educational purposes. One of his seminal publications was his last, an analysis of the Netherlands according to cultural landscapes, *Het Nederlandse Landschap* (1971). Started just after the war, it was not finished until after his retirement in 1966.

Bijhouwer showed a good understanding of international developments and was in demand as a lecturer abroad. One of his best foreign friends was Lewis Mumford, the American planner and sociologist. Working as a guest professor in the United States, he reported on his visit with a series of "American Notes" (*Bouw*, 1953) in which he analyzes aspects of and trends in American society.

Bijhouwer is considered the first modernist landscape architect in the Netherlands because he showed the peculiar ambiguity between landscape and modernism.

He was among the prominent professionals and academics who completed the transition from garden architecture to landscape architecture. He was the Netherlands' foremost landscape teacher of the 20th century and had international influence. His main legacy lies in his writings, which show the gradual evolution of the profession to embrace social issues, large=scale planning of newly reclaimed land, housing, recreation, and issues relating to the increased use of the automobile.

## Biography

Born in Amsterdam, Netherlands, 1898. His father was a teacher who lectured on horticulture; studied horticulture and garden architecture at Agricultural University, Wageningen, Netherlands, 1916–21; military service, 1921–22; assistant at Department of Plant Taxonomy and Geography, Wageningen, 1922–26; completed doctorate, geobotanic study of the Berger dunes, 1926; Rockefeller Fellowship at Arnold Arboretum, Boston, Massachusetts, botanical expedition to Cuba, 1927–28; landscape architect for Better Homes in America, 1928–29; married Evelyn Oliver, 1930; joined Department of City Development, Rotterdam, Netherlands, 1930–32; taught course in landscape types at Technical University of Delft, Netherlands, 1932; landscape adviser, Wieringermeer, Netherlands, 1933; started private practice, initially in Velsen, Netherlands, then Wageningen, 1939, Amsterdam, 1945, and back to Wageningen, 1948; lecturer on garden art at Agricultural University, Wageningen, 1936–39; reader, 1939–46, with inaugural lecture on "The Problem of Plant Grouping"; first professor in garden and landscape architecture, 1946–66, with inaugural lecture on neighborhood planning, 1947; married Gerda Marx, former Bauhaus student, 1947; guest professor in Department of Landscape Architecture, School of Design, Rhode Island, United States, 1951–52; part-time adviser in Rotterdam, 1953–56; guest professor, Massachusetts Institute of Technology, lectured at Harvard University and Technical University, Berlin, 1962; retired 1966. Died in Wageningen, 1974.

## Selected Designs

1930–36   Kralinger Hout, Rotterdam, Netherlands
1933   Landscape advice, Wieringermeer Polder, Netherlands
1942   Landscape masterplan, Noordoostpolder, Netherlands
1946   Landscape masterplan for regeneration of Walcheren (with R.J. Benthem), Zeeland, Netherlands
1947   Erebegraafplaats, Overveen, Netherlands (with L. van Weydom Claterbos and architects G.H. Holt and Auke Komter)

1955–64   Kröller-Müller sculpture garden, National
          Park De Hoge Veluwe, Otterlo,
          Netherlands
1961      Regional recreation plan for "Holland
          Green Zone" between Rotterdam and
          Amsterdam, Netherlands (with J. Vallen
          and J.W. Zaaijer)

**Selected Publications**

"Nieuwe banen," *Onze tuinen met huis en hof* 25
   (1930)
*Perspectief-constructie zonder vertekening voor
   tuinontwerpers en architecten*, 1938
"Gebouw en tuin," *De 8 en Opbouw* 9 (1938)
*Nederlandsche tuinen en buitenplaatsen*, 1942
"Cultuursteppe Nederland," *Natuur en landschap* 1
   (1946)
*De wijkgedachte: Rede uitgesproken bij de
   aanvaarding van het ambt van hoogleraar aan de
   Landbouwhoogeschool te Wageningen, op 18 Maart
   1947*, 1947
"Two Neighborhood Parks from Two Centuries:
   Contrasting Developments in Denmark and the
   Netherlands," *Landscape Architecture* 40 (1949)
"Plantensociologie en tuinarchitectuur," *De
   Boomkwekerij* 6 (1951)
"A Continental Looks Critically at American
   Landscape Architecture, with Regret for the Passing
   of 19th-Century Tradition," *Landscape Architecture*
   63, no. 2 (1952)
*Waarnemen en ontwerpen in tuin en landschap*, 1954
"Het landschapsbeeld van de nieuwe polders," *Forum*
   10 (1955)

*Leven met groen in landschap, stad en tuin* (with Mien
   Ruys), 1960
"Stedenschemering," *Polytechnisch tijdschrift* 70, no. 3
   (1960)
"It Cannot Happen Here," *Publieke werken* 31
   (1963)
"Recreatie vraagstukken," *Publieke werken* 32
   (1964)
*Het Nederlandse landschap*, 1971

**Further Reading**

Boer, W.C.J., "Changing Ideals in Urban Landscape
   Architecture in The Netherlands," in *Learning
   from Rotterdam: Investigating the Process of Urban
   Park Design*, edited by M.J. Vroom and J.H.A.
   Meeus, London: Mansell, and New York: Nichols,
   1990
Lörzing, Han, *Van Bosplan tot Floriade*, Rotterdam:
   Uitgeverij, 1992
Oldenburger-Ebbers, Carla S., Anne Mieke Backer, and
   Eric Blok, *Gids voor de Nederlandse tuin- en
   landschapsarchitectuur: Deel West: Noord-Holland,
   Zuid-Holland*, Rotterdam: De Hef, 1995
Woudstra, Jan, "Jacobus P. Thijsse's Influence on Dutch
   Landscape Architecture," in *Nature and Ideology:
   Natural Garden Design in the Twentieth Century*,
   edited by Joachim Wolschke-Bulmahn, Washington,
   D.C.: Dumbarton Oaks, 1997
Woudstra, Jan, "Landscape for Living: Garden Theory
   and Design of the Modern Movement," Ph.D. diss.,
   University of London, 1997

JAN WOUDSTRA

---

# Biltmore House

## Asheville, Buncombe County, North Carolina, United States

**Location:**   entrance off U.S. 25 at Lodge Street,
               Asheville, approximately 120 miles (193
               km) northeast of Atlanta, Georgia

The Biltmore Estate, a national historic landmark, is a
remarkable complex that embodies two men's masterpieces: the house designed by Richard Morris Hunt and
the gardens by Frederick Law Olmsted. George Vanderbilt decided to build his house on a bluff overlooking
the confluence of the French Broad and Swannanoa
Rivers, with distant views of Mount Pisgah. Soon afterward Vanderbilt consulted Olmsted, who advised him
that, as the land had been timbered and as it was
"rough," the extensive park that Vanderbilt envisaged
was not practicable. Olmsted suggested a "small" 250-
acre (101 ha) home park, gardens around the house,
farms near the rivers, and the renovation of the forest.

Hunt designed the brick-and-pebbledash lodge that
guards the entrance to the estate. The three-mile-long
(approximately 4.8 km) approach road winds through
the parkland landscape, which is carefully planned to
give no distant views because Olmsted wanted to create

the sensation of "passing through the remote depths of a natural forest." The planting includes many native species as well as stock from the Biltmore nursery, which was superintended for many years by the horticulturist Chauncey Beadle. Many of the rare plants from the nursery were grown from seeds supplied by the Arnold Arboretum, horticultural societies, botanical gardens, and nurseries both in the United States and abroad. Olmsted designed the planting of the approach road to be of year-round interest.

The approach road ends in a sharp turn that gives one a dramatic view of the house. The area at the front of the house is called the Esplanade and includes the Front Lawn, which frames the house and is lined with a double row of tulip trees, the Rampe Douce, and the grass slope known as the Vista, which is crowned by a little temple and a statue of Diana. The house and the Esplanade stand on a plateau carved out of the hillside, buttressed on the valley side by a massive retaining wall. Apparently at Richard Hunt's suggestion, the Esplanade was modeled on the gardens at the Château de Vaux-le-Vicomte in France.

The terraces near the house include the Library Terrace, shaded by wisteria, and the South Terrace, which has spectacular views across to the Blue Ridge Mountains. The formal serenity of the Italian Garden is intentionally evocative of Renaissance villas.

The Ramble, or Shrub Garden, runs down the hillside from the Italian Garden. On either side of the meandering paths are numerous specimen shrubs, some American and some from the Far East. The gate at the lower end of the Ramble leads to the four-acre (1.6 ha) Walled Garden. Olmsted originally designed this peaceful enclosed area to be like an English country-house kitchen garden, but Vanderbilt insisted on an ornamental garden instead. Part of the Walled Garden is planted with bedding plants and part with roses, with a particular emphasis on the varieties grown in George Vanderbilt's time.

The conservatory and greenhouses were designed by Richard Hunt and restored in the 1950s. In the glassed-in buildings the bedding plants are grown for the Walled Garden, potted plants are raised for the Winter Garden in the house, and hothouse plants are displayed in the conservatory. Planting for butterflies is particularly emphasized in the beds in front of the conservatory.

The Spring Garden, or Vernal Garden, lies beyond the Ramble. A grove of tall native white pines and hemlocks surrounds spring-flowering shrubs. From the Spring Garden a path leads to the Glen or Azalea Garden. The 20-acre (8 ha) garden, set in a valley below the Ramble, is renowned for the azaleas collected by Chauncey Beadle and for the other rare plants and trees, including *Torreya*, *Metasequoia*, and *Franklinia*. The azaleas include 14 native species and numerous hybrids, a colorful sight in the spring.

Olmsted designed the Deerpark, which lies to the south and west of the house, in the English Picturesque landscape tradition. In the fall the foliage colors are spectacular. The two water features of the gardens are also in the English tradition. An old millpond was enlarged to make the Bass Pond, which is just to the south of the Azalea Garden. The tranquil lagoon is near the lower drive to the west of the house and was mostly used for fishing.

Vanderbilt originally intended to plant the farmland like an English park, but Olmsted persuaded him to develop it as commercially, but responsibly, managed forest. To this end Gifford Pinchot, who had trained in France, was employed to create a land-use plan for the forest. The plan, designed according to European principles of responsible forestry, was the first in the United States and became a model for many others. Pinchot left Biltmore in 1895 and went on to found the U.S. Forest Service. Vanderbilt then employed Dr. Carl Schenk, a well-known German forester, who was particularly interested in native species of trees and designed several new woods on the estate. In 1898 Schenk founded the Biltmore Forest School, which operated until 1913. The ecological and scientific principles of forest management, which were pioneered by Vanderbilt and then established at the school by Schenk, are still important and influential. The forest surrounding the estate, donated to the nation in 1915, became the United States' first national forest.

Biltmore House, Richard Morris Hunt's masterpiece, is probably the finest example not only of the early eclectic period of American architecture but also of the American country house. The estate, Olmsted's masterpiece, is immensely influential in the history of both landscape design and forestry in the United States.

## Synopsis

| | |
|---|---|
| 1888 | George Vanderbilt begins to buy parcels of land near Asheville |
| 1888–95 | Gardens and estate laid out by the landscape architect Frederick Law Olmsted, including parkland forest, deer park in the English Picturesque landscape tradition, and many gardens |
| 1889 | Vanderbilt engages the architect Richard Morris Hunt |
| 1890 | Chauncey Beadle engaged as nursery superintendent |
| 1891–95 | Gifford Pinchot, as forest superintendent, creates land-use plan for the forest of Biltmore, the first such plan in the United States |
| 1895 | Carl Schenk engaged as forest superintendent |

| 1895 | Biltmore House completed |
| 1896–1902 | Town of Best, renamed Biltmore Village, enlarged, including hospital, school, church, and railway station |
| 1898 | Biltmore Forest School founded by Schenk |
| 1901 | Biltmore Industries founded |
| 1903 | School for Domestic Science founded |
| 1914 | George Vanderbilt dies |
| 1915 | Edith Vanderbilt deeds nearly 87,000 acres (approximately 35,200 ha) (now part of the Pisgah National Forest) to the federal government |
| 1920s | Biltmore Industries and Biltmore Village sold |
| 1925 | Edith Vanderbilt remarries and Cornelia Vanderbilt Cecil takes over the estate |
| 1930 | Biltmore opened to the public |
| 1950s | Conservatory and greenhouses restored |
| 1963 | Biltmore named a National Historic Landmark |

## Further Reading

Baker, Paul R., *Richard Morris Hunt*, Cambridge, Massachusetts, and London: MIT Press, 1980

Bryan, John Morrill, *Biltmore Estate: The Most Distinguished Private Place*, New York: Rizzoli, 1994

Carley, Rachel D., and Rosemary G. Rennicke, *A Guide to Biltmore Estate*, Ashville, North Carolina: Biltmore, 1999

Messer, Pamela Lynn, *Biltmore Estate: Frederick Law Olmsted's Landscape Masterpiece*, Asheville, North Carolina: WorldComm, 1993

Pinchot, Gifford, *Biltmore Forest*, Chicago, 1893; reprint, New York: Arno, 1970

Schenck, Carl Alwin, *The Biltmore Story: Recollections of the Beginning of Forestry in the United States*, edited by Ovid Butler, St. Paul, Minnesota: American Forest History Foundation, Minnesota Historical Society, 1955

Stein, Susan R., editor, *The Architecture of Richard Morris Hunt*, Chicago: University of Chicago Press, 1986

Stevenson, Elizabeth, *Park Maker: A Life of Frederick Law Olmsted*, New York: Macmillan, and London: Collier-Macmillan, 1977

JULIA KING

---

# Birkenhead Park

## Birkenhead, Merseyside, England

**Location:** on the Wirral Peninsula, across the River Mersey from Liverpool, approximately 3 miles (4.8 km) southwest of Liverpool city center

Birkenhead Park is one of the most important 19th-century landscapes in the United Kingdom. It established a pattern that was emulated in many parts of the world. This was not a treat reserved for the rich, nor was it graciously bestowed upon the "deserving artisan" or "laboring poor," who might have had nothing better (it was not a park donated to the masses as a sign of the beneficence of a great industrialist, as was, for example, the Derby Arboretum, dedicated by Joseph Strutt to the "artisans of Derby"). It was not even to be in an area where only one class of society lived; part of the park's very significance was that its benefit was available to all. Moreover, the landscape was laid out and beautified by Joseph Paxton, perhaps the most

important designer of the day and head gardener at Chatsworth, the seat of one of the greatest nobles in the land. It was a landscape that clearly signified a new social order, where the community itself—that admixture of rich and poor, worthy and unworthy—was on the edge of becoming as great a force of economic and political power as had been the great dynastic families of earlier centuries.

The 1833 Select Committee on Public Walks and the 1840 Select Committee on the Health of Towns were two milestones marking the British government's increasing anxiety about the conditions in the rapidly developing urban environment. When legislation was enacted allowing local authorities to borrow money to buy land for a park and finance the loan through the rates, the town commissioners of Birkenhead were the first to acquire such a loan, thus making the park the first in the world to be publicly funded. The commissioners had grand ambitions for their new town; it was to be the "city of the future." One of the most dramatic ways of signaling this ambition was to lay out a spacious public park to provide fresh air, natural and artistic beauty, and space for recreation and leisure for all the people of Birkenhead.

The chosen site was low-lying and required extensive drainage. From the beginning it was intended that the ornamental landscape would be surrounded by housing plots, the sale of which would help to finance the park—a practice that was to set the pattern for many future developments. During 1844 and 1845 much of the layout and planting was developed. By the time it was officially opened, on Easter Monday, 1847, the landscape was beginning to hint at its beautiful maturity.

The park topography is highly distinctive, especially the contrast between the mounded enclosures around the lakes and the broader stretches of meadow that provide so successful a setting for a peaceful stroll or energetic sporting activities. The lakes themselves are central features of the design, distinctive in their sinuous outline, the range of potential views originally enlarged by five strategically placed bridges.

The emphasis on variety and contrast is essentially Picturesque. The lakes and broad green meadows have the quality of fruitful English acres. They must have suggested to all those who visited—and who had "title" to—the park the comfortable prosperity of ownership. But Paxton also employed a more exotic vocabulary, a reflection of a society that was reveling in its taste for travel and learning, its imperial ambition. The park was highlighted by ornamental structures such as the Roman boathouse, the Swiss bridge, and dramatic Alpine rockwork. These structures were in addition to the lodges in varied style, from the Italianate to Gothic, which marked each entrance. Birkenhead Park offered a "mini Grand Tour" to the people of the town.

The planting, too, was highly varied. Indigenous forest trees provided the backbone of the layout. But Turkey oaks (*Quercus cerris*) were employed for their rapid growth and their handsome stature, while Monterey pines (*Pinus radiata*)—introduced from California in 1833—lent their striking silhouettes. Throughout the park the planting was intended to be colorful and even dramatic, with evergreen and broadleaf trees, fastigiate, weeping and rounded habits, flowering shrubs and, on the periphery, between park and housing, lavish ornamental bedding-out. The site today—which is still beautiful—reveals that variegated holly, dark Corsican pine (*Pinus nigra* subsp. *laricio*), purple-leafed beech (*Fagus sylvatica* f. *purpurea*), pale green swamp cypress (*Taxodium distichum*), lime green weeping willow (*Salix babylonica*), silvery pear (*Pyrus*), and poplar (*Populus*) all contributed to the scene.

A great deal has been written about the circulation system of Birkenhead Park. It is elegantly planned, with separate routes for various kinds of traffic: crosstown vehicles slicing between the two parts of the park; leisurely traffic enjoying the views from the encircling carriage drive; pedestrian footpaths winding their way through the landscape. At no point do any of these routes intrude on the views from within the park, which retains its sense of spacious beauty. This clever planning was widely influential. Most notably, Central Park in New York City similarly accommodates a variety of users with a design that maximizes ease of movement for all but does not overwhelm the landscape with intruding roads and paths. This development was directly inspired by the visit to Birkenhead of one of the designers of Central Park: Frederick Law Olmsted.

It is not surprising that Olmsted visited Birkenhead in 1852 with a mission to see the "city of the future." His description of the park in *Walks and Talks of an American Farmer in England* (1852) has been frequently quoted. Beyond the Grand Entrance, he found

> a thick, luxuriant and diversified garden. Five minutes of admiration, and a few more spent in studying the manner in which art had been employed to obtain from nature so much beauty, and I was ready to admit that in democratic America, there was nothing to be thought of as comparable with this People's Garden. . . . [W]e passed by winding paths over acres and acres, with a constant varying surface, where on all sides were growing every variety of shrubs and flowers, with more than natural grace, all set in borders of greenest, closest turf, and all kept with most consummate neatness.

There can be no doubt that Birkenhead Park offered inspiration for the development of public parks in many parts of the world. As a work of art it is outstanding. Paxton was an extraordinary designer, and this is one of his most remarkable achievements. As a social signifier—which was a prime function from the beginning—the park was also supremely important. As Olmsted observed, "all this magnificent pleasure ground is entirely, unreservedly and forever the people's own. The poorest British peasant is as free to enjoy it in all its parts as the British queen. More than that, the baker of Birkenhead has the pride of an OWNER in it."

## Synopsis

| | |
|---|---|
| 1843–47 | Sir Joseph Paxton designs and lays out Birkenhead Park for local town commission, with Edward Kemp as foreman |
| 1847 | Official opening of park |
| 1850 | Visit to Birkenhead by Frederick Law Olmsted |

**Further Reading**

Chadwick, George F., *The Works of Sir Joseph Paxton, 1803–1865*, London: Architectural Press, 1961

Chadwick, George F., *The Park and the Town: Public Landscape in the 19th and 20th Centuries*, New York: Praeger, and London: Architectural Press, 1966

Chadwick, George F., "Paxton's Design Principles for Birkenhead Park," *Landscape Design* (November 1989)

Conway, Hazel, *People's Parks: The Design and Development of Victorian Parks in Britain*, Cambridge: Cambridge University Press, 1991

Lasdun, Susan, *The English Park: Royal, Private, and Public*, London: Deutsch, 1991; New York: Vendome Press, 1992

Newton, Norman T., *Design on the Land: The Development of Landscape Architecture*, Cambridge, Massachusetts: Harvard University Press, 1971

Olmsted, Fredrick Law, *Walks and Talks of an American Farmer in England*, New York, 1852; reprint, Ann Arbor: University of Michigan Press, 1967

Ponte, Alessandra, "Public Parks in Great Britain and the United States," in *The History of Garden Design*, edited by Monique Mosser and Georges Teyssot, London: Thames and Hudson, 1991

Smith, Charles H.J., *Landscape Gardening; or, Parks and Pleasure Grounds: With Practical Notes on Country Residences, Villas, Public Parks, and Gardens*, New York, 1853

Taylor, Hilary, "Urban Public Parks, 1840–1900: Design and Meaning," *Garden History* 23, no. 2 (1995)

HILARY A. TAYLOR

# Blenheim Palace

## Oxfordshire, England

**Location:**  8 miles (12.9 km) north-northwest of Oxford, immediately west of Woodstock

Blenheim Park is one of the largest (2,500 acres) and most important landscape parks in Great Britain. It is named after the village of Blindheim, Bavaria, where John Churchill, first duke of Marlborough, won a crucial victory over the French in 1704. He was rewarded by Queen Anne with the gift of the royal manor of Woodstock and its former medieval hunting park. The park, developed over a long period or time, has undergone several major transformations but still retains elements from its medieval period. The dominant phase, however, is that of the greatest landscape park created by Britain's most famous landscaper, Lancelot ("Capability") Brown, in the 1760s and 1770s.

The park, surrounded by a stone wall, occupies a rectangular area of rolling ground and is divided by the flooded valley of the small river Glyme. Churchill's great house, Blenheim Palace (1705–19), built by the architect John Vanbrugh, is the focus of the core of the park. The main entrance is through Nicholas Hawksmoor's Triumphal Arch (1723) at the west end of the village. Inside, a scene of stunning beauty and drama greets the eye: stretching away below is a great, sinuous lake, crossed in the background by the single-arched Grand Bridge, which appears from this vantage point to be perfectly in scale. The palace appears as a picturesque object in the landscape. The sloping ground, some of which has been artificially smoothed, is dotted with plantations and clumps of trees, dominated by beech and cedar of Lebanon planted by Brown. It is this view that William Gilpin, codifier of the Picturesque, called "the grandest burst, which art perhaps ever displayed."

The park contains formal as well as informal elements. The main formal one is the Grand Avenue, two miles (3.2 km) long, which runs northwest to the park's north boundary on the main axis of the palace. At its southern end is the classical Column of Victory (1727–30), 134 feet (40.8 m) tall, with a statue of the first duke on top. At right angles to the Grand Avenue, running eastward from the palace, is a shorter avenue, the Mall, which leads to Hensington Gate. The main informal landscaping is the lake itself and the planting immediately around it.

The park has long been divided into sections of different character. The higher half, north of the lake, is known as the Great Park. Apart from the Grand Avenue, a boundary shelter belt (trees planted in rows to block wind and for privacy), and a few large clumps of trees, this area is largely farmland. To the west of the

Parterre and fountains at Blenheim Palace, Oxfordshire, England
Copyright Paul Miles Picture Collection

lower part of the lake is an area of ancient oak woodland, High Park, where little landscaping has taken place. The area around and to the south of the palace is known as the Lower Park, which contains the gardens, pleasure grounds along the southeast side of the lake, the sinuous, artificial New River below the lake, and two cascades at the ends of the lake and New River. To the southeast of the house are a ha-ha and, beyond it, an eight-acre (3.2-ha) kitchen garden surrounded by a high brick wall with four bastions. The wall was built by Vanbrugh at the beginning of the 18th century; there are two, original circular pools within and a modern maze and garden center.

There are two areas of garden. To the east of the palace is a formal garden known as the Italian Garden, with a fountain of Venus (ca. 1910) by the American sculptor Waldo Story in the center. To the west, on the site of a Victorian shrubbery, are two magnificent and theatrical water terraces, with pools, fountains, and statues. The lower terrace is dominated by Bernini's *modello* (model) for his river gods fountain in the Piazza Navona, Rome.

Henry I made a royal hunting park at Woodstock in the early 12th century. The medieval park occupied most of the southern half of the present park, and its remnants are best seen in High Park. The park was stocked with deer; Henry I also had a menagerie here, which boasted, among other animals, a porcupine. The hunting lodge, Woodstock Manor, was situated on the north side of the lake, to the east of the Grand Bridge. To its west are the remains of another medieval feature, now known as Fair Rosamund's Well. This is a stone-lined pool of the clearest water, fed by a spring, which is all that is left of a much more extensive complex of pools and buildings created by Henry II in the 13th century, supposedly for the delight of his mistress, Rosamund de Clifford.

The next great phase was the formal landscaping of Vanbrugh, with planting by Henry Wise, which started in 1705. By this time the park had fallen into disuse,

Blenheim Palace with water terraces, Oxfordshire, England
Copyright Robert M. Craig

and Woodstock Manor was mostly in ruins. Vanbrugh wished to retain it as a Picturesque feature, but Sarah, duchess of Marlborough, disliked it, and after Vanbrugh was dismissed in 1716, she had it demolished in 1723. The massive Grand Bridge (1708–12), which was to have a Palladian superstructure—vetoed by Sarah—was built across the Glyme, and great earth causeways were constructed to join it to the sides of the valley. The Grand Avenue was planted with 686 mature elms. To the east of the palace was the duchess's private garden (1708) of highly scented flowers. Beyond it, the Mall and plantations of limes and elms were created, the latter laid out with rides in formal *pattes d'oie* (straight allées that radiate forward from a single point). To the south was a large box parterre and beyond it, a 77-acre (31-ha) walled and bastioned formal wilderness, known as the "woodwork" or military garden. This was formally planted and laid out, with summerhouses, fountains, alcoves, and a grotto, which was almost immediately demolished on the duchess's orders. The

last formal landscaping was carried out about 1719 by Colonel Armstrong, the duke of Marlborough's chief engineer, who began the transformation of the Glyme by creating a small lake, a cascade, and a formal canal ending in a circular basin.

Between 1760 and 1774 Brown, commissioned by the fourth duke, took hold of the landscape, preserving the main existing elements, with the exception of the parterre and "woodwork," and molded it into a beautiful and subtle whole. His chef d'oeuvre was the creation of the 150-acre lake. Allied to this project was the smoothing of the lake's sides and the planting of clumps of trees to diversify the landscape and direct views from a network of rides. Part of the medieval causeway to Woodstock Manor was retained as an island. Brown designed two cascades, one at the foot of the lake and one at the end of his sinuous New River below it.

A few buildings were added during the late-18th century. Brown himself redesigned High Lodge, in the High Park, as a castellated Gothic folly. William Chambers

Pond with bridge, landscape by Lancelot "Capability" Brown, Blenheim Palace, Oxfordshire, England
Copyright Robert M. Craig

designed the elegant New Bridge (1773) over the New River, and three small classical temples were built in the pleasure grounds — the temples of Diana and Flora by Chambers and the Temple of Health (1789) by John Yenn. The fourth duke made gardens around the cascade at the foot of the lake, which included the fountain now on the lower water terrace, and the fifth duke embellished them from 1817 onward. Little survives of these features.

Blenheim's landscape park has been widely admired from the start, even by Brown, who remarked that the Thames would never forgive him for what he had done there, implying that his creation eclipsed the beauty of the natural one. William Mavor wrote an influential guide to the park (1789 and subsequent editions); Thomas Jefferson (1786) was impressed by the huge scale and number of gardeners (200).

By the time the ninth duke inherited in 1892, the park was deteriorating. He instigated a major campaign of replanting, including the Grand Avenue, planted with elms and featuring a central lozenge instead of an ellipse. When in the 1970s Dutch elm disease struck, the avenue was replanted with lime trees and the Mall with alternating lime and plane trees. The ninth duke also commissioned the great French landscape architect Achille Duchêne to create the Italian Garden, on the site of the former flower garden of Sarah, and the water terraces (1925–30). For the latter, the duke asked Duchêne to work in the exuberant baroque style of Bernini and stipulated that the water be brought from Rosamund's Well. The landscaping had come full circle.

### Synopsis

| | |
|---|---|
| 12th century | Henry I makes deer park |
| 13th century | Henry II adds Rosamund's Well |
| 1705–19 | Construction of Blenheim Palace by John Vanbrugh and creation of formal park by Vanbrugh and Henry Wise |

| | |
|---|---|
| 1760–74 | Capability Brown landscapes park |
| 1817 | Fifth duke embellishes cascade garden |
| 1888 | Boathouse added to lake |
| 1892–1935 | Ninth duke's major regeneration scheme, including avenue replanting; Achille Duchêne creates Italian Garden and water terraces |
| 1970s | Avenues again replanted, with lime and plane; instigation of long-term management plan for park |

**Further Reading**

Bond, James, and Kate Tiller, editors, *Blenheim: Landscape for a Palace,* Gloucester, Gloucestershire: Sutton, 1987; 2nd edition, 1997

Green, David Brontë, *Blenheim Palace,* London: Country Life, 1951
Green, David Brontë, *Gardener to Queen Anne: Henry Wise (1653–1738) and the Formal Garden,* London and New York: Oxford University Press, 1956
Jefferson, Thomas, *Garden Book, 1766–1824,* Philadelphia, 1944
Mavor, William Fordyce, *New Description of Blenheim,* London, 1789; reprint, New York: Garland, 1982
Stroud, Dorothy, *Capability Brown,* London: Country Life, 1950; new edition, London: Faber, 1975

ELISABETH WHITTLE

---

# Blondel, Jacques-François 1705–1774

## French Architect, Writer, and Design Theorist

An architect, engraver, theorist, and teacher, Jacques-François Blondel was an important proponent of the classical *jardin à la française*. Blondel's considerable influence on garden architecture is not based on actual gardens, but on his writings and published projects. In fact, very few of his garden designs were ever realized and none still exist. He wrote three influential treatises on architecture that contain considerations on gardens. His most substantial contribution to garden theory is contained in *Cours d'architecture* (Course in Architecture), a work based on the author's lectures at his own private school and the French Académie d'Architecture. At the time of Blondel's death in 1774, only four volumes of this work had appeared. His pupil Pierre Patte subsequently published two more volumes of text and three of plates, done according to Blondel's plans.

Blondel's *Cours d'architecture* was important in the development of classicism in architecture and garden design. No other French author of the 18th century shows as clearly as Blondel the continuity of principles in the *jardin à la française* up to the first part of Louis XVI's reign. Some of the designs in his early work *De la distribution des maisons de plaisance* (1737–38; On the Arrangement of Country Houses) follow the rococo *goût moderne*, but the major parts are stylistically conservative. Criticism of rococo garden design is clearer in *Architecture françoise* (1752–56) and entirely obvious in the *Cours d'architecture*. Blondel recommends the

creations of André Le Nôtre, as well as the earlier garden treatise, Antoine-Joseph Dézallier d'Argenville's *Théorie et pratique du jardinage* (1709; Theory and Practice of Gardening).

Blondel's *Cours d'architecture* is critical to French garden theory in the late 18th century because it is a remarkably persistent plea for the defense of the *jardin à la française* against the influence of the English landscape garden. Blondel bases his preference of garden styles of the French classical age and Regency period on the interpretation of the *jardin à la française* as a genuine artistic manifestation of the French national character. According to Blondel, "le vrai goût national" (the genuine national taste) is realized in regular, geometrical garden structures based on rational criteria. But he criticizes the exaggerated symmetry of *jardins à la française* as well as the irregularity and confusion of gardens in the rococo and *anglo-chinois* styles. Nevertheless, Blondel adopts some ideas from the landscape garden movement, and he mentions Thomas Whately's treatise *Observations on Modern Gardening* (1770), translated as *L'art de former les jardins modernes; ou, L'art des jardins anglois*. Within the concept of "cette belle simplicité," Blondel pleads for joining regular and irregular structures in a garden ("ni trop de régularité, ni trop de désordre"), for variety and contrast, and he emphasizes natural material and effects. The *Cours d'architecture* also contains plates which illustrate the systematic

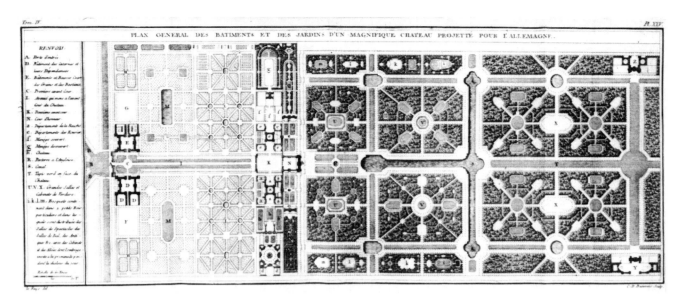

Project for palace and gardens in Germany, designed by Jacques-François Blondel
Copyright Zentralinstitut für Kunstgeschichte, Munich

description of the different elements of formal gardens. Other plates show layouts for huge garden grounds, which prove the author's preference for the classical age.

### Biography
Born in Rouen or Paris, France, 1705 or 1708. Studied with his uncle, architect Jean-François Blondel; collaborated on engravings for *Architecture françoise*, 1727; republished with comments by younger Blondel, 1752–56; worked as architect, but few projects realized; author of essays on architecture for Denis Diderot's and Jean Le Rond d'Alembert's *Encyclopédie,* 1751–65; admitted to Académie d'Architecture (2nd class), 1755; founded private school, École des Arts, 1739/40; appointed to architectural chair at Académie d'architecture, 1762. Died in Paris, 1774.

### Selected Designs
| | |
|---|---|
| 1761–70 | Urban planning of Metz, France, and church of Saint-Louis, Metz, France |
| from 1764 | Urban planning of Strasbourg, France (Place d'Armes) |
| 1766 | Project for palace for Archbishop of Cambrai, Le Cateau-Cambrésis, France |

### Selected Publications
*De la distribution des maisons de plaisance et de la décoration des edifices en général,* 2 vols., 1737–38
*Architecture françoise ou Recueil des plans, elévations, coupes, et profils des églises, maisons royales, palais,* *hôtels, et édifices les plus considérables de Paris,* 4 vols., 1752–56
*Cours d'architecture, ou Traité de la décoration, distribution et construction des bâtiments . . .* 9 vols., 1771–77

### Further Reading
Kalnein, Wend von, *Architecture in France in the Eighteenth Century,* translated by David Britt, New Haven, Connecticut: Yale University Press, 1994

Kaufmann, Emil, *Architecture in the Age of Reason,* Cambridge, Massachusetts: Harvard University Press, 1955

Lauterbach, Iris, *Der französische Garten am Ende des Ancien Régime,* Worms, Germany: Werner, 1987

Middleton, Robin, "Jacques François Blondel and the 'Cours d'architecture,'" *Journal of the Society of Architectural Historians* 18, no. 2 (1959)

Picon, Antoine, *Architectes et ingénieurs au siècle des Lumières,* Marseille: Parenthèses, 1988; as *French Architects and Engineers in the Age of Enlightenment,* translated by Martin Thom, Cambridge and New York: Cambridge University Press, 1992

Pinon, Pierre, "Blondel, Jacques François," in *Allgemeines Künstlerlexikon: Die bildenden Künstler aller Zeiten und Völker,* vol. 11, Munich: Saur, 1995

Wiebenson, Dora, *The Picturesque Garden in France,* Princeton, New Jersey: Princeton University Press, 1978

IRIS LAUTERBACH

# Boboli Gardens

## Florence, Firenze Province, Tuscany, Italy

**Location:** behind Palazzo Pitti, approximately .75 mile (1.2 km) south of central train station

The Boboli Gardens, most probably named after the Bogoli or Bogolini family who once owned the land, are the grandest formal gardens in Florence. Because so much of their design depends on the topography of the site, the basic pattern of the gardens survives in much of the same form as in the 16th century, despite changes over the years. The land the gardens lie on is behind and to the east end of the Palazzo Pitti in Florence, on the side of the city beyond the Arno, and stretches from the slope of San Giorgio and the Forte del Belvedere down to the Porta Romana to the east. The water for the many decorative features was brought in from the hills nearby in aqueducts that led also to the main part of the city and supplied fountain water throughout Florence to the general population. The Palazzo Pitti itself, a vast structure set on the site of a quarry that supplied its stone, was built by Luca Pitti beginning in 1458, perhaps after a design by Luca Fancelli.

At first nothing was done to the grounds, and they remained covered by olive groves and vineyards. But in 1549 Buonaccorso Pitti sold the palace to Eleonora of Toledo, wife of Duke Cosimo de' Medici, who saw the Pitti—away from the center of the city and with its views and gardens—as a country estate. Work began immediately to extend the palace and design the gardens. Bartolommeo Ammanati remodeled parts of the Pitti, especially the *courtile* and the windows of the wings, and Niccolò Pericoli, il Tribolo, laid out the design of the garden, to be followed after his death by Bernardo Buontalenti and then, in the 17th century, by Alfonso and Giulio Parigi.

The first part of the design, laid out by Tribolo, focused on a central axis, running up the hill from the *courtile* and included the great amphitheater and the Neptune Pond beyond it. The amphitheater, in a horseshoe form shaped as in a Roman circus, served often as an outdoor theater. If it was altered in the 17th and 18th centuries by the planting of parterres of flowers and the bringing in of statues from other parts of the garden, it has essentially kept its form. In the center is a red basin, brought from Rome and placed there in 1841, and parts of an obelisk from Luxor in Egypt, brought in 1790, with a base of sculpted turtles by Gaspero Paoletti. In the niches around the balustrade are terra-cotta urns and copies of classical statues. At the center of the Neptune Pond, halfway up the hill behind, is an island built in the 17th century. The bronze statue there of Neptune,

created by Stoldo Lorenzo in 1565–68, came originally from a small fountain to the left of this area and was moved to its present site some time in the 17th century.

At the crest of the hill is a gigantic statue of Dovizia (Abundance), conceived as a portrait of Giovanna of Austria, wife of Francesco I de' Medici, which was begun by Giambologna to be set in the Piazza San Marco but completed after his death in 1608 by Pietro Tacca and placed here in 1636. To the east of this area is a Viottolene, or Cypress Alley, which runs diagonally down to the Piazzale dell' Isolotto. Its island fountain was designed by Alfonso Parigi. Sculptures were placed regularly along this road, a detail later copied at Versailles. In the center of the Isolotto are small islands with statues of Perseus and Andromeda; in the hedge surrounding the *piazzale* are niches containing figures of bird hunters, collectors of fruit, a wine server, a David, and a Neptune. Further to the east are two statues, one of Saturn, one of Neptune, both set there in the 17th century. At the end are various classical and baroque pieces near the fountain of the Vintage, made between 1599 and 1608 on designs by Valerio Cioli. To the south of the Isolotto, at the edge of the garden, was a small zoo, which was transformed in 1785 by Grand Duke Leopold I into a hothouse for orange and lemon trees, the *Serraglio* or *Limonaia*. The building was designed by Zanobi del Rosso, who also built the Kaffehaus at the western end of the garden. The area in front of the hothouse was used for games.

Much of the garden has remained; lost, however, are the extensive botanical sections, for which many of the Medici dukes had cultivated an interest. Francesco I introduced mulberries into Tuscany by growing them here first. Later, Ferdinand I introduced both potatoes and pineapples; and when John Evelyn came here in 1644 he reported seeing roses being grafted onto orange trees and many topiary bushes. The garden is grand, but amid all this, especially in the first wave of design near the Palazzo itself, were many more playful elements, most notably the *Fountain of Bacchus* by Valerio Cioli, with the dwarf Morgante astride it (completed after 1560) and the wonderful grotto by Buontalenti (finished in 1588), with three interior chambers, filled with statues and murals. The room farthest back, with its statue of *Venus Emerging from the Bath* by Giovanni da Bologna, once had a base of green stone with four leering imps spitting up water at Venus.

During the French rule in the early 19th century, there was at one point a threat of the gardens being transformed into an English park. Nothing came of this,

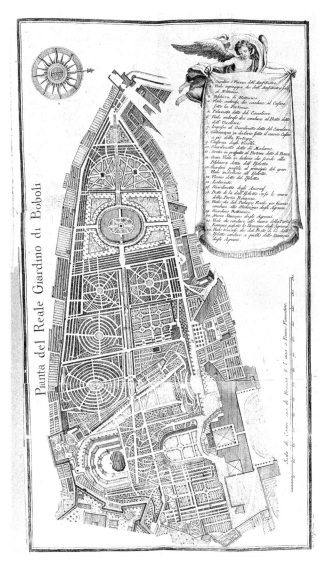

**Engraving of a map of Boboli Gardens by Gaetano Vascellini (1745–1805)**
**Courtesy of Scala/Art Resource, New York**

## Synopsis

| | |
|---|---|
| 1458– | Palazzo Pitti constructed for Luca Pitti, designed perhaps by Luca Fancelli |
| 1549 | Palazzo Pitti purchased by Eleonora of Toledo |
| 1549 | Work begun on extending palace, designed by Bartolommeo Ammannati, and creating gardens, designed by Niccolò Pericoli (known as Il Tribolo) |
| 1550 | Garden design taken up by Bernardo Buontalenti |
| after 1560 | Fountain of Bacchus constructed by Valerio Cioli |
| 1565–68 | Bronze statue of Neptune created by Stoldo Lorenzo (later set in Neptune Pond) |
| 1583–93 | Buontalenti finishes grotto |
| 1636 | Statue of Dovizia (Statue of Abundance) erected, begun by Giambologna and finished by Pietro Tacca |
| 1644 | John Evelyn visits garden |
| 1785 | Grand Duke Leopold I of Tuscany transforms zoo into Serraglio (or Limonaia), a hothouse for orange and lemon trees |
| 1790 | Obelisk brought from Luxor, Egypt |
| 1870 | House of Savoy takes possession of palace and garden |
| 1946 | Care of garden passed to Soprintendenza dei Monumenti |

## Further Reading

Borsook, Eve, *The Companion Guide to Florence*, New York: Harper and Row, and London: Collins, 1966; 4th edition, London: Collins, 1979

Gurrieri, Francesco, and Judith Chatfield, *Boboli Gardens*, Florence: Eden, 1972

Lazzaro, Claudia, *The Italian Renaissance Garden*, New Haven, Connecticut: Yale University Press, 1990

Masson, Georgina, *Italian Gardens*, New York: Abrams, and London: Thames and Hudson, 1961; revised edition, Woodbridge, Suffolk: Antique Collectors Club, 1987

however, and it was indeed at this time that the first careful restorations were carried out, to be continued by the House of Savoy, to whom ownership of the Palazzo had passed in 1870 after the unification of Italy. Since 1946 the care of the gardens has been the responsibility of the Soprintendenza dei Monumenti in Florence.

DAVID CAST

# Boer, Willem Christiaan Johannes 1922–2000

## Dutch Landscape Architect

Dutch landscape architect Wim Boer attended his local horticultural college and seemed to be destined to follow in his father's footsteps as a Boskoop tree nurseryman. His studies, however, awakened an interest in design. He continued his horticultural training with courses in garden architecture, and he ultimately became one of the foremost landscape professionals of his generation. Influential teachers who stimulated his interest in modernist architecture and landscape design included W. van Gelderen, who taught both architecture and urban design, and the garden architects G. Bleeker and Jan Thijs Pieter Bijhouwer.

Functionalism and World War II were the most significant influences on Boer's design philosophy. He was part of an emerging group of idealists who saw garden architects as independent advisers, and thus promoted a more professional approach that separated the design and nursery worlds. In a statement that divorced him from his father's tree nursery and commerce, he once noted that newly qualified garden architects were less interested in maintaining a nursery. Individuals such as Boer were more and more interested in work that would benefit the population at large, such as the care of rural and urban landscapes that had suffered considerably during the war. This view was of course strengthened by Boer's wartime experiences, when nearby Rotterdam had been burned to the ground during the first days of the war and large tracts of land in the Netherlands had been flooded.

These new ideals were associated with what was known as the school of Bijhouwer, which paid more attention to space than the total range of plants available, and more to form than color. Boer called this "functional garden and landscape architecture," and he characterized it as "the shaping, the creation of spaces, with the correct proportions between shape and mass, noticing particularly where accents have to be placed, and above all for which purpose it should serve, i.e. the function the layout will be put to" (1945). Comparing this with contemporary trends in architecture, he used a famous dictum to describe the importance of the fourth dimension as "space-time," quoting Sigfried Giedion, whose modernist manifest *Space, Time, and Architecture* (1941) was one of Boer's guiding influences.

Contact with modernists Van Gelderen and Bijhouwer proved to be instrumental in Boer's developing career. From 1947 to 1952 he worked for the town planning department in Rotterdam and was involved in the rebuilding of the city and planning its expansion. Under director C. van Traa, Rotterdam maintained a progres-

sive development policy and became the focus of Opbouw, the Rotterdam branch of the International Congress of Modern Architecture (CIAM). Lotte Stam-Beese, a former Bauhaus student with prewar Russian experience, was employed as town planner. She invited the participation of others in the town-planning process, including Boer and Bijhouwer, who proposed the use of greenspace as a structural element as well as for pedestrian and bicycle routes. Thus Boer became involved in the planning of the neighborhoods Pendrecht and Alexanderpolder, which were developed according to an orthogonal pattern reminiscent of the early paintings of the De Stijl movement. The proposals for Pendrecht were presented at the 1951 CIAM conference in Hoddesdon, England entitled "The Heart of the City." The conference had a significant impact on Boer's work. "The Core," the concept of a greenspace as a social area within a settlement, was to become a recurrent theme.

After this formative period Boer won a design competition for a cemetery in Doorn in 1952, at which point he decided to set up his own practice. During the 1940s to the mid-1980s Boer was a prominent landscape architect, most often running his practice single-handedly, but at times employing four or five people. The practice worked on some 380 projects varying from large rural and urban design projects to private, communal, and institutional gardens, as well as public parks and cemeteries. Boer also taught part-time at Boskoop and worked at his father's nursery during slack times. He continued as a member of CIAM for the design of Nagele, a village proposed in the newly reclaimed Noordoostpolder. The final design was by Aldo van Eyck, but included many of Boer's proposals. A large greenspace formed the central area where schools and churches were positioned and around which housing was arranged.

Boer concentrated his work largely on the urban environment, becoming one of the main practitioners and teachers in this field. He was quick to respond to changes in attitude. As a general design philosophy, he attempted to relate landscape to architecture and create spaces using vegetation. These were variously sized spaces in which he always emphasized multifunctional use, incidence, and variety. Asymmetry and rhythm in his planting design reinforced this approach. In his plant selection Boer showed a good knowledge of the different taxa and their individual habits, and was one of the first landscape architects to work with ecological planting. Later he became one of the first to advocate "let go," which encouraged spontaneous natural vegetation.

Plan of Nagele by Wim Boer
Courtesy of Wageningen UR Library

Boer's main achievements lie within the fields of urban design and public greenspace, and include well-known projects such as the Gijsbrecht van Aemstelpark, the Green Heart in Kampen, and the Houtkamp, Leiderdorp. He used planting as the main structural element in designs that respected existing and new traffic patterns and the scale of the surrounding architecture. The landscape framework often incorporated a series of public buildings and facilities such as a town hall, theater, sports stadium, swimming pool, skating rink, and city farm. Boulevard-style tree planting created multifunctional spaces. Pedestrian and bicycle access were of prime importance as links to different housing areas. In the design of residential areas Boer showed it was possible to achieve successful schemes using a geometric approach or by working with the existing landform. The Eurohousing in Leusden and Het Dorp, Arnhem, are contrasting examples. The former was not related to topography, soil conditions, or existing vegetation, but created a sheltered suburban atmosphere with intimate squares, playgrounds, and streets following a strict geometric plan. The second development was set within naturalistic, ecological plantings that contrasted with the architecture. On a domestic scale the garden was considered an extension of the house, and expressed the aspiration of "spatial continuity" of the De Stijl movement.

While Boer's published articles reveal the development of his design philosophy, his academic career commenced not so much on the basis of any published works but on the considerable achievements of his practice. He started teaching at the Technical University in Delft in 1955, later took a position at the Agricultural University in Wageningen, and then returned to Delft, ultimately to be appointed as professor in urban landscape architecture. In these positions he promoted modern design and thinking based on rational principles.

## Biography

Born in Boskoop, Netherlands, 1922. Son of nurseryman, studied at Horticultural College in Boskoop, 1937–40, where interest in architecture awakened; studied with architect W. van Gelderen, garden architect G. Bleeker, and landscape architect Jan Thijs Pieter Bijhouwer, at various times between 1939 and 1946; occasionally worked for state forestry service and for van Gelderen, 1940–45; employed at parks department in the Hague, Netherlands, 1945–46; employed by Bleeker to produce landscape plan for wartorn Zeeuws-Vlaanderen, 1946–47; worked at town planning department, Rotterdam, Netherlands, 1947–52; member of De Opbouw and CIAM, 1948–55; attended CIAM conference in Hoddesdon, England, entitled "Heart of the City," 1951, and presented city plan for neighborhood Pendrecht, Rotterdam; won design competition of Society for Dutch Landscape Architects for cemetery in Doorn, 1952; maintained private practice, 1952–90 (based in Rotterdam until 1965, then successively in Bergschenhoek, Capelle aan de IJssel, Berkel-Rodenrijs, and finally in Emmen since 1988), carrying out some 380 projects, varying from large rural and urban design projects to private, communal, and institutional gardens, public parks, and cemeteries; won competition for Gijsbrecht van Aemstelpark, 1959; taught part-time at Boskoop, 1952–57; lectureship in garden art at Technical University, Delft, Netherlands, 1955–63; lecturer at Agricultural University Wageningen, 1970–72; readership in urban greenspace in Delft, 1972–81, and professorship 1981–87. Died in Emmen, 2 June 2000.

## Selected Designs

1952–55   Cemetery, Doorn, Netherlands; village plan and planting design, Nagele, Noordoostpolder, Netherlands
1954–64   Development plan, Sluis, Netherlands
1955       Communal garden, Franselaan, Rotterdam, Netherlands; courtyard, HAV Bank (with architect W.M. Dudok), Schiedam, Netherlands
1957       Cemetery, Zoetermeer, Netherlands
1958       Landscaping, Dutch pavilion, Brussels World Expo, Brussels, Belgium; private

garden Ter Hofstedeweg (with architect
H. Salomonson), Overveen, Netherlands

| | |
|---|---|
| 1958–79 | The Green Heart, Kampen, Netherlands |
| 1959–62 | Gijsbrecht van Aemstelpark, Amsterdam-Buitenveldert, Netherlands |
| 1961–88 | Garden, Boer's house, Berkel-Rodenrijs, Netherlands |
| 1962–80 | De Houtkamp, Leiderdorp, Netherlands |
| 1964 | Woodland cemetery, Epe, Netherlands |
| 1966 | Het Dorp, Arnhem, Netherlands |
| 1967 | Morsebelpolder, Oegstgeest, Netherlands |
| 1970 | Eurohousing (with town planner D. Zuiderhoek and architect H. Klunder), neighborhood Rozendaal, Leusden, Netherlands |
| 1978–88 | Neighborhood park, Beverwaard, Rotterdam, Netherlands |

## Selected Publications

"Tuinarchitectuur met of zonder kweekerij en boomkwekers met tuinaanleg," *De boomkweekerij* 1 (1945)

"Gemeenschappelijke tuinen," *De boomkwekerij* 9 (1953)

"Het groen in het uitbreidingsplan," *De boomkwekerij* 10 (1954)

"De tuin in de nieuwe stad," *Algemeen handelsblad* (15 March 1960)

"Recreatie op en aan het water," *Bouw* 18, no. 13 (1963)

"Het groen in het centrum van de stad," *Beplantingen en boomkwekerij* 24 (1968)

"Tuin- en landschapsarchitectuur in de ban van het eeuwige heden," *Plan* 3 (1973)

*Stedelijk groen: I: De ontwikkelingsgeschiedenis van Tuin en Park*, 1980

"Ten geleide," in *Bolwerken als stadsparken; Nederlandse stadswandelingen in de 19e en 20e eeuw*, edited by Elisabeth Cremers, Fred Kaaij, and Clemens M. Steenbergen, 1981

"60 jaar ontwerpen in de stedelijke sfeer," *Groen* 38 (1982); as "Changing Ideals in Urban Landscape Architecture in the Netherlands," in *Learning from Rotterdam: Investigating the Process of Urban Park Design*, edited by M.J. Vroom and J.A. Meeus, 1990

*Stedelijk groen: 2: Recente ontwikkelingen*, 1982

"De ontstaansgeschiedenis van een park in Leiderdorp," *Groen* 39 (1983)

## Further Reading

Louwerse, D.C., *Wim Boer: Beschrijving en documentatie van zijn beroepspraktijk*, Wageningen, The Netherlands: Department of Landscape Architecture, 1982

Vroom, Meto J., *Buitenruimten: Ontwerpen van Nederlandse tuin- en landschaps-architecten in de periode na 1945; Outdoor Space: Environments Designed by Dutch Landscape Architects in the Period since 1945* (bilingual Dutch-English edition), Amsterdam: Thoth, 1992

JAN WOUDSTRA

---

# Bog Garden

The English word *bog* comes from the Irish *bogach*, meaning soft and so also a piece of spongy, wet, peaty ground. Under natural conditions a bog may form especially in declivities or basins as long as water continually accumulates, creating acidic, anaerobic conditions that virtually stop the decomposition of accumulating organic matter and thus allowing peat to form. A bog therefore usually comprises deep deposits of water-saturated peat. Natural bogs are characteristic of regions with high rainfall and relatively low rates of evaporation, irrespective of latitude and altitude.

A bog garden is one created in a place in which the soil is perpetually wet, but where the water table does not usually rise above the soil surface so that permanent pools form. The soil in such places, being continually waterlogged, tends to be high in organic matter (peat) and acidic. Such conditions may also be described as marshy, but no clear distinction is possible between a bog garden and a marsh garden. Bog gardens usually are sited at the edge of pools, ponds, or lakes, but they do not need to be close to water; they can also be created on a small scale in raised beds and containers. Bog gardens were not, and are not, formal areas, replenished on a regular cycle, because such gardens are not easily tilled after planting. The plants usually are informally grouped and allowed to proliferate naturally.

The earliest publication about bog gardens seems to have been written by William Robinson and was published in the first part of his new periodical *The Garden*, issued on 25 November 1871. In modified form he republished this article in the numerous editions of his influential book *The English Flower Garden*. This essay begins, "The bog-garden is a home for the numerous children of the wild that will not thrive in our harsh, base, and dry garden-borders, but must be cushioned on moss, and associated with their own relatives in moist peat soil."

Among plants Robinson recommended for the bog garden were European species native in peaty, wet habitats including bog asphodel (*Narthecium ossifragum*), royal fern (*Osmunda regalis*), and species of butterwort (*Pinguicula*) and sundew (*Drosera*). He also suggested several hardy orchids including marsh helleborine (*Epipactis palustris*) and species of lady's slipper orchids or moccasin flowers (*Cypripedium*). As he had recently returned from North America, he also commended *Trillium* species and the insectivorous pitcher plants (*Sarracenia purpurea*) and the Californian cobra lily (*Darlingtonia californica*).

Members of the heather family (Ericaceae), including various cranberries *(Vaccinium, Oxycoccus)*, some dwarf species of *Rhododendron*, and a few of the hardy European heathers (e.g., *Calluna vulgaris, Erica tetralix,* and *Erica mackaiana*), will thrive in the acidic conditions of bog gardens. However, larger shrubs, including many species and innumerable cultivars of *Rhododendron,* can only be accommodated in very extensive bog gardens.

During the 20th century, plant collectors, especially those working in temperate parts of Asia, introduced other plants that were ideal for growing in bog gardens. Thus, for example, candelabra primroses (e.g., *Primula beesiana, P. helodoxa, P. florindae*) and various globe flowers (*Trollius*) soon because features of such gardens.

Bog gardens have never been of major significance in garden design, tending to be confined to specialist gardens, including botanic gardens. To be successful they require continuous, high rainfall, as well as a ready supply of peat. Bog gardens were major features of some botanic gardens, for example, the National Botanic Gardens, Glasnevin, Dublin, Ireland, during the late 1800s and early 1900s. In the late 20th century interest in bog gardens was reawakened by the vogue for wild gardens and native plant gardens.

**Further Reading**

Bellamy, David J., *Bellamy's Ireland: The Wild Boglands,* Dublin: Country House, 1986

Robinson, William, "The Bog Garden," *The Garden* 1 (1871)

Robinson, William, *The English Flower Garden,* London, 1883; 15th edition, London: Murray, 1933; reprint, Sagaponack, New York: Sagapress, 1995

E. CHARLES NELSON

# Bois de Boulogne

## Paris, France

**Location:**  west side of Paris, approximately 1 mile (1.6 km) west of the Arc de Triomphe

The Bois de Boulogne, now one of the great "playgrounds" of Paris, is situated at what was up to the 19th century the western edge of the city. It is found between the line of the Seine and the old city walls, as indicated by the continued use of the names of the old *portes* or gates of the city on the east of the "Bois," as it is colloquially known. At the north is the Porte Maillot, then the Porte Dauphine; further south are the Portes de la Muette, De Passy, and d'Auteuil. The walls were finally removed in the 1930s when this quarter was redeveloped as a fashionable residential area. The Paris ring road, the Periphique, now cuts through the eastern edge of the Bois.

Historically a hunting park of the French kings, the Bois is now all that remains of the much more extensive earlier Foret de Rouvre. Even in Roman times the ancient city of Lutece, as it then was, was surrounded by huge forests. Francis I built a château here in 1528, the Château de Madrid, and in 1556 constructed a wall around a large proportion of the Bois. Louis XIV opened the land up for public use and under the supervision of Colbert straight roads and *rondpoints* were set out.

In 1777 a villa was built in a record 64 days as a result of a bet between Marie Antoinette and the Comte d'Artois. This was the Pavilion de Bagatelle (Bagatelle Pavilion), now used for exhibitions, concerts, and cultural events. It was originally surrounded by a *jardin anglais* of some seven hectares (17.3 acres) designed by the Scottish gardener Thomas Blaikie. This area, which

Jardin de Bagatelle at the Bois de Boulogne, Paris, France
Copyright Marco Cristofori/Das Fotoarchiv

the city. This redesign of the Bois may have been principally influenced by the style of Hyde Park in London. Another member of the team was Edouard André, who later developed an international reputation practicing in many countries and was known for his interest in and promotion of exotic plants. In particular he has been identified as introducing the Parisian principles of park design to England through his work at Sefton Park in Liverpool in 1871.

The present area of the park is generally stated to be 865 hectares (2,137 acres), and it contains within it a number of discrete features. The Bagatelle Pavilion already mentioned is now set in a formal garden of the French style created in the early 20th century by the gardener J.C.N. Forestier, keeper of the promenades of Paris, who designed a vast rose garden and an iris garden there. Toward the eastern side of the area are two lakes, the smaller known as Lac Superior and the larger, lower lake with two islands within it. The soil excavated from these lakes was used to create topographical variation in what was otherwise a relatively flat site The racecourse of Longchamps is another of the features developed within this area, when the Bois was extended to the edge of the Seine in 1857. The extensive rock features with the great cascade were created at this time. Another racecourse, for steeplechasing, also in the Bois is that of Auteiul. At the north end of the Bois is the Jardin d'Acclimatation, or Zoological Garden, originally designed to display both animals and plants for education and entertainment. This has now changed and become an area of fun fairs, a model farm, play schools, shows, and sports facilities for children. At the south of the Jardin d'Acclimatation there is an extensive municipal nursery for the city. In the center, the garden called the Pre-Catalan, is a self-contained English-style romantic park, which includes the Shakespeare Garden featuring the plants mentioned in his writings. The Bois also includes several private club sites, one of these being that of the racing Club de France, described as the most eminent sporting club in the country, and the Cercle du Bois de Boulogne, devoted principally to tennis.

From the Arc de Triomphe the 140-meter (153-yard)-wide Avenue Foch, originally named the Avenue de L'Imperatrice, leads to the northeast entrance of the Bois de Boulogne. Regarded as one of the most exclusive residential streets in Paris, this was completed in 1854.

included the Château de Madrid, was enclosed for the comte's private use.

It is to the 19th century, however, that the Bois owes its present form. Damaged first in the Revolution, it was used as a field for troop operations in 1814, and then suffered further as a result of the invasion by the Allies following the defeat of Napoléon. It was given to the city in 1852 by Napoléon III and was redesigned under the direction of Baron Haussmann, who was renowned for the redevelopment of Paris's center and the creation of the great avenues, which are such a major feature of the city center. These were all part of the great plan for the redevelopment of Paris, which among other things intended to site four great parks around the edge of the city. The actual design was the work of a team led by Jean Alphand, engineer and landscape architect. Planting design was the work of Jean-Pierre Barrillet-Deschamps, who was, under Alphand, chief gardener to

## Synopsis

| | |
|---|---|
| 1528 | François I of France builds the Château de Madrid |
| 1556 | The Bois (Woods) enclosed by a wall |
| 17th C. | Louis XIV opens the gardens for public use; Jean Baptiste Colbert supervises construction of roads and *rondpoints* |
| 1777 | Pavilion de Bagatelle built in 64 days |

| | |
|---|---|
| 1814 | The Bois used for troop operations |
| 1815 | Devastated by the Allies after the defeat of Napoléon |
| 1852 | Napoléon III gives it to the city of Paris; redesign supervised by Baron Haussmann; design by Jean Alphand and Jean-Pierre Barrillet-Deschamps |
| 1857 | The Bois extended to the Seine |
| early 20th C. | Formal gardens laid out around the Pavilion de Bagatelle, by J.C.N. Forestier |

**Further Reading**

Alphand, Adolphe, *Les promenades de Paris,* 3 vols., Paris: Rothschild, 1867–73; reprint, Princeton, New Jersey: Princeton Architectural Press, 1984

Cameron, Robert, and Pierre Salinger, *Above Paris: A New Collection of Aerial Photographs of Paris, France,* London: Deutsch, and San Francisco, California: Cameron, 1984

Chapman, Joan Margaret, and Brian Chapman, *The Life and Times of Baron Haussmann: Paris in the Second Empire,* London: Weidenfeld and Nicolson, 1957

Couperie, Pierre, *Paris au fil du temps: Atlas historique d'urbanisme et d'architecture,* Paris: Cuénot, 1968; as *Paris through the Ages: An Illustrated Historical Atlas of Urbanism and Architecture,* translated by Marilyn Low, New York: Braziller, 1968; London: Barrie and Jenkins, 1970

M.F. DOWNING

# Bolotov, Andrei Timofeevich 1738–1833

## Russian Garden Writer and Architect

Andrei Timofeevich Bolotov was the most influential and most productive writer on horticulture and garden aesthetics in czarist Russia. He also involved himself with agriculture and forestry and is acclaimed as one of the fathers of Russian botany. Apples and pears were his specialty, and many of his numerous publications were based on his own experimental work. Bolotov worked in the Russian province, most notably in the Tula region southeast of Moscow, from where he originated. However, thanks to many of his articles being published as a supplement to the largest Moscow newspaper of the time, Bolotov gained a large readership.

Considering himself a man of the Enlightenment, Bolotov was led by a twofold will to teach and to moralize. In his writings as well as in his comprehensive activities as a consultant and designer, Bolotov first and foremost addressed himself to representatives of the Russian gentry. Bolotov's reputation never withered, even during the Soviet era, but all of his design works gradually fell into ruin or were destroyed. The reestablishment of some of Russia's traditional values since 1991 has promoted the safeguarding of Bolotov's greatest single design, the Bogoroditske garden near Tula.

In 1762, Bolotov abandoned service in the Russian Imperial Army. He returned to his family estate in the village of Dvoryaninovo, situated about 160 kilometers (100 mi.) southeast of Moscow, not far from the city of Tula, which was a center of arms production because of local metal resources. In so doing he took advantage of an imperial ukase issued that very year and freeing the nobility and gentry from the obligation to serve the court. Many others also chose to retire and committed themselves to a new life at family estates in the province, which they had left when summoned to the imperial court. Forestry and agriculture then became the primary source of revenue. Next to orchards and vegetable gardens supplementing the household, gardens also became increasingly appreciated for their pleasurable as well as their recreational and didactic values. The thinking of the Enlightenment thus spread from the Western-oriented capital of St. Petersburg out into the Russian province. Bolotov was to become a key figure in this movement from the early 1770s.

Bolotov set out developing his native Dvoryaninovo into a modern and more profitable enterprise. He also ventured to embellish the grounds and the buildings at Dvoryaninovo. Fruit trees and fruit bushes were planted between the new straight alleys, and gates, ponds, glades, or small pavilions were applied as motifs at the end of the optic axes. In the groves, however, Bolotov did not strive to "attain too much symmetry," as he once stated. Parallel to this, he more and more involved himself in propagating information about horticulture, agriculture, and forestry. The subject of his early writings, many of which were published in the new magazines of the time, was practical advice, explaining at length how, for example, to plant or graft apple trees or currant bushes. He based his work on his own experience and on the botanical experiments he carried out (e.g., cross-fertilization). He was also knowledgeable about the growing specialist literature of his time. In writing, Bolotov addressed himself primarily to his peers. Economic considerations therefore influenced his recommendations of specific designs, plants, and methods, and Bolotov took much care to underline the moderate size of the gardens belonging to his readers.

As tradition had it, Bolotov also set up as head of a family with many children. Insufficient revenue forced him to accept an official post in 1773. He subsequently served as a land surveyor in the Tula region until the end of Catherine the Great's reign, in 1796. This post suited well his talents as a designer, and over the years—and still parallel to his energetic writing activities—Bolotov laid out a series of gardens and urban plans (e.g., the geometric design of the town of Bogoroditske). Similar projects to modernize some of Russia's old provincial towns were initiated by Catherine the Great in many other places.

In 1784–86, Bolotov was commissioned to embellish the grounds next to the Bogoroditske Palace (architect: I.Ye. Starov, 1771–76). The ensemble was destined for A.G. Bobrinsky, the son of Catherine the Great and Prince Orlov. Initially, a densely wooded area near the neoclassical palace was turned into a pleasure grove. Bolotov's subsequent development of the Bogoroditske garden earned him the reputation as the creator of the Russian landscape garden. Part of the garden was laid out with formal parterres, but landscape aesthetics soon came to the fore, inspired by Bolotov's reading of the German C.C.L. Hirschfeld's garden theory *Theorie der Gartenkunst* (1779–85; Theory of Landscape Gardening). The naturally sloping landscape was furnished with various architectural motifs, including an antique-inspired rotunda, an obelisk, a grotto, ruins, large-scale painted screens, and carved-out quarries.

While the general design and some architectural pieces of the Bogoroditske garden were indebted to foreign inspiration, the planting was based on local resources. The neighboring woods largely provided what was needed at this point. Birch, oak, and linden trees blended with aspen, maple, ash, willow, and bird-cherry. Birch was chosen for the imposing allée. To some degree, financial considerations may have influenced Bolotov's choice of local trees and plants. In the case of planting, however, Bolotov was very eager to propagate a specifically national attitude. He found the Russian flora "particularly beautiful," as opposed to American and other overseas trees "that the Englishmen use in their gardens."

In 1786, on completion of the garden, Bolotov and his son Pavel made a number of pencil drawings and nearly 40 watercolors. Next to being one of the most precious sources on the Bogoroditske garden, this album at the State Museum of History in Moscow is also a highly valuable source of Russian 18th-century landscape and garden aesthetics in general.

The scale and span of Bolotov's writings and editorial work in the horticultural field remain unsurpassed in a Russian context. The first guide to Russian botany is due to him, as is a study of some 660 types of apple and pear trees, filling eight volumes with text and another three volumes with watercolored depictions. For *Ekonomichesky Magazin,* Bolotov wrote or translated some 4,000 articles and notes (1780–89). This magazine grew into a large opus, comprehending some 16,000 pages. Apart from theoretical and practical gardening, Bolotov also squeezed in small notes and reflections on a wide range of other matters. The spirit of the Enlightenment literally pervaded this magazine. What *The Spectator* had meant for the formation of British garden amateurs' taste in the early 18th century *Ekonomichesky Magazin* came to signify to its Russian readership. Many concepts and recommendations were rooted in British tradition, but Bolotov's fascination with Hirschfeld and Bolotov's publishing of hundreds of pages from Hirschfeld's *Theorie der Gartenkunst* testifies to Germany's role as a filter and mediator. Several of the garden elements described and designed by Bolotov and like-minded professionals and amateurs were taken over from Hirschfeld's, Grohmann's, and Mansa's works. Bolotov also wrote his memoirs. They contain much information on the lifestyle of the gentry in the Catherine period and confirm to what extent Bolotov remained dedicated to the study of horticulture, agriculture, and forestry.

The Bogoroditske palace opened as a museum in 1992. Descendants of the 18th-century Bobrinsky family have taken an active part in the establishing of the Bogoroditske Palace Museum. Extensive restoration works have been carried out indoors as well as outdoors. The museum and its exhibition program are devoted to Russian country house culture of the late 18th and early 19th centuries, with special emphasis on the Bobrinsky family. The pleasure grounds are undergoing a step-by-step reconstruction. The line of sight toward the geometric pattern of the town of Bogoroditske has been reestablished.

**Biography**

Born 1738. Military professional; served in St. Petersburg, Russia, and Königsberg, East Prussia; retired, 1762, and settled in native Dvoryaninovo, near Tula; involved with botany, horticulture, agriculture, and forestry; extensive publishing activities in these fields, from late 1760s; worked simultaneously as consultant in garden and landscape design and in urban planning; served as land surveyor, 1773–96. Died, 1833.

**Selected Designs**
1784–86    Redesign of Bogoroditske garden, near Tula, Russia

**Selected Publications**
editor, *Selski zhitel*, 1778–79
editor, *Ekonomichesky magazin*, 1780–89
*Zhizn i prikliucheniia Andreia Bolotova: Opisannye samim im dlia svoikh potomkov* (1871–73), 1986

**Further Reading**
Floryan, Margrethe, *Gardens of the Tsars: A Study of the Aesthetics, Semantics, and Uses of Late 18th-Century Russian Gardens*, Aarhus, Denmark: Aarhus University Press, and Sagaponack, New York: Sagapress, 1996
Kovshova, L.A., "Bogoroditsky ansambl': Usadba i gorod (The Bogoroditske Ensemble: Garden and City)," Ph.D. diss., Russian Academy of Art, 1992
Liubchenko, Oleg Nikolaevich, *Yest v Bogoroditske park* (There Is a Garden at Bogoroditske), Tula: Priokskoe Knizhnoe Izdatelstvo, 1984
Liubchenko, Oleg Nikolaevich, *Andrei Timofeevich Bolotov*, Tula: Priokskoe Knizhnoe Izdatelstvo, 1988
Vergunov, Arkadi Pavlovich, and Vladislav Andreevich Gorokhov, *Vertograd: Sadovo-parkovoe iskusstvo Rossii: Ot istokov do nachala XX veka* (Vertograd: Garden and Landscape Art in Russia: From the Beginning to the Early 20th Century), Moscow: Kultura, 1996

MARGRETHE FLORYAN

# Books, Gardening

Although not the only source of information about historic gardens, printed garden literature is nevertheless a very important one. Garden books appeared in Europe beginning in the Renaissance. The early texts may be subdivided under (1) works on husbandry, (2) works on gardening, (3) works on garden design, (4) garden catalogs, and (5) garden descriptions. All books on architecture and on plants, which often contain remarkable sections on gardening, have been excluded here, as have the numerous belles lettres on gardens.

**Books on Husbandry**
Compiled works on husbandry had great importance for 16th- and 17th-century gardening. One of the earliest European garden books is Charles Estienne's *De re hortensi libellus* (1535). An innovative publisher, Estienne compiled explanations of Latin garden terms collected in the classic literature for use in Latin schools. Within a few years he published similar booklets on planting, sowing, and grafting. In 1554 he drew them together in the volume *Praedium rusticum*, which Jean Liebault translated into the French and augmented as *L'agriculture, ou La maison rustique* in 1564. Subsequently, numerous reprints and translations (including an English edition in 1600) were published up until 1702. Addressed to nobles and husbandmen, the work deals with kitchen gardens, flower gardens, and orchards.

The first English book on husbandry, which is anonymous, was compiled by John Fitzherbert in 1523. In 1557 Thomas Tusser printed his didactic poem *Five Hundred Pointes of Good Husbandrie*. The first German book on husbandry, *Rei rusticae libri IV*, originally written in Latin dialogues by Conrad Heresbach (1570) was translated into English in 1577. Gervase Markham's *The English Husbandman* (1613) also pertains to gardening. Other German husbandry works were published by Johann Coeler (1593), Georg Andreas Böckler (1678), Wolfgang Helmhard von Hohberg (1682), and Franz Philipp Florinus (1702).

Contemporaries held the Frenchman Olivier de Serres's *Le theatre d'agriculture* (1600) in high esteem. It covers all branches of gardening and garden design and contains some remarkable designs for parterres by Claude Mollet. Despite its fame and several editions, it has not yet been translated.

Italian works on husbandry with sections on gardening include works by Agostino Gallo (*Le vinti giornate dell'agricoltura e piacere della villa* [1567]), Giambattista della Porta (*Villae libri XII* [1584]), Marco Bussato (*Giardino di agricoltura* [1592]), and Vicenzo Tanara (*L'economia del cittadino in villa* [1644]).

**Books on Gardening**
A distinction has not always been made between books on gardening and books on garden design. Up to the 16th century garden books were mostly based on ancient and medieval writers such as Palladius, Pliny the Elder, Albertus Magnus, and Pietro de' Crescenzi. The

first ones included *The Crafte of Grafftynge & Plantynge of Trees* (ca. 1520), Johann Domitzer's grafting booklet, *New Pflantzbuechlin von Propffung der Baum* (1529), and Benoit Le Court's scholarly *Hortorum libri triginta* (1560), which has a philosophical and philological focus. The short *Pflantzbuechlin der Lustgaerten* (1562) gives primarily information on grafting, while Thomas Hyll's *Most Brief and Pleasant Treatyse, Teaching Howe to Dress, Sowe, and Set a Garden* (1563), his *The Gardeners Labyrinth* (1577), and Antoine Mizauld's *Historia hortensium* (1576; French edition as *Le Iardinage*, 1578) cover more topics. They are all based on classical authors. In his *L'art et maniere de semer, et faire pepinières* (1544; English edition, ca. 1569), David Brossard refers to his own experiences.

More refined and detailed works appeared after 1600. Among the most noteworthy ones are the German humanist Peter Lauremberg's *Horticultura* (1631), written in Latin, which deals at length with plants and design. The invention of the term *horticulture* is attributed to Lauremberg. The Swiss councillor Daniel Rhagor's *Pflanz-Gart* (1639) covers herb gardens, orchards, and vineries. The German writer Wolfgang Jacob Dümler's *Obsgarten* (1661) covers fruit as well as ornamental trees. Georg Viescher produced the amusing *Blumen Garten* (1645), which filled the gap left by Rhagor and Dümler by treating flower gardens, design, and greenhouse plants only; however, it has no illustrations. Other fairly comprehensive works from the period included Johann Sigismund Elsholtz's *Vom Garten-Baw* (1666) and Heinrich Hesse's *Neue Garten-Lust* (1696) and *Teutscher Gärtner* (1710). Jirí Holík's simple small *Gartenbüchlein* (1684) was printed in many editions, the last in 1772.

William Lawson was a pioneer in England with *The Country Housewife's Garden* (1617) and *A New Orchard and Garden* (1618). John Parkinson's well-known *Paradisi in Sole* (1629) is mostly a florilegium, but its text also relates it to garden literature. Leonhard Meager's practical *The English Gardner* (1670) was published repeatedly. Also influential were John Evelyn's compendious *"Sylva"; or, A Discourse of Forest Trees . . . to Which Is Annexed Pomona; or, An Appendix concerning Fruit-Trees* (1664), Stephen Blake's *The Compleat Gardener's Practice* (1664), and John Rea's *Flora Ceres and Pomona* (1665). John Worlidge followed with his popular and enlightened *Systema Horticulturae* (1677). In 1683 John Reid published the first Scottish book on gardening. Excellent British books on fruit culture were published by Samuel Hartlib (1653), Ralph Austen (1653), and John Beale (1657). In 1728 these works were surpassed by Batty Langley's *Pomona*, containing 79 fruit prints. The first English book to focus exclusively on flower gardens book was Samuel Gilbert's *The Florist's Vademecum* (1683).

The best Italian garden book of the 17th century was Giovanni Battista Ferrari's *De Florum Cultura* (1633). Written in Latin, the work contains high-quality plates by famous artists, illustrating flowers, tools, and parterre designs. Agostino Mandirola's brief *Manuale dei giardinieri* (1646), however, became more popular. A later work, Paolo Bartolomeo Clarici's *Istoria e coltura delle piante* (1726), discusses design, flower gardening, botany, and citrus culture.

In France important works included Nicolas de Bonnefons's anonymously published *Le jardinier françois qui enseigne à cultive les arbres et herbes potagères* (1651; English edition, 1658), Antoine Le Gendre's *La maniere de cultiver les arbres fruitiers* (1652; English edition, 1660), and Francois Gentil's *Le jardinier solitaire, ou Dialogues entre un curieux et un jardinier solitaire* (1704; English edition, 1706). These three books were distributed throughout Europe. Good practical information is found also in Pierre Morin's *Remarques necessaires pour la culture des fleurs* (1658). The most precise treatise on gardening, however, was Jean de La Quintinye's *Instruction pour les jardins fruitiers et potagers, avec un traité des orangers* (1690; English edition, 1693). René Rapin's *Hortorum Libri Quatuor* (1665; English edition, 1672) treated flowers, trees, water, and orchards and was, despite its Latin hexameters, published frequently and widely distributed. René Dahuron's highly useful *Traité de la taille des arbres* was published first in Germany (1692) and contained oft-reprinted illustrations. Louis Liger's *Le jardinier fleuriste et historiographe* (1704; English edition, 1706), which addresses garden layout, culture, and mythological meanings of flowers, was also printed in many editions. The popular *Le spectacle de la nature* by Abbé Noel-Antoine Pluche (1735) consists of gallant dialogues. Pastor Louis-René Le Berryais attempted to replace La Quintinye with his accomplished *Traité des jardins, ou le nouveau De La Quintinye* (1775).

Important for the understanding of French garden systems and terminology are Abbé Roger Schabol's *Dictionnaire pour la théorie et la pratique du jardinage* (1767) and Antoine Nicolas Dézallier d'Argenville's anonymously published *Dictionnaire du jardinage* (1777).

The Low Countries produced a number of popular works, including Jan van der Groen's straightforward *Den Nederlandtsen hovenier* (1669), Henri Cause's *De koninglicke hovenier* (1676), Jan Commelin's ambitious *Nederlandste Hesperides* (1676) English edition, 1683), Henrik van Oosten's *De nieuwe Nederlandse bloemhof* (1700; English edition, 1703), and Pieter La Court van der Voort's anonymously published *Byzondere aenmerkingen over het aenleggen van pargtige en gemeene landhuizen, lusthoven etc.* (1737).

The gardener's calendar become a popular phenomenon beginning in the 17th century. In 1664 John Evelyn published the first such calendar in English. John Hill gave in his *Eden* (1756–57) weekly instructions for gardeners. The best-known calendar was Philip Miller's, first published in 1732.

As the predominance of French garden design in Europe declined and the English garden ascended, English gardening literature correspondingly became dominant. In his works Richard Bradley treated gardening as a science, such as in his *New Improvements of Planting and Gardening* (1717–18). Philip Miller's *The Garden and Florists Dictionary* (1724), later *The Gardener's Dictionary* (1731), became the most widespread garden and plant dictionary of the 18th century throughout the Western world. John Abercrombie's *Every Man His Own Gardener* (1767) held the second position on the scale of popularity in England.

John Claudius Loudon's outstanding *Encyclopaedia of Gardening* (1822) contains all contemporary Western knowledge about garden design throughout the world. George Nicholson's later *Dictionary of Gardening* (1884–88) became very popular, as did the German dictionaries of Friedrich Gottlieb Dietrich (*Lexikon der Gärtnerei und Botanik* [1802–40]), Julius Bosse (*Handbuch der Blumengärtnerei* [1829]), and Theodor Rümpler (*Illustrirtes Gartenbau-Lexikon* [1882]). The annually revised *Le bon jardinier* became the most widely used garden manual of the 19th century in France.

Prior to 1800 Americans made due with a number of British works that were revised for their use. In 1804 John Gardiner and David Hepburn published a work written especially for American farmers, *The American Gardener*. In 1806 Bernard MacMahon in Philadelphia followed with *The American Gardener's Calendar*, which also contains hints on garden design. Thomas Green Fessenden updated the former as *The New American Gardener* (1828). Joseph Breck wrote on American flower gardening beginning in 1851. The American William Cobbett wrote *The American Gardener* based on English authors; it was later released under the title *The English Gardener* (1829).

The early and mid-19th century saw the first books on gardening written especially for women and children, for example, August Batsch's *Botanik für Frauenzimmer* (1798), *Le jardinier fleuriste dedié aux dames* (1819), Jane Loudon's *Companion to the Flower Garden* (1841; American edition, as *Gardening for Ladies*, 1843), and Louisa Johnson's *Every Lady Her Own Flower Gardener* (1839; American edition, 1844). During the same time a great number of small books appeared that dealt with indoor gardening (e.g., Carl Paul Bouché's *Der Zimmer- und Fenstergarten* [1808], Nathaniel B. Ward's *On the Growth of Plants in Closely Glazed Cases* [1842]) and flower language (e.g., B. Delachénay's *Abécédaire de flore* [1811], Charlotte de la Tour's *Le language des fleurs* [1818]).

Numerous books on flower gardening, ornamental trees and shrubs, and kitchen and fruit gardening have been published as monographs since the 19th century and are not listed here.

**Books on Garden Design**

Garden designs without an accompanying text were first published separately by Hans Vredeman de Vries in Antwerp (*Hortorum viridariorumque elegantes et multiplices formae* [1583]). The Saxon pastor Johann Peschel was the first to release a book on garden design, his *Garten-Ordnung* in 1597. In it he provides experience from his part-time occupation as a garden designer, illustrating the work with numerous woodcuts. His designs are of lower quality than Vredeman's, but his practical instruction was not surpassed in its details.

Engraved designs for parterres published separately include Jean Leclerc's *Parterres et compartiments divers* (ca. 1600), the anonymous *Certain Excellent and New Invented Knots and Mazes* (1623), Daniel Loris's *Le thrésor des parterres* (1629), Daniel Rabel's *Livre de différents desseigns de parterres* (1630), and Pierre Berain's *Le fidèle jardinier* (1636). Models for parterres and mazes were often annexed to treatises without comment.

In addition to well-conceived designs Jacques Boyceau's highly esteemed *Traité de jardinage* (1638) contains an excellent discussion on layout that explains the main principles of the baroque garden. Belonging to the same class are André Mollet's *Le jardin de plaisir* (1651; English edition, 1670) and Claude Mollet's anonymously published *Theatre des plans et jardinages* (1652).

Like La Quintinye's earlier writings on gardening, Antoine Joseph Dézallier d'Argenville's *La théorie et la pratique du jardinage* (1709; English edition, 1728) became the most famous book on French garden design of its time. It contains very good designs, exact explanations of terms, and also practical hints on the execution of designs, as well as the cultivation of plants. It can be compared to the slighter works by Liger and Pluche, which also treat the entire subject matter but focus chiefly on flowers.

Comprehensive books on garden design include Stephen Switzer's works dating from the transitory period between the baroque and the landscape garden, especially his *Ichnographia Rustica* (1718), and Batty Langley's *New Principles of Gardening* (1727), which also discusses practical gardening. Daniel Marot, Le Bouteux, Johann Jacob Schübler, Johann David Fülck, Franz Anton Danreiter, and Galimard excelled with baroque garden designs as models, which they published on engraved folio plates.

The landscape-garden style had existed in England for a long period before a book describing its principles was published. The young William Gilpin anonymously published his small *A Dialoge upon the Gardens . . . at Stow* (1748). In 1767 was published the poem *The Rise and Progress of the Present Taste in Planting Parks*. Not until 1768 did the first treatises come out on the subject, namely, George Mason's short *An Essay on Design in Gardening* (1768) and Thomas Whately's *Observations on Modern Gardening*. After these works the amount of literature dealing with garden design exploded. No time has produced such an abundance of often polemic literature concerning correct garden design. Authors from all professions participated in the discussion. William Chambers opened a battle with his *A Dissertation on Oriental Gardening* (1772), followed by William Mason's four-volume *The English Garden, a Poem* (1772–81). Also well known are Richard Payne Knight's *The Landscape, A Didactic Poem* (1794), Sir Uvedale Price's *Essay on the Picturesque* (1794), and Humphry Repton's *Sketches and Hints on Landscape Gardening* (1795).

Claude-Henri Watelet (*Essai sur les jardins* [1774]) was the first to write about landscape gardening in France. Other well-known publications on the subject in France are Jean-Marie Morel's *Théorie des jardins* (1776), René-Louis de Gerardin's *De la composition des paysages* (1777), and Jacques Delille's poem *Les jardins* (1782).

In Germany the philosopher Christian Cay Laurenz Hirschfeld wrote his five-volume *Theorie der Gartenkunst* (1779–95). More pragmatic is Johann Gottlieb Schoch's little-known *Versuch einer Anleitung zur Anlegung eines Gartens im englischen Geschmack* (1784). Friedrich Ludwig von Sckell advocated the landscape-garden practice in his *Beiträge zur bildenden Gartenkunst* (1818) into the 19th century. Prince Heinrich Ludwig von Pückler-Muskau's English-based *Andeutungen über Landschaftsgärtnerei* (1834) excelled with its large lithographs. Written for the common man was Eduard Schmidlin's *Bürgerliche Gartenkunst* (1843).

Humphry Repton continued to publish, with his *Observations on Theory and Practice of Landscape Gardening* (1803) in addition to other works, while John Claudius Loudon began his immense works with *Observations on the Formation and Management of Useful and Ornamental Plantations* (1804). William Sawrey Gilpin renewed in his beautifully illustrated *Practical Hints upon Landscape Gardening* (1832) his uncle's picturesque principles.

In Italy Count Ercole Silva produced *Dell'arte dei' giardini inglesi* (1799), while the rare *Mysli rózne* by the Polish countess Izabella Czartoryska (1805), with its excellent illustrations of clumps, is also interesting.

Relatively few works contain primarily plans of landscape gardens. Those that do include Pierre Panseron's *Recueil de jardinage* (1783) and Ludwig Christian Mansa's *Plans zu Anlagen englischer Gärten* (1795). In addition are mostly copperplate works containing chiefly decorations for landscape gardens, such as those

by William Halfpenny, Charles Over, George-Louis Le Rouge (the famous *Jardins anglo-chinois*), Johann Friedrich Ernst Albrecht, Johann Gottfried Grohmann, Wilhelm Gottlieb Becker, Jean Charles Krafft, Thomas Elison, Friedrich Gotthilf Baumgärtner, and others.

The French *Essai sur la composition et l'ornement des jardins* (1818), which contains many copperplates, is attributed to Guiol and became quite popular, as did Pierre Boitard's *L'art de composer et de décorer les jardins* (1834). Elegant plan drawing was first and best demonstrated by Gabriel Thouin in his *Plans raisonnés de tout les espèces de jardins* (1819–20), followed by N. Vergnaud's *L'art de créer les jardins* (1834) and Joseph Ramée's *Parcs et jardins* (ca. 1836). In Germany Rudolf Siebeck and Gustav Adolph Rohland excelled in publishing colored garden designs beginning in 1851.

In 1841 Andrew Jackson Downing published the first book on garden design in the United States, *A Treatise on the Theory and Practice of Landscape Gardening, Adapted to North America*. The Scot Charles H. Smith's remarkable *Parks and Pleasure Grounds* (1851) appeared in five editions in the United States. Frank J. Scott's compendious *The Art of Beautifying Suburban Home Grounds* (1870) recommended, in the spirit of Loudon, good designs "for persons of moderate income." Elaborate colored plans embellish Jacob Weidenmann's *Beautifying Country Homes* (1870).

British mid-19th-century eclectic garden taste can be studied through Joshua Major's *Theory and Practice of Landscape Gardening* (1852), Charles M'Intosh's *The Book of the Garden* (1853–55), Edward Kemp's *How to Lay Out a Garden* (1856), and Shirley Hibberd's *Rustic Adornments for Homes of Taste* (1856).

Several authors attempted to surpass each other by publishing comprehensive manuals. Such was the case in Germany with Gustav Meyer (*Lehrbuch der schönen Gartenkunst* [1859–60]), Eduard Petzold (*Die Landschaftsgärtnerei* [1862]), and Hermann Jäger (*Lehrbuch der Gartenkunst* [1877]). In France similar works included Alfred-Auguste Ernouf's *L'art des jardins* (1868), Alfred Gressent's *Parcs et jardins* (1877), and Edouard André's *L'art des jardins* (1879). American manuals of this period are G.M. Kern's *Practical Landscape Gardening* (1855), Horace Cleveland's *Landscape Architecture* (1873), and Samuel Parson's *Landscape Gardening* (1891).

A new, often polemic discourse began about 1870 between advocates of the so-called formal style and those of the so-called natural style. The Englishman John Arthur Hughes recommended neobaroque designs in his *Garden Architecture and Landscape Gardening* (1866), which Lothar Abel plagiarized in Vienna as *Gartenarchitektur* (1876).

On the other side, William Robinson published his first influential pamphlets, *The Wild Garden* (1870) and *English Flower Garden* (1883). The followers of Robinson regarded his books on plants as the only source books on garden design. Robinson's associate Gertrude Jekyll wrote several books on planting designs for smaller gardens, beginning with *Wood and Garden* (1899). Henry Ernest Milner's *Art and Practice of Landscape Gardening* (1890) shows a similar method of natural planting for large parks. Willy Lange advocated such ideas in Germany with his *Gartengestaltung der Neuzeit* (1907).

John D. Sedding (*Garden Craft Old and New* [1891]) and Sir Reginald Blomfield (*The Formal Garden in England* [1892]) continued to insist on an architectural layout, as did Thomas Mawson (*The Art and Craft of Garden Making* [1900]), Paul Schultze-Naumburg (*Kulturarbeiten: Gärten* [1902]), Joseph Maria Olbrich (*Neue Gärten* [1905]), Hermann Muthesius (*Landhaus und Garten* [1907]), Henry Inigo Triggs (*Garden Craft in Europe* [1913]), and Walter H. Godfrey (*Gardens in the Making* [1914]) in their charming works on arts-and-crafts-gardens.

During the years surrounding World War I, garden architects attempted to free themselves from traditional models of design and create a modernist garden style, often presumed as a national one. Examples include, in Germany, Leberecht Migge, *Die Gartenkultur des 20. Jahrhunderts* (1913), Harry Maass, *Kleine und grosse Gärten* (1926), and Hugo Koch, *Der Garten* (1927); in France, Jean C.N. Forestier, *Jardins* (1920), André Vera, *Le nouveau jardin* (1912) and *Les jardins* (1919), Raymond Charmaison, *Les jardins précieux* (1919), and Achille Duchêne, *Les jardins de l'avenir* (1935); in the United States, Frank A. Waugh, *Formal Design in Landscape Architecture* (1927); and in England, Richard Sudell, *Landscape Gardening* (1933).

More recent works on modernist garden design include those of Margaret O. Goldsmith (*Designs for Outdoor Living* [1941]), Otto Valentien (*Zeitgemäße Wohngärten* [1949]), Garret Eckbo (*Landscape for Living* [1950]), Hans Schiller (*Gartengestaltung* [1952]), and Sylvia Crowe (*Garden Design* [1958]).

## Garden Catalogs

Many Renaissance plant collectors published their garden catalogs. The first to be published independently were by Joachim Camerarius of Nuremberg (1588) and Giacomo Antonio Cortuso of Padova (1591). By 1648 more than 20 printed catalogs followed. The total number ever printed may have surpassed a thousand. Such catalogs are important for the investigation of plant history.

In 1613 Basilius Besler began with his famous *Hortus Eystettensis*, a tradition of voluminous plant books, each of which illustrated the stock of only one garden. Similar but smaller is Tobia Aldini's *Exactissima Descriptio Rariorum quarundam Plantarum, quae Continentur Romae in Horto Farnesiano* (1625). New introductions of rich gardens were documented by clear black-and-white

plates in Jan Commelin's description of the plants in the Amsterdam Botanical Garden (*Horti Medici Amstelaedamensis Rariorum Plantarum Descriptio et Icones* [1697–1701]), Johann Jacob Dillen's *Hortus Elthamensis* (1732), and Carl Linnaeus's *Hortus Cliffortianus* (1737).

The tradition of publishing select illustrated garden catalogs culminated between 1770 and 1810 in magnificent color-plate books, such as Nicolaus Joseph Jacquin's *Hortus Botanicus Vindobonensis* (1770–76), with 300 plates, and his *Plantarum Rariorum Horti Caesaeri Schoenbrunnensis Descriptiones et Icones* (1797–1804), both published in Vienna; and French works such as Pierre-Joseph Buc'hoz's *Le jardin d'Eden* (1783) and Pierre Etienne Ventenat's *Description des plantes nouvelles et peu connues, cultivées dans le jardin de J.M. Cels* (1800) and *Jardin de la Malmaison* (1803–5), the latter illustrated by the famous flower painter Pierre-Joseph Redouté.

## Garden Descriptions

Although not at first published independently, descriptions of actual gardens were sometimes parts of plant catalogs. The Italian Giacomo Antonio Cortuso (1591) and the Dutch Peter Pauw (1601) both added short descriptions and a map of their gardens to their catalogs. Salomon de Caus published the first independent description of a garden in 1620, of the castle garden in Heidelberg, decorated with 30 high-quality copperplates. In 1636 Guy de la Brosse edited a catalog that included a description and magnificent bird's-eye-view of the Jardin du Roi in Paris. In 1647 Hans Raszmussøn Block gave a description of the Danish Cronenborg garden in his *Horticultura Danica*. Johann Royer did so as well for the Brunswick garden at Hesse in 1648.

In the 18th century a number of famous gardens were portrayed by extraordinary copperplate series without a text, such as Rome by Giovanni Battista Falda, Kassel by Giovanni Francesco Guerniero (1706), Versailles by Pierre Lepautre (1716), Vienna by Salomon Kleiner, and Nancy by Emmanuel Héré (1756).

Independent garden guides first appeared in regard to Versailles, such as *La promenade de Versailles* by Mademvoiselle de Scudery (1669), the *Labyrinthe de Versailles* by Charles Perrault (1677), and the *Nouvelle description des chateaux et parcs des Versailles et de Marly* by J.A. Piganiol de la Force (1701). In 1779 Carmontelle published a work on the *Jardin de Monceau, près de Paris*, and René-Louis Girardin a book on Ermenonville in 1788. Other guides on single gardens include August Rode's work on Wörlitz (1788), W.F. Mavor's on Blenheim (1809), Johann Michael Zeyher's on Schwetzingen (1819) and Eduard Petzold's on Muskau (1856).

Several authors in the 18th century attempted to deal with landscape design by describing and commenting on existing gardens. One is particularly drawn to William Gilpin's *Dialogue upon the Gardens at Stowe*

(1748), Charles-Joseph de Ligne's *Coup d'oeil sur Beloeil* (1781), and Alexandre de Laborde's *Description des nouveaux jardins de France* (Paris 1808). Joseph Heely (*Letters* [1777]), William Gilpin (*Picturesque Tours* [1782–1809]), and Wilhelm Gottlieb Becker, writing on the Plauische Grund near Leipzig (1799) related descriptions of pictorial landscapes to thoughts on landscape design.

Annual park reports were a singularly American phenomenon. The first may have been the *Report of the Joint Committe on Public Lands in Relation to the Public Garden* (1850). The reports on New York's Central Park became famous and were followed by reports on other parks created by Frederick Law Olmsted, for example, in Brooklyn, Buffalo, and Chicago.

The public gardens of Paris, remodeled by Haussmann, were described by Adolph Alphand in 1867–72 and by William Robinson in 1869. Guides to U.S. parks include Clarence Cook's *A Description of the New York Central Park* (1869) and Sylvester Boxton's *Boston Park Guide* (1895).

Travel guides focusing on the gardens of a single country became popular in the age of tourism. Forerunners of these include Pückler-Muskau's *Briefe eines Verstorbenen* (1830), on his English garden tour, and early historical art studies on Italian gardens, such as Wilhelm P. Tuckermann's *Die Gartenkunst der italienischen Renaissance* (1884), Charles Platt's *Italian Gardens* (1894), Charles Latham's *The Gardens of Italy* (1905), and Geoffrey Jellicoe's *Italian Gardens of the Renaissance* (1925). Today, many countries and towns provide garden guides.

**Further Reading**

Dobai, Johannes, *Die Kunstliteratur des Klassizismus und der Romantik in England*, 4 vols., Bern, Switzerland: Benteli, 1974

Dochnahl, Friedrich Jakob, *Bibliotheca Hortensis*, Nuremberg, Germany, 1861; reprint, Hildesheim, Germany, and New York: Olms, 1970

Felton, Samuel, *On the Portraits of English Authors on Gardening*, London, 1828

Ganay, Ernest, *Bibliographie de l'art des jardins*, Paris: Bibliothèque des Arts Décoratifs, 1989

Hazlitt, William Carew, *Gleanings in Old Garden Literature*, London, 1887; reprint, Detroit: Gale Research, 1968

Henrey, Blanche, *British Botanical and Horticultural Literature before 1800*, London: Oxford University Press, 1975

Janson, H. Frederic, *Pomona's Harvest: An Illustrated Chronicle of Antiquarian Fruit Literature*, Portland, Oregon: Timber Press, 1996

Miltitz, Friedrich von, *Handbuch der botanischen Literatur für Botaniker, Bibliothekare, Buchhändler und Auctionatoren, mit Angabe der Preise und Recensionen*, Berlin, 1829

Raphael, Sandra, *An Oak Spring Pomona: A Selection of the Rare Books on Fruit in the Oak Spring Garden Library*, Upperville, Virginia: Oak Spring Garden Library, 1990

Rohde, Eleanour Sinclair, *The Old English Gardening Books*, London: Hopkins, 1924; new edition, London: Minerva, 1972

Séguier, Jean Francois, *Bibliotheca Botanica*, The Hague, 1740

Tongiorgi Tomasi, Lucia, *An Oak Spring Flora: Flower Illustration from the Fifteenth Century to the Present Time*, Upperville, Virginia: Oak Spring Garden Library, 1997

Wimmer, Clemens Alexander, *Geschichte der Gartentheorie*, Darmstadt, Germany: Wissenschaftliche Buchgesellschaft, 1989

Wolschke-Bulmahn, Joachim, and Jack Becker, *American Garden Literature in the Dumbarton Oaks Collection (1785–1900)*, Washington, D.C.: Dumbarton Oaks Research Library and Collection, 1998

CLEMENS ALEXANDER WIMMER

# Boris Gardens

## Sofia, Bulgaria

**Location:** central part of the city of Sofia

Boris Gardens is one of the oldest and largest parks in Sofia and a major element of the urban green system of the capital city of Bulgaria. It covers 361 hectares (892 acres), including the formal gardens (90 ha [222 acres]) and the forest park (271 ha [669 acres]). The establishment of the park is associated with the period of liberation of Bulgaria from the Ottoman domination. In 1837 Sofia numbered 18,000 inhabitants. A small central garden in front of the palace included a place for musicians and a coffee shop. The subsequent European appearance of the new capital of Bulgaria resulted from the efforts of Czech, Austrian, German, and Russian experts. Numerous public buildings and streets were built and cadastre plans drawn; the electrification of the capital was one of the first public utility developments. The major cultural institutions were created, including the national library (1879), natural history museum (1889), national theater and Sofia University (1904), and the Sofia opera (1908). The end of the 19th century saw the emerging of public gardens, long after their models, the European public parks, had been created.

The author of the first plan of Boris Gardens, the Swiss gardener Daniel Neff, was invited in 1882 by the mayor, Ivan Hadjienov, to create a large nursery garden (*pépinière*) for the parks of the capital city. The land designated in 1882 for this purpose was a former Turkish pasture situated beyond the city boundaries, used after the liberation for military drills. Neff developed his plan that same year, planted numerous trees (acacias, pagoda trees, maples, elms, limes, and mulberry trees), put up a fence, and built a house for himself on the land. Six years later he replaced some of the acacia trees with sycamores, oaks, ashes, birches, spruces, and pines. During the following ten years the park grew to include the Fish Lake and the Big Lake. New trees and plants were imported. The geometrical composition of the Boris Gardens' alley network dominates the first cadastre plan of Sofia. In January 1895 the garden was officially named after Prince Boris Turnovski.

The second period in the park's development is associated with the appointment of the municipal gardener Joseph Fray in 1906. The construction of Eagles Bridge in 1890–91 redirected the pedestrian walk toward Tzarigrad Road, thereby marking the main park entry. The intensive development of the garden during this time included the construction of a new maintenance yard and the creation of the rose garden and the horse chestnut and lime alleys, as well as the creation of the central parterres. The new plan preserved both the central composition, whereby the new alleys run parallel to the central axis, and the overall modular park structure. Along this central longitudinal axis, framed by geometrical parterres and rows of trees, the composition of the park's spaces is in a landscape garden style. The gardens were completed about 1920, at which time, several successful flower shows took place. The forest park was extended as a protective forest belt, and the park became an important element within the urban structure and in the life of the capital city.

From 1934 until World War II the Bulgarian Georgi Duhtev, educated as a landscape architect in Austria, took the position of chief gardener. This period is charac-

terized by public works—water supply and electricity supply systems, restoration of the rose garden by the replanting of 1,400 new roses, and the maintenance of the forest parts. The public bath complex Maria Luiza was constructed, and at the central part of the park, busts of eminent Bulgarians were situated. Following a proposal of the Japanese plenipotentiary minister, a Japanese garden was created with imported cherry and morello trees, Japanese roses, and euonymus and maple trees.

The park's fourth period spans World War II to the present day. Similar to all other parks in the country, together with the name change (to Freedom Park), the content of the park's composition was modified to include the typical symbols of the Communist regime. The most significant of these is the Common Partisan Grave, constructed in 1955 on the main axis of the park at the highest point of the formal gardens. Its white obelisk stands as a vertical accent above the green canopy, while the other end of this axis was marked by the ruby star of the Communist Party headquarters at the city center. Sport complexes, including the National Stadium Vassil Levski (1961) and the winter stadium, replaced the existing playgrounds. They formed a longitudinal "sport" axis and covered almost one-third of the area. During this period Delcho Sugarev made the most significant contributions to the development of the park, uniting the formal gardens and the forest park. In the 1980s Georgi Radoslavov, a landscape engineer, through an analysis of the park's archives, demonstrated the influence of the German-Austrian baroque style on the park's composition and discovered its module, preserved throughout the years in the elements of the central part. He followed the principles thus uncovered in his restoration plans.

In the 1990s the name of the park was restored to Boris Gardens, accompanied by a renewed concern about its condition. In 1997 the mayor of Sofia ordered a master plan for the formal gardens, protected for their high historic and aesthetic values and biodiversity. The renovation of the formal gardens has included minor changes in the structure and considerable replanting. Following the dendrology plan (1989) some of the oldest trees were replaced with new ones—lime trees, birch, and pine spruce. One of the most important tasks of those involved is to reduce the negative impact of the changed urban environment. The ambition of the landscape professionals and the municipality is to make the park a favorite and safe place for the citizens, restoring the brightness of its prototype—the European park.

**Synopsis**

| | |
|---|---|
| 1882 | Daniel Neff designs plan for nursery gardens |
| 1888 | Land designated for construction of park |
| 1888–89 | Construction of Fish Lake and Big Lake |

| | |
|---|---|
| 1895 | Park named after Prince Boris Turnovski |
| 1906 | Josef Fray appointed city gardener; construction of main entrance |
| 1912 | Construction of lime tree and chestnut alleys |
| 1929 | Construction of casino and rose garden |
| 1934 | Georgi Duhtev takes position of chief gardener |
| 1939 | Construction of bath complex "Maria Luiza" |
| 1940 | Construction of Japanese garden |
| 1948 | Plan for reconstruction prepared by Delcho Sugarev |
| 1955 | Common grave monument |
| 1957 | Construction of rock garden |
| 1960 | Construction of additional lakes |
| 1961 | Construction of national stadium |
| 1972 | Reconstruction of Big lake |
| 1984 | National competition for park's plan; plan from Georgi Radoslavov |
| 1989 | Dendrology plan for vegetation restoration |
| 1997 | Plan for reconstruction of historical part of gardens |
| 1989–90 | Updating of plan |

**Further Reading**

*Atlas Sofiia i Sofiiskata aglomeratsiia; Atlas Sofia and Sofia Agglomeration,* Sofia: Kartografiia EOOD, 1993

Radoslavov, Georgi, "Predstavitelnata chast na Parka na svobodata (Representative Part of the Freedoms Park)," *Arhitektura* 2 (1988)

Radoslavov, Georgi, "Classic Compositional Principles in the Construction of Prince Boris Gardens," Ph.D. diss., Lesotehnicheski Universitet, Sofia, 1995

Radoslavova, Julia, "Kniaz Borisovata gradina (Prince Boris Gardens)," *Gradina* 1 (2000)

Robev, Rashko, "Parkut prez godinite (The Park throughout the Years)," *Arhitektura* 2 (1988)

Samardjieva, Maria, "Proektantut (The Designer)," *Gradina* 1 (2000)

Stoichev, Luiben, *Parkova i landshaftna arhitektura (Parks and Landscape Architecture),* Sofia: Tehnika, 1985

Sugarev, Delcho, *Gradinsko-parkovo i peizajno izkustvo* (Garden and Landscape Art), Sofia: Zemizdat, 1976

VESSELINA TROEVA

---

# Botanical Illustration

The purpose of a botanical illustration is to provide a precise image of a plant or its parts. Botanical illustration records a plant's often ephemeral and fragile structure so that the viewer may recognize the plant shown and ascertain its identity. Ideally, an anonymous plant illustration is neither datable nor attributable to an individual hand. Botanical illustrations have very little to do with art; they pertain to the world of science, aesthetic considerations being totally inappropriate, and beauty a pleasant, though irrelevant side effect. As a rule, these naturalistic or realistic images are prepared by or for the scientist and represent a given plant very much in the same way as a preserved herbarium specimen but have the advantage of not losing color, showing the three-dimensional structure, and not being vulnerable to insect attack. *Naturalistic* is, however, a very relative term; the illustrator, after all, produces an illusion of a three-dimensional plant on a two-dimensional, flat surface and often in reduced scale. The following discussion does not address the Eastern tradition of botanical illustration, which is based on an entirely different philosophy (although some works are fully identifiable from a botanical point of view).

Accurate two-dimensional images of plants are produced by the following methods: drawing or painting, self-impression, and photography. In all methods of botanical illustration, the selection of the specimen (whether living or conserved) is a very important process. It necessitates a careful analysis of the existing variation in a population, and it is the average, statistically "normal" specimen that must be used for botanical illustration. Characteristics that are critical to identification have to be recorded with particular care—like the pubescence of the leaves, color marks on petals, or the form of the seeds. Any botanical illustration should be fully annotated with the provenance of the plant, the scientific name, and, ideally, be correlated with a herbarium specimen. Consequently, a botanical illustration is usually the result of a collaborative effort by the graphic artist and the scientist. On the voyage of the *Endeavour* commanded by Captain Cook, a scene in the "Great Cabin" is described as "we [the two scientists] sat til dark at the great table with the draughtsman opposite and showed him in what way to make his drawings, ourselves made rapid descriptions . . . while the specimen was fresh" (Joseph Banks cited in J.C. Beaglehole,

A group of *Iris reticulata* forms and hybrids and *Iris danfordiae*, from Martyn Rix and Roger Phillips, *The Bulb Book*, 1981
Photo by Roger Phillips and Martyn Rix

editor, *The Endeavour Journal of Joseph Banks, 1768–1771*). Only a few outstanding personalities—like the scientist Conrad Gessner, and illustrators Maria Sibylla Merian, George Dionysius Ehret, and Ferdinand and Franz Bauer—seem to have worked on their own. All illustrators, however, have something in common: they wish not to express themselves, but to record objects of nature in a cool, objective manner.

Botanical illustration began with the works of a scriptorium in Byzantium (now Istanbul). In the early sixth century a text by Dioscorides on *materia medica* (essentially medicinal plants) was illustrated with several hundred images of plants, many very true to nature. This manuscript painted on vellum, known as the *Codex Vindobonensis* (now in the Österreichische Nationalbibliothek, Vienna, Austria), exemplifies the common origins of botany and pharmacy and the strong interdependence of text and illustration. The images may or may not have been made from nature but copied from preexisting models. This is a fundamental problem with all botanical illustrations; perfect copies of earlier illustrations are very hard to distinguish from originals made directly from nature. For almost a millennium pharmaceutical texts were copied and recopied by hand, including the illustrations, which gradually lost their precision and deteriorated into almost meaningless figures.

The Renaissance brought about a novel approach: plant illustrators went out into the garden to produce accurate images from nature. The *Carrara Herbal* (now in the British Library, London), Martin Schongauer's *Paeony* (now in the Paul Getty Museum, Malibu, California), Leonardo da Vinci's *Bramble* (now in the Royal Collection, Windsor, England) and Albrecht Dürer's *Iris* (now in the Kunsthalle, Bremen, Germany) stand at the beginning of this new trend, but may at best be regarded as studies for oil paintings, not as independent works intended for science. However, plant illustrations made for Leonhart Fuchs (now in the Österreichische Nationalbibliothek, Vienna, Austria), for Pier Antonio Michiel (now in the Biblioteca Nazionale Marciana, Venice, Italy), and by Conrad Gesner (now in the Universitätsbibliothek, Erlangen, Germany) are independent works. Using the resources of their private gardens—in Tübingen (Germany), Venice (Italy), and Zürich (Switzerland), respectively—plants were painted using body color and, often, in the actual size. All three works used a few items copied from similar earlier works, to create illustrated manuscript encyclopedias of botanical knowledge. Fuchs, Michiel, and Gessner added numerous notes to the images, such as plant names (often in several languages), the provenance of the material, medicinal and other uses, etc.

Such works are called florilegia, being manuscript or printed books consisting largely or entirely of pictures of plants. They are outstanding documents of the history of botany and primary sources for finding out which plants were grown in a garden at a given time. Many florilegia were to follow, among them the florilegium painted for Ulysse Aldrovandi (now in the Biblioteca Universitaria, Bologna, Italy), for Karel van Sint Omaar (now in the Biblioteka Jagiellonska, Cracow, Poland), and for Conrad von Gemmingen, Prince Bishop of Eichstätt (now in the Universitätsbibliothek, Erlangen, Germany). These works are mines of information on the introduction of new species into cultivation, in particular from overseas. A notable image is the precise illustration of the dragontree (*Dracaena draco*) (see Plate 7)—a native of the Canary islands first cultivated in a garden in Lisbon—that was published by Clusius in 1576. Such botanical illustrations are of particular value because plant descriptions were often incomplete during this period.

Due to the immense production cost, these botanical encyclopedias were objects of prestige. They have always been rare and most often depended on patronage. The largest collection of such works is that owned by the kings of France. These volumes document the plants grown over many years in the Jardin du Roi in Paris (now in the Bibliothèque Centrale of the Muséum National d'Histoire Naturelle in Paris). A slightly smaller group belongs to the Prince of Liechtenstein (as of 1999, Sammlungen des Fürsten von Liechtenstein, Vaduz); and yet another famous florilegium is that painted for Franz I, Emperor of Austria (now in the Österreichische Nationalbibliothek, Vienna). Many more gardens were documented in this way, often by generations of illustrators. Some florilegia were broken up, such as the one made by Pierre-Joseph Redouté for Empress Joséphine (the first wife of Napoleon I), the fragments of which are now kept in several private collections.

Another function of botanical illustration is documenting plants collected on an expedition. One early traveling illustrator was Melchior Lorch, who accompanied the ambassador Ghislain de Busbecq to Istanbul; he may have been the first to produce an illustration of the lilac (*Syringa vulgaris*) which was subsequently sent to Prague. Many illustrators followed, among them Claude Aubriet, who went with Joseph Pitton de Tournefort to Armenia (drawings and finished watercolors in the Bibliothèque Centrale, Muséum National d'Histoire Naturelle, Paris); Sydney Parkinson, who recorded the plants collected by Joseph Banks and Daniel Solander on Captain Cook's first circumnavigation (watercolors in the Natural History Museum, London); and Ferdinand Bauer, who produced an extremely rich documentation of the plants found on John Sibthorp's first voyage to the Levant (drawings and finished watercolors in the Department of Plant Sciences, Oxford). The archives of the Real Jardín Botánico in Madrid are full of plant illustrations prepared in the Spanish colonies, and the Komarov

Botanical Institute in St. Petersburg holds drawings made by Japanese illustrators who were influenced by Western models. Traveling illustrators worked like photographers today, and they had the same problem: limited time to fix the image of often short-lived objects. Consequently, often only outline drawings were made in the field, with notes on color added either in words or in a color code. Later, finished watercolors were produced in the studio.

Over the centuries more details were recorded by the illustrator, such as single stamens, pollen grains, dissections of flowers, fruits, and seeds. Roots, which had been consistently drawn in utmost detail by earlier generations of illustrators, were later excluded. This development paralleled the improvement of optical instruments, in particular the microscope. The height of this trend was Ferdinand Bauer's watercolors of Australian plants (now in the Natural History Museum, London), which provide perfect images of plants previously unknown. In a few cases his paintings were used as the only basis for the description of new taxa, rather than the often miserable herbarium specimens. Drawing aids, such as the camera lucida—which allowed an object to be traced—were used occasionally to produce accurate images from nature. It is, however, extremely difficult to analyze the technical equipment used by a botanical illustrator because preliminary drawings were typically destroyed. Supplemental drawings to herbarium specimens—often dissections done in graphite or pen and ink—also became a tradition. Heinrich Gustav Reichenbach's orchid herbarium (now in the Naturhistorisches Museum, Vienna) is a good example of this practice.

Typically plant illustrations are unicates made using paper (and in rare instances vellum), graphite pencil, pen and ink (for preliminary studies), and watercolor or gouache (for finished works). It has become a tradition to annotate plant illustrations with their modern names, which sometimes results in several anonymous *glossae* on them. Libraries often preserve plant illustrations in bound albums, in other cases they are fixed to herbarium specimens or kept loose in Solander boxes.

Reproducing botanical images was often problematic. With the exception of work by the most accomplished masters—such as Veit Spreckle, James Sowerby, or the lithographers working for the *Historia Naturalis Palmarum* by Karl Friedrich Wilhelm von Martius—reproduction always led to inaccuracies and the loss of some information. There was often a lapse of time between the completion of drawings and the making of the printing form, and frequently different persons did the work. Early prints often were not correlated with a text, or such pairings were totally inappropriate. Leonhart Fuchs, for example, had a text from classical antiquity referring to Mediterranean flora illustrated with images showing plants from his native Swabia and Bavaria, as well as others growing in his garden.

The earliest technique used to multiply images was the woodcut, which was used to reproduce about a third of Fuchs's drawings. These woodcuts appeared as black-lined illustrations in his *De historia stirpium* (Basel, 1542), a book which opened a new era. Like many other works this book exists in an uncolored version and in a special hand-colored version. Since the colors used often were not based on the original watercolor paintings but on the colorist's fancy, the colored version is rarely superior to the normal edition and colored copies often vary enormously from each other. The number of copies made of *De historia stirpium* is unknown, but because of the use of pear wood for the blocks, several hundred could easily have been produced. In fact, cut woodblocks were often used for several editions or book productions. *De historia stirpium* is a unique work in another respect: it contains not only a portrait of the author, but also of the illustrator, Albrecht Meyer; of the man who translated the drawings on the woodblock, Heinrich Füllmauer; and of the man who cut the woodblock, Viet Speckle. This is an unparalleled gesture toward the collaborators, since often the graphic artists remain anonymous. Remarkably, some uncut woodblocks not used in this project, but with their plant drawings in ink, have survived and are held by the botanical institute of Tübingen University.

Copper-engraving subsequently allowed a more subtle reproduction of botanical detail. A vast number of botanical illustrations were multiplied in this way, such as Conrad von Gemmingen's plant illustrations, which were published after his death as *Hortus Eystettensis*. Ferdinand Bauer's watercolors of Levantine plants were engraved and printed using copper plates many years after their creation by James Sowerby and his collaborators in London. The resulting black-lined illustrations were colored using Bauer's work as a model. No more than 25 copies were printed and because of special circumstances all were colored. In most cases, however, a standard, black-lined version and a hand-colored, luxury version were done. The softness of copperplate restricts the number of "pulls," thus editions are always relatively small. Worn-out copperplates were usually melted down. Sometimes several printing inks were used, resulting in a polychrome engraving produced from a single plate. A stipple engraving is a special modification of this technique, that allows for the printing of subtle color gradations using a single plate. For some of his publications Alexander von Humboldt made use of this very expensive printing technique; his color engravings printed from a single plate were often further improved by hand-coloring. This refined printing method was also applied in many of the publications by Pierre-Joseph Redouté. Among other works, his *Les liliacées* documented the floral wealth of the gardens belonging to the upper echelons of Paris society, both of the ancien and nouveau régimes.

Lithography dramatically changed the duplication of plant illustrations. It allowed the production of an almost infinite numbers of copies from a single template using a much cheaper process. Walter Hood Fitch, for example, copied the plant sketches prepared by John Dalton Hooker in India, then transferred the outline drawing on a lithographic stone and printed them. The resulting black-lined lithographs were subsequently colored on the basis of the incompletely colored field sketches. Etching, aquatint, mesotint, and wood-engravings were other techniques which opened the gates to the more refined methods used in the late 19th and the 20th centuries.

With a few exceptions printed plant illustrations form part of printed books, like floras, monographs, and journals, with Curtis's *The Botanical Magazine*—founded in 1785 and still flourishing—being the patriarch in this field. For plant illustrations published after 1753 and before ca. 1900, a standard bibliography exists, the famous *Index Londinensis*, which summarizes this extremely diverse material. Botanical prints often are not dated or signed, and only annotated with the plant name. Many of the works published between 1753 and 1940 are listed in a standard bibliography, the second edition of *Taxonomic Literature* by Frans A. Stafleu and Richard S. Cowan. As a rule, these printed illustrations are kept in libraries (often associated with botanical institutions), which can comprise several million of these items. Because they were needed for reprints and second editions, some cut woodblocks, engraved copper plates, etc. have been preserved. Existing specimens include woodblocks cut for illustrating Pier Andrea Matthioli's works (now dispersed), the copper plates of Georg Christian Oeder's famous *Flora Danica* (now in the Botanisk Have, Copenhagen), and many of the copper plates last used for reprinting the *Hortus Eystettensis* in 1713 (now in Albertina, Vienna).

Another approach to botanical illustration is nature printing. When a plant specimen is pressed flat, it can be colored with printer's ink and used as a printing form, producing a perfect, albeit monochrome image on paper that lacks internal details. This very simple method seems to have been first used in a manuscript on *materia medica* written in the 13th century in Syria (now in the Topkapi Sarayi Kütüphanesi, Istanbul), but early examples also exist from Central Europe, like in an anonymous Rasenstück of the early 16th century (now in the Staatliche Schlösser und Gärten, Potsdam, Germany). Although a conveniently quick method, it has several drawbacks: only flat plant structures like leaves can be adequately documented and the force of the printing process destroys the objects. Therefore only a few copies can be made. Although it has been refined, this technique of plant illustration was never of great importance and has remained a speciality for the connoisseur.

The invention of photography brought a revolution to botanical illustration. A light-sensitive substance on a carrier (such as glass plate or film) automatically produces an image that is made permanent by a second process creating a negative or positive original. As with plant drawings or paintings, the resulting illustration is a unicate, but copies on paper can be made very easily and quickly. These prints can in turn be duplicated using the more conventional printing process. Some of the earliest photographic images—the short-lived sun pictures by John Wedgewood and the cyanotypes of Sir John Herschel—show silhouettes of leaves. Very soon photographing botanical objects became a quick, easy, and cheap method of producing plant illustrations, but it did not totally replace conventional botanical illustration. The Challenger Expedition of 1872–76 is believed to be the first sea voyage to use an official photographer in addition to a traditional illustrator.

When color photography emerged, few continued on the old route of hand rendering plant images. Photographic unicates (either negatives or positives such as slides) and prints are kept in photo archives that often form a special collection within a botanical library. Advancements in photography, photocopying, and computer technology have furthered the ease and speed of multiplying, storing, and distributing images. These dramatic changes are making plant illustrations more readily available than ever—and the development of botanical illustration will continue to influence the future course of botany.

## Further Reading

Blunt, Wilfried, and William Stearn, *The Art of Botanical Illustration*, London: Collins, 1950; New York: Scribner, 1951; new edition, Woodbridge, Suffolk: Antique Collectors' Club, 1994

Ford, Brian J., *Images of Science: A History of Scientific Illustration*, London: British Library, 1992; New York: Oxford University Press, 1993

Geus, Armin, "Natur im Druck: Geschichte und Technik des Naturselbstdruck," in *Natur im Druck*, edited by Geus, Marburg, Germany: Basilisken-Presse, 1995

Hulton, Paul Hope, and Lawrence Smith, *Flowers in Art from East and West*, London: British Museum Publications, 1979

Koreny, Fritz, *Albrecht Dürer und die Tier- und Pflanzenstudien der Renaissance*, Munich: Prestel-Verlag, 1985; as *Albrecht Dürer and the Animal and Plant Studies of the Rennaissance*, translated by Pamela Marwood and Yehuda Shapiro, Boston: Little Brown, 1988

Nissen, Klaus, *Die botanische Buchillustration*, Stuttgart: Hiersemann, 1951

Raphael, Sandra, *An Oak Spring Sylva*, Upperville, Virginia: Oak Spring Garden Library, 1989

Raphael, Sandra, *An Oak Spring Pomona*, Upperville, Virginia: Oak Spring Garden Library, 1990

Rix, Martyn, *The Art of the Plant World*, Woodstock, New York: Overlook Press, 1980; as *The Art of the Botanist*, Guildford, Surrey: Lutterworth Press, 1981

Tongiorgi Tomasi, Lucia, *An Oak Spring Flora: Flower Illustration from the Fifteenth Century to the Present Time*, translated by Lisa Chien, Upperville, Virginia: Oak Spring Garden Library, 1997

H. WALTER LACK

# Botanic Garden

Botanic gardens are collections of living plants that in the present day have four major functions: scientific inquiry, botanical and horticultural education, public recreation, and landscape aesthetics. A specific kind of botanic garden is the arboretum, a collection that concentrates on living woody shrubs and trees.

There is no such thing as a standard botanic garden. Descriptions of botanic gardens have changed over the last four centuries since a medical garden was established at Pisa University in 1543. Although now a worldwide phenomenon, botanic gardens still vary according to different cultures, countries, and climates. Exactly what comprises a proper botanic garden varies according to a person's interest: botanists, horticulturists, recreational park managers, and garden historians are just some of those involved. These gardens also vary in the method of administration. For instance, many botanic gardens in the United States are privately operated or funded, whereas most European and British Commonwealth gardens are run by the government or a public institution. Numerous universities or academies still retain a traditional connection with botanic gardens as places of study and research.

Whatever the form or organization, public visitors are welcome in most botanic gardens, where they can enjoy the beautiful arrangements of plants, unusual species—some of great age—water bodies, and wildlife or take advantage of museums of economic botany, libraries, greenhouses, tours, lectures, and other educational offerings. Behind the scenes, scientists and gardeners undertake investigations into taxonomy (the classification and naming of plants), germ plasm conservation, ecology, horticultural experimentation, and other pursuits. Their herbaria and publications are useful to colleagues throughout the world. Indeed, one of the great strengths of botanic gardens is the collaboration with other garden establishments and researchers within worldwide networks such as the International Association of Botanic Gardens (IABG), established in 1954, and Botanic Gardens Conservation International (BGCI), which began in 1987. At present, temperate climates contain the largest number of botanic gardens, but the numbers of gardens in the tropics and subtropics is increasing. In 1987 Europe had 459 botanic gardens (with 11,000 different taxa or types of plants), North America had 262 gardens (21,000 taxa), Central and South America only 59 gardens (but 90,000 taxa), Africa and Madagascar 46 gardens (30,000 taxa), Australia 41 gardens (25,000 taxa), and the former USSR 156 gardens (21,500 taxa). The latest *International Directory of Botanic Gardens* (1990) lists over 1,400 botanic gardens and arboretums around the world.

Edward Hyams's *Great Botanical Gardens of the World* (1969) describes the historical development of 42 of the major botanic gardens still functioning at that time and remains a useful reference that has yet to be superseded in scope and scholarship. Botanic gardens, as a garden type, have gone through many transformations over the centuries but always with a foundation of botanic or horticultural investigation into the usefulness of plants to humankind. Medicinal plants formed the basis of plant collections made in ancient times in Europe, Central America, and China. The origin of modern botanic gardens rests with the monastic institutions of the first millennium, according to Arthur Hill (1915). Two documents provide the first records of plant collection for scientific (i.e., medical) purposes. These are Emperor Charlemagne's *Capitulaire de Villis*, or decree concerning towns, ca. A.D. 800 and a drawing of an "ideal plan" for a monastery, attributed to Abbot Haito of Reichenau. The *Capitulaire* is attributed to Abbot Aniane and contains a list of 89 plants recommended for cultivation in monastery gardens, of which 73 are medicinal. Abbot Haito's drawing was sent to Abbot Gozbert of St. Gall (Switzerland), where it still exists. It includes representations of a cemetery-cum-orchard, a large kitchen garden (*hortus*) and a smaller medicinal garden (*herbularis*).

The botanic gardens of the modern era began in Renaissance Italy as systematic collections of medicinal herbs used by student apothecaries and medical physicians at the newly established universities. The earliest university *physick* (medical) garden or *hortus medicus* was at Pisa, soon followed by Padua (1543). The first director of the Pisa Orto Botanico was Luca Ghini, who is also credited with inventing that vital component of modern scientific botanical study, the herbarium. Ghini recognized the need to identify and compare plants all year round and from different places, so he dried and mounted specimens of leaves, flowers, and fruit—with suitable naming labels—which he called a *hortus siccus* (collection of dried plants). Ghini's invention helped to establish a truly scientific botany, based on observation and experimentation rather than the medieval and Renaissance custom of referring only to ancient Greek and Roman authorities such as Theophrastus and Dioscorides.

As botany became a science distinct from medicine in the late 16th century, botanic gardens diversified their plant content from purely medicinal herbs. This process was assisted by explorations of eastern Europe, the Levant, and the Americas, which began the unending flow of exotic plants into Europe. These plant introductions encouraged the refinement of plant classification systems, such as the binomial system of naming plants, introduced to Europe between 1737 and 1753 and devised by Swedish botanist Carl Linnaeus (1707–78). There is also a strong connection between plant exploration and the beginning of European imperialism in the 16th century. The pattern of introducing new plant species into Europe has been recognized by several botanical historians, beginning with German botanist Gregor K.M. Kraus (1841–1915), who distinguished six main periods based on their geographical origins. Kraus's six periods have been augmented by English botanist W.T. Stearn into nine periods: (1) European period, to 1560 (*Die Zeit der Europäer, die Eingeborenen*), (2) Near East period, 1560–1620 (*Die Zeit der Orientalen*), (3) period of Canadian and Virginian herbaceous plants, 1620–86 (*Die Zeit der canadischen-virgilischen Stauden*), (4) African Cape period, 1687–1772 (*Die Capzeit*), (5) period of North American trees and shrubs, 1687–1772 (*Die nordamerikanische Gehölze*), (6) period of Australian plants, 1772–1820 (*Neuholländer*), (7) period of tropical greenhouse plants and hardy plants from Japan and North America, 1820–1900, (8) period of West Chinese plants, 1900–30, (9) period of hybrids, 1930 onward. The discovery of new species is not over yet, especially from the floristically rich Australian, Asian-Pacific, African, and South American ecosystems, where botanical explorations and discoveries continue.

From these botanical explorations European botanic gardens received both herbarium specimens and living material, which enabled propagation and horticultural experimentation. The search for useful plants was matched by a desire for beautiful and unusual ornamen-tal species. Useful plants had an enormous economic imperative, especially in establishing colonies and supporting European imperial homelands; plants can provide food, spices, drugs, perfumes, fibers, building materials, and dyes. While great industries were founded on these plants, humanity also benefited from improved health and well being (with cinchona bark for quinine, potatoes, tea, coffee, and chocolate, to name a few). As these plants were being studied and cultivated in European botanic gardens, local botanic gardens were also established in the far reaches of the world. In 1735 the first colonial botanic garden was established at Pamplemouses, on French Mauritius. The first British economic garden was created on St. Vincent in the Caribbean in 1764, followed by Calcutta Botanic Garden, India (1787), Sydney Botanic Garden, Australia (1816), and others. In *Science and Colonial Expansion* (1979), Lucile Brockway describes the intricate relationships between colonial gardens and the success of the British Empire. National botanic gardens, particularly the Royal Botanic Gardens, Kew, provided much of the trained personnel to establish and maintain these colonial gardens. Their scientific knowledge about plants was converted into "profit and power, for the Empire and for the industrial world system of which Britain was then the leader." William Bean (1908), the former curator of Kew, writes: "As soon as the *pax Britanica* is established, and often before, he [the 'Kew Man'] appears. He founds botanic stations where useful plants are grown for distribution, and gives demonstrations of the best methods of cultivating them."

Colonial botanic gardens were created by several imperial powers. French, Spanish, and Dutch settlements in Africa, Southeast Asia, the Caribbean, and the Americas were supported by acclimatizing and experimental botanic gardens, as were British colonies in the Indian subcontinent, Southeast Asia, and Australia. Each empire followed a pattern of establishing gardens, typically in unfamiliar climates. In the British framework of administration, local government management was under the direction of the Colonial Office (in London) and Kew. This informal international network of gardens persisted even after independence and self-government in the 20th century. Botanic gardens from the Old World, the New World, and the rest of the world now belong to international associations that encourage the free trade of knowledge and experience about plants, botany, ecology, and natural environment conservation.

The landscape design approaches used at botanic gardens are connected to reigning stylistic fashions, but the practical and scientific requirements are often the dominant influence. In some old gardens overlays of several design styles can be seen (e.g., Leiden, Netherlands). In Renaissance medical and botanical gardens, the emphasis was on utilitarian arrangements consisting of straight, narrow garden beds between access paths enclosed by secure walls to prevent thefts of rare and valuable plants. As larger plants were introduced, arboretums were established, in either formal or irregular layouts. At Padua, for instance, this additional plantation was located directly outside the walls of the older utilitarian garden. By the 19th century public accessibility to botanic gardens was being popularized by such influential figures as John Claudius Loudon (1783–1843). As both a garden writer and designer, Loudon provided great impetus for establishing botanic gardens and public parks in British cities. He saw the public park as vital and health giving for the working and middle classes in grimy industrial cities, and when overlaid with botanic labeling and systematic arrangements, these places could also provide educational opportunities. Loudon's design for Derby Arboretum (1840) was a tangible example of his ideas and was a direct influence on Joseph Paxton's design for Birkenhead Park (near Liverpool, 1843), which in turn influenced the design of Central Park in New York (1858) by Frederick Law Olmstead and Charles Vaux. The design of proper botanic gardens during the 19th century contained a significant component of recreational opportunity for visitors. To cater to all the requirements of botany and aesthetics, these botanic gardens developed several compartments, including picturesque arboretums, utilitarian systematic gardens, greenhouses for propagation and display of warm climate plants, water and bog gardens, rock and alpine gardens, "wild" woodland areas, and so on. Excellent examples of this are Kew (England) and the Royal Botanic Garden, Edinburgh (Scotland).

During the 19th and early 20th centuries, several wealthy Europeans and North Americans created private collections of living plants—some even sponsoring plant hunters to find new specimens in the wild. Modern public botanic gardens such as Huntington, in Los Angeles, the Missouri Botanical Garden (both United States), and Westonbirt Arboretum (United Kingdom) began in this manner. Another development among modern botanic gardens is the annex. To accommodate the many newly discovered plants and expanded activities of botanic gardens, extensions to the older botanic gardens were required. By the 20th century these annexes were often located away from the main garden to allow a range of microclimates to be available for study (e.g., Oxford University Botanic Gardens has Nuneham Courtenay; the Royal Botanic Gardens, Sydney has gardens at Mt. Tomah and Mt. Annan). Specialized gardens, which emphasize one group of plants, such as the *palmetum* (collection of palms), are another recent development.

A major shift in the traditional role of botanic gardens in recent times was demonstrated by the preparation of the *Botanic Gardens Conservation Strategy*, finalized in 1989, after extensive work by Professor V.H. Heywood, on behalf of the Botanic Gardens Conservation Secretariat (BGCS, now BGCI) which was derived from the International Union for the Conservation of Nature (IUCN) and allied with the World Wildlife Fund (WWF). Comparing the older Western places and those elsewhere, Heywood maintains that their roles had reversed. The exotic plant collections of the Western botanic gardens were no longer their strongest attribute; instead, their herbaria, libraries, and laboratories "justify their reputation. Today, in accepting a major conservation role, it is the botanic gardens of those countries with rich floras that have a clearly defined role to play." Heywood also observes that, just as many botanic gardens are accepting a major conservation role, "some of the major tropical gardens, which have in the past occupied a brilliant role in plant introduction and domestication, have now been reduced to little more than public parks," as their scientific research programs have largely been stripped away. While the important scientific functions and facilities of these former colonial gardens are being lost, the historic, social, and aesthetically valuable aspects of these places are also at risk. The potential educational opportunities for botany and horticulture are also wasted with such disregard for old botanic gardens. The connection between science and the landscape arts is strong in botanic gardens and represents one of the few times these disparate forces come together. One important goal for botanic gardens in the future, then, is the collaboration between cultural and natural heritage conservation. Meanwhile, they remain major destinations for the general public and reinforce a popular fascination with gardening, landscape design, and the environment.

## Further Reading

Bean, W.J., *The Royal Botanic Gardens, Kew: Historical and Descriptive*, London and New York: Cassell, 1908

Bramwell, David, et al., editors, *Botanic Gardens and the World Conservation Strategy*, London and Orlando, Florida: Academic Press, 1987

Brockway, Lucile H., *Science and Colonial Expansion: The Role of the British Royal Botanic Gardens*, New York: Academic Press, 1979

Crosby, Alfred W., *Ecological Imperialism: The Biological Expansion of Europe, 900–1900*, Cambridge: Cambridge University Press, 1986

Desmond, Ray, *Kew: The History of the Royal Botanic Gardens*, London: Harvill Press, 1995

Dyer, Thiselton, "The Botanical Enterprise of the Empire," *Proceedings of the Royal Colonial Institute* 11 (1879–80)

Elliott, Brent, *Victorian Gardens*, London: Batsford, and Portland, Oregon: Timber Press, 1986

Green, Joseph Reynolds, *A History of Botany (1860–1900),* Oxford: Clarendon Press, 1909; reprint, New York: Russell and Russell, 1967

Greene, Edward Lee, *Landmarks of Botanical History,* 2 vols., edited by Frank N. Egerton, Stanford, California: Stanford University Press, 1983

Grove, Richard H., *Green Imperialism: Colonial Expansion, Tropical Island Edens, and the Origins of Environmentalism, 1600–1860,* Cambridge: Cambridge University Press, 1995

Heywood, Vernon Hilton, *The Botanic Gardens Conservation Strategy,* London: IUCN Botanic Gardens Secretariat, 1989

Hill, Arthur W., "The History and Functions of Botanic Gardens," *Annals of the Missouri Botanical Garden* 2 (February–April 1915)

Howard, Richard Alden, Burdette L. Wagenknecht, and Peter Shaw Green, compilers, *International Directory of Botanical Gardens,* Utrecht, The Netherlands: International Bureau for Plant Taxonomy and Nomenclature, 1963; 5th edition, compiled by Christine A. Heywood, Vernon Heywood, and Peter Wyse Jackson, Koenigstein, West Germany, and Champaign, Illinois: Koeltz Scientific Books, 1990

Hyams, Edward, and William MacQuitty, *Great Botanical Gardens of the World,* London: Bloomsbury Books, and New York: Macmillan, 1969

Johnson, Dale E., "Literature on the History of Botany and Botanic Gardens, 1730–1840: A Bibliography," *Huntia* 6, no.1 (1985)

Loudon, John Claudius, *An Encyclopaedia of Gardening,* 2 vols., London, 1822; new edition, 1835; reprint, New York: Garland, 1982

McCracken, Donal P., *Gardens of Empire: Botanical Institutions of the Victorian British Empire,* London: Leicester University Press, 1997

Prest, John M., *The Garden of Eden: The Botanic Garden and the Re-Creation of Paradise,* New Haven, Connecticut: Yale University Press, 1981

Sim, J.C.R., "Conservation of Historic Botanic Gardens," Master's thesis, Institute of Advanced Architectural Studies, University of York, 1990

Stafleu, Frans Antoine, "Botanic Gardens before 1818," *Boissiera* 14 (1969)

Stafleu, Frans Antoine, *Linnaeus and the Linnaeans: The Spreading of Their Ideas in Systematic Botany, 1735–1789,* Utrecht, The Netherlands: Oosthoek, 1971

Stearn, William Thomas, "The Origin and Later Development of Cultivated Plants," *Journal of the Royal Horticultural Society* 90 (1965)

Stearn, William Thomas, "Sources of Information about Botanic Gardens and Herbaria," *Biological Journal of the Linnean Society* 3 (1971)

JEANNIE SIM

---

# Botanic Station

Though more than 120 botanic gardens existed in the Victorian British Empire, there was no formal botanical network. Some botanic gardens were run by the Colonial Office or by the India Office. Others were controlled by planters' horticultural, agricultural, or acclimatization societies and often received annual colonial government grants. As the 19th century drew to a close, municipalities increasingly established botanic gardens or took over existing ones. Some botanic gardens, such as Georgetown in British Guiana or Calcutta in India, had satellite gardens, and both Ceylon and Jamaica had botanical departments controlled by the Colonial Office. The nearest there came to "imperial botanical federation" was the attempt made in the 1880s and 1890s to establish networks of botanic stations in two tropical parts of the British empire: the West Indies and West Africa. Malacca (established in 1886) and Zomba in British central Africa (1891) also had gardens that were described as botanic stations.

In the early 1880s, when the sugar industry in the West Indies went into depression, both the Colonial Office and the Royal Botanic Gardens at Kew were anxious to diversify the economy of the area away from the near monoculture of sugar production. In October 1884 Dr. Daniel Morris, the director of Jamaican botany, proposed a network of satellite botanic stations centered on the Jamaica Botanical Department. The key to this enterprise was that the stations should be small, one or two acres, and that they should grow only "economics": plants of possible economic value to either planters or small indigenous farmers. Botanic stations were to be properly fenced, have an adequate water supply, and be near the seat of government and the chief port.

Implementation of the scheme was difficult and slow. In 1886 botanic stations were established on St. Lucia and at Dodd's Reformatory on Barbados, the latter at 90 acres (36.5 ha) being more of an experimental farm. The departure of Morris in March 1886 to become assistant director of Kew did not help matters. Worse was the colonial inter-island rivalry among the press, planters, and their legislatures, all resentful of Jamaica being the headquarters of the scheme. Besides, many islands wanted full botanic gardens like Trinidad (established in 1818) and Jamaica, which had four: Bath (1779), Castleton (1862), Cinchona (1868), and Hope (1873). In 1896 Grenada defied Kew and established its own botanic garden. The other problem facing the imperial authorities was how the network was to be funded.

In 1887 the momentum of establishing botanic stations shifted to West Africa, where the energetic governor, Captain Alfred Moloney, supported by the Colonial Office and Kew, started a botanic station at Ebute-Metta at Lagos. Fewer white planters made the task easier than in the West Indies, and other botanic stations followed: Aburi on the Gold Coast (1888); Asaba (1888; moved to Abutshi in 1889), N'kisi (1889), and Old Calabar (1891) in the Royal Niger Protectorate; Kotu (1894) in the Gambia; Pademba Road, Freetown (1895) in Sierra Leone; and Olokemeji (1901) in Lagos.

The concept in West Africa was to encourage the growing of such plantation crops as coffee, rubber, cocoa, cola nut, and cotton, as well as to train the sons of African chiefs who would then introduce new agricultural methods into the villages. The appointment of several African curators proved a success, although the introduction of additional black curators both in the West Indies and West Africa was largely stymied due to racial prejudice at Kew.

The new governor of the Windward Islands, Sir Walter Hely-Hutchinson, and the arrival in the West Indies of Morris on a "fact-finding" mission reinvigorated the botanic station scheme there, and stations were established in 1889 at St. Johns (site moved in 1894) and on Dominica, and in 1890 on Monserrat, St. Kitts-Nevis, and St. Vincent. The transfer of Moloney from Lagos to British Honduras led to the setting up of a botanic station in the American mainland colony. Moloney had employed a black West Indian curator at Lagos, James McNair, whom he now brought to British Honduras to run the botanic station there.

A royal commission into agriculture in the West Indies recommended the establishment of an imperial commissioner for agriculture. In August 1898 Morris returned to the Caribbean in this capacity. New botanic stations were laid out on Tobago and further away on Bermuda, and in 1900 on the Virgin Islands, but the emphasis now was on general agriculture rather than purely crop husbandry. Agricultural inspectors were appointed and several agricultural schools established.

Some of the botanic stations of the West Indies and West Africa survived into the 20th century, often saved by the fact that they were not what they were meant to have been: utilitarian, unattractive, and regimented plots. Many were very attractive. The station on St. Vincent occupied the site of what had been Britain's oldest imperial botanic gardens (founded in 1765 and abolished in 1822), and it still had nutmeg trees that had been planted in the 18th century. And despite being sited on the town dump beside a swamp, the botanic station at Castres on St. Lucia soon had a fine rose garden.

While botanic stations were not as prestigious as imperial botanic gardens, they had some able curators. West Africa could boast Harold Bartlett, Horace Billingham, William Crowther, Henry Millen, James McNair, and the ill-fated George Woodruff (one of several in West Africa to die of blackwater fever), while the West Indies boasted John Gray and Henry Powell.

**Further Reading**

McCracken, Donal P., *Gardens of Empire: Botanical Institutions of the Victorian British Empire*, London: Leicester University Press, 1997

DONAL P. MCCRACKEN

# Botanischer Garten Berlin-Dahlem.
## *See* Berlin-Dahlem, Botanischer Garten

BOX    177

# Box

Hardly any other individual plant has had such importance for the artistic framing and adornment of the garden as box (*Buxus sempervirens*) throughout the 5,000-year history of gardens in occidental countries and throughout the world. Box is perhaps the oldest adornmental detail in a garden. The interest in box in landscape gardening has also always been great, although there have been fluctuations in its application. Today's interest in box is partly connected to a general interest in historical gardens and historical plants, for which box is frequently used both for restoration of gardens and for new pastiches. But box is also suitable for completely new expressions, growing naturally as well as severely clipped, due to its plasticity and its natural richness in growth variation.

The *Buxus* genus is part of the *Buxaceae* family, together with the *Notobuxus, Sarcococca, Styloceras,* and *Pachysandra* genera. The *Buxaceae* family includes about 100 species, and the *Buxus* genus about 70. They grow wild in central and eastern Europe, in North Africa, Asia Minor, and as far away as China and Japan. Box can also be found in the West Indies, Cuba (approximately 35 species), and Central America. The historical use of box is solely connected to the *Buxus sempervirens* species. The area of distribution for naturally growing as well as wild populations of box covers a wide belt from southern Europe in the west (Spain, France, Italy, Greece), across North Africa, along the coastal areas of the Middle East across Turkey, and toward the mountain regions of the Caucasus in the east.

Box existed (and partly still does) where agriculture first was established around 9000 B.C. in the eastern half of the fertile crescent in highlands with high rainfall in north Mesopotamia, in the steppes north of the Euphrates (today the northeast parts of Iraq and Syria), and in Lebanon. In the highlands box grows on the mountain sides together with oaks, Oriental plane trees, Lebanese cedars, genuine cypresses, and poplars.

In its wild state box grows as a bush or small tree. When cultivated it can reach a height of up to 8 meters (8.7 yd.); in the wild in the Caucasus it can reach 16 meters (17.5 yd.). Carl Linnaeus gave the species its present scientific name and described it in *Species Plantarum* (1753). At present there are approximately 200 registered named varieties of *Buxus sempervirens*. *Buxus microphylla* from Japan, cultivated since 1860, has through the species *koreana* during the 20th century expanded the possibilities of box cultivation through its greater hardiness, primarily in the United States and Canada. Other species in the genus are mostly of dendrological interest and are later introductions.

The possibly natural existence of box (*B. sempervirens*) in the British Isles has been much debated. Research has corroborated the existence of pollen grain to about 5000 B.C. and remains of charcoal to about 2000 B.C. However, the most common opinion today argues that box grew in England before the Ice Age but that the variety was completely wiped out by the inland ice. For that reason the present natural existence of box would be a result of later introductions, through the agency of the Romans during the Roman Empire, among others. The forests of tall and old box in Box Hill in Surrey, south of London, represent the foremost "wild" collection in the country. The world's tallest box hedges, more than 300 years old, can be found in Ireland, at Birr Castle, 129 kilometers (80 mi.) south of Dublin.

The Sumerian epic of *Gilgamesh* (ca. 2000 B.C.) contains a description of the city of Uruk by the river Euphrates in southern Iraq that refers to the vast gardens in the city and the extensive forests outside the city, and specifically to the willow and box groves on the flat land by the river. Evidence of conscious collecting and planting of box is found in a text from the 12th century B.C. written by the Assyrian king Tiglathpileser I: "Cedars and Box I have carried off from the countries I conquered, trees that none of the kings my fore-fathers possessed: these trees I have taken and planted in my own country, in . . . Assyria."

The qualities of boxwood, particularly its weight due to its high density (1.4 km/cubic dm), contributed to the early wide range of uses of boxwood. In the *Iliad* Homer writes that box was used for the yokes for the horses in the army of the king of Troy. In 1957 an almost intact table made from boxwood dating back to the ninth century B.C., with inlays of juniper and a knob of walnut, was found at the excavations of the tomb of King Midas. In ancient Greece and Rome boxwood was used for tables, flutes and other instruments, combs, spoons, jewel boxes, intarsia, and veneer, among other objects. Boxwood has been much coveted as a material for wood engraving for the illustration of gardens.

The Bible includes a number of verses that refer to box. The most often quoted is from Isaiah 41:18–19, written during the Babylonian captivity in the sixth century B.C.: "I will open rivers in high places, and fountains in the midst of the valleys: I will make the wilderness a pool of water, and the dry land springs of water. I will plant in the wilderness the cedar, the shitta tree, and the myrtle, and the oil tree; I will set in the desert the fir tree, and the pine, and the box tree together." Another passage from Isaiah, Isaiah 60:13, also refers to box: "The glory of Lebanon shall come unto thee, the fir tree, the pine tree, and the box together, to beautify the place of my sanctuary, and I will make the place of my feet glorious."

The first scientific reference in literature to box was written by the fourth-century B.C. Greek botanist

The Queen's Garden, Het Loo, Apeldoorn, Gelderland, Netherlands
Copyright Kjell Lundquist

Theophrastus, who was Aristotle's student and colleague. In his botanical treaties Theophrastus observed the qualities of boxwood. Beginning in the reign of Emperor Augustus in Rome, box was planted and clipped (topiary) at the villas of many influential Romans. One of them was the first-century A.D. Roman official and author Pliny the Younger, whose descriptions of two of his country houses, one by the coast outside Rome, the other in the Apennines in the upper Tiber Valley, are important sources of knowledge for Roman villas and gardens. He discusses how to shape box and refers to specific forms. Concerning the garden at the villa in the Apennines, for instance, he writes: "In front of the colonnade is a terrace laid out with box hedges clipped into different shapes from which a bank slopes down, also with figures of animals cut out of box," and also that box was "clipped into innumerable shapes, some being letters which spell the gardeners' names or his master's." The J. Paul Getty Museum in Malibu, California, contains a reconstruction of a Roman villa with a peristyle garden, the Villa dei Papiri in Herculaneum, with more than 1.6 kilometers (one mi.) of cut box.

The information given by the 12th-century Arab botanist Al-Awwam on agriculture in Andalusia (southern Spain) is one example of the continuous, traditional, and surely extensive use of box in clipped hedges during the Middle Ages in southern Europe. Al-Awwam is moreover one of the first writers to encourage gardeners to consider a garden from the point of view of shape and form and to suggest principles of form. Box appears on more than half of the known lists of plants in (northern) Europe during the Middle Ages. The species came into use as a living but clipped border to beds at the end of the Middle Ages, probably in the Netherlands, although there is no evidence of it before 1500.

Starting in Italy with simple geometric parterre patterns during the 15th and 16th century, gardens gradually contained increasingly elaborate box adornments. In the context of garden history, the name *box* is associated primarily with these Renaissance gardens. Leon Battista Alberti, Italian architect and art theorist, almost literally quoted both Pliny the Younger and Vitruvius in his book *De re aedificatoria* (1452) concerning the importance of garden symmetry and regular patterns. The art of parterre gardening spread to northern Europe by way of the many

BOX  179

pattern books published during the late 16th and early 17th centuries. The Netherlands and England showed a particular preference for this art. Box played the leading part in many Renaissance gardens, and especially in parterres, both in the form of topiary work such as ships, temples, wild and domestic animals, birds, giants, people, urns and vases, labyrinths, and monograms and later also as low clipped border hedges, framing expensive new bulbous plants, such as tulips, hyacinths, and anemones from the Middle East. In the small stretches of woodland (*bosco*) outside the formal parts of the gardens in Italy, box was often planted to grow freely as undergrowth.

The use of box exploded during the baroque, starting in France, in the axially arranged parterres framed by low hedges of many kinds. At the beginning of the 17th century, box played a major role in the construction of parterres. One of the first box parterres with curves was planted in the Luxembourg Garden in Paris around 1619. In this ideal embroidery parterre (*parterre de broderie*), developed and well illustrated by both Claude and André Mollet in their works, skillfully arranged curves of severely and low clipped box contrasted with colored ground material. The clipping of box refined in arabesques, ornaments, and palmettes became an art of gardening itself. The finest parterres were planted with *Buxus sempervirens* 'Suffruticosa', originating in the Netherlands. Low beds framed with box, so-called *plates-bandes*, often encircled the *parterres de broderie*, but they were also used detached as borders. In these beds severely formed and clipped evergreen trees and bushes (juniper, yew) were planted; newly introduced bulbous plants, perennials, and annuals were also displayed there.

In northern Europe (Sweden, Russia) box was at times replaced with lingonberry (*Vaccinium vitis-idaea*), due to the inadequate hardiness of box, according to a recommendation by André Mollet in *Lustgård* (1651; *The Garden of Pleasure*). The peak of parterre construction and the use of box was reached during the second half of the 17th century in practically all of Europe and lasted for some decades into the 18th century. Box also reached North America during that time. The first planting there is considered to have been carried out by Nathaniel Sylvester in his garden on Shelter Island, in New York City, just after 1652.

Box played a minor role in gardens from the second half of the 18th century and during the whole period of landscape parks. Wherever it grew it was preferably growing freely. As early as 1722 the London gardener Thomas Fairchild wrote in *The City Gardener* concerning the use of evergreens such as yew, holly, ivy, box, privet, and English laurel to "improve wastelands." The formation should be designed as "Wilderness-Work rather than in Grass platts and Gravel Works." In some places the past was kept alive, however. In 1796 Benjamin Latrobe

visited George Washington's garden in Mount Vernon and noted: "For the first time since I left Germany I saw here a parterre, clipped and trimmed with infinite care into the form of a richly flourished Fleur-de-Lis: The expiring groans, I hope, of our grandfathers' pedantry."

Box began returning in its traditional clipped and framed application as early as the beginning of the 19th century. Humphry Repton and Hermann Fürst von Pückler-Muskau gave several examples of this in their designs. Primarily, box was used in several different "historicizing" geometric expressions and styles during the whole 19th century, well described in contemporary writings by the Scottish garden universalist John Claudius Loudon. In this respect certain gardens became living landscape gardening encyclopedias, wherein the visitor could walk between the box expressions of Tudor gardens and in Italian, French, and Dutch geometries.

Box gained acceptance in the space-intense and craftsmanlike gardens of the Arts and Crafts movement during the second half of the 19th century and turn of the 20th century. Once again it was used for clipped border hedges but also for pleasurable and popular figure trimming. With the neoformalism at the end of the 19th century (as evidenced in Reginald Blomfield's *The Formal Garden in England* [1892]), box's importance was accentuated. Cemeteries in southern Scandinavia during this time, in the cities as well as in the countryside, were in general dominated by box-framed graves in an apparent Renaissance style. Box was used popularly and especially cherished as a border hedge for several decades in the early 20th century in the countrysides in northern Europe.

Public gardens that expressed modernism, and especially functionalism, used box only as an exception. Box also did not have a place in the many natural garden designs of the 1970s and 1980s, which themselves expressed a reaction of the constraint of shape of earlier decades. Box has, however, always survived in private gardens and with classically aware garden lovers, and it has once again played an increasingly major role at the turn of the 21st century. The knot parterre in the garden of garden writer Rosemary Vereys, in Barnsley House in England, is one of many well-known examples. Box today is used in public designs as well as in stylish gardens and avant-garde compositions and is appreciated both for its history and its plasticity. Few plants can be said to be more in vogue, more in demand, and more utilized. One expression of contemporary interest is the organization The American Boxwood Society, founded in 1961, and which publishes the quarterly journal *The Boxwood Bulletin*.

**Further Reading**

Blomfield, Reginald Theodore, and F. Inigo Thomas, *The Formal Garden in England,* London, 1892; 3rd edition, New York: Macmillan, 1901; reprint, New

Maryhill, Lund, Sweden
Copyright Kjell Lundquist

York: AMS Press, 1972; reprint, London: Waterstone, 1985

*The Boxwood Bulletin* (1961– )

Gothein, Marie Luise Schroeter, *Geschichte der Gartenkunst,* Jena, Germany: Diederichs, 1914; 2nd edition, 1926; as *A History of Garden Art,* 2 vols., edited by Walter P. Wright, translated by Mrs. Archer-Hind, London: Dent, and New York: Dutton, 1928; reprint, New York: Hacker Art Books, 1979

KJELL LUNDQUIST

# Boyceau, Jacques de la Barauderie 1560s–ca. 1633

## French Author and Garden Designer

Little is known concerning Jacques Boyceau's biography and professional career. He was clearly more a "gentleman gardener," whose experience with design and practice of gardening began only at the age of about 40 or 50, than he was a man of practical education and knowledge as were, for example, his contemporary colleagues, the members of the Mollet family. So, which part exactly Boyceau—"Intendant des jardins du Roi" from 1620 until this charge was placed into his nephew's hands probably about 1630—played in the planning of the royal gardens is rather open to question. In most cases, older, already existing gardens had to be reorganized. Boyceau must have been responsible for the work to be executed, but whether the whole layout of a garden such as the Luxembourg can be attributed to him is unknown; the archival documents do not mention his name in such an important role. However, Boyceau's *Traité du jardinage* (1638; Treatise on Gardening) contains parterre designs for the gardens of Fontainebleau and the "first" castle of Versailles, the Hôtel du Luxembourg, the Tuileries, the Louvre, and the Château Neuf at Saint-Germain-en-Laye. Whether all of these plans were realized is unknown. From 1610 Boyceau had been asked for parterre designs from outside the court, for example, by the art collector Nicolas-Claude Fabri de Peiresc with whom Boyceau exchanged letters on botanical questions. These designs, however, are known only through written sources.

Boyceau's importance for the history of garden architecture consists less in his practical work, which can not be traced very clearly, than, above all, in his contribution to garden literature. His *Traité du jardinage*, written in the author's old age, sums up his experience in the field of garden architecture. About 55 plates offer parterre designs, and about four show the layout of bosquets (the number of plates differs insignificantly from one exemplar to the next). Most plates show *parterres de broderie* of an utmost ornamental elegance and formal variety. Boyceau was not the inventor of the *parterre de broderie*, but his designs—perhaps engraved by the younger Claude Mollet—are among the most refined examples of the genre.

Boyceau does not name older treatises on garden architecture in his own work, but he must have known certain publications, such as the treatise by Charles Etienne, revised by Jean Liébault (first French edition, 1567), and the one by Olivier de Serres (1600), which include the basic ideas of garden art but still concentrate on the purpose of utility more than of pleasure. Only from the beginning of the 17th century did pleasure gardens become the focus of garden literature. Together with Boyceau, two members of the Mollet family are of great importance for the formation of the classical French garden style. In the second decade of the 17th century, the practically experienced gardener Claude Mollet, whom Boyceau must have known personally, wrote his treatise on garden architecture, which was to be published only in 1652. His son André's treatise appeared in 1651. Together with Claude and André Mollet's works, Boyceau's *Traité du jardinage* differs from earlier sources in its accentuation of theoretical and artistic values of garden art. But compared with Claude and André Mollet's treatises, Boyceau often

PL. 34

The parterre design, *parterres de broderie*, from Boyceau, *Traité du jardinage*, 1638
Courtesy of Zentralinstitut für Kunstgeschichte, Munich

neglects practical details. Perhaps this is due to Boyceau's formation as a gentleman gardener.

The strength of Boyceau's treatise lies on the side of theory and of classification. Systematically and using clearly defined rational criteria, in a cultivated language, Boyceau describes the ideal interplay of nature and art in pleasure gardens, as well as the characteristic elements of the garden—parterres, allées, bosquets, fountains—linked to each other in a system of hierarchic references and expressing categories such as relief, monumentality, and grandeur. Boyceau's *Traité du jardinage* (written later but published earlier than Claude Mollet's treatise) was the first important step in the development of the *jardin à la française*. As the later editions prove, it was influential until the beginning of the next century. André Le Nôtre never wrote down his maxims on garden architecture, and only in 1709 did Antoine-Joseph Dézallier d'Argenville's *Théorie et pratique du jardinage* (Theory and Practice of Gardening) take over the role of "bible" in French garden architecture.

### Biography

Born probably at Saint-Jean-d'Angely, near La Rochelle, France, 1560s. Member of nobility of Saintonge and a Huguenot; first mentioned for military bravery during the conquest of Luçon, 1587; early friendship with Charles de Biron probably brought him into contact with court of King Henri IV, in whose service Boyceau first mentioned in 1602; appointed *Gentilhomme ordinaire de la chambre du Roi*, a post he held until his death; precisely when Boyceau left his career as courtier and military man to take up gardening as a profession not known; first documented activity in garden design, 1610; worked primarily in the royal service for Maria de Medici and Louis XIII after Henri IV's assassination; received post of *Intendant des jardins du Roi*, after 1620, which he held until in his old age, when his nephew Jacques de Menours assumed the post. Last will enlarged, October 1633; probably died soon afterward, mid-1630s and before 1637, in Paris.

## Selected Designs

| | |
|---|---|
| 1610 | Parterre design, Duc de la Force's garden, Périgord, France |
| 1612 | Parterre design and other activities, Hôtel du Luxembourg, Paris, France |
| 1620s–30s | Other activities as *Intendant des jardins du Roi* for the royal gardens: Fontainebleau, Seine-et-Marne, France; Château-Neuf, Saint-Germain-en-Laye, Yvelines, France; Tuileries, Paris, France; Versailles, Yvelines, France |
| 1623 | Parterre design for Nicolas-Claude Fabri de Peiresc's garden in Belgentier, Provence, France |
| 1623 | Parterre design, Tuileries, Paris, France |
| 1626 | Parterre design, garden of the archbishop of Aix-en-Provence, France |

## Selected Publications

*Traité du jardinage selon les raisons de la nature e de l'art*, 1638 (prepared for publication posthumously by the artist's nephew, Jacques de Menours)

## Further Reading

Conan, Michel, [Postface,] in *Le jardin de plaisir* (1651), by André Mollet, Paris: Éditions du Moniteur, 1981

Hazlehurst, F. Hamilton, *Jacques Boyceau and the French Formal Garden,* Athens: University of Georgia Press, 1966

Karling, Sten, "André Mollet and His Family," in *The French Formal Garden,* edited by Elisabeth B. MacDougall and F. Hamilton Hazelhurst, Washington D.C.: Dumbarton Oaks Trustees, 1974

Lauterbach, Iris, "Le *Traité du Jardinage* de Jacques Boyceau," in *Traité du jardinage selon les raisons de la nature et de l'art* (1638), by Jacques Boyceau, Nördlingen, Germany: Verlag Dr. Alfons Uhl, 1997

Strandberg, Runar, "Jacques Boyceau: His Theory of Landscape Gardening and Some of His Creations," *Konsthistorisk tidskrift* 37 (1968)

Wimmer, Clemens Alexander, *Geschichte der Gartentheorie,* Darmstadt, Germany: Wissenschaftliche Buchgesellschaft, 1989

IRIS LAUTERBACH

# Bradley, Richard 1688–1732

## English Horticulturist and Plant Biologist

Richard Bradley, the leading English author on horticultural subjects during the reign of George I, had a varied career as garden designer, horticulturist, agricultural consultant, university lecturer, artist, and journalist. Though he pioneered the teaching of plant physiology at the University of Cambridge, criticism by his successor John Martyn seriously damaged his posthumous reputation. Bradley's later biographers have assessed his achievements more favorably. He is now recognized as a pioneer in the science of applied biology as well as an authoritative writer on horticultural, agricultural, and culinary themes. He is also highly regarded today for his achievements in cultivating succulent plants.

Bradley made several original contributions to the understanding of plant biology. His observations on the role of insects in pollinating plants led to a better understanding of the sexuality of plants. His experiments on cross-fertilization were described in his book *New Improvements of Planting and Gardening . . .* (1717). He documented the transmission of plant viruses by grafting, thanks to his close acquaintance with another pioneering horticulturist, Thomas Fairchild of Hoxton. Bradley was also the first to describe the germination of fungal spores and to explain the circulation of sap in the xylem and phloem of woody plants. These discoveries were of profound importance to 18th century English gardeners. Later successes in naturalizing exotic plants owed much to Bradley's popularization of improvements in the design of greenhouses, providing better methods of temperature control. His most enduring invention, the kaleidoscope, was proposed as a means of designing geometric patterns for landscaped gardens.

The most significant book published by Bradley was undoubtedly his *Historia Plantarum Succulentarum . . . The History of Succulent Plants,* which appeared in parts between 1716 and 1727. Each part was dedicated to a wealthy patron. The 50 engravings were taken from Bradley's original drawings. He also published an account of the cultivation requirements of succulents in *New improvements . . . .* The advice it contains remains horticulturally sound, as it places great emphasis on re-creating the conditions in which these plants are found in nature.

Bradley's career as a horticultural and landscape consultant blossomed thanks to a visit to Amsterdam in 1714 as agent for the horticulturists James Petiver and Samuel Reynardson and the nurseryman Fairchild. He supplied plants to several other wealthy estate owners, including the Duchess of Beaufort. James Brydges, first Duke of Chandos, briefly employed him in laying out a physic garden and stove (hothouse) at Cannons, near Edgware, a commission later continued by the ill-fated Alexander Blackwell. Another of his friends and patrons, the merchant Robert Balle, owned an estate (Campden House) in Kensington, which Bradley may have managed.

Bradley suffered a financial disaster in 1720 or 1721 "at Kensington," the nature of which is unknown. Though he failed to secure an academic position at Oxford, despite the support of the Duke of Chandos and Sir Hans Sloane, he succeeded not long afterward in being appointed the first professor of botany at the University of Cambridge. His hopes of establishing a botanical garden there remained unfulfilled, however, and he consequently lost the esteem of his university colleagues.

Though he wrote on a wide range of subjects, his most influential books were those on culinary and horticultural matters. He popularized English regional cuisine, leading to an expansion in the repertoire of 18th century kitchen gardeners, and his gardening books stimulated the fashion for cultivating exotic plants and helped to promote the most advanced methods of horticulture.

## Biography

Date of birth uncertain, ca. 1686–1688. Not known to have attended university; practiced medicine during visit to Netherlands; worked for several leading London botanists and horticulturalists, 1710–20; elected Fellow of the Royal Society, 1712; traveled to Netherlands and France, and sent plants and seeds to England for Mary Somerset, Duchess of Beaufort, and for several London garden owners and nurserymen; wrote, illustrated, and published his most significant work, *Historia Plantarum Succulentarum,* between 1716 and 1727; pursued career as author of books on plant physiology, gardening, farming, cookery, and estate management; invented Kaleidoscope as garden design tool; became first Professor of Botany at Univerisity of Cambridge, 1724, delivering lectures in applied plant physiology and *materia medica*; published first English dictionary of botany in 1728. Died in Cambridge, England, 5 November 1732.

## Selected Publications

"Observations and Experiments Relating to the Motion of the Sap in Vegetables," *Philosophical Transactions of the Royal Society* 29 (1714)

*Short Historical Account of Coffee,* 1714

*History of Succulent Plants,* 1716–27

*New Improvements of Planting and Gardening, both Philosophical and Practical,* 1717

*Gentleman and Gardeners Kalendar, Directing What Is Necessary to Be Done in Every Month, in the Kitchen Garden, Fruit-Garden, Nursery, Management of Forest Trees, Green-house, and Flower-Garden,* 1718

*Philosophical Treatise of Husbandry and Gardening: Being a New Method of Cultivating and Increasing All Sorts [Kinds] of Trees, Shrubs, and Flowers,* 1721

*Philosophical Account of the Works of Nature,* 1721

*General Treatise of Husbandry and Gardening; Containing a New System of Vegetation,* 1721–23

*Survey of Ancient Husbandry and Gardening, Collected from Cato, Varro, Colum(b)ella, Virgil, and Others,* 1725

*Dictionarium Botanicum; or, A Botanical Dictionary for the Use of the Curious in Husbandry and Gardening,* 1728

## Further Reading

Davidson, Caroline, "Editor's Introduction," in *The Country Housewife and Lady's Director,* by Richard Bradley, 6th edition, edited by Davidson, London: Prospect Books, 1980

Rowley, Gordon, "Introduction," in *Collected Writings on Succulent Plants,* by Richard Bradley, London: Gregg Press, 1964

Egerton, Frank N., "Richard Bradley's Understanding of Biological Productivity: A Study of Eighteenth-Century Ecological ideas," *Journal of the History of Biology* 2 (1969)

Egerton, Frank N., "Richard Bradley's Illicit Excursion into Medical Practice,"*Medical History* 14 (1970)

Egerton, Frank N., "Richard Bradley's Relationship with Sir Hans Sloane," *Notes and Records of the Royal Society* 25 (1970)

Hamshaw, Thomas, "Richard Bradley, an Early Eighteenth Century Biologist," *Bulletin of the British Society for the History of Science* 1, no. 7 (1952)

Henrey, Blanche, *British Botanical and Horticultural Literature before 1800,* 3 vols., London and New York: Oxford University Press, 1975

Pulteney, Richard, *Historical and Biographical Sketches of the Progress of Botany in England, from its Origin to the Introduction of the Linnaean system,* 2 vols., London: Cadell, 1790; see especially vol. 1

Roberts, William, "R. Bradley, Pioneer Garden Journalist," *Journal of the Royal Horticultural Society* 64 (1939)

Rowley, Gordon, "Richard Bradley: A Disincornufistibilated Servant if Botany," in *Gordon Douglas Rowley's A History of Succulent Plants,* by Rowley, Mill Valley, California: Strawberry Press, 1997

Tjaden, W.L., "Richard Bradley F.R.S., 1688–1732, Succulent Plant Pioneer," *The Bulletin of the South African Succulent Plant Society* 8ff (1972–76)

Walters, Stuart Max, *The Shaping of Cambridge Botany,* Cambridge and New York: Cambridge University Press, 1981

JOHN EDMONDSON

# Brandt, Gudmund Nyeland 1878–1945

## Danish Landscape Architect

Gudmund Nyeland Brandt was the foremost Danish landscape architect practicing at the beginning of the 20th century. His designs for cemeteries, public gardens, and private estate gardens and his theoretical work and teaching were important forerunners of the "golden age" of Danish garden art (1920–60).

Brandt's approach to landscape design was rooted in highly skilled horticultural knowledge coupled with a deep appreciation of classicist space. Like many Danish landscape architects at the beginning of the 20th century, Brandt was influenced by the work of the English designers Sir Edwin Lutyens and Gertrude Jekyll and their reworkings of themes from Florentine villa gardens. His own gardens were organized into roomlike spaces by rows of trees and hedges. Brandt was also influenced by William Robinson's writing on woodland gardens and the use of herbaceous plants in flower gardens, as well as by the German writer Willy Lange.

As a result of his writings and teaching at the Royal Danish Academy of Fine Arts, Brandt became the most influential Danish landscape architect of the 1910s. His own garden at Ornekulsvej in Ordrup, like many English Arts and Crafts gardens, is structured as a series of garden rooms recalling Italian Renaissance gardens. Indeed, this garden with its long grass, bowling green–like space connecting all the rooms is a sort of miniaturized Villa Gamberaia. The design also draws from the forms of Danish vernacular landscapes and includes an orchard, wood, stream, meadow, and a flower garden.

Brandt's Hellerup Coastal Park (1912) is a small neoclassical composition of well-defined rectangular spaces determined by hedges and rows of trees enclosing tennis courts, lawns, a rose garden, and a perennial flower garden. The elements are similar to some of Lutyens's designs, but what makes Brandt's design significant is the free composition of the formal elements to serve a diversity of public uses on a small scale.

At Marienlyst Palace at Elsinore, Brandt formulated a Danish restoration philosophy that eschewed a complete reconstruction of the original appearance of Nicolas-Henri Jardin's 1769 plan, since he believed that "this could easily destroy contemporary values without achieving corresponding future benefits." He retained the outer, enclosing linden avenues and within their structured space devised a simple tripartite scheme of two hedge-enclosed lawns flanking a central section of hedge-enclosed symmetrical Greek-key pattern parterres. By contrast, Brandt's design for the Historical Botanical Gardens at Gåsetårnet was intended "to create a measure of old-fashioned atmosphere," based on historical models, that is almost an exercise in pastiche.

Brandt's mastery of classically derived spaces is beautifully demonstrated in the formal grass terracing and linden avenues of the Katedralskole at Viborg and at Ordrup and Mariebjerg cemeteries. Both cemeteries are divided into roomlike spaces by formal rows of trees and high clipped hedges. Considerable diversity was created within this formal structure. At Ordrup the "Common Grave" is treated as a formal mown promenade flanked by gently sloping banks planted with high grasses, bulbs, and scattered shrubs. This pioneered the Danish technique of contrasting mown with long grasses.

The larger and more complex design of Mariebjerg Cemetery consists of two rectangular areas nested within each other and defined by avenues. Two broad parallel axial avenues, each planted with a different tree species, provide a strong sense of orientation. The rectangles are divided into smaller rectangular spaces by high hedges. The simple design, whose origins can be traced back to baroque gardens, provides considerable variety. Quarters were assigned to grave and urn burial. The anonymous section is laid out with hexagonal patterns of sets in mown grass. The simple dignity of this scheme makes it one of the most memorable of Scandinavian cemeteries.

Brandt's design for Villa Svastika inserted a number of formal elements such as long axial alleys, hedged walks, and flower gardens into a broad sweeping natural landscape of park spaces and forested areas that invoked Robinson's wild gardening. It also recalls Humphry Repton's later designs. Brandt referred to this concealed horticulture as "a motley jewel amidst neutral green." He used the vocabulary of classic formal walks and enclosed garden elements in a loose manner that anticipated his students' completely abstract designs. In the flower garden Brandt organized the square and rectangular flower beds, reflecting pool, pergola, and garden pavilion into an abstract design remarkably similar to a Mondrian composition.

In 1930 Brandt wrote about "the coming garden," a forward-looking garden that first appeared at the jubilee horticultural exhibition in Dresden. For the German landscape architects Leberecht Migge and Hermann Mattern, the coming garden was either a powerful social statement or a retreat from social pressures of National Socialism. In contrast, Brandt's coming garden was a broader cultural concept of a nature garden that rejected anthropomorphic dominance to become a place where humans would become partners with the rest of nature.

In 1945 Brandt and the architects Poul Henningsen and Hans Hansen prepared a master plan for the Tivoli Gardens in Copenhagen. One of the projects associated with this was a fountain terrace placed along the edge of a low-lying inlet of Lake Tivoli. With its long, narrow, diagonal beds, diverse flower planting, and shallow wooden fountain basins set against a long undulating brick wall with wooden benches, it introduced the postwar Danish delight in formal geometries set against full plantings.

Brandt's distinctive contribution to Danish landscape design owes much to the classicist spatial clarity of Edwin Lutyens's designs and to William Robinson's and Gertrude Jekyll's writings about the value of plants and techniques of wild and herbaceous planting. Brandt used the past not in a scholarly manner but as a creative basis for addressing contemporary social problems of spatial organization that asserted the role of plants. These influences were allied to a strong artistic appreciation of Danish vernacular landscapes, in which he reinterpreted poetically the landscape of wood, common, meadow, hedgerow, path, fence, and ditch and turned away from rational town life to seek "infinite" space and celebrate the character of the individual plant.

*See also* Tivoli

## Biography

Born in Denmark, 1878, son of the well-known gardener, Peter Christoffer Brandt. Studied philosophy at Copenhagen University, graduating 1898; studied in England, France, and Germany, 1898–1901; apprentice at nursery in England and Jardin des Plantes in Paris; appointed leader of new Ordrup Cemetery in Copenhagen, 1901; designed extension to Ordrup Cemetery, 1918; taught in Architecture program at Royal Danish Academy, Copenhagen, from 1924, where his students included many distinguished landscape architects of the following generation, including C.Th. Sørenson, Troels Erstad, and Aksel Andersen. Died in Gentofte, Denmark, 1945.

## Selected Designs

| | |
|---|---|
| 1912–18 | Hellerup Coastal Park, Hellerup, Copenhagen, Denmark |
| 1914 | G. N. Brandt Garden, Ornekulsvej, Ordrup, Copenhagen, Denmark |
| 1919–21 | Marienlyst Palace, Elsinore, Denmark |
| 1919–30 | Ordrup Kirkegård, Ordrup, Copenhagen, Denmark |
| 1925 | Katedralskole, Viborg, Denmark; Villa Svastika, Rungsted, Denmark |
| 1926–36 | Mariebjerg Kirkegård, Mariebjerg, Copenhagen, Denmark |
| 1943 | Broadcasting Company Headquarters, Copenhagen, Denmark; Springvandsterrasse, Tivoli Gardens, Copenhagen, Denmark |

## Selected Publications

*Stauder,* 1918

"Haveservittutter," *Havekunst* 3 (1922)

"Der komende Garten," *Wasmuth's Mondtshefte für Baukunst* 14 (1930)

"Tivoli's springvandsterrasse," *Havekunst* 23 (1943)

## Further Reading

Bülow-Hübe, Erik, "Nogle nifere Danske Haver," *Ark M* 1 (1933)

Erstad, Troels, "En Haver i Ordrup Krat," *Havekunst* 22 (1942)

Groening, Gert, and Joachim Wolschke-Bulmahn, "Changes in the Philosophy of Garden Architecture in the 20th Century and Their Impact upon the Social and Spatial Environment," *Journal of Garden History* 9, no. 2 (1989)

Hauxner, Malene, *Fantasiens have: Det moderne gennembrud i havekunsten og sporene i byens landskab,* Copenhagen: Arkitektens Forlag, 1993

Lund, Annemarie, "Mariebjerg Cemetery," *Arkitektur DK* 34, no. 4 (1990)

Lund, Annemarie, *Guide til Dansk havekunst år, 1000–1996,* Copenhagen: Arkitektens Forlag, 1997; as *Guide to Danish Landscape Architecture,*

1000–1996, translated by Martha Gaber Abrahamsen, Copenhagen: Arkitektens Forlag, 1997

Ørum-Larsen, Asger, "Havekunstneren G.N. Brandt," *Landskab* 66, no. 2 (1985)

Sørenson, C.Th., "Junihaven ved Svastika og re andre Haver," *Havekunst* 7 (1927)

Stephensen, Lulu Salto, *Garden Design in Denmark: G.N. Brandt and the Early Decades of the Twentieth Century,* Chichester, West Sussex: Packard, 2000

DAVID C. STREATFIELD

# Branitz

## Cottbus, Germany

**Location:**  80 miles southeast of Berlin

Along with Hermann prince Pückler-Muskau's first garden in nearby Muskau, Branitz represents the epitome of mid-19th-century German gardening. The intricate flower beds set an international standard that was not questioned until modernism, whereas Pückler's virtuosity in composing with trees has remained largely uncontested. A unique cosmic iconography was embedded in the setting around Branitz's three earthen pyramids.

After the sale of Muskau, Pückler in 1846 began to lay out a garden at the old family estate of Branitz. The fields and meadows surrounding the palatial manor house (1772) had been neglected for many years, but Pückler spared no effort; he bought up additional plots as previously at Muskau and also had the village moved. Work, including repeated alterations of existing elements, continued until his death in 1871. In 1868 the chief gardener, G. Bleyer, was appointed garden director. The 70-hectare (173 acre) garden was completed in 1910 by Pückler's nephew. Descendants of Pückler lived at Branitz until 1945.

A comprehensive redesign of the manor house and the immediately surrounding area took place between 1846 and 1852. In the garden Pückler closely followed the principles defined and tested by his great example, Humphry Repton. A direct impact from Pückler's travels to England, Italy, Switzerland, and Egypt can also be seen. His wife, Lucie (née Hardenberg), took an active part in the project, in practice confirming Pückler's praise of women's sense of color, but her share in the overall works at Branitz still lacks proper analysis and evaluation.

The prominent Dresden-based architect G. Semper designed the imposing granite terrace around the manor house. Surviving archival sources describe the subsequent staging of a complex and colorful planting scheme. Originally the 16 cast-zinc vases on the terrace border were planted with blue hydrangeas, a result of Pückler's fascination with blue hues and their specific play of light. By 1865 the scheme encompassed orange trees in bowls alternating with vases dominated by geraniums, fuchsias, and hydrangeas, among others; red geraniums ornamented the entire upper-terrace edge, and a herbaceous border with climbing roses flourished beneath the terrace; ferns and dracaenas were placed on gilded tables at the entrance door. The basic features of this planting have been recently re-created. A broad flight of steps, flanked by two griffins, faced the western part of the pleasureground (Repton's term, which Pückler adopted). A gilded fence originally enclosed the latter.

East of the manor house, between the Tudor-style cavalier house and stable, a pergola designed by G. Semper was erected. By turns it was planted with grape vines and roses. Cast-zinc vases and sculptures, some of which were painted or gilded, mixed with a colorful display of perennials. Terra-cotta reliefs with mythological motifs after the distinguished Danish sculptor B. Thorvaldsen were inserted in the so-called Italian Wall framing the pergola. A large-scale bed, planted with flowers and grasses and featuring a copy of the Venus Capua in its center, was placed between the entrance and the pergola.

The landscaping of the grounds stretching further east toward the old smithy was completed between 1846 and 1853. Groups of trees were composed onto this plain, called the Smith's Meadow, and the sight of the

Grabpyramide at Branitzer Park, Cottbus, Germany
Copyright Johann Scheibner/Das Fotoarchiv

pond was further enhanced through a varied planting. A blue bridge offered a nice view toward the manor house. Later a pavilion, named after Queen Augusta, was added. Matching Pückler's taste for colorful ornamental patterns, a railing with stained glass enclosed the pavilion.

A series of utilitarian facilities, including a greenhouse and an orchard, were added to this part of the garden beginning in 1849. The planting of fruit trees and bacciferous shrubs in the orchard was much indebted to Repton's teachings. A unique feature at Branitz was the Tea Garden, which had initially been laid out for Pückler to entertain his guests. In 1860 it was renamed the Civil Garden and opened to the citizens of Cottbus. People could meet in the pavilions, and light meals were offered free of charge. Not least, the playground was much praised at the time.

More separate gardens were created on the westward side of the manor house, for example, the Blue Garden with hydrangeas and a bust portraying Pückler's father-in-law, the Rose Hill (later renamed Flower Hill), the

Blue Kiosk, and the Black Pond with yet another Venus statue. The large flower beds reflected Pückler's luminous palette, for example, the Crown Bed in blue, lilac, rose, and yellow hues with the princely initials surmounted by a crown. Cast-zinc basketlike borders or figures encircled most of the beds. Circular rings in two to four different colors constituted the most characteristic pattern. Reconstruction of the pleasureground has largely been based on the descriptions made by Pückler's gardeners and on garden archaeological surveys.

As a fervent propagator in theory and practice of the aesthetic significance of visual axes, pathways, and waters, Pückler concentrated on these elements in his layout of the area west of the pleasureground (1849 and following). He put much emphasis on the creation of artificial hills and additional ponds to obtain more variety on the vast and sandy, largely grass-covered plain. Yet the composition with trees was the genre in which he truly excelled. In view of achieving a certain magnificence from the very beginning, Pückler preferred trees of an advanced age. He bought such in large quantities yet never failed to appreciate the uniqueness of each tree. He had fairly large and primarily national specimens moved and planted with great success. Densely planted groves and large and small groups of trees alternated with solitaires. Spatial sequences of great dynamic power and aesthetic value thus came into being. The bridle roads and footpaths were modeled so as to support these schemes and to act as "silent guides" to specific garden vistas.

The construction of three earthen pyramids in the westernmost corner of the garden was in perfect tune with Pückler's aspirations toward a universal language, flavored by a biographical note. One pyramid (1854–56) was placed amid the Pyramid Pond; it was here that Pückler and his wife were later buried. Next followed the Step Pyramid (1863) and, on the opposite side of the Snake Pond, Hermann's Hill (unfinished).

Pückler's fascination with Egyptian mysticism, Greek mythology, and Islamic tradition accounts for the intricate iconography of this setting. The pyramids were constructed according to astronomical calculations based on Pückler's personal data. A cyclic journey passing through the life ages, across the waters, over to the tumulus and back to nature again, would thus become apparent as the sun rose and then set on his birthday.

Branitz contrasts with the stylistic profusion, anecdotal content, and sentimental qualities of numerous German landscape gardens of an earlier age. In essence, the garden embodies Pückler's attempt at creating a cosmic order.

## Synopsis

| | |
|---|---|
| 1846 | Prince Pückler-Muskau takes over Branitz |
| 1846–53 | Repton-inspired layout of the pleasureground and first initiatives in the landscape garden |
| 1849–50 | Modeling of first visual axis |
| 1853–71 | Creation of the earthen pyramids |
| 1945 | Nationalization of the Branitz property; inauguration of museum and public garden |
| 1978–82 | Restoration of the manor house |
| 1991–95 | Extensive restoration of the garden |

## Further Reading

*150 Jahre Branitzer Park: Garten-Kunst-Werk: Wandel und Bewahrung,* Cottbus, Germany: Fürst-Pückler-Museum, Park und Schloß Branitz, 1998

Fried, C., V. Herold, and S. Kohlschmidt, editors, *Im Spiegel der Erinnerung: Hermann Fürst von Pückler-Muskau: Gartenkünstler, Schriftsteller, Weltenbummler,* Berlin: Fürst-Pückler-Museum, Park und Schloß Branitz, 1995

MARGRETHE FLORYAN

# Bridge

A bridge is a structure built over a natural or manmade feature such as a highway or railroad to provide a way across for pedestrians or vehicles. Its practical function is extended by an aesthetic one, as well as by the symbolism of representing gateways to other worlds and the attainment of new goals; in the Orient they are read as depictions of the infinite and immortality. They are at their most original and appealing, yet least practical, in the garden or designed landscape.

Garden bridges are found as garden decorations in many countries, but only in China and Japan and in the English landscape garden do they become more than just decorations but integral garden elements. This comes from a common desire to withdraw from the material world to be in the presence of nature. The inspired intricacies of the Oriental garden were created for gentlemen scholars and Buddhist monks in the upper echelons of feudal society. The extensive vistas of the English landscape garden were made for a wealthy and classically educated aristocracy. Both groups, in their own ways, believed that a person who loved nature over worldly interests was a person of deep spiritual cultivation.

The Oriental garden evolved slowly over a long period, whereas the English landscape garden was invented, suddenly, early in the 18th century as a reaction to the soulless and ultraformal French classic-style garden. Inspiration came from poetry and classical mythology, given form by the Romantic painters of the Roman Campagna, realized against a background of the most productive agriculture in Europe and profitable overseas investment.

Bridges have symbolic or celestial value in transposing one's essence from one world to another. The audacious act of bridging water was believed to offend its spiritual guardians, so the act of crossing evolved into a rite of passage. The move to new worlds created what has been called a circuit garden, where the promenader

Palladian Bridge at Stowe, Buckinghamshire, England
Copyright Clay Perry/Garden Picture Library

moves from one natural element to another, challenging the designer to choreograph a succession of views to lure one deeper into the garden. Bridges played an important role because they were the gateways to new experiences—actual and metaphysical—of nature: the mountains, the vigorous yang or male element, and the still yin or female element revealed in the waters.

Among the finest survivors in China are found, restored, at the Summer Palace, Beijing, which began as a pleasure residence for the emperor Wan Yung Leang in 1153. Like many garden bridges they are miniaturizations of functional structures that are found refined in the Seventeen-Arch Bridge, whose subtle upward curve is supported on an equally sensitive increase in the arch

size. A silk painting of the Summer Palace, the Yüen Ming Yüen (Ming dynasty, 1368–1644), shows a similar bridge crossing a lake. The Loukou Bridge, near Beijing (1192), praised by Marco Polo, has its massive cutwaters and solid arches offset by a balustrade punctuated by decorative stone lions, elements found in the exquisite Yutai or Jade Girdle Bridge. This is built of white marble with a steep two-way counter curve to the deck so that different prospects are presented, kinetically, as pedestrians ascend and descend.

The semicircular bridge form was considered ideal because its reflection made a perfect circle, the symbol of divine perfection. Its form was exported and is found in the Eye-Glass Bridge in Nagasaki (1634). Semicircles were also incorporated into more elaborate bridge structures, such as the Five-Pavilion Bridge in Slender West Lake, Yangzhou.

Not all Oriental bridges were semicircular, as the aristocratic gardens at Suzhou prove. The simplest are mere stone slabs, as in the Lingering Garden and the Garden of Cultivation. More elaborate is the rock-hugging bridge found in the Master of Nets Garden; others have complex zigzagged decks to take advantage of views, for example, the Humble Administrator's Garden and Mountain Villa with Embracing Beauty Garden. Some bridges are roofed, including part of the Small Flying Rainbow Garden and the Humble Administrator's Garden, the latter with an elaborately carved balustrade.

Stone is the material of choice, but wood is frequently employed for variety, flexibility, and economy, especially in the Japanese garden. The little hump-backed moss-covered bridge in the Daigoji Temple, Kyoto, follows the circle type, but many others have segmental arches, their profiles more gently curved and often of wood, as in the Shinden Zukari Garden. Others have a graceful form yet exude dynamic energy; simple detailing adds to this effect at the Upper Tea House, Shugakuin Detached Palace, Kyoto. The simplest are flat stone slabs, roughly trimmed, found in Taizo-in, Myoshinji Temple, and the Abbot's Garden, Daisen-in, in Kyoto. The stubby piers, held low to the water, enhance the sense of suspension and intensify the mirror-black reflections.

In England the scale of bridges is greater, and progress through the circuit of landscape pictures was achieved by horseback or carriage, rather than on foot. William Shenstone's The Leasowes (1745–63) famously employed a circuit garden to surprise the visitor, an idea underlying many landscape garden layouts. Bridges were important not only because they enhanced views over water but also because they provided natural stopping points to view the water or for romantic trysts.

A popular form was the Palladian Bridge, inspired by Andrea Palladio's *Third Book of Architecture,* his chaste Roman classicism appealing to English bridge builders. The first was erected at Wilton House (1735–37), for the ninth earl of Pembroke—the "architect earl"—with Roger Morris and John Devall. Like many others, this bridge spanned a stream deliberately widened to justify building the bridge. Others are found at Stowe (1738) and, enjoying a spectacular setting, Prior Park, Bath (ca. 1740). Palladio's circular arch bridge appears at Stourhead Garden (1762), extended to five arches and paved with turf; in its day it evoked comparison with the art of Poussin. Another is the Oxford Bridge at Stowe (1761). Several of Palladio's proposals for wood truss bridges could be found at Stowe, Stourhead, Painshill, and the Royal Botanic Gardens, Kew.

Architects have contributed landscape bridges in England, including Robert Adam, at Compton Verney and Kedlestone. Sir John Vanbrugh's bridge at Blenheim, Oxfordshire (ca. 1710), is arguably the grandest, but its fine proportions are due more to Lancelot "Capability" Brown, who raised the level of the lake (1764), submerging its lower level. Garrett's "huge affair" at Castle Howard, the great "Roman Bridge" (ca. 1744), was thrown over a little stream in a frantic attempt to compete with the scale of Nicholas Hawksmoor's giant mausoleum (1729). Another architect, James Paine, was responsible for a number of elegant stone bridges, notably that at Chatsworth (1761), which actually carries vehicular traffic over the river Derwent.

Many metal garden bridges can still be found that reflect the state of bridge building during the industrial revolution. That at Stourhead, by Maggs and Hindley (1860), bridges the cascade between the upper and middle lakes. It has a single, delicate span of cast iron with a reverse curve section to ease the deck gradient.

Chinese style in architecture and interior decoration became popular in England and other countries by the end of the 18th century and into the Victorian era. Biddulph Grange has "China" (1842), a garden with Chinese pavilions and bridges. A chinoiserie bridge, at Alton Towers (1814), connects an island with a copy of the ToHo Pagoda in Canton. The Chinese bridge at Birkenhead Park (1843) is the one on which Frederick Law Olmsted took shelter while visiting this remarkable suburb created by Sir Joseph Paxton. The restored Paca House Garden, Annapolis, Maryland, contains a small chinoiserie bridge. The delicate, wisteria-draped Japanese Bridge by Claude Monet at Giverney (ca. 1890) spans his water lily lake.

The late 18th-century Picturesque style called for rustic bridges, many short-lived, such as that at Méréville connecting the cliff-top classical temple and Andrew Jackson Downing's proposal for a bridge spanning a gorge at Blithewood, New York (ca. 1840). Olmsted and Calvert Vaux used bridges extensively and with great imagination in their public parks to separate pedestrians and carriages and add to the parks' interest and delight. Typical of their work in this regard are the bridges found in the "Emerald Necklace," Boston (1878–95) (with H.H. Richardson's bridges), and those in Central Park, New York City (1858). The rich variety of forms and materials was inspired by the example of past bridge builders.

**Further Reading**

Alberti, Leon Battista, *De re aedificatoria,* 1452; as *The Architecture of Leon Battista Alberti in Ten Books*, 3 vols., translated by James Leoni, London, 1726; *On the Art of Building in Ten Books,* translated by Joseph Rykwert, Neil Leach, and Robert Tavernor, Cambridge, Massachusetts: MIT Press, 1988

Boyer, Marjorie Nice, *Medieval French Bridges: A History*, Cambridge, Massachusetts: Mediaeval Academy of America, 1976

Cullen, Gordon, *Townscape*, London: Architectural Press, and New York, Reinhold, 1961

Fugl-Meyer, Helge, *Chinese Bridges*, Shanghai: Kelly and Walsh, 1937

Mao, I-sheng, *Bridges in China, Old and New: From the Ancient Chaochow Bridge to the Modern Nanking Bridge over the Yangtze*, Peking: Foreign Languages Press, 1978

O'Connor, Colin, *Roman Bridges*, Cambridge: Cambridge University Press, 1993

Palladio, Andrea, *I quattro libri dell'architettura di Andrea Palladio*, 4 vols., Venice: Appresso Dominico de Franceschi, 1570; as *The Four Books on Architecture*, translated by Robert Tavernor and Richard Schofield, Cambridge, Massachusetts: MIT Press, 1997

Ruddock, E.C., "Bridge," in *The Dictionary of Art*, 34 vols., edited by Jane Turner, New York: Grove, and London: Macmillan, 1996

Watson, Wilbur Jay, *Bridge Architecture*, New York: W. Helburn, 1927

Weale, John, *The Theory, Practice, and Architecture of Bridges of Stone, Iron, Timber, and Wire*, 5 vols., London, 1843–50

JOHN MARTIN

---

# Bridgeman, Charles d. 1738

## English Landscape Architect

Charles Bridgeman was perhaps the most important landscape architect in England in the first half of the 18th century. If he is less known than some of his contemporaries or followers, it is in part due to the very success and popularity of the tradition of landscape design he helped establish that led to so many of his plans being continuously redeveloped and redesigned by the heirs of his first patrons. Little is known of Bridgeman's origins or training. He first appears at Blenheim in 1709, working under the architect John Vanbrugh and Henry Wise, the royal gardener. A plan he drew up of the estate shows that he was already a skillful surveyor, and it is possible he had already worked for Wise and his partner, George London.

It is not clear what Bridgeman did at Blenheim, but he continued to collaborate with Vanbrugh on several further commissions, at Stowe from 1716 on for Viscount Cobham, at Eastbury in 1718 for Bubb Dodington, and in the 1720s at Claremont for the first duke of Newcastle. Possibly, as Horace Walpole suggested, he worked also at Chiswick, and, as early as 1715, there is much there, in the radiating pathways, wiggly walks, temples, and round ponds, that is found in much of his other work.

Bridgeman was one of the many artists around Lord Burlington and Alexander Pope, who included Bridgeman's name in the first version of his poem *Epistle to Lord Burlington*. In 1726, perhaps on the suggestion of the architect James Gibbs, Bridgeman was elected steward to the St. Luke's Club, a position of considerable reputation and authority; and he appears in several of the portraits of virtuosi and clubmen, most notably one painted in 1735 by Gawen Hamilton, *A Club of Artists* (National Portrait Gallery).

In 1724 Bridgeman received his first royal commission from the Prince of Wales, later George II, to improve the gardens at Marble Hill House, London. It was perhaps through this connection that, upon the death of Joseph Carpenter in 1726, he was appointed partner to Wise in managing the royal gardens. A year later, writing a report with Wise, he recommended that more money be spent on them. Two years later, in 1728, Wise retired, and Bridgeman assumed sole control of the gardens at Hampton Court, Kensington, St. James Park, and Richmond. This appointment also brought him into contact with the Board of Works and the architect there, Henry Flitcroft; in the 1720s he worked with Flitcroft on gardens at Bower, Woburn Abbey, Amesbury, Boughton, and Montague House, London. In the early 1730s he worked also with William Kent at Rousham, and in 1728 he received commissions from Sarah, duchess of Marlborough, for both Blenheim and Wimbledon House. This was a considerable amount of work.

Bridgeman seems never to have been especially interested in the theory of design or indeed either in any of the new discoveries of such horticulturists as Philip Miller or Hans Sloane. But his importance, coming also at a time of great prosperity and social change, was to suggest a move beyond the purely formal traditions of the French and Dutch gardens, established at Hampton Court by André Le Nôtre and Daniel Marot, to the more natural garden, *le jardin anglais,* that was to become so much a topic of intellectual and artistic interest in England and Europe throughout the 18th century, even if he did not, as Kent did later, pursue the idea of the associational qualities of garden design.

Bridgeman often worked with water, as at Chicheley Hall, Buckinghamshire, in 1722, where he designed a U-shaped canal—all that now survives there of his work—and notably also at Kensington Gardens, where the Round Pond (1728) and the Serpentine River (1731) remain essentially as he designed them. He also introduced from France the idea of the ha-ha, a concealed ditch that serves to divide the garden from the surrounding countryside while not disturbing the view beyond, inspired perhaps from the text of Antoine Joseph Dézallier d'Argenville. As Walpole noted, the ha-ha allowed the garden "to assort with the wilder country without."

Of all Bridgeman's designs, Rousham and Stowe were perhaps the most successful. Rousham, Oxfordshire, was done for General James Dormer, a friend of Pope and Swift; Stowe, Buckinghamshire, was created for Viscount Cobham. At Rousham, for which a plan of about 1715 survives, Bridgeman enlarged what was a relatively small garden by using paths that wandered though wooded areas. Although Kent, who worked there between 1738 and 1740, changed much of the design, transforming many of the straight walks and geometrically planned areas of wood, part of Bridgeman's plan survives still, including the serpentine through the wilderness to the so-called Cold Bath, the Elm Walk—Bridgeman was especially fond of elm trees—and the Venus Vale (although there Kent added statues to suggest an iconography for the garden as a whole).

At Stowe, working from about 1715 on, Bridgeman was able, as at Rousham, to extend the sense of the whole area, mixing the formal and the informal, parterres and straight avenues, and rides and ponds and lakes. He introduced within this an asymmetry that was in part deliberate, in part defined by the shape of the estate; all this was surrounded with a ha-ha. Between 1727 and 1730 Bridgeman extended the grounds, doubling the size and bringing in several seminatural features and a large irregular lake, to the west of the Octagon Lake where he had worked earlier. But everything was soon changed by Kent, transforming Stowe to a greater extent even than he did Rousham.

It was also Kent who made changes at Claremont. Bridgeman's designs at Richmond, Blenheim, and Wimbledon were redesigned in the 1760s by Lancelot "Capability" Brown, and in 1804 the gardens at Woburn Abbey were redesigned by Humphry Repton.

*See also* Kensington Gardens; Kew, Royal Botanic Gardens; Rousham House; Stowe

### Biography

Date and place of birth unknown. Worked for architect John Vanbrugh and royal gardener, Henry Wise, 1709; collaborated with Vanbrugh at Stowe for about a decade, beginning 1716; received first royal commission at Marble Hill House, London, 1724; became partner with Henry Wise in management of royal gardens, 1726; elected to St. Luke's Club of Artists, 1726; upon Wise's retirement in 1728, Bridgeman appointed royal gardener to George II, responsible for grounds at Hampton Court, Kensington, St. James's Park, and Richmond, among other royal estates; worked with William Kent at Kensington, Richmond, and Stowe, 1730s. Died in Kensington, England, 19 July 1738.

### Selected Designs

| | |
|---|---|
| 1716–1726 | Collaborated with Vanbrugh and Wise at Stowe, Buckinghamshire, England |
| 1718 | Collaborated with Vanbrugh and Wise at Eastbury, Dorset, England |
| 1720s | Collaborated with Vanbrugh and Wise at Claremont, Surrey, England |
| 1724 | Improvements at Marble Hill House, London, England |
| 1728 | Round Pond, Kensington Gardens, London, England |
| 1731 | Serpentine River, Kensington Gardens, London, England |
| 1720s–30s | Rousham House, Oxfordshire, England |

### Selected Publications

*A Report of the Present State of the Great Level of the Fens . . .* , 1725

### Further Reading

Hunt, John Dixon, and Peter Willis, editors, *The Genius of the Place: The English Landscape Garden, 1620–1820,* London: Elek, and New York: Harper and Rowe, 1975

Rorschach, Kimerly, *The Early Georgian Landscape Garden* (exhib. cat.), New Haven, Connecticut: Yale Center for British Art, 1983.

Willis, Peter, *Charles Bridgeman and the English Landscape Garden,* London: Zwemmer, 1977

Willis, Peter, "Charles Bridgeman and the English Landscape Garden: New Documents and Attributions," in *English Architecture Public and Private: Essays for Kerry Downes,* edited by John Bold and Edward Chaney, London and Rio Grande, Ohio: Hambledon Press, 1993

DAVID CAST

# Brooklyn Botanic Garden

## Brooklyn, New York, United States

**Location:** approximately 5 miles (8 km) south of downtown New York City

The Brooklyn Botanic Garden, located in the middle of one of the largest cities in the world, is an example of environmental restoration. This public garden was created in 1910 on 39 acres (15.8 ha) leased from the city of New York—a site that was strewn with glacial boulders and that had been previously used mainly as a dump for trash, building rubble, and ashes. The original site was expanded, and today the Brooklyn Botanic Garden extends to 52 acres (21 ha) and encompasses dozens of specialty gardens and collections, with 8,500 taxa from around the world. Brooklyn Botanic Garden's mission from its inception has been to combine botanical collections and horticultural displays with education and research.

At the garden's northernmost end, the three-acre (1.2-ha) Osborne Garden is an Italian-style garden with a formal green framed by azaleas, rhododendrons, flowering crabapples, and wisteria. The nearby Louisa Clark Spencer Lilac Collection features about 150 lilac species and cultivars.

One of the world's first ecological gardens, the Native Flora Garden covers two acres and features plants indigenous to the New York metropolitan region arranged in nine plant communities: serpentine rock, dry meadow, kettle pond, bog, pine barrens, wet meadow and stream, deciduous woodland, limestone ledge, and a border mound with representatives of the region's coniferous forests. The Native Flora Garden complements Brooklyn Botanic Garden's long-standing New York Metropolitan Flora research program through which staff botanists are conducting research

Viewing Pavilion and Torii in the Japanese Garden, Brooklyn Botanic Garden, ca. 1921
Photo by Louis Buhle, courtesy of Brooklyn Botanic Garden

to identify and catalog the plant biodiversity of the tristate metropolitan region.

Created in 1927, the Cranford Rose Garden features more than 5,000 bushes of nearly 1,200 varieties, including wild species, hybrid teas, grandifloras, floribundas, polyanthas, hybrid perpetuals, climbers, ramblers, and miniatures, as well as a companion planting of clematis. The Cherry Esplanade and adjacent Cherry Walk contain more than 40 varieties of Oriental flowering cherries, including 76 double-flowering 'Kwanzan' cherry trees.

The nearby Japanese Hill-and-Pond Garden, designed by Japanese landscape designer Takeo Shioto and opened to the public in 1915, illustrates one of the oldest forms of Japanese gardens, the hill-and-pond style. The three-and-a-half-acre (1.4 ha) garden consists of artificially constructed hills, a waterfall, a pond with an island, artfully placed rocks, wooden bridges and stone lanterns, a viewing pavilion, a torii, and a wooden Shinto shrine. Plants include those traditionally found in Japanese gardens, such as Japanese flowering cherries, Japanese iris, Japanese tree peonies, Japanese maples, and sacred lotus, while most of the largest canopy trees—white pines, American beech, and bald cypress—are native to northeastern North America.

Early plans for the Brooklyn Botanic Garden included a section for culinary and medicinal plants, but it was not until the Great Depression that the Herb Garden was constructed by laborers from the U.S. government's Works Project Administration. The Brooklyn Botanic Garden's landscape architect, Harold A. Caparn, created the plans; the central knot design is based on a design in Thomas Hill's *The Gardener's Labyrinth* (1577). The garden contains more than 300 kinds of medicinal and culinary herbs.

The Shakespeare Garden presents more than 80 plants mentioned in Shakespeare's works in a lush, informal English cottage-garden setting. Plants are labeled with their common or Shakespearean names, along with their references in the playwright's works. The nearby Fragrance Garden was designed in 1955 by landscape designer Alice Recknagel Ireys for sight-impaired visitors. It features plants with fragrant flowers or foliage in raised beds at a level easily accessible to people in wheelchairs; identification plaques are in both Braille and plain text.

About one-third of the Brooklyn Botanic Garden is devoted to the Plant Family Collection, which includes beds of trees, shrubs, and herbaceous plants systematically arranged according to family and evolutionary development. The most primitive plants are represented by the ferns growing alongside the Japanese Garden pond. Nearby conifers are descendents of the ancient gymnosperms. The presentation of flowering plants starts with the magnolias featured in and around Magnolia Plaza. The display continues to trace the evolution of flowering plants, with grouped plantings of heaths, roses, legumes, honeysuckles, the composites or daisies, and numerous other families.

Many of the glacial boulders originally found on the Brooklyn Botanic Garden site were moved and used in constructing the Rock Garden in 1917. Technically not a rock garden in the traditional sense of the term, this garden features not just alpine plants but also low-growing plants arranged in woodland, alpine meadow, and scree settings, as well as habitats for acid-loving and drought-tolerant plants.

The two large pools of the Lily Pool Terrace display hardy and tropical water lilies, sacred lotuses, and other aquatic plants. The pools are bordered on the west by the Mixed Perennial Border—a lush American-style garden of trees, shrubs, and herbaceous perennials and bulbs—and on the east by the colorful Annual Border.

In the glasshouses of the Steinhardt Conservatory, the C.V. Starr Bonsai Museum features more than 550 specimens of indoor and outdoor bonsai. The Robert W. Wilson Aquatic House displays tropical water lilies and various aquatic plants, including papyrus, water hyacinths, water lettuce, cannas, carnivorous plants, rice, and water chestnuts. By means of plant specimens and interpretive text and graphics, the Stephen K-M. Tim Trail of Evolution traces the development of plant life from its origin to the present day. The Helen Mattin Warm Temperate Pavilion houses plants representing warm temperate and Mediterranean regions, while the Tropical Pavilion re-creates a tropical rain forest, complete with waterfall, stream, and plants from the main tropical regions of the world. The Desert Pavilion houses plants from warm deserts and other arid regions.

**Synopsis**

| | |
|---|---|
| 1897 | New York state legislation reserves 39 acres (11.2 ha) for a botanic garden |
| 1910 | Brooklyn Botanic Garden founded; Charles Stuart Gager first director; architects McKim, Mead, and White design beaux-arts administration building and Palm House |
| 1911 | Native Flora Garden laid out |
| 1914 | Children's Garden program begins |
| 1915 | Japanese Hill-and-Pond Garden completed by landscape designer Takeo Shiota |
| 1916 | Rock Garden constructed |
| 1925 | Bonsai collection started with donation of 32 dwarfed potted trees from the Coe Collection; Shakespeare Garden opens |
| 1927 | Construction of Cranford Rose Garden begins |
| 1933 | Magnolias planted |
| 1936 | Rose Arc Pool completed |
| 1938 | Herb Garden opens |
| 1939 | Osborne Garden opens |

1941   *Prunus serrulata* 'Kwanzan' planted on Cherry Esplanade
1955   Fragrance Garden, designed by landscape architect Alice R. Ireys, opens
1956   Plant patent received for 'Red Jade' weeping crabapple, developed at Brooklyn Botanic Garden
1977   Plant patent received for *Magnolia* × 'Elizabeth', the first yellow magnolia, developed at Brooklyn Botanic Garden; 500-year-old lantern, gift of New York's sister city Tokyo, placed near the Japanese Hill-and-Pond Garden
1988   Steinhardt Conservatory completed
1989   Education Building completed; Palm House is renovated as a special-events center
1992   Rock Garden restored; Research Center opens
1993   Lily Pool Terrace renovated
1994   Mixed perennial border added to Lily Pool Terrace
1995   Refurbished Fragrance Garden reopens; Bluebell Wood, a mass planting of 45,000 bluebells (*Hyacinthoides hispanica* 'Excelsior') blooms for the first time
1999   Children's Garden house, yard, and field reopen after major renovations
2000   Japanese Hill-and-Pond Garden and Shakespeare Garden reopen after major restorations

**Further Reading**

Canty, Donald, "Reconstructing a Victorian Legacy," *Architectural Record* 177, no. 13 (1989)

*For the Love of a Garden: Memories of the Brooklyn Botanic Garden,* New York: Brooklyn Botanic Garden, 1997

Kissam, Betsy, Janet Marinelli, and Christine M. Douglas, *Brooklyn Botanic Garden,* New York: Brooklyn Botanic Garden, 1997

Martin, Douglas, "Restoring the Glory of a Japanese Jewel," *New York Times* (21 February 1999)

Martin, Douglas, "Tracking and Cataloguing the Wild Flora," *New York Times* (21 July 1996)

Pesch, Barbara B., editor, *The Garden at 75: Brooklyn Botanic Garden,* New York: Brooklyn Botanic Garden, 1985

Raver, Anne, "In a World of Wonders, Here Are Six That Stand Out: Brooklyn Botanic Garden," *New York Times* (21 April 1999)

Raver, Anne, "Human Nature: Under a Canvas of Snow, a Garden of Imagination," *New York Times* (3 February 2000)

Raver, Anne, "Human Nature: Revealing a Japanese Garden as Serene Melting Pot," *New York Times* (18 May 2000)

ANNE GARLAND

---

# Brown, Jocelyn 1898–1971

## Australian Landscape Designer

Unlike her Melbourne-based contemporary Edna Walling, whose career has been well documented, the Australian Jocelyn Brown is not well known as a landscape designer. Her work, however, deserves recognition. Brown's gardens, which spanned the 1930s to the 1950s, reflected the growing, post-Depression interest in horticulture and house-and-garden fashions by the affluent middle class. Her popular gardening and garden-design articles, which she illustrated herself and which appeared each month in *The Home* magazine, were aimed at a predominantly female readership, both educated and well versed in the principles of "good taste," for whom gardening was a respectable occupation. In a 1941 article, "Leaves from the Garden," she explained her viewpoint:

Always one gets back to those fundamental laws of art in trying to achieve a perfect garden design. The successful and satisfying planting scheme will embody good proportion, scale, line, contrast and unity. If any one of these is absent, the cultured eye will be conscious of loss.

Brown's articles often contained sketch plans of her own gardens or sketches for a typical suburban garden, with detailed planting plans and planting lists, which readers could copy or use as models for their own gardens.

Born Jocelyn Giles, Brown grew up surrounded by the subtropical vegetation of southern Queensland, but in 1914 she moved to the temperate climate of Sydney,

New South Wales, to study art and begin a career as a commercial artist and draftswoman. Here she met Alfred Brown, a New Zealander on his way to the battlefields of France. Wounded and invalided out of the army, Alfred Brown commenced studies in architecture and worked with Louis de Soissons, who was responsible for the town design at Welwyn Garden City, in England. Here Jocelyn and Alfred were married in 1920, and here they lived for the next three years. During this time Jocelyn Brown absorbed both town-planning theory and the ideology of the Arts and Crafts movement, becoming aware of the then radical garden-design theories of William Robinson and Gertrude Jekyll. All this was to influence her own landscape-design thinking.

Returning to Australia, Alfred Brown set up in practice as an architect while Jocelyn continued her career as a commercial artist. In addition, she redesigned the gardens around the various houses in which they lived and also collaborated with her husband on several of his architectural commissions, thus establishing herself as a professional landscape designer. Although she had no formal qualification, she was elected a fellow of the Institute of Landscape Architects (United Kingdom)—the first Australian to gain such membership. Although she considered herself a professional, she did not aggressively promote herself as a designer but preferred instead to work with her husband or accept commissions from other architects. After all, this was an era when a full-time career for a woman, especially one with two sons, was not easy to sustain.

Jocelyn Brown not only designed many Sydney gardens, mostly in the more affluent suburbs, but also advised owners of rural properties on the layout of the grounds around their homesteads, thus demonstrating her competence in handling both small- and large-scale design projects. Her strength, however, lay in planting design rather than structural design, and she would often play Jekyll to Alfred's (or some other architect's) Lutyens, suggesting plantings to complement various structures and spaces. Although many of her suburban sites were surrounded by natural bushland, and some of the rural properties had retained remnants of the original woodland vegetation, Brown chose predominantly exotic rather than indigenous species for these gardens. Some of her favorite trees were colorful deciduous species, such as sweet gum (*Liquidambar styraciflua*) and claret ash (*Fraxinus oxycarpa* 'Raywood'), spectacular flowering species, in particular, Brazilian rosewood (*Jacaranda mimosifolia*), and conifers such as deodar cedar (*Cedrus deodara*). She was not averse to certain striking Australian plants, such as wattles (*Acacia* spp.), Illawarra flame (*Brachychiton acerifolius*), lemon-scented gum (*Corymbia citriodora*), and bottlebrushes (*Callistemon* spp.), but these were usually not species endemic to the particular locality, being planted as specimens rather than with any ecological association in mind. Brown's work of course predated the era of an ecological approach to landscape design.

During the interwar years, Australian middle-class women were not only interested in gardening and growing flowers; they also considered flower arrangement one of the essential household arts, and Brown capitalized on this special interest. She was familiar with the ideas of Constance Spry, fashionable London florist and author of the book *Flower Decoration* (1934), and she admired the principles embodied in Japanese flower arrangement. Brown adopted many of these ideas for the floral decorations in her own house, using not only flowers but other materials such as leaves, branches, fruits, and bark, which she collected in her garden. She acknowledged the important therapeutic values of both gardening and flower arrangement, particularly for women trapped in the drudgery of suburban life. As she wrote in a 1941 article entitled "Many Are Culled but Few Are Chosen: Grow Selected Flowers for House Decoration":

> In tending plants and flowers the cares of the world are forgotten and the complete mental rest of a few hours gardening renews one's strength to face the realities of life. So also with the hours spent in arranging flowers.

Both in her own gardens and those she designed for others, Brown paid particular attention to the selection of species that would give a year-round supply of flowers and complementary foliage for use in the house. Several of her articles published in *The Home* describe in detail—illustrated by delicate line drawings—how various materials could be combined to make a satisfying arrangement and also include a list of plants recommended for picking.

The careers of Jocelyn Brown in Sydney and Edna Walling in Melbourne had much in common, yet, curiously, they did not ever meet, correspond, or even acknowledge each other's work. The most productive years for both were the 1930s and 1940s; both were influenced by the writings of Gertrude Jekyll, and both wrote articles for popular journals of the day: Brown for *The Home*, published in Sydney, and Walling for the *Australian Home Beautiful*, published in Melbourne. Both women also made important contributions to Australian garden design; unfortunately, while many of Walling's gardens survive, lovingly cared for by their owners, few of Brown's designs remain intact.

## Biography

Born in Maryborough, Queensland, Australia, 1898. Trained and worked as commercial artist and draftsperson in Sydney, New South Wales, Australia,

1914–20; traveled to England and lived with husband, an architect, in Welwyn Garden City, Hertfordshire, England, 1920–23, and influenced by ideas of Ebenezer Howard, William Robinson, and Gertrude Jekyll; worked as commercial artist in New Zealand, 1923–30; worked as commercial artist and garden designer in Australia throughout 1930s and 1940s; wrote and illustrated monthly articles on gardening and garden design for *The Home,* 1939–42; gave lectures on landscape design at newly formed Department of Town and Country Planning, University of Sydney, 1950; first Australian to be elected fellow of Institute of Landscape Architects (United Kingdom), 1952. Died in Appin, New South Wales, Australia, 1971.

## Selected Designs

| | |
|---|---|
| 1930 | Comely, Woollahra, New South Wales, Australia |
| 1937–41 | Fountains, Killara, New South Wales, Australia |
| 1940 | St. Aubins, Scone, New South Wales, Australia; Blue Mist, Killara, New South Wales, Australia |
| 1941–45 | Greenwood, St. Ives, New South Wales, Australia |
| 1945–50 | The Hermitage, Camden, New South Wales, Australia |
| 1950 | Yarran, Darling Downs, Queensland, Australia; Checkers, Cargo, New South Wales, Australia |
| 1950–71 | Appin Water, Appin, New South Wales, Australia |
| 1956 | Coolibah, Young, New South Wales, Australia |

## Selected Publications

"Rock Gardening Is an Art," *The Home* (1939)
"Replanning the Garden," *The Home* (1940)
"How We Use Colour Schemes in the Garden," *The Home* (1940)
"Architecture in the Garden," *The Home* (1940)
"Many Are Culled but Few Are Chosen: Grow Selected Flowers for House Decoration," *The Home* (1941)
"Planting for Autumn Colour," *The Home* (1941)
"Leaves from the Garden," *The Home* (1941)
"Making the Most of a Small Garden," *The Home* (1942)
"Garden Design with Trees," *The Home* (1942)

## Further Reading

Baskin, Judith, and Trisha Dixon, *Australia's Timeless Gardens,* Canberra: National Library of Australia, 1996
Bligh, Beatrice, *Cherish the Earth: The Story of Gardening in Australia,* Sydney: Ure Smith, 1973
Proudfoot, Helen, *Gardens in Bloom: Jocelyn Brown and Her Sydney Gardens of the '30s and '40s,* Kenthurst, New South Wales: Kangaroo Press, 1989
Proudfoot, Helen, "Jocelyn Brown and Her Sydney Gardens of the '30s and '40s," *Australian Garden History* 1, no. 3 (1989)
Proudfoot, Helen, "Jocelyn Brown's Garden Book," *Australian Garden History* 8, no. 2 (1996)
Tanner, Howard, and Jane Begg, *The Great Gardens of Australia,* Sydney and Melbourne: Macmillan, 1976

ALLAN CORREY

# Brown, Lancelot 1716–1783

## English Landscape Designer

Lancelot Brown was an 18th century landscape designer renowned for removing boundary walls and hedges, creating vast expanses of water and rolling green parkland, and incorporating the "borrowed landscape" of the surrounding countryside into his large-scale garden designs. He is thought to have been responsible for "improving" at least 150 estates in this way, earning his nickname "Capability" Brown through a tendency to assure his clients that their landscapes had "great capabilities." Although Horace Walpole said of him, "so closely did he copy nature that his works will be mistaken for it," Brown was criticized by some for the trail of destruction he left in his wake. For example, he destroyed many grand formal gardens and even entire villages, as at Bowood, to create his natural-looking landscapes. Brown was not, however, the instigator of the landscape movement in England.

During the 18th century there began a reaction against the rigid formal geometry of the French garden that had been inspired by the great designer André Le

Nôtre. The new landscape ideal was embodied in Ashley Cooper's call for "things of a natural kind" but was not in practice any more "natural" than the formal gardens it supplanted. It involved transforming the countryside by the creation of carefully positioned lakes, hills, valleys, trees, and classical buildings to imitate the picturesque landscape paintings of Claude Lorrain, Poussin, and Rosa, who were much admired at the time. This style was not, however, initiated by landscapers or artists but by writers and poets, such as Alexander Pope, Joseph Addison, and Stephen Switzer, royal gardener and author on gardening matters. Nor did this informal landscape style solely draw inspiration from contemporary fashions in literature and art—it was also seen as symbolic of contemporary liberal Whig politics. Land enclosure and progress in science and agriculture also provided the opportunity for open tracts of land to be brought within the control of wealthy landowners, who saw the landscape garden as the ideal setting for their country houses. It was the landscape designers Charles Bridgeman, with his introduction of the ha-ha, a sunken fence to replace the visible boundary wall, and William Kent, with his artfully "natural" layouts, who began to change the face of the English countryside during the first half of the 18th century.

Brown left his native Northumberland in 1732, at 16 years old, to become apprenticed to Sir William Loraine, a local landowner, with whom he acquired his practical gardening skills. Sir William also considered him sufficiently capable to entrust him with the laying out of part of his grounds. This led to other successful landscape commissions, and in 1739 Brown moved south, working as a gardener at Wotton, Oxfordshire, for Sir Richard Greville, son-in-law to Lord Cobham, at nearby Stowe Park, already one of the finest estates in the country. Impressed by the work Brown had done at Wotton, Lord Cobham soon appointed him gardener at Stowe. In 1740 Brown started work in the kitchen garden, progressed to the pleasure grounds, and was very quickly promoted to head gardener. This appointment gave him the opportunity to develop his own landscaping ideas while putting into effect the designs of William Kent and James Gibbs, who were already involved with "improving" the Stowe landscape in the new informal style. Although working under Kent's direction, much of Stowe's "natural" landscape is attributed to Brown, in particular the Grecian Valley, where he created the open, rolling landscapes for which he was to became famous. Although the Grecian Valley is natural looking, 18,000 cubic meters (23,540 cubic yards) of soil were moved during its construction and semimature trees were planted along the undulating valley sides.

While working at Stowe, Brown was encouraged by Lord Cobham to take on private commissions and had improved the nearby Wakefield Estate and advised on the layout of the grounds of Warwick Castle. However, Brown was still largely unknown. Walpole wrote of the scheme at Warwick, "It is well laid out by one Brown who has set up on a few ideas of Kent and Mr. Southcote." When Lord Cobham died in 1748, Brown felt sufficiently confident and experienced to consider moving to London to set up his own private practice. This he did in 1751, quickly forming a friendship with Henry Holland, an architect and building contractor, who encouraged him to design houses as well as gardens. Brown was then able to put into practice his growing belief that a house and garden should be designed as a unity, in total completing 19 important commissions of this kind. Brown had a unique ability to quickly and accurately assess a landscape and make proposals for improvement. He would then either present the landowner with designs to be carried out by the estate workers or supervise the works himself.

The earliest surviving Brown plans, dated 1750 and 1751, are for the grounds of Packington Hall. However, an important early commission was for a new house and gardens at Croome Court, where he worked intermittently until the 1770s. The old house was demolished and a Palladian house built, with interior decoration by the celebrated Robert Adam. Brown also developed a complex scheme of garden buildings, including a lodge, ice house, and church in Gothic style. The land required extensive drainage, and by damming an existing stream and culverts, Brown created a shimmering serpentine lake, the expanse of water contrasting dramatically with the surrounding undulating lawns. Brown's treatment of water can be considered his greatest achievement. As at Croome, his method for creating a lake was to dam an existing stream, thus flooding the surrounding valley. This he did as part of his landscaping schemes at estates as diverse as Burghley, Longleat, Kiddington, Blenheim, Audley End, Syon Park, and Alnwick Castle.

Brown's most famous commission was probably for the fourth duke of Marlborough at Blenheim Park. Here, during the 1760s and 1770s, Brown turned Henry Wise's formal gardens into idealized countryside, leaving nothing of the original landscape but the kitchen garden, a phenomenal 4.8 km (three-mile) avenue, and Sir John Vanbrugh's controversial bridge over the River Glyme. Vanbrugh had constructed an elaborate bridge on the grounds, a bridge quite out of proportion to the small river that it spanned. One of Brown's first tasks was to dam the stream, forming two great lakes joined by a neck of water, thus providing a magnificent setting worthy of Vanbrugh's bridge. The damming of the river also provided the opportunity to create a splendid rockwork cascade, to conceal the fact that the water landscape was man made rather than natural.

Although Brown's expertise was primarily as a designer, not a horticulturist, one of his unique skills was his ability to visualize what plantings would look like in the future. Perimeter belts to "conceal the bounds" and judiciously placed clumps of trees were essential elements of his designs, hiding, screening, and revealing successive landscape features. The majority of trees chosen were native deciduous oaks, elms, beeches, ashes, and limes, but Brown occasionally used evergreens. For example, at Kirklington Park he experimented with the large-scale use of evergreen trees, in particular conifers recently introduced from North America, together with the Scotch pine (*Pinus sylvestris*), once native to England and reintroduced from Scotland. Although he never saw them at maturity, Brown's bold tree groupings would eventually change the look of the English countryside.

During the 1750s Brown was involved in major landscaping works at Belhus, Moor Park, Ragley, Longleat, and Wrest Park, to name but a few. At the end of the decade, although supported by influential friends, attempts made to secure him a royal appointment were unsuccessful. It was not until 1764, after the accession of George III, that Brown was given the position of Surveyor to His Majesty's Gardens and Waters at Hampton Court. With this appointment came £2,000 per year and a house, Wilderness House, on the grounds of Hampton Court. Perhaps surprisingly, in view of his landscaping works elsewhere, Brown chose not to "improve" the formal gardens of Hampton Court, his main addition being the Black Hamburg grape planted in the vinery. (This plant is still thriving and each year produces an abundant crop of black grapes, for sale to visitors.) It has, however, been suggested that Brown replaced most of the terrace steps in the Privy Garden with gravel and grass steps. In nearby Richmond Old Park, he replaced Merlin's Cave (a grotto constructed by Kent for Queen Caroline) and part of the formal gardens with a more informal landscape. This included the Rhododendron Dell, now part of the Royal Botanic Gardens, Kew.

On his royal appointment, Brown and his family immediately moved to Wilderness House, although he later bought a grand house for himself in Huntingdonshire. The opportunity to acquire this house, the Manor of Fenstanton, came in 1767 while making a new landscape park for the earl of Northampton at Castle Ashby. Partly to pay Brown's fees, the earl needed to raise money and agreed to sell Fenstanton, which Brown promptly bought for £13,000. Here, when work permitted, he delighted in living the life of a country gentleman. However, by the mid 1760s Brown's workload had increased to the extent that he took on two assistants, Samuel Lapidge and Michael Milliken, the latter employed by the Crown to work under Brown's direction at Hampton Court and Richmond. Lapidge was able to relieve Brown of some of the traveling necessary to visit and survey the many estates and landowners requiring his services.

During this period one of Brown's most interesting commissions was at Broadlands for Lord Palmerston. In the years preceding his inheritance of the property, Palmerston had completed the Grand Tour, during which he became interested in Italian art and architecture. He employed Brown to redesign his house as an Italianate villa and to transform the grounds. With the help of his close associate, Henry Holland, a portico was built onto the house, windows were replaced, an orangery added, and the building faced in white brick. The house was set against trees and sweeping lawns down to the River Test—all at a cost of £21,000. A second interesting project was for Robert Clive, who on his return from India bought Claremont in Surrey. Both Brown and Sir William Chambers prepared designs for the house and landscape, but Brown's proposals were accepted, and again with Henry Holland, he constructed a grand Palladian house with a portico and Corinthian columns, framed by magnificent cedars and surrounded on all four sides with sweeping lawns.

In 1770 official recognition came to Brown when he was made High Sheriff of Huntingdonshire. This was an annual appointment made by George III and thus conveyed the message that Brown, although from a humble background, was to be considered a successful designer and a gentleman. In 1771, as Brown's sons were not going to join him in the business, Brown made Henry Holland's son his partner. Holland benefited considerably from this association, receiving many commissions through his recommendations and becoming one of the most influential architects of the time.

During the 1770s, despite a worsening of the asthma that had affected him throughout his life, Brown continued to travel extensively and take on new commissions. He worked on the Fellows' Garden at St John's College, Cambridge, replacing a bowling green and formal gardens with lawns and trees, receiving "a piece of plate of the value of £50" for his efforts. He also presented an overall plan for college land on both sides of the River Cam, but because his design involved unifying the college gardens and diverting the river, the work was not carried out. Other notable later works included those at Nuneham Courtenay, a landscape already extensively altered by the first earl of Harcourt, who had removed a village and church to open up the views from his new Palladian villa. On his father's death in 1777, the second earl commissioned Brown to landscape a further 405 hectares (1,000 acres), which resulted in plans to extend the lawns from the house into the deer park and to construct a winding walk through the plantations, in order to give splendid views over the Thames.

Brown created an enormous body of work, but although many of his plans still exist, unlike many of his contemporaries, he was not a writer and left no published account of his theories. His general principles were, however, outlined in a letter written to the Reverend Thomas Dyer in 1775. Brown wrote that good landscape design should be

> a perfect knowledge of the country and the objects in it, whether natural or artificial, and infinite delicacy in the planting etc so much Beauty depending on the size of the trees and the colour of their leaves to produce the effect of light and shade.

Brown's style and methods were widely copied during his lifetime, but after his death in 1783, there was no obvious successor. It was not until the emergence of Humphry Repton in the next decade that a landscaper of sufficient talent was able to carry on Brown's work and bring his own unique landscape style to English gardens.

*See also* Blenheim Palace; Chatsworth Gardens; Hampton Court Palace and Bushy Park; Kew, Royal Botanic Gardens; Nuneham Courtenay; Prior Park; Stowe

## Biography

Born in Kirkharle, Northumberland, England, 1716. Apprenticed to Sir William Loraine, 1732; became gardener at Wotton for Sir Richard Grenville, 1739; gardener at Stowe Park for Lord Cobham, 1741; moved to London to set up private practice, 1751; appointed as Surveyor of Gardens at Hampton Court, 1764; became High Sheriff of Huntingdonshire, 1770. Died in London, 6 February 1783.

## Selected Designs

| | |
|---|---|
| 1741–51 | Stowe, Buckinghamshire, England |
| 1750–70s | Croome Court, Worcestershire, England |
| 1757 | Longleat, Wiltshire, England |
| 1758 | Wrest Park, Bedfordshire, England |
| 1759 | Alnwick Castle, Northumberland, England |
| 1760 | Castle Ashby, Northamptonshire, England |
| 1761–68 | Bowood, Wiltshire, England |
| 1763–64 | Blenheim Palace, Oxfordshire, England |
| 1763–74 | Luton Hoo, Bedfordshire, England |
| 1769–70s | Claremont, Surrey, England |
| 1778–9 | Nuneham Courtenay, Oxfordshire, England |
| 1781 | Heveningham Hall, Suffolk, England |

## Further Reading

*Capability Brown and the Northern Landscape,* Newcastle upon Tyne: Tyne and Wear County Council Museums, 1983

Clifford, Joan, *Capability Brown: An Illustrated Life of Lancelot Brown, 1716–1783,* Aylesbury, Buckinghamshire: Shire, 1974

Hyams, Edward, *Capability Brown and Humphry Repton,* London: Dent, and New York: Scribner, 1971

Stroud, Dorothy, *Capability Brown,* London: Country Life, 1950; new edition, London: Faber, 1975

Thacker, Christopher, and John Bethel, *England's Historic Gardens,* London: Headline, and Toronto, Ontario: McGraw-Hill Ryerson, 1989

BARBARA SIMMS

# Buildings, Garden

Because gardens are places of work, pleasure, and retreat, there have probably always been structures of some type to provide a place for rest or for shelter from sun or rain. Garden buildings can be as simple as a bower made of living plants or as grand as a miniature Pantheon. It may be argued that the Taj Mahal is a form of garden building, yet garden architecture has been dismissed by some architectural historians as trivial and by garden historians and designers as irrelevant. This attitude is gradually changing, evidenced by the large number of publications now devoted to the subject.

Garden buildings were often highly imaginative, sometimes fantastic, which is why they are also sometimes referred to as *follies.* And as architectural historians have begun to understand, garden buildings have also frequently been used for serious architectural experimentation because they are generally small and relatively inexpensive to build. Similarly, buildings often provide the framework or focus of a garden; in extreme cases they define the garden. This is especially true in highly geometric designs, such as those found in Islamic and Renaissance gardens. At the Villa Lante, Bagnaia, for example, the house itself consisted of a pair of pavilions (casinos) that dominate the garden. In addition, without conservatories and other buildings used to protect and propagate plants, certain horticultural developments might never had occurred.

It is likely that simple arbors—vine-covered bowers or tunnel-arbors (pergolas)—were the first forms of garden architecture. Images of arbors appear in Egyptian wall

Temple of British Worthies, Stowe, Buckinghamshire, England
Copyright Paula Henderson

paintings and in Persian sculpted reliefs. This ancient form of architecture has been popular through the centuries, in spite of its fragility. More permanent structures were associated with Greek culture, particularly stoas or long colonnades that surrounded open spaces. These were adapted into Roman architecture as peristyles and in the Italian Renaissance as loggias. The perfect link between interior and exterior space (they were usually part of a solid wall of the house, then open on the court or garden side), grand colonnades were also one of the major architectural forms in baroque gardens.

The great gardens of the ancient Romans established the importance of elaborate architectural forms in gardens. The emperor Hadrian at his villa at Tivoli (A.D. 118–38), for example, attempted to re-create some of the most impressive architectural monuments that he had encountered during his campaigns, including the Stoa Poikile at Athens and the temple of Serapis. Although imperial in scale, Hadrian's villa reflects the same attitude toward architectural ornament found in the letters of Pliny the Younger. Renaissance garden designers sought to imitate both, and at the Villa d'Este (also at Tivoli), Cardinal Ippolito II d'Este had Pirro

Ligorio create a miniature *Rometta*, constructed on a terrace and representing the seven hills of Rome with its most important architectural monuments. Early English landscape gardens, such as Stourhead and Stowe, were equally architectural.

While influenced by both antique and Renaissance precedents, the designers of these gardens were also enthralled by the classical landscape paintings of the 17th century—particularly those of Claude Lorrain and Nicholas Poussin (collected by many of the most important patrons)—whose evocative and highly imaginative views of the ancient Roman landscape (filled with temples, ruins, bridges, etc.) provided a perfect picturesque model. Western garden buildings were often built in a classical style or could be inspired by more exotic forms; bridges, for example, could be based on Palladian models (as in many 18th-century English gardens) or on Chinese prototypes (in eclectic gardens of the 19th century, such as Biddulph Grange in Staffordshire).

The form of a garden building was often determined by symbolic associations, and it was through architecture (and sculpture) that iconographic programs in gardens were developed. At Stourhead, for example, the buildings (mostly designed by the Palladian architect Henry Flitcroft) were laid out in such a way that a proper circuit of the landscape (as specified by its creator, Henry Hoare II, in the mid-18th century) emphasized the parallels between the experience of the garden and the route of Aeneas in Virgil's *Aeneid*. The visitor would begin at the Doric Temple of Flora. Over the door was an inscription in Latin that warned, "Begone! You who are uninitiated, begone!" suggesting that the garden was a mysterious, sacred ground, not to be visited by the unworthy or, as Hoare himself put it, the uneducated. The visitor would then begin the walk around the manmade lake. Arriving at the grotto, the visitor descended (and still does descend) into the dark, damp, tufa-covered building, encountering there statues of a sleeping nymph and of an ancient river god, the latter pointing upward and away from the grotto. Those familiar with the classical text would remember that it was the river god who told Aeneas that he would found the greatest city in the world. No surprise, then, that the next building along the path is a miniature—but still impressively large—copy of the Pantheon, the most famous and best-preserved of all ancient Roman buildings. Few gardens were as literary as Stourhead, yet garden buildings often elicited intellectual responses by contemporary visitors that are completely lost today.

The garden as microcosm (an idea that permeated garden design from the medieval period), meant that there should be a place for all God's creatures. Aviaries were common in ancient gardens (the Roman scholar Varro described a large aviary or *ornithon* at his villa near Cassino, which became an important model) and many later gardens. Aviaries could be very large for splendid, ornamental birds. They could also be very small—simple cages for songbirds might be inserted into an arbor or attached to a small building. For example, the pavilion in the center of the garden at the château at Gaillon, as shown in the 16th-century engravings of Androuet du Cerceau, had cages built into the angles of the pavilion so that the birds would be hidden but their songs could be heard. Aviaries were found in many later gardens as well, precursors of the common birdhouse found in so many gardens today.

Roman emperors also had menageries for wild beasts, and gifts of exotic animals were common between rulers in later periods. Fynes Moryson (*An Itinerary,* 1617) writes of the menagerie at one of the Medici villas near Florence in the late 16th century, where the duke kept "fierce wild beasts in a little round house." English kings kept lions in the Tower of London and from the early 17th century had a proper menagerie in St. James's Park. The zoological component of many early gardens culminated in the modern-day zoo, although they are sometimes so unnatural as to be almost unrecognizable as gardens.

Perhaps even more important than buildings for animals were conservatories (*orangeries,* when designed to overwinter citrus trees), forcing houses, and other buildings constructed to protect plants. When purely functional, these were simple structures with large south-facing windows. One of the largest was the orangery at Versailles, enlarged by Jules Hardouin-Mansart in the 1680s and meant to complement the facade of the great château. By the 18th century in England, orangeries were frequently very handsome structures, designed by the most important architects. In the 19th century builders of conservatories benefited from the achievements of the industrial revolution, particularly the use of cast iron in building. Joseph Paxton, designer of the great conservatory at Chatsworth for the duke of Devonshire (ca. 1840), for example, adapted a glasshouse design for the Great Exhibition of 1851 (Hyde Park, London). The famous Crystal Palace at the exhibition, made of prefabricated iron and glass, became a model of modern design and the precursor of skeleton-frame construction.

It was not unusual for garden buildings to anticipate later developments in architecture. In the middle of the 18th century, a number of garden buildings used the most recent architectural publications to experiment with forms of neoclassicism (e.g., the Temple of Concord and Victory at Stowe). At the same time, Sir William Chambers designed a remarkable number of buildings for the Royal Botanic Gardens, Kew (published in 1763 as *Plans of the Gardens and Buildings at Kew*), including a Chinese pagoda (Chambers was one of the few architects who had actually been to China), a ruined arch, a miniature cathedral, an "Alhambra," a mosque, and numerous classical and Gothic buildings.

Such an encompassing attitude toward architectural style anticipated the eclecticism of the 19th century. Some garden buildings were built purely as symbols and not meant to be used. When placed at a distance, silhouetted against the sky, they were known as "eye catchers." At Rousham House in Oxfordshire (1730s), one of the earliest landscape gardens and designed by William Kent, the view from the garden was enhanced by a ruined rustic mill on the hillside opposite, transformed by the addition of Gothic windows and flying buttresses, a contrast with the classical buildings and sculpture within the garden itself. Eye catchers were often ruins (sometimes to suggest that the owner of the land was from an ancient family and not a parvenu), but columns (sometimes with statues to commemorate a hero), obelisks (symbolic of the rays of the sun), and towers were equally common. These towers might be at the end of a long walk, and a splendid view would be the reward for climbing to its upper rooms or roof.

Although many gardens throughout history had fine garden buildings, few could compete with the gardens at Stowe in Buckinghamshire, begun in the early 18th century by the aptly named Temple family (whose family motto, *Templa Quam Dilecta,* means "how beautiful are thy temples"). For more than 50 years the most important architects of the period, including Sir John Vanbrugh and James Gibbs, created in excess of 40 garden buildings at Stowe. Among the first was Vanbrugh's classical domed rotunda. William Kent added numerous buildings in the 1730s, many commemorating the political heroes of Lord Cobham. The Temple of British Worthies, for example, was modeled on a Roman shrine with busts of British monarchs, men of letters, philosophers, artists, and politicians. There was a Temple of Ancient Virtue and a Temple of Modern Virtue, the latter in ruins because Cobham felt that there was no modern virtue in early Georgian England.

At Stowe and many other gardens, temples were the primary architectural form. They could be dedicated to gods or goddesses (with their various associations flattering the owner or guests), or they could be dedicated to heroes (often Hercules), to states of mind (the virtues), or as at Stowe, to political ideals (a temple dated 1783 at Parlington in Yorkshire was even dedicated to "Liberty in North America").

In addition to temples, many other types of buildings were found in gardens: bridges, artificial ruins, Chinese buildings (the one at Stowe has recently been restored), "Turkish tents" (one has been recently restored to the late 18th-century garden at Le Desert de Retz near Paris), grottoes, and hermitages. Grottoes are one of the most delightful forms of garden architecture and the perfect fusion of nature and artificiality so admired in garden design. The original inspirations were natural caves, which in ancient times often had mystical or religious associations, and the Roman *nympheum,* with statues of nymphs, river gods and other mythological figures. Most grottoes imitated the dark, damp quality of natural caves and were embellished with rough, weathered stone and sometimes elaborate shellwork.

The most spectacular Renaissance grotto to survive is at the Medici villa at Castello (1546), where the shell- and stone-encrusted structure retains its original sculpture of animals, both real and fantastic, although they no longer spout water from a variety of sources (as reported by the 16th-century French writer Michel de Montaigne). Grottoes were found in many Renaissance gardens, often with automated figures and complex hydraulic systems, especially those of the early 17th-century French engineer Salomon de Caus. The spectacular Grotte de Thetis at Versailles (1667–69), with its statues of Apollo, nymphs, and tritons, became yet another metaphor for the Sun King, Louis XIV, who could retire to the dark grotto and emerge refreshed and "enlightened." Many English landscape gardens also contained grottoes.

Thomas Wright, who published the highly imaginative *Arbours and Grottoes* in the 1750s, was also the designer of some of the most delightful hermitages in the period (his Root House survives at Badminton in Gloucestershire). Unlike most garden architecture of the 18th century, the inspiration for the hermitage was not classical but biblical. A religious recluse—the hermit—was meant to inhabit the hermitage, a wild, rustic hideaway. Advertisements for hermits—men who would live in the damp, cold hermitage and who would not be allowed to bathe or communicate with others—largely went unanswered. As a result the role of the hermit would be played by a servant. In some cases a wax or stuffed figure sufficed.

As evocative and amusing as many garden buildings were, the primary function of garden architecture was to provide a pleasant retreat or refuge within the garden. The ways in which these buildings were used, provide insights into how the gardens themselves were used. Some were very functional: boathouses and fishing lodges, bath houses, and even the delightfully ornamental "necessaries" (outdoor latrines) at the corners of colonial American gardens (re-created in many gardens in Colonial Williamsburg).

Banqueting (or, today, picnicking) was one of the most common activities in garden buildings. The Romans built platforms in trees for banquets. At Pratolino, an enormous tree house was constructed in the branches of a giant oak (known as La fontana della Rovere); others were found at Castello and Petraia. The practice of building tree houses spread throughout Europe and remains, of course, one of the joys of modern gardens for children. In Elizabethan England most garden buildings were referred to as *banqueting houses* (the Italian term *gazebo* and French *pavilion* were not used until later). At that time a banquet was a small, intimate meal of sweets (marzipan made into fantastic shapes, gingerbread, meringues, and other "conceited" dishes) washed down with Ipocras (mulled wine). Some of these banqueting houses—often octagonal in plan—were built on artificial mounts or terraces, providing a vantage point to look into the gardens or over the surrounding landscape. Elsewhere, buildings such as these were referred to as *gloriets* (*gloriette* in French and *glorieta* in Spanish) or *belvederes* (Italian for "beautiful view").

The grandest belvederes were the elegant retreats built in baroque and rococo gardens in Germany and eastern Europe (for example, the belvedere at Charlottenburg in Berlin). Thomas Jefferson built a much smaller version at Monticello in Virginia, placed at the edge of his vegetable garden and overlooking the agricultural landscape below.

Garden buildings as a place for clandestine meetings became something of a poetic cliche, and "bowers of bliss" were suggestive of the sexual overtones of the garden, implicit in the fall of Adam and Eve. Medieval literature and manuscript illuminations, especially the *Roman de la Rose*, are full of references to courtly love, while in other societies the romance was frequently more lusty than honorable. Mogul and Rajput manuscripts often show wealthy princes cavorting with voluptuous young women in the shelter of magnificently ornamented pavilions.

Buildings were also used for theatrical and musical entertainments. The great amphitheater in the Boboli Gardens behind the Pitti Palace in Florence and the semicircular water theater at the Villa Aldobrandini at Frascati could be flooded for mock sea battles or naumachiae. In Persian and Mogul gardens (such as the Shalimar Gardens in Lahore), small platforms of the finest marble were built for musicians so that the princes and their court could listen to music as they strolled through the exquisite water gardens. Similar pleasures on a much more democratic level were provided by musicians in the bandstands built originally in the 19th century; such bandstands are still used in many public gardens and parks today.

Gardens have always been places for reflection and thought. Greek philosophers met under the colonnades or stoas. Medieval and Renaissance philosophers discussed weighty matters in cloistered walks; the French often built small chapels in their gardens. The Japanese erect "moon-watching pavilions" to provide places to sit and contemplate the beauty of the reflection of the moon in pools of water.

By its very nature the garden is a metaphor for life. Plants emerge in spring and die in the winter. The evocation of death, then, is also something that inspired architecture. Memorials—urns, pyramids, and shrines—were built in many gardens. Some of the greatest Mogul gardens were created around tombs—the Taj Mahal (from 1631) being the most famous. In the 18th century the earl of Carlisle built a splendid mausoleum in the park at Castle Howard, probably suggested by Sir John Vanbrugh (who had wanted the duchess of Marlborough to build one in honor of her husband at Blenheim) but ultimately completed by Nicholas Hawksmoor and based on ancient Roman mausoleums on the Via Appia Antica. Others followed, and the blend of memorial temple and rolling landscape served as the perfect model for 19th-century urban cemeteries. The cemetery of Pere-Lachaise, just east of Paris, was one of the first and retained many of the formal features of French gardening. Mount Auburn Cemetery in Boston, Massachusetts (1831), was one of the first in the United States and served as both a public park and a memorial garden.

It is not possible to discuss all types of garden architecture here. At their most basic, garden buildings provide shelter. Garden buildings could also be capricious, entertaining, and amusing; and on a more serious note, they could elevate the garden beyond horticulture and pleasure to provide spiritual and intellectual inspiration. Whatever their purpose and appearance, garden buildings have rarely been trivial and almost never irrelevant to the gardens in which they were built.

*See also* Amphitheater/Theater; Aviary; Bridge; Greenhouse; Ruins

**Further Reading**

Brown, Jane, *The Art and Architecture of English Gardens: Designs for the Garden from the Collection of the Royal Institute of British Architects, 1609 to the Present Day*, London: Weidenfeld and Nicolson, and New York: Rizzoli, 1989

Enge, Torsten Olaf, and Carl Friedrich Schröer, *Gartenkunst in Europa, 1450–1800*, Cologne, Germany: Taschen, 1990; as *Garden Architecture in Europe, 1450–1800*, translated by Aisa Mattaj, Cologne, Germany: Taschen, 1990

Fariello, Francesco, *Architettura dei giardini*, Rome: Ateneo, 1967

*Georgian Arcadia: Architecture for the Park and Garden*, London: Colnaghi, 1987

Jones, Barbara Mildred, *Follies and Grottoes*, London: Constable, 1953; 2nd edition, revised and enlarged, 1974

Miller, Naomi, *Heavenly Caves: Reflections on the Garden Grotto*, New York: Braziller, and Boston and London: Allen and Unwin, 1982

Mosser, Monique, and Georges Teyssot, editors, *L'architettura dei giardini d'Occidente*, Milan: Electa, 1990; as *The Architecture of Western Gardens*, Cambridge, Massachusetts: MIT Press, 1991; as *The History of Garden Design*, London: Thames and Hudson, 1991

Mott, George, and Sally Sample Aall, *Follies and Pleasure Pavilions: England, Ireland, Scotland, Wales*, London: Pavilion, and New York: Abrams, 1989

Plumptre, George, *Garden Ornament*, London: Thames and Hudson, and New York: Doubleday, 1989

Robinson, John Martin, *Temples of Delight: Stowe Landscape Gardens*, London: National Trust, 1990

Saudan, Michel, and Sylvia Saudan-Skira, *De folie en folies: La découverte du monde des jardins*, Geneva: Bibliotheque des Arts, 1987; as *From Folly to Follies: Discovering the World of Gardens*, New York: Abbeville Press, 1988; Cologne, Germany, and London: Taschen, 1997

PAULA HENDERSON

# Bulb

The word *bulb* as generally used is a generic term for the underground storage organs developed by many monocotyledonous plants. It is often used for structures that botanically speaking are corms, rhizomes, or even tubers. Regardless of their morphological origin, each form has evolved in response to an environment that is characterized by a season of extreme drought or unacceptable heat when survival of the species depends on considerable reduction of transpiration. Usually this means complete loss of aerial parts and the concentration in the subterranean "bulb" of the food stores necessary for regrowth when conditions become suitable. That such organs are a medium for natural vegetative reproduction also provides an important horticultural dimension.

True bulbs such as those of *Narcissus* (daffodils), *Galanthus* (snowdrops), *Tulipa* (tulips), and *Allium* (onions) consist of a basal disc of tissue that can be shown to be a flattened vertical stem. On this is arrayed a series of overlapping fleshy leaf bases with vestigial buds in their axils. The central bud grows into the main flower stem with its surrounding foliar leaves, while other buds may take two or more years to produce flowers. A single large daffodil bulb may consist of a central mother bulb with two or three attached daughter bulbs, all capable of flowering. Left alone such a bulb will build up a steadily increasing colony. Most bulbs are enclosed by a papery tunic that helps to prevent desiccation and damage; those of *Lilium* (true lilies) are tunicless, and their loose aggregations of swollen leaf bases are more vulnerable. They cannot successfully be stored dry and should never be bought in this condition.

Crocuses and gladioli are characterized by corms. Here the food store is concentrated in a fleshy stem base enclosed by a tunic and surmounted by a number of buds of which the bigger produce the season's flower and develop the next years corm on top of the old ones. Swollen horizontal stems such as those of flag irises are known as rhizomes; although their raison d'être and morphology resemble true bulbs, like lilies they seldom become fully dormant. The distinct stem tubers of potatoes and Jerusalem artichokes and root tubers of dahlias are dicotyledonous responses to the need for food storage and, in turn, asexual reproduction.

The bulbous form is encouraged by Mediterranean climates, typically of mild wet winters followed by hot dry summers. In the lands of the Mediterranean basin itself, the first rains of autumn stir the bulbs into sudden action: usually this consists of new fibrous root growth often with no signs of aerial tissue until early spring. However, a few species are immediately triggered into flower: most colchicums (meadow saffron), a few crocus species, and even narcissus species, whose vegetative growth then follows the usual pattern, emerging as conditions permit and going to rest before the summer's heat. The leaves of some species begin to appear in early winter but remain unextended if conditions become inclement. Further east in Asia Minor the more extreme climate causes autumnal root growth, semidormancy in the icy winter, and an explosion of flower and leaf growth in the short spring that precedes an arid summer.

That tulips especially originate in such areas makes them particularly suited for cultivation in cool temperate regions, even into regions with an average annual minimum temperature of minus 40 degrees Celsius (104 degrees F), so long as their natural pattern of growth is respected: autumn root growth has to have taken place before the ground freezes, while in warmer regions winter dormancy must be respected.

Interestingly, the same pattern of growth has evolved in response to the apparently very different habitat of eastern North American woodlands and parts of temperate Asia. Here the tree canopy is the determinant, and forest-floor bulbs such as *Erythronium* (trout lilies) have to arrange and complete their life cycle during the short seasons of illumination each side of a hard winter.

The Mediterranean climatic pattern is also dominant in other areas of the world: parts of California, Chile, South Africa, and southeast Australia. In each plant response has been similar, with trees and shrubs having leathery antidessicant foliage and a herbaceous ground flora characterized by underground storage organs. Unfortunately, few species are winter hardy in cool temperate regions. Nonetheless, the especially rich South African flora has provided several valuable garden genera such as *Crinum, Nerine, Crocosmia*, and *Gladiolus*. Of these the latter exhibits complete winter dormancy and is thus treated as a seasonal annual in cool climates, the corms being lifted in autumn, stored dry in frost-free conditions and replanted the following spring. True bulbs from South Africa, such as nerine, seem not to become fully dormant; even when leaf growth disappears, typically in summer, fleshy roots are maintained. Autumn flowers and the immediate development of overwintering foliage preclude dry-condition storage. Most such species, therefore, together with bulbs such as South American *Hippeastrum* (amaryllis), are treated as conservatory plants in temperate climates.

It may be presumed that the first bulbs to be brought into cultivation were those that provided food. All early cultures used forms of onion and garlic (*Allium* species are native throughout the north temperate world, although not all are bulbous), and references to these plants can be traced back to the first Egyptian dynasty (3200 B.C.). Classical Greek and Roman authors, including Hippocrates and Pliny the Elder, describe a number of onion cultivars—oval, round, white, yellow, red, strong, mild—which indicates that selection had long taken place. Cultivation for medical or religious reasons can also be found in early times; for example, depictions of the Virgin Mary holding a Madonna Lily (*Lilium candidum*) predate the Middle Ages. Admiration for what are still the most important garden bulbs, tulips and daffodils, was widespread in the Middle East, which was, of course, the epicenter of wild species distribution. In the 16th century thousands of tulip bulbs were dug up annually from the wild for planting in Turkish Royal Gardens, and selections were made over time to concentrate on what were considered ideal forms: extreme, narrow "lily-flowered" types were especially prized, in contrast to the rounded flowers preferred in western Europe.

In 1562 a few tulip bulbs were sent to Carolus Clusius at the Leiden Botanic Garden, which began Holland's major industry of flower bulb production that continues to this day. Dutch enthusiasm for the new plants reached the frenzy known as Tulipomania between 1634 and 1637, when tulip bulbs, particularly new forms, changed hands for vast sums. Because of their rarity and price, tulips, hyacinths, and daffodils are invariably depicted in contemporary illustrations of 17th-century gardens growing well-spaced in formal beds or containers. The current concept of swaths of naturalized bulbs reflects both availability and changes of taste that date to the late-19th-century edicts of William Robinson and Gertrude Jekyll.

Today spring bulbs are available as cut flowers before winter begins and as pot plants by Christmas, the bulbs having been pretreated to break their natural dormancy pattern. Millions of tulips, daffodils, hyacinths, and less-hardy bulbs are planted each autumn throughout the temperate world; spring would be inconceivable without them.

**Further Reading**

Fritsch, Felix Eugene, and E.J. Salisbury, *Plant Form and Function,* London: Bell, 1938

Grey-Wilson, Christopher, and Brian Mathew, *Bulbs: The Bulbous Plants of Europe and Their Allies,* London: Collins, 1981

Rix, Martyn, and Roger Phillips, *The Bulb Book: A Photographic Guide to over 800 Hardy Bulbs,* edited by Brian Mathew, London: Pan, 1981; as *The Random House Book of Bulbs,* New York: Random House, 1989

ALLEN PATERSON

# Bulgaria

Bulgaria is situated on the northeastern part of the Balkan peninsula and covers an area of 110,993 square miles (287,500 square km). Its high woody mountains, fertile valleys, meandering rivers, and protected bays, as well as its crossroad location between Europe and Asia, attracted settlers from different nations, leaving traces of various civilizations.

Travel notes and archaeological remains provide evidence for ancient and medieval gardens. In the plan of Seuthopolis, a typical Thracian town (400 B.C.), the houses were built around a courtyard with a colonnade. Traces from a well prove the existence of a garden. At one of the well-preserved Roman towns, Nicopolis ad Istrum, founded in A.D. 102, the streets were covered with stones, and there were water supply and sewerage systems. Villa Abritus (Razgrad), property of a landowner, is reminiscent of Pliny the Younger's Tuscan villa on a smaller scale. A rectangular atrium, 25 meters by 125 meters (27 by 137 yd.), with Ionic colonnades was surrounded by residential buildings and paved with marble stones.

The First Bulgarian Kingdom (681–1018) was created following the cultural traditions of Thracians, Greeks, and Romans. In its capital Pliska and later in Preslav (893–927) the churches, monasteries, and palaces were built between the inner and the outer wall. During the tenth century, known as the Golden Age, Joan the Exarch describes palaces decorated with marble, gold, and silver. Supposedly the gardens matched in wealth and beauty those in Byzantium and Persia.

After the liberation from the Byzantine yoke, the capital of the Second Bulgarian Kingdom (1186–1391), Veliko Turnovo, was founded around the meanders of the river Jantra. The Tsarevets Hill is a natural fortress, while the Trapezitsa Hill accommodates a religious center with 17 churches. Terrace gardens were built between the steep streets and buildings all the way down to the river.

During the Ottoman domination (1391–1878) the population moved to the mountains for shelter and protection. Civil construction decreased, while houses hid behind high stone walls. The fields, pastures, meadows, and forests provided the natural background of the settlements. The Bulgarian Renaissance (18th–19th century) was marked by economic development, cultural revival, and struggle for national liberty and religious independence. Midsize towns such as Gabrovo, Plovdiv, Trjavna, Koprivshtitsa, Arbanasi, Turnovo, and Kotel came into prominence. Houses increased in size and, with their asymmetrical, small yards (0.1–0.2 ha [.25–0.5 acres]), became a center for the intimate, cultural, and business life of the family. The house garden was enclosed, depended in size on the relief, smaller on steep slopes and larger on flat terrain, and was divided into representative flower, fruit, and farm parts. The main alley connected the gate with the house entrance and was surrounded by flower beds lined with box shrub. The veranda and vines, climbing around a wooden pergola, connected the house with the exterior. A fountain and well performed both aesthetic and utilitarian functions.

The monastery courtyards differed from those in the rest of Europe. Typical elements of each garden included cobblestone pavements and a few skillfully positioned ornamental trees, climbing flower shrubs, herbs, flowers around the church, and a fountain. The Rila, Bachkovo, Drjanovo, and Preobrazhenski monasteries are examples of creating perfect harmony with the landscape.

The period between the two world wars was the most prosperous one during the 20th century. Construction of public gardens began first in Sofia, to be followed by a number of towns Plovdiv (1878, 1892), Burgass (1881), Varna (1883), Stara Zagora (1891), Shumen (1897), and Vidin (1907–8). In 1884 the Swiss Lucien Shevallace turned the royal fruit and vegetable garden into the first botanical garden on the Balkans. In 1888 Prince Ferdinand placed the foundation of the first zoo on the Balkans. At first all gardens were created without plans. Later Austrian, German, Czech, and French gardeners were invited to train the first Bulgarian professional gardeners, who included Georgi Duhtev, Ivan Stoychev, Delcho Sugarev, Alexander Ginev, and Georgi Petrov, among others.

The parks of the royal residences were created at the end of the 19th century. Their geographical location (from zero up to 2,000 meters [6,562 ft.] above sea level) explains their biological diversity. Evcsinograd (1888) carries both the glamour of the French geometrical park and the charm of the English landscape park. The park has the richest collection of over one hundred species of palm trees. The park in Balchik (1926–36) prides itself with the richest collection of over 600 kinds of cacti, rare magnolia, and cotoneaster.

After World War II the existing parks were extended and new ones were built. In Sofia the West, North, and South Parks linked the city center with the surrounding mountains. The South Park was designed under the

impressive leadership of Marta Kolarova, Valentina Atanasova, Ekaterina Dimitrova, and Iskra Shtetinska. Its formal part (1981–83) represents a rich water composition on two levels. The upper one is a row of fountains on the axis of the main entrance of the Palace of Culture. The southern end of the park is occupied by the zoo (Nedelcho Radoslavov [1973]) and the National Botanic Gardens (Luiben Stoychev [1980–85]).

In the contact zones of the cities, the forest parks, created with the support of the local population, serve the needs of weekend recreation. Most famous are Ayzmo (Stara Zagora), Kayluka (Pleven), Sinite kamuni (Sliven), Izvorite (Kotel), Kenana (Haskovo), and Lipnic (Russe). Memorial parks have been created on the sites of major historical events.

From the 1960s to the 1980s development of parks and gardens included landscaping of the large housing estates, representative open spaces in the reconstructed city centers, and the greening of the seaside resorts. The second generation of the seaside resorts—smaller scale, low rise vacation homes (Rusalka, Elenite, and Dujni)—were interpreted in the best Bulgarian Renaissance traditions. The landscape parks of the Communist government residences were designed by the best professionals on the most beautiful sites in the country (Sandanski, Boyna, Bankya, Arbanasi, Perla).

The turn of the 21st century has seen attempts to preserve the existing parks from the aggressive constructions after land and property restitution, fund-raising for parks reclamation, and progressive legislation development for protecting the great variety of picturesque landscapes.

*See also* Boris Gardens

**Further Reading**

Alecsiev, Alexander, "Botanicheskata gradina pri BAN: Dobur stopanin li e bulgarinut?" *Gradina* 4 (2000)

Angelova, Julia, "Morskata gradina vuv Varna," *Gradina* 6–7 (2000)

Diankov, Tenko, "Aiazmoto v Stara Zagora: Edin park—Ecologichen fenomen," *Gradina* 2 (2000)

Iordanova, Marina, and Doncho Donchev, editors, *Geografia na Bulgariia: Fizicheska geografiia, sotsialno-ikonomicheska georgrafiia* (The Geography of Bulgaria: Physical Geography, Socio-Economic Geography), Sophia: Akademichno Izd-vo "Prof. Marin Drinov," 1997 (with a summary in English)

Karakashev, Krustan, "Parkoustroistvoto v arhitekturata na otminavashtoto stoletie" (Parks Design in the Last Century), *Arhitectura* 2 (2000)

Karakashev, Krustan, "Stolichniiat Zoopark," *Gradina* 5 (2000)

Kostov, Rozalin, "Plovdiv: Zelenoto nasledstvo tursi novo Vazrajdane," *Gradina* 11 (1999)

Kuleliev, Jordan, "Evesinograd—Tsarstveniiat," *Gradina* 5 (1998)

Kuleliev, Jordan, "Park—Dvorets Balchik," *Gradina* 7 (1999)

Marinov, Vladimir, "Parkut Krichim—Loynoto imenie na Ferdinand," *Gradina* 7 (1998)

Meine, Curt, editor, *Bulgaria's Biological Diversity: Conservation Status and Needs Assessment*, 2 vols., Washington, D.C.: Biodiversity Support Program, 1998

Robev, Rashko, "Natsionalnoto gradinsko-parkovo nasledstvo i obshtestveniiat jivot v Bulgaria (The National Garden and Parks Heritage and the Public Life in Bulgaria)," *Arhitectura*, nos. 4 and 5 (1996)

Stoichev, Luiben, *Parkova i landschaftna arhitectura* (Parks and Landscape Architecture), Sofia: Tehnika, 1985

Sugarev, Delcho, *Gradinsko-parkovo i peizajno izkustvo* (Garden and Landscape Art), Sofia: Zemizdat, 1976

Tashev, Peter, *Istoriia na gradoustroiistvoto* (History of Urban Planning), Sofia: Tehnika, 1973

VESSELINA TROEVA

# Bullard, Helen Elise 1896–1987

## United States Landscape Architect

Helen Elise Bullard acquired an early interest in trees and plants from her father, a physician who maintained an apple orchard close to the family home in Schuylerville, New York. Immediately after receiving a bachelor of science in landscape architecture from Cornell University in 1919, Bullard became a residential landscape designer for an Ohio nursery company, where she headed the firm's department of Small Home Grounds.

During the 1920s, Bullard moved first to Cambridge, Massachusetts, and then to New York City, working for two of America's most prominent landscape architects, Warren H. Manning and Annette Hoyt Flanders. Because of her knowledge of plants, Bullard's duties for Manning and Flanders often involved the preparation and supervision of planting plans. However, the 35 weeks she spent from 1921 to 1923 in Calumet, Michigan, implementing plans prepared by Manning for the Calumet and Hecla Mining Company, illustrate Bullard's wide range of talents. Here she supervised a group of mine laborers who blasted holes in the native rock and planted mountain ash trees (*Sorbus americana*), and twice she directed "Community Day" activities—volunteer work events that Manning often included as part of his public design projects. The first of Calumet's Community Days occurred in 1922. As part of this event, Bullard helped supervise local citizens and thousands of school children transplant 30 varieties of fern and 60 varieties of wild flowers from nearby wooded areas to a Manning-designed park. One year later she oversaw the distribution of plants from the park to local gardens and helped direct 700 residents in a pageant that depicted the history of copper mining activities in Michigan's Upper Peninsula. After joining Annette Hoyt Flanders in 1927, Bullard's time was devoted almost entirely to the design and supervision of plans for large Long Island estates.

Since few private estate commissions were available following the onset of the Great Depression, Bullard left the office in Flanders in 1930 and began her career as a public servant. During the next eight years her work often included projects directly supervised by Robert Moses, who was then park commissioner for New York City. For the first five years Bullard was employed as a landscape architect by the Long Island State Park Commission, working on planting designs for parks such as Sunken Meadow and Jones Beach, and developing planting plans for the Southern State, Grand Central, and Montauk parkways. In 1935, Bullard moved to the New York City Parks Department, where she directed the annual flower planting program for the five boroughs and prepared planting plans for the grounds of the Hayden Planetarium in Manhattan Square Park, and the Morris-Jumel Colonial Garden in Roger Morris Park. From 1936 to 1938, Bullard again worked closely with Moses preparing site plans and landscape details for the 1939–40 New York World's Fair. In a 1938 *New York Times* article, Bullard stated that she was developing flower beds that would contrast with the yellow, red, and blue "rainbow" colors of the fair's buildings, and was choosing varieties of flowers noted "for their abundant bloom, ability to survive a Long Island summer, and long blooming season."

Ms. Bullard reportedly hoped to return to designing private estate gardens at some time, but a 1938 offer from the New York State Department of Public Works in Albany led to her continued involvement in the public sector. During more than a quarter century that she subsequently spent working for the state, Bullard developed and supervised designs for over 50 projects. Although little information about Bullard's designs has been located, evidence from the 1930s indicates that she clearly was a proponent of modernism. "Landscape design has for the most part to date utilized straight beds and pattern gardens, and modern principles for this field are still undeveloped," she announced in 1938, "but with modern buildings we cannot depend on the classic forms." Despite a lack of precedents to guide her efforts at the time, Bullard concluded that plantings need to "be designed in directional lines to give the feeling of motion."

## Biography

Born in Schuylerville, New York, 1896. Graduated from Cornell University, B.S. in landscape architecture, 1919; worked in Sydney, Ohio, for the Small Homes Grounds Department of Wagner Park Nursery, 1919–21; employed by the Warren H. Manning firm in Cambridge, Massachusetts, as landscape architect, 1921–27, including supervision of industrial grounds and public parks in Calumet, Michigan; designed private estates for Annette Hoyt Flanders in New York City, 1927–30; began public career with onset of Great Depression, preparing landscape designs for Long Island State Park Commission, 1931–35, New York City Parks Department, 1935–36, and 1939 New York World's Fair, 1936–38; joined New York State Department of Public Works, Division of Construction, as landscape architect, 1938; developed plans for at least 50 institutions before retiring in 1964. Died in Schuylerville, New York, 1987.

## Selected Designs

| | |
|---|---|
| 1921–23 | Industrial grounds and public parks, Calumet, Michigan, United States |
| 1927–30 | Private estates on Long Island, New York, United States |
| 1931–35 | State parks and parkways on Long Island, New York, United States |
| 1935 | Colonial garden, Morris-Jumel Mansion, Roger Morris Park, New York City, New York, United States |
| 1935 | Hayden Planetarium, New York City, New York, United States |
| 1936–38 | 1939 New York World's Fair, New York City, New York, United States |
| 1938–64 | Public parks, state of New York, United States |

## Further Reading

Alanen, Arnold R., and Lynn Bjorkman, "Plats, Parks, Playgrounds, and Plants: Warren H. Manning's Landscape Designs for the Mining Districts of Michigan's Upper Peninsula, 1899–1932," *The Journal of the Society for Industrial Archeology* 24, no. 1 (1998)

Petersen, Anne, "Women Take Lead in Landscape Art," *New York Times* (13 March 1938)

LYNN BJORKMAN AND ARNOLD R. ALANEN

---

# Burbank, Luther 1849–1926

## United States Horticulturist and Plant Breeder

Luther Burbank, often referred to as the "Plant Wizard," exerted a major influence on the development and breeding of plants in the first quarter of the 20th century. He devoted his career to plant breeding and hybridization and throughout his lifetime developed over 800 kinds of plants, including 200 new varieties of flowers, fruits, trees, vegetables, and grasses.

Burbank was raised on a farm in Lancaster, Massachusetts. While working around the family farm helping his father, he first became fascinated with growing plants. This experience taught him that better plants could be grown by starting with only the best plants and then crossbreeding each to produce a new variety. After his father died he raised vegetables with his brother and mother to make ends meet, and he continued experimenting with plant breeding.

In 1870, at the age of 21 and eager to put his experiments to work, Burbank purchased a 17-acre parcel of land outside Lunenberg, Massachusetts, and began what would become a 55-year career in plant breeding. Although he was not the first practitioner of plant breeding, Burbank perfected the craft. His specific methods consisted of crossbreeding multiple native and foreign plant species to cultivate seedlings and then

Luther Burbank home and garden
Photo by Lenny Siegel, courtesy of Luther Burbank Home and Gardens

grafting these seedlings to develop new and better breeds. In essence he pioneered hybridization by being the first person to create plants to order. He turned plant breeding into such an art that he could build any plant to fit any set of specifications, and he had a knack for developing the plants that people wanted.

Burbank had his first practical success in 1871, when he developed the Russet Burbank potato, which is known today as the Idaho potato. The finished product was made after he found a potato seed ball and planted some of its seeds. After harvesting a healthy crop of large potatoes, he then replanted the harvest and produced a large crop of the finest potatoes possible. He then sold some of the seeds to a seed catalog, and soon his potato was being grown all over the country. The Burbank potato was such an important discovery that it was even brought to Ireland to help fight the potato blight. It is still grown and remains a staple of American agriculture.

Burbank's work developed out of Charles Darwin's theory of evolution, and he was one of the first people to put Darwin's theories to practical use. His embracement of the theory of evolution came at a time when it was still controversial. As a result it is considered extremely important in the field of applied genetics because his plant breeding innovations were so revolutionary; his methods and innovations continue to be put into practice. Burbank based his methods on the belief that he could guide and quicken the evolution process. Realizing that natural selection depends on pollen spreading from one plant to another, he set out to transfer the pollen himself to create better plants. He believed that, by using only the fittest plants, he could breed stronger and larger plants. Like Darwin, his experiments numbered in the thousands. He always worked on a large scale and would often simultaneously conduct as many as 3,000 experiments on millions of plant varieties from all over the world.

Seeking a milder climate in which to conduct his plant experiments, Burbank moved to Santa Rosa, California, in 1875, where he bought a large farm in Sebastopol. There he established a greenhouse, experimental farms, and a nursery. After moving to Santa Rosa he became even more productive and spent the next 50 years creating new breeds and perfecting his hybridization methods. Throughout the years he produced seven new raspberry varieties, over 40 plum varieties, apples, peaches, berries, cherries, nectarines, pears, prunes, almonds, walnuts, grasses, grains; new varieties of tomato, corn, pepper, chive, squash, pea, and asparagus; and many new flowers, particularly lilies. He also became internationally renowned due to some of his more unique creations, such as the fire poppy (*Papaver Californicum*), the plumcot (*Prunus armeniaca*, a cross between a plum and an apricot), and the Shasta daisy (*Leucanthemum × super-*

*bum*, which he created by cross-pollinating the Japanese daisy and the English daisy). He even created a spineless cactus that was used as cattle feed.

The success of his new hybrids—and his 52-page catalog listing over 100 of the varieties, *New Creations in Fruits and Flowers* (1893)—received enormous attention from horticultural and botanical professionals worldwide and was eventually translated into several languages and published in several subsequent editions.

Burbank's work is considered influential not only because it stimulated a broader movement in plant breeding but also because it brought to the public a new understanding of horticulture, how crops are developed, and the new concept of producing better plants. Prior to his work, the idea that humans, not just God, could create plants was considered almost blasphemous. Burbank's work changed all that and garnered both public interest and support for plant breeding.

By 1915 both Burbank and his work were so influential that he was visited by Thomas Edison and Henry Ford, who came to his Santa Rosa home to learn about his production methods. Edison asked, "'Mr. Burbank, how do you make things grow so big?' 'Well, you see,' Burbank said, 'some big cannery man, perhaps, sends me specifications and I get to work and give him what he wants'" (quoted in Kraft).

Burbank's work even led to an amendment to U.S. patent law, the Plant Patent Act of 1930, which permitted the protection of new and distinct varieties of asexually reproduced plants and made new varieties of plants patentable for the first time. As Edison stated in support of the act, "This will, I feel sure, give us many Burbanks." After the act was passed, Burbank posthumously received 16 plant patents. As evidence of how he literally dominated the field of plant breeding, according to Peter Dreyer, "Burbank was listed in Webster's dictionary as a transitive verb: 'To modify and improve (plants or animals), esp. by selective breeding.'"

Burbank's development of new vegetable and fruit varieties is considered his greatest contribution, and he literally revolutionized the fruit industry. We still eat his foods today, including the Santa Rosa plum, Flaming Gold nectarine, and July Elberta peach, as well as dozens of others. In addition, his birthday, March 7, is officially designated as California's Arbor Day. His home, now known as the Luther Burbank Home and Gardens, is a registered national, state, and city historic landmark.

## Biography

Born in Lancaster, Massachusetts, 7 March 1849. Worked alongside his father on family farm; to make ends meet, took up vegetable and flower growing; took up plant breeding, 1870; created Burbank potato (*Solanum tuberosum* 'Burbank'), 1871; relocated to Santa Rosa, California, 1875; developed more than 800 new and improved varieties of plants, flowers, fruits, and vegetables, more than 40 plums, ten new varieties of berry, and Shasta daisy (*Leucanthemum* × *superbum*), 1875–1920s. Died in Santa Rosa, California, 11 April 1926.

## Selected Publications

*New Creations in Fruits and Flowers*, 1893
*The Training of the Human Plant*, 1906
*How Plants Are Trained to Work for Man*, 1921
*The Harvest of the Years*, 1927
*Partner of Nature*, 1939

## Further Reading

Bacon, Paul, *Luther Burbank: Creating New And Better Plants*, Chicago: Encyclopaedia Britannica Press, 1961

Beaty, John Y., *Luther Burbank, Plant Magician*, New York: Messner, 1943

Beeson, Emma Burbank, *The Early Life and Letters of Luther Burbank*, San Francisco: Harr Wagner, 1927

Dreyer, Peter, *A Gardener Touched with Genius: The Life of Luther Burbank*, New York: Coward McCann and Geoghegan, 1975; new and expanded edition, Santa Rosa, California: Luther Burbank Home and Gardens, 1993

Kraft, Ken, and Pat Kraft, *Luther Burbank: The Wizard and the Man*, New York: Meredith Press, 1967

Quackenbush, Robert, *Here a Plant, There a Plant, Everywhere a Plant, Plant! A Story of Luther Burbank*, Santa Rosa, California: Luther Burbank Home and Gardens, 1982

JUDITH GERBER

# Burle Marx, Roberto 1909–1994

## Brazilian Landscape Architect

Roberto Burle Marx was Brazil's most famous landscape architect who created a distinctive garden style within the modernist design philosophy. His artistic garden expressions gave Brazil a unique garden identity that is celebrated as one of the most exemplary modern landscape styles. Referred to as the *Burle Marx style*, his landscapes are characterized by asymmetrical spatial rhythms that seem to reflect Brazilian culture, rooted in passion and emotional expressiveness, as well as the mysteries of the wild landscape, including the tropical Amazon, coastal beaches, and the east-central plain of Brasília. Burle Marx's artistry for garden design used modern art as a prototype within the matrix of living ecological systems. As J. William Thompson notes, "If ever there was a marrying of art and science, he accomplished it." Burle Marx's extensive knowledge of South American tropical plants and plant associations was assembled into abstract garden compositions. In his own words, "[T]he garden is a complex of aesthetic and plastic intentions; and the plant is, to a landscape artist, not only a plant . . . but it is also a color, a shape, a volume, or an arabesque in itself."

One can grasp the significance of Burle Marx's garden creations more clearly by examining its historical context. During the late 19th century public parks and estate gardens in Brazil imitated the French and Portuguese baroque styles in architecture and garden layout, which included Victorian flower gardens and exotic plantings. Additionally, the French engineer Glaziou introduced the English romantic gardenesque style to Brazil. Although he sympathized with Glaziou's romantic landscape translations, which used native South American flora, Burle Marx noted that "Glaziou brought both the good . . . features of this English garden, [and] it was obvious that some of the worst would be copied as well as the best." As the new theories of visual composition emerged through the vision of 20th-century artists such as Pablo Picasso and Wassily Kandinsky and architects such as Walter Gropius and Le Corbusier, design professionals were redirected away from the European classical aesthetic. Brazil's international modernist architects—Oscar Niemeyer, Jorge Machado Moreira, and Gregori Warchavchik—and garden designer Burle Marx became paramount in this movement.

As a 20th-century Renaissance man Burle Marx not only designed gardens but also used his genius in painting, sculpting, flower arranging, jewelry, and fabric design, as well as the creation of stage sets and costume design. He inherited his mother's love for both gardening and music; she was an accomplished opera singer. Music became a constant inspiration and metaphor for his gardens. As one scholar notes, one can see "obvious musical qualities in his garden designs, both in their often flowing lines and in their harmony of color and

Fountain wall at Sitio Santo Antônio da Bica, Campo Grande
Copyright Paul Miles Picture Collection

form, not unlike the lyrical qualities in works of Matisse, where the abstract configurations of form and space express the artist's intentions" (Adams). The family's musical heritage led older brother Walter to became a professional composer and conductor, while the amateur singer Roberto by several accounts sang often and well for the many guests who stayed at his famous garden estate, the Sitio Santo Antônio da Bica, Campo Grande—19 miles (30.6 km) south of Rio. Burle Marx acquired the property, originally a coffee plantation, in 1949 for use as his home, studio, and garden laboratory. He used the variety of terrains and microclimates for horticultural experiments primarily related to plant community habitats. Within this garden Burle Marx created the most important collection of tropical plants in the world. The site also included a main house, a restored 17th-century chapel, and a sculptural granite wall composed of fragments of demolished 18th- and 19th-century buildings set within a pond and collection of bromeliads. The estate is now owned and managed by a foundation supported by the government.

Burle Marx was born in São Paulo. In 1913 the family moved to Rio de Janeiro. He was raised with a Victorian sensibility within a richly cultured environment in which he learned to speak Portuguese, Italian, French, Spanish, English, and German. Roberto's mother, Cecilia Burle Marx, was Brazilian with French and Dutch descent. His father, Wilhelm Marx, was a businessman of Jewish heritage, born in Trier, Germany. It was assumed by the family that he was a distant relative of Karl Marx. At the age of 19, in 1928, Roberto traveled to Berlin to study painting and music. While in Berlin, at the Berlin-Dahlem Botanic Garden he began to learn about Brazilian native plants (through a greenhouse collection of tropical plants). In 1930 he returned to Rio de Janeiro and enrolled in the Escola Nacional de Belas Artes—the school of fine arts—to study painting, architecture, and landscape design. Here he met architect and urban designer Lúcio Costo (who designed the plan for Brasília), who gave Burle Marx his first commission, a private home in Copacabana, Rio de Janeiro.

Sitio Santo Antônio da Bica, Campo Grande
Copyright Paul Miles Picture Collection

As an artist Burle Marx explored several movements within modernism, including cubism, geometrism, concretism, and according to Walker and Simo, surrealism, which in fine art explores dreamlike, unnatural juxtapositions of elements. Walker and Simo's analysis of Burle Marx's gardens emphasizes the surreal aspects of his compositions that largely dealt with planar forms: "As did Le Corbusier, he places objects on a plane not to glorify the object but to express the plane itself. And however enriched with patterning and planting, the plane remains taut. In this he is the first modernist to extend the greatness of Le Nôtre."

Burle Marx's childhood interest in gardening and native flora continued to grow. With his mentor, the distinguished botanist Henrique Lahmeyer de Mello Barreto, head of Rio's zoological garden, Burle Marx began to travel throughout the Brazilian landscape, including Amazonian jungles, deserts, and swamps. He identified and collected plants for study and use in his garden designs. This was a monumental task as the native flora include over 50,000 species. Ultimately, his "intimate knowledge of the tropical American landscape . . . served as a central thesis for a spectrum of subjects ranging from today's Amazon development programs to the propagation of house plants" (Gregory). Through his efforts as a self-trained botanist, at least 25 plant species are named for Burle Marx. He developed a passion for the beauty and ecological character of Brazil's natural environment and supported the protection of the Amazon rain forest well before Ian McHarg's book *Design with Nature* (1969) helped to popularize the environmental movement. Burle Marx used his knowledge of plants and native habitats as a constant source of inspiration for his garden creations, which were not meant to be imitations of the natural landscape but artistic dialogues between hard and soft materials. In the words of former apprentice Anthony Walmsley, his designs "are deliberately composed landscapes, finding their correspondence with nature through analogy and inference." Burle Marx used natural elements (plants, earth, water, sky) as if they were living pigments of paint on canvas. And he used architectural features (mosaic pavings, recycled columns, bas-relief wall panels) as sculpture within the garden setting. His imaginative garden layouts are interlocking patterns of spatial sequences characterized by his genius to orchestrate rhythms of color, texture, and form within curvilinear and rectangular modern gestures. The 1948 Odette Monterio (now Fernandes) residence in Corrêas near Petrópolis, a mountain resort north of Rio, shows well his signature style, which "claims its pedigree from the paintings of Miro, the sculptures of Arp, and the cut-outs of Matisse" (James).

In 1934 Burle Marx moved to Recife, in northern Brazil, where he became the curator of parks in Pernambuco. Three years later he returned to Rio to start his own practice. In 1938 he became a member of the design team headed by Le Corbusier for the creation of the gardens of the Ministry of Education and Health. In the realm of public projects, it is Flamengo Park (1954) and the Copacabana Beach promenade (1970) that receive world acclaim. In Burle Marx's 60-year career he designed over 3,000 public and private gardens in many nations, including Brazil, Germany, Japan, France, South Africa, Switzerland, the United States, and Venezuela. In 1991 garden plans and photographs of Burle Marx's work were featured in a retrospective exhibition entitled *The Unnatural Art of the Garden* at the Museum of Modern Art in New York City. He was the first landscape architect ever to have received this honor.

## Biography

Born in São Paulo, Brazil, 1909. Traveled to Berlin, Germany, 1928, where he studied painting and music, and was introduced to native Brazilian plants at Berlin-Dahlem Botanic Garden; returned to Rio de Janeiro, Brazil, 1930; studied at National Academy of Fine Arts; became curator of parks in Recife, for Pernambuco state, northern Brazil, 1934; established private practice, Rio de Janeiro, 1937; worked with Le Corbusier on gardens of Ministry of Education and Health, Rio de Janeiro, 1938; designed more than 3,000 public and private gardens in Brazil, Germany, Japan, France, South Africa, Switzerland, the United States, and Venezuela. Died near Rio de Janeiro, Brazil, 1994.

## Selected Designs

1938   Ministry of Education and Health, Rio de Janeiro, Brazil
1942   Conjunto da Pampulha, Belo Horizonte, Brazil
1948   Odette Monteiro residence, Correas, Brazil; Diego Cisneros residence, Caracas, Venezuela; Burton Tremaine residence, Santa Barbara, California, United States
1951   Roche Laboratory, Rio de Janeiro, Brazil
1953   United States Embassy, Rio de Janeiro, Brazil; Parque do Ibirapuera, São Paulo, Brazil
1954   Museu de Arte Moderna, Rio de Janeiro, Brazil
1955   Labor Temple Planting Project, Los Angeles, California, United States
1956   Parque del Este, Caracas, Venezuela
1957   Schultess family residence, Havana, Cuba
1958   Olivetti factory (play area), Buenos Aires, Argentina
1961   Parque do Flamengo (land fill), Rio de Janeiro, Brazil; Eixo Monumental, Brasilia, D.F., Brazil
1962   Parque de las Americas, Santiago, Chile
1963   UNESCO internal patios, Paris, France; Jardim das Nacoes, Vienna, Austria; Brazilian Pavilion (sculpture), Tokyo, Japan
1965   Palacio Itamaraty, Brasilia, D.F., Brazil; Fernandez Concha residence, Lima, Peru
1966   Residential area of Parque Norte, San Isidro, Argentina; Hotel Dorado Hilton, San Juan, Puerto Rico
1967   United States Embassy, Brasilia, D.F., Brazil; Conjunto Santa Barbara, San Juan, Puerto Rico
1968   Placio dos Leoes, São Luís, Maranhão, Brazil; Brazilian Embassy, Washington, D.C., United States
1969   Hotel Nacional, Rio de Janeiro, Brazil
1970   Copacabana Beach, Rio de Janeiro, Brazil; Ministry of Defense, Brasilia, D.F.; Parque Central, Caracas, Venezuela
1971   Urban renovation of South area, Buenos Aires, Argentina; Sport center Chacra Saavedra, Buenos Aries, Argentina; Belgian Embassy, Brasilia, D.F., Brazil
1972   Brasilia Square, Quito, Equador
1973   Centro Administrativo da Bahia, Salvador, Bahia, Brazil
1974   Edgar Stores Limited, South Africa
1976   Estacao Morelos y Carabobo, Caracas, Venezuela; Residence of Enrique Delfino, Caracas, Venezuela
1977   Maglay Cannizaro residence, Caracas, Venezuela
1978   Rio de Janeiro International Airport, Rio de Janeiro, Brazil
1979   World Organization for Intellectual Property, Geneva, Switzerland; Organizacao dos Estados Americanos, Washington, D.C., United States; Lincoln Center, Punta del Leste, Uruguay; IBM Brasil, Rio de Janeiro, Brazil
1980   Xerox Brasil, Rio de Janeiro, Brazil; Country Club Izcaragua, Caracas, Venezuela; Banco Central, Barbados
1981   Miami port (study), Miami, Florida; Laro da Carioca, Rio de Janeiro, Brazil
1982   Citibank, Rio de Janeiro, Brazil; Paseo del Lago, Maracaibo, Venezuela; Alcoa, São

Luís, Maranhão, Brazil; Banco Central do Paraguai, Assuncao, Paraguay; Oleta River leisure center (study), Miami, Florida

1983 Banco do Nordeste do Brasil, Fortaleza, Ceara, Brazil

1986 Parque Nacional Canaima, Venezuela; Sherwin Williams do Brasil, São Paulo, Brazil; Botanic Garden (preliminary plan), Louisville, Kentucky, United States

1988 Biscayne Boulevard, Miami, Florida; Henry Lord Boulton residence, Caracas, Venezuela; Plant Exhibition (preliminary plan), Osaka, Japan

1992 Theater Rosa Luxemburgo square, Berlin, Germany

## Selected Publications

"A Garden Style in Brazil to Meet Contemporary Needs, with Emphasis of the Paramount Value of Native Plants," *Landscape Architecture* 44, no. 4 (1954)

"Santiago Caracol: Headquarters of the United Nations Economic Commission for Latin America," *Progressive Architecture* 47 (December 1966)

"Testimonial to Rino Levi," in *Rino Levi,* by Rino Levi, 1974

*Arte e paisagem: Conferências escolhidas,* 1987

## Further Reading

Adams, William Howard, *Roberto Burle Marx: The Unnatural Art of the Garden,* New York: Museum of Modern Art, 1991

Bardi, Pietro Maria, *The Tropical Gardens of Burle Marx,* New York: Reinhold, 1964

Carelli, Emile, "Roberto Burle Marx: Peintre du paysage," *L'architecture d'aujourd'hui* 262 (April 1989)

Eliovson, Sima, *The Gardens of Roberto Burle Marx,* New York: Harry M. Abrams/Sagapress, 1991

Frota, Lélia Coelho, *Burle Marx: Landscape Design in Brazil,* São Paulo, Brazil: Câmara Brasileira do Livro, 1994

Gregory, Frederick L., "Roberto Burle Marx: The One-Man Extravaganza," *Landscape Architecture* 71, no. 3 (1981)

James, Jamie, "Revisiting Burle Marx, Hero of the Modern Garden," *Garden Design* 76, no. 85 (1999)

Otis, Denise, "Artist of the Garden: The Extraordinary Landscape Designs of Brazil's Roberto Burle Marx," *House and Garden* 158, no. 9 (1986)

Thompson, J. William, "In Memoriam: Burle Marx," *Landscape Architecture* 84, no. 9 (1994)

Walker, Peter, and Melanie Simo, *Invisible Gardens: The Search for Modernism in the American Landscape,* Cambridge, Massachusetts: MIT Press, 1994

Walmsley, Anthony, "Burle Marx, South America: Appraisal of a Master Artist," *Landscape Architecture* 53, no. 4 (1963)

LAURI MACMILLAN JOHNSON

# Busch Family

## German Nurserymen, Gardeners, Designers, and Surveyors

### Busch, Johann ca. 1725–1795

Johann (John) Busch was born into a gardener's family probably in the service of the Prussian court in the Altmark in about 1725. He received his initial training in gardening and forestry on the grounds of Baron Grote's manor in Schnega near Lüneburg. After a probable apprenticeship at Hannover-Herrenhausen, he made a trip to the Netherlands and Great Britain in 1744, where he must have come in contact with Philip Miller, the English botanist and curator of the Chelsea Physic Garden. In May 1750 he married Anne Plant in London, who bore him eight children, including Joseph, his successor, and Catherine, who married the architect

Charles Cameron. In 1753 he moved to Hackney, where he opened a nursery.

In 1758 Daniel August Schwarzkopf, later to become gardener at Kassel-Wilhelmshöhe, recommended Busch's nursery to his patrons Christian Daniel von der Schulenburg and Friedrich August von Veltheim. Together with Otto von Münchhausen, these men created the German landscape garden by integrating foreign forest trees into a natural layout. Seeds and sometimes plants could be ordered from Busch, who acted as intermediary, getting American seed-boxes from John Bartram via Peter Collinson. At the end of the 1760s he was the most important English source for foreign plants and seeds in German gardens and forests. His trees could be found in many early landscape gardens such as those at Schwöbber (1760), Rheinsberg (1760), Karlsruhe (1765), and Darmstadt (1765), and he maintained contacts with forest specialists such as Carl Christoph Oelhafen von Schoellenbach, Johann Georg von Langen, Friedrich August von Burgsdorff, and Hans von Carlowitz.

Essential to his success were the translation of Miller's *Gardeners Dictionary* into German in 1750 and 1751 and Münchhausen's *Der Hausvater* (1765–71), which introduced the concept of a landscape garden strongly focused on forestry. Busch offered a wide selection of different species and, in addition, was able to correspond with his clients in their native language. Some gardeners were sent to him for training as botanical gardeners, among them Johann E.A.B. Petri, Johann Andreas Graefer, D.A. Schwarzkopf, and Neuholtz. Most of this information may be found in the correspondence collected at the Harbke archive (County Archive Sachsen-Anhalt, Wernigerode).

In 1771 Busch won the competition for a position as court gardener for Kolomenskoye, near Moscow, ahead of Thomas Cloase (Hampton Court) and a gardener known only as Reeve from Bristol. That same year he sold his nursery to the German Conrad Loddiges, who developed it into the world's largest nursery.

He was sent to Tsarskoye Selo, site of one of the Russian royal family's summer palaces, where, since 1768, Catherine II had been intending to remodel her baroque gardens according to Münchhausen's designs. The work had started in 1770 under the architect Vassili Neyelov and his sons Ivan and Piotr. When Busch took over in the spring of 1772, the gardens were developed in the *anglo-chinois* style, as a 1778 print shows. Most of the garden design, especially the architecture, was heavily influenced by the empress herself, who in turn was guided by William Chambers's thoughts and supported by Voltaire. With the appointments of Charles Cameron and Giaccomo Quarenghi in 1779, the concept of the garden was simplified, made more spacious and more English in character. A familiar and very representative 1789 print shows the state of the garden in 1785-86. Along with the architects, Busch collaborated with his Peterhof colleague James Meader (active from 1779 to the 1790s) and the botanist Peter Simon Pallas. In Russia he was a mediator between English, Russian, and German plant lovers, was responsible for promoting the empress's modern idea of a landscape garden, had great success in greenhouse production, and was one of the first in Russia to cultivate tea. He also hosted several well-known visitors, such as Joseph II of Austria, the Princess of Darmstadt, Potemkin, the Earl of St. Vincent, Ambassador James Harris, and other notables. Being a botanical gardener, his main achievements were the translation of the traditional English landscape garden into the inclement weather and botanically difficult situation in Russia. The successful "experiment" of Tsarskoye Selo was followed by a rash of English gardens all over Russia.

In 1786 Busch traveled to England and Germany, leaving his position to his son Joseph. In 1789 he moved to England for good, where he built a house (today Busch House) on the grounds of Sion House in Isleworth near London. He died in May of 1795. He was still in contact with several nurserymen, including John Bell, possibly Joseph Banks, and the Duke of Northumberland, who seems to have supplied several of the Russian gardeners. According to the Scottish author and designer John Claudius Loudon, Busch is supposed to have introduced *Alnus incana*, several kinds of *Rhododendron*, and the flourishing currant to England.

*See also* Tsarskoye Selo

**Biography**

Born in Germany, ca. 1725. Apprenticeship in Schnega (Lüneburg) and perhaps in Hannover-Herrenhausen; journey to Netherlands and England, 1744; probably studied under Philip Miller; married, 1750; opened own nursery in Hackney, London, ca. 1753; procured seeds and plants for German market, to 1771; instructed German gardeners; gardener to Catherine II of Russia, working in Tsarskoye Selo and Pulkovo, 1771; initially worked with architect Neelov, then, after 1779, with G. Quarenghi and C. Cameron; chiefly responsible for planting, layout, and procuring plants and fruits; moved to England, 1789 built a house in Ilseworth, Middlesex. Died in Ilseworth, Middlesex, 1795.

**Selected Designs**

| | |
|---|---|
| 1771–75 | Work on Pulkovo, St. Petersburg |
| 1771–89 | Work on Tsarskoye Selo |
| 1780– | Work at Gatshina, possibly as a surveyor |
| 1784 | Work at Babolovski |
| 1785–89 | Work at Pella as a surveyor |

**Selected Publications**

*Catalogus von Bäumen und Pflanzen, so in Lustwälder gepflanzet werden . . .* , 1759

# Busch, Joseph 1760–1838

The first time Joseph Busch came to light as a major gardener was on his journey to England and Scotland in 1783, carrying a recommendation from Peter Simon Pallas, to meet Joseph Banks and the nurseryman John Bell at Isleworth. He was described by his colleague James Meader as being shy and humble. Nevertheless, he did well representing his father during the latter's absence in 1786, also working at the new residence, Pella.

Catherine II was very impressed by his skill, so much so that he was named his father's successor in 1789. He was responsible for Babolovski Park and Pulkovo as well and also partly for the park-village Sophia in Tsarskoe Selo. He undertook minor alterations in Tsarskoye Selo and in the 1790s was primarily engaged in laying out the gardens around Alexander Palace, a residence built by Giaccomo Quarenghi between 1792–96, including lakes, a cascade, flower borders, and a ha-ha. In 1793 Busch married Sarah Gordon (died, 1803); the couple had three children. Busch fathered four more children with his second wife Mary Ann Pitt. Alexander I granted him a dacha in 1800 and a pension of 2000 rubles in 1809. He probably spent the French occupation (1811–16) in London, where his sister Catherine, wife of Charles Cameron, died in 1817. He left his position in Tsarskoye Selo in 1816–18, selling his shell and mineral collection to the Lyceum (a school for the offspring of the Russian nobility) there, and started to lay out the grounds around the imperial villa constructed by Carlo Rossi at Jelagin Island near the city center of St. Petersburg. The work ended in 1826, leaving grounds that reveal a picturesque style reminiscent of that of the English landscape designer Humphry Repton: flowers in the pleasure garden, greenhouses, and varied topography.

In 1826 Busch retired with a pension of 4000 rubles. Between 1828–30 he worked on the grounds of the Theater at Stone Island opposite Jelagin Island. In 1830 he started to design the Forest Academy at St. Petersburg with its well known aboretum. After his official retirement in 1836, he died in St. Petersburg on 24 March 1838. His work in Rotchesalm (1795), Michailovski Palace (St. Petersburg), and Petrovksi Park (Oranienbaum) are apocryphal.

Busch inherited the widespread contacts, especially to his German colleagues and Conrad Loddiges, from his father. Moreover he was very interested in botany. According to the *Botanical Cabinet,* he introduced *Serratula* species from Persia (1804), *Robinia jubata* (1796), and also *Lillium bushianum,* which was first cultivated at Loddiges's nursery in 1829.

He must have had several pupils, although only two gardeners are known to have worked with him in Tsarskoye Selo, Thomas William Grey (1789) and Charles Manners (1810). Although his work is rather limited in scope, he seems to have carried on in his father's tradition: bringing the rather romantic style of gardening into the Russian gardens, especially using smaller patterns, often supplemented by flowers.

*See also* Tsarskoye Selo

## Biography

Born in London, 1760. Moved to Russia with his family, 1771; apprenticed to his father, 1778; journeyed to England and Scotland, 1783; substituted for his father during father's absence, 1786, succeeding him in 1789; surveyor of Tsarskoye Selo, Babolovski Park, and Pulkovo; highly esteemed by Emperor Alexander I; flight to England during the French occupation; returned to Russia, ca. 1816; started to lay out Jelagin Island, 1817; retired 1826 but still engaged to design the grounds around the theater at Stone Island, 1828–30, possibly Michailovski Palace, and St. Petersburg Wood Academy, 1830; pensioned in 1836. Died in St. Petersburg, 1838.

## Selected Designs

| 1790s | Alexander Palace, Tsarskoye Selo, Russia |
| | Sophia, Tsarskoye Selo, Russia |
| 1817–30s | Jelagin, St. Petersburg, Russia |
| 1828–30 | Theater garden at Kammenii-Ostrov, Stone Island, St. Petersburg, Russia |
| 1830 | Forest Academy, St. Petersburg, Russia |

## Selected Publications

"Obst in Rußland," *Neues Allgemeines Garten Magazin* (1827)

## Further Reading

Bronshtein, Samuel Solomonovich, *Arkhitektura goroda Pushkina* (Architecture of the Town of Pushkin), Moscow: Gosudarstvennoe Arkhitekturnoe Izdatelstvo Akademii Arkhitektury SSSR, 1940

Call, Martin, "History of the First Introduction of the Modern Style of Laying Out Grounds into Russia, with Some Account of the Imperial Residences of Tzarsco Celo and Taurida: By One of the Imperial Gardeners," *The Gardeners Magazine* 2, no. 8 (July 1827)

*Catherine the Great and Tsarskoe Selo* (exhib. cat.), Aalborg: Aalborg Historical Museum, 1992

Cross, Anthony, "Catherine the Great and Whately's Observations on Modern Gardening," *Study Group on Eighteenth-Century Russia* 18 (1990)

Cross, Anthony, "The English Garden in Catherine the Great's Russia," *Journal of Garden History* 13, no. 3 (1993)

Cross, Anthony, "Russkie Sady: Britannskie sadovniki (Russian Gardens: British Gardeners)," in *Pamiatniki istorii i kul'tury Sankt-Peterburga* (Monuments of Saint Petersburg's Cultural History), by Anna V. Kornilova, St. Petersburg: Beloe i Chernoe, 1997

Demidova, Danai, "Der Park auf der Jelagin-Insel in St. Petersburg," *Die Gartenkunst* 4, no. 2 (1992)

Dimsdale, Elizabeth, Baroness, *An English Lady at the Court of Catherine the Great: The Journal of Baroness Elizabeth Dimsdale, 1781,* edited by Anthony Cross, Cambridge: Crest, 1989

*Elagin Dvorets; Le Palais Y'elaguine,* St. Petersburg: Izdanie Imperatorskago S-P-Burskago o-ba Arkhitektorov, 1913

Iakovkin, Il'ia F., *Istoriia Sela Tsarskago v trech gastech sostavleniia is den arkhiva pravleniia Sela Tsarskago* (History of Tsarskoe Selo in Three Volumes Drawn from the Archives of Tsarskoe Selo), 3 vols., St. Petersburg, 1829–31

Köhler, Marcus, "'—Thinking Himself the Greatest Gardener in the World,' der Pflanzenhändler und Hofgärtner Johann Busch," Ph.D. diss., Free University of Berlin, 1997

Lemus, Vera V., *Pushkin, muzei i parki*, Leningrad: Lenizdat, 1980; as *Pushkin: Palaces and Parks*, translated by Boris Grudinko, Leningrad: Aurora Publishers, 1984

Nemchinova, D., *Elagin ostrov* (Jelagin Island), Leningrad: Iskusstvo Leningradskoe Otd-nie, 1982

Petrov, Anatolii Nikolaevich, *Pushkin: Dvortsy i parki* (Pushkin: Palaces and Parks), Leningrad: Iskusstvo, 1964

*Sadovo-parkovoe iskusstvo Leningrada* (The Art of Leningrad Gardens and Parks; exhib. cat.), Leningrad: Stroiizdat Leningradskoe Otdelenie, 1983

Shvidkovskii, Dmitri Olegovich, *The Empress and the Architect: British Architecture and Gardens at the Court of Catherine the Great*, New Haven, Connecticut: Yale University Press, 1996

Solman, David, *Loddiges of Hackney, the Largest Hothouse in the World*, London: Hackney Society, 1995

Vil'chkovskii, Sergei, *Tsarskoe Selo*, St. Petersburg: Golike i Vil'borg, 1911

Vitiazeva, V.A., *Nevskie ostrova: Elagin, Krestovskii, Kamennyi* (Neva Islands: Elagin, Krestovskii, Kamennoi), Leningrad: Khudozhnik RSFSR, 1986

MARCUS KÖHLER

---

# Bushy Park. *See* Hampton Court Palace and Bushy Park

---

# Buttes Chaumont

## Paris, France

**Location:**   19th arrondissement, near Métro stations Buttes Chaumont and Botzaris

The Parc des Buttes Chaumont, located in the northeastern section of Paris, opened to the public on 1 April 1867, in conjunction with the opening of the celebrated Exposition Universelle. The park exemplified the exposition's themes of art and industry, befitting its intended role as one of the main attractions of the exposition. (Due to its distance from the city center, however, this role went mainly unfulfilled.) At the park, the conceptual ideas influencing the art of Picturesque landscape design are manifested by the design team's use of contemporary French industry in the technology and materials.

Located in one of the working-class suburbs annexed in 1859, the 62-acre (25-ha) park was a major element in Napoléon III's urban-design campaign. Baron Georges Haussmann, the prefect of the Seine, oversaw numerous projects throughout the city, all of which supported Napoléon III's desires to create an image of Paris

that outshone other European capitals of the time. The projects introduced verdant park spaces and sophisticated boulevards and squares. The city of Paris and local investors benefited from the cachet of increased beauty and the rise in real estate values for properties adjacent to the improvements. In addition, Napoléon III's motives acknowledged the contemporary idea that urban green spaces helped cleanse the city and offered the calming and salubrious influences of "nature" to the citizenry. In these goals the Parc des Buttes Chaumont can be seen in a larger international context of urban parks that include Birkenhead Park (Liverpool, ca. 1845); Central Park (New York City, ca. 1857–65), and Prospect Park (Brooklyn, New York, ca. 1866–67).

A design team headed by the chief engineer and landscape designer J.-C.-A. Alphand created the Parc des Buttes Chaumont. Horticulturist Jean-Pierre Barillet-Deschamps and the architect Gabriel Davioud also contributed significantly to the park's design and appearance. It owes some of its conceptual intent to the

Buttes Chaumont, Paris, France
Copyright Juan Luis de las Rivas Sanz

landscaped gardens of Great Britain that Napoléon III had seen but also much to precedents Alphand derived from Gabriel Thouin's *Plans raisonnées de toutes les espéces de jardin* (1819; Analytical Plans for All Gardening Spaces) as well as from the work of Prince Pückler-Muskau in Germany, whose treatise *Andeutungen uber landschaftsgartnerei* (1834; Hints on Landscape Gardening) Alphand knew well. More directly, the park's design responds to or is informed by three key factors: the site itself, the conceptual ideas of the Picturesque, and the technology employed to produce the park. These three ideas are present in all significant aspects of the park, including the treatment of the topography, the circulation system, the planting, and

the details of material and construction for drainage, water features, bridges, and structures.

Reflecting the Parisian topography, the site boasts one of the highest points in the series of hills and ridges surrounding the lower basin of the Seine and the Isle de la Cité. The site comes into the historical record as the location of the Montfaucon gallows, where many well-known Parisian citizens met their deaths. It also served as a battlefield and later as the location for at least six windmills. In addition, the site's geologic formation of stone and gypsum sustained for many years a quarrying operation. Prior to its acquisition by the city of Paris in 1862, the residual quarry spaces were a dump for the city's "night soils."

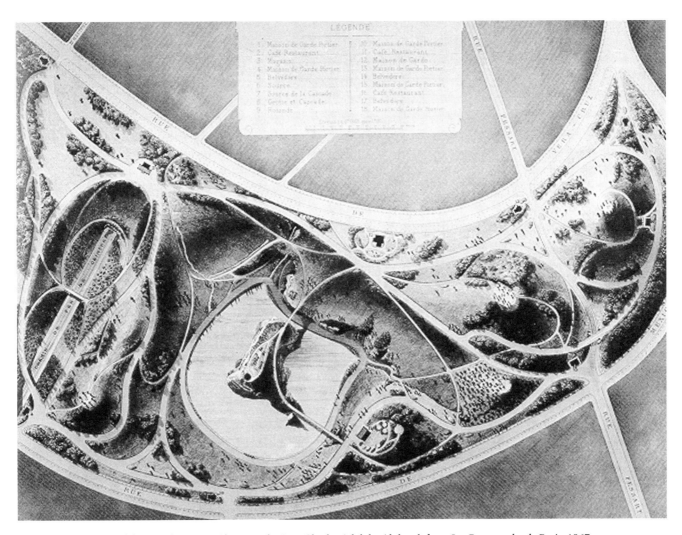

Plan of the Parc des Buttes Chaumont by Jean-Charles Adolphe Alphand, from *Les Promenades de Paris*, 1867
Courtesy of Ann E. Komara

The design team scripted a Picturesque park whose features and layout celebrated the physical vestiges of this site. The quarried landscape became a smoothly sculpted series of four high points whose slopes undulate across the site as they dip to the two-acre (0.8 ha) lake. The quarry cuts and remnants inspired an island in the lake crowned with a copy of the Temple of Sibyl at Tivoli, a celebrated grotto filled with stalactites and a water cascade, and two sets of fissured rock "seams" that appear as natural channels for the elaborate new water rills and small pools.

Planted boulevards bound the site, and the main entrances to the park reflect some of the preexisting street pattern. Within the park, however, Alphand scripted a new circulation system of macadam carriage roads, bridges, and underpasses, concrete promenades, and crushed stone walking paths that he carefully overlaid on the reformed landscape. The experience of the park is largely perceived by moving along these routes—up and down, across and around the site in sweeping arcs through an ever-changing series of choices and directions. As the visitor moves through the park, the vistas and scenes shift as the eye is directed from lush plantings to open lawn spaces and features within the park, then to panoramas and distant views of the surroundings.

These constructed views, so much a part of the Picturesque idiom, are fully enhanced by Barillet-Deschamps's planting and use of decorative horticulture. Barillet-Deschamps trained at the Jardins des Plantes and then set himself up as a landscape architect at Bordeaux. Alphand brought him to Paris around 1860, and they worked closely together on several parks. Barillet-Deschamps's work characteristically featured specimen trees positioned at key intersections of the paths, sweeping masses and clumps of shrubs and lawns, and detailed planting beds at the water rills and entrances. The plant palette at the Parc des Buttes Chaumont reflects the city nursery cultivation system initiated by Alphand and Barillet-Deschamps. Trees included many exotic and imported varieties, such as hardy orange, Lebanon cedar, ginkgo, tulip tree, monkey puzzle tree, and Japanese pagoda tree. Native species were interspersed to cover slopes, hide sections of shoreline, and line certain promenades. Hothouse-cultivated tender annuals were also planted, including begonia, coleus, fuchsia, and hibiscus. The planting scheme overall served to frame spaces, direct sight lines, and provide focal points.

In addition to the sophisticated palette of exotica, the designers made use of contemporary technology to create the park. The most notable innovations show up in the park's circulation and hydrologic systems. Elaborate drainage systems directed the water through the site and into one of the new sewers installed by the engineer Eugène Belgrand. The elaborate water features were fabricated and the lake created with a newly introduced cement that could be cured wet and withstand water. The water supplied by the Canal de L'Ourcq to the north was brought via hydraulic pump to an off-site reservoir and then pumped into the site. Iron-reinforced concrete appears throughout the park, in everything from handrails made to simulate wood to the structured concrete work of the grotto and the island. The suspension bridge itself, as well as the rockery created to mask the supporting side-cable connections, also feature and show off contemporary materials and technologies. In short, the work of Alphand and his design team at the Parc des Buttes Chaumont is a highly successful melding of Picturesque landscape aesthetics, site reclamation for urban park development, and modern materials and technology.

## Synopsis

| | |
|---|---|
| 13th C. | Gallows of Montfaucon constructed on site |
| 15th C. | Under name "Central Quarry," extraction operations for stone and gypsum used in plaster of Paris began; windmills appeared atop buttes |
| 18th C. | City of Paris began dumping waste and refuse into site |
| 1860 | Quarrying ceased |
| 1862 | City of Paris declares use of public funds to acquire site; 27 hectares (67 acres) acquired for creation of park |
| 1863 | Alphand and team begin designing park |
| 1864 | Earth moving and site construction began shaping features and form of park, including circulation routes and water systems |
| 1865 | Planting commences; Napoléon III visits site |
| 1867 | Construction of reservoir for water supply finished; park inaugurated 1 April |
| 1869 | Davioud oversees completion of Temple of Sibyl atop island |
| 1871 | Communards occupy park as final stronghold in uprising; ammunition stored in Grotto catches fire |
| 1988 | City of Paris reopens newly restored Grotto and waterworks, which had been closed since World War II due to deterioration |
| 1999 | City of Paris reopens restored suspension bridge |

## Further Reading

Alphand, Adolphe, *Les promenades de Paris: Histoire-description des embellissements-dépenses de création et d'entretien des Bois de Boulogne et de Vincennes, Champs-Élysées-parcs-squares-boulevards-places plantées, etude sur l'art des jardins et arboretum,* 3 vols., Paris, 1867–73; reprint, Princeton, New Jersey: Princeton Architectural Press, 1984

Conan, Michel, and Isabelle Marghieri, "Figures on the Grass: The Public Gardens of Paris," *Landscape* 31, no. 1 (1991)

Ernouf, Alfred Auguste, *L'art des jardins,* Paris, 1868; 3rd edition, 1886

Grumbach, Antoine, "The Promenades of Paris," *Oppositions* 8 (Spring 1977)

Jarrassé, Dominique, "Le bouquet de Paris: Les jardins publics parisiens au XIX siècle," *Monuments Historiques* 42 (December 1985–January 1986)

Marceca, Maria Luisa, "Reservoir, Circulation, Residue: J.C.A. Alphand, Technological Beauty, and the Green City," *Lotus International* 30 (1981)

Merivale, John, "Charles-Adolphe Alphand and the Parks of Paris," *Landscape Design* 123 (August 1978)

Meyer, Elizabeth K, "The Public Park As Avante-Garde (Landscape) Architecture: A Comparative Interpretation of Two Parisian Parks, Parc de la Villette (1983–1990) and Parc des Buttes Chaumont (1864–1867)," *Landscape Journal* 10, no. 1 (Spring 1991)

Pinkney, David H., *Napoleon III and the Rebuilding of Paris,* Princeton, New Jersey: Princeton University Press, 1958

Robinson, William, *The Parks, Promenades, and Gardens of Paris: Described and Considered in Relation to the Wants of Our Own Cities,* London, 1869; reprint, London: Murray, 1976

Schenker, Heath Massey, "Parks and Politics during the Second Empire in Paris," *Landscape Journal* 14, no. 2 (1995)

Strauss, M. Paul, "M. Alphand et les travaux de Paris," *Revue Politique et Litteraire: Revue Bleue* 48 (1891)

ANN E. KOMARA

# Byzantium

The Byzantine enthusiasm for gardens is apparent everywhere. Depictions of vegetation abound in churches, whether as formal paradisiacal compositions (chiefly in the sixth and seventh centuries) as background to biblical scenes, or simply as decorative elements; and significantly, trees and flowers were also portrayed in polychromatic marble veneer. Manuscripts are often veritable gardens in themselves with vegetal section dividers, canon tables festooned with flowers and often supporting trees, fountains, and birds, while their illuminations show vegetation even in the unlikely setting of the desert. Most Byzantine literary genres delight in descriptions of plants, both in the wild and under cultivation, and agricultural and horticultural metaphors, such as marriage as a form of grafting. Gardening was considered a gentlemanly pursuit: the scholarly patriarch Photios carried out horticultural experiments in the ninth century, and various emperors, perhaps influenced by Roman and contemporary oriental belief in gardens as symbols of power, concerned themselves with designing palatial landscapes, most notably the impatient Constantine IX Monomachos (1042–55). There were localities in and around the capital known as "Little Park," "Cypress Plantation," "Beautiful Field," and so forth, and in late 13th- and early 14th-century Macedonia, even male peasants could boast floral first names such as "Flowery," "Rose," and "Clover," while "Gardener" is found as an occupational surname (earlier, an Isaurian saint had been known as "Konon the Gardener"). This enthusiasm for gardens was a Roman inheritance fortified by Christianity. The biblical injunction of Jeremiah, "Plant gardens and eat their produce" (29:5–29:28; the word *garden* is a Greek addition to the Hebrew) and the agricultural imagery of many New Testament parables ennobled the monastic kitchen gardens, while the tradition of the Garden of Eden as the original God-given home of mankind, along with the early Church Fathers' emphasis upon the glories of God's natural creation, ennobled the aesthetically designed pleasure gardens.

Nonetheless, precise knowledge of Byzantine gardens is so elusive that until the 1990s no substantial attempt had been made to delineate them. Art can provide not a single depiction devoted simply to a garden but only details, and these often borrowed, in other scenes. Moreover, after the early centuries, most representations of trees and flowers are simply generic or even at times completely fanciful. Byzantine literature, although indulgent towards paradise and the imaginary gardens in romances, vouchsafes only five descriptions more than just a few lines long of real gardens, all with an eye to literary artistry rather than factual portrayal; and as in the visual arts, references are often generic rather

than specific. Even the *Geoponika*, a lengthy agricultural manual with horticultural sections, must be read with caution since it is a 10-century compilation of the wisdom largely of late antiquity, although one chapter does specifically address the Constantinopolitan climate. Continued occupation of most Byzantine settlements has resulted in scanty archaeological evidence apart from the tracing of irrigation and terracing, most notably in monastic gardens in Judaea and, to a lesser extent, in the gardens of the capital itself.

A chronological survey of Byzantine gardens is, in the present state of knowledge, impossible. What evidence we have, however, renders it safe to assume that in the early centuries the tradition of Roman gardens persisted, at least for the upper classes. While barbarian invasions into the western parts of the empire forced owners to transform their rural villas with extensive gardens into fortified strongholds, those in the generally more settled areas of the east could afford to be less defensively minded. However, Persian and later Arab and Turkish incursions had their increasing effect there too, and in Middle and Late Byzantium, few large gardens are known, and these are mainly in and around the capital. Meanwhile the Roman peristyle garden had disappeared, and many smaller houses did not boast even a small courtyard.

About the gardens of peasants' houses virtually nothing is known. It seems that they could either adjoin the house or be on the periphery of the village, and they were primarily utilitarian. It is, however, hard to imagine that some did not have a few pots of herbs and a trellis of vines to provide fruit and shade. Monasteries had their own productive gardens, while market gardens, often leased from monasteries but at a distance from them, supplied cities in their vicinity. The range of vegetables was extensive (although not all were available in any one locality) and mention may be found of cabbage, kale, kohlrabi, broccoli, lettuce (many kinds), spinach, orach, endive, rocket, artichoke, leek, celery, bean (many kinds), chick-pea, chickling, lentil, asparagus, pumpkin, cucumber and other gourds (including melon), turnip, parsnip, beetroot, mangold-wurzel, carrot, rape, purslane, chicory, onion, garlic, radish, lupine, mallow, and eggplant. Gardens devoted solely to the growing of herbs are not mentioned, but the following herbs occur in the *Geoponika* and other literary sources: basil, marjoram, rosemary, savory, coriander, saffron, dill, rue, fenugreek, cress, mallow, fennel, mint, borage, costmary, squill, mustard, tarragon, parsley, cumin, smilax, salsify, and monk's rhubarb. Byzantine interest in herbs is shown also by the numerous and frequently illustrated manuscripts of the 1st-century A.D. herbal of Dioscorides.

Pleasure gardens were chiefly in the cities and nearby estates. Urban houses, except those of the rich, usually possessed little vegetation apart from herbs and perhaps small trees in pots or tubs in the small serviceable courtyard and additional trees in tubs to create roof gardens, of which later illuminated manuscripts especially give not inconsiderable witness. The 10th-century poet John Geometres gives two epistolary descriptions of his own garden in the center of Constantinople, but unfortunately he writes of it only in general terms, being concerned to prove it superior to the Homeric garden of Alcinous. He does boast, however, that it is not sunken (thus suggesting that some gardens were) and also specifies a vine on a trellis, a pear tree and a triple-crowned bay. His garden is not central in his house but separated from the road only by a wall over which hang fruit-laden branches enjoyed by passersby. A garden described in a poem by the early 14th-century statesman and scholar Theodore Metochites belongs rather to a mansion. It contains a chapel, bath, lawns, artificial watercourses, antique statuary, and Theodore's particular pride, a circular, shaded path paved and sprinkled with lime dust for walking and riding.

Most is known about palatial gardens, although specific information is, again, sparse. Like the country villas of Roman grandees, the Great Palace in Constantinople was a complex of buildings (public and residential, churches, baths, and pavilions) interspersed with colonnades, an orchard, a pool, a sports ground, and pleasure gardens, all set on terraces sloping down to the Sea of Marmora. The gardens could be small and secluded, like the Mesokepion, but the Mangana, measuring some half-mile in length, was large and open. Although these gardens contained lawns, flowerbeds, and trees, the sources expatiate on the fountains and automata (mechanical figures of birds and animals usually activated hydraulically), which had their origin in the Greco-Roman world and were in the 9th and 10th century the subject of rivalry between the imperial and caliphal courts. The Mystic Fountain of the Trikonchos Palace within the Great Palace spouted water—or spiced wine at receptions—through the jaws of bronze lions. One fountain in the Mesokepion poured water through a perforated sculpted pinecone, while another used as conduits both a similar pinecone and bronze cocks, goats, and rams. There were also trees of gilded bronze whose branches were filled with birds enabled hydraulically to emit appropriate sounds.

Again following Roman tradition, nobles and especially emperors had suburban palaces, notably on both sides of the Bosporos and along the Sea of Marmara. These were intended to provide relief in summer from the heat and bustle of the city. Historical anecdotes, however, also support a belief in the claim of the *Geoponika* that "the circumambient air, because it is infected by the exhalations of the plants, may make the house salubrious" and aid in "recuperation from diseases." Imperial game parks, some such as the Philopation and that at Aretai even within sight of the capital, provided not only sport but often also relaxation in buildings in a garden setting.

Finally, just as gardens and groves might be associated with pagan temples, so urban churches sometimes provided a fountain and were surrounded by lawns, flowerbeds, alleys of trees, and paths for the enjoyment of the public.

The layout of pleasure gardens was to some extent dictated by the watercourses, but there is no evidence for the Islamic quadripartite arrangement of the *chaharbagh* representing the four rivers of paradise. These gardens were designed to be enjoyed from both inside the grounds themselves and from within their associated buildings. If the gardens were big enough, care was taken that strolling visitors should encounter different vistas. Michael Psellos, in a somewhat satirical account of the enthusiasm of Constantine IX, refers to the transportation of good soil to barren sites, the removal of hills, the creation of new hills, and the transplanting of growing trees to create a grove. On slopes terracing was used and can actually be traced today in the Mangana garden of the Great Palace now below the Ottoman Topkapı Saray in Istanbul. Although trees were often arranged in straight rows, individual trees and clumps can also be found, while Saint Theodore of Stoudios (759–826) deliberately planted new trees between standing ones to create a crescent. Mention is made of gardens in palaces and of massed flower beds and "hanging gardens" around churches, but the *Geoponika* advises that different species be kept separate. Nevertheless, varied flowers were commonly planted between and under trees to take advantage of the shade, and irrigation channels were created in an attempt to keep the flowers from withering.

There is almost no evidence of which trees and flowers were grown in which known gardens, and it is also unclear to what extent fruit and merely ornamental or shade-giving trees were found together. Of trees and shrubs the *Geoponika* mentions pine, fir, cypress, black and white poplar, cedar, willow, tamarisk, oak, ash, elm, beech, plane, bay, myrtle, mastich, terebinth, arbutus, box, juniper, vine, olive, apple, pear, sorb, peach, apricot, citron, quince, damson, cherry, pomegranate, fig, date palm, jujube, medlar, carob, mulberry, hazelnut, almond, walnut, pistachio, and sweet chestnut, while later sources add orange, lemon, plum, and sloe. Most frequently referred to in literature are olive, myrtle, plane, and, especially, the vine, while the *Geoponika* gives information on what grows best in what soils. Flowers are far less numerous in variety. The rose was especially prized, since it could bloom at any season of the year and could be grown in rows in the ground, spiraling up trees, and in baskets or pots. Also popular were violet, narcissus, lily, and crocus, while iris, pimpernel, and for ground cover, periwinkle are also found. Ivy too was used decoratively.

The principal aims of horticulture were the extension of the growing seasons, improvement of stock by grafting, increase of yield, and enhancement of sweetness, fragrance, and color. In its arboricultural chapters the *Geoponika* sanely details propagation from seed, suckers, or cuttings (pollination was not understood); manuring; pruning; transplanting; and protecting from pests. It does, however, also include some wishful thinking: recipes are given for producing myrtle-flavored grapes (grafted onto myrtle) and white mulberries (grafted onto white poplar), trees bearing fruit with markings similar to inscriptions made on the kernels from which trees were grown, or fruit in the shape of birds, human faces, etc. (created by means of molds). The principal source of information on topiary work is manuscript illumination, which, unless it is a mere artistic convention, shows that the favored design was of two strata of outstretched branches, one at the crown and one beneath, separated by a length of bare trunk. There is no evidence for attempts to emulate classical Roman topiary excesses.

The *ekphraseis* (literary descriptions) of gardens in the romances of the 12th, 14th, and 15th centuries, where they are almost de rigueur as erotic symbols, are clearly dependent to a considerable extent upon real palatial gardens. They may thus give us a fair idea of what the Byzantines valued in their pleasure gardens. The most commonly recurring elements are: trees whispering in the wind and intertwining their branches to form shady arbors; roses and other flowers, often vernal and unfading; a gentle breeze to rustle leaves, sway branches, and waft scents; singing birds; an enclosing wall; a fountain, often elaborate and sometimes with automata; pavilions; statues; mosaics and paintings in buildings; and a shrine (a survival from pagan romances) or chapel.

## Further Reading

Barber, C., "Reading the Garden in Byzantium: Nature and Sexuality," *Byzantine and Modern Greek Studies* 16 (1992)

Brubaker, L., and A.R. Littlewood, "Byzantinische Gärten," in *Der Garten von der Antike bis zum Mittelalter,* edited by M. Carrol-Spillecke, Mainz, Germany: Von Zabern, 1992

*Geoponika,* edited by H. Beckh, Leipzig, 1895; as *Geoponika: Agricultural Pursuits,* translated by T. Owen, 2 vols., London, 1805–6

Hirschfeld, Yizhar, *The Judean Desert Monasteries in the Byzantine Period,* New Haven, Connecticut: Yale University Press, 1992

Koder, Johannes, *Gemüse in Byzanz: Die Versorgung Konstantinopels mit Frischgemüse im Lichte der Geoponika,* Vienna: Fassbinder, 1993

Littlewood, A.R., "Romantic Paradises: The Rôle of the Garden in the Byzantine Romance," *Byzantine and Modern Greek Studies* 5 (1979)

Littlewood, A.R., "Gardens of Byzantium," *Journal of Garden History* 12, no. 2 (1992)

Littlewood, A.R., "Gardens of the Palaces," in *Byzantine Court Culture from 829 to 1204,* edited by Henry Maguire, Washington, D.C.: Dumbarton Oaks Research Library and Collection, 1997

Maguire, Henry, "A Description of the Aretai Palace and Its Garden," *Journal of Garden History* 10 (1990)

Maguire, Henry, "Imperial Gardens and the Rhetoric of Renewal," in *New Constantines: The Rhythm of Imperial Renewal in Byzantium, 4th–13th Centuries,* edited by Paul Magdalino, Aldershot, Hampshire: Variorum, and Brookfield, Vermont: Ashgate, 1994

Schissel von Fleschenberg, Otmar, *Der byzantinische Garten,* Vienna: Hölder, Pichler, Temkpsky, 1942

Wolschke-Bulmahn, Joachim, "Zwischen Kepos und Paradeisos: Fragen zur byzantinischen Gartenkultur," *Das Gartenamt* 4 (1992)

A.R. LITTLEWOOD

# C

## Calcutta Botanic Garden

### Calcutta, India

**Location:** on the north bank of the river Hooghly at Sibpur, Calcutta

The Calcutta Botanic Garden was founded in 1787 on a 310-acre (125.5 ha.) riverside site at the suggestion of an army officer, Colonel Robert Kyd. He became its honorary superintendent, contributing to it his own valuable collection of exotic plants. The garden's principal purpose was to introduce economic plants so as to improve the region's agriculture and also to cultivate spices in an attempt to break the Dutch monopoly of the then valuable spice trade. Eventually, the garden was to become the greatest of British imperial botanic gardens and an important center for the study of the flora of India and other tropical countries.

In 1793 Kyd was succeeded as superintendent by the first of a line of medical doctors who were also botanists. Dr. William Roxburgh, a proponent of the Linnaean layout of botanic gardens, published the first catalog of the garden's 3,500 plants, *Hortus bengalensis* (A Horticultural Flora of Bengal), in 1814 and is known as the "Father of Indian Botany" on account of his posthumously published *Flora Indica* (The Flora of India), the first systematic account of Indian native plants. There was a two-year interregnum under another Scot, Dr. Francis Buchanan Hamilton, before the Dane Dr. Nathaniel Wallich became superintendent in 1817. Wallich was a great plant hunter who explored Nepal, Assam, Burma, Java, and Singapore for new plants. He discovered in Assam and introduced to Calcutta *Amherstia nobilis*, now one of the most widely planted ornamental trees in the tropical world. He also pioneered the introduction of many Asiatic plants, including rhododendrons, to European gardens. In the late 1820s Wallich had the difficult task of steering the botanic garden through the cash-strapped period of the first Anglo-Burmese War, but the garden's herbarium and library suffered. Wallich published two important books illustrated by Indian artists, *Tentamen Florae Nepalensis Illustratae* (1824; A Tentative Illustrated Flora of Nepal) and the three-volume *Plantae Asiaticae Rariores* (1829–32; Rare Plants of Asia).

Wallich was succeeded in 1846 by Dr. Hugh Falconer, a paleontologist, and in 1855 by Thomas Thomson (joint author with Sir Joseph Hooker of the first volume of the *Flora of British India*). The garden's curator and second-in-command during this period was John Scott, a noted correspondent of Charles Darwin. Although the garden was then poorly funded, it made one notable contribution to the Indian economy. In 1851 Robert Fortune returned from his epic trip to China bringing 17,000 tea-plant seeds from Shanghai to the Calcutta Botanic Garden for distribution. These formed the basis of the Indian tea industry. Between 1861 and 1868 the garden was revived under the superintendence of Dr. Thomas Anderson. Professor of botany at Calcutta's university, Anderson was also appointed the first Conservator of Forests in Bengal and established an arboretum of indigenous trees in the botanic garden.

The garden was largely destroyed by two cyclones in 1864 and 1867 but was reconstructed under the supervision of Dr. (later Sir) George King. The layout had developed on an ad hoc basis, but now the gardens were comprehensively relandscaped with an integrated system of islanded lakes, occupying one-ninth of the garden's total area and set in undulating parklike terrain varied with plants arranged in natural groupings. King also raised the level of that part of the garden's terrain that was susceptible to periodic flooding by the river Hooghly. In 1878 a satellite garden, the Lloyd Botanic

Garden, was laid out in Darjeeling—its high elevation and rainfall make it to this day an important location for the study of East Himalayan plants. Other satellites were the chinchona plantations at Mungpoo and Munsong. (Chinchona produces quinine, the Victorian miracle cure for malaria.) An 1875 conservatory was followed in 1888 with a series of hothouses manufactured in London by Messrs. Fletcher and Lowndes. In 1882 a new herbarium building was built, which was recorded in 1890 as containing 50,000 mounted specimens. The garden also undertook the publication of scholarly botanical research, including the magnificent journal *Annals of the Royal Botanic Gardens, Calcutta* and from 1893, the series *Records of the Botanical Survey of India.*

In 1897 a military doctor, Major (later Sir) David Prain succeeded as superintendent. He had previously been keeper of the garden's library and herbarium. Prain built on King's work, devising a new geographical plan for the garden's future plantings. The plan was described in 1938:

> The scheme adopted 34 years ago was to treat the garden as a map of the world on Mercator's projection, representing the tropical floras. The plants of India and Burma are to occupy the central triangular area of the large western part of the garden, this area being again subdivided in accordance with the geographical subdivisions of the Indian Empire. To the west and south-west of the large central Indian area are the divisions for north-west Asia, Europe, the Americas, Africa and Madagascar, and to the east of it the divisions for north-east Asia, China, Japan, the Philippines, Siam and Annam, the Malaya Peninsula and Archipelagio and Australasia, the last five being separated from the central Indian divisions by the special collections of palms, screw-pines and bamboos.

Prain was appointed director of the Royal Botanic Garden, Kew, near London in 1905 and was succeeded by A.T. Gage (1906–23) and C.C. Calder (1922–37), who further improved the garden. The first Indian to be appointed superintendent was Dr. Kalipada Biwas in 1937. By 1938 there were about 15,000 trees and shrubs representing 2,500 species in the open garden, as well as several thousand herbaceous species in the palm houses, orchid houses and ferneries. Over ten miles (16.1 km) of tarmacadam roads traversed the garden, and for some time part of the garden also fulfilled the purpose of a zoological garden.

Many important plants, both economic and ornamental, were introduced to India through the agency of the garden. As long ago as 1814, the mahogany tree had been introduced from Jamaica, and the nutmeg tree from the Molucca Islands, as well as coffee and pimento. Later, cinnamon trees were imported from Ceylon, the camphor tree from the Cape of Good Hope, where it had been grown by the Dutch, the benzoin tree from Sumatra, and the culilawan from Amboyna in Java. Among the many economic plants imported successfully were flax, hemp, tobacco, henbane, vanilla, India rubber, cardamom, tapioca, and cocoa.

Today the giant banyan tree, planted around the time of the garden's foundation continues to be one of the principal living features of the garden as does the Royal Palm Avenue in front of the River Gate. The large Palmetum and the Victoria waterlily tank are also noteworthy. The library contains more than 25,000 volumes, and the herbarium continues to be the largest and best in India.

**Synopsis**

| | |
|---|---|
| 1787 | Foundation of garden by British East India Company |
| 1793–1813 | Superintendence of William Roxburgh, "the father of Indian botany" |
| 1851 | Introduction of tea-plant (*Camellia sinensis*) seeds from Shanghai |
| 1867 | Virtual destruction of garden by major cyclone |
| 1871–97 | Comprehensive redesign under superintendence of George King |
| 1878 | Foundation of satellite Lloyd Botanical Garden in Darjeeling |
| 1937 | Appointment of Kalipada Biwas, first Indian superintendent |

**Further Reading**

*Annals of the Royal Botanic Garden, Calcutta,* Calcutta, 1887

Desmond, Ray, *The European Discovery of the Indian Flora,* Oxford and New York: Clarendon Press, 1992

McCracken, Donal P., *Gardens of Empire: Botanical Institutions of the Victorian British Empire,* London and Washington, D.C.: Leicester University Press, 1997

Nayar, M.P., editor, *Network of Botanic Gardens,* Calcutta: Botanical Survey of India, 1987

PATRICK BOWE

# Cameron, Charles ca. 1741–ca. 1811

## Scottish Architect and Landscape Architect

The architect and landscape architect Charles Cameron, of Scottish descent, went to Russia in 1779 to serve as the court architect for Catherine the Great (1729–96) for three decades. Catherine wrote to Voltaire in 1772:

> I now love to distraction gardens in the English style, the curving lines, the gentle slopes, the ponds in the forms of lakes . . . and I scorn straight lines and twin allees. I hate fountains which torture water in order to make it follow a course contrary to nature . . . anglomania rules my plantomania. (Quoted in Shvidkovsky)

As a youth in London, Cameron served a seven-year apprenticeship to his father, a successful builder. He also learned a great deal from studying the many books in his father's collection, including Colen Campbell's fifth edition of *Vitruvius Britannicus*.

Cameron claims to have studied under Isaac Ware. More than likely, Cameron only learned what he could through Ware's friendship with his father. He also helped Ware with the Lord Burlington collection of architectural engravings by Palladio, measured drawings of Roman baths that Ware was preparing for publication (Rae). When Ware died in 1766, with the book unfinished, Cameron decided to go to Rome and remeasure the baths in order to "correct and improve" upon Palladio's measured drawings. He left for Rome in 1768 and remained there for one year, returning to London to publish his *The Baths of the Romans* in 1772. The book includes many of his own drawings and an essay on Roman architectural history. The text, in English and French, gained him much acclaim even though he only produced 50 copies. Catherine the Great hired him on the basis of his knowledge of all things Roman. She boasted that she had hired "a great designer trained in the antique manner" (quoted in Rae). In fact, Cameron had built nothing of any significance in England.

Cameron was the architect and interior designer of the palace and a portion of the grounds of Tsarskoye Selo and the Palladian palace at Pavlovsk. After Catherine's death Cameron was retained by her successor, Alexander I (1777–1825). Between 1803 and 1805 Cameron designed a number of important civic buildings in the capital, St. Petersburg.

Tsarskoye Selo (Imperial Village) is considered one of the world's greatest landscape parks. It lies 14 miles (22.5 km) south of St. Petersburg. Within this forested setting there are two royal palaces, the Yekaterinsky (Catherine Palace), in the Italian baroque style, and the neoclassical Alexandrovsky (Alexander Palace) for Alexander I. The French Grand Manner gardens of the former took up 225 acres (91 ha), while the latter measured 440 acres (178 ha). Catherine Palace was massive, with its garden facade measuring over 300 yards (274 meters) in length.

The enlightened empress was a devotee of the *jardin anglais,* or English landscape garden style. In 1771 she hired John Bush, a German-born landscape gardener who moved to England in 1744, and Vasily Ivanovich Neyelov, a Russian architect, who had studied garden design for six months in England. Between 1771 and 1780 they remodeled the park into a semblance of the English landscape garden—the first on Russian soil. Its grounds included a Palladian bridge, fashioned after the one at Wilton, England; a small shrine, called the Creaking Pavilion; a classical concert hall; a Turkish kiosk; and a small pond featuring several islands, called the Archipelago.

Cameron was hired to design several Chinese-style buildings in the manner of those depicted in Sir William Chambers's books of 1763 and 1772. These comprised the Chinese Village, the largest collection of buildings in Europe executed in that style. He also melded the geometric basins into the "natural" style Great Pond. Around that he added many monuments and obelisks, each emblematic of an important event or person in Russian history. He unified the entire ensemble of monuments already in place with his own additions via the meandering Triumphal Path.

Cameron built several structures, most important of which was the elevated Cameron Gallery, between the formal gardens and the romantic landscape garden, with commanding views of both. In the distance could be seen the model village of Sofia, also designed by Cameron.

J.C. Loudon, who visited Russia in 1813, devoted two pages to Cameron's Tsarskoye Selo in his *Encyclopedia of Gardening* (1822), pronouncing its layout and maintenance "equal to any in Europe." He called Pavlovsk "the best specimen of the English style in the [Russian] empire."

Cameron worked at Pavlovsk for Grand Duke Paul I. This palace and grounds, three miles (4.8 km) from Tsarskoye Selo, consisted of a 1,500-acre (607 ha) park, within which Cameron designed a Doric-style Temple of Friendship, the Apollo colonnade, an aviary, the Temple of Three Graces, a rustic thatch-roofed dairy, a hermitage, and a picturesque charcoal maker's hut. These sat amid dense forest greenery and spacious grassy strolling spaces; there are 15 miles (24.2 km) of paths. This place was altered many times over the years after Cameron was dismissed. Vincenzo Brenna, Pietro Gonzaga, Carlo Rossi, and Andrei Voronikhin each built structures and attempted to improve on nature in the park.

Cameron was the mentor for several aspiring young Russian architects, each of whom went on to achieve distinction in the field: Ivan Rostovtsev, Pavel Lukin, Alexsander Shmidt, Fedor Utkin, and Nikolai Rogachev.

Paul I, who never appreciated Cameron's genius because the latter never mastered the Russian language, dismissed him following the death of Catherine. He was rehired by Alexander I when Paul was assassinated in 1801. From 1803 to 1805 Cameron was the architect-in-chief to the Admiralty; he also designed many buildings for the army. Much of Cameron's career and personal life is a mystery since his possessions were all sold at auction upon his death.

*See also* Pavlovsk

## Biography

Born in Scotland, ca. 1741. Received no formal education in architecture, but honed his architectural skills while in Rome, 1768–69, measuring the Roman baths; published a collection of his etchings and measured drawings, and a selection of the plans by Andrea Palladio, titled *Baths of the Romans,* 1772; hired by Catherine the Great as her personal architect, 1779; designed many buildings for her imperial estate, Tsarskoye Selo, and her son Paul I's residence, Pavlovsk, and remodeled grounds of both in English landscape garden style; after Catherine's death, served as architect-in-chief to the Admiralty, 1803–5, when he retired. Died in St. Petersburg, Russia, 1811.

## Selected Designs

| | |
|---|---|
| 1780–87 | Tsarskoye Selo, including palace interior remodeling, Agate Pavilion, Pente-Douce, baths, colonnade (Cameron Gallery), Pyramid, Chinese bridges, the town of Sofia, St. Sofia Cathedral, Chinese Village, Temple of Memory, Post Station, and park, with its many bridges, ponds, paths and plantings, Pushkin, near St. Petersburg, Russia |
| 1781–87 | Palladian palace and grounds, including Temple of Friendship, aviary, obelisk, Memorial to Parents, Apollo colonnade, Music Pavilion, Elizabeth Pavilion, House of the Vicar, farm, dairy, a hermit's cell, and several bridges and cascades, Pavlovsk, near St. Petersburg, Russia |
| 1786–88 | Bakhtchisarai Palace, Crimean peninsula, Ukraine |
| 1796–1801 | Lialitchi Palace, Triumphal Arch in Novgorod-Seversky, and four pavilions for the Branicki family near Kiev, all in Ukraine |
| 1803–5 | Port and shipbuilding facilities, factories, lighthouses, hospitals, warehouses, and powder magazines; laid out port towns of Riga, Latvia; Revel (now known as Tallinn), Estonia; Nikolaev, Ukraine; Kherson, Ukraine; and Archangel, Russia |
| 1804–5 | St. Andrew's Cathedral, Kronstadt, Russia |
| 1805–6 | Maritime Hospital, Oranienbaum, near St. Petersburg, Russia |

## Selected Publications

*The Baths of the Romans Explained and Illustrated, with the Restorations of Palladio Corrected and Improved,* 1772

## Further Reading

Alexander, John T., *Catherine the Great: Life and Legend,* New York: Oxford University Press, 1989

Kennett, Audrey, and Victor Kennett, *The Palaces of Leningrad,* London: Thames and Hudson, and New York: Putnam, 1973

Rae, Isobel, *Charles Cameron: Architect to the Court of Russia,* London: Elek Books, 1971

Shvidkovskii, Dmitri Olegovich, *The Empress and the Architect: British Architecture and Gardens at the Court of Catherine the Great,* New Haven, Connecticut: Yale University Press, 1996

WILLIAM A. MANN

---

# Canada

It is usually possible to generalize satisfactorily about a country's gardens by reference to its geographical position and therefore its climate. To try to do so with Canada, however, is virtually meaningless due to the country's large size. Its southern boundary with the United States follows the 49 degree parallel eastward from Vancouver for nearly 2,000 miles (3,219 km) until, meeting Lake Superior, it dips steeply southeast, using the center of the

Great Lakes as the international boundary. Thus, in Lake Erie the 42 degree north latitude is reached, amazingly on a line with Marseilles and southern Oregon. Northward Canada continues to the tip of Ellesmere Island, one thousand miles (1,609 km) above the Arctic Circle.

Not surprisingly, human population and horticultural activities are concentrated along a relatively narrow band close to the Canadian/U.S. border. This still, however, encompasses a wide climatic range. On the west coast a mild maritime climate provides at Victoria on Vancouver Island, the province's capital, an average of 285 frost-free days. All other provincial capitals are far less benign; Edmonton, Alberta, for example has only 106 such days and a typical prairie climate characterized by long hard winters and hot dry summers. Farther east the continental climate of southern Ontario is somewhat moderated by the expanses of the Great Lakes. Here the Niagara Peninsular enjoys a zone 6 climate, which permits commercial orchards of peach, apricot, pear, and apple, as well as a flourishing wine industry.

The expected maritime effect of the Atlantic Ocean on such eastern provinces as Quebec and Newfoundland is almost completely nullified by the arctic Labrador Current, which delays the onset of spring and thus reduces the potential garden flora.

It is this latter climate that was first encountered, with evident disappointment, by early settlers. "Nothing," wrote John Young in one of his *Letters of Agricola* (1822), "affects philosophers with so much surprise, on the discovery of America, as the different laws to which it was subject with respect to the distribution of heat and cold." Nonetheless, the foundation of New France in the late 16th century quickly brought European garden forms and garden plants to the new land. No doubt some of the native peoples whom the newcomers encountered had an agriculture-based lifestyle, which on a small scale could be seen as horticulture, but Canada's garden aesthetic is essentially western European in origin and development.

The formality of the traditional French *potager* translated well here. Its enclosure, necessary in an unknown and possibly hostile land, and its divisions for different crops produced the pattern that can be recognized in the first illustrations of Canadian gardens. They appeared as early as 1604 in Samuel de Champlain's map of the Isle de St. Croix (in modern Nova Scotia) and later at Louisbourg on Cape Breton. A restoration of the latter may be seen today. Religious foundations soon followed, and especially in the colony's capital, Quebec. Founded in 1608, they maintained a considerable presence into the mid-19th century. Such gardens, for food, for the flowers necessary for religious observations, and for recreation, exist still at the 17th-century Sulpician seminary in Montreal. Some indication of their sophistication can be obtained from the observations of a visitor to Quebec's Hotel Dieu in 1749. Peter Kalm, a pupil of Carl Lin-

naeus, wrote of seeing "vegetables of all kinds, numerous fruit trees—pears, apples and cherries." Such gardens seemed set to continue and spread, but the second half of the 18th century changed Upper Canada (as it became) from its Gallocentricity to Anglo-Saxon domination. The Treaty of Paris of 1763 at the end of the Seven Years' War transferred ownership of French Canada and all its lands east of the Mississippi River to Britain, but less than 25 years later the United States's Declaration of Independence left Britain with only its northern possessions.

From that time, with an increase of immigrants from England and the relocation of loyalists from the south, British garden styles became paramount, as indeed became the case, with local variants, across the Western or Westernized world. The ideal of the Picturesque soon reached Upper Canada, with seats or garden pavilions placed to enjoy views artfully framed by trees, native or introduced. Such idealization was later apt to be depicted of the prairies to encourage colonization farther west, even when there were no actual trees to be seen.

In the early 19th century Reptonian ideas can be detected at the estates of prosperous merchants and of the governing elite around Montreal and York (modern Toronto). More significant and more lasting were the trends set by John Claudius Loudon and his wife Jane, aimed at a rapidly increasing middle class in Britain. The suburban *Gardener* and *Villa Companion* (John Claudius Loudon) of 1838 and *Gardening for Ladies* (Jane Loudon) of 1840 were soon as popular in North America as in England; they promoted somewhat eclectic designs and ranges of plants but also personal, hands-on gardening. Canada's promotion from colony to dominion status emphasized cultural ties with England, whose fashions throughout the Victorian and Edwardian years in gardening, as in other art forms, continued to dominate. The influence of William Robinson and Gertrude Jekyll, so strong in England, was soon seen in Canada. Ironically, many of the herbaceous species they used so enthusiastically in their sophisticated designs were indigenous to eastern North America, to be brought back across the Atlantic as garden plants. Canadians, however, did not accept all these plants with enthusiasm, still viewing with some derision, for example, the use of goldenrod (*Solidago*) in well-known English gardens.

A dependence on European trends is not surprising: settlers in a new land naturally look back to the Old Country, and success is demonstrated by creating a "home from home." In gardens this goal was early hindered in the lack of suitable plants and nurseries providing them, but by the early 19th century more were available. In York (modern Toronto) William Custead's catalog of 1829 offered trees, shrub, bulbs, and seeds, as well as tender greenhouse material.

The development of public parks coincided with the movement toward home gardening. Here again, J.C.

Loudon was influential, being credited with designing the earliest British public park in Derby in 1840. In Halifax, Nova Scotia, an existing private estate provided the site for the first Canadian public gardens in 1841. Large landscaped cemeteries also took on an amenity role, with Mount Royal in Montreal and Mount Pleasant in Toronto being especially renowned. The latter's fine collections of trees and shrubs planted in the early 20th century still act as a living textbook for students of horticulture and landscape architecture.

The public parks movement developed as cities increased in size and sophistication. Frederick Law Olmsted, renowned for his creation of Central Park, New York, worked on Mount Royal Park, Montreal, and, most significantly, on the Niagara Parkway Gardens in the 1880s. The Niagara Parks Commission, set up to administer this internationally famous site, added a school of horticulture in 1933, whose teaching collections are now designated as botanical gardens.

Capitals of the prairie provinces were not to be outdone. Most significant were the gardens established around the Houses of Parliament at Regina, Saskatchewan (known today as the Wascana Centre), and those at Saskatoon's university campus. The designer was Thomas Mawson, an Englishman, who, while traveling across Canada in 1912, obtained so many contracts that he set up an office in Vancouver with his two sons and a nephew. The then recently completed Canadian Pacific Railway that Mawson used for his transcontinental journey itself took a significant lead in promoting horticulture across the land beginning in the 1880s. By 1912, 1,500 railway stations had gardens that were supported by a staff planning unit with plant nurseries. Records of Canadian Pacific Railway station gardens provide a linear guide to successful plant growing in every climate zone that Canada experiences.

Emphasis in railway gardens and elsewhere was placed upon the colorful summer effects provided by tender annuals. This is still a Canadian habit, the traditional date for planting countrywide being 24 May—a national holiday, Queen Victoria's birthday, and the date after which spring frosts are rare. But the need for a broader garden, amenity, and economic flora was recognized early as the country was opening up, and in the last decades of the 19th century, research stations based on the existing pattern in England were established to this end. Morden and Dropmore Research Stations, both in Manitoba, concentrated on herbaceous perennials and woody plants that would accept the prairie provinces climate, where average daily minimum temperatures in winter are between 5 degrees and 13 degrees below zero Fahrenheit (15 and 25 degrees below zero Celsius). Trees for wind shelter, hardy top fruit, and ornamental shrubs were sought from comparable climates, particularly Eastern Europe and Russia. Breeding programs followed. The

Dominion Experimental Farm and its arboretum in Ottawa maintained a nationwide brief in similar terms; *Weigela, Philadelphus, Forsythia, Malus, Rosa,* and *Syringa* are among the woody genera favored. A number of *Syringa × prestoniae* cultivars celebrate their originator in Ottawa, Isabella Preston, and have been popular throughout the temperate world for half a century.

Ottawa's arboretum, as a demonstration of what can be successfully grown in a given area, is paralleled by a string of 20th-century botanic gardens across the country. Although they vary vastly in size, from a few acres to many hundreds, they are linked by their contemporary roles, an amalgam of research, education, and public amenity. Several are university departments, set up to support traditional botany, as at Edmonton and Vancouver. Montreal is a municipal foundation and Royal Botanical Gardens, although growing from the Hamilton, Ontario, parks department, it is now an autonomous cultural institution. In recent years such bodies have had a major impact on the promotion and development of home gardening in their own provinces and often beyond through educational outreach programs and their established and expanding plant collections. All have plant specializations that reflect or capitalize on their position and climate. At the University of British Columbia Botanic Garden in Vancouver, a seagirt peninsula still possessing some relict native forest is the site of an important Asian garden gathering together established as well as new wild-collected taxa from the temperate Far East. The Royal Botanical Gardens, Hamilton, possesses a world-famous *Syringa* collection with almost a thousand different species and cultivars. Collections under glass demonstrate and interpret the flora of other parts of the world. Hamilton concentrates on those areas with a Mediterranean climate (its own latitude making the link), while Montreal has adapted an ex-World Fair cycle stadium into a biodome to show a diversity of plant zones from tropics to tundra.

Home gardening has expanded greatly beginning in the last decades of the 20th century, encouraged by horticultural societies, garden clubs, and specialist plant societies. Plant introduction programs promoted by certain botanic gardens having links with the commercial trade help to extend the gardeners' palette. So too does a more sophisticated and traveled gardening public that has begun to demand more than summer annuals from garden centers and nurseries. Nurseries in turn access new plants from abroad; hardy herbaceous perennials especially, both exotic and native, have assumed considerable importance in current garden design. Such plantsmanship is even reflected in trends at departments of landscape architecture in universities such as Guelph, Toronto, and British Columbia.

European gardening traditions of France and Great Britain brought by settlers to a new land over four centuries have provided the largest influence in Canada.

However, other ethnicities have begun to add their styles and emphases. Important classical Japanese gardens exist in Montreal, Edmonton, and Vancouver, where the Sun Yet Sen Garden adds a significant Chinese dimension. Also of interest are the tiny town gardens where recently established expatriate communities from Asia and Europe have put down their first roots and added their contribution to Canada's continually expanding garden aesthetic.

*See also* Ontario, Royal Botanical Gardens

**Further Reading**

Eaton, Nicole, and Hilary Weston, *In a Canadian Garden*, Markham, Ontario: Viking, and New York: Rizzoli, 1989

Harris, Marjorie, *The Canadian Gardener: A Guide to Gardening in Canada*, Mississauga, Ontario: Random House of Canada, 1990

Paterson, Allen, *Designing a Garden: A Guide to Planning and Planting through the Seasons*, Camden East, Ontario: Camden House, 1992

Track, Norman S., *Canada's Royal Garden: Portraits and Reflections*, Toronto, Ontario: Viking, 1994

Von Baeyer, Edwinna, *A Preliminary Bibliography for Garden History in Canada*, Ottawa, Ontario: National Historic Sites and Parks Branch, Parks Canada, Environment Canada, 1983; revised edition, as *A Selected Bibliography for Garden History in Canada*, 1994

ALLEN PATERSON

# Cane, Percy S. 1881–1976

## English Landscape Architect and Writer

Percy Cane was an English landscape architect and writer who decided on his future career after a visit to Harold Peto's gardens at Easton Lodge, Essex. His international private practice was based in London from 1919 to 1972, and he carried out commissions throughout Britain, as well as in France, Austria, Greece, the United States, and Ethiopia. Cane's clients came from all walks of life, although predominantly from the wealthy middle classes. Both country house gardens and gardens in the prosperous commuter belt were typical of his working milieu. He also designed public parks and gardens for hospitals and worked on corporate commissions.

The artist Harold White illustrated Cane's design proposals from the 1920s to the 1950s. Christopher Tunnard, landscape architect and pioneer of the modern movement in gardens, and Frank Clark, landscape designer, author and teacher, were both articled to Cane from 1932 to late 1934.

In *Modern Gardens British and Foreign* (1926–27), Cane described successful garden design as "the harmonious relation of the garden to the house, and of the gardens to the surrounding scenery." In *Garden Design* (1930) he stressed again that the style of a garden should be determined by "the architectural character of the house and the natural scenery of the surrounding countryside" and that there should be "a harmonious connecting link between the two."

Cane had a sound knowledge of plants and an ability to absorb architectural styles and present sensitive designs with appropriate planting, producing workable and attractive gardens that retained their popularity. He greatly admired the aesthetics and carefully prescribed rules of Japanese gardens and wrote with authority about them. Among his favorite plants were the free spreading *Juniperus chinensis* 'Pfitzeriana', the finely cut foliage of *Acer palmatum* 'Dissectum Atropurpureum', and the large flowered white cherry, *Prunus* 'Taihaku'.

Cane skillfully combined formal and informal design features to produce a unified whole. Characteristic hallmarks of his work are immaculate, spreading lawns bordered by glades; paved rose gardens, each bed filled with one variety of hybrid tea; elegant, stone terraces surrounding the house, often including formal pools; rock gardens with flowing streams, planted with junipers, azaleas, maples, and cherries; dramatic flights of wide, shallow steps; and semicircular seats terminating vistas or placed at the end of long straight herbaceous walks, lavishly planted with perennials. In the 1950s and 1960s, these were adapted to contain chiefly shrubs to give the same effect.

Cane coined the use of the word *glade* and gave it a particular significance in the context of his garden designs as a manageable alternative to labor-intensive bedding schemes. Despite their informal appearance, his glades were meticulously proportioned with gently curving borders of ornamental trees—maples, laburnums, and cherries—and shrubs, including berberis, broom, lilac, Pfitzer juniper, viburnum, philadelphus, and weigela.

Steps of the Heath Bank at Dartington Hall, Devon, England
Copyright Charlotte Johnson

of Horticulture; ran thriving international private practice based in London, 1919–72; exhibited regularly at Chelsea Flower Show, 1921–53; eight gold, three silver-gilt medals, Chelsea Flower Shows; Royal Horticultural Society Veitch Memorial Medal, 1963. Died in Wallingford, Oxfordshire, England, 1976.

### Selected Designs

| | |
|---|---|
| 1926 | Ivy House, Hampstead, London, England |
| 1927–29 | Llanerch Park, North Wales |
| 1928–29 | Hascombe Court, Godalming, Surrey, England |
| 1929 | Bodens Ride, Ascot, Berkshire, England |
| 1935 | King's House, Burhill, Surrey, England |
| 1939 | British Pavilion, New York World's Fair, New York, United States |
| 1945–71 | Dartington Hall, Devon, England |
| 1947–48 | Falkland Palace, Fife, Scotland |
| early 1950s | Hungerdown, Seagry, Wiltshire, England |
| 1953–64 | Wetfields, Oakley, Bedfordshire, England |
| 1955 | Imperial Palace, Addis Ababa, Ethiopia |

### Selected Publications

*My Garden, Illustrated* (1916–20)
*Modern Gardens, British and Foreign*, 1926–27
*Garden Design* (1930–38)
*Garden Design of Today*, 1934
"The Gardens of Dartington Hall," *Journal of the Royal Horticultural Society* 79 (1954)
*The Earth Is My Canvas*, 1956
"Garden Design in Relation to Labour and Maintenance Costs," *Journal of the Royal Horticultural Society* 82 (1957)
*The Creative Art of Garden Design*, 1967

### Further Reading

Gunn, Fenja, "Gardens of Their Time and Ours," *Country Life* 188 (28 July 1994)
Gunn, Fenja, "Reviewing Percy Cane," *The Garden* (September 1996)
Hellyer, Arthur, "A Percy Cane Period Piece: The Garden at Westfields, near Bedford," *Country Life* 170 (2 July 1981)
Snell, Reginald, *From the Bare Stem: Making Dorothy Elmhirst's Garden at Dartington Hall*, Devon: Devon Books, 1989
Webber, Ronald, *Percy Cane, Garden Designer,* Edinburgh: Bartholomew, 1975
Webber, Ronald, "Percy Cane: International Garden Designer," *The Garden* (July 1976)

After World War II, Cane worked at Dartington Hall, Devon, where his work survives in excellent condition. Westfields, Bedfordshire, has all the characteristic Cane features at their best: a glade of flowering trees and shrubs, a rock and water garden of Westmorland stone, and a formal lily pool flanked by wide herbaceous borders and a paved rose garden.

### Biography

Born in Bocking, near Braintree, England, 1881. Educated privately; worked for Crittals window manufacturers, 1903–08; studied at Chelmsford College of Science and Art, part-time at Architectural Association, London, and Chelmsford County School

CHARLOTTE ANN JOHNSON

# Canglang Ting

## Suzhou, Jiangsu Province, China

**Location:** Renmin Road, southern district of Suzhou, approximately 50 miles (95 km) west of Shanghai

Located near the Confucian temple in the southern part of the city, Canglang Ting (the Surging-Wave-Pavilion Garden) is the oldest of all classical gardens in Suzhou. During the Song dynasty (960–1279) Su Shun-qing (1045) built a waterfront pavilion named Canglang Ting and later expanded it into a garden. According to historical accounts the original garden featured scenes of wilderness with tall man-made mounds covered with ancient trees and bamboo groves.

Following many eventful times of change, growth, desolation, and rebuilding over the centuries, Song Luo, a high governmental official of the Qing dynasty (1644–1911), rebuilt the garden in 1695. One of his key decisions was to move the Canglang Ting Pavilion, the garden's namesake, to the top of a man-made mountain. Open halls, covered corridors, and other buildings were built to face the pool in the north, while a zigzag stone bridge constructed over the water leads to the garden entrance gate. By that time foundations had already been laid for the plan of Canglang Ting as it is today.

The garden covers an area of approximately 1.1 hectares (2.71 acres). Its layout centers on a mound. While the water, which surrounds the garden on three sides, provides external scenes, buildings inside the garden proper, placed around the mountain and connected by long and zigzag corridors, form a continuous whole. For example, a double corridor along the northern periphery unifies and links the waterscapes outside and the mountain view inside by some 100 latticed windows of a variety of intricate designs.

Crossing the stone bridge and entering the garden gate, one immediately meets a tall mountain, which runs from west to the east. Piled stones cover and protect the slopes of the earthen mound on all sides. Along the slope of the mound are paths with steps. There are stone paths winding about in circles on the hill, and there is a dim and gloomy forest of trees, with indocalamus covering the soil beside the paths. The scenery appears very natural in this section of the garden. It is in fact one of the best rockery scenes in all of the gardens of Suzhou.

Encircling the hill is a winding corridor that rises and dips with the topography, and there are pavilions and waterside pavilions at key locations. At the highest point of the earthen mound is the Canglang Ting Pavilion, a simple and elegant square-shaped structure.

Noteworthy are the couplets on its stone pillars by the Song poet Liang Zhang-ju, which read: "The refreshing breeze and the bright moon are priceless; the nearby water and the distant mountain strike a sentimental note." The tablets not only help enhance the enjoyment of the garden scenes but also embody the theory of design in the context of Chinese landscape gardening.

The greatest concentration of garden architecture occurs in the south of the earthen mound. Notable halls in this cluster of buildings include Ming Dao Tang (Comprehending-the-Doctrine Hall) and Wu Bai Ming Xian Ci (Shrine of 500 Sages). In addition, Kan Shan Lou (Looking-at-the-Hill Two-Storied Building) was built for distant sceneries. To the south of the Shrine of 500 Sages, in Cuilinglong (the Delicate Emerald Hall) and its environs, tiny buildings wind about amid the bamboo grove. Here, in an obvious interpretation of a line of a verse by Su Zimei (a pseudonym of Su Shun-qing)—"Sunlight penetrating through the bamboo like an emerald delicately wrought,"—a refreshing and secluded environment is thus created.

From this point on one walks along a corridor around the southwestern corner of the small pool and then turns north and passes by Yubei Ting (the Imperial-Tablet Pavilion). Then one returns to the garden gate. To the west of the gate are several buildings, including Ouxiang Shuixie (Lotus-Root-Fragrance Waterside Pavilion), Wenmiaoxiangshi (Smelling-the-Wonderful-Fragrance Chamber), and Yaohua Jingjie (Land of Glistening-Jade). They form a courtyard by themselves.

The northern part of the mountain faces the pool. To the west is a waterside pavilion called Mianshui Xuan (Facing-the-Water Pavilion), while to the east is a square-shaped pavilion called Guanyu Chu (Place for Watching the Fish). A double corridor joins the two pavilions; on its walls tracery windows link the scenery inside and outside the garden.

The garden encompasses altogether 20 buildings, 22 plateaus and tablets, 23 parallel couplets (a Chinese literary form in which two lines of rhyming verses are written/carved on two parallel wooden or stone tablets), 153 stelae, and 12 valuable old trees, including maidenhair trees, Chinese elms, and common camellia.

### Synopsis

1044    Garden built on ruined villa owned by imperial brother-in-law Sun Cheng-you; named Canglang Ting, by the poet Su Shun-qing

1131    Ownership to General Han Shi-zhong

Canglang Ting garden, Jiangsu Province, China
Copyright Zheng Ke Jun

| | |
|---|---|
| 1546 | Major repairs by Buddhist monk Wen Ying |
| 1695 | Further reconstruction by high governmental official Song Luo, who relocates the Canglang Pavilion to top of man-made mountain |
| 1828 | As part of renovation, Tao Shu builds Shrine of 500 Sages |
| 1860 | Taiping Rebellion army destroys Shrine of 500 Sages |
| 1873 | Shrine of 500 Sages rebuilt by Zhang Shu-sheng, who also adds new constructions, such as Kan Shan Lou (Looking-at-the-Hill Two-Storied Building and Mingdao Tang (Comprehending-the-Doctrine Hall) |
| 1927 | Extensive repairs financed by Wu Zi-chen |
| 1954 | Placed under the jurisdiction of Garden Bureau of Suzhou; following extensive repairs, garden opened to public by PRC government |
| 1982 | Listed in Jiangsu Province Cultural Relics Register |

## Further Reading

Jiang, Yin-qiu, *Canglang Ting xin zi* (A New Record of Canglang Ting), Suzhou, China: Jiangsu Provincial Library Publications, 1929

Liu, Tun-chen, *Su-chou ku tien yüan lin*, Beijing: Chung-kuo Chien Chu Kung Yeh Ch'u Pan She, 1979; as *Chinese Classical Gardens of Suzhou*, translated by Chen Lixian, edited by Joseph C. Wang, New York: McGraw Hill, 1993

Wang, Xi-ye, "Canglang Ting," *Suzhou yuanlin* (Gardens of Suzhou) 2 (1996)

XU DEJIA AND JOSEPH C. WANG

# Caribbean Islands and West Indies

The Caribbean Islands stretch in an arc of 2,500 miles (4,032 km) from the same latitude as Florida south to Venezuela. The topography of the islands varies from flat, sandy terrain to high volcanic mountains, and thus there is great variety in climate and rainfall. There is an abundance of sunshine, but there are both droughts and torrential rains, and wind in the form of hurricanes can be most destructive. The rainfall can vary from the 40 inches (103 cm) of flat, sandy Antigua to the 120 inches (308 cm) of mountainous Dominica. But the rate of growth is good, and so the destruction of the growth of years can in fact be replaced comparatively quickly. The volcanoes in some of the islands are still active, and although over time volcanic activity produces good soil, it can also destroy islands, as occurred recently in Montserrat.

Several of the nations of Europe have played their part in the discovery and development of the islands, although traces of the original Arawak and Carib Indian inhabitants are still observable. Probably the greatest influence is that of Africans brought over as slaves, who,

for the last 170 years, have called the islands their own. The Spaniards and Portugese were the first Europeans to arrive, closely followed by the Dutch, then the English and French. In past centuries some of the islands changed hands as a result of wars and treaties while others remained in the possession of a single nation. St. Vincent and Dominica bear traces of their Indian past, although technically belonging mostly to England, with periods as French possessions. Barbados has always been British, Martinique and Guadeloupe always French. Cuba was Spanish. This dominance of a single nationality has led to tremendous influence on each island, even to the characteristics of its gardens and the disposition of its towns.

Many of the islands have botanic gardens. The oldest of all is that of St. Vincent, started in 1765 by the governor of the island. The interest in plants from exotic climes was at its height, and there was a dawning realization that plants from other continents might flourish as cash crops in the New World. It was during this period that breadfruit was brought from the Pacific to the West Indies

Slat house, Barbados
Copyright Jill Collett

in the hope it would feed the labor force. The botanic gardens were used to establish the newly imported plants and propagate them so that they might be distributed to the local planters, thereby encouraging new crops. Allspice, nutmeg, cocoa, coffee, and bananas were all imported, and experiments in growing cotton, arrowroot, and new strains of sugarcane were conducted.

During the 19th century, after the upheavals attendant on the abolition of slavery, there was a sense of alarm in England over the poverty of the West Indies. The botanic gardens played their part as teaching gardens for local inhabitants, as well as serving as laboratories for the growing of new experimental crops. The modern botanical gardens still contain the old trees and plants of the 19th century, but they now strive to grow their own native endangered species. There is growing concern over the destruction of habitat and of potentially useful plants that have not yet even been discovered. The ecological movement varies greatly from island to island. Grenada has already declared its extensive rain forest a national park, as have Dominica and St. Lucia. These islands are encouraging ecotourism with the creation of guided hiking trails to view the forests and some of the creatures that live in them, such as parrots, monkeys, agoutis, and iguanas. Other islands were denuded of their forests many years ago.

Farming still plays a large economic part in the life of the islands. There are still sugar estates as there have been from the 17th century, but these demand large, cleared, fairly even areas of land. On many of the islands, with their steep mountainsides, good soil occurs only in pockets. Crops such as cassava, sweet potato, peppers, tomatoes, carrots and bananas are grown in the smaller fields, while plantains are cultivated in bigger areas. Cocoa, nutmeg, and coffee grow in plantations shading each other.

The present-day gardens of the islands vary as much in character as the islands themselves. There are green lawns, a tremendous use of flowering shrubs, and lovely creeping, climbing plants. There are pools and lakes and water lilies. There are orchids and collections of palms. But it is seldom that one sees a herbaceous border, and the layout of the garden is very much influenced by the contours of the land, the depth of the soil, and the availability of water. Shade is valuable, created by large trees or shade- or "slat" houses. In these are grown ferns and orchids and other shade-loving plants. There is great skill in growing plants, and many are the verandas and porches that boast their burden of potted plants, as well as small gardens crammed with plant treasures. Hotel gardens are often designed by specialist landscape designers and make use of shrubs, trees, lawns, and in places, ground-cover plants. Private estates have gardens surrounding the houses, running seamlessly into the farmland beyond.

Commercial flower cultivation is also part of life. Much of the produce is exported—orchids and anthuriums, for example—but some is sold locally, and plant nurseries are now to be found where only a few years ago plants were only to be had by exchanging with friends.

**Further Reading**

Bannochie, Irish, and M. Light, *Gardening in the Caribbean,* London: Macmillan, 1993

Bourne, M., G.W. Lennox, and S.A. Seddon, *Fruits and Vegetables of the Caribbean,* London: Macmillan Educational, 1988

Fermor, Patrick Leigh, *The Traveller's Tree: A Journey through the Caribbean Islands,* London: Murray, 1950

Grove, Richard, *Green Imperialism,* Cambridge and New York: Cambridge University Press, 1995

North, Marianne, *A Vision of Eden: The Life and Work of Marianne North,* Exeter, Devon: Webb and Bower, and New York: Holt Rinehart and Winston, 1980

JILL COLLETT

# Caserta, La Reggia di

## Caserta, Campagnia, Italy

**Location:**  approximately 18.5 miles (30 km) north-northeast of Naples

The garden of Caserta was thought of as a Neapolitan answer to Versailles, which was also built by the Bourbons. The results were rather unusual. Architecturally, the incredibly large palace resembles the shape of the Escorial, using elements of the late Renaissance at the exterior and realizing quasi stage designs for the staircase, which was characterized by Chierici as "a rather severe classical spirit."

Luigi Vanvitelli, who published some splendid plates illustrating his ideas, proposed a rich baroque garden behind the palace, extended by an alley with waterworks. In front of the castle he envisioned an oval with a radial system of axes similar to those of Saint Peter's in Rome.

The rectangular garden with a semicircular parterre and flanking bosquets was never executed in the elaborate style shown on the plates. Because of the costs, work was started next to the palace, leaving out the alleylike cascade garden. The design itself goes back to Dézallier D'Argentville's *La théorie et la pratique du jardinage* (1709) and designs such as those supplied by Robert de Cotte for Buen Retiro (Spain) in 1714–15. The planned journey for Vanvitelli to see Versailles (1752) was never realized because he feared facing the original. In fact, the garden at Caserta as it was planned, found, as did the palace, a unique solution: the flower borders and ornaments were never executed, so that the *parterre à l'anglais* must have been one of the main features. Along with it, there are only two bosquets dedicated to special mythological subjects. The highly elaborate system of mythological themes at Versailles was answered by a common assortment of statues. An Italian particularity—the *giardino segreto*—was followed in the designs, including the fruit, orange, and vegetable gardens. Whereas in Versailles the vistas are prolonged to infinity—because of the flat terrain—the treatment of sight lines is quite different in Caserta, owing to the lay of the land.

The most remarkable achievement in the garden was not artistic but technical: the aqueduct, planned from 1753 onward, later supplied the garden with water from a distance of over 30 miles (48.3 km). The Ponte di Valle (579 yards [529 m] long and 61 yards [56 m] high)—a bridge—is the largest aqueduct erected since Roman antiquity.

The second stage in the garden's history started when Carlo Vanvitelli delivered some designs for the cascade garden, enlarging the central axis of the palace beyond the former borders to a mountain two miles (3.2 km) away. The cascade begins beyond the Hercules Bridge (Ponte di Hercole) at the Upper Fish Pond (Peschiera Superiore). Over the Cascade of Dolphins (or Canalone) from 1779, the axis reaches the Fountain of Aeolus (Fontana di Eolo). Because of an intervening public street, the cascade passed via the Sala Bridge (Ponte di Sala) to the Ceres fountain (Fontana di Cerere, or Zampiliera) of 1783. The end of the cascade is dominated by the Venus Fountain (Fontana di Venere) and the adjacent Grotto of Diana. The idea of a cascade had also been realized at Villa Lante (Bagnaia), Villa Aldobrandini, and Ludovisi (Frascati), Villa d'Este (Tivoli), and Villa Farnese (Caprarola). The wildly exaggerated form of this Renaissance concept is found only in the baroque gardens of Kassel-Wilhelmshöhe (Germany) and Caserta.

**The Grand Cascade in the garden with statues of Diana and Actaeon by Luigi Vanvitelli, Palazzo Reale, Caserta, Italy**
Copyright Alinari/Art Resource, New York

The sculptors engaged to carry out the designs included the most famous names active in Naples at the time: Salomone, Solari, Brunelli, and Persico. The fountains were rightly celebrated as outstanding examples of rococo statues at the height of this style because of the way in which they combined classicism and naturalism.

A plan of 1783 shows that there must have been a park next to the cascade garden—possibly for hunting—ornamented with some edifices such as a Capucinian Cell, a Vaccaria, and the Tower of San Leucio. The village of San Leucio, which was founded at the edge of the park, thought to be for the manufacture of silk, never fulfilled its intended function, but resembled park villages such as Sophia near Tsarskoye Selo or even the rural elements of the Versailles Hameau.

The third stage of the garden came in 1785 when Queen Maria Carolina, sister of Maria Antoinette of France, decided to have as an annex to the cascade garden a landscape garden. Although the idea of the garden can be traced back to France, the garden itself was decidedly English. William Hamilton was the appointed *direttore del progetto,* which enabled him to change the plan from a landscape garden to a botanic garden, in which Maria Carolina and her children were eventually to take botanical lessons. This must have been the reason to ask the naturalist Joseph Banks for a well-trained gardener. The unspoken idea behind the whole project must have been the unique opportunity to cultivate exotic foreign plants in the wild under Mediterranean conditions, a concept that could not be realized in Kew Gardens. Johann Andreas Graefer, a gardener born in 1746 in Helmstedt (Germany) and trained with Philip Miller and Johann Busch, was recommended. He was a trained nurseryman who had gained gardening experience at Croome Court and ran a seed trade with the Londoner James Gordon and Company (in the 1770s), later with James Vere, a specialist in Japanese plants at Kensington Gore. Although the conditions under which he started were rather inadequate, Graefer set up a garden that was painted by Philipp Hackert in—surely idealized—wonderful gouaches. Only gardens such as Kew Garden can be compared with these illustrations of a garden combining botanical and aesthetic concepts to such a degree of perfection. Reflecting Hamilton's and Winckelmann's preoccupation with antiquity, the first antique *spolia* were arranged in the garden: what had to be constructed with great effort in northern countries was already in place in Naples. The appreciation of local antiquities first came to flower in the *parco archeologico* at the end of the 19th century. The unique position of the garden is also underlined by the fact that this is possibly the first landscape garden on the Italian peninsula.

Graefer also made some botanical excursions that were important for the publication of his works *Descriptive Catalogue of Herbaceous and Perennial Plants* (1789) and *Flora dell'isola di Capri* (1791). It is surely his merit to have cultivated some of the plants which he found at Caserta. The maze called Bosco di San Silvestro must have been planted exclusively with native plants of the *macchia.*

Beginning in 1798 the garden was maintained in a rather provisional state. Although Graefer's successors, his sons, kept the garden, Francesco I made the first alterations, predominately by leaving Vanvitelli's design unfinished and bringing in ideas of romantic gardening. The garden remained royal property until 1921, when the state took over the garden and palace. The archival material concerning bills is immensely rich; unfortunately, however, good plans are not extant.

## Synopsis

| | |
|---|---|
| 1751 | Purchase of land and wood by Don Carlos de Borbón from duke of Caserta at village La Torre (since 1752, known as Caserta); first alterations made in existing groves, but estate remained hunting ground |
| 1752 | Castle built, designed by Luigi Vanvitelli, while Old Wood replanted and changed into bosquets and semicircle at end of parterre; construction of waterworks |
| 1756 | Publication of Vanvitelli's *Dichiarazione dei disegni del Real Nuovo Palazzo,* with explanation of layout and baroque iconography |
| 1759–69 | Cessation of work due to Don Carlos becoming Carlos III, King of Spain; his successor, Ferdinando IV, not enthroned as King of Naples until 1769 |
| 1769 | Waterworks completed; construction of Peschiera Grande (Grand Fish Pond), designed by Vanvitelli, under supervision of architect Francesco Collecini |
| 1770 | Well-furnished straw building dedicated on island in Grand Fish Pond; construction of Castelluccia (octagonal edifice) |
| 1771 | 3,000 chestnut trees transplanted from Belvedere to Old Wood |
| 1773 | Death of Luigi Vanvitelli, succeeded by his son Carlo |
| 1774 | Exterior of palace finished |
| 1775–87 | Several land purchases beyond boundaries of existing garden (Ponte di Ercole) |
| 1777 | Layout of cascade garden begun |
| 1778 | Model for fountain of Aeolus, by Andrea Violani; also model for fountain of bridge of Sale, by Gaetano Salomone |

| | |
|---|---|
| 1779 | Salomone's model for waterfall basin; collaboration on Fountain of Aeolus |
| 1779–85 | Construction of fountain of Juno and Aeolus, sculpted by Paolo Persico, Andrea Violani, Angelo Brunelli, and Gaetano Salomone |
| 1779–87 | Cascade garden constructed |
| 1783 | Ceres Fountain, created by Gaetano Salomone, and cascade garden ready to work |
| 1785 | Queen Maria Carolina decides to have landscape garden laid out beside cascade |
| 1785–89 | Cascade and fountain of Diana, created by Paolo Persico, Angelo Brunelli, and Pietro Solari |
| 1786 | Arrival of gardener Johann Andreas Graefer and creation of botanic garden; introduction of non-native plants (e.g., *Cameliae* and camphor tree) |
| 1787 | Subdivision into a *giardino di erbaggi* and *giardino botanico* |
| 1789 | Casino built at end of cascade |
| late 1780s | S. Leucio founded as ideal village on borders of park |
| 1790 | Arrival of gardener Edward Holt from Kew |
| 1790–91 | Monopteros built into maze Bosco di S. Silvestro, and dovecote, pyramid, *antique spoliae*, and Bath of Venus now in existence |
| ca. 1793 | Casino di Graefer built as *loggia* for *divertisements* |
| 1798–1802 | Problems caused by riots and French occupation; Graefer leaves Caserta to work for Lord Nelson in Sicily |
| 1800 | Botanical plantations near Belvedere |
| 1803 | Publication by Graefer's son (and successor) Giovanni of *Synopsis Plantarum Regii Viridarii Casertani*, describing 551 genera in gardens |
| 1819 | Castelluccia transformed into toy castle for royal princes |
| 1826 | L'Apria (cistern by L. Vanvitelli) comes to English garden with statue of Venus (1761) |
| 1838 | Formal flower garden built by architect De Lillo to right of palace |
| 1876 | Publication of Niccola Terracino's botanical guide, *Cenno Intorno al Giardino Botanico della Real casa in Caserta* |
| 1921 | Garden becomes state property |

**Further Reading**

Caroselli, Maria Raffaella, *La reggia di Caserta: Lavori, costo, efferti della construzione*, Milan: Giuffré, 1968

Chierici, Gino, *La Reggia di Caserta*, Rome: La Libreria dello Stato, 1930; reprint, 1984

Chigiotti, Guiseppe, "The Design and Realisation of the Park of the Royal Palace at Caserta by Luigi and Carlo Vanvitelli," *Journal of Garden History 5*, no. 2 (1985)

Defilippis, Felice, *Il palazzo reale di Caserta e i Borboni di Napoli*, Naples: Di Mauro, 1968

Gentile, Aniello, editor, *Caserta nei ricordi dei viaggiatori stranieri*, Naples: Società Editrice Napoletana, 1980

Gentile, Aniello, editor, *Benevento nei ricordi dei viaggiatori italiani e stranieri*, Naples: Società Editrice Napoletana, 1982

Knight, Carlo, *Il Giardino Inglese di Caserta*, Naples: Eklund, 1986

Knight, Carlo, and Antonio Gianfrotta, *Il Giardino Inglese nella Reggia di Caserta*, Naples: Sergio, 1987

MacDougall, Elisabeth Blair, *Gardens of Naples*, New York: Train/Scala Books, 1995

Maderna, V., "Gli scultori della Reggia di Caserta negli anni della direzione di Carlo Vanvitelli," in *Le arti figurative a Napoli nel Settecento*, edited by N. Spinosa, Naples: Società Editrice Napoletana, 1979

Maderna, V., and F. Petrelli, "Gli scultori a Caserta," in *Civiltà del '700 a Napoli, 1734–1799* (exhib. cat.), edited by Denise Maria Pagano and Mariella Utili, Florence: Centro Di, 1979

Margozzi, Mariastella, editor, *Reggia di Caserta: La scultura dell'Ottocento*, Rome: Editalia, 1992

Nicolini, Luigi, *La Reggia di Caserta (1750–1775): Ricerche storiche*, Bari, Italy: Laterza, 1911

Patturelli, Ferdinando, *Caserta e San Leucio, descritti dall' architetto*, Naples, 1826; reprint, Naples: Athena Mediterranea, 1972

Petrelli, F., "Gli scultori della Reggia di Caserta negli anni della direzione di Luigi Vanvitelli," in *Le arti figurative a Napoli nel Settecento*, edited by N. Spinosa, Naples: Società Editrice Napoletana, 1979

Sigismondo, Giuseppe, *Descrizione della città di Napoli e i suoi borghi*, 3 vols., Naples, 1788–89; reprint, Sala Bolognese: Forni, 1989

Vanvitelli, Luigi, *Dichiarazione dei disegni del Reale Palazzo di Caserta*, Naples, 1756; reprint, as *Il Palazzo Reale di Caserta*, edited by Marco Nocca, Rome: Audino, 1992

Vanvitelli, Luigi, *Le lettere di Luigi Vanvitelli della Biblioteca Palatina di Caserta*, edited by Franco Strazzullo, 3 vols., Galatina, Italy: Congedo, 1976–77

MARCUS KÖHLER

# Castle Howard

## North Yorkshire, England

**Location:** approximately 15 miles (24 km) northeast of York

Generally regarded as one of the earliest examples of the style known as the English landscape garden, the house and grounds at Castle Howard were begun in 1699 when Charles Howard, third earl of Carlisle, resolved to build himself a new home at Henderskelfe in Yorkshire, close to the prosperous and important city of York.

Carlisle initially chose William Talman as his architect but dismissed him in favor of Sir John Vanbrugh, whose decision to reposition the proposed house on a north-south axis was to have profound consequences for the development of the grounds. Early proposals for formal gardens at Castle Howard, attributed to the leading nurseryman George London, show designs that included formal parterres, canals, and plantations. These were declined, and instead Carlisle, with Vanbrugh and Nicholas Hawksmoor, favored a more innovative development of the grounds, shunning the geometrical styles influenced by prevailing French and Dutch fashions.

Ray Wood, an ancient woodland to the east of the house, was fashioned into a series of serpentine walkways and ornamented with lead sculptures, water features, and pavilions. Early accounts by visitors reveal this woodland garden to have been executed by 1710, although it was to fall into disrepair and vanish by the middle of the 18th century.

By 1715, with the building of the mansion largely complete, a plain grass parterre was laid out to the south of the house and filled with statues, obelisks, urns, and a column, with a symmetrical wilderness fashioned out of fir trees beyond, which can be seen in the bird's-eye view in volume 3 of Campbell's *Vitruvius Britannicus* (1725).

Attention was given to the wider landscape, too, with the erection of Vanbrugh's Temple of Diana (now known as the Temple of the Four Winds). Modeled on Palladio's Villa Rotonda at Vicenza, it was begun in the 1720s and completed in 1739. A second temple by Hawksmoor, known as the Temple of Venus, was constructed in the 1730s, but this no longer survives. Other features by Vanbrugh included his Obelisk (1714–15), the Pyramid Arch (1719; expanded in the 1750s), and his Mock Fortifications (1720s). Buildings by Hawksmoor included the Carrmire Gate (late 1720s), the Pyramid (1728), and a smaller pyramid in Pretty Wood (date unknown).

Hawksmoor's most important building was the Mausoleum. On the outside it is a tall cylinder with a colonnade surmounted by a shallow cap above a clerestory; inside there is a chapel on the upper level with a crypt and vaults below. Begun in 1729 it was finished in the 1740s to a different design after a triumvirate of gentleman architects had intervened in the execution of the building. These were Henry Howard, future fourth earl of Carlisle, his brother-in-law, the architect Sir Thomas Robinson, and Richard Boyle, third earl of Burlington, the influential patron of Palladian architects. Their alterations included a bastion wall surrounding the edifice and the addition of a set of steps on the east side (modeled on those at Burlington's own villa in Chiswick, Middlesex).

In addition to the water features in Ray Wood, the exploitation of abundant natural water sources led to the creation of the South Lake (1724) and the fashioning of New River (1732), which was spanned by New River Bridge (1744).

Comparable English gardens of the period include Stowe, Buckinghamshire (1713–50), where Vanbrugh also worked, as well as Studley Royal, North Yorkshire (1715–30), and Duncombe Park, North Yorkshire (begun 1713). The landscaping operations at Castle Howard were completed in under half a century, and early descriptions of the grounds unanimously praise the natural or extensive landscaping together with the buildings and monuments surrounding the house.

The early 18th-century gardens were altered little during the following century, with the exception of the South Parterre, where the wilderness and most of the obelisks and statues were removed. In the 1790s the Great Lake to the north of the house was fashioned with an adjoining pond.

The next significant period of change occurred in 1850 with the arrival of William Andrews Nesfield, premier landscape architect of the early Victorian period. Commissioned by the seventh earl of Carlisle, Nesfield added a new pond to the Great Lake, known as the Reflecting Pond. At the same time, to the south of the house, he began work on an elaborate, geometrical *parterre de broderie,* consciously modeled on the 17th-century designs of Le Nôtre and other French baroque designers. A color lithograph of the parterre appeared in Adveno Brooke's *The Gardens of England* (1857). Two fountains were also installed with the assistance of the engineer James Easton. The first, known as the Atlas Fountain, was shown at the Great Exhibition in London before being dismantled and brought by rail to Castle Howard, where it was situated in the center of Nesfield's parterre. A second fountain, known as the Prince

Plate 1. Säynätsalo Town Hall, 1949, Säynätsalo, Finland
Photo by M. Kapanen, copyright Alvar Aalto Museum

Plate 2. Spring and summer plantings in a garden designed by Gustav Allinger for the Jubilee Horticulture Exposition, Dresden, 1926
From *Die Gartenschönheit* 8, no. 4 (1927), courtesy of Joachim Wolschke-Bulmahn

Plate 3. Tunnel of Trees, Halsey Court
Copyright Clay Perry/Garden Picture Library

Plate 4. Laying out of the Mogul emperor Babur's Garden of Fidelity, near Jalalabad, Afghanistan, from the *Babur Name*, 1508
Copyright Victoria and Albert Museum, London/Art Resource, New York

Plate 5. Flower bed design by Wilhelm Legeler, 1839
Copyright C.A. Wimmer

Plate 6. *Wien, vom Belvedere aus gesehen* (Vienna, Viewed from the Belvedere), by Bernardo Bellotto
Courtesy of Kunsthistorisches Museum, Vienna

Plate 7. *Dracaena draco*, anonymous watercolor on paper, ca. 1570
Courtesy of Biblioteka Jagiellońska, Kraków

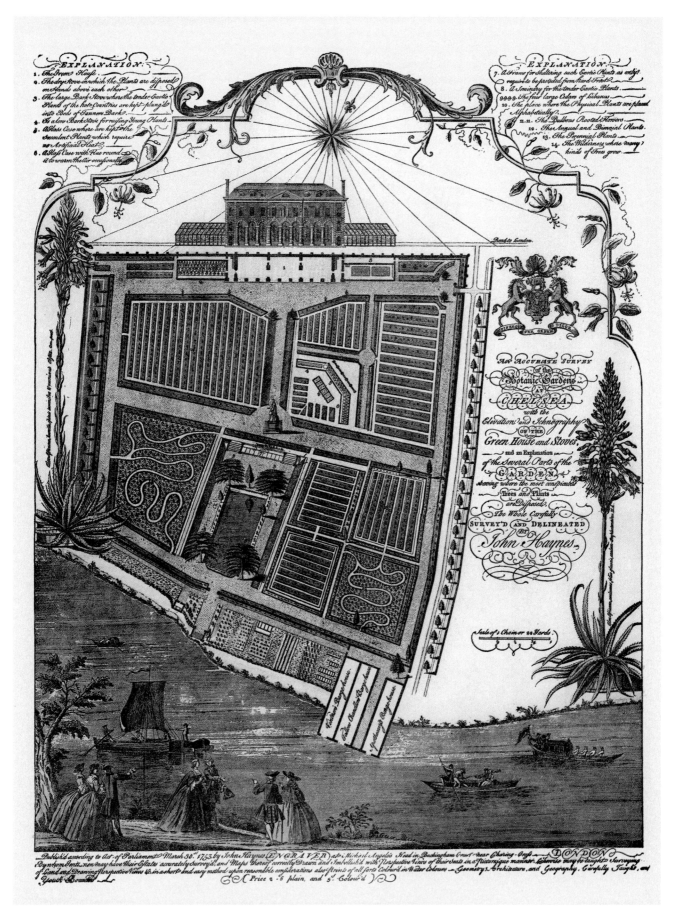

Plate 8. Drawing of Chelsea Physic Garden, London, England, ca. 1751
Courtesy of Chelsea Physic Garden Company

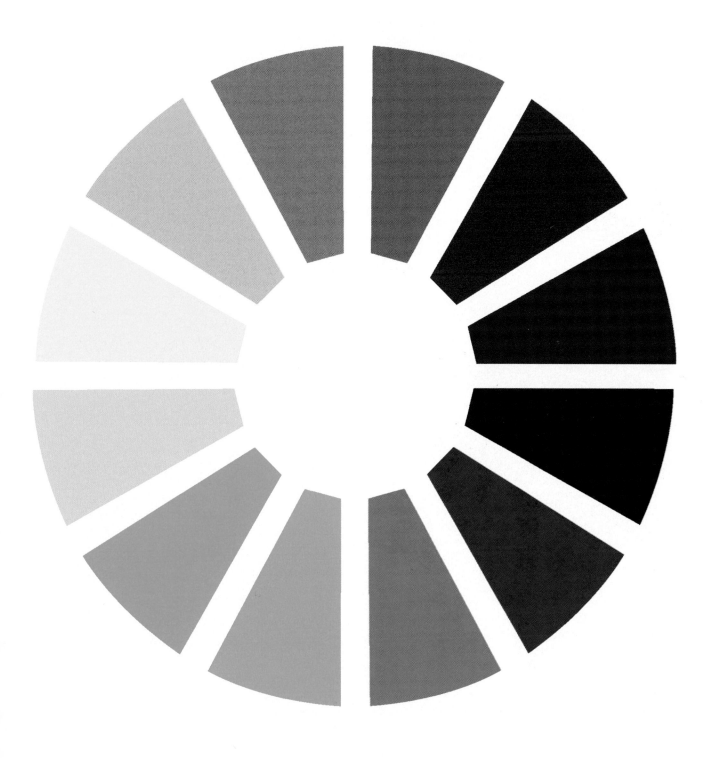

Plate 9. Example of a color wheel, used as a guideline when arranging color schemes in gardens
Copyright Chicago Botanic Garden

Plate 10. Cottage garden at Merriment Gardens, Sussex, England
Copyright J.S. Sira/Garden Picture Library

Plate 11. Variety of plants used to create visual interest, Denver Botanic Gardens, Denver, Colorado, United States
Copyright Lauri Macmillan Johnson

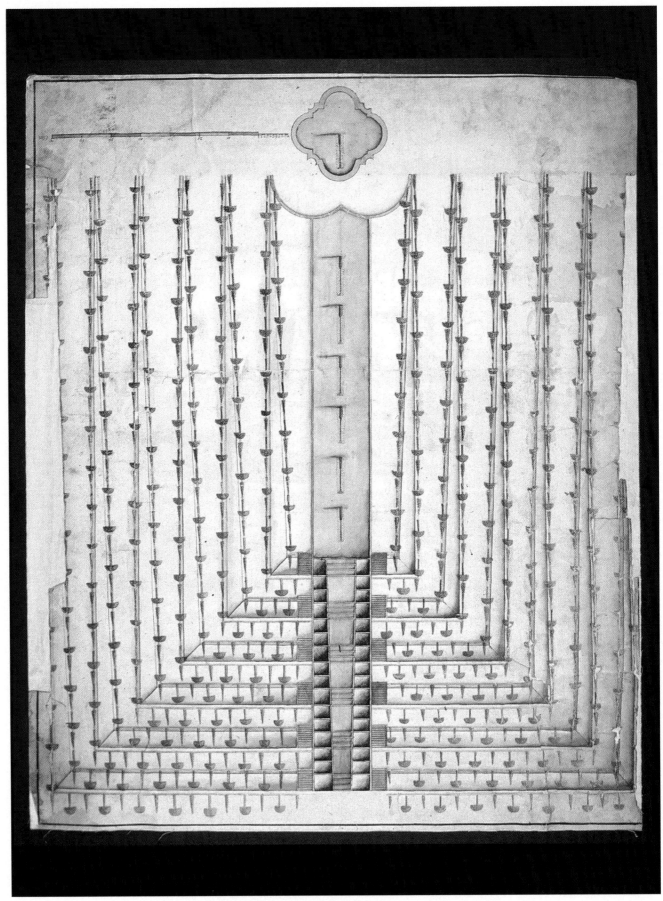

Plate 12. Plan for the gardens at Frederiksberg Castle by Krieger, ca. 1720
Courtesy of Statens Arkiver, Rigsarkivet, Denmark

of Wales Fountain, was placed in the South Lake, which was formalized in a geometrical fashion. These improvements were completed by 1853 at enormous cost. Ten years later Nesfield advised on the extension of the South Waterways with the creation of a cascade, a basin, and a waterfall, which connected the South Lake with New River beyond.

Nesfield's landscaping was largely erased in 1893 by the ninth countess, who objected to his parterre on aesthetic grounds but also the expense of maintaining it. The parterre was replaced with a grass terrace and yew hedges. Trees and shrubs were also planted on the shores of the lake, and in time these grew to obscure the vista across the waterways. After years of neglect in the 20th century, the fountains, lakes, and waterways were comprehensively restored between 1985 and 1992.

Ray Wood, which had been clear felled during World War II, was replanted under the direction of George Howard and James Russell in the 1960s; today the wood boasts an unparalleled collection of rhododendrons, Pieris, wild roses, magnolias, hydrangeas, viburnums, maples, and rowans. In 1979 James Russell also began designing the Castle Howard Arboretum, which today is jointly administered in trust with the Royal Botanic Gardens, Kew.

Although Castle Howard is rightly famed as an 18th-century landscape, it bears significant traces of Victorian involvement as well as important late 20th-century developments.

## Synopsis

| | |
|---|---|
| 1699 | Charles Howard, third earl of Carlisle, begins new family home and chooses Sir John Vanbrugh as architect |
| 1710 | Ray Wood fashioned into woodland garden with meandering walkways and other features |
| 1715 | Castle Howard largely built; South Parterre begun |
| 1720s | Vanbrugh's Temple of Four Winds begun |
| 1724 | South Lake created |
| 1729 | Hawksmoor's Mausoleum begun |
| 1732 | New River fashioned |
| 1744 | Mausoleum completed |
| 1770 | South Parterre modified |
| 1797 | Great Lake to north of house fashioned |
| 1850 | William Andrews Nesfield begins work at Castle Howard |
| 1864 | Extension of South Waterways |
| 1893 | Removal of Nesfield's parterre |
| 1940s | Ray Wood clear felled, grounds and buildings in acute disrepair |
| 1960s | Ray Wood replanted by James Russell |
| 1979 | Castle Howard Arboretum started |
| 1985 | Commencement of restoration of fountain, lakes, and waterways |

## Further Reading

*Castle Howard,* S.l.: Castle Howard Estate, 1997

Downes, Kerry, *Hawksmoor,* London: Zwemmer, 1959; New York: Praeger, 1969; 2nd edition, London: Zwemmer, and Cambridge, Massachusetts: MIT Press, 1979

Downes, Kerry, *Vanbrugh,* London: Zwemmer, 1977

Hawthorne, Lin, "A Woodland Paradise at Castle Howard," *Northern Gardener* (Summer 1996)

Hunt, John Dixon, "Castle Howard Revisited," in *Gardens and the Picturesque: Studies in the History of Landscape Architecture,* by Hunt, Cambridge, Massachusetts: MIT Press, 1992

Hussey, Christopher, *English Gardens and Landscapes, 1700–1750,* New York: Funk and Wagnalls, and London: Country Life, 1967

Murray, Venetia, *Castle Howard: The Life and Times of a Stately Home,* New York and London: Viking Press, 1994

Pevsner, Nikolaus, *The Buildings of England: Yorkshire, the North Riding,* Harmondsworth: Penguin, 1966

Ridgway, Christopher, "The Restoration of the Lakes and Waterways at Castle Howard," *Country Life* 173, no. 30 (27 July 1989)

Ridgway, Christopher, "Design and Restoration at Castle Howard," in *William Andrews Nesfield: Victorian Landscape Architect,* edited by Ridgway, York, North Yorkshire: Institute of Advanced Architectural Studies, 1996

Ridgway, Christopher, "Using the Archive," *European Gardens* 2 (Summer 1996)

Ridgway, Christopher, "Making Heroes Fit for a Landscape," *Country Life Art and Antiques* (6 May 1999) (special issue)

Saumarez Smith, Charles, *The Building of Castle Howard,* Chicago: University of Chicago Press, and London: Faber, 1990

Simmons, John, "Castle Howard Arboretum Trust," *Newsletter of the Tree Register of the British Isles* 7 (1997–98)

Simmons, John, "He Could See the Wood for the Trees," *Country Life* 193, no. 13 (1 April 1999)

CHRISTOPHER RIDGWAY

# Catesby, Mark 1682–1749

## English Collector, Artist, Author, and Horticulturist

Mark Catesby's achievements as a collector and botanical artist during the 1700s are reflected today in his commemoration in the genus *Catesbaea* and in five species: *Gentiana catesbaei*, *Lilium catesbaei*, *Sarracenia catesbaei*, *Trillium catesbaei*, and *Leucothoe catesbaei*. The plates in Catesby's *The Natural History of Carolina, Florida and the Bahama Islands*, a work which W.T. Stearn describes as "a pioneer contribution to the natural history of the West Indies as well as to that of the southern United States" (Stearn, 1958), were cited by J.F. Gronovius in the *Flora Virginica* (1739–43) as well as by Linnaeus throughout his works, especially in the *Species Plantarum* (1753) and the *Systema Naturae* (1759). In addition, Linnaeus founded 21 taxa (species and varieties) on Catesby's botanical plates.

Catesby speaks in the preface to the *Natural History* of his "early Inclination to search after Plants," an interest he pursued during the two periods of his life that he spent in North America, when he collected and drew the flora of those areas he visited, namely Virginia, Carolina, Florida, and the Bahama Islands. He noted that "Both in Carolina and on [the Bahama] Islands, [he] made successive Collections of dry'd Plants and Seeds," sending "some dried specimens of plants and some of the most specious of them in tubs of earth, at the request of some curious friends," among whom were the botanists Samuel Dale, William Sherard, and J.F. Gronovius, collectors and gardeners Hans Sloane and Peter Collinson, and nurseryman Thomas Fairchild. Catesby took special care in his methods of preserving and sending specimens and seeds, remarking later in the preface to the *Hortus Britanno-Americanus* that he had "been particular in . . . directing how [plant specimens] are to be collected, packed up, and secured, so as to preserve them in good condition during their passage, which are matters of utmost consequence, though less known even than their culture." Catesby's specimens survive today in the Department of Plant Sciences, University of Oxford (Sherard and Du Bois herbaria) and in the Natural History Museum, London (Sloane, Dale and General herbaria), and were referred to in several botanical memoirs during the century that followed their collection.

Catesby's horticultural contributions in introducing North American shrubs, trees, and herbaceous plants into English gardens, were recognised by the gardener Thomas Knowlton: "The infinity of new Trees, Shrubs, etc. now of late introduced by [Catesby] into Gardens from North America fill me with the greatest Wonder and Astonishment imaginable" (Knowlton to Richard Richardson, July 18, 1749). Following Catesby's return to England in 1726, his contacts in America, the most important of which was the Pennsylvanian naturalist John Bartram, continued to send him plants and seeds. Some of these were reared in Fairchild and Gray's nurseries, some by Catesby in his own garden in Fulham, and some in the gardens of his horticulturally minded friends, such as Peter Collinson at Peckham. In his *Hortus* Catesby describes 85 trees and shrubs with greater detail than in his *Natural History*, noting, "By a long acquaintance with the trees and shrubs of America, and a constant attention since for several years to their cultivation here, I have been enabled to make such observations on their cultivation, growth and culture, as may render the management of them easy to those who shall be desirous to enrich their country, and give pleasure to themselves, by planting and increasing these beautiful exotics." It is difficult to number precisely how many American plant and tree species Catesby introduced into English gardens at this time. However, he can confidently be credited with introducing *Catalpa bignonioides*, *Callicarpa americana*, *Wisteria frutescens*, *Calycanthus floridus*, *Quercus phellos*, and two species of North American rose, *Rosa carolina* and *R. foliosa*. The herbaceous plants he is credited with include *Lilium superbum*, *Liatris squarrosa* and *Liatris spicata*, *Canna glauca*, *Coreopsis lanceolata*, and *Phlox paniculata*.

In his *Natural History* plants are depicted in 156 of the 220 plates, sometimes in combination with birds and other animals, and sometimes on their own. Catesby claimed that his illustrations of plants were "taken from living Plants, fresh and just gathered." While a significant number of the non-botanical images were in fact copied from other illustrations rather than done from life, it remains true that the majority of plant illustrations were based on actual specimens, which if not always fresh, were at least dried specimens collected and preserved by Catesby himself. Indeed, features of a number of his botanical drawings, such as one showing a stalk bent over in order to display the whole specimen, appear to be influenced directly by his methods of preserving and displaying plant specimens. Catesby had no artistic training and few predecessors in the field to influence him. He therefore developed his own style, claiming that he depicted plants "in a Flat tho' exact manner, [as this] may serve the Purpose of Natural History better in some Measure than in a more bold and Painter like way." His "exact manner" (all of his plants are clearly identifiable) combined with his striking sense of composition, and the fact that he produced the first large format color plates of the flora of North America, ensure him a notable place in the history of botanical illustration.

## Biography
Born probably in Castle Hedingham, Essex, England, 1682. Had no formal training, but likely to have been educated locally in Sudbury, Suffolk; traveled in Virginia, 1712–19 (visiting Jamaica in 1714), exploring, collecting plant specimens, and drawing flora and fauna; returned to London and met William Sherard; sponsored by Sherard, Hans Sloane, Richard Mead, and others, traveled in Georgia, Carolina, and the Bahama Islands, 1722–26; resettled in London, 1726, and employed as horticulturist in two nurseries specializing in American exotics: Thomas Fairchild's in Hoxton (later taken over by Stephen Bacon) and Christopher Gray's in Fulham; etched his own drawings of American flora and fauna, publishing them by subscription between 1729 and 1747, as parts of his *Natural History*. Died in London, 1749.

## Selected Publications
*The Natural History of Carolina, Florida, and the Bahama Islands*, 2 vols., 1731–43
*Hortus Britanno-Americanus; or, A Curious Collection of Trees and Shrubs, the Produce of the British Colonies in North America: Adapted to the Soil and Climate of England . . .*, 1763; as *Hortus Europae Americanus*, 1767

## Further Reading
Britten, James, *The Sloane Herbarium: An Annotated List of the Horti Sicci Composing It: With Biographical Accounts of the Principal Contributors,* edited and revised by James Edgar Dandy, London: British Museum, 1958
Clokie, Hermia Newman, *An Account of the Herbaria of the Department of Botany in the University of Oxford*, London: Oxford University Press, 1964
Coats, Alice M., *The Quest for Plants: A History of the Horticultural Explorers*, London: Studio Vista, 1969; as *The Plant Hunters: Being a History of the Horticultural Pioneers, Their Quests, and Their Discoveries from the Renaissance to the Twentieth Century*, New York: McGraw-Hill, 1970
Frick, George Frederick, and Raymond Phineas Stearns, *Mark Catesby: The Colonial Audubon*, Urbana: University of Illinois Press, 1961
Gorer, Richard, *The Growth of Gardens*, Boston and London: Faber and Faber, 1978
Henrey, Blanche, *British Botanical and Horticultural Literature before 1800*, London and New York: Oxford University Press, 1975
Howard, Richard A., and George W. Staples, "The Modern Names for Catesby's Plants," *Journal of the Arnold Arboretum* 64 (October 1983)
McBurney, Henrietta, *Mark Catesby's Natural History of America: The Watercolours from the Royal Library, Windsor Castle*, London: Merrell Holberton, and Houston, Texas: Museum of Fine Arts Houston, 1997
Myers, Amy R.W., and Margaret Beck Pritchard, editors, *Empire's Nature: Mark Catesby's New World Vision*, Chapel Hill: University of North Carolina Press, 1998
Stearn, William T., "Publication of Catesby's Natural History of Carolina," *Journal of the Society for the Bibliography of Natural History* 3 (1958)

HENRIETTA MCBURNEY

---

# Cautley, Marjorie Sewell 1892–1954

## United States Landscape Architect

Marjorie Sewell Cautley was one of the first female landscape architects in the United States to successfully expand her practice of private garden and estate design to include community planning. Her most influential work focused attention on landscape design and site planning for lower-cost communities. She combined site planning and planting design to create community open spaces and private gardens suited to the growing middle class, as well as urban redevelopment areas.

Cautley received a bachelor's degree in landscape architecture from Cornell University's School of Agriculture in 1917. Immediately afterward she went to work for Warren H. Manning in Billerica, Massachusetts. His office was flourishing with estate, public park, suburban development, and community planning commissions. In 1918 Sewell supervised the construction of a hotel for World War I workers in Dalton, Illinois, for Julia Morgan, a California architect. After the war Cautley moved to New Jersey to open her own practice. She began her practice when women were not welcome in the professions and few could compete for public projects. Beatrix Farrand's work on college campuses and Helen Bullard's employment with the Long Island State Parks Commission are notable exceptions. At various times throughout her career Cautley used either her maiden name, Sewell, or married name, Cautley.

Cautley's early work experiences helped her move from the private garden design projects typically associated with early 20th-century female landscape architects to site planning and construction supervision of public commissions generally restricted to men. Cautley excelled at creating low-cost landscape designs reflecting the horticultural characteristics and requirements of plants, as well as providing residential and community open space in lower-cost housing developments.

During the 1920s and 1930s the nation's demands for low-cost housing outside of dense urban centers swelled dramatically. Architects, planners, and landscape architects responded with plans translating upper-class suburban ideals to small-scale suburban lot developments. Cautley joined the movement when hired by Henry Wright and Clarence Stein, members of the Regional Planning Association of America (RPAA). The RPAA conceptualized a regional city idea strongly based on Ebenezer Howard's Garden City of Tomorrow. Wright and Stein studied Howard's model and others as they developed plans and built prototype communities emphasizing proper housing and outdoor spaces for moderate-income families. Cautley designed and supervised construction of low-cost landscape plans supporting the community focus of four innovative community housing developments. Sunnyside Gardens' single-family apartments and flats (1924–28) enclosed central open spaces designed for private community use. Cautley used inexpensive plants, hardy in adverse urban conditions, to define small private gardens, green courtyards, and recreation areas within the interior blocks. She took great care to construct a landscape to meet the high-use demands of future residents while minimizing the site's maintenance needs.

Sunnyside was a testing ground for the development of Radburn in Fairlawn, New Jersey (1928–30). Radburn is perhaps the single most influential project of the Greenbelt Town Movement in the United States. Again, Wright and Stein located a site and developed a master plan focused on a high quality of living in a lower-cost community. The super-block development pattern featured houses facing a central park accessible from each residential unit within this "new town for the motor age." Cautley designed and supervised construction of a planting scheme providing small lawns and gardens for each house and a park with programmed recreation open space winding through the center of an entire super-block. Shade trees and shrubs transplanted from neighboring woods line open play fields, and wide sidewalks follow the natural contours of the land. Cautley desired to preserve the beauty of the landscape and the regional vegetation that was rapidly disappearing under the expanding suburban growth of New York City. Individual properties connected to the park by garden alleyways were planted in garden groupings with unique themes. Young plants were selected and placed in anticipation of their mature size and form. Cautley worked to minimize the maintenance demands of the public areas as well as the new house properties. Most of the latter were to be purchased by first-time home buyers unfamiliar with landscape maintenance needs.

Housing and site planning for small suburban lots was a growing concern during the small-house era of the 1920s and 1930s. Architects and landscape architects published a number of popular magazine articles describing how potential home owners could create low-cost houses on new suburban lots. Cautley wrote a series of articles illustrating how classic house styles could be sited and landscaped for the needs of a contemporary family. In 1935 she published an eclectic manuscript, *Garden Design: The Principles of Abstract Design as Applied to Landscape Composition,* detailing her design principles, describing their application to small suburban sites, and providing detailed plant lists categorized by site context, use, and color. The book also provided general guidance on small-lot subdivision design. Her illustrative lot plans directly critiqued the cookie-cutter lots and houses characteristic of the 1930s suburban development patterns and practices. Few books of its time offered such clear commentary and advice on such a wide range of design and applications.

Cautley continued to work on community-centered projects similar to Radburn and Sunnyside Gardens. Her early work with Wright and Stein addressing larger societal issues influenced the direction of her professional career. After the worst of the Great Depression passed, Cautley entered the University of Pennsylvania and obtained a master's degree in city planning (1943). Her thesis combined her site-planning expertise with concerns of urban blight, residential development, and open space into a redevelopment proposal for a blighted Philadelphia neighborhood. Unlike many of her contemporaries, Cautley detailed her proposal with site-specific arguments, tying together housing proposals with nearby employment areas, parks and open spaces with adequate neighborhood and municipal policing, and free-time activities with a neighborhood structure emphasizing community social activities and opportunities rather than vices. Her proposal took the ideals expressed in earlier garden suburb developments and related them to the redevelopment needs of existing, neglected urban neighborhoods. Cautley's ideas would not be widely taken up again until the 1980s and 1990s, long after the ravages of urban renewal devastated many city neighborhoods.

## Biography
Born in California, 1892. Attended School of Agriculture, Cornell University, Ithaca, New York; received B.S. in landscape architecture, 1917; apprenticed with Warren H. Manning, Billerica, Massachusetts, and Julia Morgan, Dalton, Illinois, before establishing private consulting office in New Jersey, 1919; most productive work period 1920s and 30s included landscape plans for Regional Planning Association of America's community prototypes, Sunnyside Gardens, Queens, New York, 1924–28, and Radburn in Fairlawn, New Jersey, 1928–30, as well as traditional garden estate designs; received M.A. in city planning, University of Pennsylvania, 1943; taught in architecture and planning department, Massachusetts Institute of Technology, Cambridge, Massachusetts, and Columbia School of Architecture, New York; wrote numerous articles and book illustrating use of garden design and community planning principles on small properties to create pleasant living environments. Died in New Jersey, 1954.

## Selected Designs
| | |
|---|---|
| 1921 | Roosevelt Common, Tenafly, New Jersey, United States |
| 1924–28 | Landscape, Sunnyside Gardens, Queens, New York, United States |
| 1928–30 | Landscape (with architects Henry Wright and Clarence Stein), Radburn in Fairlawn, New Jersey, United States |
| 1930–35 | Landscape (with architects Henry Wright and Clarence Stein), Phipps Garden Apartments, Sunnyside Gardens, Queens, New York, United States |
| 1934–36 | Landscaping for recreational park projects, Kingston State Park and Wentworth Lake State Park, New Hampshire, United States |
| 1935 | Hillside Homes (with architect Henry Wright), New York City, New York, United States |

## Selected Publications
"A City Garden," *Architecture* (April 1922)
"New Houses of Old Flavor," *Country Life in America* (1922) (a series of seven articles)
"A Group of Houses Planned and Planted as a Unit," *House Beautiful* (January 1929)
"Planting at Radburn," *Landscape Architecture* (October 1930)
"New Hampshire's Planned Park Projects," *American City* (May 1934)
"Landscaping the Housing Project," *Architecture* (October 1935)
*Garden Design: The Principles of Abstract Design as Applied to Landscape Composition*, 1935
"Border Colors," *House and Garden* (July 1937)
"Camouflage Planting," *American City* (April 1943)
"How Blighted Areas in Philadelphia and Boston Might Be Transformed," *American City* (October 1943)
"Small City Parks for Community Use: How Neighborhood Parks Meet Public Needs," *American City* (May 1944)

## Further Reading
Birnbaum, Charles A., and Robin S. Karson, editors, *Pioneers of American Landscape Design*, New York: McGraw Hill, 2000
Krall, Daniel W., "Early Women Designers and Their Work in Public Places," in *Proceedings for Landscape and Gardens: Women Who Made a Difference*, compiled by Miriam Easton Rutz, East Lansing: Michigan State University, 1987
Mann, William A., *Space and Time in Landscape Architectural History*, Washington, D.C.: Landscape Architecture Foundation, 1981; revised edition, as *Landscape Architecture: An Illustrated History in Timelines, Site Plans, and Biography*, New York: Wiley, 1993
Newton, Norman T., *Design on the Land: The Development of Landscape Architecture*, Cambridge, Massachusetts: Harvard University Press, 1971
"Review of Garden Design by Marjorie Sewell Cautley," *Architecture* (August 1935)

TERRY L. CLEMENTS

# Cemetery

By definition a cemetery is simply a burial ground. Cemeteries provide for the disposal of the dead by either interment or cremation, each of which may be expressed in different ways. They are typically nonde-nominational, although this is not always the case. Unlike the burial grounds associated with churches, cemeteries are not used for any other religious events, such as daily worship, weddings, or christenings. As a consequence they are much more clearly focused in their purpose. Unlike churchyards, which may have been used and reused for many hundreds of years and tend to evolve organically with time, cemeteries are usually planned and designed. Their period of use is often more clearly defined, and therefore they may be seen as a more coherent expression of a culture's changing response to providing for and managing death. Care must be taken, however, when looking to establish the differences between church and cemetery, as this distinction is not always made in other languages.

Some of the best-known ancient monuments relate to death and dying, signifying cultural and regional differences, with pyramids in Egypt, hunebeds in northern Europe, and tumuli or burial mounds that can be found elsewhere in Europe. Some traditions are culturally linked, but all are subject to fashion. In ancient Rome it was the tradition to have cemeteries just outside city walls along major routes; later, graves were incorporated in sacred groves, following Greek examples. In ancient mythology the Elysium represented an alternative for dying and was a place where chosen heroes were sent by the gods. This delightful landscape was said to contain evergreen meadows and streams and has remained a powerful archetype in planning cemeteries; it has also been used in a range of different landscape settings, including 18th-century landscape parks.

Early Christianity set different examples: Jesus was buried in a sepulchre (a tomb cut into rock) in a garden, and Constantine the Great, the first Roman ruler (306–37 A.D.) to be converted to Christianity, is said to have started the practice of burial in churches. By the Middle Ages most burial took place in churchyards; these were regularly cleared of bones to make space for new burials. Bones were stored in charnel houses, which are still common in some mountainous regions today, where extensions of cemeteries are difficult, and also occur as ossuaries in southern Europe. The rise of Protestantism discouraged charnel houses, and so bones were then reburied elsewhere in the cemetery. This practice, however, changed with the growing notion of grave ownership. New burials now took place on top of existing graves, which were left in place. This practice accounts for the significant change in levels between the churchyard and the adjacent landscape.

By the 17th century the condition of churchyards in European cities had become unsavory. The situation was exacerbated by various epidemics, which placed a tremendous strain on existing burial resources. Similarly, the practice of burial inside the church had led to an intolerable situation. It is reported that churchgoers actually fainted due to the stench from within the church. Even so, the practice continued, as it was an important source of revenue for the church. When the connection between the existing burial practice and the spread of disease was made, intellectuals throughout Europe called for a reform of these practices. One of the earliest commentators was Joseph Furttenbach who wrote in *Architectura recreationis* (1640; Architecture Restored) of the need for reform. Change, however, was slow. The fashion of in-church burial was exported to England with the arrival of William III and Mary in 1689. However, by this time dissenters had already created their own cemetery that was not attached to a church, at Bunhill Fields in the City of London.

The inspiration for new cemeteries came from the Far East, where Europeans had founded large cemeteries to cope with the high death rate. Sir John Vanbrugh drew inspiration from these and submitted a formal design for a cemetery, which was enclosed by a wall and planted with avenues of different trees in order to provide individual character. He took the cemetery at Surat, India, as an example and recommended the "Lofty and Noble Mausoleums," which were to become such a feature of his landscape designs, particularly Castle Howard, Yorkshire, with which he later became involved.

These colonial cemeteries served as an encouragement for more hygienic and more magnificent cemeteries in Great Britain. The Old Calton Burial Ground in Edinburgh was established around the middle of the 18th century and contained both mausoleums and house tombs. The Clifton Old Cemetery in Belfast was established in 1774 by the earl of Donagall, who had donated the land. Both cemeteries were laid out in a formal manner on a rectangular pattern, with little or no provision for planting, similar to other cemeteries in the Netherlands and France.

The Netherlands also saw a significant move toward the development of new general cemeteries, which were located on the outskirts of the town. Their peripheral location addressed the health concerns associated with over-crowded churchyards and provided access to cheaper and freely available land. In 1779 a model cemetery Ter Navolging ("to serve as a model") was established in Scheveningen. The design drew its inspiration from the practice of burial inside the church and was laid out as a church in the open air with the memorial stones laid flat and with no provision for planting. As John Claudius Loudon noted: "The first attempt to establish a public and park-like cemetery was in the Low Countries, by an edict of the enlightened and benevolent emperor Joseph. This example was soon followed in France and Italy" (*Encyclopaedia of Gardening* [1834]). Perhaps the most notable example was Montmartre Cemetery, Paris, which was laid out in a disused quarry and designed in a formal landscape style by Jacques Molinos in 1799. However, it was remodeled into an essentially urban cemetery in the 1820s and 1830s.

The world-renowned example of a garden cemetery that became a paradigm and symbol of the 19th-century movement for religious and sanitary reform and design was Père Lachaise in Paris. Père Lachaise was established following Napoléon's 1804 decree, which prohibited burial grounds in built-up areas. Designed by Alexandre-Théodore Brongniart, it incorporated a series of formal avenues culminating in a *rond point*, with a winding path up a steep slope. The *rond point* was planted with Italian poplars, a reference to those on the Île des Peupliers at Ermenonville surrounding Rousseau's grave. Père Lachaise provided a clear stimulus for the creation of nondenominational cemeteries all over the Western world and encouraged a wave of cemetery building, particularly during the 1820s and 1830s. In Italy, for example, this led to the creation of the Venetian Cemetery in 1837, composed of the islands San Michele (which had first been dedicated as a cemetery in 1807) and San Cristoforo.

In the Netherlands an 1825 royal decree prohibited burial within town centers and in churches beginning 1 January 1829. This resulted in a wave of new cemeteries being completed that year. Soestbergen, near Utrecht, and one in Zutphen were both designed by Jan David Zocher, Jr., and the General Cemetery, Leeuwarden, was designed by Lucas Pieterszoon Roodbaard. All of these were completed in the landscape style, with winding walks and informal shrubberies. In Germany there was a similar interest in new cemeteries, which is reflected in the growing body of literature relating to both technical and design issues. Early examples include Friedrich Ludwig von Sckell's *Beitraege zur bildenden Gartenkunst* (1818; Contributions to Garden Art) and a book entirely dedicated to the topic by Johann Michael Voit, *Über die Anlegung und Umwandlung des Gottesacker in heitere Ruhegärten der Abgeschiedenen* (1825; About the Layout of God's Acres in Cheerful Restgardens of the Departed). This was well before the earliest British literature on the subject, John Claudius Loudon's *On the Laying Out, Planting, and Managing of Cemeteries: And on the Improvement of Churchyards* (1843).

England followed in this development, with the first nondenominational cemetery opened in 1821, The Rosary at Norwich. The Liverpool Necropolis at Low Hill followed shortly after in 1825. In 1829 the St. James's Cemetery, Liverpool, was completed in a disused quarry, evidently inspired by Montmartre. It was designed by the architect John Foster, with plantings by John Shepherd, the first curator of the Liverpool Botanical Garden. The planting softened the harshness of the rock faces and emphasized the picturesque effect. Perhaps one of the best-known cemeteries of this period was designed by Richard Forrester at Kensal Green, London, for the General Cemetery Company and completed in 1833. Forrester's design was in a modified landscape manner with few formal elements, such as avenues, being given central emphasis. The Necropolis,

Glasgow, was established at the same time and opened in 1832; although spectacular in topography and range of monuments, it contained only minimal planting.

Other well-known cemeteries of this period included the General Cemetery, Sheffield (1836), designed by the architect Samuel Worth and the landscape gardener Robert Marnock. Loudon visited the cemetery, and it is speculated that he used it as an example of how to design a cemetery on hilly ground. Other cemeteries of this period explored very different approaches in their design and laying out. Norwood Cemetery, London (1837), took the informal landscape park as a model. More picturesque or sublime effects were achieved at Highgate, London, designed in 1839. Abney Park Cemetery, London (1840), planned with a collection of plants from the nurseryman George Loddiges, set a new example for a cemetery as an arboretum. The Coventry Cemetery, designed in 1847 by Joseph Paxton, consisted of a simple geometric layout with the use of terraces, which was widely followed as a model.

The planting of cemeteries is as subject to fashion as are their design and layout. Perhaps one of the most authoritative works on this subject is by Loudon (*On the Laying Out, Planting, and Managing of Cemeteries and on the Improvement of Churchyards,* 1843), who recommended arboretum-like layouts with a great variety of plants. His book includes extensive lists of trees and shrubs and also "lawn plants," perennials that could be planted in grass. He disliked bedding in cemeteries, but it appears to have been common practice. The list included many plants with a strong symbolic significance, for example, the weeping forms of ash, holly, and willow. His legacy can still be seen today in many historic cemeteries.

The tradition for barren functional cemeteries in the United States ceased with the establishment of the New Burying Ground (later Grove Street Cemetery), New Haven, Connecticut (1796), founded by James Hillhouse, which displayed gridded avenues designed by Josiah Meigs. The first "rural cemetery" and prototype for many others was established at Mount Auburn, Boston (1831). Its designer, General Henry A.S. Dearborn, based the design on Père Lachaise, with buildings designed by Dr. Jacob Bigelow. Laid out under the auspices of the Massachusetts Horticultural Society, the cemetery doubled as an experimental garden and provided an important recreational function. Among others, it became a model for Green-Wood, New York (1838), designed by the civil engineer David B. Douglas and extended not long afterward by Zebedee Cook, a cofounder of Mount Auburn, and Almerin Hotchkiss, the new superintendent. While similar in approach, Laurel Hill, Philadelphia (1836), designed by the architect John Notman, is said to have been inspired by Kensal Green Cemetery, London.

Further examples of the rural cemetery include Spring Grove, Cincinnati, Ohio (1845), designed by local architect Howard Daniels. This launched his career as a landscape designer; he went on to design many more cemeteries and a prize-winning competition entry for Central Park, New York. The new superintendent of Spring Grove in 1855 was Adolph Strauch, a former student of Prince Pückler Muskau. He initiated a "landscape lawn plan," which eliminated cluttering fences and subjected the use of memorial stones to strict regulations, in order to enable the creation of spreading lawns and vistas, interspersed by monuments and lakes. This type of design became very influential and was copied elsewhere, ultimately becoming acknowledged as the "American system." Many existing rural cemeteries were converted on the basis of Strauch's lawn plan. Examples include Graceland in Chicago (1860), designed in the rural style by the landscape architect Horace William Shaler Cleveland and William Le Baron Jenny, which was converted using the American system by Ossian Cole Simonds, who then went on to become superintendent in 1881. Simonds became a national advocate of this system when he founded the Association of American Cemetery Superintendents in 1887.

One of the best-known 20th-century examples of the lawn plan is Forest Lawn, Los Angeles (established 1906). In 1916 Dr. Hubert Eaton was asked to extend the cemetery and create a highly regulated memorial park. The following year he hired Frederick Hansen to design the park. This set a prototype that was occasionally copied elsewhere, for example, Greenlawn Memorial Park, Surrey, Great Britain (1938).

In Germany the ideas of the British garden cemetery and the American rural cemetery were translated into the park cemetery. The supposedly largest park cemetery in the world is Ohlsdorf Cemetery, Hamburg, 400 hectares (988 acres) designed by Johann Wilhelm Cordes (1877). The park cemetery was highly influential; similar schemes were implemented in Stettin, Mainz, Cologne-Merheim, and Hanover-Stöcken.

The introduction of crematoriums from the middle of the 19th century brought new opportunities and required different treatments, in both memorial gardens and columbaria. One of the first crematoriums was incorporated at Père Lachaise in 1861, designed by Jean-Camille Formigé. Other European examples include Gotha, Germany (1878), North Cemetery in Stockholm (1897), and Golders Green in London (1902), which included a new memorial garden designed by William Robinson. In the Netherlands the first crematorium was built at the Westerveld Cemetery in 1913. Designed by the architect M. Poel, it was incorporated into an existing cemetery designed in 1888 by L.P. Zocher and J.J. Kerbert. One of the most striking features of this cemetery, which is set on the edge of the dunes, are the carefully integrated columbaria, which were designed by the architect W.M. Dudok in 1925.

In contrast to the Protestant countries, which produced cemeteries in the landscape style, Catholic countries in southern Europe generally favored a layout on a grid system, where the central feature of the walks forms a cross in plan, with a church or chapel at the middle point. An example of this style is the Central Cemetery, Vienna, designed in 1874 by Mylius and Bluntschli. The debate between a formal or informal layout was nowhere more clear than in the various design competitions for cemeteries in Germany, where different hybrid versions between landscape and geometrical layouts were produced. While regular in layout, plantings often formed an important aspect and helped to structure and strengthen the design.

The 20th century brought with it greater diversity in the expression of cemetery design, which reflected new and very different ideologies. This has been particularly well expressed in the German-speaking world, where cemeteries became a special branch of horticulture and where, since the 1914 Landesausstellung in Bern, they have been regularly included as exhibits at garden festivals. The famous debate between architects and garden designers of the architectural garden versus landscape style also transferred to cemetery design, with the architect Max Läuger designing the architectural Osterholz Cemetery, Bremen, in 1900. This differed from the regular 18th- and 19th-century formal cemeteries, in that the main buildings were off center and also in the extensive provision of semipublic open space. The designer also anticipated the need for future expansion, providing for this eventuality through the creation of different character areas, with varied planting. Mariebjerg, north of Copenhagen, Denmark, is one of the best-known examples of this approach. Laid out from 1929 by G.N. Brandt, it probably drew inspiration from Osterholz Cemetery in its architectural approach. However, the layout was simpler and yet more surprising for the variation within the different compartments.

In 1907 the first Woodland Cemetery designed by Hans Grässel opened in Munich. The design proved to be extremely popular, striking a chord with the contemporary ideology and responding to a changing culture. From this success Grässel was employed to design a new woodland or forest cemetery in Schaffhausen, Switzerland, which was completed in 1909. His approach has become one of the most popular ways of establishing new cemeteries in Germany. The most famous of these woodland cemeteries was laid out in Sweden. Designed by the partnership of the architects Erik Gunnar Asplund and Sigurd Lewerentz, Stockholm's new South Cemetery in Enskede has become a potent symbol for the Nordic cemetery and of modernist landscape design. The proposal originated in 1915 as the winning entry for a competition for a new cemetery. Perhaps much of the scheme's success can be attributed to the continued involvement of the architects. Asplund helped to oversee the implementation of the design until his death in 1940.

During the ideology-ridden era between the two world wars, German nationalism sought ways of expressing connections with the ancient past by establishing so-called Places of the Ancestors (Ahnenstätte). This included Hilligenhoh and Seelenfeld (ca. 1930) by Rudolf Bergfeld, and the Grove of Saxons (Sachsenhain) near Verden by Wilhelm Hübotter (1935). These cemeteries included large boulders associated with ancient Nordic burials, as well as naturalistic vegetation.

Following the two world wars the Imperial War Graves Commission (established in 1917) and American Battle Monuments Commission (established in 1923) had the task of commemorating those who had died in battle. The war cemeteries, of which there are many throughout the world, have left a legacy in terms of quality of design and management.

The war cemeteries produced during World War I and II were evidence of a new era, with an equality and unity in design not seen before. The remarkable consistency and their management generally make them emotional spaces, even today. The British cemeteries of World War I were designed by Edwin Lutyens and Herbert Baker and included architectural elements by Reginald Blomfield. The designs were unified by the simple Portland headstones, all of the same size, in neat rows with associated strips of planting. The American World War II cemetery in Normandy (landscape designed by Markley Stevenson) displays a similar clarity and unified simplicity in design. The layout is based on a Latin cross. Headstones are marked by either a Star of David for those of the Jewish faith or a simple cross for all others. The headstones are aligned in perfect rows within an immaculately maintained lawn. German war cemeteries were typically less unified in their approach and implementation.

Some of the most moving cemeteries are those for resistance fighters executed during World War II, such as the Erebegraafplaats Zeeweg, Overveen, Netherlands (1947), designed by J.T.P. Bijhouwer and L. van Weydom-Claterbos, which is situated within a dune landscape completely integrated within a natural environment, and the Memorial Grove, Ryvangen, Copenhagen (1946 by Aksel Andersen; altered and extended in 1977 by Ole Nørgård), which is both artistic and well integrated within an existing grove of elm trees (now diseased).

In the quest for new expressions of cemetery design, the Igualada Cemetery, designed by Enric Miralles and Carme Pinós (1985), near Barcelona, Spain, is perhaps one of the most exciting and challenging of contemporary designs. Opened in 1990 the cemetery is located in an excavated hollow on the edge of an industrial estate. The design is unusual in its acknowledgment of its own finite life. The cemetery is constructed from concrete, steel, and wood, and there is an explicit acceptance that it will decay over time and that the surrounding vegetation will ultimately engulf the site, thereby challenging the notion that death is the end.

The growth in environmental awareness that began toward the end of the 20th century has had a significant impact on burial practice. Those who are concerned about the environment have become increasingly skeptical of the environmental costs associated with traditional burial and cremation. In Great Britain there has been a dramatic growth in the provision of "green burial" sites. These are frequently extensions of local authority cemeteries but may also be in privately owned nature reserves and farmland. Green burial has at its core an environmental response to the disposal of the dead and has also been seen as a way of protecting land from development. The aim is that through burial there should be an improvement of the environment, not further pollution. Green burial typically involves no other form of memorial than plants, which it is hoped will mature into either native woodland or meadow.

### Further Reading

Bracco, Patrick, "Le cimtière du Père La Chaise," *Monuments historiques* 124 (December 1982–January 1983)

Bradfield, J.B., *Green Burial: The D-I-Y Guide to Law and Practice*, London: Institute for Social Inventions, 1993; 2nd edition, London: Natural Death Centre, 1994

Constant, Caroline, *The Woodland Cemetery: Toward a Spiritual Landscape: Erik Gunnar Asplund and Sigurd Lewerentz, 1915–61*, Stockholm: Byggförlaget, 1994

Curl, James Stevens, "The Design of the Early British Cemeteries," *Journal of Garden History* 4, no. 3 (1984)

Downing, Andrew Jackson, "Public Cemeteries and Public Gardens," in *Rural Essays*, by Downing, edited by George William Curtis, New York, 1853; reprint, New York: Da Capo Press, 1974

Fürttenbach, Joseph, *Architectura recreationis*, Augsburg, Germany, 1640; reprint, in *Architectura civilis (1628), Architectura recreationis (1640), Architectura privata (1641)*, 3 vols. in 1, Hildesheim, Germany, and New York: Olms, 1971

Karsten, Jørgensen, "Equality and the Modern Way of Death," *Topos* 2 (1993)

Loudon, John Claudius, *On the Laying Out, Planting, and Managing of Cemeteries and on the Improvement of Churchyards*, London, 1843; reprint, Redhill, Surrey: Ivelet Books, 1981

Robinson, William, *God's Acre Beautiful: or, The Cemeteries of the Future,* London and New York, 1880; 3rd edition, London and New York, 1883

Rugg, Julie, "A Few Remarks on Modern Sepulture: Current Trends and New Directions in Cemetery Research," *Mortality* 3, no. 2 (1998)

Sckell, Friedrich Ludwig von, *Beiträge zur bildenden Gartenkunst,* Munich, 1818; 2nd edition, 1825; reprint, Worms, Germany: Werner, 1982

Tishler, William H., editor, *American Landscape Architecture: Designers and Places,* Washington, D.C.: Preservation Press, 1989

Valentien, Otto, *Der Friedhof: Gärtnerische Gestaltung, Bauten, Grabmale,* Munich: Bayerischer Landwirtschaftsverlag, 1953

Voit, Johann Michael, *Über die Anlegung und Umwandlung des Gottesacker in heitere Ruhegärten der Abgeschiedenen,* Augsburg, 1825

Wolschke-Bulmann, Joachim, "The Nationalization of Nature and the Naturalization of the German Nation: 'Teutonic' Trends in Early Twentieth-Century Landscape Design," in *Nature and Ideology: Natural Garden Design in the Twentieth Century,* edited by Wolschke-Bulmann, Washington, D.C.: Dumbarton Oaks, 1997

Zabalbeascoa, Anatxu, *Igualada Cemetery: Enric Miralles and Carme Pinós,* London: Phaidon, 1996

ANDREW CLAYDEN AND JAN WOUDSTRA

---

# Central Park

## New York City, New York, United States

**Location:**  center of Manhattan Island

A green reservoir in the center of the city, Central Park is an island of nature, defined by the boundary walls that form a rectangular enclosure paralleling the bordering grid of streets and avenues of New York City. Allowing people a relatively safe space for reflection and refreshment, the park provides an antidote to the surrounding urban intensity.

Created between 1850–76, the design of Central Park marked a transition from the previous formality of American park designs to the introduction of the English landscape school into the United States. The designers, Frederick Law Olmsted and Calvert Vaux, also incorporated the Victorian influences of their own times, in which industrialization and urbanization were developing rapidly. Olmsted and Vaux believed that an urban park should offer respite from the pressures of city life, and in his writings Olmsted described the necessity of a park within a gridded city: "It should present an aspect of spaciousness and tranquillity with variety and intricacy of arrangement, thereby affording the most agreeable contrast to the confinement, bustle, and monotonous street division of the city." Ironically, with the place of urban escape being located at the center of the city, New Yorkers find themselves turning inwards, both literally and metaphorically, to escape the intensity of the surrounding urban environment.

Not only a space for personal reflection, Central Park has long served as New York's grand green stage for large-scale celebrations and demonstrations. Numerous places were planned throughout the park where New Yorkers could engage in the social and pleasurable custom of public promenading. Nineteenth and early 20th-century society turned out in Central Park to see and be seen in many different guises. These included the fashionably theatrical custom of parading Sunday finery and Easter hats along the Grand Promenade and at Bethesda Fountain, enjoying evening concerts at the Bandshell, boating on the lake or dining at the Boat House, promenading along the Main Drive in fashionable carriages, and picnicking in the sun in Sheeps' Meadow or playing lawn tennis in the courts provided. Sheeps' Meadow was used in the 1960s for anti-Vietnam War demonstrations and later served as the site for Philharmonic Orchestra concerts. In the last decades of the 20th century, disco roller-skating along the Grand Promenade superseded the traditional form of promenading. The rectangular reservoir was replaced early in the century by playing fields, and childrens' playgrounds have always been numerously supplied throughout the park. The miniature sailboat pond has been popular with young and old in both past and current times, and fishing is and has been a leading form of recreation in Olmsted's parks. The Bowling Green has provided the elderly with an enjoyable sport, and ice skating and cross-country skiing are seasonal sports enjoyed by many.

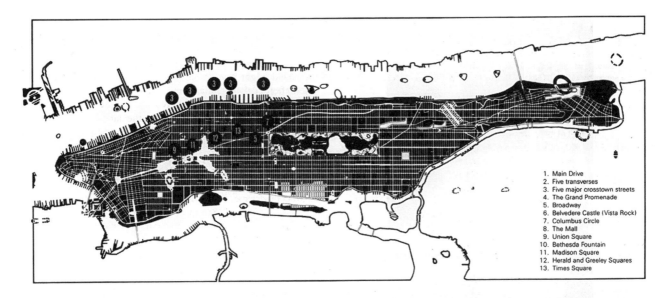

1. Main Drive
2. Five transverses
3. Five major crosstown streets
4. The Grand Promenade
5. Broadway
6. Belvedere Castle (Vista Rock)
7. Columbus Circle
8. The Mall
9. Union Square
10. Bethesda Fountain
11. Madison Square
12. Herald and Greeley Squares
13. Times Square

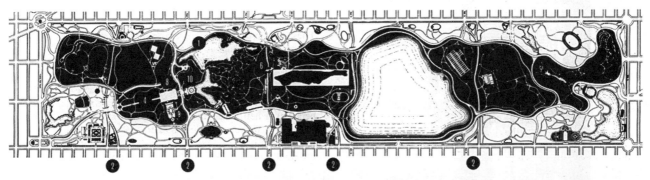

Map of Manhattan Island and detail of Central Park with the rectangular "reservoir" at its center
Copyright Lorna McNeur

Naturally, walking, jogging, roller-skating, and cycling have always been accessible pastimes for much of the population. As a democrat, Olmsted believed that people of all classes should have access to every aspect of the park. The designers were aware that the long, thin shape of the park (0.5 mile wide by 2.5 miles long [0.8 km wide by 4 km long]) allowed for it to be accessible to a number of different neighborhoods comprising working-class, middle-class, and wealthy people of numerous nationalities, ages, and persuasions living in the city. Here is a green urban space that meets the needs of such a significant cross section of urban dwellers that it can be considered as complex in its design as the city itself.

Olmsted often refers in his writings to the park and the city simultaneously, implying their potential interchangeability. Because of the unusually long and thin rectangular shape of the park plan, Olmsted explains that, paradoxically, he found it necessary to consult the plans of cities in order to create his design for the park: "The form and position of Central Park are peculiar . . . such that prece-

dent with dealing with it is rather to be sought in the long and narrow boulevards of some of the old continental European cities, than in the broad parks with which from its area in acres, we are most naturally led to compare it."

He began the design of the park by organizing the major road systems in a configuration similar to that of the existing major road structure of New York. In writing on his design intentions for Central Park, Olmsted explains in the section entitled "The System of Walks and Rides" that "it must be necessary to lay out all the principal drives, rides and walks of the Park in lines having a continuous northerly and southerly course, nearly parallel with each other and with the avenues of the city . . . ." A comparison of the plan of Central Park and New York City (specifically Manhattan) reveals just how similar the road structures actually are.

The Main Drive within Central Park is a continuous loop through the park describing a shape that is long and thin and is similar in contour to the island of Manhattan. The 1:5 proportions of both Central Park and the island of Manhattan are identical. The north-south orientation of the main drive parallels the avenues, while the crosstown streets of the park, called transverses, are a continuation of the major crosstown streets of the city. Olmsted's comparison of the park's transverse roads and the city's major crosstown streets reveals the similarities of both the form and the function of these parallel roadways: "Each of these will be the sole line of communication between one side of town and the other, for a distance equal to that between Chambers street and Canal street." The primary road system in Central Park incorporates the city grid but is disguised with curves to reinforce the romantic landscape.

Other highly significant similarities include the fashionably theatrical Grand Promenade within Central Park that parallels the diagonal orientation of the celebrated route of Broadway within the city. In discussing the potential traffic problems of the Grand Promenade, the transverses, and the Main Drive, Olmsted makes a comparison with Broadway and the crosstown streets. He explains that "If we suppose but one crossing of Broadway to be possible in this interval, we shall realize that these transverse roads are destined to become . . . crowded thoroughfares." Here again, Olmsted is visualising the parallel relationships between the Grand Promenade and Broadway, along with the incorporation of the city grid within the romantic landscape. Recognizing the traffic problems occurring at the conjunction of Broadway and the grid, Olmsted aimed to avoid the same in his design of the Grand Promenade and the warped grid within the Park. His solution to this potential congestion in the park was to drop the height of the transverses below ground level (while leaving them open to the sky), thus creating a feature similar to the so-called ha-ha in English landscape gardens, an excavated or "sunken" fence that gives the illusion of a continuous landscape at ground level.

In looking at the plan of Central Park within the context of New York City, it is interesting to note that the location of the once existing rectangular reservoir within the park (part of the original design) was analogous to the placement of Central Park within Manhattan itself. Stepping further back to view both the park within its urban context and the city within its landscape, one can see that the compressed relationship of the park to its defining walls is similar in nature to that of Manhattan island and its watery borders. For Olmsted, the need for Central Park was a direct result of its context within the "densely populated central portion of an immense metropolis." Central Park, he wrote, provides "a means to certain kinds of REFRESHMENT OF THE MIND AND NERVES which most city dwellers greatly need." As an urban park it was designed to respond to its numerous types of inhabitants in equally as complex a way as does the city to its citizens.

It can be seen that Central Park and New York City have very strong similarities both in form and in function. Ironically, in Olmsted's efforts to create a romantic landscape as a means of escape from the pressures of metropolitan life, he also used as a role model the very city that it was necessary to escape. A park as rich and complex as the city surrounding it; could it be that Central Park is a city clothed in foliage?

**Synopsis**

| | |
|---|---|
| 1840s | Initial ideas raised about need for a park as New York City grows |
| Early 1850s | Public discussion and debate begins in newspaper editorials, letters to editors, and legislative testimonies; debate heightens with intense political struggles over use of land for private real estate or public park |
| 1851 | First site chosen for Central Park at Jones Wood through legislative act |
| 1853 | Through act of legislature, final site chosen for what is now Central Park; commissioners of estimate and assessment appointed for feasibility study |
| 1858 | Board of commissioners of Central Park assembled; design competition advertised; Olmsted/Vaux "Greensward" plan for Central Park wins competition; site clearance begins (rubbish, stones, and open surface drains); first tree planted in Park |
| 1859 | Construction of park south of 79th Street completed |
| 1861 | Carriage road in public use |
| 1865 | Drive and ride completed; school boys allowed to play in Park; enclosing walls continued |
| 1867 | Construction of Belvedere Castle begun |
| 1869 | Dairy and Merchants' gate commenced |
| 1873 | Number of visitors in park this year over 10 million |
| 1878 | Building of Central Park, with its principal features, completed |

**Further Reading**

Fabos, Julius Gy, Gordon T. Milde, and V. Michael Weinmayr, *Frederick Law Olmsted, Sr.: Founder of Landscape Architecture in America*, Amherst: University of Massachusetts Press, 1968

Fein, Albert, *Frederick Law Olmsted and the American Environmental Tradition*, New York: Braziller, 1972

Kelly, Bruce, Gail Travis Guillet, and Mary Ellen W. Hern, editors, *Art of the Olmsted Landscape*, 2 vols.,

New York: New York City Landmarks Preservation, Arts Publisher Commission, 1981

Olmsted, Frederick Law, *Forty Years of Landscape Architecture: Central Park,* edited by Frederick Law Olmsted, Jr., and Theodora Kimball, New York: Putnam, 1928; reprint of vol. 2, Cambridge, Massachusetts: MIT Press, 1973

Olmsted, Frederick Law, *Landscape into Cityscape: Frederick Law Olmsted's Plans for a Greater New York City,* edited by Albert Fein, Ithaca, New York: Cornell University Press, 1967

Olmsted, Frederick Law, *The Papers of Frederick Law Olmsted,* 6 vols., edited by Charles Capen McLaughlin et al., Baltimore, Maryland: Johns

Hopkins University Press, 1977– ; see especially vol. 3, *Creating Central Park, 1857–1861*

Rosenzweig, Roy, and Elizabeth Blackmar, *The Park and the People: A History of Central Park,* Ithaca, New York: Cornell University Press, 1992

Sennett, Richard, *The Conscience of the Eye: The Design and Social Life of Cities,* New York: Knopf, 1990; London: Faber and Faber, 1991

Sennett, Richard, *Flesh and Stone: The Body and the City in Western Civilization,* New York: Norton, and London: Faber and Faber, 1994

LORNA ANNE MCNEUR

---

# Červený Dvůr

## Český Krumlov district, South Bohemian region, Czech Republic

**Location:**   2 miles (3.2 km) southeast of Chvalšiny, 5 miles (8 km) northwest of Český Krumlov, and approximately 85 miles (137 km) south of Prague

The natural landscape park in Červený Dvůr at Chvalšiny ranks among the most important historic parks in the Czech Republic. As the archival evidence shows, each particular developmental stage of the park (architectural as well as scenic) maintained a high standard, ranking Červený Dvůr among the important parks in Europe. The park's layout resembles the German parks of Prince Hermann Pückler-Muskau, such as Muskau and Branitz. Presumably, Theodor Heinrich Rehder, son of Jacob H. Rehder (head gardener to Prince Pückler) took part in creating the park's structure. The main feature of the park's structure is the dramatic contrast that exists between open areas with trees shaped in chains and dark forest sceneries, in the exact arrangement of solitary trees in regard to the surrounding space, in the location of solitary trees at the end of long views, and in the use of the surrounding nature (hills of Blanský Forest, Šumava) in the park's general scheme. The park as it exists today originated about 1850 as a result of the transformation of a pretentiously designed and richly fitted baroque garden.

The marvelous landscape beneath Klet', in the area of the Blanský Forest, had been used by the Český Krumlov nobility for rest and entertainment since the end of the 16th century. At this point in time the Rosenbergs established on the site of the present castle the so-called

New Chvalšiny Court together with a pheasantry. The castle was built under the Eggenbergs in the second half of the 17th century, and the Schwarzenbergs enlarged it in the mid-18th century to meet the requirements of a summer residence for a powerful aristocratic house.

During the second half of the 18th century, the pheasantry was transformed into an elaborately designed baroque garden. A trapezium-shaped garden demarcated by an enclosing wall was symmetrically broken up into eight radial stairways leading from the central fountain into closed bosquets with various contents. In the center of the layout the main axis, where various water designs were located (pools with water fountains), led toward the castle. Water was also represented in various other places, for example, a 200-meter-long (219 yd.) water cascade with a cave, a styled blind branch of the river, a water canal with a poplar island, a beaver lake, and ponds for cultivation of water fauna. In addition, the garden included Chinese and Dutch pavilions, a natural theater, rosarium, Schneckenberg (Snail Hill), and a summer riding school.

At the beginning of the 19th century, the pathway was simplified, although the fundamental stairway remained. Inside the bosquets irregularly laid paths provided a Romantic element. In the middle of the 19th century, under Prince Jan Adolf II Schwarzenberg, the baroque garden was elaborately transformed into a natural landscape park. The garden modification was driven not only by the prince's repeated visits to England but also by the deteriorating state of the garden. The structure of the newly formed natural landscape park was to a significant degree influenced by the spaciousness and ground plan of the baroque garden. Only the central axis remained as the main layout and central view of the park. All water features were left on the axis, with the exception of the trapezoid pond, which was adapted as a lake with an island. The enclosing wall was pulled down and the area of the park was on the east and west sides enlarged to the present size of 117 hectares (289 acres).

Although the previous network of paths was eliminated, irregular paths in many sections originated from the baroque design. The basis of the new system of paths was an outer and inner walking circular route, together with a representative route leading to the castle, which contains a central green and offers numerous views of the castle, as well as at the opposite opened part of the park. The core of the composition is a central grassy space, formed by means of solitary trees and groups into numerous sceneries with an impressive dramatic atmosphere. The efficiency of the middle part stresses the monumental scenery of the southern slope of the Blanský Forest, which rises immediately above the park and by so doing becomes an integral part of the entire layout. A score of new structures contributed to the formation of particular Romantic sceneries, ingeniously bound with panoramas: a neo-Gothic building called the Pheasantry, a Swiss Cottage, a porter's lodge, a rose arbor connected with a shadow corridor to the rose garden, an obelisk transported to the southern part of the park, and a Holy Virgin's pillar built in a neo-Gothic style.

The rudiments of the plantation had been already laid in the original pheasantry, from which also probably came some of the huge trees (spruces, oaks). The prevailing tree species in this central part is oak (*Quercus robur*), followed by linden (*Tilia cordata, T. platyphyllos*), alder (*Alnus glutinosa*), maple (*Acer platanoides, A. pseudoplatanus*), and ash (*Fraxinus excelsior*). Conifers are represented by spruce (*Picea abies*) and pine (*Pinus sylvestris*); the regular plantation also includes larch (*Larix decidua*). The characteristic of the rear section differs due to a higher representation of maple; the border also includes a higher occurrence of hornbeam (*Carpinus betulus*) and birch (*Betula alba*); based on some huge stumps, it is clear that a few elms (*Ulmus* sp.) also grew there until recently. Newly introduced plants occur only rarely, especially in the castle surroundings. They include *Acer rubrum, Pinus strobus, Gleditsia triacanthos, Platanus × acerifolia, Fraxinus excelsior* 'Pendula', and *Picea pungens* var. *argentea*.

The natural landscape image of the park has been preserved without any significant changes. The castle area was owned by the Schwarzenbergs until 1940; in 1949 it became state property. In 1966 a psychiatric hospital was established in the castle, which still exists today.

The park is not yet accessible to the public, although special excursions are allowed.

## Synopsis

| | |
|---|---|
| 1591 | Vilem of Rosenberg begins building New Chvalšiny Court |
| 1598 | Petr Vok of Rosenberg creates enclosed pheasantry at New Chvalšiny Court |
| 1672 | Marie Ernestina Eggenberg builds castle |
| 1748–81 | Under Prince Josef Adam Schwarzenberg, castle paint work and decoration completed, and side wing added |
| 1750–84 | Breeding of beavers, Chinese pheasants, ducks, Bengal stags, and Egyptian pigs |
| 1761 | Water jets put into operation |
| 1764–69 | Construction of enclosing wall |
| 1784 | Construction of cave |
| 1786 | Construction of obelisk in corner of garden |
| 1787–89 | Establishment of Chinese and Dutch pavilions, planting of Canadian and common poplars |
| 1838–40 | Construction of Swiss Cottage, which included stable for cow breeding of Swiss origin, salon, and two cabinets; establishment of neo-Gothic Pheasantry for seasonal guests |
| 1839 | Enclosing wall pulled down |
| 1844 | Powerful storm caused considerable damage to garden |
| 1845 | Obelisk moved to Cross Field in southern part of Park |
| 1850 | Prince Jan Adolf II Schwarzenberg has baroque garden transformed into natural landscape park; summer houses pulled down and cave closed |
| 1949 | Castle became state property |
| 1966 | Psychiatric hospital established in castle |
| 1989 | Surveys completed to compare park layout in Červený Dvůr with that of Hermann Pückler's parks |
| 1998 | Surveys and comparisons with landscape plan from 1910, followed by replanting in accordance with original layout |

## Further Reading

Dokoupil, Zdeněk, *Historické zahrady v Čechách a na Moravě* (Historic Gardens in Bohemia and Moravia), Prague: Nakladatelství Československých Výtvarných Umělců, 1957

Hieke, Karel, *České zámecké parky a jejich dřeviny* (Czech Castle Parks and Their Tree Species), Prague: Stání Zemědělské Nakladatelství, 1985

Pacáková-Hošt'álková, Božena, et al., *Zahrady a parky v Čechách, na Moravě a ve Slezsku* (Gardens and Parks in Bohemia, Moravia, and Silesia), Prague: Libri, 1999

MARIE PAVLÁTOVÁ AND MAREK EHRLICH

# Chambers, William 1723–1796

## British Architect and Landscape Gardener

Although Sir William Chambers is remembered principally as a leading 18th-century architect, his work at the Royal Botanic Gardens, Kew for Augusta, dowager Princess of Wales (1757–63), shows him to have been an innovative and talented landscape gardener. The plans and drawings for Kew, together with their subsequent publication, and three drawings for royal gardens in Sweden appear to be all that remain of his designs as a landscape gardener. However, Chambers contributed many notable garden temples to established landscapes, while his publications ensured a wider influence.

Ironically, the royal patronage in England that Chambers enjoyed and that established the success of his architectural career was more fruitful in terms of landscape gardening than in palace design; a great number of alternative drawings for a new royal palace at Richmond exist, but none were ever executed, while the Royal Botanic Gardens, Kew, is a lasting testament to his talents as a landscape gardener, with 5 of the original 25 buildings, including the notorious Pagoda, still standing. The buildings at Kew showed a far greater versatility of style than is to be seen in the rest of his work. His architecture is generally in a Franco-Italian inspired neoclassical style, a consequence of his studies at Blondel's École des Arts in Paris followed by five years of study in Italy.

Chambers's sketches of Chinese buildings and gardens, made on his voyages when in the employ of the Swedish East India Company, seem to have brought him to the attention of Frederick, Prince of Wales. It was fortuitous that Chambers, having decided to leave his Swedish employment in order to study architecture in Paris, spent a few months in London. This was in 1749 when the prince was having garden temples built in the chinoiserie style at Kew, and Chambers appears to have been consulted. Following the Prince of Wales's death

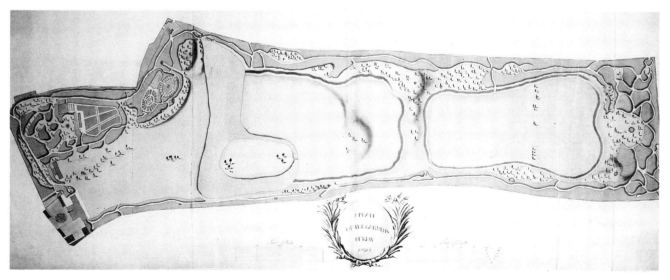

**Plan of the gardens at the Royal Botanic Gardens, Kew, London, England**
**Courtesy of British Library**

two years later, Chambers sent an unsolicited proposal for a mausoleum. The drawings are particularly interesting as they can be seen as a precursor to his garden temples; the mausoleum would have stood in a similar landscape setting. Indeed, one drawing shows the mausoleum as a ruined section set in a landscape with trees and shrubbery growing out of the dome. The design was not executed, but it may have led to the formal commission to lay out the gardens at Kew. This came from Frederick's widow in 1757, the year that Chambers published his *Designs of Chinese Buildings*.

Chambers had made his drawings of China as a record, in the same way that he drew French buildings with their gardens as part of his studies in France, but the French drawings were not appropriate to the current fashion for chinoiserie. When Chambers returned to London from Rome, the Chinese style was still much in vogue, and with his unique portfolio of drawings, Chambers was the acknowledged authority. He was in the enviable position of being able to publish before establishing a practice. He took the opportunity, but it was his *Plans, Elevations, Sections, and Perspective Views of the Gardens and Buildings at Kew* (1763) that formed a more realistic record of his work and ideas.

*Designs of Chinese Buildings* includes an essay on gardening that formed the basis for Chambers's later *Dissertation on Oriental Gardening* (1772). It was initially more influential in France, where there was a fashion for the Anglo-Chinese garden long after it had been supplanted in England by Lancelot "Capability" Brown's landscape garden. The influence in England came later, with the introduction of the picturesque movement. Brown was undoubtedly the more successful of the two in terms of the landscape garden, and Chambers's dissertation was a veiled, but well-understood, attack on Brown's work. It was not intended to promote the imitation of Chinese gardens in England and proved an embarrassment to Chambers, who was obliged to publish a further edition with an explanatory discourse. However, his ideas on variety and color in garden planning continued to be an influence throughout the 20th century.

Chambers was astute enough to dedicate his first book to George, Prince of Wales, and shortly afterward he was appointed architect to the dowager Princess of Wales and architectural tutor to her son, the future George III. His role as tutor seems to have been influential both in his choice of buildings at Kew and the publication of his *Treatise on Civil Architecture* (1759). His choice of buildings at Kew provides firsthand examples of different architectural styles from around the world, while his *Treatise on Civil Architecture* focuses on an analysis of the five orders of classical architecture and became the standard English treatise on the subject.

Chambers maintained his family connections in Sweden and periodically sought commissions and appointments there. His design for a new royal palace at Svartsjo appears, as was his design for the mausoleum, to have been unsolicited. It was in any event rejected, but it helped secure him the honor of Knight of the Order of the Polar Star, which he received in 1770 and which was a source of great pride to him, although it was by no means the equivalent of an English knighthood. He continued to pursue the royal family, sending English and French copies of his *Dissertation on Oriental Gardening* to Gustav III. Chambers was eventually rewarded with two commissions: one from Queen Lovis Ulrica, the Queen Mother, for the garden at Svartso and one from the king to design a new garden at the royal palace at Ulriksdal.

At Svartsjo Chambers was limited by the Queen's small budget and her desire to retain the original formal garden. Thus, he restricted his work to an area to the east of the formal garden, where he introduced winding paths and garden temples. At Ulriksdal the drawing shows a wide pathway around the perimeter of the garden, several temples or garden follies, and an odd boot-shaped pond with an island—all features to be found also at Kew. This design was not executed, but Chambers's influence can be seen in a garden designed by the king at Ekolsund.

Ambition was presumably the determining factor in Chambers's decision to practice in England rather than return to Sweden on completion of his studies. He had already met many of his future English patrons on their Grand Tour in Rome, and his design for a mausoleum for Frederick, Prince of Wales, is evidence of his desire to seek the patronage of the British royal family. His pursuit of the Swedish royals took longer, and the commissions were less fruitful, but it is to the royal patronage of both countries that we owe our record of Chambers's work as a landscape gardener.

*See also* Kew, Royal Botanic Gardens

**Biography**

Born in Gothenburg, Sweden, 23 February 1723, son of Scottish merchant. Worked as merchant seaman, architect, writer, and landscape architect and designer of furniture, silver, ormolu, ceramics, clocks, and George III's state coach; educated England; returned to Sweden to work for Swedish East India Company; first voyage to Bengal, 1740–42; sailed to Canton, 1743–45; returned to China, 1748–49; studied modern languages, mathematics, art, and civil architecture; sketched Chinese buildings and traveled in Europe; abandoned merchant marine in favor of architecture, 1749; studied in Paris at Blondel's École des Arts; traveled extensively in Italy, 1750–55; studied with Clérisseau and Pecheux in Rome; submitted design for mausoleum for Frederick, Prince of Wales in 1752; began architectural practice in England

and employed as architectural tutor to Prince of Wales, 1755; employed at Kew by dowager princess, 1757; appointed to Office of Works with Robert Adam as joint architect to George III, 1761; remodeled Buckingham House and created many unexecuted designs for new royal palaces at Richmond and Kew; exhibited designs at Society of Arts, 1761–68; first treasurer of Royal Academy of Arts, 1768; Knight of the Polar Star, Sweden, 1770; commissions included public buildings, town and country houses, and garden temples in Great Britain. Died in London, England, 8 March 1796.

## Selected Designs

| | |
|---|---|
| 1763 | Kew Gardens, London, England |
| 1774 | Gardens at Svartsjo, Sweden |
| 1775 | New royal pleasure garden (not executed), Ulriksdal, Sweden; Bladon Bridge, Temples of Flora and Diana, and Tuscan gateway, Blenheim, Oxfordshire, England |
| 1776 | Casino, Marino House, Dublin, Ireland |

## Selected Publications

*Designs of Chinese Buildings, Furniture, Dresses, Machines, and Utensils,* 1757
*Treatise on Civil Architecture,* 1759; 2nd edition, 1768
*Plans, Elevations, Sections, and Perspective Views of the Gardens and Buildings at Kew in Surrey,* 1763
*Dissertation on Oriental Gardening,* 1772; 2nd edition, 1773

## Further Reading

Harris, John, *Sir William Chambers: Knight of the Polar Star,* London: Zwemmer, and University Park: Pennsylvania State University Press, 1970
Harris, John, and Michael Snodin, editors, *Sir William Chambers: Architect to George III,* New Haven, Connecticut: Yale University Press, 1996
Snodin, Michael, editor, *Sir William Chambers,* London: Victoria and Albert,1996

ANNE PURCHAS

# Chantilly

## Chantilly, France

**Location:** approximately 20.5 miles (36 km) north of Paris and 5 miles (7 km) west of Senlis

The castle of Chantilly lies to the east of the town of the same name, which was sited to the west of the castle park and has subsequently spread over a considerable part of the castle gardens. The castle was originally a fortified building of the medieval period, a triangular structure built on a rock in a large body of water that served as a moat. Beside this was added in the mid-16th century the building known as the Petit Chateau, on its own island with a small formal garden. A narrow channel of water ran between the two, which were joined by a bridge. The present castle was rebuilt in the 19th century, the original having been razed in the French Revolution.

This was the ancient estate of the Montmorency family, for a number of generations *connetable* (high constable) of France. The most famous member to serve in this office was Anne, duc de Montmorency (named for his godmother, Anne of Brittany), who served as constable in the middle years of the 16th century, dying in 1567. His equestrian statue stands on the great mid-16th-century terrace on the eastern side of the chateau. It was

from this side that the original main approach and entrance to the castle were laid out and the great raised terrace, built to emphasize these, constructed (1538). A later access was created across the pond from the southwest in the same century and another from the north.

A plan by Androuet Du Cerceau of 1570 shows a complex of rectangular gardens laid out on the west bank of the water, opposite the castle, and the small river Nonette just north of the castle running east to west into the Oise. The renowned architect André Le Nôtre was called to Chantilly in 1662 by Louis II de Bourbon, prince de Condé, known as the Grand Condé, a cousin of Louis XIV who proved invaluable to the latter as an outstanding military commander. The estate upon which he planned to make his improvements extended over 2,500 acres (1,012 ha). Chantilly is often spoken of as Le Nôtre's major achievement, and he was involved in its development for about 20 years. The central feature of his wonderfully bold design was the existing grand terrace. The other essential element in the success of the work was the presence of water, both still and flowing, evidenced by the large pond within which the castle was sited and the river to the north.

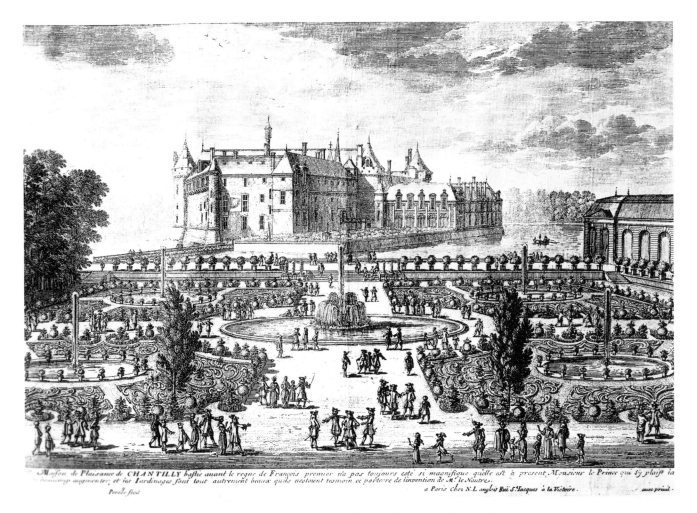

*Mason de Plaisance de CHANTILLY bastie auant le regne de François premier n'a pas tousjours esté si magnifique quelle est à present, Monsieur le Prince qui s'y plaist la beaucoup augmenter; et les Iardinages sont tout autrement beaux quils nestoient tesmoin ce parterre de l'inuention de M.r le Nautre.*

*Perelle fecit*
*a Paris chez N.L anglois Rüe S.t Iacques à la Victoire .*
*auec priuil .*

Engraving of the gardens at Chantilly, Oise, France, by Adam Perelle
Copyright Giraudon/Art Resource, New York

In order to create a new grand formal layout Le Nôtre could be said to have set the castle to one side. He created a new access from the south, aligned not on the castle but on the raised grand terrace immediately to the east of it. The castle thus becomes a mere element, though an important one, in a much larger composition. This begins along the Rue du Connetable, which starts the axis several kilometers south of the castle. Crossing the pool, the Etang de Sylvie, the axis enters a formally laid out and symmetrical grass esplanade, shaped like an ornate shield and with smooth vertical stone walls forming the banks, projecting southward into the water. The esplanade leads by a gentle ramp up to the Grand Terrace. From here, the entrance to the castle on the left is at right angles to the axis. To the right a path leads to the wooded Parc de Sylvie. Continuing northward on the same line, a great stairway leads down to the Grand Parterre, flanking a short but wide north-south canal called the Manche. The Manche is a branch of the east-west Grand Canal, which closes off further physical access to the north at this point. The northern end of the Manche is marked on the north side of the Grand Canal by a semicircular feature, the "Vertugadin," in which were placed the busts of the 12 Caesars. The visual line of the axis is carried beyond this to the north by an avenue in the great park.

The Grand Parterre, in which water is again a major element, is flanked on either side by avenues, the so-called philosophers walks, running north and south. Beyond these, east and west, were areas of open grass. On each side of the Manche are five pools with fountains, now laid out with simple lawns but where previously there would have been extensive ornamental and shrub planting. This is virtually all that remains of Le Nôtre's great design. Replacing the original 16th-century garden on the west bank of the Etang de Sylvie, Le Nôtre created a new formal garden that, complemented by Jules Hardouin Mansart's later orangery building, became known as the Orangery garden. Further to the west, a series of formal gardens and walks, laid out in about 1675, continued for a distance of more than a kilometer. These formal gardens were noted at the time for their collections of flowers, particularly tulips, hyacinths, and other bulbs. As well as André Le Nôtre, Le Quintinie, the king's gardener, was employed here. The orangery was swept away in the early 19th century to make way for a *jardin anglais*—a garden in the English landscape style. This was the fate of designs in a number of historic French gardens. Within this garden, now restored, is still to be found a rustic hamlet, the Hameau, set around a green of the same period. Over the rest of the formal 17th-century gardens, the modern town of Chantilly has expanded eastward to engulf almost the entire area.

The Grand Canal, created east-west along the line of the river Nonette with a straight length of 1.8 kilometers (1.1 mi.), and with a further one-kilometer extension at an oblique angle to the west, is the principal water feature. A little west of the castle and to the south of the Grand Canal, another canal ran virtually parallel to the latter. Between the two was a long promontory of lawns, described as water meadows, narrowing to the west. Continuing further west a thin strip of land known as the Canardière, one and three-quarters kilometers long and about 400 meters wide (437 yd.) and bounded both north and south by water, was divided into rectangular spaces with ornamental features and walks. Only the outline of these features remains.

East and south of the castle the Parc de Sylvie, a wooded area with straight avenues cutting through it, still exists with the Maison de Sylvie and its small parterre garden at the southern extremity. Although so much of this once great garden, said to rival Versailles in magnificence, is now lost, Le Nôtre's masterstroke of design—his grand axial layout—remains for visitors to see and admire.

## Synopsis

| 1522–67 | 250-acre (101 ha) park enclosed, formal gardens created west of castle |
| --- | --- |
| 1538 | Raised terrace constructed |
| ca. 1560 | Petit Chateau built |
| 1659 | Park extended to 2,500 acres (1,012 ha) |
| 1662–85 | André Le Nôtre employed |
| 1663–80 | New formal gardens created west of castle |
| 1666 | Grand Parterre laid out |
| 1670 | Maison de Sylvie reconstructed |
| 1671–72 | Grand Canal excavated |
| 1673 | Esplanade set out |
| 1682–86 | Mansart's Orangery constructed |
| 1773 | Hameau constructed |
| 1774 | English Garden created east of the Grand Parterre |
| 1817–19 | Orangery garden and adjoining formal gardens replaced by Jardin Anglais |
| 1875–82 | Chateau reconstructed |

## Further Reading

Adams, William Howard, *The French Garden, 1500–1800,* New York: Braziller, and London: Scolar Press, 1979

Bazin, Germain, *Paradeisos, ou, L'art du jarin,* Paris: Chêne, 1988; as *Paradeisos: The Art of the Garden,* London: Cassell, and Boston: Little Brown, 1990

Fox, Helen Morgenthau, *André le Nôtre, Garden Architect to Kings,* New York: Crown, 1962; London: Batsford, 1963

Ganay, Ernest, comte de, *André le Nostre, 1613–1700,* Paris: Vincent, Fréal, 1962

Marie, Alfred, *Jardins français classiques des XVIIᵉ et XVIIIᵉ siècles,* Paris: Vincent, Fréal, 1949

Woodbridge, Kenneth, *Princely Gardens: The Origins and Development of the French Formal Style,* New York: Rizzoli, and London: Thames and Hudson, 1986

M.F. DOWNING

# Chapultepec Park

## Mexico City, Distrito Federal, Mexico

**Location:** Paseo de la Reforma, 3 miles (4.8 km) west-southwest of the Palacio Nacional and Mexico City center

As the largest woodland park in the largest city in the Americas, Chapultepec is an important center for modern recreational activities in Mexico City. Dominated by a bluff surmounted by a castle, the 2,100-acre (850-ha) park includes a zoo, a lake, and several museums, including the world-famous National Museum of Anthropology and the Museum of Modern Art.

Chapultepec's importance dates back seven centuries or more, to a time long before Mexico City was Tenochtitlan, capital of Aztec Mexico. *Chapultepec* means "hill of the grasshopper," and the promontory first received notice in native historical annals as the refuge of Toltecs; in fact, the Toltec king Huemac was purported to have died in the promontory's Cincalco Cave in A.D. 1162. About 1250 the Mexica Aztecs sought refuge on the hill. They were still a wandering group, dependent on the tolerance of settled peoples in the Basin of Mexico, but so warlike and committed to human sacrifice that they quickly offended those who adopted them.

Driven from Chapultepec, the Mexica eventually founded their own capital, Tenochtitlan, about three miles (approximately 4.8 kilometers) to the northeast, on an island in Lake Texcoco. The island is now buried beneath the oldest part of Mexico City—the Zócalo plaza and cathedral—and both the modern city and the Mexican nation took their name from the Mexica Aztecs. As Tenochtitlan began to grow in the early 1400s, the city supplied its potable water needs by building an aqueduct to bring water from the abundant springs at Chapultepec. Chapultepec's attractions as a parkland began to be developed at that time. In the 1420s Nezahualcoyotl, the great landscape architect, civil engineer, and ruler of the city of Texcoco, designed the first royal palace at Chapultepec for his cousins, the kings of Tenochtitlan, at the same time that he supervised the construction of the aqueduct system.

Nezahualcoyotl is also credited with early plantings of the *ahuehuetl* tree around the promontory. The *ahuehuetl* is a fast-growing cypress (*Taxodium* 'Montezuma Cypress', Mexico's national tree) and was thought by the Aztecs to be a symbol of royalty because of the dignity of these great sheltering evergreens. Planting them in a royal pleasure park was appropriate to the park's role and suited the purposes of the upstart Mexica to establish quickly a substantial-looking capital.

In the 1430s the Mexica precipitated a quarrel with their overlords, trying to wrest from them control of the Chapultepec springs, as well as control over an extensive tribute network. They succeeded in both, and thus was established the core area of the Aztec Empire that would extend by 1519 over much of modern Mexico. The Aztec kings made Chapultepec into their dynastic memorial as well as their pleasure retreat. The trip from the main palace at the city's center to Chapultepec would have been made by canoe along the canals crisscrossing the city and across the reaches of Lake Texcoco.

On the cliff faces of the promontory, Aztec kings had their portraits carved; these bas reliefs served as dynastic monuments. Throughout the late 15th century Chapultepec's gardens were developed. The high altitude of the Basin of Mexico (lake level was about 7,300 feet [2,225 m] above sea level) made for a challenging horticultural environment, but the ability to grow rare plants lent considerable status to Aztec lords, who outdid each other with increasingly elaborate garden designs.

In the early 1500s Chapultepec became the special refuge of King Motecuzoma Xocoyotzin, or Motecuzoma II. Several years before Cortés arrived in the Aztec capital, Motecuzoma had been receiving news of the Spaniards' explorations along the Gulf coast. Motecuzoma interpreted these portents of doom correctly and retreated to Chapultepec to enter the paradise of the storm god through Cincalco Cave. According to legend, Huemac's spirit, the guardian of the cave, refused him admittance. Accepting his fate, Motecuzoma welcomed Cortés and his entourage, hosting them in true royal style for over half a year, including festive visits to pleasure parks and game reserves. After this alliance fell apart, the Spaniards conquered the Mexica and destroyed Tenochtitlan, but Chapultepec's status as desirable real estate was unchanged, being as prized by the Spanish elite as it had been by Mexica lords.

Chapultepec was the subject of repeated court cases as one conquistador after another claimed it. In 1537 Viceroy Antonio de Mendoza petitioned the king to protect Chapultepec and its water supply. The second viceroy, Luis de Velasco, had a new viceregal palace built where Motecuzoma's old pleasure palace had stood. In addition, a wall was built around the forest of the parkland, which protected the region for the viceroys, from encroachment by natives who might use the springs or hunt the game (deer, rabbits). It was the custom for the viceroy and his entourage to spend Saturdays at the park.

Even in the 1550s many vestiges of the Aztec park were perceptible. The pools formed by the springs were thought by the Aztecs to be spiritually purifying and remained part of the recreational facilities, and the rock-cut features such as terraces, sculpture, and plantings were still visible. Some of the cypress trees were nearly 200 feet (60 meters) tall, and in the 1570s several of them were cut in order to erect a cross in the city that would be visible from a great distance, providing a focal point as dramatic as the still-hulking ruins of the Great Temple Pyramid of Tenochtitlan.

By the mid-1700s a historian noted that, of all the fabulous Aztec palaces and pleasure parks, only Chapultepec remained because the viceroys had preserved it for themselves. Nonetheless, the bas-reliefs were being destroyed by artillery target practice. In the late 1700s the promontory was surmounted by a castle that could serve as either a palace or a fortress; it became the home of Maximilian and Carlotta, would-be rulers of Mexico, in the mid-1800s.

Chapultepec Park is now open to all people, and its castle is the Museum of Mexican History. The heights of the promontory can now be reached by elevator: the entrance is at Cincalco Cave.

## Synopsis

| | |
|---|---|
| 1100s | Chapultepec promontory became a refuge for Toltec and Chichimec migrants |
| 1162 | Toltec king Huemac dies at Chapultepec promontory |
| 1250s | Mexica Aztecs establish camp on Chapultepec promontory but are driven away by enemies |
| 1300s | Mexica Aztecs establish their capital, Tenochtitlan |
| 1420s | Nezahualcoyotl of Texcoco establishes Mexico's earliest known pleasure palace, at Chapultepec, for the rulers of Tenochtitlan |
| 1454 | Nezahualcoyotl directs reconstruction of the Chapultepec aqueduct system that supplies Tenochtitlan with potable water |
| 1460s | Motecuzoma I (ruled 1440–69) initiates custom of bas-relief portraits of Mexica rulers on the promontory |
| 1467 | Aqueduct officially opened, celebrated by human sacrifice |
| 1480 | Axayacatl, ruler of Tenochtitlan 1469–81, has portrait carved on Chapultepec promontory |
| 1502 | Ahuitzotl, ruler of Tenochtitlan 1486–1502, has portrait carved on Chapultepec promontory |
| 1510s | Motecuzoma II, ruler of Tenochtitlan 1502–20, has portrait carved on Chapultepec promontory |
| 1521 | Conquest of Mexico by the Spanish |
| 1530s | Court cases concerning claims on Chapultepec by various Spaniards |
| 1537 | Royal protection sought for viceregal rights to Chapultepec and its water supply |

## Further Reading

Braniff Torres, Beatriz, and María Antonieta Cervantes, "Excavaciones en el Antiguo Acueducto de Chapultepec," *Tlalocan* 5 (1966)

Cervántes de Salazar, Francisco, *Life in the Imperial and Loyal City of Mexico in New Spain, and the Royal and Pontifical University of Mexico (1554),* translated by Minnie Lee Barrett Shepard, Austin: University of Texas Press, 1953

Dibble, Charles E., editor, *Códice Xolotl,* Mexico City: 1951; 2nd edition, 2 vols., Mexico City: Universidad Nacional Autónoma de México, Instituto de Investigaciones Históricas, 1980

Durán, Diego, *Historia de las Indias de Nueva-España y islas de Tierra Firme (1579–81),* 2 vols., Mexico City, 1867–80; reprint, Mexico City: Consejo Nacional para la Cultura y las Artes, 1995; as *The History of the Indies of New Spain,* translated by Doris Heyden, London and Norman: University of Oklahoma Press, 1994

Evans, Susan Toby, "Aztec Royal Pleasure Parks: Conspicuous Consumption and Elite Status Rivalry," *Studies in the History of Gardens and Designed Landscapes* 20 (2000)

León-Portilla, Miguel, "Chapultepec en la literatura nahuatl," *Revista de la Universidad de México* 24 (1970)

Nuttall, Zelia, "The Gardens of Ancient Mexico," *Annual Report of the Board of Regents of the Smithsonian Institution* (1923, 1925)

Torre, Mario de la, editor, *Chapultepec: Historia y presencia,* Mexico City: Smurfit Cartón y Papel de México, 1988

SUSAN TOBY EVANS

# Charlottenburg

## Berlin, Germany

**Location:** 7 miles (11.3 km) west of Berlin city center

Elector Friedrich III of Brandenburg decided in 1694 to build a new summer residence for his brilliant and well-educated wife, Sophie Charlotte of Brunswick-Lüneburg. Here, baroque ideas could be developed unhampered. After the death in 1695 of the Dutch architect Johann Arnold Nering, who made the first pal-

ace and garden plan, the electress altered the whole layout; she wished to live on the ground floor so that she would be able to go directly into the garden from every room. Despite her Dutch connections she decided to turn to her cousin Elisabeth Charlotte of Orléans for advice on the plans for her garden. This princess, Louis XIV's sister-in-law, possessed one of the French landscape designer André Le Nôtre's most famous gardens at St. Cloud, and she sent the experienced gardener Siméon Godo (Godeau), of whose earlier career little is known. The design that Godo worked out on the spot was sent by Sophie Charlotte to Paris to be submitted to Le Nôtre himself. In the summer of 1696 Le Nôtre completed a corrected design, which, along with Godo's drawings, has since been lost. During the following summer the first ground was broken on the land allotted to the garden north of the palace; in 1698 the groundwork was completed, the avenues laid out, and the greater part of the trees and flowers planted. Consequently, it was necessary to rebuild the palace to connect it with the existing avenues. It was inaugurated in 1699. The garden was an example of French garden design of the highest order, which at that time had no equal elsewhere in Germany.

All Brandenburg castles were situated on rivers and channels and accessible by boat, named in Dutch *trekschuit* (towboat). Originally one approached the palace from the Spree River in the north toward a *pièce d'eau* (large formal pond) modeled after the Lac de Suisses at Versailles. The *pièce d'eau* contained a splendid yacht and several gondolas. Next, one reached the *parterre de broderie melé des massifs de gazon* (formed by box, gravel, and flower and grass borders) and ornamented by topiary yews and gilded or marblelike painted sculptures and vases. The main and cross axes were enlarged by *tapis de gazon* (lawn carpets), and a fountain was planned to accentuate the center. An *allée double* of lime trees bordered the sides and hid the bosquets with other fountain saloons and some Dutch-styled trelliswork ornaments. The terrace before the palace was decorated by putti, vases, and orange trees in a finely tuned rhythm. At both ends were enormous trelliswork saloons; one was covered by honeysuckle, the other was of elaborate carpentry. Two private gardens for the king and the queen prolonged the enfilade of the palace.

From the central hall of the palace, three axes led into the landscape. The main axis, 100 meters (109 yards) wide, extended about 9 kilometers (5.6 miles) into the woods and fields; the left one led to the fortress in Spandau and the right one to the Niederschönhausen Palace. Such direct links seem to be unprecedented. The court games area in the northwest contained two long basins for water games and races, two bowling greens, and a pall-mall course. Frederick the Great built the New Wing instead of the intended eastern orangery and created a hidden rococo garden in front of it in 1742.

Johann August Eyserbeck from Wörlitz remodeled parts of the garden in 1788–99, namely the garden in front of the New Wing, the parterre, and the former pheasantry in the west. He also excavated new channels, creating the Belvedere Island and the Louise Island. The latter was named after Queen Louise, who is buried

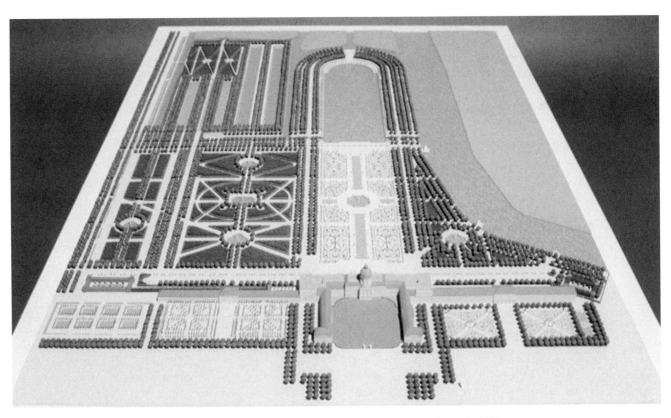

Plan for the garden at Charlottenburg, Berlin, Germany, as it was in 1742
Copyright C.A. Wimmer

in the Charlottenburg mausoleum, which was built after her death in 1810 by Karl Friedrich Schinkel at the end of a spruce allée. The former was the site of the belvedere, built by Carl Gotthard Langhans in 1788 and intended to be a scenic vantage point. Both islands were reachable only by ferry. Two cast-iron bridges (dating from 1799 and 1802) are other important structures from this period. The very interesting wooden Gothic lodge (1788), reminiscent of the Holy Sepulcher in Jerusalem, and the Otahiti wickerwork cabinet (before 1790) on the Spree River are now demolished.

George Steiner, Eyserbeck's successor, redesigned the eastern bosquet and the former *piéce d'eau*, now the carp pond, in an English landscape style (1802) and created the Louise Square in the south of the New Wing (1806). In 1822 John Claudius Loudon ranked Charlottenburg Park among "the principal examples of the English style in Prussia."

Finally, Peter Joseph Lenné redesigned the western bosquet (1819) and the alder woods on the former game area (1822) and the Princess's Flower Garden in front of the New Wing (1834). He laid out a viewing mount on the northern boundary from which one could gaze into the distant landscape and created a long axis, now replanted, toward the cupola of the palace. Between 1823 and 1840 several bronze sculptures were placed throughout the garden. They were partly replicas of antiques and partly designed by Christian Daniel Rauch (the two personifications of Victory). King Friedrich Wilhelm IV reconstructed the western bosquet in the geometric style in 1841. After his time, few improvements were carried out.

The buildings were largely demolished in 1944 during World War II. The parterre was restored in 1952–67 in a baroque manner and not in its original form, while the rest of the garden was simplified in a modern taste. In the north, a mound was built out of rubble; play areas for children were included here. In 1979 a marble obelisk has marked the actual end of the main axis, which is now interrupted by a railway embankment. In 1989, following the historic documentation of a garden conservancy team, the Louise Island was reconstructed with three bronze sculptures. Other areas are still waiting for reconstruction.

## Synopsis

| | |
|---|---|
| 1696–99 | Construction of the garden by Siméon Godo (Godeau) |
| 1702–9 | Enlargement of the castle by Johann Friedrich Eosander; construction of an orangery |
| 1742 | Creation of the New Wing and a private garden by Georg Wenzeslaus von Knobelsdorff |
| 1788–99 | Transformation partly into a landscape garden by Johann August Eyserbeck |
| 1801–18 | Continuation of remodeling by George Steiner |
| 1819–34 | Landscape garden completed by Peter Joseph Lenné |
| 1841 | Some parts redesigned geometrically |
| 1944 | Buildings severely damaged by bombing during World War II |
| 1952–58 | Garden remodeled according to modern requirements; creation of a neo-baroque parterre |
| 1989 | Reconstruction of Eyserbeck's Louise Island |

## Further Reading

Wimmer, Clemens Alexander, *Die Gärten des Charlottenburger Schlosses,* Berlin: Senator für Stadtentwicklung und Umweltschutz, 1985

Wimmer, Clemens Alexander, and Martin Schaefer, "Charlottenburg's French Garden," *Journal of Garden History* 5, no. 4 (1985)

CLEMENS ALEXANDER WIMMER

# Chashma Shahi

## Kashmir, India

**Location:**  approximately 400 miles (645 km) north-northwest of Delhi, approximately 5 miles (8 km) from Srinagar, near Dal Lake

The Chashma Shahi was first built in 1632 under the instruction of the emperor Shah Jahan (the builder of the Taj Mahal), although an early inscription attributes the garden directly to the emperor himself. The actual builder was probably Ali Mardan Khan, the governor of Kashmir, who established a number of fine rest houses (*sarai*) along the Pir Panjal route from Kashmir down to the plains of India. He was a Persian by background and was previously the governor of Kandahar under Shah Safi. Due to some strong disagreement, he surrendered the city to Shah Jahan, who immediately rewarded him with the position of comptroller of works in Delhi. Ali Mardan

Khan was responsible for a number of notable projects, such as building canals in order to bring water to Delhi's Red Fort as well as the Shalamar Gardens at Lahore.

Chashma Shahi (Royal Spring) is the smallest Mogul garden and is located about 5.5 miles (8.8 km) from Srinagar and less than a mile from Nishat Bagh (another famous Mogul garden). According to a Persian verse inscription on the gateway, the date for this wonderful miniature garden is 1632–33. The verse inscription reads "Guftamash bahr-e-chashma tarikhe./Guft bar go Kausar-e-Shahi" (I asked "What is the date of this spring?"/I was told, "Say Kausar-e-Shahi"). The phrase "Kausar-e-Shahi" (Royal Spring) yields the date 1042 Hijri, or A.D. 1632–1633 (*Kausar* is another word for *chashma* [spring]).

The original garden was small and stood molded to the contours of the nearby mountain. The design of the garden derived from a strong spring at the top of the garden (the Chashma Shahi), still famous for its cool, pure water that bubbles up through a marble lotus basin (now reconstructed). The flow of the water led down from here by a small cascade and a canal and filled a wide rectangular tank with a single jet. Nearby, on an approximately 20-foot- (six-meter-) high retaining wall, stood the principal (and second) stone pavilion. Below, another water chute dropped down the center of the wall to supply another water garden. Of the buildings presently in situ, the two pavilions, the surrounding wall, and the side entrance are recent, although built on Mogul bases. The cascades, plinths of the pavilions, watercourses, tanks, and fountains are genuine Mogul works. The lowest terrace has a tank in the center with five fountains in a quincunx pattern. Flights of steps on each side of the pavilion lead up to the second terrace and to the ground floor of the pavilion itself. From here the view of Dal Lake is truly breathtaking. In the spring the garden is exceptionally beautiful; the hill slopes are golden with blossoming rapeseed and red and white almond blossoms, transforming the tiny paradise garden into the very image of tranquility. Shah Jahan in one of his visits is supposed to have remarked in a Persian couplet "If heaven can be found on the face of this earth,/ Then it is here, it is here, it is here."

The entire composition of the garden is greatly accented by the full use of levels. The main pavilion has a particularly enchanting setting. One side projects a cloistered feeling, with its pool, canal, and upper pavilion. On the other side are the drop of the retaining wall and a spectacular view of Dal Lake.

Recently the garden has been restored and expanded, with dramatic changes in the various levels, careless planting of overpowering trees and shrubs, and a strong sense of asymmetry. At times one gets a feeling of a Tudor or an Italian Renaissance garden rather than a Mogul work. However, the Mogul qualities of the garden are certainly visible in the cascades, the plinths of the two pavilions, and the canals, tanks, and fountains. The two pavilions are themselves recent, and the upper garden has been expanded into a wide terrace. The lower level has been made into an extensive flower garden (a feature likely absent in the original Mogul garden). The approach to the garden is by a steep flight of steps that leads to an arch, the present entrance to the lowest water garden. Neither the steps nor the arch are likely original; however, they do lend force and character to the entire design.

**Synopsis**

1632  Chashma Shahi (Royal Spring) garden built, probably by Ali Mardan Khan, governor of Kashmir

**Further Reading**

Kak, Ram Chandra, *Ancient Monuments of Kashmir,* London: The India Society, 1933

Moynihan, Elizabeth B., *Paradise As a Garden: In Persia and Mughal India,* New York: Braziller, 1979; London: Scolar Press, 1980

Villiers-Stuart, Constance Mary, *Gardens of the Great Mughals,* London: Black, 1913; reprint, New Delhi: Cosmo, 1983

NIRMAL DASS

# Chatsworth Gardens

## Chatsworth, Bakewell, Derbyside, England

**Location:**  approximately 10 miles (16 km) west of Chesterfield, or approximately 40 miles (64.4 km) southeast of Manchester

The lost medieval village of Chatsworth lay below the gritstone moorlands on the east bank of the River Derwent in the region known as the Derbyshire Peak. Here, between Baslow and Beeley, stood the manor house, mill, and deer park of the Leche family at the beginning of the 16th century.

In 1549 Sir William Cavendish and his wife Elizabeth (Bess) of Hardwick bought Chatsworth and in 1551 began to build the first country house with park and gardens in the north of England. Bess finished it in 1585. William Senior's estate survey (1617) depicts the park on either side of the Derwent and the three-storied courtyard house approached by means of a drive from the medieval road bridge to the south. A garden containing a prospect house (a small building on a mount overlooking the garden and park), two obelisks, and what may have been a fountain was on the south front; to the northwest, between the house and the river and set among orchards, were formal fish ponds, which also served to absorb the floodwaters of the tortuous Derwent.

Two architectural features of this garden and park still survive. The first is a garden mount and fishing tower (ca.1572) originally standing in the northernmost pool. The tower is now erroneously named "Queen Mary's Bower," following the belief of 18th- and 19th-century romantics that Mary Queen of Scots was imprisoned here. The other surviving structure, overlooking the valley, is the Hunting Tower, or Stand, probably the work of Robert Smithson and completed by 1570. It was a lookout for deer and a rendezvous after the hunt.

Bess's great-great-grandson, William, fourth earl of Devonshire (1640–1707) totally remodeled the house and gardens following visits to France and Holland. Having assisted the accession of William and Mary in 1688, he was created first duke of Devonshire in 1694. He began his vast changes in 1685, when he created a Dutch-style canal in the fish pools. William Talman began to recreate Bess's house in the baroque style (1687), and George London and Henry Wise laid out the south parterre and sea-horse fountain (1688). The French-style waterworks consisted of more than 20 fountains fed by moorland ponds. The largest water cascade in England was created in 1694 by Grillet, a pupil of the celebrated architect André Le Nôtre and was extended in 1703 and crowned with a cascade

The cascade at Chatsworth, Derbyshire, England
Copyright Robert M. Craig

house by Thomas Archer. The famous copper weeping willow (1692) was not, as is claimed, a *joco-d'aque* but a Versailles-inspired conceit. An engraving (1699) by Knyff and Kip shows the formal gardens with a bowling green and house, a greenhouse (orangery), pheasantries, Flora's garden, fountains, statues by Caius Gabriel Cibber, and urns by Samuel Watson. Finally, the duke created a second canal (1702) beyond the south parterre.

The great cost and the transient style of the first duke's gardens shortened their life. The English landscape designer Lancelot ("Capability") Brown swept much of them away. He relandscaped the park with clumps of trees and woods on the perimeter. The fishponds were filled in and the river straightened and widened to reduce flooding. Queen Mary's Bower and the Stand were left as parkland follies.

James Paine created a new entry to the house in 1761 with new stables (1763) and a new bridge, all on the north side. The old mill and road bridge were demolished and replaced by new ones to the south. Within the gardens Brown laid down lawns over the parterres and terraces, sparing the cascade, the sea-horse fountain, and the southern canal. Cibber's statue of Flora was taken, along with the bowling house, and Flora's temple was created by placing the statue within it.

Brown's new creation held little interest for the fifth duke and by the early 19th century was somewhat unkempt. The sixth duke found the house small, outdated, and inconvenient. In 1820 he employed Jeffry Wyatt, later Sir Jeffry Wyatville, to provide a new north wing culminating in a belvedere. Wyatt included a new orangery and on the old west front laid out a parterre of box and golden yew. The Broad Walk from Flora's temple is also his.

Joseph Paxton, appointed head gardener in 1826, transformed Chatsworth into one of the world's great botanical gardens and is perhaps best remembered for his revolutionary glasshouse designs, precursors of his Crystal Palace of 1851. By the sixth duke's death (1858) Paxton had created some 25 glasshouses at Chatsworth. His "Conservative Wall" (1848) for camellias and peaches is 311 feet long. The house in which he first brought the lily 'Victoria Amazonica' to flower (1849) has gone, as has his Great Conservatory, designed (1836–40) in consultation with Decimus Burton and demolished in 1920. Paxton successfully grew the banana *Musa cavendishii* and established a famous orchid collection, some of which bore his and the Cavendish names. Plants from around the world were grown—a manuscript of 1845 lists some 3,500 species.

Tree collections were especially important; Paxton planted the pinetum (1829) and the arboretum (1835), and on a smaller scale he built the world's first rockery for primitive flowerless plants such as lichens, mosses, and liverworts.

Paxton's romantic use of huge rocks transformed the gardens. The ruined aqueduct (1840) was inspired by that at Wilhelmshöhe, near Kassel; the rock garden (1842) contained the Strid, based on the natural river chasm on the duke's Yorkshire estate at Bolton Abbey, while the "rocking stone" and caves were derived from nearby Rowtor Rocks. In an alcove in the rocks he recreated the copper weeping willow fountain and crowned his achievements by placing in the canal his Emperor Fountain (1844), whose jet once reached 294 feet, the world's highest.

After two World Wars the gardens again declined, but the 11th duke and his duchess have done much to restore the old and create new features. The Display Greenhouse (1974) has a range of temperate, Mediterranean, and tropical plants. Here the 'Victoria Amazonica' and *Musa cavendishii* still flourish. New gardens have been created; on the site of the Great Conservatory is the Lupin garden and the Maze (1969), while on the west front, a pool and parterre of golden box (1960) illustrate the plan of Chiswick House. Fittingly, parallel serpentine beech hedges were laid out (1953) drawing the eye to the elevated bust of the 6th duke.

**Synopsis**

| | |
|---|---|
| 1549 | Chatsworth purchased by Sir William Cavendish and his wife, Elizabeth of Hardwick |
| 1551–85 | Construction of first country house with park and gardens in north of England |
| 1570 | Hunting Tower (or Stand) completed, probably by Robert Smithson |
| ca. 1572 | Garden mount and fishing tower completed (erroneously referred to as "Queen Mary's Bower") |
| 1685 | House and gardens remodeled by William, fourth Earl of Devonshire |
| 1688 | South parterre and sea-horse fountain laid out by George London and Henry Wise |
| 1692 | Copper weeping willow fountain built, cascade |
| 1694 | Largest water cascade in England created by Grillet |
| ca. 1760 | Lancelot "Capability" Brown relandscapes park, lays down lawns over parterres and terraces |
| 1820 | Jeffrey Wyatt employed by sixth Duke of Devonshire to build new orangery and lay out parterre on old west front |
| 1826 | Joseph Paxton appointed head gardener |
| 1826–58 | Paxton creates 25 glasshouses, including Great Stove (1836–40), plants pinetum and arboretum, and builds world's first |

rockery for primitive, flowerless plants
such as lichens, mosses, and liverworts
1844        Paxton builds the Emperor Fountain
1953–74     Extensive restoration and new building
completed by the eleventh Duke of
Devonshire

**Further Reading**

Brighton, Trevor, "Chatsworth's Sixteenth-Century
Parks and Gardens," *Garden History* 23, no. 1 (1994)

Devonshire, Deborah Cavendish, Duchess of, *Chatsworth
Garden,* Derby: Derbyshire Countryside, 1996

Devonshire, Deborah Cavendish, Duchess of, and Gary
Rogers, *The Garden at Chatsworth,* London: Lincoln,
1999; New York: Viking Studio, 2000

Devonshire, William, 6th Duke of, *Handbook of
Chatsworth and Hardwick,* London, 1844

Lemmon, Ken, "Bringing His Grace's Orchids by
Canal," *Country Life* (7 August 1986)

Loudon, John Claudius, "General Results of a
Gardening Tour," *Gardener's Magazine* 7 (1831)

Loudon, John Claudius, "Recollections of a Tour Made
in 1839," *Gardener's Magazine* 15 (1839)

Paxton, Joseph, "Miscellaneous Intelligence,"
*Horticultural Register* 1 (1832)

Paxton, Joseph, "The Chatsworth Arboretum,"
*Gardener's Magazine* 11 (1835)

Paxton, Joseph, "The Emperor Fountain at
Chatsworth," *Magazine of Botany* 11 (1844)

Paxton, Joseph, "Chatsworth," *Journal of Horticulture
and Cottage Gardener* (7 November 1865, 1
December 1870, 5 and 12 February 1874)

Paxton, Joseph, "Chatsworth," *Gardener's Chronicle* (5
September 1874)

Paxton, Joseph, "Four Hours at Chatsworth," *Journal
of Horticulture and the Home Farmer* (March 1909)

JOHN TREVOR BRIGHTON

# Chelsea Physic Garden

## Chelsea, London, England

**Location:** on Thames between Royal Hospital Road,
Swan Walk, and Chelsea Embankment,
approximately 1 mile (1.6 km) southwest of
Victoria station

The Chelsea Physic Garden, London, founded in 1673
and located between Paradise Row, or what is now the
Royal Hospital Road, Swan Walk, and the Chelsea
Embankment is, after Oxford, the oldest botanical garden in England. It was established by the Society of
Apothecaries, who leased the site from Charles Cheyne
for a house to store their ceremonial barge between
royal processions. The river frontage, the gravel subsoil,
and the recognized clear air of Chelsea immediately suggested that the grounds be used for some more practical
purposes; by the following year a director had been
appointed for the garden, and the walls and first plantings were in place. The plants were transferred from
other sites owned by the society in Westminster and
Lambeth. A greenhouse was erected in 1681; in 1683
the famous four cedars of Lebanon were in place,
among the first in the country.

The early years were difficult, for the society was
small and impoverished. But in 1722 Hans Sloane, who
was interested in the garden and had succeeded Cheyne
as lord of the manor of Chelsea, presented them the site
for a nominal rent of £5 per annum; in gratitude a
statue by Michael Rysbrack, now there in a copy, was
erected in 1737 in the center of the garden. On Sloane's
recommendation, Philip Miller was appointed gardener
in 1722, a position he held until his death in 1771.

The first garden had been divided into a series of
square and rectangular plots—what were called systematic order beds—the center marked by an open area
defined by planted trestles, the irregular sides filled with
trees. To this Miller added a greenhouse and two hothouses where, for the first time, he was able to germinate
the seeds of certain tropical plants never before bred in
England (see Plate 8). The fame of the garden spread
throughout Europe; on his journey to England in 1736,
the Swedish botanist Carl Linnaeus made a point to
visit, establishing a professional relationship with Miller
that led to exchanges of specimens and the cultivation of
ever more exotic plants. Miller had also visited Holland
and was in constant correspondence with Dutch botanists. The work Miller did was immensely important not
only for discoveries about fertilization and pollination
but also for all his publications, based on work at
Chelsea, most notably the *Gardener's Recreation,* the
first volume of which appeared in 1731. The work

became a standard manual that went through eight editions during Miller's lifetime and established in England the system of plant nomenclature devised by Linnaeus. When the first volume appeared there were perhaps a thousand plants noted as in cultivation; by the time Miller died this number had increased to over 5,000.

Among the many young men trained by Miller was Sir Joseph Banks, explorer and natural historian, who became the most significant contributor of stock to the garden, bringing many specimens back from his journeys to such exotic places as Newfoundland, Iceland, Australia, and Tierra del Fuego. In 1772 Banks brought back from Iceland several tons of volcanic rock out of which, together with some stones salvaged from the Tower of London, the first rock garden in Europe was made, which still exists, if now much altered and damaged.

Miller was in correspondence with such botanists working in America, including Mark Catesby and John Bartram. Many other distinguished scientists were also associated with the garden, including William Hudson, *praefectus horti* there from 1765 to 1771, who in 1762 had written the *Flora Anglica*; William Curtis, author of the *Flora Londinensis* (1777); Georg Ehret, author of *Plantae et papiliones rariores* (1748–62); and later, John Lindley, who in 1836 produced a catalog of the contents of the garden and in 1841 founded the journal *Gardeners' Chronicle*.

By the 1840s the fortunes of the garden had declined badly. In 1853 the situation was so critical that the Society of Apothecaries, in great need of funds, approached Lord Cadogan, the successor to Sloane, with a view to giving up all responsibility for the garden. Nothing final was done, but the director was discharged, the gardeners dismissed, and the hothouses closed. A few years later, in 1863, through the efforts of Nathaniel Ward, a distinguished botanist and treasurer of the Society of Apothecaries, attempts were made to revive the garden and its work. Ward was able to move the herbaria to the British Museum for safer keeping. In 1870 the Chelsea Embankment was built, cutting off the garden from the Thames. However, an area was added on the other side and sufficient compensation was paid for the land lost to allow many of the programs of the garden to be revived. In 1899 a significant change took place in the running of the garden; the Trustees of the London Parochial Charities took over the organization, recognizing the usefulness of the work there for their students and thereby providing an income in addition to the funds from various other related organizations, including the Treasury, the Royal Society, and London University. Much now was spent on new buildings, such as a lecture room and laboratory, greenhouses, and pits. The director was also able to replenish much of the stock and lay out a new code of regulations.

When in 1902 the garden was formally reopened by Lord Cadogan, it was reconstituted, if in a more modest way than previously, again as a site for scientific research and education. The garden survived the damage of the world wars, and was closed to all visitors. In 1974, however, it was opened to members of the Royal Horticultural Society. Since 1983 the garden has been run by a private board of trustees dedicated to maintaining both its historical character and its function as a center of research. New sources of income have come from relationships with pharmaceutical companies, ensuring both the educational status of the garden and its continued use as a site for research on plants as sources of herbal medicine.

## Synopsis

| | |
|---|---|
| 1673 | Society of Apothecaries lease site from Charles Cheyne, initially to store ceremonial barge |
| 1674 | First plantings made and director appointed |
| 1681 | Greenhouse erected |
| 1683 | Famous four cedars of Lebanon *(Cedrus libani)* planted |
| 1722 | Hans Sloane presents site to Society of Apothecaries for nominal rent |
| 1722 | Philip Miller appointed gardener |
| 1736 | Carl Linnaeus visits |
| 1836 | John Lindley produces catalog of garden's plants |
| 1853 | Fortunes of garden decline to point where gardeners dismissed and hothouses closed |
| 1862 | Herbaria moved to British Museum for safe keeping |
| 1871–74 | Road built separating garden from Thames, compensation helped revive many programs |
| 1899 | Garden taken over by City Parochial Charities, which found funding for replanting and research programs |
| 1902 | Garden reopened by Lord Cadogan for students of botany |
| 1974 | Garden open to members of the Royal Horticultural Society |
| 1982 | Garden became independent with private board of trustees (Chelsea Physic Garden Company) and opened to general public |

## Further Reading

Bainbridge, J., "London Journal," *Gourmet* 43 (1983)

Blunt, Reginald, *In Cheyne Walk and Thereabout*, Philadelphia, Pennsylvania: Lippincott, 1914

Elliott, C., "The Apothecaries' Plot," *Horticulture* 95 (1998)

Field, Henry, *Memoirs, Historical and Illustrative of, the Botanick Garden at Chelsea, Belonging to the Society of Apothecaries of London*, London, 1820; revised edition, *Memoirs of the Botanic Garden at Chelsea, Belonging to the Society of Apothecaries of London*, revised by Robert Hunter Semple, London, 1878

Le Rougetel, H., "A Horticultural Exchange: Philip Miller and the Chelsea Garden," *Country Life* 166 (1978)

Minter, Sue, *The Apothecaries' Garden: A New History of Chelsea Physic Garden*, Stroud, Gouchestershire: Sutton, 2000

DAVID CAST

# Chenonceaux

## Indre et Loire, France

**Location:**  8 miles (12.9 km) south of Amboise; 20 miles (32.2 km) east of Tours

The Château of Chenonceaux (or Chenonceau) is widely considered one of the most attractive of the historic houses in France. Although the overall structure of the gardens established in the 16th century remains, they are largely 19th century in their style. The château was built in the 16th century when the valley of the Loire and its tributaries were the social, political, and economic center of France, with important royal residences at various times in Chinon, Amboise, and Blois.

The unique arrangement of the château is that it is built not beside but across the water of the river Cher, a tributary of the Loire, which gives it its fairy-tale quality. It consists of a small square keep built about 1512, standing in the river close to its north bank. To this is attached a bridge that at one time crossed the river and led to gardens on its south side. The connection with the south was later severed and an elegant two-story gallery constructed on the bridge. The château thus appears to float over the river. The romantic quality of Chenonceaux is enhanced by the fact that it was here that Henri II of France established his mistress, Diane de Poitiers, in 1551. She began developing the gardens and from 1551 to 1557 had the large terrace and garden on the north bank created. Despite its visual qualities Chenonceaux was never a place of central significance in the history of French Renaissance gardening. Its most important period was from 1560 to 1585 when Henri II's widow, Catherine de Médicis, lived and entertained there during the reigns of her three sons (François II, Charles IX, and Henri III), who it could be said ruled under her direction. It was in that period that J.A. Du Cerceau produced his plans for the development of the gardens across the river from the château, in the area northwest of the site, and for the Fontaine du Rocher.

The gallery over the bridge, completed later, may have been the only stage of the adventurous plan for the massive expansion of the château produced by Du Cerceau in 1577, after which the bridge created for Diane was severed.

Before Chenonceaux came into Diane's possession, the château had been built by Thomas Bohier on the site of an earlier building of the Marques family. This family had earned the king's wrath, and their home was razed in the early 15th century as punishment for entertaining an English garrison. In 1432 Jean Marques II had been allowed to build a new "Donjon," and this—the Marques Tower, which still stands—is the oldest structure on the site. The earliest garden recorded was the Pavilion Garden, created by Bohier after 1512, north and slightly west of the château and behind the present pavilion on the right-hand side of the avenue leading to the château that forms the main axis facing south toward the château. Diane's garden, begun in 1551 on the north bank of the river east of the axis, formed a large, two-and-a-half acre rectangle with a raised terrace or levee surrounding it and a moat on three sides connected to the river on the fourth. In the 16th century this was divided into 24 rectangular plots; it is thought that, at least in Diane's time, the gardens were devoted to growing fruits and vegetables. The present internal layout of the Diana Garden, completed by Henri and Achille Duchêne in the 19th century, is, as Germain Bazin notes, "completely anachronistic."

Henri II sent Philibert de l'Orme to work on Chenonceaux for Diane, and it is to de l'Orme that the concept of the central axis is attributed. From the north the great avenue of elms led toward the château, with the axis continuing across the bridge over the river and finishing in a formal garden on the south side. A plan by J.A. Du Cerceau shows elaborate proposals for a vastly increased area of building formed from symmetrical

The Château of Chenonceaux
Copyright Dirk Eisermann/Das Fotoarchiv

extensions flanking the chateau to the north on either side and completed by a range of buildings enclosing a rhombus-shaped forecourt all centered on the axis. How much this was based on De L'Orme's ideas and how much this was merely Du Cerceau's fancy is unclear, but present-day aerial photos show the outline of the rhomboidal forecourt, and on its west side a short range of functional buildings still follows the line of buildings on Du Cerceau's plan. When Henri II was killed while hunting in 1559, Catherine took possession of Chenonceaux, continuing the work that had been begun, including the gardens south of the river. She spent a large portion of her time there and hosted a number of great spectacles at Chenonceaux, including grand fetes in 1561, 1563, and 1577. She created the Fontaine du Rocher northwest of the château as a site for these events, where now the Garden of Catherine is found. The Fontaine du Rocher was a large rock structure from which a number of fountain jets erupted. There was also an elaborate structure of trelliswork enclosing it and

creating shaded walks. The fountain is gone, as is the trelliswork shown in one of the drawings by J.A. Du Cerceau assumed to be dated about 1565. This is a bird's-eye sketch showing how two new gardens might look, one to the northwest and the other south of the river. Later Du Cerceau produced a drawing for a vast symmetrical enlargement of the château with new wings and a series of courtyards, the first of which would be surrounded by buildings including, on the west side, the existing pavilion; but apparently nothing came of this. After the death of Catherine in 1589 Chenonceaux passed to the widow of Henri III, who lived in mourning there for the rest of her life. For more than a century the château fell into disrepair, being restored in the mid-18th century by Claude Dupin—the "Farmer General"—and his wife. No obvious signs of their work remain. In the 19th century a Madame Pelouse kept the château and reputedly spent a great deal on its restoration, including commissioning the Duchênes. It was taken over by the present owners in 1913.

**Synopsis**

**Further Reading**

Adams, William Howard, *The French Garden, 1500–1800,* New York: Braziller, and London: Scolar Press, 1979

Bazin, Germain, *Paradeisos, ou, L'art du jardin,* Paris: Chêne, 1988; as *Paradeisos: The Art of the Garden,* London: Cassell, and Boston: Little Brown, 1990

Hansmann, Wilfried, *Loire Valley,* London: Webb and Bower, Exeter and Michael Joseph, 1986

Mosser, Monique, and Georges Teyssot, editors, *L'architettura dei giardini d'Occidente,* Milan: Electa, 1990; as *The Architecture of Western Gardens,* Cambridge, Massachusetts: MIT Press, 1991; as *The History of Garden Design,* London: Thames and Hudson, 1991

Woodbridge, Kenneth, *Princely Gardens: The Origins and Development of the French Formal Style,* New York: Rizzoli, and London: Thames and Hudson, 1986

M.F. DOWNING

# Children and Gardening

Children's participation in the act of gardening can be traced back to Pharaonic Egypt (980–525 B.C.). Garden laborers included children, and representations of children gardening have been found in excavated tombs. A drawing from one of these tombs shows a child figure scaring a bird with a sling device, a typical garden task for children. Other tasks performed by children were watering, picking, and planting. Horticultural appreciation was highly regarded within Egyptian culture. The garden and its plants were symbolic of both life and afterlife. Yet, actual gardening work was primarily restricted to adults and children belonging to the lower classes.

In classical Greece (461–146 B.C.) even the children of economically stable families tended gardens and fields. Children were expected to perform work otherwise assigned to slaves. Both young boys and girls tended small animals and picked berries and nuts, while older boys performed field work. Field work done by children included clearing stones, breaking up dirt clods, picking, and planting. This was done not only to free up slaves for other work, but to teach children about their accountability to the family as an economic unit. Gardening and field work were forms of child rearing, and thus part of a child's socialization into Greek society.

Excavations of villas built at Pompeii and Tunisia offer an expanded view of life in the family garden during the Roman Empire (27 B.C.–476 A.D.). Private courtyard gardens were transformed into spaces for gardening, dining, and entertainment. Children not only tended to gardens, but played in these spaces. Children's actual gardening was most likely limited to the kitchen gardens containing lettuce, asparagus, beans, carrots, onions, peas, and sprouts, as well as herb plants. Oleander (*Nerium oleander*), laurel (*Kalmia latifolia*), and lily types (*Agapantnus orientalis, Convallaria majalis, Gloriosa superba*) are some of the most common plants identified in domestic, ornamental gardens; however, these plants contain deadly poison. Fencing found around the more formal gardens and deeper pools suggest that these garden spaces were off-limits to children.

Domestic gardens in medieval times continued to provide a place where the youngest children intermingled play with domestic duties that included gardening. A calendar for the year of 1280, entitled the *Occupations of the Months,* displays a child and adult preparing the soil during the month of March. The child is picking up a large dirt clod, a common gardening task performed by children. For the lower classes in England during the 16th century, children between infancy and seven years stayed home playing games, tending small animals, and gardening for the family. At age eight, children would prepare for adult life by working. Boys were shepherds, reapers, mill hands, or servants. Girls watched younger children, collected fire wood, and assisted their parents in the fields during harvest time.

The notion of children gardening in preparation for a life of agricultural work was also followed by the Puritans and Mennonites who settled in North America during the 17th century. In Puritan society children under the age of seven could be idle; however, older children were expected to partake in more productive activities like gardening. According to Puritan law, every father was responsible for instructing his sons in husbandry or trade. Likewise, Amish children did not receive toys from their parents. Playing with toys was viewed as a shallow and foolish endeavor. Instead, Amish children were given a lamb or garden plot to tend. These elements of daily domestic life were thought to help unify children with the adult world.

While the importance of the family garden has been radically altered in the industrial era, children's tasks in tending domestic gardens have remained remarkably unchanged. However, new ideas about the garden itself would change why gardening was performed by children. These changes grew from new theories of education and an expanding middle class that was eager to overcome the social and economic barriers of a previous age.

The Age of Enlightenment ushered methods of scientific inquiry into the garden. Gardens at universities and monasteries became educational laboratories where knowledge was gleaned from sensory experience and reasoning. Children were also introduced to this new view of the garden. At age four, Carl Nils (Linnaeus) was taught to identify flowers in his father's rectory in Sweden. Later, the child was given his own plot in which to experiment. John Locke in *Some Thoughts Concerning Education* (1692–93) encouraged parents and tutors to include gardening as part of the manual arts for children. Locke notes that gardening is important for all children whether they grow up to be people of study or business. Hence, there was an expansion of the role of gardening in children's lives. Gardening was not simply about skill development in preparation for adult life, it became a mode of direct physical inquiry and discovery about the world.

Jean Jacques Rousseau would direct these ideas more specifically to children and their education. In *Émile* (1762), Rousseau's critique on authoritarian education, he observed the wonders and opportunities available to the child running barefoot through the garden. Rousseau noted that formalized games, like shuttle cock, trained the child's body with no risks. He contrasted such games with picking cherries from a tree, where a consciousness of gravity, equilibrium, risk, and desire provided a range of physical and cognitive questions. The child must ask: how shall I climb the tree? Should I get a ladder? How long must the ladder be? How will I not fall? Rousseau concludes that cherry picking would also be useful in providing the child with survival skills.

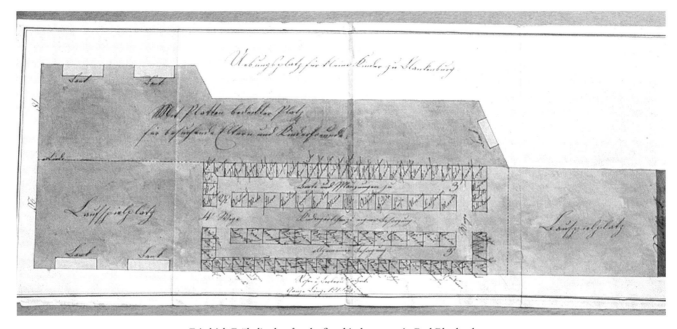

Friedrich Fröbel's plan for the first kindergarten in Bad Blankenburg
Courtesy of Bibliothek für Bildungsgeschichtliche Forschung des Deutschen Instituts für Internationale Pädagogische Forschung

Educators Johann Heinrich Pestalozzi and Friedrich Froebel both attempted to actualize the theories of Locke and Rousseau in educational systems for children. Pestalozzi's first school, Neuhof (new farm), included experimental farming as part of the manual training of children from poor families. However, the work of Friedrich Froebel is most significant for synthesizing actual learning experiences with gardening. In 1839 Froebel opened the first kindergarten in Bad Blankenburg, Germany. Froebel's original kindergarten contained an actual garden that was tended by the children (ages three to six years old) and their teachers (kindergartners). Other kindergartens established in Germany under Froebel's direction also contained gardens. The kindergarten gardens were typically planted with vegetables, flowers, and field plants. The gardens not only provided food for the school, but were designed to reflect Froebel's pedagogy as informed by the theories espoused by Locke and Rousseau.

In his garden designs Froebel attempted to represent a Lockean relationship between individuals and the whole. This relationship prescribed the location of the planting beds. The communal plots always encompassed the children's plots, so that the children felt embraced by the adult world and at the same time individually linked to this world. The inclusion of children's individual plots in Froebel's designs reflects Rousseau's respect for the individual inclinations of a child. In the kindergarten garden, children could do what they pleased in their own plots; yet, this freedom was always conditioned by nature. For Froebel, gardening provided a tangible artifact of a child's divine essence.

Landscape gardener and author John Claudius Loudon would also use the garden as a vehicle for learning. Loudon was deeply interested in bringing the art of gardening to the growing middle classes and educating a skilled labor force of gardeners. Like Linnaeus, Loudon was given his own garden plot at a very young age. Childhood experiences of laying out the paths and beds of his garden initiated a lifelong love of gardening. In both Loudon's *An Encyclopedia of Gardening* (1822) and the *Suburban Gardener and Villa Companion* (1836–38) he was cognizant of the child's role in gardening. In a section from the *Encyclopedia* concerning birds in the garden, Loudon refers to the ancient practice of "putting a boy to watch" as the best method of bird scaring. Loudon also included children's gardens in the planning of private gardens in the *Suburban Gardener*.

The rise of popular gardening magazines reflected the growing number of domestic gardeners in both England and the United States. Along with gardening, Victorian girls took great interest in gardening crafts. Gertrude Jekyll in *Children and Gardens* (1908) wrote of her childhood gardening experiences. Providing plan, section, and elevation drawings of her early garden designs, she also described the crafts she made from her garden. Gardening crafts like primrose balls, daisy chains, and flower garlands were often products of a girl's own garden, and were made by children in Europe, the United States, and New Zealand.

The gardening world of middle and upper class children differed drastically from the agricultural work required of poor children. In the 19th century work gangs that hired children sometimes employed individuals as young as four years old. Typically, children walked to large-scale farming operations where they would clear fields, scare birds, stack hay, and rake corn. The presence of children in the fields was not controversial. However, when children began working in urban factories, the consequences of child labor became hotly contested in industrialized cities.

By the end of the 19th century, the notion that the quality of children's lives shaped their adult character was in conflict with the landscape of rapid urbanization, immigration, and child labor. The education of children became a key issue in urban reform. Education reformers such as John Dewey believed that learning was a social process that required children to cooperatively do things such as weave, draw, cook, and garden. Children's gardening programs occupied a special place in the reform movement because of the appeal to those who lamented the loss of an agrarian society. Children's gardening programs were seen as an opportunity to instill the moral and practical skills associated with rural life. Often promoted by specific political groups, children's gardening programs were part of both the allotment garden and school garden movements.

The first allotment gardens emerged in Great Britain in the 18th century; the first to integrate children's gardening were the Schrebergärtens founded in Leipzig, Germany, in 1870. Schrebergärtens were located in empty urban lots, playgrounds, and derelict lands outside major cities. These gardens were tended by children as part of an outdoor calisthenics program established by Dr. Daniel Schreber, a physician and pedagogue who promoted totalitarian child-rearing practices. Under National Socialism, Schrebergärtens were thought to purify children and connect their blood with the German soil. After World War II, the emphasis on children was dropped. Allotment gardens in other parts of Europe and North America were primarily concerned with providing gardening opportunities for urban tenants, especially during wartime. While children have sometimes been part of community gardening movements in large cities during the 1960s and 1970s, allotment gardening has primarily been a recreational hobby for adults.

Some of the first school gardens in Europe were established to augment natural history and science courses. Embracing romantic notions of learning and gardening, early school gardens provided a tangible means for understanding abstract phenomena. However, by the late 19th century, European school gardens were used to provide vocational skills, as well as to introduce children to the economic profits of agriculture. By 1890 all major countries in Europe recognized school gardens as part of the curriculum. In Sweden, Austria, Germany, Belgium, and Russia, gardens were mandatory at schools. In England a teacher's salary was often determined by the productivity level of their school garden.

Providing vocational skills and training for immigrants in the city and keeping American rural children on the farm were the salient goals of the school garden movement in the United States. Child labor laws and mandatory education laws brought unprecedented numbers of children into the public school system. Some of the earliest gardens were located at housing projects in Boston, New York, and Philadelphia. By the beginning of the 20th century, gardens were incorporated into the yards of both urban and rural public schools.

School gardens in the United States were sponsored by women's groups and progressivists and were relevant to both the City Beautiful and Country Life movements. Children's "decoration gardening" sought to galvanize local pride by planting ornamental flowers at school entrances, local parks, and street medians. Children's vegetable gardens and orchards were located in the back or side yards of schools and served scientific and economic purposes. A typical vegetable plot for a class was approximately 150 square feet (14 sq. m) and contained radishes, lettuce, onions, and spinach. Children were instructed how to properly stake-out, till, hoe, plant, water, prune, and harvest fruits and vegetables. Records were maintained for each plot over a course of several years to determine which crop was most successful. The crops were sold to local restaurants or given to the children's families. Companies such as the National Cash Register Company of Ohio promoted school gardening with publications and awards.

It was thought that gardening at school taught children valuable skills and the economic benefits of individual ownership, cooperation, and love of country life. Yet the logic of the school garden movement was flawed. Technological advances in agriculture and the proliferation of grocery stores made small-scale hand gardening virtually obsolete. Gardening was hardly a marketable skill in light of new types of vocational training such as automotive work. Additionally, teachers began to protest that gardening was taking too much time away from increasingly demanding academic curricula.

By the late 1930s school gardens were abandoned and sports fields took their place in the school yards. During the mid-20th century some schools, particularly in England, the Netherlands, and Japan, still maintained gardening and nature study programs. However, newly constructed schools rarely contained spaces for gardens or gardening programs. At the end of the 20th century, children's gardening at home and at childcare centers gained popularity. Parents began to view outdoor activities such as gardening as healthy and inexpensive alternatives to television and commercial entertainment centers.

## Further Reading

Calvert, Karin, *Children in the House: The Material Culture of Early Childhood, 1600–1900,* Boston: Northeastern University Press, 1992

Golden, Mark, *Children and Childhood in Classical Athens,* Baltimore, Maryland: Johns Hopkins University Press, 1990

Greene, Maria Louise, *Among School Gardens,* New York: Charities Publications Committee, 1910

Hanawalt, Barbara A., "Childrearing among the Lower Classes of Late Medieval England," *Journal of Interdisciplinary History* 8, no. 1 (1977)

Heffernan, Maureen, editor, "Children, Plants, and Gardens: Educational Opportunities," in *Proceedings from the American Horticultural Society National Symposium,* Chevy Chase, Maryland: American Horticultural Society, 1994

Herrington, Susan, "Friedrich Fröbel's Kindergarten: Beyond the Metaphor," *Studies in the History of Gardens and Designed Landscape International Quarterly* 18, no. 4 (1998)

Hopkins, Eric, *Childhood Transformed: Working-Class Children in Nineteenth-Century England,* Manchester and New York: Manchester University Press, 1994

Jashemski, Wilhelmina F., *The Gardens of Pompeii: Herculaneum and the Villas Destroyed by Vesuvius,* New Rochelle, New York: Caratzas Brothers, 1979

Jekyll, Gertrude, *Children and Gardens,* London: Country Life, and New York: Scribner, 1908; reprint, Woodbridge, Suffolk: Antique Collectors' Club, 1982

Sutton-Smith, Brian, *A History of Children's Play: New Zealand, 1840–1950,* Philadelphia: University of Pennsylvania Press, 1981

Wahmann, Birgit, "Allotments and Schrebergärtens in Germany," in *The Architecture of Western Gardens: A Design History from the Renaissance to the Present Day,* edited by Monique Mosser and Georges Teyssot, Cambridge, Massachusetts: MIT Press, 1991

Weir, Lebert Howard, *Europe at Play: A Study of Recreation and Leisure Time Activities,* New York: Barnes, 1937

SUSAN HERRINGTON

# China

Modern China is a vast territory, extending over some 60 degrees of longitude, and exceptionally diverse in its geography. As well as the rice terraces and river scenery of popular imagination, it includes some of the highest peaks in the Himalayas, great swathes of the Gobi Desert, and rich pockets of subtropical rainforests. Essentially, the country slopes downward from northwest to southeast, with the Qinghai-Tibet plateau and high grasslands of Inner Mongolia Autonomous Region giving way first to lower mountain ranges, the loess plateau and the fertile Sichuan basin, and eventually to the low coastal area. The latter encompasses the lower reaches of China's great rivers, which, despite the sustained efforts of the government, remain prone to regular and devastating flooding. Arable land is comparatively scarce and intensively cultivated to support the vast population (at the beginning of the 21st century, approximately 1.2 billion). The climate in the south ranges from temperate (Kunming, in the southwest, is known as "the city of eternal spring") to tropical and supports an enormous diversity of plant life. Historically, urban centers have concentrated along the temperate eastern seaboard, and this is where many of China's best-known classical gardens lie. Especially famous are those in the city of

The garden of Hsi-Ma-Kuang, an example of a Chinese garden with overhanging rocks, from the journal *Le jardin Anglo-Chinois*, 1770–87

Suzhou, on the shores of the Grand Canal. Further north the climate is mainly harsh and dry, with hot summers and extremely cold winters. Extant imperial gardens are mainly concentrated in this northern area, centered on Beijing, China's capital since the late 13th century.

Historically, Chinese gardens have reflected the need to set aside and beautify special places in a naturally hostile environment. Designers have taken advantage of the particular skills developed in that environment, notably water conservancy and flood control. With farmland at a premium, gardens have been concentrated in urban centers and stamped with the tastes and concerns of the imperial court and its scholar-officials. Perhaps more than elsewhere, the area demonstrates a long and close connection between gardens and political legitimacy. The earliest dynasties' hunting grounds included ceremonial spaces to reinforce the ruler's relationship with the land and his status as the Son of Heaven. From medieval times the centralized bureaucracy necessary to control such a diverse territory meant exiling scholar-officials to the edges of the empire. A marked consistency of design emerged across the empire, as gardens came to represent a corner of home and imperial order. Structural elements (rocks, water, architecture), which could be introduced to any environment, assumed great importance, to the relative neglect of botanical diversity. The sophisticated later imperial culture sought new ways of combining elements in the pursuit of elegance and fashion but preserved traditional choices of plants and forms of garden architecture. In modern times rapid industrialization, urbanization, and political change have raised new questions for Chinese gardeners, and the issues of environmental protection, biodiversity, and "greening" urban living space are posing new challenges for garden enthusiasts and policy makers.

## Shang and Zhou Dynasties

The earliest records of gardenlike space in China relate to the Shang dynasty (ca. 16th–11th century B.C.). The Shang comprised an itinerant court of royal and noble families: the emperor's progression through his territories in east-central China seems to have served the twin purpose of sacred ritual and spreading the burden on his subjects of supporting the sophisticated tastes of the court. The court intermittently regrouped at one favored site, a hunting ground based in Yi district (an area covering the north part of modern Henan and the south of Shanxi). It was an enclosed space, known as a *you*, used for breeding fish, birds, and livestock. Inscriptions on divination bones from the period include numerous references to imperial hunts undertaken for pleasure in the deliberately stocked park.

Evidence also indicates that this early hunting ground was used as a focal ceremonial space. In the center of the *you* was a large raised earthen platform, upon which the emperor would perform the sacred rituals of divination. The emperor's authority derived from his ability to interpret the will of the Shang god, Di, through whose intercession he ruled. He was responsible for predicting the weather and the solstices and for determining auspicious dates and places for the court's progress. The manmade platform at the heart of the *you* was the emperor's vantage point, from which he could observe the stars and the weather, make sacrifices, and perform the rituals of divination. It represents the earliest example of manmade architecture in the garden, which has been a defining feature of Chinese garden design ever since.

The warrior Zhou dynasty who conquered the Shang (ca. 1123 B.C.) refined the *you* and created a scattering of hunting parks across their lands. Different types known as *ling you*, *ling tai*, and *ling chi* are mentioned in China's first known literary work, the *Shi Jing* (ca. 600 B.C.; Classic of Poetry). This proliferation of parks parallels the emergence of a feudal system, and the local lord's stewardship of a *you* (which technically remained the property of the emperor) was an expression of his political status. Myths dating from Zhou oral tradition suggest a mythic attachment to certain plants and trees cultivated in the *you*; examples include the peach tree (seen as a ladder to heaven), the mulberry (where the world's ten suns come to rest at the end of each day), and the yarrow or milfoil, whose stalks were used for the complex divination rituals described in the *Yi Jing* (Classic of Change).

## Qin and Han Dynasties

The end of the Zhou Dynasty marked the start of a period of fracturing and political disorganization. For many, the Warring States period raised the philosophical question of whether to participate in society, in line with Confucian ideology, or to retreat to a Taoist ideal of hermitism. This question became a recurrent theme shaping the subsequent development of the garden.

Emperor Qin Shi Huang (r. 221–210 B.C.), from whose name the word "China" is derived, is credited with establishing a settled and centralized country from this mass of fractured states. With greater stability, the *you* (hunting ground) was replaced by the *yuan* (park). The famous park of Shang Lin Yuan (since destroyed) encapsulates the transition. Founded by the Qin and later improved by the Han, Shang Lin Yuan was vast: like the *you*, it included forests, fields for grazing animals, and areas for breeding deer, horses, and elephants. Naval exercises in the lake retained a political element. But there were also pleasure boating, rare fish and birds bred as curiosities, and architecture, with elegant pavilions dotting the landscape. Surviving only in literature, the idyll of Shang Lin Yuan influenced the future development of garden design.

Gardens continue to have a close relationship to sacred places during this period. Mystical sites, especially those with dynastic significance, were transformed into garden spaces with artificial ponds or new trees added to enhance their beauty. Naming the new space to recall legend or literature was common, as at Hu Gui.

With a clearer definition of China, interest developed in the world beyond the empire. In particular emperors became obsessed with finding the mythical mountain islands of Penglai, Fangzhang, and Yingzhou, on whose slopes grew herbs that would bring immortality. In 219 and 210 B.C. Qin official Xu Fu was sent on expeditions to find these magical plants. He landed in Japan and, fearful of the emperor's anger if he returned without the secret of the Immortals, remained there. His disappearance only fueled fantasies and led to the feverish development of projects to re-create the Three Mountains of the Immortals in China, with the three-mountains-one-lake garden model first created by Han dynasty emperor Wudi at Jian Zhang and later imitated throughout the empire. Another paradise model was the home of the gods, Yanzhou, mythically located in the high Kunlun mountain range in the far northwest. Legend told of natural wells of fresh water there and jewel trees in wonderful shapes. This related to the Taoist vision of a jade and gold paradise, and both informed the rich architecture and taste for the exotic of imperial gardens.

Structure and layout were emerging as the key elements of the Chinese garden by this period. Especially notable is the great symbolic attachment to the elements of mountain and water (the two words make up the Chinese word for landscape, *shan-shui*) and to the balance between them in a garden. Confucius, not generally given to commenting on nature, reflected that "the wise find joy in water; the benevolent find joy in mountains." Based on traditional dualist theories, the equilibrium between wood or rock (mainly *yang*, or male, in influence) and water (mainly *yin*, or female) in a garden was considered crucial. Both elements are contained in the traditional Chinese character for *yuan*, a pictogram comprising an enclosure containing a manmade structure, an enclosed piece of water, and plants. With significant advances in construction engineering during the Han period, the mythic garden could be made real. Lakes were dug and artificial mountains built to imitate places of great natural beauty elsewhere in the country. Later, stone was brought from one part of the empire to create rock gardens in another. Powerful scholars and officials such as General Liang Jie of the Eastern Han (25–220 A.D.) built scaled-down imitations of famous mountains to ornament their private gardens.

## End of Han Dynasty through Sui Dynasty

The fall of the Han dynasty in the third century, however, brought confusion, corruption, and danger to the ruling classes. This period consolidated the role of the Chinese garden as retreat, a place for disgusted scholars or disgraced officials to retire in peace. Private gardens became more numerous, and some clear divisions can be seen between the styles prevalent in different regions as the kingdom became less centralized. In the north, dominated by the Wei, earlier techniques were retained, and a fashion took hold for "piling mountains" (*die shan*) in ever more elaborate and fanciful configurations. In the more fertile south, influenced by Taoist and Buddhist ideology, the Jin intelligentsia developed a taste for more "natural" gardens, used as a living space rather than an exhibition. The famous poet of the Eastern Jin, Tao Qian, popularized a pastoral ideal with his lyrical writings. When relative peace was restored under the Sui dynasty at the end of the sixth century, both traditions fed into the design of the new imperial gardens (*Xi Yuan*) in the capital, Luoyang. Xi Yuan was a garden in which to wander: huge and impressive, with set pieces such as three-mountains-one-lake. But in its winding paths and secluded scenic spots, it reflected the experience of the private scholar gardens.

## Tang and Song Dynasties

Scholars had ample time to work on their gardens in the Tang and Song dynasties, when it was common to exile temporarily those who had fallen out of favor, often to the far south and west of the empire. The exotic settings of Yunnan, South Guangzhou, or Hainan Island allowed lush, fast-growing gardens in which the owner could contemplate his fate. Liu Zong Yuan, exiled in 805 for his involvement in a failed reform movement, bought land in Hunan Province and was closely involved in the construction of his scenic garden:

> I added to the height of the terrace, lengthened the railed walks and led the spring up to a height so that it fell into the lake with the sound of waters meeting. This place is especially appropriate for viewing the moon at mid-autumn, in that one may see from here the loftiness of the heavens.

Garden design became closely allied to other literati pursuits, particularly poetry composition and landscape painting. The conventions of poetry and painting influenced garden design, and vice versa. In all three modes Tang scholars idealized a peaceful setting with a lone figure in quiet contemplation of nature. The mood was characteristically wistful. The eighth-century poet Wang Wei, who built beautiful gardens on his estate at Chang'an, is typical of the Tang poets in his sparse and elegant descriptions of an idealized garden landscape. The dominant features are rock and water, with one lifting note of color: falling cassia flowers, red peach blossom, a single blooming lotus. This preference for an

View through covered bridges at Zhuo Zheng Yuan
Copyright Robert M. Craig

uncluttered vista, with relatively few plant types or colors, is characteristic of the Chinese garden.

Wang Wei's garden was also recorded in his scroll paintings, which mimic the effect of a walk through the garden, broken up into consecutive scenes (*jing*). Books of such painted scenes were common; they could be used to describe and transmit ideas for a garden, and increasingly, landscape paintings were used as the basis for design. The depiction of the garden in separate *jing* encouraged the development of complex layouts, leading the viewer along a narrow winding path from one clearing to the next, each offering a different, single focal feature.

The symbolic use of plants gained currency in these literati gardens and defines the plants most used in Chinese gardens even today. In particular were those representing the four scholarly virtues: bamboo for its straightness, pine for its resilience, plum blossom because in blooming early in the year it leads the way for others, and the Chinese orchid, small and green but very fragrant. (The orchid's scent in the garden was meant to recall the effect of scholars on history, individually perhaps forgotten but their influence obvious to later generations—doubtless a comforting thought for officials in exile.) The lotus was prized for its purity, rising white and unblemished out of the surrounding mud. Similar influences appeared in architecture, with the

round moon gate especially popular; the autumn moon festival (referred to by Liu Zong Yuan) recalls distant friends and is traditionally a time for reunion.

Political references, especially in the naming of garden elements, were not unusual. Liu called his "Fool's Garden," composed of a Fool's Bridge, Fool's Pond, and so on. With rather bitter irony, he dedicated it to the "righteous" emperor and eunuchs who had ousted him. Similarly, the Song dynasty Fisherman's Garden refers to the legend of the Warring States period: a palace adviser, disgusted with the corrupt court of the king of Chu, fled to the fisherman's pond. Water here is a cipher for the condition of society, and the adviser must decide how "clean" the water in the pond is: clean enough to wash his hat and return to the king or dirty enough to wash his feet, forget the court, and go to sleep. In the legend the wretched adviser drowns himself, but in the Song garden is The Pavilion of Washing One's Hat, suggesting the Confucian choice of engagement with society. Many officials clearly took the "hat-washing" route, for suburban and urban private gardens, close to the center of power, began to proliferate from this period onward. Records indicate that by the late Tang period there were over one thousand gardens in the city of Luoyang alone. Rapid population growth and urbanization contributed to the trend; by the 13th century the

Southern Song city of Lin'an (Hangzhou) was the largest in the world, with thousands of private gardens scattered in and around its suburbs.

Imperial and private garden design fed off one another, with elaborate construction in small gardens and intimate spaces created in palatial parks. There was a fashion for unusually shaped, eroded rocks from Tai Hu Lake, most famously used at Gen Yue by Emperor Wei Zong in the 12th century. The profusion of rocks in other gardens (especially Shi Zi Lin) reflects how design trickled down from the imperial level to smaller gardens. The craze became pervasive—it was said that the emperor had Tai Hu rocks removed from roads and bridges to satisfy his garden plans and took apart the empire in the process.

## Yuan, Ming, and Qing Dynasties

The invading inheritors of the sophisticated Song dynasty took on much of its culture, including in garden design. The Mongol Yuan dynasty (1206–1368) showed some of its nomadic heritage in the great pleasure dome of the Great Khan at Shang-tu (Xanadu), which Marco Polo described as a great hunting ground similar to the ancient *you*, its ornate central pavilion "constructed with such ingenuity, that the whole may be taken asunder, removed, and again set up, at his majesty's pleasure." But in the cities more sophisticated Song preoccupations still dominated and shaped the new capital at Kanbalu (Beijing). Kublai Khan erected in the 13th century the vast artificial hill behind the Forbidden City (now Jingshan Park) and had it covered with fully grown trees uprooted from the surrounding area and brought to the park by elephants; he also made significant improvements at Beihai Park.

Reverence for the old and traditional has been a major feature of Chinese garden design in the modern period. The basic patterns for garden design were already well established by the beginning of the Ming dynasty (1368–1644), and this tendency became more pronounced as the Confucian system, prizing heritage and age, became entrenched. For example, ancient principles of geomancy (in Chinese, *feng shui*; literally, wind and water) governed layout: blocking "spirit walls" near entrances were meant to prevent evil from entering the garden, and concealed entry and exit points for water stopped luck from "draining out" of the area. The ancient tradition of imitative architecture saw a revival, with the Three Mountains of the Immortals appearing in new gardens. Old trees were much admired, with long-lived varieties such as cypress, pine, and gingko, or those with a naturally gnarled appearance, commonly used. In the late Ming and Qing (1644–1911) dynasties, garden design flourished as an aristocratic pursuit, and the traditional techniques were refined and codified. Almost all the classical gardens visible in modern China today date from this period.

Ji Cheng's *Yuan Ye* (1634; The Craft of Gardens) is an important contemporary document of garden design and practice. Ji envisaged a close engagement with the business of planning the garden, remarking that seven-tenths of the effect lies with the "gentlemanly" design and only three-tenths with the craftsmen who will execute it. Plants occupy no place in his treatise, which is devoted to composition and the desired overall effects of elegance and interest. This focus reflects contemporary preoccupations. Many of Ji's principles of "gentlemanly" design are visible throughout later Ming and Qing dynasty gardens.

One important influence is the link to landscape painting and the significance of the scenic. The garden must appear natural and be at ease with its surroundings. The technique of "borrowing" scenery from surrounding landscapes became popular (e.g., Ji Chang Yuan, Xie Qu Yuan), as did framing the *jing* with windows, lattices, moon gates, or overhanging trees. There was a fashion for offering "sets" of *jing* based on the four seasons or different scholarly accomplishments (e.g., Ge Yuan, Xiequyuan). In the imperial garden architectural painting developed so that a real scene was supplemented by scenes painted in lozenges on a pavilion or walkway. Covered corridors, offering long lines of *jing* both real and painted, were considered especially sophisticated; one of the most dramatic is the long walkway at the Summer Palace (Yi He Yuan) outside Beijing.

Connected to the influence of landscape painting is the development of a refined awareness of effects of space and depth in the garden. The best of Ming and Qing gardens use multiple techniques, including borrowed scenery, curved walls, complex layout, and reflecting water, to achieve the sense of "the big in the small, and the small in the big." To enhance a sense of perspective, large-leafed plants are often set nearer to the viewer, with small-leafed ones further away. Multiple points of interest could be used to break up a vista, a technique that has been linked to the similar use of scattered vanishing points in Chinese landscape painting, which contrasts with Western technique.

Gardeners also hoped to evoke "the real in the unreal, and the unreal in the real"; sophisticated gardens might include curious or fantastical elements designed to elicit wonderment (*qu*). This objective fostered a fashion for *pen jing* cultivation (adopted by the Japanese as *bonsai*), for miniature gardens and pot planting, as well as the continued demand for unusually shaped or colored rocks.

Pastoral influences were still important. Recent scholars have noted how late Ming gardens such as Zhuo Zhen Yuan (Garden of the Artless Administrator) and Yanshan Yuan devoted large amounts of space to fruit trees, even in the urban gardens of socialites and literati where self-sufficiency was neither necessary nor realistic. In China's classic 18th-century novel *Hong Lou Meng* (Dream of Red Mansions), the young hero Pao-yu voices rebellion against the rather precious pastoral motif:

A farm [rustic lodge] here is obviously artificial and out of place here with no villages in the distance, no fields nearby, . . . no source for the stream at hand. When you insist on an unsuitable site and hills where no hills should be, however skilfully you go about it, the result is bound to jar.

The garden in *Hong Lou Meng* reflects the concept of a garden in the Ming and Qing dynasties as the setting for the pleasures of polite society. Beautifully laid out and adorned with flowers, poetry, and graceful women, it is a metaphor for the privileged, closeted world of its aristocratic patrons and a setting for their social aspirations and power struggles. It also reflects contemporary practice; as urban living became more common, the ideal of a secluded rural retreat gave way to more social garden rituals such as the tea garden, the literary party, and seasonal festivals. Urban gardens, especially in southerly cities such as Suzhou, were sometimes separate from the site of a residence. They might be open to the public in the mornings, with social events hosted later in the day. The 17th-century Ming scholar Qi Biaojia wrote of the endless round of garden entertainment that "left any domestic business to be attended to under the lamplight."

In practice the aristocratic concept of garden living became ever more separate from the actual process of making a garden. The gentleman owner's role was to select a designer and perhaps contribute to deciding layout or particular features to be included. When the garden was complete the owners would add their personal stamp through the inscriptions, poetic couplets, and titles that invariably graced each pavilion, hill, or lake. Lord Qia Cheng in *Hong Lou Meng* has his advisers compete for this honor, noting that, "Without a single name or couplet, . . . the garden, however lovely with its flowers and willows, rocks and streams, cannot fully reveal its charm." The eventual lines would be inscribed on a plaque or standing stone, often in the calligraphy of its author. This technique parallels the common practice of adorning a landscape painting with a calligraphic verse or quotation and demonstrates how admired classical accomplishments were brought together in private garden design.

Under the Qing dynasty a huge investment was also made in building and improving imperial parks. The wealthy Manchu emperors, perhaps because of their nomadic heritage, showed a predilection for large naturalistic gardens away from the capital, which could house the entire court and a supporting army for months at a time. Emperors Kang Xi and Qian Long in particular spent huge amounts of money on improvements to the Summer Palace (Yuan Ming Yuan) and the Summer Resort at Chengde and while traveling frequently ordered notes and paintings to be made of favored scenery or unusually shaped rocks to be transported back to Beijing to improve their own gardens.

Political and dynastic concerns are evident both in the parks' practical uses and their iconography. The giant lake at Yi He Yuan was used for naval exercises as well as for pleasure boats and doubled as a means of flood control. Symbolic animals reflect the ever-present quest for immortality (deer) or at least longevity (cranes, tortoises). The multiple references to longevity (*yangshou*) at the Summer Palace mainly refer to Qian Long's mother and reflect the Confucian expectation of filial piety. Ancestor worship and Buddhist practice were influential. After the Qing conquered Beijing in 1644, Emperor Shunzhi commissioned the famous White Dagoba in Beihai Park to demonstrate his religious devotion and wish for the empire's unification. Under his successors many ancient temple gardens near the capital were restored; they were once again used for sacrifices, as at Ritan Yuan (Altar of the Sun) in Beijing; and prayer halls and dagobas (a variety of Lamaist monument) proliferated in imperial parks.

Many of these gardens were destroyed in the tumultuous years of the Taiping Rebellion (1853–64) and the Second Opium War (1857–60). British and French forces effectively razed the Summer Palace and its gardens in 1860. The Dowager Empress Cixi reconstructed the site, thereby diverting funds from a plan to rebuild the decimated navy. The furious military establishment appears not to have been appeased by her inclusion of a splendid marble boat in the lake of the restored park.

Botanical interest remained a low priority in these great years of Chinese park and garden design. There is little evidence of plant catalogs being used or new varieties sought. In *Hong Lou Meng* Pao-yu speaks of garden plants whose names have been forgotten and new ones casually invented, at variance with the increasingly scientific thinking of the Western world at the time. The great plant-collecting expeditions undertaken in China by the likes of Reginald Farrer and George Forrest found little inspiration in the gardens of Suzhou and Peking. Instead, they fled as quickly as possible to the edges of the empire, to Tibet and Yunnan, to explore the richness of tropical and alpine varieties apparently unknown to local gardeners. The main repository of botanical knowledge in imperial China was instead the medical profession. Apart from symbolic flowers, the plants the educated Pao-yu can identify include *Alpinia officinarum* (used as an expectorant), snakeroot (for treating venomous bites), and *Glycyrrhiza* (licorice, used in a host of preparations). The first extant Chinese pharmacopoeia dates from the tenth century, and works such as Li Sui Zheng's *Bao Cao Gan Mu* (1599; Compendium of Materia Medica) continued to add to the list of known

Memorial to Sun Yat Sen at Nanking
Courtesy of Mary Evans Picture Library

native plants, their sources, and properties. But the rise of the garden as a literati pursuit beginning in the Tang period had placed a wedge between this body of botanical knowledge and the development of garden design.

## 20th Century

During the turbulent decades following the fall of the last emperor, traditional gardens suffered neglect, occupation, and in some cases destruction. In the 1930s in Suzhou the ancient gardens of Shi Zi Lin became barracks for Japanese soldiers. Under Communist rule many were restored and reopened as public parks. The practice of naming or appending quotations to beautiful sites persisted, many being adorned by the flamboyant calligraphy of Chairman Mao. To accommodate communal leisure activities, labyrinthine paths were broadened and more paved open spaces created. A large central lake was usually the major feature, with boating or skating facilities according to the season, and surrounding space supported a host of activities from kite flying to mah-jongg and impromptu choir practices. More recently, urban parks have been supplemented with fairground entertainments, where roller coasters, shooting ranges, and illuminated fountains are placed among the artificial hills and lakes. Meanwhile in Hong Kong and Singapore, overseas Chinese saw traditional culture preserved in the fantastical parks built by Chinese magnate Aw Boon Haw, peopled with figures from Buddhist and Taoist legend and including examples of traditional arts.

Private gardens fell out of favor under Mao. During the Cultural Revolution (1966–76) the leadership sought to suppress "the evil wind of growing flowers" in favor of increased agricultural production. The effects of this stigmatization of horticulture are still perceptible today. Moreover, for many who were sent to the countryside for re-education during that period, or who have come to live in cities since, working a bed of plants still connotes peasant labor. Private gardens on the mainland remain unusual.

As an export the classical grace of the Chinese garden has proved popular all over the world. Since the institution in 1979 of Deng Xiaoping's policy of "reform and opening up," more international exchange has been possible. Joint projects with Chinese and foreign organizations include the Astor Court Garden in New York's Metropolitan Museum of Modern Art (1979), a series of gardens in five German cities (1983–93), a Chinese botanical garden in Edinburgh, Scotland (1996), and the recent Portland Project in Oregon (2000). The 1999 International Horticultural Exhibition was held in Kun-ming, Yunnan Province, and has supported a development of botanical research in the region. New gardens inspired by traditional models have been constructed on the mainland, as at Beijing's Da Guan Yuan (Great View Garden, based on the garden in *Hong Lou Meng*), and the postmodern Fang Ta Yuan (Square Tower Garden) near Shanghai.

Environmental concerns are partially changing the emphasis of the traditional Chinese concept of a garden, encouraging a greater focus on flora and biodiversity. Some foreign influences are visible, particularly in the move to "green" urban space with flower planting (as at Tiananmen Gate in Beijing). The haphazard mass tree-planting programs of the 1950s are gradually being replaced by admittedly scattered projects to promote biodiversity and protect sites of natural beauty, often through joint ventures with foreign or international organizations. In the increasingly industrial landscape of the People's Republic, the need for green "special places" is as great as ever. One much-cited example is the "scenic reserve" at Jiuzhaigou in Sichuan Province. With China's great reverence for historical continuity, perhaps it is appropriate that Jiuzhaigou, with its great expanses of natural scenery and protected wildlife, should resemble a return to the fecund *you* of the earliest emperors.

*See also* Ban Mu Yuan; Bei Hai Park; Canglang Ting; Gen Yue; Ge Yuan; Gu Yi Yuan; Hu Qiu; Ji Chang Yuan; Liu Yuan; Shi Zi Lin; Wang Chuan Bie Ye; Wangshi Yuan; Xie Qu Yuan; Xi Yuan; Yi Yuan; Yuan Ming Yuan; Zhan Yuan

**Further Reading**

Cheng, Liyao, *Imperial Gardens*, New York: Springer-Verlag, 1998
Cheng, Liyao, *Private Gardens*, Vienna and New York: Springer-Verlag, 1999
Chi, Ch'eng, *The Craft of Gardens* (1634), translated by Alison Hardie, New Haven, Connecticut: Yale University Press, 1988
Chiu, Che Bing, and Berthier, Gilles Baud, *Yuanming Yuan,* Paris: Éditions de l'Imprimeur, 2000
Clunas, Craig, *Fruitful Sites: Garden Culture in Ming Dynasty China,* London: Reaktion, and Durham, North Carolina: Duke University Press, 1996
Grayling, A.C., and Whitfield, Susan, *A Literary Companion to China,* London: John Murray, 1994
Haw, Stephen G., *A Traveller's History of China,* New York: Interlink, and Moreton-in-Marsh, Gloucestershire: Windrush Press, 1995; 2nd edition, 1998
Inaji, Toshiro, *Teien to jukyo no "ariyo" to "misekata, misekata,"* Toyko: Sankaido, 1990; as *The Garden as Architecture,* translated by Pamela Virgilio, New York: Kodansha International, 1998
Johnston, R. Stewart, *Scholar Gardens of China: A Study and Analysis of the Spatial Design of the Chinese Private Garden,* Cambridge and New York: Cambridge University Press, 1991
Keswick, Maggie, and Charles Jencks, *The Chinese Garden: History, Art and Architecture,* New York: Rizzoli, and London: Academy Editions, 1978
Liu, Tun-chen, *Su-chou ku tien yüan lin,* Beijing: Chung-kuo chien chu kung yeh ch'u pan she, 1979; as *Chinese Classical Gardens of Suzhou,* translated by Chen Lixian, edited by Joseph C. Wang, New York: McGraw-Hill, 1993
Peng, Yigan, *Zhongguo gudian yuanlin fenxi* (Analysis of the Classical Chinese Garden), Beijing: Beijing Architecture and Building Press, 1986
Wang, Joseph Cho, *The Chinese Garden,* Oxford and New York: Oxford University Press, 1998
Wong, Young-tsu, *A Paradise Lost: The Imperial Garden Yuanming Yuan,* Honolulu: University of Hawaii Press, 2001

GILLIAN CULL

# Chinampas

## Xochimilco, Mexico

**Location:** approximately 10 miles (16.1 km) south of Mexico City

*Chinampas* are gardens and orchards developed as insular and peninsular reclamations on the lake landscape of the Mexican altiplano. The history of the Mexican garden is rooted in the *chinampas*, whose flowers and vegetables have sustained the region for two millennia. As one of the most intensive and productive agricultures ever practiced, the *chinampas* supported the expansion of the great Tenochca Empire. In 1987 the extant *chinampa* landscape of Xochimilco, which means "place of flower gardens" in *náhuatl*, was designated a World Heritage Site by the United Nations Educational, Scientific, and Cultural Organization (UNESCO).

According to legend the Aztecs were directed by the god Huitzilopochtli and guided by the priest Tenoch on a long pilgrimage from the real or mystical island of Aztlán (place of herons) to the Valle de México on the Meseta del Anáhuac. The Aztecs, who spoke *náhuatl* and changed their name to *méxica*, settled at Chapultepec in 1299. After the rupture of regional alliances and their expulsion from this ancient forest, they sought refuge on the shores of Lake Texcoco. There they witnessed the fulfillment of the prophecy by Huitzilopochtli to found Tenochtitlán in 1325. While searching for food, a group of *méxica* observed an eagle eating a serpent. As it had been foretold, the eagle was perched on a prickly pear (*Opuntia* sp.) that was rooted in a rock of a small island.

Tenochtitlán and the annex market city of Tlatelolco were developed on *chinampas* at the lake site over the next two centuries. By the time the Spaniards arrived under the command of Hernán Cortés, the *chinampas* had reached their greatest extent, and causeways and canals connected the urban center to the valley.

The natural lacustrine communities within the valley landscape comprised the saltwater lakes of Texcoco at the center and Zumpango and Xaltocán to the north, and the freshwater lakes of Xochimilco and Chalco to the south. The capital was also served by an aqueduct fed from the springs in the ancient forest of Chapultepec.

Farming towns, such as Xochimilco, Acalbixca, Tlaxialtemalco, Atlapulco, Cuitláhuac, Tulyehualco, Mixquic, Tetelco, and Tezompa, developed along the shores and islands of the southern lakes, which were fed by spring water that flowed through the canals among the *chinampas* to the western portion of Lake Texcoco,

which was diked to prevent saline intrusion. *Chinampas* were also cultivated in the latter sector around the island of Ixtacalco and along the shores of Huitzilopochco and Ixtapalapa.

The Spanish chronicles on the conquest of México describe in awe the magnificent urban forests, groves, gardens, and *chinampas* in the domains of the emperor at Tenochtitlán, Chapultepec, Ixtapalapa, and Huastepec. However, only a fragment of the lake garden landscape has survived in the *chinampas* of Mixquic and Xochimilco. Tenochtitlán and Tlatelolco were razed and the lakes drained to build and expand Mexico City.

To develop *chinampas*, canals are initially dug to create a drainage and transportation network. The resulting grid plots are then filled in a multiple ridge pattern a few feet above water with mud dredged from the lake bottom during excavation. The Spanish word *chinampa* is derived from *chinamitl*—*náhuatl* for "reed fence"—in reference to the wattle used to crib the mud. The edges of the orchards are finally planted with *ahuejotes* (willow, *Salix bonplandiana*) to anchor the *chinampas* with their roots. When the surface of the *chinampas* reaches elevations not practical for irrigation and cultivation, the ground is cut to fill new *chinampas*.

To fertilize the orchards, rafts of aquatic plants are towed along the canals and spread over the packed mud to create compost layers that are then covered with fresh sediment. Although maize is planted in the *chinampas*, other crops are first grown in nurseries where mud is placed over weeds to create seedbeds. When the mud has sufficiently hardened, it is cut into small blocks called *chapines*. Each *chapín* is then seeded, enriched with manure, and covered with reeds. The seedlings are later transplanted to the orchard in the *chapines*. The *chapines* may be planted on rafts to transport the seedlings to the *chinampas*. This practice probably gave rise to the misconception that the *chinampas* were floating gardens.

Abundant harvests are possible due to an intensive but sustainable agriculture that involves seepage irrigation, organic fertilization, and seedbed cultivation. The subsurface irrigation efficiently delivers virtually permanent moisture to crop roots with little evaporation. The muck, compost, and manure are ecologically renewable resources in the lake landscape, and the use of *chapines* enables an intensive cycle of production that significantly saves time and space. In addition, through the selection of healthy seedlings, the method also improves crop yield.

The *chinampas* of Xochimilco continue to provide produce for Mexico City, yielding abundant crops of maize (*Zea mays*), squash (*Cucurbita* spp.), beans (*Phaseolus* spp., *Vigna* spp.), chilies and peppers (*Capsicum annum*, *C. frutenscens*), and tomatoes (*Lycopersicon* spp.), as well as flowers such as marigolds (*Tagetes* spp.) and dahlias (originally, *Dahlia pinnata*, *D. coccinea*), the national flower of Mexico.

An example of a *chinampas* in Xochimilco, Mexico
Copyright J.A. Bueno

Since the late 1980s an ecological, hydrological, and agricultural reclamation has been undertaken within the federal district of México to protect the aquifer, prevent inundations, and preserve the *chinampas* of Xochimilco. As part of the effort, 1,730 acres (700 ha) dedicated to agriculture have been reclaimed. A crafts market has been added, and the market and embarcadero have been revitalized.

The development of Xochimilco Ecological Park in 1993, designed by Mario Schjetnan of Grupo de Diseño Urbano, complements the reclamation effort. This multipurpose facility comprises recreational, educational, and commercial opportunities within 670 acres (271 ha), including botanical and ornamental gardens, as well as ecological, archeological, and agricultural exhibits. Also developed are a plant and flower market and a lagoon with an embarcadero for the colorfully painted and florally decorated barges, called *trajineras*, that are ridden to visit the *chinampas*.

## Synopsis

| | |
|---|---|
| 1116 | Aztecs leave real or mythical Aztlán |
| 1267 | Aztecs arrive in the Valle de México |
| 1299 | Aztecs, who changed their name to *méxica*, settle in Chapultepec |
| 1300 | Approximate date for Xochimilco settlement |
| 1325 | The *méxica* found Tenochtitlán |
| 1352 | The *méxica* defeat *xochimilca* |
| 1364 | The *méxica* build Tenochtitlán |
| 1375 | The *méxica* again defeat *xochimilca* |
| 1427–40 | Reign of King Itzcóatl, who defeats Azcapotzalco to control Valle de México |
| 1428 | Kingdoms of Tenochtitlán, Tetzcoco, and Tlacopán found Tenochca Empire |
| 1440–69 | Reign of Emperor Motecuhzoma I, who extends control beyond Valle de México and builds Chapultepec aqueduct |
| 1486–1502 | Reign of Emperor Ahuítzotl, who builds Coyoaca'n aqueduct |
| 1502–20 | Reign of Emperor Motecuhzoma II, who wages wars with the *tlaxcala* |
| 1519 | Spaniards arrive in November at Tenochtitlán under command of Hernán Cortés |
| 1520–21 | Reign of Cuauhtémoc, last emperor of Tenochca |
| 1520 | The *méxica* repel Spaniards from Tenochtitlán on 7 June (*la noche triste*) |
| 1521 | Spaniards and the *tlaxcala* besiege Tenochtitlán, 30 May |
| 1521 | Spaniards and the *tlaxcala* conquer Tenochtitlán, 13 August |
| 1700s | Spanish colonial government drains most of Lake Texcoco |
| 1987 | UNESCO declares the extant *chinampas* of Xochimilco a World Heritage Site; ecological, hydrological, and agricultural reclamation of Xochimilco started |
| 1993 | Xochimilco Ecological Park opens to the public |

## Further Reading

Armillas, Pedro, "Gardens on Swamps," *Science* 174, no. 4010 (1971)

Carrasco Pizana, Pedro, *Estructura político territorial del Imperio Tenochca: La triple alianza de Tenochtitlán, Tetzcoco y Tlacopán*, Mexico: Colegio de México, 1996; as *The Tenochca Empire of Ancient México: The Triple Alliance of Tenochtitlán, Tetzcoco, and Tlacopán*, Norman: University of Oklahoma Press, 1999

Coe, Michael D., "The Chinampas of Mexico," *Scientific American* 211, no. 1 (1964)

Cortés, Hernán, "Carta segunda" (30 October 1520) and "Carta tercera" (15 May 1522), in *Cartas de relación de la conquista de México*, Benito Juárez: Espasa-Calpe Mexicana, 1945; 16th edition, Madrid: Espasa-Calpe, 1995

Darch, J.P, "Drained Fields in the Americas: An Introduction," in *Drained Field Agriculture in Central and South America*, edited by Darch, Oxford: B.A.R., 1983

Departamento del Distrito Federal, *La obra hidráulica en el programa de rescate*, México, n.d.

Díaz del Castillo, Bernal, *Historia verdadera de la conquista de la Nueva España*, edited by Alonso Remón, Madrid, 1632; reprint, 3 vols., Chiapas, Mexico: Gobierno del Estado, 1992; as *The True History of the Conquest of Mexico*, London, 1800; reprint, La Jolla, California: Renaissance Press, 1979

Haas, Antonio, *Jardines de México*, New York: Editorial Jilguero/Rizzoli, 1993

"Parque Ecológico Xochimilco," *Landscape Architecture* (November 1994)

Parsons, Jeffrey, "Chinampa Agriculture and the Aztec Urbanization in the Valley of Mexico," in *Prehistoric Intensive Agriculture in the Tropics*, edited by Ian S. Farrington, vol. 38, Oxford: B.A.R., 1985

Thompson, J. William, "Aztec Revival," *Landscape Architecture* (April 1999)

JUAN ANTONIO BUENO

# Chinoiserie

The term *chinoiserie* derives from the French *chinois,* or Chinese, and refers to art objects produced in Europe with Chinese or pseudo-Chinese decorative motifs. Although the term is commonly reserved for porcelain objects manufactured to fill a gap in consumer demand for fine china, chinoiserie also includes the textiles, lacquerware, metalwork, and garden designs that took their inspiration from Chinese models.

The vogue for chinoiseries began in the second half of the 17th century, peaked in the 1750s when trade with China reached its height, and began to wane in the early 19th century. James Cawthorne's lighthearted verse of 1756 reveals the attitude of Chinese enthusiasts:

Of late, 'tis true, quite sick of Rome and Greece,
We fetch our models from the wise Chinese;
European artists are too cool and chaste,
For Mand'rin is the only man of taste.

European trade routes established a small but steady stream of Chinese spices, silk, ivories, and other commodities dating back to antiquity. Marco Polo's tales of his adventures at Kublai Kahn's court (1295) fired the European imagination and desire for exotic objects and ideas. In 1544 the Portuguese first established direct trade with China, which expanded exponentially with the foundation of the British East India Company (1600) and the Dutch Verenigde Oost Indische Compagnie (1602). Collectors displayed the blue-and-white import porcelains from China as rare and precious objects in *wunderkammern,* or "rooms of wonders," alongside mineral specimens, fossils, and art objects. Chinese and Japanese goods were channeled through India, and objects from all three countries poured into Europe, resulting in blurred distinctions between national styles. As a result the term *chinoiserie* sometimes refers to any "Oriental" object and lacks the implied geographic specificity of the reference to China.

The reigning image of Chinese gardens in Europe at this time was one that blended the opulent nature of exotic plants with the whimsy and freedom of garden plans. Europeans focused especially on those features of Chinese gardens that stood in direct opposition to the European paradigm of the highly regular garden as a metaphor for God's law expressed in nature. Under the influence of theoretical writing on Chinese gardens, such as William Temple's *Upon the Gardens of Epicurus* (1685), J.B. Fischer von Erlach's *Plan of Civil and Historical Architecture* (1721), and perhaps most important, William Chambers's *Dissertation on Oriental Gardening* (1772), landowners began incorporating Chinese ideas and forms in two principal ways, one structural and the other decorative.

Chinese garden theory penetrated to the level of the plan in the disposition of irregular walking paths, surprising views, and interesting objects of contemplation. Fans of Chinese garden techniques such as Temple and Chambers opposed their own culture's attitudes toward nature—where humankind's dominion over nature, granted by God to Adam in the Bible, was expressed metaphorically in gardens through the use of rigid garden paths and trees and shrubs trimmed to geometrical precision—favoring that of the Chinese, where scattered, asymmetrical arrangements were viewed as a vehicle for personal expression and creativity. Temple introduced the term *sharawaggi* to describe the scattered and disordered but ultimately pleasing placement of elements such as rocks, streams, and pavilions in the Chinese garden, writing, "Their greatest reach of imagination is employed in contriving figures where the beauty shall be great . . . but without any order or disposition of parts."

These informal gardens with a mixture of sources became known as *jardins anglo-chinois* and were well suited to the cultural needs of an aristocracy seeking increasing freedom from the dictates of style and behavior represented by the oppressive European courts of the 17th century. With the development of new forms of social leisure, such as those portrayed in Antoine Watteau's *fête galante* paintings, new garden forms provided the intimate and informal setting for lighthearted, frivolous pursuits such as moon viewings, garden teas, and aimless wandering.

The most noticeable additions to European gardens, however, were the scattered Chinese buildings, such as pagodas or pavilions, found across Europe. From Drottningholm to Palermo, from Madrid to St. Petersburg, the 18th-century traveler delighted in these fanciful and exotic forms. Stylistically sympathetic with the rococo aesthetic, pagodas, such as the one built by Chambers at the Royal Botanic Gardens at Kew in 1761, were thought to give the landscape a "whimsical air of novelty that is very pleasing," as Horace Walpole commented in 1750. Kew's fame spawned a rash of pagodas in other gardens, including those at Amboise, Potsdam, Chanteloup, Scoonenberg, Montbéliard, Munich, Oranienbaum, and Tsarskoye Selo. These structures were often more concerned with decorative detail in the form of bright colors, latticework, and dragons than in technically accurate construction. Erected quickly and with flimsy materials, few structures remain standing today.

While Chambers praised Chinese gardeners, who sought to generate emotional responses to the land through irregular contours, creative displays of exotic vegetation, and the thoughtful disposition of buildings,

**Chinese pagoda at the Royal Botanic Gardens, Kew, built by William Chambers, 1761, from Osvald Sirén,** *China and Gardens of Europe of the Eighteenth Century,* **[1950], 1990**
**Courtesy of Dumbarton Oaks**

statuary, and fountains, it is important to note that much of his *Dissertation* places a Chinese mask on his own gardening theories. European writers on Chinese gardens, few of whom had actually visited China (Chambers is one exception, having traveled to China in 1743–45 and 1748–49), rarely distinguished between imperial and literati gardens and did not recognize that "the Chinese garden" as it existed in their minds was an accretion of historically and stylistically nonspecific ideas rather than a reality.

The reception of the introduction of Chinese elements into European gardens was mixed. Remarking on the habit of placing buildings from a variety of styles and types within a garden, Sir John Parnell complained in his journal of 1769 that, "where different nations are thus introduced into an improvement, they shou'd at least be hid from one another, by a hill, wood or clump of trees." Other critics, concerned with nationalist purity, denied any influence of Chinese garden theory on European designs. Lord Shaftesbury, a sinophobe, claimed that the admiration of wild nature found in the new informal garden style in Europe had no Chinese precedent.

After the French Revolution the *jardin anglo-chinois* fell out of favor as a throwback to a corrupt era. The fascination with Chinese gardens in the 19th century grew more scientific, and the focus shifted to botany and the importation of Chinese species of rare plants. Gilbert Slater published a catalog of Chinese plants, and Robert Fortune introduced 190 species into Europe, including the white wisteria and forsythia (*F. viridissima*). By the end of the 19th century, more than 200,000 Chinese species were preserved in Europe, and the popularity of irises, peonies, and rhododendrons continued to grow. Most recently, the Astor Garden Court at the Metropolitan Museum of Art in New York City re-creates a Ming dynasty scholar's garden for rest and meditation.

**Further Reading**

Chambers, William, *Dissertation on Oriental Gardening*, London, 1772; reprint, 1983

*Chinoiserie: Fantasy in the Age of Reason*, Ann Arbor: University of Michigan Museum of Art, 1971

Clunas, Craig, *Fruitful Sites: Garden Culture in Ming Dynasty China*, London: Reaktion Books, and Durham, North Carolina: Duke University Press, 1996

Fischer von Erlach, J.B., *Entwurff einer historischen Architectur*, Vienna, 1721; 2nd edition, Leipzig, 1725; as *A Plan of Civil and Historical Architecture*, translated by Thomas Lediard, London, 1737; reprint, Ridgewood, New Jersey: Gregg Press, 1964

Gruber, Alain, "La chinoiserie dans l'art européen," *L'oeil*, 350 (September 1984)

Halfpenny, William, and John Halfpenny, *New Designs for Chinese Temples, Triumphal Arches, Garden Seats, Pailings, etc.,* London, 1750; reprint, London: Sayer and Brindley, 1973

Hirschfeld, C.C.L., *Theorie der Gartenkunst*, Leipzig, 1777; reprint, 5 vols., Hildesheim and New York: Olms, 1985

Honour, Hugh, *Chinoiserie: The Vision of Cathay*, London: Murray, and New York: Harper and Row, 1961

Impey, Oliver R., *Chinoiserie: The Impact of Oriental Styles on Western Art and Decoration*, New York: Scribner, and London: Oxford University Press, 1977

Jacobson, Dawn, *Chinoiserie*, London: Phaidon, 1993

Jarry, Madeleine, *Chinoiserie: Chinese Influence on European Decorative Art, 17th and 18th centuries,* New York: Vendome Press, and London: Wilson, 1981

Lovejoy, Arthur, "The Chinese Origin of Romanticism," in *Essays in the History of Ideas*, Baltimore: Johns Hopkins Press, 1948

Maverick, Lewis A., *China: A Model for Europe*, San Antonio, Texas: Andersen, 1946

Morris, Edwin T., *The Gardens of China: History, Art, and Meaning; Chung-hua yüan lin* (bilingual English-Chinese edition), New York: Scribner, 1983

Sieveking, Albert Forbes, editor, *Upon the Gardens of Epicurus, with Other XVIIth Century Garden Essays,* London: Chatto and Windus, 1908

Sirén, Osvald, *China and Gardens of Europe of the Eighteenth Century*, New York: Ronald Press, 1950

Watelet, Charles Henri, *Essai sur les jardins*, Paris, 1764; reprint, Geneva: Minkoff Reprint, 1972

Wiebenson, Dora, *The Picturesque Garden in France*, Princeton, New Jersey: Princeton University Press, 1978

PAMELA J. WARNER

# Christchurch

## Canterbury, South Island, New Zealand

**Location:** approximately 190 miles (317 km) southwest of Wellington

Christchurch, New Zealand, has cultivated the character of a "garden" city for many years and actively promotes itself as "Christchurch—The Garden City." In 1997 this was acknowledged by the International Parks Congress held in Madrid, which voted Christchurch the best garden city in the world. Its reputation derives from a number of factors. These include the favorable temperate climate, soils, and high water table; the overall city plan, with its numerous avenues and the picturesque Avon river; the presence of a number of notable public and private gardens across and around the city; active promotion of civic amenity by successive councils and other bodies; and a widely shared "culture" of gardening, centered on two long-established societies and a large number of garden clubs.

Christchurch was established in 1850, one of a number of planned settlements in New Zealand in the mid-19th century. It was notable for the combination of social and religious goals pursued by its founder, the Canterbury Association. The aim was to re-create a traditional English community, and it was a reaction to rapid industrialization and social upheaval in Europe. This aim was not achieved, but it did leave two important legacies to the contemporary garden city: a formally planned city, based on a grid, with significant public reserves, and the beginnings of a myth that Christchurch is particularly "English" in character—respectable, ordered, civilized. The "Garden City" ideal forms part of this myth of Englishness.

A major feature of the city is the large expanse of Hagley Park and the Christchurch Botanical Gardens. Designated as a public reserve in 1856, Hagley Park is characterized by extensive boundary plantings and intersecting avenues of European deciduous trees, with open areas of amenity grass. Victoria Lake was created as part of the setting for the 1906–7 International Exhibition, and other areas have been developed as sports fields and a golf course. A large meadow is retained in North Hagley and provides the venue for public concerts. Hagley Park is situated immediately to the west of the original city grid, and the river Avon passes through the park. A major loop of the river provides a natural boundary to the Christchurch Botanical Gardens.

The origins of the Christchurch Botanical Gardens came soon after the initial colonial settlement. Its establishment was proposed at a public meeting in 1864, in conjunction with the formation of the Canterbury Horti-

cultural and Acclimatisation Society. The new gardens were intended to support the objectives of the society and were located on the site of a tree nursery run by the government gardener Enoch Barker, who laid out the first stage of the gardens. Since then, a succession of curators have developed the botanical gardens to become one of Christchurch's most important civic attractions.

The character of the Christchurch Botanical Gardens is dominated by a large number and wide range of exotic trees, many now mature, creating an open woodland setting that encloses several formal lawns, shrub borders, and display gardens. The overall style is best described as late Victorian/Edwardian gardenesque, with a layout that expresses the incremental process of development. The botanical character of the gardens reflects a long-standing emphasis on the introduction and cultivation of exotic plants for urban amenity and acclimatization. The collection represents an important scientific resource that illustrates how Northern Hemisphere trees adapt to new conditions—growth rates, habit, life span, etc. Many of the specimens in the gardens also have historical value, having been planted as commemorative trees. The botanical gardens also contain a wide range of indigenous species, particularly within the Cockayne Memorial Garden, as well as built features in a variety of styles, such as the recently restored Peacock Fountain.

Mona Vale is also another important site within Christchurch. Located along the banks of the Avon just upstream from Hagley Park, Mona Vale was originally laid out as a private garden at the beginning of the 20th century and further developed in the 1940s. Following a period of decline it came into public ownership in 1969, partly funded by public appeal. The restored English Domestic Revival homestead is surrounded by lawns, a rose garden, lily pond, an iris garden, rhododendron and azalea borders, and a fernery originally built for the 1906–7 International Exhibition. Mona Vale typifies more than any other site the gardenesque qualities that appear to be sought by visitors and favored by many Christchurch residents. The Ilam homestead is another notable garden featuring extensive rhododendron and azalea borders. Developed by Edgar Stead, whose expertise was recognized by his role as an international judge at the Chelsea Flower Show, the garden became world renowned in the 1920s and 1930s. It is now the University of Canterbury Staff Club, approximately 0.9 miles (1.5 km) upstream from Mona Vale.

Lying between the two gardens, Riccarton Bush is a prominent and ecologically significant reserve. It comprises a unique remnant of the former kahikatea (white pine, *Podocarpus dacrydioides*) forests that grew on wetter parts of the Canterbury Plains prior to human settlement. The Deans family settled the area before the arrival of the Canterbury Association migrants and ensured the conservation of part of the bush following the establishment of Christchurch. The Deans's homestead and garden now form part of the Reserve. To the north of Riccarton Bush, and between Mona Vale and Ilam, the suburb of Fendalton is an area of large private homes, many of which are surrounded by mature trees and shrubberies, which collectively provide a gardenesque character to the northwest approach to the city from the airport. A number of these (including Mona Vale, Parkdale, and Rotoroa) were laid out or influenced by Canterbury's leading designer of the early 20th century, Alfred Buxton.

Buxton's employee and then successor Edgar Taylor also laid out a number of private Christchurch gardens and designed several formal public parks and gardens around the city. One of his most historically significant projects was the Edmonds Factory Garden. A central feature of the garden, the floral display based on a stylized sunrise, appeared from the 1950s onward on the cover of a book said to be New Zealand's all-time bestseller, the *Edmonds Cookery Book*. The "sure-to-rise" style (the phrase refers to one of the Edmonds bakery products) of vivid floral displays and smoothly manicured lawns has for many years provided an inspiration for the garden competitions that form another important element of Christchurch. The original Edmonds Garden was initiated in 1923 around a new factory building on Ferry Road, to the east of the city, in a late Victorian gardenesque style, but part was remodeled by Edgar Taylor in 1935 in a formal neoclassical style. More recent additions are more naturalistic. Although the factory has been demolished, a portion of the garden has been re-created as a historic reserve.

A number of private gardens in the rural areas around Christchurch also contribute to its reputation as a Garden City. The most notable is Ohinetahi, in Governors Bay, some 7.5 miles (12 km) south of the city center. The first European garden on the site was laid out about 1853, soon after the initial colonial settlement, by the botanist T.H. Potts. The house and garden were largely abandoned in the late 19th century, finally bought in 1977 by Sir Miles Warren and Pauline and John Trengrove, who over the succeeding 20 years restored and redesigned both house and garden. The main garden is formal and European in inspiration, with a central lawn, pleached hornbeam walk, and a series of smaller enclosed gardens. This is complemented by a more romantic woodland garden in the adjoining gully. A notable feature is the number of contemporary sculptures located throughout the garden.

Although notable gardens make a vital contribution, the overall character of Christchurch as a Garden City owes much to the cumulative activities of many thousands of enthusiastic private gardeners. An important part of this garden culture derives from the activities of the Canterbury Horticultural Society (whose origins are linked with the establishment of the Botanical Gardens in the mid-19th century), and the Christchurch Beautifying Association. The Beautifying Association was formed in 1897 and included in its early membership many influential opinion leaders, such as the architect Samuel Hurst Seager, an early advocate for town planning in New Zealand and promoter of a garden suburb on Clifton Hill; Harry Ell, member of Parliament and promoter of the Summit Road along the Port Hills south of Christchurch, an early scenic parkway; and Leonard Cockayne, who pioneered plant ecology in New Zealand.

The activities of the association were influenced by the ideals of both the City Beautiful movement in the United States and the Garden City movement in the United Kingdom. The association lobbied the city council to improve public amenity and initiated a number of projects through volunteer work, promoted the title "Garden City," and introduced garden and street competitions. Among the public amenity projects promoted and undertaken by the Beautifying Association and its members over the past 100 years have been the development of walks and planting along the banks of the river Avon through the city, development of parks and reserves such as the Millbrook Reserve, and the planting of street trees throughout the city. There have also been a number of gifts made to the city, such as the Peacock Fountain, now restored in the botanical gardens, and a floral clock in Victoria Square.

Garden competitions have been a continuing and influential factor in the Garden City ideal. They have been held throughout the 20th century, based on strict criteria and with a number of cups and trophies for different categories. Competitions were most influential during the 1950s to 1970s and continue to the present. An important aspect of the Christchurch Beautifying Association competitions has been the emphasis on the appearance of private gardens from the street, which has strengthened their contribution to the Garden City ideal. However, the competition tradition has tended to favor more conservative garden styles (the Edmonds Garden, for example), and in recent years its overall influence has probably been overtaken by fashions promulgated through the mass media and garden centers. The civic dimension of garden competitions was reinforced in the 1950s by the introduction of a street competition by the Beautifying Association, in which the appearance of an entire street is judged and recognized, as is the contribution of private gardens to the streetscape.

Christchurch garden and street competitions are underpinned by the long-standing tradition in the city of horticultural and garden clubs. The Canterbury Horticultural Society has been a focus of plant knowledge and cultivation, particularly of introduced species and native cultivars, since the earliest days of European settlement. It holds annual exhibitions and competitions, including garden competitions, in addition to a year-round educational program. The Canterbury Horticultural Society is also the parent organization for approximately 50 local garden clubs based in different parts of the city. Local garden clubs originated in the early years of World War II, which also coincided with the centennial celebrations for the Canterbury settlement. They have provided both a focus for sharing knowledge and a significant social role and have been particularly important for the many women gardeners in the city.

Recent years have seen major growth in another related phenomenon, garden tours. Organized by both local communities and private entrepreneurs, garden tours provide an opportunity to visit private gardens not normally open to the public. These include a number of homestead gardens in the rural areas around Christchurch, many of which are modeled on the English cottage and country garden tradition and extend the Garden City ideal into the wider region.

The Christchurch City Council has increasingly adopted a central role in the maintenance and promotion of the Garden City ideal. Although it was the lack of effective municipal action during the 19th century that led to the initial formation of the Beautifying Association, several phases of local government reorganization have since concentrated responsibility for planning and management of most streets and public reserves within the city, including the botanical gardens, on the city council. It now provides coordination as well as funding and managing parks, street trees, and promotional activities, including a self-drive tour of gardens in and around the city. Another significant factor has been the influence of graduates and staff from the horticultural and landscape architectural programs at Lincoln University (formerly Canterbury Agricultural College and Lincoln College).

In contrast, the influence of the indigenous Maori culture of New Zealand on and within the Garden City ideal has been conspicuous largely by its absence. The relationship between Maori and European settlers in New Zealand is complex and has been frequently contentious. The low-lying wetlands, which are now largely drained and occupied by Christchurch City, were formerly used extensively for hunting and gathering by Maori, while some productive gardens were established on the adjoining higher land of the Banks Peninsula. A significant political shift over the past two decades has resulted in much wider recognition of Maori rights and values. In particular the recent legal settlement between the government of New Zealand and Ngai Tahu, the tribe that now has primary status in the Christchurch area, of claims arising from the initial process of colonization clearly reestablishes Maori as key development partners and significant landowners in the city. The most likely impact on the Garden City character of Christchurch is to reinforce the current move toward greater recognition and celebration of the qualities of indigenous plants and the fauna they support.

The evolving political relationship between Maori and the contemporary descendants of European settlers highlights the changing nature of the Garden City ideal in Christchurch. For much of its first 150 years, the citizens of Christchurch have emphasized British, and to a lesser extent North American, approaches to gardens. Particularly in the earlier phases, this was expressed through a focus on introduced plants and planting styles, attempting to re-create familiar, northern traditions in the Southern Hemisphere. However, there has always been an interest by some in the use and cultivation of indigenous plants, and today there is growing emphasis on a search for a more regionally based identity. This creates some tensions, for example, over the use of indigenous species within formal public parks, gardens, and reserves, exemplified in the debates generated by the city's program of waterways and wetland restoration. The growing commercial role of the Garden City ideal in city promotion and tourism adds further challenges. However, the history of the past 150 years shows that the association of Christchurch with gardens and gardening is deep-seated, resilient, and adaptable to new opportunities and needs.

## Synopsis

| | |
|---|---|
| 1843 | Deans family settles at Deans Bush (subsequently Riccarton Bush) |
| before 1850 | Mahinga Kai (place of food gathering) for Maori |
| 1850 | Founding of Christchurch by Canterbury Association, intended as re-creation of traditional English community |
| 1853 | Ohinetahi garden first laid out by T.H. Potts |
| 1856 | Hagley Park designated as public reserve |
| 1863–64 | Initial steps to create Christchurch Botanical Gardens on site of tree nursery run by government gardener Enoch Barker |
| 1864 | Founding of Canterbury Horticultural and Acclimatization Society |
| 1897 | Founding of Christchurch Beautifying Association to encourage private gardens and neighborhood parks |
| 1906–7 | New Zealand International Exhibition in North Hagley Park; Victoria Lake created |

| 1920s–30s | Street Trees Movement |
|---|---|
| 1923 | Edmonds Garden laid out around factory building on Ferry Road |
| 1935 | Edgar Taylor plan for remodeling of Edmonds Factory Garden |
| 1940 | Mona Vale garden created |
| 1950s–70s | High point of garden competitions |
| 1969 | Mona Vale purchased for public use |
| 1977 | Ohinetahi remodeling commenced by Sir Miles Warren and Pauline and John Trengrove |
| 1980s–90s | Active promotion of Garden City as tourist attraction |
| 1997 | Christchurch voted Best Garden City at International Parks Congress in Madrid, Spain |

**Further Reading**

Barnett, M.J., H.G. Gilpin, and L.J. Metcalf, editors, *A Garden Century: The Christchurch Botanic Gardens, 1863–1963*, Christchurch, New Zealand: Christchurch City Council, 1963

Bradbury, Matthew, editor, *A History of the Garden in New Zealand*, Auckland, New Zealand, and New York: Viking Press, 1995

Challenger, S., "Landscapes and Gardeners in Early New Zealand," *Bulletin/Royal Society of New Zealand* 21, no. 2 (1983)

Eldred-Grigg, Stevan, *A New History of Canterbury*, Dunedin, New Zealand: McIndoe, 1982

*Gardenfo: Christchurch Botanic Gardens* 1–32 (1993–2000)

*Gardens to Visit in Mid and North Canterbury and Christchurch City*, Christchurch: 1998

Gower, Sidney William, compiler, *Christchurch, The Garden City of New Zealand*, Christchurch: Christchurch Beautifying Association, 1968

Hight, James, and C.R. Straubel, editors, *A History of Canterbury*, 3 vols., Christchurch: Whitcombe and Tombs, 1957–71

McBride, B., "The (Post)colonial Landscape of Cathedral Square: Urban Redevelopment and Representation in the 'Cathedral City,'" *New Zealand Geographer* 55, no. 1 (1999)

Strongman, Thelma, *The Gardens of Canterbury: A History*, Wellington, New Zealand: Reed, 1984

Strongman, Thelma, "The Use of Native Plants in Canterbury Gardens from Raoul until the Present," in *Etienne Raoul and Canterbury Botany, 1840–1996*, edited by Colin J. Burrows, Christchurch: Canterbury Botanical Society, and Manuka Press, 1998

Strongman, Thelma, *City Beautiful: The First 100 Years of the Christchurch Beautifying Association*, Christchurch: Clerestory Press, 1999

Tipples, Rupert, *Colonial Landscape Gardener: Alfred Buxton of Christchurch, New Zealand, 1872–1950*, Canterbury: Department of Horticulture and Landscape, Lincoln College, 1989

SIMON SWAFFIELD

# Church, Thomas Dolliver 1902–1978

## United States Landscape Architect

Thomas Church was one of the best-known American modernist landscape architects. In his California practice he pioneered the design of modernist small gardens in response to the greatly changed social and economic circumstances of the Depression. This new garden was much smaller than the professionally designed gardens of the late 19th and early 20th century, had a reduced staff, and a much smaller budget. Church's training in the mid 1920s in the Beaux-Arts tradition, followed by travel to the major aristocratic gardens of Italy and Spain, would appear to have been poor preparation for these new, more modest conditions. Yet he derived fun-

damental principles that became an important part of his eclectic and nonideological design approach.

His origins as a native Californian also influenced his professional development. Because of its prior history as an area not strongly committed to European design traditions, California was also better placed than many other regions to forge new approaches. Its isolation from eastern influences also fostered a willingness to accept the new and unconventional. In southern California in the 1920s, architects such as Frank Lloyd Wright, Rudolph Schindler, and Richard Neutra had developed integrated houses and gardens along the lines of European modernist designs. In Santa Barbara, Lockwood de Forest had designed several simple abstract gardens that anticipated later modernist concerns.

In the San Francisco Bay area, the earlier work of idiosyncratic architects such as Bernard Maybeck, Julia Morgan, and Ernest Coxhead was characterized by simplicity, integration of interior and exterior spaces, and sensitive adaptations to hillside sites. In addition, the membership of many socially prominent local families in the Swedenborgian Church ensured that the qualities of modest simplicity embodied in these designs were not valued solely by the intelligentsia.

Church's academic training and this sympathetic social milieu provided the ideal opportunity for creative garden design in northern California. Church's practice can be divided into three phases. From 1929 until 1937 his designs were simplified versions of historicist precedents such as French baroque parterres and Spanish gardens. In the second phase, from 1937 until 1960, he developed a new abstract aesthetic around the concept of "visual endlessness" with multiple visual foci. He used innovative materials such as corrugated asbestos-cement panels, light steel columns, heart redwood blocks, and poured concrete in abstract forms similar to those seen in cubist paintings and sculpture. In this period his practice remained largely residential. In the last phase, from 1960 until 1977, his practice included a number of large commercial and institutional projects, and in his garden designs, he frequently reverted to pronounced but simple formalist tendencies.

Church redefined the garden as space with four functional zones. The entrance zone established relationships to the street and often included parking and entry courts. The service zone was usually kept as small as possible and included the service entrance, storage areas for tools, lath houses, and vegetable plots. The social zone was directly related to the living rooms of the house and provided areas for outdoor entertaining, and the recreation zone provided space for swimming and play for children. The client's intended use of their outdoor space determined whether all zones were present. Owing to the comparatively small size of these gardens, swimming pools frequently occupied a prominent position.

Church's designs differ from those of later California designers in their restraint and superb craftsmanship. As he said, "All is calculated to give complete restfulness to the eye. If the eye sees too many things it is confused and the sense of peace is obliterated." His designs employed a simple abstract vocabulary of paved areas of concrete or brick, wooden decking, small lawn panels, and areas of ground cover; boldly textured plants and carefully pruned trees provided contrast to these geometric shapes. The design of the garden on the Dewey Donnell (Sonoma, California) ranch, an iconic

modernist garden, employs these characteristics. Such designs celebrate the complete and relaxed integration of interior and exterior spaces and were conceived as "outdoor rooms" for the relaxed and diverse lives of his upper-class clients.

Church's simply written, eminently approachable, and nondidactic books and articles in *House Beautiful* magazine, together with the frequent inclusion of his work in *Sunset Magazine,* introduced him to a wide audience and played a major role in the broad acceptance of the modernist garden as an outdoor room. Each garden was a unique work of art, appropriate to the client, program of uses, site, and budget. His skills as a site planner are also evident in his work for several university campuses, especially the University of California, Santa Cruz. But his command of larger-scale design commissions, created in conjunction with impersonal committees, were not always successful. His forte was unquestionably the private garden.

Church differed from later modernist landscape designers in his lack of adherence to a radical agenda of social ideas or aesthetics. His work was not based on a strongly defined or defended theory. Rather, his designs were a highly pragmatic reaction to client needs and site circumstances. He was influenced by his study of Italian and Spanish gardens and by a number of individuals. Fletcher Steele's work inspired him to break Beaux-Arts rules. Church also studied the work of his friend de Forest, which was notable for its abstract simplicity and regional character.

A 1937 trip to Scandinavia with architect William Wurster introduced Church to the eclectic, subtle, and humanistic modernism of the Finnish architect Alvar Aalto, with its incorporation of references to vernacular traditions. The fluid abstract forms of Aalto's buildings, furniture, and glassware are similar to the forms of many Church gardens. Church's fascination with Aalto was reinforced by the fact that for many years Church and his wife ran a shop in San Francisco that was the sole American franchise for Aalto's furniture.

Church was also affected by developments in modern art. In the late 1930s and 1940s he was associated with a number of Bay Area sculptors whose work he incorporated in his gardens, the most notable being Florence Alston Swift and Adaline Kent. There is, however, no evidence that he took any interest in major modern artists, such as Jóan Miro and Jean Arp, whose work has sometimes been cited as an influence on his designs.

*See also* Stanford University

**Biography**

Born in Boston, Massachusetts, 1902. Moved to Ojai, California, with family; started undergraduate work at University of California, Berkeley, in law; transferred to landscape architecture after taking a course in history of landscape architecture; graduate work in landscape architecture, Harvard University, 1924–26; traveled in Italy and Spain on a Sheldon Travelling Scholarship; taught landscape architecture at Ohio State University, 1927–29; moved to California, opened office at resort community of Pasatiempo, near Santa Cruz, designing small gardens around golf-course; moved to San Francisco, 1932; retired, 1977; designed well over 2,000 gardens, mostly in San Francisco Bay region, 1930–77; campus landscape architect for University of California, Berkeley, University of California, Santa Cruz, and Stanford University. Died in 1978.

## Selected Designs

| 1937 | Jerd Sullivan Garden, San Francisco, California, United States |
| 1939–41 | Exhibition Gardens, Golden Gate International Exhibition, Treasure Island, San Francisco, California, United States |
| 1941–50 | Park Merced, San Francisco, California, United States |
| 1948 | Dewey Donnell Ranch, Sonoma, California, United States |
| 1949–59 | Technical Center, Detroit, Michigan, United States |
| 1956 | Corydon Wagner Garden, Tacoma, Washington, United States |
| 1959 | Stanford Medical Center, Stanford, California, United States |
| 1962 | Campus Plan, University of California, Santa Cruz, United States |
| 1962 | Sunset Magazine headquarters, Menlo Park, California, United States |
| 1971–74 | Longwood Gardens, Kennett Square, Pennsylvania, United States |

## Selected Publications

"The Small California Garden, Chapter 1: A New Deal for the Small Lot," *California Arts and Architecture 5* (1933)

*Gardens Are for People: How to Plan for Outdoor Living*, 1955; 3rd edition, with Grace Hall and Michael Laurie, 1995

*Your Private World: A Study of Intimate Gardens*, 1969

## Further Reading

Calkins, Carroll, "Thomas Church: The Influence of His 2,000 Gardens," *House Beautiful* 109, no. 3 (1967)

Laurie, Michael M., "The Gift of Thomas Church," *Horticulture* 63, no. 9 (1985)

Messenger, Pam-Anela, "Thomas Church and His Role in American Landscape Architecture," *Landscape Architecture* 67, no. 3 (1977)

Messenger, Pam-Anela, "Thomas Church and Garden Design in the West," *Pacific Horticulture* 40, no. 1 (1979)

Messenger, Pam-Anela, "El Novillero Revisited," *Pacific Horticulture* 43, no. 2 (1982)

Reiss, Suzanne, editor, *Thomas Church, Landscape Architect*, 2 vols., Berkeley, California: Regional Oral History Office, Bancroft Library, University of California, 1978

Simo, Melanie, "Regionalism and Modernism: Some Common Roots," in *Keeping Eden: A History of Gardening in America*, edited by Walter T. Punch, Boston: Bulfinch Press, 1992

Streatfield, David C., "Thomas Church and the California Garden 1929–1950," in *Festschrift, a Collection of Essays on Architectural History*, edited by Elisabeth Walton Potter, Eugene, Oregon: Northern Pacific Coast Chapter, Society of Architectural Historians, 1978

Streatfield, David C., *California Gardens: Creating a New Eden*, New York: Abbeville Press, 1994

Streatfield, David C., "Modernist Gardens 'On the Edge of the World,'" in *Masters of American Garden Design III: The Modern Garden in Europe and the United States*, edited by Robin Karson, Cold Spring, New York: The Garden Conservancy, 1994

Treib, Marc, "Aspects of Regionality and the Modern(ist) Garden in California," in *Regional Garden Design in the United States*, edited by Therese O'Malley and Marc Treib, Washington, DC: Dumbarton Oaks Research Library and Collection, 1995

DAVID C. STREATFIELD

# Cleve. *See* Kleve

# Cleveland, Horace William Shaler 1814–1900

## United States Landscape Architect

Horace William Shaler Cleveland was an important pioneer in the development of landscape architecture during the 19th century. Together with other prominent figures in the profession, including Andrew Jackson Downing, Frederick Law Olmsted, and Robert Morris Copeland, he synthesized important literary explorations regarding landscape and civilization in the design of parks, park systems, suburban communities, and urban boulevards. Many of Cleveland's ideas were grounded in the work of such prominent literary figures as Henry Wadsworth Longfellow and Ralph Waldo Emerson.

Born in Lancaster, Massachusetts, Cleveland attended an experimental school managed by his mother, Dorcas Hiller Cleveland. Based on the principles of Swiss educational theorist Johann Heinrich Pestolozzi, the innovative education included field trips to the surrounding landscape, careful observation of the real world, and map-making skills that would later guide Cleveland in his artful manipulation of the landscape. During these years Cleveland also became a bibliophile, embracing the work of Washington Irving and several English writers.

As a young adult Cleveland journeyed west to Illinois on a survey expedition to study and record observations in the wild region he would later describe as a "dream land." Upon returning to Massachusetts, he stayed for a time at the home of his brother Henry Cleveland, a renowned scholar who met regularly with a literary organization known as the "Five of Clubs" that included Longfellow, who was completing his novel *Hyperion*. Cleveland later wrote to Longfellow that the book guided him throughout his lifetime and that its words had "come home to me like the echo of the surging of my own heart."

Not attending Harvard as had his scholarly brother, Cleveland decided to meld his love for ideas with the pursuit of a more practical enterprise. In the 1840s he purchased acreage near Burlington, New Jersey, to pursue scientific farming. Like other early landscape architects, he engaged in pomological research ostensibly geared to improving the plight of American farmers. However, he also likely engaged in landscape design experiments. In 1854 he formed a partnership in landscape and ornamental gardening with Robert Morris Copeland. One of their first important projects was the design of Sleepy Hollow Cemetery in Concord, Massachusetts—later the final resting place of Ralph Waldo Emerson, Henry David Thoreau, Louisa May Alcott, and Nathaniel Hawthorne. Emerson was on the cemetery board that enlisted their services, and Cleveland

knew the transcendental leader's cousin George Barrell Emerson, a former teacher at the Lancaster school.

As work progressed at the cemetery, Ralph Waldo Emerson delivered "An Address to the Inhabitants of Concord at the Consecration of Sleepy Hollow." In it, he revealed the designers' intent for the cemetery. A review of Emerson's words makes it clear that Cleveland and Copeland designed in a natural style and avoided superfluous decoration. That stark aesthetic is consistent with the aesthetic theories of both Emerson and Horatio Greenough, which were familiar to Cleveland. More important, with the design of Sleepy Hollow, Cleveland and Copeland also likely worked with the idea of connecting public open spaces into a town and country continuum. The cemetery, said Emerson, "fortunately lies adjoining the Agricultural Society's ground, to the New Burial Ground, to the Court House and Town House, making together a large block of public ground, permanent property of town and country—all of the ornaments of either adding so much value to all."

Further emphasizing their concern for regional open space systems, Cleveland and Copeland made recommendations for Boston's Commonwealth Avenue as a link connecting the Common and Public Garden with the countryside landscape on the periphery of the city. For its time, their idea of connecting public open spaces within an urban environment was a visionary concept that Olmsted, Charles Eliot, and other landscape architects would develop with greater sophistication.

Cleveland and Copeland amicably dissolved their partnership prior to the Civil War. In 1869 Cleveland moved his practice west, where for a time he formed a loose partnership with William Merchant Richardson French, the brother of Daniel Chester French. From his Chicago office Cleveland designed that city's Drexel Boulevard, worked on the South Parks, Graceland Cemetery, and an array of projects in other Midwestern states and beyond. In his work he remained true to the natural aesthetic he had promoted years earlier with his work at Sleepy Hollow.

Cleveland also was concerned with accommodating the rapid growth of burgeoning Midwestern cities. He reasoned that something of the existing environment should be left intact as an armature around which new cities might grow. He also further developed the idea of connecting public open spaces, an idea he discussed in *The Public Grounds of Chicago, How to Give Them Character and Expression* (1869) and *Landscape Architecture as Applied to the Wants of the West* (1873). In 1886 he moved his office to Minneapolis. There he designed the Minneapolis Park System and the Omaha Park and Boulevard System. The Minneapolis system is considered the crowning achievement of his long career. He designed parkways linking the Mississippi River and a number of lakes to a small park at the center of the city.

During the late 1880s Cleveland was successful in helping preserve the area around Minnehaha Falls in Minneapolis. He designed the landscape with a light hand, allowing the site's naturalness to read through. He also directly related the design to American literature because Minnehaha Falls—as well as Minnehaha's character—were featured in Longfellow's classic work *The Song of Hiawatha*.

## Biography

Born in Lancaster, Massachusetts, 16 December 1814. Worked as surveyor and scientific farmer, 1830s and 1840s; started landscape and ornamental gardening practice in Massachusetts with Robert Morris Copeland, 1854; worked briefly with Frederick Law Olmsted before moving to Chicago, 1869, where he practiced with William M.R. French; began publishing series of important books, pamphlets, and articles; moved to Minneapolis, 1886, and designed Twin Cities metropolitan park system; planned array of estates, parks, cemeteries, subdivisions, resorts, and institutional projects from Maine to the Great Plains and from the upper Midwest to the deep South; retired, 1895. Died in Chicago, 5 December 1900.

## Selected Designs

1855–56    Sleepy Hollow Cemetery (with partner Robert Morris Copeland), Concord, Massachusetts, United States
1870    Juneau Park, Milwaukee, Wisconsin, United States; Highland Cemetery, Junction City, Kansas, United States
1872–86    Washington Park and Drexel Boulevard, Chicago, Illinois, United States
1872    Capitol Square, Madison, Wisconsin, United States
1872    Highland Park Plat, Highland Park, Illinois, United States
1880    Natural Bridge, West Virginia, United States
1881    Oak Hill Cemetery, Lake Geneva, Wisconsin, United States
1885–95    Twin Cities Metropolitan Park System, Minneapolis-St. Paul, Minnesota, United States
1886    Jekyl Island Resort, Jekyl Island, Georgia, United States
1891    Madison Park, Quincy, Illinois, United States

1892–93    Omaha Park and Boulevard System, Omaha, Nebraska, United States

## Selected Publications

"Landscape Gardening," *Christian Examiner* (1855)
*Public Grounds of Chicago: How to Give Them Character and Expression,* 1869
*Public Parks, Radial Avenues, and Boulevards: Outline Plan of a Park System for the City of St. Paul,* 1872
*Landscape Architecture, As Applied to the Wants of the West: With an Essay on Forest Planting on the Great Plains,* 1873; reprinted, 1965
*A Few Hints on the Arrangement of Rural Cemeteries,* 1881
*Aesthetic Development of the United Cities of St. Paul and Minneapolis,* 1888
*Social Life and Literature 50 Years Ago,* 1888

## Further Reading

Blegen, Theodore Christian, *Horace William Shaler Cleveland: Pioneer American Landscape Architect,* Minneapolis, Minnesota: Bruce, 1949
Haglund, Karl, "Rural Tastes, Rectangular Ideas, and the Skirmishes of H.W.S. Cleveland," *Landscape Architecture* (January 1976)
Hubbard, Theodora Kimball, "H.W.S. Cleveland: An American Pioneer in Landscape Architecture and City Planning," *Landscape Architecture* 20, no. 1 (January 1930)
Nadenicek, Daniel Joseph, "Nature in the City: Horace Cleveland's Aesthetic," *Landscape and Urban Planning* 29 (1993)
Nadenicek, Daniel Joseph, "Sleepy Hollow Cemetery: Transcendental Garden and Community Park," *Journal of the New England Garden History Society* 3 (Fall 1993)
Nadenicek, Daniel Joseph, "Sleepy Hollow Cemetery: Philosophy Made Substance," *Emerson Society Papers* 4 (Spring 1994)
Nadenicek, Daniel Joseph, "Civilization by Design: Emerson and Landscape Architecture," *Nineteenth Century Studies* no. 10 (1996)
Nadenicek, Daniel Joseph, "The Other Side of Progress: Cleveland, Longfellow, and the Superintendents of Society," *Nature and Technology: Selected CELA Annual Conference Papers* 7 (1996)
Nadenicek, Daniel Joseph, "Emerson's Aesthetic and Natural Design: A Theoretical Foundation for the Work of Cleveland," in *Nature and Ideology: Natural Garden Design in the Twentieth Century,* edited by Joachim Wolschke-Bulmahn, Washington, D.C.: Dumbarton Oaks Research Library and Collection, 1997
Neckar, Lance, "Fast-Tracking Culture and Landscape: Horace William Shaler Cleveland and the Garden in the Midwest," in *Regional Garden Design in the*

*United States,* edited by Therese O'Malley and Marc Treib, Washington, D.C.: Dumbarton Oaks Research Library and Collection, 1995

Tishler, William H., "H.W.S. Cleveland," in *American Landscape Architecture: Designers and Places,* edited by Tishler, Washington, D.C.: Preservation Press, 1989

Tishler, William H., "Horace Cleveland: The Chicago Years," in *Midwestern Landscape Architecture,* edited by Tishler, Urbana: The University of Illinois Press, 2000

Tishler, William H., and Virginia Luckhardt, "H.W.S. Cleveland: Pioneer Landscape Architect to the Upper Midwest," *Minnesota History* (Fall 1985)

Volkman, Nancy J., "Landscape Architecture on the Prairie: The Work of H.W.S. Cleveland," *Kansas History* 10 (Summer 1987)

DANIEL NADENICEK AND WILLIAM H. TISHLER

---

# Climber

Of all the primary requirements for plant growth—food, water, warmth, air, and light—light is perhaps the most essential. Without it even photosynthesis cannot take place. The quest for sufficient light thus propels the development of most plant forms, culminating in the vast structure of a forest tree that reaches above and dominates all surrounding types of vegetation. The latter in turn have to adapt their own forms to obtain light; forest-floor species, for example, succeed by being active early in the year before the trees' leaf canopy closes in to cut off direct sunlight.

The desirable superiority of height that woody plants obtain of course demands a time commitment that can militate against success as many years may pass before the plant reaches sexual maturity and seed production. Some plants therefore have evolved mechanisms to attain height without the need to develop a great weight-bearing structural framework: these are climbers. All plant life-forms are represented in climbers, from annuals that attain no more than half a meter in height, which in short turf is sufficient, to woody lianas reaching to the tops of tropical forest trees.

Many climbers are valuable garden plants as ornamental clothing for walls and fences; suitable examples can be found for every aspect in all but the most inclement climatic zones. Success in cultivation is helped by understanding the climbing method of each chosen plant, which determines the type of support that needs to be supplied.

Climbing roses are among the simplest. They are in fact scramblers, merely opportunists. In the wild long quick-growing shoots push up through the surrounding vegetation, which acts as a simple prop. The rose shoots have no way of actually holding on but have evolved prickles that are downward-pointing so that, once a shoot has attained the branches of some support, only the worst weather will tear it down. (Rose species that are nonclimbing have straight prickles.) *Rubus* spp. (blackberry, bramble) are similarly adapted scramblers with shoots that flower, fruit, and die in their second year. In the wild such growth develops impenetrable tangles. This indicates clearly the annual pruning pattern necessary in cultivation. *Elaeagnus* × *ebbingei,* a common garden shrub, supports its scrambling habit by stiff, backwood-pointing lateral branches. A large heap of interlacing growth can result.

True climbers have more specific adaptations either of morphology or of method of growth. A number of plants have evolved tendrils, wirelike extensions that hold fast to almost anything they touch. Their origin differs. In the Papilionaceae (pea family) the terminal leaflets of a typical compound leaf—as in sweet pea—become the tendril while a form of culinary pea has all its leaves transmuted to tendrils, and extended stipules and winged stems have to take on the photosynthetic role. With *Gloriosa superba* and *Fritillaria thunbergii,* each leaf tip elegantly elongates into a delicate tendril sufficient to hold on to surrounding vegetation.

Tendrils of woody climbers are much more robust and frequently become themselves woody and, once attached, utterly unmovable. Those of *Passiflora* and grape (*Vitis vinifera*) are derived from lateral shoots.

Young tendril growth is sensitive to being rubbed by any object with which it comes into contact; this provokes rapid cell division on the side opposite to that touched, causing the curling growth effect. Tendrils of Boston ivy and Virginia creeper (*Parthenocissus*) are made especially effective by the addition of adhesive pads on their tips.

In *Clematis* and Canary creeper (*Tropaeolum canariense*) there are no distinct tendrils, but the petioles of young leaves exhibit similar irritancy and twist around potential supports. Ivy, trumpet vine (*Campsis*), and climbing hydrangea (*Hydrangea anomala petiolaris*) are

Wisteria and arbor climbers
Copyright Linda Oyama Bryan, courtesy of Chicago Botanic Garden

fences and for training over arbors and arches. A close sequence of arches could provide a cool shady walk in hot climates. Such features are also depicted in medieval books of hours. Trellises, either freestanding as garden divisions or against walls, provided support for the chosen plants. By the 17th century treillage, especially in formal French gardens such as those at Versailles, became an important feature in its own right, not always clothed with plants. Where plants were employed, they were not necessarily climbers requiring support but also species that could accept a rigorous training and pruning regime.

It was recognized early that plants growing against walls gained protection from inclement weather, an advantage that led to a number of garden innovations. On sheltered south- and west-facing walls, tender plant species flourish that would fail in the open ground; early blossoms of fruit trees are thus protected from wind and to some extent from late frosts. It was then but a short step to providing some additional physical protection, first of fabric and then, as technology progressed, glass and the invention of the greenhouse. Support methods also moved on: wooden pegs or chicken or sheep knuckle bones were set into walls being built so that canes, rope, or netting could be attached. Old garden walls often carry the relics of these early methods and the later methods of hand-forged nails and specially designed vine eyes—flattened metal pegs set or driven into supports with holes though which wires could pass. Wire netting or plastic mesh made tight with straining bolts is the modern method—horizontal and vertical support in one.

Most traditional trained fruits are not true climbers; exceptions are blackberry and its hybrids such as loganberry and tayberry. The rampant twiner kiwi fruit (*Actinidia chinensis*) is now common in warm temperate gardens, and throughout the world one finds grapevines. In the ornamental garden *Celastrus* and *Ampelopsis* are grown for their fruiting effect, but most garden climbers are chosen for their flowers. Annuals include sweet pea (*Lathyrus odoratus*) and nasturtiums (*Tropaeolum* spp.), *Adlumia fungosa* is an unusual biennial of the fumitory family, and species of *Aconitum* and *Humulus* are herbaceous perennials. Popular woody ornamentals, in addition to those already mentioned, include wisteria—the Japanese *Wisteria floribunda* is a counterclockwise twiner; its Chinese relation *W. sinensis* grows clockwise—and many honeysuckles (*Lonicera*), jasmines (*Jasminum*), and clematis.

It should always be remembered that the climbing plant form is one in search of success and even dominance, which normal supports and small gardens cannot necessarily contain. For example, Russian vine (*Polygonum baldschuanicum*) planted to conceal an outhouse can instead overwhelm it completely, and *Rosa filipes* 'Kiftsgate', capable of producing eight-meter-long shoots in a year, can fell the tree that it has used as support.

examples of the relatively few temperate-world plants that climb by means of adventitious roots (many more exist in the tropics). Such roots enable them to scale rock faces and tree trunks. When ivy reaches the top of its support, increased illumination causes the ability to climb to be exchanged for an arborescent type of growth capable of flowering and fruiting.

Twining is the final major climbing form. Rapidly elongating shoot growth makes sweeping movements until it meets a suitable vertical support, at which point, as with tendrils, the outer wall grows more quickly to give a twisting effect. Species are constant in the direction of climb: Morning glory (*Convolvulus*) and runner beans (*Phaseolus coccineus*) do so in a counterclockwise direction; honeysuckle (*Lonicera*) and hops (*Humulus*), clockwise. Hop is also aided by small bristly prickles that prevent growth from slipping down the support.

The value of climbers in the garden has been appreciated at least since classical times as covering for walls and

**Further Reading**

Crandall, Chuck, and Barbara Crandall, *Flowering, Fruiting, and Foliage Vines: A Gardener's Guide,* New York: Sterling, 1995.

Fritsch, Felix Eugene, and E.J. Salisbury, *Plant Form and Function,* London: Bell, 1938

ALLEN PATERSON

# Clusius, Carolus 1526–1609

## French Botanist

Carolus Clusius began life as Charles de l'Écluse in Arras (Artois), France. He was the oldest child of Michel de l'Écluse, the lord of Watènes, an aristocrat and councillor at the provincial court in Arras. The family is described as being rich during the years that Carolus was growing up. As the oldest child, Carolus received the title seigneur de Watènes when his father died in 1573. Clusius immediately passed this title on to his younger brother.

As a young man Clusius traveled widely and acquired both legal and botanical training at several different schools. He was first trained as a lawyer under Gabriel Mudaeus and received his licence in law from the University of Louvain in Belgium. His interest in botany was awakened in 1551 when he studied with Guillaume Rondelet, a professor at the University of Montpellier in France. Botany soon became Clusius's passion, and his interest in practicing law waned. Clusius's knowledge and prestige in the plant world grew so much that he eventually became an eminent botanist and later in life was asked by the Holy Roman Emperor to serve as the director of the Imperial Garden in Vienna.

It was during the time that Clusius was studying at the University of Montpellier that his family was forced to leave their home because of religious war. Clusius and his family were Protestants during a time when the majority were practicing anti-Protestant persecutions. His father would lose his considerable fortune because of this persecution, and some of his family were put to death or tortured for their beliefs during this time.

From 1561 to the 1580s Clusius traveled, worked, and studied in England, France, Germany, Czechoslovakia (now the Czech Republic and Slovakia), and Austria. Clusius was ever wary of religious turmoil and his precarious finances. Both of these forced him to move often and to become adept at finding work or patronage. During this time Clusius wrote and translated for Rembert Dodoens and several other botanists and acted as a tutor for the sons of noblemen. Clusius also had an interest and involvement in cartography; he prepared two major maps of southern France and Spain. He also worked at the Imperial Medicinal Herb Garden in Prague, where he cultivated all types of plants. He knew eight languages and rose above personal misfortune (including ill health) and persecution to pursue his love of botany.

In his later years Clusius settled in Leiden, in the Netherlands, where he taught botany and introduced several significant plants to European gardens and agriculture. From his travels and personal contacts Clusius introduced the potato, the chestnut, and most significant, the tulip. It is not widely known that Clusius was responsible for introducing the potato into Germany, Austria, France, and several other countries. He also introduced various types of *Ranunculus, Anemone, Iris,* and *Narcissus* into cultivation. In total Clusius was responsible for the promotion of many plants and at the time was said to have written about 600 plants that were new to cultivation.

Clusius lived to be 83 and died in Leiden. His most notable written work was the *Rariorum Plantarum Historia* (1601; History of Rare Plants). This book is one of the outstanding collections of plant illustrations from the Renaissance era, documenting 100 new plants. Just before his death, Clusius published another important work, the *Exoticorum Libri Decem* (1605; Ten Books of Exotics) on exotic flora. The two books contain all of Clusius's original contributions to botany and natural history and are still valuable references.

The years between 1520 and 1566 were called the golden age of power and grandeur for Suleiman the Magnificent, sultan of the great Ottoman Empire. It was a time of great conquest and expansion. It was also the time that Ogier Ghislain de Busbecq first saw tulips, which were originally a wildflower bred by the Turks. De Busbecq was the ambassador to the Ottoman Empire for the Holy Roman Emperor, Ferdinand I. De Busbecq lived in Constantinople (now Istanbul), the seat of power, and had access to new treasures arriving from far lands. He was a keen gardener and the first Westerner to see tulips and subsequently to mention their existence in writings. In the early 1570s de Busbecq brought back a collection of tulip bulbs and seeds to Vienna. He called the tulips "Tulipa Turcarum" (of the Turks) and gave some to his friend Clusius, whom he helped get appointed as the superintendent of the Royal Botanical Garden in Vienna for a 14-year span, from 1573 to 1587. The first tulips that de Busbecq brought were long stemmed with red flowers. Clusius in turn was successful in raising the first European tulips and started crossing the original ones with others that had subsequently arrived from seafaring traders.

Clusius was just beginning to make progress with his tulip breeding when he had to flee Vienna for religious reasons. He went to Holland, where people were more tolerant of his religious beliefs. In the Netherlands he became the Hortulanus or prefect of a new botanical garden or Hortus Academicus at the University of Leiden in 1593. Clusius accepted the post in 1590 after the curators of the University of Leiden obtained permission from the lord mayors of the city to create a small study garden for medicinal, edible, or ornamental plants. An area was made available in a vacant lot to the rear of the university. The Hortus Academicus at Leiden was the first botanical garden in western Europe to focus on ornamental plants rather than medicinal or herbal plants. Clusius divided the garden into four main areas each designated with a letter, with each plant given a number. Clusius first introduced plants from his travels through Europe. As a result of his valuable contributions, he was given an appointment as professor of botany, a position he held for the remainder of his life.

Fortunately, when Clusius fled Vienna he took his tulip bulbs and plant collection. It is believed that Carolus planted the first known tulips in Holland, assisted by the Hortus Academicus curator Dirk Outgaertszoon Cluyt. Cluyt was a skilled botanist and pharmacist in the town of Delft, located south of The Hague. Both the bulbs and Clusius thrived in the Dutch climate, and an industry was born. By the time he moved to his new university post, Clusius had already been experimenting and cross breeding tulips for many years while in Vienna. His special interest was in medicinal applications for the tulips. Clusius was very protective of his bulbs and refused to give away bulbs or even sell them. Some people, realizing the potential of a tulip industry and frustrated by Clusius's refusal to sell any bulbs, stole part of his collection. This was probably the start of the tulip industry in the Netherlands.

One of Clusius's original tulip hybrids created in 1595 was called 'Duc van Tol Red and Yellow.' This bulb is still grown and can be seen in the living tulip museum, Hortus Bulborum, in Limmen. Perhaps because of Clusius's university background and the scientific nature of the first

bulbs, the Dutch have been meticulous about cataloging and preserving important tulip species, hybrids, and cultivars. Many of these can be seen in the tulip museum today.

In the early 1990s, in celebration of the 400th anniversary of the arrival of the tulip in Holland, a re-creation of Clusius's original garden (at two-thirds its original size of 1,200 square meters [1,435 sq. yd.]) was unveiled. This has not been built on the original site, but is still in the Hortus Academicus at Leiden. The garden is designed according to historic plans and includes tulips grown by Clusius as well as other plants from that era. Also in the garden are potato, tomato, corn, marigold, and tobacco plants, which were discovered in the New World during Clusius's lifetime. As a result of Clusius's initial breeding and promotion of the tulip, the bulb industry is now worth $750 million (U.S.) per year to the Dutch economy. Over 3 billion tulips are produced and exported around the world each year.

*See also* Leiden, Universiteit Hortus Botanicus

**Biography**
Born in Arras, France, 1526. Traveled widely and trained initially as lawyer; studied botany with Guillaume Rondelet, University of Montpellier, France, from 1551; traveled, worked, and studied in England, France, Germany, Czechoslovakia, and Austria, 1561–80s; superintendent of Royal Botanical Garden, Vienna, Austria, 1573–87, where he cultivated some of the first tulips to reach Europe from Constantinople (brought back by Austrian ambassador to Constantinople, Ogier Ghiselin de Busbecq); fled religious persecution and settled in Netherlands, taking his tulip bulbs with him, 1587; appointed prefect of Hortus Academicus botanical garden, University of Leiden, Netherlands, 1593; taught botany in Leiden, 1593–1609; also credited with introducing potato into Germany, Austria, and France. Died in Leiden, Netherlands, 1609.

**Selected Publications**
*Rariorum aliquot stirpium per Hispanias,* 1576
*Rariorum Plantarum Historia,* 1601
*Exoticorum Libri Decem,* 1605

**Further Reading**
Arber, Agnes, *Herbals, Their Origin and Evolution, a Chapter in the History of Botany, 1470–1670,* Cambridge: Cambridge University Press, 1912; 2nd edition, rewritten and enlarged, 1953
Hunger, Friedrich Wilhelm Tobias, *Charles de l'Escluse (Carolus Clusius): Nederlandsch Kruidkundige, 1526–1609,* Amsterdam: Nijhoff, 1927; reprint, 1943
Morren, Edouard, *Charles de l'Escluse: Sa vie et ses œuvres, 1526–1609,* Liège, Belgium: s.n., 1875

Phillips, Roger, and Nicky Foy, *A Photographic Garden History*, London: Macmillan, 1995

Reed, Howard S., *A Short History of the Plant Sciences*, New York: Ronald Press, 1942

Roze, Ernest, *Charles de l'Escluse d'Arras*, Paris, 1899; reprint, S.l.: Landré et Meesters, and Kew Books, 1976

Anne Marie Van Nest

# Cobbett, William 1762–1835

## English Political Journalist and Garden Writer

William Cobbett was the most famous English political journalist of the first third of the 19th century. He was the scourge of a most corrupt and authoritarian government and a master of direct and accessible prose, a forerunner of modern journalism. What is often forgotten, and almost completely neglected in works on him, is that he was also a gardener and garden writer. He brought to these activities the same practical intelligence and commitment that he devoted to politics.

Cobbett's father was a farm laborer who became a small farmer, and Cobbett acknowledged his debt to him for a lifelong passion for gardening. At the age of 11 Cobbett was working as a gardener's boy, clipping box edgings and weeding flowerbeds in the garden of the bishop of Winchester at Farnham Castle. Upon hearing of the beauties of the Royal Botanic Gardens at Kew, Cobbett decided to go and work there. He walked the entire distance, 30 miles (approximately 48 kilometers) as the crow flies, and was given food and lodgings by the Scottish gardener, who also set him to work. During this period of his life Cobbett also worked in the ancient kitchen garden at Waverley Abbey in Surrey, picking strawberries.

Because of his own childhood enthusiasm for gardening, Cobbett made sure his children had opportunities to garden. They each had a flowerbed, a little garden, and a plantation of trees, as well as their own hoes and spades. He was an admirer of Rousseau, believing in practical education, not formal schooling. He encouraged his children to read gardening books, one of which his eldest son read 20 times in order to learn how to raise melons. This stood Cobbett in good stead when he was imprisoned for criminal libel in Newgate Gaol. He carried on running his farm and garden with the help of his eldest son, who was 11, and his daughter; he explains in *Advice to Young Men* (1829) how he was still able to enjoy his own garden produce during his two years in prison:

We had a hamper with a lock and two keys, which came up once a week, or oftener, bringing me fruit and all sorts of country fare. . . . The hamper brought me plants, bulbs, and the like, that I might see the size of them; and always every one sent his or her most beautiful flowers, the earliest violets, and primroses, and cowslips, and bluebells; the earliest twigs of trees; and, in short, every thing they thought calculated to delight me.

Cobbett's first gardening book, *The American Gardener*, was written mainly in Long Island, New York, during 1819. The previous year he had vowed to write a gardener's guide in an attempt to turn every farmer into a gardener. He had noticed the lack of flowers in the United States: birds without songs and flowers without scent. His model was the English cottage garden. He was particularly struck by the laborers' gardens in the south of England, which, as he describes in *A Year's Residence in the United States of America*, "form so striking a feature of beauty," with "the garden, nicely laid out and the paths bordered with flowers, while the cottage door is crowned with a garland of roses or honey-suckle." Cobbett's credo is succinctly expressed in *The American Gardener*: "For my part, as a thing to keep and not to sell; as a thing, the possession of which is to give me pleasure, I hesitate not a moment to prefer the plant of a fine carnation to a gold watch set with diamonds."

*The English Gardener* (1829) is a revised and much expanded version of his first book. Although it contains the same number of vegetables and herbs, for example, the number of flowers discussed increases from about 60 to 140. It begins in Cobbett's inimitable style: "I make no apologies for the minuteness with which I shall give my instructions; for my business is to *teach* that which I know; and those who want no teaching, do not want my book." Cobbett contributed to two other books related to gardening. The first was William Forsyth's *A Treatise on the Culture and Management of Fruit Trees* (1802), to which Cobbett added an introduction and notes specially adapted for the United States. Cobbett had been an eyewitness to Forsyth's methods of curing diseased trees and felt that his book would help the cultivation of fruit in the United States. The second was a book on planting trees, entitled *The Woodlands* (1825). Typically, Cobbett claimed that it contained everything the reader might need to know about the subject, from the gathering of the seed to the rearing up and the cutting down of the tree.

Although John Claudius Loudon referred to Cobbett's ignorance of botany and physiology, he greatly admired the journalist's writing style. It is what Cobbett is still remembered for, as when he writes about spinach: "Every one knows the use of this excellent plant. Pigs, who are excellent judges of the relative qualities of vegetables, will leave cabbages for lettuces, and lettuces for spinage" (*The English Gardener*).

In his politics Cobbett may have looked back to a golden age of rural self-sufficiency, but his style of garden writing looked forward to the immense market for practical gardening books and magazines that developed in the second half of the 19th century, and he heralded the era of the amateur gardener. He was also a market gardener, and by 1827, in his nursery in Kensington, he had more than a million seedling forest trees and shrubs and about 3,000 young apple trees. He championed sweet corn and the acacia tree, both of which he introduced in large quantities from the United States.

Cobbett is remembered most for his political writing, but his support for workers and farm laborers was linked with his love of gardening and with the idea of producing for use and beauty, something that he felt was being destroyed by the industrial revolution. He managed to combine gardening and politics. As he wrote in 1819 in the *Political Register* two days before the Peterloo massacre of demonstrators in Manchester, "If I wrote grammars, if I wrote on agriculture; if I

sowed, planted, or dealt in seeds; whatever I did had first in view the destruction of infamous tyrants."

## Biography

Born in Farnham, Surrey, England, 1762. Worked as small boy on father's farm, bird-scaring, weeding wheat, hoeing peas, reaping, and ploughing; worked as gardener's boy in garden of bishop of Winchester, from 1773; joined British Army, 1784; worked in United States as pro-British, anti-French satirist, 1792–1800; returned to England and, as political radical, edited *Political Register*, 1802–35; attacked flogging of soldiers and prosecuted for criminal libel, 1809; sentenced to two years in Newgate Gaol, London, 1810; returned to New York, 1817–19, where he wrote *The American Gardener*; returned to England and established nursery in Kensington, before 1827; published *The English Gardener*, 1829; elected MP for Oldham, 1832. Died in London, 1835.

## Selected Publications

*Cobbett's Weekly Political Register*, 1802–35
*A Year's Residence in the United States of America*, 1818–19
*The American Gardener*, 1821
*Cottage Economy*, 1822
*The Woodlands*, 1825
*The English Gardener*, 1829
*Advice to Young Men and (Incidentally) to Young Women*, 1829
*Rural Rides*, 1830

## Further Reading

Forsyth, William, *A Treatise on the Culture and Management of Fruit Trees*, New York and London, 1802; 7th edition, London, 1824

MARTIN HOYLES

---

# Coffin, Marian 1876–1957

## United States Landscape Architect

Marian Cruger Coffin was one of the most successful landscape architects of the country-house era in the United States, designing approximately 50 large estate gardens in the northeast, primarily in New York and Delaware. At the height of her career (1910–35), Coffin counted among her clientele millionaires such as Childs Frick, Marshall Field, Edward F. Hutton, Frederick

Frelinghuysen, and Henry F. du Pont. Coffin was one of the first women to obtain a professional education in landscape architecture and establish her own firm in New York City. In 1930 she received the Architectural League of New York's gold medal of honor in landscape design. In 1946 she received an honorary doctorate of letters from Hobart and William Smith Colleges in

Geneva, New York, at which time she was described as "an artist whose medium is the living earth."

Coffin was born into a patrician New York family but was raised by her mother after her father abandoned the family. They lived with maternal relatives in New York City and Geneva, New York, and Coffin was largely tutored at home. (She continued to live with her mother throughout her life.)

In order to be self-supporting, Coffin decided when in her early 20s to pursue a career in landscape gardening, a field newly opened to women. With some difficulty she attended the Massachusetts Institute of Technology (MIT) in Cambridge, Massachusetts, between 1901 and 1904 as a special student, entitled to take the necessary courses but not to receive a degree. This was an arrangement made by the college to assist students training for a particular career. Not the only woman in her class, she received an excellent education in landscape architecture based on MIT's architectural program and the Beaux-Arts methodology of spatial composition prevalent at the time. The director of her program, the architect Guy Lowell, advocated the design principles of the Italian Renaissance revival in the United States. Coffin's interest in plants was molded by intensive studies in horticulture at the Arnold Arboretum of Harvard College. She later excelled at integrating both formal and naturalistic styles of landscape design through the use of meticulously composed plantings.

When Coffin completed her education in 1904, few design firms were willing to hire a woman, so she and her mother returned to New York City, where Coffin set up an office in their quarters and relied on social connections to obtain her first clients. She was soon working on residential projects. She attracted larger commissions by aggressively publishing short photographic essays on her designs in popular magazines such as *Country Life in America* and *House and Garden*. One of her strongest supporters during this period was the millionaire connoisseur Henry Francis du Pont of Winterthur, Delaware. Du Pont was a family friend who shared Coffin's passion for horticulture while both were students in Boston and became a lifelong friend. In 1911 du Pont directed his friend William Marshall Bullitt of Louisville, Kentucky, to employ her for his estate landscape, and in 1916 he urged H. Rodney Sharp to have her lay out the gardens of Gibraltar, Sharp's estate in Wilmington, Delaware (1916–24).

Gibraltar, which is now a public garden, remains the finest extant example of her work. Coffin demonstrated her knowledge of plant composition at Gibraltar, where she incorporated existing specimens of American elm (*Ulmus americana*) and black walnut (*Juglans nigra*) into the four terrace levels below the mansion and added long-lived Southern magnolia (*Magnolia grandiflora*) and Kentucky coffee tree (*Gymnocladus dioica*). When Coffin returned in 1924 to design the bald cypress allée

for Gibraltar, she used native *Taxodium distichum* underplanted with flame-colored azaleas, boxwood, and American smokebush (*Cotinus obovatus*) to showcase garden statuary and an Italianate pavilion.

Du Pont invited Coffin to landscape the grounds of his summer home, Chestertown House (1924–28), in Southampton, Long Island, New York, and the gardens of his palatial house-museum, Winterthur, near Wilmington, Delaware (1928–32). During a massive remodeling of the mansion at Winterthur, Coffin and her architectural associate, James M. Scheiner, laid out the walks, drives, terraces, pavilions, bathhouses, swimming pool area, and iris garden. It was the largest single commission of her career. In 1955, at the age of 79, Coffin returned to Winterthur for one last collaborative effort. She designed the April Garden (today known as the Sundial Garden), two oval lawns surrounded by the pastel colors of April-flowering trees and shrubs. Du Pont always directed the planting schemes with Coffin as consultant.

Coffin believed that her work at Winterthur was one of her finest achievements, along with the formal garden she had designed for Mrs. Childs Frick at Clayton (1924) in Roslyn, New York. The "Georgian Garden" at Clayton was an elegant four-part enclosed garden in keeping with the Fricks' Georgian Revival mansion. (Today it is the Nassau County Museum of Fine Art, and the garden is being restored.)

Coffin also had institutional clients such as the University of Delaware (1918–1940s) and the New York Botanical Garden (1942–57), where she designed the Robert Montgomery Conifer Collection, the Havemeyer Lilac Collection, and a pavilion for the Rose Garden, an area originally designed by Beatrix Farrand.

Coffin worked to achieve the highest professional standards and to educate others in the subtleties of landscape design. She joined the American Society of Landscape Architects in 1906 and was elected a Fellow in 1918. She offered young women the opportunity to apprentice in her office to help overcome the sexual discrimination she believed persisted in the field. Landscape architect Clara Stimson Coffey trained with her before establishing her own successful firm in New York. During the depression, when many small firms went out of business, Coffin survived by moving her office from New York City to her home in New Haven, Connecticut, and by retaining her staff on a contract basis. She sought out public projects and authored a book entitled *Trees and Shrubs for Landscape Effects* (1940), in which she describes her approach to landscape design. Coffin also wrote many short journal articles.

Coffin was able to combine well-trained skill in the design of spatial compositions with her love of plants and horticulture. She died in her home in New Haven at the age of 81, having still been working on several landscape projects earlier that year.

## Biography

Born in New York City, New York, 16 April 1876. Educated in landscape architecture at the Massachusetts Institute of Technology, 1901–4; toured European gardens, 1904; opened own practice in New York City, ca. 1904; designed small residential properties before 1910, then larger estate commissions until 1957; worked with several institutions (Delaware College, Newark, Delaware; Foxcroft School, Middleburg, Virginia; and New York Botanical Garden). Died in New Haven, Connecticut, 2 February 1957.

## Selected Designs

| | |
|---|---|
| 1911 | Oxmoor estate of William M. Bullitt, Louisville, Kentucky, United States |
| 1916–24 | Gibraltar estate of H. Rodney Sharp, Sr., Wilmington, Delaware, United States |
| 1918–19 | Bayberryland estate of Charles Sabin, Southampton, New York, United States |
| 1918–40 | Delaware College (University of Delaware), Newark, Delaware, United States |
| 1920 | Belfry estate of Gordon Knox Bell, Katonah, New York, United States |
| 1920–26 | Pavilion estate of Stephen H.P. Pell, Fort Ticonderoga, New York, United States |
| 1922 | Hillwood estate of Edward F. Hutton (now C.W. Post College), Wheatley Hills, New York, United States |
| 1925 | Clayton estate of Childs Frick (now Nassau County Museum of Fine Art), Roslyn, New York, United States |
| 1928 | Oaks estate of Edgar Bassick, Bridgeport, Connecticut, United States |
| 1928–55 | Winterthur estate of Henry F. du Pont, Greenville, Delaware, United States |
| 1942–57 | New York Botanical Garden, Bronx, New York, United States |
| 1950 | Mt. Cuba estate of Lammot du Pont Copeland, Greenville, Delaware, United States |

## Selected Publications

*Trees and Shrubs for Landscape Effects*, 1940

## Further Reading

Fleming, Nancy, *Money, Manure, and Maintenance: Ingredients for Successful Gardens of Marian Coffin, Pioneer Landscape Architect, 1876–1940*, Weston, Massachusetts: Country Place Books, 1995

*Gardens Designed by Marian Cruger Coffin, Landscape Architect, 1876–1957* (exhibit catalog), Geneva, New York, 1958

Griswold, Mac, and Eleanor Weller, *The Golden Age of American Gardens: Proud Owners, Private Estates, 1890–1940*, New York: Abrams, 1991

Libby, Valencia, "Marian Cruger Coffin (1876–1957), the Landscape Architect and the Lady," and "The Formal Garden at Clayton," in *The House and Garden*, Roslyn, New York: Nassau County Museum of Fine Art, 1986

VALENCIA LIBBY

# Collecting, Plant

Understood here in the restricted sense as the gathering of plants or parts of them, either living or dead, by people, plant collecting is undertaken for various reasons—for food, fuel, ornament, clothes, building, medicine, and only comparatively recently, for cultivation and science. Plant collecting and its ultimate consequences, agriculture and horticulture, made a profound change possible—sedentary life—which quickly led to the emergence of towns and cities, monumental buildings, professional classes, stratification of economic and political power, centralized government, priestly classes, standing armies, writing, and metallurgy. The selection of suitable variants for further use was parallel to this and resulted in today's universal availability of highly productive plant genetic resources, which form the principal basis of food for humankind.

As descendants from forest-living and fruit-eating primates, the early hominids must have possessed rich botanical knowledge. By defecating in their home area, they seem to have concentrated selected edible-fruited species, thereby unconsciously creating "protogardens," a phenomenon known as the Eden Syndrome. Forest people in the Malay Peninsula spread, at least until the end of the 19th century, rambutans (*Nephelium lappaceum*), in this way leaving rambutan groves at their deserted encampments. The prerequisite for the domestication of fire, now regarded as the shibboleth of humankind, is the knowledge of what kind of plant material is inflammable. In order to keep fire alive, suitable supplies must have been collected beforehand. Since forest people today use plants for ornament, clothes, building shelters, and medicine, it can be conjectured that the same was also true in the very remote past.

The vast amount of general biological knowledge, collected by trial and error, available at an early date, and passed on orally from generation to generation, is still evident today, for example, in the Australian aborigines. Considering this and the inborn curiosity of humans, it is not surprising that several lifestyles were practiced: hunter, fisherman, herder, gatherer, and protofarmer. These various lifestyles were different solutions to the same problem (although many people, past and present, tend to look down on forest people as "primitive" and "wild").

Grass seeds (potential cereals), legumes (potential pulses), root and tuber crops, fruits and nuts, and cucurbits have been widely harvested for untold millennia. This was no generalized phenomenon, however, but rather a series of parallel events happening in different regions at different periods of time and on the basis of different plants. The next step was the deliberate planting of potential crop plants and the selection of suitable variants: the reasons for this are complex, and no coherent theory explains the change, which opened the gate to a novel way of life of agriculture and horticulture. Pumpkins (*Cucurbita pepo*) in Central America, sweet potatoes (*Ipomoea batatas*) in South America, diploid wheat (*Triticum aestivum*), barley (*Hordeum vulgare*), and lentils (*Lens culinaris*) in the Near East are among the patriarchs of crops, all five having first been cultivated about ten millennia ago. Many more were to follow—among them maize (*Zea mays*) in Central America, hemp (*Cannabis sativa*) in China, grape (*Vitis vinifera*) in the Caucasus area, and the date palm (*Phoenix dactylifera*) in the Near East, all further improved by selection. Some of these crops, such as the seeds of the cocoa (*Theobroma cacao*), were so highly valued that they were used as money. Many were also regarded as having divine origin—Chinese mythology, information from cuneiform tablets in the Near East, Greek theogony, Inca legends, and Aztec stories agree on this point.

The transfer by humans of these cultivated plants to other regions had enormous consequences: the crops from the fertile crescent became the basis of agriculture in the Levant and subsequently on the continent of Europe, enabling this part of the world to support a much larger population than before. Sea-faring Polynesians took with them their crops, such as coconut (*Cocos nucifera*), sugarcane (*Saccharum officinale*), and taro (*Colocasia esculenta*), and by cultivation created the very substance to feed on in the islands of the Pacific newly populated by them, which before had been without any edible plants. Coffee (*Coffea arabica*) was brought from a small area in Ethiopia to the Yemen and cultivated, gradually becoming a ubiquitous commodity. Finally, the Columbian exchange brought numerous crops from the Old World to the New World and vice versa, with far-reaching consequences, including the introduction of hexaploid wheat, barley, oats (*Avena sativa*), and many fruit trees to the Western Hemisphere, and maize, potato (*Solanum tuberosum*) and sunflower (*Helianthus annuus*) to the Eastern Hemisphere. This had vast socioeconomic consequences and completely changed the demography of the world.

Tobacco (*Nicotiana tabacum*), long enjoyed only in Mesoamerica, became a great success also in the Eastern Hemisphere, and the same holds true for coffee in the West, to name just two examples. Agriculture in Australia developed only with the arrival of European settlers and is based exclusively on crops introduced from the four other continents; the same applies for agriculture in southern Africa.

The amount of selection done before these deliberate transfers varied enormously: maize had undergone profound changes in pre-Columbian America, whereas beans (*Phaseolus vulgaris*) brought to Europe still possessed many wild characters and were developed further there.

In the same manner, ornamental plants were taken into cultivation and transferred over considerable distances, an early example being the introduction of *Mimusops laevigata* from Ethiopia into Egypt, where this monumental tree was grown three millennia ago. The citron (*Citrus medica*) is the first tree from the Far East to reach the Mediterranean area, with remnants found in tombs of the third century A.D. An endless procession of ornamental plants followed, producing the tantalizing potpourri typical of modern gardens.

The first expedition sent out for the purpose of collecting living material was that in ca. 1500 B.C. by Queen Hatshepsut to the land of Punt (Somalia, Yemen). Fragrant trees (?*Boswellia sacra*, ?*Commiphora gileadensis*) were the trophies brought back: their unloading from a sailing boat is carefully documented in a temple at Deir El Bahari near Thebes in modern Egypt. A long series of plant hunters followed, among them Captain William Bligh, who, on his second voyage, successfully brought the breadfruit tree (*Artocarpus altilis*) from the Pacific to the Caribbean Islands. Many discoveries were side effects of nautical undertakings, such as the sighting of the well-known Norfolk pine (*Araucaria heterophylla*) of Norfolk Island during Captain Cook's second voyage. A few early cases are well documented, such as the introduction of the horse chestnut (*Aesculus hippocastanum*) from Istanbul to Florence, Padua, and Vienna by Marcantonio Barbaro and Ghislain de Busbecq, both ambassadors at the Porte in the 16th century. By contrast, many other plant introductions are poorly documented and scarcely under-

Midwest Plant Collecting Collaborative gathering plants in the Russian far east
Photo by Galen Gates, copyright Chicago Botanic Garden

stood, such as that of many ornamental plants from Mexico, first illustrated in oil paintings done in Prague for Emperor Rudolf II, or of the numerous bulbous plants imported from the Ottoman Empire depicted in the herbals and florilegia of the 16th and 17th centuries.

Plant introductions often reflect the political situation. When, for example, the Cape region was a Dutch colony, numerous ornamental plants were brought into cultivation and disseminated via botanical gardens and plantsmen in the Low Countries. With the colonization of Australia specimens of its extremely diverse flora were collected and studied by generations of mainly English botanists, and English botanical gardens and trade companies played an important role in their dissemination. China and Japan opened up only late to European plant hunters; among several competing nations the English were particularly successful—John Gould Veitch introduced among others Boston ivy (*Parthenocissus tricuspidata*) into cultivation, a climber now

so common, that it is often believed to be native in Europe or temperate North America.

Similarly, dead plant material was collected early and brought from distant countries; for the mummification of Ramses IV, for example, lichens were collected, almost certainly in modern Greece. Knowledge of medicinal plants must have also existed very early, for example, the flower collars of the priests assisting at the funeral of Tutankhamun contain the psychoactive fruits of mandragora (*Mandragora officinalis*). From an early date trade with spices—for example, dried plant material of pepper (*Piper nigrum*), cinnamon (*Cinnamomum verum*), and nutmeg (*Myristica fragrans*) from India and Malaysia—had been an important economic factor. Trade with other plant products was of no less importance: opium poppy (*Papaver somniferum*) was unmistakably illustrated in the Codex Vindobonensis (A.D. 512) and the effects of opium described; sugar from sugar cane, first imported from the Levant into Europe, later from the Canaries, and finally from the Caribbean Islands, was a luxury good sold for centuries only in pharmacies.

Plant collecting for science also started early: living specimens, often seeds, fruits, and bulbs, were gathered in the wild and subsequently cultivated in botanical gardens, with the institutions in Pisa, Padua, Florence, and Rome founded in the 16th century being the oldest in existence. A few monumental trees still survive in the Padua Botanic Garden from this early period. Dried plant specimens were glued into manuscripts to illustrate the prescriptions prepared by the apothecaries of the late 15th century; examples of these early herbaria are kept in the Biblioteca Angelica in Rome and other libraries.

The modern botanical gardens and seed banks, on the one hand, and the modern herbaria on the other are the direct successors of these Renaissance institutions. Whereas the methodology has scarcely changed, specimens brought into cultivation for research or preserved dry or in spirits are now fully annotated with the coordinates of the collecting sites, photographed, and their ecological conditions carefully recorded. As a rule both living and permanently preserved specimens are collected on modern expeditions, an early example being Joseph Pitton de Tournefort's journey in the Levant: he brought back seeds, among them the Oriental poppy (*Papaver orientale*) from eastern Anatolia, cultivated upon his return in the Jardin du Roi in Paris, and numerous herbarium specimens now kept in the Muséum Nationale d'Histoire Naturelle in Paris. Other examples are Alexander von Humboldt's expedition to Central and South America, who introduced *Lobelia splendens* into cultivation, and Joseph Dalton Hooker's tour to Assam and Sikkim, bringing back *Rhododendron falconeri*, which was soon to ornament parks and gardens. Often, however, the situation is more complex: many species were long known to science only as dried material or as illustrations but not as living specimens, including the tiger lily (*Lilium tigrinum*), first drawn by Engelbert Kaempfer in Japan and introduced into Western gardens from China more than a century later by William Kerr. The inverse situation also exists: the lilac (*Syringa vulgaris*) was long known in cultivation and had been often described, but it was not until 1795 that it was first collected in the wild—in modern Bulgaria by John Sibthorp. Considering the changing fashions in horticulture, the spectrum of species in cultivation will continue to change. There is no end of new introductions, the perennial *Corydalis* species with sky-blue flowers from China being a very recent example.

The diversity of plant life is so immense that even today unknown organisms are constantly being found, collected, studied, and subsequently described as new to science. Their number is particularly high in tropical zones, in scarcely explored areas of the temperate zones, and among cryptogamic plants, such as fungi, algae, mosses, and lichens. Similarly, new cultivars of well-known plants are selected, multiplied, and offered on the agricultural and horticultural market. Considering the sophisticated methods of modern biology, in particular hybridization, genetic engineering, and in vitro propagation, it is certain that man-made changes will continue to alter very many plants now in cultivation.

**Further Reading**

Bridson, Diana, and Leonard Forman, *The Herbarium Handbook*, Richmond, Surrey: Royal Botanic Gardens, Kew, 1989; 3rd edition, 1998

Coats, Alice M., *The Quest for Plants: A History of the Horticultural Explorers*, London: Studio Vista, 1969; as *The Plant Hunters: Being a History of the Horticultural Pioneers, Their Quests, and Their Discoveries from the Renaissance to the Twentieth Century*, New York: McGraw-Hill, 1970

Germer, Renate, *Flora des pharaonischen Ägypten*, Mainz, Germany: Von Zabern, 1985

Harlan, Jack R., *Crops and Man*, Madison, Wisconsin: American Society of Agronomy, 1975; 2nd edition, 1992

Huxley, Julian S., *New Bottles for New Wine: Ideology and Scientific Knowledge*, London: Royal Anthropological Institute of Great Britain and Ireland, 1950; as *New Bottles for New Wine: Essays*, New York: Harper, 1957

Simmonds, N.W., editor, *Evolution of Crop Plants*, London and New York: Longman, 1976; 2nd edition, edited by J. Smartt and Simmonds, Harlow, Essex: Longman Scientific and Technical, and New York: Wiley, 1995

Spongberg, Stephen A., *A Reunion of Trees*, Cambridge, Massachusetts: Harvard University Press, 1990

Tam, Geraldine King, and David J. Mabberley, *Paradisus: Hawaiian Plant Watercolours*, Honolulu, Hawaii: Honolulu Academy of Arts, 1999

Zohary, Daniel, and Maria Hopf, *Domestication of Plants in the Old World*, Oxford: Clarendon Press, and New York: Oxford University Press, 1988; 3rd edition, 2000

H. WALTER LACK

# College Campus

The practice of setting an institution of higher education in landscaped grounds traditionally has occurred primarily in the United States and Canada. The term *campus* (Latin for "field") can refer to all of a university's buildings and grounds or, in a more limited sense, only to the landscaped grounds. Such grounds have not been common in other countries. When they are included in the building of new universities in countries such as China, Brazil, or Saudi Arabia, the word *campus* is often incorporated into the local language to describe them.

During the end of the Middle Ages, universities were established in cities such as Padua, Bologna, Prague, and Paris, serving dominant urban elites. Contrary to the practice on the Continent, in England, a pastoral society of grazing lands dominated by a rural aristocracy, the universities of Oxford and Cambridge were established in hamlets far from London.

The colleges that composed Oxford and Cambridge had open grounds located around them and interior courtyards. Even today the Oxford college of Christ Church has a sheep meadow attached to it, and Magdalen has a deer park. In medieval times the grassy lawn was recognized as an especially English garden element, and it distinguished the quadrangles of England's colleges. Bartholomew notes in his garden compendium (1265) that such lawns should be level and open, and that shading trees and vined walls should appear only along the borders.

The Puritan leaders in the United States, many of whom trained for the clergy at Cambridge, followed this practice. In establishing in 1636 the first U.S. college, Harvard, the founders located it in a distant village, named Cambridge, across the river from Boston. Harvard's grounds, however, were not a campus in the sense of a landscaped area. Indeed, sheep and cattle wandered the field, cropping the grass.

The planning of a campus, meaning the physical integration of school buildings and grounds, only occurred with the University of Virginia in the early 19th century. Founded by Thomas Jefferson as an "academical village," the library, residential, and classroom buildings and their grounds were planned to operate as an efficient, attractive unit. Part of this unity Jefferson achieved by laying a sweeping lawn as the central axis of the complex. However, the aesthetics of the complex were concentrated on the architecture of the buildings and not the design of the grounds.

Education has always been a vehicle for upward social mobility in the United States. The 19th century witnessed an intense building and expansion of grade schools, colleges, universities, and libraries. Before the Civil War the new institutions of higher education, rising behind the westward advancing frontier, were designed only in relation to their buildings. They had a uniformity of building materials, brick or stone, and of architectural styles: classical, colonial, or local. Designing the grounds was given little more attention than during Puritan times.

However, the 19th century also witnessed a growing movement for landscaping. It especially emphasized, under the influence of the Romantic movement that dominated so many intellectual and academic circles, design along natural as opposed to formal lines. After the Civil War an increasingly urban and middle-class population began to be accustomed to city parks, the landscaped mansions of the newly wealthy, county courthouses and state capitols in well-tended squares, and cemeteries in park-like grounds.

During this period, too, there was once again a surge in the building of new universities. These, however, mostly appeared in major cities and had endowments that allowed them considerable embellishment of their buildings and grounds. Landscaped grounds became an assumed element of the university complex.

The schools emerging with such a characteristic included Johns Hopkins University, the University of Chicago, Cornell, Stanford, and the University of California at Berkeley. At the University of Chicago, Henry Ives Cobb literally recreated the buildings and quadrangles of Oxford University. The inspired leader of the park movement in the United States, Frederick Law Olmsted, left his distinctive mark on the design of the grounds of Stanford and Berkeley. He also made suggestions for Bryn Mawr, Cornell, Gallaudet, Massachusetts at Amherst, Michigan State, and Smith.

Older universities, such as Harvard, Yale, and Princeton, gave renewed attention to their grounds and incorporated landscaping into them. Princeton became a singularly more verdant and seasonally hued environment under the design leadership of its president in the latter half of the 19th century, James McCosh. This transformation was continued through the early 20th century by the dedicated and innovative landscape architect Beatrix Jones Ferrand.

The 20th century saw the emergence of the classic American college campus: a wide stretch of well-tended lawn crossed by meandering paths and dotted by large, deciduous trees casting graceful shadows and framing elegant buildings of traditional, often Gothic, design. This campus became the environmental expression and embodiment of the dignity and serenity of learning. This image, although quite vivid until today, witnessed several variations in the post–World War II period.

The GI Bill vastly increased the number of college students, requiring the expansion of college complexes.

Further expansion was necessary two decades later with the postwar baby boom. These factors stimulated the building of modernist structures, which is especially evident in community colleges. Fountains, plazas, and sculpture became imaginative elaborations on the traditional campus.

As the U.S. population shifted south and new universities were built or old ones expanded, new images of the American campus emerged. They were dotted with palm trees, livened by exuberant floral gardens, and blessed with regular sunshine, their students and faculty strolling in casual clothes. In the West, one of the most striking new campuses, the University of California, Santa Cruz, was designed by John Carl Warnecke. Situated on almost 2,000 acres (810 ha), Santa Cruz is actually a campus dominated by landscape, with college buildings nestled in groves of pine and redwood and roads winding through rolling meadows and woods. The great expansion of colleges and universities worldwide has been heavily influenced both in concept and design by the modern U.S. campus experience.

The universities of the United States, together with their libraries and laboratories, are among the richest assets of the world. Their resources are as exceptional as those of U.S. hospitals, museums, or corporations. Hundreds of thousands of students and scholars from around the world seek and use them every year, and the value of these institutions are singularly enhanced by the unique landscaping that graces them.

**Further Reading**

"The American Campus as a Work of Art and Utility," in *Facilities Management: A Manual for Plant Administration*, 2nd edition, edited by Rex O. Dillon and Teresa Burnau Evans, Washington, D.C.: Association of Physical Plant Administrators of Universities and Colleges, 1989

"The Campus: A Place Apart" (videorecording), Princeton, New Jersey: Films for the Humanities, 1986

"The Campus Infrastructure," in *Facilities Management: A Manual for Plant Administration*, 2nd edition, edited by Rex O. Dillon and Teresa Burnau Evans, Washington, D.C.: Association of Physical Plant Administrators of Universities and Colleges, 1989

Hitchcock, Susan Tyler, *The University of Virginia: A Pictorial History*, Charlottesville: University Press of Virginia, 1999

Schmertz, Mildred F., editor, *Campus Planning and Design*, New York: McGraw-Hill, 1972

Turner, Paul Venable, *Campus: An American Planning Tradition*, New York: Architectural History Foundation, 1984; revised edition, 1995

EDWARD A. RIEDINGER

# Collinson, Peter 1694–1768

## English Cloth Merchant and Plant Collector

Peter Collinson was one of London's most influential horticulturists during the early 18th century, thanks to his wide circle of friends and business contacts among botanists, nurserymen, explorers, and wealthy estate owners. Born in London into a family of woolen drapers, his grandmother fostered his love of gardens and plants from an early age. Brought up as a Quaker, Collinson became a prosperous cloth merchant; his drapery business numbered among its customers many members of the English aristocracy. But his most significant achievement was the successful importation of many newly discovered plants from temperate North America into Britain, first and foremost for his own garden.

Collinson's principal supplier was the American-born Quaker farmer and botanist John Bartram. Collinson maintained a long and lively correspondence with Bartram and acted as his agent, forwarding consignments of seeds to various wealthy English aristocrats and estate owners for their gardens and plantations. Recipients included Baron Petre at Thorndon, the Duke of Richmond at Goodwood, the Duke of Norfolk at Worksop, Charles Hamilton at Painshill, the Duke of Bedford at Cheam, John Blackburne at Orford, and the Duchess of Portland at Bulstrode. He also shared his choicer "novelties" with several London nurserymen and seed collectors, notably Lord Petre's former gardener James Gordon of Mile End, who, "with a sagacity peculiar to himself, has ra[i]sed a vast variety of plants from all parts of the world."

Collinson's business included the export of woolen cloth to the American colonies; he also supplied plants, bulbs, and seeds to several of his American correspondents. He was a close friend of Sir Hans Sloane, president of the Royal Society and a distinguished botanist, and Dr. John Fothergill, one of London's leading physicians. As well as contributing dried plant specimens to Sloane's herbarium and living ones for Fothergill's garden, Collinson was an avid collector of books, flower paintings, fossils, minerals, and shells. Another friend, the linen merchant John Ellis, had helped refine techniques for the long-distance transportation of seeds and cuttings, which contributed to Collinson's success in importing plants from North America.

Through his generosity to his botanical friends, Collinson promoted both their explorations and their publications. The naturalist artist Mark Catesby's magnificently illustrated account of *The Natural History of Carolina* was produced with the aid of an interest-free loan from Collinson, and Bartram was able to afford to abandon his farm and mount expeditions of several months' duration to gather seeds, bulbs, and cuttings for dispatch to Collinson. Bartram's efforts were eventually rewarded by his appointment as King's Botanist; his son William was also encouraged in his career as explorer and natural history artist by Collinson, who flatteringly (though inaccurately) compared his work to that of the great flower artist Georg Dionysius Ehret.

Collinson's garden at Ridgeway House, Mill Hill, was described by Cadwallader Colden, the Irish-born American physician, as "the most compleat Garden of American Plants that is in Great Britain." Though in later life his garden was plundered on several occasions, causing him great anxiety and annoyance, his meticulous cataloging of the living collections, together with the drawings he commissioned from botanical artists such as Ehret and William King, have preserved a very clear impression of its contents.

Many of the plants first introduced into cultivation in England by Collinson were painted by Ehret on behalf of his wealthy patrons, several of whom were also Collinson's customers. William Aiton, curator of the Royal Botanic Gardens, Kew, credited Collinson with many new introductions in *Hortus Kewensis*, the catalog of the living plant collections published under his name. The University of Oxford Botanic Garden and Chelsea Physic Garden also received specimens from Collinson, who consulted the Sherardian professor of botany at Oxford, Johann Jacob Dillenius, and the Chelsea curator Philip Miller regarding their identification.

Collinson's "genius for friendship and correspondence," as the biographer Arthur Raistrick describes it, led to extensive contacts with European botanists. Principal among these was Carl Linnaeus, who named the genus *Collinsonia* after him. He also corresponded with Carlo Allioni, Johannes Fridericus Gronovius, Albrecht von Haller, Jacob Theodore Klein, G. Leclerc (Comte de Buffon), Peter Simon Pallas, and Christopher Jacob Trew (Ehret's longest-standing patron). These contacts partly grew from Collinson's role as an active fellow of the Royal Society, London's premier scientific learned society. The Swedish botanist Daniel Carlsson Solander, later to accompany Joseph Banks on James Cook's first voyage to Australia and the south Pacific, was one of his many protégés.

Collinson exchanged garden plants with a circle of Philadelphia Quakers that included James Logan (William Penn's secretary and later chief justice of the state of Pennsylvania), a keen horticulturist. He was responsible for exciting Benjamin Franklin's interest in electricity and for several publications on that subject; both were active in trying to maintain good relations between Britain and its American colonies. Collinson played a major role in establishing a library in Philadelphia by purchasing and forwarding books from a subscription organized by Franklin and by sending gifts of additional books such as Miller's pioneering *Dictionary of Gardening*.

Collinson's horticultural legacy was a major increase in the diversity of plants grown in English and European gardens. His frenetic importation of hardy North American plants led to the development of a variant of the picturesque, "wild" landscape garden, the American garden. His grandmother's garden in Peckham, Surrey, where he lived as a child from the age of two, had a profound influence on him. In a memorandum written in later life, he recalls its "fine cutt greens" and "clip'd yews," so it must have been representative of the more formal garden style prevalent at the turn of the 18th century. By greatly extending the repertoire of cultivated plants and trees, Collinson made a contribution to the horticultural sophistication of the Georgian period as significant in its own way as that of the celebrated landscape designer Lancelot "Capability" Brown.

## Biography

Born in London, 14 January 1694. Went to live with grandmother in Peckham, Surrey, 1696, where he learned to like gardens and plants; assisted father in mercer's shop, 1711; influenced by Thomas Story's accounts of rich plant life in North America, 1714; started to catalog living plant collections, 1722; elected Fellow of the Royal Society, 1728; initiated correspondence with John Bartram of Philadelphia, 1734; received Carl Linnaeus at his premises in Gracechurch Street, London, 1736; elected as Fellow of the Society of Antiquaries, 1737; moved to Ridgway House, Mill Hill, inherited from wife's father, created a botanical garden with collection of American plants. Died in London, 1768.

## Further Reading

Berkeley, Edmund, and Dorothy Smith Berkeley, editors, *The Correspondence of John Bartram, 1734–1777*, Gainesville: University of Florida Press, 1992

Blunt, Wilfrid, *The Compleat Naturalist: A Life of Linnaeus,* New York: Viking Press, and London: Collins, 1971

Brett-James, Norman George, *The Life of Peter Collinson,* London: Dunstan, 1926

Darlington, William, *Memorials of John Bartram and Humphry Marshall with Notices of Their Botanical Contemporaries,* Philadelphia, Pennsylvania, 1849; facsimile edition, New York: Hafner, 1967

Dillwyn, Lewis, *Hortus Collinsonianus: An Account of the Plants Cultivated by the Late Peter Collinson . . . Arranged Alphabetically according to Their Modern Names, from the Catalogue of His Garden, and Other Manuscripts,* Swansea, Wales, 1843

Fothergill, John, *Some Account of the Late Peter Collinson,* London, 1770

Fothergill, John, *Some Anecdotes of the Late P. Collinson, by the Late Dr. John Fothergill, from the Original Manuscript in a Letter to a Friend,* London, 1875

Fox, Richard Hingston, *Dr. John Fothergill and His Friends: Chapters in Eighteenth Century Life,* London: Macmillan, 1919

*John Ellis,* part 1, *Merchant, Microscopist, Naturalist, and King's Agent,* by Julius Groner, and part 2, *A Biologist of His Times,* by Paul F.S. Cornelius, Pacific Grove, California: Boxwood Press, 1996

Lambert, Aylmer Bourke, "Notes Relating to Botany, Collected from the Manuscripts of the Late Peter Collinson, Esq., FRS.," *Transactions of the Linnean Society of London* 10 (1811)

Raistrick, Arthur, *Quakers in Science and Industry,* London: Bannisdale Press, and New York, Philosophical Library, 1950; new edition, Newton Abbot, Devon: David and Charles, and New York: Kelley, 1968

Swem, Earl G., "Brothers of the Spade: Correspondence of Peter Collinson, of London, and of John Custis, of Williamsburg, Virginia, 1734–1746," *Proceedings of the American Antiquarian Society* (1949)

JOHN EDMONDSON

# Colonialism and Gardening

Colonial gardens combined plants from both the mother country and the surrounding environment. They provided food products, medicinal herbs, and pleasurable sights for colonists and also influenced the cultivation of crops in established nations.

Writers chronicling the discovery and exploration of the Americas described the New World as the First Garden, or the Garden of Eden. They used this comparison to convince would-be colonists to make the trip to this earthly paradise. The idea of the New World as the First Garden was a figurative characterization because settlers had the opportunity to eat the fruit of the tree of knowledge without the biblical repercussions experienced by the original inhabitants of Eden. The information the settlers acquired about plant life came from the native peoples of the Americas and from a system of trial and error. The Hurons, for instance, taught 16th-century explorer Jacques Cartier that a tonic derived from pine trees could help him and his men avoid scurvy. Like colonial gardens, Native American gardens contained plants to be used for medicinal, food, and aesthetic purposes. Native American food crops—especially beans, corn, and potatoes—were the basis for a worldwide food revolution. Colonists also learned for themselves which American plant items were welcome additions to the colonial table. Wild American fruits that became favorites were then uprooted and transplanted to more convenient locations.

Seventeenth-century colonial American gardens were overwhelmingly practical, furnishing food and medicine. Their pragmatic purposes were nowhere more apparent than in the New England colonies. Sources reveal that these gardens catered to the production of vegetables and medicinal remedies. Pennsylvania Quaker gardens also provided plants used for sustenance and cures, but, unlike those to the north, they often used flowers for pleasure. New Amsterdam gardens in the 17th century benefited from the horticultural and agricultural knowledge of the Dutch. Like Quakers, Dutch gardeners welcomed the color and beauty of flowering plants, especially roses. Southern colonists focused their efforts on the creation of kitchen gardens and orchards; however, 17th-century southern settlements were isolated, and the landscape that surrounded these plantations has been described as scrubby. The emphasis on monoculture, especially tobacco production, hampered the development of gardens in the region.

The economic, cultural, and social vitality of 18th-century colonial America enlivened gardening. The Navigation Acts of the 18th century guaranteed a British market for colonial ships and naval stores. Compared to England, the colonies had access to innumerable trees. Lumbering, the production of naval supplies, and shipbuilding became crucial to the economies of New England and North Carolina in the 18th century.

The quest for cures also affected the development of colonial gardening. This exploration was not unique to the British North American colonies. French physicians in 18th-century Saint Domingue (modern-day Haiti) questioned slave herbalists about the remedies they used to treat a wide variety of ailments. Physicians, for instance, learned that slaves practiced wound therapy using medicinal herbs. *Digitaria insularis* and *Eupatorium odoratum* were key elements in the care of contusions, lacerations, and bruises.

As they had done in the previous century, Quakers continued to affect colonial horticulture. The leading Quaker botanist in the 18th century was John Bartram, who established the Bartram Botanic Garden at Kingessing (near Philadelphia, Pennsylvania) in 1728. Botanical gardens also existed in other colonies throughout the world. The Dutch established colonial botanical gardens in Capetown, Ceylon, and Indonesia. The British developed similar gardens in Saint Vincent, Jamaica, India, and Australia that served as extensions of the Royal Botanic Gardens at Kew, which contained specimens from these satellite gardens. The Jardin du Roi in Paris, likewise, collected samples from botanical sites in Saint Domingue, Guadeloupe, Martinique, and Cayenne.

Botanists such as Bartram traveled throughout the colonies in search of plants. Bartram personally was responsible for sending many American trees, shrubs, and flowers to Europe. He and other naturalists benefited from the invention and popularization of the Linnaean binomial system, which allowed them to communicate effectively and accurately with scholars in other parts of the globe. Bartram, for instance, regularly corresponded with Peter Collinson, a Quaker merchant in London who led the exchange of plants from colony to mother country.

Immigration into the British North American colonies in the 18th century also had a positive effect on colonial plant production. Palatine German immigrants, who became known as the Pennsylvania Dutch, were responsible for Pennsylvania's reputation as the "breadbasket" of the colonies because of their tremendous production of grains. Their fruit cultivation also helped to rank them as the foremost colonial agriculturists of the 18th century.

The forced movement of Africans to the New World also affected the history of colonial gardening. Plantation agriculture and slavery were key aspects of the colonial economy. Sugar, rice, coffee, tobacco, and indigo cultivation depended on the unpaid labor of slave men and women. Slave owners saved money that might have been spent on food for these slaves by having them tend garden plots known as common grounds. Enslaved men and women also farmed ravine or mountain grounds without the consent of the slave master or kept slave houseyard gardens near their quarters. Slave gardens helped to improve the poor nutritional status of slaves throughout the British mainland colonies and the Caribbean, allowing slaves to supplement the meager rations they received from their masters with staples, such as potatoes and cassava, and fresh vegetables from their gardens. In addition, enslaved women had the opportunity to sell surplus vegetables, as well as medicinal herbs, at local markets. In the West Indies slave yards sometimes contained trees to be used for decorative and useful purposes. Coconut, banana, and plantain trees were the most popular plants. Slaves consumed coconuts as food and used them for fiber and as containers. The practice of sweeping the yard, an act performed by slaves in both America and the Caribbean, was a gardening tradition that may have survived from West Africa. Bondsmen in both locations also kept small pens of chickens and pigs.

Like those of 17th-century America, the gardens of the 1700s provided both food and medicine. Vegetable gardens remained overwhelmingly "colonial," meaning that they contained a majority of plants that originally were grown in the colonist's country of origin. However, the gardens of the 18th century differed from those of the previous century in that there was more emphasis placed on planting for pleasure. In fact, American colonists who possessed both time and money studied landscape gardening. American gardeners emphasized pleasure and utility, two elements that had been the foundation of colonial gardening since its inception.

Plant production in the Americas was not only practical and pleasing but also ultimately political. Thomas Jefferson's Monticello and George Washington's Mount Vernon were manifestations of republican gardening, an agrarian philosophy that aimed to recapture the pastoral tradition of ancient Rome. Washington's reputation as the American Cincinnatus, or the virtuous farmer-soldier, statesmen, and leader, exemplified this political ideology. Jefferson's high regard for the citizen-farmer became a driving force during the early years of the republic. As president, Jefferson made his agrarian philosophy a practical reality by purchasing the Louisiana Territory and lowering federal land prices. He hoped that the qualities that exemplified colonial gardening—pragmatism and pleasure—would be the legacy inherited by future generations of Americans.

**Further Reading**

Adams, William Howard, *Nature Perfected: Gardens through History,* New York: Abbeville Press, 1991

Hedrick, U.P., *A History of Horticulture in America to 1860,* New York: Oxford University Press, 1950

Leighton, Ann, *American Gardens in the Eighteenth Century: "For Use or for Delight,"* Boston: Houghton Mifflin, 1976

McClellan, James E., *Colonialism and Science: Saint Domingue in the Old Regime,* Baltimore, Maryland: Johns Hopkins University Press, 1992

Pulsipher, Lydia Mihelic, "The Landscapes and Ideational Roles of Caribbean Slave Gardens," in *The Archaeology of Garden and Field,* edited by Naomi F. Miller and Kathryn L. Gleason, Philadelphia: University of Pennsylvania Press, 1994

Westmacott, Richard Noble, *African-American Gardens and Yards in the Rural South,* Knoxville: University of Tennessee Press, 1992

KAROL K. WEAVER

# Color

Getting color combinations of plants right can be most difficult. Unlike interior design, wherein the designer has full control over the materials, colors, and environment, all of which remain constant, gardening involves a continuously evolving medium—plants—the colors of which fade and change with age, situation, and varying light conditions.

Color can be introduced into gardens in two ways, most obviously through the selection of plants with attractive flowers and interesting foliage but also by means of pigmented objects and structures. There has been a long-standing tradition of applying vivid color to such garden features as statues and follies (for example, the Turkish tent in Le Désert de Retz in France), as well as to bridges (e.g., the Chinese bridge in Biddulph Grange in the U.K.) and pergolas. The 20th century has seen several examples of gardens where structural elements such as walls have been brightly painted, adding a distinctive color note. Purple, red, orange, blue, and pink are some of the colors used on walls by the Mexican designer Luis Barragán. Traditional in hotter climates, brightly painted garden features have become increasingly popular in cooler regions.

Color theories for planting schemes were not developed until the 19th century. Prior to that they were not especially relevant, as the color palette available was very limited. Gardeners had to rely on species or the occasional naturally occurring sport (genetic variant), which was mostly white or sometimes a paler or darker version of the dominant color. One exception could be found in the handful of florists' flowers. Florists had been hard at work expanding the color range of a limited selection of plants such as tulips, auriculas, and ranunculus, particularly during the 17th and 18th, and into the 19th century.

Because of the restricted color range, the aim of garden designers was to use as many different colors as possible, with no two plants of the same color being next to each other, thus creating as much variety as possible.

Some consideration for the effects of colors can be found in the 18th century, when William Mason suggested the planting of little groups of three flowers of the same height and flowering period adjacent to each other, for example in the primary colors of red, yellow, and blue. In 1779 James Meader published a catalog of trees and shrubs arranged according to their position in a planting scheme. No mention was made of the flower color; instead, details on foliage color were included.

The 19th century was the period when horticulture reached its prime. European and North American plant hunters were conquering hitherto unexplored parts of the world, sending back an ever-increasing stream of plants. In response to this massive influx and with the help of new technology, the nursery trade flourished. Continuing the work of florists, nurserymen were not only multiplying these novelties, they were selecting new varieties, steadily increasing the available color range.

Initially, the tender plants used for "bedding out" were most fashionable with nurserymen and gardeners alike, who were striving to expand the existing color range. It was not until the second half of the 19th century that nurseries across Europe started to breed and select perennials specifically for different color strains and improved flower forms. These new cultivars were used in the increasingly popular herbaceous borders, a trend that reached its peak around the turn of the century.

In the course of the 19th century, several color theories were adopted by gardeners, though initially they were mainly applied to the popular massed schemes of bedding plants, as the large areas of bright color needed to have some order imposed on them. It was not until the last quarter of the century that the theories began to be applied to the arrangement of herbaceous perennials.

Sir Isaac Newton (1642–1727) had found that white solar light consists of simple or homogenous color rays, which become visible when the light is passed through a prism. In analogy with the seven tones of the diatonic scale, Newton divided the light rays into seven colors: red, orange, yellow, green, blue, indigo, and violet. Attempts to draw parallels between music and light continued throughout the 19th century, resulting in a certain amount of confusion in the terminology applied to colors. When Newton's seven colors were arranged in a full 360-degree circle, each individual color was represented by its own individual proportion as seen in the rainbow. These could be divided as follows: violet 80 degrees, indigo 40 degrees, blue 60 degrees, green 60 degrees, yellow 48 degrees, orange 27 degrees, and red 45 degrees. With the colors thus arranged, it was possible to work out the contrasting color by finding the one that lay directly opposite a given color in the circle. The colors contrasted as follows: black with white (and vice-versa), red with green, orange with blue, yellow with indigo, green with reddish violet, blue with orange, indigo with orange yellow, and violet with bluish green. Even people not so confident in their grasp of the different color theories could use this as a guideline when arranging color schemes.

Johann Wolfgang von Goethe (1749–1832) also divided the different hues into relative proportions but in such a way that when the values of a primary color and its complimentary secondary color were added up, they made a total of 12. These allocated values were yellow (nine), red (six), blue (four), orange (eight), green (six), and violet (three). Johannes Itten (1888–1967) referred to this as contrast of extension. The more brilliant the color, the smaller amount of it was needed. The aim was for colors to be used in the right proportions when composing a picture.

George Field (ca. 1777–1854) decreed that white solar light consisted of only three colors, the primaries, yellow, red, and blue. All other colors, according to Field, were a combination of these three. Sir David Brewster, who originally had been a follower of Newton's theories, conceded that by the 1850s most writers on color had accepted this new way of thinking. Field's theories were backed up by the findings of Georges-Louis Leclerc Buffon. Buffon discovered that when one placed a colored object on a white or black background and looked at it intensely for a short while, upon removal of the object, a patch of the contrasting color seemed to appear in the place where the object had been. In case of blue, the color that appeared was orange, in case of yellow, it was purple, and for red the color seen was green, and vice-versa. David Ramsay Hay (1798–1866) described these as accidental colors or contrasting colors to the primaries, with which they were said to harmonize in opposition. Hay observed that to obtain the right hues of secondary colors, the primaries could not be mixed half-and-half, but had to be mixed in specific proportions. Orange was made up of three parts yellow and five parts red, purple consisted of five parts red and eight parts blue, while green had three parts yellow and eight parts blue.

Of all the color theorists, the one most quoted is Michel-Eugène Chevreul (1786–1889). His work *De la Loi du Contraste Simultané des Couleurs* was translated into English by Charles Martel as *The Principles of Harmony and Contrast of Colors* (1854). Chevreul recognized the theory that white light consisted of the three primary or simple colors, which, when combined, produced secondary or compound colors. He also found that when white light was shone onto a reflective surface, it appeared white, while when it was shone onto an absorbent surface, it appeared black. Surfaces that were part reflective and part absorbent showed only the color rays not absorbed. Colors became complementary if, when put together in the right proportions, they formed white light again.

Throughout much of the 19th century, gardening literature mostly referred to color schemes based on complementary colors, which opposed each other in the color circle (see Plate 9). Towards the latter part of the century a shift in opinion is noticeable, as people started to use the law of harmony. Contrary to the previously discussed law of contrast involving opposing colors, the law of harmony relies upon colors that blend into one another. Harmonizing colors are those adjoining each other on the color wheel—for example, yellow and orange or red and violet. The harmonizing colors were considered the easiest to identify, the effect being that of a gentle transition.

Although the color theories were known to many gardeners in many different countries, not everybody considered them the most important design criteria in the arrangement of flowers. In Germany for example, Hermann Jäger considered the luminosity of flowers to be of greater relevance than the actual color. He thought it was important for gardeners to follow their own instincts; color was a matter of mood and taste rather than a science. Jaeger contended that trying out new combinations each year was more adventurous and more likely to improve the garden than was clinging to the same tried and tested combination year after year as Prince Hermann Pückler-Muskau had suggested.

Luminous colors such as white, yellow, yellowish red, and other bright colors were best planted at a distance, as their luminous qualities made them clearly visible when viewed from far away. Near the paths or at the front of a planting, dark- as well as cold-colored flowers could be used. Warm colors were considered the most luminous. Going through the spectrum, from purple to green shades, the luminosity of colors decreased, dark blue being the weakest. The lighter tints of a cold color were more luminous than the darker ones because there was a higher proportion of white in them. White was considered the most luminous, as it could be seen the furthest away and even at night. Following white came, in order of decreasing luminosity, whitish yellow, orange-yellow, golden yellow, middle yellow, orange, orange-red, carmine, dark pink, pink, bright blue, dark blue, and purple.

In addition to the luminosity of the flower, the surface qualities of the leaf and petal also had to be taken into account, namely whether they were shiny or not. Matte surfaces absorb light, whereas shiny surfaces reflect it. Thus shiny-surfaced petals tend to be more visible than those with a matte surface.

Gertrude Jekyll (1843–1932) is the one person in gardening history who has probably had the greatest and longest-lasting influence on the use of colors throughout Britain and abroad. The American garden writer Mrs. Francis King considered Jekyll's *Colour in the Flower Garden* the second most important book for dedicated American gardeners after Liberty Hyde Bailey's *Cyclopedia of American Horticulture*. In *Planting Design* Florence Bell Robinson frequently referred her readers to Jekyll's work. Interpretations of her color schemes for the flower garden can still be found in numerous gardens across Europe and North America, and the principles she developed continue to be applied. Her articles on color in the flower garden in the gardening press during 1882 generated a considerable response. It was apparent that the average gardener was baffled by the differing theories and was badly in need of guidance on how to plant effectively. This task Jekyll took upon herself in her writings, including her chapter on color in William Robinson's *The English Flower Garden* (first published in 1883), her numerous articles, and her book *Colour in the Flower Garden* (first published in 1908; later issued as *Color Schemes for the Flower Garden*). Although her ideas were not the norm at the time, their regular exposure in her numerous publications caused them to catch on. During the period leading up to World War I, it appears that her theories were becoming increasingly popular. Her efforts on the color front continued well after her initial successes, and she continued to write about the subject in articles and in book introductions such as that to George F. Tinley and William Irving's *Color Planning of the Garden* (1924). The book listed plants by color and was lavishly illustrated with color plates.

Jekyll pointed out that planting a herbaceous border was in fact no different from painting a picture, except in size. The flowers and the sunlight were to create the image, and therefore the border required careful planning rather than just amalgamating a series of lines or evenly distributed dots of color, as had been the practice previously. She recommended planting in harmony rather than contrast (Jekyll used the term harmony to indicate colors adjoining one another in the spectrum), with a decided color scheme. She also advocated using generous groups of plants rather than the small clumps that had been seen so often earlier in the 19th century. Furthermore she recommended the use of warm colors in hot, sunny spots, reserving the cooler ones for the shady places, a rule not universally accepted. Some garden designers, Jäger among them, felt that the cooler colors retained their purity better in bright sunlight, whereas the warm colors were better suited to shade.

Jekyll's rules could be applied as easily to bedded-out plants as to a permanent scheme of perennials. She was not entirely against the old system of using contrasting colors; she thought that there was a place for them in the garden but that they should be used only sparingly.

In all but the last edition of Robinson's *The English Flower Garden*, the chapter on color was written by Jekyll, together with "JD," repeating once again her views on the use of color. Readers were not only told that harmonies of rich and brilliant colors were the rule, they were also told about grading colors and creating sequences of such combinations. It was not only the color of the flower that had to be taken into account, however; the foliage and the background (grass and shrubs) also had to be considered as part of the whole display, and flower colors had to harmonize with those as well. Jekyll's favorite color scheme for a border was a progression from the cool, calm colors through the hot, fiery colors and then receding again into the cool colors. She explained that once the eye was saturated with the grays and blues at the start of the border, it avidly progressed to the soft yellow tones, moving on to stronger yellows, oranges, and scarlet reds. At this point the eye would again be saturated, this time with strong colors, and being in need of a soothing, calm color would readily move on to purple and gray tones again.

Blues were best treated quite separately, adding delicate contrasts of warm whites and pale yellows or simply set on their own in a mass of dark foliage. Whites were to be used as an aid to a particular color or to make a transition between difficult colors but never were they to be dotted about the border, as this was considered visually unsatisfactory. All whites were to be grouped together into one large patch.

Although the legacy of Jekyll's artistic approach to planting has been particularly noticeable throughout 20th century Britain, it can also be found abroad. Monochrome planting schemes, such as the white gardens in Sissinghurst and Crathes castle and the red border at Hidcote, are a legacy of this period, as are the schemes based on the law of harmony, such as in Sissinghurst's cottage garden or Tony Lord's design (ca. mid 1980s) for the borders at Hardwick Hall.

The first decades following World War II saw major cutbacks in most gardens, resulting in the disappearance of many herbaceous borders. To bring low-maintenance color into the garden, shrubs and conifers with gray, yellow, and red foliage were used in shrub borders to create an evergreen or semi-evergreen display, with little seasonal variety.

During the 1980s, however, herbaceous perennials started to come back into favor, often mixed with shrubs and roses. The preference was for crisp, cool pinks, blues, purples, silver, and whites—fresh but often tame colors—which gardeners of the 1990s abandoned for "impure" colors such as bronze and coppery oranges, salmon and peachy pinks, plums, smoky yellows, and metallic blues, with foliage plants such as bronze fennel being used to create a transparent screen, bringing these together. Strong colors such as bright yellows, vivid oranges, and scarlet reds, as well as bright blues, became popular as the century drew to a close. Nori and Sandra Pope's color schemes at Hadspen Garden in Somerset were widely acclaimed as being in the forefront of the new approach to color combinations, featuring a carefully orchestrated progression of colors strongly influenced by music. While the Popes were being influenced by music, Giles Clement in the Parc André Citroen in Paris was inspired by metals, creating small theme gardens with subjects such as copper, bronze, and silver, all reflected in the foliage and flower color of the plantings.

While the British have retained the artistic approach to planting using color, shape, and texture as main criteria, gardeners in other countries have used nature more as a source of inspiration, in their planting as well as in their color combinations. The German nurseryman Karl Foerster (1874–1970), for example, was keen on matching plant with habitat, having less regard for color effect. Influenced by both the British and German approaches, the Dutch designer Mien Ruys (1904–99) developed her own unique style. Although color associations were of relevance in her designs, they were not necessarily the dominating feature. In the distinctive style of the Dutch designer Piet Oudolf, who created large-scale herbaceous planting schemes in various European parks and gardens during the 1990s, form, texture, shape, and plant association took precedence over color associations, even though he employed a restricted color palette.

Other designers such as Roberto Burle Marx and the team of James van Sweden and Wolfgang Oehme have allowed themselves to be inspired by art in their use of color patterns. Marx's designs reflect the hot tropical environments in which he has been accustomed to work, whereas van Sweden and Oehme's colors tend to reflect the influence of their native North American prairie environments.

Although each generation of gardeners comes up with new ideas and sources of inspiration, and fashions in color come and go, the principles remain the same: they are mostly variants on either the law of contrasting colors, based on the use of colors that oppose each other on the color wheel, or the law of harmony, based on the pairing of colors adjacent to each other on the color wheel.

*See also* Bed and Bedding System; Jekyll, Gertrude

**Further Reading**

Bending, Steven, "William Mason," *Journal of Garden History* 9, no. 4 (1989)

Elliott, Brent, "A Spectrum of Colour Theories," *The Garden* 118, no. 12 (1993)

Hobhouse, Penelope, *Colour in Your Garden*, London: Collins, 1985

Itten, Johannes, *Kunst der Farbe*, Ravensburg, Germany: Maier, 1961; as *The Art of Color*, translated by Ernst van Haagen, New York: Van Nostrand Reinhold, 1961; new edition, 1973

Jekyll, Gertrude, "Colour in the Flower Garden," *The Garden* 22, no. 177 (1882)

Jekyll, Gertrude, *Colour in the Flower Garden*, London: Country Life, 1908; reprint, Portland, Oregon: Sagapress/Timber Press, 1995

King, Francis, *The Well-Considered Garden*, New York: Scribner, 1915

Meader, James, *The Planter's Guide*, London, 1779

Pope, Nori, and Sandra Pope, *Colour by Design: Planting the Contemporary Garden*, London: Conran Octopus, 1998

Robinson, Florence Bell, *Planting Design*, London: Whittlesey House, and New York: McGraw Hill, 1940

Robinson, William, *The English Flower Garden*, London, 1883; 15th edition, London: Murray, 1933; reprint, 1995

ISABELLE VAN GROENINGEN

# Container

The oldest evidence for the use of plant containers is from ancient Egyptian wall paintings. These pots, used to mark significant positions in the garden, were probably constructed by lining the inside of a basket with clay. After the clay dried or was fired, the basket was destroyed, leaving the textured impression of the weave on the outside of the pot. This is most likely the origin of the basket-weave pattern, which has recurred

Garden urns, designed by Daniel Marot ca. 1703
Courtesy of Dumbarton Oaks Research Library and Collections

throughout history and is still used in pottery today. The cultivation of plants in pots, however, is an intuitive phenomenon and would have occurred with the emergence of agriculture. Greek vase paintings show how old vessels were reused as plant containers; this makeshift approach can be seen today in the recycling of such objects as discarded toilet bowls and car tires as planters. It is likely that more perishable materials such as leather and canvas may also have been experimented with as plant containers.

Flowerpots have been items of low priority to archaeologists, and there appear to be few surviving early examples. Excavations in the Mediterranean have revealed Roman examples, all of which were constructed of clay and had a generally rounded shape and holes in the bottom for drainage. Drainage holes are, in fact, the general distinguishing feature of flowerpots. Other containers excavated in Pompeii had holes in the sides and are thought to have been used to transport plants, which

were then planted while still in the pots, leaving the roots to emerge later. Little further evidence survives of flowerpots until the Middle Ages. Illustrations and archaeological finds show a range of pots, the most popular fairly similar to the simple Roman examples but also some that were substantially more elaborately shaped and painted. The ornamental stone vase uncovered in the garden of the first century B.C. historian Sallust in Rome in 1566 sparked an interest in similar vessels.

While some remarkable flowerpots were produced in western Europe in medieval times, a great incentive came with an increased interest in exotic plants from the Americas and the East Indies in the period between ca. 1650 and 1730. This coincided with an era of great enthusiasm for the building of greenhouses (today commonly called orangeries) and stoves (a heated chamber or hothouse) to display these exotic, and usually tender, plants. Elaborate and diversely shaped pots on pedestals, highly decorated, were seen as an appropriate way

Increased interest in flowerpots during the 17th century encouraged the production of vases in more durable mediums, including stone, marble, lead, and bronze. These containers were normally painted in a similar manner to the earthenware pots or, in some cases, gilded. The more ordinary larger "greens" were planted in tubs or cases (boxes). These were produced in various inventive forms that varied locally; they were typically painted on the outside and pitched with tar within. Sometimes they were charred on the inside in an attempt to render the wood less penetrable and retard decay. Wooden boxes were also the favorite way of transporting larger evergreens, such as oranges, lemons, pomegranates, olives, and jasmines, from Italy to northern European countries. During the 19th century one of the most popular container materials was cast iron, mainly produced according to classical models. A decline in large gardens led to decline in orangeries and thus in larger containers. These were revived, however, after World War II, when containers filled with seasonal plantings again became fashionable. This trend was sparked by the development of the concrete planters (known as Stockholm planters) used by the parks department in Stockholm, Sweden, and the introduction of the Tivoli bowls, originally designed as fountains by G.N. Brandt in Copenhagen, Denmark, during the war.

The majority of plant containers were utilitarian, however, used for propagation rather than display, and were made of clay. In England these pots were produced in a cast—a specified amount of clay—and the names for the different-sized pots reflected the number of pots derived from a single cast. The smallest pot sizes were eighties or sixties, moving up to forty-eights, thirty-twos, twenty-fours, sixteens, twelves, eights, and twos. While a sixty pot had an inside measure of about two inches (5 cm), a two would have been approximately 18 inches (46 cm). As the size of a cast varied locally, however, so did the measurements of the various pots. This lack of standardization was one of the problems of English flowerpots. The other was the difficulty of transportation. While the weight of pots produced in America and most European countries was carried by the rim, the English pots were without supporting rims, making them more vulnerable to breakage, as the full weight of a stack would be carried by the pots at the bottom. The shape of the rim normally follows local custom, as does the arrangement for the provision of drainage at the bottom of the pot.

The English potmakers never resolved the lack of standardization, and the debate continued until the beginning of the 20th century. Beginning in the 19th century, there were experiments to produce different types of flowerpots. Patents were issued for a variety of materials: gutta-percha and India rubber (1855), cork (1856), iron (1861), slate (1870), zinc (1874), glass (1875), asphalt

Woman with flower pots, ca. 1890
Courtesy of Mary Evans Picture Library

of exhibiting rare and expensive plants from distant parts of the world. These often heavily modelled pots were typically produced in molds consisting of four or five parts. Lead armatures were sometimes added. These pots were particularly popular in the Low Countries and Germany and also had a brief vogue in England and colonial America. Another range of pots popular for preserving orange trees and plants in the house were the so-called Dutch ware, or Delft, and were used indoors as well as in the more distinguished gardens. In France there was a similar fashion, in which Nevers-style flowerpots with their distinctive coiled handles were positioned in fireplaces, and other decorated pots were used in gardens. Cachepots—decorative receptacles in which plain clay flowerpots could be concealed—were used from the 17th century onward.

(1895), sheet metal (1897), coconut shell (1901, used for hanging baskets), celluloid (1907), and various artificial compositions. It was not until after World War II that plastics gradually overtook the traditional clay, with a preference for plastic becoming evident in the early 1960s; polypropylene, polystyrene, and polythene are the most popular materials today. These are produced in various shapes and in a range of colors, including those that imitate clay. On the other hand, there has been a search for biodegradable pots, with Root-o-pot by Jiffy pots, launched initially in the United States in the mid-1950s, becoming the first commercial success. These pots were composed of 75 percent sphagnum peat and 25 percent wood pulp. Increased environmental concerns have led to research into recycled materials, resulting in the introduction of paper pots and Roottrainers. The latter, developed to increase root growth, are stored as flat packs and folded to form long, grooved cells.

## Further Reading

Currie, C.K., "The Archaeology of the Flowerpot in England and Wales, circa 1650–1950," *Garden History* 21, no. 2 (1993)

Davis, John Patrick Stuart, *Antique Garden Ornament: 300 Years of Creativity,* Woodbridge, Suffolk: Antique Collectors' Club, 1991

Elliott, Brent, "Perfecting the Pot," *The Garden* 120, no. 3 (March 1995)

Hume, Audrey Noël, *Archaeology and the Colonial Gardener,* Williamsburg, Virginia: Colonial Williamsburg Foundation, 1974

Keeling, Jim B.M., *The Terracotta Gardener,* London: Headline, and North Pomfret, Vermont: Trafalgar Square, 1990; revised edition, as *The New Terraccotta Gardener: Creative Ideas from Leading Gardeners,* London: Headline, 1993

Lindijer, Tony, and Sabine van Vlijmen, *Om de tuinpot geleid: 17e eeuwse tuinpotten uit Haarlem,* Haarlem, The Netherlands: Archaeologisch Museum Haarlem, 1993

Moorhouse, Stephen, "Late Medieval Pottery Plant-Holders from Eastern Yorkshire," *Medieval Archaeology* 28 (1984)

Renaud, J.G.N., "Bloempotten en tuinvazen," *Vrienden van de Nederlandse ceramiek* 27 (1962)

Sanecki, Kay, "A Potted History," *Country Life* 187 (16 September 1993)

Yellin, Joseph, and Jan Gunneweg, "The Flowerpots from Herod's Winter Garden at Jericho," *Israel Exploration Journal* 39, nos. 1–2 (1989)

JAN WOUDSTRA

---

# Container Gardening

The first container gardening was the result of early trading and pillaging activities. Thousands of years ago, as people moved from one location to another, they transported their food plants in containers. Conquering warriors also transported plants when they returned from foreign countries with exotic plant treasures. Using pottery eating or drinking vessels as a means to move many of these plants proved successful. The more powerful the ruler, the more countries they conquered and the more exotic their gardens became. The technique of growing small shrubs in large earthenware pots in a garden was developed in the Western world by King Ramses III of Egypt (1198–1167 B.C.). The practice was later adopted by the invading Romans, who took the idea back home, along with many new plants.

The influx of exotic plants continued during the conquering era of Alexander the Great. On a trip to Asia Minor in early 300 B.C., he collected seeds of a plant that would become important for container gardening throughout Europe: he discovered lemons (*Citrus limon*) and subsequently sent seeds to Aristotle's students at the Lyceum in Athens, Greece. This treasured fruit was not hardy and needed to be moved to a protected site indoors during the winter. Containers were ideal for this. During this period citrus and other tender plants were extremely popular in Greek courtyard gardens, which featured large terra-cotta pots.

During the next hundred years the Roman gardens in Pompeii flourished and included the use of containers as part of a formal garden design. The courtyards of Pompeian gardens often contained potted plants situated around a central pool. Casa dei Vettii, still present southeast of Naples, is a peristyle garden bearing tribute to the influences of the Greek colonies in southern Italy. Pompeian gardens made excellent use of small spaces and included many elements that would later inspire the great Roman garden designers. It is speculated that the large terra-cotta pots excavated from Pompeian gardens of this era were specifically designed for growing citrus plants. They had a hole in the bottom for drainage and three on the sides that are thought to be "breathing holes" for the roots. Early Romans also used an impressive number of containers on their rooftop gardens. Innovative ideas solved the problem of transporting water to these sites. These Romans were also the first to use window boxes as containers for growing plants.

During the 13th-century garden designers in Europe used containers to grow plants both above and below the soil level. Containers were of all shapes and sizes. As the technology progressed, stone and metal containers joined the traditional terra-cotta pot as growing vessels. Round or square wooden tubs were also made to grow citrus trees, palms, and other special plants.

The use of containers reached a high point during the Renaissance era in Europe. One garden of note in Italy is the 16th-century Tuscan garden at Villa Gamberaia. It includes a wonderful *giardino segreto* (secret garden) that is an enclosed, rectangular sunken garden. The restored garden room is now filled with citrus plants growing in classic terra-cotta pots mossy from age. Citrus plants in containers line one entire side of the garden, creating a hedgelike wall.

The baroque era brought theatrics and experimentation to the regimented, symmetrical evergreen parterres of the typical Renaissance garden. Symmetrically placed, square, wooden planters painted white or dark green were still favored, but gardens during the late 17th and early 18th centuries began to include more ornate pots designed to impress visitors. The architecture of the container often was more important than the plant it contained. The European ruling class looked at the garden as a status symbol.

The French design and style was highly emulated during the 17th century, and Louis XIV's Palace of Versailles was deemed the greatest garden in the world. The garden was designed over a 20-year period by André Le Nôtre. It was a huge and expensive project that employed an army of laborers and would become the greatest work of the designer. Le Nôtre used many of the principles developed during the Italian Renaissance and expanded them to larger-than-life size. He enlarged terraced parterre gardens, full of architectural beauty, to a grandiose scale. One such terrace at Versailles was the sunken orangery. Louis XIV personally wrote a garden guide directing visitors to walk along an upper terrace so that the full grandeur of the orangery below could be appreciated from the best vantage points. The orangery contained an exotic collection of hundreds of tender plants that were moved outdoors for the summer and protected indoors during the winter. This impressive collection included full-size palm trees, numerous orange trees, pomegranates (*Punica granatum*), myrtle (*Myrtus communis*), and oleander (*Nerium oleander*) growing in ornate wooden tubs. Trimmed evergreens in containers completed the picture by adding an upright conical shape to the design. The orange trees were particularly important to the king because the orange fruit symbol-

ized his power as the Sun King. Stone containers from this era were typically heavily ornate and often did not contain plants. If they did, the plants were not impressive or were of a subdued color. The French formal gardens at Vaux-le-Vicomte, the first garden designed by Le Nôtre, and which have been preserved, contain stone urns on plinths interspersed with statues. The urns, used for their architectural or sculptural effects, contain a simple pink flowering plant that complements the color of the brick inside the ornate boxwood *parterre de broderie* (embroidered parterre).

The Baroque era in Italy saw garden designers using large plants in containers as accents for their parterre terraces. The formal parterres found in the garden Isola Bella, Lago Maggiore, Piedmont, Italy, can still be viewed today, are an example of this style. Large terracotta pots containing citrus trees adorn the corners of

*Penjing,* a container garden in the Chinese Gardens at Montreal Botanic Gardens
Copyright Anne Marie Van Nest

each boxwood parterre. The garden also contains potted plants adorning the balustrades of the ten terraces. Isola Bella was built on one of the Borromean Islands on Lake Maggiore and was designed to resemble a ship.

Gardening during the Victorian era in the 19th century was a hobby of extravagances. The garden was a symbol of social worth, moral righteousness, and imposed aristocratic taste. Exuberance abounded. Design principles of the time required that gardens display humankind's ability to conquer nature. Gardens were thus filled with all types of ornaments and decorations; a taste for embellishment was a sign of refinement. The manufacturing boom quickly satisfied the growing demand for garden ornaments, and the 19th century saw the first mass production of terra-cotta flower pots and saucers. Cast-iron urns in classically inspired shapes were essential to the Romantic landscape. Some gardens included urns in excess of one meter (1.1 yd.) wide. Urns were often left empty during the early days of the Romantic era, placed in remote areas of the garden as a surprise for adventurous visitors. The empty urns were intended to represent ancient artifacts. After 1860 garden urns took on a more decorative look and were considered to be accents to contain plants. These planted urns appeared in the center of carpet beds, symmetrically placed on a terrace or as accent pieces in the center of the lawn. Often they would be filled with bright annuals, dusty miller (*Senecio cineraria*), and cascading English ivy (*Hedera helix*). Containers during this era were used to accentuate the axial architecture of the garden and were often placed at intersections of paths. Others were used to add architectural interest to the boxwood, yew, and turf parterre plantings. Containers of myrtle (*Myrtus communis*) were often used in topiary form to line the paths surrounding ornate parterres. The clipped myrtles often had a round-shaped head and were planted in a wooden box or tub. These plants were permanently grown in containers, moving from the conservatory to the parterre with the changing seasons. This technique has changed little since the days of the grand Italian and French Renaissance gardens. Similarly, symmetry was important to the integrity of the design.

The shape of plant-growing containers may have changed, but their use was still important in the early 20th century. Simple, modernistic containers holding flowering plants were found in urban areas. The modern movement to use plants in containers started in Stockholm, Sweden, and quickly spread throughout Europe. The trend toward higher density living reduced the amount of green space in the city. Plants in movable large containers solved this problem and have become a fixture in the modern city streetscape.

The use of containers to create miniature gardens is a centuries-old art. In the garden at Powis Castle, Welsh-

pool, Powys, Wales, for example, an early English interpretation (1860) of an Italian Renaissance era garden, urns containing upright growing annuals are framed in brick niches along one of the many terraces. Rustic troughs filled with flowering alpines accent a gravel path leading to one of the more natural areas of this garden. Troughs typically are shallow rectangular stone receptacles that contain miniature or dwarf plants. Troughs were also used at Levens Hall Gardens in Kendal, Cumbria, England, created in the 18th century. Here, rough-hewn stone troughs contain delicate annuals. The use of stone troughs evolved from the desire to grow alpine plants in stone sinks. As the use of stone sinks grew out of fashion, practical-minded gardeners used them for growing plants. These miniature rock gardens are ideal for displaying tiny plant treasures.

The ancient art of *penjing* (Chinese bonsai) concentrates on the growing of miniature plants. These are used to decorate tables and stands found in courtyard gardens in China. *Shansui penjing* (Chinese landscape bonsai) expands the growing of dwarf plants, in a shallow container, to create a miniature landscape complete with buildings, figures, stones, moss, and water. Japanese bonsai originated from the Chinese *penjing*. A special decorative, shallow container is used to grow plants in miniature sizes. Bonsai literally means "grown in a tray." The containers themselves are often works of art covered with decorative glazes and fashioned in a rectangular, oval, or square shape, often with beautiful rims and feet.

Container gardening is still immensely popular. It allows gardeners to bring plants to areas where they would normally not be able to grow. Containers are now available in a diverse selection of shapes, sizes, materials, and colors, giving gardeners a versatility not experienced previously.

**Further Reading**

Currie, C.K., "The Archaeology of the Flowerpot in England and Wales, circa 1650–1950," *Garden History* 21, no. 2 (1993)

Davis, John Patrick Stuart, *Antique Garden Ornament: 300 Years of Creativity,* Woodbridge, Suffolk: Antique Collectors' Club, 1991

Elliott, Brent, "Perfecting the Pot," *The Garden* 120, no. 3 (March 1995)

Hume, Audrey Noël, *Archaeology and the Colonial Gardener,* Williamsburg, Virginia: Colonial Williamsburg Foundation, 1974

Keeling, Jim B.M., *The Terracotta Gardener,* London: Headline, and North Pomfret, Vermont: Trafalgar Square, 1990; revised edition, as *The New Terraccotta Gardener: Creative Ideas from Leading Gardeners,* London: Headline, 1993

Lindijer, Tony, and Sabine van Vlijmen, *Om de tuinpot geleid: 17e eeuwse tuinpotten uit Haarlem,* Haarlem,

The Netherlands: Archaeologisch Museum Haarlem, 1993

Moorhouse, Stephen, "Late Medieval Pottery Plant-Holders from Eastern Yorkshire," *Medieval Archaeology* 28 (1984)

Renaud, J.G.N., "Bloempotten en tuinvazen," *Vrienden van de Nederlandse ceramiek* 27 (1962)

Sanecki, Kay, "A Potted History," *Country Life* 187 (16 September 1993)

Yellin, Joseph, and Jan Gunneweg, "The Flowerpots from Herod's Winter Garden at Jericho," *Israel Exploration Journal* 39, nos. 1–2 (1989)

ANNE MARIE VAN NEST

# Copeland, Robert Morris 1830–1874

## United States Landscape Architect

Robert Morris Copeland, a 19th-century landscape architect, designed numerous rural cemeteries and private estates and made sweeping regional design suggestions for the Boston area. His innovative idea of incorporating large parcels of connected park landscapes into an urban environment was ahead of its time.

Born in Roxbury, Massachusetts, Copeland sailed to California in 1849 to seek his fortune in the gold rush. When he found he would not strike it rich, he returned home to enter Harvard, where he later graduated with a degree in liberal arts ca. 1852.

Following his graduation, Copeland became a scientific farmer at Beaver Brook Falls near Lexington, Massachusetts. Scientific farming was clearly a training ground for landscape architecture—both Frederick Law Olmsted and Horace Cleveland were first scientific farmers before practicing landscape design. Copeland became a leading expert on the topic, ultimately publishing *Country Life: A Handbook of Agriculture, Horticulture, and Landscape Gardening* (1859), which addresses both the technical aspects of farming and the art of landscape design. Copeland's goal in writing the book was to convince those "who earn . . . their bread with the sweat of their brow, and look upon their calling as a treadmill of drudgery and endurance, . . . that within the round of their daily duties they have every thing which can expand the mind and ennoble the soul." In early 1854 he delivered a Concord, Massachusetts, Lyceum address entitled "The Useful and the Beautiful," which dealt with the subject of melding practical enterprise and art. Copeland was invited to the Lyceum by the transcendental leader Ralph Waldo Emerson and Simon Brown, editor of the *New England Farmer.*

Those important connections enabled Copeland to secure work when he entered a practice in landscape and ornamental gardening with Horace Cleveland in 1854.

Their first job was likely the State Farm at Westborough, Massachusetts, probably lined up by Brown. Copeland and Cleveland immediately began designing a number of private estates and rural cemeteries, including the Samuel Colt Estate in Hartford, Connecticut, and Sleepy Hollow Cemetery in Concord, Massachusetts. In 1855, as a member of the Concord Cemetery Board, Emerson helped secure the Sleepy Hollow Cemetery Commission for Copeland and Cleveland. In creating Sleepy Hollow Cemetery, the designers considered how the space was linked to other public open spaces. The following year they again considered the importance of linking public spaces when they made recommendations about Commonwealth Avenue as a significant recreational space and a connector linking the Common and Public Garden of Boston to open spaces on the periphery of the city. Those opinions were offered to the "Committee under the Resolves" charged with regulating and monitoring the development of land created with the filling of Boston's Back Bay. With those recommendations in hand, the committee reported:

> It is believed that an ornamental avenue of this character . . . with stately dwelling-houses upon each side, connecting the public parks in the center of a busy city with the attractive and quiet, although populous country is a thing not possible of construction elsewhere in the world; and those places where some thing of the same kind already exists have been rendered famous in the consequence.

Copeland and Cleveland severed their partnership prior to the Civil War. Copeland served in the Union Army during the war and attained the rank of major. Unfairly dishonorably discharged in 1862, he spent the next several years of his life working to clear his name. In that effort he solicited a number of character witnesses, including Ralph Waldo Emerson. He also met with President Lincoln to discuss the matter.

After the Civil War Copeland returned to the practice of landscape architecture. During the late 1860s and early 1870s, he designed landscapes in New York, Pennsylvania, and several New England states. Significant projects during those years include the Frederick Billings Estate in Woodstock, Vermont, today Marsh-Billings National Historical Park, and the Oak Bluffs community on Martha's Vineyard.

Beginning in 1869 Copeland published several articles in the *Boston Daily Advertiser* (Charles F. Dunbar, his brother-in-law, was the editor of that newspaper) promoting a large park system for Boston. By 1872 Copeland had developed those ideas into a schematic plan for the larger regional landscape in and around Boston. This was published, along with explanatory text, in *The Most Beautiful City in America: Essay and Plan for the Improvement of the City of Boston* (1872). Copeland continued to refine the concept until his death in 1874. His obituary clearly articulated the driving interest at the end of his life: Copeland "had done much in the laying out and ornamenting private grounds, . . . [but] his ambition was for work at a grander scale." While Frederick Law Olmsted is usually given credit for conceiving Boston's connected park system, clearly the idea had evolved for a number of years, and Copeland was one of its principal promoters.

## Biography

Born in Roxbury, Massachusetts, 1830. Sailed to California during gold rush before entering Harvard, graduating ca. 1852; engaged in scientific farming and established landscape and ornamental gardening practice with Horace Cleveland, 1854; projects included estates and cemeteries primarily in Massachusetts, and unsuccessful entry in Central Park competition; after service in Civil War, established flourishing practice with commissions in New York, Pennsylvania, and several New England states; developed visionary public open space plan for Boston, 1872. Died in Boston, 1874.

## Selected Designs

1855      Oak Grove Cemetery, Gloucester, Massachusetts, United States (with Horace Cleveland)

1855–56    Sleepy Hollow Cemetery, Concord, Massachusetts, Unites States (with Horace Cleveland)

1866–71    Oak Bluffs, Martha's Vineyard, Massachusetts, United States

1869      Frederick Billings Estate, Woodstock, Vermont, United States

1872      Boston Metropolitan Open Space Plan, Boston, Massachusetts, United States

## Selected Publications

"What a Garden Should Be," *New England Farmer* 6 (February, March, April, May, June, July 1854)

"The Useful and the Beautiful," *New England Farmer* 6 (October 1854)

*A Few Words on the Central Park* (with Horace Cleveland), 1856

*Country Life: A Handbook of Agriculture, Horticulture, and Landscape Gardening*, 1859

*The Most Beautiful City in America: Essay and Plan for the Improvement of the City of Boston*, 1872

## Further Reading

Hough, Henry Beetle, *Martha's Vineyard, Summer Resort, 1835–1935,* Rutland, Vermont: C.E. Tuttle Publishing, 1936

Nadenicek, Daniel Joseph, "Civilization by Design: Emerson and Landscape Architecture," *Nineteenth-Century Studies* 10 (1996)

Nadenicek, Daniel Joseph, William H. Tishler, and Lance M. Neckar, "Robert Morris Copeland," in *Pioneers of American Landscape Design II*: An Annotated Bibliography, edited by Charles A. Birnbaum and Julie K. Fix, Washington, D.C.: U.S. Department of the Interior, 1995

"Park and Garden Pioneers: R. Morris Copeland," *The Park International* (January 1921)

Weiss, Ellen, "Robert Morris Copeland's Plans for Oak Bluffs," *Journal of the Society of Architectural Historians* 34 (March 1975)

Weiss, Ellen, *City in the Woods: The Life and Design of an American Camp Meeting on Martha's Vineyard,* New York: Oxford University Press, 1987

Zaitzevsky, Cynthia, *Frederick Law Olmsted and the Boston Park System,* Cambridge, Massachusetts: Belknap Press, 1982

DANIEL JOSEPH NADENICEK AND WILLIAM H. TISHLER

# Córdoba, Great Mosque of

## Córdoba, Córdoba Province, Spain

**Location:**  south side of Córdoba, within old Islamic walled city, approximately 121 kilometers (75 mi) northeast of Seville

The Great Mosque of Córdoba contains the first documented mosque courtyard garden in Islamic history. Although Islamic gardens are often interpreted as earthly anticipations of paradise, the responses to the plantings in this mosque in the ninth through the 11th century indicate that medieval jurists did not regard such gardens as symbols of paradise but instead as contrary to correct religious practice.

This congregational mosque was built by rulers and regents of the Umayyad dynasty in stages from A.D. 786–87 to 988. The first structure, which replaced a Visigothic church, was a rectangular enclosure consisting of a large open courtyard and a roofed prayer hall of 11 aisles. The courtyard was little more than a dusty walled area with a fountain for ritual ablutions. In 836 the prayer hall was enlarged by eight bays to the south, and in 951 'Abd al-Rahmān III al-Nasir extended its courtyard to the north and built a tall new minaret overlooking the courtyard's interior. Prior to constructing the minaret, al-Nāsir surrounded the inner face of the courtyard with an arcade of horseshoe arches. In 987–88 the courtyard reached its final dimensions of approximately 120 by 60 meters (131 by 66 yd.), when the regent Almanzor (al-Mansur)

Courtyard of the Mosque of Córdoba
Courtesy of D. Fairchild Ruggles

extended the prayer hall and courtyard eastward by eight aisles.

Today the courtyard is popularly known as the Patio de los Naranjos (Court of Orange Trees), and indeed this courtyard, as well as those of smaller mosques in Córdoba, was planted with trees since the first decade of the ninth century or earlier. The water for the mosque's fountain and irrigation during the long dry summer came from an underground tank filled with rainwater. The water was raised to ground level by means of a camel-driven wheel and distributed via shallow channels dug in the soil. Between 961 and 976 the supply of water was augmented by a large canal dug from the mountains, and in 991–92 larger, deeper cisterns were excavated in the courtyard floor.

It is not known whether the courtyard was originally planted with fragrant orange trees, as is the case today; whatever the genus, the trunks were probably planted in straight rows aligned with the columns of the prayer hall. Today the courtyard is paved; stone-lined irrigation channels lead to the shallow depressions where single trees are planted. Although the precise date of these pavements is uncertain, it is plausible that something similar was installed when the trees were first planted, because of the need for regular irrigation.

In the 11th century, a leading Muslim jurist was asked whether trees were permissible in a place of prayer. The jurist cited prior judgments opining that any vegetation whatsoever in a mosque courtyard was reprehensible and should be removed. Clearly, neither this jurist nor the authorities he consulted regarded mosque gardens as symbols of paradise. Thus, contrary to the widespread assumption among modern historians that the courtyard plantings in Islamic mosques, tombs, and palaces were intended as evocations of the Koranic paradise—a place of shady, fruit-laden trees and four flowing rivers—it is quite clear that at this early phase in Islamic garden history, trees and gardens had little or no recognized paradisiac connotation.

**Synopsis**

| | |
|---|---|
| 786–87 | First mosque built at site by ʿAbd al-Rahmān I |
| before 807–88 | Trees planted in courtyard, creating first documented mosque courtyard garden |
| 951 | ʿAbd al-Rahmān III al-Nāsir extends courtyard northward and builds new minaret |
| 961–76 | Canal dug, bringing irrigation water to courtyard |
| 987–88 | Almanzor (al-Mansūr) extends mosque and courtyard eastward by eight aisles |
| 991–92 | New cisterns dug in courtyard floor |
| 1236 | Mosque converted to church |

**Further Reading**

Creswell, K.A.C., *A Short Account of Early Muslim Architecture*, London and Baltimore, Maryland: Penguin, 1958; enlarged edition, revised by James W. Allan, Aldershot, Hampshire: Scolar Press, 1989

Ruggles, D. Fairchild, *Gardens, Landscape, and Vision in the Palaces of Islamic Spain*, University Park, Pennsylvania: Pennsylvania State University Press, 2000

D. FAIRCHILD RUGGLES

# Cottage Garden

In their billowing yet controlled informality, cottage gardens are distinctly British. While seemingly natural, cottage gardens are entirely artifice and require a great deal of work, both in design and maintenance. The guiding principle is to eventually have the plant material blend and grow together, as if by nature (see Plate 10). This requires some knowledge of growing habits or the result will soon be a wild, overgrown weedy jumble.

Not until Elizabethan times did the English working class begin growing subsistence vegetables in their small gardens. In the late 17th century foreign influence brought a taste for hybridized flowers and an appreciation for vegetable dishes. The close association of France and England carried over into the garden, with the English copying the French. By the time of James I, country houses for the wealthy were beginning to appear throughout the country, each with a formal garden. Garden writer John Worlidge commented that the English had become so fond of gardens that it was hard to find a cottage without one.

Before the system of enclosures was in place in the 18th century, cottagers were in the precarious predicament of holding their land only as long as it suited their landlord. Their gardens could disappear overnight. The 18th century brought not only a sense of more permanence but also several voices of reform. Scottish landscape architect John Claudius Loudon, with his publication *The*

*Gardener's Magazine,* promoted the idea that given a specified amount of space one could grow enough food to easily feed the average family. Through the efforts of Loudon and other contemporary reformers, cottagers began being granted more land to cultivate. Ironically, Loudon was also promoting a defined formality in the garden. But by the end of the 18th century, even members of the gentry were embracing cottage gardening as a simpler, back-to-nature lifestyle. Modern cottage gardening is more an offshoot of this movement than a tie to the subsistence gardening of the original cottage gardeners.

Toward the end of the 19th century, one of the chief proponents of the natural style was William Robinson. Although Robinson generally worked on larger-scale gardens, he loathed formality and helped to spread the emerging cottage style to the upper class in England through his commissions. Similarly, his disciple Gertrude Jekyll furthered the idea of informality in her designs, advocating the so-called natural garden style as a reaction to the carpet bedding of annuals then seen in most upperclass gardens. Robinson felt that only in cottage gardens could flowers be seen growing in a pleasing, natural way. The motto for his magazine *The Garden,* borrowed out of context from Shakespeare's *The Winter's Tale,* was: "This is an art/Which does mend nature: change it rather: but/The art itself is Nature." Jekyll took this style of gardening a step further, putting the casual form into a carefully designed plan. She incorporated plant color, form, and relationships in her design and credited cottage gardening with teaching her restraint. Her rules concerning color in the garden are still followed.

The original cottage-style garden was probably created in the front yard of a British cottage. Most likely, it would have been a combination of flowers, vegetables, and fruits, with culinary and medicinal herbs grown near the house and a path through the center to the front door. The garden was probably much more functional than ornamental, with color coming from the blossoms on the herb plants. Flowers for ornamental purposes were a later development. The flowers that were there had to fend for themselves; there was little time to devote to the garden, and that time was spent on the vegetables. For the same reason probably little space was devoted to shrubbery, except for berries.

Vegetables were in the garden for practical reasons and as such were planted in conventional rows. The flowers were tucked in wherever they fit and allowed to self-seed and wander. Throughout the garden perennial flowers were favored, along with self-sowing annuals, because both cut down on labor by requiring no replanting in the spring. Since new plants had to be added wherever space allowed, the rules of design were often ignored. Unlike perennial borders or carpet bedding, the garden had no large groupings of single plants. Foliage was not a prized component of the early cottage garden.

Although some garden borders could be found in the use of a single type of flower to edge with, by and large the restraint posed by the need to grow vegetables gave the garden its sense of order and refinement. Although grown in rows, the vegetables were still considered decorative, adding contrast in color, form, and texture.

Most gardens continued to have an enclosure of some type, either a wall or hedge, but the formality of clipped box hedges was replaced with paths lined with pinks (*Dianthus plumarius*), lady's mantle (*Alchemilla mollis*), or a similarly low-growing, sprawling plant allowed to spill over the edges. Gates and doorways were given special emphasis. Gates often had vine-covered arches or a topiary accent. The gate's primary purpose was to keep the farm animals out of the garden, but it was also viewed as an enticement into the garden. Doorways also were often framed with climbers and potted plants. The door, the end of the path, was seen as the focal point.

Fruit trees were often planted against the cottage itself or espaliered, a craft the cottager undertook with pride. Climbers, especially roses, were allowed to crawl freely over walls, roofs, and arbors, helping to unify the architecture with the surroundings. The cost of materials kept hardscaping to a minimum. Paths were made out of local material, often local stone or discarded old bricks or pavers. Originally, beehives were a regular feature in the cottage garden, but as beekeeping has faded as a hobby, the beehives have disappeared.

The custom of exchanging plants between gardeners accounts for the similarity in cottage-garden plant material and explains how it was possible to preserve so many old varieties. Many estate gardeners would bring home a division of a plant from the employer's garden. If it grew well for him, he would pass it on to neighbors. Time and expense prohibited cultivating plants from cuttings or potted seedlings.

The cottage garden was intended to be an intimate space, intrinsic to the cottage itself. There were no sweeping lawns, borrowed landscapes, or vistas. If the garden bordered the roadside, flowers were grown in front, with the vegetables somewhat hidden to the rear. If the garden was more private, flowers would line the path, and the vegetables would flank either side. As the need to grow one's own produce declined, smaller gardens could be devoted entirely to flowers.

The modern cottage gardens are often considered recreated rather than authentic, as few gardeners are still willing to allow the garden to create itself and instead impose their own design aesthetic on what should be free flowing. Vegetables are rarely intermingled with flowers, if grown at all. Lawns now dominate front yards, and the flowers have been relegated to borders or out of the front yard entirely. One of the problems faced by modern gardeners is how to make container grown plants spaced in clumps look natural. Gardeners in past times did not have the luxury of buying seedlings or plants and laying out an instant garden. Growing from seed took longer, but the garden acquired the more natural look required for a successful cottage garden.

Today, there is no definitive cottage garden format, but certain design elements are characteristic. Choosing among these elements allows gardeners to lend their garden its distinct character. While it may look like a jumble, and some gardens are, there is usually an underlying structure that starts with a feature plant used as a focal point. Many times the feature plant changes with the season, for example, peonies in the spring followed by delphiniums in the summer and asters in the fall. Crucial to the lushness associated with cottage gardens are what are referred to as filler plants. Many plants can be used as filler, but generally sprawling plants such as forget-me-nots, hardy geraniums, *Lysimachia,* mountain bluet (*Centaurea montana*), and catmint (*Nepeta mussinii*) are used. Finally, the edging plants can do double duty as filler since the desired look is to have the edges spilling into the paths. Placement of paths, for function, organization, and guiding people to other parts of the garden, is key to the unstructured structure of a cottage garden.

As for what defines a cottage plant, there are as many answers as there are cottage gardeners. Traditional cottage-garden plants include old roses, delphiniums, hollyhocks, poppies, lilacs, lilies, hardy geraniums, lady's mantle, catmint, and valerian (*Centranthus ruber*), the charm coming in the unique combinations of each garden. As hybrids and foreign plants were introduced to England, gardeners incorporated them into their cottage gardens. Still favored, however, are plants that retain their wild or uncultivated look and flowers that reproduce freely, particularly by self-seeding. Most modern gardens considered to be in the cottage style are still mixes of old-fashioned perennials, especially roses, with highlights from late spring through summer, forming a lush, romantic, natural look of abundance, usually spilling over the borders and barely in containment. The close planting and limited space of a cottage garden prevent such plants from taking over or becoming invasive, yet they keep the garden full and informal.

Although the cottage garden should ideally be allowed to grow into itself, knowledge of a plant's growing habits is still critical. Slow starters will be choked out by the more aggressively invasive spreaders and self-seeders, and the garden will lose its variety and opulence. Despite the lushness of the cottage garden, the gardener still has to plan for a sequence of bloom, which can vary with weather. The lack of formality combined with the lack of bloom caused by bad weather will give the cottage garden an unkempt appearance. Other keys to a successful cottage garden are the fragrance of the flowers and a plant's suitability as a cut flower. One of the main reasons for failure in this style of gardening is that many people either do not have the space to create a balanced mix or start with a too-narrow border. To accomplish the drifts advocated by Jekyll requires a border at least two-and-a-half meters (2.7 yd.) wide to successfully blend the colors and textures of the plant material.

Cottage gardening is often branded as too sentimental, and perhaps for that reason it has not been greatly employed in the rest of Great Britain, except to some degree in the southeast portion of Scotland. It has found a ready welcome in the United States and Canada, where an abundance of natural plant material available in much of North America's wide variation of zones and climates and an affinity for informal domiciles fit well with the principles of the cottage garden. But by the same token, the ideals set forth by Jekyll have often proved too confining and frustrating for U.S. gardeners with the country's extreme swings in temperature.

Cottage gardens were traditionally tended by people who viewed gardening as a necessity as much as recreation, generally with the husband tending the vegetables and the wife caring for the flowers. Unlike most garden styles that are developed by prominent professionals, the cottage style evolved out of practicality. While garden styles change with the times, cottage gardening innately suits cottages so well that it may endure much longer.

**Further Reading**

Genders, Roy, *The Cottage Garden and the Old-Fashioned Flowers,* London: Pelham Books, 1969

Hensel, Margaret, *English Cottage Gardening for American Gardeners,* New York: Norton, 1992

Jekyll, Gertrude, *Colour in the Flower Garden,* London: Country Life, 1908; reprint, edited by Graham Stuart Thomas, Portland, Oregon: Sagapress/Timber Press, 1995

Lloyd, Christopher, and Richard Bird, *The Cottage Garden,* New York: Prentice-Hall, 1990

Robinson, William, *The English Flower Garden: Style, Position, and Arrangement,* London, 1883; 15th edition, as *The English Flower Garden and Home Grounds of Hardy Trees and Flowers Only,* London: John Murray, 1933; reprint, as *The English Flower Garden,* edited by Graham Stuart Thomas, Sagaponack, New York: Sagapress, 1995

Scott-James, Anne, *The Cottage Garden,* London: Allen Lane, 1981; New York: Penguin, 1982

MARIE IANNOTTI

# Cramer, Ernst 1898–1980

## Swiss Landscape Architect

Ernst Cramer, one of the most renowned European garden architects after 1945, had a strong influence on present-day landscape architecture. He learned the profession of a gardener at Froebels Erben, a renowned firm in Zürich. He was instructed by the landscape architect Gustav Ammann, a close friend of Richard Neutra and one of the most important Swiss garden architects at the time. Ammann promoted a modern architectural style in garden architecture, but the general tendency was toward the informal style of the so-called *Wohngarten* (domestic garden style). This style became very popular when German garden architects such as Harry Maasz and Guido Harbers published their influential books on informal gardens as a natural extension of the private indoor space. When Cramer started his own business in 1929, he mostly designed private gardens for wealthy clients and perfected a romantic, rather picturesque style. He was especially interested in the rustic gardens that were built in the southern part of Switzerland in the canton of Ticino. He not only created many remarkable gardens in the *Wohngarten* style with a broad variety of Mediterranean plants in Ticino, but he also successfully imported the popular southern style to the Zürich region.

Threatened by the beginning of World War II, Swiss architecture and garden architecture had a strong tendency toward a conservative traditional style, the so-called *Heimatstil* (traditional Swiss country style). Nonetheless, a group of progressive designers, architects, and artists, most of them members of the influential Swiss "Werkbund," tried to develop the idea of a modern society, living in a modern environment. Cramer was a member of the Zürich section of the Werkbund, headed by the Bauhaus member Johannes Itten and the Swiss sculptor Max Bill, and became more and more interested in a modern method of garden design. About 1950, when the world was generally looking for a new way of life after the war, Cramer dramatically changed his style and started designing modern architectural gardens. His friendship and cooperation with many modern Swiss artists and his strong interest in modern architecture reinforced his will to find a new language in garden architecture. In particular, the temporary exhibition projects of Cramer are among the most remarkable creations of modern garden architecture in Europe. Most impressive were his contributions to national and international garden exhibitions, for example, the first national garden show in Zürich, G/59 (1959), and the international garden exhibition in Hamburg (1963). The abstract basic conception of his gardens, the renunciation

of superfluous decoration, and the use of concrete and geometrically shaped elements caused considerable irritation among his professional colleagues and added to his international reputation.

Cramer's Garten des Poeten (Poet's Garden), built for the 1959 Zürich show, was portrayed by Elizabeth B. Kassler in her classic book *Modern Gardens and the Landscape* (1964). This garden was probably the most important work in Cramer's professional career. At the age of 61 the garden architect had been asked to design a poet's garden for the first national garden show in Switzerland. He knew the difficulty of competing with the abundance of colors, forms, flowers, and shrubs at such an event. His proposal was in strong contrast to the general picturesque garden design. He worked with minimal means and maximum abstraction instead of imitating nature. Kassler described the design: "Triangular earth mounds and a stepped cone were precisely edged, grass-sheathed, and doubled by a still pool. The garden was not so much a garden as a sculpture to walk through—abstract earth shapes independent of place, with sharp arises foreign to the nature of their material." Just a few years later a new radical form of art called Land Art or Earthworks came on the U.S. art scene, creating impressive, almost archaic geometrical earth sculptures, which are among the most important sources of inspiration for present-day landscape architects.

Cramer's journey to Brazil in 1960 and his admiration for the architecture of Oscar Niemeyer were most important for the garden architect's further development. Coming back from his first trip overseas, he designed the Theatergarten (theater garden) for the 1963 international garden exhibition in Hamburg. Again, he created a "garden" without any plants but instead worked with huge, nearly 11-meter-high (12-yd.) concrete slabs and prefabricated concrete elements to create a sculptural space. In its strict architectonic appearance the garden resembled very much the central congress building in Brasilia built by Niemeyer. Only a few years later Cramer changed his style again and added modernistic biomorph shapes to his design. These related to the works by Roberto Burle Marx and the rather expressionistic details of Niemeyer's architecture. One of the most important projects from that late period was created for the central Post and Administration building in the city of Vaduz in Liechtenstein. Here, Cramer combined abstract several meter-high concrete sculptures resembling ski jumps, with a colorful concrete pavement laid out in an informal pattern of undulating lines. Even though it was not meant to be temporary, the project was dismantled a few years ago.

Many other remarkable projects by Ernst Cramer built in close cooperation with some of the most important Swiss modern architects and two gardens designed for houses by Richard Neutra do still exist. Among Cramer's clients were some of the most influential Swiss families, as well as companies such as the Roche and Ciba chemical companies. With his remarkable life's work Cramer not only prepared the ground for an intensive discussion about the contemporary influence of minimalist art and Land Art on landscape architecture. With his courageous gardens he also helped shape the profile of modern Swiss landscape architecture and strongly influenced the work of young successors such as Willi Neukom, Fred Eicher, and Dieter Kienast from Switzerland.

## Biography

Born in Zürich, Switzerland, 1898. Apprenticed as gardener at Froebels Erben, Zürich, instructed by garden architect Gustav Ammann, 1914–17; traveled to Germany, France, and Switzerland, 1918–22; attended Swiss school of horticulture Gartenbauschule Oeschberg, 1922–23; founded private office for garden architecture, Zürich, and worked as teacher in several schools of horticulture, 1929; founded firm Cramer and Surbeck, together with garden architect Ernst Surbeck, Zürich, 1945–50; participated in international building exhibition Interbau, Berlin, 1957; completed radical abstract Garten des Poeten at Swiss garden exhibition G/59, Zürich, 1959; journeyed to Brazil to see work of Oscar Niemeyer, 1960; participated in international garden exhibition IGA 63, Hamburg, Germany, 1963; taught landscape architecture at Athenaeum Ecole d'Architecture, Lausanne, Switzerland, 1972–80; completed approximately 1,400 projects of all sizes and scales, mostly in Switzerland and neighboring countries, working together with renowned Swiss architects and Richard Neutra. Died in Rüschlikon, Zürich canton, Switzerland, 1980.

## Selected Designs

| | |
|---|---|
| 1933 | Garden Vogel-Sulzer (rustic garden style), Itschnach, Zürich canton, Switzerland |
| 1942–48 | Garden Dr. Forrer-Sulzer (rustic garden style), Moscia, Ticino canton, Switzerland |
| 1945–48 | Garden Göhner (rustic garden style), Morcote, Ticino canton, Switzerland |
| 1955–59 | School Bernarda, Menzingen, Zug, Switzerland |
| 1957 | Garden, building exhibition Interbau, Berlin, Germany |
| 1959 | Garten des Poeten (Poet's Garden), garden exhibition G/59, Zürich, Switzerland |
| 1963 | Theatergarten (Theater Garden), international garden exhibition IGA, Hamburg, Germany |
| 1964–66 | Public place, Sulzer office building, Winterthur, Zürich canton, Switzerland |
| 1964–74 | Open spaces, housing area Grüzefeld, Winterthur, Zürich canton, Switzerland |
| 1965 | Garden, Casa Ebelin Bucerius (with architect Richard Neutra), Brione, Ticino canton, Switzerland |
| 1965 | Garden, Haus Rentsch (with architect Richard Neutra), Wengen, Bern canton, Switzerland |
| 1968–72 | Open spaces, Bruderholzspital hospital, near Basel, Switzerland |
| 1972–78 | Public space, central Post- and Administration building, Vaduz, Liechtenstein |
| 1974–78 | Open spaces, Roche chemical industry, Sisseln, Switzerland |

## Selected Publications

"Wo stehen wir heute im Gartenbau?" *Werk* 3 (1946)
"Gärtnerische Planungen," *Schweizer Garten* 2 (1953)
"Die Pflanze macht den Garten!" *Das ideale Heim* 9 (September 1953)

## Further Reading

*Anthos* 2 (1987) (special issue on Cramer)
Baumann, Albert, *Neues Planen und Gestalten für Haus und Garten: Friedhof und Landschaft,* Munich: Fischer, 1953; 2nd edition, 1954
Bucher, Annemarie, *Vom Landschaftsgarten zur Gartenlandschaft: Gartenkunst zwischen 1880 und 1980 im Archiv für Schweizer Gartenarchitektur und Landschaftsplanung,* Zurich: Hochschulverlag AG an der ETH, 1996
Jonas, Walter, and F. Steinbrüchel, *Das Inter-Haus: Vision einer Stadt,* Zurich: Origo, 1962
Kassler, Elizabeth Bauer, *Modern Gardens and the Landscape,* New York: Museum of Modern Art, 1964; revised edition, 1984
Weilacher, Udo, *Zwischen Landschaftsarchitektur und Land Art,* Basel, Switzerland, and Boston: Birkhäuser, 1996; as *Between Landscape Architecture and Land Art,* translated by Felicity Gloth, Basel, Switzerland, and Boston: Birkhäuser, 1996
Weilacher, Udo, *Visionäre Gärten: Die modernen Landschaften von Ernst Cramer,* Basel, Switzerland, and Boston: Birkhäuser, 2001; as *Visionary Gardens: The Modern Landscapes of Ernst Cramer,* Basel, Switzerland, and Boston: Birkhäuser, 2001

UDO WEILACHER

# Croatia

From its beginnings (seventh–tenth centuries) until the present day, Croatia, as both a central European and Mediterranean country, has developed under two kinds of cultural influences: central European—by way of Austria and Hungary—and Italian, which came from across the Adriatic Sea. Garden art is abundant in Croatia and compares favorably with garden architecture in other parts of Europe. Unfortunately, garden architecture in Croatia is not well known, and many gardens and parks are impoverished or have disappeared during the 20th century, and the designers of these parks and gardens are mostly unknown. Croatia forms part of two phytobioclimates: continental and Mediterranean. Because of this it has two different types of flora: the flora on the Adriatic Sea is Mediterranean, and in northern Croatia one finds plants from central Europe.

Garden art in present-day Croatia can be traced to antiquity. Although nothing is known about gardens in Greek cities on the Adriatic Sea (fourth century B.C.) (cities include Issa, today's Vis on Vis Island; Pharos, Stari Grad on Hvar Island; Tragurion, Trogir; and Epetion, Stobreč near Split), we can follow the history of gardens through country villas (*villa rustica*) in the north and south of Croatia from the time of the Roman Empire (second–fifth centuries B.C.). Garden art from the Middle Ages is best represented in the monastery cloister; many are still preserved today, especially those on the Adriatic Sea (Ston, Hvar, Split, Mljet, etc.). The cloister garden of the Old Town's Franciscan monastery is one of the best-known monastic gardens of Dubrovnik, dating from the 14th century. In the Middle Ages and Renaissance, gardens were built mostly on the Adriatic Sea, especially in the area of Dubrovnik.

In continental Croatia, medieval gardens were small and utilitarian and were constructed near feudal towns (fortifications). A majority of these medieval fortifications have either disappeared or are in ruins today. Some were later (mostly in the 19th century) converted into castles surrounded with romantic gardens. During the Renaissance in Italy and in Dubrovnik, country houses and villas were built and garden art flourished. In northern Croatia, however, fighting against the Turks (from the 15th to the 17th century) prevented such development. In this atmosphere utilitarian gardens were built near monasteries, fortifications, and Renaissance military towns, following the scheme of Renaissance ideal towns (such as Karlovac from the 1579, which is shaped as an hexagonal star).

Baroque gardens from the 18th century are preserved only in traces because they were transformed during the 19th century (for example, the garden of St. Francis Church in Zagreb and the menagerie-hunting garden around the Valpovo Castle). The largest garden conceived in the baroque style is an Episcopal park, Maksimir, in Zagreb, but it was completed as a distinctly Romantic park.

During the 19th century numerous gardens and parks were developed in Croatia; many of them still exist today. There were three types of parks: private gardens around castles in northern Croatia, public parks and promenades in towns, and spa gardens (for example, Spa Lipik in Slavonia).

Gardens around castles in northern Croatia (about 100 are still preserved) are comparable with similar smaller gardens in central European countries (Austria, Hungary, Slovakia, and the Czech Republic). Castles were built from the 18th century until the beginning of the 20th century, concentrated north of Zagreb. Landscapes parks arose in the 19th century (the most important are Našice, Valpovo, Trenkovo, and Stubički Golubovec). Romantic gardens date from the second half of the 19th century (for example, Trakošćan, from 1861, and Opeka). At the beginning of the 20th century, historicist parks (Donji Miholjac, Oroslavje) arose. In these parks were planted indigenous trees such as yew (*Taxus baccata*), lime (*Tilia platyphiyllos*), hornbeam (*Carpinus betulus*), oak (*Quercus petraea* and *Quercus robur*), common maple (*Acer campestre*), ash (*Fraxinus excelsior* and *Fraxinus ornus*), and maple (*Acer platanoides*). Other trees found frequently in those parks included spruce (*Picea abies*), abies (*Abies nordmanniana*), pine (*Pinus strobus*), Oregon pine (*Pseudotsuga menziesii*), gingko (*Gingko biloba*), plane (*Platanus orientalis*), horse chestnut (*Aesculus hippocastanum*), southern catalpa (*Catalpa bignonioides*), copper beech (*Fagus sylvatica*), and tulip tree (*Liriodendron tulipifera*).

Associations for the creation of public gardens, parks, and promenades appeared in Croatia beginning in the middle of the 19th century. Medieval and Renaissance

Squares of the "Green Horseshoe," Zagreb, Croatia
Copyright Mladen Obad Ščitaroci

fortifications were demolished, and parks and promenades were created in their place. Town gardens arose in the town of Osijek (eastern Slavonia) already in 1750. During the 18th and 19th centuries, other military and public parks were also built in Osijek. Garden architecture in Osijek arose in the empty area of the military fortification in the middle of town. Parks in the town of Karlovac (northern Croatia) were created in the area of the starlike fosse of this Renaissance town at the end of the 19th century. The first public garden in Zadar (Adriatic Sea) was opened in 1829. The first public promenade in Zagreb (capital of Croatia) was a southern promenade, initiated in 1813 and finished in 1908–12. The most important and impressive park complex in Zagreb was created as a part of town planning during the second half of the 19th century. At the foot of the medieval and Renaissance upper town was created, as a center of a lower town, an array of seven squares with one park (botanical garden). This array is well known as a "green horseshoe." Several landscape artists had this idea, but the most important was Milan Lenuci, the main town planner. This unique realization was created under the influence of Vienna's Ringstrasse and today represents a recognition and representative quality for Zagreb. The green horseshoe today frames a historical nucleus of Zagreb and is a monument of architecture, town planning, and garden architecture dating from the end of the 19th century. It represents a peculiarity of urban utopia that believed in incorporating the concepts of harmony and beauty as part of its concept of an idealized town.

*See also* Dubrovnik Renaissance Gardens; Maksimir

**Further Reading**

Maruševski, Olga, and Sonja Jurković, *Maksimir,* Zagreb: Školska Knjiga, 1992

Obad Šćitaroci, Mladen, *Perivoji i dvorci Hrvatskoga zagorja,* Zagreb: Školska Knjiga, 1989; as *Castles, Manors, and Gardens of Croatian Zagorje,* Zagreb: Školska Knjiga, 1992; 3rd edition, 1996

Obad Šćitaroci, Mladen, "Maksimir: A Romantic Episcopal Park in Zagreb, Croatia," *Journal of Garden History* 14, no. 2 (1994)

Obad Šćitaroci, Mladen, "The Renaissance Gardens of the Dubrovnik Area, Croatia," *Garden History* 24, no. 2 (1996)

Ogrin, Dušan, *The World Heritage of Gardens,* London: Thames and Hudson, 1993

MLADEN OBAD ŠĆITAROCI
AND BOJANA BOJANIĆ OBAD ŠĆITAROCI

---

# Crowe, Sylvia 1901–1997

## English Garden Designer

From an early age Sylvia Crowe was drawn to the landscape. Her initial intention on entering training at Swanley Horticultural College in Kent was to follow her father's second profession as a fruit farmer. Four years in Italy followed her training, and she returned to pursue garden design, an interest she is reputed to have acquired at the age of seven. Crowe trained with Edward White in London and then began work at the Cutbush Nurseries in Barnet, Hertfordshire, just north of London. A strong influence on her design development at this time was the man who, besides his nursery work, was the editor of *The Studio,* Shirley Wainwright. War service followed, first as a driver with the First Aid Nursing Yeomanry and later the Auxiliary Territorial Service, where she displayed practical skills as a vehicle mechanic.

The end of World War II saw a time when redevelopment and change in the English landscape was on everyone's mind. The small landscape profession was alive to the challenges facing it and at the same time adamant that its role would not be just the design of gardens but the shaping of the broader landscape of the future. It was Sylvia Crowe's particular qualities as one of a small group of talented but largely untried professionals that were to be crucial to the development of the profession and its role in the early postwar years. Though trained in small scale-design, she had the foresight and the ability to articulate the needs of the broader landscape and large scale developments both in her own design work and in her theoretical writing.

Crowe's first task of this kind was the planning of the New Town of Harlow, north of London, into which she was brought by the architect consultant Frederick Gibberd in 1948. This was quickly followed by a consultant role to another New Town, this time east of the capital, Basildon. Harlow, developing in an agricultural landscape with its own developed visual character, provided an opportunity to integrate the town into its rural context by the creation of a series of green fingers or wedges that penetrated its fabric. By contrast Basildon was sited in an area that had been despoiled by low quality developments and demanded a much more radical approach to the reconstruction of the landscape.

In the same year that she took on these consultancies, Crowe was appointed as consultant to the Central Electricity Generating Board, which was embarking on a major program of renewing and updating the whole national power generation structure. This involved the creation of major new generating plants, frequently, as at Trawsfynydd, north Wales, in highly sensitive positions. Crowe's approach was to ameliorate the impact these giant structures would have on the landscape, and as a result Trawsfynydd became not a blot but an asset to the scene. It is a tribute to Crowe's design ability but also her powers of persuasion that this and many other advances in the design contribution of the profession have come about.

Crowe always advocated the landscape point of view. At Trawsfynydd she buried some of the functional elements, screened others, and swept away some that could be dispensed with. The resulting simplified composition, in scale with the natural landscape setting, supported by woodland planting, became a model for the future approach to the development of such large new industrial elements in the landscape.

In forestry, too, Crowe took a leading role in bringing a civilizing influence into the work of the Forestry Commission of the United Kingdom. It was not merely the monotony of monocultures for which their planting was criticized. The imposition of mechanical boundaries particularly in upland areas was seen as particularly damaging visually. Crowe devised an approach to planting, and in the longer term to the patterns of felling, which she persuaded the commission was compatible with operational needs and a reasonable commercial return. This has been the basis of much subsequent planting and management by the commission.

Another field to which Crowe contributed was the design of roads. Although her actual work on the ground here was comparatively limited, it still influenced subsequent design ideas, as seen in her proposals for the major interchange in the Hotwells area of Bristol.

Those who are not familiar with Crowe's work on the ground discern her philosophy from the range of her writing. Like her design it is engagingly straightforward, full of common sense, and, devoid of whimsy, it celebrates the best that humankind, drawing on nature's beneficence, can achieve. It contains no overt symbolism, but if that is lacking the celebration of the combined efforts of people and nature is implicit. This was very much the case in the design she completed for the office of the Scottish Widows Insurance Fund in Edinburgh, which carries the landscape of the celebrated rugged hill Arthur's Seat right into the design of the roof

garden. Another of her acclaimed smaller works is the garden of the Commonwealth Institute in west London.

Crowe was active in the development of the British Institute even while still on war service. After the war, when the suggestion of the creation of the International Federation of Landscape Architects was proposed in 1948, she took on the role of the first honorary secretary, having been closely involved in the first conference in London. In addition to years of service in numerous landscape architecture institutions, she traveled extensively and lectured all over the world.

## Biography
Born Banbury, Oxfordshire, 15 September 1901. Studied at Swanley College, Kent, 1920–22, and later as pupil to Edward White, landscape architect in London; job at Cutbush Nurseries Barnet under Shirley Wainwright, editor of *The Studio*, until war service; after return to private practice in London, shared an office with Brenda Colvin; consultant to Harlow and Basildon New Towns, Essex, 1948–49; consultant to Central Electricity Generating Board, 1948–68; consultant to forestry commission, 1963–76; consultant to Southern and South West Water Boards; prepared master plans for Washington New Town Company, Durham and Warrington Lancashire; published extensively; founder, member of International Federation of Landscape Architects, 1948; president, Institute of Landscape Architects 1957–59; president, International Federation of Landscape Architects, 1969; chairman, Tree Council 1974–76. Died 30 June 1997.

## Selected Designs
| | |
|---|---|
| 1958–61 | Trawsfynydd power station, North Wales; Magdelen College rose garden, Oxford, England; Commonwealth Institute garden, London, England |
| 1963 | University College quadrangles, Oxford, England |
| 1966 | Commonwealth Gardens, Canberra, Australia |
| ca. 1970 | Rutland Water, Rutland; Wimbleball Reservoir |
| 1970 | Belbridge Reservoir, Lamberhurst, Kent, England |
| 1976 | Scottish Widows Fund offices, Edinburgh, Scotland |

## Selected Publications
*Tomorrow's Landscape*, 1956
*Garden Design*, 1958
*The Landscape of Power*, 1958
*The Landscape of Roads*, 1960
*Forestry in the Landscape*, 1966
*Landscape Planning: A Policy for an Overcrowded World*, 1969

*The Landscape of Forests and Woods,* 1978
*The Pattern of Landscape* (with Mary Mitchell), 1988

**Further Reading**
Collins, Geoffrey, and Wendy Powell, editors, *Sylvia Crowe, a Monograph,* Landscape Design Trust, Surrey: LDT Redhill, 1999

Harvey, Sheila, editor, *Reflections on Landscape: The Lives and Work of Six British Landscape Artists,* Aldershot, Hampshire: Gower Technical Press, and Brookfield, Vermont: Gower, 1987

MICHAEL DOWNING

# Cultivar

Linnaeus first distinguished between species and varieties by marking them with Greek letters in his *Species Plantarum* (1753). Despite this, he was not definitively sure which plants were to be regarded as species and which as varieties. In the second edition of *Species Plantarum* of 1762, he lists many sorts as species again. Linnaeus believed that only God can create species, whereas man and the environment can produce varieties. No differences were made between subspecies, varieties, forms, and cultivated varieties (commonly called cultivars). Therefore, the garden catalogs in and some time after the time of Linnaeus listed cultivars as varieties. Today, variation phenomena originating in nature must be identified as varieties and forms, whereas such phenomena that are the result of human intervention are described as cultivars. For example, the purple beech (*Fagus sylvatica* f. *purpurea*) is a form, being first found in a wood in Switzerland in the 17th century. Cultivars, on the other hand, may be bred by selection or by hybridization.

In his *Sylva Sylvarum* (1627), Francis Bacon laid a theoretical base for the alteration of plants by man, but it was not known at that time how plant alterations come into being in nature. Cultivars could only be bred from selection, and the gardeners spent a great deal of time collecting differing plants. In this way, they created a great number of cultivars from such species as fruit trees, vegetables, roses, oranges, bulbs, auriculas, anemones, African marigolds, peonies, and carnations. Philip Miller reported in 1768 that the great number of rose cultivars grown in English gardens were mostly derived from seed by chance. The selection was easier from hybrids found in nature, because their descendants split up into many forms. This was the case with the tulip, the auricula, the iris, the marigold, and the oldest garden roses. Great numbers of hybrids of tulips, narcissus, and carnations were seen as early as the 16th century. Very old shrub cultivars are *Rosa gallica* 'Versicolor'

(1583), *Sambucus nigra* 'Laciniata' (1597), and *Viburnum opulus* 'Roseum' (1551). As the Europeans did, so did Oriental gardeners. Besides Turkish bulb cultivars, some Asian rose and *Hibiscus* cultivars were introduced into Europe before 1700.

Variegated herbs and shrubs were extensively demanded in the second half of the 17th century. The English especially preferred cultivars of holly, periwinkle, and other evergreen shrubs. It seems that holly varieties were the first plants named after their finders or breeders. Robert Morrison was the first to find the variegated sycamore in about 1675; he was a collector of variegated plants, many of which can be found in the Oxford Botanical Garden today.

The greatest number of cultivars offer different flower colors and double flowers. In addition, Miller listed 92 variegated forms from 66 woody species in 1741. Some shrubs had different fruit color. Only one cultivar with red (purple beech), laciniated (elder), crisp (woodbine), column-shaped (lombardian poplar), and weeping character (willow) was known to Weston in 1770. The purple beech, known since 1680, was used before 1800, but few, other than *Populus nigra* 'Italica' and *Salix babylonica* were widely adopted. Globose cultivars and cultivars of conifers were unknown in the 18th century.

Joachim Jung (1587–1657) of Hamburg first found the generic parts of plants, but he never published his theories. Some botanists discovered the possibility of hybridizing plants by the end of the 17th century. Nehemiah Grew reported to the Royal Society of London on the sexuality of plants in 1671, as did John Ray in 1690 and Richard Bradley in 1731 in his popular gardening book. Rudolph Jacob Camerarius published *De sexu plantarum* in Tübingen in 1694 and argued that hybrids existed. Among botanists, all these theses were controversial, and few became popular. The *Sexus Plantarum* was mostly regarded as blasphemous. Few exceptions are reported. Thomas Fairchild crossed carnations in about 1715, and Philip Miller hybridized white and red cabbage in 1721. In Berlin in 1749, Johann Gottlieb Gleditsch fertilized an 80-year-old *Chamaerops humilis* (dwarf fan palm) with pollen from Leipzig. The Suabian professor J. Georg Gmelin claimed to have conducted experiments in hybridization in 1747, and his pupil Joseph Gottlieb Koelreuter began such experiments in 1759 at St. Petersburg. Since this time, some florists experimented in hybridization of hollyhocks (*Alcea rosea*), gilly-flowers (*Matthiola incana*), and other species. Thomas Andrew Knight, a brother of Richard Payne Knight, originated vegetable and fruit hybrids before 1795 by means of manual fertilization. Systematic hybridization however, was practiced very rarely before the 19th century. The theories on evolution by Lamarck (1809), Baden-Powell (1855), and Charles Darwin (1858) increased the popularity of hybridization.

Pansies, pelargoniums, ranunculus, fuchsias, roses, and rhododendrons belong to the first genera hybridized systematically in the early 19th century. Estienne Soulange-Bodin introduced the very first magnolia hybrid, *M. × soulangeana*, in 1826. England (Low, Standish), Belgium (Mackoy, Verschaffelt) and France (Cels, Leroy) were leading countries in hybridization. The number of rose and lilac cultivars extended to hundreds in the 19th century. France became famous for the rose hybrids, and the greatest lilac cultivator was Victor Lemoine at Nancy.

The introduction of plants from Asia forced by Siebold and Regel, brought Asian cultivars to Europe too, such as chrysanthemums, peonies, camellias, roses, hydrangeas, maples, and cherries.

Shortly after 1800, some eccentric tree cultivars were developed, such as the monstrous *Robinia pseudoacacia* 'Tortuosa' (1810), *Ulmus glabra* 'Crispa' (1808), or *Fagus sylvatica* 'Pendula' (1811). The colored-leaved plants appeared much later than the variegated ones, for example, the golden ash (*Fraxinus excelsior* 'Aurea', 1804), the purple hazel (*Corylus maxima* 'Fuscorubra', 1823), and the purple sycamore maple (*Acer pseudoplatanus* 'Purpureum', 1828). They came to a peak about 1850. Additionally, plants with more than two colored leaves were introduced from 1850 onward, especially warmhouse plants.

Cultivars of conifers also originated after 1850. Dwarf and blue conifers appeared. *Picea glauca* 'Conica', found by Rehder in 1904, gave a clipped appearance without having been clipped.

Dahlias, verbenas, and phlox were crossed early in the 19th century. The most hardy flowers, however, were crossed only from 1870 onwards, such as *Delphinium, Lilium, Hemerocallis, Hosta, Iris*, and *Gladiolus*. Another new field for hybridizers opened with the bedding plants from South America, *Canna, Petunia*, and *Begonia* in the first half of the 19th century, and *Alternanthera* and *Coleus* in the second.

Shirley Hibberd wrote on plant fashion in 1869: "Fashion is certainly capricous; and in the cultivation of plants we are well accustomed to see this or that particular subject or class elevated for a time to the highest popularity, only to prepare the way for something else which shall take its place, and eclipse in public favor." Today, many formerly highly esteemed cultivars are lost.

In the beginning, the names of the varieties were formed analogously to other plant names with long Latin phrases, e.g. *Ligustrum vulgare* var. *foliis aureovariegatis*, later shortened as *aureovariegatus*, now spelled 'Aureovariegatus'. As the number of hybrids increased, fantasy names in modern languages were common, such as *Syringa* 'Charles X'. Rose varieties were named after persons already in the late 18th century. Long Latin names, nevertheless, continued to be formed, such as *Chamaecyparis pisifera* var. *filifera nana aurea*. Siebold imported Japanese cultivar names into Europe in the mid-19th century. New Latin cultivar names have been forbidden since 1959. Today, a new cultivar name must be single-phrased and borrowed from a modern language.

**Further Reading**

Besler, Basilius, and Gérard G. Aymonin, *L'herbier de quatre saisons*, Paris: Mazenod, 1987

Greene, Edward Lee, *Landmarks of Botanical History*, 2 vols., edited by Frank N. Egerton, Stanford, California: Stanford University Press, 1983

Hibberd, Shirley, *New and Rare Beautiful-Leaved Plants*, London and Boston, 1870

Hurst, C.C., "Notes on the Origin and Evolution of Our Garden Roses," in *The Old Shrub Roses*, by Graham Stuart Thomas, London: Phoenix House, 1955; Boston: Branford, 1956

Miller, Philip, *The Gardener's Dictionary*, London, 1731; 8th edition, London, 1768; reprint, London: Miller, 1960

Morton, Alan G., *History of Botanical Science: An Account of the Development of Botany from Ancient Times to the Present Day*, London and New York: Academic Press, 1981

Weston, Richard, *The Universal Botanist and Nurseryman*, 4 vols., London, 1770–77, see especially vol. 1

CLEMENS ALEXANDER WIMMER

# Curtis, William 1746–1799

## English Botanist and Author

Botanist William Curtis was one of the original fellows of the Linnaean Society and is important for his many publications on botany and insect life. The son of a tanner, he was born in Alton, Hampshire, England and at the age of 14 was apprenticed to his grandfather, an apothecary. He moved to London six years later to finish his medical education and soon was associated with an apothecary, whose practice he took over. Meanwhile he became known as a demonstrator of botany at the medical schools of London, having established a garden for research at Bermondsey; later he had even larger gardens at Lambeth Marsh and Brompton. In 1771 Curtis wrote his first pamphlet on botany; in 1772 he produced a translation of Carl Linnaeus's *Fundamenta Entomologiae*. Also in 1772, having worked with Philip Miller (gardener and curator of the Chelsea Physic Garden), he was appointed *praefectus horti* at the Chelsea Physic Garden.

In 1775 Curtis began the publication of *Flora Londinensis,* a comprehensive study of wild flowers, as well as some mosses and fungi, growing within ten miles of the capital. Although the study made Curtis famous, subscriptions to the first edition were not enough to cover its costs, and he turned for support to Lord Bute (Prime Minister of England in the 1760s), to whom the volumes are dedicated. The first edition was completed in 1798; three hundred copies were printed in parts containing about six plates. The parts were published separately and the plates were unnumbered so that they could be bound in any order. There was a total of some 432 plates, hand-colored engravings that were usually lifesize; many were designed by William Kilburn, while others were done by James Sowerby and Sydenham Edwards. An accompanying text contains a synonymy, description of the plant, account of its habitat, and list of the localities where Curtis had seen it. Later, between 1817 and 1828, an enlarged edition was published, with 647 plates and additional text by William Hooker; plants were added from other areas of the British Isles, including the first descriptions of some previously unidentified Scottish plants.

In 1781 Curtis began publication of *The Botanical Magazine,* which was a great financial boon to the botanist. The journal's success is evidenced by the fact that it is still in publication. In a small pamphlet, *A Short History of the Brown-Tail Moth* (1782), Curtis demonstrates the very practical value of his work. By studying the caterpillar form of this moth, he shows there is no reason to be concerned for local vegetation by the caterpillar's large population increase in London. Curtis also continued to print catalogs of his collections of plants. His books on grasses, beginning with *Practical Observations on . . . British Grasses* (1787), were of great value to farmers. Revised editions of these works were published as late as 1834. Curtis died in 1799 and was buried in Battersea Church. His collected *Lectures on Botany,* which were edited by his son Samuel Curtis, were published posthumously in 1803–4.

### Biography

Born in Alton, Hampshire, England, 1746. Apprenticed at 14 to his uncle, an apothecary; moved to London to finish medical training, ca. 1766; established research garden at Bermondsey, London, 1771; demonstrator of botany at medical schools of London; elected *praefectus horti* at Chelsea Physic Garden, 1773; began publication of *Flora Londinensis,* 1775; founded the *Botanical Magazine,* 1787. Died in Brompton, London, 1799.

### Selected Publications

*Flora Londinensis,* 2 vols., 1775–98; 2nd edition, 1817–28
*A Short History of the Brown-Tailed Moth,* 1782
*Practical Observations on the British Grasses,* 1787

### Further Reading

Chatwin, Charles, *The Geological Work of William Curtis,* Alton, Hampshire: Curtis Museum, 1955
*Exhibition in Commemoration of the Bicentenary of the Birth of William Curtis,* Alton, Hampshire: Curtis Museum, 1946
Rix, Martyn, *The Art of the Plant World: The Great Botanical Illustrators and Their Work,* Woodstock, New York: Overlook Press, 1980

DAVID CAST

# Czech Republic

The Czech Republic is situated in the middle of Europe. This old settled territory of the former kingdom of Bohemia had developed a dense network of seigniorial residences, monasteries, and towns in which during the Middle Ages the first castle gardens were established, partly as spaces for intimate life and serious discussions, and partly as gardens of medicinal plants, fruits, and vegetables. Thus arose small gardens on castle fortifications or in the paradise yards of the monasteries, encircled by groined vault corridors. The architectural framework of these gardens has often been preserved, and in many places the gardens are now being restored.

The advent of the Renaissance style in the 16th century changed the character of residences and their gardens. Emperor Charles IV had spent some time in the medical plant garden of the Italian apothecary Angelo in Prague. One of the first Renaissance gardens in the Czech lands was the Royal Garden in Prague, founded in 1535 outside the castle, beyond the Deer Moat, with Queen Ann's summerhouse, in front of which was established a flower *giardinetto* with a bronze singing fountain. Later, the garden was complemented with a game hall and rearranged by Vredeman de Vries as a plane garden articulated into ornamental fields with clipped hedges and sculptural decoration. The *giardinetto* was restored in the 20th century.

In the second half of the 16th century, plane gardens were established around the Italian casino-type summerhouses in Krásný Dvůr and Kratochvíle. The garden around the summerhouse was enclosed by walls with towers or pavilions in the corners. Kratochvíle, the summer residence of the Rožmberks, was enclosed by a moat. The preserved space of the garden was restored in the 1990s. The castle garden of Jan Šembera of Boskovice at Bučovice, which had been built by Pietro Ferrabosco on a plane in front of the castle, beginning in 1567, was conceived as part of the fortification and enclosed by a moat. It was articulated by regular fields with fountains in the intersections of axes, and its composition was not yet connected with the castle. The garden was restored in the 1960s and endowed with box-tree ornaments. It provides a significant example of the Renaissance garden of the central European region.

A number of gardens were established in connection with the Renaissance reconstruction of the seigniorial residences. In Telč the castle garden of Zacharias of Hradec was enclosed about 1560 by an arcaded walk decorated by a figural relief of Neptune's triga on the side of the castle and by an arcaded walk in the castle's first story. In Jindřichův Hradec, at the end of the 16th century, a small garden was annexed to the castle of the lords of Hradec, on the castle's fortifications, and connected with the castle by an arcaded walk. The dominant feature of the irregular triangular garden is a monumental garden pavilion, a rotunda with a high conical tower and a richly decorated hall. The gardens on the fortifications of the former fortified castles reconstructed into Renaissance castles and mansions were also established throughout the 16th century, often in simpler forms.

A terraced garden was created in the 16th century for the castle of Jiří Březnický of Náchod at Lysice. On the lower terrace was developed an open ball-game field with a single-story walled gangway, which is still preserved in the form of an empire colonnade, although the inner playground was replaced by a flower parterre. On the central terrace was a menagerie; the upper terrace contained a Dutch garden of bulbous flowers. The vegetable garden on the plane below the terraces was later transformed into an English park.

A paramount work of the late Renaissance was the extensive garden of Julius Henry, duke of Saxony, at Ostrov nad Ohří, created in 1623 around his castle, beyond the city's fortifications. The garden extended on a river and its branches and took up an area bigger than that of the city. It was a system of several gardens, each arranged on a different regular pattern without mutual linkage of their original compositions, that only gradually developed. The abundance of details, labyrinths, fountains, sculptures, and pavilions is characteristic of the end of the Renaissance. In its time, however, it was regarded as the eighth wonder of the world and was even included in M. Merian's *Cosmographia* (1642), so that its detailed picture was preserved.

Wealthy citizens created small "pleasure gardens" within the cities, in which they planted linden and walnut trees as well as carnation and cypress. In 1501 the founder of the new Renaissance town of Nové Město nad Metují subdivided special garden lots for the individual houses in the town. In 1558 Jošt of Rožmberk published the *Booklet on Grafting Pleasure Garden Trees* in Olomouc. The rational husbandry of that time had changed the landscape by establishing extensive seigniorial game enclosures and comprehensive pond systems, in particular in South Bohemia and South Moravia, which still determine to a considerable extent the character of the landscape.

The beginning of baroque gardens in central Europe falls into the period of the Thirty Years' War, which resulted in the defeat of the Czech lands, followed by the advent of a new nobility, who were rewarded for political and military merits with lands and who wanted to demonstrate their wealth. The first baroque garden was established in Prague in 1623 by Generalissime

Albrecht of Valdštejn, who had many houses in Prague's Lesser Town demolished in order to build his palace and garden. Between 1625 and 1629, the Italian Andrea Spezza built a grand loggia at Valdštejn, whose colossal triple arcade opens to a plane parterre decorated with sculptures by Adrien de Vries, with a fountain in the middle. Espaliers of clipped hornbeams close the parterre in front of the loggia and continue into the back garden, whose espalier axis is closed by the arcade wall of a riding school, in front of which, along the garden's whole width, is situated the pool. The Valdštejn garden was restored in 1954–55. A significant early mannerist garden was the Flower Garden in Kroměříž.

Spatial garden layouts in the French style, particularly the axial bosquet compositions, were also developed during this period. Beginning in 1678 Count Eggenberg developed in Český Krumlov, behind the castle and riding school, a garden accessible through a two-story bridge crossing the moat. The garden's main axis passes through the square *parterre de broderie* with pools in the middle, ascends along the flanks of a monumental sculptured fountain to the terrace, and heads uninterrupted—bordered on both sides by square bosquets—to a pool with a square islet in the middle, whose five trees create a vista point. In the bosquets are arranged various decorative features and labyrinths. After 1750 the Bellarie summerhouse was built in place of the bosquets on one side of the axis.

At the beginning of the 18th century, Count Kounic, the imperial envoy to Paris, developed an extensive park at his castle in Slavkov. On an artificial terrace above the little town, in front of the castle, a parterre with three fountains was created and richly decorated with sculptures by Giovanni Giuliani. The main axis descends in cascades from the terrace to a plane garden into a long channel from which it runs, in the form of long alleys, into the landscape. The channel was subsequently divided into a system of pools corresponding to the square composition of bosquets.

French axial garden layouts, with extensive *parterres de broderie* on the terraces, clipped espaliers, rich sculptural decoration, and fountains, appeared in the 18th century at almost all countryside residences. In some places they have disappeared, for example, in the Liechtenstein residence of Lednice, where they were replaced by new features, and some have been preserved in a modern form, for example, at the Colloredo residence at Dobříš, or in a simplified version, for example, the Serénnyi residence of Milotice or the Vrtba residence of Hořovice.

The Italian-style terrace gardens also found application, particularly where ground conditions were favorable. After 1689 an extensive garden with an orchard was established at Count Václav Vojtěch of Šternberk's castle at Trója, in the suburb of Prague, by Jiří Seeman. The garden's central axis passes from the entrance diagonally through a square *parterre de broderie,* crosses the central fountain, ascends through a ramp to a high terrace decorated with large ceramic vases, continues to a monumental double stairway, with a grotto in the middle and decorated with statues representing the fight of the gods with the Titans, and leads to a lookout platform in front of the portal of the castle hall. Adjacent to the garden in its transversal axis is an orchard, with a circular labyrinth in the middle. The garden was restored in the 1980s.

The dramatic terrain of the historical Prague, with the castle's hill rising above the valley of the Vltava River, forced the builders of palaces in the adjacent quarters, in particular in the Lesser Town, to the difficult foundation of gardens on steep slopes, but with splendid views of the city below. Thus, from the second half of the 17th century to the end of the 18th century, an ensemble of terrace gardens developed. To these belong the palace gardens of the Counts Lobkovic, Schönborn, and Černín. The axes of these terraces lead to the palaces at their foot. The palace gardens of the Counts Fürstenberg, Kolowrat, Ledebour, and Palfy below Prague Castle were limited to narrow terraces and are thus more an architecture of walls and pavilions than a green garden. The main feature of these gardens is the central stairway leading from the palace at the lowest place to the outlook terrace or pavilion at the top, from where opens the panoramic view of the city below. The garden of Count Vrbna, established about 1720 by František Maxmilián Kaňka, is particularly inventive. Three terraces with a *sala terrena* and an aviary, which are inserted into the composition of the palace's architecture, culminate in an outlook terrace bordered by a balustrade with sculptures of Mathias Braun and in the architecture of the balcony of the fourth terrace, which open the view of the city's panorama. These gardens were restored in the 1990s.

The garden in Slavkov (Austerlitz) demonstrates that incorporating large water elements into a garden was not unknown in the Czech lands during this period. Sophisticated water supply devices made it possible to create artificial water systems to fill the gardens with moving water features. The garden of the castle of the counts of Questenberg in Jaroměřice nad Rokytnou was established during the reconstruction of the castle after the design by Jakob Prandtauer during the period 1709–37. The garden was founded after the preserved design by Jean Trehet of 1715. The axis of the *parterre de broderie* in front of the castle, with a fountain in the middle, crosses the river via a bridge and continues to a triangular isle created by artificial river branches. On the isle, behind the *parterre de broderie,* was situated a garden theater, behind which the axis continued, in the form of an alley, up into the landscape. The flanks of the parterres are enclosed by high bosquets. An orchard with circular plantings links to the garden. The river's breadth was increased to 22 meters (24 yd.) in order to enable gondolas to pass, and remarkable decorative stone benches were hewn. The garden was restored in the mid-20th century.

Italian-style terraced water gardens were also created. A small garden, for example, was created at the castle of the Count of Žerotín in Velké Losiny, at the foot of the Jeseník Mountains, between 1731 and 1738. Its main feature was a high cascade of water steps above a decorative parterre, culminating in a richly sculptured, almost theatrical, decoration. The garden is documented by a preserved contemporary model. While this feature was destroyed by the garden's later conversion into an English park, a small terraced garden of the mid-18th century has been preserved in Smilkov. The stairway and the sculpted scenery above the pool, which are endowed with many cypresses and statues, evoke an Italian atmosphere.

Garden areas were also developed at old monasteries that during the baroque period had frequently been reconstructed into extensive architectural ensembles. In addition to traditional orchards and medicinal plant gardens, decorative gardens were established, the most representative one being usually the abbatial garden. New features were added: for example, in the Benedictine cloister of Rajhrad, a vineyard with a grotto, in the Cistercian cloister of Žd'ár, an intimate *giardinetto* in front of the summer prelature and a water garden at the fish hatchery below the pond, and in the Premonstratensian cloister of Teplá, a deer garden with a summerhouse and a *viridarium* (evergreen garden). The intimate medieval paradise gardens, hidden in the historical quadrature of the arcaded walk, had always been preserved.

In the baroque garden the relation between the garden and the landscape was significant. Garden architecture modified nature according to certain artistic aims and attempted to engrave these aims on the landscape as a whole: the axes of gardens continued in the form of alleys into the free landscape, the through vistas directing the view toward architectural dominants that frequently were built just for this purpose. To provide a bird's-eye view of the landscape, intimate "hanging gardens" were developed at baroque castles as part of the residence, for example, in Rychnov nad Kněžnou, in Vranov, the most expressive one being that of Count Thun's castle in Děčín. The terrace, built after 1688, opens its entire long side to views of the landscape and is dominated by a *gloriette* in form of a high stairway decorated with sculptures and leading to a gate that acts as an observation point.

At Kuks, in a monumental arrangement of the Labe valley, on the river's upper course, baroque art stepped out of the garden and into the Czech landscape. In 1694 Count František Antonín Špork created a spa on one side of the valley and in 1697 a hospital on the opposite side. He connected both buildings with a common axis: from the castle, surrounded by spa buildings and a chapel above the spring, a stairway with a water cascade descended the slopes of the valley to Diana's Bath. The Labe River was straightened into a water channel and bridged over, and a race course with 40 statues, two obelisks, and a summerhouse were developed along the river. On the valley's opposite side the axis of the stairway culminated in a terrace with a graveyard church surrounded by eight statues of Beatitudes, and in the hospital terrace with a group of 12 allegoric statues of Virtues and 12 allegoric statues of Vices, all of them created by Mathias Braun. In 1711 a large checkered hospital garden was established behind the hospital and the whole landscape composition was closed by a windmill as an axial dominant. Thus were created a profane world of pride on one side of the valley and a spiritual world of repentance on the other. In the surrounding landscape the count created four hermitages, each with a garden, and in 1726–33, in the nearby Betlem forest, he had life-size statues and reliefs of biblical figures and episodes chiseled directly into the rocks by Braun's workshop.

The baroque goal of connecting the garden to the landscape significantly affected the character of the Czech lands of Bohemia and Moravia. In many estates, for example, in Červený Dvůr of the Schwarzenbergs, during the period 1748–49 the garden parterre was linked with an extended game enclosure, which was divided by a network of hunting paths that formed various figures. This format also occurred at dozens of other game enclosures, becoming a convention of large estates of the time.

The Romantic park abandoned the symmetry of the baroque garden. At first, it brought to life the images of Romantic literature through numerous buildings evoking a sentimental mood. After 1750 the count of Hodice developed at his castle in Rudoltice a landscape of the ancient Arcadia, with innumerable garden buildings, artificial caves, and hundreds of fountains, all enlivened with costumed villeins representing idyllic scenes. The park, admired by both Voltaire and Frederick the Great, dissolved with the death of its creator.

At Červený Hrádek, the baroque summer residence of the Schwarzenbergs, in 1769 artificial caves, isles, an obelisk, and a Chinese pavilion were built, exotic animals kept, and poplars planted. Count Rudolf Černín, after his return from a tour of England in 1783, commissioned the design of a 100-hectare (247-acre) park at his castle in Krásný Dvůr, which was completed after ten years. Meadows with 100-year-old oaks—including Bohemia's oldest oak (with a circumference of 925 cm [361 in.])—and a stream valley with a system of five ponds formed its basis. The park's axis is an approximately 2.4-kilometer (1.5-mi.) long hornbeam alley closed by an obelisk. The alley also contains a Chinese pavilion and, on the top, a Gothic temple as lookout. Červený Hrádek and Krásný Dvůr rank among the first and oldest Romantic parks of central Europe.

In the third quarter of the 18th century, the baroque park at Červený Hrádek was romanticized and endowed with a new fashionable feature: the planting of introduced, mostly North American, tree species. In 1785 already 177 taxa of these were known here, *Cedrus libani* being planted here from 1769. The park, extending at the foot of the Krušné Mountains 400 meters (437 yd.) above sea level, was expanded to 300 hectares (741 acres) and passes unfenced into the landscape. From here comes the mourning form of *Picea excelsa* 'Rothenhausii'.

The park of Count Chotek at Veltrusy, founded 1785 on an isle in the Vltava River, is an example of a *ferme ornée*, an ornamental farm, designed by Richard van der Schott. A branch of the Vltava River dammed to allow pleasure boat trips through the park surrounding cultivated fields: work in the fields became the decoration of the landscape's aesthetic image, in which both decorative and utility areas formed a unified artistic composition. The ring way along the channel's arm and the meadows were decorated with a series of buildings that reflected the period's mood, including the Temple of the Friends of the Countryside and Gardens, General Laudon's pavilion on the bridge across the channel, and an Egyptian cabinet cut in the rock and accessible by boat under the bridge with a Sphinx. Memorials were erected here to both van der Schott and Christian Hirschfeld, the author of the then popular work *History and Theory of the Art of Garden-Making* (1784). The park was formed by deliberate cultivation of the flood plain forest, in which selected native tree species were accentuated, and specimens of oak, together with *Liriodendron tulipifera*, *Sophora japonica*, and *Platanus*, among others, were used.

Kačina was the second park laid out by Count Karel Chotek, in 1789, at his new castle, which was built later (1802–22). From a flat hilltop the castle dominated a wide plane landscape that still exhibited the formal elements of classicism: a trident of mostly lime tree alleys diverging from the castle into the landscape and a game reserve interwoven by a star of alleys with a vase in the middle. The main poplar alley descended from the castle to a vast pond with isles and continued on to the village. The main vista through the park to the castle's monumental frontage aimed at the vast water mirror of the pond, which no longer exists. The basic character of the park resulted from the landscaping and planting of predominantly native tree species, which formed the backstage for the extensive greens, the fenceless transition of distant views into the landscape being ensured by ha-has. The park, with an area of 200 hectares (494 acres), was laid out with the aid of the botanist N.J. Jacquin who, about 1800, founded a botanic garden there. The castle presently serves as an agricultural museum that is preparing a collection garden of dendrology and medicinal plants.

The Podzámecká garden in Kroměříž and, in particular, in the extensive pond landscape near Lednice, the summer residence of the princes of Liechtenstein, who lived in the neighboring town of Valtice, underwent significant transformations into the Romantic style. At that time the center of the landscape park was the Temple of the Sun, from which diverged a star of eight poplar alleys enclosed, via vistas, by natural and built features. By converting the branches of the Dyje River into a system of ponds, architect Fanti and the imperial gardener van der Schott created in 1805–11 an extensive Romantic landscape park on an area of 270 hectares (667 acres), in which 36,000 exotic plants, imported from North America, were planted. Monumental buildings completed the composition of the plane landscape: from the outlook minaret above the pond in the castle's axis of 1802 to the artificial ruin of Jan's Castle up to the Temples of Apollo, Diana, and the Three Graces and the colonnade of the Memorial to Father and Brothers. The monumental buildings became vista points of the wide prospects of the park landscape and gave it its sense and order.

During the reconstruction of the Hluboká Castle in the mid-19th century, the princes of Schwarzenberg created an extensive landscape park at the castle, on a hilltop over the Vltava River. By 1864 a park, with distant through vistas to the castle and to the plane pond landscape, was established under the direction of Rudolf Vácha. The landscaping work carried out by Princess Eleonore connected the castle complex with game enclosures, forests, farmyards, and ponds via alleys, preserves, and solitary trees. The richness of tree species was extraordinary; the park was the first one into which many tree species from North America were introduced.

Beginning in the mid-19th century a series of older parks were enlarged and converted into arboretums. By 1842, for example, Count Černín had established in Chudenice a park with an arboretum called the American Garden. It began as a nursery of decorative conifer and broad-leaved tree species for the parks of the Černín estates. The arboretum still contains a 150-year-old *Pseudotsuga taxifolis* with a trunk circumference of 510 centimeters (199 in.) and a height of 44 meters (48 yd.); and from here comes the slender *Picea excelsa* 'Harrach'. The arboretum was laid out on a checkered network, and catalogs of plants and trees have been kept since the arboretum was established.

In Buchlovice, in front of the castle once belonging to the Petřvaldskýs, is an originally Italian terraced garden that was converted in the mid-18th century into a French-style garden. In the mid-19th century the garden was extended to about 20 hectares (49.5 acres) and converted into a landscape park intended for an extensive collection of tree species. The collection includes a large selection of *Picea*, *Abies*, *Chamaecyparis*, *Thuja*, *Pinus*, and *Metasequoia,* as well as several *Fagus, Quercus, Philodendron,* and rare shrubs. The contemporary collection of 650 species and varieties of *Fuchsia* is also significant.

The landscape park of Konopiště, at the castle of Archduke Franz Ferdinand d'Este, the successor to the Austrian imperial throne who was shot dead in 1914 in Sarajevo, belongs to the largest and dendrologically most significant parks. This extensive park (225 hectares [556 acres]) was developed between 1888 and 1910 by connecting a smaller baroque garden with a 100-hectare (247-acre) game enclosure in which fallow deer and white deer had been kept. The park includes a rose garden (1906–13; it still exists in a modified form), the parterre of which was filled with 1,500 tall-trunked and 7,000 brush roses of 200 species, as well as rich sculptural decoration. The park's composition makes use of the natural vividly modeled ground and open vistas to the pond and the castle above it. Native tree species formed the basis of the plantings, to which exotic species were added. Thus the park made up an extensive collection especially of spruces (*Picea*), low cypresses (*Chamaecyparis*), thujas, and junipers, as well as *Abies procera, A. lasiocarpa* 'Arizonica', and *Pinus banksiana,* among others. The collection of broad-leaved trees includes oak, maple, and beech trees, as well as the rare *Almus glutinosa* 'Imperialis' and 'Pyramidalis', *Betula verrucosa* 'Dalecarlica' and 'Purpurea', *Cladrastis lutea,* and *Fraxinus pennsylvanica* 'Aucubaefolia'.

The extensive (200 hectare [494 acre]) Průhonice castle park was created by Count Arnošt Emanuel Silva-Tarouca in 1885–1917, in cooperation with the dendrologist Camillo Schneider, in the valley of a stream that gradually passed into three ponds. A passionate collector, the count created the park as a beautiful analogy of the Bohemian landscape to be used as a Dendrological Society center for introduced tree species. This tradition has been continued in the nearby botanical garden in Průhonice, founded in 1962 for the Academy of Sciences, and in the dendrological garden developed in 1974–89

Neo-baroque parterre in winter, Hluboká nad Vltavou, Czech Republic
Photo by Marek Ehrlich

after the design made by the local Research Institute of Decorative Horticulture of the Academy of Agricultural Sciences. The castle park contains extensive collections of spruce, fir, and pine trees, *Cedrus libani,* low cypresses (*Chamaecyparis*), maple, oak, birch, and cotoneaster. The park became famous especially for its extensive groups of rhododendrons (more than 700 cultivars) and azaleas (more than 200 cultivars). The development of landscape parks in the Czech lands saw its culmination at the beginning of the 20th century at Průhonice castle park, whose famous tradition still continues.

With the onset of the Enlightenment, public parks began appearing in the cities. In 1786 Emperor Joseph II opened the first public park in the Czech lands, in Brno. The classical layout of new towns built near springs still persisted, such as Františkovy Lázně (1792) and Mariánské Lázně (1805). In Mariánské Lázně Václav Skalník developed the composition of a square in the center of the spa. By creating a park at another spring, he laid the foundation of a park system of the contemporary spa, which follows the river flowing through the valley. In difficult ground conditions Skalník created in 1830 a park in the deep valley of the spa  Karlovy Vary, where chestnut tree alleys had been planted in 1756. These parks were completed by an extensive system of forest promenades with a series of landscape vista points. Efforts to create parks in the towns became more pronounced with the removal of the fortification walls. In the former moats promenade alleys arose, as did continuous ring parks endowed with music pavilions, memorials, and cafés, surrounded on the perimeter by the public buildings. Such ring parks began to be developed in Brno in 1793, more quickly after the destruction of the fortress in 1845, in Plzeň from 1803, in Olomouc in 1820, in Opava in 1834, and in České Budějovice in 1875. Such parks were also developed in a series of smaller towns, for example, Písek. The abolished Spilberk fortress in Brno was gradually converted, beginning in 1861, into a planned park with a system of ring paths offering views of the city and the landscape of South Moravia. In Prague the inner fortification ring was not converted into a park; however, a park belt was developed on the top of the hillsides above the Vltava River, on the Letná plane, on the slopes of the Petřín Hill, and on the fortification wall of Vyšehrad, which offered panoramic views of the city. Josef Thomayer, the director of City Parks and a significant developer of such parks in the second half of the 19th century, participated in the development of all these Prague parks, imprinting on them an individual character through his classicizing concept, making particular use of the lowered flower parterre. Of the other parks developed by Thomayer, the most significant are the Charles Square in Prague (1884), the city park Michalov in Přerov (1903), and the fortification ring in Hradec Králové (1905). During the 19th century new city parks were established in most cities, usually in connection with the city shooting ranges of the revolutionary year 1848, and became the basis of the system of urban public green spaces.

At the beginning of the 20th century the period of development of large, mostly aristocratic gardens with decorative parterre arrangements in the spirit of historicism, such as those established at the end of the 19th century in Dobříš and Lednice, was over. New artistic views began to prevail, which were reflected in the art of garden making. From the first decade of the 20th century, the modernistic garden with pergolas at the Otto Villa in Prague, designed by Otakar Novotný, the garden of the Bata villa in Zlín, enclosed by a colonnade, designed by Jan Kotěra, and the square in Brno-Královo Pole, with a play meadow designed by Leberecht Migge, the pioneer of modern garden design, deserve to be mentioned, even if today these gardens are debased. Also deserving of mention is the Cubist house and renewed garden of 1913 in Prague designed by Josef Chochol.

The first quarter of the 20th century can be characterized by two gardens: the gardens of the castle in Nové Město nad Metují and the gardens of the presidential residence in Prague. During the reconstruction of the castle in Nové Město nad Metují for the industrialist Bartoň of Dobenín, Dušan Jurkovič designed in 1913 an Art Nouveau–inspired garden on its former terraces and fortification walls, while still respecting its historic values. The garden is connected with the area of French-style clipped bosquets by a colored timber bridge. The gardens of the presidential residence in Prague were created between 1921 and 1931 on the terraces of the former castle fortification wall, designed by Josip Plečnik. The Garden on the Wall, which makes up a promenade connecting unique vistas to historical Prague, accentuated by architectural features—fountains, obelisks, and statues—and the Garden on the Bastion, which provides an access space to the ceremonial hall of the castle and to the outlook into the moat with a series of individual artistic details of stairs and balustrades and with columns of *Thuja occidentalis* 'Malonyana'. Plečnik also arranged some water features of the park of the president's summer residence in Lány.

The expressive functionalistic architecture of interwar Czechoslovakia was surrounded by functional and simple garden architecture that, through wide entrances and terraces, open into the garden, tying it together with the house's interior. The most outstanding designers of modern gardens in the 1920s and 1930s were the architects Otakar Fierlinger in Prague and Otto Eisler in Brno. Arnošt Wiesner designed the first roof garden in Czechoslovakia in 1923, on a flat roof of an insurance company in Brno, as a space for employees to relax. Functionalistic gardens are characterized by their great spaciousness and restraint, for example, the sloping garden below the Müller Villa in Prague (1929–31), designed by Adolf Loos, with the participation of Camillo Schneider, Karl Foerster, and Hermann Mattern, and the spacious open garden of the Tugendhat Villa (1930), designed by Mies van der Rohe with the aid of Markéta Müllerová.

Functionalism contributed significantly to the urban-planning concept of city parks as systems of green spaces. In addition to English-style garden cities, such as the Ořechovka and Záběhlice quarters in Prague, new "garden towns" were also created, such as Zlín, around the "factory in gardens" of the Bata Company, as well as a series of Bata Company satellite towns, of which 8 were built in Czechoslovakia and 14 in three continents, between 1930 and 1941. The urban-planning concept of these towns, which was developed in Zlín, was based on a square in the town center, which passed into a longitudinal park axis surrounded on both sides by residential quarters of standardized family houses. One side the park axis led into the factory area, while the other side led into the recreation area of the town. According to this concept, four new Bata factories with residential quarters were built in the Czech lands, for example, in Otrokovice. But the primary example is Zlín, in which Masaryk Square's monumental grassy carpet was laid out. It ascends through a poplar alley from the Labor Square to a glass block of the original memorial to Tomáš Bata, as the central axis of composition of the urban center. Extensive company residential estates of standardized family houses were situated in a uniform fenceless garden landscape, in which the common lawns were differentiated by individual flower plantings. It was in this spirit that even the Forest Cemetery was conceived. The concept of the Zlín garden town was designed and implemented by František Lydie Gahura in the years 1921–34.

Extensive park systems for the health resorts of Luhačovice and Poděbrady also occurred during this period. In Luhačovice the spa park is situated in the axis of a deep forest valley, through which a small river flows and which is bordered by a colonnade and spa buildings. In Poděbrady a system of plane parks connects the spa with the railway station. After World War II, at the end of the 1940s, the art of garden making was revived in the landscaping of places of national tragedies, including Lidice as an extensive Czech landscape in the place of the burned-down community and Ležáky as a contrasting countryside idyll in the place where victims of Nazi terror were executed. Both arrangements were the work of Ladislav Žák, the author of the book *The Habitable Landscape* (1947). In both cases the natural landscape was potentiated in a creative way.

During the 40 years of Communism, although historic gardens were restored, new creative work succeeded only as an exception. One such park is the extensive belt-shaped Park of Friendship in the Prosek residential estate in Prague. Its spine is formed by a water course with cascades and a central fountain, bordered by willows and leading into a small lake. The garden layout of the stone courtyard of the former Valdštejn riding school in Prague is also interesting, with many water and sculptural features. Both gardens were designed by Otakar Kuča in the 1970s.

The same period also saw the creation of new botanical gardens: The City Botanic Garden in Prague-Trója was founded in 1965 by Jan Jágr. It is still under construction, on the slopes of the Vltava River valley. The arboretum of the Mendel Agricultural and Silvicultural University in Brno was conceived by Ivar Otruba in 1970 in a natural amphitheater above the city. It has marked natural sculptural features. Both gardens are collection gardens intended for teaching and study.

Shortly after the so-called Velvet Revolution in the 1990s, free creation manifested itself in several new parks meant to be the gardens for meditation and developed by private initiative. The garden of meditation in Plzeň is the reflection of the years of suffering. It includes grassy areas closed by a backstage of trees, with statues along the way leading to the chapel. The Potoční park, also in Plzeň, is situated in a rocky area. The spaces of meditation inspired by archaizing stones and statues arose through the regeneration of the area after the design by Pavel Šimek and colleagues. The southern slopes of the Jeseník Spa represent an extensive mountain meadow 600 meters (656 yd.) above sea level, modeled in several waves through which wind the *Way of Life*, expressed by 11 stone stations created by the sculptor Jan Šimek, up to the closing "gate" with a panoramic view of the Jeseníky Mountains. In Štramberk, after the design of Ivar Otruba, the White Mountain forest park, with a *Sunny Way* accompanied by statues in a dramatic limestone site, is being developed. In the Czech environment contemporary garden design tries to potentiate the expression of the natural landscape and in the city express new ideas in cooperation with the other creative arts.

*See also* Kroměříž; Ledebour Garden; Lednice-Valtice Cultural Landscape; Milotice; Prague Castle Gardens; Průhonický Park; Vrtba Garden

**Further Reading**

Bašeová, Olga, *Pražské zahrady* (Prague Gardens), Prague: Panorama, 1991

Bowe, Patrick, *Gardens in Central Europe,* New York: M.T. Train/Scala Books, 1991

Dokoupil, Zdeněk et al., *Historické zahrady v Čechách a na Moravě* (Historic Gardens in Bohemia and Moravia), Prague: Nakl. Československých Výtvarných Umělců, 1957

Fierlinger, Otakar, *Zahrada a obydlí* (Garden and Habitation), Prague: Laichter, 1938

Freimanová, Milena, editor, *Člověk a příroda v novodobé české kultuře* (Man and Nature in Modern Czech Culture), Prague: Národní Galerie, 1989

Hieke, Karel, *České zámecké parky a jejich dřeviny* (Czech Castle Parks and Their Tree Species), Prague: Státní Zemědělské Nakl., 1985

Hieke, Karel, *Moravské zámecké parky a jejich dřeviny* (Moravian Castle Parks and Their Tree Species), Prague: Státní Zemědělské Nakl., 1985

Kříž, Zdeněk, *Významné parky Severomoravského kraje* (Significant Parks of the North Moravian Region), Ostrava: Profil, 1971

Kříž, Zdeněk, Dušan Riedl, and Jan Sedlák, *Významné parky Jihomoravského kraje* (Significant Parks of the South Moravian Region), Brno: Blok, 1978

Kuča, Otakar, "Zahrady a parky v českých zemích (Gardens and Parks in the Czech Lands)," *Architektura ČSSR* 29 (1970)

Kuča, Otakar, *Zur Entwicklung der europäischen Park- und Gartenlandschaft,* Berlin: s.n., 1974

Maiwald, V., *Geschichte der Botanik in Böhmen,* Vienna: Fromme, 1904

Novák, Zdeněk, "Monuments of Garden Architecture in the South Moravian Region," *Acta Průhoniciana* 57 (1988)

Pacáková-Hošťálková, Božena et al., *Zahrady a parky v Čechách, na Moravě a ve Slezsku* (Gardens and Parks in Bohemia, Moravia, and Silesia), Prague: Libri, 1999

Petrů, Jaroslav, "Rudolfinské zahrady na Moravě (Rudolfinian Gardens in Moravia)," *Zahrada—park—krajina* (Garden—Park—Landscape) 3 (1998)

Riedl, Dušan, "Funkcionalistická zahrada v někdajšom Československu (A Functionalist Garden in the Former Czechoslovakia)," *Projekt* 38 (1976)

Wirth, Zdeněk, "Česká zahrada (The Czech Garden)," *Styl* 18 (1933–34)

Wirth, Zdeněk, *Pražské zahrady* (Prague Gardens), Prague: Poláček, 1943

DUŠAN RIEDL

# D

## Daisen-in

### Kyoto, Japan

**Location:** northeastern Kyoto

The so-called dry gardens (*kare-san-sui*) of Japan are a distinctive type of small landscape for which that country is justifiably famous. The garden courtyards at Daisen-in, a subtemple of the Daitoku-ji Temple of Kyoto, are among the most impressive of these dry gardens. The dry garden is most often considered in the West to be one made completely of inorganic materials, typically boulders and raked gravel. In fact, the name comes solely from the physical absence of water—many dry gardens, including those at Daisen-in, have abundant plant material ranging in size from small trees to mosses. In addition to the lack of water, dry gardens are typically quite small, really courtyards, and enclosed from distracting views by screening devices, especially stuccoed walls. They are typically located adjacent to housing, particularly the *hojo* (abbot's residence) in a temple complex, where they serve as settings for meditation.

Dry gardens entered the Japanese design palette in the late 15th century, during the Muromachi era, associated with the rise of Zen Buddhism in Japan. Zen is a form of Buddhism in which one attains personal enlightenment through direct personal experience, rather than through the study of religious texts, meditation being the principal way to gain appropriate reflective experience. Dry gardens provide a calming setting without distractions on which to look during meditation. Like almost all Japanese gardens, designs for dry gardens are based on abstracted, diminutive versions of the landscape of the island nation.

Daisen-in was begun in 1513 by the temple's first abbot, Kogaku Soko (also known as Shuko or Kogaku-Zenji), who is credited as the designer. The dry garden at Daisen-in differs in design from better-known examples, such as Ryoan-ji or Entsu-ji, because the garden itself wraps completely around the *hojo*, rather than just being a single court off one side of the building. One must physically or visually move around three sides of the building to fully view and interpret the design. The garden's principal visual focus is located at its northeast corner, where a composition of rocks, plants, and gravel emphasizes the visual and symbolic starting point of the garden. From there, the design moves out in two directions, toward west and south, in courtyards encircling the *hojo*. The south garden is generally considered to be the principal meditative view. Compared with other Japanese dry gardens, Daisen-in is visually complex. It contains multiple plant species and numerous rocks of various scales, and the gravel has several patterns ranging from free-falling to raked lines. In addition, a panel with a bell-shaped window separates the garden into two quite distinct parts, although this separation is less dramatic when viewed on end from within parts of the *hojo* than when seen obliquely from the adjacent porch.

Although dry gardens are intended to have multiple meanings as interpreted by the viewer, one agreed-upon interpretation of the symbolism has developed at Daisen-in. The miniaturized landscape scenes depicted in the garden have been interpreted to illustrate the course of a waterway as it progresses from wild mountain streams to the still inlet and channel waters surrounding islands. This depiction was, of course, based on landscapes familiar in Japan. More interestingly, the symbolic intent of this miniaturization has been interpreted as the story of a human journey through life from the early years as an energetic youth (represented by the mountain stream) through the more settled middle years (represented by bays and protected waters) to the eventual slowing and end of life (represented by the expansive, cosmos-like open ocean). In this scheme rocks represent both the impediments and challenges found in life, as well as the vehicles to overcoming them. One rock whose form looks much like that of a boat is particularly suggestive of this life-journey symbolism.

The garden's details carry out the beauty of this symbolic representation. Plants, including pines shaped into ideal forms, clipped camellias, and nandina, represent a variety of landscape zones from cool mountains to humid southern coasts. Likewise, stones depict the variety of rocky scenery found in nature, from massive plateau-topped boulders to slender striated pinnacles. As in other gardens throughout Japan, such as Ryoan-ji and Gingkaku-ji, stones were chosen for their mass and outline form, making the local granite an ideal design material. With its modulated color and uniform texture, gravel provides a unifying element to the design, but it too is treated in different ways. To depict wild mountain streams, the gravel is left unorganized; as it moves into lakes and lowlands, raked wavelike patterns are used; and upon reaching the "ocean" the pattern is one of broad curves. This subtlety of detail creates an infinite number of viewing experiences within the small space of this marvelous *kare-san-sui*.

The visceral experience of dry gardens is highly individual. In addition, culture and education influence appreciation, so that people from the West may have a different experience at a dry garden than those from Japan. Nonetheless, comparisons can be made between the dry gardens. From historical descriptions, Daisen-in appears to follow one of the earliest models for dry gardens in that it is composed with both plants and inorganic materials. In this, as well as its easily interpreted story line, it differs from its more famous contemporary Ryoan-ji, which is composed solely of 15 boulders set against a background of raked gravel. Daisen-in also differs from some later dry gardens in that it does not make use of "captured scenery" (landscape views outside the garden itself), the design approach used at Entsu-ji. There, scrub hedges and pine trees with their lower branches removed frame a view to Mount Hiei, the tallest mountain close to Kyoto. In contrast to other dry gardens, such as Saiho-ji or Honen-in, where moss, a plant so typical of Kyoto, is the dominant ground cover, the design at Daisen-in uses a variety of organic and inorganic materials to create a richly patterned ground plain. Despite the quality of these and other exceptional dry gardens, Daisen-in remains one of the most treasured and visited in all of Japan.

## Synopsis

| | |
|---|---|
| 1319 | Daitoku-ji founded |
| 1509 | Daisen-in subtemple founded |
| 1513 | Dry garden begun |
| ca. 1950 | Temple restored |
| 1961 | Bell-shaped window constructed or reconstructed |

## Further Reading

Bring, Mitchell, and Josse Wayembergh, *Japanese Gardens: Design and Meaning*, New York: McGraw-Hill, 1981

Harada, Jiro, *Japanese Gardens*, Boston: Branford, and London: The Studio, 1956

Keane, Marc Peter, *Japanese Garden Design*, Rutland, Vermont: C.E. Tuttle, 1996

Kuck, Lorraine E., *The World of the Japanese Garden: From Chinese Origins to Modern Landscape Art*, New York: Walker/Weatherhill, 1968

Mizuno, Katsuhiko, *Meitei; Masterpieces of Garden Art in Kyoto* (bilingual Japanese-English edition), 5 vols., Kyoto: Kyoto Shoin, 1991–92

Pregill, Philip, and Nancy Volkman, *Landscapes in History: Design and Planning in the Western Tradition*, New York: Van Nostrand Reinhold, 1993; 2nd edition, as *Landscapes in History: Design and Planning in the Eastern and Western Traditions*, New York and Chichester, West Sussex: Wiley, 1999

Slawson, David A., and Zoen, *Secret Teachings in the Art of Japanese Gardens: Design Principles, Aesthetic Values*, Tokyo and New York: Kodansha, 1987

NANCY VOLKMAN

# Darwin, Charles Robert 1809–1882 and Down House

## English Naturalist
## Downe, near Bromley, Kent, United Kingdom

**Location:**   16 miles (25.8 km) south-southeast of central London

Charles Darwin is too well known to require a detailed biography. He was born on 12 February 1809 at The Mount, Shrewsbury, Shropshire. In 1825 he enrolled at the University of Edinburgh to study medicine but left in April 1827 without completing his studies. With the intention of becoming an Anglican clergyman, Darwin entered Christ's College, Cambridge, in October 1827, but again he did not graduate. At Cambridge he took up the study of natural history, especially botany, and became a close friend of the Reverend J.S. Henslow, professor of botany. It was Henslow who encouraged Darwin's natural history studies and who persuaded Darwin to think about traveling, to explore unknown regions, and to accept the commission to join Captain Robert FitzRoy on a voyage to survey the coast of South America. The now famous voyage of the HMS *Beagle*, which lasted from 4 November 1831 until 2 October 1836, not only provided Darwin with the opportunity to study the geology of South America and to collect natural history specimens but also provoked him to consider the origin of species.

On returning to England Darwin set about writing up his *Beagle* journal and studying his specimens. He lived sometimes at Shrewsbury but also frequently went to London, where he stayed with his brother. On 29 January 1839 Charles married Emma Wedgwood, and they set up home in Upper Gower Street, London, a few hundred yards from Regent's Park. Dogged by illness, Darwin disliked London but needed to be near the city so that he could pursue his research. He was financially independent and did not need to have a full-time, salaried position, so the idea of moving into the countryside near London was appealing.

The Darwins purchased Down House, a former parsonage, in the summer of 1842. It was in a quiet, rural village in Kent, 16 miles (25.8 km) from central London. The house itself was plain, "square and unpretending," in a rather exposed position on the top of a ridge. There were some stunted, old trees beside the house, but they gave no shelter. A small holding, comprising a hay field of 15 acres (6 ha), was attached. Down House and its garden were in no way distinguished, but in terms of garden history they are of outstanding significance because of the work that Darwin, undoubtedly one of the world's greatest naturalists, did there. It was at Down that he wrote his most important and famous book, *On the Origin of Species by Means of Natural Selection* (1859), as well as almost all his other books.

Down House was Darwin's place of retreat, where he could work and think without being distracted. He desired absolute seclusion, without passers-by peering in. The kitchen garden was bordered by a high wall along its northern boundary. In 1846 Darwin rented an additional one-and-a-half acre (0.7 ha) strip of land, which he replanted with trees and shrubs, and established his Sandwalk, a path one-quarter of a mile (0.4 km) long, where he habitually walked at midday.

During the winter of 1862–63, Darwin had a hothouse built, which was stocked with exotic plants, including orchids, from the Royal Botanic Gardens,

DOWN HOUSE, FROM THE GARDEN.

Charles Darwin's Down House, from the garden, ca. 1880s
Copyright North Wind Picture Archives

Kew. He had begun studying the pollination of orchids some time earlier. His book *On the Various Contrivances by Which Orchids Are Fertilised by Insects* was first published in May 1862 before the hothouse was finished. So it was at Down House that Darwin experimented and observed and wrote up his results. He tested the capacity of sea water to kill the seeds of kitchen garden plants, among them lettuce, cress, and carrots. He and his children tracked the flights of humble-bees, discovering that they stayed on a fixed track year after year. He was puzzled why flowers of plants belonging to the same species sometimes had quite different structures. He wondered how climbing plants climbed and how the parts of some plants moved. He cultivated numerous plants, indoors and outdoors, in order to investigate these mysteries. And last, it was at Down House that he experimented with and observed earthworms, the subject of his last book, *The Formation of Vegetable Mould through the Actions of Worms* (1881).

Darwin "died, as he had lived [since 1842] in the quiet retirement of the country home which he loved; and the sylvan scenes amidst which he found the simple flowers and animals that enabled him to solve the great enigma of the Origin of Species" (*The Standard*, 22 April 1882). His wish was to be buried in St. Mary's churchyard at Downe, beside his children who had predeceased him, in the shadow of an ancient yew, but he was interred instead in Westminster Abbey on 26 April 1882.

In 1999 Down House and its environs were nominated to the United Nations Educational, Scientific, and Cultural Organization by the United Kingdom as a site deserving World Heritage Status.

## Biography
Born in Shrewsbury, Shropshire, England, 1809. Studied at University of Edinburgh, 1825–27 and at University of Cambridge, 1827–31; sailed on HMS *Beagle*, November 1831; returned to England, October 1836; married Emma Wedgewood, February 1839; purchased Down House, July 1842, and lived there from September 1842 until his death; rented additional land, replanted it, and established Sandwalk (for his daily walk of .25 mile), 1846; hothouse built for exotic plants from the Royal Botanic Gardens, Kew, 1862–63. Died at Down House, Downe, Kent, England, 1882.

## Selected Publications
*On the Origin of Species by Means of Natural Selection*, 1859

*On the Various Contrivances by which British and Foreign Orchids Are Fertilised by Insects*, 1862; 2nd edition, as *The Various Contrivances by which Orchids Are Fertilised by Insects*, 1877
*Movements and Habits of Climbing Plants*, 1865
*Variation of Animals and Plants under Domestication*, 1868
*Insectivorous Plants*, 1875
*Effects of Cross and Self Fertilisation in the Vegetable Kingdom*, 1876
*Different Forms of Flowers on Plants of the Same Species*, 1877
*Power of Movement in Plants*, 1880
*Formation of Vegetable Mould through the Actions of Worms, with Observations on Their Habits*, 1881

## Further Reading
Allan, Mea, *Darwin and His Flowers: The Key to Natural Selection*, New York: Taplinger, and London: Faber, 1977
Burkhardt, Frederick, and Sydney Smith, editors, *The Correspondence of Charles Darwin*, 10 vols., Cambridge and New York: Cambridge University Press, 1983–97
Desmond, Adrian J., and James Richard Moore, *Darwin*, New York: Viking Penguin, and London: Joseph, 1991

E. CHARLES NELSON

# De Caus Family

## French Engineers and Architects

If one compares the lives and works of the two de Caus brothers, Salomon and Isaac, it has to be noted that Salomon was the more original whereas his younger brother holds a more derivative position. It is an accident of history that there survives an example of a magnificent grotto of Isaac and not of Salomon: Isaac's famous grotto at Woburn Abbey in Bedfordshire, built for Lucy Harington, countess of Bedford, around 1625, is perhaps the best example for the reception of the grotto marvels at Pratolino that survive in England, surpassed only by the "water scherzos" at the Villa Suburbana, Hellbrunn (near Salzburg, Austria).

Salomon de Caus was a man of many interests—an architect, engineer, artist, and theorist in both art and music. The most creative period of Salomon de Caus's life was spent in the service of the elector palatine Friedrich V. De Caus's *Hortus Palatinus* (1620) was the outcome of his activities as an engineer and garden architect in the pleasure garden at Heidelberg. A book typical of the mannerist period, it is the first printed description in the German language of an important aristocratic garden. It is known that Rubens held this fascinating work in high esteem. *Hortus Palatinus* is the only publication that documents Salomon de Caus's skill in the art of gardening.

Already in 1615 de Caus had published an influential treatise, *Les raisons des forces mouvantes*, consisting of three books: on hydraulics, on fountains and grottoes, and on the fabrication of water organs. In the second book, entitled *Livre second ov sont desseignées plusieurs Grotes et Fontaines propres pour l'ornement des palais maisons de plaisances et Jardins,* one plate depicts four Italianate garden squares with quite simple patterns of lawn segments. The design of this plate clearly goes back to the author's journey to Italy from 1595 to 1598. The majority of the illustrations of this treatise show inventions for grottoes, artificial mountains, and gigantic sculptured figures, one of which has a small grotto in its head—a typical mannerist invention that de Caus had seen at Villa Pratolino (north of Florence, where it still can be visited today).

About a dozen of the designs for moving figures and automatic organs of the *Livre premier* of the *Les raisons des forces mouvantes* are derived from Heron of Alexandria's *Pneumatica,* dating from the first century (a translation was published by Giovanni Aleotti in 1589). A group of de Caus's grotto inventions, part of the *Livre second,* can be associated with the English projects of de Caus, executed for members of the royal family between 1610 and 1612.

Unfortunately, no overall garden plans of Salomon de Caus survive, with the exception of one published in 1612 in a rare handbook entitled *Perspective,* written for his drawing lessons for Princess Elizabeth, daughter of King James I of England. This design, probably for Richmond Park, is quite conventional with its unsophisticated square, accentuated by a fountain in the middle of the cross of paths. For Anne, queen of Denmark, de Caus built a parnass at Somerset House in Greenwich, showing a fountain and a grotto with integrated *volière* (aviary), and again a fountain for Robert Cecil at Hatfield House. He is also said to have built a gallery for paintings at Richmond House for the young prince of Wales and the south facade of Wilton House (altered). (The so-called English wing of Heidelberg Castle is no longer attributed to de Caus but to Jakob Wolff the Younger.)

Most of Salomon de Caus's engraved designs for representative grottoes show a contrast between a simple facade and a splendid interior, accentuated by several water basins in front of rusticated wall niches. As a main attraction there is usually either a group of automatically moving figures or a ball, pushed up by a fountain. Only one original drawing is known to survive that can be attributed to de Caus, showing the grotto of the pleasure garden at Stuttgart. Heinrich Schickhardt has mentioned de Caus in the context of a grotto at Brussels, but it was probably not built at all.

The three-story building at the eastern end of the Heidelberg pleasure garden also was never built. The Thirty Years' War (1618–48) prohibited the execution of this building, probably conceived as a *Wunderkammer* and offering a general view of the garden with cas-

From Salomon de Caus, *Von gewattsamen Bewegungen: Beschreibungen etlicher, so wol nüzlichen als lustigen Machiner,* 1615 Courtesy of G. Gröning and J. Wolschke-Bulmahn

tle, the town, and the Rhine valley. It is a matter of speculation whether all of the grottoes with hydraulic automatons that de Caus presented in *Hortus Palatinus* were built.

Salomon de Caus had a reputation both as music theorist and as inventor of all kinds of machines, which worked by the pressure of water, the heating of air, or both together; his work also cannot be overlooked as a forerunner in the history of the locomotive. His masterwork was the water organ at the Hortus Palatinus: music meant to emulate ancient Greek music was played to accompany the bathers in a warm-water pool.

Together with his brother Salomon, Isaac de Caus shared the profound knowledge of hydraulics; he also was skilled in designing grottoes, hydraulic machines, and sculptures. Isaac de Caus's name appears in the Royal Works Accounts for the first time for the years 1623/24, for creating "a Rocke in the vaulte under the banquetting house," which is one of the most revolutionary Palladian buildings by Inigo Jones; some years later Isaac is said to have worked with his brother Salomon at Corhambury (for Sir Francis Bacon) and Camden House near Kensington. The Italian-shaped Moor Park (Hertfordshire), according to Sir Roy Strong, was probably planned by Isaac as it made extensive use of grottoes, fountains, and hydraulics.

Isaac de Caus's most important work, without any doubt, was the garden planning for Wilton House (Wiltshire) during the 1630s, which "combines in one experience the layout of villas of the Brenta with the grotto marvels of Pratolino, the disposition and details of the traditions of Henry IV's St. Germain-en-Laye and Marie de' Medici's Palais du Luxembourg with the museum garden of the Roman aristocracy" (Strong). In the magnificent book *Hortus Pembrochianus* (ca. 1645) Isaac de Caus documents the alterations done for the earl of Pembroke, which, among other things, show a surprisingly modern variation of the knot parterre. Of this pleasure garden nothing remains except the carved facade of the grotto (now a garden house).

Isaac de Caus wrote a treatise entitled *New and Rare Inventions of Waterworks* (1659; first published in 1644 in Paris as *Nouvelle Invention de lever l'eau*), which is nothing more than a selective translation of his brother's *Les Raisons des forces mouvantes* (1615); in contrast to Salomon's book, *New and Rare Inventions* does not describe water organs or musical problems in detail. Like Salomon, Isaac, too, returned to France at some unknown date, but certainly not before the outbreak of the civil war in 1642.

## De Caus, Salomon 1576–1626
### French Architect, Hydrologist, Artist, and Art Theorist

### Biography
Born in Dieppe, France, 1576. Moved to England with his parents and brother Isaac because of religious unrest in France, 1590; journey through Italy, 1595–98; in service of Archduke Albrecht of Habsburg at Brüssel and worked under the architect Henri Meerte, 1606; returned to England, 1610; until spring 1613, worked as engineer and architect at Richmond for Henry, Prince of Wales; publication of his first book, 1612; in service of Queen Anne at Somerset House (parnass), at Greenwich (fountains) and other places; in service of the Elector Palatine, Friedrich V at Heidelberg Castle, 1614; until autumn 1619, architect, engineer, and supervisor of works at the Pleasure Garden at Heidelberg; in correspondence with the town council of Rouen, France, 1618 (worked on designs for a bridge over the river Seine); remained at Heidelberg even when the elector left for Prague to become king of Bohemia, October 1619; departure from Heidelberg for Paris, where he became supervisor of streets, squares, and fountains in the service of Louis XIII, 1620. Died in Normandy, 18 February 1626.

### Selected Publications
*La perspective, avec la raison des ombres et miroirs,* 1612
*Institution harmonique,* 1615
*Les raisons des forces mouvantes,* 1615
*Hortus Palatinus,* 1620
*La pratique et démonstration des horloges solaires,* 1624

## De Caus, Isaac 1590–1648
### French Architect and Garden Designer

### Biography
Born in Dieppe, France, 1590. With parents and elder brother Salomon, fled to England because of religious unrest in France; in service of Royal family at Whitehall (Banqueting House), 1623–24; architect of surviving grotto at Woburn Abbey, ca. 1625; worked for other aristocrats, perhaps for Lucy Harington at Moor Park (Hertfordshire) and Covent Garden (London); designer and surveyor of new garden project at Wilton House for the Earl of Pembroke, 1632–38; designed a house including part of the garden at Stalbridge Park, Dorset, for Richard Boyle, First Earl of Cork, 1638; outbreak of Civil War, 1642; De Caus left England for France, ca. 1640s. Died in Paris, 22 February 1648.

### Selected Publications
*Nouvelle invention de lever l'eau,* 1644
*Hortus Pembrochianus,* ca. 1645
*New and Rare Inventions of Waterworks,* 1659

### Further Reading
Maks, Christina Sandrina, *Salomon de Caus, 1576–1626,* Paris: Imprimerie Jouve, 1935
Patterson, Richard, "The 'Hortus Palatinus' at Heidelberg and the Reformation of the World," *Journal of Garden History* 1 (1981)
Strong, Roy C., *The Renaissance Garden in England,* London: Thames and Hudson, 1979
Whalley, Robin, and Anne Jennings, *Knot Gardens and Parterres: A History of the Knot Garden and How to Make One Today,* London: Barn Elms, 1998
Zimmermann, Reinhard, *Kommentar* (on de Caus's *Hortus Palatinus*), Worms, Germany: Werner'sche Verlagsgesellschaft, 1986

THOMAS SCHELIGA

# Denmark

Danish landscape and garden history has evolved within a rather undramatic natural setting. The configuration of the ground having been formed by the big glacier movements of the last ice age, Denmark boasts no significant ridges, everywhere the sea is nearby, and the flora benefits from the predominantly mild insular climate. From a historical and political viewpoint, Denmark is an integral part of the Nordic community, yet geographically it is more closely related to the rest of the European continent. Geographically favorable for encounters, travels, and other kinds of exchange, these circumstances form an important backdrop for Denmark's horticultural tradition, which largely harmonizes with that of its southernmost neighbors.

Archaeological findings testify to onions, beans, and cabbage having been cultivated in the region around 4,000 B.C. However, it was not until the Middle Ages that a proper horticulture came into being. In this, the monasteries played a crucial role, with friars from the south serving as specialists. Religious considerations were decisive for the selection of certain plants and gave preference to a cruciform garden layout, with the monastery well placed in the center. Medicinal herbs, vegetables, and fruits were emphasized, but aesthetic aspects were not neglected. Noteworthy is the widespread cultivation of hops instead of grapes. Gradually this practice spread out to castles and towns, and royal ordinances repeatedly encouraged the layout of orchards and hops gardens. Following the Reformation, in 1536 the monasteries devolved upon the Crown. From then on, metaphysical values did not have any appreciable impact on Danish garden design.

German and French patterns played an important role in the development of the Renaissance garden in Denmark (Koldinghus, 1562). As far as practical gardening was concerned, Dutch manpower was at a premium. Owing to these continuous foreign contacts, Danish gardeners succeeded in keeping pace with European standards, as far as plants were concerned, whereas a certain conservatism manifested itself in the continued use of square beds planted with utility as well as ornamental plants and bordered by low planks or hedges. The earliest Danish garden plan dates from 1649 and shows the Royal Garden of Rosenborg in Copenhagen. Begun in 1606, this garden boasted 1,400 species, including vegetables, herbs, and fruit trees, all planted in square modules. In 1647 the gardener to Lundehave (Kronborg), H. Raszmussøn Block, published the first Danish garden treatise, *Horticultura Danica* (Horticulture of Denmark). The astronomer Tycho Brahe's garden at Uranienborg (1580s) has recently been restored.

The introduction of absolute monarchy in 1660 formed, as it had previously in France, the ideological setting for the successful application of baroque garden doctrines. The first attempt to apply the planting patterns and the spatial scheme as laid down by André Le Nôtre has survived in the plans for Queen Sophie Amalie's garden (1667–85). A visual and axial relationship was established between palace and garden, and pools, bosquets, and avenues were incorporated. Chantilly served as the immediate model for the *parterre de broderie*. Kindred, though less opulent, projects were also carried out by the nobility (Nysø, 1680s). Bosquets, as well as alleys reaching far out into the surrounding farmland, were particularly favored. Traces of such alleys remain clearly detectable in today's landscape (Bregentved, 1747–70s). At Clausholm a unique Italianate terrace garden was constructed in the 1690s. The zenith of baroque garden design in Denmark was reached by J.C. Krieger (1683–1755) in the gardens of Frederiksberg, Frederiksborg, Fredensborg, and Ledreborg.

As the ideals of the English landscape garden gained ground on the Continent, Danish garden patrons also sought to comply with the new teachings. This development was accompanied by large-scale forestry and agrarian reforms, and the landscape was thereby gradually furnished with the neat geometric pattern that still characterizes it today. In the spirit of the Enlightenment, the Royal Danish Agricultural Society advocated unaffected aesthetics and rational horticulture. The French *jardin anglo-chinois* proved a favorite model (Dronninggaard, 1781–86), but often a distinct sentimental touch was added to the botanical and architectural tableaux (Liselund, 1791–1800). Such models thrived particularly in Germany. The North-German duchies forming part of the Danish monarchy, German culture was a conspicuous element of Danish society of the time. Numerous German garden terms were assimilated, and professionals frequently crossed the frontiers. The work and writings of C.C.L. Hirschfeld, professor at the university in Kiel, are exemplary of this Danish-German intertwining.

In the course of the 19th century, the landscape garden ideals were interpreted on a variety of scales. The remarkable remodeling of extensive royal forest grounds at Jaegersborg and Fredensborg into wide plains planted with beech coulisses took place in the 1850s (R. Rothe, 1802–77). In response to new social conventions, the city park genre prospered, as it did abroad (Odense, 1865–75). On softly undulating grass-grown grounds, deciduous clumps made the scenes continuously shift, and winding paths guided the walkers to exotic solitaires or big, flowering shrubs. Still waters became a standard motif and, as in the fairy tale, white

Dolmen, Søndermarken, print by Elias Meyer
Courtesy of Royal Library, Copenhagen, Department of Maps, Prints, and Photographs

swans completed the scenery. H.A. Flindt (1822–1901) was one of the most prolific garden designers of the time, working all over the country and mastering several genres (København Botanisk Have). E. Glaesel (1858–1915) should be mentioned for his expansion and remodeling dozens of country house gardens, whereas E. Erstad-Jørgensen (1871–1945) excelled in the layout of large villa gardens with monumental solitaires and a wealth of bedding plants.

A more formal design again asserted itself in the gardens of the early 20th century. The trends of British and German turn-of-the-century aesthetics and, slightly later, German Bauhaus came to the fore. In the projects realized by G.N. Brandt (1878–1945), neoclassicism went hand in hand with a distinct sense of using plants, even within minor layouts, to create a sequence of interesting garden spaces. The design works by the following generation gave rise to the label "the Golden Age" of

Danish garden design. Its foremost representatives were C.Th. Sørensen, G. Boye, and E. Langkilde.

Since the 1950s, the tasks confided to landscape and garden planners have continued to outdistance earlier practices. The Nørgård couple, S. Hansen, A. Bruun, and J. Aagaard-Andersen have made substantial contributions at a time when apartment blocks, schools, sporting grounds, cemeteries, allotment gardens, factories, and motorways entered the designers' field. A marked simplicity, sturdiness, rationality, and unpretentiousness have remained at a premium since the rise of functionalism. To this can be added a distinctly poetic aspect in the landscape designs of S.-I. Andersson. Concurrently with the aesthetic solutions having become more and more disparate, a pronounced ecological awareness is bringing moral and symbolical values back into the field. Within the past few decades, several Danish landscape architects have created large-scale projects abroad.

*See also* Frederiksberg; København Botanisk Have; Liselund; Tivoli

**Further Reading**

Andersson, Sven-Ingvar, *Havekunst i Danmark; Landscape Art in Denmark; Gartenkunst in Dänemark* (trilingual Danish-English-German edition), Copenhagen: Arkitektens, 1990

Bruun, Svend, et al., *Danmarks Havebrug og Gartneri til Aaret 1919,* Copenhagen: Gyldendal, 1920

Christensen, Annie, *Haverne dengang,* Copenhagen: Rhodos, 2000

Elling, Christian, *Den romantiske Have,* Copenhagen: Gyldendal, 1979

*Landskab: Tidsskrift for planlaegning af have og landskab; Review for Garden and Landscape Planning* (1981– ) (with summaries in English)

Lange, Johan, *Kulturplanternes indførselhistorie i Danmark,* Frederiksberg: DSR, 1999

Lange, Johan, Hans Mathiesen, and Finn Sørensen, editors, *Fra kvangård til humlekule,* Frederiksberg, Denmark: Havebrugshistorisk Selskab, 1987–

Lund, Annemarie, *Guide til dansk havekunst år 1000–2000,* Copenhagen: Arkitektens, 2000; earlier edition as *Guide to Danish Landscape Architecture, 1000–1996,* translated by Martha Gaber Abrahamsen, Copenhagen: Arkitektens, 1997

Lund, Hakon, *De kongelige lysthaver,* Copenhagen: Gyldendal, 1977

MARGRETHE FLORYAN

# Derby Arboretum

## City of Derby, England

**Location:** about 1.2 miles (2 km) from city center, south of Osmaston Road (A514)

Derby Arboretum has immense historical importance in the development of public parks. Initially offering free entry two days per week, it was the forerunner of England's public parks movement. The site was presented to the town of Derby by Joseph Strutt, who also commissioned J.C. Loudon to prepare the design for its construction. Essentially a level site, it had no external views "worthy of being taken"; therefore, the ground plan had to create its own vistas internally. Mounds of earth were introduced into the scheme to prevent visitors from seeing too much of the arboretum from any single point. Loudon included two main walks, one running north to south and another forming a cross axis running east to west. Subsidiary serpentine walks were created on the periphery to provide further interest.

Two matching Italianate pavilions were provided, one at each end of the cross axis, by the architect E.B. Lamb, with a fountain by Handyside at the crossing point. At the northern end of the main axis was the original entrance lodge and gates, also by Lamb. Apart from the replacement of the western pavilion by a reading room in the 1940s, these structures still survive today. Other slightly later buildings that can still be seen are the Rosehill Lodge by Lamb and the Arboretum Square Lodge by Dewsbury.

To sustain interest, Loudon decided that an arboretum was most appropriate; therefore, a collection of over 1,100 different hardy trees and shrubs was included in the design, which utilized his gardenesque style of planting. Because part of the philosophy behind the construction of the arboretum was to encourage public education, botanical information and geographical origins were provided for every plant in the collection. Loudon further instructed that no tree or shrub should be duplicated, and all should be removed if and when they outgrew their space. A list of the plants together with a set of his *Arboretum et Fruticetum Britannicum* (1838; The Trees and Shrubs of Britain) were kept on site for interested visitors to refer to.

The Anderson and Glenn survey of the Derby Arboretum, commissioned by Derby City Council and conducted in 1996, found that it contained 268 mature trees, of which nearly half were London planes (*Platinus × hispanica*) or limes (*Tilia × euchlora* and *T. petiolaris*). Photographic evidence held in the city archives indicates that these two dominant groups were introduced early

in the life of the park, thus quickly eroding Loudon's important concept of horticultural variety within the original plantings. This botanical reduction has made as important a contribution to the substantial drift from the principles clearly laid out by the designer as has the destruction of some historic boundary treatments and buildings. Indeed, comparison of the 1996 survey with Loudon's tree list of 1840 indicate that only about 11 percent of the trees correspond to or are likely to be plantings contemporary with the opening of the park. Most of these occur within two distinct areas of concentration. One, in the southeastern part, contains the likely remains of Loudon's original collection of oaks, namely, *Quercus rubra*, *Q. robur*, *Q. petraea*, *Q. cerris*, and *Q. frainetto*. Adjacent to these is a fine *Pyrus communis* that also appears on the plan of 1840. The other area is to the northeast of the site and contains mature specimens of *Morus nigra*, *Pterocarya fraxinifolia*, *Juglans nigra*, *Corylus colurna*, *Liriodendron tulifera*, and *Castanea sativa*. Scattered about the other areas are likely contemporary plantings that include an old *Magnolia accuminata*.

In 1845, two years after the death of Loudon, the arboretum was enlarged by the purchase of a further two-and-a-quarter hectares (5.6 acres). In the conveyance document it was the stated intention that this land was to be for similar purposes as the original site of 1840. There was, however, no longer the genius of the original designer available, and the resultant lime avenues on the three new boundaries fell quite short of the brilliant innovation Loudon had brought to the park. This part is now used for games, together with a further small extension that acts as a play area.

The land around the arboretum was rapidly developed in the 19th century, and the site became enclosed by housing. Postwar housing clearance and development of open-plan public housing in the 1960s and 1970s at the northern end of the site have encroached upon the setting of the arboretum, in particular Grove Street Lodge, where entrance gates and railings have been removed. These changes, together with the removal and disuse of some of the buildings and the overpowering scale of the mature London planes and limes, means that the Derby Arboretum has changed substantially from Loudon's initial concepts, comparison of which is possible because of the detailed account he recorded of his design philosophy in the 1840 volume of his *Gardener's Magazine*. Despite these horticultural and boundary changes, the footprint of the 1840

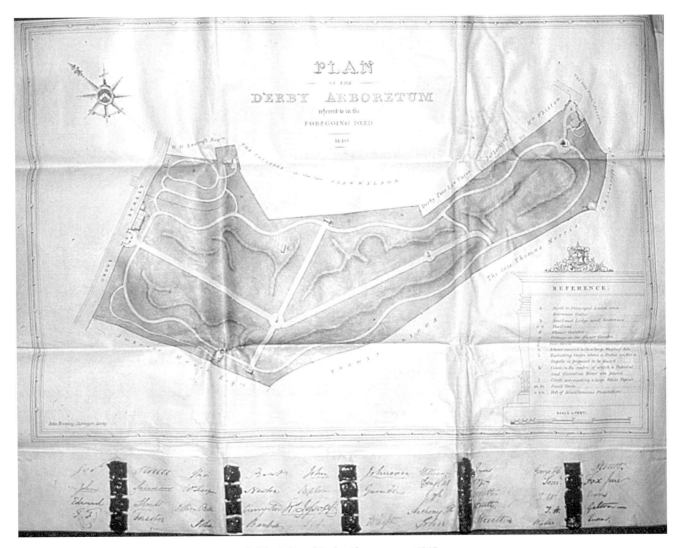

Original plan of Derby Aboretum, ca. 1840
Photo by John Glenn, copyright Anderson and Glenn

plan is substantially intact, and the majority of the original mounds remain, albeit lower than shown in the Loudon plan. This gives the arboretum immense historical status as a rare survival of Loudon's executed work.

**Synopsis**

1839    Philanthropist Joseph Strutt provides finance for the project and commissions J.C. Loudon to design it

1840    Derby Arboretum opened to the public and becomes property of Borough of Derby by deed of settlement

1846    Additional 2.25 hectares (5.6 acres) of land, adjacent to south western side of arboretum, purchased to extend park, to which a further entrance lodge by architect E.B. Lamb was added

1850    New entrance lodge and orangery designed by Henry Dewsbury added to eastern boundary, complete with statue of Joseph Strutt

1881    Elimination of admission fee, making all days free to the public

1892    Arboretum extended further to south and west; bandstand constructed on 1845 extension

1936    Concert stand (destroyed by fire, 1995) erected in northern sector of park, necessitating removal of small percentage of original mounds

1940–45    Arboretum mounds used for building air-raid shelters and for food production during the "Dig for Victory" campaign

1970s    1840 northern boundary wall, railings, and gates destroyed during open plan housing development of Grove Street

1980s   Old frame-yard area to west of site added to arboretum

1996   Derby City Council appoints Glenn Anderson Associates to prepare restoration proposals for arboretum

1998   Heritage Lottery Fund makes an offer of substantial funding for restoration of park

**Further Reading**

Loudon, John Claudius, "The Derby Arboretum, and Probable Influence of Mr. Strutt's Example; with Some Remarks on the Advantages that Would Result from Uniting Horticulture with Botany in Public Gardens," *Gardener's Magazine and Register of Rural and Domestic Improvement,* 16 (1840)

Loudon, John Claudius, *The Derby Arboretum: Containing a Catalogue of the Trees and Shrubs Included in It,* London, 1840

Simo, Melanie Louise, *Loudon and the Landscape: From Country Seat to Metropolis, 1783–1843,* New Haven, Connecticut: Yale University Press, 1988

JOHN GLENN

# Design Fundamentals

Since the earliest times, humankind has been concerned with the design layout of gardens and outdoor places for the purposes of function, pleasure, and beauty. Garden design and landscape architecture have progressed through the ages with a number of identifiable styles. French noble gardens of the 17th century, for example, possessed elements of formality and symmetrical balance. The grand style of these baroque landscape

Balance of elements through symmetrical layout, fountain detail, Missouri Botanical Garden, St. Louis, Missouri, United States
Copyright Lauri Macmillan Johnson

Contrast between plants and sky in a private garden, Buena Vista, Colorado, United States
Copyright Lauri Macmillan Johnson

expressions of power emphasize axial vistas and optical illusion in an exaggeration of depth in space. André Le Nôtre's garden layouts from this period reflect the spatial order of mathematical theorists René Descartes and Blaise Pascal. These extravagant landscapes, such as Versailles and the earlier Vaux-le-Vicomte (completed in 1661), include geometrical patterns such as radial avenues, cross axes, straight tree-lined allées, linear canals, and elaborate parterres.

In contrast, the 18th-century English Romantic style as exemplified by Lancelot "Capability" Brown's redesign of the grounds at Stowe, Buckinghamshire, England, was founded on contemporary art and literature based on the conviction of the beautiful and sublime qualities of natural conditions. These composed pastoral scenic landscapes, designed by William Kent, Brown, and Humphry Repton, consist of curved forms with irregular-shaped lakes and rolling topography. Although not ecological in approach, as works of art they inspired a movement toward asymmetrical design. William Hogarth's 1753 *The Analysis of Beauty* intro-

duced the theory that beauty is achieved through the geometry of the "serpentine line." Writers such as Alexander Pope, Joseph Addison, Richard Steele, and Richard Payne Knight as well as the Romantic painters Gaspar Poussin, Salvatore Rosa, and Claude Lorrain, promoted the beauty of natural topography and irregular forms. As a result of these efforts, a serpentine Picturesque garden style emerged. Undulating meadows, ponds, and land forms, as well as clumped trees, created the stage for these visual landscapes. Grazing cattle and architectural follies such as ha-ha walls, pagodas, Greek temples, and allegorical artifacts were used to provide areas of special interest. The French grand and English Romantic styles are representative examples of what is often described as the two basic styles of outdoor space—formal and informal.

Formal space is regarded as architectural and symmetrically balanced through mirror-image repetition along a real or implied axis; the right side of the space is the same as the left side. Formal gardens suggest human dominance over nature and are inspired by classical

Diminishing details at Longwood Gardens, Kennett Square, Pennsylvania, United States
Copyright Lauri Macmillan Johnson

Greco-Roman standards of beauty, proportion, and sci-entific reason. Examples through history include the Islamic (Moorish) paradise gardens such as the rectan-gular or square enclosed courtyards of the Alhambra, Granada, Spain. The layout is geometric and the para-dise garden or *chahar-bagh* (fourfold water garden) is symbolic of the four quarters of the universe or four riv-ers of heaven. Equilateral parts are often divided with four pathways that join at a central water fountain. Egyptian, Greek, and Roman courtyards, as well as Ital-ian Renaissance and colonial American gardens, usually displayed symmetrical balance in design. These formal garden compositions continue to inspire contemporary designers and are used with variations in modern (to a lesser extent) and postmodern interpretations as seen in the work of landscape architects such as Dan Kiley, Peter Walker, and George Hargreaves. (The pretense of modern garden design was to eliminate the reference to historical styles and to respond to the users and the con-ditions of the site as well as the theories of the modern art movement. Postmodern garden design intentionally refers to the styles of the past.)

Informal space is organic and asymmetrical; spaces have a "felt" order. The informal garden draws inspira-tion from nature through its re-creation or artistic abstraction. The traditional Japanese garden (such as Ryoanji, Kyoto, Japan [rebuilt 1488]) is a primary example; forces of nature held religious and sacred value and were represented within the garden. These highly controlled yet informal gardens are organic and balanced through occult or asymmetric approaches. The asymmetrically balanced garden (or visual compo-sition) can imply an imagined axial line in which non-identical elements of shape, color, and texture have equal play along either side of the invisible axis. Occult balance, derived from Eastern design philosophy, sug-gests order without the use of an axis. Void empty space, or negative space, as it is termed in visual art, can play an equally strong role in the balance of the compo-sition. An open meadow—the void—can be balanced by the single tree placed along the meadow's edge.

Brazilian landscape architect Roberto Burle Marx employs occult balance and modern abstract curved patterns in his landscape works of art to create dynamic

Direction in a garden pathway, Dumbarton Oaks, Washington, D.C., United States
Copyright Lauri Macmillan Johnson

. . . art is the beginning of vision. . . . One artist attempts the new understanding through color, another through form, another by new and strange uses of materials, another through pattern, or by new proportions and aspects of old familiar things. All use the principles of balance, rhythm, and harmony. . . . The results make one feel (when the works are masterpieces) that one has a new understanding . . . of movement, color, vibration, space, or what not.

**Design Theory**
Landscapes are defined by many salient qualities: the sights, sounds, and smells that have the power to evoke strong feelings and emotions. Manmade landscapes from history often reflect the "spirit of place." As René Dubos reflects:

> Like individual human beings, landscapes and civilizations display distinctive characteristics. While they change in the course of time, they retain a uniqueness derived in large part from the set of conditions under which they emerged and also from the factors which influenced their subsequent evolution. The phrases *genius loci* and *spirit of place* symbolize the forces or structures generally hidden beneath the surface of things which determine the uniqueness of each place.

The spirit of place is created through the natural conditions of the environment, aesthetic interpretation, and cultural influences. Changes in taste and style mirror the cultural conditions of the time. Therefore, theories of design in visual art, architecture, and garden design developed as a reflection of cultural context. Egyptian and Greek art and architecture were ruled by deep concern for beauty found in mathematical perfection. Proportion as determined through a ratio known as the "golden mean" was endorsed by Greek mathematician Pythagoras in the sixth century B.C. and became the standard for classical design through the Renaissance. Italian Renaissance architect Leon Battista Alberti (*De Re Aedificatoria* [1452]), and his Vitruvian theory of beauty as a harmony of all the parts, became a fundamental influence on design. Architects Sebastiano Serlio and Andrea Palladio in the 16th century also developed rules of design in architecture; these were later described in the 19th century in *Sir Banister Fletcher's A History of Architecture*, first published in 1896 (Musgrove).

The human form held fascination for design theorists as a key to unlocking the secrets of harmony in design. As summarized in Zube, Brush, and Fabos, proportional

combinations of color and texture in three-dimensional compositions. His artistic manipulation of plants, water, pavement, and so on have been compared (by others as well as himself) to an artist's application of paint on canvas: "I decided to use natural topography as a field of work as the elements of nature, mineral, and vegetable, as materials for the plastic construction, as the other artists worked on canvas with paint and brush."

Modern art and the use of occult balance inspired the work of modern garden designers and landscape architects such as Marx, Fletcher Steel, Thomas Church, Garrett Eckbo, and Lawrence Halprin. Steel's 1930 milestone article "New Pioneering in Garden Design" discusses the experimentation of the modern artist with the prospect that garden designers would follow:

A focal point or accent (distant bridge) within a garden composition, Missouri Botanical Garden, St. Louis, Missouri, United States
Copyright Lauri Macmillan Johnson

Relationship between figure (volume of room) and ground (doorways, walls, plants), Missouri Botanical Garden, St. Louis, Missouri, United States
Copyright Lauri Macmillan Johnson

A path directing movement of people through outdoor spaces and visual movement, as the viewer's eye follows the lines of the staircase, Longwood Gardens, Kennett Square, Pennsylvania, United States
Copyright Lauri Macmillan Johnson

Overlapping used to create depth and interest, Missouri Botanical Garden, St. Louis, Missouri
Copyright Lauri Macmillan Johnson

Repetition of plants for a ground plane planter, garden at Arizona Center, Phoenix, Arizona, United States
Copyright Lauri Macmillan Johnson

systems for application in the creative arts were explored by Polyclitus (fifth century B.C.), who used ideal ratios within the basic dimensions found in the human body. Leonardo Da Vinci's picture of a man enclosed in a circle depicts Vitruvius's theory of design fundamentals based on the navel as a central point and key to the perfection of human proportion. Le Corbusier's method of proportion in the 20th century (*The Modulor I* [1954]; *Modulor II* [1958]), represented by the ideal man with one arm raised, also marks the navel as a starting point in determining a set of ratios describing the golden mean.

The Bauhaus (School of Design) as directed by Walter Gropius in the 20th century incorporated theories of contemporary art in painting and what became known as the "plastic arts" (three-dimensional art) in the education of design students. The fusion of creative collaboration among allied designers (industrial design, architecture, interior design, and furniture design) was

the precedent. They abandoned Renaissance theories of perspective and three-dimensional space created through Euclidean geometry in favor of the new aesthetic of space and volume as presented through modern art. Modernism in architecture arose from the experimentation of the Cubist, Futurist, and De Stijl movements. Artists including Paul Cézanne, Georges Braque, and Pablo Picasso led the exploration of composition as movement through space and time. Garden designers inspired by the modernist movement were guided by an unprecedented set of visual design standards that encouraged "plastic" manipulation of spaces in organic and rectangular/angular occult patterns.

Contemporary garden design theories have evolved to include a range of paradigms, including sustainable or ecological design, historic and cultural preservation, and postmodern translations of past classical, Romantic, and modern styles. What follows are some of the concerns

Rhythm created by the repeated patterns in the Rose Arbor, University of Pennsylvania, United States
Copyright Lauri Macmillan Johnson

related primarily to visual aspects of design. It is also important to investigate other references describing frameworks such as design function and use and site and cultural analysis techniques, as well as economic considerations. The visual design fundamentals described here (usually termed the *principles* and *elements* of design) remain one aspect in the generation of enduring gardens.

### Landscape Spaces and Spatial Sequences

Like sculpture, gardens are three-dimensional compositions that are viewed from many angles. The deliberate placement of earth, water, sky, plants, and man-made materials serves to create outdoor rooms. Overhead structures, ground surfaces, and vertical masses are some of the features that define physical or visual boundaries within the garden. These walls of outdoor space possess texture, color, volume, size, and other qualities that fashion the essence of the garden.

Garden design is the composite arrangement of interlocking spaces and spatial sequences within a carefully articulated composition. The size and relationship of spaces, circulation pathways, and other functions are organized as a progression of visual and physical experiences. As one moves through the environment scenes unfold and sensations are felt. This succession and unfolding of scenes is similar to the art of filmmaking, as a filmmaker leads the viewer through a series of frames in order to tell a story and produce a set of controlled visual effects and related emotions. Similarly, garden designers create a medley of settings that reveal themselves as one travels through the series of outdoor spaces. These garden conditions create visual interest and excitement. The arrangement of spatial sequences within the landscape is an art form of the highest level.

The father of landscape architecture in the United States, Frederick Law Olmsted, exhibited masterful

Effect of transparency used to create depth and accents, Monmouth Battlefield State Park, Manalapan, New Jersey, United States
Copyright Lauri Macmillan Johnson

control of spatial sequencing in his 1858 design for New York City's Central Park. As described by Pregill and Volkman, "The Olmsted and Vaux plan was not simply a circulation plan. . . . It provided a carefully orchestrated sequence of spaces." Pedestrians and carriages (now automobiles) were separated both visually and physically through level changes, stone-wall placement, and beautiful plant compositions. As people walk through the picturesque Romantic landscape, strong sight lines direct views toward magnificent landscape features such as Bow Bridge or the naturalistic lake. These dramatic focal points are framed by vertical elements, predominantly plants, while undesirable views, now skyscrapers, are screened by hills planted with evergreens. The arrangement of spaces within the park, including Bethesda Terrace, the wooded natural area called the Ramble, and the open lawn or Great Meadow, as it was originally named, create a well-integrated whole landscape.

## Design Principles

Artistic principles (e.g., unity, balance, and proportion) guide the placement of elements (e.g., forms, textures, and colors) in the creation of two- and three-dimensional composition. Design principles are the organizational precepts or theories of all visual art. In garden design the assemblage of earth, water, plants, and bricks must have function, meaning, and visual attraction. The rules of composition primarily address visual aspects of design. The principles and elements presented as follows provide a vocabulary for the visual aspects of place design. As Sylvia Crowe argues in her classic book *Garden Design* (1958), "Through all the variations, due to climate, country, history and the natural idiosyncrasy of man, which have appeared in the evolution of the garden through successive civilizations, certain principles remain constant however much their application may change."

Forms abstracted from natural forms found in the High Sierra Mountains, Ira's Fountain, Portland Oregon, United States
Copyright Lauri Macmillan Johnson

Lines creating interest and suggestive of movement, Denver Botanic Gardens, Denver, Colorado, United States
Copyright Lauri Macmillan Johnson

Balance is an ordering of elements in the design. It implies stability and equilibrium. The École des Beaux-Arts tradition emphasized symmetrical layout patterns: mirror-image repetition along an axis to create indisputable balance. Radial symmetric patterns consist of identical elements placed around a central point or position. Asymmetrical or occult balance gives a sense of order without identical duplication.

Contrast implies opposition or difference within the elements of design. This can be seen in the lightness and darkness of objects. Contrasting forms, colors, shapes, and textures will enhance the visual excitement of the environment. A flowering shrub will be accented if it is placed against a wall of contrasting color. Contrast is used to create variety and visual impact.

Diminishing detail is the means of creating the appearance of depth in the visual field or garden through the variation and definition of detail. Close-appearing objects show detail clearly, whereas objects in the distance have less description or information (their form disappears into an outline). This principle can be used to exaggerate the sense of perspective by changing the size of objects to make the distance appear shorter or longer.

Direction is the relation of a shape or form to the orientation of environment. Direction suggests movement. Some forms are static (the circle) and alone do not suggest direction. A linear or triangular shape or form, on the other hand, will suggest direction. A ground-plane grid pattern (perhaps a paving pattern) placed on a diagonal may imply visual direction and movement.

Emphasis, attraction, or focal points within the garden are special areas of curiosity. These accent points will engage viewers. They are the distinctive places within the garden composition, perhaps areas that are brightly colored or that include dynamic works of art. They may

Mass planting, Parque Ecólogico Xochimilco, Xochimilco, Mexico
Copyright Lauri Macmillan Johnson

Ground planes, Denver Botanic Gardens, Denver, Colorado, United States
Copyright Lauri Macmillan Johnson

possess unusual materials or other contrasting expressions of tone, texture, or shape. They could hold symbolic meaning and provide places for contemplation. Water features have historically provided attraction in the garden.

Figure-ground relationships within a composition include a dialogue between figure—object, positive space, dominant shape—and ground; that is, the background, neutral, or contextual framework for the placement of the figure. Figure and ground work together, one reacting to the other to produce a dynamic united effect. Sometimes the figure and ground can become subordinate depending on the viewer's perception. In garden design the figure could be the open air or space, and the objects within the landscape (trees, walls, etc.) could be the background or negative space within the composition.

Movement can be objective—an actual change in the visual field or environment—or subjective—the percep-

tion of a change in position or time. In landscape design movement is a critical component that can refer to visual eye movement and circulation through the outdoor spaces. The designer will orchestrate both within the layout of the garden. Views will be directed through sight lines and framing/screening techniques. Circulation pathways involve the movement of people through a series of spaces designed for a variety of visual and physical experiences.

Overlapping is a layering of objects to create depth and visual interest. In garden design this layering is often exhibited in plant compositions. For example, large evergreen trees could be planted as the background for smaller flowering deciduous trees and shrubs. This overlapping effect creates a greater sense of depth and adds visual interest.

Proportion refers to the mathematical relationship among the real dimensions of the object or space. Often,

Vertical planes, wall in Mexico City, Mexico
Copyright Lauri Macmillan Johnson

a ratio or comparison among objects is used to describe the relationship of one object, mass, or material to another. The golden mean or golden section is a mathematical proportion used by the early Greeks. The creators of the Parthenon, for example, used this mechanism of proportional order. It was believed that key numerical relationships within the golden mean disclose the harmony of the universe. The proportion of the human body was studied through number relationships and algebraic equations of the golden mean. The golden mean was represented through a rectangle or logarithmic spiral that could grow or subdivide indefinitely with magnifications or divisions retaining the same proportional properties. These proportions are best described in the work of mathematician Leonardo of Pisa, also called Fibonacci: his treatise *Liber abaci* (1202) describes number sequences that have come to be called Fibonacci numbers. The proportions of a credit card follow these principles and provide an example of a golden rectangle.

Repetition is a pattern created by the same or similar form or object. A repetitive pattern can have radial balance or a more irregular occult progression.

Rhythm involves eye movement often marked by expected recurrence. The repetition of similar forms, colors, etc., composes visual rhythm. For example, ground-paving materials could repeat modular units according to various visual themes or patterns. Plant groupings can also appear in patterns that reflect a sense of rhythm. Rhythm relates to proportion and is understood by ratios and organic forms in nature. Visual rhythm can repeat in predictable familiar forms or be more aligned with the spontaneous nature of avant-garde music.

Scale refers to how we perceive the size of an element or space, relative to ourselves—to the dimensions and proportions of the human body (human scale). Spaces can be a wide range of sizes. For example, they could be large monumental football-field-size spaces or tiny child-size places. Landscape spaces must be designed with consideration for the scale appropriateness of the proposed activity.

Transparency is used to create depth and accent. Used in coordination with overlapping techniques, transparency can control views through the framing of vistas for enhancement or illusion. For example, tree branches or fences with openings, placed in the foreground, frame the "borrowed" landscape of the distance.

Unity is a cohesiveness that is attained when all the elements of a garden—the colors, textures, and forms—are perceived as parts of a whole harmonious system. Unity is the "glue" of design. It can be achieved through spatial layout of repeated forms or materials such as plant species as well as through other ordering devices, such as balance, rhythm, and proportion.

Variety refers to the variation and contrast within the visual composition (see Plate 11). Incorporated with unity, variety is as an essential component of design. Change in color, texture, and form can create interest within the garden. This visual excitement or liveliness is similar to dissonance in music; it is the "spice" of design. Variety in the landscape can be attained through differences such as the size of spaces, spatial sequence, plant species, and other materials. While variety creates interest, too much variation will be visually chaotic and confusing.

## Design Elements

Design elements, the building blocks of design, interact with one another in harmony or discord. The designer manipulates the elements through study sketches until final resolution or equilibrium is attained among all factors (visual, artistic, functional, ecological, and cultural).

Color is the hue or pigment of an object, the effect of light upon matter. Light rays of the spectrum fall upon a surface; that surface absorbs some rays and reflects other rays. The reflected rays are seen by the eye as color. When a color absorbs all other colors and reflects red, the color red results. Hue is the difference between color (e.g., blue versus red). Intensity or chroma corresponds to saturation and refers to the purity of hue. When the color red is pure it has full intensity. When red is mixed with a neutral color (black, white, or gray), the intensity is reduced. Tone is the perception of reflected surfaces. Value is the lightness and darkness of tones, the amount of light a surface can reflect.

Forms are the result of the total mass of an object or space. The visual properties of forms include shape, size, color, texture, and direction. Forms imply three-dimensional objects or masses. Forms can be natural and organic—informal; or they can be symmetrical and highly ordered—formal.

Light or illumination from the sun or artificial sources contributes dramatically to the feeling and experience of a place. As light moves and changes intensity during the day and throughout seasons, the visual qualities of the environment will be affected.

Lines within the garden define edges or boundaries, suggest movement, and add interest. Lines are articulated through a change in material, texture, color, or shape. For example, a line appears at the edge of a lawn. Additionally, pathways along the ground plane also appear as lines. Lines of sight are invisible lines directing or framing the views of the "borrowed" landscape of the distance.

Masses are forms that are perceived as a solid volume. In architecture and landscape architecture mass is evaluated largely by proportion, context, and scale. Plant massing is a term used to describe a grouping of plants, usually of similar species, to define and unify space as well as provide visual interest.

Planes are used to define spaces within the garden and include ground planes, vertical planes, and overhead planes. These "walls" of the landscape can be architectural structures or natural features. The plane orientations and their various combinations of treatments provide unlimited opportunities for consideration. Ground planes can be hard, paved surfaces or soft, natural materials, depending on the intended purpose. The degree of slope and topographic contour of the ground plane(s) offer additional variables with which to work. The ground plane offers designers a canvas of opportunity for expression in color, form, texture, and line with patterns of flowers, grasses, stones, tiles, paint, etc. Vertical planes are the spatial dividers and can be made of earthen forms, plant masses, solid walls, lattice or open-air structures, or single vertical elements such as trees. Variations in texture, form, color, and size must be considered. Overhead planes are the "roofs" of landscape spaces used to protect and create various degrees of enclosure. Overhead planes can be thought of as the open sky or the more tangible materials such as tree canopies, overhead trellises, and solid architectural structures.

Points are static directionless positions in space; they imply stability. Within three-dimensional space this element is best regarded as a focal point or place to where the eye is directed as a result of its unique characteristics.

Shapes imply two-dimensional patterns. Within the garden they are lines and edges of spaces. These shapes could be amorphous and natural or derivations of geometric patterns, including circles, squares, rectangles, and triangles. Shapes are manipulated and combined into patterns that begin to structure the site.

Texture refers to the surface characteristics of a form that affect both the tactile and light-reflective qualities of the surface.

Volumes of spaces are created through man-made and natural materials. The volume of an outdoor space implies the form and mass of the objects within the garden as well as the open air or the void created by these masses (vegetation, walls, etc.) Volumes of spaces within spatial sequences should change to create visual and functional variety and interest.

Texture within a desert planting to create visual interest, Arizona-Sonora Desert Museum, Tucson, Arizona, United States
Copyright Lauri Macmillan Johnson

Overhead planes, Missouri Botanical Garden, St. Louis, Missouri, United States
Copyright Lauri Macmillan Johnson

Volumes of spaces created through man-made arches, Parque Ecólogico Xochimilco, Xochimilco, Mexico
Copyright Lauri Macmillan Johnson

## Further Reading

Crowe, Sylvia, *Garden Design,* London: Country Life, 1958; New York: Hearthside Press, 1959; 3rd edition, Woodbridge, Suffolk, and Wappinger's Falls, New York: Garden Art Press, 1994

Doczi, Gyorgy, *The Power of Limits: Proportional Harmonies in Nature, Art, and Architecture,* Boston: Shambhala, 1994

Dubos, René, *A God Within,* New York: Scribner, 1972

Fletcher, Banister, *A History of Architecture for the Student, Craftsman, and Amateur: Being a Comparative View of the Historical Styles from the Earliest Period,* London and New York, 1896; 20th edition, edited by Dan Cruickshank, Oxford and Boston: Architectural Press, 1996

The Garden Conservancy, the American Society, and Longwood Gardens, *Roberto Burle Marx: Legend and Legacy,* symposium announcement, 1996

Jencks, Charles, *Post-Modernism: The New Classicism in Art and Architecture,* New York: Rizzoli, and London: Academy Editions, 1987

Le Corbusier, *Le Modulor: Essai sue une mesure harmonique a l'echelle humaine applicable universellement a l'architecture et a la mécanique,* Boulogne, France: L'Architecture d'Aujourd'hui, 1950; as *The Modulor: A Harmonious Measure to the Human Scale Universally Applicable to Architecture and Mechanics,* translated by Peter de Francia and Anna Bostock, London: Faber and Faber, and Cambridge, Massachusetts: Harvard University Press, 1954

Le Corbusier, *Modulor 2, 1955: La parole est aux usagers: Suite de "Le Modulor 1948,"* Boulogne, France: L'Architecture d'Aujourd'hui, 1955; as *Modulor 2, 1955 (Let the User Speak Next): Continuation of "The Modulor,"* translated by Peter de Francia and Anna Bostock, London: Faber and Faber, and Cambridge, Massachusetts: Harvard University Press, 1958

Pregill, Philip, and Nancy Volkman, *Landscapes in History: Design and Planning in the Western Tradition,* New York: Van Nostrand Reinhold, 1993; 2nd edition, as *Landscapes in History: Design and Planning in the Eastern and Western Traditions,* New York: Wiley, 1999

Scott, Robert Gillam, *Design Fundamentals,* New York: McGraw-Hill, 1951

Steel, Fletcher, "New Pioneering in Garden Design," *Landscape Architecture* 20, no. 3 (April 1930)

Zube, Ervin H., Robert O. Brush, and Julius Gy Fabos, editors, *Landscape Assessment: Values, Perceptions, and Resources,* Stroudsburg, Pennsylvania: Dowden Hutchinson and Ross, 1975

LAURI MACMILLAN JOHNSON

---

# de Vries, Hans Vredeman 1526–ca. 1606

## Dutch Artist, Architect, and Garden Designer

Hans Vredeman de Vries is the author of the first independent series of garden designs published in early modern Europe. Whether he should be considered a practicing garden architect as well as an architectural theorist is still unclear. He was trained in Flanders and lived for many years in Antwerp, then the most important communication center in northern Europe. At the age of 60 he had to leave for religious reasons and went to Germany. In Frankfurt he must have met an agent of Duke Julius of Brunswick-Luneburg, who was at that time looking for a capable engineer for canal and floodgate building and fortifications work as well as the construction of a new pleasure garden for his residence at Wolfenbüttel. De Vries's training as a soldier made him just the right man for these various duties.

Between 1555 and 1605 he published more than 50 series of etchings, including thousands of illustrations showing town gates, canals, and floodgates as well as all sorts of ornaments. About 500 of these engravings are architectural sketches; 28 of them are pure garden designs, and some 20 more are combined with architectural projects such as *Scenographiae* (1560), *Artis perspecitvae* (1568), *Architectura* (1577), *Variae architecturæ formae* (1601).

Around 1583 de Vries prepared his definitive series of Mannerist etchings *Hortorum viridariumque formae* (Forms of Gardens and Orchards) in Antwerp, creating the first printed Western pattern book exclusively for ornamental gardens. It is certainly no coincidence that the second edition (1587) of *Formae* was published at the same time de Vries was involved in the layout of the *Mühltorgarten* at Wolfenbüttel. From 1586 to 1590 he is known to have been in Wolfenbüttel before he had to escape from his creditors via Brunswick, Hamburg, and

Danzig to Prague. De Vries and his son Paul painted several halls inside Prague Castle for Emperor Rudolph II (destroyed during Empress Maria Theresa's reign). About this time he possibly went to Denmark for a short period. In 1601 he returned to the Netherlands. In vain he tried to get a chair at the University of Leiden and probably died embittered in about 1606.

The second edition of *Formae* gained eight engravings. These always present the gardens in axial alignment with rough representations of palatial buildings. None of the editions of *Formae* include text describing de Vries's garden inventions as became usual in the next century. Only subtitles in capital letters, such as "DORICA," "IONICA," "CORINTHIA," indicate a connection between these imaginative gardens with the classical orders. The Doric order stands for power and heroism, femininity is expressed by the Ionic order, and the Corinthian order means grandeur, purity (Vitruve), and even the state of exclusivity. While the ornamental beds of the Doric pattern are comparatively simple and clearly arranged, the Corinthian group shows exclusively miniature labyrinths of great elegance. It is confusing that these mazes, which have only a decorative function (they have no hedges), also appear within the Ionic order. More precise interpretations of the individual garden orders cannot be made convincingly.

The ornamental beds consist solely of paths and sharp-edged compartments of lawn or soil and are quite thinly planted with precious individual plants. Especially tall plants such as iris, summer lilies, and martagone are typical for the Mannerist period. The almost total absence of box trees in *Formae* is conspicuous except for in borders, broderies, and knot patterns. So there is a significant distinction between de Vries and the Franco-Italian late Renaissance garden which culminates in André Mollet's *Le Jardin de Plaisir* (Stockholm, 1651). Also, there is no reason to think of Androuet du Cerceaus's splendid volumes of *Les plus excellents bastiments de France* as models for de Vries. At best the tunnel arbors could have influenced de Vries's bizarre compositions of covered passageways which are arranged around garden courts like palatial loggias. Only a few designs for gardens included in the architectural treatise show box trees cut in spherical or oval shapes (e.g., *Artis perspectivae*, 1568). Characteristic features of the high baroque Dutch garden are foreshadowed: the miniature forms, the repeated dispersion, and the multifarious accumulation of vertical structures—things seen in the reconstructed gardens at Het Loo Palace near Apeldoorn.

The bare trunks of the thin young trees with oval shaped treetops on de Vries's engravings are strange to modern viewers. The growing tree symbolizes youth. Such trimmed, immature trees are to be found in nearly all garden books in mannerist Europe and are therefore not specific to de Vries's *Viridarium* (Orchard). The question remains if de Vries indicated in the title of the series just kitchen gardens in general, which often appear in simple forms at the side or in the background. Real tree plantations are very rare in his designs, but in his *Formae* they sadly enough appear in two of the layouts, called *Corinthia*.

De Vries probably designed a garden portico in trellis work for the great garden to the west of the Dammfeste, as the residence west of Wolfenbüttel was named for the so-called Mühltorgarten. An engraving from 1654 bears a striking resemblance to his other portico designs. It has been proved that he was in charge of saw works and potted plants at the Mühltorgarten, but it cannot be expected that de Vries was able to implement his *Formae* and *Artis perspectivae* designs at Wolfenbüttel because he was dependent on Duke Julius's strong ideas. For the pleasure garden at Hessen Castle, a Guelph subresidence, de Vries presumably designed a fountain, a painted ceiling with floral ornaments symbolizing vanity, and an altar triptych for the palace chapel. These are the only surviving large-scale commissioned art works by de Vries, except for an altar piece at Danzig. The fountain was altered later and given a larger bowl than initially intended.

De Vries's importance at the Wolfenbüttel residence can be compared with that of Salomon de Caus's for the court at Heidelberg, with the difference that de Vries was only able to contribute his advice to an already planned garden project. It still has to be proven to what extent de Vries influenced gardens of the higher nobility in Danzig and Prague, and possibly in Denmark and England. Erik de Jong's research on Hans Puechfeldner's drawings, which largely follows de Vries's compositions and details, substantiates this theory for Prague. It has even been claimed that de Vries's specific form for tunnel arbors was the model for the trelliswork at Ambras Castle in Tyrol.

It is certain that his designs inspired the so-called *parterre de pièces coupées*, which ornaments pathways without making them impassable and which was highly fashionable until the French Regency period (1715–23). This phenomenon was popular outside of the Dutch baroque garden.

On the other hand, a tendency towards spacious grandeur that was fashionable in France overtook the miniature patterns of de Vries as well as the delicate playfulness of Cerceau; André Le Nôtre's noble garden creations are evidence of this new taste. In contrast, in Germany and apparently also in Bohemia, Moravia, and Poland, generations adhered to the Dutch Mannerism as de Vries had set forth in his *Formae*. This influence was often mediated by Hans Furttenbach's less elegant pattern books (e.g., the reconstructed gardens at Idstein near Frankfurt; former Hradschin gardens in Prague, Lobzów near Cracow).

CORINTHIA

Engraving from the *Hortorum Formae,* Antwerp, ca. 1583, showing an example of a garden in the Corinthian style
Courtesy of Herzog August Bibliothek Wolfenbüttel

De Vries's influence in England seems to have been restricted to architectural ornaments, but admittedly very few significant views of English gardens from 1570 to 1630 have survived. It has not yet been analyzed whether or not the baroque *parterre anglais* can be attributed to de Vries's *Formae.* The English parterre also consists mostly of path patterns contrasting with lawn beds.

## Biography

Born in Leeuwarden, Friesland, Netherlands, 1526. Educated as glass painter by R. Gerbrant, in Leeuwaarden; studied painting with town painter of Kampen, Netherlands; under guidance of Pieter Cocke van Aelst, worked at Malines, Belgium, and Antwerp, Belgium; involvement in works of triumph porticoes for emperors Charles V and Philip II, 1549; began studies of Serlio's and Vitruvius's theories, ca. 1550; first publications in Antwerp; undertook commission for Carlo Dorici at Malines, 1561; returned to Antwerp, 1563–64; fled from duke of Alba's troops to Aix-la-Chapelle, spring of 1570, and to Liège, Belgium, 1573; two years later returned to Antwerp, became leader of fortification works, 1577; participated in Antwerp town hall competition in August 1585; after renewed victory of Catholics, left for Frankfurt; in service of Julius, duke of Brunswick-Luneburg, at Wolfenbüttel, Germany, for several years, as painter, architect,

DORICA

Engraving from the *Hortorum Formae,* Antwerp, ca. 1583, showing an example of a garden in the Doric style
Courtesy of Herzog August Bibliothek Wolfenbüttel

water-engineer, and supervisor of gardening work; may have been involved in designing new Lustgarten (pleasure garden) west of residence; in Brunswick, Germany, 1590, for some months just when Gewandhaus (cloth merchants hall) built; in Hamburg, Germany, 1591; in Danzig, 1592–95; back in Hamburg, followed Emperor Rudolph II to Prague in 1596; via Hamburg, returned to Netherlands, ca. 1600; lived at son's house in Amsterdam, ca. 1601; in Hamburg, 1604. Died in Amsterdam, Netherlands, ca. 1606.

## Selected Publications
*Scenographiae,* 1560
*Artis Perspecitvae,* 1568
*Architectura oder Bauung der Antiquen,* 1577
*Hortorum viridariorumque elegantes et multiplices formae,* 1583; 2nd edition, ca. 1587
*Variae Architecturae Formae,* 1601

## Further Reading
Fuhring, Peter, compiler, and Ger Luijten, editor, "Vredeman de Vries, Part 1, 1555–1571," and "Vredeman de Vries, Part 2, 1572–1630," *Dutch and Flemish Etchings, Engravings, and Woodcuts, 1450–1700* 47–48 (1997)
Herman, Jean, "Hans Vredeman de Vries," *Gazette des Beaux Arts* 93 (1979)

Hopper, Florence, "The Dutch Classical Garden and André Mollet," *Journal of Garden History* 2, no. 1 (1982)

Irmscher, Günter, "Hans Vredeman de Vries als Zeichnet," *Kunsthistorisches Jahrbuch Graz* 21–22 (1985–86)

MacDougall, Elisabeth B., and Naomi Miller, editors, *Fons Sapientiae: Garden Fountains in Illustrated Books, Sixteenth-Eighteenth Centuries: Catalog,* Washington, D.C.: Dumbarton Oaks Collection, 1977

*Macmillan Encyclopedia of Architects,* New York: Free Press, and London: Collier Macmillan, 1982

Mander, Carel van, *Het schilder-boeck,* Haarlem, Netherlands: Wesbvach, 1604; reprint, 2 vols., New York: Broude International, 1980

Mehrtens, Ulbe Martin, "The 'Hortorum Formae' of Johan Vredeman de Vries," in *The History of Garden Design: The Western Tradition from the Renaissance to the Present Day,* edited by Monique Mosser and

Georges Teyssot, London: Thames and Hudson, 1991

Mielke, Hans, *Hans Vredeman de Vries*, Berlin: Reuter, 1967

Mielke, Hans, et al., "Hans Vredeman de Vries," in *Fünf Architekten aus fünf Jahrhunderten* (exhib. cat.), Berlin: Gebrüder Mann, 1976

Scheliga, Thomas, "A Renaissance Garden at Wolfenbüttel, North Germany," *Garden History* 25, no. 1 (1997)

Schoy, Auguste, *Hans Vredeman de Vries*, Brussels: Hayez, 1876

Strong, Roy C., *The Renaissance Garden in England,* London: Thames and Hudson, 1979

Veen, Pieter A. Ferdinand van, "Introduction," in *Hortorum Viridariorumque Elegantes et Multiplices Formae* (1587), by Hans Vredeman de Vries, Amsterdam: Van Hoeve, 1980 (introduction in English, Dutch, and French)

Thomas Scheliga

---

# Dioscorides, Pedanius ca. 40–ca. 90

## Greek Physician

Dioscorides was born in the first half of the first century A.D. in Roman Cilicia at Anazarbus, a town by the river Pyramus on trade routes to Cappadocia and Syria. Manuscripts of his work add the name Pedanius, which probably indicates that he received Roman citizenship. He states in the dedication to his *De materia medica* that he was encouraged to study drugs by his teacher Areios of Tarsus; later authorities add that he studied also at Alexandria, but this has not been confirmed. Extensive travels took him to many parts of the Roman Empire, from possibly as far west as Spain to Egypt and Syria, and he almost certainly visited Petra, outside the empire, and may have penetrated even farther east. The later biographical statement that he was a physician to the Roman legions is probably based solely on his own statement, which could be interpreted to mean no more than that he led a soldier-like life through his travels. If he did serve in the Roman army, it is likely to have been for only a short while. He had been trained in medicine by Areios, and although it is not known to what extent he may have been in practice, he could certainly be described as the ancient equivalent of a medical researcher.

Sometime between A.D. 50 and 80, Dioscorides completed his treatise on "the preparation, properties, and testing of drugs," today usually referred to by its Latin title, *De materia medica* (On Medical Materials). Spurious tracts also exist that deal with poisons, "female herbs," and related subjects; the text *Peri Haplon Pharmakon* (*On Simple Drugs*) may be a genuine, albeit youthful, production. *De materia medica* is divided into five books, whose contents according to Dioscorides's own prefatory summaries are aromatics, oils, salves, and trees; animals and their products, pot, and "sharp" herbs; roots, juices, other herbs, and seeds; further herbs and roots; and wines and minerals. In total Dioscorides lists slightly more than 1,000 natural (approx. 700 vegetal) products for which he knows over 4,700 medical usages. His normal practice for each plant, either wild or domesticated, is to give information with exemplary clarity and conciseness under the following heads (when relevant) and usually in the same sequence: name (and synonyms) with illustration; habitats; description (usually excellent, with precise detail and emphasis on the outstanding features); drug properties (e.g., analgesic, astringent, diuretic, dilating); medicinal uses (quite specific and sometimes meshed with previous category); side effects; dosages; collection (including optimal time and immediate environment), preparation, and storage; adulteration and tests for its detection; veterinary purposes (of products unsuitable for human use); nonmedical and (far less common) magic usages; and specific habitats for greatest abundance or efficacy.

In his pharmacognosy Dioscorides drew from many sources. Although the Hippocratic corpus mentions incidentally only about 130 drugs, many treatises specifically devoted to drugs had been written by the first century A.D., some by *rhizotomoi* (root cutters), who were a kind of superior herbal healer. Dioscorides seems to have thought most highly of the works of Crateuas, who was personal physician to the Pontic king Mithridates VI (famous for experimenting with poisons) and who was perhaps the first to add illustrations to his verbal descriptions. Dioscorides knew also, although perhaps only through an intermediary, of treatises by Aristotle's scholarly successor, Theophrastus, whose interest was, however, more botanic than pharmacologic. There was also an oral tradition of beneficent and baneful plants among the rural population and *pharmakopolai* (druggists), which Dioscorides tapped.

In his preface Dioscorides justifies his own opus on three grounds. First, he is far more comprehensive than previous writers. Second, whereas other writers have fallen into error by trusting secondhand information and not engaging in thorough investigation or experimentation to test the potency of drugs, he has attempted to verify personally all information that he has culled from elsewhere. This claim is certainly supported by his work, in which he is careful to distinguish between what he knows through autopsy and what he has merely heard; in an age of growing addiction to the supernatural, he also demonstrates his rationalism by never vouching for the few magic usages he feels obligated to include. The third reason is the most interesting and marks Dioscorides as a scientist of the highest order: he arranges his descriptions, under the broad headings previously mentioned, not in alphabetical order or in accordance with botanic similarities but in accordance with what can be termed "drug affinity"—that is, he groups together natural products that have similar physiologic effects on the body. Thus he comes close to a chemical classification, although his is based rather on meticulous medical observation and testing. Notwithstanding his belief in the superiority of this approach, it was too complex and subtle for users (and modern scholars until Riddle), and ironically some manuscripts of his work are arranged alphabetically.

Although unknown to his Roman contemporary Pliny the Elder, Dioscorides was much admired and used by the Pergamene physician Galen, and it was through Galen's works as well as his own treatise that Dioscorides was the primary source of pharmacologic knowledge until about 1600. Of the numerous Byzantine copies of *De materia medica*, at least 13 are illustrated, the oldest and most lavish being a codex from the early sixth century with 383 botanic descriptions (Vienna, Nationalbibliothek, cod. med. gr. 1). That the work had a practical and not merely antiquarian value is shown by the addition in manuscripts of supplementary and, occasionally, adversely critical comments by Byzantine physicians. *De materia medica* (and some of the spurious tracts) was translated into Latin and in this form, although rarely illustrated, was never completely lost during the Dark and Middle Ages in the West. The invention of movable type inspired an avalanche of editions, commentaries (most in Latin), and translations into vernacular languages in the 16th century. It had been translated also into Armenian and was first introduced into the Islamic world in the mid-ninth century by Hunayn ibn Ishaq (physician at the court of the caliph al-Mutawakil), who translated it into Syriac and supervised a version into Arabic. At least a dozen illustrated Arabic manuscripts of the work survive, and it formed the basis of treatises by Avicenna and others.

## Biography

Born at Anazarbus, Roman Cilicia (now Anavarza, Turkey), first half of first century A.D. Studied under Areios of Tarsus; wrote five-volume work on pharmacology for which he traveled extensively and invented "drug affinity system," ca. A.D. 50–80; was leading authority on subject in West until late 16th century; was highly regarded in Islamic World. Died ca. 90 A.D.

## Selected Publications

*De materia medica*, ca. A.D. 50–80; as *Pedanii Dioscuridis Anazarbei De Materia Medica Libri Quinque*, 3 vols. 1907–14; as *The Greek Herbal of Dioscorides: Illustrated by a Byzantine A.D. 512*, translated by John Goodyer, 1933

## Further Reading

Dubler, César Emil, *La "Materia Médica" de Dioscorides: Transmisión Medieval y Renacentista*, 6 vols., Barcelona: Tipografía Emporium, 1953–59

Gerstinger, Hans, *Dioscurides: Codex Vindobonensis Med. Gr. 1 der Österreichischen Nationalbibliothek*, Graz, Austria: Akademische Druck, 1970 (reproduction of illustrated manuscript with accompanying volume)

Riddle, John M., "Dioscorides," in *Catalogus Translationum et Commentariorum: Mediaeval and Renaissance Latin Translations and Commentaries*, vol. 4, edited by Paul Oskar Kristeller, Washington, DC: Catholic University of America Press, 1980

Riddle, John M., "Byzantine Commentaries on Dioscorides" *Dumbarton Oaks Papers* 38 (1984)

Riddle, John M., *Dioscorides on Pharmacy and Medicine*, Austin: University of Texas Press, 1985

Sadek, Mahmoud Mohamed, *The Arabic Materia Médica of Dioscorides*, St-Jean-Chrystome, Québec: Éditions du Sphinx, 1983

Scarborough, J., and V. Nutton, "The *Preface* of Dioscorides' *Materia Medica:* Introduction, Translation, Commentary," *Transactions and Studies of the College of Physicians of Philadelphia* 4, no. 3 (1982)

A.R. LITTLEWOOD

# Diseases, Combatting of. *See* Pests and Diseases, Combatting of

# Dornava

## Ptuj, Slovenia

**Location:**   Approximately 140 km (87 mi.) northeast of capital, Ljubljana

Dornava manor is located in eastern Slovenia, close to the Dornava settlement, northeast of the town of Ptuj. Originally, the manor and its garden were situated on the alluvial plain of the Drava River and its tributary Pesnica. The expansive fertile plain surrounded by rolling hills was well suited for the luxurious residence of the counts of Attems, one of the most powerful aristocratic families in Styria in the later part of the Austro-Hungarian monarchy. Count Josef Tadeus Attems extended the existing manor (a former estate of the noble families Herberstein and Sauer) into a manor between 1753 and 1755. The rebuilt manor consisted of three wings with rich baroque elements, ornamented facades, and illusionistic frescoes by J.C. Waginger. The manor with its garden presented an outstanding baroque complex in Slovenia, comparable with contemporary manors in Central Europe.

The garden followed the central axis of the manor and was more than two kilometers (1.2 mi.) long. The composition was determined by two sculptures located at the edge of the estate. It was initiated by the statue of the Blessed Virgin (*Immaculata*) in the south, extended over three diverse garden sections, and concluded by the statue of John of Nepomuk at the edge of the Pesnica River in the north. The garden extended through a double lime tree alley to the front courtyard surrounded by a rustic pillar fence decorated with stone figures, cartouches, and rococo vases.

The spatial axis led through the hall, through the inner courtyard, and from there through an ornamented portal to the Neptune's parterre with a central fountain, which consisted of the Neptune's statue on rock surrouded by a group of figures. The parterre was marked by rich statuary elements, particularly by 12 stone dwarfs, which were a characteristic feature of the Dornava garden and presented a unique baroque garden sculpture in Slovenia. The dwarfs were inspired by the etching collection *Il Calloto resuscitato; oder, Neu eingerichtetes Zwerchen Cabinet,* which presented a caricature of the contemporary states of the society, and further by Central European models, especially by Austrian dwarf gardens (*Zwerggärten*). The group of dwarfs was the earliest sculptural composition of Dornava, dating from the period before the Attems renovation (1715–20). It could have been located in a bosquet or in a more richly planted section of the third parterre. Another group of six sages of the antiquity was located around the fountain: Seneca, Aristotle, Diogenes, Hippocrates, Homer, and Theophrastus. Other ornaments—including stone putti, vases, allegories of the seasons, and two statues of saints—probably originated from the workshop of F.J. Straub from Graz.

The garden composition was extended to the north through a lawn parterre with a central alley leading to the orangery and the garden house. The alley of horse chestnuts, which became fashionable in Slovenia in the 19th century, was planted probably already in the 1850s. The parterre was further followed by an orchard. The sequence of diverse garden sections was continued with a portal ornamented with statues and extended into a bosquet with three paths in the goose-foot motif.

Extensive archaeological research is planned for the future to reveal more data of the inventory of the plants and trees of the garden. Minor excavations performed so far revealed the area of the original garden and the remains of conifers, planted in the front courtyard. The preserved orangery and garden house indicated the presence of pot plants, including citrus trees and other delicate foreign species that were kept there during harsh sub-Pannonian winters. Joseph Tadeus Attems possesed a large collection of orange and lemon trees, which existed also in the period of the Pongratz family, who took over the estate of Dornava in 1901. The last gardener of the Pongratz family, the Czech Vaclav Vavra, cultivated numerous perennial and annual ornamental plants for the beds of the parterre.

During World War II, the garden was devastated, the trees were cut down, and the vegetation was removed. After the war, the complex suffered great damage on account of inconsiderate interventions: the garden was inappropriately maintained, a mental institution for children was established in the manor, and farm buildings were constructed in close vicinity. In recent years, efforts have been made to remove the institution to a new building and to turn the manor into a museum of Slovenian baroque art. Intensive restoration of the statues in the garden presents an important step in the renovation of the garden. The statues are to be exhibited in the museum and copies of them erected in the garden. The attained independence of Slovenia in 1991 opened up new possibilities for a thorough reconstruction of the Dornava complex.

## Synopsis

| | |
|---|---|
| late 17th C. | Fenced garden with orchard and bosquet-like forest exists beside hunting lodge belonging to counts of Sauer |
| before 1708 | Manor rebuilt and extended into Baroque manor; central hall painted with illusionistic frescoes by J.C. Waginger |
| 1715–20 | Group of 12 dwarfs sculpted by unknown sculptor, located in bosquet |
| 1740s | Group of seven classical sages sculpted and located in Neptune's parterre |
| ca. 1750 | Stone putti, vases, allegories of the seasons, two statues of saints added |
| 1753–55 | Manor rebuilt and enlarged by Count Josef T. Attems; garden remodeled with axial composition of diverse garden parterres, lime tree alley, fenced courtyards, and designed bosquet, leading to river |
| 1850– | Small park in English style with exotic trees added on western side of manor |
| 1941–46 | Trees and ornamental vegetation mostly devastated or removed |
| after World War II | Major interventions in garden and manor; lack of maintenance; mental institution for children established in manor, farm buildings constructed next to it |
| 1990s | Intensive restoration of garden statuary; thorough restoration and revitalization of Dornava complex in progress |

## Further Reading

Guggenbauer, Gustav, "Zwerggärten," *Zeitschrift für oberösterreichische Geschichte, Landes und Volkskunde* 12 (1931)

Janisch, Josef Andreas, *Topographisch-statistisches Lexikon der Steiermark, mit historischen Notizen und Anmerkungen,* 3 vols., Graz, Austria, 1878–85; reprint, Graz, Austria: Sammler, 1978

Mušič, Marjan, "V obrambo velikopotezne baročne kompozicije v Dornavi," in *Arhitektura in cas: Eseji in razprave,* by Mušič, Maribor: Obzorja, 1963

Reichert, Carl, editor, *Einst und jetzt: Album Steiermarks,* 3 vol., Graz, Austria, 1863–64

Šumi, Nace, "Dornavska graščina," *Zbornik za umetnostno zgodovino* 5–7 (1959)

Vrišer, Sergej, "Posvetna baročna plastika v severovzhodni Sloveniji," *Kronika* 9 (1961)

Weigl, Igor, "Dornavski pritlikavci," *Argo* 33–34 (1992)

ALENKA KOLŠEK

# Douglas, David 1799–1835

## Scottish Plant Collector

David Douglas was an outstanding scientific traveler and plant hunter who earned his reputation by making several expeditions to the largely unexplored territory of western North America, in particular the Pacific coastal regions and mountainous forest regions of the Rocky Mountains from San Francisco in the south to the Yukon in the north. His major contribution to the history of gardens was the introduction of thousands of new plants at the beginning of the 19th century, a time when interest in horticulture was gathering momentum and the thirst for new plants was insatiable.

Douglas was one of a number of plant collectors sponsored by the Horticultural Society of London (founded in 1804 and later to become the Royal Horticultural Society), including Theodore Hartweg, Robert Fortune, and others. Seeds and plants received from collectors and distributed to nurseries and botanical gardens laid the foundations for commercial nurseries such as Loddiges in Hackney and botanical institutions such as the Royal Botanic Gardens, Kew (founded in 1840).

Douglas, an adventurous and single-minded Scot, began his career working in the gardens at Scone Palace, the botanically interesting garden of Valleyfield, and the Glasgow Botanic Garden before being selected (through the auspices of Professor Joseph Hooker) by Joseph Sabine of the Horticultural Society for arduous plant-collecting expeditions to North America.

After a preliminary expedition to New York and the eastern United States in 1823, Douglas embarked between 1824 and 1835 on a series of journeys to the coastal regions of western North America. He explored the Columbia River, the Snake and Willamette Rivers, and the country of Oregon and the forest of California, uncharted territory inhabited by Native Americans. He explored areas that only a handful of travelers had previously visited, including Archibald Menzies in 1792 and Meriwether Lewis and William Clark, who had crossed the Great Divide and reached the Pacific Ocean paddling canoes down the Columbia River, between 1804 and 1806. Douglas was the first to explore the area extensively, making hazardous journeys over terrain inhabited by Native American tribes often at war with each other; he sometimes went for days without food and often traveled in poor health, and later, with failing eyesight.

Seeds and plants introduced by Douglas fell into three categories, each useful for different types of planting. Giant conifers such as the Douglas fir (*Pseudotsuga menziesii*), Monterey pine (*Pinus radiata*), and *Pinus coulteri* provided the backbone for the exotic tree and shrub gardens in the milder areas of the west coast of Scotland and Devon and Cornwall. One of Douglas's introductions, the Sitka spruce (*Picea sitchensis*, transformed forestry plantations, especially in Scotland. Some of the first seeds of the Douglas fir were sent by Douglas to his brother-in-law, gardener at Drumlanrig Castle, in 1832.

Shrubs such as *Garrya elliptica*, *Ribes speciosum* (flowering currant) and *Mahonia aquifolium*, *Gaultheria Shallon* and *Cornus stolonifera*, *Rubus parviflorus*, and *Vaccinium ovatum* became the mainstay of the shrubbery in Victorian gardens.

Herbaceous perennials and annuals Douglas introduced included *Lupinus* sp., *Delphinium menziesii*, *Mimulus moschatus*, phlox, penstemons, antirrhinums, *Eschscholzia californica*, *Limnanthes*, *Clarkia elegans*, and godetia. These became the main ingredients of large country house and suburban villa gardens, as well as cottage gardens in the Victorian period. Over 670 species were collected in all.

Douglas's journals, although not all survive, give accounts of his journeys, and his dissertations on North American pines and oaks are valuable contributions to botanical literature. He was honored in his lifetime by the Zoological Society, the Royal Horticultural Society, and the Linnaean Society.

A memorial garden in his honor has been founded at Scone, and there is a David Douglas Memorial Society in Scotland.

**Biography**
Born in Scone, Perthsire, Scotland, 1799. Apprentice gardener, age 11, on earl of Mansfield's estate, Scone Palace, 1811; worked at Valleyfield garden near Dunfirmline for Sir Robert Preston, 1818, where he had access to Sir Robert's botanical library; worked at Glasgow Botanical Garden, 1820; selected, through recommendation of Joseph Hooker, by Joseph Sabine of Horticultural Society of London, to travel to North America on plant hunting expeditions; traveled to New York and Canada, returning home with cargo of plants, 1823; sailed to Washington and Oregon, explored Columbia River, traveling more than 2,000 miles (3,219 km) on foot, horseback, or canoe, 1824; explored Snake and Willamette Rivers, Blue Mountains, and Pacific coastal regions, 1826; returned to Portsmouth, honored by Linnaean Society, Zoological Society, and Geological Society, 1826; genus *Douglasia* named after him; embarked on expedition to Oregon, surveyed Columbia River and visited Hawaii and Honolulu,

1829; landed in San Francisco and explored California, 1831; visited Hawaii, 1832, and dispatched collection of seeds and plants to London; returned briefly to Columbia River area, but same year returned to Hawaii. Died (accidental death) in Hawaii, 1834.

## Further Reading

Coats, Alice M., *The Quest for Plants: A History of the Horticultural Explorers*, London: Studio Vista, 1969; as *The Plant Hunters: Being a History of the Horticultural Pioneers, Their Quests, and Their Discoveries from the Renaissance to the Twentieth Century*, New York: McGraw-Hill, 1970

Davies, John, editor, *Douglas of the Forests: The North American Journals of David Douglas*, Edinburgh: Harris, 1980

Morwood, William, *Traveller in a Vanished Landscape*, London: Gentry Books, 1973

DIANA BASKERVYLE-GLEGG

---

# Downing, Andrew Jackson 1815–1852

## United States Landscape Gardener and Horticulturist

Andrew Jackson Downing was the premier practitioner, author, and editor in landscape gardening, horticulture, and rural architecture in the United States from the early 1840s until his death in 1852. His *Treatise on the Theory and Practice of Landscape Gardening Adapted to North America* (1841) was the first American book devoted exclusively to the subject, and *Fruits and Fruit-Trees of America* (1845) soon became the standard pomological work. As editor of the monthly magazine *Horticulturist* from 1846 to 1852, Downing addressed a wide range of "rural arts," including architecture because residential structures in particular were meant to be component parts of the general scene. His *Cottage Residences* (1842) and *The Architecture of Country Houses* (1850) stress that architectural beauty must be considered jointly with the beauty of the landscape.

Downing was born and spent his 36 years on the west bank of the Hudson River in Newburgh, New York, and the spectacular natural setting of the Highlands was a significant factor in the life of this landscape gardener who promoted an American version of the British Picturesque style. He lived and worked in the midst of the type of landscape that he recommended to his readers, where nature assists in the creation of lovely homes and gardens.

*A Treatise on the Theory and Practice of Landscape Gardening* should be recognized as part of the response to intensifying demands for an American national literature. For a young country anxious to justify itself, a native-born work on the art of landscape gardening was proof that Americans were ready to enjoy a civilized society. The improvement of house and garden was turned into a patriotic act as Downing forged a bond between landscape gardening and popular cultural issues of the period, including the love of rural life, ideals of domesticity, stability, and the freehold concept. There were also practical reasons for the book's success; British works were predicated upon a climate, society, income, and cost of labor and material wholly different from those in the United States. As the title implies, the *Treatise* addresses landscape gardening as a fine art. Although there are significant differences among the 1841, 1844, and 1849 editions and, ultimately, concessions to the singularly wild and unfinished aspects of the American population and scenery, each edition remains true to Downing's highest aspirations: to guide country gentlemen in the creation of ideal homes and extensive pleasure grounds.

Downing could not have attempted the *Treatise* without borrowing from the Old World, especially Britain, whose taste in rural embellishment many felt to be unrivaled. Initially, he was particularly indebted to the Scotsman John Claudius Loudon's theory of imitation in landscape gardening. Downing quickly realized, however, that the adoption of Loudon's notion that the modern or natural style could be acknowledged as art only through the employment of numerous exotic plants made little practical or aesthetic sense in a country so rich in indigenous trees and shrubs. Changes in the two later editions of the *Treatise* were mainly influenced by Archibald Alison's concept of expression as set forth in *Essays on the Nature and Principles of Taste* (1790), the one-volume collection of Humphry Repton's writings brought out by Loudon in 1840, Sir Thomas Dick Lauder's edition of *Sir Uvedale Price on the Picturesque* (1842), and John Ruskin's theory of "Typical Beauty" in *Modern Painters II* (U.S. edition, 1848). Throughout all editions Downing maintains that the end and aim of landscape gardening are to embody the "ideal of a rural home"; to that end, the new "starting ground" for American landscape gardening rests in the *Horticulturist,* in which Downing attempts to achieve a harmony between the ideal and the real.

Downing's stature was such by 1846 that publisher Luther Tucker asked him to be editor of the new *Horticulturist and Journal of Rural Art and Rural Taste: Devoted to Horticulture, Landscape Gardening, Rural Architecture, Botany, Pomology, Entomology, Rural Economy, &c.* Downing penned 74 editorials during his six-year tenure, and whatever the month's particular topic, he continually wove in his views on such subjects as the value of country living, taste, economy, American progress, and republicanism. One-quarter of the editorials specifically address landscape gardening, and many more do so peripherally. The editorials written after the 1849 *Treatise* are an essential addendum to Downing's theory and practice of landscape gardening.

In the summer of 1850 Downing embarked on his first and only trip abroad and acquired not only a partner in architect Calvert Vaux but a firsthand knowledge of England and a fresh understanding of his own country's worth. These insights, along with Downing's growing practical experience and editorial contact with correspondents throughout the United States and its territories, effected a change in the *Horticulturist.* A chronological look at the editorials shows that, while encouraging Americans to live a life refined by the rural arts, Downing increasingly advocates republican simplicity and frugality linked with the best use of the country's existing natural vegetation. The *Horticulturist,* in contrast to the *Treatise,* sets its sights on more moderate establishments. Downing seeks to imbue his readers with a concept of landscape gardening shaped by the American economy—specifically, the high cost of labor and the limited means of the majority of its population. The journal's readership did not consist primarily of country gentlemen but of men and women with a wide range of aspirations and monetary resources. Many were novices, and Downing repeatedly warned them about the perils of improving without expert professional guidance. He also held forth on "the moral effects of the fine arts," and his vision for this included parks.

Downing is commonly linked with his fellow editor William Cullen Bryant as the writers who fired the popular imagination to the idea of freely accessible, green open spaces for American cities. In 1844 it was Bryant who, as editor of the *New York Evening Post,* first proposed "A New Public Park"—"an extensive pleasure ground for shade and recreation." Writing from England one year later, Bryant describes the "lungs of London," the numerous and spacious parks in the city of London that contributed to public health and happiness. When Downing added his voice to the public

parks campaign in the October 1848 *Horticulturist,* his "Talk about Public Parks and Gardens" was not limited to the situation in New York. Subscribers to his journal included residents of Boston and Philadelphia, and they too were concerned with a large and constantly increasing population crowded together in sunless streets. The public park was portrayed as a healthy outdoor drawing room where all classes could meet, sip tea and coffee, and walk about. Downing's July 1849 editorial "Public Cemeteries and Public Gardens" addresses the phenomenal popularity of the rural cemeteries in the three leading cities. He observes that, in the absence of great public gardens, cemeteries such as Greenwood, Mount Auburn, and Laurel Hill had been serving to some degree as a substitute due to the great attraction of these sites' natural beauty. The high number of visitors to these cemeteries proved the need for a "general holiday-ground" filled with plant collections, drives, and promenades. Downing's 1851 "The New-York Park" editorial argues for the reservation of at least 500 acres (202.4 ha) to act as a green oasis for the city's body and soul. The park's social aspect was of critical importance to Downing, who believed that, through the refining influence of intellectual and moral culture, every laborer was a possible gentleman. Six years after Downing's death, the "Greensward Plan" by Calvert Vaux and Frederick Law Olmsted won the design competition held for New York's Central Park.

A seminal figure in landscape architecture, Downing has equivalent standing in the history of horticulture. In the ten years preceding the publication of the *Treatise,* he gained extensive professional experience as a horticulturist, first in partnership with his brother Charles and then as sole proprietor of his Newburgh nursery, and he quickly assumed a leadership position in American horticultural societies. Believing that everything previously issued in the United States on the subject of fruit was full of errors, Downing devoted several years to completing the 600-page *Fruits and Fruit-Trees of America.* The volume was generally acclaimed, and Downing was praised for his untiring research and industry (although W. Miller states in his 1915 *Standard Cyclopedia of Horticulture* that A.J.'s brother Charles did the bulk of the work). In 1847 the leading horticultural societies adopted the "Rules for American Pomology" as suggested by Downing in the *Horticulturist.* The code reformed nomenclature and the description of new varieties of fruit, and Downing's *Fruits and Fruit-Trees* (already in its seventh edition) was designated the standard American authority in deciding the names of fruits already known and described. A great percentage of the *Horticulturist* was devoted to the discussion and illustration of hundreds of new and improved varieties of fruit and related topics such as the best manures for fruit trees.

The *Horticulturist* also provided a forum to plead for the establishment of agricultural schools in the United States that could offer a complete scientific and practical education to farmers. Thirteen years before George Perkins Marsh published *Man and Nature* (1864), Downing reminded his readers that the pursuit of "a ruinous system of husbandry" had turned once-fertile plains in the Old World into desert wastes. He warned that the common American practice of wearing out one good soil and abandoning it for another to the west must stop before the prairies became as barren as the exhausted farms of Virginia. Downing also supported the founding of what he termed a "practical school for gardeners," arguing that an experimental garden would offer newly arrived immigrants the opportunity to naturalize their knowledge. Progress in horticulture, he believed, was being hampered by foreign-born practitioners (mostly British) who stubbornly adhered to old customs based on an entirely different climate. Mulching was one of the most beneficial practices introduced into American horticulture, Downing noted, because the dry climate made it difficult to preserve moisture around the roots of plants.

Downing was equally at home as editor and as "An Old Digger," the pseudonym under which he wrote 11 pieces full of plain sayings and wholesome advice for the *Horticulturist*. The "Old Digger" was very fond of peas and informed readers about the best early peas, the best soil for peas, and how to cook peas; among other topics, he also lectured on how to put down "rascally" insects in the orchard. It was not in his professional landscape gardener voice that Downing offered these practical hints; rather, he spoke like an experienced gardener, an old family retainer who didn't have to mince words even with the country gentleman who paid his wages.

Downing's practice prospered after the *Treatise* appeared in 1841; he wrote to a friend soon after its publication that he was busily employed in laying out grounds and was optimistic that landscape gardening would become a recognized profession in the United States. (It was not until the early 1860s that Vaux and Olmsted began to sign reports as "landscape architects.") Downing's personal and professional papers have not been found, and there are few references to specific commissions in scattered correspondence. The two projects with the most documentation are Springside in Poughkeepsie, New York, and the Public Grounds in Washington, D.C.

In 1851 Matthew Vassar engaged Downing (assisted by Vaux) to design several buildings and to improve the grounds with walks and drives at his country place Springside. Vaux describes the estate in *Villas and Cottages* (1857), noting that each structure had been studied in reference to "its position and artistic importance" within the gently undulating landscape. That same year,

at the request of U.S. President Millard Fillmore, Downing designed the L-shaped area extending from the president's house along the Mall to the foot of Capitol Hill. The National Park was composed of six distinct scenes: the President's Parade, Monument Park, the Evergreen Garden, Smithsonian Park, Fountain Park, and a botanic garden with three greenhouses. The public grounds would have fulfilled many of Downing's aspirations: expressing on a grand scale what he considered the national style in landscape gardening (i.e., the natural style), remedying the country's lack of a national garden, and promoting an American taste for public pleasure grounds. Downing was in the midst of supervising the improvements to the Capitol grounds when he drowned in a Hudson River steamboat accident on 28 July 1852. Afterward, a new superintendent allowed the larger sense of the design to be lost, and although the 1851 plan guided work on the Mall until the turn of the century, no trace of it remains.

Downing united in a rare degree talents as a writer, horticulturist, and practitioner, yet his most important legacy is in his roles of author and editor. He was a master of an articulate yet unaffected style of writing and an acute social observer who understood the psychology of an emerging nation. Able to shift smoothly between directions on "How to Make Strawberry Beds" and an editorial on "The Philosophy of Rural Taste," Downing not only addressed the practical needs of his American audience but convinced a great number of his countrymen and women of the value of beauty in daily life, whether it be homes and gardens, schoolhouses, country villages, parks, or cities.

**Biography**

Born in Newburgh, New York, 1815. Nurseryman in partnership with his brother Charles until 1837 and then sole proprietor of Newburgh, New York, Botanic Garden and Nursery; active in horticultural societies; began contributing articles to horticulture and agriculture magazines, early 1830s; built residence in Newburgh, 1838–39; practiced as a professional landscape gardener, from early 1840s; began editorship of the *Horticulturist*, 1846; sold nursery, 1847; toured England and made a brief visit to Paris, 1850; returned to U.S. with British architect Calvert Vaux, and in partnership with Vaux opened a "Bureau of Architecture" in Newburgh, 1850; in the two years before his death, received approximately a dozen major commissions including Matthew Vassar's Springside, Poughkeepsie, New York, 1850–52; invited by President Millard Fillmore to design the Public Grounds at Washington, D.C., 1850; plan of the National Park adopted and work begun, 1851; British architect Frederick Clarke Withers joined firm as an assistant, 1852. Drowned in a steamboat accident on the Hudson River in 1852.

## Selected Designs

Downing's personal and professional papers have never been located; therefore, a comprehensive list of his design work is difficult to establish.

1838–52   A.J. Downing's residence and grounds, Newburgh, New York, United States

1842   New York State Lunatic Asylum grounds, Utica, New York, United States

1847   Grounds of Medary, Harry Ingersoll residence, Philadelphia, Pennsylvania, United States

1848   New Jersey State Lunatic Asylum grounds, Trenton, New Jersey, United States

1849   Grounds of Alverthorpe, Joshua Francis Fisher residence, Jenkintown, Pennsylvania, United States

1851   Grounds of Brookwood, Charles Henry Fisher residence, Philadelphia, Pennsylvania, United States

1852   Algonac, Warren Delano residence and grounds, Newburgh, New York, United States (with Vaux)

1852   Springside, Matthew Vassar residence and grounds, Poughkeepsie, New York, United States (with Vaux)

1852   David Moore residence and grounds, Newburgh, New York, United States (with Vaux)

1852   Public Grounds, Washington, D.C., United States (with Vaux). Incomplete at death and plan was not carried out

## Selected Publications

*Treatise on the Theory and Practice of Landscape Gardening adapted to North America: With a View to the Improvement of Country Residences*, 1841; 9th edition, 1875

*Cottage Residences: or, A Series of Designs for Rural Cottages and Cottage-Villas, and Their Gardens and Grounds, Adapted to North America*, 1842; 5th edition, 1873

*Fruits and Fruit-Trees of America; or, The Culture, Propagation, and Management, in the Garden and Orchard, of Fruit Trees Generally: With Descriptions of All the Finest Varieties of Fruit, Native and Foreign, Cultivated in This Country*, 1845; 2nd edition, revised and corrected and with appendixes by Charles Downing, 1883

editor, *Horticulturist and Journal of Rural Art and Rural Taste: Devoted to Horticulture, Landscape Gardening,*

*Rural Architecture, Botany, Pomology, Entomology, Rural Economy, etc.*, 3 vols., 1846–49

*Architecture of Country Houses: Including Designs for Cottages, Farm Houses, and Villas, with Remarks on Interiors, Furniture, and the Best Modes of Warming and Ventilating*, 1850

*Rural Essays*, edited by George William Curtis, 1853

## Further Reading

Alex, William, and George B. Tatum, *Calvert Vaux: Architect and Planner*, New York: Ink, 1994

Downs, Arthur Channing, Jr., "Downing's Newburgh Villa," *Bulletin, Association for Preservation Technology* 4, nos. 3–4 (1972)

Greiff, Constance M., *John Notman: Architect, 1810–1865*, Philadelphia, Pennsylvania: Athenaeum of Philadelphia, 1979

Haley, Jacquetta M., editor, *Pleasure Grounds: Andrew Jackson Downing and Montgomery Place*, Tarrytown, New York: Sleepy Hollow Press, 1988

Major, Judith K., "The Downing Letters," *Landscape Architecture* 76, no. 1 (1986)

Major, Judith K., *To Live in the New World: A.J. Downing and American Landscape Gardening*, Cambridge, Massachusetts: MIT Press, 1997

O'Malley, Therese, "'A Public Museum of Trees': Mid-Nineteenth-Century Plans for the Mall," *Studies in the History of Art* 30 (1991)

Schuyler, David, *Apostle of Taste: Andrew Jackson Downing, 1815–1852*, Baltimore, Maryland: Johns Hopkins University Press, 1996

Sweeting, Adam W., *Reading Houses and Building Books: Andrew Jackson Downing and the Architecture of Popular Antebellum Literature, 1835–1855*, Hanover, New Hampshire: University Press of New England, 1996

Tatum, George B., and Elisabeth Blair MacDougall, editors, *Prophet with Honor: The Career of Andrew Jackson Downing, 1815–1852*, Washington, D.C.: Dumbarton Oaks Research Library and Collection, 1989

Toole, Robert M., "Springside: A.J. Downing's Only Extant Garden," *Journal of Garden History* 9, no. 1 (1989)

Vaux, Calvert, *Villas and Cottages: A Series of Designs Prepared for Execution in the United States*, New York: Harper, 1857; reprint, New York: Da Capo Press, 1968

JUDITH K. MAJOR

# Drottningholm

## Lovön, Stockholm, Sweden

**Location:** island of Lovön on Lake Mälaren, about 5 miles (8 km) west of Stockholm city center

The name Drottningholm (literally "Queen's Island") originated in the 16th century after the property, then known as Torvesund, was acquired by the crown and John III had a stone castle built. Built between 1680 and 1700 for the dowager queen, Hedvig Eleonora, the palace and several plans for the garden were designed by Nicodemus Tessin the Elder.

The overall design of the garden, which represents an evolution of over 300 years, is mostly the work of Tessin's son, the architect and garden designer Nicodemus Tessin (called the Younger), who was educated in France, where he went to Versailles and met Le Nôtre, whose style he intended to introduce into Sweden. Tessin was Le Nôtre's foremost non-French pupil. His plan for the garden was adopted in 1681, and in the 1690s he collaborated with Johan Hårleman, a royal gardener.

The castle was erected on a raised terrace reached by a magnificent staircase, whose axis extended into the parterre with its landmark Hercules Fountain, followed by a sequence of eight basins forming a kind of *parterre d'eau*. The spreading allées, parterres, and fountains are reminiscent of Versailles. The garden (800 by 180 meters [875 by 197 yd.]) is entirely enclosed by a double avenue of limes, and there is a water parterre situated on a lower level between a *parterre de broderie* (now grass) and bosquets.

Next to the park is the rococo chinoiserie built between 1753 and 1769. It is a small Chinese pagoda or tower with attendant buildings that followed the mid-18th-century custom of having chinoiserie in gardens. One visitor, Sir Nathaniel William Wraxall (*Cursory Remarks Made in a Tour through Some of the Northern Parts of Europe* [1775]), noted:

> In the gardens [at Drottningholm] the queen dowager has lately built a little palace of pleasure, in a semi-circular form, composed of several compartments fitted up in that taste which we usually call the Chinese; though, unless a few Mandarins and Vases of China form this style, of which we know

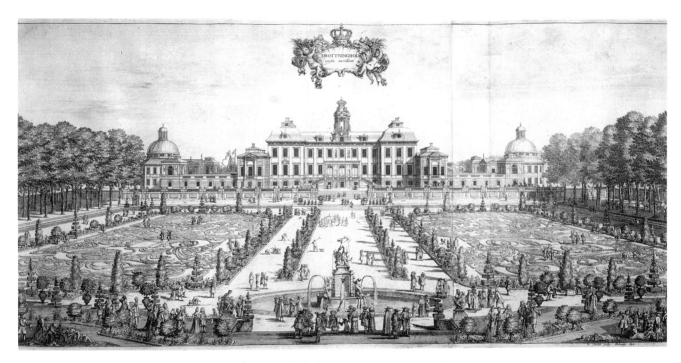

Engraving of Drottningholm from *Suecia Antiqua et Hodierna*, 1692
Photo by Bengt Melliander, courtesy of Lund University Library

scarce any thing, it may just as well be called an European structure, where whimsy and caprice form the predominant character, and spread a grotesque air through the whole.

In 1777 the Swedish government purchased the palace as a royal residence. This small palace, with its attendant buildings, has its own park created in a freer style, as well as an English park landscaped by Gustav III and Fredrik Magnus Piper that was completed in 1781. The year before, the king commissioned Piper to redesign a substantial section of the gardens in the less formal English park style and proposed a design for the rearrangement of the baroque parterres. This was vetoed by Gustav, himself an amateur garden designer, who admired classicism from his travels in Italy. From his observations in Italy, he was inspired to imitate in his landscaping designs "at Drottningholm a number of things I have seen." On one trip to Rome (1783) the king wrote the governor of Drottningholm that he saw "a thousand pieces which I could sketch for my garden but which I am sure to forget unless I draw them." At the end of the 1760s, while still crown prince, Gustav drew a rather clumsy copy of Tessin the Younger's design for the area north of the parterre. For the trees Gustav imagined "planting elms as being a tree which prospers with us and grows to quite a considerable height." In the western part of the garden, Piper was allowed to lay out a large-scale landscape with several lakes and an island, first conceived as Diana's Isle. After the king's death the architect converted it into a circular memorial hill surmounted by a granite pedestal, Monument Island, the central point of the pleasure ground and a delightful vista from the formal garden, although archival records indicate that it was never finished as Piper intended. Many of his original details for the gardens are found in the "List of completed plans and designs and those in course of preparation for the Royal Pleasure Grounds" (1796) and a "Draft of General Plan of the Grounds of the Park at Drottningholm with Improvements" (1797).

At Drottningholm the water canals that Piper designed were approximately 16 meters (17 yd.) wide, three or four times the width of other canals. This was typical of canals in Sweden; their main function was mazy and obstructive in a country with 96,000 natural lakes, but they were considered essential to an English-style landscape. This is seen in Monument Island, which cannot be reached directly from any of the places from which it may be seen—the Gothic Tower, the formal garden, or the palace—and there is usually more than one bridge to cross. It is difficult to see the water's shape or direction, and there is very little sense of river. However, Piper used the lawn to distinctive advantage at Drottningholm, where lawns were made in woods. It first required the removal or turfing over of rocks in

worn areas, such as the north end of the formal garden by the statue of Castor and Pollux, where the rock can be seen wearing its way back through the turf.

The large open area forming the parterre section resulted from extensive blasting and infill operations. The last of the small rock that had formerly stuck up in the same place and could not be shifted with gunpowder from the arsenal was concealed with an elegant backdrop of cascades, an outstanding example of a compensatory measure to bring the rocky Swedish landscape into line with French landscaping fashion.

The water parterre was restored in 1961, but the garden as a whole has been under continuous restoration. The palace and its gardens are open to the public from May to September each year.

**Synopsis**

| | |
|---|---|
| 1661 | Drottningholm purchased by Dowager Queen Hedvig Eleonora |
| 1662 | Nicodemus Tessin the Elder commissioned to work on the palace |
| 1664–67 | Parterre garden laid out by Nicodemus Tessin the Elder |
| 1681 | Plan adopted for gardens by Nicodemus Tessin the Younger |
| 1744 | Palace given as wedding present to Lovisa Ulrika of Prussia |
| 1753–69 | Small palace and attendant buildings built |
| 1777 | Drottningholm Palace and its grounds purchased by the Swedish government |
| 1780 | Fredrik Piper appointed artistic supervisor |
| 1781 | English-style park completed |
| 1796 | "List of completed plans and designs and those in course of preparation for the Royal Pleasure Grounds" drawn up by Piper |
| 1797 | Piper submits "Draft of General Plan of the Grounds of the Park at Drottningholm with Improvements" |

**Further Reading**

Gollwitzer, Gerda, "The Influence of Le Notre on the European Garden of the Eighteenth Century," in *The French Formal Garden*, edited by Elisabeth B. MacDougall and F. Hamilton Hazlehurst, Washington, D.C.: Dumbarton Oaks Trustees, 1974

Joyce, David, editor, *Garden Styles: An Illustrated History of Design and Tradition*, London: Pyramid Books, 1989

Ogrin, Dušan, *The World Heritage of Gardens*, London: Thames and Hudson, 1993

Olausson, Magnus, "National or International Style? From Nicodemus Tessin the Younger to Fredrik

Magnus Piper," *Journal of Garden History* 17 (1997)

Phibbs, John, "Pleasure Grounds in Sweden and Their English Models," *Garden History* 21 (1993)

Sirén, Osvald, *China and Gardens of Europe of the Eighteenth Century,* New York: Ronald Press, 1950

MARTIN J. MANNING

# Dubrovnik Renaissance Gardens

## Dubrovnik area, Croatia

**Location:** Area surrounding Dubrovnik at Adriatic east coast, southern part of Croatia

The Mediterranean part of Croatia is known in the field of garden history for the Renaissance gardens of southern Dalmatia, especially in the area around Dubrovnik. Dubrovnik (the Croatian name) or Ragusium (the Roman name) was first mentioned about 667 as a new medieval settlement, and it existed as a free town and state from 1358 to 1808. Dubrovnik was most famous and powerful during the 15th and 16th centuries. It was the main seaborne trade center for the Balkans and the mediator between the Balkans, Italy, and other Mediterranean states. The oldest descriptive town plans of Dubrovnik are from 1272 and 1296, meaning that planned development of the town and the surrounding area had been deeply rooted and accepted in Dubrovnik centuries before the Renaissance.

The landed gentry and the rich plebeians of Dubrovnik began to build villas outside the walls of the city (at the mainland stretching from Cavtat to Orašac) and on the islands (Koločep, Lopud, and Šipan), and the whole area was named Astarea (boundaries were made in 1366). Each villa formed a complex that included a garden and the surrounding landscape.

Although Renaissance villas and gardens were built all over the Dalmatian area, their number is insignificant in comparison with those in the Dubrovnik area. The best known are the Hanibal Lucić Villa in Hvar, the Petar Hektorović fortified villa, Tvrdalj, in Stari Grad on Hvar Island, the Foretić Villa in Korčula, and the Jerolim Kavanjin Villa in Sutivan on Brač Island.

The Dubrovnik Renaissance garden was a specific type within European garden art during the Renaissance. It was not a copy of the Italian Renaissance garden but rather the result of a fusion of Italian Renaissance ideas with the specific historical, cultural, social, and natural characteristics of the Dubrovnik area.

The medieval experience of building domestic and monastic gardens preceded the Renaissance gardens of Dubrovnik. The main idea behind the Dubrovnik Renaissance garden arose from the unity of country life and agriculture. The villas and gardens of Dubrovnik were for both agricultural use and pleasure. About 300 villas standing in lush gardens with fountains are known to have existed, and some 70 gardens are still preserved today. Of these, some 20 have remained virtually unchanged. The majority of villas with gardens were built during the 16th century, appearing at the same time as the villa gardens in Italy.

The Dubrovnik Renaissance garden is an architectural garden: it is constructed of stone; plants are secondary, and the ground plan is geometrical, mostly rectangular. A geometrical layout is more accurate on the gentle slopes than on the steep ones. An axial and symmetrical composition is not always the rule as in Italian gardens. The villa and the architectural elements of the garden give shape to an architecturally and functionally complete composition. The Renaissance garden of Dubrovnik is rather small, about 5,000 square meters (5,980 sq. yd.), for two main reasons: bad natural conditions (stony land and lack of water and soil) and limited space (small territory and numerous properties).

The Dubrovnik Renaissance garden has several specific elements: inscriptions on the stone entrance, paths, the vine pergola, the terrace, garden furniture, and water in the garden. Latin inscriptions on the stone entrances or on the monuments in the garden confirm the cultural value of the gardens. The vine pergola is a traditional part of the Dubrovnik garden from ancient times through the Middle Ages and Renaissance, and it remains an important architectural element of the garden today. The pergola integrates villa and garden and enables the interior of the house to include the garden itself. The garden is divided by paths covered with pergolas into a few rectangular or square compartments. The paths through the geometrical network of the garden follow its ground plan precisely.

The garden terrace has also been a traditional architectural element of the Dubrovnik garden from ancient

Trsteno-Fontaine, Dubrovnik Renaissance Gardens, Croatia
Copyright Mladen Obad Šćitaroci

times and was one of the essential characteristics of the Renaissance garden of Dubrovnik. The specific attributes of the terraces are the pavilion and chapel. The position of the garden terraces is either along the boundary wall, in the middle of the garden, or both. Garden furniture in the garden was always made of stone and included benches, seats, tables, fountains, urns, and vases.

Water was used sparingly in the Renaissance garden due to the lack of springs. There were only a few villas with aqueducts (e.g., Trsteno from 1492), and the use of the town waterworks, built in 1436, was prohibited. As a result, gardens made use of reservoirs filled by rainwater to supply water for the plants and fountains. Fountains were mostly located in niches in walls. The garden of the Gučetić Villa in Trsteno has one of the best known and biggest fountains in Dubrovnik gardens, dating from the 18th century. A fishpond filled up with

seawater and linked by a channel to the sea was an inevitable part of a garden. Water channels built into the walls of terraces conducted rain to reservoirs and irrigated the planted parts of gardens.

Plants, including orange tree, lemon tree, lime tree, dog-rose, and vine and aromatic herbs, were cultivated in gardens from the Middle Ages. Their delightfulness originates from the fragrance and appearance of plants such as myrtle (*Myrtus communis*), sweet bay, rosemary (*Rosmarinus officinalis*), Mediterranean cypress (*Cupressus sempervirens*), jasmine (*Jasminum* sp.), oleander (*Nerium oleander*), rose (*Rosa* sp.), lily (*Lilium* sp.), carnation, and violet. Dubrovnik merchants and sailors brought back different plants that were unknown in Dubrovnik. The texture of the countryside with its vineyards, orchards, and olive groves and the texture of the utilitarian plants and fruit trees within the garden are quite similar.

One peculiarity of the Dubrovnik garden is that it is a garden near the sea. The most precious garden still preserved today is Trsteno, located about 12 miles (19 km) northwest of Dubrovnik. Count Gučetić (Gozze) built the garden from 1494 to 1502 and included all the main characteristics of the Renaissance garden. An exceptional quality of the garden is its single-axis composition, a rarity among the Dubrovnik Renaissance gardens. At the time Trsteno was conceived, a single-axis composition of villa and garden was also uncommon in Italy.

## Synopsis

| | |
|---|---|
| 1494 | Family Gučetić (Gozze) villa (single-axis composition of garden) in Trsteno few km northwest from Dubrovnik |
| 1520 | catastrophic earthquake in Dubrovnik destroys many villas |
| 1521 | Sorkočević summer residence in Lapad (part of town Dubrovnik outside walls) on bank of Omble river |
| 1527 | Gundulić villa in Gruž (part of town Dubrovnik outside walls) |
| 1548 | Skočibuha villa in Suđurđ on Šipan island |
| 1574–88 | Vice Stjepović-Skočibuha summer residence near three churches |

## Further Reading

Obad Šćitaroci, Mladen, "The Renaissance Gardens of the Dubrovnik Area, Croatia," *Garden History* 24, no. 2 (1996)

MLADEN OBAD ŠĆITAROCI
AND BOJANA BOJANIĆ OBAD ŠĆITAROCI

---

# Du Cerceau, Androuet ca. 1520–ca. 1584

## French Architect and Engraver

Currently the date of birth and death of Jacques Androuet Du Cerceau can only be guessed at. Estimates of his date of birth have been suggested from some years before 1515 to as late as 1520. The date of his death is likewise unknown but is generally thought to have been just after the completion of his last published work, which appeared in 1584. This lack of certainty epitomizes our knowledge of the man, about whose work apart from his publications there are still many unanswered questions. He is known as an architect and engraver, although it is for the latter that he is most generally recognized. It seems he set up an engravers' workshop in Orléans sometime between 1539 and 1545, the year when he was granted the monopoly of the sale of his engravings by Francis I. Du Cerceau published a number of volumes of his illustrations of architecture and of gardens featuring the major châteaus in the Île-de-France and the valleys of the Seine and the Loire. The best-known of these are the two volumes of *Les plus excellent batiments de France* (1576, 1579; The Finest Buildings of France). He was in fact the first author of an architectural handbook in France. The first of his volumes on architecture, the *Livre d'architecture* (Book of Architecture), was published in 1559. His other published works featured designs for triumphal arches in his first publication, *Arcs* (1549), a collection of fantastic designs in *Temples* a year later, and in 1566 a book devoted to *Grotesques*.

Du Cerceau was a Huguenot, and his engraving workshop was destroyed by the Catholic faction in the religious wars. Although he had royal protection first from François I and then from Henri II and worked for both the queen of Navarre and Renée of France, the king's aunt, he would have been less than welcome in many aristocratic French Catholic homes. After the destruction of his workshop, he went to Montargis in the service of Renée, to whom he dedicated his volume of *Grotesques*. At Montargis he seems to have fulfilled a number of functions and was described in the records as "almoner and architect." During his service with Renée he sought help from King Charles IX to enable him to travel and complete more of his illustrations of châteaus. After her death in 1575 he joined the service of her daughter and son-in-law, the duc and duchesse de Nemours, and it was to the duke that he dedicated his last book, the *Edifices antiques Romain* (1584; Buildings of Classical Rome). Little else is known of the last nine or so years of his life.

While at Montargis, Du Cerceau took charge of the reconstruction of the château, then in poor condition. Other sites with which he is associated as an active architect include those of Charleval, near Rouen, and Verneuil, on the river Oise. The latter was the property of the duc de Nemours, where a sophisticated design attributed to Du Cerceau was never apparently completed, nor, according to Woodbridge, was it likely to be capable of completion on the ground. Yet another site that some authorities credit to the architect, and for which he produced no less than nine different engravings, was the château of Gaillon. These châteaus are all included in *Les plus excellent batiments de France*.

Du Cerceau's drawings of château gardens, like those of his buildings, beg a number of questions. It can be assumed that for Montargis and Verneuil the drawings he produced represent his design proposals. In other cases it has been suggested that much that he showed represented the true state of what was there in overall design terms, with perhaps some fanciful additions of detail. In the case of drawings such as that for Chenonceaux, where he produced an illustration of a grand scheme, it seems that the ideas were his; whether they were seriously intended to be built, or indeed whether any attempt to build them was undertaken, however, is not at all clear.

Du Cerceau's illustrations of châteaus and their gardens in his published volumes and original drawings are nonetheless an invaluable source of information for the French Renaissance, particularly in the 16th century, illustrating the layout of the gardens of the period and their relationship to the castles they adorned. His use of bird's-eye perspectives was a novel feature in the period. He also developed a technique of supplementing his main plan with a detail or details focusing on particularly interesting parts of a design that he then presented as enlargements. His drawings are thought to be an accurate representation of the major features of the places represented, sometimes including considerable detail of what was on the ground. He has, however, been accused in some instances of being more interested in representing symmetry rather than accuracy and of straightening out in his drawings what was not straight on the ground. It is also suggested that he may have overelaborated his drawings with his own design ideas. In other cases his work may either have been fanciful exercises, imagining what might have been, or even his own complete design ideas produced for the client.

Like many educated men of the period, Du Cerceau was interested in what could be learned from antiquity, particularly from an architectural point of view, and the promulgation of this knowledge appears to have been one of the objectives of his publications. Another was the provision of pattern books of designs for a wide range of elements, from his triumphal arches to tombs, temples, grotesque features, and a wide range of ornaments. Perhaps the most important contribution of these publications was his design ideas for dwellings, from great houses, the châteaus of royalty and nobility, to "Petit Habitations." His illustrations and the design ideas they contained were clearly an important influence for several generations, and not only in France, as his drawings were also found in other parts of Europe.

His sons, Jean II and Baptiste, were both distinguished architects, as was his grandson Saloman de Brossee, the child of his daughter Julienne, ensuring his continued legacy not only from his published work but from that of his descendants well into the next century.

*See also* Chenonceaux

## Biography

Born between ca. 1515 and 1520. Established engraving workshop, Orléans, France, between 1539 and 1545; published many volumes of illustrations of architecture and gardens, featuring major châteaus in Île-de-France and valleys of Seine and Loire rivers, 1549–84; a Huguenot, his engraving workshop destroyed by Catholics in religious wars; entered service of Renée of France, aunt of King Henri II, in Montargis, France, 1566; entered service of duke and duchess of Nemours, 1575. Died ca. 1584.

## Selected Publications

*Arcs*, 1549
*Temples*, 1550
*Livre d'architecture*, 1559
*Monuments antiques*, 1560
*Second livre d'architecture*, 1561
*Grotesques*, 1566
*Les plus excellents bâtiments de France*, 2 vols., 1576–79
*Edifices antiques Romain*, 1584

## Further Reading

Blunt, Anthony, *Art and Architecture in France, 1500 to 1700*, London and Baltimore, Maryland: Penguin, 1953; 5th edition, New Haven, Connecticut: Yale University Press, 1999

Geymüller, Heinrich Adolf, Freiherr von, *Les Du Cerceau, leur vie et leur oeuvre d'après de nouvelles recherches*, Paris, 1887

Toesca, Ilaria, "Drawings by Jacques Androuet Du Cerceau the Elder in the Vatican Museum," *Burlington Magazine* 98, no. 98 (1956)

Woodbridge, Kenneth, *Princely Gardens: The Origins and Development of the French Formal Style*, New York: Rizzoli, and London: Thames and Hudson, 1986

M.F. DOWNING

# Duchêne Family

## French Landscape Architects

Henri and Achille Duchêne were two of the most important landscape architects at the turn of the 19th century. They were leading specialists in the redesign and restoration of gardens in the classical French style. Together they worked on over 350 parks and gardens.

Henri Duchêne was born in Lyon, France. Similar to Aldolphe Alphand, he was an engineer turned horticulturist. Henri came to Paris in 1854 and started some years later to work for the city at the side of M. Darcel, the chief engineer of the Ponts et Chaussées. Henri collaborated closely with Darcel on projects such as the squares and promenades in the city of Paris. In 1877 Henri left the service of the city and began to plan parks and gardens for a prestigious private clientele. It was from working in Alphand's team that he was able to make his first campaign into a landscaped and horticultural style highly favored not only by the emperor but also by the public and other well-known landscape architects such as Edouard André. The Alphand style, which Henri practiced at first, was the Picturesque or landscape garden. In 1882 he started to design parks and gardens in the classical French style. He designed gardens in the style of the past, restored them, or reconstructed gardens that often had been destroyed to be transformed into landscape gardens. In 1899 he fell ill with hemiplegia but managed to work until his death in 1902 in Lorient, France.

Henri's son Achille Duchêne began his career at the age of 12, working with his father. He traveled a great deal and started an imposing career amplifying the work his father had introduced. In 1892 he married Gabrielle Laforcade, daughter of Jean Laforcade, chief gardener of the city of Paris. Achille collected many books on literature, architecture, and the art of gardening in his enormous library, which he developed with the help of Ernest de Ganay, one of the best garden historians of France. One of the most prolific contributors to the *Gazette Illustrée des Amateurs de Jardins*, Achille was also very active in societies and committees. At the Society of the Landscape Architects of France, over which he presided together with Ferdinand Duprat, he created a movement toward the art of gardens and set the International Office for the Documentation on the Art of Gardening in place. He was the president of honor on the committee of the art of gardening of the Société Nationale d'Horticulture de France. He also produced several publications on the art of gardens.

Achille Duchêne established himself as the leading professional exponent of the traditional French classical style not only in the matter of restoration but also in creating new gardens. Vaux-le-Vicomte, Champs-sur-Marne, Courances, and Nordkirchen in Germany were just a few objects of his restoration work. Voisins, Ile-de-France, is one of his best-known new creations. Sometimes he also integrated architectural gardens into existing landscape gardens, such as Blenheim Palace in Oxfordshire, England. Social upheavals at the beginning of the 20th century and the decrease in great private fortunes led Achille Duchêne to turn to communal gardens. In his work *Les jardins de l'avenir* (1935; Gardens of the Future), he showed his own conception of gardens for education, recreation, rest, sports, games, and enjoyment.

Both Henri and Achille Duchêne designed and redesigned gardens in the formal French style during a time when the fashion of the landscape gardens was starting to fade and the style was returning to formal design. Moreover, the interest and demand for gardens of the Renaissance and baroque was also starting to grow. The Duchênes' fame and work went beyond the borders of France to Europe and even worldwide. They worked in France, Belgium, Luxembourg, Great Britain, the Netherlands, Germany, Switzerland, Italy, Spain, Morocco, Romania, Russia, the United States, and Argentina. Because father and son worked together on the same projects for so many years, it is difficult to assess their individual contributions. But it is correct to say that the Duchênes were among the most famous landscape architects at the turn of the 19th century.

*See also* Blenheim Palace; Chenonceaux; Vaux-le-Vicomte

## Duchêne, Henri 1841–1902

### Biography

Born in Lyon, France, 1841. Started work as engineer; moved to Paris, 1854, and worked on squares and promenades there with M. Darcel, chief engineer of Ponts et Chaussées; started private practice designing parks and gardens, 1877; switched from Alphand style (Picturesque) to classical French style, 1882; also became known for restoring converted landscape gardens to original formal style; succeeded by his son Achille Duchêne in his design practice. Died in Lorient, Morbihan, France, 1902.

### Selected Designs

1875–1939    Vaux-le-Vicomte, Seine-et-Marne, France

1890–1914   Courances, Ile-de-France, France
1895–99     Champs-sur-Marne, Seine-et-Marne,
            France
1897–1903   Breteuil, Ile-de-France, France

## Duchêne, Achille 1866–1947

### Biography

Born 1866. At age 12, worked for father, landscape
architect Henri Duchêne, 1878, restoring converted
landscape gardens to original formal style and designing
some original gardens in formal style as well; married
Gabrielle Laforcade, daughter of chief gardener of the
city of Paris; contributed extensively to gardening
periodicals such as *Gazette illustrée des amateurs de
jardins;* active in societies and committees promoting
gardening as art; published *Les jardins de l'avenir,*
1935. Died in France, 1947.

### Selected Designs

1878–1939   Vaux-le-Vicomte, Seine-et-Marne, France
1890–1914   Courances, Ile-de-France, France
1895–99     Champs-sur-Marne, Seine-et-Marne,
            France
1897–1903   Breteuil, Ile-de-France, France
1900–1932   Blenheim Palace, Oxfordshire, England
1903–25     Voisins, Ile-de-France, France
1906–14     Nordkirchen, North Rhine-Westphalia,
            Germany

### Selected Publications

"Quatre siècles de jardins à la Francaise," *La vie à la
    campagne* 84 (March 1910)
*De l'art des jardins du XV<sup>e</sup> au XX<sup>e</sup> siècle,* with Marcel
    Fouquier, 1911
*Des divers styles de jardins,* with Marcel Fouquier, 1914
"Le parc de Nordkirchen," *Gazette illustrée des
    amateurs de jardins* (1914)
Pour la reconstruction des cités industrielles, 1919
"Formal Parks and Gardens in France," *Journal of the
    R.H.S.* (1929)
"Des changements de styles dans l'art des jardins et la
    rénovation des jardins à la francaise," *Jardins
    d'aujourd'hui* (1932)
*Les jardins de l'avenir: Hier, aujourd'hui, demain,* 1935

### Further Reading

Duchêne, Henri, and Achille Duchêne, "A Return to
    Formalism," in *The Modernist Garden in France,*
    edited by Dorothée Imbert, New Haven, Connecticut:
    Yale University Press, 1993
Frange, Claire, et al., *Le style Duchêne: Henri and
    Achille Duchêne, architectes paysagistes, 1841–1947,*
    Neuilly, France: Éditions du Labyrinthe, 1998
Molinier, Jean-Christophe, "Achille Duchêne: Inventor
    of a Distinctive Style," in *Jardins de ville privés:
    1890–1930,* Paris: Association Duchêne, 1991

BEATE RÄCKERS

---

# Dumbarton Oaks

## Washington, District of Columbia, United States

**Location:** 1703 32nd Street NW, in Georgetown,
approximately 2 miles (3.2 km) northwest
of the White House

The property that holds the Dumbarton Oaks
Research Library, Collection, and Garden was acquired
in 1920 by diplomat Robert Woods Bliss and his wife
Mildred, who hoped to fulfill their dream of having a
country house in the city. Beginning in 1921 the owners
remodeled the Federal-style house to accommodate
their extensive library and art collection and entirely
transformed the grounds over the next 20 years. In
1940 the Blisses conveyed the house, gardens, and their
collections to the Trustees of Harvard University. The
library and collection contain important research
resources in the areas of Byzantine studies, pre-
Columbian studies, and the history of landscape architecture. Related collections of Byzantine and pre-
Columbian art and rare books and prints illustrating
the history of landscape design are on public display.

The garden was designed by Beatrix Jones Farrand, a
distinguished landscape architect and charter member of
the American Society of Landscape Architects. Beginning in 1921 and over the next 26 years, Farrand transformed the property, which had once been a farm, into
one of the most imaginative gardens in the United States.
The entire composition reflects Farrand's clear understanding of the topographic subtleties of the site. "Never
did Beatrix Farrand impose on the land an arbitrary concept," wrote Mildred Bliss, but instead "listened to the

Melissande's Allée or Lover's Lane at Dumbarton Oaks Garden
Photo by Eleanor M. Mc Peck

light and wind and grade of each area." The garden is marked by richness of architectural detail and sense of delicacy and restraint in planting, qualities associated with all of Farrand's best work.

Given the complexity of the site, marked by steep grades falling off to Rock Creek, Farrand seized the opportunity to reconcile both formal and informal elements within the over all scheme. Gardens nearest the house reflect the formal character of the manor house. The upper terraces are conceived as outdoor rooms for entertaining. The descending series of walled terraces to the east—the Box (or Urn) Terrace, the Rose Garden, the Fountain Terrace—were conceived separately and experienced individually, but always with the idea of having another garden within view. Orchards, secluded seats, meandering walks, and informal groups of trees or shrubs appear at lower levels. Finally, a naturalistic park, now owned by the National Park Service, lies beyond a gate at the bottom of the steep slope descend-

ing from the house to Rock Creek. Rarely is the entire composition understood at once.

Lending complexity to the whole is the principle of asymmetry. Although the house commands an impressive north vista, Farrand placed it deliberately off axis, with the principal terraces extending to the east and to wooded areas below. Often, when resolution is expected, a sudden turn in the walk leads to some unanticipated part of the garden.

The poetic dimension of the garden, whose intricate structure unfolds gradually, offers moments of revelation. Carefully measured steps descend through box walks to pools of water. Willows sway above the swimming pool, and forsythia spirals downward to unseen streams below. One of the most evocative places in the garden is the Lover's Lane pool with its open-air theater, an interpretation of the Arcadian Academy in Rome. Finally, there is the descent to the lowest part of the garden, beyond an iron gate to a stream, a rustic arbor, a

Brick path leading to lower garden at Dumbarton Oaks Garden
Photo by Eleanor M. McPeck

best work survives as living evidence of her genius as a designer.

## Synopsis

| | |
|---|---|
| 1920 | Property known as Oaks acquired by Robert Woods Bliss and wife, Mildred, from Mrs. Henry Fitch Blount |
| 1921 | Reconstruction of federal-style house on site begun under direction of Frederick H. Brooks; Beatrix Jones Farrand commissioned to design gardens and serve as landscape consultant |
| 1921–47 | Garden laid out, designed by Beatrix Jones Farrand |
| 1940 | Garden, house, and collection deeded by Blisses to trustees of Harvard College; approximately 27 acres, comprising lower valley of property, deeded to National Park Service |
| after 1959 | Urn Terrace and Pebble Garden redesigned by Ruth Havey |
| 1962 | Pre-Columbian Wing added, designed by Philip Johnson |
| 1963 | Garden Library opened, designed by Frederick Rhinelander King |
| 1976 | Proposal to construct underground library in North Vista rejected |
| 1999 | Proposal to construct underground library in North Vista revisited |

## Further Reading

Balmori, Diana, Diane Kostial McGuire, and Eleanor M. McPeck, *Beatrix Farrand's American Landscapes: Her Gardens and Campuses,* Sagaponack, New York: Sagapress, 1985

Masson, Georgina, *Dumbarton Oaks: A Guide to the Gardens,* Washington, D.C.: Dumbarton Oaks Trustees, 1968

McGuire, Diane Kostial, and Lois Fern, *Beatrix Jones Farrand (1872–1959): Fifty Years of American Landscape Architecture,* Washington, D.C.: Dumbarton Oaks Trustees, 1982

McPeck, Eleanor M., "Beatrix Farrand," in *American Landscape Architecture: Designers and Places,* edited by William H. Tishler, Washington, D.C.: Preservation Press, 1989

Whitehill, Walter Muir, *Dumbarton Oaks: The History of a Georgetown House and Garden, 1800–1966,* Cambridge, Massachusetts: Harvard University Press, 1967

ELEANOR M. MCPECK

stone bridge. The garden's power to evoke on so many levels other passages, other moments in time is what makes Dumbarton Oakes and enduring work of art.

Farrand's original design is still substantially intact, although several elements were redesigned by Ruth Havey, including the Urn Terrace and the Pebble Garden, after Farrand's death in 1959. The Pre-Columbian Wing, designed by Philip Johnson, was added in 1962. The discreetly sited Garden Library, designed by Frederick Rhinelander King, opened in 1963. A proposal to construct an underground library beneath the North Vista was rejected by the trustees in 1976. A more recent proposal would locate the new library on a site behind the existing gardener's cottage. Fortunately, the garden that Farrand considered her most deeply felt and

# Duncombe Park

## Helmsley, North Yorkshire, England

**Location:**  approximately 45 miles (73 km) northeast of Leeds, near river Rye

Duncombe Park, located at the western border of Helmsley, sits high on a plateau above a wooded vale and the winding river Rye. The garden terrace, for which it is best known, is a crescent-shaped lawn terminated at either end with temple follies. It embraces the Ryedale view to the east and the picturesque vista to the north toward the tower of Helmsley Church and the massive stone walls of the ancient castle. This extraordinarily beautiful and sublime prospect embodies a concept that was continued and complemented by the later development of the west-facing arc of Rievaulx Terrace above the ancient Cistercian Rievaulx Abbey, approximately three miles (4.8 km) to the northwest. Duncombe Terrace is an elegant yet simple gesture of appreciation for the natural and romantic landscape and secures its place in history as an important transitional work between an era of great formal gardens and the beginning of the English landscape garden.

In 1689 Sir Charles Duncombe purchased Helmsley from the estate of the second duke of Buckingham for an unprecedented £90,000. Duncombe was a wealthy commoner who had made his fortune as a London goldsmith and banker in the years following the Restoration of Charles II. His acquisition afforded him the Helmsley seat in Parliament, which he held until 1697. He later became Lord Mayor of London (1708). He preferred his other properties closer to the city and, although he may have identified the present site as a desirable location for a house, he did little to improve the North Riding estate. Duncombe was unmarried when he died in 1711, and the estate went to his nephew Thomas Browne, who took the name Duncombe and immediately set out to establish a home on the property.

In defining the layout for the house and grounds, it is likely that Thomas Duncombe consulted with noted architect Sir John Vanbrugh, who between 1699 and 1726 was developing plans for Castle Howard about 12 miles (19 km) southeast of Helmsley. The writer and landscape gardener Stephen Switzer, who was also involved at Castle Howard, may have given advice as well. In 1713 William Wakefield, a talented amateur architect, assumed responsibility for the design and construction of Duncombe Park, but the house design published in *Vitruvius Britannicus* (vol. 1, 1715; vol. 3, 1725) clearly shows his mentor Vanbrugh's influence in the use of Doric pilasters (Castle Howard) and the raised central clerestory (Seaton Delaval). In 1843 Sir

Charles Barry designed the Italianate wings of the mansion for William Duncombe, the second Baron Feversham. The square additions, housing the servants' apartments (south) and the stables (north), are each connected to the mansion with a curved, enclosed colonnade. Barry's scheme reinforces the symmetry of the house, establishes a well-defined arrival court, and harmonizes with Wakefield's earlier work. William Andrew Nesfield, a landscape gardener who had collaborated with Barry at Harewood House, designed the boxwood parterre garden associated with the additions. The mansion was largely destroyed by fire in 1879 and rebuilt to the original design, with alterations to the garden portico. The grounds are what distinguish Duncombe Park from all the other estates of North Riding, representing "one of the most extensive and boldest landscaping enterprises of England" (Pevsner).

The approach from Helmsley through the deer park gives view to the elevated Ionic temple on the left and gracefully rises toward the mansion's west front at the edge of an open field. Another entrance (now closed to the public but viewed from the Thirsk-Pickering Road) is near the village of Sproxton, approximately three miles (4.8 km) southwest of Helmsley. This drive passes through the Nelson Gate (ca. 1806) and over the Mill Bridge.

The central axis of the house enters through the west gates of the forecourt and continues through the two-story central hall. It exits the house at the grand Doric portico, descending two flights of stairs and traversing the broad north-south walk on the east garden front. From here it moves across the great lawn panel, about 100 square yards (84 sq. m), bounded by gravel walks and ancient deciduous plantations north and south. On the northern perimeter of the north plantation lies a Yew Walk, approached by a diagonal path in a northeasterly direction from the house. At the east edge of the lawn, a sculpture of Father Time leans over a sundial inscribed with the words "Non Tardis Appereor." The sculpture, a composition attributed to John van Nost (1715), receives the axis and announces the intersection of the gently curving half-mile-long (0.8 km) great terrace, a concave embrace of the verdant Rye valley. To the north an Ionic temple and to the south a Tuscan temple terminate the graceful sweep of leveled grass that follows the crest of the escarpment. Just below the terrace a line of yews once traced the contour and defined the border of the lower woodland plantings.

The Ionic rotunda is attributed to Vanbrugh. It was designed and constructed between 1714 and 1724 while

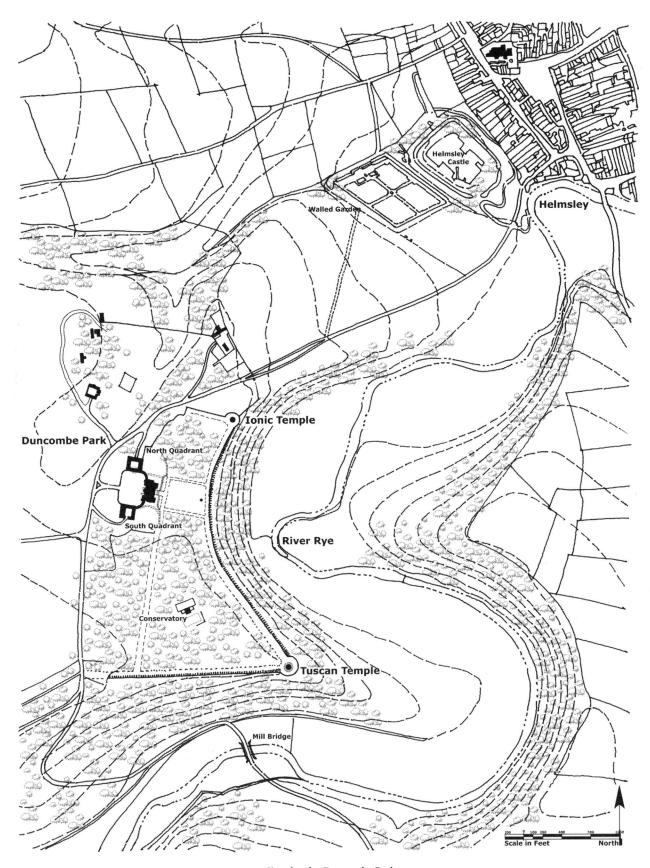

Helmsley Castle

Helmsley

Walled Garden

Ionic Temple

Duncombe Park

North Quadrant

South Quadrant

River Rye

Conservatory

Tuscan Temple

Mill Bridge

Scale in Feet

North

Site plan for Duncombe Park
Copyright Jack Sullivan

he was working at Castle Howard. The open temple, capped with a lead dome, is the same design that Vanbrugh contributed to Stowe in Buckinghamshire (1719–20). The temple frames the glorious view to the north and east, incorporating in the composition the distant heather-covered moors, the Helmsley scene in the middle ground, and the deer park at the fore.

The temple stands upon a bastion supported by a rusticated masonry revetment, a wall that parallels the Helmsley approach, defines and enhances its course, and retains the higher wooded ground and Yew Walk to the south. The irregular serpentine shape of this wall suggests that it was constructed to preserve large specimen trees in the process of easing the grade for the entrance drive. It is similar in appearance to Switzer's description (in *Iconographia Rustica* [1718]) of "raised fortification work" and anticipates the ha-ha, or sunk fence, that Charles Bridgeman later designed for Stowe. As such, it is probably the earliest example of a device for physically separating the garden from the park yet establishing the visual continuity of the landscape garden.

In a description of the walk along the terrace, Arthur Young wrote in *A Six Month Tour through the North of England* (1771), "Nothing can be more truly beautiful than the bird's eye assemblage of objects, which are seen from hence." He described a view that "is beheld with a moving variation . . . with fresh objects breaking upon the eye as you advance" toward the Tuscan temple. Sir Thomas Robinson of Rokeby designed for Thomas Duncombe II the enclosed circular Doric or Tuscan temple at the southeastern end of the terrace. An avowed Palladian classicist, Robinson attempted to correct the proportions of Hawksmoor's mausoleum (1729) at Castle Howard. He had criticized the design for its tall, slender columns and close column spacing. Duncombe Park's Doric temple (ca. 1730), a much smaller structure, stands upon a bastion where the escarpment turns sharply to the west and proceeds along a straight line above the river's meandering course. Below the temple promontory is the river's natural cascade. Further downstream is the earlier site of the kitchen garden, which was moved in the late 1750s to a walled garden adjacent to Helmsley Castle. Young noted that "the temple commands such various scenes of the sublime and beautiful as to form a theatre worthy of the magnificent pencil of nature."

The grass walk along the southern escarpment ends at a gate that opens to the agricultural fields west of the mansion. To the north of the walk, a plantation of magnificent oak and ash contains a wildflower habitat and winding trails that lead to a prominent clearing. On the northwest side of the sunken lawn is a conservatory (ca. 1851–52) that was designed by Charles Barry, Jr., and R.R. Banks. It briefly served as Michael Rochford's incubator for exotic tropical houseplants while he was head gardener at Duncombe Park between 1851 and 1856. Today it offers an intimate secret hideaway within the stately grounds. The roofless apses on either side of the main tripartite block enclose colorful floral gardens and screen the tennis court behind.

Duncombe Park was given over to a girls' school soon after World War I. In 1987 the sixth Baron Feversham and Lady Feversham decided to live on the estate and began work to restore the house and gardens. Duncombe Park is now open to visitors and affords a rare glimpse of the early landscape garden as it was originally proposed. As seen from the grand terrace, the remaining stone fortification at Helmsley Castle captures the golden light of the setting sun. The contemporary scene, framed with temple and woods, reflects the spirit and beauty of the 18th-century poetic garden.

**Synopsis**

| | |
|---|---|
| 1689 | Charles Duncombe purchases Helmsley and becomes member of parliament |
| 1711 | Charles's nephew Thomas (Browne) Duncombe inherits Helmsley estate |
| 1713 | William Wakefield, Yorkshire amateur architect, designs mansion with advice from Sir John Vanbrugh |
| 1713–18 | Duncombe Terrace created by Thomas Duncombe |
| 1714–24 | Vanbrugh designs Ionic rotunda (contemporary with design for Stowe) at one end of Duncombe Terrace walk |
| 1730 | Thomas Robinson designs Doric or Tuscan temple, at other end of terrace walk |
| 1758 | Thomas Duncombe II completes Rievaulx Terrace, 3 miles (5 km) away to the northwest |
| 1843 | Italianate additions designed by Charles Barry, boxwood parterre gardens by William Andrews Nesfield |
| 1879 | Original Duncombe mansion badly destroyed by fire |
| 1891 | Reconstruction of mansion begun |
| 1920–87 | Duncombe Park used as girls' school |
| 1987 | Lord and Lady Feversham move into Duncombe Park and begin restoration |

**Further Reading**

Campbell, Colen, *Vitruvius Britannicus*, 3 vols., London, 1715–25; reprint, 1 vol., New York: Blom, 1967

Drake, Francis, *Eboracum; or, The History and Antiquities of the City of York*, 2 vols., London, 1736

Fleming, Laurence, and Alan Gore, *The English Garden*, London: Joseph, 1979

Hussey, Christopher, *The Picturesque: Studies in a Point of View*, London and New York: Putnam, 1927;

reprint, Hamden, Connecticut: Archon Books, and London: Cass, 1967

Hussey, Christopher, *English Country Houses,* 3 vols., London: Country Life, 1956–65; see especially vol. 1, *Early Georgian, 1715–1760*

Hussey, Christopher, *English Gardens and Landscapes, 1700–1750,* London: Country Life, 1967

Langdale, Thomas, *A Topographical Dictionary of Yorkshire,* Northallerton, North Yorkshire, 1809; 2nd edition, 1822

Lees-Milne, James, *English Country Houses: Baroque, 1685–1715,* London: Country Life Books, 1970

Pevsner, Nikolaus, *Yorkshire: The North Riding,* London: Penguin Books, 1966

Tipping, Henry Avray, and Christopher Hussey, *English Homes, Period IV,* 2 vols., London: Country Life, and New York: Scribner, 1920–28; see especially vol. 2

Whistler, Laurence, *The Imagination of Vanbrugh and His Fellow Artists,* London: Art and Technics, 1954

Willis, Peter, *Charles Bridgeman and the English Landscape Garden,* London: Zwemmer, 1977

Young, Arthur, *A Six Months Tour through the North of England,* 4 vols., London, 1770; 2nd edition, corrected and enlarged, 1771; reprint, New York: Kelley, 1967

JACK SULLIVAN

# E

## Eckbo, Garrett 1910–2000

### United States Landscape Architect

Garrett Eckbo claims that his entry into the profession of landscape architecture was inspired by his boyhood interest in plants and art. By some miracle of intuition in 1933 he discovered the program in landscape design at the University of California, Berkeley, where it had been taught since 1913. After his graduation he worked for a major nursery in Los Angeles and reputedly designed 100 gardens in a single year.

In 1936 Eckbo won a scholarship to the Harvard Graduate School of Design, where he found landscape architecture entrenched in traditionalism and a reverence for Frederick Olmsted, while architecture had been transformed by the radical modern theories of the Bauhaus, through the teachings of Walter Gropius, László Moholy Nagy, and Gyorgy Kepes. With two fellow students (James Rose and Dan Kiley), Eckbo defected to the new ideas. Even before finishing his degree, he published an article in *Pencil Points*, entitled "Small Gardens in the City" (September 1937), in which bilateral symmetry and conventional rules of design are rejected in favor of "forms which come out of the situation," combined with artistic expression. He argues that landscape design in the mid-20th century should reflect current technology, art, and the spirit of the new age. Eckbo believes that garden design, having fewer constraints than modern house design, can be viewed in the same way as a sculptor approaches a new block of stone or a painter a blank canvas. The implied freedom for the designer is tempered only by the implications of functionalism and a more broadly based affluent lifestyle. He suggests that the garden, as a background for life, should be more than an outdoor living room: it should be a place of delight, fantasy, imagination, and adventure.

With this break from the traditional understanding of what a garden should be, Eckbo developed a philosophy and process of design that he claims has served him well for landscape projects of all sizes and scales. Eckbo's garden plans of the 1940s and 1950s have been compared to the paintings of Kandinsky and Miró, and the gardens illustrated in his first book, *Landscape for Living* (1950), indicate a concern for the sculptural structuring of space. Similar characteristics can be found in later commercial projects, such as the Union Bank Plaza in Los Angeles (1964).

In 1945 Eckbo formed a partnership with Robert Royston and Edward Williams. (Francis Dean joined in 1948.) Eckbo was in charge of a Los Angeles office of the firm until 1963. The practice, later dubbed EDAW, expanded and in addition to private gardens included campus design, schools, and parks. After 1970 large-scale design and planning came to dominate the practice in response to state and national concerns for urban renewal and environmental protection. The large practice became international in scope. The list of commissions is virtually endless. In 1979 Eckbo formed a separate practice, which lasted in various forms until 1989.

Eckbo's influence on the profession was extended through the publication of four major books and his work as a teacher at the University of Southern California (1948–56) and the University of California, Berkeley (1963–78). In recognition of his contribution to the profession, Eckbo received the American Society of Landscape Architects Medal of Honor in 1975.

Beyond completed projects, teaching, and writing, Eckbo's major contribution was changing the way landscape architects think about design as a response to the need for human comfort, the site environment, and the potential contribution of art as a source of form.

## Biography

Born Cooperstown, New York, 1910. Raised in California; B.S. in Landscape Architecture, University of California at Berkeley, 1935; Master of Landscape Architecture, Harvard Graduate School of Design, 1938; over 50 years of diverse professional practice in various partnerships (Robert Royston; Dean, Austin, and Williams), writing, and teaching (1939–90). Received numerous awards, including American Society of Landscape Architects Medal of Honor, 1975, and Certificate of Achievement, Harvard University, 1976.

## Selected Designs

| 1939–45 | Farm Security Administration and Defense housing projects in California and western United States |
| 1955–65 | Private gardens, mainly in the Los Angeles area, United States |
| 1955[–65] | Ambassador College, Pasadena, California, United States |
| 1958 | Alcoa Forecast Garden, Los Angeles, California, United States |
| 1959[63] | Downtown Pedestrian Mall, Fresno, California, United States |
| 1960[64] | Union Bank Square, Los Angeles, California, United States |
| 1961[65] | Mission Bay Park, San Diego, California, United States |
| 1962[–78] | University of New Mexico campus, Albuquerque, New Mexico, United States |
| 1963[75] | Shelby Farms, Memphis, Tennessee, United States |

## Selected Publications

*Landscape for Living,* 1950
*The Art of Home Landscaping,* 1956; revised edition, 1978
*Urban Landscape Design,* 1964
*The Landscape We See,* 1969

## Further Reading

French, Jere Stuart, *The California Garden: And the Landscape Architects Who Shaped It,* Washington, DC: The Landscape Architecture Foundation, 1993

*Garrett Eckbo: Philosophy of Landscape; Garetto Ekubo: Rando sukepu no shiso* (bilingual English-Japanese edition), Tokyo: Purosesu Akitekuchua, 1990

Laurie, Michael, *An Interview with Garrett Eckbo, January 1981,* edited by Karen Madsen, Watertown, Massachusetts: Hubbard Educational Trust, 1990

Streatfield, David C., *California Gardens,* New York: Abbeville Press, 1994

Treib, Marc, editor, *Modern Landscape Architecture: A Critical Review,* Cambridge, Massachusetts: MIT Press, 1993

Treib, Marc, and Dorothée Imbert, *Garrett Eckbo: Modern Landscapes for Living,* Berkeley: University of California Press, 1997

Walker, Peter, and Melanie Louise Simo, *Invisible Gardens: The Search for Modernism in the American Landscape,* Cambridge, Massachusetts: MIT Press, 1994

MICHAEL LAURIE

---

# Ecology

All gardens are ecological, whether the designers know about ecology or not. For example, the great artistic Californian gardens of Garrett Eckbo and Thomas Church, while known for their modernistic designs, contain exquisite examples of the application of ecological knowledge sympathetic to the client, site, and surrounding environments. While ecology is a relatively new construct of science, the development of gardens is much more ancient: garden designers in ancient China applied the principles of *feng shui,* garden designers of the Old and New Kingdoms in Pharaonic Egypt prepared functional gardens for food production, and the creators of the bottomland gardens during classic Mayan times studied and were interested in ecological applications to design for both functional and aesthetic reasons. For most of civilization's history, science has provided very little useful information for garden design. During the last 150 years, however, science has made significant strides in studying the environment, being able to more accurately describe the age of the earth and the evolution of life forms and to characterize the relationship of these life forms to each other and to related physical phenomena. During its formative period ecology (the study of the *oikos*—a Greek name for "home") originated in the study of natural history and was considered a branch of biology. Ecology has now grown beyond natural history and biology to include economics, political science, urban design, environmental psychology, medicine, engineering, and many other disciplines and professions. In this vein ecology has much to contribute to garden design and landscape architecture.

While ecology can make contributions to garden design, it is important to distinguish the art of garden design from the science of ecology. Ecology addresses the relationships of environmental phenomena to each other, especially involving living organisms; art addresses the practice of "deciding what should be done." Therefore, ecological information can provide input into the design of a garden but does not dictate what should be accomplished in a design. In addition, scientific ecological information can never be complete, as there is always something more to study. In addition, it is not always easy to translate ecological information into meaningful design prescriptions. Sometimes great ecological discoveries are not relevant to garden design. For example, concepts in evolutionary ecology may have little importance in practical garden design. At best, ecological information translates into principles or normative design theories with a series of statements beginning with "The designer should consider . . ." Jens Jensen, a designer of parks and gardens in the American Midwest in the early 20th century, strongly believed that one should derive design solutions based on sound ecological study. He was a student of the environment and translated ecological and natural history observations into heuristic/normative design ideas in an ecologically sensitive manner.

One of the exciting recent contributions of ecology to design is in the area of landscape ecology. In this scientific area the patterns of the landscape are studied in great detail to understand the composition of the landscape and its capacity to support plants and animals in a meaningful and economically wise manner. Principles and concepts in landscape ecology can be employed for large regions, for a small rock containing lichens, or for a tidal basin area with sea anemones and can thus be applicable to garden design. The dominating landscape cover type (such as forest, grassland, paving, or cropland) is considered to be the matrix. Within the matrix are patches (flower beds, a small ornamental tree, a deck) and networks of other cover types (walkways, a stream, a gravel road, a hedgerow), thus forming patterns within the garden. Each cover type contains a structure such as a high canopy or an exposed substrate plain. This structure provides habitat, microclimates, and aesthetic spatial features that one can use in design. The connectivity of cover types and the size, shape, and interspersion of patches are issues for the garden designer to consider.

Some landscape ecological information translates into direct programmatic items for the garden designer to consider. For example, some herons and bald eagles prefer not to be disturbed when raising young; thus, a specific distance may be required to separate transportation networks and housing from patches of land with nesting habitat. In another example, patches of wetlands with a certain minimum size may be required to support specific wildlife types; or two small unconnected patches can be made more beneficial with the inclusion of a connecting network forming a larger contiguous patch. Landscape ecology may well be most applicable when considering wildlife habitat.

To assess landscapes for their landscape ecological potential, one needs to divide the landscape into various meaningful cover types. The cover types are really vegetation associations (sometimes called plant communities). The identification of plant communities, for example a maple/basswood (*Tilia*) mesic forest, extends beyond what one may normally consider. Ecologists have identified a series of vegetation associations affiliated with humans. For example, a landscape with one- and two-story buildings containing at least one tree per acre (0.4 ha) is considered to be the urban savanna association. Urban landscapes with three-story or higher buildings are in the cliff detritus association. Most gardens are in the urban savanna association, a landscape characterized by extremely wide diversity of vegetation and abundant plant growth that accommodates wildlife species that thrive in edge conditions. Because an abundance of urban savanna can fragment a large block of a single matrix such as a forest, species that require large blocks of a uniform cover type can be disadvantaged. This is why the urban savanna landscape may require balance by incorporating nature preserves with large blocks of forest, prairie, or wetland especially for interior species. It is also important to remember that each of these environmental associations is not necessarily a discrete entity, and one can find a gradual continuum of associations where one combination of plants blends into another. In other settings the edges between associations may be more discrete and the blending less evident. It is often helpful to consider each stand of vegetation as unique, yet containing properties that may be similar to other related stands.

Plants and animals within each of these associations have strategies often well suited to a particular set of environmental conditions. For example, in mesic environments where the water, light, soils, and temperature are ideal for many plants, and which are often the growing conditions of a garden, the plants that perform best are the competitors. Competitors are able to capture resources away from other plants and dominate the environment. Beech, maple, and basswood trees are examples of competitors. This is why it is difficult to grow turf beneath maple trees; they capture resources such as light and moisture, taking them away from the turf. Other plants pursue ruderal strategies (living in disturbed areas). Disturbances are classified as phenomena that physically destroy vegetation, such as by trampling, mowing, browsing, wind erosion, and fire. Ruderals grow quickly, setting seed before the next disturbance, and are often very weedy plants. A third growth strategy is a stress-tolerator strategy, whereby plants and animals attempt to survive in special environments that limit their growth, such as hot temperatures, cold temperatures, drought, flooding, high or low soil pH, and a variety of other physical conditions. Stress-tolerating plants can often perform quite well in a mesic garden provided competition and disturbances are controlled. For example, *Larix*, a tree that is found growing in bogs, can grow quite well in the garden landscape by controlling competition—removing or pruning plants that would shade the tree—and by controlling fire, a disturbance. Some stress tolerators require particular stresses to survive, such as many acid bog plants and alpine tundra rock garden plants. These plants do not have a mesic preference. A number of plants have strategies between the three basic ones. For example, a bur oak tree is a partial stress tolerator (drought), partial disturbance tolerator (fire), and a partial competitor (shading grasses and shrubs).

In planning and designing a garden, it is helpful to map the potential vegetation strategy and survival environments of a site, assigning stressful, ruderal, and competitive conditions. This environmental mapping can aid in assessing the capacity and constraints of the landscape to sustain vegetation. Garden designers and landscape architects who are knowledgeable concerning the life histories and preferences of plant material can match the environments with the appropriate vegetation for planting, illustrating the connection between ecology and natural history. Knowing the palette of vegetation, especially vegetation preferences within a particular region, is so important that states such as California and Nebraska require a special plant-material exam for the registration of landscape architects.

While the aesthetic beauty and physical characteristics of plants are important in garden design, ecological understanding has become an important part of the required knowledge base for garden designers as well. The Brazilian gardens of Roberto Burle Marx are as emblematic in the application of ecological knowledge to design with plants as the designs are artistic. Frank Waugh, an educator and landscape architect, presented one of the first published site cross-sections concerning the ecological interpretation of human-influenced landscape ecological settings, the ecology of roadsides. His work is illustrative of the importance and ability of designers to transcribe ecological phenomena into useful design information. The late Ian McHarg, while addressing the environment at the landscape-planning level, also illustrated how ecological information is translated into design information about environmental structure, suitability, capability, processes, sustainability, and the siting of facilities. John Tillman Lyle transcribed information for the planning and design of environments across scales and is best known for his vision for the Center for Regenerative Studies, a contemporary ecological garden in California.

Unlike architecture, which often looks best upon initial construction, gardens usually look their best with age. As trees grow and plants mature, the environmental conditions of the site may change, affording new opportunities in the garden and removing others. These changes in structure and composition are succession and regression occurrences. In response, some garden designers attempt to plan an area so that the installed vegetation will eventually fill a space without the need for new plants or the removal of crowded plants. Other designers attempt to halt succession by regularly removing tree seedlings. Still others intend to develop woodland shade gardens once a tree canopy has formed. Thus, any garden design project should carefully take into account the environmental context of the site, including environmental change. In addition, the effects of hurricanes, wildfires, floods, insect damage, and other disturbances and stresses should be thoughtfully considered.

In the design, implementation, and management of a garden, it is often helpful to consider that the substrate (soil, bark, rocks), topography, and especially vegetation, wildlife, and humans interconnect and that their functions affect the intent of the space. For example, a windbreak can contribute to the development of a successful magnolia garden, and a sloping hillside with canopy trees to the west can allow the development of an azalea garden that is cool and shaded during the warmest time of the day. In addition to the functions, the interaction of the materials and energy in the garden follows processes that are important to consider. For example, in a maple/basswood forest setting, autumn leaves recycle calcium for the trees. Removing the leaves in the woodland breaks the ecological flow of materials within the forest. When designing a space, it is useful to examine and learn about the functions and processes affiliated with the site. Such knowledge can allow the garden designer to be more efficient and effective with the management of the landscape. For this reason, many garden designers have committed their professional efforts to specializing their work for specific regions, enabling them to build a vast ecological knowledge base for the design of gardens in their region of choice.

Ecological gardening often includes practices in which pesticides are not used, extensive soil modification is discouraged, irrigation is not employed, organic materials are recycled, and locally adaptive native plants are preferred over exotics. This practice also includes activities whereby invasive exotic plants such as buckthorn (*Rhamnus*) or loosestrife (*Lythrum*) are controlled or removed. Some gardeners (both professional and amateur) view gardening as the practice of getting highly ornamental exotics to grow near the limits of their environmental boundaries and to use any means possible (fertilizers, pesticides, soil amendments, and other gardening devices) to succeed. Ecological gardening is the opposite of this approach.

Today many gardeners and garden designers are able to create specialized ecological gardens affiliated with their region of choice. Because a region or a specific site may contain a variety of environments, garden designers learn to design an array of ecological garden types. For example, in the American Midwest designers can create designs for numerous types of wetland, woodland, savanna, and prairie. In addition, they can design gardens for songbirds, butterflies, and other wildlife types. Public examples of these gardens can be observed at the Missouri Botanical Gardens, the Chicago Botanic Garden, and the Minnesota Landscape Arboretum.

One of the greatest lessons that has been gleaned from ecological science is the importance of diversity across scales. Some designers actually use measures and indicators of diversity to assess their designs, meaning that diversity should occur at the vegetation association level as well as in the selection of individual plants within a shrub bed. Ecology at the beginning of the 21st century has much to offer gardeners and garden designers, but it also means that there is more to learn and to apply as gardens are created.

## Further Reading

Bakker, Elna S., *An Island Called California: An Ecological Introduction to Its Natural Communities,* Berkeley: University of California Press, 1971; 2nd edition, revised and expanded, 1984

Chabot, Brian F., and Harold A. Mooney, editors, *Physiological Ecology of North American Plant Communities,* New York and London: Chapman and Hall, 1985

Diekelmann, John, and Robert Schuster, *Natural Landscaping: Designing with Native Plant Communities,* New York: McGraw Hill, 1982

Eliovson, Sima, *The Gardens of Roberto Burle Marx,* New York: Abrams/Saga Press, and London: Thames and Hudson, 1991

Forman, Richard T.T., and Michel Godron, *Landscape Ecology,* New York: Wiley, 1986

French, Jere Stuart, *The California Garden: And the Landscape Architects Who Shaped It,* Washington, D.C.: Landscape Architecture Foundation, 1993

Grese, Robert E., *Jens Jensen: Maker of Natural Parks and Gardens,* Baltimore, Maryland: Johns Hopkins University Press, 1992

Grime, John Philip, *Plant Strategies and Vegetation Processes,* Chichester, West Sussex, and New York: Wiley, 1979

Hale, Gill, *The Feng Shui Garden: Design Your Garden for Health, Wealth, and Happiness,* Pownal, Vermont: Storey Books, and London: Aurum, 1998

Lyle, John Tillman, *Design for Human Ecosystems: Landscape, Land Use, and Natural Resources,* New York: Van Nostrand Reinhold, 1985

Lyle, John Tillman, *Regenerative Design for Sustainable Development,* New York and Chichester, West Sussex: Wiley, 1994

McGinnies, William Grovenor, *Discovering the Desert: Legacy of the Carnegie Desert Botanical Laboratory,* Tucson: University of Arizona Press, 1981

McHarg, Ian L., *Design with Nature,* Garden City, New York: Natural History Press, 1969; new edition, New York and Chichester, West Sussex: Wiley, 1992

Mitsch, William J., and James G. Gosselink, *Wetlands,* New York: Van Nostrand Reinhold, 1986; 2nd edition, 1993

Myers, Ronald L., and John J. Ewel, editors, *Ecosystems of Florida,* Orlando: University of Central Florida Press, 1990

Reynolds, James F., and John D. Tenhunen, *Landscape Function and Disturbance in Arctic Tundra,* Berlin and New York: Springer, 1996

Ricklefs, Robert E., *The Economy of Nature: A Textbook in Basic Ecology,* New York: Chiron Press, 1976; 4th edition, New York: Freeman, 1997

Watts, May Theilgaard, *Reading the Landscape: An Adventure in Ecology,* New York: Macmillan, 1957; revised and expanded edition, as *Reading the Landscape of America,* 1975

Waugh, Frank A., "Ecology of the Roadside," *Landscape Architecture* 21, no. 2 (1931)

Wilber, Donald Newton, *Persian Gardens and Garden Pavilions,* Rutland, Vermont: Tuttle, 1962; 2nd edition, Washington, D.C.: Dumbarton Oaks, 1979

JON BRYAN BURLEY

# Edinburgh, Royal Botanic Garden

## Inverleith, Edinburgh, Scotland

**Location:**   Inverleith, approximately 1 mile (1.6 km) north of Edinburgh city center, between Arboretum Place (West Gate) and Inverleith Row (East Gate)

The Royal Botanic Garden, Edinburgh is the second oldest botanic garden in Great Britain, after the Oxford Botanic Garden (established 1621), and has a living plant collection representing about 7 percent of the world's flowering plants, as well as conifers, cycads, ferns, and their allies—nearly 17,000 species in all. In addition to the living collection, famous in particular for its rock and heath gardens, arboretum, and Sino-Himalayan collection, the Royal Botanic Garden, Edinburgh, has an important library and herbarium and is engaged in significant research, education, and conservation programs. Its main site (31 ha [76.6 acres]) is at Inverleith, in Edinburgh, but it also incorporates three specialty gardens at separate sites in Scotland: the Younger, Logan, and Dawyck Botanic Gardens (50, 12, and 25 ha [123.5, 29.6, and 62 acres] respectively).

The Royal Botanic Garden, Edinburgh, originated in a small physic garden developed near Holyrood in 1670. The garden was moved twice before its final relocation to the site at Inverleith and the history of its development reflects changing attitudes toward the value and purpose of studying botany and the cultivation and display of plant collections. Its original importance lay in the 17th-century link between botany and medicine, which was based on the herbalism of medieval times. In the early 18th century it became famous not only for its science but also for the skill of its horticulturalists. Its curators and keepers necessarily developed great expertise in moving mature plants. Most notably, William McNab relocated the garden, trees and all, to its Inverleith site in the 1820s; he and others created naturalistic settings for the great collections of plant material gathered by a succession of Scottish explorers, from Archibald Menzies in the 18th century to George Forrest and Reginald Farrer in the early 20th century. Several innovative glasshouses have been part of the garden's history, from the first in 1713 to the last major construction in 1967. The garden's educational importance has continued since its inception, but by the 19th century the focus had shifted from medicine to taxonomy and horticulture, backed throughout by a high level of research. In the late 20th century, new emphasis was placed on the conservation of rare and endangered species, from Scotland and elsewhere, and on public and school education programs.

The garden was started in 1670 by Andrew Balfour and Robert Sibbald, Edinburgh physicians educated in continental Europe who knew the medicinal value of plants. They established their botanic garden because of their horror at the ignorance of the local apothecaries and chirurgeons, creating a 161.6 square meter (193.3 sq. yd.) plot in St. Anne's Yards, south of Holyrood Abbey. The original collection of 800 to 900 plants came from the physicians' private gardens and from gardens of friends. Additions soon made a new garden necessary, and in 1675 land was acquired adjoining Trinity Hospital at the mouth of the Nor' Loch (now occupied by Waverley Station). This plot became known as the Physick Garden. Measuring 91.5 by 58 meters (100 by 63.5 yd.), it contained about 2,000 plants arranged in subdivisions containing order beds, flowering displays, medicinal plants, aquatic plants, and an arboretum. Sibbald and Balfour achieved prominence as Edinburgh physicians and Sibbald was appointed first professor of medicine at the University of Edinburgh. James Sutherland was appointed "Intendant" of the Physick Garden, and he introduced a number of new species to Great Britain. The university created a chair of botany for Sutherland in 1695 and he not only became active in teaching, but was also responsible for the King's Royal Garden at Holyrood. In 1699 he was appointed King's Botanist to William III, and in 1710 he became Regius Professor of Botany to Queen Anne, apparently the first time such titles had been bestowed.

Concerns about urban pollution and the desire for a better site led to the development of a new 2 hectare (5 acre) garden west of Leith Walk; the entire plant collection was successfully transferred there under Regius Keeper John Hope in 1761. Hope, a brilliant botanist and educator, and an admirer of Linnaeus and his revolutionary natural classification system, successfully obtained a modest but permanent income from the crown for the upkeep of the new garden.

By 1820 the garden site had again become inadequate and was encroached upon by urban development; the contents of the garden were again moved, this time to the location at Inverleith. The move took over two years, under Robert Graham (Regius Keeper) and McNab (Curator). The latter's horticultural skill and, in particular, his invention of a transplanting machine that successfully relocated mature trees, meant that virtually none of the more than 4,000 species in the collection were lost. James McNab succeeded his father as curator and oversaw the building of the new (now the Temperate) Palm House, as well as a much-acclaimed rock garden on a site extension acquired from the Royal Caledonian Horticultural Society. The purchase of another 12.5 hectares (31 acres), including Inverleith House and grounds, allowed the development of an arboretum.

In 1889 the Royal Botanic Garden, Edinburgh, was placed under crown control with Regius Keeper Isaac Bayley Balfour in charge of the early development of the modern garden. After more than 30 years of heated debate on the subject, the garden was finally opened to the public on Sundays (it had previously been open only on weekdays and Saturdays, in deference to the Sabbath Alliance) and over 27,000 people visited it on these first Sundays in April 1889. Balfour initiated classes in horticulture and forestry, which were free in return for labor in the garden, as well as a major taxonomic research program. He appointed George Forrest to undertake a series of plant collecting expeditions to western China and the Himalayas, resulting in the introduction of hundreds of new plants into cultivation, including some 300 rhododendrons as well as primulas, magnolias, gentians, mecanopsis, and lilies. In addition, Forrest brought back over 30,000 herbarium specimens. Under Balfour's direction, McNab's rock garden, much admired for 30 years or more but now described as "chaotic" and "hideous" by plant collector Reginald Farrer, was rebuilt using a more naturalistic design. Subsequently, under William Wright Smith's keepership, new heath, woodland, and peat gardens were developed, the latter in particular to accommodate part of the Sino-Himalayan collection.

Smith also established the Royal Botanic Garden, Edinburgh's first specialty garden, the Younger Botanic Garden, which provided mild and moist conditions more suitable for rhododendrons and conifers. It was acquired from the Forestry Commission's Benmore Estate, Argyll, in the west of Scotland. Subsequently two more specialty gardens were added: the Logan Botanic Garden in Galloway (1969), a mild, subtropical site on Scotland's southwest extremity, and the Dawyck Botanic Garden in Peebles (1978), a drier and colder site with a remarkable tree collection dating from the 17th century.

Upon Smith's death in 1956, the posts of Regius Keeper of the Garden and Regius Professor of Botany, which had been vested in one person since 1738, became distinct again. Harold Fletcher as keeper oversaw the building of a new herbarium and library in 1964 and, in 1967, the construction of a new range of exhibition plant houses designed by G. Pearce, an architect with the Department of Buildings and Public Works, which were hailed as the most innovative since Burton's Palm House at the Royal Botanic Gardens, Kew, built in the 1840s. The main plant house (128 by 18.25 m [140 by 20 yards]) was designed with an external support system that left the large interior free of

James McNab's Rock Garden, ca. 1890, Royal Botanic Garden, Edinburgh, Scotland
Courtesy of Royal Botanic Garden, Edinburgh

structures, for plant display, and for sophisticated automatic climate modification systems. In 1960, under Fletcher, the garden also became, briefly, the first home of the Scottish National Gallery of Modern Art; the collection was housed in Inverleith House and on the surrounding lawns, to glorious effect. In 1986, however, the gallery's collection was moved to new premises.

Recent innovations include a Chinese hillside (1998) and a new layout for the heath garden (1999). The Royal Botanic Garden, Edinburgh, continues its scientific, conservation, and educational roles with the Conifer Conservation Program and the Scottish Rare Plant Project and new courses in biodiversity, taxonomy, and horticulture, all launched under David Ingram as keeper.

## Synopsis

| | |
|---|---|
| 1670 | Garden started by physicians Andrew Balfour and Robert Sibbald as medicinal plant garden, 40 square feet (ca. 3.72 sq. m) square, at St. Anne's Yards beside |

James McNab's transplanting machine
Courtesy of Royal Botanic Garden, Edinburgh

Holyrood Abbey, Edinburgh, Scotland

| | |
|---|---|
| 1675 | Land leased for extended physic garden attached to Trinity Hospital, for experiments and supply of specimens to medical students, under care of James Sutherland |
| 1699 | Sutherland appointed King's Botanist to William III; formal royal status for garden |
| 1713 | First glasshouse constructed |
| 1763 | Collections from Holyrood and Trinity Hospital transferred to larger, 2 hectare (5 acre) site off Leith Walk; Regius Keeper John Hope obtains permanent crown funding for the garden |
| 1820–23 | Under Regius Keeper Robert Graham and Curator William McNab, garden moved to part of present site at Inverleith, in Edinburgh, covering 6 hectares (14.5 acres) |
| 1858 | Palm House built, tallest in Britain |
| 1864 | Garden extended by acquisition of 4-hectare (10-acre) experimental garden from Royal Caledonian Horticultural Society (RCHS), including hall that became RBGE Herbarium |
| 1871 | Curator James McNab completes first rock garden on RCHS site |
| 1876 | Inverleith House and grounds, some 12.5 hectares (31 acres), purchased and subsequently planted as arboretum |
| 1888–89 | Under Regius Keeper Bayley Balfour, garden placed entirely under control of crown (Commissioners of Her Majesty's Works and Public Buildings) |
| 1889 | Garden opened to public on Sundays for first time |
| 1892 | Horticulture and forestry classes initiated, with free tuition in return for labor |
| 1904–32 | Thousands of new rhododendrons, primulas, magnolias, gentians, mecanopsis, and lilies introduced through Chinese and Himalayan plant-collecting expeditions of George Forrest and others |
| 1908–14 | Rock garden demolished and rebuilt to new design, basis for today's version |
| 1929 | Part of policies of Benmore Estate, Argyll, purchased to become Younger Botanic Garden Benmore, first specialist garden of RBGE |
| 1935 | Heath garden constructed |
| 1939 | Peat garden constructed for part of Sino-Himalayan collection |
| 1958 | 4.6-hectare (11-acre) site north of Inverleith Place acquired as temperate nursery |
| 1960 | Inverleith House becomes first home of Scottish National Gallery of Modern Art; gardens used for outdoor sculpture |
| 1964 | New Herbarium and Library opened |
| 1967 | Opening of new and innovative exhibition plant houses, designed by G. Pearce of the Department of Buildings and Public Works |
| 1969 | Logan Botanic Garden, Galloway, Scotland, becomes second specialist garden of RBGE; responsibility for RBGE transferred to Department of Agriculture and Fisheries for Scotland (DAFS), within Scottish Office |

1978     Dawyck Botanic Garden, near Peebles, Scotland, becomes third specialty garden of RBGE

1991     Conifer Conservation Program launched, based at RBGE

1998     Chinese hillside opened on Inverleith site

1999     Innovative heath garden layout completed

**Further Reading**

Bown, Deni, Alan P. Bennell, and Norma M. Gregory, editors, *4 Gardens in One: The Royal Botanic Garden, Edinburgh*, Edinburgh: HMSO, 1992

Fletcher, Harold Roy, and William H. Brown, *The Royal Botanic Garden, Edinburgh, 1670–1970*, Edinburgh: HMSO, 1970

Hyams, Edward, and William MacQuitty, *Great Botanical Gardens of the World*, London: Nelson, and New York: Macmillan, 1969

*List of Medicinal Plants Cultivated in the Open Air in the Royal Botanic Garden of Edinburgh, May 1846*, Edinburgh, 1846

*The Royal Botanic Garden, Edinburgh* (guidebook), Edinburgh: HMSO, 1970

CATHARINE WARD THOMPSON

---

# Education: Garden Design

The first gardens were not made but discovered. No one tended these gardens; they grew on their own accord. Antiquity has many references to such places: in the Old Testament, for example, we read about the Garden of Eden. The meaning of the word *garden* can be traced to the Hebrew word *gan,* implying a fence or enclosure. The word *Eden* means delight. The English word *garden,* therefore, is a combination of two words suggesting an enclosure for pleasure or delight. The craft of agriculture—the very development of an artful skill in the fabrication of materials—is the basis of garden craft and design. With the domestication of plants, the first gardens were created.

In Greek mythology there were deities responsible for agricultural prosperity and general fertility, and the god Priapus was responsible for gardens. In medieval Christian times (476–1400) gardeners found their patrons in St. Phocas and St. Fiacre. With the collapse of the Roman Empire, gardens and garden art dwindled, and the only people who practiced the garden craft and created small gardens were monks. Several documents from monasteries of that period describe the work of the gardener's life. Walafrid Strabo (809–49) begins a poem with general remarks: "A gardener's life is a quiet one, but needs hard work." The poem describes the work of gardening, from the building of raised beds for the plants in spring to seeding and watering. The plants used in these monastery gardens had culinary, herbal, or medicinal uses that would fully justify their place in the small garden. The documents provide a picture of the state of the gardening in western Europe around A.D. 800. The shape of the garden was square or rectangular in form. The education for the garden craft was handed down through apprenticeship, as was done with all crafts of the time. The same is true for the next historical period.

From the Renaissance period until the late 19th century, much of the notable work studied in landscape architecture history was designed by gardeners who were the owners themselves or that was commissioned by the client to someone trained in architectural engineering or art. The celebrated French 17th-century designer André Le Nôtre, a son and grandson of notable gardeners, for example, began his gardening career at the Tuileries Gardens in Paris. He worked there in a subordinate position for several years before he was allowed to develop gardens on his own. During this period the garden evolved into an art form, no longer meeting only the function of food production.

In the middle of the 19th century, many countries in Europe established agricultural schools for educating students in the craft of small-fruit production and general agriculture and horticulture. Technical gardening was not an independent subject. Russell Page's experience provides a good example of the education of a gardener. He became a professional garden designer in 1928 after studying painting at the University of London and in Paris. He designed a great variety of gardens in Europe, the Middle East, and North and South America, ranging from small cottage and town gardens to elaborate layouts. Like most gardeners before him, he learned the elements of his trade from a head gardener working near his childhood home. In his book *The Education of a Gardener* (1962) Page describes his garden education as a self-study full of hands-on experiences: "I started to understand something about plants by handling them. . . . My apprenticeship to the art of garden composition was also on a small but very practical scale." He learned by doing and by traveling to France and meeting with amateurs of architecture, decoration, sculpture, and furniture, slowly learning to appreciate some of the French style. To expand his garden education he spent time reading garden books. From the readings and visits to many gardens, he made sketches of all kinds of objects "not so much to accumulate a formal documentation, as to train my eye and mind to look and register more carefully." Later he collaborated with Sir Geoffrey Jellicoe, a noted English landscape architect and one of the founders of the Institute of Landscape Architects in England. Page's professional career illustrates the education of the premier gardeners of the time.

In Europe today many universities train students in the art of gardening and landscape design, which emanates from gardening tradition. It relies heavily on horticulture knowledge particularly as it applied to working with private and public gardens. Thus, in many countries landscape designers are hired for their practical horticultural knowledge as well as their expertise in garden design.

In the United States less formalized educational activities are offered to gardeners, with the exception of the degrees in ornamental horticulture offered by many of the land-grant universities. The Garden Club of America, founded in 1913, offers courses in landscape design and gardening. This organization established education in both horticultural and design aspects of landscape as one of its key goals. Many projects are organized in the form of competitions, thereby giving unknown designers opportunities to demonstrate their abilities in garden design. Education for garden design can take other forms as well: garden literature of the 1890s and early 1900s did much to promote rural "villa"-style living. Histories of various areas, especially England, France, and Asia, became favorite books. Marie L. Gothein's book *A History of Garden Art* (1910) was by far the most comprehensive and scholarly work on garden history of its time.

Another type of literature also began to emerge at the beginning of the 20th century—the professional text. Frank Waugh's *Landscape Gardening* (1914) can be considered the prototype for many later works. Other books of this period include Tomas Mawson's *Art and Craft of Garden Making* (1901) and Florence Robinson's *Planting Design* (1940). Many other books followed.

The modern recreating public seeks what could be called educational recreational activities, and over the last two decades there have been many places to learn about the natural environment and gardening. New arboretums have been constructed and older ones enlarged. Botanical gardens have become popular visitor amenities in larger park systems throughout the United States and elsewhere. These botanical gardens demonstrate the latest horticultural innovations and provide instructions for the public on ground management and gardening. Most have display gardens oriented toward suburban home owners. Many of these gardens offer continuing education programs composed of courses, lectures, workshops, and tours that focus on garden planning and design. The courses are building blocks and are taken in sequence.

The Master Gardener program was initiated in 1972 in Seattle, Washington, in response to the public demand. The program was established to assist the Extension Service, a service authorized in 1914 by the federal government. In the early years all the states introduced extension services for agriculture, horticulture, and home economics. The Master Gardener program was introduced to meet present demands for answers to garden design and management questions. David Gibby, a county agent in King County, Seattle, is credited for designing the Master Gardener program to meet the demand for reliable gardening information. In return for training in various phases and levels of gardening, the participants dedicate volunteer time to teach others the art of home gardening. This program was so successful in the state of Washington that within a few years the program became active in 48 states, the District of Columbia, and three Canadian provinces. Volunteer activities differ in each county of each state. In most counties Master Gardeners spend much of their time answering questions regarding garden development and planning.

A different sort of public education comes from several television programs that offer viewers shows to help educate them in creating and constructing various elements in the garden: patios, arbors, fences, pools, etc. Viewers can follow the landscape-design gardener's and the contractor's progress from the early stages of construction to the completion of the project.

All of these forms of education serve to promote good garden experience and influence designs by residential landscape architects, gardeners, landscape contractors, and home owners.

**Further Reading**

Bell, Susan G., "Women Create Gardens in Male Landscapes: A Revisionist Approach to Eighteenth-Century English Garden History," *Feminist Studies*16 (Fall 1990)

Best, Clare, and Caroline Boissett, editors, *Leaves from the Garden: Two Centuries of Garden Writing*, London: Murray, 1986; New York: Norton, 1987

"The Curious History of Herbaceous Borders," *Economist* 343, no. 8023 (28 June 1997)

Dietsch, Deborah K., "A Garden of Hope and Recovery," *Architectural Record* 177, no. 13 (November 1989)

Griswold, Mac, and Eleanor Weller, "Green Grandeur: American Estate Gardening in the French Style, 1890–1910," *Magazine Antiques* 140, no. 3 (September 1991)

Hill, May B., "Grandmother's Garden," *Magazine Antiques* 142, no. 5 (November 1992)

Huxley, Anthony J., *Illustrated History of Gardening*, New York: Paddington Press, 1978; London: Macmillan, 1983

Martin, Carol, *Cultivating Canadian Gardens: The History of Gardening in Canada*, Ottawa, Ontario: National Library of Canada, 1998

O'Malley, Therese, "Appropriation and Adaptation: Early Gardening Literature in America," *Huntington Library Quarterly* 55, no. 3 (Summer 1992)

Pollan, Michael, "Digging Into the Past," *House Beautiful* 133, no. 10 (October 1991)

Stearn, William T., "The Garden History Society's Tenth Anniversary and Some Historians of Garden History," *Garden History* 4, no. 3 (Spring 1977)

Stocker, Carol, "1,000 Years of Progress in Horticulture," *Boston Globe* (30 December 1999)

Strong, Roy, *A Celebration of Gardens*, London: Harper Collins, and Portland, Oregon: Sagapress/ Timber Press, 1991

Wheeler, David, editor, *Penguin Book of Garden Writing*, New York and London: Viking, 1996

ALON KVASHNY

# Education: Landscape Architecture

The landscape architecture discipline has experienced three periods of formal educational development. These periods overlap and are most evident in North America but can also be detected internationally. The first period was dominated by agricultural and horticultural concerns. The English landscape gardening approach became institutionalized in American land-grant colleges in the late 19th century. Aesthetic and planning issues dominated the second era of development. The establishment of a landscape architecture program at Harvard University in 1900 forged closer ties with architecture and helped birth the field of city planning. Beginning in the 1960s increasing environmental concerns distinguished the third period. Led by the Department of Landscape Architecture and Regional Planning at the University of Pennsylvania, ecology was advanced as a theoretical basis for the discipline. Current thinking advocates the synthesis of art and science, of design and planning, and of cultural and natural concerns.

Information about land, water, and plants was crucial for the success of colonial farmers in North America. Agricultural and horticultural societies were formed beginning in the late 18th century as a means to provide educational opportunities for their members. These societies advocated a more learned approach to farming and eventually for agricultural colleges. The idea of agricultural colleges grew during the 19th century, championed by, among others, Andrew Jackson Downing and Frederick Law Olmsted, Sr.

As a result of this movement, Senator Justin S. Morrill of Vermont sponsored legislation in 1862 to create a national system of agricultural land-grant colleges. Certain granted lands were appropriated to each state to provide for the endowment, support, and maintenance of at least one college developed to teach agriculture and what were then called the "mechanic arts" (engineering, in more contemporary terms). Landscape gardening was a required course at these new institutions as early as 1863. Michigan State Agricultural College, now Michigan State University was one of these colleges.

Landscape gardening was taught at Michigan State during this time by lectures and illustrative material on the college grounds. Reference material included all the leading American and English authors on the subject, such as Downing and William Kent. The Michigan approach was repeated at other 19th-century land-grant colleges that became the University of Illinois, Iowa State University, Cornell University, and the University of Massachusetts.

The relationship between landscape architecture and the land-grant colleges is further underscored by the involvement of Frederick Law Olmsted, Sr. In addition to advocating their foundation, he (and later his sons) became involved in their campus design and planning. Olmsted was even offered the presidency of Iowa State Agriculture College (now Iowa State University). After Olmsted declined, Iowa State selected Adonijah Strong Welch, who taught a course in landscape gardening and made suggestions concerning the design of the first buildings and grounds at the new college.

The Olmsteds also played a pivotal role in transforming landscape gardening to landscape architecture and in establishing academic programs more strongly linked to design and planning. The Olmsted office in Brookline, Massachusetts, was both a design practice and a teaching studio. The senior Olmsted attracted many bright young men to learn the new art. Among his brightest prodigy was Charles Eliot, the son of the president of Harvard University. The younger Eliot had led a multidisciplinary, comprehensive ecological study of Mount Desert Island in Maine during the 1880s and was responsible, with the Olmsted firm (then Olmsted, Olmsted, and Eliot), for the metropolitan Boston park system plan in the 1890s. Known as the "Emerald Necklace," Eliot's plan combined recreational and open-space needs with functional concerns for flood control, water supply, and sewage disposal. In 1897, at age 38, Eliot died of spinal meningitis.

In honor of his son, President Eliot founded the landscape architecture program at Harvard in 1900, one year after the establishment of the American Society of Landscape Architects (ASLA). The Harvard department has had an enduring influence on the field ever since. Its first head was Frederick Law Olmsted, Jr. (who helped found the ASLA with his half-brother John Charles Olmsted). About the same time (in 1894) the American Academy in Rome was founded by architect Charles McKim, in part stemming from the enthusiasm for interdisciplinary collaboration that had prevailed in the 1893 design of the World's Columbian Exposition in Chicago (which involved the elder Olmsted, the architect Daniel Burnham, the sculptor Augustus Saint-Gaudens, and others). In 1915 the Rome Prize fellowship in landscape architecture was established at the American Academy.

With Harvard and the American Academy providing the lead, landscape architecture grew in stature in the early 20th century. However, there were tensions between the new aesthetically based programs and the older horticulturally focused schools, as well as, increasingly, between a design and a planning orientation. Many landscape architects with strong social consciences, including Frederick Law Olmsted, Jr., were increasingly attracted to the growing field of city planning. As a result, according to the historian Norman Newton, "single-track eclecticism" took over landscape architecture practice and many academic programs, including Harvard's.

Within the Harvard program a modernist rebellion also fermented. During the late 1930s the principal rebels were Garrett Eckbo, Dan Kiley, and James Rose. Their quest for a more modern and more creative approach to landscape design coincided with the arrival of Walter Gropius at Harvard in 1937. Gropius helped institutionalize the Bauhaus philosophy of design within this leading American academic institution. Arguably, modernism in landscape architecture education coalesced through the work of Hideo Sasaki, who moved between the University of Illinois and Harvard, as both student and teacher. During the 1950s Sasaki's teaching and practice returned landscape architecture, in scope and scale, to that established in the previous century by the Olmsteds—urban parks, new communities, campuses, and increasingly, corporate headquarters.

During the 1960s the way people viewed their relationship to the earth changed fundamentally. Since World War II the specter of nuclear destruction clouded the future. In the quest to prevail in the arms race, the Soviet Union and the United States raced to the moon. Something unexpected happened. Images of the earth from space were transmitted into living room televisions and breakfast newspapers. On 20 July 1969 Neil Armstrong stepped on the moon and altered our view of earth. From that barren orb it became clear that the earth is alive and that boundaries are human impositions. The world we inhabit is both fragile and beautiful.

Even before the *Apollo* images were broadcast, voices for protecting the earth had been raised. Aldo Leopold in the first half of the 20th century had urged people to view land as community, and Rachel Carson demonstrated the dangers of poisoning our nest in her classic *Silent Spring* (1962). To this chorus Ian McHarg urged that we "design with nature." His 1969 book by the same name provided a new theory for landscape architecture and altered other fields as well, notably planning, architecture, and the environmental sciences.

From his University of Pennsylvania base, McHarg married a traditional landscape architecture technique with contemporary concepts from ecology for his new theory. Map overlays had been used by landscape architects since the Olmsteds and Eliot. McHarg suggested that information be collected in a systematic, chronological order to reveal interactions, relationships, and patterns. Natural phenomena, such as climate and geology, influence processes such as water flow and soil development, which in turn affect the location of plants and animals. McHarg suggested that, by conducting such an ecological inventory of a place, opportunities and constraints for various possible land uses can be identified. The values of people living in the place can then be used to determine how these opportunities and constraints indicate a range of suitabilities for potential land uses.

This approach influenced how environmental-impact assessments are undertaken and provides the underlying theory for geographic information systems (GISs). GISs are used for displaying, analyzing, and storing spatially related data in map overlays. The initial technological and theoretical advancement of GISs largely came from landscape architecture planning faculty such as Carl Steinitz (Harvard), Bruce MacDougall (University of Pennsylvania, then the University of Massachusetts), Julius Fabos (University of Massachusetts), Lewis Hopkins (University of Illinois), and Thomas Dickert (University of California, Berkeley).

In many ways the international evolution of landscape architecture education mirrors that in the United States, only slightly later and with some notable distinctions. Early 20th-century programs were mostly established at agricultural, horticultural, or forestry schools such as the Agricultural University of Norway (1919) and the

Tokyo University of Agriculture (1924), and the German schools provided an early synthesis of design, town planning, and ecology before taking an ugly turn in the 1930s and 1940s.

After World War II at first a trickle and then a flood of programs were established, many still founded in colleges of agricultural and/or forestry but increasingly concerned with town planning and urban conservation orientation due to the postwar reconstruction efforts. As in North America, the most significant growth in programs has occurred since the 1960s with the rise of global concerns about the environment. Many new programs were established with ecological-centered curricula. Other older horticulture- or design-based programs were adapted and enlarged to address environmental challenges.

The landscape architecture program at the Agricultural University Wageningen in The Netherlands provides an example. Drawing on a rich Dutch landscape tradition, the Wageningen program was led for many years by the brilliant designer J.T.P. Bijhouwer. One of his students, Meto Vroom, pursued his graduate degree at the University of Pennsylvania with McHarg during the 1950s. When Vroom became professor and chair at the Agricultural University Wageningen, he introduced many concepts from North America into the curricula, including those about ecological design from McHarg and Massachusetts Institute of Technology planning professor Kevin Lynch's ideas about site planning and the image of the city.

The ecological revolution promulgated by McHarg at the University of Pennsylvania went beyond influencing techniques and technology. In fact the ecological perspective advocated a fundamental shift in the way we design and plan. Ecology is the study of how all living creatures, including people, interact with each other as well as with their physical and biological environments. Such understanding is essential for sustainable development and regenerative design.

The future is bright for landscape architecture education. The number of programs continues to grow: The need for people who can indeed "design with nature" has never been more pressing. The challenge is for landscape architecture educators to draw on their rich tradition and history, while developing new theories for building regenerative communities in the 21st century.

## International Establishment of Landscape Architecture Degree Programs

| | |
|---|---|
| 1900s | United States |
| 1910s | Norway |
| 1920s | Germany, Japan |
| 1940s | Netherlands, United Kingdom |
| 1950s | Bulgaria, China, Czech Republic, Poland |
| 1960s | Australia, Belgium, Croatia, Denmark, Hungary, Turkey |
| 1970s | France, India, Israel, Korea, Philippines, Portugal, South Africa, Spain, Sweden, Switzerland, Thailand |
| 1980s | Finland, Indonesia, Italy, Malaysia, Mexico, New Zealand, Sri Lanka |
| 1990s | Argentina, Austria, Latvia, Saudi Arabia |

## Further Reading

Cunningham, Deirdre F., editor, *Guide to International Opportunities in Landscape Architecture Education and Internships*, Versailles-Cedex, France: International Federation of Landscape Architects, 1999

Newton, Norman, *Design on the Land: The Development of Landscape Architecture*, Cambridge, Massachusetts: Harvard University Press, 1971

Palazzo, Danilo, *Sulle spalle di giganti: Le matrici della pianificazione ambientale negli Stati Uniti*, Milan: Franco Angeli, 1997

Rybczynski, Witold, *A Clearing in the Distance: Frederick Law Olmsted and America in the Nineteenth Century*, New York: Scribner, 1999

Steiner, Frederick R., and Kenneth R. Brooks, "Agricultural Education and Landscape Architecture," *Landscape Journal* 5, no. 1 (1986)

Thompson, George F., and Frederick R. Steiner, editors, *Ecological Design and Planning*, New York: Wiley, 1997

Walker, Peter, and Melanie Simo, *Invisible Gardens: The Search for Modernism in the American Landscape*, Cambridge, Massachusetts: MIT Press, 1994

FREDERICK STEINER

# Edwardian Period

The Edwardian period in the history of the English garden (known as *la belle epoque* in art history) extended roughly from 1890 to the onset of World War I in 1914. There was, however, an overlap between the gardens of the late Victorian period and the Edwardian period, and the trends that became set in the 1880s established the fundamental principles of design for the next 30 years.

Garden design, like architecture and the decorative arts of the time, was influenced by the ideas of two major figures in the cultural life of the age—John Ruskin and William Morris. Both established principles of aesthetics that influenced the informal landscape style of William Robinson, as well as the group of architects who were laying out gardens in the vernacular style of the Arts and Crafts movement. A love of nature and a belief in the importance of following natural principles were the pivot of Ruskin's thoughts on gardens. Robinson, in his highly successful books *The Wild Garden* (1871) and *The English Flower Garden* (1883), steered the taste of the educated classes away from the extravagant artificiality of the High Victorian garden, with its emphasis on the bedding out system.

Harold Peto's own garden at Iford Manor begun in 1899—terraced and on a hillside—was reminiscent of Italian gardens in which house, garden, and countryside are interrelated and the informal planting is set against a backdrop of mellow stone walls and antique sculpture. (The garden has been restored over a period of 35 years and is open to the public.)

The partnership of Sir Edwin Lutyens and Gertrude Jekyll from 1898 to 1914 created gardens in which hard and soft landscaping complemented each other; the house was given a formal setting, and informality took over farther away from the house, merging the garden into the countryside. Some of the finest gardens ever made were laid out by Lutyens and Jekyll during the early years of the 20th century, including their gardens in the vernacular Arts and Crafts movement Surrey style, such as Orchards, Surrey, in 1898, Folly Farm near Reading (1906), and Hestercombe, Somerset.

While the large houses of the affluent upper classes demanded sweeping lawns and grand balustraded terraces, gardens for smaller country houses could be on a more intimate scale, often laid out in a series of small compartments typical of the Arts and Crafts movement nostalgia for the medieval enclosed garden. Each room had a separate theme, often filled with cottage garden plants such as lavender (*Lavandula angustifolia*) and catmint (*Nepeta* sp.), and with aubretia (*Aubretia × cultorum*) covering dry stone walls made of rubble or rough-cut pieces of stone. The axial layout with terminating focal points, pergola-covered walks, and sunken gardens with plats and parterres filled with flowers (often roses) was typical of small and large gardens. The gardens of Inigo Triggs in Surrey, Sussex, and Hampshire, including the Platts Petersfield and Ashford Chace, Steep, are good examples of this style.

Architectural embellishments included walls decorated with finials and coronas, such as at Athelhampton in Dorset by Inigo Thomas (1891), and brick or stone summer houses in 17th-century style with tiled roofs. A good example of an Arts and Crafts movement garden is Rodmarton Manor in the Cotswolds (begun 1909).

Soft landscaping in this style included topiary work, especially yew hedges, sometimes gabled to echo the house (as at Godinton Park, Ashford, Kent [1906]) and sometimes buttressed (Moundsmere [1908]). Clipped shapes—cones, obelisks, and spheres of yew and box—punctuated the formal layouts of many garden architects. Athelhampton, Dorset, is an outstanding example, but the need for vertical emphasis in formal layouts meant that such features were universally used.

Many gardens combined influences from a variety of sources—French, Italian, Arts and Crafts—and incorporated them into one. Hidcote Manor, Gloucestershire (begun by an American Lawrence Johnston in 1907 and now owned by the National Trust), combines the style of Arts and Crafts compartments such as the cottage garden and bathing pool garden with straight vistas in the French style. The classical simplicity of the bathing pool garden, with its circular pool and sculpture, is distinctly Italian. The Italian style in its pure form was only partially successful in England, an example being the gardens of Renishaw Hall laid out for the Sitwells in 1897.

Planting in Edwardian gardens was dominated by the demand for color, especially in June, to satisfy owners of country houses who entertained during the season. The herbaceous border was the showpiece (depicted in the many watercolor paintings of the period), often backed by tall yew hedges. Double herbaceous borders flanking grass or stone paths terminating in a seat or sculpture were the *pièce de résistance* of the grand Edwardian garden. Packed with flowers, they included hollyhocks, phlox, sunflowers, heleniums, poppies, and many other flowering plants. Jekyll's garden at Munstead Wood had borders for different months of the year, starting with June and going on to July and late summer. Purists who were admirers of the Pre-Raphaelite painters restricted their flowers to the "old-fashioned" kind seen in their paintings—madonna lilies, sunflowers, clove-scented carnations, and sweet briar roses.

The social and economic upheavals of World War I effectively ended the Edwardian style of garden made for the affluent and the discerning in a leisured age. Reduction of labor was the greatest single factor in the decline of these gardens, which were among the most labor intensive gardens ever made. The books of Jekyll and other writers of the age are its greatest legacy to the gardener of today.

**Further Reading**

Brown, Jane, *The English Garden in Our Time: From Gertrude Jekyll to Geoffrey Jellicoe,* Woodbridge, Suffolk: Antique Collectors' Club, 1986

Ottewill, David, *The Edwardian Garden,* New Haven, Connecticut: Yale University Press, 1989

DIANA BASKERVYLE-GLEGG

---

# Egypt: Ancient

The gardens of ancient Egypt 2600–350 B.C. developed in an especially favorable environment, since the river Nile delivered a fresh covering of fertile soil every year. Most gardens were economic units consisting of orchards of fruit trees and vines, with pools for storing water and irrigation channels for its distribution. They provided fruit and wood, vegetables to eat, papyrus for paper, and flowers for perfume and decoration. A second type of garden was the grove planted around royal funerary temples. These were estates for the dead, where magical places were painted on tomb walls and where the goddess perpetually gave food and water. Somewhere nearby, however, was a real estate supporting the priests who kept the cult of the dead person alive.

Water was scarce in these gardens, since rain was a rare occurrence. Egypt had three seasons: inundation, winter, and summer. Work was possible at the end of the inundation, when planting could begin; cultivation went on during winter; and harvesting occurred at the end of winter and beginning of summer.

The society was hierarchical, with the ruler and his court of administrators at the top. Only occasionally did central control break down and local rulers take power, more or less independently of the king. As a result, nearly all of the remains of gardens that have been discovered were created for Egyptian rulers. Gardens have been discovered near the pyramids and temples dedicated to dead rulers, around the palaces and temples of living rulers and their courtiers, and in the precincts of temples, where the national gods were worshipped. Illustrations on the walls of officials' tombs show the idealized gardens, which they hoped to enjoy after death, as well as the avenues and walled gardens that surrounded the temples. The plants most frequently illustrated and mentioned are sycamore fig (*Ficus sycomorus*), common fig (*Ficus carica*), grape (*Vitis vinifera*), date (*Phoenix dactylifera*) and doum (*Hyphaene coriacea*) palm, pomegranate (*Punica*), olive (*Olea*), and mandrake (*Mandragora officinalis*). The wreaths laid on the dead included wild flowers such as poppy (*Papaver rhoeas*) and cornflower (*Centaurea depressa*),

as well as waterlilies and papyrus (*Cyperus papyrus*), and leaves from trees that are now rare in Egypt, such as *Mimusops laurifolia*. Foods left in tombs were grapes, figs, almonds, seeds including coriander (*Coriandrum sativum*), and the legume fenugreek (*Trigonella foenumgraecum*).

The earliest garden found to date is a grove of trees beside the Fourth Dynasty pyramid of Seneferu at Dahshur (ca. 2613 B.C.). Illustrations of men working in orchards and vegetable plots have been found carved on the walls of tombs of the Sixth Dynasty at Saqqara. Men pulling up onions and lettuces from vegetable patches divided into squares with raised edges, were painted in tombs at el-Bersheh and Beni Hasan in Middle Egypt dating from about 1800 B.C. Two wooden models of tomb gardens, with miniature sycamore fig trees around a pool, were left with models of farm life in a courtier's tomb at Deir el-Bahari. Here, opposite the modern town of Luxor, was a temple dedicated to the perpetuation of the memory of the king Mentuhotep (ca. 2055–2004 B.C.). With its grove of tamarisks on either side of an avenue of sycamore fig trees, the arrangement recalls a grove beside the pyramid of Seneferu, and shows that trees had a symbolic significance. They represented the trees that were depicted growing from the grave of Osiris, the god of the dead and of resurrection after death.

Five hundred years later, Queen Hatshepsut (ca. 1479–1458 B.C.) built a temple beside that of Mentuhotep. This building swept down the hillside in colonnaded terraces to two pools filled with papyrus plants. The papyrus was grown in honor of Hathor, the deity who protected the dead buried in the cliffs around Deir el-Bahari. She could appear as a woman or as a cow, who would enjoy eating the papyrus provided. On the terraces Hatshepsut may have arranged pots of myrrh trees, which her trading mission had brought back from Ethiopia. The myrrh was needed for its resin, which was burned in front of divine statues in the temples for the delight of the gods. Later kings followed her example and built themselves memorial temples with lakes and avenues in front of them. The lakes were used for a

Vegetables in a rectangular bed shaded by a vine, Middle Kingdom, ca. 1800 B.C., from a wall painting at Beni Hasan
Copyright Rubicon Press (redrawn from original by Juanita Homan)

ceremony in which a statue of the king is placed in a shrine mounted on a boat. A similar ceremony was painted in tombs of some of the courtiers, in which they represented themselves as the passenger in the boat.

The courtiers' tombs were hewn out of the mountainside west of the temples. Some of the owners may have tried to imitate their rulers by planting gardens outside the entrances, but to be sure that they had gardens in perpetuity, they painted illustrations on the inner walls. These gardens contained the thing most needed for continuing life after death: a perpetual supply of food provided by the presence of the tree-goddess called Hathor and Isis, who emerged from a sycamore fig tree to pour water into the deceased's hands and give him bread. A pool ensured the supply of water for drinking and to nourish the fruit trees in the garden. Fruit was piled high on tables, and wine in jars stood ready to be consumed.

On the opposite side of the river at Karnak, the temple dedicated to the god Amun was approached by long avenues of sycamore fig trees, as was illustrated in the temple and in Theban private tombs. In the sacred precinct were gardens surrounding ceremonial palaces and a walled garden full of vines and fruit trees.

A garden city was created by Akhenaten (1352–1336 B.C.) at el-Amarna in Middle Egypt. A park-like sacred area called the *Maru-Aten* (seeing place of the sun's globe) was created just south of the city, with a central, oval-shaped lake, avenues of trees, small temples, and beds for plants. In the center of the city, the main building had sunken gardens and a vineyard. The gardens were decorated with tiles painted with individual plants and with three-dimensional bunches of grapes molded in Egyptian faience along the top of the walls. Inside the garden buildings, the walls were painted with scenes of life in the city and with ceremonies of the king and queen worshipping the sun. Some of the most important officials had gardens beside their houses that enclosed small temples dedicated to the worship of the king. Further north, was another enclosure with a temple, pool, tethering places for animals, and a sunken garden. The workers who lived on the outskirts of the city had their own vegetable gardens.

**Further Reading**

Eigner, Dieter, "Gartenkunst im alten Ägypten," *Gartenkunst* 7, no. 1 (1995)

Hugonot, Jean-Claude, *Le jardin dans l'Égypte ancienne*, Frankfurt and New York: Lang, 1989

Lichtheim, Miriam, *Ancient Egyptian Literature*, 3 vols., Berkeley: University of California Press, 1973–80

Rohde, Eleanour Sinclair, *Garden-Craft in the Bible,*
London: Jenkins, 1927; reprint, New York: Books for
Libraries Press, 1967

Rosellini, Ippolita, *I monumenti dell'Egitto e della
Nubia,* 3 vols., Pisa, Italy: Presso N. Capurro,

1832–44; reprint, Geneva: Editions de Belleslettres,
1977

Wilkinson, Alix, *The Garden in Ancient Egypt,*
London: Rubicon, 1998

ALIX WILKINSON

# Egypt: Medieval

"Dull and uninspired" is how one medieval garden historian describes the medieval gardens of Egypt. Nevertheless, the ancient Egyptian oasis garden, along with the Islamic *paradeisoi,* laid the foundation for Western garden and landscape styles—in fact, the Egyptian style is considered to be the foundation of the formal school of landscape design—and medieval gardens in Egypt can hold their own against gardens anywhere. The famed Arab botanist and superintendent of the gardens of Toledo, Ibn Bassal, traveled extensively throughout medieval Egypt, cataloging and returning with a number of plants from Egypt, including carob, pomegranate, dill, cotton, iris, lotus, and water lilies for the gardens of Spain. In his *Book of Agriculture* (ca. 1080), Ibn Bassal favorably comments on the northern African methods of irrigation, fertilization, and sterilization in his recommendations for the gardens of Moorish Spain. An earlier work, *Book of Plants,* by Abu Hanifah al-Dinawari (ca. 820–95), also recommended northern African horticultural practices.

The Egyptian garden style was innovative in both design and utilitarian purpose. The oldest oasis garden on record is dated ca. 1400 B.C. The pharaohs improved upon the Assyrian methods of irrigation and drainage and sought to incorporate man-made oases into the landscape. Ramses III introduced the growing of small shrubs in earthenware, a practice later adopted by the Romans and medieval Europeans. The cultivation of flowering plants specifically for the garden was a chief contribution of the ancient Egyptians. None of this was lost in the medieval gardens of Egypt.

The Greeks followed the pharaohs, and Grecian features such as statues and urns were incorporated, particularly so in Alexandria. After the Greeks came the Romans, building Babylon Fortress, now Coptic Cairo, and with them came Roman garden styles. For our intent and purposes, the Egyptian medieval garden has its beginnings in A.D. 640, when Muslim Arabs arrived. As the Muslim influences became felt, Hellenistic and Roman influences waned. Islam prohibits the display of all statues, seeing them as "graven images" prohibited by Allah. The Arab Muslim influence, however, was a double-edged sword. As the Greek and Roman influences diminished, the ancient Egyptian oasis garden style was reborn. The Islamic style and Egyptian style each have their roots in the ancient gardens of Mesopotamia. Perhaps the major difference between the two is that the Islamic *paradeisoi* in physical layout was modeled after the "cosmic cross." The second chapter of Genesis states, "in the middle of the garden were the Tree of Life and the Tree of Knowledge of Good and Evil. A river watering the garden flowed from Eden, and from there it divided; it had four headstreams" (Gen. 2:9, 10 NIV). The four branches of the stream flowing from the axis mundi and the two mystical trees made up the cosmic cross that gave shape and form to the Islamic *paradeisoi.* The scarcity of water made the four traditional Islamic watercourses impractical. Nevertheless, ponds and pools have been part of the traditional Egyptian oasis garden from ancient times, and attempts were made to reduplicate the cosmic cross, sometimes at great cost and effort.

The medieval oasis garden was a formal, symmetrical, walled garden that deliberately placed plants for both utilitarian and ornamental uses. The garden provided a substantial portion of the family's daily diet. Shade, almost nonexistent in this sunny climate, was created by the use of high walls and strategically placed shade trees. A common feature of the garden was a tilapia or perch-stocked pond, serving a threefold purpose. Tilapia, a bottom-feeding fish, recycled pond-bottom waste. The water, nutrient rich with fish waste, was used to irrigate the garden by providing the necessary fertilizer. Fish scraps also served in this purpose. Finally, the stocked ponds provided the family with a source of protein. Plants were grown in small grids in a soil and sand mixture.

Seasonal and scarce in Egypt, water was often transported to the garden from a considerable distance. Those gardens alongside the routes of the ancient irrigation canals generally depended on waterwheels, water screws, and most often the *shaduf* (invented by the Assyrians ca. 2200 B.C.). The *shaduf* was a long pole pivoted on a high support between watercourse and garden. It had a bucket on one end and a counterbalanced weight or another bucket on the other. To utilize every drop of water, the ancient Egyptians also developed a system of drainage that refed the irrigation system, a system still in use in some areas of Egypt.

Plants in the Egyptian garden included figs, pomegranates, dates, carob, and grapevines (providing fruit, a leafy green, and shade); vegetables such as lettuce and bulbs; herbs such as chamomile and dill; and small flowering, often artificially propagated, ornamentals (often medicinal). Reeds, irises, and water lilies were found in the pools. As shade was an essential part of the garden, flowering and scented shade trees were important and the scent consequently served the function of perfuming the home. The most popular trees were the flowering tamarisk, acacia, and willow. Many medieval Egyptian romantic stories were set in such a garden.

Around A.D. 880, a new book appeared entitled *Nabataean Agriculture*. Soon reaching every part of the Arabic world, including Egypt, it become a major sourcebook of agriculture. Written by Ibn al-Wahsiyya al-Kaldani, *Nabataean Agriculture* purported to have discovered and updated the horticultural secrets of the ancient Nabataeans. The book was later shown to be a hoax. How much influence this book had on medieval Egyptians can only be speculated, but we do know that the Copts incorporated Nabataean motifs in their art, and it has been suggested that the Copts also applied the principles of al-Kaldani's work to their gardens; if so, their gardens were planted, harvested, and laid out according to lunar cycles and alchemical rites, the basic themes of *Nabataean Agriculture*. The early medieval Copts, relying heavily on Arabic and Greek sources, developed an extensive pharmacopoeia, growing and propagating the herbs necessary for their medicines. Some ideas advanced were the use of celery as a contraceptive, bananas as an aphrodisiac, and juniper berries as a cure for asthma. Although never held in high esteem by Europeans or Moors, many of these remedies are still in use in Egypt.

## Further Reading

Anthes, Rudolf, *Die Maat des Echnaton von Amarna*, Baltimore, Maryland: American Oriental Society, 1952

Behrens-Abouseif, Doris, "Gardens in Islamic Egypt," *Der Islam* 69 (1992)

Bowman, Alan K., and Eugene Rogan, editors, *Agriculture in Egypt: From Pharaonic to Modern Times*, Oxford: Oxford University Press, 1999

Hobhouse, Penelope, *Plants in Garden History*, London: Pavilion Books, 1992; as *Penelope Hobhouse's Gardening through the Ages*, New York: Simon and Schuster, 1992

Manniche, Lise, *An Ancient Egyptian Herbal*, Austin: University of Texas Press, and London: British Museum, 1989; reprint, London: British Museum Press, 1999

Petruccioli, Attilio, editor, *Il giardino islamico*, Milan: Electa, 1994

FRANK MILLS

---

# Egypt: Modern

With the Libyan desert in the west and the Gulf of Suez to the east, less than one-tenth of the land in Egypt is settled or under cultivation. The remaining 90 percent is classified as arid desert punctuated by oases, with the Nile River, whose course runs through Abu Simbel in the south to the fertile delta region of Cairo, fulfilling most of the country's water requirements. Significantly, the Nile, and its manipulation through draining and leveling, has been a dominant force for gardening in a country where most vegetation is confined to the river's tributaries and alluvial plains. An additional benefit is a climate moderated by northern winds in both the summer and the winter, allowing for an unusual yearlong growing season that has proven hospitable to plants from both temperate and tropic areas.

History, of course, has had great bearing on modern Egyptian gardens. The legacy of pharaonic Egypt placed a high importance on the tripartite features of water, shade, and enclosure—later trademarks of Islamic gardens as well. Indeed, both the strict allocation of water and the geometry of garden designs were expressive of a hydraulic society highly organized in its engineering endeavors. Thick privacy walls often enclosed gardens with private ponds to which water was drawn by waterwheels; these ponds, fertilized by tilapia and perch, in turn provided rich aquaculture water for the garden's plants and vegetables, including date palm, banana, pomegranate, fig, jujube, water lily, and papyrus. Vines, fruits, and flowers were dominant in gardens as well as trees such as sycamore and "false plane" (*Acer pseudoplatanus*), ordinarily a challenge to grow in flood regions.

In later centuries, the influence of Islam and incursions by the French and British had a palpable effect on Egyptian garden design. Following the defeat of the Mamelukes by Selim the Grim in 1517, the Ottoman Empire established a firm foothold in Egypt, and the domed mosques and Islamic character of Constantinople were replicated quickly in Cairo and surrounding areas. Elements of the paradisical garden accompanied these developments, and arcaded courtyards with cells opening to a central fountain provided an ideal setting for the ritual ablutions of the resident Sufi monks. Surviving examples include two *takiyyas* (Sufi monasteries) in Cairo, that of Suleiman II and Sultan Mahmud II.

The French occupation of 1798–1801 imported a European aesthetic in terms of both architecture and garden design. Napoléon Bonaparte's initial observations of traditional Egyptian gardens suggest that an imposition of order was necessary: "The garden was filled with fine trees but there was not a single path," he wrote in his description of Qasim Bey's palace, his headquarters during the occupation (Brookes, 1987). Curiously, the haphazard planting of most Egyptian gardens more closely resembled European gardening traditions of the time than the Islamic models. With the resurgence of the Ottoman Empire and the consequent expulsion of the French, the Macedonian ruler Muhammad Ali (1769–1849) secured control in 1805 and wedded his preference for European styles with traditional Islamic emblems. This combination of styles can be seen at Shubra Palace in Cairo, with its large pools and loggias, and also at the rococo Manyal palace on Rawdah Island, which benefited in subsequent years from the policy of beautification implemented by Muhammad's son Ibrahim.

French influence became even more pronounced under Khedive Ismail Pasha (r. 1863–79), a later successor who pursued a strident policy of westernization. Inspired by landscape architects such as Pierre Grant and Barrillet Deschamps, Ismail laid out the Azbakiyya Gardens as well as the gardens of the royal homes at Gazirah and Giza. Both palace gardens still exist today. The Gazirah gardens, founded in 1886 with 49 acres (19.8 ha) and reported to contain over one million plants in 1924, have since been reduced to eight acres (3.2 ha). Similarly the palace garden in Giza, now the Orman Gardens and Zoo, features pebbled mosaic paths, circuitous waterways, a rock garden planted with succulents, and an impressive rose garden, albeit on a much smaller scale from its original dimensions.

The Qubba Palace survives as another celebrated palace garden built by Ismail's son, Khedive Tewfik, during his reign (1879–90). It was here—several miles north of downtown Cairo—that the palace overlooked a reported 70 acres (28 ha) of gardens that included an acclimatization chamber for foreign plants, trees, and shrubbery. In 1960 the Qubba botanical garden was established as both a research facility and a guest house for foreign dignitaries. It is significant that the garden still fulfills one of its original purposes by acclimatizing specimens from around the world, and its collections comprise 3,500 different species from 72 families of monocotyledons, dicotyledons, and gymnosperms. Two other subgardens within the complex include a succulent garden and a rose garden with 257 varieties of rose.

The last of the larger extant botanical gardens in Egypt, Aswan Botanical Garden on Kitchener's Island, was founded in the early 20th century by Lord Herbert Kitchener, an unpopular British consul who owned the eponymous island and imported plants and trees from throughout Southeast Asia and India. In 1982 the garden was transferred to the Egyptian Ministry of Agriculture, and its tropical collection, including 20 varieties of fruit trees, has been one of its most enduring attractions.

Although Egypt's larger public gardens have been adequately maintained and in some cases enhanced, the private gardens of the 19th and early 20th centuries suffered from neglect, and efforts to cultivate European-style swards and shrubbery often strained labor and cash allowances for private garden owners. Unsurprisingly, lush vegetation radiating from a central pool formed the essence of most of these gardens, which are now, for the most part, dilapidated examples of an occasionally awkward fusion of exotic, pleasure-garden abundance and Western landscaping.

**Further Reading**

Abu-Lughod, Janet, *Cairo: 1001 Years of the City Victorious,* Princeton, New Jersey: Princeton University Press, 1971

Behrens-Abouseif, Doris, *Azbakiyya and Its Environs from Azbak to Ismail, 1476–1879,* Cairo: Institut Français d'Archéologie Orientale, 1985

Brookes, John, *Gardens of Paradise: The History and Design of the Great Islamic Gardens,* New York: New Amsterdam, and London: Weidenfeld and Nicolson, 1987

Hassan, Fayza, "How Green Was This Valley," *Al-Ahram Weekly* (22–28 October 1998)

Jabarti, A, *Tarikh muddat al-Faransis bi-Misr,* Leiden, The Netherlands: Brill, 1975; as *Napoleon in Egypt: Al Jabarti's Chronicle of the French Occupation, 1798,* translated by Shmuel Moreh, Princeton, New Jersey: Wiener, 1993

Moynihan, Elizabeth B., *Paradise As a Garden: In Persia and Mughal India,* New York: Braziller, 1979; London: Scolar Press, 1980

Osman, Colin, *Egypt: Caught in Time,* Reading, Berkshire: Garnet, 1997

Prest, John M., *The Garden of Eden: The Botanic Garden and the Re-Creation of Paradise,* New

Haven, Connecticut: Yale University Press, 1981

Raafat, Samir, "Koubbeh Palace: Egypt's Official Guesthouse," *Cairo Times* (2 February 2000)

Thompson, Colin, *The Paradise Garden*, New York: Knopf and London: Cape, 1998

Kristin Wye-Rodney

# El Escorial

## San Lorenzo de El Escorial, Madrid, Spain

**Location:** Approximately 25 miles west-northwest of Madrid

The monastery of San Lorenzo el Real de El Escorial reflects the Golden Age of Spain and the personality of its founder, Philip II (1527–98), who became king of Spain and the New World upon the retirement of his father, Emperor Charles V, to the Hieronymite Monastery of Yuste at Cáceres in Extremadura. As a monument, El Escorial is foremost a symbol of the imperial power of Spain in Europe and America at the time. It also portrays Spain and the king as the preeminent defenders of the Roman Catholic Church during the Counter-Reformation. Its architectural style and building program manifest the austere taste and religious fervor of the king. But it is in the cloister patio, parterre terraces, and tree groves that his humanist interest in botany and passion for gardens are reflected.

Although only partly a votive monument, Philip II decided to build and name El Escorial in commemoration of his victory over Henri II of France at Saint Quentin on 10 August 1557—the feast of St. Lawrence (San Lorenzo in Spanish). Traditionally, the layout of the monument represents the gridiron employed in the martyrdom of this saint. Philip II searched for the ideal site from 1558 until 1562. He found it—exposed to the sun and protected from the cold mountain winds—at the foot of Monte Abantos on the southern slopes of the Sierra de Guadarrama northwest of Madrid, which he chose as the capital in 1561.

In 1559 the king summoned the philosopher, mathematician, and classical scholar Juan Bautista de Toledo, who had been an assistant to Michelangelo, to design the vast complex that would eventually house the royal palace and pantheon, college and library, Hieronymite monastery, and basilica dedicated to St. Lawrence. However, the king was personally involved in the supervision of all development and construction, including the gardens. Juan de Herrera, Toledo's assistant, became project architect in 1572. Although Toledo had executed the overall design for the project, Herrera was charged with the completion and overall harmony of the project, including portions not designed by Toledo. The king also engaged Marcos de Cardona, Juan Anglés, Jerónimo de Algora, and the brothers Juan and Francisco Holbecq as gardeners.

The monument is sited on the hillside with terrace gardens buttressed above the lower ground to the east and south. Against the higher ground the palace and basilica entrances face north and west along the arrival esplanade called La Lonja, which was originally partly grassed. Within the monument are 17 courtyards, including the basilica atrium or Patio de los Reyes (Court of the Kings of Judah), the royal house courtyard or Patio de las Máscaras (Court of the Masks), seven identical courtyards of the college and monastery, and the monastery cloister or Patio de los Evangelistas (Court of the Evangelists).

The Patio de los Evangelistas was designed in 1586 by Herrera, who modified the gallery facades originally proposed by Toledo. It is a symbol of paradise underscored by theological and philosophical numerology. Within the harmony of the perfectly square Renaissance architecture, the four rivers of Eden and Gospels of Christianity, as well as the four virtues and elements of antiquity, are represented by a layout reminiscent in form and flora of Islamic pavilion gardens, such as the Jardín Alto that fronts the Salón Rico at Umayyad Madīnat al-Zahrā' in Córdoba.

The courtyard is enclosed by the arcaded galleries of the cloister. On the two levels and four sides of the courtyard, 12 columns, which represent Christ's Apostles, engage the gallery pilasters—Doric at ground level, Ionic on the main level. It is comprised of a square subdivided by crisscrossing paths into 16 squares, where 12 square parterres box four square pools. At the center the dome of an octagonal *templete*, or pavilion, shelters the crossing paths. From niches on the blind sides of the *templete*, statues of the Evangelists by the sculptor Juan Bautista Monegra diagonally face the pools, which are fed from fountains at the inner corners of the water parterres.

Originally, the courtyard parterres were planted with flowers within hedges of lavender (*Santolina chamaecyparissus*) and myrtle (*Myrtus communis*) from Talavera de la Reina. After the great fire of 1671, boxwood (*Buxus sempervirens*), a native species from the Serranía de Cuenca, was planted to replace the Mudejar tradition of color and fragrance in the severely damaged parterres.

During the 16th and 17th centuries flowers cultivated since antiquity and the Middle Ages, such as roses (*Rosa × alba, R. damascena, R. gallica*), irises (*Iris pseudacorus, I. pumila, I. xiphium, I. germanica*), carnations (*Dianthus caryophyllus*), and lilies (*Lilium candidum*), were still favored in the gardens of Spain. According to the friar Juan de Sigüenza, the latter adorned Philip II's dining table at El Escorial. The king also owned the *Iris* by Dürer (ca. 1508) and *Spring* by Arcimboldo (1563). Philip II's favorite flower was the musk rose (*R. moschata*).

The introduction of American, Anatolian, and Balkan plant species greatly influenced the development of ornamental gardens in western Europe during the 16th century. Cherry laurel (*Prunus laurocerasus*), hyacinth (*Hyacinthus orientalis*), fritillary (*Fritillaria imperialis*), scarlet lily (*Lilium chalcedonicum*), and tulips (*Tulipa*) were among the imported Asian and eastern European shrubs and herbs. The American species included the tuberose (*Polianthes tuberosa*), beauty-of-the-night (*Mirabilis jalapa*), garden nasturtium (*Tropaeolum majus*), sunflower (*Helianthus annus*), and passionflower (*Passiflora caerulea*). These plants were among the 3,000 species described by the physician and naturalist Francisco Hernández, whom Philip II entrusted with the first modern scientific expedition of natural history to America from 1570 to 1577.

The garden terrace physically and spiritually mediates the order of the Renaissance architecture and the harmony of the natural landscape in a medieval parterre layout, reminiscent of Christian cloister and Islamic courtyard gardens. These upper gardens for the king, queen, and monks act as monumental *miradores* (high terraces) in the transition from monastery to the landscape of groves and orchards below, and pastures and fields beyond. The flowers, as symbols of human virtue and divine grace, connect the works to the creation.

The garden terrace is retained by a massive arcaded wall. Six pairs of stairs lead to the groves and orchards below, through grottoes under the terrace, without disruption of the tectonic unity. Niches were created in the wall facing the groves and orchards to allow the cultivation of orange trees.

The five square and seven rectangular parterres on the terrace, which is overlooked by the monastery and royal apartments, are divided into quadrants by paths that almost meet at 12 central square fountains. Originally, the vibrant parterres were hedged with southernwood (*Artemisia abrotanum*), which was later replaced with the boxwood. The pattern of color was compared to fine Middle Eastern carpets by Sigüenza. Against the wall, protected from the mountain winds, oranges and lemons were grown, and roses, jasmines, and passion fruit vines were fanned on wood trellises, as chosen by Philip II. In the 18th century Juan de Villanueva replaced them with metal *rejas,* or grilles.

In 1592 the physician Juan Alonso de Almela listed some 75 species and varieties of plants from Europe, Asia, and America as grown in the garden terrace parterres. Flowering and fragrant herbs, shrubs, and vines on the list included jonquil and narcissus (*Narcissus jonquilla, N. poeticus, N. tazetta*), marigolds (*Tagetes patula, T. erecta*), Spanish broom (*Spartium junceum*), common lilac (*Syringa vulgaris*), roses, and poet's jasmine (*Jasminum officinale*). Among the culinary and medicinal plants there were thyme (*Thymus*), rosemary (*Rosmarinus officinalis*), savory (*Satureja*), marjoram (*Origanum*), and absinthe (*Artemisia absinthium*). Also listed were celery (*Apium graveolens* var. *dulce*) and peppers (*Capsicum*).

Francisco de Mora designed a large reservoir to irrigate the groves and orchards and to stock carp and tench. The groves produced a great diversity of nuts and fruits, including almonds, chestnuts, and walnuts, as well as apricots, cherries, grapes, quinces, sloes, pears, plums, peaches, and pippins; 10,000 fruit trees had been planted in 1580. Almela also itemized the orchard produce, which included garlic, onions, parsley, coriander, mint, chard, lettuce, cabbage, spinach, borage, chicory, carrots, parsnips, turnips, eggplants, and wide beans.

## Synopsis

| | |
|---|---|
| 1557 | King Philip II of Spain defeats Henry II of France at the battle of Saint Quentin |
| 1558 | Philip II begins search for a building site for El Escorial |
| 1559 | Juan Bautista de Toledo is summoned by Philip II to design El Escorial |
| 1561 | Philip II selects Madrid as capital of Spain |
| 1562 | Philip II finds ideal site for El Escorial, at Monte Abantos in the Sierra de Guadarrama |
| 1563 | Toledo starts work on El Escorial and Juan de Herrera is named his assistant |
| 1570–77 | Entrusted by Philip II, Francisco Hernández leads first modern scientific exploration of America; describes over 3,000 American plant species in *Historia de las plantas de Nueva España* (before 1582) |

| | |
|---|---|
| 1572 | Juan de Herrera becomes project architect |
| 1576 | Charles de l'Écluse (also known as Carolus Clusius) publishes *Rariorum aliquot stirpium per Hispanias observatarum historia,* most significant book on Iberian flora of the 16h century |
| 1583 | Francisco de Mora, a disciple of Herrera, becomes project architect |
| 1584 | Work is substantially completed on El Escorial |
| 1586 | Juan de Herrera designs the Patio de los Evangelistas |
| 1590 | José de Acosta publishes *Historia a natural y moral de las Indias,* which incorporates American nature into European science |
| 1592 | Juan Alonso de Almela lists 75 species and varieties of plants growing in the garden terrace parterres of El Escorial |
| 1592 | Gregorio de los Ríos publishes *Agricultura de jardines,* the first book on gardening written in Castilian |
| 1671 | Bartolomé Zumbigo rebuilds monastery for Charles II after fire |
| 1771–73 | Juan de Villanueva builds Casa del Príncipe and Casa del Infante, gardens for the sons of Charles III (the future Charles IV and his brother Gabriel) |
| 1781–84 | Juan de Villanueva enlarges Casa del Príncipe |
| 1875 | Augustinians occupy monastery |
| 1963–86 | Quadricentennial celebrations prompt restoration of the monument |

**Further Reading**

Alonso de Almela, Juan, "Descripción de la octava maravilla del mundo, que es la excelente y santa casa de San Lorenzo el Real (1594)," in *Documentos para la historia del Monasterio de San Lorenzo el Real de El Escorial,* by Eusebio Julián Zarco Cuevas, vol. 6, Madrid: Imprenta Helénica, 1932

Añón, Carmen, "El Real Monasterio de El Escorial," in *Jardín y naturaleza en el reinado de Felipe II,* edited by Carmen Añón and José Luis Sancho, Madrid: Sociedad Estatal para la Conmemoración de los Centenarios de Felipe II y Carlos V, Unión Fenosa, 1998

Bueno, Juan Antonio, "The Patio: Origin, Development, and Transformation of the Hispanic Courtyard," *Annual Meeting Proceedings* (American Society of Landscape Architects) (1997)

George, Michael, and Consuelo M. Correcher, *The Gardens of Spain,* New York: Abrams, 1993

López Piñero, José María, and María Luz López Terrada, "La botánica en el reinado de Felipe II," in *Jardín y naturaleza en el reinado de Felipe II,* edited by Carmen Añón and José Luis Sancho, Madrid: Sociedad Estatal para la Conmemoración de los Centenarios de Felipe II y Carlos V, Unión Fenosa, 1998

López Terrada, María José, "Las plantas ornamentales," in *Jardín y naturaleza en el reinado de Felipe II,* edited by Carmen Añón and José Luis Sancho, Madrid: Sociedad Estatal para la Conmemoración de los Centenarios de Felipe II y Carlos V, Unión Fenosa, 1998

Murray, Peter, *Architecture of the Renaissance,* New York: Abrams, 1971; revised edition, as *Renaissance Architecture,* Milan, Italy: Electa, and New York: Rizzoli, 1985; London: Faber/Electa, 1986

Sancho, José Luis, *Visitor's Guide: Monastery of San Lorenzo el Real de El Escorial,* Madrid: Patrimonio Nacional and Aldeasa, 1997

Sigüenza, José de, *La fundación del Monasterio de El Escorial* (1605), Madrid: Turner, 1986

JUAN ANTONIO BUENO

# Eliot, Charles William 1859–1897

## United States Landscape Architect

Charles Eliot's fame derives not from any specific designs but from his conception and organization of America's first regional park system, the Metropolitan Park Commission (since 1919, the Metropolitan District Commission) of Boston, Massachusetts. The approximately 20,000 acres (8,097 ha) of open spaces preserved by his pioneering efforts form a series of woodlands, wetlands, and urban parks, many connected by scenic parkways, that circle the city. As an American practitioner of the then fledgling profession of landscape architecture,

Eliot defined it broadly as the "art of arranging land and landscape for human use, convenience, and enjoyment." Had he lived more than 37 years, his production would no doubt have been more varied, but public open spaces surely would have dominated his work.

Born into an affluent family, Eliot spent long summers on the coasts of Maine and Massachusetts, where he roamed the countryside. Although no degree program in landscape architecture existed during his student days, he took courses in agriculture and horticulture at Harvard University's Bussey Institute. This educational experience, coupled with his earlier country summers, helped him to appreciate landscapes, both natural and human-made. The Eliot family championed high standards of intellectual attainment and civic service; Charles's father became president of Harvard University in 1869, and Charles spent much of his life in the president's house at the edge of the campus. He would use his many advantages of birth and education for the public good. In this he followed the traditions of the noted American landscape architect Frederick Law Olmsted. As design professionals, both believed that rural scenery had a profoundly elevating effect upon the moral character of their fellow citizens and thus promoted social harmony. Although Eliot wrote in less passionate terms than Olmsted, he described almost tenderly how a working-class father and son gathering berries or a group of people enjoying a picnic in the public parks were proof that his efforts to secure public lands were making a better world. As "this innocent pleasuring is now likely to go on here for many generations," he wrote in 1924, "something worthwhile has been accomplished."

Olmsted had been responsible for the series of urban parks that are the "jewels," which, connected by a string of pleasure drives and parkways, form an "emerald necklace" within the city limits of Boston. While this example must have influenced Eliot, his design for a similar necklace of large tracts of land in the politically independent towns of Boston's suburbs derives also from a scheme to build a great "ring road" through the then rural lands surrounding the city. This latter proposal was made by Robert Morris Copeland (1830–74), who is well known as the author of *Country Life: A Handbook of Agriculture, Horticulture, and Landscape Gardening* (1859 and later editions) and less well known for his later work *The Most Beautiful City in America: Essay and Plan for the Improvement of the City of Boston* (1872). Eliot was fortunate that there were like-minded citizens willing and able to support his ideas for an extensive system of public lands. Many such individuals belonged to the Appalachian Mountain Club, a Boston-based group that regularly organized trips to sites of natural or historic interest in Massachusetts. Its membership included many men influential in government circles. Of great help to the cause of public

lands was the journalist Sylvester Baxter of Malden, who had written frequently and persuasively to urge the preservation of open spaces of scenic beauty. This nurturing climate made it possible for the park system to be established by the state legislature in the summer of 1893, only a few years after Eliot's initial proposal.

Several basic principles guided Eliot in his conception and implementation of the parks. Unlike the great national parks such as Yellowstone and Yosemite, which preserved unique geological, biological, or historical treasures, the lands to be preserved near Boston were not the wonderlands of the West. Farming, logging, and fire had left woodlands of second or third growth. Yet they were large tracts that offered beautiful views to inspire the lover of nature, much as paintings in a museum inspire the lover of art. Eliot's primary goal was safeguarding the scenery of the reserved lands. In setting boundaries for the properties to be acquired, Eliot expected that each parcel would form a topographical unit, including the contiguous lands necessary to frame the scenery being preserved. He was sensitive to the possibility of conflicting public and private property rights and preferred to use roads to separate the reservations from neighboring private land. In part because of high costs, he avoided locations already developed or having clear development potential. Again unlike the parks of the Far West, his lands lay within an 11-mile radius of Boston's densely populated urban core. Public access was a major goal. Unvisited, the scenery had no value.

Eliot proposed that roads be built to give access, to allow park employees to supervise the land and to act as fire breaks. He envisioned public horse-drawn wagons for visitors who did not have their own carriages. Parkways were expected to link Boston with the reservation lands. Road building as an end in itself was to be avoided. Thus a proposal for a carriage road to the top of the highest hill, Great Blue Hill, was rejected, despite its potential popularity. Eliot fully expected the land to be managed. "Keepers" and "watchmen" would be employed with the special intent of preventing forest fires. Arborists would prune and "surgically treat" important trees. He realized that there would have to be some facilities for visitors, and he suggested that in urban parks sports equipment as well as refreshments could be provided by concessionaires.

The public reservations of Massachusetts were Charles Eliot's great design legacy. His tragic death, however, produced another legacy. In 1900 his father established at Harvard University the world's first comprehensive study program in landscape architecture, which was devised by Olmsted's son, Frederick Law Olmsted, Jr.

## Biography

Born in Cambridge, Massachusetts, 1859. Attended Harvard College, but his most relevant courses were taken at Harvard's Bussey Institution in agriculture and horticulture; began apprenticeship in the office of Frederick Law Olmsted, 1883; traveled extensively in the Southern and Eastern United States observing landscapes; studied landscapes in Europe with a particular emphasis on public parks, 1885–86; opened his office in Boston, 1886; worked to create Trustees of Public Reservations, 1890–91; appointed landscape architect to Metropolitan Park Commission, 1892, shaping its development until his death; Metropolitan Park Commission (after 1919, the Metropolitan District Commission) officially established by the Massachusetts state legislature, 1893; joined the firm of F.L. Olmsted, which became Olmsted, Olmsted, and Eliot, 1893. Died in Hartford, Connecticut, 1897.

## Selected Designs

| 1887 | John Parkinson estate, Bourne, Massachusetts, United States |
| 1887 | Plan for Longfellow Memorial Park, Cambridge, Massachusetts, United States |
| 1888 | White Park, Concord, New Hampshire, United States |
| 1890 | Development report for Garfield (unbuilt), Salt Lake City, Utah, United States |
| 1891 | Establishment of Trustees of Public Reservations, Massachusetts, United States |
| 1893 | Development and conservation plan for Nahant, Massachusetts, United States |
| 1893 | Plan for Metropolitan Park Commission, various locations near Boston, Massachusetts, United States |

## Selected Publications

Charles Eliot's papers are preserved in the Charles Eliot Collection, Frances Loeb Library, Graduate School of Design, Harvard University, Cambridge, Massachusetts.

"The Landscape Gardener," *Garden and Forest* 2 (13 February 1889)
"The Waverly Oaks," *Garden and Forest* 3 (5 March 1890)
*A Report upon the Opportunities for Public Open Spaces in the Metropolitan District of Boston Massachusetts, Made to the Metropolitan Park Commission*, 1893
"The Boston Metropolitan Reservations," *New England Magazine* 15 (September 1896)
*Vegetation and Scenery in the Metropolitan Reservations of Boston*, 1898

## Further Reading

Eliot, Charles William, *Charles Eliot, Landscape Architect*, Boston and New York: Houghton Mifflin, 1902; reprint, Amherst: University of Massachusetts Press, Library of American Landscape History, 1999
Morgan, Keith N., *Held in Trust: Charles Eliot's Vision for the New England Landscape*, Bethesda, Maryland: National Association for Olmsted Parks, 1991
Morgan, Keith N., *Charles Eliot, Landscape Architect: A Research Guide*, Jamaica Plain, Massachusetts: Institute of Cultural Landscape Studies, Arnold Arboretum of Harvard University, 1999

RICHARD KENWORTHY

# Enclosure

The purpose of an enclosure is to give security, privacy, or shelter. These functions can be provided by a physical barrier, a visual barrier, or both. The design basis for a physical barrier is its function, and the usual objective is to create the barrier with the least possible material. It is necessary, therefore, to determine what kind of access the barrier is meant to prevent. If, for example, a barrier is to be erected to prevent a car running off a road and into a garden, must it also exclude dogs? The answers to such questions can produce widely different solutions. Barriers can also be used to delineate property ownership.

Visual barriers function to conceal the view of an object, either to give privacy or to hide the object from the scene, but they also have a much wider and more fundamental use, that of defining space. Visual barriers can enclose spaces for particular functions and make them particular places to a far greater degree than a physical barrier can; thus, a fence around a bowling green will keep people off of it, but a hedge, by visual enclosure, makes it an environment, a room, with its own identity. In their wider use as space-defining objects, visual barriers are one of the raw materials of landscape design. As such they have an unlimited range of application from large-scale landscape design, where trees can be combined with landforms to make broad spatial compositions, through urban design, where visual barriers can be an extension of architecture to create the different space zones of a town, to the formation of small-scale, intimate local spaces, as in garden design.

Two broad groups of materials are used for garden enclosures: plants and manmade structures. Plants provide enclosure that is constantly changing in form, color, and texture; with manmade structures there is no modification of form, and the only changes that may take place are surface ones of texture and color, through processes of weathering or the application of color. Plants cannot be left unattended, and if their form has been shaped, as in a hedge, there must be periodic attention to clipping, pruning, or training; manmade structures, on the other hand, often require little maintenance, such as a brick wall. People most often choose plants for their aesthetic effect or for the innate love of growing things but use a whole range of manmade structures, such as fences, primarily for functional reasons. Because barriers formed by natural materials may take some time to establish, the two groups are sometimes combined, as when a hedge is planted against a chain-link fence.

Plants are primarily used for visual enclosure and for shelter. As physical barriers they are limited to hedges, used as an alternative to fences or walls. Their choice over manmade structures is based on their association with other organic material, the desire to obtain contrast between manmade works and nature, or simply the desire for natural things. One must take into account the time interval before the plants are either effective visual or physical barriers and the limited length of life before they need to be replanted. In some instances plants may involve considerable maintenance costs if their form is only constant when clipped, pruned, or trained. Of the two broad plant groups, evergreen and deciduous, the choice, planting conditions being similar, is primarily aesthetic. Evergreen plants give the most complete visual enclosure, except in broadscale or dense planting, such as a wood or copse. Deciduous plants provide complete changes of form, color, and texture over the seasons but often require more upkeep in urban settings, where, for example, leaves have to be disposed of. Evergreen and deciduous plants used for enclosure can be placed into the three broad groups of trees, shrubs, and hedges, providing a vast range of material from which to choose. The first selective processes are ecological ones. Beyond this, limiting the species to those that are indigenous to an area will preserve the character of the environment. The selection of new species is based on those that give the most effective enclosure: functional expression is the objective. Beyond this, it is largely a matter of the composition of the landscape, such as considering whether a hedge should unobtrusively follow the contours of the landscape or whether a tree screen may break the silhouette. Each design poses its own particular set of problems.

Trees can be used for space defining, view screening, or wind screening. Space defining is the art of landscape enclosure, and trees combined with the landform provide its raw materials. Trees may be used to distract attention from the unpleasant view. Tree screening to hide ugly structures or disfigured landscape, as with planting for visual enclosure, is primarily an aesthetic problem, and little need be noted here, except to mention that many alternatives exist to the common technique of masking the object with a row of fast-growing trees. Shelterbelts or windbreaks are formed by belts of trees singly or in systems, or by small blocks of trees of various shapes.

Hedges are alternatives to both fences for physical enclosure and walls for physical and visual enclosure. As windbreaks they are more effective than solid walls because they are permeable. Hedges are the complement to trees and land shaping in the art of landscape enclosure. They define space for different functional uses, such as playing fields, and in gardens they provide the partitions and dividing screens that give the design structure. Hedges meant to provide a physical barrier are generally strong-growing plants with thorns; those meant to form a visual screen tend to be evergreens; and those for windbreaks are sturdy and dense in growth.

The yew (*Taxus baccata*) makes a particularly effective evergreen hedge. Its strong compact growth and dense texture make possible shaping it into precise forms that may on the one hand take on the architectural character of walls and on the other hand the exuberance of topiary work. Its dark color makes a beautiful contrast with ground covers such as grass and pavings, as well as an admirable background for flowers.

Deciduous hedges, said to be introduced by the Romans, provide a tough impenetrable fence for field enclosure and form an integral part of the English agricultural scene. Large-scale mechanized farming and the high cost of maintenance has resulted in many miles of hedges being dug up, with a consequent loss of shelter for crops, animals, and wildlife. Two deciduous species of particular value as visual screens because they retain their leaves in winter are the beech and hornbeam. Both are slow starters but make a fine hedge up to six meters (6.5 yd.) high. Beech does well on light and chalky soils, and hornbeam often succeeds where the former is unsatisfactory, as on heavy clay.

Walls for enclosure can form complete physical and visual barriers with a long life. They are an essential part of urban and village design; in open landscape they provide an alternative to fences and hedges only in those areas where stone is found in abundance. The most important historic use of walls is for defense. Walls for enclosure may be divided roughly into four main types: walls higher than eye level, walls for partial enclosure, dwarf walls, and retaining walls. Walls higher than eye level, used to form a complete physical and visual barrier, are often associated with architecture, such as screen walls linking dwellings together and giving continuity of facade. Walls for partial enclosure, below eye level in height but still providing visual obstruction, are generally used as an alternative to hedges or fences, such as the 18th- and 19th-century garden wall. Dwarf walls are used where a strong physical barrier of architectural qualities is required as an alternative to trip fences or low hedging. They are often associated in design with pavings or combined with other barriers, such as a metal fence over a dwarf wall. Retaining walls are used to form changes in level, either for formal reasons, as an alternative to land shaping, or for functional purposes.

Rubble walls, used as boundary fences, are a characteristic of those areas of the countryside where timber is scarce and stone readily available.

Brick walls, being composed of small prefabricated units laid in horizontal courses, are less flexible in form than stone. In particular, they cannot assume changes in level without stepping the top of the wall, which means they cannot flow with the landform, as can stone walls or hedges. Apart from their association with farm buildings, they are mainly an urban building form. The appearance of a brick wall is dependent on the color and texture of the brick itself, the type of mortar joint, and the bond.

Concrete walls can be divided into two groups: in situ and block. In situ walls seldom occur in landscape design except as retaining walls. Block walls are of three main types: plain blocks, profiled blocks, and exposed aggregate blocks, composed of aggregates chosen for their color and texture, which are exposed by removing the cement skin. The advantage of exposed aggregate blocks over the other two types is that the blocks weather well because the greater part of the surface is of a natural material.

Retaining walls afford the following problems: the construction of the wall itself to withstand the earth pressure, the expansion of the wall along its length, and the drainage of moisture from the retained earth. Most forms of block construction are suitable for retaining walls, but where there is considerable earth pressure, concrete, either in situ or reinforced, has largely supersede traditional materials such as blue brick or granite blocks because of the cost.

The ha-ha, that unexpected ditch by which the 18th-century landscape architect could tear down the enclosing wall or hedge to let the garden seemingly extend into the countryside, is in essence a retaining wall sunk into the ground. It is not, as is generally supposed, an English invention but was devised by the French as a means of obtaining an uninterrupted view of the open countryside at the end of formal allées. The ditch is approximately one to two meters (1–2.2 yd.) deep, with the wall on the garden side sloping down to its foot. The ha-ha was little used during the 20th century, but the revival of large-scale landscape design, coupled with the modern inventions of muck-shifting machinery and ready-mixed concrete, make it a practical method of enclosure without visual obstruction.

Fences and railings as garden enclosures perform numerous functions. Their prime use is as a physical barrier. They are of various types, including chained wire or strained line wire, woven-wire fences, chain-link fences, wood post and rail, metal continuous bar, vertical bar railing, Palisade fences, trip fences, and guard rails.

Bollards are vertical barriers that, being freestanding objects, are one of the most unobtrusive ways of preventing access; they have no great height and no horizontal line is drawn across the scene. Their common use is to prevent vehicles encroaching on pedestrian areas by narrowing a space.

**Further Reading**

Dézaillier d'Argenville, Antoine-Joseph, *La théorie et pratique du jardinage*, Paris, 1709; as *The Theory and Practice of Gardening*, translated by John James, London, 1712; reprint, Farnborough, Hampshire: Gregg, 1969

Fairbrother, Nan, *The Nature of Landscape Design*, New York: Knopf, and London: Architectural Press, 1974

Switzer, Stephen, *The Nobleman, Gentleman, and Gardener's Recreation*, London, 1715; new edition, as *Ichnographia Rustica: The Nobleman, Gentleman, and Gardener's Recreation*, 3 vols., London, 1718; reprint, New York: Garland, 1982

Thacker, Christopher, *The History of Gardens*, Berkeley: University of California Press, and London: Croom Helm, 1979

Whitehead, George E., *Garden Design and Construction*, London: Faber, 1966

JANA DAS

# Enghien

## Hainaut, Belgium

**Location:**  approximately 18 miles (29 km) southwest of Brussels

Enghien was established in the 11th century on the route from Brussels to Tournai and until 1606 remained within the French border. The French king Henri IV sold Enghien to Prince Charles d'Arenberg in 1606. The superb park at Enghien was the creation of Antoine d'Arenberg, 6th of the 12 sons of Charles d'Arenberg and Anne de Croy. Antoine, known as Père Charles, renounced worldly ambitions to become a Capuchin monk but in fact devoted himself largely with the help of his nephew Philipe-François, first duc d'Arenberg, to imposing a compartmentalized design on the vast park at Enghien. Unfortunately, the French Revolution wreaked its havoc, and the château where the 18th-century duke entertained Voltaire, who repaid the hospitality by amusing the company after dinner with the famous *contes,* was burnt down. The stone cottage built on the grounds by the same duke later for Jean-Jacques Rousseau is, however, still standing.

The garden, mostly unmentioned in the guidebooks, is still open to the public but apart from the few features that have been carefully restored, now lacks its former glory. Mlle de Montpensier said of it in 1650 that it was "the most beautiful garden in the world." Although the history of the Arenberg family is reasonably well known, and archival sources for its leading figures remain extant, knowledge of the garden at its prime comes almost exclusively from what can be gleaned from a series of 17 engravings of aspects of the garden by Romeyn de Hooghe, published by Nicolaes Visscher in Amsterdam in 1685 under the title *Villa Angiana, vulgo het Perc von Anguien.* In addition, a series of 1782 drawings by the French painter Charles de Wailly show ideas for the New Herculaneum that Wailly wanted to construct at Enghien.

The major features of the park as laid out by Antoine d'Arenberg were, to judge by the plan left by G.-L. Le Rouge (*Details de nouveaux jardins à la mode,* 1776]), a large hedge maze dating from about 1650 to which steps led down from a parapet, and an *étoile,* or heptagonal garden with a center from which radiated beyond

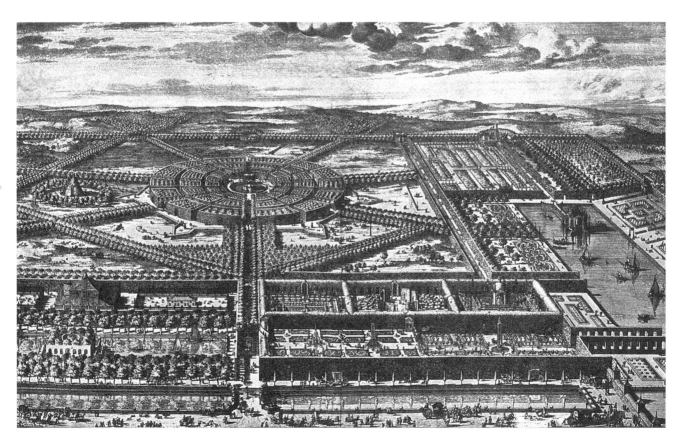

Rendering of the Castle Garden at Enghien, mid-17th century

the formal *étoile* seven rides, each bordered by different species of tree. The maze or labyrinth, in which all paths led to the center and in which it was not intended that anyone should get lost, occupied a huge circle touching the outer edges of a rhomboid garden, the long sides of which were bordered by avenues. The labyrinth paths continue above and below the labyrinth itself to surround small formal beds in geometrical patterns roughly symmetrical around a central axis that the labyrinth interrupts.

At the center of the labyrinth stood a large domed Fountain of Amphitrite, the wife of Poseidon, drawing attention to the way in which water was exploited as a feature of the garden. The *étoile* was itself moated, and there was an L-shaped canal as well as two lakes, which still remain, surrounded by excellent statuary. Between the labyrinth rhomboid and the *étoile,* and enclosed within two of the rides radiating from the center of the *étoile,* a semicircular path with radial paths extending beyond the semicircle to small formal plots, tops off the rhomboid garden, as if by an arch.

The seven segments of the heptagonal garden, with each perimeter side bisected at right angles by its ride radiating from the center, are filled with a reasonably intricate medley of geometrical shapes created by paths, with an inner heptagon whose perimeter sides are at right angles to paths leading from the center to the angles between the seven outer heptagon sides, so that any impression of concentricity is avoided; many of the shapes formed by the paths are diamond based, often with radial paths to a center within the diamond.

Le Rouge's plan gives the overall impression that not very much space has been very cleverly used, although we know that the plan does not tell the whole story and that the garden was in fact vast. One of Hooghe's engravings, for example, shows a reasonably large garden compartment devoted entirely to experiments with different forms of topiary.

Most of the garden appears to have been taken up by parterres, each with four *cabinets,* with some parterres containing orange trees or flowers. It also included an amphitheater, and there is still a "triumphal arch" or slave gate. Two of the pavilions have recently been carefully restored. The park at Enghien was certainly once one of the great European gardens, not as large or flamboyant as Versailles, Hampton Court, or even Potsdam but a smaller masterpiece in what was inevitably an ephemeral medium.

**Synopsis**

| | |
|---|---|
| ca. 1606 | Château sold by Henri IV to Charles de Ligne |
| early 17th C. | Park of Enghien created by Antoine d'Arenberg |
| late 18th C. | Château of Enghien burned down during French Revolution and park badly damaged |
| present day | Château and park restored |

**Further Reading**

Hooghe, Romeyn de, *Villa Angiana, vulgo het perc van Anguien,* Amsterdam, 1685

Mosser, Monique, and Daniel Rabreau, *Charles de Wailly: Peintre architecte dans l'Europe des Lumières* (exhib. cat.), Paris: Caisse Nationale des Monuments Historiques et des Sites, 1979

ANTHONY H.T. LEVI

# England

England is a small island with subtle landscape variations, from the rocky coasts of the southwest in Cornwall to the flatland expanses of the east coast in East Anglia to the Pennine moorlands of Yorkshire and Northumberland. The maritime climate is cool and moist with considerably less bright sunshine than in Continental or Mediterranean countries.

Garden art in England dates to Roman times but primarily evolved from medieval gardens. Medieval gardens were small, the size of a house extension, and functional, designed to produce herbs, fruits, some vegetables, and a few medicinal plants. Some flowers, particularly roses and lilies, were cultivated for ceremonial use. The earliest know English treatise on gardening is John Gardiner's *The Feate of Gardening,* thought to be copied about 1440 from a text of about 1400. It contains nine parts, mentioning in all 97 plants, with some, such as hazel and ash, recommended for making tools. Important gardens of this period were Romsey Abbey at Hampshire, Woodstock (the first recorded English work of large-scale landscape gardening), Kingsholm by Gloucester, Kingbury by Dunstable, Havering-atte-Bowers (Essex), and at the palaces of Westminster and Windsor.

The end of the War of the Roses and the subsequent reign of the Tudors (1480–1603) ushered in a period of regeneration in England. As the need for fortification diminished, the medieval *hortus conclusus* transformed into pleasure gardens and became an essential aspect of palace planning. Major garden development occurred during the reign of Henry VIII, motivated by his ambition to outshine those of his rival, François I of France. Royal gardens were created at Hampton Court Palace (1531–34), Whitehall (completed in 1545), and Nonsuch Palace (1538–47). While they contained many typical English aspects, decorative motifs from France mingled with those of the Italian model.

Typical garden elements of the Tudor period included the mount, built to enjoy a view rather than detect the approach of potential enemies. The mount at Hampton Court Palace had a foundation of a quarter of a million bricks and was covered with soil and hawthorns, with a three-story building at the summit. As also done at Hampton Court, the early Tudor gardens were often subdivided by hedges, often tall and with arches giving access to other plots. The plots typically consisted of a series of rounds or squares, themselves split into rectangular or triangular segments. Another popular feature was the use of heraldic symbols and beasts, such as the lion and the unicorn, carved in wood or stone and brightly painted or completely gilded.

At its most grandiose and fully developed, the Tudor mansion had gardens on several sides, such as at Nonsuch Palace, near Cheam in Surrey. Although Nonsuch was pulled down by the duchess of Cleveland, Barbara Villiers, mistress of Charles II, there is an early 18th century description of its plan by the antiquarian Daines Barrington. Barrington notes that, in addition to the leisure ("great") and kitchen gardens, Nonsuch at the end of the 16th century also had an enclosed ten-acre (4 ha) "wilderness" and a privy garden. The privy garden at Nonsuch contained "pyramids, fountains, and basons of marble."

At the same time as Italian neoclassical garden ornamentation and design were being absorbed along with angular patterns from French models, English gardening was being affected by the new Italian interest in botany. In 1545 Padua became the site of the first garden dedicated to the scientific study of plants. In 1548, shortly after the first Huguenot and Dutch Protestant refugee gardeners and vegetable growers had arrived in southwest England, William Turner's *The Names of Herbs in Greek, Latin, English, Dutch and French, with the Common Names that Herbaries and Apothecareis Use* was published. The father of English botany, Turner had founded his own garden at Kew in 1547.

The reign of Elizabeth I in the second half of the 16th century shifted the emphasis to the gardens of the aristocracy, transplanting to the great country house the early Tudor palace formula. The practice of garden art extended down the social scale, reflected in the stream of garden literature beginning with Thomas Hill's *The Profitable Arte of Gardening* (1568). The most famous garden of the Elizabethan age was that commissioned by Lord Burghley at Theobalds. It consisted of a sequence of enclosed courtyards with gardens, displaying the hallmark of the early English gardens, the knotted (as opposed to embroidered) parterre. Knot gardens were often used for ornamental purposes at residences with small garden areas and by 1600 were contrived in all manner of patterns of dwarf box or rosemary, the gaps filled with flowers or gravel.

Discussion of English gardens under James I, who acceded to the throne in 1603, has long been dominated by Francis Bacon's essay "Of Gardens" (1625), although what Bacon outlines is a fantasy, not a manual. Still, Bacon's principles allow a glimpse of the ideal, which requires "things of Beautie" to be in season for "all the Moneths of the Yeare" and provides a long list of plants and perfumes too idealized to have been practical. Bacon's vision was in some respects premature. His dismissal of topiary work and colored earths represents little more than a repudiation of medieval practice. His desire that the garden should encompass a mound, banqueting houses, and fountains accords with contemporary taste on the grand scale, but his "natural wildness" was still in advance of its time. His refusal to acknowledge that statues and figures added distinction to the true pleasures of a garden was counter to the Renaissance principles that were to be incorporated into the early 17th-century baroque.

Several detailed records survive of actual Jacobean gardens. The most imposing was at Hatfield, with plans drawn up in 1609 for Robert Cecil, Burleigh's son and earl of Salisbury. The Frenchman Salomon de Caus designed the waterworks, said to have been inspired by the Tuileries and the gardens of Saint-Germain. De Caus constructed an artificial serpentine stream with colored pebbles and exotic seashells, which was then dammed to create an island. Anne of Denmark and Henry, Prince of Wales, also employed de Caus to redesign their gardens at Somerset House, Greenwich Palace (both ca. 1609), and Richmond Palace (1610–12). De Caus introduced new features to England, including a profusion of Italian motifs, grottoes, water machines, fountains, and sculptures, as well as the architectural alignment of house and garden. No less important was his brother or nephew Isaac de Caus, whose English career began in the 1620s.

Isaac de Caus's most celebrated and influential design was the garden created for Lord Pembroke at Wilton (begun 1632). It was an outstanding mannerist work, adjoining the Palladian house designed by Inigo Jones. Although essentially in the de Caus manner, the profusely designed grotto, a *parterre d'eau,* and a terraced amphitheater cut into a slope are pronouncedly Italianate in character and indicate that the guidelines were

Viscount Downe's garden at Dingley Park, Northamtonshire, England
Courtesy of Mary Evans Picture Library

laid down by Inigo Jones; the work foreshadows the landscape gardens of the 18th century.

By the mid-17th century there is evidence, notably from the *Garden Book* (1659) of Thomas Hanmer, that British developments were strongly influenced by French and Dutch practice. Orchards, walks, and gardens for which exotic imports were much sought after were enhancing great houses, long approached by avenues through parks. Views, prospects, and vistas were being opened up, hedges were uprooted, and the knots and borders near the house, no longer walled, gave way to arabesques of flowers, sometimes in the shapes of animals or birds, beyond which might be planted trimmed evergreens with stone ornaments set between them.

Gardens were divided according to the functions of the different parts, but labyrinths, gravel walks, and allées with fountains and cascades were still popular. Hanmer specified rectangular gardens of approximately 180 to 280 meters (197 to 306 yd.) in length, with a width two-thirds of the length, although most of the squirearchy had to make do with something smaller. Greenhouses, often heated by a stove outside, where plants could be protected from frost, were becoming a necessity, although some plants could be potted and left outside or covered with straw.

The dominating figures in England during the mid-17th century were Inigo Jones and the Frenchman André Mollet. Jones studied landscape painting in Italy from 1613 to 1614 and imported into England the neoclassical Palladian style from Venice. Axial or radial allées lined with limes or perhaps yew were beginning to be planted, but in garden design Jones may well have stimulated a new fashion for vistas and evergreens. Mollet made two visits to England, both times invited by the court. He laid out the gardens of St. James's Palace and of Wimbledon House. For the latter Jones reshaped the building, while Mollet remodeled the gardens, introducing baroque parterres, allées, bosquets, and terraces.

In 1664 John Evelyn, best known as a diarist, published *"Sylva"; or, A Discourse on Forest Trees,* which would remain the standard work for over a century. Although conceived in the context of providing the navy with timber, the book was used regularly by landowners intent on improving their landscapes. Evelyn virtually introduced the yew into English gardens for topiary. The Mediterranean cypress, extensively planted earlier in the century, was proving vulnerable to cold, whereas the yew was resistant "to all the efforts of the most rigid winter." In fact, the harsh winter of 1683–84 killed off almost all the cypress planted in England. Later editions of *Sylva* contain a proposal for a large garden beyond the pleasure, fruit, and vegetable gardens, laid out in a way clearly derived from the practice of André Le Nôtre, with eight tree-lined allées radiating from a central circle to the edge of the square. A second diagonal of tree-lined allées in each quadrant split each of the four interior quadrants into four triangular plots.

Peace with France was made in 1697, and French influence again became paramount in the creation of English gardens. Perhaps surprisingly, in view of the cultivation of flowers in the Low Countries during this period, the reign of William and Mary from 1689 saw in England a strong upsurge in the fashion for evergreens. It also saw the creation by George London of the great fountain garden in front of Christopher Wren's new eastern facade at Hampton Court. The garden had a canal, seven fountains surrounded by scroll-like beds, with both axial and radial avenues, and numerous stone ornaments and statues. Henry Wise effectively became Queen Anne's garden manager and with London formed a partnership of England's most celebrated garden designers in the formal style. They jointly redesigned the gardens of Hampton Court for William III, introducing a new baroque ground plan. Two more gardens they designed in the baroque style were Melbourne Hall and Chatsworth. By the turn of the 18th century, English baroque gardening had reached its mature stage, both in its repertory of features and in its formal patterns.

The rise of English landscape gardening in the 18th century arose from a whole set of complex circumstances, social, economic, and political. It was a time of urbanization of the population following the industrial revolution. The English countryside changed its appearance primarily due to the parliamentary enclosure acts of the 1660s, which enabled wealthy landowners to enclose their open land; a total of 1.2 million hectares (2.96 million acres) was enclosed over the 18th century. This new world power wanted preeminence in more than its vast military and economic power. Understandably, the reigning baroque fashion, imported from England's greatest rival, France, was little suited to display British grandeur. Therefore, a new, original style was sought. The first half of the 18th century was essentially a period of improve-

ment, and the environment was rich for the seeds of the new ideals to take root and prosper.

Many writings of the time exhibit the growing discontent with the French formal style. In his essay *The Moralist* (1710) Ashley Cooper, third earl of Shaftesbury, expressed his preference for natural forms over artificial gardens associated with princely courts. Joseph Addison in *The Spectator* (1711–12) emphasized the superiority of the natural landscape found in the countryside. He also launched an idea that won enthusiastic approval: the transformation of an entire estate into a kind of garden complex. Alexander Pope in *The Guardian* (1713) urged a return to the "amiable simplicity of unadorned nature," rejecting the balance, regularity, and artificiality of formal gardens and elaborate topiary work.

Stephen Switzer's publications began in 1715 with *The Nobleman, Gentleman, and Gardener's Recreation,* followed by nine other books on related subjects and a monthly magazine called *The Practical Husbandman and Planter,* which became well received sources of advice for the new trend in design. The success of these works is a measure of his influence among those wishing to embark on the improvement of their estates. Switzer's views may well have influenced Charles Bridgeman, who became one of the leading professionals of the transitional period. A showpiece of Bridgeman's work is Stowe (1713), where he created a magnificent central vista, surrounded by masses of trees, although it was completely remodeled by William Kent a few decades later. Bridgeman was probably the first to use the ha-ha, which many believe was crucial to the development of the landscape garden. The ha-ha did away with the need to wall the garden and gave the illusion from the house of an unbroken continuity between the cultivated formal garden area near the house and the rougher natural meadows beyond.

William Kent was a major figure during this period. He lived in Italy for a long period, training to become a painter, for which he demonstrated mediocre talent. However, his training gave him a deep feeling for the works of the great landscape painters, which was to prove invaluable when he turned his attention to architecture and garden design. In the garden at Chiswick House created for his patron Lord Burlington, Kent arranged a large number of elements in a relatively restricted space, without any strict controlling symmetry between the various parts. Lord Cobham then invited Kent to Stowe, which was constantly enlarged over a number of years. With each development reflecting the growth of aesthetic theory, Stowe remained for nearly a century the most significant and influential model of garden style. Kent was called in to remodel Bridgeman's earlier 11-hectare (27.2-acre) garden and to create a design for a recently added area. He thoroughly broke up the original formal structure, especially the straight lines of vegetation and regular shapes of pools. Some of his details were major breakthroughs in English garden design, in particular the Elysian Fields, a truly Arcadian landscape.

Kent arranged his compositions as a counterpoint to the vegetation to conform to a painting's compositional ideals of the classical landscape. Pictorial compositions in the manner of Claude Lorrain and Nicolas Poussin were referred to as Picturesque. The term passed to the garden as an explicit reference to the scenes represented in the major arts, confirming the affinity between poetry, theater, painting, and the newly flourishing art of the garden. Fillippo Pizzoni in his book *The Garden* (1997) notes that this relationship with the major arts meant that the garden would explicitly represent historical or mythological texts: "By singling out painting as their model and literary references as their informing criterion, the theorists of the new art furnished the garden—still regarded as an artificial creation—with an invaluable *raison d'être*." In his gardens Kent conferred the greatest importance and centrality upon the "stage," with humankind as the protagonist and nature providing backdrops and sideshows.

The gardens at Stowe continued to be extended and updated in the mid-1740s when Lord Cobham commissioned Lancelot "Capability" Brown to carry out some of Kent's later designs. This experience gave Brown much of his theory of landscape, which was more radical and unlike his predecessors'. Much more of a purist, he considered the "capabilities" of the site most important and regarded the symbolic structures and intellectual references as distinctly superfluous. His landscapes consist of gently rolling lawns, curving lakes melting into the background, mighty masses of tree clumps, and fringes of tall vegetation. His compositions no longer implied any symbolic concern: he stood for the pleasing panoramic effect, uncluttered by pointless architectural elements. Brown's most important work was at Blenheim Palace in Oxfordshire, the property of the duke of Marlborough. Brown became the central figure of the landscape movement in the middle of the 18th century and dominated the profession for 35 years. Unfortunately, his dominance resulted in many valuable formal gardens being destroyed.

About the same time Brown started at Stowe, an increasing number of landowners began to build landscaped parks, to their own designs, finding inspiration in the pictorial and literary principles of an earlier generation. One early and remarkable example was the park at Stourhead, begun by Sir Henry Hoare around the 1740s. Perhaps the masterpiece of the landscape movement, it is an ideal Arcadian landscape, organized around a lake with a number of skillfully chosen and placed programmatic features of classical inspiration. Other notable examples of landscapes inspired by paintings and literary works include Painshill by Sir Charles Hamilton and The Leasowes by William Shenstone.

The third and last figure to make a lasting impression in landscape gardening was Humphry Repton. First to call himself a landscape gardener, Repton began his career as a garden designer around 1790. His designs were broadly in the style of Brown, the main differences being that Repton created denser thickets and more closely planted clumps of trees and drew the inspiration for his follies from the rustic and rural, rather than from the classical world. Later in his career he moved away from the rigid compositions of Brown and urged the reinstatement of geometric gardens and terraces immediately surrounding the house, this in the era following Brown's dominance and excessive "pastoralism" to a period of compromise between informal and formal. Repton also wrote several authoritative books on the theory of landscape design and found himself involved in a controversy with Sir Uvedale Price, Richard Payne Knight, and William Gilpin, who attacked the monotony of pastoral landscapes and championed Picturesque wild landscapes. They shaped the philosophy of the Romantic untamed landscape, soon to spill over to the European continent. The *jardin anglais* was the adaptation of the English landscape garden style on the European continent.

By the 1830s the Picturesque style was in decline. John Claudius Loudon proposed the idea of the Gardenesque style, which took into account the specific properties of individual plants, especially exotic species, which he planted in arrangements designed to allow each specimen to develop its full potential. His planting schemes became extremely influential and fashionable partly due to his various publications, including the periodical *Gardener's Magazine* (1826–44). His wife, Jane Loudon, also published many books and periodicals about the garden, particularly concerning the cultivation of flowers and the practical aspects of gardening. Their joint editorial activity—one of the first examples of gardening journalism with such success in Great Britain—also contributed to the passion for plants and flowers.

The search through the riches of the past use of the French, Dutch, and particularly Italian styles guided design in the mid-19th century. The most important feature reintroduced from the Italian classical garden was the terrace, which offered another way of experiencing the space around the house, as well as a vantage point from which to enjoy the garden and the view. Sir Charles Barry was responsible for many such layouts in the 1840s and 1850s. He introduced the popular "Italian" garden, an English version with formal symmetrical layouts and huge flower beds. The success of the Italian garden was not just the replacement of one style by another but part of the idea that all garden styles were equally valid and applicable, that each should be judged by its own rules.

Victorian gardens focused on three essentials: the large scale, novelty, and color. Gardens were stuffed with ideas, structures, plants, and colors, much like the superabundance within the interiors of homes. Advances in propagation meant that plants could be raised in greenhouses for bedding out in the summer, virtually unknown prior to the 1830s. Tens of thousands of tender and half-hardy exotic plants were planted into intricate patterns of beds during the summer—often brilliantly gaudy.

The invention of the Wardian case by Dr. Nathaniel Bagshaw Ward opened the way for a flood of new plant introductions from overseas, satisfying the Victorian appetite for novelty. Introductions from temperate regions such as parts of the United States, New Zealand, China, and the Himalayas adapted easily to British conditions and produced great families of hybrids. The most exotic introductions were tender plants brought back from more tropical regions of the world that would never survive the British climate.

The role of the gardener became more important as the person who could change the appearance of the garden annually through the bedding out, as well as developing systems to grow the exotics and get them to flower. Artificial environments were needed, and with the abolition of the tax on glass in 1845, most home owners could now afford a glasshouse. The Great Stove at Chatsworth, designed and built between 1836 and 1840 by head gardener Joseph Paxton, was the largest area enclosed by glass in the world and became the prototype for Paxton's famous Crystal Palace. Both garden and glasshouse began to be developed for the public as well as for the private owner. The Crystal Palace demonstrated the attractions of the glasshouse for the public not only for horticulture but for entertainment. The culmination of all this development was the opening of the Royal Horticultural Society's gardens in Kensington. Laid out to celebrate the society's elevation to royal status, the gardens incorporated all the most fashionable designs of the period. Initial admiration, however, turned to criticism and represented a growing tide of opinion looking for change, which was to sow the seeds of the 20th-century garden.

For centuries the gardens of the upper classes had been built on an unshakable confidence in land and the security of a country estate. The agricultural depression that began in the 1880s, and which would recur until World War II, combined with growing democracy to undermine this confidence and bring about a reassessment. Land prices fell, and many of the vast landed estates were broken up and sold. Massive countrywide industrialization led to a call for protection of the countryside. In 1875 the National Trust was founded to preserve the natural beauty and artistic heritage of Great Britain. In 1897 the periodical *Country Life* first appeared, reflecting the new interest in English rural culture. It was in this setting that the Arts and Crafts movement came into being.

The Arts and Crafts movement arose out of opposition to the factory system and advocated small-scale handmade craftsmanship. It looked back to Tudor and medieval times for its stylistic influence, paying renewed attention to the concept of the cottage garden, with its vegetables, fruits, and flowers. The Irishman William Robinson strongly espoused this concern for nature and rejection of mass-produced goods. In a series of publications the outspoken Robinson firmly maintained the need for greater respect for nature, for informal design, and for the cottage garden. His most lasting suggestion was that a garden should combine in an uncontrived manner seasonal interest throughout the year with a degree of natural self-sufficiency and native, or at least hardy, plants.

This "natural" informal style provoked the opposition of many designers who favored the formal approach. Most prominent among Robinson's opponents was the architect Reginald Blomfield, who stated his position in his book *The Formal Garden in England* (1892). Blomfield combined elements of Italian and French gardens in a way that was well suited to the tastes of the Edwardians. Thomas Mawson's *The Art and Craft of Garden Making* (1900) also espoused a sensitivity toward the formal garden. The first English professional garden designer to build an international practice, he ended his career as the first president of the Institute of Landscape Architects in 1929, four years before his death. In *The Art and Craft of Garden Making*, Mawson explained that he aimed for "formality near the house, merging into natural by degrees, so as to attach the house by imperceptible graduations to the general landscape." In this Mawson saw himself maintaining continuity with Humphry Repton in the early 19th century, and he laid out what has become an enduring principle of garden design through the 20th century.

The partnership of Gertrude Jekyll and Edwin Lutyens at the turn of the 20th century achieved lasting results. Trained as a painter, Jekyll was an amateur plantswoman and was directly inspired by Robinson's theories. She applied her eye for color to the arrangement of plants in a border and demonstrated how the small-scale intimacy of the cottage garden ideal could be adapted to, or developed for, any scheme. Lutyens had been trained as an architect and was equally immersed in Arts and Crafts ideals. Their work was a synthesis of formal layout and natural planting. Lutyens's genius for architectural form together with Jekyll's mature understanding of the crafts and an enthusiasm for vernacular and old-fashioned plants produced a succession of captivating designs.

Following World War I the models that had proven successful prewar were no longer valid. Progress, whether technical or scientific, appeared unstoppable. The realities of the 20th century were altogether more complex. Garden design drew from the avant-garde and attempted a revival of the classical garden; yet the formal gardens of the early 20th century failed to make any great impact. World War II also cast a shadow over the world of the garden. In the postwar era the garden occupied a distinctly secondary position, mainly because designers were turning their attention almost exclusively to the urban environment. A garden became a matter of personal expression, of the individual's response to the times; thus the modern garden resulted in a great variety of design. The gardens created in England in the first half of the 20th century have a strongly personal feel, with the owners oftentimes the designers.

Vita Sackville-West and the architect Laurence Johnston were both passionate gardeners and had a deep personal involvement in the making of their gardens. From 1907 onward, Johnston developed the garden at Hidcote Manor in Gloucestershire. He continued the traditions of Jekyll, developing new styles of planting and emphasizing the division of a garden into enclosures, each with its own character and appearance. The example of Hidcote—where flowering shrubs grow together with roses, herbaceous plants combine with bulbs, colored creepers train over evergreen hedges, and flowers are allowed to grow where they have seeded themselves—was an important source of inspiration for Sackville-West in her garden at Sissinghurst in Kent. Like Hidcote, Sissinghurst is a garden of open-air "rooms," some planted to achieve maximum effect at a given season, and others based on specific color schemes. Hidcote and Sissinghurst have all the elements typical of the 20th-century English garden: a regular structure of walls, expanses of water, squared evergreen hedges, and pathways softened and to some degree confused by an overlay of plants, which are allowed to grow freely.

The careers of Sylvia Crowe, Brenda Colvin, and Geoffrey Jellicoe demonstrate the development of the profession of landscape architect in the 20th century. Crowe began her career with private garden design during the 1930s and expanded to monumental landscaping projects, such as siting reservoirs and electrical power lines. In her book *Garden Design* (1958) she suggested that the source of inspiration for the contemporary gardener is limitless but that certain principles of composition remain unchanged "because they are rooted in the natural laws of the universe." Her work was wide ranging: she consulted on two New Towns, Harlow and Basildon, and planned a park for Canberra, Australia. Her gardens include those for the Commonwealth Institute, London, and a roof garden for the Scottish Widows' Fund and Life Assurance Society offices in Edinburgh.

Colvin was an early champion of informal wildflower planting and encouraged the idea of the garden as a haven. In her book *Land and Landscape* (1948), she gave early voice to environmental concerns now universally accepted. As a consultant she was responsible for the military town of Aldershot, as well as for a number of reservoirs, land reclamation schemes, power stations, and urban design projects. Notable gardens include the Manor House, Sutton Courtenay, Oxfordshire, and her own garden, Little Peacocks, Filkins, Gloucestershire.

Jellicoe's career encapsulates all the diversity and dilemmas that have arisen around contemporary garden design. Trained as an architect, he made a particular study of Italian Renaissance gardens, publishing *Italian Gardens of the Renaissance* (1925) at the age of 25. The essence of Jellicoe's work is his vision of gardens and landscape as an evolutionary process and humankind's relation to the natural landscape, addressed in his book *The Landscape of Man* (1975), written with his wife, Susan Jellicoe. Jellicoe designed private gardens and city parks. One of his last projects was the garden at Sutton Place, where he created a series of gardens with a strongly symbolic content: the Moss Garden, the Paradise Garden, the Music Garden, the Fish-Pool Garden, and the Surrealist Garden, forming an allegorical stroll through life and creation.

Early in his career Jellicoe worked in partnership with Russell Page, and the divergence of their paths illustrates the broad spectrum of postwar garden design. Page's book *The Education of a Gardener* (1962) describes the fundamental principles underlying his work, which lies in his understanding of plants—their shapes, characteristics and combinations—and his instinctive feeling for the "genius" and possibilities of a particular place. Page had an international practice with gardens in the United Kingdom, Belgium, Egypt, France, Germany, Portugal, Spain, Switzerland, the West Indies, and the United States.

The contemporary English gardener is informed by divergent sources. The Chelsea Flower Show, a model flower show, provides a national platform for new plants of horticultural curiosity and competitions for garden design. The garden center, as common as the supermarket, caters to everyday practical gardening needs. The Royal Horticultural Society and various botanical gardens ensure academic progress in the study and breeding of plants of all kinds. Gardening journals cover all aspects of the subject from the academic to the practical. As it has been throughout the successive periods, the well-designed English garden is based on the choice of plants, their groupings, and their use with architectural features and even water.

*See also* Biddulph Grange; Birkenhead Park; Blenheim Palace; Castle Howard; Chatsworth Gardens; Chelsea

Physic Garden; Derby Arboretum; Duncombe Park; Hampton Court Palace and Bushy Park; Hestercombe; Hidcote Manor Garden; Kensington Gardens; Kew, Royal Botanic Gardens; Leasowes; Levens Hall; Munstead Wood; Nuneham Courtenay; Oxford Botanic Garden; Painshill; Prior Park; Rievaulx Terrace; Rousham House; Sissinghurst Castle Garden; Stourhead; Stowe; Studley Royal and Fountains Abbey; Tresco Abbey Gardens; Wisley

## Further Reading

Conan, Michel, *Dictionnaire historique de l'art des jardins,* Paris: Hazan, 1997

Fleming, Laurence, and Alan Gore, *The English Garden,* London: Joseph, 1979

Hadfield, Miles, *Gardening in Britain,* London: Hutchinson, and Newton, Massachusetts: Branford, 1960; 3rd edition, as *A History of British Gardening,* London: John Murray, 1979

Hunt, John Dixon, *The Figure in the Landscape: Poetry, Painting, and Gardening during the Eighteenth Century,* Baltimore, Maryland: Johns Hopkins University Press, 1976

Hunt, John Dixon, *William Kent: Landscape Garden Designer,* London: Zwemmer, 1987

Hunt, John Dixon, and Peter Willis, *The Genius of the Place: The English Landscape Garden, 1620–1820,* London: Elek, and New York: Harper and Row, 1975

Jackson-Stops, Gervase, editor, *An English Arcadia, 1600–1990: Designs for Gardens and Buildings in the Care of the National Trust,* Washington, D.C.: American Institute of Architects Press, and London: National Trust, 1992

Jackson-Stops, Gervase, and James Pipkin, *The Country House Garden: A Grand Tour,* London: Pavilion, and Boston: Little Brown, 1987

CANDICE A. SHOEMAKER

# Eremitage

## Bayreuth, Bavaria, Germany

**Location:** approximately 1 mile (1.6 km) east of Bayreuth

The garden at the Eremitage on the eastern outskirts of Bayreuth retains the air of rural seclusion that first drew the margraves of Bayreuth to the site in the early 17th century. On a wooded plateau high above the river that encircles it, it consists of groves of beech wood interspersed with walks and water features, subdivided into charming vignettes of scenery around decorative buildings and grottoes. The present layout is essentially that completed by Wilhelmine, sister and confidante of Frederick the Great and herself margravine of Bayreuth from 1731 to 1758.

Margrave Christian Ernst adapted the site of the Eremitage, which had been acquired in 1616, as a hunting preserve in 1665. His improvements included a grotto built over a natural spring. The first significant ornamental overlay was made by Margrave Georg Wilhelm in 1712–16. Intent on developing the site as a hermitage retreat in the woods, he commissioned Johann David Räntz to design a small summer residence, now the Altes Schloss. This single-story building, with its grotto-like rustic exterior stonework, was set in a framework of clipped limes radiating out from the side and rear facades, while the entrance looked out over a simple geometric parterre. This early garden was the work of Wolf Gabriel Lück. Other solitary huts were scattered through the woods for court members and guests to indulge in the simple life. No advantage was taken in their placement of the views into the surrounding countryside; introspection was the key to the experience.

In 1735 Wilhelmine's husband succeeded to the title as Margrave Friedrich and promptly handed over the Eremitage to his creative wife. She developed it into a cultural center of courtly life, essentially a summer residence, while scrupulously retaining the atmosphere of an informal woodland retreat. The bulk of Wilhelmine's additions, largely the work of the architect Joseph Saint-Pierre, were made from 1743 onward.

The modern visitor approaches the site along a horn-beam tunnel, with a baroque layout of hedge cabinets and geometric water features to the south. The inner garden is entered via the rock of Parnassus. This great lump of rugged limestone, sprouting with shrubs, was formed at the same time as the Altes Schloss in 1718 and originally evoked a classical scene more thoroughly; an early illustration shows statues of Apollo and the nine Muses cavorting underneath Pegasus at its peak. A rustic arch passes under Parnassus and leads to the Altes Schloss itself, extended by Wilhelmine to form an ornamental building with suites of rococo chambers grouped around a central garden courtyard. In front of the building is the parterre of turf panels, at the end of which a delicate rococo cascade descends the long fall to the river valley below.

Immediately to the west, although visually quite separate, is the Neues Schloss, whose construction began in 1749. The central Temple of Apollo is decorated in an arresting style, with columns, busts, and walls encrusted with colored minerals and gold leaf to create a rich and tactile effect. Curving wings, originally occupied as orangery and aviary, flank the temple and embrace the swelling curves of a formal pool, within which sandstone statuary groups shoot slender interlocking arcs of water at intervals.

Nearby are two ornamental structures built in a "ruinated" style during the 1740s. A crumbling classical facade half hidden by the woodland edge is the memorial to Wilhelmine's favorite dog, Folichon. The adjacent Theater of Ruins consists of an open stage within the apparently ancient remains of stone arches and columns, again blending with the trunks and foliage of the beech wood. This feature is strongly reminiscent of the theater at Wilhelmine's other rural garden of Sanspareil, between Bayreuth and Bamberg. A small bark-clad chapel further complements the air of mournful decay.

A short walk brings the visitor to the Lower Grotto, which is approached across a rustic bridge over a shady pool. This grotto was the province of the margrave rather than his wife, essentially subdividing the garden into male and female zones. The Lower Grotto, dark and cool compared with Wilhelmine's open and sunny sections of the garden, is overlooked by a balcony and a hermitage from which the knowing could watch the uninitiated receive a soaking from the labyrinth of sudden water jets around the central basin.

The clean lines, simple decoration, and cottage garden of the house called Monplaisir, a *ferme ornée* surviving from Georg Wilhelm's time, create a refreshing contrast to the constantly shifting atmospheric scenery of the grounds. Elsewhere in the grounds of the Eremitage, hornbeam tunnels, treillage pavilions, and service buildings are now scattered at random intervals.

In remodeling the Eremitage for her own purposes, Wilhelmine added overlays of taste and sentiment to a garden already intended for solitary retirement. She found the existing format the ideal basis for her distinctive combination of rococo refinement, appreciation of nature, and a desire to withdraw from courtly life accentuated by private grief. The garden was a key venue for her creative skills in music, theater, and art and was much admired by her younger brother, Frederick the Great, to whom it was informally dedicated as a temple of friendship.

After Wilhelmine's death in 1758 the grounds of the Eremitage went into decline, despite periods of favor during the 19th century. Parts of the estate, including Monplaisir, were sold off, and damage during World War II destroyed suites of rooms in the Neues Schloss. Since then, however, an exemplary program of research and repair has seen the Eremitage emerge as an exceptional rococo garden that, despite its geographical isolation, in many ways anticipates the later tastes for the Picturesque and Romantic across Europe.

## Synopsis

| | |
|---|---|
| 1616 | Site of Eremitage purchased by Margrave of Bayreuth |
| 1665 | Margrave Christian Ernst establishes hunting preserve and constructs grotto over natural spring |
| 1712–16 | Margrave Georg Wilhelm establishes court hermitage with Altes Schloss and outlying huts, as well as house later known as Monplaisir |
| 1735 | Margrave Friedrich succeeds and gives Eremitage to wife Wilhelmine |
| 1736 | Remodeling of Altes Schloss begins |
| 1737 | Initial work on eventual Lower Grotto |
| 1743 | Theatre of Ruins begun |
| 1749 | Neues Schloss begun |
| 1755 | Folichon's Grave built |
| 1819 | Bark Temple built |
| late 19th C. | Eremitage used by Ludwig II as residence when attending Richard Wagner's operas |
| 1945 | War damage to Neues Schloss |
| 1949 | Restoration work begins |

## Further Reading

Bachmann, Erich, and Seelig, Lorenz, *Eremitage zu Bayreuth*, Munich: Bayerische Verwaltung der Staatlichen Schlösser, Gärten und Seen, 1987

Hennebo, Dieter, "Tendencies in Mid-Eighteenth-Century German Gardening," *Journal of Garden History* vol. 5, no. 4 (1985)

Krückmann, Peter, *Das Bayreuth der Markgräfin Wilhelmine*, Munich: Prestel, 1998

Reinhardt, Helmut, "German Gardens in the 18th Century: Classicism, Rococo and Neoclassicism," in *The History of Garden Design*, edited by Monique Mosser and Georges Teyssot, London: Thames and Hudson, 1991

STEVEN DESMOND

# Ermenonville

## Ermenonville, Oise, France

**Location:**   approximately 28 miles (45 km) northeast of Paris

In 1766 the marquis de Girardin inherited Ermenonville and completely remodeled his family's formal gardens into the then popular Picturesque style. A celebrated example of this genre in 18th-century France, Ermenonville remains one of the best examples of the Picturesque garden from this period. In his *Essay on Landscape* (1777), the marquis declared, "It is not as an architect or a gardener, but as a poet and as a painter, that landscape must be composed, so at once to please the understanding and the eye."

The style of landscape gardening promoted by the marquis in his essay is commonly called an English, or Anglo-Chinese, garden, but the passion to imitate nature was not limited to England; these landscape gardens were popular in France as well. From the mid-18th century until the Revolution, the Picturesque gradually became a favorite among the French aristocracy. Influenced by the philosophy of Jean-Jacques Rousseau, informality crept into French garden plans. Some formal landscapes were entirely revamped into naturalistic designs, while others retained the traditional formal garden near the château and added informal areas farther away.

The moated château at Ermenonville sat on the main highway, a convenience dating back to the Middle Ages when travelers paid a toll to gain access across the marshy land. When the marquis inherited the property, he removed the old walls and redesigned the formal gardens. Influenced by his own travels to England, where he had seen Picturesque gardens, and by Rousseau's *Julie; ou, La nouvelle Héloïse* (1761, *Julie; or, The New Eloise*) Girardin refashioned his landscape by having an artist sketch pictures of the proposed views. These scenes were then constructed in the landscape.

Wherever possible, Girardin used the site's inherent amenities. The existing terrain was varied, the perfect situation for the creation of an informal garden. The extant rolling topography provided an excellent setting for a garden featuring curvilinear paths and constantly changing views. Girardin converted canals and marshes into naturalistic lakes complete with cascades, islands, and grottoes. The property was transformed from a stiffly formal landscape to one consisting of forests, meadows, and farms. Critical to the concept of providing pictures in a natural setting, the marquis dotted the landscape with structures, both classical and rustic, to enhance views from inside the château and to create a variety of picturesque views from various promontories within the landscape.

South of the château, the marquis laid out a circuit walk around the lake. The Temple of Philosophy, an artificial ruin, sat on a hill above the lake in a portion of the garden called the Grand Parc. The promenade, encircling the lake, provided constantly changing views of the temple. Another important feature in this section of the park was the Tomb of Rousseau, a sarcophagus situated on the Island of Poplars. Young poplars are continually planted on the island in a circular pattern, in keeping with the original design, which gave the island its name. It was, incidentally, not through his love of the garden but through his love of music that the marquis had the occasion to meet Rousseau. Hired to give music lessons to the marquis's children, Rousseau arrived at Ermenonville on 20 May 1778. He spent the last six weeks of his life there enjoying the gardens that his philosophy had inspired.

To the north of the château, Girardin built a water mill, a small village with barns and thatch-roofed cottages, and a cabin, where Rousseau spent his last days. Girardin created these accoutrements to enhance the rustic character of the garden. To complete the rural motif, he provided a *rond-point,* a circular clearing in the woods, where the village people could hold dances. Thus, the peasant was not only admitted into the garden but also invited to enjoy it. The imagery of rustic structures and the merry peasant at play added to the appeal of the marquis's pleasure garden.

The gardens of Ermenonville were designed by the marquis himself, in the French Picturesque tradition. On an estate historically occupied by aristocrats, the formal garden was replaced by a naturalistic one, evocative of the artistic and literary traditions of the day. The garden's circulation was carefully designed to maximize the views of picturesque objects in the landscape. True to the philosophy that shaped the garden's form, the love of rural simplicity was manifest in the naturalistic landscape of the garden and its rustic design features.

Ermenonville was a popular destination for many of Rousseau's disciples, and although privately owned, it often functioned as a public park. Because it was so often frequented by followers of Rousseau, the lovely gardens inspired many of its visitors, including Marie-Antoinette, to create landscapes in the Picturesque manner. Today, even though Rousseau's remains were moved to the Panthéon in Paris, visitors are still attracted to his original burial site. The portion of the garden called the Grand Parc, south of the château, is

*mely del. et sculp*

ERMENONVILLE,

*Tombeau de J.J. dans l'Isle des Peupliers*

*Tombeau de J.J. dans l'isle des Peupliers* (Tomb of J.J. Rousseau on the Isle of Poplars), Ermenonville
Courtesy of Bibliothèque Nationale de France

owned by the Touring Club of France and is open to the public. The château is now a hotel, and the gardens to the north are part of the hotel patrons' landscape. Although greatly reduced in size and lacking some original features, the park's Picturesque charm is still evident.

## Synopsis

| | |
|---|---|
| 1766–76 | Gardens redesigned by marquis de Girardin in Picturesque style |
| 1776 | Temple of Philosophy built |
| 1778 | Jean-Jacques Rousseau arrives at Ermenonville to spend last six weeks of his life; Tomb of Rousseau built on Island of Poplars, designed by Hubert Robert |
| 1794 | Rousseau's body exhumed and moved to Panthéon, Paris |
| 1938 | Touring Club of France purchases Jean-Jacques Rousseau Park, south of château |

## Further Reading

Girardin, René Louis, Marquis de, *De la composition des paysages*, Geneva and Paris, 1777; as *An Essay on Landscape*, translated by Daniel Malthus, London, 1783; reprint, New York: Garland, 1982

Girardin, Stanislas, *Promenade; ou, Itinéraire des jardins d'Ermenonville*, Paris, 1788; as *A Tour to Ermenonville*, London, 1785; reprint (with *An Essay on Landscape*), New York: Garland, 1982

Gothein, Marie Luise Schroeter, *Geschichte der Gartenkunst*, Jena, Germany: Diederichs, 1914; 2nd edition, 1926; as *A History of Garden Art*, 2 vols., edited by Walter P. Wright, translated by Mrs. Archer-

Hind, London: Dent, and New York: Dutton, 1928; reprint, New York: Hacker Art Books, 1979

Laborde, Alexandre, *Description des nouveaux jardins de la France et de ses anciens châteaux*, Paris, 1808–15 (with descriptions in French, English, and German)

Mathieu, René, *Ermenonville*, Paris: Touring-Club de France, n.d.

*Trois jours en voyage; ou, Guide du promeneur à Chantilly, Mortefontaine et Ermenonville*, Paris, 1828

Volbertal, J.H., *Aux environs de Paris: Un domain célèbre: Ermenonville, ses sites, ses curiosités, son histoire*, Senlis, France: Imprimeries Réunis de Senlis, 1923

Wiebenson, Dora, *The Picturesque Garden in France*, Princeton, New Jersey: Princeton University Press, 1978

CONSTANCE A. WEBSTER

# Este, Villa d'

## Tivoli, Lazio, Italy

**Location:**  at Tivoli, 17 miles (27 km) east of Rome

The Villa d'Este at Tivoli, created under Cardinal Ippolito d'Este of Ferrara between 1550 and 1572, is perhaps the most spectacular garden in the whole of Italy. Poetic and literary descriptions and especially the well-known engraving by Etienne Du Pérac assured the garden's popularity throughout Europe until well into the 17th century, when the garden itself was poorly tended and the royal garden at Versailles began to command attention. Representing the humanist culture of one of Europe's most powerful nobles, the Villa d'Este is now carefully restored, a striking reminder of the particular fascination that the domain of the garden held for late 16th-century Italian culture.

Despite the project's enormous scale and expense, the cardinal spent only two or three summers at the villa. Son of Alphonso I and Lucrezia Borgia, he was made governor of Tivoli as a result of the papal enclave that gathered in 1549 following the death of Pope Paul III. Lying approximately 17 miles (27 km) to the east of Rome, Tivoli was set in a landscape rich in antique ruins of numerous and important Roman villas and temples, among them the temples to Hercules Victor and Hercules Saxanus, the villas of Emperor Hadrian and Quintillius Varus, and the well-known circular temple of the Tiburtine Sibyl (also known as the Temple of Vesta).

Of the cardinal's erudite court, the antiquarian Pirro Ligorio played the most significant role in the design of the garden. Ligorio accompanied the cardinal during his first visit to the region and set about a large number of excavations, including one of Hadrian's Villa. With Ligorio as his close adviser, the cardinal began to purchase land in the vicinity of the Franciscan monastery attached to Santa Maria Maggiore, part of which was traditionally rented to the ecclesiastical governors of Tivoli. The medieval cloisters overlooked the Valle Gaudente, whose steep west-facing slopes were to be transformed into the terraces of the Villa d'Este gardens. The cardinal planned to rebuild the courtyard, substantially extend the residence facing the garden, and demolish a large section of the old town, including several churches, retaining only the old defensive wall to define the western boundary of the garden.

Between 1555 and 1563 little work was carried out on the villa. With the election of Pope Paul IV in 1555, the cardinal was removed from the governorship of Tivoli and banished to Lombardy. Although Pope Pius IV restored the cardinal to the governorship in 1560, he subsequently sent him to serve as papal legate to France. During these difficult years Ligorio was architect to Pope Pius IV but returned to the service of the cardinal in 1567.

Work proceeded on the garden, and the natural landscape of the hillside was transformed; a plateau was built along the lower edge, and the height of the southeast corner was increased, culminating in a large rocky mound behind the Tiburtine Sibyl at the Oval Fountain. According to Du Pérac's engraving the lower cross axis was marked by a line of fishponds stretching between the Water Organ and the Fountain of Neptune (which was never built). Nature's creativity was represented by the two figures of Neptune (ruler of the oceans) and Diana of Ephesus (goddess of nature), or Mayer Matuta, who surveyed Neptune's domain from the top of a clifflike facade in the central niche of the Water Organ.

The second prominent cross axis in Du Pérac's engraving cuts across the hillside at a higher level and is marked by the so-called Line of a Hundred Fountains, which stretches uninterrupted between the Oval Fountain to the east and the miniature Rome of the Rometta,

View of the Rometta Fountain, Villa d'Este, Tivoli, Lazio, Italy
Photo by Alastair Carew-Cox

built out from the ancient town wall, to the west. The Oval Fountain is a vision of Tivoli represented as a new Mount Helicon—home of the Muses—looking toward Rome, the great patron of the noble arts. Seen in this way, the upper cross axis articulates the geographical relationship between Tivoli and Rome and themes associated with poetry and the arts.

A further set of themes emphasized by Du Pérac concerns the legendary figure of Hercules. At the heart of the garden is the Fountain of the Dragon. Structured like a cave and cut deep into the garden's steep slope, it is the scene of a most powerful drama whose meaning unifies and gathers the most erudite of distant references involved in the pagan imagery. It can first be interpreted as an allegory of the paradigmatic life of Hercules, where the choice between the relatively easy path to the

Grotto of Venus (Voluptas) and the relatively steep path to the Grotto of Diana (Virtu) high up in the southwest corner of the garden reflects Hercules's legendary choice between virtue and vice.

The layers of such allegorical meaning conveyed in the garden are further developed by geometric alignments that exist between key fountains of the garden and the Tiburtine landscape. These have such a startling consistency that there seems to be little possibility of their being casual or coincidental. Quite the contrary, it appears that the principal fountain elements were determined by a matrix of alignments that thread across the ancient landscape. The Grotto of Diana is located by a diagonal line struck from the Temple of Hercules Saxanus through the position of the Water Organ (built adjacent to the Church of San Pietro della Carita). This diagonal line bisects the central axis of the garden at the principal niche of the Fountain of the Dragon, and from this point a second diagonal joins the new bay in the boundary wall to the central hall in the Villa of Augustus. Extrapolated in the other direction from the niche in the Fountain of the Dragons, the same line locates the entrance on the central axis of the secret garden and the line of the Grotto of Venus in the villa. Furthermore, if a line is extrapolated from the Grotto of Neptune (which lies below the Temple of the Sibyl) perpendicular to the central axis of the garden, the positions of the octagonal pavilion of the lower garden, and the center of the bay in the town walls are located. Finally, the skewed central axis appears to be generated by its alignment with the town's Roman amphitheater.

The creative thinking that characterized Ligorio's archaeology, and which was the driving force behind the striking departure in garden design in the 16th century, depended on the development of the art of perspective and scenography. Here, perspective allows the garden setting to be grasped in its full depth, as a visual experience whose geometrical consistency embodies a sequence of thematic relationships that build the identity of the garden in its historicity. The result is an emphasis on a meaning that is specific to the context and its history, pertaining not only to the confines of the garden itself but to the Tiburtine region and to Rome, Tivoli's ancient rival. There is a complex attempt to ground the highly artificial landscape of the garden and villa in classical mythology and more specifically, in local Tiburtine history, learning oriented to *comtemplatio* and *admiratio* of history.

On the death of Ippolito in 1572, the garden remained largely incomplete. It was inherited by his nephew, Luigi Cardinal d'Este, who carried out significant work on the garden until his death in 1586. The last Este cardinal to possess the Villa d'Este was Rinaldo II, in 1687. On his resignation there followed a long period of neglect and disarray. The villa first passed into the hands of the Habsburgs of Austria and finally to the Italian government after World War I. There is at present an extensive program of restoration to recover this exquisite water garden as a striking reminder of the breathtaking *bella maniera* of the 16th-century imagination.

## Synopsis

| | |
|---|---|
| 1549 | Ippolito II, Cardinal d'Este, becomes governor of Tivoli and begins to purchase land for Villa d'Este |
| 1550–72 | Villa d'Este garden created by Cardinal Ippolito II, designed principally by Pirro Ligorio |
| 1555–60 | Work on garden suspended during Cardinal Ippolito II's exile to Lombardy |
| 1560 | Cardinal Ippolito II sent as Papal Legate to France |
| 1567 | Ligorio returns to service of Cardinal Ippolito II and work on garden is started again |
| 1572 | Cardinal Ippolito II dies and work on garden continued by his nephew, Luigi, Cardinal d'Este |
| 1586 | Luigi, Cardinal d'Este, dies |
| 1687 | Death of last Este cardinal in possession of Villa d'Este; garden fell into long period of neglect |
| 1918 | Italian government acquires villa |

## Further Reading

Coffin, David R., *The Villa d'Este at Tivoli*, Princeton, New Jersey: Princeton University Press, 1960

Dernie, David, *The Villa d'Este at Tivoli*, London: Academy Editions, 1996

Lamb, Carl, *Die Villa d'Este in Tivoli: Ein Beitrag zur Geschichte der Gartenkunst*, Munich: Prestel, 1966

DAVID DERNIE

---

# Evelyn, John 1620–1705

## English Writer and Translator of Gardening Books

"I was born (at Wotton, in the County of Surrey) about twenty minutes past two in the morning, being on Tuesday the 31st and last of October." Thus begins the celebrated diary of John Evelyn, who was in fact well known both to his contemporaries and to posterity for a variety of attributes. John Evelyn lived through particularly turbulent times in English history: the reign of Charles I; the Civil War between the Cavaliers and

Roundheads, which resulted in the Commonwealth when no monarch was on the throne; the Restoration of Charles II; the reigns of James II and William III; and the beginning of the reign of Queen Anne.

Evelyn's diary, for which he is most generally known, records his continental travels from 1642 to 1647 and devotes much attention to gardens and the arts generally. During this period of travel he married and then, leaving his wife in Paris, returned to England until July 1649, when he went back to Paris for another three years. Due in part to his connections at court and among the nobility, his diary presents a rational, if not totally unbiased, record of the times. He was a fair, honest, and balanced individual, although undisguisedly, at least through his diary, a Cavalier. What is striking about this record is the matter-of-fact way in which it intermixes issues of state and episodes of danger and enormity with the simple activities of everyday life. He commented upon not only the gardens of France and Italy but also the gardens he saw on his travels around England.

On his return to England in March of 1652, Evelyn settled at Sayes Court, Deptford, east of London, which belonged to his father-in-law, in order to protect it from the ravages of parliamentarians. In the same month he went down to his elder brother George's home at Wotton to advise him on the design of his garden. Wotton was the old family home. Scholars have suggested that it was laid out in the Italian style, in contrast to the French influence that dominated Evelyn's own garden at Sayes Court, which he began designing the same year.

In 1662 Evelyn was sworn in as a member of the original Council of the Royal Society, which had been established under the auspices of Charles II. While this is now the premier learned scientific society in the United Kingdom, its early members took a keen interest in the design, layout, and plants of their gardens. One of the earliest presentations to the society was by Evelyn, the historic "Discourse on Forest Trees," which he gave on 15 October 1662. It was published two years later under the title *"Sylva"; or, A Discourse on Forest Trees, and the Propagation of Timber in His Majesty's Dominions: As It Was Delivered in the Royal Society on the 15th Day of October 1662.*

In the aftermath of the Civil War and the ravages that many estates underwent in the Commonwealth, there was a great need to rebuild the stocks of timber, which were especially needed for the construction of the fleet on which England depended for both defense and commerce. Care for the land and maintenance of estates was seen as an important duty by all landowners. Thus, while the exhortation of *Sylva* may not have been necessary for all, the advice and information would have been greatly valued. Evelyn's diary notes that he presented the volume to the Royal Society on 16 February 1664, and on the following day he also presented it to the king, to whom it

was dedicated, as well as to the lord treasurer and the lord chancellor. This seems to have been the first publication emanating from the Royal Society, and a very important and influential one it was. Later editions of the work also contained *Pomona; or, An Appendix Concerning Fruit Trees* and the *Kalendarium Hortense.* These works appear to have been part of a much larger project, the *Elysium Britannicum,* for which an outline scheme was found among Evelyn's papers. Had it been completed, the work would have been a substantial encyclopedia. As it was, *Sylva* was published and enlarged on a number of occasions (2nd edition, 1671; 3rd edition, 1679) and was the standard work on the subject into the 19th century. The dedication to the king in the third edition states, "I need not acquaint Your Majesty how many millions of timber trees (besides infinite others) have been propagated and planted throughout your vast dominions at the instigation and sole direction of this work because Your Gracious Majesty has been pleased to own it publickly for my encouragement."

Earlier, in 1658, Evelyn had produced a translation of a volume by Nicholas de Bonnefons, which he entitled *The French Gardener.* After *Sylva* Evelyn engaged in a translation of another French work, this time by La Quintinie, which Evelyn presented as *The Complete Gardener.* The English translation was published in 1693, by which time at least some in England were beginning to consider design concepts that did not conform to the traditional ideas of order and symmetry propounded by La Quintinie. Nevertheless, La Quintinie's writing on forestry, horticulture, and fruit growing was to be an important influence for many years after his death.

Evelyn, as an amateur, was quite prepared to give advice and even prepare plans for the gardens of his friends and acquaintances. For his friend Henry Howard, earl of Arundel and later duke of Norfolk, Evelyn designed a philosophers' garden at Albury Park. He also advised on the planting of the park at Euston Hall in Suffolk for the earl of Arlington and on the layout of Cassiobury Park, in Hertfordshire, where the earl of Essex had previously created a forest park.

*See also* Luxembourg Gardens

**Biography**

Born in Wotton, Surrey, England, 31 October 1620. Traveled extensively in France, Italy, and Germany, 1642–47; lived in Paris, 1649–52; laid out his brother George's garden in Wotton, 1652; delivered *Discourse on Forest Trees* to Royal Society, October 1662. Died in Wotton, 27 February 1705.

**Selected Designs**

1652    Italian-style gardens at the family residence
        in Wotton, Surrey, England

| 1667 | Natural philosopher's garden at Albury Park, Surrey, England |
| 1671–80 | Consulted on French style of gardens and parks for Euston Hall, Suffolk; Cassiobury Park, Hertfordshire; and Cornbury House, Oxfordshire |

**Selected Publications**

*Elysium Britannicum* (written in 1650s; never published)

*The French Gardener*, a translation from the French by Nicolas de Bonnefons, 1658

*"Sylva"; or, A Discourse on Forest Trees*, 1664; 5th edition, 1825

*The Compleat Gard'ner*, a translation from the French by Jean de la Quintinie, 1693

**Further Reading**

Bowle, John, *John Evelyn and His World: A Biography*, London and Boston: Routledge and Kegan Paul, 1981

Evelyn, John, *The Diary of John Evelyn*, edited by E.S. de Beer, 6 vols., Oxford: Clarendon Press, 1955

Ponsonby, Arthur, *John Evelyn: Fellow of the Royal Society, Author of "Sylva,"* London: Heinemann, 1933

Willy, Margaret, *English Diarists: Evelyn and Pepys*, London: Longmans Green, 1963

M.F. DOWNING

# F

## Fairchild, Thomas 1667–1729

### English Nurseryman and Author

In the late 17th and early 18th century, the English plantsman, florist, and scientist Thomas Fairchild established one of the most influential commercial nurseries in Europe. Among his most significant scientific achievements, Fairchild pioneered the artificial hybridization of plants. To the practical gardener, it is probably his early contribution to city gardening that is most valued; to the landscape historian, it is probably his role as a major commercial supplier of important species and varieties of tree, shrub, bulb, and herbaceous flower.

It was only in the late 17th century that plant nurseries such as Fairchild's became established in Britain on a commercial basis. The *Oxford English Dictionary* dates the first use of the term nursery in this modern sense to 1672. Fairchild's nursery opened in Hoxton, a village close to the City of London, in 1692. At this time it was one of only seven commercial nurseries in the London area, each of which appears to have developed particular specialities. Fairchild's became the principal London-based commercial grower of North American tulip trees (*Liriodendron tulipifera*) and Indian bean trees (*Catalpa bignonioides*) and stocked possibly the largest collection of fruit trees of any nursery in Europe. His nursery also raised new varieties of garden flowers, including lilies, and established the practice of forcing plants to flower even in the winter months. As the nursery's reputation grew, Fairchild became regarded as a truly great plantsman and one of the great florists of the early 18th century.

Fairchild's success as the main commercial supplier of certain North American trees was helped by his friend and eventual witness to his will, the English naturalist illustrator, plant collector, and author Mark Catesby, who lived in Virginia. Catesby traveled widely in North America, mainly at the expense of the English Quaker botanist Peter Collinson. The seed he supplied to Fairchild was not the first to arrive in Britain from the New World—trees such as the tulip tree had been grown in Britain since Elizabethan times—but Fairchild, along with his neighbor William Derby, raised and distributed large quantities for the first time.

Besides North American trees, Fairchild's nursery developed a strong reputation in shrubs, herbaceous plants, bulbs, aloes and other succulent plants, and grapes—of which the nursery's catalog listed 50 different types. Lilies were also a speciality. After Fairchild's death, his letter on the culture of the "Guernsea Lilie" was printed in *The Practical Husbandman,* and "The Late Mr. Fairchild's White Lily" was engraved for *The Compleat Florist.* Most remarkable of all was Fairchild's fruit tree collection, described in 1721 by the first horticultural journalist, Richard Bradley, a professor of botany at Cambridge, who produced a *Monthly Register of Experiments and Observations in Husbandry and Gardening, with a General Treatise of Husbandry and Gardening* (1721–24). In Bradley's words, Fairchild's nursery offered "the greatest collection of fruits that I have yet seen, and so regularly disposed . . . that I do not know any person in Europe to excel him in that particular."

For Bradley's *Monthly Register* Fairchild produced a list of all the plants in flower at the nursery month-by-month over the course of a year. The historical importance of this document lies in the fact that it provides a more precise idea than is available from any other source of which plants could be induced to flower in England at this time. It confirms that good plant nurseries—and certainly Fairchild's—were no longer restricted to the normal growing season of February to September, as had been the case 20 years earlier at Henry Wise's London nursery.

Dried specimen of Thomas Fairchild's Mule in the Oxford University Herbarium
Courtesy of Oxford University Herbarium, Oxford, England

Occasional scientific studies were published by Fairchild, such as his study of the circulation of sap in plants, which was printed in *Transactions of the Royal Society*. However, Fairchild's principal contribution to science was made in 1717, when he transferred pollen from the anthers of a sweet William flower to the style of a carnation flower. This experiment with the role of pollen in the sexual nature of flowers—a subject then only recently understood and hotly debated resulted in fertile seed that germinated to produce the world's first artificial plant hybrid. The original specimen is still preserved in the herbarium of Oxford University. It is named, appropriately, "Mr Fairchild's Mule" (*Dianthus caryophyllus* × *D. barbatus*). Following Fairchild's pioneering work, artificial hybridization opened up a multitude of opportunities in crop production, horticulture, and floristry.

In 1722 Fairchild published *The City Gardener,* the first book devoted to the problems and practices of town gardening. It explored the effects of air pollution on plants and suggested ways in which gardeners could overcome the effects of harmful city smoke. Recommendations were made on the selection of trees and herbaceous plants with the ability to withstand a smoky atmosphere, such as the new London plane tree. Today this tree is perhaps the most ubiquitous in central London and not without good reason, for London's smoke-control legislation, although originally drafted during Fairchild's youth, did not appear on the statute book until the modern period.

*The City Gardener* also focused attention on the landscaping of urban spaces. Fairchild urged that cobbled town squares and vacant city plots be landscaped with a greenery of "wilderness-work" rather than the formality of "Grass Platts and Gravel Walks." For such planting schemes Fairchild suggested evergreens (such as holly, ivy, box, privet, and bay) and deciduous shrubs (such as laburnum, lilac, philadelphus, and viburnum) that were suitable for the city environment, along with flower beds edged with colorful staples such as sunflowers, asters, and sweet Williams. Fairchild is sometimes credited as author of another book, *Catalogus Plantarum* (1730), as his name appears at the head of the Society of Gardeners who are credited on the title page. This catalog of trees and shrubs was published a year after Fairchild's death, however, and although he made a significant contribution, so too had other members of the Society of Gardeners, who had conceived the project in 1725.

Fairchild died in 1729 at the age of 63. The nursery passed to his nephew Stephen Bacon. Following subsequent changes in ownership, it finally closed in 1740, and so ended, after a little less than 50 years, one of the most remarkable and significant plant nurseries of all time.

In his will Fairchild left money to the local poor and specified only the most inexpensive and humble burial for himself "in some corner of the Churchyard . . . where the poore people are buried." A sum was also set aside to cover the cost of a sermon, or "annual vegetable lecture," to be preached in perpetuity every Whit Tuesday, "setting forth the wonderful works of God in creation." It is possible that Fairchild was troubled by his success in raising a hybrid plant that was not part of God's creation. A new headstone was erected in tribute to Fairchild in 1846. This monument, inscribed with a lengthy biography, is today set in a small open space on the site of the old burial ground. Fairchild's annual sermon continues to this day and is now associated with the guild service of the Worshipful Company of Gardeners.

## Biography

Born in England, 1667. Fairchild obtained a piece of ground at Hoxton village, close to London, in 1692 and began to grow exotic trees, fruit trees, vines, bulbs, flowers, and succulents, establishing gardens that became famous as the "City Gardens"; corresponded with Mark Catesby and asked him to import the seeds of North American trees into Britain; established himself as the main British commercial grower of North American tulip trees and Indian bean trees, ca. 1700; he produced the first artificial plant hybrid known to science, 1717: a sterile cross of a carnation and sweet William, given the name "Mr. Fairchild's mule" (*Dianthus caryophyllus* × *D. barbatus*); grew possibly the largest collection of fruit trees of any nursery in Europe and demonstrated the forcing of flowers throughout the year for commercial purposes, ca. 1720; wrote *The City Gardener* (1722), the first book devoted to town gardening, which recommended plants and trees that would withstand air pollution (for example, the London plane tree), and promoted schemes of "wilderness" planting for urban spaces. Died in Shoreditch, London, 1729.

## Selected Publications

*The City Gardener,* 1722
*Catalogus Plantarum*: *A Catalogue of Trees and Shrubs,* 1730 (co-authored within the Society of Gardeners)

## Further Reading

Harvey, John Hooper, *Early Nurserymen,* London: Phillimore, 1974
Hobhouse, Penelope, *Plants in Garden History,* London: Pavilion Books, 1992; as *Penelope Hobhouse's Gardening through the Ages,* New York: Simon and Schuster, 1992
Leapman, Michael, *The Ingenious Mr Fairchild,* London: Headline, 2000

Leighton, Ann, *American Gardens in the Eighteenth Century*, Boston: Houghton Mifflin, 1976

Walters, Stuart Max, *The Shaping of Cambridge Botany: A Short History of Whole-Plant Botany in Cambridge from the Time of Ray into the Present*

*Century*, Cambridge and New York: Cambridge University Press, 1981

DAVID SOLMAN

# Farrand, Beatrix Jones 1872–1959

## United States Landscape Architect

In addition to the influence of Charles Sargent during her apprenticeship at the Arnold Arboretum, Beatrix Farrand drew inspiration for her style of garden design from her experience at the Italian villas and English Elizabethan gardens she visited on her European tour of 1895. The popularity of the formal garden at this time was largely due to Charles Platt's *Italian Villas and Their Gardens* (1895) and later her aunt Edith Wharton's book on the same subject (1905).

Early commissions, for example for William Garrison of Tuxedo, New York (1896), and others completed in an architectural style, were so highly regarded that Farrand was invited to be a founding member of the American Society of Landscape Architects (1899), the only woman in a small but noteworthy group that included John Olmsted and Charles Eliot.

Farrand was not only a distinguished designer and plantswoman but she was also well connected socially. In the first 17 years of professional practice, she completed 38 private gardens for clients whose names filled the social register of the day, including Rockefeller, Whitney, and Morgan. During the same years she completed ten public projects, including her first campus work for Princeton University and a rose garden for the White House. Although always regarded as an East Coast designer, Farrand also received opportunities via her husband's, Max Farrand, position as director of the Huntington Library (1924), in California, including several major gardens and the Cal Tech campus in Pasadena (1928). Apart from the campus work, few of the great gardens Farrand designed are extant. Two major exceptions are Dumbarton Oaks—the Robert Wood Bliss residence in Washington, D.C. (1921–47)—and the Eyre Garden for John D. Rockefeller in Seal Harbor, Maine (1926–50).

The term *campus* to describe a university gained currency during Farrand's development as a landscape architect. By the 1890s it was considered appropriate that the ideal university should be set in nature. The older established schools, such as Yale and Princeton, unable or unwilling to relocate, withdrew into a quadrangle format with collegiate-Gothic-style buildings surrounding a central green space. Farrand considered such enclosed areas suitable for circulation with grass and a few trees. Shrubs and other plantings were kept to the sides or on the walls. In 1912 she planted Princeton's new Graduate School, and between 1922 and 1939 she was employed by other universities and colleges, including Yale, Oberlin, the University of Chicago, Vassar, and Hamilton, as designer and frequently for extended periods of consultation related to maintenance and perpetuity.

The design for the Eyre Garden was commissioned by the Rockefellers in 1926. Farrand's involvement with it lasted until 1950 (with a break, 1935–45). It was perhaps unique because the client had a particular program in mind: within a large estate to provide a secluded setting for Mrs. Rockefeller's collection of oriental sculptures and a walled flower garden. The Asian theme was critical to the client, and Farrand detailed the wall with gates in an exhaustive series of sketches and full-scale paper mock-ups resulting in the final selection of a circular moon gate in an otherwise straightforward wall topped with Chinese tiles. Outside the walled garden but directly connected to it was a straight walk lined with large Korean figures in pairs, framed by the surrounding forest (the Guardian Walk). The collaboration resulted in an elegant design of great emotional and aesthetic impact and suggests Farrand's skill at working with a client's perspective and the opportunities offered by the site.

In addition to the gardens' interest as examples of Farrand's skill in design and planting is the length of time she was involved with the gardens and her clients, which illustrate her understanding of time and the role of the client as a participant in the design process. Both are critical in the production of lasting and satisfying landscape architecture. Her concern for management and time is clearly illustrated in the *Plant Book* prepared by her in 1941 for Dumbarton Oaks. It is a remarkable document and one that has never been equaled for its clear statement of design objectives, rationale for plant selection, and understanding of time and the need for renewal, the last of which is the fourth dimension of private and public landscapes.

In the late 1930s, as a culmination to their long working lives, the Farrands retired to their summer home in Bar Harbor, Maine, where they established an institution known as Reef Point Gardens (1939). It was intended to be horticulturally educational and included a small working library and a group of European garden prints that Farrand had collected over the years. In contrast to the projects for which she is most famous, Reef Point was informal in design, influenced strongly by the nature of the site and ecological considerations, perhaps a reflection of changing interests and directions in the field of landscape architecture in postwar years.

*See also* Dumbarton Oaks; Huntington Library and Botanic Gardens

## Biography

Born in New York City, New York, 1872. Studied for three years at the Arnold Arboretum (1892–95) under its director, Charles Sargent; also strongly influenced by her aunt Edith Wharton, who introduced her to Italian gardens; traveled in Europe in 1895; her professional practice, from 1891 to 1949, included 200 garden and university commissions, mainly on the East Coast, but also in California. Died in Bar Harbor, Maine, 1959.

## Selected Designs

| | |
|---|---|
| 1896 | Residence of William Garrison, Tuxedo Park, New York, United States |
| 1901 | The Mount, residence of Edward and Edith Wharton, Lenox, Massachusetts, United States |
| 1898 | Residence of Pierpont Morgan, New York City, New York, United States |
| 1921–47 | Dumbarton Oaks, residence of Robert Wood Bliss, Washington, District of Columbia, United States |
| 1922–45 | Yale University, New Haven, Connecticut, United States |
| 1926–50 | The Eyrie garden, residence of John D. Rockefeller, Jr., Seal Harbor, Mt. Desert Island, Maine, United States |
| 1928–38 | California Institute of Technology, Pasadena, California, United States |
| 1933–38 | Dartington Hall, Devonshire, England |
| 1939–46 | Oberlin College, Oberlin, Ohio, United States |

## Selected Publications

*Beatrix Farrand's Plant Book for Dumbarton Oaks,* 1980

## Further Reading

Balmori, Diana, Diane Kostial McGuire, and Eleanor M. McPeck, *Beatrix Farrand's American Landscapes: Her Gardens and Campuses,* Sagaponack, New York: Sagapress, 1985

McGuire, Diane Kostial, and Lois Fern, editors, *Beatrix Jones Farrand (1872–1959): Fifty Years of American Landscape Architecture,* Washington, D.C.: Dumbarton Oaks, 1982

MICHAEL LAURIE

# Ferme Ornée

The *ferme ornée,* or "the farmlike way of gardening," was a variation of the English landscape garden, which became popular in the mid-18th century, was copied on the continents of Europe and North America, and persisted until the mid-19th century. It had literary roots in the works of Alexander Pope and Joseph Addison, fulfilling the latter's injunction in the *Spectator* of June 1712:

But why may not a whole Estate be thrown into a kind of Garden by frequent Plantations that may turn as much to the Profit, as the Pleasure of the Owner. Fields of Corn make a pleasant Prospect, and if the Walks were a little taken care of that lie between them, if the natural Embroidery of the Meadows were helpt and improved by some small Additions of Art, and the several Rows of Hedges set off by Trees and Flowers, that the Soil was capable of receiving, a man might make a pretty Landskip of his own Possessions.

Pope's rubric in the *Moral Essays* (1731), "Tis use alone that sanctifies Expense, / And Splendour borrows all her rays from sense," was also realized in a landscape that provided an environment for fish and fowl, pasture for sheep and cattle and, more unusually, embraced corn lands. The patchwork of hedgerows and small woods, which typified lowland England, was enshrined in this form of gardening.

The movement was promoted especially by the prolific garden writer Stephen Switzer, who gave definition to the ideas of Addison and Pope in the catchphrase "rural gardening," which promoted estate management that was both pleasurable and profitable. In the *Practical Husbandman* (1733) Switzer used the term *ornamental farm* and later in *Ichnographia Rustica* (1742) mentions that "This taste . . . has also for some time been the Practice of the best Genius's of France, under the Title of La Germe Ornée. And that Great Britain is now likely to excel in it, let all those who have seen the Farms and Parks of Abbs-Court, Riskins, Dawley-Park, now a doing."

Dawley in Middlesex was the estate of the Tory leader Viscount Bolingbroke, who exploited the concept of the *ferme ornée* to embarrass his political opponents, the Whigs. By converting his park into a series of tenant holdings and renaming it Dawley Farm, he deliberately embraced the simple life to draw attention to the profligacy of the Whigs, many of whom possessed massive formal landscapes. Switzer had already noticed the antique precedents of the *ferme ornée* in the works of Virgil, Horace, and Pliny the Younger, which naturally recommended the idea to his contemporaries. Bolingbroke's ally, Lord Bathurst, a close friend of Pope, owned Riskins (now Richings, in Buckinghamshire) where sheep grazed in the avenues and corn and turnips grew within the pleasure grounds. Pope dedicated two of his *Moral Essays* to Bolingbroke and Bathurst. Apps Court, near Walton on Thames, was the creation of George Montague, first earl of Halifax. It was less well known, but Switzer referred to Montague as a "good husbandman and planter," implying that Montague epitomized those landowners the writer admired, seeking profit as well as pleasure from their estates.

The *ferme ornée* was made famous by two celebrated mid-18th-century gardens—Philip Southcote's Woburn Farm in Surrey and William Shenstone's the Leasowes in Shropshire. Joseph Spence recorded that Southcote had come upon the idea of the *ferme ornée* independently, while traveling in Italy from Rome to Venice, where he noticed that intensive cultivation gave the fields "the air of a garden." This was enhanced by the grassy margins left around the fields for pasture. At Woburn there was an interplay of native shrubs and exotic flowers. Hedges were retained with wide margins, planted with herbaceous perennials and bulbs and edged with pinks. Sheep and cattle grazed the grass, the poultry had use of a temple for their roost, and in the remoter parts of the pleasure grounds, small fields of corn or grazing mingled with walks and plantations. The naïveté, which impressed visitors at Woburn, was contrived to achieve even greater effect at the Leasowes.

Shenstone, a poet who moved in elevated circles, had to support himself from his small farm and an income of £300 per year. Thus, the theory of profit and pleasure was put to the test, and in Shenstone's case the latter was tarnished by the lack of the former. When he took over his farm in 1745, he was already familiar with the *ferme ornée* at Mickleton, Gloucestershire, which belonged to the family of his friend Richard Graves. Shenstone's ambition was to follow nature, enhancing the inherent qualities of his little valley, eschewing costly monuments, and highlighting the varied scenes of his landscape with the artful use of footpaths and emblematic inscriptions. Robert Dodsley's *Description of the Leasowes* (1764) reproduced a plan of the farm, which shows the irregular field boundaries typical of the ancient enclosed landscapes of the West Midlands. Similarly, Shenstone's own watercolors convey the impression of conventional farmland, with small fields, scattered clumps of trees, and a pair of haystacks close to the farm buildings. When the poet James Thompson visited the Leasowes in 1746, he complimented Shenstone on his achievement and suggested extending the garden into a little valley on the west. Shenstone replied that it was not a "regular garden" but a farm: "The French have what they call a *parque ornée* and I give my place the title of *ferme ornée*."

Shenstone's last years were troubled with debt, which proved that the *ferme ornée*, for all its arcadian purity, was best suited as the plaything of rich men. In his lifetime Shenstone provided advice on the laying out of Enville in Staffordshire, where, it seems, he persuaded Henry Grey, fourth earl of Stamford, to follow the model of the Leasowes. But with a better income, Stamford could afford many more substantial monuments, pushing Enville closer to the show gardens at Hagley. Such conspicuous expenditure undermined the simplicity that was at the heart of the concept of the *ferme ornée*.

Toward the end of the century it looked as if interest in the *ferme ornée* was declining as a particular exemplar of the landscape garden. William Gilpin certainly did not appreciate its point when he visited the Leasowes in 1772. He detected too much artifice, disliked the hedgerows, and thought the water lacked brilliancy. Humphry Repton was equally unsympathetic and throughout his career promoted a strictly ornamental form of pleasure ground, banishing arable lands from his parks. In *Fragments* (1816) he poured scorn upon the concept of the *ferme ornée*: "I never have admitted the word *Ferme orné* into my ideas of taste, any more than a butcher's shop, or a pigsty adorned with pea-green or gilding."

Not all advocates of the picturesque were out of sympathy with the *ferme ornée* concept. Sir Uvedale Price's management of the Foxley estate in Herefordshire was firmly based on the principle of profits and pleasure, and one of the central themes of his *Essays on the Picturesque* (1794) was to promote efficient estate management that provided an aesthetic bonus. Recent studies of his farming strategy by Daniels and Watkins have demonstrated that he was successful on both counts. Price was much admired by John Claudius Loudon, who took the tenancy of Tew Lodge in Oxfordshire in 1808 to prove conclusively that, notwithstanding Repton's rarefied concept of the picturesque, it could be combined with productive farming. Reflecting on his achievement, Loudon was especially pleased with his new roads, which "appear like rides through an arable *ferme ornée.*" Loudon rescued the idea of the *ferme ornée* and included it in the *Encyclopaedia of Gardening* (1822), regarding it as a distinct form of farming associated with the villa landscapes of the Home Counties. Good examples, he thought, could be found in Surrey, Kent, and the Isle of Wight. He also outlined the characteristics of the *ferme ornée:*

> The *ferme ornée* differs from a common farm in having a better dwelling-house, neater approach, and one partly or entirely distinct from that which leads to the offices. It also differs as to hedges, which are allowed to grow wild and irregular, and are bordered on each side by a broad green drive, and sometimes by a gravel-walk and shrubs. It differs from a villa farm in having no park. A dry hilly soil is best suited for this description of residence.

Loudon may well have realized that the *ferme ornée* had already been exported to the Continent and the United States. Although both Switzer and Shenstone believed the term was imported from France, it is not mentioned in any French source until 1774. The translation of Thomas Whately's *Observations on Modern Gardening* (1771) celebrated Woburn and the Leasowes, and the influential marquis de Girardin acknowledged his debt to Shenstone at Ermenonville, where the marquis combined farming with picturesque beauty in the Pricean manner. He erected a statue to Shenstone on his estate. In a corrupted form the *ferme ornée* makes its appearance in the Hameau (1785) at Le Petit Trianon with its cowsheds, dairies, rustic houses, vegetable gardens, and orchards.

Thomas Jefferson visited the Leasowes in 1786, more than 20 years after Shenstone's death, only to discover that poetical gardening was difficult to sustain without the poet. Jefferson was not impressed, calling it a "grazing farm with a path around it." His impression of Woburn, however, was more favorable. He appreciated the ornamental walk through the intermixed pleasure ground and garden. Jefferson carried the idea of the *ferme ornée* to Monticello in Virginia and about 1790 realized that his gardening principles were closely allied with what he had seen at Woburn and the Leasowes. Flowering peaches acted as fences to his fields, and fishponds were both functional and ornamental. He even planned a more thorough *ferme ornée,* intermingling husbandry and gardening. In a very real sense the *ferme ornée* was the perfect vehicle for American gardening in the 18th and 19th centuries, providing improvers with a reason to combine utility and pleasure.

Today the name has fallen into disuse, but in principle the *ferme ornée* lives on where ever there is an aspiration to produce beauty out of fecundity.

*See also* Leasowes

**Further Reading**

Daniels, Stephen, and Charles Watkins, "Picturesque Landscaping and Estate Management: Uvedale Price at Foxley, 1770–1829," *Rural History* 2, no. 2 (1991)

Hatch, Peter J., *The Gardens of Thomas Jefferson's Monticello,* Charlottesville, Virginia: Thomas Jefferson Memorial Foundation, 1992

Hunt, John Dixon, and Peter Willis, editors, *The Genius of the Place: The English Landscape Garden, 1620–1820,* London: Elek, and New York: Harper and Row, 1975

Jacques, David, *Georgian Gardens: The Reign of Nature,* London: Batsford, and Portland, Oregon: Timber Press, 1983

Leighton, Ann, *American Gardens in the Eighteenth Century: "For Use or for Delight,"* Boston: Houghton Mifflin, 1976

Loudon, John Claudius, *An Encyclopaedia of Gardening,* 2 vols., London, 1822; new edition, 1835; reprint, New York: Garland, 1982

Simo, Melanie Louise, *Loudon and the Landscape: From Country Seat to Metropolis, 1783–1843,* New Haven, Connecticut: Yale University Press, 1988

DAVID WHITEHEAD

# Fernery

A fernery is a living collection of ferns and fern allies typically found within constructions that protect the plants from outside weather conditions. At times during the 19th century, a fernery, fern garden, or fern house was called a *filicetum* (after the Latin *filix*, meaning fern or bracken). In cool climates ferneries often have glazed roofs and walls to trap the sun's warmth and are also called hothouses, glasshouses, or conservatories. In warm climates ferneries are not glazed but are shaded by timber laths or shade cloth and are also called shade-houses (or bush-houses in Australia). A variation on the walk-in fernery is the early 19th-century invention, the Wardian case—a glazed container that simulates the humid conditions of a hothouse and can be transported across oceans in boats for scientific purposes or positioned on a table within a residence for decorative purposes. Later in the 1890s this kind of container was called a *terrarium*, whose popularity was rekindled in the 1970s. Neither container was ever exclusively for ferns. Ferneries can also be created outside using hardy ferns suitable to the local climate: for instance, the tropical fernery under the shady canopy of large trees at Peradeniya Botanic Gardens, Sri Lanka, during the 19th century and the contemporary cool-temperate fernery at Highgrove, England, in the *stumpery*.

The term *fernery* came into existence around the 1840s in England, as the botanical study of ferns became popular. This was soon followed by horticultural interest in fern collections and garden design using foliage plants. Some of the early publications that sparked the "fern fever" that followed include George William Francis's *An Analysis of the British Ferns and Their Allies* (1837) and Edward Newman's *A History of British Ferns and Allied Plants* (1840) and *A Handbook of British Ferns* (1848), as well as articles in the numerous gardening magazines that arose during this time in England, such as the *Magazine of Natural History, Gardener's Magazine,* and *Gardeners' Chronicle*. These botanists described the cultivation of ferns in Wardian cases and outside in ferneries created in specially designed glens or rockeries.

After field botanists began the craze for ferns, nursery operators (especially Loddiges and Sons, London, and specialists such as W. and J. Birkenhead, Manchester) and gardeners took part in the second phase of popularity for ferns (or "pteridomania"). More books and articles heightened the excitement: Shirley Hibberd wrote several influential works relating to foliage and fern growing, including *Rustic Adornments for Homes of Taste* (1856) and *The Fern Garden* (1869); Benjamin Samuel Williams wrote *Select Ferns and Lycopods* (1868); and E.J. Lowe cultivated and wrote about ferns from the 1840s, culminating in *Fern Growing* (1895). The British and European fascination with ferns spread to the colonies and beyond. Fern collections in ferneries were particularly well represented at botanic gardens (e.g., Jardin des Plantes, Paris). Colonial botanists, such as F.M. Bailey in Queensland (Australia), rivaled their colleagues in England with publications about native ferns, cultivation, and fernery construction. The 19th-century fern mania reached its zenith with the establishment of the British Pteridological Society (1891) and the American Fern Society (1893), both of which remain strong to this day.

The 19th-century fern craze was not just a gardening phenomenon. Living ferns were used in many ways in

FERN CULTURE FOR DECORATIVE PURPOSES.

*Frontispiece.*                    *p.* 210.

**Example of fern cultivation for decorative purposes**
**Courtesy of Mary Evans Picture Library**

Victorian England: outside in the garden, in ferneries, or inside decorating hall and table (indeed, in all the important rooms). The ornamental use of ferns inside houses supported the need for ferneries, which supplied the inside stock and provided a suitable environment for old specimens to be rested and propagated. In warm climates these decorative functions for ferns extended to the verandas and veranda gardening (using potted plants on stands or hanging from rafters). Indeed, sometimes the veranda was converted to a permanent, well-stocked fernery with suitable wind protection and lounging chairs for the appreciation of the ferns.

As with earlier writers, H.F. Macmillan (1935) recommended growing ferns by observing their natural state: usually luxuriating in humus or fibrous soil over rock, occupying shady banks or gullies by the side of streams. Many of the largest and most beautiful ferneries have these characteristics in common: moist, shady conditions; constructions of rock or rockeries (sometimes with large shells in Australia); and artificial streams and ponds. Ferneries often contain fern allies, which include the club mosses and some water plants. The addition of tree ferns (*Dicksonia antarctica* and *Cyathea*) and the epiphytic staghorn and elkhorn ferns (*Platycerium*) allowed garden designers greater choice in the form and arrangement of ferneries. Apart from prosaic collections of rows of pots, fantasy worlds of nature were possible with ferns above, below, and on the walls. The delicate, lacy fronds of ferns combined with shade make a welcome retreat whatever the climate. Thus, ferneries can be used for scientific enquiry, decorative production, relaxation, and pleasure.

Two unusual outside ferneries show the range of possible solutions for the fern grower. In the early 1860s, curator Walter Hill created Fern Island in the low-lying alluvial part of the Brisbane Botanic Gardens, Queensland. This was an eclectic mixture of native and exotic plants, ferns, tree ferns, palms, and tropical foliage plants. Surrounding the island's modest moat of water was a grove of giant clumping bamboo that enclosed the area in a secret world of delight. By 1936, after several planting overhauls, the lagoon was finally filled in and Fern Island was lost. There was a happier ending in Victoria. In the mid-1870s, William Guilfoyle, curator of the Royal Botanic Gardens, Melbourne, created Fern Gully as part of his beautiful redevelopment of the gardens. Located in a small creek valley leading to the lake, this gully was planted out with tree ferns and ground and epiphytic ferns emulating the character (if not the exact composition) of the natural plant communities in the Dandenong Ranges. Many of these plants came from subtropical Queensland. The wild flavor of the planting, ground form, and rustic rockwork created a enchanting world, popular with visitors ever since.

Perhaps the most intriguing and beautiful fernery anywhere is the vaulted structure at Rippon Lea developed by Frederick Sargood between 1874 and 1903 on his large suburban mansion estate in Melbourne (Australia). This fernery contained two parts: a tall vaulted roof "hardy fernery" (approximately 37 meters by 9 meters [40 yd. by 10 yd.]) and a smaller (approximately 24 meters by 9 meters [26 yd. by 10 yd.]), lower glazed fernery for tender plants. The hardy fernery was curved in plan and designed to provide shade; the finely detailed wrought iron framework was sheathed with timber laths to create a luscious vaulted form, with plenty of internal height for growing tree ferns. To increase the ambient heat inside, the lower fernery or close house had glass roof panels set in a timber frame with straight sloping sides. These two ferneries were contiguous, containing rustic rockwork, banks, paths, artificial streams, and a fishpond, which helped to set the scene for the naturalistic display of plants. Today, only the curved fernery remains, having been recently restored and replanted. Rippon Lea is now the property of the National Trust of Australia (Victoria) and is open to visitors all year.

The popularity of ferns for gardeners did not disappear in the 20th century, although the fashion of decorating the house with ferns, especially with glass cabinets or terrariums, has waned considerably. The cost of upkeep on large timber shadehouses or glazed conservatories also took a toll on ferneries, but ardent devotees maintain their passionate interest and collections. Other surviving ferneries are Tatton Park, Cheshire (England) and Morris Arboretum of the University of Pennsylvania (United States).

## Further Reading

Allen, David Elliston, *The Victorian Fern Craze: A History of Pteridomania,* London: Hutchinson, 1969

Bailey, Frederick Manson, *Handbook to the Ferns of Queensland,* Brisbane, Queensland, 1874

Bailey, Frederick Manson, *The Fern World of Australia with Homes of the Queensland Species,* Brisbane, Queensland, 1881

Cooke, Mordecai Cubitt, *A Fern Book for Everybody: Containing All the British Ferns, with the Foreign Species Suitable for a Fernery,* London, 1868

Elliott, Brent, *Victorian Gardens,* London: Batsford, and Portland, Oregon: Timber Press, 1986

Hall, N.A., "W. and J. Birkenhead: 'Ferns a Speciality,'" *Garden History* 11, no. 1 (1983)

Hibberd, Shirley, *Rustic Adornments for Homes of Taste,* London, 1856; reprint, London: Century, 1987

Hibberd, Shirley, *The Fern Garden: How to Make, Keep, and Enjoy It; or, Fern Culture Made Easy,* 2nd edition, London, 1869

Howe, Bea, "Victorian Cult of the Fern," *Country Life* 152 (1962)

Jones, David Lloyd, and Stephen C. Clemesha, *Australian Ferns and Fern Allies,* Terrey Hills, New

South Wales: Reed, 1976; revised edition, Chatswood, New South Wales: Currawong Press, 1989

Lowe, Edward Joseph, *Fern Growing: Fifty Years' Experience in Crossing and Cultivation, with a List of the Most Important Varieties and a History of the Discovery of Multiple Parentage, etc.,* London, 1895

Macmillan, Hugh Fraser, *A Handbook of Tropical Gardening and Planting, with Special Reference to Ceylon,* Colombo, Ceylon: Cave, 1910; 6th edition, as *Tropical Planting and Gardening,* revised by Henry Sackville Barlow, I.C. Enoch, and R.A. Russell, Kuala Lumpur, Malaysia: Malayan Nature Society, 1991

Thompson, George Malcolm, *The Ferns and Fern Allies of New Zealand: With Instructions for Their Collection and Hints on Their Cultivation,* Melbourne, 1882

Ward, N.B., "On Growing Ferns and Other Plants in Glass Cases, in the Midst of the Smoke of London; and on Transplanting Plants from One Country to Another by Similar Means," *Gardener's Magazine and Register of Rural and Domestic Improvement* 10 (1834)

Wee, Yeow Chin, *Ferns of the Tropics,* Singapore: Times Editions, 1997; Portland, Oregon: Timber Press, 1998 (contains a list of contemporary fern societies around the world)

Williams, Benjamin Samuel, *Select Ferns and Lycopods: British and Exotic,* London, 1868; 2nd edition, 1873

JEANNIE SIM

# Film, Garden in

Gardens in film traditionally play supporting roles, but on occasion they can become principal settings or even critical characters. While gardens are obviously landscapes, not all landscapes are gardens, although landscapes can be gardenlike, a distinction based on the degree of human involvement, design intent (or lack thereof), scale, focus, and viewpoint. Each possesses dynamic spatial and temporal qualities, although experientially they are dissimilar—in cinematography one sees only what the camera reveals. The spectator has few spatial choices, whereas in reality one possesses complete freedom of movement in a full three-dimensional environment. Gardens are also cultural artifacts—physical metaphors that condense and package the social, moral, aesthetic, and environmental values of their creators.

Garden backgrounds can also enframe film narratives, acting as catalysts that not only reinforce a scene but also convey cultural information, especially in historical dramas. A portion of Stanley Kubrick's *Barry Lyndon* (1975) is set in the 18th-century English garden at Stourhead to establish a sense of period authenticity and spatial reality. The garden's allegorical theme of the individual's journey through life visually and metaphorically reinforces the film's narrative thrust.

As settings, gardens can focus the viewer's attention by contracting visual space to create a sense of intimacy that can promote or prevent a meeting of minds. In *Kismet* (Vincente Minnelli, 1955) future lovers meet as "strangers in paradise" in an enclosed Persian garden, while *Camelot* (Joshua Logan, 1967) shows a secret tryst in an abandoned medieval garden aviary, metaphorically portraying Lancelot and Guinevere as caged by their desire for each other. In *South Pacific* (1958) Logan also uses an intimate garden setting, Emile Du Bec's terrace overlooking the sea, to set up the confrontation that will throw Nellie Forbush's racial prejudices into high relief. Mrs. Eliza Higgins's elegant conservatory in *My Fair Lady* (George Cukor, 1964) also sheds light on the passionate conflicts dividing Eliza and Henry and recalls Eliza's humble Covent Garden flower-girl origins. Garden settings, however, can also encourage reconciliation or resolution of conflict, as occurs between Elizabeth Bennet and Mr. Darcy at the end of Robert Z. Leonard's 1940 version of Jane Austen's *Pride and Prejudice.* They also embody, conceal, or unveil secrets, as in Francis Hodgson Burnett's much-filmed *The Secret Garden* (1949, 1987, 1993).

Gardens, like the larger landscapes of which they are tenants, should never be viewed as mere scenery. Geographer John Brinckerhoff Jackson pointed out that they are always artificial or synthetic, rather than naturally occurring. Each provides a locus or place in which human activities converge. This is true regardless of whether a space is "dilated," i.e. expansive, or contracted, as may be seen in the agricultural panoramas and walled courtyards in *The Good Earth* (Sidney Franklin, 1937). Balance is achieved between these two extremes depending on how a scene is filmed, such as altering the viewpoint of the camera—and thereby the audience—or regulating its movement in a certain way. This allows a dramatic contraction of what begins as dilated space in *My Name Is Nobody* (Tonino Valerii, 1974), when a mob of horsemen attack a lone cowboy on foot and the camera pulls back and pans down to focus the viewer's attention on their intended victim.

A critical distinction between landscape and landscape on film is the role played by nature, traditionally not part of cinematographic reality until locational shooting and Technicolor became common during the 1940s. Up to this time nature served primarily as background decor until the portable camera made possible more dramatic and intimate visual relationships. These backgrounds accurately reflected both the filmmaker's and the viewer's cultural biases, as well as economic and technological necessities. The work of landscape architect and set designer Florence Yoch in Hollywood is a prime example. The landscaped settings of *The Garden of Allah* (Richard Boleslawski, 1936), *Romeo and Juliet* (George Cukor, 1936), *The Good Earth* (Sidney Franklin, 1937), *Gone with the Wind* (Victor Fleming, 1939), and *How Green Was My Valley* (John Ford, 1941) were all her creations on studio back lots or in the nearby San Fernando Valley.

Gardens on film also reflect narrative social and economic realities. The "wealth of the manor" and elevated social status of the owner/character are displayed by the picture-postcard grounds of Manderley in Alfred Hitchcock's *Rebecca* (1940) or by the lofty mountaintop setting of Xanadu in Orson Welles's *Citizen Kane* (1941). Their squashed contemporary opposites are represented by the stereotypical suburban gardens of *Edward Scissorhands* (Tim Burton, 1990), which reflect the banality of the houses they enclose—claustrophobic epicenters of nowhere and nothingness.

Garden images, both on film and in reality, are the products of human imagination and depend on quite predictable cues and responses for their effects. The long vistas of Tara in *Gone with the Wind* were actually collages of multiple live-action shots, matte background paintings, and individual landscape elements photographed against a blue screen and merged into a single, memorable landscape image by a device known as an optical printer, still in use today. In the late 1930s and early 1940s, location shooting introduced a heightened sense of spontaneity and realism. Director John Huston took advantage of the mobility made possible by improvements in transportation by taking the entire cast and crew to equatorial Africa to film the classic *The African Queen* in 1951.

Some film sites have begun to acquire considerable archaeological or archival interest, as in the case of Cecil B. DeMille's 1923 silent epic *The Ten Commandments*. The remains of his huge replica of the ancient Egyptian city of Thebes have been recently rediscovered in the sand dunes bordering the tiny coastal town of Guadalupe, California, although their exact location has been kept a carefully guarded secret from the sightseeing public and would-be looters. Ironically, increased use of digital imaging in the 1990s has revived interest in "manufactured" settings. George Lucas's *Star Wars: The Phantom Menace* (1999) employed more than 2,000 effects shots to create otherwise impossible-to-achieve landscapes.

In the past gardens have often been viewed as symbols of God or the imprint of humanity upon nature, although in contemporary times wild nature itself is often perceived as God's garden. Dual structures of good and evil, however, are visible in films such as *The Bible* (John Huston, 1966), in which evil in the form of temptation first reveals itself in the Garden of Eden. Paradise, however, is never lost in the long succession of Tarzan movies, starting with Scott Sidney's 1918 silent *Tarzan of the Apes* and continuing down to the present day in "Episode 48," the Disney Studio's 1999 animated film version of the Edgar Rice Burroughs novel. Paradise, however, may sometimes need to be concealed for its own protection, as is the case with Frank Capra's *Lost Horizon* (1937), in which Shangri-la, and its isolated Valley of the Blue Moon, with its promise of extended life and preservation of precious cultural treasures in the aftermath of global conflict, manages to survive over the centuries by remaining a "garden" in hiding.

Gardens as symbols for evil also appear frequently. In *Suddenly, Last Summer* (Joseph L. Mankiewicz, 1959), a sinister garden is dominated by a carefully tended herbaceous carnivore, a metaphor for the state of mind—and ultimately, the fate—of its owner, while its comic parallel, the extraterrestrial Audrey, is "closely encountered" in *Little Shop of Horrors* (Roger Corman, 1960). Stanley Kubrick terrorizes viewers in *The Shining* (1980), with its maze garden that recalls and reimages the labyrinthine interior structure of both the narrative and the hotel. Clint Eastwood conjures up a cemetery setting to serve as a conduit for voodoo magic in *Midnight in the Garden of Good and Evil* (1997), while Ridley Scott's *Alien* (1979) delivers a malignant "nursery" in a derelict spaceship that can be perceived as a sort of embryonic medieval Paradise garden in which evil is contained within rather than without. This alien "Garden of Eden" could be a representation and embodiment of what Carl Jung would name the unconscious.

Spatially and in narrative terms the garden is often associated with the notion of a center, which it surrounds, protects, or isolates. In Hitchcock's *Rebecca* the manicured gardens of Manderley serve as a safe haven and barrier to intruders and in their ruined and abandoned state conceal its disgrace from an ignorant and unforgiving world. In this and other instances garden and narrative are so intertwined that one feeds off the other. In Jean Cocteau's ravishing *Beauty and the Beast* (1946), a hidden, magical garden in the form of a dense wood has spatial reality but little visual depth, thereby permitting both concealment and escape. The sense of isolation and drama is intensified by John Ford's much-imitated setting, Utah's Monument Valley, in *Stagecoach* (1939). The immobile, overwhelming landscape strengthens the resolve of the main characters by raising the stakes (and the difficulty) of their quest for survival, both as a group and as individuals. This is also evident in the British television series *The Prisoner* (1966–67), in which no one escapes from the fake "village," constructed for their confinement.

In a related sense gardens can also function in the same manner as water surrounding an island. Old before his time, Henry Pulling hides from life among his dahlias in *Travels with My Aunt* (George Cukor, 1972). Shipwrecked visitors discover a haven promising temporary safety in *The Most Dangerous Game* (Ernest B. Schoedsack, 1932), while a narrow gorge provides both a refuge for the fugitive and a child's garden of Eden in *Mad Max beyond Thunderdome* (George Miller, 1985). But for some "Robinson Crusoes," gardens can be cages from which there is *No Escape* (Martin Campbell, 1994). Such landscapes, therefore, can as easily be places of deadly peril as of shelter or solace, as in Merian C. Cooper's classic *King Kong* (1933). Thus the island/garden/landscape metaphor simultaneously encompasses both ideas: that is, the refuge that becomes metaphorically and—as in *The Mysterious Island* (Cy Endfield, 1961)—literally a prison.

Modern films have increasingly infused gardens with technological values, most often in science fiction. In *When Worlds Collide* (1951) Rudolph Mate offers an entire planet as "paradise regained," a new, if risky, Eden for humanity. Influenced by the Cold War, *The Twilight Zone* episode "Time Enough at Last" (John Brahm, 1959) offers a dead, bombed-out landscape, emptied of humanity. This influence lasted throughout the 1970s, when a succession of films depicted bleak futures in which nature is destroyed and gardens are relics of the past, sometimes existing only in pastoral images used to ease the dying out of life, as in *Soylent Green* (Richard Fleischer, 1973). Ultimately, the garden becomes a machine, an artificial shelter created and maintained for the benefit of the pathetic humans who huddle in the domed cities of *Logan's Run* (Michael Anderson, 1976). Only after escaping their restrictive

environment do the main characters discover that nature has taken a fitting revenge by reclaiming what was once hers alone. Finally, gardens go at last where no one has gone before in Douglas Trumbull's *Silent Running* (1971), in which the last remains of terrestrial ecology are embalmed in space-faring geodesic domes.

Cinematographic images are layered visual environments. It is critical to examine each component (such as setting) in relation to other components (such as characters). One cannot exist without establishing a visual connection with others. Hitchcock's understanding of the visual mechanics of cinematographic imagery is evident in his layering of many elements into a single visual reality supplying such a rich array of images that all cannot be grasped at once. In *The Birds* (1963) a solitary pickup truck crawls across a dry California field, raising almost no dust in its leisurely passage. Upon discovering the farmer's gruesome remains, however, the terrified driver flees the scene, sending up a vast plume in her flight from this metaphorical garden of death. Such visual complexity greatly enriches the cinematographic experience by its subtlety, unexpectedness, and, in this instance, force of contrast.

Gardens, too, are layered environments—culturally, aesthetically, and experientially. One moves through them in much the same manner one progresses through a film narrative. The concept of space-time is paramount in both, for they are designed as three-dimensional experiences involving movement along a fourth-dimensional temporal axis or time line. Whether cinematographic in nature, or encompassing the eternal cycle of changing seasons, these experiences have much in common. In George Pal's *The Time Machine* (1960) the fast-changing, overlapping images of the inventor's garden as he travels through time create a visually overwhelming set of dynamic impressions for the viewer. Thus, gardens in film bear the same relationships to the viewer that they have to the larger landscapes of reality, and those who experience them.

**Further Reading**

Helphand, Kenneth, "Landscape Films," *Landscape Journal* 5, no. 1 (1986)

Yoch, James J., *Landscaping the American Dream: The Gardens and Film Sets of Florence Yoch, 1890–1972,* New York: Abrams, 1989

ROBERT A. BENSON AND DANIEL DOZ

# Finland

We have some knowledge of gardens and gardening in the region now known as Finland that dates back to ancient times. For example, Stone Age people cultivated the annual *Trapa natans* in the lakes as early as in the third millennium B.C., and they seem also to have made plantings of hazel bushes. During the Bronze Age people built large burial mounds of stones on hill tops, thus creating land art that is still impressive today. The oldest mazes, also of stones, along the southern and western sea coast of the region, were probably constructed at that time as well. Iron Age sites are often indicated by the presence of *Verbascum nigrum* and *Filipendula vulgaris*, useful plants for ancient people and otherwise rare.

People cultivated hops and peas as garden crops during the early Middle Ages, as well as broad beans and a special early turnip, 'Navet Jaune de Finlande', which remained staple food for centuries. Monks and merchants brought new plants from abroad. Merchants from Lübeck and other Hanseatic towns are also credited with introducing foreign fruit trees. A herbal of the Naantali Monastery records a number of medicinal plants, many of which are indigenous, but it also includes anise, horseradish, mustard, rue, and sweet cicely, which are foreign to Finland and which were probably among the plants introduced during the late Middle Ages. The earliest references to specific gardens date from the 15th century. More detailed information about garden plants and gardeners survives from the 16th century.

The Botanic Garden of the University of Turku was founded in 1640. The first flora of the Turku area, published in 1673, includes a number of garden plants, including *Aesculus hippocastanum*, barberry, roses, lilies, tulips, narcissi, sunflowers, and marigolds, as well as herbs, vegetables, and fruit trees. Another source records successful cultivation of grapes, certainly in vineries. Gardens seem to have been an established feature of noblemen's manors in the 17th century, and professional gardeners were employed by them. The design of the gardens was certainly simple, fish ponds and fruit trees being the most important features.

All manner of gardening began to decline from the 1680s onward due to a long series of misfortunes: the radical reorganization of taxation, famines, the notorious Cold Winter of 1709, wars, and outbursts of plague. It was only after the Peace of Turku in 1743 that people were able to turn to gardening again. One of the leading figures in this revival was Pehr Kalm, professor of economics at the University of Turku. He traveled to the northeastern United States and Canada in 1748–51, and he introduced an American hawthorn (*Crataegus grayana*) and Virginia creeper (*Parthenocissus inserta*) which are still ubiquitous in Finnish gardens today.

Kalm also lectured in horticulture and garden design at the university. He favored simple geometric layouts and considered English landscape gardens a waste of arable land. The interest in landscape gardening nevertheless grew steadily, and quite a number of private gardens in the new style were established during the second half of the 18th century. Monrepos, near Wiburg, was the best known because it was open to the public. Public promenades were still designed in the rectilinear baroque manner; the most important of these were in Heinola and Vaasa.

The interest in gardening grew steadily in the 19th century. A wealth of trees and flowering shrubs from different countries were introduced. Glasshouses became popular, meaning that well-to-do landowners could fill their gardens with agaves, palms, succulents, and other tender plants during the summer. Thus, their pleasure grounds did not essentially differ from those in the mid-European countries despite the harsh climate. Träskända and Aulanko were considered the most beautiful; the latter, with its 260 hectares (642 acres), was probably also the largest landscape garden in all of Scandinavia.

After the disastrous Fire of Turku in 1827, modern town planning began to gain ground. Wide tree-lined streets and market squares became common. Most towns boasted of lake- or seaside promenades in addition to the public parks. Private gardens in the new parts of the towns were conspicuously large. They often contained linden and maple trees, a summerhouse, an ornamental well, a *berceau* of lilacs, and plenty of flowers. The planting and laying out of cemeteries became common. Much of the work for the greening of the towns was undertaken by committees founded by private individuals. The landscaping of the canal areas and the land surrounding the railway stations was exemplary and helped to spread the knowledge of gardening among country people. Professional training of gardeners was started in the 1840s; Nora Pöyhönen began the training of women gardeners in 1892. Her school was probably unique in the world at that time. The growth of towns led to the building of villas in the country for summer use. These were often surrounded with large gardens, simply designed and merging imperceptibly into well-tended woods. The essentially Finnish features were the panoramic views of the sea or of lakes, with the ubiquitous backdrop of coniferous forests. Garden houses or prospect towers were built on hills and promontories, and bowling alleys and croquet and tennis lawns were ubiquitous.

At the beginning of the 20th century the new architectural style became popular. The best-known garden architects were Paul Olsson and Bengt Schalin. Carefully

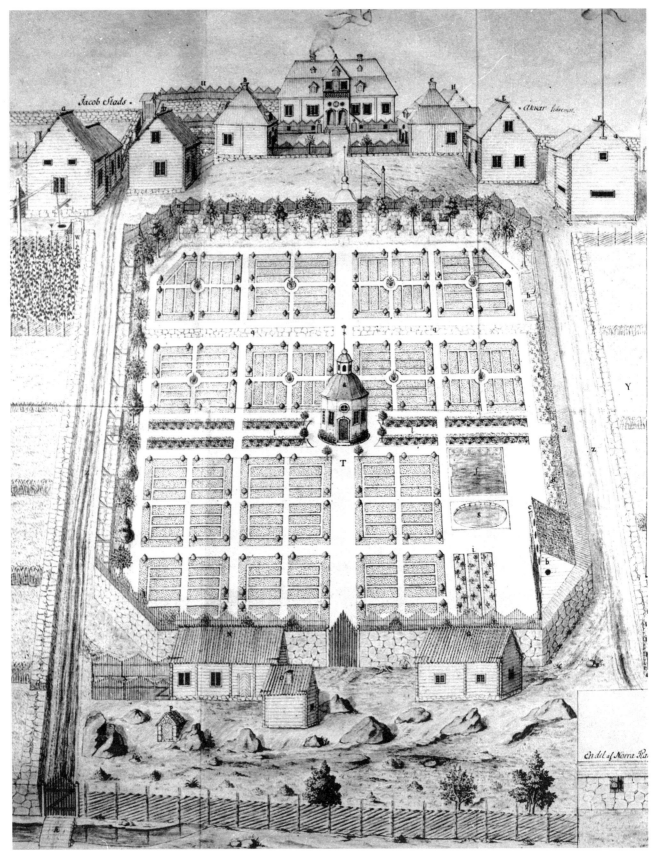

Pietarsaari Rectory, Garden, 1777
Photo by Jens-Ole Hedman, courtesy of City Museum of Pietarsaari

composed flower gardens were surrounded by woodland parks. Rock gardens became very popular, the granite outcrops of the country serving as austere and natural backgrounds to them. With the growth of affluence larger country farmsteads were surrounded with tree plantings, lawns with flower beds, tree-lined approaches, and fir hedges. The development of the modern movement was cut short by World War II, which also put an end to large private gardens. The postwar period has been characterized by the rapid development of landscape architecture. The laying out of war cemeteries, sports facilities, and roads led to large-scale planning of new satellite towns, Tapiola being the best known of them. Jussi Jännes was possibly the best-known landscape architect of the postwar period. Katri Luostarinen was another prominent figure with a large number of public commissions, even beyond the Arctic Circle. Many of the earlier landscape architects studied abroad, but landscape architecture is now being taught at the Helsinki University of Technology.

## Further Reading

Eskola, Taneli, *Water Lilies and Wings of Steel: Interpreting Change in the Photographic Imagery of Aulanko Park*, Helsinki: University of Art, 1997

Hagman, Max, et al., "Mustila Arboretum as a Centre for Introducing and Breeding Shrubs and Trees," in *Proceedings of the 90th Anniversary Jubilee Symposium of Mustila Arboretum*, Helsinki: Yliopistopaino, 1993

Lilius, Henrik, *Esplanadi 1800-luvulla, Helsinki; Esplanaden på 1800-talet, Helsingfors; The Esplanade during the 19th Century, Helsinki* (trilingual Finnish-Swedish-English edition), Rungsted Kyst, Denmark: Nyborg, 1984

Lilius, Henrik, *Suomalainen puukaupunki; Trästaden i Finland; The Finnish Wooden Town* (trilingual Finnish-Swedish-English edition), Rungsted Kyst, Denmark: Nyborg, 1985

*Mitteilungen der Deutschen Dendrologischen Gesellschaft* 36 (1926) (special issue on Finland)

Pallasmaa, Juhani, editor, *Villa Mairea*, Helsinki: Alvar Aalto Foundation, 1998

"Practical Education Abroad: The School of Gardening and Cookery for Women in Haapavesi, Finland," *Agricultural Economist and Horticultural Review* (December 1913)

Ruoff, Eeva, "Das finnische Monrepos: 'Ein Garten für das Herz, ein Garten für den Geist,'" *Die Gartenkunst* 4, no. 1 (1992)

Ruoff, Eeva, "Plant Trials of Pehr Kalm in Turku, 1751–1779," in *Atti del Convegno internazionale "I 400 anni dell'orto botanico di Pisa"; Proceedings of the International Symposium: "The 400 Years of the Pisa Botanic Garden,"* Pisa, Italy: Università di Pisa, 1993

Ruoff, Eeva, *Kultaranta; Gullranda; A Summer Home in Finland* (trilingual Finnish-Swedish-English edition), Porvoo, Finland: WSOY, 1996

Sælan, Thiodolf, "Finlands botaniska litteratur till och med år 1900," *Acta Societatis pro fauna et flora fennica* 43, no. 1 (1916)

EEVA RUOFF

# Flower Show. *See* Garden Show and Flower Show

# Fontainebleau

## Seine-et-Marne, France

**Location:** in center of the town of Fontainebleau, south of Paris and 7 miles (11.2 km) south of Melun

The gardens of Fontainebleau rank with those of the Tuileries in Paris, and not far behind those of Versailles, in their importance to the history of royal garden making in France. Their framework was laid down in the first major phase of development in the 16th century; subsequent periods of alteration added new features and layers but never entirely destroyed this original layout.

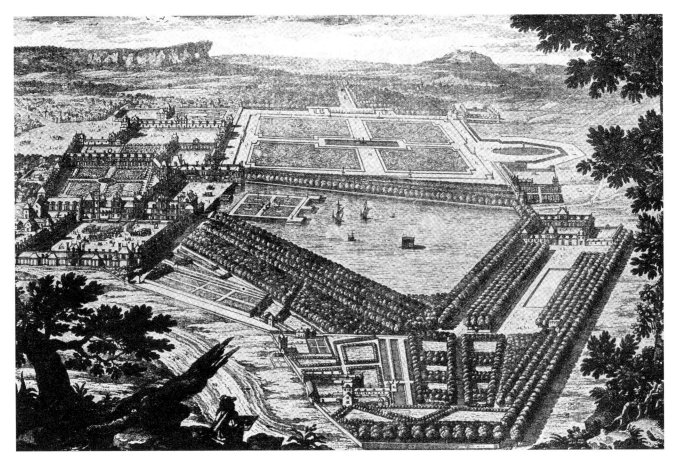

17th-century view of Fontainebleau from an engraving by Israel Silvestre

To a large extent the nature of the gardens was dictated by the ground, which is flat, low-lying, and poorly drained. The solution for this marshy area was to harness the water for ornamental use; thus, throughout their existence water has been a dominant feature in the gardens. This is even reflected in the name of the château and town—originally Fontaine Belleau (Fountain of Beautiful Water)—a spring within the gardens, in the area between the lake and the Jardin des Pins.

The Forêt de Fontainebleau attracted the French kings as a hunting ground, and from the 12th century they had a hunting lodge here. Hunting was evidently not of the tame variety; John Evelyn, visiting Fontainebleau on 7 March 1644, describes the forest as "prodigiously encompassd with hidious rocks. . . . It abounds with Staggs, Wolves, Boares and sometimes more savage bea[s]ts." The legacy of the medieval château is evident in its irregular plan. The first major phase of rebuilding and garden development was instigated by François I (r. 1515–47) beginning in 1528. The king enthusiastically embraced Italian Renaissance culture, importing Italian artists, architects, and sculptors to effect the transformation of Fontainebleau into what Giorgio Vasari called "a

new Rome." A large garden was laid out south of the new château. Its main feature was the large carp pond, the Etang des Carpes, probably adapted from a medieval one, which extended southward from the Cour de la Fontaine. In the center of the court was a fountain on which Michelangelo's *Hercules*, which had been given to Henri II, was placed in 1529. Next to the lake was an elm-lined causeway to the Porte Dorée and the village of Avon. To the east a large area, the Grand Jardin, was laid out in simple, tree-lined, rectangular compartments surrounded by moats, with two large areas set aside for games. To the west of the lake was an irregular-shaped area, formerly an orchard, which in 1535–38 was leveled and laid out with a network of small canals and walks. It became known as the Jardin des Pins after the large number of *Pinus pinaster* planted there. Beyond this was a compartmented area, part ornamental, part utilitarian. To the north of the château was a small private garden, leading off the royal apartments, for which Vignola made bronzes of Laocoon, Apollo Belvedere, and the sleeping Ariadne circa 1540 (all now in the Louvre Museum, Paris).

Here, then, was a grand garden of the typical compartmented late Renaissance style to be found elsewhere at the time in France, for instance at the Tuileries and the royal châteaus in the Loire Valley, albeit embellished with some very fine statuary. In 1543, however, it acquired a feature not seen in France before—a classical architectural grotto, the Grotte des Pins. This survives, restored, and is situated at the southwest end of the château. It is attributed to the Italian architects Francisco Primaticcio and Sebastiano Serlio, who were then working at Fontainebleau. Primaticcio went on to build the Grotte de Meudon for Cardinal de Lorraine in 1552. The Grotte des Pins has a monumental facade of three arches held up by four great Atlases, similar to that of the Sala dei Giganti in the Palazzo del Té, Mantua (1530–35). Inside, the walls are decorated with shells and mosaics, with Juno and Minerva on the ceiling fresco; in the center is an elaborate fountain.

After Henri II's death in 1559, his widow, Catherine de Médicis, ambitious and scheming mother of the succeeding Valois kings, undertook further work at Fontainebleau in 1560–63. She concentrated on the private garden, which was renamed the Jardin de la Reine, giving it a surrounding moat, an elaborate wooden gallery, sculpture, and parterres. Theatrical fetes to celebrate the reconciliation of Catholics and Huguenots were staged by Catherine in the gardens during February and March 1564. Water was used to its full effect; sirens greeted Neptune, drawn by sea horses, in a canal, and a mock assault on an enchanted island took place on the lake. As at the Tuileries fete, festivities included a *rocher*, which opened to disclose a nymph. The court was also entertained at Catherine's highly ornamented pleasure house, Mi-Voye, built in 1562 in the park to the east. This had canals, fountains, a dairy, and a menagerie with a few cows, hence its nickname, La Vacherie. It is an early precursor of the royal and aristocratic recreational dairies of the 18th century.

Henri IV (r. 1589–1610) was the last French king to take a great interest in Fontainebleau. He instituted some revolutionary changes to the gardens, which were accompanied by further building works to the château. The first major work was the building of the Jardin de l'Etang in 1594. This was a square island on the north side of the lake, in front of the Cour de la Fontaine. It was laid out with a parterre in four compartments, designed by Claude Mollet. The design, in box, was not flowing, like those of the following generation of Mollets, but was revolutionary in treating the parterre as a single entity. *Hercules* was moved from the Cour de la Fontaine to the center of this new garden. At the south end of the lake, Henri IV, who was keen to establish an indigenous silk industry, planted a tunnel of white mulberry trees.

At the same time the Grand Jardin of François I was transformed into the Parterre du Tibre. This involved the creation of two central east-west canals and one north-south canal, with a great Tiber fountain by Vignola at their intersection. The Tiber statue had been made for Francis I; it consisted of a colossal bronze figure, and next to it Romulus and Remus and the wolf. The statue was placed on a rockwork fountain made by the Francini brothers, Alessandro and Tommaso. The rectangular beds were replaced by four large, geometric parterres, each with a central fountain by the Francini brothers. This new layout attempted to achieve a balanced and dignified scheme that would be in harmony with the château buildings.

Henri IV also made changes to the Jardin de la Reine, the area of the gardens that was altered most frequently. The east side was enclosed by a new and artistically influential building, the Galerie de Diane, and a fountain with a bronze statue of Diana surrounded by dogs and stags' heads, by Pierre Biard, was installed in 1603. The emphasis on Diana the huntress may in part have been symbolic—Fontainebleau was full of metaphor and this was the emblem of Diane de Poitiers, Henri II's mistress and archenemy of his wife, Catherine de Médicis, between whom and Henri IV no love had been lost. The north side of the garden was enclosed by an elaborate aviary.

Henri IV's most lasting and revolutionary contribution to the gardens was the building in 1609 of the grand canal, which survives and runs eastward from the end of the Grand Parterre, as the Parterre du Tibre became known. Although canals were a characteristic element of French Renaissance gardens, this is an early date for such a colossal one, which measures 1,145 by 39 meters (1,252 by 42 yd.) and is 2 meters (2.2 yd.) deep at the near end and 4 meters (4.4 yd.) deep at the far end. It is said to have been inspired by that at Fleury, west of Fontainebleau, where one of similar size was built in 1607–9. At the same time the wooded Petit Parc was established to the north of the canal; to the south were meadows and elm-lined walks. Thomas Coryate, visiting in May 1608, saw ostriches in the gardens and noted that cormorants were kept to fish the lake in the Asiatic manner.

The only change of note during the reign of Louis XIII (r. 1610–43) was the addition of bronze dolphin fountains at either end of the canal. It was during the subsequent reign of Louis XIV (r. 1643–1715) that the gardens were brought into line with the latest fashion by its main protagonist, André Le Nôtre, appointed royal gardener in 1643. His first work at Fontainebleau, in 1645–47, was to design a *parterre de broderie* for the Jardin de Diane. This was redesigned by Charles Mollet in 1671. The aviary on the north side was replaced with an orangery, designed by Le Mercier, in 1647. Illustrations show that the garden was full of orange trees in "Versailles" tubs; some from this period survive to this day.

Visitors to Fontainebleau in the mid-17th century who recorded their impressions included John Evelyn, Robert Montagu, Sir William Temple, and Louis Huygens, son of the secretary to the princes of Orange. Huygens visited in 1655 and was full of praise. He noted the Parterre du Tibre, the canal, and the lake, which he thought particularly fine. Temple admired the orange trees set out in tubs; Montagu visited and wrote a full description in November 1650. Evelyn's account is particularly interesting and detailed. An intriguing feature he mentions is a hermitage in the forest: "Upon the Summite of one of these gloomy Precipices, intermingled with Trees and Shrubbs and monstrous protuberances of the huge stones which hang over and menace ruine, is built an Hermitage." He saw the aviary just before it was demolished. It had a cupola and "also great trees and bushes, it being full of birds who dranke at two fountaines." In the Cour de la Fontaine were "divers Antiquities, and statues, a Mercury especialy." Evelyn mentions a fountain at the end of the canal that had three jets in the form of a fleur-de-lis "of an exceeding height." He was impressed with the setting: "The White and horrid rocks at some distance in the Forest yeald one of the most august and stupendious prospects imaginable."

Major changes came in 1661–64, when Le Nôtre redesigned the Parterre du Tibre and simplified the Jardin de l'Etang. Monumental cascades at the head of the canal were built by François and Pierre Francini. In 1662 the Jardin de l'Etang was converted to a dignified *parterre de pelouse*. Le Nôtre replaced the Parterre du Tibre with his Grand Parterre, the largest of its kind in the country. The gardens were given greater coherence and unity by the orientating of the parterre on the grand canal. A raised terrace was made, the small canals of the Parterre du Tibre were filled in, walls were demolished, and the area was extended to the south. Flowing patterns of box in four compartments depicted the interwoven initials of Louis XIV and his queen, Marie-Thérèse. The parterre was best seen from the upper windows of the château. In the middle was a square pool with a central *rocher* fountain known as "Le Pot Bouillant," whose jet rose five meters (5.5 yd.) in the air. The Tiber fountain was removed to a circular pool to the south. Rows of clipped trees cleverly disguised the irregularities of the plan. As with other of Le Nôtre's schemes, the layout was not symmetrical but balanced. This layout survives today, the parterre, shorn of its *broderie* detail, surrounded by walks of pollarded limes.

The cascades, finished in 1664, became a major feature of the gardens. They were similar in conception and appearance to those at Vaux-le-Vicomte, invisible from the château, with cascades and jets falling into superimposed bowls around a rectangular basin. Grilled portals at the bottom of flanking ramps were framed by minigrottoes and water poured from a rocaille background. Unfortunately, only the back wall, restored in 1812, survives; the remainder was destroyed in 1723.

The only significant change made to the gardens in the 18th century was the destruction of the Jardin de l'Etang in 1713. A hermitage and attendant garden were built for Madame de Pompadour by Gabriel in 1749, but these are outside the grounds of the château. Napoléon I, seeing Fontainebleau as symbolizing the ancient seat of royalty, spent 12 million francs on its restoration. Work on the gardens took place in 1811–12 and included a pavilion, still standing, on the island in the lake, the restoration of the remains of the cascades, and the complete transformation of the Jardin de Diane and the Jardin des Pins into informal *jardins anglais* by Napoléon's architect, Hurtault. In the Jardin de Diane informal paths were laid out, and the Diana fountain, placed off center, was restored with marble steps and iron balustrading. In 1830–38 Louis-Philippe demolished the ruined orangery, filled in the surrounding moat, and gave the garden its present form. Hurtault planted the Jardin des Pins informally, using many exotic trees, such as tulip trees (*Liriodendron tulipifera*), *Sophora* spp., *Catalpa* spp., and swamp cypresses (*Taxodium distichum*), some of which survive.

It is somewhat difficult now to conjure up the magnificence of the gardens that were used to such effect in the fete of 1564 and that so impressed visitors in the 17th century. Some areas have been altered, and much of the lavish detail has gone. How tantalizing it is that features that would have added so much interest and character, such as the hermitage in the forest, Mi-Voye, the Jardin de l'Etang, the aviary, and its successive orangery, are gone. However, elements of all periods remain, the grand canal and Grotte des Pins being particularly important in that they were revolutionary in their time and of great influence to future garden making.

**Synopsis**

| | |
|---|---|
| 1528 | François I rebuilding begins |
| 1529 | Michaelangelo's *Hercules* placed on fountain in Cour de la Fontaine |
| 1543 | Grotte des Pins built by Primaticcio and Serlio |
| 1560–63 | Alterations to the gardens for Catherine de Médicis, particularly in the Jardin de la Reine. A pleasure house, Mi-Voye, made for Catherine in the park in 1562 |
| 1564 | Famous *fête* held by Catherine de Médicis in the gardens |
| 1590–1609 | Henri IV implements changes to gardens, especially Jardin de la Reine (Jardin de Diane) and Grand Jardin (Parterre du Tibre). Petit Parc established east of Parterre du Tibre |

| | |
|---|---|
| 1594 | Jardin de l'Etang built for Henri IV |
| 1609 | Building of grand canal |
| 1645–47 | André le Nôtre alterations to Jardin de Diane, including design of *parterre de broderie*, subsequently redesigned in 1671 by Charles Mollet |
| 1647 | Aviary on north side of Jardin de Diane replaced by orangery by Le Mercier |
| 1661–64 | Redesign of Jardin de l'Etang (1662) and Parterre du Tibre (Grand Parterre) by André le Nôtre; building of cascades by François and Pierre Francini |
| 1713 | Jardin de l'Etang demolished |
| 1811–12 | Major alterations to Jardin de Diane and Jardin des Pins by Hurtault for Napoléon I; pavilion built on island in lake |
| 1830–38 | In Jardin de Diane, Louis-Philippe demolishes orangery, fills in moats and gives garden its present form |

**Further Reading**

Adams, William Howard, *The French Garden, 1500–1800,* New York: Braziller, and London: Scolar Press, 1979

Evelyn, John, *The Diary of John Evelyn,* 6 vols., edited by E.S. de Beer, Oxford: Clarendon Press, 1955

Hazlehurst, F. Hamilton, *Gardens of Illusion: The Genius of André Le Nostre,* Nashville, Tennessee: Vanderbilt University Press, 1980

Samoyault, Jean Pierre, "Le Nostre et le jardin de la reine de Fontainebleau en 1645–1646," *Bulletin de la Société de l'histoire de l'art français* (1974)

Woodbridge, Kenneth, *Princely Gardens: The Origins and Development of the French Formal Style,* New York: Rizzoli, and London: Thames and Hudson, 1986

Yates, Frances Amelia, *The Valois Tapestries,* London: Warburg Institute, University of London, 1959; 2nd edition, London: Routledge and Kegan Paul, 1975

ELISABETH WHITTLE

# Forest Lodge

## Stirling, South Australia

**Location:**   approximately 12 miles (18 km) southeast of Adelaide, in the Adelaide Hills

Forest Lodge is a hill-station style garden developed in the Adelaide Hills in the 1890s and extended with northern Italian and Mediterranean characteristics in the 1930s and 1940s. During the late Victorian period many wealthy Adelaide families constructed summer residences in the cool, acid-soil Adelaide Hills to escape the heat on the plains. An extensive garden was also laid out with each residence, illustrative of the period fashion for plant cultivation and propagation.

In 1889 John Bagot (1849–1910) purchased 23.5 acres (9.5 ha) of land at Stirling in the Adelaide Hills on which he built Forest Lodge. A member of an influential pioneering family of pastoralists, he married Lucy Josephine Ayers, daughter of colonial premier and philanthropist Sir Henry Ayers, in 1878. While the Gothic-style freestone house was under construction in 1890, to a design by architect Ernest Bayer, the garden was laid out and planted in a Victorian manner in circles and semicircles and surrounded by a deep conifer forest. The design and planting of the garden were the work of the German gardener Ernst Wilhelm Menzel (1847–1917). Menzel, originally from Munich, acquired a reputation in the Adelaide Hills for his knowledge of conifers and garden design. He cleared the upper slopes for the garden but retained the lower half as forest, thereby providing protection from the weather and creating a visual contrast between garden and forest. Many of the plants and trees were obtained by Bagot in 1891 during his travels through Japan, North America, and Europe and were sent back to Adelaide with planting instructions. Menzel obtained other specimens through Australian, English, and German nurseries.

Influential Adelaide architect Walter Hervey Bagot (1880–1963), the couple's only son, inherited the property in 1910, and upon his death, his son, barrister John Hervey Bagot (1910– ), inherited the property. Brought up with a fervent interest in shrubs and trees, Walter studied architecture at King's College in London before returning to practice in Adelaide. His designs are marked by a careful use of light and space and the development of a strong relationship between natural and built forms. Bagot believed that "buildings need the caressing of trees to relieve their hardness." He served on the boards of both the Adelaide Botanic Gardens and National Park, Belair. Walter, introduced to northern Italy in 1891, developed a deep affinity for this landscape and its design traditions and sought to apply these in his design projects, especially in his town residence, Nurney House, while also influencing the design of Broadlees, Crafers, and the University of Adelaide campuses at North Terrace and Waite.

The drive at Forest Lodge passes through Italian-style, urn-topped stone gates and ascends to the house through a forest of mature conifers. A path leads off to the west, next to the gardener's cottage, to a long rhododendron walk and a rose garden. In the latter, along narrow, rectangular stone-edged walks and terraces, are azaleas, camellias, magnolias, Japanese maples, palms, macrozamias, and rhododendrons. The drive opens up to a large, grassy glade, featuring three copper beech trees planted in 1914, one for each of John Bagot's three children. The glade, surrounded by tall conifers, opens up to introduce the house. The gravel drive ends in a circular hedge of *Ilex exedra* set with stone *herms* and a bronze fountain of a "Boy and Swan," acquired from the Ayers estate, in a bed of false dragonhead. Adjacent is a private garden screened by clipped *Euonymus* hedges, Italian cypresses, and Irish yews. Originally a flower parterre, it was converted by Walter Bagot into an enclosed croquet green in 1911. A verandah of delicate Gothic cast-iron, cloaked in roses, links the house to the green, the glade, and several gravel paths that lead into the garden. Behind the house is a tennis court, built in 1924, and a series of sheds. Rustic, fern-detailed, cast-iron furniture and weathered, hand-painted statutary, imported from northern Italy, were positioned along the pathways and under cypress, including *Cedrus,* and *Chamaecyparis* species and paired Italian cypresses. Old terracotta pots, also imported from northern Italy, placed parallel to the paths and at steps, support flowering azaleas, geraniums, and succulents, while grassy banks support marguerite daisies. A path leads from this garden through a conifer forest and down to the railway station.

From the glade, marble steps descend from terraces into the conifer and eucalyptus forest that sweeps down a small valley enclosed by two spurs to a number of circuitous Victorian stone-edged walks. Plantations and clusters of hollys, azaleas, camellias, rhododendrons, cordylines, and dracaenas, with weeping elms in the path triangles, are shaded by the forest cover. Farther down the valley are its most grandiose features, which include a circular cast-iron Victorian fountain, also acquired from the Ayers estate, that spills into a watercourse characterized by Victorian elements: cement urns, a large fern-studded grotto, clumps of bamboo, and an arched-timber, red-painted Japanese bridge. The bridge was ordered following Bagot's 1891 visit to Japan; it replaced an earlier timber bridge. A now dilapidated shadehouse constructed of timber, tea tree, and wire was erected in 1900 to one side of the Japanese bridge. From the bridge a grand vista, devised by Walter Bagot in 1917, leads down the slope to an enormous terracotta Medici tazza featuring a relief of the "Judgment of Ajax" set on a classical base and emphasized by a now-fallen column-like white-shafted eucalyptus. The tazza, a memorial to Bagot's forebears, also features the family crest. Walking down marble steps edged by *Gordonia,* the visitor enters the grass sward avenue of regularly planted Italian cypresses, grown from seeds obtained in Florence, paralleled by Douglas firs and California redwoods on either flank, which edge the forest.

The garden structure is relatively intact and has not been affected by brushfires that often ravage the Adelaide Hills. It reputedly contains the "most complete public or private collection" of conifers in Australia and remains a fine example of a late Victorian garden in the gardenesque style with northern Italian modifications and additions.

## Synopsis

| | |
|---|---|
| 1889 | Land purchased by John Bagot |
| 1890–91 | Garden laid out by German gardener Ernst Menzel, house under construction |
| 1890–91 | Bagot tours Japan, North America, and Europe, acquiring plants and trees for the garden |
| 1910 | Walter Bagot inherits the property and redesigns portions of the gardens |
| 1911 | Croquet lawn created from the parterre garden |
| 1914 | Copper beech trees (*Fagus sylvatica* f. *purpurea*) planted |
| 1917 | Italian cypress *allée* established |
| 1963 | John Bagot inherits the property |

## Further Reading

Bagot, Tempe L., "Forest Lodge: A Garden in the Adelaide Hills," *Australian Garden History* 6–7 (1987)

Beames, Rodney Owen, and J. Anthony E. Whitehill, *Some Historic Gardens in South Australia,* Adelaide: National Trust of South Australia, 1981

*Gardens in South Australia 1840–1940: Guidelines for Design and Conservation,* Adelaide, South Australia: Dept. for Environment, Heritage, and Aboriginal Affairs, and the Corporation of the City of Adelaide, 1998

Jones, David S., *Designed Landscapes of South Australia,* Adelaide, South Australia: School of Architecture, Landscape Architecture and Urban Design, The University of Adelaide, 1997

Tanner, Howard, and Jane Begg, *The Great Gardens of Australia,* South Melbourne, Australia: Macmillan, 1976

DAVID JONES

# Formal Garden Style

Formal garden style is based on symmetry and geometry rather than on the irregular forms of nature. Formality can be seen to represent the underlying harmony existing in nature or the perfection of paradise. An example of the latter is the Islamic garden with its *chahar bagh*—four-square garden—representing the four rivers of paradise in the Koran. Formal garden style is evident in the earliest gardens and was arguably the first real garden "style." Ancient Egyptian gardens, for example, were enclosed and crossed by channels or pools of water in regular, geometric forms, and Egyptian temples were approached through parallel groves of trees planted along a straight axis. This strong relationship between the garden and architecture would remain an essential quality of most formal gardens. The Romans added the use of sculptures, fountains, topiaries, and magnificent garden buildings (porticoes and splendid retreats), all of which were mentioned by Pliny the Younger in the highly influential *Letters* he wrote describing his two villas in the last quarter of the first century A.D. Pliny also recommended the use of box (*Buxus*) for borders and topiary forms, which would become the botanical staple of later formal gardens.

Renaissance architects from Leon Battista Alberti (*De re aedificatoria libri* x [1485]) on developed the ideas of Pliny the Younger, creating gardens that were controlled and regular. Italian gardens were often built on the sides of hills with terraces cascading down from the house, as at the Villa d'Este, Tivoli (1560–75). Although there is a strong axis from the house down through the garden at Villa d'Este, there remains a sense of enclosure and compartmentalization, consisting of many smaller gardens with labyrinths, mazes or knots, orchards of trees, and elaborate configurations of tunnel arbors.

A far greater sense of unity was the accomplishment of the French, who established the paradigm of formal garden style in the late 17th century, first at Vaux-le-Vicomte (1656–61) and then at Versailles (from 1661), both designed by André Le Nôtre. At the center of the composition—either actually or visually—was the house or château. Radiating from the house were long allées or avenues of carefully planted trees or clipped hedges (*palissades*) that seemed to stretch infinitely into the distance. The parterres or garden compartments were laid out in evergreen material in swirling, embroidered designs (*parterres de broderie*) whose form was emphasized by contrasting sand, gravel, or brick dust. Water was contained in long canals or geometric basins, all aligned or at right angles to the main axis of the house and garden. Sculptures and fountains were carefully placed at the center of the axis, at the center or corners of the parterres, or most dramatically, as the culmination of a long avenue. Other vertical motifs included yews clipped into pyramidal forms. Otherwise, trees were placed beyond the garden to act as a distant frame.

The essential elements of Le Nôtre's style could be applied to gardens of vast scale or even to very small gardens. In eastern Europe and Germany, numerous large gardens were created in imitation of Versailles (Herrenhausen, Hanover) in the first half of the 18th century. In the Netherlands French elements were combined with traditional Dutch layouts to create intimate but still grand gardens, such as Het Loo in Apeldoorn (1686–95), designed for William of Orange and his wife Mary by Daniel Marot, a French Huguenot. The Dutch alternative was transferred to England by William and Mary, now king and queen of England (at Hampton Court, also designed by Marot). At the same time the more expansive French model was imitated widely by wealthy English landowners, apparent in the panoramic bird's-eye views by Leonard Knyff and Johannes Kip (published in *Britannia illustrata,* from 1715). The original garden at Blenheim Palace, created for the first duke of Marlborough from 1705, had long avenues of trees and a fortified garden, emphasizing the military successes of the conqueror of Louis XIV. Most of these gardens, including Blenheim, would disappear by the end of the 18th century, victims of a monumental change of taste.

The reaction against formal garden style has been associated with the idea that people became uncomfortable with the extreme control over nature, seen to parallel the

Formal garden, Hampton Court Palace, London, England
Copyright John Riley/Garden Picture Library

evils of absolute monarchy in the reign of Louis XIV. The English landscape garden, a much more natural garden style that abhorred symmetry and geometry, was, in contrast, associated with ancient English liberties. Another plausible explanation for the (temporary) demise of formality is that formal gardens are extremely labor intensive. It would be wrong, however, to think that either of these styles existed in absolute isolation. One need only look carefully at views of Italian Renaissance gardens with their peripheral *boschi* (or wildernesses) and the irregular bosquets at Versailles. Recent scholarship has also shown that 18th-century English gardens quite often had geometrically arranged flower gardens hidden in some area near the house.

By the early 19th century greater formality was reintroduced successfully by Humphry Repton, whose designs included regular beds of flowers, arcaded approaches, and terraces framing the house, yet still set in an open landscape. Eclecticism in architecture was complemented by revivals of so-called Italianate, French, Renaissance, Tudor, and even Moorish gardens, all of them highly formal in style. At the end of the century, a heated debate over the virtues of "formal" (architectural) and "natural" (horticultural) garden style was held by William Robinson (*The Wild Garden* [1870] and *The English Flower Garden* [1883]) and Sir Reginald Blomfield (*The Formal Garden in England* [1892]), each proclaiming the superiority of one style over the other.

In the end a fusion of styles triumphed, particularly in the partnership of the architect Sir Edwin Lutyens and the garden designer Gertrude Jekyll (Hestercombe, Somerset [1904–9]). Inspired by the work of the latter, Vita Sackville-West would write in the 1940s that the ideal garden consisted of maximum formality in design with maximum informality in planting. Sackville-West's influential garden at Sissinghurst, Kent, consisted of a series of "rooms" (based on Lawrence Johnston's Hidcote Manor in Gloucestershire) or geometric compartments, each planted spectacularly.

Gardens of the late 20th century continued to be influenced by these ideas, and even today formal garden style is popular with garden designers across the social scale. Geometric plans, symmetry and axiality, clipped trees, and topiary forms of box, yew, and holly all play a major role in many gardens, large and small.

*See also* Le Nôtre, André

**Further Reading**

Laird, Mark, *The Formal Garden: Traditions of Art and Nature,* London: Thames and Hudson, 1992

Van der Horst, Arend Jan, *Art of the Formal Garden,* London and New York: Cassell, 1995

PAULA HENDERSON

---

# Fortune, Robert 1812–1880

## Scottish Gardener and Plant Collector

Robert Fortune's value to horticulture undoubtedly lies in his travels to China, his collection of many and varied plants, his books (which make interesting reading even today), and his contribution in establishing the tea trade.

Other men had traveled in China previously and left records, but Fortune must have been one of the earliest to have done so widely and diversely. China, until the Treaty of Nanking in 1842, had not welcomed visitors and positively discouraged curiosity about the land. In spite of this, plants had been collected and sent to Europe, enough to whet the appetite for more. Fortune found many of the Chinese hostile and suffered several robberies. He endured dreadful attacks of fever, and on several occasions he was attacked by pirates as he sailed from one port to another. Because he was armed, he was able to save not only himself but his boat and crew. Luckily the British Consul and friendly Chinese helped him find plant nurseries and contact traders coming from the north, where the terrain and flora were different from the south.

Fortune was the first plant collector to travel with the Wardian case. Invented a few years earlier by Nathaniel Ward, it resembled a small greenhouse, completely sealing the plants (which survived on their own moisture) and revolutionizing plant commerce. Almost all Fortune's plants traveled safely to England to flourish in the Horticultural Society's garden at Chiswick. His collections certainly had a great impact on English gardens. He found *Anemone japonica* growing on graves. He found moutans in colors not yet seen in England—lilac, purple, "some nearly black," and a white with a yellow center. He also found chrysanthemums being cultivated in large numbers near Shanghai. He discovered *Cryptomeria japonica,* which he admired, and from his descriptions he also found what we now call the *Gingko biloba.* He described too what we would call "bonsai" and training of trees. He found the yellow azalea, with which he was very pleased, and also what he called *Magnolia fuscata* and *Olea fragrans.* There were many more, such as the winter jasmine, weigela, dicentra, numerous rhododendrons, and double deutzia.

Tea had been a popular drink in Europe since the 17th century. Its cultivation and preparation had been a closely guarded secret from the Europeans, but on his travels Fortune took the opportunity to observe its manufacture. It had been thought that two different types of tea were manufactured. In fact Fortune observed that it was a difference in the preparation of the leaves that explained the contrast and even in some cases dyeing of the leaves. After his return to England in 1846 and his two years as curator of the Chelsea Physic Garden, he was employed by the East India Company in 1848 to return to China to collect tea plants and seeds and even to collect "Chinese trained in tea production." His first cargo reached Calcutta in 1850, and Fortune arrived later with 2,000 tea plants, 17,000 seedlings, and six competent tea manufacturers. He returned again to China in 1853 and 1856, this time to collect "black tea." But it was Fortune who settled the controversy over different species of tea: it is now known that all tea comes from the species *Camellia sinensis*, with varieties according to the area in which it is grown.

## Biography

Born at Blackadder Town, Berwickshire, Scotland, 1812. First job at the Royal Botanic Gardens, Edinburgh, Scotland, 1839; went south to the Horticultural Society's garden, Chiswick, London, 1841, where he was in charge of the Hot House Department; chosen by John Lindley, secretary of the Horticultural Society, and given instructions and a list of desired plants for a trip to China; sailed for Hong Kong and arrived in July 1843; in spite of numerous misadventures (including robbery, assault, and shipwreck), succeeded in collecting many beautiful and hitherto unknown plants; returned to London and appointed curator of the Chelsea Physic Garden, 1846; after two years, he was asked by the East India Company to return to China to collect tea plants and study the management of tea, still a closely guarded secret of the Chinese; this first trip was not as successful as his second trip in 1853; made yet another journey to the Far East, 1860–62, collecting mostly in Japan; lived the last years of his life in Kensington, London, writing his books and also writing for the gardening journals of the era. Died in London, 1880.

## Selected Publications

*Three Years' Wanderings in the Northern Provinces of China*, 1847
*A Journey to the Tea Countries of China*, 1852
*Visits to the Capitals of Japan and China*, 1857
*A Residence among the Chinese*, 1857
*Yedo and Peking: A Narrative of a Journey to the Capitals of Japan and China*, 1863

## Further Reading

Lyte, Charles, *The Plant Hunters,* London: Orbis, 1983
McCracken, Donal P., *Gardens of Empire: Botanical Institutions of the Victorian British Empire*, London: Leicester University Press, 1997

JILL COLLETT

---

# Frames and Pits

Frames and pits, both cold and heated, allow gardeners to germinate seeds, protect seedlings, make cuttings, grow exotics, and force out-of-season delicacies. Halfway between a bed on the open ground and a bed in a heated glasshouse, frames were first used in European gardens in the 16th century. They began as nothing more than flat-topped heaps of fresh, fermenting horse manure surmounted by layers of good loam; these heaps were known as "hotbeds" and had their origins in the gardens of Moorish Spain.

The beds faced south to benefit from the sun. They could be any length but were never more than five or six feet (1.5 or 1.8 m) across. Their height was four or five feet (1.2 or 1.5 m) to start with, but the beds sank as fermentation progressed. The manure warmed the soil and hastened the germination and growth of seeds. The heat was originally contained, and the seedlings protected, with covers of canvas, matting, or large leaves, supported on poles. The coverings were removed in daytime unless the weather was very severe.

In the 17th century, hotbeds were chiefly used for growing melons. They were also sown with winter salad greens and cucumbers. Later they were used to raise pineapples, forced vegetables, exotic flowers, cuttings, and strawberries. Seedling oranges were grown on hotbeds and picked when only a few inches high to put into salads.

Hotbeds and their necessary heaps of dung were grouped together in their own enclosure, which was known first as "the melonry" or "melon ground" and later as "the frame yard." Reed fences, hedges, and walls helped to maintain tidiness and fend off cold winds.

Hotbed protection was further improved in the 17th century by the use of six-by-four-foot (1.2 m) glazed wooden "frames," "sashes," or "lights"—all names by which the beds came to be measured and known; gardeners still speak of a "seven-light frame," for example. Individual plants could also be protected by "cloches," or "bell-jars"—great glass bells first manufactured by Italian glassblowers in the late 16th century. Their use on the open ground, as well as on hotbeds, rapidly spread throughout Europe and was shortly followed by the development of square cases of leaded glass. Wickerwork coops and earthenware pots were also used for protection if the sun was too hot or if frost threatened. Whole rows of produce, again on the open ground, were protected with oiled paper "cloches" stretched over wooden frames. "Continuous cloches" of glass panes held in place by wire clips, and polythene film stretched over plastic hoops, are modern developments.

The heat declines in a hotbed after a few weeks; it is boosted with fresh dung heaped as "linings" round the outside. Later in the 17th century, dung was laid in brick-lined pits, and soil was put inside the pits in portable wooden boxes. In the 1670s the Dutch pioneered the use of glass-roofed pits heated by the fermenting, crumbled oak bark that was discarded after leather tanning; also known as "tanners-bark," this relatively clean material provided moist, constant heat—ideal for growing pineapples—and maintained its warmth longer than horse manure. Tan-beds could also be reactivated merely by stirring more bark into the bed.

Pine pits and melon frames improved considerably during the 18th century. Attempts were made to augment dung- or bark-heat with hot-air flues or steam. In 1794 a brick forcing pit with outer trenches for linings of fresh manure was invented by James McPhail, a gardener who had found that both melons and cucumbers did well as long as the air was warm, making "bottom heat" unnecessary. His pits, three feet deep, had beds of earth (covered with frames as usual) in square containers. The containers had pigeonholed, flued walls front and back, opening into trenches walled in with bricks. The trenches were filled with fresh dung, which transmitted its heat to the flues and the air above the beds by means of the pigeonholes. This pit had several advantages over the old hotbed. The dung needed no preparation, as the heat passed indirectly to the plants; the heat of the beds never rose above 35 to 36 degrees C (96 to 97 degrees F) on the outside or over 26 to 29 degrees C (80 to 85 degrees F) on the inside and, being within a pit, remained steady no matter what the weather; the linings, being in a trench, retained their heat better than outside linings and were easy to replenish; the earth in the beds did not sink as much as in beds based on dung, and no taint from the dung could reach the fruit, which could now be grown all year round. Previously, the season for forced hotbed cucumbers ran from February to October and for melons from May to October.

Forcing in this type of pit rapidly became the preferred method of producing early salads, melons, and cucumbers and also of raising pineapples. And pits were now designed with steps down so gardeners could stand inside them and work more comfortably. The introduction in the 1820s of pipes heated by hot water disposed of the unreliability and untidiness of dung heat. With the invention of hot-water heating, pits and frames began to be heated by the same boilers as the glasshouses. The frame yard, which had once occupied any convenient, sheltered area with access to the stables or a farmyard, was now brought within the glasshouse range.

By the end of the 19th century, the gardener was able to control exact amounts of heat, light, ventilation, and humidity. Sashes were still made of wood, which was lighter than iron to lift, but ventilation, always a problem in glazed, heated structures, was now mechanized, so that with the turn of one handle, the entire roof ridge of a frame could be levered open. Rectangular ventilators, set in the walls, could be opened or closed individually by hinged or sliding panels. Humidity was dispensed either by perforated steam pipes or from evaporating pans cast onto the heating pipes. Frames and pits (even if unheated), as well as cloches, are still useful today.

**Further Reading**

Abercrombie, John, *The Complete Forcing-Gardener; or, The Practice of Forcing Fruits, Flowers, and Vegetables to Early Maturity and Perfection,* London, 1781

Anderson, James, *The New Practical Gardener and Modern Horticulturist,* London, 1874

Bonnefons, Nicolas de, *Le jardinier français: Qui enseigne a cultiver les arbres et herbes potageres,* 4th edition, Paris, 1653; as *The French Gardiner: Instructing How to Cultivate All Sorts of Fruit Trees and Herbs for the Garden,* translated by John Evelyn, London, 1658

Bradley, Richard, *A General Treatise of Husbandry and Gardening,* 2 vols., London: Woodward and Peele, 1721–26

Bradley, Richard, *New Improvements of Planting and Gardening,* 3rd edition, 3 vols. in 1, London, 1719–20; 7th edition, London, 1739

Evelyn, John, *Kalendarium Hortense; or, The Gard'ners Almanac,* London, 1666; 6th edition, 1676; reprint of 1666 edition, London: Stourton, 1983

Forsyth, William, *A Treatise on the Culture and Management of Fruit Trees,* New York: Sargeant, 1802; 7th edition, London, 1824

Hill, Thomas, *The Gardener's Labyrinth,* London, 1577; reprint, edited by Richard Mabey, Oxford and New York: Oxford University Press, 1987

McPhail, James, *A Treatise on the Culture of the Cucumber,* London, 1794

Meager, Leonard, *The English Gardner; or, A Sure Guide to Young Planters and Gardners,* London, 1688

Miller, Philip, *The Gardener's Dictionary,* 2 vols., London, 1731–39; 8th edition, revised, 1768

Parkinson, John, *Paradisi in Sole Paradisus Terrestris; or, A Garden of All Sorts of Pleasant Flowers,* London, 1629; reprint, as *A Garden of Pleasant Flowers (Paradisi in Sole: Paradisus Terrestris),* New York: Dover, 1976

Reid, John, *The Scots Gard'ner,* Edinburgh, 1683

Thompson, Robert, *The Gardener's Assistant*, London, 1859; new edition, revised and extended by Thomas Moore, 1890

White, Gilbert, *Garden Kalendar, 1751–1771: Reproduced in Facsimile from the Manuscript in the British Library*, edited by John Clegg, London: Scolar Press, 1975

Whitmill, Benjamin, *Kalendarium Universale; or, The Gardiner's Universal Calendar*, 5th edition, London, 1751

Wood, Samuel, *The Forcing Garden; or, How to Grow Early Fruits, Flowers, and Vegetables*, London, 1881

SUSAN CAMPBELL

# France

Louis XIV and the formal gardens at Versailles, built in the classical style by André Le Nôtre, have always dominated perceptions of the French garden, but the history of the garden in France is rich and varied. From the Renaissance to the 20th century, the French garden went through various stylistic changes, influenced by and influencing other cultures. The formal garden with its allées, parterres, water features, and statuary, although characteristically French, is by no means the only kind of garden that has been created in France. The French garden has evolved as a reflection of the political, social, and cultural institutions that have created a climate for change, resulting in a rich legacy for study and enjoyment.

### Renaissance Gardens

The emergence of the French Renaissance château and its formal pleasure garden evolved from several sources. From the time that the monarchy was born in France during the Middle Ages, the power and influence of kings, queens, and courtiers was woven into the fabric of French culture. The omnipotence of the king provided a strong milieu for the development and proliferation of a courtly style. Even though there are few physical remains of the medieval garden in France, certain distinct characteristics from the Middle Ages prevailed in the architecture and gardens of the early Renaissance. Vestiges of the formal medieval cloister and castle gardens created a framework on which to build even grander gardens that would expand into the landscape, underscoring the power of the aristocratic owners. Finally, the impact of the Italian Renaissance on garden design helped to catapult the garden from an intimate domestic dependency to a venue for artistic achievement and grandeur.

During the Renaissance the French court had no fixed residence. As the need for living in fortified castles became obsolete, kings and nobles enjoyed country life year-round. The Loire Valley was a favorite place to stay. The pleasure of the hunt was important to French royalty. Images of country life, architecture, and gardens were well documented in paintings, miniatures, and illuminated manuscripts, such as *Les Très Riches Heures du Duc de Berry* (1413–16), which illustrates courtly life and depicts the enclosed pleasure gardens within castle walls, featuring geometric beds, flowers, and fountains.

The 16th-century engravings of Jacques Androuet du Cerceau's *Les Plus Excellents Bastiments de France* offer a rich resource for royal taste in architecture and gardens. The châteaus in the Loire Valley, depicted in Androuet du Cerceau's work, evoke a stylistic unity, derived from the availability of wood, stone, and water; roofs were slate and featured high dormers. Walled gardens within the confines of the defensive castle, set on a hill or surrounded by a moat, were formal, often laid out in a checkerboard pattern, planted with clipped box in arabesques and geometric shapes, surrounded by gravel paths. A strong organization between gardens and castle was absent. Gardens were initially contained in courtyards and gradually moved into the larger landscape. They represented nature tamed.

The landscape in central France was flatter, colder, and wetter than that of villas in Italy; it was easier to grow flowers and to create still water than cascades. Water was confined to small decorative fountains; it was reflective rather than active. The moat continued to be an important feature, although ornamental, and canals were used as long, linear elements in the garden. Elevated walks, reminiscent of battlement walks along walls of medieval castles, continued to exist, stressing the inward character of the garden. The French used parterres, a combination of herbs, flowers, and evergreens planted in patterns to be viewed from raised walks and the upper stories of the château. Superb examples from the early Renaissance include Amboise, Blois, and Chenonceau, all located in the Loire Valley.

At first, little of the Italian Renaissance spirit was comprehended by the French. In 1498 Charles VIII (r. 1493–98) went to Italy on a military campaign and returned with paintings and sculpture, as well as Italian

The largest and most important château of its day, Blois served as a royal residence for the longest period. Resting on medieval foundations, it had three wings dating from the 16th and 17th centuries, built by Louis XII, François I, and the duke of Orléans. The garden was built on ramparts outside the palace walls by Italian designer Mercogliano, with a series of large terraces on three separate levels, and no connecting steps from level to level. Each was enclosed and related neither to the other garden terraces nor to the château. The gardens could, however, be viewed from the gallery in the François I wing. Blois is a good example of the struggle to change from medieval, cloistered garden spaces that provided charm and quiet intimacy to a more expansive Renaissance concept in which the aristocracy controlled nature with confidence. Although access from the palace is awkward, the design reflects an interest in extending the garden into the larger landscape, away from the confines of the castle walls.

Deer hunting had long been a popular pastime among royalty, requiring enormous tracts of forested land. These hunting parks were built not only for sport but also to display the wealth and refinement of the owner through good design. The châteaus and formal gardens constructed in these large landscapes were the epitome of the opulence enjoyed by the monarchy. The château and gardens at Chenonceau, built in the Cher River, evolved over several decades and were surrounded by a vast hunting park. Several women influenced the design. The château was begun in 1515 by Thomas Bohier, the finance minister of François I. Bohier's wife, Catherine de Briçonnet, oversaw the construction of the château while her husband was away. Diane de Poitiers, mistress of Henri II, received the property as a gift in 1551. She lined the entrance with an allée and built a garden on a rectangular plinth above the flood line. When Henri died, his queen, Catherine de Médicis, took Chenonceau away from Diane and constructed her own garden. The individual gardens are formal, but there is no overall scheme tying the various elements together.

In the mid-16th century, the publication of literature on antique art increased travel to Italy, and the influence of the Italian school at Fontainebleau led to the evolution of a greater knowledge of classicism that refined architecture and landscape design. Philibert de l'Orme, the king's architect, had visited Italy and mastered the High Renaissance. Commissioned to build a hunting lodge for Henri II and his mistress in 1546, he created Château d'Anet for Diane de Poitiers. De l'Orme's plan called for the unification of the house and garden on a single axis. The design was a significant departure from earlier château developments, in which gardens had been squeezed into available space within castle walls or placed in the landscape with little attention to creating an axial relationship to the château. The symmetrical

Example of a formal French style garden, ca. 1738
Courtesy of Mary Evans Picture Library

artists, to decorate his castle and grounds at Amboise. A formal garden was placed along the battlement walk with views toward the river. Thus began the French Renaissance, a time when châteaus, built with vestiges of the medieval period, were overladen with Italian decoration and the completely enclosed garden became more open to the landscape. Louis XII (r. 1498–1515) added a new wing to Amboise and further embellished the garden and then moved the court to Blois. His successor, François I (r. 1515–47), continued to invite Italian artists and craftsmen to Amboise, including Leonardo da Vinci. He built an underground passage to link Amboise with Leonardo's château, Clos Lucé. Although much of the palace has been destroyed and the garden became only a simple bosque, Amboise was the birthplace of the Renaissance in France.

plan for Anet represented a breakthrough in garden design that would last for 200 years and would characterize the great achievements of the 17th century.

In 1566 Catherine de Médicis commissioned de l'Orme to build the Tuileries Palace (now demolished) and Gardens; she conceived the idea of connecting the palace to the Louvre with a gallery. It was within this complex of palaces and gardens that several influential gardeners, including Claude and André Mollet, Jean Le Nôtre, and Jacques Boyceau, elevated, through their artistic achievements and expertise, their vocation to a profession. Boyceau is credited with the development of the *parterre de broderie,* formal garden designs inspired by fashionable silken brocades and embroideries. He employed this new garden art, in parterres in the shapes of Ms and crowns honoring Marie de Médicis, regent from 1610 to 1617, at the Luxembourg Palace and Gardens. In 1638 Boyceau's *Traité du jardinage selon des raisons de la nature et de l'Art* (Treatise on Gardening According to the Rules of Nature and Art) was published. In his treatise he recommends training for the professional practice of gardening.

Under Louis XIII (r. 1610–42) the divine right of kings was established. His hunting lodge at Versailles, begun in 1624, was located in a marshy wooded lowland, about 16 miles (25.7 km) west of Paris. The palace was designed by Philibert Le Roy, with gardens by Boyceau and Jacques de Menours. The house and garden were placed on a single axis flanked by large parterres. From a relatively modest beginning, Versailles, the greatest achievement of the French monarchy, would flourish later in the century to become one of the world's most famous gardens.

## André Le Nôtre and the Classical Style Garden

In the 17th century the French emerged as a powerful influence in the world of garden design as never before. The development of increasingly larger tracts of relatively flat land gave rise to the creation of long vistas stretching the eye toward infinity. The *parterre de broderie* reached the level of a new art form, and the greatest genius of the day created optical illusions in these grand landscapes that would be imitated by royalty throughout the Western world and would later become a model for urban design. The genius was André Le Nôtre, who was born into a family of gardeners at the Tuileries and who took the art and profession of garden design to an unprecedented height. Later in his career he visited Italy to study sculpture and architecture. His work was the epitome of high-style garden design, simply called *le jardin à la française,* or the French-style garden. Although Le Nôtre lived during what we call the baroque period, a term used to describe art, architecture, music, and gardens, his gardens are also called "classical" because of the strong sense of unity and order they evoked in the landscape and for their thoroughness and clarity of design.

Le Nôtre's first major work, and probably his greatest, was at Vaux-le-Vicomte in Melun, 18 miles (30 km) southeast of Paris. The palace and gardens, built from 1656 to 1661, sat on 12,000 acres (4,858 ha). Considered to be the most refined achievement in 17th-century French garden design, three villages were displaced to build it and the course of a river altered. It was intended to be an enormous theater for grand fetes, the first of which was a party for 6,000 people. The buildings were designed for Nicolas Fouquet, Louis XIV's finance minister, by Louis Le Vau, with interiors by Charles Le Brun and gardens by Le Nôtre. The garden features many of the elements most characteristic of the 17th-century French formal garden: *parterres de broderie, rond-point* (a circular opening with radiating avenues), *patte d'oie* (goose foot), *tapis vert* (a lawn panel), bosquets, statuary, urns, allées, terraces, balustrades, canals, fountains, gravel paths, plants pruned into geometric shapes, and a grand axis.

On 17 August 1661 Fouquet gave a reception for Louis XIV (r. 1643–1715) in the château and gardens at Vaux. The young king was infuriated by the grand style Fouquet afforded himself and was immediately suspicious of his handling of finances, including his lavish expenditures at Vaux. Fouquet was arrested 19 days later; he spent the rest of his life in prison. His property was confiscated, and the designers of Vaux were taken into the service of the king to create a grander display at Versailles. Over time Vaux-le-Vicomte fell into ruin. In 1875 the owner, Alfred Sommier, began the restoration of the château and gardens, returning Vaux to its former grandeur.

The general concept for the design of Versailles was similar to Vaux but larger. Laid out on an east-west axis that bisected the palace facade, the central view extended to the grand canal and reached toward the horizon. A cross-axis ran north and south parallel to face of the building. Unity was achieved by the precise geometry so characteristic of Le Nôtre.

Versailles was sacked during the Revolution: furnishings were removed, statuary stripped of its gilt, and the gardens neglected. The building was saved from demolition by Louis-Philippe and became the Museum of the History of France in 1857. The gardens were restored after World War I with funding from John D. Rockefeller.

André Le Nôtre was the king's landscape architect from 1661 until his death in 1700 and as such was responsible not only for the work at Versailles but also for new designs and revisions at other royal estates. He was greatly admired abroad, where his work was emulated. In France the classical style lingered into the 18th century through the work of his protégés, including his nephew Claude Desgots. His legacy remains the best known and most important contribution to the history of the garden in France. Some of his other projects included Sceaux, Saint-Cloud, Rambouillet, Maintenon, Saint-Germain-en-Laye, Les Tuileries, Chantilly, and Fontainebleau. Although these have not been completely restored to their 17th-century grandeur, the geometry, the optics, and the genius are apparent. Many are still in large hunting parks, which have been designated national forests.

## 18th-Century Picturesque Garden

In the 18th century the formality that had dominated European garden design throughout the history of Western civilization came to an end. The strict formality and geometry of the French formal garden had fallen out of favor, and there was a shift in taste toward a more naturalistic form of landscape gardening. The landscape or picturesque garden (*jardin paysager, jardin anglais,* or *anglo-chinois*) came into vogue as an expression of the poetry, philosophy, and artistic traditions of the day. Examples included Ermenonville, Désert de Retz, Mortefontaine, and hamlets built on the grounds of Chantilly and the Petit Trianon.

Commissioned by Louis XV (r. 1715–74) in 1768, the original plan for the Petit Trianon by Antoine Richard shows formal parterres surrounding the palace with an English garden to the north. In 1775 the landscape was further embellished when Richard Mique designed *Le Hameau,* or the Hamlet, for Marie-Antoinette. Modeled after an Austrian village, this little park had rustic buildings placed in an asymmetrical layout in a naturalistic setting overlooking a lake. The whole scene conveyed a pastoral mood, much like a stage set, that delighted the young queen and her entourage.

Picturesque gardens were symbolic of freedom and of untamed nature; they glorified the idyllic lifestyle of the peasant, unencumbered by the responsibilities brought on by titles and wealth. The incongruity of aristocrats frolicking in these pastoral settings contributed further to the demise of this style of landscape gardening. Because of its popularity with the ancien régime, the picturesque fell out of favor after the Revolution. Less than a decade later the negative connotation of these landscapes was forgotten. The landscape garden with its irregular plantings, curvilinear pathways, naturalistic lakes, and eye-catchers (objects such as temples scattered throughout the landscape) enjoyed a revival during the Consulate (1799–1804) and the First Empire (1804–15) and became fashionable motifs for 19th-century public parks.

## First Empire Gardens

Although the gardens built during the First Empire have received little attention, and indeed have even been considered by some to be without merit, landscape design under the Bonapartes stood at the nexus of France's emergence into the modern world. These gardens reflected sentiments about landscape design that would continue not only in estate design but also in the public sector. They also served as excellent contrasting complements to the classicism that prevailed in architecture.

The neoclassical style in architecture, so highly favored by Napoléon, has been criticized as being imitative, copying directly from ancient examples. During the First Empire architectural detailing became more eclectic, with details inspired not only by antique motifs such as sprays of palm, wreaths, meanders, and the Greek orders but also by symbols of the military, especially of the Egyptian campaign. Some of these icons found their way into the garden.

Taste in garden design during this period also appeared to be merely imitative at first glance. Many of the gardens that were restored or redesigned during the empire were simply a revival of the picturesque, a style popular among the Bonapartes. The basic tenet of the picturesque style was the imitation of nature. Within this setting a series of eclectic objects dotted the landscape. Other characteristics of gardens built during the empire included a continuation of some formality near the château, with lawn parterres surrounded by flowers; expansive, barren entrance courts, especially preferred by Napoléon for security reasons; the use of exotic plant materials, including an improved and longer-lasting rose, as well as an abundance of imported flowers that could be grown in hothouses; and the use of new building materials, namely iron, for the fabrication of decorative fences, railings, and bridges previously made of wood or stone.

During their brief tenure as European aristocrats, the Bonapartes altered some of the best-known gardens on the Continent. In France these included Malmaison, the Trianons, Compiègne, Fontainebleau, Saint-Cloud, and Rambouillet. Many of those revised garden schemes no longer exist, as time and taste have erased their memory, but aspects of some, particularly those associated with Napoléon, have been preserved and restored as testament to an important and highly influential period of landscape design.

## Urban Parks Movement

The appreciation of the Bonapartes for the picturesque, that highly emotional response to an idealized imitation of nature, continued to obsess landscape designers in Western Europe and the United States throughout the 19th century, on private estates as well as in public park design. Napoléon's nephew Louis Napoléon, who had been in exile in England, returned to France and was proclaimed president in 1848 and later Emperor Napoléon III (1853–68). He, too, had a penchant for the picturesque and wanted to create a series of parks in

Paris such as the ones Queen Victoria had commissioned in London. With the engineer Baron Georges Eugène Haussmann, he proposed to sweep away most of medieval Paris with grand boulevards, lined with allées of trees, recalling the grand axis at Versailles, the epitome of the classical style. He also wanted to create a series of public parks throughout the city designed in the style called *parc paysager,* or landscape park.

The emperor's plan for the Paris park system included 24 small neighborhood parks within the city, based on the English "key park" tradition, except that the Paris parks would not be locked but open to the public. On the north-south axis, Buttes-Chaumont and Parc Montsouris served a larger population. At the east and west edges, even larger parks were developed—the Bois de Vincennes, a former military parade ground and the Bois de Boulogne, a former royal hunting park. Although many of these landscape parks were essentially green, some contained flower gardens. Similar to the Victorian concept of creating carpet beds, annuals were planted along borders, and the practice of mosaiculture, using bedding plants to create a clock or coat-of-arms, for example, was popular.

The 19th-century urban parks movement, a collective reaction to the industrialization and democratization of the Western world, inspired a great deal of discourse on park design, and the Paris parks were a popular subject. Books, reports, and correspondence are evidence of the compelling interest that park designers had in each other's work, leading to the mutual exchange of information and ideas that helped to unify the look of the 19th-century urban park. Adolphe Alphand and Baron Ernouf's *Traité Pratique et Didactique de l'Art des Jardins: Parcs, Jardins, Promenades* (A Practical and Didactic Treatise on Garden Art: Parks, Gardens, Promenades), published in 1868, was a seminal work on the history and theory of garden art and contains descriptions of the major Paris parks; it was reprinted as Alphand's *Promenades de Paris* (1867–73). In *Parks and Gardens of Paris* (1878), English landscape gardener William Robinson conducts an exhaustive examination of Paris parks, which included French horticultural practices, as well as studies in fruit and vegetable culture. Frederick Law Olmsted, codesigner of New York's Central Park, visited the Bois de Boulogne several times and wrote about it in his annual reports.

The landscape architect Edouard André, author of *L'Art des Jardins* (1879) and one of the designers of the Bois de Boulogne, wrote a treatise on garden history and design, citing both European models and parks and gardens that he had visited in North and South America. André advocated the *style composite,* a composite or mixed style, consisting of combining a *jardin regulier,* a formal garden, with a *jardin paysager,* or landscape garden, an idea that would eventually be accepted.

### Return to Formality

From the beginning of the Third Republic in 1870, national pride and a renewed interest in French heritage inspired designers to create formal gardens. Two landscape architects, Henri Duchêne and his son Achille, were at the forefront of the revival of the classical style, especially the work of André Le Nôtre. Many gardens that had been neglected or revamped into landscape gardens in the 18th and 19th centuries were restored or redesigned as the *jardin à la française* by the Duchênes. Their first major restoration was at Vaux-le-Vicomte. Besides restoring historic gardens, they also designed new formal gardens in France, Russia, the United States, Australia, and South America. Achille Duchêne's 1925 design for the Water Garden at Blenheim Palace borrowed heavily from Versailles. The Duchênes designed some smaller gardens for town houses in Paris and suburban gardens. Achille was keenly aware of the changes that were occurring in modern society and wrote about making gardens for recreation, socializing, and education. The fervor with which the Duchênes promoted the principles of André Le Nôtre became a primary influence on new modern gardens, based on geometry and art.

Monet's garden at Giverny, restored in the 1980s and opened to the public, combined the order and formality of the French traditional garden with the 19th-century taste for the landscape garden. Monet acquired the pink-and-green farmhouse, located in Normandy, approximately 55 miles (88 km) northwest of Paris, in 1883. The four-acre (1.6-ha) garden, designed in the composite or mixed style, provided a setting for the artist's two passions, gardening and painting. Near the house the Clos Normand was laid out in rectangular beds with exuberant flowers spilling onto the paths, while the Water Garden, which inspired his famous water lily series, was laid out in the informal style. Monet's artistic handling of the landscape at Giverny combined the best achievements of French garden history.

### Twentieth-Century Developments

After World War I many estates were subdivided into smaller parcels, giving rise to opportunities for a new garden aesthetic. During a relatively short time period, between the world wars, the modernist or Art Deco garden emerged. Leading designers of this period included J.C.N. Forestier, the Vera brothers, Robert Mallet-Stevens, Pierre-Emile Le Grain, and Gabriel Guévrékian. At the Paris Exposition for the Decorative Arts in 1925, models for new gardens were displayed. Some gardens, based on the Art Deco style found in architecture, fabrics, and jewelry, followed the principles of the traditional classical design but used more abstract geometry and color. Others, inspired by Cubist paintings, broke the rules of classicism, creating asymmetrical spaces, works that looked more like an abstract painting. The designers explored the use of new materials, such as concrete and glass.

In 1937 another exposition featuring gardens was held in Paris. The chief architect was Jacques Gréber. The event marked the end of the modernist garden. Even though Gréber himself was a garden designer, the emphasis of the exposition was on floral decoration around buildings and horticulture, not on design, art, or creativity.

Since World War II, the modern garden and its nemesis, the floral garden, have been revived. Parc Floral in the Bois de Vincennes, built for an exposition, features characteristics from both garden types, functioning as an urban display garden with horticulture as its focus. Much of the design—water features, berms constructed of lawn as well as cut stone, and even flower beds—is a reflection of the abstract forms derived from modern paintings. The late 20th century saw an increased interest in using flowers in public gardens. At the Luxembourg Gardens, where restoration of the *parterres de broderie* was not practical, the lawn parterres with flower borders, traditionally planted with annuals, began to feature perennials.

Throughout the 20th century historic parks and gardens were constantly restored and reconstructed. At Versailles, where the gardens are now a public park, allées were replaced, statuary regilded, and bosquets restored. Many national historic gardens, although still privately owned, were opened to the public, some on a limited basis; and many that were state-owned became public parks. The Tuileries received a facelift during the 1990s, retaining the form and spirit of André Le Nôtre's 17th-century redesign while accommodating new needs for underground parking and a better connection to the Pyramid at the Louvre. The grand axis from the Louvre though the gardens, which even Le Nôtre envisioned extending to a *rondpoint*, was extended to the Arch of Triumph in the 19th century and then to La Défense, a new town built in the early 1970s, terminating at Johan Otto von Spreckelsen's white marble cube, L'Arche, inaugurated in 1989.

In the late 20th century more property became available for public open space, as some large factories and industries moved out of Paris, creating new opportunities for innovative design. New buildings and plazas replaced the famous meat market at Les Halles. Parc de La Villette, in the northeastern part of the city, was built on the former site of a meatpacking plant. The design features a series of red follies superimposed in a grid on the overall plan, which includes playgrounds, gardens, and large lawn spaces for play, a rarity in Paris. The park is located in the midst of several cultural institutions: a university, science museum, and music conservatory. Canals from former industrial use cross the site, a reminder of past activity. The design for Parc Bercy at a place previously used for wine shipping retains the layout of former streets that accessed the Seine. These angled street paths cross the park under a grid of trees, a new order superimposed on the old.

Finally, the design for Parc André Citroën, an abandoned automobile factory site in southeastern Paris, features a long central lawn space, or *tapis vert,* leading to a fountain flanked on each side by conservatories. The park's formal central spine, reminiscent of the axial plans of the classical gardens of the 17th century, is surrounded by garden rooms with horticultural themes and opportunities for privacy, similar to the bosquets of Versailles. The designers of all of these late-20th-century projects employed some formal elements at each site—using the grid, the allée, or the central axis—recalling the strength of the classical garden and continuing to adhere to the formality so strongly associated with the French. Even though the formal features have been disguised in modern trappings, without a clear reference to historical precedent, formality has continued to be a major source of inspiration to the designers of the gardens and landscapes of France.

*See also* Anet; Bois de Boulogne; Buttes Chaumont; Chantilly; Chenonceaux; Ermenonville; Fontainebleau; Giverny; Jardin des Plantes; Les Cèdres; Luxembourg Gardens; Marly; Montpellier Botanic Garden; Parc Monceau; Père Lachaise Garden Cemetery; Rambouillet; Sceaux; Tuileries; Vaux-le-Vicomte; Versailles

**Further Reading**

Adams, William Howard, *The French Garden, 1500–1800,* New York: Braziller, and London: Scolar Press, 1979

Alphand, Adolphe, *Les promenades de Paris*, 2 vols., Paris, 1867–73; reprint, Princeton, New Jersey: Princeton Architectural Press, 1984

André, Édouard François, *L'art des jardins*: *Traité général de la composition des parcs et jardins*, Paris, 1879

Androuet du Cerceau, Jacques, *Les plus excellents bastiments de France*, 2 vols., Paris, 1576–79; reprint, Paris: Sand and Conti, 1988

Arneville, Marie Blanche d', *Parcs et jardins sous le premier empire*, Paris: Tallandier, 1981

Berger, Robert W., *In the Garden of the Sun King: Studies on the Park of Versailles under Louis XIV,* Washington, D.C.: Dumbarton Oaks Research Library and Collection, 1985

Blunt, Anthony, *Art and Architecture in France, 1500 to 1700,* London and Baltimore, Maryland: Penguin, 1953; 5th edition, revised by Richard Beresford, New Haven, Connecticut: Yale University Press, 1999

Blunt, Anthony, *Philibert de l'Orme,* London: Zwemmer, 1958

Ernouf, Alfred Auguste, and Adolphe Alphand, *L'art des jardins: Parcs, jardins, promenades,* Paris, 1868

Gothein, Marie Luise Schroeter, *Geschichte der Gartenkunst,* 2 vols., Jena, Germany: Diederichs, 1914; as *A History of Garden Art,* edited by Walter P. Wright, translated by Mrs. Archer-Hind, London and Toronto, Ontario: Dent, and New York: Dutton, 1928; reprint, New York: Hacker Art Books, 1979

Hautecoeur, Louis, *Histoire de l'architecture classique en France,* Paris: Picard, 1943; new edition, 7 vols, 1965

Hazlehurst, F. Hamilton, *Jacques Boyceau and the French Formal Garden,* Athens: University of Georgia Press, 1966

Hazlehurst, F. Hamilton, *Gardens of Illusion: The Genius of André Le Nostre,* Nashville, Tennessee: Vanderbilt University Press, 1980

Imbert, Dorothée, *The Modernist Garden in France,* New Haven, Connecticut: Yale University Press, 1993

Jellicoe, Geoffrey Alan, and Susan Jellicoe, *The Landscape of Man: Shaping the Environment from Prehistory to the Present Day,* New York and London: Thames and Hudson, 1975; 3rd edition, 1995

Mosser, Monique, and Georges Teyssot, editors, *L'architettura dei giardini d'Occidente,* Milan: Electa, 1990; as *The Architecture of Western Gardens,* Cambridge, Massachusetts: MIT Press, 1991; as *The History of Garden Design,* London: Thames and Hudson, 1991*

Newton, Norman, *Design on the Land: The Development of Landscape Architecture,* Cambridge, Massachusetts: Harvard University Press, 1971

Péreire, Anita, and Gabrielle van Zuylen, *Gardens of France,* New York: Harmony Books, 1983

Robinson, William, *The Parks, Promenades, and Gardens of Paris,* London, 1869; 2nd edition, revised, as *The Parks and Gardens of Paris,* London, 1878

Walton, Guy, *Louis XIV's Versailles,* Chicago: University of Chicago Press, and London: Viking, 1986

Ward, William Henry, *The Architecture of the Renaissance in France: A History of the Evolution of the Arts of Building, Decoration, and Garden Design under Classical Influence from 1495 to 1830,* 2 vols., New York: Scribner, and London: Batsford, 1911; 2nd edition, 1926; reprint, 1 vol., New York: Hacker Art Books, 1976

Wiebenson, Dora, *The Picturesque Garden in France,* Princeton, New Jersey: Princeton University Press, 1978

Woodbridge, Kenneth, *Princely Gardens: The Origins and Development of the French Formal Style,* New York: Rizzoli, and London: Thames and Hudson, 1986

CONSTANCE A. WEBSTER

# Frederiksberg

## Copenhagen, Denmark

**Location:** suburb of Copenhagen, west of the city center

Frederiksberg is one of Copenhagen's largest public gardens, covering some 160 acres (65 ha). Its history largely parallels that of numerous other European royal summer residences established in the absolutist period. Although the grounds were extensively remodeled in the landscape garden manner around 1800, some of the innovative features introduced in the garden's early periods are still visible.

Located on a ridge overlooking the capital, the countryside, and the sea, the area had been farmed for several generations when, in 1651, Frederik III invited Dutch peasants to settle there. As in the earlier Dutch colony on the island of Amager, just south of Copenhagen, the inhabitants grew vegetables for the royal court. In 1662 Queen Sophie Amalie ordered a country house, a menagerie, and a garden to be created, the latter so that her young daughters might enjoy life in the countryside. The exact chronology of these works remains to be established. The garden layout was strictly axial, stretching from the riding ground in the east to the formal bosquets and the pheasant warren in the west. Large fishponds and a fountain were placed midway between the two. Compared to Queen Sophie Amalie's other pleasure gardens, the one in the so-called New Dutch Village was modest and somewhat old-fashioned.

In 1680 Crown Prince Frederik (later Frederik IV) took over the property. As a consequence of his horticultural initiatives, a new and prosperous chapter of Danish garden history was to begin. The farmland surrounding what then became known as Frederiksberg (literally "Frederik's hill") was regained, and Frederik's ambition to have a *villa suburbana* and a garden, in concordance with the European garden aesthetics of the time, led the crown prince to hire the Swedish architect Nicodemus Tessin the Younger. A detailed garden plan (1697) by Tessin's hand exists, testifying to his virtuous handling of French and Italian models, such as the Villa Aldobrandini Frascati, Lazio, Italy. And although Tessin was not to carry out the project, some of his proposals, such as the addition of a perpendicular axis and the erection of a nymphaeum, were echoed in the final design (1697–1708) generally attributed to H.H. Scheel, a Danish military engineer. Some of the elements, however, owed their existence to the crown prince himself. He had traveled widely in Italy and France; the open-air theater at Frederiksberg—the first of its type in Denmark—may indeed have been inspired by André Le Nôtre's theater in the Tuileries. Large quantities of trees and plants were imported from Holland as well.

At the same time that the garden was created, a new palace (1699–1703, designed by the architect Ernst Brandenburger) was erected on top of the hill at the southern end of a new north-south axis. The crown prince's Italianate taste immediately came to the fore in this villa-like construction as well as in the cascades and fountains dominating the slope. Yet on the whole, Scheel's layout was marked by a mixture of the then current aesthetic paradigms. The French garden theorist A.-J. Dézallier d'Argenville prescribed parterres near the main building, and therefore *parterres de broderie* were laid out on Frederiksberg's slope. The nymphaeum marked the transition to level ground, and here eight squares, each consisting of eight triangular bosquets, unfolded. To make the geometrics fit with the existing scale, the borders were occupied by carefully composed *cabinets de verdure* holding the outdoor theater, a spiral hill, and a retreat intended for the public when the royal family was in residence. The final stage of the design created by Scheel and the crown prince concerned the extensive grounds lying to the south of the new palace, an area called the Søndermarken. Here a *patte d'oie*, modeled after that at Versailles, was laid out (1708) so that the Søndermarken could serve as a *bosquet sauvage*.

A new garden plan was drawn up around 1720 (see Plate 12). The water supply had been a serious problem from the very beginning, and the cascades and the fountains had become dilapidated. The slanting parterre garden also looked somewhat inappropriate. To remedy the situation, a series of remarkable alterations were devised by J.C. Krieger, one of Denmark's foremost architects at the time. Krieger suppressed the parterres, remodeled the cascades, terraced the entire slope, and saw to it that lime trees were planted in several rows parallel to the new cascades. Finally, he placed an octagonal pavilion where the two main axes met. Krieger's innovations became Frederiksberg's distinctive mark. Although the cascades disappeared before the second main remodeling of the gardens around 1800, the terraced slope has remained practically unaltered.

Throughout the 18th century, the gardens were to provide an ideal setting for royal festivities. Numerous rulers from abroad were also welcomed at Frederiksberg. As fashion prescribed, illumination and fireworks were in frequent use. In the 1730s some changes were made to the buildings and grounds, and following the destruction of the old main building by fire in 1753, the two partly rebuilt side wings were placed so as to frame the main entrance to the gardens from the city. The wings continued to house the orangery (1744, designed by N. Eigtved) and the stables.

As in elite circles across Europe, alternative ways of life and fashions found favor at Frederiksberg toward the last quarter of the century. In the mid-1780s new features in the Søndermarken showed the influence of the cosmopolitan world of the landscape garden. An antique-inspired rotunda, a Norwegian cabin, and a hermitage were combined in with the new landscaping. In 1797–1800 the pleasure garden was remodeled under the guidance of gardener Peter Petersen. Pools and fountains were transformed into winding canals, and ponds dotted with small islands appeared. The majority of the existing allées were cut down. Undulating lawns were sown, and typical Danish trees alternating with North American species, imported from Hamburg and Lübeck, were planted. The Chinese pavilion (1799–1800, designed by A. Kirkeru), the burial mound, the Swiss cabin, and the Apis Temple (1801–4, designed by N. Abildgaard) were erected to act as visual surprises and emblems rich in connotations. A forest nursery was founded in support of a nationwide campaign encouraging the planting of fruit trees.

For all these innovations, the diagonal axes of the former baroque garden were saved in the form of wide clearances. They are still the key reminders of Frederik IV's grandiose garden. In 1868 the palace was turned into a military academy. Copenhagen's zoological garden (1859; enlarged, 1949) was placed on the fringes of the Frederiksberg gardens. Since 1884 the Royal Danish Garden Society has been housed in the former orangery; its model gardens attract hundreds of thousands of garden lovers every year.

## Synopsis

| | |
|---|---|
| 1651 | Frederik III establishes a Dutch farming colony on the site |
| ca. 1662 | Queen Sophie Amalie has a country house and garden constructed |

| | |
|---|---|
| 1680 | Crown Prince Frederik (IV) acquires the estate |
| 1697–1709 | Layout of formal gardens, including first green theater in Denmark, designed by H.H. Scheel, with certain elements after Nicodemus Tessin the Younger |
| 1699–1703 | Construction of new *villa suburbana,* designed by Ernst Brandenburger |
| 1708 | Søndermarken laid out as *bosquet sauvage* |
| ca. 1720 | New cascades and terraces planted with lime alleys, designed by J.C. Krieger |
| 1797–1800 | Remodeling of the gardens in the landscape manner by P. Petersen |
| 1884 | The Royal Danish Horticultural Society moves into the old orangery |

**Further Reading**

Hartmann, Jørgen B., "Frederiksberg," in *Danske Slotte og Herregaarde,* edited by Aage Roussell, vol. 2, Copenhagen: Hassings Forlag, 1963–68

Lund, Hakon, *De kongelige lysthaver,* Copenhagen: Gyldendal, 1977

MARGRETHE FLORYAN

# Froebel Family

## Swiss Landscape Architects and Plantsmen

For three generations, members of the Froebel family designed important gardens and landscapes in Switzerland, and for almost 100 years the family maintained a highly successful nursery that specialized in rare and unfamiliar plants.

Theodor Froebel was educated by his uncle Friedrich Froebel. After practicing horticulture in Germany, he came to Switzerland in 1834 and took a position as head gardener at the University of Zürich in 1835 to lay out and plant the new botanic garden there. In the same year, he designed the first rock garden for alpine plants in Switzerland at the University of Zürich, and he founded the first nursery garden in Zürich with Heinrich Würth. After Würth had left the nursery to collect plants in Australia, Froebel established his own *Kunstgärtnerei,* a bureau for designing landscape gardens, which he led until 1890.

Theodor Froebel designed a large number of parks and gardens primarily in eastern Switzerland in a refined landscape garden style. Zürich has long been dominated by the private and public parks laid out by Froebel. The playground for children that he included in his design for the Stadthausanlage of Zürich was the first of its kind in a Swiss public park, and it was probably inspired by the work of teacher and uncle Friedrich Froebel, who was the founder of the kindergarten.

Theodor Froebel's nursery became famous for its large selection of rare and little-known plants, especially alpine plants and hellebores. He also hybridized many plants, such as *Dephiniums,* of which he introduced 18 cultivars of his own. He made many selections of aesthetically pleasing and especially floriferous trees and shrubs (e.g., linden, *Cydonia japonica,* and *Clematis*). He published several articles in horticultural journals on the plants he had hybridized or introduced. His son and grandson carried on his work as designer and plantsman.

Theodor's son Otto Froebel worked and traveled in Belgium, France, England, and other European countries before joining his father's nursery and landscape gardening firm. In addition to running his father's nursery, he designed a large number of private and public parks, often in the rich, French-influenced "composite style" that was popular close to the end of the 19th century. However, he also fought vehemently for the conservation of the existing natural vegetation in some park schemes.

Otto Froebel was extremely knowledgeable about plants, and he is known to have used 17 different kinds of *Picea,* for example, in addition to other conifers and additional plants, in a relatively small park. Despite his use of numerous plant types, his designs were nevertheless considered very harmonious. He introduced dozens of plants that were new to the nursery trade, such as *Picea omorika,* now ubiquitous in Europe. He loved flowers and excelled in hybridizing *Anthuriums* (the nursery introduced about 60 *Anthurium* hybrids of his between 1885 and 1907), *Begonias, Cypripediums,* and water lilies (*Nymphaea*). His nursery catalog from the year 1899 comprises approximately 5,000 plants or cultivars.

Otto Froebel won numerous medals and prizes for his plants at various exhibitions, including a first class certificate from the Royal Horticultural Society in London for *Begonia froebelii* in 1876 and the Prix Estella and 21 further prizes at the Swiss Exposition in Geneva in 1896. In order to curb the collecting of alpine plants in the wild,

Botanic Garden of the University of Zürich, planted by Theodor Froebel, 1835–41
Courtesy of Zentralbibliothek Zürich

which had already led to the destruction of many habitats at that time, at his nursery he grew alpine plants only from seed. He devoted much of his time to jury and committee work in order to raise the standards of horticulture, the nursery trade, and the education of gardeners.

Otto's son Robert worked and traveled widely in France, Germany, and England, but after the death of his father, he led the family firm very successfully for the following 20 years. He pioneered design ideals of the new formal garden in Switzerland, designed numerous private gardens, and specialized in laying out sports fields and grounds for schoolhouses, hotels, and hospitals, reducing the nursery branch of the firm.

The 1933 ZUGA (Zuercher Gartenbau-Ausstellung) garden exhibition in Zürich was the glorious finale to the long history of the Froebel firm. The preceding years of worldwide financial depression had served as a warning that the days of fastidious workmanship and quality of design would soon be over. Robert Froebel refused to lower the standards of the family firm, and he therefore closed it in 1934, nearly 100 years after his grandfather had come to Zürich.

The Froebels are commemorated in the name of Froebel-Strasse in Zürich in an area where they had one of their nurseries.

## Froebel, Theodor 1810–1893

### Biography

Born in village of Griesheim, Thuringia, Germany, 1810. Educated by uncle Friedrich Froebel, founder of kindergartens; after practicing in botanic and royal gardens in Germany, came to Switzerland, 1834; took position of head gardener at University of Zürich, 1835, and laid out and planted new botanic garden there with first rock garden for alpine plants in Switzerland; founded first nursery garden in Zürich (with H. Würth), 1835; established and directed his own *Kunstgärtnerei* (bureau for designing landscape gardens) and nursery until 1890; designed large number of parks and gardens in refined landscape garden style, mainly in eastern Switzerland; hybridized many plants; published several articles in horticultural journals on plants he hybridized or introduced. Died in Zürich, 1893.

## Selected Designs

| | |
|---|---|
| 1835–41 | Botanic Garden of University of Zürich, Zürich, Switzerland |
| 1840s | Green belt surrounding Old Town of Winterthur, Switzerland |
| 1850 | Stadthausanlage, Zürich, Switzerland |
| 1855 | Garden of Villa Wesendonck (now Rieterpark), Zürich, Switzerland |
| 1863 | Stadelhofer Park, Zürich, Switzerland |
| 1864 | Garden of Villa Martinsburg (now new Botanic Garden of University of Zürich), Zürich, Switzerland |
| 1866 | Sihlhölzli, Zürich, Switzerland |

# Froebel, Otto 1844–1906

## Biography

Born in Zürich, Switzerland, 1844. Worked and traveled in Belgium, France, England, and other European countries before joining nursery and landscape-gardening firm of his father; designed large number of private and public parks; introduced dozens of plants new to nursery trade; founded first florist's shop in Zürich and excelled in hybridizing flowers; numerous medals and prizes for plants at various exhibitions, including first class certificate from Royal Horticultural Society, London, for *Begonia froebelii*, 1876, Prix Estella, and 21 other prizes at Swiss Exposition in Geneva, 1896. Died in Zürich, 1906.

## Selected Designs

| | |
|---|---|
| 1881–87 | Quaianlagen with Arboretum and Zürichhorn Park (together with Evariste Mertens), Zürich, Switzerland |
| 1885 | Garden of Villa Brandt, Zürich, Switzerland |
| 1890 | Park of Family Blanc, Chambéry, Savoy, France |
| 1890s | Gardens of several villas in Neumünster-Allee, Zürich, Switzerland |
| 1896 | Wiedikon Church Park, Zürich, Switzerland |
| 1896–97 | Garden of Villa Egli, Zürich, Switzerland |
| 1898 | Garden of Villa Schwarzenbach, Rüschlikon, Canton Zürich, Switzerland |
| 1899 | Parks of Hotels Reichenbach and des Alpes, Meiringen, Canton Bern, Switzerland |
| 1900 | Park of Theodosianum, Zürich, Switzerland |

## Selected Publications

"Ueber Alpenpflanzen und deren Kultur," *Jahrbuch des Schweizerischen Alpenklubs* 20 (1884/85)

"Gartenbau," in *Chronik der Kirchgemeinde Neumünster,* 1889

"Die Helleborus," *Der Garten* (1891)

*Illustrierter und erläuternder General-Katalog über sämtliche Kulturen der Firma* no. 124 (1899)

# Froebel, Robert 1878–1966

## Biography

Born in Zürich, Switzerland, 1878. Only son of Otto Froebel; worked and traveled widely in France, Germany, and England; after death of father in 1906, led family firm for 20 years; designed numerous private gardens and specialized in laying out sports fields and grounds for schoolhouses, hotels, and hospitals; firm designed ZUGA garden exhibition, Zürich, 1933; firm closed, 1934. Died in Zürich, 1966.

## Selected Designs

| | |
|---|---|
| 1907 | Formal show garden, Garden Exhibition, Zürich, Switzerland; garden of Villa Müller-Renner, Winterthur, Switzerland |
| 1915 | Garden of Villa Zuberbühler, Zurzach, Switzerland |
| 1920 | Garden of Villa Geiser, Langenthal, Canton Bern, Switzerland |
| 1925 | Grounds of the Tennis Club, Winterthur, Switzerland |

## Further Reading

"100 Jahre Gärtnerei Froebel (1835–1935)," *Schweizer Garten* 5 (1943)

Krausch, Heinz-Dieter, and Clemens Alexander Wimmer, "Ein Katalog der Gärtnerei Otto Froebel vom Frühjahr 1899 und seine Bedeutung für das Zierpflanzensortiment in der Schweiz," *Mitteilungen der schweizerischen Gesellschaft für Gartenkultur* 16, no.3 (1998)

Olbrich, Stephan, "Theodor Froebel," *Schweizerischer Gartenbau* 6, no. 20 (1893)

Ruoff, Eeva, "Die frühen Jahre der Kunstgärtnerei Froebel in Zürich," *Mitteilungen der Gesellschaft für Gartenkultur* 3, no. 2 (1985)

Ruoff, Eeva, "Kunstgärtner und Pflanzenzüchter," *Turicum* 4 (1990)

Schröter, Carl, "Otto Froebel," *Jahrbuch der Naturforschenden Gesellschaft in Zürich* (1906–7)

EEVA RUOFF

# Fronteira, Palácio

## Lisbon, Portugal

**Location:**  Lisbon, approximately 4 miles (6.5 km) northwest of the city center, in the Benfica neighborhood, by Monsanto Park

The mellowed house and gardens of the Palace of Fronteira have allured admiring visitors for over three centuries. The setting presents a *quinta* (Portuguese country home) of unique cultural integration. The house was built in the style of the Italian Renaissance, set in gardens of the French Renaissance, and accented with colorful Portuguese tiles.

The area of the house and gardens comprises an almost uniformly square setting of nearly 2.5 acres (1 ha). The residence occupies the northwest quadrant, with the portico entrance on the north side. Gardens stretch along the eastern half and the southwestern quadrant. The latter forms an oblong protrusion from the square setting, a diagonal extension of the house having been built along the southwestern edge of the terrain.

The house and gardens were built as a country retreat, begun probably in 1667 or 1668. Construction began at the order of João Mascarenhas, second count of Torre and first marquis of Fronteira. The gardens were completed before the house, whose original purpose was more that of a hunting lodge than a residence. The Mascarenhas family contributed extensively to the history of Portugal and its empire. The father of the first marquis was crucial in expelling from Portugal its Spanish overlords, while the marquis was instrumental in consolidating the power of the new Portuguese royal dynasty.

The Fronteira house was built according to Italian Renaissance models of the previous century and ornamented inside with elegant detailed decoration and outside with formal Franco-Italian gardens. The house design, with double loggias along the north and east sides of the three-story structure, was mainly conceived from drawings of the 16th-century Italian architect Sebastiano Serlio.

Portugal has not had an extensive tradition of grand domestic architecture. Its most noted buildings are usually religious or public. The Palace of Fronteira represented, however, one of the most distinguished families of the Portuguese realm and was built in a bucolic enclave near Lisbon amid the country homes of other aristocrats. The site became the Mascarenhas family seat after the Lisbon earthquake of 1755. In moving to the Benfica house, they added an extension stretching to an older, outside chapel, establishing the essential pattern of house and gardens that one sees today. (The Palace of Fronteira has over the centuries also been referred to as the Palace of Benfica and the Palace of São Domingos of Benfica.)

The salons, bedrooms, and noted library of the palace are decorated in a rich but restrained baroque manner. Singular to the interior are accents of blue Portuguese tiles (*azulejos*) and ceramics. Numerous windows reveal vistas of the gardens, the most noted elements of the site. From the south exit of the house, one encounters a complex of several small, intimate gardens. They lie in cool shade from trees towering overhead, one a gigantic bunya-bunya (*Araucaria bidwillii*). To the right is the chapel. It is reached by a terrace whose western wall presents a progression of blue tiles and classical statuary framed in spring by Judas tree (*Cercis siliquastrum*) blossoms. To the left and rising into the background extends an array of small fountains, hedges, bending palms and ferns, flower beds, and wandering paths. Lichen and moss have crept everywhere.

Under shading trees all slumber in this aged bower. Here the gardens hold their most romantic character, where Fronteira has its peculiarly mysterious feeling, a sense of the "aging of antiquity." The shadows of thick foliage are penetrated by hazy beams of sunlight; meandering byways in the half-light reveal ivy-covered walls, draping wisteria, and moldering statues; and water spouts gently from fountains.

In spectacular counterbalance are the main gardens, occupying in open air more than half the east side of the Fronteira site. At the south end of this area stands an elevated terrace with blue tiles covering its back and side walls. Two spacious balustraded stairways lead up to pavilions at each end of the terrace. Along the back of this terrace is a gallery of the busts of Portuguese monarchs set in richly colored alcoves. The vista from this elevation is first of a rectangular pool, actually a watering tank, that horizontally fronts the terrace. Classical marine statues float on the surface. Tiled tableaux line the containing walls that enfold inset grottoes.

As one gazes out from this terrace, there beckons the climax of the Fronteira gardens, a complex of parterre arrangements stretching from the pond. The sculptured hedging is divided into four measured quadrants, each of different geometric design. Each quadrant is further divided into four parts. Small water fountains lie at the center of each subdivision, and a large one at the center of the entire complex. While the previous gardens give a feeling of quiet intimacy, the parterre complex strikes with hypnotic splendor.

Fronteira marks the advance of Italian and French influence in Portuguese landscape architecture, reflecting the decline of Roman and Moorish influence. However, remnants of the latter remain at Fronteira in the chapel, recalling a temple to the *lares*, Roman household gods, and in the parterre design evoking Islamic art. Although the Fronteira site physically occupies a relatively small area, it singularly concentrates a wide array of vistas and sentiments.

## Synopsis

| | |
|---|---|
| 1667–68 | House and gardens begun by João Mascarenhas, the first marquis of Fronteira |
| 1669 | Duke Cosimo de' Medici visits Fronteira, commenting on it with admiration |
| 1737 | Death of third marquis of Fronteira, an army general who served throughout the Portuguese empire, whence plants were brought for the family gardens |
| 1755 | After earthquake of Lisbon, Mascarenhas family moves to Fronteira, gardens redesigned |
| 1844 | The poetry of Leonor de Almeida, the fourth marchioness of Alorna, posthumously published; she maintained a brilliant salon at Fronteira and, as a great admirer of nature, wrote a long poem on the pleasures of botany |
| 1987 | Foundation established to preserve and restore Fronteira Palace and to promote cultural events at the locale |

## Further Reading

Binney, Marcus, and Nicolas Sapieha, *Country Manors of Portugal: A Passage through Seven Centuries*, New York: Scala Books, and Woodbridge, Suffolk: Antique Collectors' Club, 1987

Binney, Marcus, et al., *Houses and Gardens of Portugal*, New York: Rizzoli, and London: Cartago, 1998

Bowe, Patrick, and Nicolas Sapieha, *Gardens of Portugal*, London: Tauris, and New York: Scala Books, 1989

Neves, José Cassiano, *Jardins e palácio dos marqueses de Fronteira*, Lisbon: Ediçoens Gama, 1941; 3rd revised edition, by Vere Mendes and Fernando Mascarenhas, Lisbon: Quetzal Editores, 1995; as *The Palace and Gardens of Fronteira: Seventeenth- and Eighteenth-Century Portuguese Style*, Wappinger's Falls, New York: Antique Collector's Club, 1995

Segall, Barbara, *Garden Lover's Guide to Spain and Portugal*, New York: Princeton Architectural Press, 1999

EDWARD A. RIEDINGER

---

# Fruit

Fruits have been cultivated for nearly 6,000 years. The date palm (*Phoenix dactylifera*) in the East and the apple tree in the West were cultivated before wheat and barley, respectively. Fruits have been planted throughout the world where settled communities based on agriculture were located. The earliest of these settlements were in Egypt and between the Tigris and Euphrates Rivers in Syria.

Although the primary reason for including fruit plants in gardens has always been practical, many have ornamental characteristics as well. For example, the apple tree (*Malus* spp.), native to a vast area of the temperate zone from Britain in the northwest to the Himalayas in the southeast, has soft-green leaves and is covered with white or pink blossoms in the spring followed by tiny green fruits that develop over the season into red, yellow, or green mature apples in late summer to fall. Citrus fruits (*Citrus* spp.), native to China, Southeast Asia, and India, are small to medium (one to three meters [1.1 to 3.3 yd.]) evergreen trees with highly fragrant small blooms at different times, depending on the type. Blueberry (*Vaccinium* spp.) bushes, native to North America, are one to 5.5 meters (1.1 to six yd.) tall, depending on variety, with dark-green leaves that turn yellow to scarlet in the fall. The pinkish-white bell-shaped blooms hang in clusters in spring, becoming dark-blue berries ready for harvest by mid- to late summer.

The style of the earliest Egyptian gardens (eighth to third century B.C.) was a collection of walled, rectangular spaces covering many acres. Each section was devoted to a special culture with a pool in the center for fish. Shade and fruit trees were planted together. The fruits included date palms, figs, pomegranates, and grapes (*Vitis vinifera*). The Assyrians and Persians interacted with the Egyptians, adopting ideas from them that were then taken up by the Greeks and Romans.

In Homer's *Odyssey*, the regal garden of Alcinous is described as consisting of an orchard of pears, pomegranates, apples, figs, and olives; a vineyard; and garden beds for other plants. The entire area was surrounded by a hedge and included fountains.

Records of monastery gardens in fourth- to sixth-century Europe include descriptions of vegetable plots, vineyards, and orchards tended inside and outside walls and flowers grown for use as decoration in the church. A plan preserved in the library of the Benedictine Monastery of Saint Gall in Switzerland includes a main cloister garden, a vegetable garden in 18 beds, and an orchard of fruit and nut trees. Fruits included apple, cherry, fig, medlar (*Mespilius germanica*), mulberry, peach, pear, plum, and quince.

## Europe

During the Middle Ages (late 13th to mid-16th century) the garden and orchard were intermingled, as described by Albert the Great in *De naturis rerum* (On Nature). At one end, facing south, were pear, apple, plum, and other trees interplanted with vines (including grapes), herbs, and flowers. The great herbalist Gerard wrote in 1597 about the Cornelian cherry (*Cornus mas*) growing in his garden. Timber and decorative trees grew together with fruit trees. Raspberry, elderberry, blackberry, and gooseberry (*Ribes grossularia*) grew thickly and profusely in the wild, so they were not cultivated in gardens at that time. After the Crusades oranges, lemons, and pomegranates were brought back from the East.

Two writers of the late Middle Ages (Petrus Crescentius, *Opus ruralium commodorum* (Book of Rural Occupations), and Giovanni Boccaccio, "Third Day" in the *Decameron*) described gardens as square sections for herbs and flowers enclosed by moats, rose hedges, fruit tree hedges, or high walls. Boccaccio added that near the middle of the garden is a "plat of fine grass, enamelled with a thousand kinds of flowers, closed about with the greenest and lustiest of orange and citron trees, the which, bearing at once old fruits and new, and flowers, afforded the eyes a pleasant shade and were no less greatful to the smell."

A description of the Villa of Castello in Florence, Italy, by the French essayist Michel de Montaigne, who visited there in 1580, said it was a symmetrically walled enclosure with orange and lemon trees grown in pots and espaliered fruit trees on sunny walls. *Espalier* is the technique of training a tree flat against a wall or trellis in a variety of symmetrical shapes (fan, horizontal or cordon, oblique) requiring consistent pruning. The method not only is decorative but also provides higher yields. Since standard apple and pear trees reach 12 meters (13.1 yd.) at maturity, making them difficult to manage in an enclosed closely planted space, it is not surprising that techniques were devised to keep them smaller.

During the 16th century in France, records show that many varieties of apple, cherry, fig, grape, peach, pear, and plum were grown. Fruit trees were trained on sun-warmed walls and latticework fences that enclosed squares of vegetables in the potager. Engravings of the 16th and early 17th centuries show a separation of pleasure gardens from the utilitarian area.

The French gardeners were acknowledged masters of growing more tender and unusual fruits. They developed the practice of training fruit trees to be small enough to be covered if necessary to protect them from frost. These small trees, known as dwarfs, were created by pruning and heading down standard trees or by grafting a chosen fruit variety (scion) on to a rooted stem (rootstock) that would reach a lower height (usually a wild type). Grafting is an ancient practice known to the Mesopotamians, to the Chinese 2,000 years before Christ, and to the Greeks and Romans. The art of dwarfing fruit trees was a specialty of medieval French monasteries.

In England records of the earliest gardens were those created by the Romans during their occupation. These included cherry, pear, mulberry, and walnut trees as well as vegetables, herbs, and flowers. The word *orchard* comes from the Anglo-Saxon *ortgeard* or *wortgeard*, literally "plant yard," not just a place for fruit trees, which is how the word is used today.

During the Tudor period in England, the intermingling of ornamental and useful plants continued to be practiced—herbs, vegetables, and fruits. These gardens, enclosed in walls or fences, followed the monastery pattern.

During the Renaissance, garden design became more elaborate. Practices in Holland such as water fountains, statues, topiary, terraces, labyrinths, and knots spread to England. In the 16th century, French Huguenots fleeing religious oppression came into Surrey and Middlesex, bringing with them the traditional methods of French market gardening, including the use of dwarf and espalier fruit trees. Garden books of the time list apricot, peach, nectarine, cherry, plum, quince, apple, and pear and describe the trees as being "spread upon the walls by the help of tacks and other means to have the benefit of the immediate reflexe of the sunne" (Amherst, 1896). Strawberry (*Fragaria vesca* and *F. moschata*) and other small bush fruits, such as gooseberry (*Ribes uva-crispa*), were grown on the ground between fruit trees.

To grow a successful crop of grapes in England, they must have protection. The Romans used forcing houses glazed with mica and planted the vines against the southern walls of their houses. Grapes continued to be grown in the open and sometimes produced a satisfactory crop, but more often they were planted against a brick or stone wall. The first plans for forcing houses in England were published in Stephen Switzer's *Practical Fruit Gardener* (1724). The true glasshouse made it possible to grow grapes (dessert varieties), which became more popular than oranges. The demand for grapes led to commercial production under glass and the foundation of the glasshouse industry in England.

In the 17th century, kitchen gardens in England were still situated near the house, and dwarf fruit trees were sometimes used as decorative plants in parterres. However, by the 18th century and into the 19th century, landscape style was becoming naturalistic, rejecting straight lines and walls. Since the kitchen garden was laid out in symmetrical squares with walls, the trend began to separate the fruit and vegetable area from the rest of the garden. Tall hedges of holly, yew, or laurel were planted to screen the kitchen garden from view from the house, and usually the main growing area was surrounded by brick or stone walls varying in height from 3.7 to 4.6 meters (four to five yd.). These protected plants from thieves and animals, supported glass and other structures, and provided the desired surface for training fruit trees.

## United States

In the United States, the same practice of growing fruits, vegetables, herbs, and flowers together near dwellings in a fenced area was followed by the Native Americans and the early settlers. The Native Americans grew grapes (*Vitis labrusca* and *V. rotundifolia*), persimmons (*Diospyros virginiana*), cherries, crab apples, strawberries (*Fragaria virginiana* and *F. chiloensis*), mulberries, gooseberries (*Ribes divaricatum* and *R. hirtellum*), juneberries, pawpaw (*Asimina triloba*), raspberries, plums, blueberries, and cranberries. Settlers brought Old World fruits and vegetables with them and wild American species were improved and placed under cultivation using Old World methods as well as those practiced by Native Americans.

On the East Coast, settlers introduced such fruits as apple, pear, quince, peach, apricot, orange, lemon, pineapple, and olive. On the West Coast, the Franciscan fathers had established 21 missions by 1823 and planted fruit collections at all of them. In the same year, William Prince, who operated a nursery in Flushing, Long Island, offered 114 apple varieties in his catalog as well as 107 varieties of pear, 74 varieties of peach, 48 varieties of plum, and 53 varieties of cherry. By the end of the 18th century, the kitchen garden and the pleasure garden had been separated, the vegetables and herbs usually planted behind the house.

In the late 20th century in the United States, the style of intermingling food plants and decorative plants throughout the home landscape returned. Called "edible landscaping," the style involves grouping vegetables, berries, herbs, fruits, nuts, and ornamental plants in attractive and harmonious ways to provide food and beauty. Another system of growing food plants with other plants developed in the early 1970s by Bill Mollison and David Holmgren is "permaculture." This is the "conscious design and maintenance of agriculturally productive ecosystems which have the diversity, stability, and resilience of natural ecosystems . . . providing food, energy, shelter, and other material and nonmaterial needs in a sustainable way" (Mollison, 1988).

## China, Japan, and Russia

Traditional Chinese gardens are representational of the natural landscape, including formed hills, cascades of water, bridges, large rocks brought from long distances, and small pavilions placed strategically to enjoy the created scenes. Fruits were grown in a separate area with rice or other crops or gathered from the wild. When plant explorer Frank Meyer visited China in 1911, he reported plantings of *Actinidia,* apple, apricot, cherry, citrus, fig, grape, haw, jujube, kumquat, lychee, loquat, peach, pear, persimmon, plum, and pineapple.

In Japan, where arable land is limited, level ground was used for the most important crop: rice. Fruit trees were planted on spare ground near rural cottages and on embankments, steep slopes, and temple grounds and only in the early 1900s planted in gardens or orchards. The most popular fruit, jujube (*Ziziphus jujuba*), has been grown for 4,000 years, often planted on the ground between rice paddies. Today there are more than 400 varieties. The second most popular fruit, persimmon (*Diospyros kaki*), was the most widely grown fruit in the Orient until the 20th century, when the apple was introduced. It has been cultivated for centuries in both Japan and China with about 2,000 cultivars known today.

Asian pears are popular in both Japan and China. The Japanese cultivars are derived from *Pyrus pyrifolia;* the Chinese ones are hybrids of *P. ussuriensis* and *P. bretschneideris.* Another common fruit is kiwi fruit (*Actinidia* spp.), which has been harvested from the wild for centuries and for the most part still is today.

Nanking cherry (*Prunus tomentosa*) is the most common fruit plant in the gardens of the Russian Far East. In Manchuria it has been grown as a hedge, as a windbreak, and for its fruit. A highly ornamental plant, the bark is an attractive orange-brown, peeling away in paper-thin strips. The pink buds unfold to white blooms very early in spring before the leaves emerge, literally covering the branches. During the summer, the tree is covered with soft-green, downy leaves, and the fruit turns bright red.

## Tropical and Subtropical Regions

In tropical regions of the world, a whole different group of fruits is native. This includes avocado, banana, date, cherimoya, carambola, guava, mango, lychee, papaya, pomegranate, and pineapple. In these areas in Central and South America, Africa, and Asia, the crucial factor in agricultural activity is rainfall; there is no frost or cold season as in the temperate zone. Near the equator, there is no dry season. Moving away from the equator there is an area with two rainy and two dry seasons alternating. Farthest from the equator is a region of minimum rainfall with one rainy season, usually monsoons.

Early writings in Sanskrit suggest that the improvement of the mango (*Mangifera indica*) through vegetative propagation may have been practiced in early times. The tree was planted in gardens and orchards in ancient India. Akbar, the Mogul emperor, planted 100,000 mango trees between 1556 and 1605 near Darbhanga, India.

In sub-Saharan Africa, the traditional garden style is intercropped, multistoried layers of annual and perennial vegetable plants and herbs with fruiting shrubs and trees. Many plants are evergreen and produce fruit year-round. For example, a garden in West Africa has banana and papaya trees as the top story with an understory of vegetables and herbs, including eggplant, bush greens, lettuce, cabbage, tomato, okra, pigeon pea, and cassava.

In Central America the avocado has been grown as a dooryard tree for centuries. The cherimoya, which originated in the highlands of Peru and Ecuador and naturalized in the cool highlands of Central America and Mexico, is also grown as a garden tree. The Aztecs, Mayas, and Incas all had great areas of well-tilled land where they raised corn, beans, squashes, melons, fruits, and other food plants.

**Further Reading**

Berrall, Julia S., *The Garden: An Illustrated History,* New York: Viking Press, 1966

Campbell, Susan, *Charleston Kedding: A History of Kitchen Gardening,* London: Ebury Press, 1996

Creasy, Rosalind, *The Complete Book of Edible Landscaping,* San Francisco: Sierra Club Books, 1982

Harrison, S.G., G.B. Masefield, and Michael Wallis, *The Oxford Book of Food Plants,* London: Oxford University Press, 1969

Hyams, Edward, and Alan A. Jackson, editors, *The Orchard and Fruit Garden: A New Pomona of Hardy and Sub-Tropical Fruits,* London: Longmans, 1961

Mollison, Bill, *Permaculture: A Designers' Manual,* Tyalgum, New South Wales: Tagari, 1988

Popenoe, Wilson, *Manual of Tropical and Subtropical Fruits, Excluding the Banana, Coconut, Pineapple, Citrus Fruits, Olive, and Fig,* New York: Hafner Press, 1974

Reich, Lee, *Uncommon Fruits Worthy of Attention: A Gardener's Guide,* Reading, Massachusetts: Addison-Wesley, 1991

Rockley, Alicia Margaret Tyssen-Amherst Cecil, Baroness, *A History of Gardening in England,* London, 1895; reprint, Detroit, Michigan: Singing Tree Press, 1969

STEVIE DANIELS

# Fruit Garden

American landscape designer Andrew Jackson Downing wrote in 1845 that a fruit tree was "the most perfect union of the useful and the beautiful that the earth knows." This double attraction has governed the use of fruit plants in gardens. The Bible's description of the Garden of Eden gives prominent mythological place to the apple tree, whose fruit gave humans knowledge of good and evil. In other cultures as well, mythological descriptions of paradise mention fruit trees with magical properties: golden apples of immortality, apples that kept the gods youthful, and fruit trees guarded by dragons, angels, or birds. All evidence suggests that the earliest actual gardens, like the mythological ones, contained fruit trees. Gardens, as places of controlled nature, may in fact have begun as plantings of fruit trees.

The earliest gardens of Persia and the Middle East used fruit trees as the main plants, along with cypresses (which, as evergreens, represented immortality) and roses. Depending on the climate the most often used trees were the pomegranate and sour cherry, and later the sour orange, which was introduced from southeast Asia and spread into the Middle East. Other important fruit trees included the peach, apricot, plum, apple, pear, quince, and chestnut. Grapevines were also common.

The concept that fruit trees represented paradise spread from the Islamic world into Europe and was widespread by the ninth century, where it manifested in monasteries as the "cemetery orchard." There, the dead were buried among fruit trees, which symbolized the paradise in which they now lived and also provided fruit for and refreshed the senses of the living. Because these orchards tended to be the only places in a monastery with private corners, ecclesiastical inspections included firm instructions to lock the inner cemetery doors overnight, from vespers to prime, to keep out unauthorized visitors.

Orchards were one of the three standard types of pleasure garden described in the Bolognese Piero de' Crescenzi's gardening text *Ruralium commodorum liber* (1305; Book of Rural Interests). Orchards were common throughout Europe, valued not only for providing fruit but also for their pleasant shady alleys for walking beneath flowering trees. According to Crescenzi orchards were to be bounded by walls, wattle fences, moats, or flowering hedges of hawthorn, roses, and fruit trees. The area within was plowed, raked, made flat, and marked out with cord, then planted with fruit and nut trees in rows five to six meters (5.5 to 6.6 yd.) apart, with vines in between. Trellises, tunnel-arbors, and seat arbors of poles were also constructed. Paths between the trees were at right angles and surfaced with sand or turf.

The walls surrounding an orchard were important for keeping out animals and for denoting legal boundaries, which could be cited in cases of theft (a common problem). By law an orchard had to have a minimum of 12 trees, so the smallest orchards were probably approximately 18 by 24 meters (20 to 24 yd.). The largest known, at a Welsh priory dating to 1199, reached 4.9 hectares (12 acres), which implies anywhere from 400 to 1,000 trees.

The most common orchard trees of medieval Europe were apple, pear, and cherry, but also found were mulberry, plum, fig, almond, quince, medlar, chestnut, and walnut. Trees might be grafted on the premises or obtained ready-grafted from commercial nurseries.

In Elizabethan times it was common to place fruit trees in the center or around the edges of the flower garden for vertical accents. Vines on trellises and arbors sheltered sitting places. Bush fruits such as currants and gooseberry were often planted in garden borders along with flowers and herbs. These ideas were transported to America, where colonial gardens often feature fruit trees along the sides of formal gardens with central box-edged parterres. Likewise, in the palace gardens of William of Orange, miniature clipped apple trees were used in parterres.

At Versailles orange and lemon trees in characteristic square, white "Versailles tubs" provided vertical accents in the formal gardens. The tubs were wheeled indoors into sunny, heated rooms, or "orangeries," for the winter. Orangeries later developed into the glass-walled, cathedral-like conservatories of the Victorian age.

Despite this longstanding formal tradition, however, most plantings where fruits or vegetables mingled with flowers were located in more informal or smaller gardens; indeed, such a mixing is part of the cottage-garden tradition. Beginning in the Renaissance, orchards began to be seen more as utilitarian food gardens and less as pleasure gardens or intimations of paradise. Although there had been a strong tradition of using fruit trees in the formal and ornamental parts of the garden, a contrary tendency began to segregate them. On larger estates the "productive" parts of the garden were usually separated from the purely ornamental; fruit trees were segregated into orchards and vegetables into kitchen gardens, both located in the back or far corners of properties. Thus, in colonial America smaller trees (pears, peaches, apricots, plums, cherries) were planted in flower borders on small properties but in separate orchards on larger ones. At Versailles the kitchen garden or *potager du roi* featured espaliered fruit trees acting as the "walls" between the different vegetable beds. Examination of pictures and photographs of ordinary houses and farms shows that in the Victorian era fruit trees were increasingly located in the rear, and in the early 20th century the place for fruit trees was in the service yard along with vegetable gardens, trash cans, and wood piles.

Beginning in the later 20th century, with more concern for the environment and fresh foods, along with the increasingly popular idea of providing food for wildlife, some general gardening books have begun to urge home owners to try "edible landscaping," advocating including food plants with the pure ornamentals. In general, however, fruit plants seem to be considered mostly as curiosities or footnotes in the modern garden; books on ornamental gardening rarely include edible plants or include them in separate chapters. The segregation of productive from ornamental is still common.

**Further Reading**

Clifford, Derek, *A History of Garden Design,* London: Faber and Faber, 1962; New York: Praeger, 1963; 2nd edition, 1966

Cowell, Frank Richard, *The Garden As a Fine Art,* Boston: Houghton Mifflin, and London: Weidenfeld and Nicolson, 1978

Cox, Jeff, *Your Organic Garden with Jeff Cox,* Emmaus, Pennsylvania: Rodale Press, 1994

Favretti, Rudy J., and Joy Putman Favretti, *Landscapes and Gardens for Historic Buildings,* Nashville, Tennessee: American Association for State and Local History, 1978; 2nd revised edition, 1991

Landsberg, Sylvia, *The Medieval Garden,* London: British Museum Press, 1995; New York: Thames and Hudson, 1996

Moynihan, Elizabeth B., *Paradise As a Garden: In Persia and Mughal India,* New York: Braziller, 1979

Taylor, Patrick, *Period Gardens: New Life for Historic Landscapes,* New York: Atlantic Monthly Press, and London: Pavillion Books, 1991

EMILY N. GOODMAN

# Furniture, Garden

Pleasure gardens were a place of rest and retreat, just as kitchen gardens and orchards were meant for work. In both, permanent seats (or "roosting places," as they were called in late medieval England) were both useful and welcome.

Seats were evident in the earliest gardens. A carved stone relief of about 645 B.C. (British Museum) shows King Ashurbanipal and his queen sitting on elegant chairs under a grape arbor in the royal park at Nineveh. Pliny the Younger (first century A.D.) in his *Letters* wrote of a "semicircular couch" set into "an alcove of white marble, shaded with vines and supported by four small Carystian columns." Pliny's bench would have been a permanent feature of the garden, meant to complement architectural and sculptural forms as well as provide a resting place. Pliny may also have had wicker work furniture in his garden, as furniture made from woven willow was described by his uncle Pliny the Elder and had been used at least since the time of the ancient Egyptians. The widespread availability of the materials for wicker furniture has meant that it has remained popular from antiquity up to the modern day.

Although no early examples of garden furniture survive, many illuminated manuscripts show medieval gardens with permanent furniture, as well as portable pieces brought from dwellings. In addition to wood and stone seats, there were "turf seats" with hollow bases of brick, wattle, or wood that could be filled with soil. The seat itself would be planted with chamomile, violets, thyme, and other herbs and flowers, whose scents would be released when sat upon. (This delightful concept was revived by Vita Sackville-West at Sissinghurst in the 1930s.) There are illustrations too of tables used for alfresco banquets and games. A late 14th-century illuminated manuscript in the Bodleian Library (Oxford) shows a king and queen seated on benches, playing chess on a gaming table in their enclosed castle garden.

Turf seat at Sissinghurst Castle, Kent, England
Copyright Paula Henderson

Illustrations of Italian and northern European Renaissance gardens show grand tables (circular, octagonal, and rectangular) laid out for splendid feasts to be consumed under an arbor or in a summerhouse. (A table survives inside the grotto of Hell's Mouth in the Sacro Bosco at Bomarzo, Italy.) In Italy stone benches, beautifully carved with classical detail, were often made of the best white marble. Where fine stone was unavailable—in England, for example—wooden seats were painted in imitation of stone. Perhaps the most popular form was the simple flat bench with trestle supports, but more elaborate seats with high backs and carved legs were also common. Sometimes these seats were fitted with concealed spouts, so that the unwary garden visitor would be drenched with water as he or she sat down. A rare survival of this type of water trick (Italian, *giochi d'acqua*) may be seen in the late 17th-century garden at Villa Barbarigo, near Padua.

Elegant stone seats were frequently used as a focal point in a formal garden, overlooking geometrically arranged parterres or placed at the end of a long walk. Seats were also used structurally in less formal gardens. At The Leasowes (Warwickshire) the influential mid-18th-century garden of the poet William Shenstone, seats (often with poetic inscriptions) were placed strategically along the path through the garden to encourage visitors to sit down and contemplate a particular view.

In the 18th century garden furniture echoed the work of the great cabinetmakers, whose designs could be carried out in stone or wood. The more exotic decorative styles of the mid-18th century were particularly apposite to the garden: Chinese, Chippendale, rococo, and "Gothick" styles were all used for garden furniture. Windsor chairs, popular "below-stairs" seating, were often moved into the landscape or into a garden building for the new ritual of afternoon tea.

Architects also provided designs for garden furniture. Batty Langley published popular books (e.g., *New Principles of Gardening* [1728]) that included designs for pavilions and seats, the most charming of which were the slightly fantastic rustic seats for hermitages and grottoes. Sir William Chambers, one of the most important neoclassical architects in England, designed buildings and furniture in a wide variety of architectural styles, published in *Designs of Chinese Buildings* (1757) and in *Plans of the Garden Buildings at Kew* (1763). At the end of the 19th century, the architect Sir Edwin Lutyens, often working with Gertrude Jekyll, designed a solid wooden bench with a curved back that has remained popular to this day.

In the 19th century the great developments in the manufacture of industrial materials were applied to making garden ornaments (fountains, sculpture, sundials) and furniture. The factories in northern England, particularly the Coalbrookdale Foundry (Shropshire), produced extensive catalogs of cast-iron furniture. Some of the most beautiful pieces employed organic forms with bench backs of flowing lilies-of-the-valley, ferns, blackberries, and other floral forms. They also supplied more typical architectural forms in classical and medieval styles. Although relatively inexpensive at the time, original pieces are now valuable and sold through auction houses and specialist dealers. Wirework garden furniture was also popular, although because of its greater fragility it was more often used in conservatories rather than outdoors. Ceramic seats, painted and glazed to look like tree stumps, added another whimsical touch to the garden or conservatory.

Modern garden furniture reflects the more relaxed attitude of the 20th century, a time when convenience, comfort, and cost often became more important than style. The ever-popular hammock has a surprisingly long history, having evolved from the hanging beds on ships used by sailors from the 16th century (the word is Caribbean in origin). So, too, the steamer deck chair—collapsible and with replaceable canvas seats—inspired the ubiquitous folding chairs and tables of wood or aluminum. At the low end of the seating market are the cheap, molded plastic tables and chairs that are seemingly immune to weather damage and can be stacked and easily stored. In the United States especially, the rise of the barbecue and emphasis on outdoor life has encouraged the development of purpose-built picnic tables and benches, used in private gardens as well as in public parks.

**Further Reading**

Edwards, Paul, *English Garden Ornament,* London: Bell, 1965; South Brunswick, New Jersey: Barnes, 1967

Henderson, Paula, "Adorning the Arbour," *Country Life* (8 March 1990)

Israel, Barbara, *Antique Garden Ornament: Two Centuries of American Taste,* New York: Abrams, 1999

Jekyll, Gertrude, *Garden Ornament,* London: Country Life, and New York: Scribner, 1918; reprint, Woodbridge, Suffolk: Antique Collector's Club, 1994

Morris, Alistair, *Antiques from the Garden,* Woodbridge, Suffolk: Garden Art Press, 1996; 2nd edition, 1999

Wilkinson, Elizabeth, and Marjorie Henderson, *The House of Boughs: A Sourcebook of Garden Designs, Structures, and Suppliers,* New York: Viking, 1985

PAULA HENDERSON

# Furttenbach, Joseph 1591–1667

## German Architect and Writer

Joseph Furttenbach was the first German architectural writer to consider the design of gardens equal in importance to architecture. Although German, he was educated in Giulio Parigi's Academy of War and Art in Florence, Italy. This educational experience would be a tremendous influence on his future work as both a theorist and a practitioner in his native country. For over 40 years, Furttenbach served as an architect and later councilor for Ulm, a medieval trading city on the Danube River. When he arrived in Ulm during the midst of the Thirty Years' War, resources for the execution of buildings and gardens were extremely limited. He built only one garden, which was at his own residence, but wrote numerous treatises on the design of gardens for both domestic and institutional spaces. His audience was the newly emerging middle class, those who were experiencing greater economic independence as the power of the feudal lords gradually declined.

Through his writings, particularly in *Architectura Civilis*, *Architectura Universalis*, *Architectura Recreationis*, and *Architectura Privata*, Furttenbach introduced Germans to Italian garden design. The Renaissance had arrived late in Germany, and Furttenbach provided bourgeois dilettantes with visions of Renaissance life in Italy through his publications. For Furttenbach, the garden played a unique role in humanist thought because it provided a living space for speculative inquiry, nature appreciation, and connoisseurship. The garden also served as a repository for exotic plants, the hallmark of the academically learned and upwardly mobile new class. Furttenbach also envisioned gardens at social institutions as fertile resources for both the aristocratic and bourgeois classes. Gardens at schools and at hospitals were designed as sites for both education and enjoyment.

His treatises typically contained elevated perspective sketches of ideal garden designs. This positioning of the viewer above the garden, perhaps on a balcony or looking out a window, helped to reinforce the physical intimacy between the house and garden that he admired in Italian gardens. His ideal gardens often stressed the Italian-style layout of paths, beds, trees, and sculptural elements. Emulating the Villa Medici, Furttenbach used the garden beds, walks, galleries, and trees (typically firs or Italian cypresses) in a consistent, repeated pattern of rectilinear sections. As a foil for this pattern, he placed within each section statues, pools, grottoes, and other sculptural elements. These garden elements were represented in plan and sectional drawings in his treatises, and they were often duplications of details that he had studied in Italian gardens.

Still tied to a medieval past, Furttenbach's ideal gardens were usually surrounded by a fortified wall. At the center of the garden, pathways often formed the shape of a cross as seen in medieval cloister gardens. His gardens were conceived of as flat spaces, more characteristic of the Danube river basin where Futtenbach lived rather than of the hilly Italian terrain that served as his inspiration. Furttenbach knew very little about the actual selection and care of plants, and he was often assisted in this by his brother Abraham, who provided specific plant types to suit his designs. Furttenbach himself was more concerned with the effect of the garden as a whole than with the specific plants.

Garden theaters were elements typically found in Italian gardens, and Furttenbach's interest in the design of stage sets can be traced to his education in Florence. He was instrumental in creating the first stage set in Germany to have moveable wings like those of the Italian stage. Likewise, in Furttenbach's gardens, the elements

Frontispiece of Joseph Furttenbach's *Architectura recreationis*, 1640
Courtesy of Gert Gröning and Joachim Wolschke-Bulmahn

became props, the galleries and bedding were treated much as scenery, and the garden visitors were conceived of as actors navigating their own destiny.

The Thirty Years' War devastated German cities such as Ulm. After the war, Furttenbach began to drop the Latinization of his treatise titles in favor of German. In works such as *Gewerbstatt-Gebäu* and *Mannhafter Kunst-Siegel*, Furttenbach exhibited an emerging concern for the social dimension of his gardens. These later books demonstrated an orientation towards reform; the creation of gardens was seen as part of rebuilding educational and social institutions. Furttenbach's design work, with its emulation of Italian gardens and duplication of their details, was far from original. However, his relentless commitment to gardens as an art form helped to establish garden design within the larger sphere of architectural discourse and ushered in a new group of garden patrons in Germany.

## Biography

Born in Leutkirch, Germany, 1591. Studied at Academy of War and Art in Florence, 1607–17, with interests in architecture, garden design, engineering, fireworks, and stage-set design; moved to Ulm, Germany, 1621; became city architect, 1631, and later city councilor, 1636; through numerous publications, Furttenbach proposed gardens for private dwellings and social and educational institutions that integrated elements from Italian-style gardens, thus introducing Italian Renaissance to German readers. Died in Ulm, Germany, 1667.

## Selected Designs

1628    Fürstlicher Lustgarten (not executed)

1640    Idealgarten (not executed)
1640    Das erste Vergnügen gärtnert (not executed)
1641    Furttenbach's garden in Ulm, Germany
1663    Schul-Paradeiss-Gärtlin (not executed)

## Selected Publications

*Newes Itinerarium Italiae,* 1627
*Architectura Civilis,* 1628
*Architectura Universalis,* 1635
*Architectura Recreationis,* 1640
*Architectura Privata,* 1641
*Gewerbstatt-Gebäu,* 1650
*Mannhafter Kunst-Spiegel,* 1663

## Further Reading

Dietzel, Senta, *Die Gartenentwürfe Furttenbachs,* Nuremberg, Germany: Frommann, 1928

Hennebo, Dieter, and Alfred Hoffmann, *Geschichte der deutschen Gartenkunst,* 3 vols., Hamburg: Broschek, 1962

MacDougall, Elisabeth B., editor, *Fons Sapientiae: Garden Fountains in Illustrated Books, Sixteenth–Eighteenth Centuries* (exhib. cat.), Washington, D.C.: Dumbarton Oaks Collection, 1977

Nehring, Dorothee, "The Garden Designs of Joseph Furttenbach the Elder," in *The Architecture of Western Gardens,* edited by George Teyssot and Monique Mosser, Cambridge, Massachusetts: MIT Press, 1991

SUSAN HERRINGTON